Oxford School
Dictionary

Chief Editor: Andrew Delahunty

OXFORD
UNIVERSITY PRESS

OXFORD
UNIVERSITY PRESS

Great Clarendon Street, Oxford OX2 6DP

Oxford University Press is a department of the University of Oxford.
It furthers the University's objective of excellence in research,
scholarship, and education by publishing worldwide in

Oxford   New York

Auckland   Cape Town   Dar es Salaam   Hong Kong   Karachi
Kuala Lumpur   Madrid   Melbourne   Mexico City   Nairobi
New Delhi   Shanghai   Taipei   Toronto

With offices in

Argentina   Austria   Brazil   Chile   Czech Republic   France   Greece
Guatemala   Hungary   Italy   Japan   Poland   Portugal   Singapore
South Korea   Switzerland   Thailand   Turkey   Ukraine   Vietnam
Oxford is a registered trade mark of Oxford University Press
in the UK and in certain other countries

British Library Cataloguing in Publication Data

Data available

ISBN-13: 978-0-19-274350-3

10 9 8 7 6 5

Printed in China by Golden Cup

Paper used in the production of this book is a natural,
recyclable product made from wood grown in sustainable forests.
The manufacturing process conforms to the environmental
regulations of the country of origin.

Oxford
OWL

For school
Discover eBooks, inspirational
resources, advice and support

For home
Helping your child's learning
with free eBooks, essential
tips and fun activities

www.oxfordowl.co.uk

Contents

Preface

The *Oxford School Dictionary* has been specially written for students aged 10 and above. It is particularly useful for students who are about to start secondary school and who need an up-to-date, student-friendly dictionary that they can use at home or at school. The dictionary is specially designed for students and includes a range of curriculum vocabulary, covering subjects such as Science, Information and Communication Technology, and Geography.

The *Oxford School Dictionary* can also be used very effectively in conjunction with the *Oxford School Thesaurus* which offers further support in creative writing and vocabulary building.

The *Oxford School Dictionary* gives all the information students need for exams in an accessible and easy-to-use format. Use of the dictionary will help students to develop their English language skills and equip them with the best reading, writing and speaking skills for years to come.

The publishers and editors are indebted to all the advisors, consultants and teachers who were involved in the planning of this dictionary. Special thanks go to Andrew Delahunty, Chief Editor.

Introduction

➤ **How does a word get into a dictionary?**
The simple answer to this question is that people use it. If enough
people use a word, it will eventually appear in print and online, and
dictionary compilers (lexicographers) will spot it. Thousands of new
words are invented every year but only a few become generally
known and make their way into the permanent record of a dictionary.
Thousands of slang or informal terms are coined and discarded every
year but if everybody learns them, then the dictionary will record them.

➤ **What do you use a dictionary for?**
If your answer to this is 'To look up spellings' or even 'To check the
meaning of a word', then you are missing out on a great deal that a
dictionary has to offer.

Dictionaries tell you how to pronounce a word, what word class it is,
what its plural is, where in the world it has come from, and what other
words are associated with the word you are looking up.

In addition to these, the *Oxford School Dictionary* gives you even more
language support to help you at home and at school. The **Vocabulary
Toolkit** section offers guidance on such topics as prefixes and suffixes,
confusable words and phrases, phrases from different languages, and
idioms and proverbs. There are **spelling, punctuation, grammar** and
usage panels throughout which provide useful tips, help and guidance
that will make a difference to your vocabulary, your writing and
your spelling.

Panels in this dictionary

Punctuation
You will find a panel at each of these words.

- apostrophe
- bracket
- colon
- comma
- dash
- exclamation mark
- full stop
- hyphen
- inverted commas
- question mark
- quotation marks
- semicolon

Grammar
There is a panel giving grammar support at each of these words.

- a
- active and passive
- adjective
- adverb
- adverbial
- be
- clause
- command
- comparative
- conjunction
- contraction
- determiner
- direct speech
- do
- exclamation
- have
- noun
- number
- phrase
- plural
- possessive
- prefix
- preposition
- pronoun
- punctuation
- question
- quotation
- relative pronoun
- sentence
- shall
- statement
- suffix
- superlative
- synonym
- tense
- the
- verb
- which
- word class

Spelling
You will find notes at tricky **words** to help you improve your spelling.

symmetry *NOUN*
 the quality of being symmetrical or well-proportioned

 SPELLING
 The 'i' sound is spelt with a y in **symmetry**.
 Do not forget to double the **m**.

Usage
Usage notes give extra information and context.

inflammable *ADJECTIVE*
 able to be set on fire

 USAGE
 This word means the same as **flammable**.
 If you want to say that something is
 not able to be set on fire, use **non-flammable**.

How to use this dictionary

word origins are given to increase language knowledge →

up-to-date examples help to make meaning clear →

word forms are given in full →

includes common phrases →

headwords are in blue to find words easily →

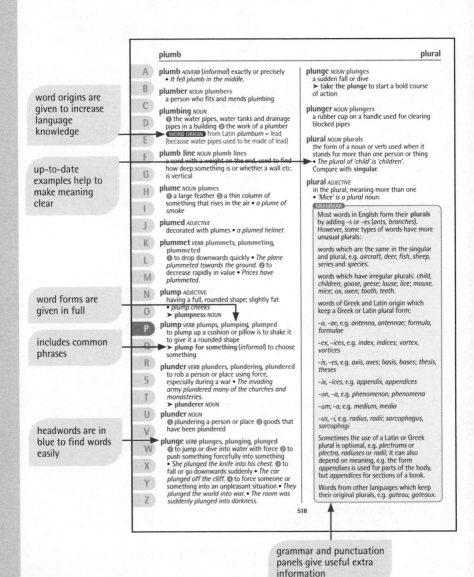

A B C D E F G H I J K L M N O P Q R S T U V W X Y Z

plumb ADVERB (*informal*) exactly or precisely • *It fell plumb in the middle.*

plumber NOUN plumbers
a person who fits and mends plumbing

plumbing NOUN
❶ the water pipes, water tanks and drainage pipes in a building ❷ the work of a plumber
WORD ORIGIN from Latin *plumbum* = lead (because water pipes used to be made of lead)

plumb line NOUN plumb lines
a cord with a weight on the end, used to find how deep something is or whether a wall etc. is vertical

plume NOUN plumes
❶ a large feather ❷ a thin column of something that rises in the air • *a plume of smoke*

plumed ADJECTIVE
decorated with plumes • *a plumed helmet*

plummet VERB plummets, plummeting, plummeted
❶ to drop downwards quickly • *The plane plummeted towards the ground.* ❷ to decrease rapidly in value • *Prices have plummeted.*

plump ADJECTIVE
having a full, rounded shape; slightly fat • *plump cheeks*
➤ **plumpness** NOUN

plump VERB plumps, plumping, plumped
to plump up a cushion or pillow is to shake it to give it a rounded shape
➤ **plump for something** (*informal*) to choose something

plunder VERB plunders, plundering, plundered
to rob a person or place using force, especially during a war • *The invading army plundered many of the churches and monasteries.*
➤ **plunderer** NOUN

plunder NOUN
❶ plundering a person or place ❷ goods that have been plundered

plunge VERB plunges, plunging, plunged
❶ to jump or dive into water with force ❷ to push something forcefully into something • *She plunged the knife into his chest.* ❸ to fall or go downwards suddenly • *The car plunged off the cliff.* ❹ to force someone or something into an unpleasant situation • *They plunged the world into war.* • *The room was suddenly plunged into darkness.*

plunge NOUN plunges
a sudden fall or dive
➤ **take the plunge** to start a bold course of action

plunger NOUN plungers
a rubber cup on a handle used for clearing blocked pipes

plural NOUN plurals
the form of a noun or verb used when it stands for more than one person or thing • *The plural of 'child' is 'children'.* Compare with **singular**.

plural ADJECTIVE
in the plural; meaning more than one • *'Mice' is a plural noun.*
GRAMMAR
Most words in English form their **plurals** by adding -s or -es (*ants, branches*). However, some types of words have more unusual plurals:

words which are the same in the singular and plural, e.g. *aircraft, deer, fish, sheep, series* and *species.*

words which have irregular plurals: *child, children; goose, geese; louse, lice; mouse, mice; ox, oxen; tooth, teeth.*

words of Greek and Latin origin which keep a Greek or Latin plural form:

-a, -ae, e.g. *antenna, antennae; formula, formulae*

-ex, -ices, e.g. *index, indices; vortex, vortices*

-is, -es, e.g. *axis, axes; basis, bases; thesis, theses*

-ix, -ices, e.g. *appendix, appendices*

-on, -a, e.g. *phenomenon, phenomena*

-um, -a, e.g. *medium, media*

-us, -i, e.g. *radius, radii; sarcophagus, sarcophagi*

Sometimes the use of a Latin or Greek plural is optional, e.g. *plectrums* or *plectra, radiuses* or *radii;* it can also depend on meaning, e.g. the form *appendixes* is used for parts of the body, but *appendices* for sections of a book.

Words from other languages which keep their original plurals, e.g. *gateau, gateaux.*

518

↑ grammar and punctuation panels give useful extra information

scherzo   try also ce-, ci-, cy-, ps- or sc-   **scoop**

scherzo (say **skairts**-oh) *NOUN* scherzos
a lively piece of music **WORD ORIGIN** Italian,
= joke

schism (say skizm or sizm) *NOUN* schisms
the splitting of a group into two opposing
sections because they disagree about
something important

schizophrenia (say skid-zo-**free**-nee-a) *NOUN*
a kind of mental illness in which people
cannot relate their thoughts and feelings to
reality
➤ **schizophrenic** *ADJECTIVE & NOUN*

scholar *NOUN* scholars
❶ a person who has studied a subject
thoroughly ❷ a person who has been
awarded a scholarship **WORD ORIGIN** from
Latin *scholaris* = to do with a school

scholarly *ADJECTIVE*
showing knowledge and learning

scholarship *NOUN* scholarships
❶ a grant of money given to someone to help
to pay for their education ❷ serious study of
an academic subject and the knowledge you
get

scholastic *ADJECTIVE*
to do with schools or education; academic

school *NOUN* schools
❶ a place where teaching is done, especially
of pupils aged 5-18 ❷ the pupils in a school
❸ the time when teaching takes place in a
school • *School ends at 4.30 p.m.* ❹ a group
of people who have the same beliefs or style
of work ❺ a large group of fish, whales or
dolphins

school *VERB* schools, schooling, schooled
to teach or train a person or animal • *She was
schooling her horse for the competition.*

schoolchild *NOUN* schoolchildren
a child who goes to school
➤ **schoolboy** *NOUN*
➤ **schoolgirl** *NOUN*

schooling *NOUN*
education at a school

schoolteacher *NOUN* schoolteachers
a person who teaches in a school
➤ **schoolmaster** *NOUN*
➤ **schoolmistress** *NOUN*

schooner (say **skoon**-er) *NOUN* schooners
❶ a sailing ship with two or more masts ❷ a
tall glass for serving sherry

science *NOUN* sciences
❶ the study of the physical world by means
of observation and experiment ❷ a branch
of this, such as chemistry, physics or biology
WORD ORIGIN from Latin *scientia* = knowledge

science fiction *NOUN*
stories about imaginary scientific discoveries
or space travel and life on other planets,
often set in the future

science park *NOUN* science parks
an area set up for industries using science or
for organizations doing scientific research

scientific *ADJECTIVE*
❶ to do with science or scientists • *scientific
instruments* ❷ studying things in an
organized, logical way and testing ideas
carefully • *a scientific study of the way we
use language*
➤ **scientifically** *ADVERB*

scientist *NOUN* scientists
❶ an expert in science ❷ someone who uses
scientific methods

scimitar (say **sim**-it-ar) *NOUN* scimitars
a curved oriental sword

scintillating *ADJECTIVE*
❶ sparkling ❷ lively and witty • *The
conversation was scintillating.*
WORD ORIGIN from Latin *scintilla* = spark

scion (say **sy**-on) *NOUN* scions
a descendant, especially of a noble family

scissors *PLURAL NOUN*
a cutting instrument used with one hand,
with two blades joined so that they can close
against each other
SPELLING
There is a tricky bit in scissors—it begins
with sc.

scoff *VERB* scoffs, scoffing, scoffed
❶ to laugh or speak in a mocking way about
something you think is silly • *She scoffed
at my superstitions.* ❷ (*informal*) to eat
something greedily or to eat it all up
➤ **scoffer** *NOUN*

scold *VERB* scolds, scolding, scolded
to speak angrily to someone because they
have done wrong; to tell someone off
➤ **scolding** *NOUN*

scone (say skon or skohn) *NOUN* scones
a soft flat cake, usually eaten with butter

scoop *NOUN* scoops
❶ a kind of deep spoon for serving ice cream

a
b
c
d
e
f
g
h
i
j
k
l
m
n
o
p
q
r
s
t
u
v
w
x
y
z

611

definitions are clear
and accurate

word classes are
given to build
grammatical skills

pronunciations are
given for difficult
words

spelling and usage
notes help to
improve spelling
and show how
words are used in
English

related words show how groups
of words are connected with
one another

a *DETERMINER* (called the indefinite article and changing to **an** before most vowel sounds)
❶ one (but not any special one) • *Can you lend me a book?* ❷ each; per • *I go there twice a month.*

> **GRAMMAR**
>
> The word *a* (or *an*) is known as the **indefinite article**. You use it before a singular noun or noun phrase when the person or thing you are talking about has not yet been mentioned or you want to refer to them in a general way:
>
> *I saw a cave and a dragon in my dream.*
>
> *Jupiter is a gas planet.*
>
> *A* is used before words which begin with a consonant (*a beetle, a text*), and *an* before those which begin with a vowel (*an ant, an email*). Abbreviations take either *a* or *an* depending on whether they begin with the *sound* of a consonant or a vowel: *a DVD*, but *an MP*; *an IQ test*, but *a UFO*.
>
> See also the panels on **the** and on **determiners**.

aback *ADVERB*
> **taken aback** surprised and slightly shocked • *Rose was taken aback by this request.*

abacus (say **ab**-a-kus) *NOUN* **abacuses**
a frame with rows of beads that slide on wires, used for counting and adding

abandon *VERB* **abandons, abandoning, abandoned**
❶ to stop doing something when it becomes impossible • *The search for the missing climbers was abandoned after two days.*
❷ to leave someone or something without intending to return • *He abandoned his family and went off to Australia.*
> **abandonment** *NOUN*

abandon *NOUN*
a careless and uncontrolled manner • *She danced with wild abandon.*

abandoned *ADJECTIVE*
left and no longer wanted or used • *an abandoned car*

abashed *ADJECTIVE*
feeling guilty and embarrassed

abate *VERB* **abates, abating, abated**
to become less or die down • *The storm showed no sign of abating.*
> **abatement** *NOUN*

abattoir (say **ab**-at-wahr) *NOUN* **abattoirs**
(*British*) a place where animals are killed for food; a slaughterhouse

abbess *NOUN* **abbesses**
the head of a convent

abbey *NOUN* **abbeys**
❶ a monastery or convent ❷ a church that was once part of a monastery • *Westminster Abbey*

abbot *NOUN* **abbots**
the head of an abbey of monks

abbreviate *VERB* **abbreviates, abbreviating, abbreviated**
to shorten a word or phrase • *abbreviated text messages*

abbreviation *NOUN* **abbreviations**
a shortened form of a word or words, especially one using the initial letters, such as St. or USA • *She uses lots of abbreviations when she texts.*

abdicate *VERB* **abdicates, abdicating, abdicated**
a queen or king abdicates if they give up the throne
> **abdication** *NOUN*

abdomen (say **ab**-dom-en) *NOUN* **abdomens**
❶ the lower front part of a person's or animal's body, containing the stomach, intestines and other digestive organs ❷ the rear section of an insect's body
> **abdominal** (say ab-**dom**-in-al) *ADJECTIVE*

abduct *VERB* **abducts, abducting, abducted**
to take a person away by force and against their will; to kidnap someone
> **abduction** *NOUN*
> **abductor** *NOUN*

abet *VERB* **abets, abetting, abetted**
to help or encourage someone to commit a crime

abeyance (say ab-**ay**-ans) *NOUN*
> **in abeyance** not being used at the moment • *More serious punishments are being held in abeyance.*

abhor *VERB* **abhors, abhorring, abhorred**
(*formal*) to hate or dislike something very

A

much **WORD ORIGIN** from Latin *abhorrere* = shrink away in horror

abhorrence *NOUN*
hatred or strong dislike • *She could not disguise her abhorrence of the man.*
➤ **abhorrent** *ADJECTIVE*

abide *VERB* abides, abiding, abided
❶ you can't abide something when you detest it or can't bear it • *I really can't abide garlic.* ❷ to abide by a promise or agreement is to keep it and do what you said you would • *He promised to abide by the rules.*

abiding *ADJECTIVE*
lasting or permanent • *The idea soon became an abiding passion.*

ability *NOUN* abilities
❶ ability is being able to do something • *Tiredness affects your ability to concentrate.* ❷ an ability is a special skill or talent • *students of mixed abilities*

abject (say **ab**-jekt) *ADJECTIVE*
❶ hopeless or pitiful • *They were living in abject poverty.* ❷ grovelling or humiliating • *an abject apology*

ablaze *ADJECTIVE*
❶ on fire and burning fiercely • *The whole building was soon ablaze.* ❷ full of bright light or colours • *The hall was ablaze with candlelight.*

able *ADJECTIVE*
❶ having the power or skill or opportunity to do something • *I was not able to move.* ❷ skilful or clever • *John is a very able musician.*
➤ **ably** *ADVERB*

able-bodied *ADJECTIVE*
fit and healthy; not disabled

abnormal *ADJECTIVE*
not normal; unusual • *abnormal weather conditions*
➤ **abnormally** *ADVERB*
➤ **abnormality** *NOUN*

aboard *ADVERB & PREPOSITION*
on or into a ship or aircraft or train

abode *NOUN* abodes (*formal*)
the place where someone lives • *Welcome to my humble abode.*

abolish *VERB* abolishes, abolishing, abolished
to put an end to a law or custom • *Slavery was abolished in Britain in 1807.*

abolition (say ab-ol-**ish**-on) *NOUN*
getting rid of a law or custom • *the abolition of slavery*

abominable *ADJECTIVE*
very bad or unpleasant • *an abominable crime*
➤ **abominably** *ADVERB*

abomination *NOUN* abominations
something that disgusts you

aborigine (say ab-er-**ij**-in-ee) *NOUN* aborigines
one of the original inhabitants of a country
➤ **aboriginal** *ADJECTIVE & NOUN*
➤ **Aborigine** a member of the people who were living in Australia before European settlers arrived
WORD ORIGIN from Latin *ab origine* = from the beginning

abort *VERB* aborts, aborting, aborted
to put an end to something before it has been completed • *They had to abort the space flight because of technical problems.*

abortion *NOUN* abortions
an operation to remove an unborn child from the womb before it has developed enough to survive

abortive *ADJECTIVE*
unsuccessful • *an abortive attempt*

abound *VERB* abounds, abounding, abounded
❶ things abound when there are a lot of them • *Fish abound in the river.* ❷ a place abounds in things when there are a lot of them there • *The river abounds in fish.*

about *PREPOSITION*
❶ near in amount or size or time; approximately • *She's about five feet tall.* • *Come about two o'clock.* ❷ on the subject of; in connection with • *I don't want to talk about it.* ❸ all round; in various parts of • *A dog was running about the yard.*

about *ADVERB*
❶ in various directions • *They were running about.* ❷ not far away • *There were wild animals about.*
➤ **be about to** to be going to do something • *We were just about to leave.*

above *PREPOSITION*
❶ higher than • *There was a window above the door.* ❷ more than • *The temperature was just above freezing.*

above *ADVERB*
at or to a higher place or point • *Look at the stars above.*

above board *ADJECTIVE & ADVERB*
honest; without deception
WORD ORIGIN from card-players cheating by
changing their cards under the table

abrasion *NOUN* abrasions
an area of skin that has been scraped

abrasive *ADJECTIVE*
❶ something abrasive rubs or scrapes things
• *an abrasive wheel* ❷ a person is abrasive
when they are harsh or hurtful in what they
say • *an abrasive manner*

abreast *ADVERB*
❶ side by side • *They walked three abreast.*
❷ to keep abreast of a situation is to have all
the most recent information about it

abridged *ADJECTIVE*
using fewer words than the original and
therefore shorter • *an abridged paperback
edition*

abroad *ADVERB*
(*British*) in or to another country

abrupt *ADJECTIVE*
❶ sudden and unexpected • *his abrupt
departure* ❷ rather rude and unfriendly
• *She has quite an abrupt manner.*
➤ **abruptly** *ADVERB*
➤ **abruptness** *NOUN*

abscess (say **ab**-sis) *NOUN* abscesses
an inflamed place where pus has formed in
the body

abscond *VERB* absconds, absconding,
absconded
to go away secretly, especially after doing
something wrong • *The cashier had
absconded with the money.*

abseil *VERB* abseils, abseiling, abseiled
(*British*) to lower yourself down a steep cliff
or rock by sliding down a rope

absence *NOUN* absences
not being in the place where you are
expected • *No one noticed his absence.*

absent (say **ab**-sent) *ADJECTIVE*
not in the place you should be; not present
• *absent from school*

absent (say ab-**sent**) *VERB* absents, absenting,
absented
➤ **absent yourself** to stay away from
somewhere you should be

absentee *NOUN* absentees
a person who is not present when they are
expected to be

absent-minded *ADJECTIVE*
having your mind on other things; forgetful
➤ **absent-mindedly** *ADVERB*

absolute *ADJECTIVE*
complete; not restricted • *absolute power*

absolutely *ADVERB*
❶ completely ❷ (*informal*) yes, I agree

SPELLING
Absolutely = absolute + ly. Don't forget
to keep the e after the t.

absolute zero *NOUN*
the lowest possible temperature, calculated
as -273.15°C

absolution *NOUN*
in Christianity, a priest's formal statement
that someone's sins are forgiven

absolve *VERB* absolves, absolving, absolved
❶ to clear a person of blame or guilt • *The
train driver was absolved of any blame for
the crash.* ❷ to release a person from a
promise or obligation

absorb *VERB* absorbs, absorbing, absorbed
❶ to soak up a liquid or gas ❷ to receive
something and reduce its effects • *The
buffers absorbed most of the shock.* ❸ to
take up a person's attention or time • *They
were completely absorbed in what they were
doing.*
➤ **absorption** *NOUN*

absorbent *ADJECTIVE*
able to soak up liquids easily • *absorbent
paper*

abstain *VERB* abstains, abstaining, abstained
❶ to keep yourself from doing something you
enjoy ❷ to choose not to use your vote

abstinence *NOUN*
going without something, especially from
alcohol

abstract (say **ab**-strakt) *ADJECTIVE*
❶ to do with ideas and not with physical
things • *Truth, hope and danger are all
abstract.* ❷ an abstract painting or sculpture
shows the artist's ideas or feelings rather than
showing a recognizable person or thing

abstract (say **ab**-strakt) *NOUN* abstracts
❶ a summary of a longer piece of writing
❷ an abstract painting or sculpture

abstract (say ab-**strakt**) *VERB* abstracts,
abstracting, abstracted (*formal*) to take
something out or remove it • *He abstracted
some cards from the pack.*

a
b
c
d
e
f
g
h
i
j
k
l
m
n
o
p
q
r
s
t
u
v
w
x
y
z

abstracted *ADJECTIVE*
with your mind on other things; not paying attention

abstraction *NOUN*
thinking deeply about something and not paying attention • *He gazed with an air of abstraction through the window.*

absurd *ADJECTIVE*
ridiculous or foolish • *I've never heard anything so absurd.*
➤ **absurdly** *ADVERB*

absurdity *NOUN* **absurdities**
something that is ridiculous or foolish • *She laughed at the absurdity of the question.*

abundance *NOUN*
a large amount of something, often more than you need • *There was an abundance of food and drink.*

abundant *ADJECTIVE*
things are abundant when there are plenty of them • *Fish are abundant in the lake.*
➤ **abundantly** *ADVERB*

abuse (say ab-**yooz**) *VERB* **abuses, abusing, abused**
❶ to use something badly or wrongly; to misuse something ❷ to hurt someone or treat them cruelly ❸ to say unpleasant things about a person or thing

abuse (say ab-**yooss**) *NOUN* **abuses**
❶ a misuse of something • *the abuse of power* ❷ physical harm or cruelty done to someone ❸ words that offend or insult a person • *a torrent of abuse*

abusive *ADJECTIVE*
rude and insulting • *abusive remarks*

abysmal (say ab-**iz**-mal) *ADJECTIVE*
extremely bad • *The weather was abysmal.*

abyss (say ab-**iss**) *NOUN* **abysses**
a deep dark hole or pit that seems to go on for ever **WORD ORIGIN** from Greek *abyssos* = bottomless

AC *ABBREVIATION*
alternating current

academic *ADJECTIVE*
❶ to do with education or studying, especially at a school or college or university ❷ theoretical; having no practical use • *an academic point*
➤ **academically** *ADVERB*

academic *NOUN* **academics**
a university or college teacher

academy *NOUN* **academies**
❶ a school or college, especially one for specialized training ❷ a society of scholars or artists • *The French Academy of Sciences* **WORD ORIGIN** from *Akademeia*, the name of the garden where the Greek philosopher Plato taught his pupils

accede (say ak-**seed**) *VERB* **accedes, acceding, acceded**
❶ to accede to a request or suggestion is to agree to it ❷ to accede to the throne is to become queen or king

accelerate *VERB* **accelerates, accelerating, accelerated**
to become quicker; to increase speed • *The plane was accelerating for take-off.*

acceleration *NOUN* **accelerations**
❶ the rate at which the speed of something increases ❷ the rate of change of velocity

accelerator *NOUN* **accelerators**
the pedal that a driver presses to make a motor vehicle go faster

accent (say **ak**-sent) *NOUN* **accents**
❶ the way a person pronounces the words of a language • *She has a French accent.* ❷ the emphasis or stress used in pronouncing a word • *In 'cuckoo', the accent is on the first syllable.* ❸ a mark placed over a letter to show how it is pronounced, e.g. in *résumé*

accented *ADJECTIVE*
spoken with a foreign accent • *He spoke in heavily accented English.*

accentuate (say ak-**sent**-yoo-ayt) *VERB* **accentuates, accentuating, accentuated**
to make something more obvious • *His pale complexion was accentuated by his black moustache.*

accept *VERB* **accepts, accepting, accepted**
❶ to take a thing that is offered or presented to you ❷ to say yes to an invitation or offer
SPELLING
Take care not to confuse with **except**.

acceptable *ADJECTIVE*
good enough to accept; satisfactory • *We think it is an acceptable offer.*

acceptance *NOUN*
❶ accepting something, such as an invitation or offer ❷ agreeing with something and approving of it

access (say **ak**-sess) *NOUN*
❶ a way to enter or reach something
❷ the right to use or look at something

access *VERB* accesses, accessing, accessed
to read and use the information that has been stored in a computer

accessible *ADJECTIVE*
able to be reached or understood easily
• *The style is accessible and easy to read.*
➤ accessibility *NOUN*

accession *NOUN* accessions
reaching a rank or position; becoming king or queen • *The monarchy was restored with the accession of Charles II.*

accessory (say ak-**sess**-er-ee) *NOUN*
accessories
❶ an extra thing that goes with something
❷ a person who helps someone else to commit a crime

accident *NOUN* accidents
something unexpected that happens, especially when something is broken or someone is hurt or killed
➤ by accident by chance; without meaning to

SPELLING
Accidentally = accident + ally. Don't forget the a and the double l before the y.

accidental *ADJECTIVE*
happening or done by accident • *accidental damage*

accidentally *ADVERB*
to do something accidentally is to do it by mistake or without meaning to • *Hal had accidentally pressed the wrong button.*

acclaim *VERB* acclaims, acclaiming, acclaimed
to praise someone or something enthusiastically • *Her plays are highly acclaimed.*

acclaim *NOUN*
enthusiastic praise • *The book was published to huge acclaim.*

acclamation *NOUN*
loud and enthusiastic approval

acclimatize (also **acclimatise**) *VERB*
acclimatizes, acclimatizing, acclimatized
to become used to a new climate or new surroundings

accolade (say ak-ol-**ayd**) *NOUN* accolades
praise or a prize given to someone for something they have done

WORD ORIGIN from Latin *collum* = neck (because in the past, when a man was knighted, the king put his arms round the man's shoulders)

accommodate *VERB* accommodates, accommodating, accommodated
❶ to provide someone with a place to live, work or sleep overnight ❷ to help someone by providing what they need • *We were able to accommodate everyone with skis.*

accommodating *ADJECTIVE*
willing to help or cooperate • *Thank you for being so accommodating.*

accommodation *NOUN*
somewhere to live, work or sleep overnight

SPELLING
There is a double c and double m in **accommodation**.

accompanist *NOUN* accompanists
a pianist or other musician who plays to support a singer or another musician

accompany *VERB* accompanies, accompanying, accompanied
❶ to go somewhere with somebody
❷ to happen or appear with something else
• *The cheers were accompanied by a few boos.* ❸ to play music, especially on a piano, that supports a singer or another musician
➤ accompaniment *NOUN*

accomplice (say a-**kum**-pliss) *NOUN*
accomplices
a person who helps another in a crime or bad act

accomplish *VERB* accomplishes, accomplishing, accomplished
to do something successfully • *He hoped to accomplish the journey in six days.*

accomplished *ADJECTIVE*
skilled or talented • *She was an accomplished painter.*

accomplishment *NOUN* accomplishments
something you have achieved or are good at

accord *NOUN*
agreement or consent
➤ of your own accord without being asked or told to do it
➤ with one accord (*formal*) doing the same thing at the same time • *With one accord they sprang to their feet.*

accord *VERB* accords, according, accorded
❶ to be consistent with something • *This theory does not accord with the facts.*

a b c d e f g h i j k l m n o p q r s t u v w x y z

A

❷ (formal) to give or grant something • *He was not accorded the respect he deserved.*

accordance NOUN
➤ **in accordance** with in agreement with • *This is done in accordance with the rules.*

accordingly ADVERB
❶ in the way that is suitable • *I've given you your instructions and I expect you to act accordingly.* ❷ because of what has just been said; therefore • *Accordingly, the name was changed.*

according to PREPOSITION
❶ used to show where a piece of information comes from • *According to Josie, he's really clever.* ❷ used to show how one thing relates to another • *Apples are priced according to their size.*

accordion NOUN accordions
a portable musical instrument like a large concertina with a set of piano-type keys at one end, played by squeezing it in and out and pressing the keys

accost VERB accosts, accosting, accosted
to go up to a person and speak to them, especially in an annoying way

account NOUN accounts
❶ a description or story about something that has happened ❷ a statement of the money someone owes or has received; a bill ❸ an arrangement to keep money in a bank or building society ❹ an arrangement to use a computing or social media service • *an email account*
➤ **on account** of because of
➤ **on no account** under no circumstances; certainly not
➤ **take something into account** to consider or include it when making a decision or calculation

account VERB accounts, accounting, accounted
➤ **account for** to explain why something happens • *I can't account for this defeat.*

accountable ADJECTIVE
responsible for something and having to explain why you have done it • *The company should be held accountable for the pollution it has caused.*
➤ **accountability** NOUN

accountant NOUN accountants
a person whose job is to record and organize the money a person or organization spends and receives
➤ **accountancy** NOUN

accounting NOUN
the business of keeping financial accounts

accredited ADJECTIVE
officially recognized • *an accredited health inspector*

accumulate VERB accumulates, accumulating, accumulated
❶ to collect things or pile them up
❷ to increase in quantity • *Snow accumulates throughout the long winters.*
➤ **accumulation** NOUN

accumulator NOUN accumulators
a large battery that can be recharged

accuracy NOUN
being exactly right or correct • *I was impressed with the accuracy of his guesses.*

accurate ADJECTIVE
correct or exact • *an accurate map*

accurately ADVERB
correctly or exactly • *Solar eclipses can be accurately predicted.*

accusation NOUN accusations
a statement accusing a person of a crime or doing something wrong

accuse VERB accuses, accusing, accused
to say that a person has committed a crime or done something wrong • *He accused her of lying about it.*
➤ **accuser** NOUN

accustom VERB accustoms, accustoming, accustomed
to be accustomed to something is to be used to it • *She was accustomed to getting her own way.*

ace NOUN aces
❶ a playing card with one spot ❷ (in tennis) a serve that is too good for the other player to reach ❸ a very skilful person • *a flying ace*

acetylene (say a-**set**-il-een) NOUN
a gas that burns with a bright flame, used in cutting and welding metal

ache NOUN aches
a dull continuous pain

ache VERB aches, aching, ached
to have an ache • *He was tired and his feet ached.*

achieve VERB achieves, achieving, achieved
to succeed in doing or producing something • *Modern go-karts can achieve speeds of more than 150 km per hour.*
➤ **achievable** ADJECTIVE

achievement *NOUN* achievements
something good or worthwhile that you have succeeded in doing • *These paintings are among the greatest achievements in the history of art.*

> **SPELLING**
> There is an ie in **achievement**.

acid *NOUN* acids
a chemical substance that contains hydrogen and neutralizes alkalis. The hydrogen can be replaced by a metal to form a salt.
➤ **acidity** *NOUN*

acid *ADJECTIVE*
❶ sharp-tasting; sour ❷ looking or sounding bitter • *an acid reply*
➤ **acidly** *ADVERB*

acidic *ADJECTIVE*
❶ very sour ❷ containing acid

acid rain *NOUN*
rain made acid by mixing with waste gases from factories etc.

acknowledge *VERB* acknowledges, acknowledging, acknowledged
❶ to admit that something is true ❷ to let someone know that you have received or noticed something • *They wrote back to acknowledge my application.* ❸ to express thanks or appreciation for something • *He raised his hand to acknowledge the applause.*
➤ **acknowledgement** *NOUN*

acme (say **ak**-mee) *NOUN*
the highest degree of something • *the acme of perfection*

acne (say **ak**-nee) *NOUN*
inflamed red pimples on the face and neck

acorn *NOUN* acorns
the seed of the oak tree

acoustic (say a-**koo**-stik) *ADJECTIVE*
❶ to do with sound or hearing ❷ an acoustic guitar or other musical instrument does not use an electric amplifier

acoustics (say a-**koo**-stiks) *PLURAL NOUN*
❶ the qualities of a hall or room that make it good or bad for carrying sound ❷ the properties of sound

acquaint *VERB* acquaints, acquainting, acquainted
to tell somebody about something • *Please acquaint me with the facts of the case.*
➤ **be acquainted with someone** to know someone slightly

acquaintance *NOUN* acquaintances
❶ a person you know slightly ❷ getting to know someone • *I am delighted to make your acquaintance.*

acquiesce (say ak-wee-**ess**) *VERB* acquiesces, acquiescing, acquiesced
to agree to something, even though you might not like it completely
➤ **acquiescence** *NOUN*

acquire *VERB* acquires, acquiring, acquired
to get or be given something • *She has acquired a good knowledge of astronomy.*

acquisition *NOUN* acquisitions
❶ something you have got or been given recently • *My latest acquisition is a surfboard.* ❷ the process of acquiring something • *a child's acquisition of language*

acquit *VERB* acquits, acquitting, acquitted
to decide that somebody is not guilty of a crime • *The jury acquitted her.*
➤ **acquittal** *NOUN*
➤ **acquit yourself well** to perform or do something well

acre (say **ay**-ker) *NOUN* acres
an area of land measuring 4,840 square yards or 0.405 hectares
➤ **acreage** *NOUN*

acrid *ADJECTIVE*
having a strong bitter smell or taste • *acrid smoke*

acrobat *NOUN* acrobats
a person who performs spectacular gymnastic feats for entertainment
➤ **acrobatic** *ADJECTIVE*
➤ **acrobatics** *PLURAL NOUN*
WORD ORIGIN from Greek *akrobatos* = walking on tiptoe

acronym (say **ak**-ron-im) *NOUN* acronyms
a word or name that is formed from the initial letters of other words and pronounced as a word in its own right • *Nato is an acronym of North Atlantic Treaty Organization.*

across *PREPOSITION & ADVERB*
❶ from one side to the other • *Swim across the river.* • *Are you across yet?* ❷ on the opposite side • *the house across the street*

acrostic *NOUN* acrostics
a word puzzle or poem in which the first or last letters of each line form a word or words

acrylic (say a-**kril**-ik) *NOUN*
a kind of fibre, plastic or resin made from an organic acid

a
b
c
d
e
f
g
h
i
j
k
l
m
n
o
p
q
r
s
t
u
v
w
x
y
z

acrylics *PLURAL NOUN*
a type of paint used by artists

act *NOUN* acts
❶ something someone does ❷ a pretence • *She is only putting on an act.* ❸ one of the main divisions of a play or opera ❹ each of a series of short performances in a programme of entertainment • *a juggling act* ❺ a law passed by a parliament

act *VERB* acts, acting, acted
❶ to do something; to behave in a certain way • *Try to act normally.* ❷ to perform a part in a play or film etc. ❸ to function or have an effect • *He stuck out his feet to act as brakes.*

action *NOUN* actions
❶ doing something • *Now is the time for action.* ❷ something you do • *Can you explain your actions that night?* ❸ a battle; fighting • *He was killed in action.* ❹ a lawsuit
➤ **out of action** not working or functioning
➤ **take action** to decide to do something

action replay *NOUN* action replays
(*British*) playing back a piece of sports action on television, especially in slow motion

activate *VERB* activates, activating, activated
to activate a machine or process is to start it working • *The alarm is activated by movement.*
➤ **activation** *NOUN*

active *ADJECTIVE*
❶ taking part in many activities; energetic ❷ functioning or working; in operation • *an active volcano* ❸ (*in grammar*) describing the form of a verb when the subject of the verb is performing the action. In 'The shop *sells* DVDs' the verb is active; in 'DVDs *are sold* by the shop' the verb is passive.
➤ **actively** *ADVERB*

GRAMMAR

Verbs can be either **active** or **passive**; these two choices are sometimes called **active voice** and **passive voice**.

A verb is active when the subject of the verb performs the action: *The sun rises in the East; My father wrote these words.* In these sentences, the verbs (*rises* and *wrote*) are active because their subjects (*the sun* and *my father*) are performing the actions. But when the verb takes an object (*these words* in the second sentence), you can turn the sentence round and say *These words were written*

by my father. Now, the verb (*were written*) is passive, because the subject of the sentence is *these words*, and the subject and object are the other way round. You use the passive voice when you want the object to be the main topic of the sentence (i.e. in the previous example, when you want to focus on *the words*, and not *your father*).

If a verb does not take an object (like *rises* in the first example), it can only be active; you cannot turn *The sun rises in the East* into a passive sentence because there is no object to make into the subject.

In passive sentences, the performer of the action often comes after the word *by*: *The mystery was solved by our neighbour; The penalty will be taken by the Welsh captain.* But sometimes the performer is unknown, or is not identified: *All the tickets have been sold; That file has been deleted.*

activist *NOUN* activists
a person who takes action to try to bring about change, especially in politics

activity *NOUN* activities
❶ an activity is an action or occupation • *outdoor activities* ❷ activity is doing things or being busy • *The streets were full of activity.*

actor *NOUN* actors
a person who acts a part in a play or film etc.

actress *NOUN* actresses
a woman who acts a part in a play or film etc.

actual *ADJECTIVE*
really happening or existing

actually *ADVERB*
really; in fact • *Actually, I think you are wrong.*

acumen (say **ak**-yoo-men) *NOUN*
the ability to make good judgements and take quick decisions

acupuncture (say **ak**-yoo-punk-cher) *NOUN*
pricking parts of the body with needles to relieve pain or cure disease
➤ **acupuncturist** *NOUN*

acute *ADJECTIVE*
❶ sharp or strong • *acute pain* ❷ having a sharp mind
➤ **acuteness** *NOUN*

acute accent NOUN acute accents
a mark over a vowel, as over é in *résumé*

acute angle NOUN acute angles
an angle of less than 90°

acutely ADVERB
very or very strongly • *He was acutely embarrassed.*

AD ABBREVIATION
Anno Domini (Latin = in the year of Our Lord), used in dates counted from the birth of Jesus Christ

adamant (say **ad**-am-ant) ADJECTIVE
determined not to change your mind

Adam's apple NOUN Adam's apples
the lump at the front of a man's neck
WORD ORIGIN from the story that when Adam (the first man, according to the Bible) ate an apple, which God had forbidden him to do, a piece of it stuck in his throat

adapt VERB adapts, adapting, adapted
❶ to change something so that it is suitable for a new purpose ❷ to become used to a new situation • *She gradually adapted to her new life.*

adaptable ADJECTIVE
able to adapt to or become suitable for different situations • *The red fox is one of the most adaptable animals.*

adaptation NOUN adaptations
❶ a play or film that is based on a novel etc. ❷ changing to suit a new situation • *New species come about because of adaptation.*

adaptor NOUN adaptors
a device that connects parts of electrical or other equipment

add VERB adds, adding, added
❶ to put one thing with another ❷ to make another remark • *'And get back soon,' he added.*
➤ **add up** ❶ to make or work out a total ❷ (*informal*) to make sense; to seem reasonable • *The things they said just don't add up.*

addenda PLURAL NOUN
things added at the end of a book

adder NOUN adders
a small poisonous snake **WORD ORIGIN** from Old English; originally called *a nadder*, which later became *an adder*

addict NOUN addicts
a person who does or uses something that

they cannot give up
➤ **addiction** NOUN

addicted ADJECTIVE
not able to give up a habit or drug • *He is addicted to computer games.*

addictive ADJECTIVE
causing a habit that people cannot give up
• *an addictive drug*

addition NOUN additions
❶ the process of adding ❷ something added
• *You are a welcome addition to our team.*
➤ **in addition** also; as an extra thing

additional ADJECTIVE
extra; as an extra thing • *There is a small additional charge for using of the swimming pool.*
➤ **additionally** ADVERB

additive NOUN additives
a substance added to another in small amounts for a special purpose, e.g. as a flavouring

addled ADJECTIVE
muddled or confused • *His brain was addled with all the questions.*

address NOUN addresses
❶ the details of the place where someone lives or of where letters or parcels should be delivered to a person or firm ❷ (*in computing*) a string of characters which shows a destination for email messages or the location of a website • *What's your email address?* ❸ a speech to an audience

address VERB addresses, addressing, addressed
❶ to write an address on a letter or parcel
❷ to make a remark or speech to somebody
• *He stood up to address the crowd.*

SPELLING
There is a double **d** and double **s** in **address.**

adenoids PLURAL NOUN
thick spongy flesh at the back of the nose and throat, which can make breathing difficult

adept (say a-**dept**) ADJECTIVE
very good or skilful at something • *He was adept at sign language.*

adequate ADJECTIVE
enough or good enough
➤ **adequately** ADVERB
➤ **adequacy** NOUN

adhere VERB adheres, adhering, adhered
❶ to stick to something ❷ to adhere to a belief or rule is to keep to it

adherence (say ad-**heer**-ens) NOUN
keeping to a particular belief or rule

adherent (say ad-**heer**-ent) NOUN adherents
a person who supports a certain group or theory etc.

adhesive ADJECTIVE
sticky; causing things to stick together

adhesive NOUN adhesives
a substance used to stick things together; glue

ad hoc ADJECTIVE & ADVERB
done or arranged only when necessary and not planned in advance • *We had to make a number of ad hoc decisions.*

Adi Granth (say ah-di-**grunt**) NOUN
the holy book of the Sikhs

ad infinitum (say in-fin-y-tum) ADVERB
without limit; for ever (**WORD ORIGIN**) Latin, = to infinity

adjacent ADJECTIVE
near or next to • *I waited in an adjacent room.*

> **SPELLING**
> There is a **d** before the **j**, and the 's' sound is spelt with a **c** in **adjacent.**

adjective NOUN adjectives
a word that describes a noun or adds to its meaning, e.g. *big, honest, strange*

> **GRAMMAR**
> **Adjectives** are words that describe a person, place or thing, e.g. *tall, pale, delicious, jagged, unique, untrue.* They can come before a noun (e.g. *a tall giraffe, a jagged cliff*), or they can come after a verb like *be, become* or *grow* (e.g. *The soup was delicious; My companion became pale; The weather grew cold*). Some adjectives can only be used in one position: e.g. *afraid* can only be used after a verb, and *utter* can only be used before a noun. You can say *The crew were afraid* but not *an afraid crew*; and you can say *It was an utter disaster* but not *The disaster was utter.*
>
> **Non-gradable** adjectives classify people and things, e.g. *Australian (an Australian actor)* or *square (a square envelope).* These are 'all-or-nothing' adjectives because actors are either Australian or not Australian, and things are either square or not.
>
> **Gradable** adjectives describe a quality that people or things may have, e.g. *tall (a tall teenager)* or *smelly (a smelly cheese).* These adjectives are called **gradable** because the amount to which people or things have a particular quality may vary; e.g. some teenagers are taller than others, and some cheeses are smellier than others.
>
> See also the panels on **comparative forms** and **superlative forms.**

adjoin VERB adjoins, adjoining, adjoined
to be next or nearest to something • *a little room adjoining the stage*

adjourn (say a-**jern**) VERB adjourns, adjourning, adjourned
❶ to break off a meeting until a later time
❷ to break off and go somewhere else • *They adjourned to the library.*
➤ **adjournment** NOUN

adjunct (say **aj**-unkt) NOUN adjuncts
something added that is useful but not essential

adjust VERB adjusts, adjusting, adjusted
❶ to change something slightly, especially because it is not in the right position • *He adjusted his tie in the mirror.* ❷ to adjust to something new is to get used to it • *It took a moment for her eyes to adjust to the dark.*
➤ **adjustable** ADJECTIVE

adjustment NOUN adjustments
a small change that you make to something

ad lib ADVERB
done or spoken without any rehearsal or preparation (**WORD ORIGIN**) from Latin *ad libitum* = according to pleasure

ad-lib VERB ad-libs, ad-libbing, ad-libbed
to say or do something without any rehearsal or preparation

administer VERB administers, administering, administered
❶ to give or provide something • *The doctor administered the antidote.* ❷ to make sure that something is carried out properly • *He was known for administering justice fairly.*
❸ to control or manage the affairs of a business, organization or country

administration NOUN administrations
❶ the work of running a business or

governing a country ❷ the group of people who run an organization; the government of a country ❸ administering something • *the administration of justice*

administrative *ADJECTIVE*
to do with running a business or country

administrator *NOUN* administrator
a person who helps to run a business or organization

admirable *ADJECTIVE*
worth admiring; excellent
➤ **admirably** *ADVERB*

admiral *NOUN* admirals
a naval officer of high rank
(WORD ORIGIN) from Arabic *amir* = commander

admiration *NOUN*
a feeling of thinking that someone or something is very good • *I am full of admiration for what she's done.*

admire *VERB* admires, admiring, admired
❶ to think that someone or something is very good ❷ to look at something and enjoy it
• *He paused to admire the view.*

admirer *NOUN* admirers
a person who likes someone or something very much • *My sister has many admirers.*

admissible *ADJECTIVE*
able to be allowed or accepted as being valid
• *admissible evidence*

admission *NOUN* admissions
❶ permission to go in • *Admission to the show is by ticket only.* ❷ the charge for being allowed to go in ❸ a statement admitting something; a confession • *He is guilty by his own admission.*

admit *VERB* admits, admitting, admitted
❶ to allow someone or something to come in ❷ to say reluctantly that something is true; to confess something • *We admit that the task is difficult.* • *He admitted his crime.*

admittance *NOUN*
permission to go in, especially to a private place

admittedly *ADVERB*
as an agreed fact; without denying it
• *Admittedly the place is a bit expensive, but the food's great.*

admonish *VERB* admonishes, admonishing, admonished
to tell someone that you do not approve of

what they have done or to warn them
➤ **admonition** *NOUN*

ado *NOUN*
➤ **without more** or **further ado** without wasting any more time

adolescence (say ad-ol-**ess**-ens) *NOUN*
the time between being a child and being an adult

adolescent *NOUN* adolescents
a young person at the age between being a child and being an adult

adolescent *ADJECTIVE*
at the age between being a child and being an adult

adopt *VERB* adopts, adopting, adopted
❶ to take a child into your family as your own child ❷ to accept something; to take something and use it • *They adopted new methods of working.*
➤ **adoption** *NOUN*

adorable *ADJECTIVE*
lovely; sweet and attractive • *adorable kittens*

adore *VERB* adores, adoring, adored
to love a person or thing very much
➤ **adoration** *NOUN*

adorn *VERB* adorns, adorning, adorned
to decorate something or make it pretty
• *Photos adorned the mantelpiece.*
➤ **adornment** *NOUN*

adrenalin (say a-**dren**-al-in) *NOUN*
a hormone produced when you are afraid or excited. It stimulates the nervous system, making your heart beat faster and increasing your energy and your ability to move quickly.

adrift *ADJECTIVE & ADVERB*
a boat is adrift when it is drifting and out of control • *He was set adrift in a small boat.*

adroit (say a-**droit**) *ADJECTIVE*
clever and skilful **(WORD ORIGIN)** from French
à droit = according to right

adulation *NOUN*
a lot of admiration or flattery

adult (say **ad**-ult) *NOUN* adults
a fully grown person or animal

adultery *NOUN*
a sexual relationship between a married person and someone who is not their husband or wife
➤ **adulterous** *ADJECTIVE*

a
b
c
d
e
f
g
h
i
j
k
l
m
n
o
p
q
r
s
t
u
v
w
x
y
z

advance *NOUN* advances
❶ a forward movement ❷ a development or improvement • *the latest advances in medicine* ❸ a loan of money or a payment made before it is due
➤ **in advance** beforehand; ahead

advance *ADJECTIVE*
given or arranged beforehand • *advance warning*

advance *VERB* advances, advancing, advanced
❶ to move forward • *The army advanced towards the city.* ❷ to make progress • *Technology has advanced at great pace over the decades.*
➤ **advancement** *NOUN*

advanced *ADJECTIVE*
at a high level; highly developed
• *an advanced maths course*

advantage *NOUN* advantages
❶ something useful or helpful ❷ (in tennis) the next point won after deuce
➤ **take advantage of someone** to treat someone unfairly when they are not likely to complain
➤ **take advantage of something** to make good use of something or benefit from it
➤ **to advantage** making a good effect • *The painting can be seen to its best advantage here.*
➤ **to your advantage** that helps or benefits you

advantageous (say ad-van-**tay**-jus) *ADJECTIVE*
giving an advantage; beneficial

Advent *NOUN*
the period just before Christmas, when Christians celebrate the coming of Christ

advent *NOUN*
the arrival of a new person or thing • *the advent of computers*

adventure *NOUN* adventures
❶ an exciting or dangerous experience
❷ doing exciting and daring things • *She had a love of adventure.*
➤ **adventurer** *NOUN*

adventurous *ADJECTIVE*
liking to do exciting and daring things

adverb *NOUN* adverbs
a word that adds to the meaning of a verb or adjective or another adverb and tells how, when or where something happens, e.g. *gently, soon* and *upstairs*
➤ **adverbial** *ADJECTIVE*

GRAMMAR

Adverbs answer questions such as *when?, where?, why?, how?,* and *how much?* Some adverbs go with adjectives: for example, *The map is very old* tells you how old the map is, and *a fairly expensive car* describes a car that is quite (but not very) expensive. Other adverbs go with verbs: for example, *The dog ate ravenously* tells you how the dog was eating, *It rains here frequently* tells you how often it rains, and *Hammering was heard downstairs* tells you where hammering was heard. Adverbs like these are often formed by adding *-ly* to an adjective, e.g. *ravenously, frequently.* Notice that adverbs can also go with other adverbs: *Sam smiled rather sheepishly.*

If an adverb refers to a whole sentence, it usually comes at the beginning: *Honestly, I didn't know where to look; Clearly, we had a long wait ahead.*

See also the panels on **comparative forms** and **superlative forms**.

adverbial *NOUN* adverbials
a group of words that functions as an adverb. Examples of adverbials are *last night* in the sentence *We saw him last night* and *more or less* in the sentence *She had more or less finished.*

GRAMMAR

A group of words that functions as an adverb is called an **adverbial**: for example, in the sentence *We email each other whenever we can,* the underlined phrase answers the question *when?* and is an adverbial (equivalent to *often* or *regularly*).

adversary (say **ad**-ver-ser-ee) *NOUN* adversaries
an opponent or enemy

adverse (say **ad**-vers) *ADJECTIVE*
bad or harmful • *adverse weather conditions*
➤ **adversely** *ADVERB*

adversity *NOUN* adversities
trouble or misfortune

advert *NOUN* adverts
(*British*) (*informal*) an advertisement

advertise *VERB* advertises, advertising, advertised
❶ to give out information about the good features of a product or service in order

to get people to buy it or use it ❷ to make something publicly known • *The meeting which was advertised for the evening of November 7th.* ❸ to give information about someone you need for a job • *A local firm was advertising for a secretary.*
> **advertiser** *NOUN*

advertisement *NOUN* **advertisements**
a public notice or announcement, especially one advertising goods or services in newspapers, on posters or in broadcasts

advice *NOUN*
❶ telling someone what you think they should do ❷ a piece of information • *We received advice that the goods had been sent.*

> **SPELLING**
> Advice is a noun, e.g. • *a word of advice,* and advise is a verb, e.g. • *I advise you to forget the whole thing.*

advisable *ADJECTIVE*
that is the wise or sensible thing to do • *It may be advisable to drink bottled water when you are abroad.*
> **advisability** *NOUN*

advise *VERB* **advises, advising, advised**
❶ to tell someone what you think they should do ❷ to inform someone about something
> **adviser** *NOUN*
> **advisory** *ADJECTIVE*

advocate (say **ad**-vok-ayt) *VERB* **advocates, advocating, advocated**
to speak in favour of something; to recommend something • *We advocate changing the law.*

advocate (say **ad**-vok-at) *NOUN* **advocates**
❶ a person who recommends or publicly supports something • *She was a strong advocate of women's rights.* ❷ a lawyer presenting someone's case in a law court

aerial *NOUN* **aerials**
a wire or rod for receiving or transmitting radio or television signals

aerial *ADJECTIVE*
from or in the air or from an aircraft • *an aerial photograph*

aerobatics *PLURAL NOUN*
a spectacular display by flying aircraft
> **aerobatic** *ADJECTIVE*

aerobics *PLURAL NOUN*
exercises to improve your breathing and strengthen the heart and lungs
> **aerobic** *ADJECTIVE*

aerodrome *NOUN* **aerodromes**
(*British*) an old word for an airfield or small airport

aerodynamic *ADJECTIVE*
designed to move through the air quickly and easily

aeronautics *NOUN*
the study of aircraft and flying
> **aeronautic** *ADJECTIVE*
> **aeronautical** *ADJECTIVE*

aeroplane *NOUN* **aeroplanes**
(*British*) a flying vehicle with wings and at least one engine

aerosol *NOUN* **aerosols**
a container that holds a liquid under pressure and can let it out in a fine spray

aerospace *NOUN*
the industry of building aircraft, vehicles and equipment to be sent into space

aesthetic (say iss-**thet**-ik) *ADJECTIVE*
to do with beauty or art

afar *ADVERB*
far away • *The din was heard from afar.*

affable *ADJECTIVE*
polite and friendly
> **affably** *ADVERB*
> **affability** *NOUN*

affair *NOUN* **affairs**
❶ an event or matter • *Dinner time was a gloomy affair.* ❷ a brief romantic relationship between two people who are not married to each other

affairs *PLURAL NOUN*
the business and activities that are part of private or public life • *Keep out of my affairs.* • *current affairs*

affect *VERB* **affects, affecting, affected**
❶ to have an effect on someone or something; to influence them • *What we eat can affect our health.* ❷ to pretend to have or feel something • *She affected ignorance.*

> **SPELLING**
> Affect is a verb and is different from effect, which is a noun, e.g. • *the effects of climate change.*

affectation *NOUN* **affectations**
unnatural behaviour that is intended to impress other people

affected *ADJECTIVE*
unnatural and meant to impress other people

• *She was talking in a loud and affected voice.*

affection NOUN **affections**
a strong liking for a person

affectionate ADJECTIVE
showing affection; loving
➤ **affectionately** ADVERB

affidavit (say af-id-**ay**-vit) NOUN **affidavits**
a statement that someone has written down and sworn to be true, for use as legal evidence

affiliated ADJECTIVE
officially connected with a larger organization

affinity NOUN **affinities**
a close similarity, relationship or understanding between two things or people • *Italian has an affinity with Spanish.*

affirm VERB **affirms, affirming, affirmed**
to state something definitely or firmly
➤ **affirmation** NOUN

affirmative ADJECTIVE
that says 'yes' • *an affirmative reply*
Compare with **negative**.

affix (say a-**fiks**) VERB **affixes, affixing, affixed**
to affix something is to stick it on to something else • *A wax seal was affixed to the bottom of the document.*

affix (say **aff**-iks) NOUN **affixes**
a prefix or suffix

afflict VERB **afflicts, afflicting, afflicted**
to be afflicted with something unpleasant, such as a disease or problem, is to suffer from it • *He is afflicted with shyness.*
➤ **affliction** NOUN

affluent (say **af**-loo-ent) ADJECTIVE
having a lot of money; wealthy
➤ **affluence** NOUN

afford VERB **affords, affording, afforded**
❶ to have enough money to pay for something ❷ to be able to do something without suffering bad consequences • *We can't afford to make any more mistakes.* ❸ to have enough time to do something

afforestation NOUN
the planting of trees to form a forest

affray NOUN **affrays**
(*formal*) a fight or riot that takes place in public

affront VERB **affronts, affronting, affronted**
to insult or offend someone • *She looked affronted by this suggestion.*

affront NOUN **affronts**
an insult

afield ADVERB
at or to a distance; away from home • *Her travels took her as far afield as India.*

aflame ADJECTIVE & ADVERB
in flames; glowing • *His cheeks were aflame with embarrassment.*

afloat ADJECTIVE & ADVERB
floating; on the sea • *Somehow we kept the boat afloat.*

afoot ADJECTIVE
happening or likely to happen • *Great changes are afoot.*

aforesaid ADJECTIVE
mentioned previously

afraid ADJECTIVE
frightened or alarmed
➤ **I'm afraid** I am sorry; I regret • *I'm afraid I won't be able to come.*

afresh ADVERB
again; in a new way • *We must start afresh.*

African ADJECTIVE
to do with Africa or its people

African NOUN **Africans**
an African person

African Caribbean NOUN **African Caribbeans**
a person of African descent living in or coming from the Caribbean
➤ **African-Caribbean** ADJECTIVE

Afrikaans (say af-rik-**ahns**) NOUN
a language developed from Dutch, used in South Africa

Afrikaner (say af-rik-**ah**-ner) NOUN **Afrikaners**
a white person in South Africa whose language is Afrikaans

Afro-Caribbean NOUN & ADJECTIVE
African Caribbean

aft ADVERB
at or towards the back of a ship or aircraft

after PREPOSITION
❶ later than • *Come after dinner.* ❷ next in position or order • *Which letter comes after H?* ❸ trying to catch; following • *Run after him.* ❹ as a result of • *After the way he behaved, I won't invite him again.* ❺ in

imitation or honour of • *She is named after her aunt.* ❻ about or concerning • *He asked after you.*

after *ADVERB*
later • *They met again the summer after.*
➤ **after all** even though you thought something different would happen • *They've decided to stay at home after all.*

afterbirth *NOUN*
the placenta and other membranes that come out of the mother's womb after she has given birth

aftermath *NOUN*
events or circumstances that come after something bad or unpleasant • *Hundreds of families needed help in the aftermath of the earthquake.* (**WORD ORIGIN**) from *after* + *math*, which is a mowing of new grass. An *aftermath* was originally the new grass that grew up after the old grass had been mowed.

afternoon *NOUN* **afternoons**
the time from noon or lunchtime to evening

aftershave *NOUN*
a pleasant-smelling lotion that men put on their skin after shaving

afterthought *NOUN* **afterthoughts**
something you think of or add later

afterwards *ADVERB*
after that; at a later time

again *ADVERB*
❶ another time; once more • *Let's try again.*
❷ as before • *You will soon be well again.*

SPELLING
The end of **again** is spelt **ain**.

against *PREPOSITION*
❶ touching or hitting • *He was leaning against the wall.* ❷ opposed to; not in favour of • *It is against the law.* • *They voted against the proposal.* ❸ in order to protect you from • *Vitamin C helps to protect us against infection.*

age *NOUN* **ages**
❶ how old you are; the length of time a person has lived or a thing has existed ❷ a special period of history or geology • *the Bronze Age* • *the ice age*
➤ **ages** *PLURAL NOUN*
(*informal*) a very long time • *We've been waiting for ages.*
➤ **come of age** to reach the age when you have an adult's legal rights and obligations (normally 18 years)

age *VERB* **ages, ageing, aged**
to become old or to make someone old

aged *ADJECTIVE*
❶ (say ayjd) having the age of • *a girl aged 9*
❷ (say **ay**-jid) very old • *an aged man*

age group *NOUN* **age groups**
people who are all about the same age
• *Anyone in the 10-12 age group would enjoy this book.*

agency *NOUN* **agencies**
an office or business that provides a special service • *a travel agency*

agenda (say a-**jen**-da) *NOUN* **agendas**
a list of things that people have to do or talk about at a meeting • *What is the next item on the agenda?* (**WORD ORIGIN**) Latin, = things that have to be done

agent *NOUN* **agents**
❶ a person or business that organizes things for other people • *a travel agent* ❷ a spy
• *a secret agent*

agglomeration *NOUN* **agglomerations**
a mass of things collected together

aggravate *VERB* **aggravates, aggravating, aggravated**
❶ to make a thing worse or more serious
• *Pollution can aggravate asthma.*
❷ (*informal*) to annoy someone
➤ **aggravation** *NOUN*
(**WORD ORIGIN**) from Latin *gravare* = make something heavy

aggregate (say **ag**-rig-at) *ADJECTIVE*
combined or total • *the aggregate amount*

aggregate *NOUN* **aggregates**
a total amount or score

aggression *NOUN*
starting an attack or war; aggressive behaviour

aggressive *ADJECTIVE*
likely to attack people; forceful • *an aggressive dog*
➤ **aggressively** *ADVERB*

aggressor *NOUN* **aggressors**
the person or nation that started an attack or war

aggrieved (say a-**greevd**) *ADJECTIVE*
resentful because you think you have been treated unfairly • *There was an aggrieved tone in her voice.*

aghast ADJECTIVE
shocked and horrified • *She stared at him aghast.*

agile ADJECTIVE
moving quickly or easily
➤ **agilely** ADVERB

agility NOUN
the ability to move quickly or easily • *She scrambled up the rocks with great agility.*

agitate VERB agitates, agitating, agitated
❶ to make someone feel upset or anxious ❷ to shake something about
➤ **agitation** NOUN

agitated ADJECTIVE
showing that you are anxious or nervous • *He was getting increasingly agitated.*

aglow ADJECTIVE
glowing • *His face was aglow with enthusiasm.*

agnostic (say ag-**nost**-ik) NOUN agnostics
a person who believes that it is impossible to know whether God exists
➤ **agnosticism** NOUN

ago ADVERB
in the past • *She died three years ago.*

agog ADJECTIVE
eager and excited (WORD ORIGIN) from French *en gogues* = in a happy mood, ready for fun

agonizing (also **agonising**) ADJECTIVE
❶ causing great pain or suffering • *an agonizing death* ❷ an agonizing choice or decision is one that you find very difficult to make

agony NOUN agonies
very great pain or suffering

agoraphobia (say ag-er-a-**foh**-bee-a) NOUN
abnormal fear of being in open spaces
(WORD ORIGIN) from Greek *agora* = market place, + **phobia**

agree VERB agrees, agreeing, agreed
❶ to agree with someone is to think or say the same as they do • *I agree that we need to act quickly.* ❷ to agree to do something is to say that you are willing to • *She agreed to come.* ❸ to suit a person's health or digestion • *Spicy food doesn't agree with me.* ❹ to correspond in grammatical number, gender or person. In 'They were good teachers' *they* agrees with *teachers* (both are plural forms) and *were* agrees with *they*; *was* would be incorrect because it is singular.

agreeable ADJECTIVE
❶ willing to agree to something • *We shall go if you are agreeable.* ❷ pleasant or enjoyable • *a most agreeable surprise*
➤ **agreeably** ADVERB

agreement NOUN agreements
❶ having the same opinion • *Are we in agreement?* ❷ an arrangement that people have agreed on

agriculture NOUN
cultivating land on a large scale and rearing livestock; farming
➤ **agricultural** ADJECTIVE

aground ADVERB & ADJECTIVE
stuck on the bottom in shallow water • *The ship had run aground.*

ah EXCLAMATION
a cry of surprise, pity, admiration, etc.

ahead ADVERB
❶ further forward; in front • *The road ahead was blocked.* ❷ before; more advanced • *They arrived a few minutes ahead of us.* ❸ winning • *Our team was ahead by five points.*

ahoy EXCLAMATION
a shout used by sailors to attract attention

aid NOUN aids
❶ help • *She walks with the aid of a stick.* • *His friends rushed to his aid.* ❷ something that helps someone to do something more easily • *a hearing aid* ❸ money, food, etc. sent to another country to help it • *overseas aid*
➤ **in aid of** for the purpose of; to help something

aid VERB aids, aiding, aided
to help someone

aide NOUN aides
an assistant

Aids NOUN
a disease caused by the HIV virus, which greatly weakens a person's ability to resist infections (WORD ORIGIN) from the initial letters of 'acquired immune deficiency syndrome'

ail VERB ails, ailing, ailed (old use)
to make a person ill or troubled • *What ails you?*

ailing ADJECTIVE
❶ ill; in poor health • *her ailing grandfather* ❷ in difficulties; not successful • *the ailing ship industry*

ailment *NOUN* ailments
a slight illness

aim *VERB* aims, aiming, aimed
❶ to point a gun or other weapon at a target ❷ to throw or kick a ball etc. in a particular direction ❸ to try or intend to do something • *We aim to leave after breakfast.*

aim *NOUN* aims
❶ aiming a gun or other weapon • *She took careful aim.* ❷ a purpose or intention • *The aim of the expedition was to reach the South Pole.*

aimless *ADJECTIVE*
without a definite aim or purpose • *They wandered around in an aimless manner.*
➤ **aimlessly** *ADVERB*

air *NOUN* airs
❶ the mixture of gases that surrounds the earth and which everyone breathes ❷ the space around and above things • *She through a ball into the air.* ❸ an appearance or impression of something • *an air of mystery* ❹ a grand or haughty manner • *He puts on airs.*
➤ **by air** in or by aircraft
➤ **in the air** probably going to happen soon • *A feeling of change was in the air.*
➤ **on the air** on radio or television

air *VERB* airs, airing, aired
❶ to put clothes etc. in a warm place to finish drying ❷ to allow air to circulate round a room ❸ to express an opinion or complaint • *People will have a chance to air their views.*

airborne *ADJECTIVE*
❶ an aircraft is airborne when it has taken off and is in flight ❷ carried by the air • *an airborne virus*

air-conditioning *NOUN*
a system for controlling the temperature, purity, etc. of the air in a room or building
➤ **air-conditioned** *ADJECTIVE*

aircraft *NOUN* aircraft
an aeroplane, glider or helicopter etc.

aircraft carrier *NOUN* aircraft carriers
a large ship with a long deck where aircraft can take off and land

airfield *NOUN* airfields
an area equipped with runways etc. where aircraft can take off and land

air force *NOUN* air forces
the part of a country's armed forces that is equipped with aircraft

airgun *NOUN* airguns
a gun in which compressed air shoots a pellet or dart

airily *ADVERB*
in a casual way that shows you are not treating something as serious • *'Oh, nothing,' she replied airily.*

airline *NOUN* airlines
a company that provides a regular service of transport by aircraft

airliner *NOUN* airliners
a large aircraft for carrying passengers

airlock *NOUN* airlocks
❶ a compartment with an airtight door at each end, through which people can go in and out of a pressurized chamber ❷ a bubble of air that stops liquid flowing through a pipe

airmail *NOUN*
letters and parcels carried by air

airman *NOUN* airmen
a man who is a member of an air force or of the crew of an aircraft

airport *NOUN* airports
a place where aircraft land and take off, with passenger terminals and other buildings

air raid *NOUN* air raids
an attack by aircraft, in which bombs are dropped

airship *NOUN* airships
a large balloon with engines, designed to carry passengers or goods

airstrip *NOUN* airstrips
a strip of ground prepared for aircraft to land and take off

airtight *ADJECTIVE*
not letting air in or out • *an airtight container*

airy *ADJECTIVE*
❶ with plenty of fresh air • *The room was cool and airy.* ❷ casual and not treating something as serious • *He dismissed her with an airy wave of the hand.*

aisle (rhymes with mile) *NOUN* aisles
❶ a passage between rows of seats, pews in a church or shelves in a supermarket ❷ a side part of a church

ajar *ADVERB & ADJECTIVE*
slightly open • *Please leave the door ajar.*

akimbo *ADVERB*
➤ **arms akimbo** with hands on hips and elbows out

a
b
c
d
e
f
g
h
i
j
k
l
m
n
o
p
q
r
s
t
u
v
w
x
y
z

akin ADJECTIVE
related or similar to • *a feeling akin to regret*

alabaster (say **al**-a-bast-er) NOUN
a kind of hard white stone

à la carte ADJECTIVE & ADVERB
ordered and paid for as separate items from a menu (WORD ORIGIN) French, = from the menu

alacrity NOUN
speed and willingness • *She accepted the invitation with alacrity.*

alarm NOUN **alarms**
❶ a warning sound or signal; a piece of equipment for giving this ❷ a feeling of fear or worry • *He cried out in alarm.* ❸ an alarm clock

alarm VERB **alarms, alarming, alarmed**
to make someone frightened or anxious • *I'm sorry, I didn't mean to alarm you.*
➤ **alarming** ADJECTIVE
(WORD ORIGIN) from Italian *all' arme!* = to arms! (a call to go and fight)

alarm clock NOUN **alarm clocks**
a clock that can be set to ring or bleep at a fixed time to wake someone who is asleep

alas EXCLAMATION
a cry of sorrow

albatross NOUN **albatrosses**
a large seabird with very long wings

albino (say al-**been**-oh) NOUN **albinos**
a person or animal with no colouring pigment in the skin and hair (which are white)

album NOUN **albums**
❶ a book with blank pages in which you keep a collection of photographs, stamps, autographs, etc. ❷ a collection of songs on a CD, record or other medium (WORD ORIGIN) Latin, = white piece of stone etc. on which to write things

albumen (say **al**-bew-min) NOUN
the white of an egg

alchemy (say **al**-kim-ee) NOUN
an early form of chemistry, the chief aim of which was to turn ordinary metals into gold
➤ **alchemist** NOUN
(WORD ORIGIN) from Arabic *al-kimiya* = the art of changing metals

alcohol NOUN
❶ a colourless liquid made by fermenting sugar or starch ❷ drinks containing this liquid (e.g. wine, beer, whisky), that can make people drunk

alcoholic ADJECTIVE
containing alcohol

alcoholic NOUN **alcoholics**
a person who is seriously addicted to alcohol
➤ **alcoholism** NOUN

alcove NOUN **alcoves**
a section of a room that is set back from the main part

alder NOUN **alders**
a kind of tree, often growing in marshy places

alderman (say **awl**-der-man) NOUN **aldermen**
a senior member of an English county or borough council

ale NOUN **ales**
a type of beer

alert ADJECTIVE
watching for something; ready to act
• *Security guards need to be alert at all times.*
➤ **alertness** NOUN

alert NOUN **alerts**
a warning or alarm
➤ **on the alert** on the lookout for danger or attack; watchful • *Be on the alert for any sign of trouble.*

alert VERB **alerts, alerting, alerted**
to warn someone of danger etc.; to make someone aware of something • *A knock on the door alerted her to their arrival.*
(WORD ORIGIN) from Italian *all' erta!* = to the watchtower!

A level NOUN **A levels**
(in the UK except Scotland) an exam in a subject taken by school students aged 16-18, or the course leading up to it; short for Advanced Level

alfresco ADJECTIVE & ADVERB
in the open air • *an alfresco meal*

algae (say **al**-jee) PLURAL NOUN
plants that grow in water, with no true stems or leaves

algebra (say **al**-jib-ra) NOUN
mathematics in which letters and symbols are used to represent quantities
➤ **algebraic** (say al-jib-**ray**-ik) ADJECTIVE
(WORD ORIGIN) from Arabic *al-jabr* = putting together broken parts

algorithm NOUN **algorithms**
a process or set of rules a computer uses to make calculations or to solve a problem

alias (say **ay**-lee-as) NOUN aliases
a false or different name • *He was travelling under the alias 'John Brown'.*

alias ADVERB
also named • *Clark Kent, alias Superman*

alibi (say **al**-i-by) NOUN alibis
evidence that a person accused of a crime was somewhere else when it was committed

alien (say **ay**-lee-en) NOUN aliens
❶ in stories, a being from another world ❷ a person who is not a citizen of the country where he or she is living; a foreigner

alien ADJECTIVE
❶ foreign ❷ not natural or familiar • *Cruelty is alien to her nature.*

alienate (say **ay**-lee-en-ayt) VERB alienates, alienating, alienated
to make someone less friendly or sympathetic towards you • *His comments have alienated a lot of local people.*

alight ADJECTIVE
❶ on fire • *The roof was soon alight.* ❷ bright or shining • *Her face was alight with joy.*

alight VERB alights, alighting, alighted
❶ to get out of a vehicle or down from a horse etc. • *The lady alighted from her carriage.* ❷ to fly down and settle • *The bird alighted on a nearby branch.*

align (say al-**yn**) VERB aligns, aligning, aligned
to arrange things so they are in the correct position or form a straight line • *Make sure the wheels are aligned properly.*
➤ **alignment** NOUN

alike ADJECTIVE
like one another • *The twins are very alike.*

alike ADVERB
in the same way • *He treats everybody alike.*

alimentary canal NOUN alimentary canals
the tube along which food passes through the body

alive ADJECTIVE
❶ living ❷ you are alive to something when you are well aware of it • *She is alive to all the possible dangers.*

alkali (say **alk**-al-y) NOUN alkalis
a chemical substance that neutralizes an acid to form a salt
➤ **alkaline** ADJECTIVE

all DETERMINER
the whole number or amount of • *All my friends came.* • *No one had seen her all day.*

all PRONOUN
❶ everything • *That is all I know.*
❷ everybody • *So, are we all agreed?*

all ADVERB
❶ completely • *She was dressed all in white.*
❷ to each team or competitor • *The score is fifteen all.*
➤ **all there** (*informal*) having an alert mind
➤ **all the same** in spite of this; making no difference • *I like him, all the same.*

Allah NOUN
the Muslim name of God

allay (say a-**lay**) VERB allays, allaying, allayed
to calm or relieve an unpleasant feeling • *Even these assurances did not allay her fears.*

all-clear NOUN
a signal that a danger has passed

allegation (say al-ig-**ay**-shon) NOUN allegations
a statement accusing someone of doing something wrong, made without proof

allege (say a-**lej**) VERB alleges, alleging, alleged
to accuse someone of doing something wrong without being able to prove it • *He alleged that I had cheated.*
➤ **alleged** ADJECTIVE
➤ **allegedly** (say a-**lej**-id-lee) ADVERB

allegiance (say a-**lee**-jans) NOUN allegiances
loyal support • *an oath of allegiance*

allegory (say **al**-ig-er-ee) NOUN allegories
a story in which the characters and events represent or symbolize a deeper meaning, e.g. to teach a moral lesson
➤ **allegorical** (say al-ig-**o**-rik-al) ADJECTIVE

alleluia EXCLAMATION
praise to God

allergic ADJECTIVE
you are allergic to something that is normally safe when it makes you feel ill or unwell • *He is allergic to pollen, which gives him hay fever.*

allergy (say **al**-er-jee) NOUN allergies
a condition of the body that makes you react badly to something that is normally safe

alleviate (say a-**lee**-vee-ayt) VERB alleviates, alleviating, alleviated
to alleviate a pain or difficulty is to make it less severe
➤ **alleviation** NOUN

alley *NOUN* **alleys**
❶ a narrow street or passage ❷ a place where you can play skittles or tenpin bowling

alliance (say a-**leye**-ans) *NOUN* **alliances**
an agreement between countries or groups who wish to support each other and work together

allied *ADJECTIVE*
❶ joined as allies; on the same side • *allied forces* ❷ of the same kind; closely connected • *stories of allied interest*

alligator *NOUN* **alligators**
a large reptile of the crocodile family
WORD ORIGIN from Spanish *el lagarto* = the lizard

alliteration *NOUN*
the repetition of the same letter or sound at the beginning of several words, e.g. in *whisper words of wisdom*
SPELLING
There is a double **l** in **alliteration**, and only one **t** before the **er**.

allocate *VERB* **allocates, allocating, allocated**
to give things to a number of people
• *Everyone has been allocated a locker.*
➤ **allocation** *NOUN*

allot *VERB* **allots, allotting, allotted**
to give a number of things to different people
• *You have all been allotted tasks.*

allotment *NOUN* **allotments**
a small rented piece of public land used for growing vegetables, fruit or flowers

allow *VERB* **allows, allowing, allowed**
❶ to let someone do something • *Smoking is not allowed.* ❷ to decide on a certain amount for a particular purpose • *She was allowed £20 for travel expenses.*
➤ **allowable** *ADJECTIVE*
SPELLING
Allowed means to be permitted to do something, e.g. *Running in the corridors is not allowed.* Aloud means in a voice that can be heard, e.g. *He read the letter aloud.*

allowance *NOUN* **allowances**
an amount of money that is given regularly for a particular purpose
➤ **make allowances** to take something into consideration and excuse it • *We must make allowances for his age.*

alloy *NOUN* **alloys**
a metal formed by mixing two or more metals etc.

all right *ADJECTIVE & ADVERB*
❶ satisfactory ❷ in good condition ❸ yes, I agree
SPELLING
All right is two words, not one.

all-round *ADJECTIVE*
(*British*) able to do many different things well; general • *an all-round athlete*
➤ **all-rounder** *NOUN*

allude *VERB* **alludes, alluding, alluded**
to mention something briefly or indirectly
• *He alluded to an incident the previous day.*

allure *VERB* **allures, alluring, allured**
to attract or fascinate someone
➤ **allure** *NOUN*

alluring *ADJECTIVE*
attractive or fascinating • *The offer was an alluring one.*

allusion *NOUN* **allusions**
a reference made to something without actually naming it

ally (say **al**-eye) *NOUN* **allies**
❶ a country that has agreed to support another country ❷ a person who cooperates with another person

ally *VERB* **allies, allying, allied**
to form an alliance • *Saruman the wizard allied himself with Sauron.*

almanac *NOUN* **almanacs**
an annual publication containing a calendar and other information

almighty *ADJECTIVE*
❶ having complete power ❷ (*informal*) very great • *an almighty row*
➤ **the Almighty** a name for God

almond (say **ah**-mond) *NOUN* **almonds**
an oval edible nut

almost *ADVERB*
near to being something but not quite • *I am almost ready.*

alms (say ahmz) *PLURAL NOUN* (*old use*)
money and gifts given to the poor

almshouse *NOUN* **almshouses**
a house founded by charity for poor people

aloft *ADVERB*
high up; up in the air • *He held the lamp aloft.*

alone *ADJECTIVE & ADVERB*
without any other people or things; without help

along *PREPOSITION*
following the length of something • *Walk along the path.*

along *ADVERB*
❶ on or onwards • *Push it along.*
❷ accompanying somebody • *I've brought my brother along.*

alongside *PREPOSITION & ADVERB*
next to something; beside • *The boat drew alongside.*

aloof *ADVERB*
apart; not taking part • *We kept aloof from their quarrels.*

aloof *ADJECTIVE*
distant and not friendly in manner • *She seemed aloof.*

aloud *ADVERB*
in a voice that can be heard

> **SPELLING**
> Aloud is different from **allowed** • *He read the letter aloud.* • *Running in the corridors is not allowed.*

alpha *NOUN*
the first letter of the Greek alphabet, equivalent to Roman *A, a*

alphabet *NOUN* **alphabets**
the letters used in a language, arranged in a set order **WORD ORIGIN** from **alpha**, **beta**, the first two letters of the Greek alphabet

alphabetical *ADJECTIVE*
to do with the alphabet • *The names are listed in alphabetical order.*
➤ **alphabetically** *ADVERB*

alpine *ADJECTIVE*
to do with high mountains • *alpine plants* **WORD ORIGIN** from the Alps, mountains in Switzerland

already *ADVERB*
by now; before now

Alsatian (say al-**say**-shan) *NOUN* **Alsatians**
a German shepherd dog

also *ADVERB*
in addition; besides

altar *NOUN* **altars**
a table or similar structure used in religious ceremonies

> **SPELLING**
> Take care not to confuse with the verb **alter**.

alter *VERB* **alters, altering, altered**
to make something different in some way; to become different • *We've altered our plans.*

> **SPELLING**
> Take care not to confuse with the noun **altar**.

alteration *NOUN* **alterations**
a change you make to something • *The jacket needed a few alterations.*

altercation (say ol-ter-**kay**-shon) *NOUN* **altercations**
a noisy argument or quarrel

alter ego (say ol-ter **ee**-go) *NOUN* **alter egos**
another, very different, side of someone's personality • *Superman's alter ego, Clark Kent* **WORD ORIGIN** Latin, = other self

alternate (say ol-**tern**-at) *ADJECTIVE*
❶ coming in turns, one after the other • *The snake had alternate rings of red and black.* ❷ one in every two • *We meet up on alternate Fridays.*

> **USAGE**
> The words **alternate** and **alternative** have different meanings. See the note at **alternative**.

alternate (say **ol**-tern-ayt) *VERB* **alternates, alternating, alternated**
to use or come in turns, one after the other • *She alternated between excitement and nerves.* • *Blue stripes alternate with red ones.*
➤ **alternation** *NOUN*

alternately *ADVERB*
in turns, one after the other • *The sky looked alternately bright, then cloudy.*

alternating current *NOUN* **alternating currents**
electric current that keeps reversing its direction at regular intervals

alternative *ADJECTIVE*
for you to choose instead of something else
• *Is there an alternative route?*
➤ **alternatively** *ADVERB*

USAGE
Do not confuse alternative with alternate. If there are *alternative colours* it means that there is a choice of two or more colours, but *alternate colours* means that there is first one colour and then the other.

alternative *NOUN* **alternatives**
one of two or more things that you can choose between • *Technology has given us alternatives to fossil fuels.*
➤ **no alternative** no choice

alternative medicine *NOUN*
types of medical treatment that are not part of ordinary medicine. Acupuncture, homeopathy and osteopathy are all forms of alternative medicine.

although *CONJUNCTION*
though; in spite of the fact that

SPELLING
There is only one l in **although**.

altimeter *NOUN* **altimeters**
an instrument used in aircraft etc. for showing the height above sea level

altitude *NOUN* **altitudes**
the height of something, especially above sea level • *an altitude of 10,000 metres*

alto *NOUN* **altos**
❶ an adult male singer with a very high voice ❷ a female singer with a low voice

altogether *ADVERB*
❶ with all included; in total • *There were six of us altogether.* ❷ completely • *The stream dries up altogether in summer.* ❸ on the whole • *Altogether, it was a good concert.*

SPELLING
Altogether is different from all together, which means together in a group
• *They wanted to be all together for the photographs.*

altruistic (say al-troo-**ist**-ik) *ADJECTIVE*
unselfish; thinking of other people's welfare
➤ **altruism** *NOUN*

aluminium *NOUN*
a lightweight silver-coloured metal

always *ADVERB*
❶ at all times • *He has always been very strict.* ❷ often or constantly • *You are always crying.* ❸ whatever happens • *You can always sleep on the floor.*

Alzheimer's disease *NOUN*
a serious disease of the brain which affects mainly older people and makes them confused and forgetful **WORD ORIGIN** named after a German scientist, A. *Alzheimer*

a.m. *ABBREVIATION*
before 12 o'clock midday **WORD ORIGIN** short for Latin *ante meridiem* = before noon

amalgam *NOUN* **amalgams**
❶ an alloy of mercury ❷ a mixture or combination

amalgamate *VERB* **amalgamates, amalgamating, amalgamated**
to mix or combine things

amass *VERB* **amasses, amassing, amassed**
to heap up or collect something • *By the time he died, he had amassed a fortune.*

amateur (say **am**-at-er) *NOUN* **amateurs**
a person who does something for pleasure, not for money as a job • *an amateur painter*
WORD ORIGIN from Latin *amator* = lover

amateurish *ADJECTIVE*
not done or made very well; not skilful

amaze *VERB* **amazes, amazing, amazed**
to surprise somebody greatly; to be difficult for somebody to believe • *It amazes me that anyone could be so stupid.*

amazed *ADJECTIVE*
very surprised • *He was amazed to discover the truth.*

amazement *NOUN*
a feeling of great surprise • *She stared at him in amazement.*

amazing *ADJECTIVE*
very surprising or remarkable; difficult to believe

ambassador *NOUN* **ambassadors**
a person sent to a foreign country to represent his or her own government

amber *NOUN*
❶ a hard clear yellowish substance used for making jewellery and ornaments ❷ a yellow traffic light shown as a signal for caution, placed between red for 'stop' and green for 'go'

ambidextrous *ADJECTIVE*
able to use either your left hand or your right hand equally well **WORD ORIGIN** from Latin

ambo = both + *dextrous* = skilful (related to dexterity)

ambiguous *ADJECTIVE*
having more than one possible meaning; unclear • *His reply was ambiguous.*
➤ **ambiguity** *NOUN*

> **SPELLING**
> Do not forget the **u** before the **ous** in ambiguous.

ambition *NOUN* ambitions
❶ a strong desire to do well and be successful ❷ something you want to do very much • *Her ambition is to be world champion.*

ambitious *ADJECTIVE*
❶ wanting very much to do well and be successful ❷ difficult or challenging • *an ambitious plan*

amble *VERB* ambles, ambling, ambled
to walk at a slow easy pace • *We ambled down to the beach.*

ambrosia (say am-**broh**-zee-a) *NOUN*
something delicious **WORD ORIGIN** in Greek mythology, ambrosia was the food of the gods

ambulance *NOUN* ambulances
a vehicle equipped to take sick or injured people to hospital **WORD ORIGIN** from French *hôpital ambulant*, a mobile military hospital; from Latin *ambulare* = walk

ambush *NOUN* ambushes
a surprise attack from a hidden place

ambush *VERB* ambushes, ambushing, ambushed
to attack someone after lying in wait for them

amen *EXCLAMATION*
a word used at the end of a prayer or hymn, meaning 'may it be so'

amenable (say a-**meen**-a-bul) *ADJECTIVE*
willing to accept or try out a suggestion or idea

amend *VERB* amends, amending, amended
to change something slightly in order to improve it

amend *NOUN*
➤ **make amends** to make up for having done something wrong

amendment *NOUN* amendments
a change that is made to a piece of writing, especially to a law

amenity (say a-**men**-it-ee or a-**meen**-it-ee) *NOUN* amenities

a pleasant or useful feature of a place • *The town has many amenities, such as a sports centre and a multiplex cinema.*

American *ADJECTIVE*
❶ to do with the continent of America ❷ to do with the United States of America
➤ **American** *NOUN*

amethyst *NOUN* amethysts
a purple precious stone **WORD ORIGIN** from Greek *lithos amethystos* = stone against drunkenness (because people believed that they would not get drunk if there was an amethyst in their drink)

amiable *ADJECTIVE*
friendly and good-tempered
➤ **amiably** *ADVERB*

amicable *ADJECTIVE*
done in a friendly way, without argument
➤ **amicably** *ADVERB*

amid, amidst *PREPOSITION*
in the middle of; among

amino acid (say a-**meen**-oh) *NOUN* amino acids
an acid found in proteins

amiss *ADJECTIVE*
wrong or faulty • *She knew something was amiss.*
➤ **not go amiss** to be useful or pleasant • *Another piece of cake wouldn't go amiss.*
➤ **take something amiss** to be offended or upset by something • *Don't take what I'm about to say amiss.*

ammonia *NOUN*
a colourless gas or liquid with a strong smell

ammunition *NOUN*
a supply of bullets, shells, grenades, etc. for use in fighting

amnesia (say am-**nee**-zee-a) *NOUN*
loss of memory

amnesty *NOUN* amnesties
a general pardon for people who have committed a crime **WORD ORIGIN** from Greek *amnestia* = forgetfulness (because the crimes are legally 'forgotten')

amoeba (say a-**mee**-ba) *NOUN* amoebas
a microscopic creature consisting of a single cell which constantly changes shape and can split itself in two

A
amok *ADVERB*
➤ **run amok** to rush about wildly in a violent rage
WORD ORIGIN from Malay (a language spoken in Malaysia), = fighting mad

among, amongst *PREPOSITION*
❶ surrounded by; in the middle of • *There were weeds among the flowers.* ❷ between • *Divide the sweets among the children.*

amoral (say ay-**mor**al) *ADJECTIVE*
not based on moral standards; neither moral nor immoral

amorous *ADJECTIVE*
showing or feeling love or passion • *amorous glances*

amorphous (say a-**mor**-fus) *ADJECTIVE*
shapeless • *an amorphous mass*

amount *NOUN* amounts
❶ a quantity ❷ a total

amount *VERB* amounts, amounting, amounted
➤ **amount to** ❶ to add up to • *The damage amounted to $3 million.* ❷ to be equivalent to • *Their reply amounts to a refusal.*
WORD ORIGIN from Latin *ad montem* = to the mountain, upwards

amp *NOUN* amps
❶ an ampere ❷ (*informal*) an amplifier

ampere (say **am**-pair) *NOUN* amperes
a unit for measuring electric current
WORD ORIGIN named after the French scientist A. M. *Ampère*

ampersand *NOUN* ampersands
the symbol &, which means 'and'
WORD ORIGIN from the phrase *and per se and* = '& by itself means and' (Latin *per se* = by itself). The symbol '&' was added to the end of the alphabet in children's school books, and when they came to it, pupils reciting the alphabet would say the phrase; they thought it was the name of the symbol

amphetamine *NOUN* amphetamines
a drug used as a stimulant

amphibian *NOUN* amphibians
❶ an animal able to live both on land and in water, such as a frog, toad, newt and salamander ❷ a vehicle that can move on both land and water **WORD ORIGIN** from Greek *amphi* = around + *bios* = life

amphibious *ADJECTIVE*
able to live or move both on land and in water

amphitheatre *NOUN* amphitheatres
an oval or circular building without a roof and with rows of seats round a central arena
WORD ORIGIN from Greek *amphi* = all round, + **theatre**

ample *ADJECTIVE*
❶ quite enough • *We've got ample time.*
❷ large • *This car has an ample boot.*

amplifier *NOUN* amplifiers
a piece of equipment for making a sound or electrical signal louder or stronger

amplify *VERB* amplifies, amplifying, amplified
❶ to make a sound or electrical signal louder or stronger ❷ to give more details about something • *Could you amplify that point?*
➤ **amplification** *NOUN*

amplitude *NOUN*
(*in science*) the greatest distance that a wave, especially a sound wave, vibrates

amply *ADVERB*
generously; with as much as you need or even more • *You will be amply rewarded.*

amputate *VERB* amputates, amputating, amputated
to cut off an arm or leg by a surgical operation
➤ **amputation** *NOUN*

amuse *VERB* amuses, amusing, amused
❶ to make a person laugh or smile ❷ to amuse yourself is to find pleasant things to do

amusement *NOUN* amusements
❶ a game or activity that makes time pass pleasantly ❷ being amused

amusement arcade *NOUN* amusement arcades
(*British*) an indoor area where people can play on automatic game machines

amusement park *NOUN* amusement parks
a large outdoor area with fairground rides and other amusements

amusing *ADJECTIVE*
making you laugh or smile

an *DETERMINER*
see a

anachronism (say an-**ak**-ron-izm) *NOUN* anachronisms
something wrongly placed in a particular historical period or regarded as out of date • *Bows and arrows would be an anachronism in modern warfare.* **WORD ORIGIN** from Greek *ana* = backwards + *khronos* = time

anaemia (say a-**nee**-mee-a) NOUN
a lack of red cells or iron in the blood, that makes a person pale and tired
➤ **anaemic** ADJECTIVE

anaesthesia NOUN
❶ the use of anaesthetic during medical operations ❷ the state of being unable to feel pain

anaesthetic (say an-iss-**thet**-ik) NOUN anaesthetics
a substance or gas that makes you unable to feel pain

anaesthetist (say an-**ees**-thet-ist) NOUN anaesthetists
a person trained to give anaesthetics
➤ **anaesthetize** VERB

anagram NOUN anagrams
a word or phrase made by rearranging the letters of another • *'Strap' is an anagram of 'parts'.*

anal (say **ay**-nal) ADJECTIVE
to do with the anus

analgesic (say an-al-**jee**-sik) NOUN analgesics
a substance that relieves pain

analogous (say a-**nal**-o-gus) ADJECTIVE
similar in some ways to something else and so able to be compared with it • *In the poem sleep is thought to be analogous to death.*

analogy (say a-**nal**-oj-ee) NOUN analogies
a comparison or similarity between two things that are alike in some ways • *the analogy between the human heart and a pump*

analyse VERB analyses, analysing, analysed
❶ to examine and interpret something • *This book analyses the causes of the war.* ❷ to separate something into its parts

analysis NOUN analyses
❶ a detailed examination of something ❷ a separation of something into its parts
➤ **analytical** ADJECTIVE

analyst NOUN analysts
a person who analyses things

anarchist (say **an**-er-kist) NOUN anarchists
a person who believes that all forms of government are bad and should be abolished

anarchy (say **an**-er-kee) NOUN
❶ lack of government or control, leading to a breakdown in law and order ❷ complete disorder

anathema (say an-**ath**-em-a) NOUN
something that you detest • *All blood sports are anathema to me.*

anatomy (say an-**at**-om-ee) NOUN
❶ the study of the structure of the bodies of humans or animals ❷ the structure of an animal's body
➤ **anatomical** ADJECTIVE
➤ **anatomist** NOUN

ancestor NOUN ancestors
anyone from whom a person is descended
➤ **ancestral** ADJECTIVE

ancestry NOUN ancestries
your ancestry is the people from whom you are descended • *She was proud of her ancestry.*

anchor NOUN anchors
a heavy object joined to a ship by a chain or rope and dropped to the bottom of the sea to stop the ship from moving

anchor VERB anchors, anchoring, anchored
❶ to fix or be fixed by an anchor ❷ to fix something firmly • *Make sure the table is securely anchored.*

anchorage NOUN anchorages
a place where a ship can be anchored

anchovy NOUN anchovies
a small fish with a strong flavour

ancient ADJECTIVE
❶ very old ❷ belonging to the distant past
• *ancient history*

ancillary (say an-**sil**-er-ee) ADJECTIVE
helping or supporting the people who do the main work • *doctors, nurses and ancillary staff*

and CONJUNCTION
❶ together with; in addition to • *We had cakes and ice cream.* ❷ so that; with this result • *Ask them and they may be able to help.* ❸ to • *Go and bring another chair.*

android NOUN androids
(in science fiction) a robot that looks like a human being (**WORD ORIGIN**) from Greek *andros* = man

anecdote NOUN anecdotes
a short amusing or interesting story about a real person or thing

anemone (say a-**nem**-on-ee) NOUN anemones
a plant with cup-shaped red, purple or white flowers (**WORD ORIGIN**) from Greek, = windflower (from the belief that the flower opens when it is windy)

A B C D E F G H I J K L M N O P Q R S T U V W X Y Z

anew *ADVERB*
again; in a new or different way • *We must begin anew.*

angel *NOUN* **angels**
❶ an attendant or messenger of God
❷ a very kind or beautiful person
WORD ORIGIN from Greek *angelos* = messenger

angelic (say an-**jel**-ik) *ADJECTIVE*
kind or beautiful; like an angel • *an angelic smile*

angelica *NOUN*
a sweet-smelling plant whose crystallized stalks are used in cookery as a decoration

anger *NOUN*
a strong feeling that you want to quarrel or fight with someone

anger *VERB* **angers, angering, angered**
to make a person angry

angle *NOUN* **angles**
❶ the space between two lines or surfaces that meet; the amount by which a line or surface must be turned to make it lie along another ❷ a point of view • *She considered the problem from all angles.*

angle *VERB* **angles, angling, angled**
❶ to put something in a slanting position • *Ben angled his phone so Kate could see the screen.* ❷ to present news or a story from one point of view

angler *NOUN* **anglers**
a person who fishes with a fishing rod and line
➤ **angling** *NOUN*

Anglican *ADJECTIVE*
to do with the Church of England
➤ **Anglican** *NOUN*

Anglo-Saxon *NOUN* **Anglo-Saxons**
❶ an English person, especially of the time before the Norman conquest in 1066 ❷ the form of English spoken from about 700 to 1150; Old English **WORD ORIGIN** from Old English *Angulseaxe* = an English Saxon (contrasted with the Old Saxons on the Continent)

angry *ADJECTIVE* **angrier, angriest**
feeling that you want to quarrel or fight with someone
➤ **angrily** *ADVERB*

anguish *NOUN*
severe suffering or misery • *a cry of anguish*
➤ **anguished** *ADJECTIVE*

angular *ADJECTIVE*
❶ an angular person is bony and not plump • *his thin, angular face* ❷ having angles or sharp corners • *a design of angular shapes*

animal *NOUN* **animals**
❶ a living thing that can feel and usually move about • *Horses, birds, fish, bees and people are all animals.* ❷ a cruel or uncivilized person

animate *VERB* **animates, animating, animated**
❶ to make a thing lively ❷ to produce something as an animated film
➤ **animator** *NOUN*

animated *ADJECTIVE*
❶ lively and excited ❷ an animated film is one made by photographing a series of still pictures and showing them rapidly one after another, so they appear to move

animation *NOUN*
❶ being lively or excited ❷ the technique of making a film by photographing a series of still pictures

animosity (say an-im-**oss**-it-ee) *NOUN* **animosities**
a feeling of strong dislike and anger towards someone • *There was a lot of animosity in his voice.*

aniseed *NOUN*
a sweet-smelling seed used for flavouring things

ankle *NOUN* **ankles**
the part of the leg where it joins the foot

annals *PLURAL NOUN*
a history of events, especially when written year by year

annex *VERB* **annexes, annexing, annexed**
❶ to take control of another country or region by force • *Rome first annexed Cyprus in 58 BC.* ❷ to add or join a thing to something else

annexe *NOUN* **annexes**
a building added to a larger or more important building

annihilate (say an-**y**-il-ayt) *VERB* **annihilates, annihilating, annihilated**
to destroy something completely
➤ **annihilation** *NOUN*
WORD ORIGIN from Latin *nihil* = nothing

anniversary *NOUN* **anniversaries**
a day when you remember something special that happened on the same day in a previous year

annotate (say **an**-oh-tayt) *VERB* annotates, annotating, annotated
to add notes of explanation to something written or printed
➤ **annotation** *NOUN*

announce *VERB* announces, announcing, announced
to make something known, especially by saying it publicly or to an audience

announcement announcements *NOUN*
a statement that tells people about something publicly or officially • *Ladies and gentlemen, I'd like to make an announcement.*

announcer *NOUN* announcers
a person who announces items in a radio or television broadcast

annoy *VERB* annoys, annoying, annoyed
❶ to make a person slightly angry ❷ to be troublesome to someone

annoyance *NOUN* annoyances
❶ the feeling of being annoyed • *He bit his lip in annoyance.* ❷ something that annoys you • *Wasps are a great annoyance at a picnic.*

annual *ADJECTIVE*
❶ happening or done once a year • *her annual visit* ❷ calculated over one year • *our annual income* ❸ living for one year or one season • *an annual plant*
➤ **annually** *ADVERB*

annual *NOUN* annuals
❶ a book that comes out once a year ❷ a plant that lives for one year or one season

annuity (say a-**new**-it-ee) *NOUN* annuities
a fixed annual allowance of money, especially from a kind of investment

annul *VERB* annuls, annulling, annulled
to cancel a law or contract; to end something legally • *Their marriage was annulled.*
➤ **annulment** *NOUN*

anode *NOUN* anodes
the electrode by which electric current enters a device. Compare with **cathode**.

anoint *VERB* anoints, anointing, anointed
to put oil or ointment on someone or something, especially in a religious ceremony

anomaly (say an-**om**-al-ee) *NOUN* anomalies
something that does not follow the general rule or that is unlike the usual or normal kind

anon *ADVERB* (old use)
soon • *I will say more about this anon.*

anon. *ABBREVIATION*
anonymous

anonymous (say an-**on**-im-us) *ADJECTIVE*
without the name of the person responsible being known or made public • *an anonymous donation*
➤ **anonymously** *ADVERB*
➤ **anonymity** (say an-on-**im**-it-ee) *NOUN*

anorak *NOUN* anoraks
a thick warm jacket with a hood
WORD ORIGIN from an Inuit word

anorexia (say an-er-**eks**-ee-a) *NOUN*
an illness that makes a person so anxious to lose weight that he or she refuses to eat

anorexic *ADJECTIVE*
suffering from anorexia

another *DETERMINER & PRONOUN*
a different or extra person or thing • *another day* • *choose another*

answer *NOUN* answers
❶ a reply ❷ the solution to a problem

answer *VERB* answers, answering, answered
❶ to give or find an answer to a question or for a person asking it ❷ to respond to a signal • *Holly went to answer the phone.*
➤ **answer back** to be rude or cheeky in replying to someone
➤ **answer for something** to be punished for something or have to explain it
➤ **answer to the name of** to be called • *His dog answers to the name of Roxy.*

SPELLING
There is a silent w in **answer**.

answerable *ADJECTIVE*
having to explain your actions to someone; responsible for something

answering machine *NOUN* answering machines
a machine that records messages from people who telephone while you are out

answerphone *NOUN* answerphones
(*British*) a telephone answering machine

ant *NOUN* ants
a very small insect that lives as one of an organized group

antagonism (say an-**tag**-on-izm) *NOUN*
an unfriendly feeling; hostility • *She could not understand his antagonism towards her.*
➤ **antagonistic** *ADJECTIVE*

antagonist *NOUN* antagonists
your opponent in a fight or contest

a b c d e f g h i j k l m n o p q r s t u v w x y z

antagonize (also **antagonise**) _VERB_
antagonizes, antagonizing, antagonized
to do something to make someone angry with
you • _He didn't want to antagonize her any
further, so he kept quiet._

anteater _NOUN_ anteaters
an animal that feeds on ants and termites

antelope _NOUN_ antelope or antelopes
a fast-running animal like a deer, found in
Africa and parts of Asia

antenatal (say an-tee-**nay**-tal) _ADJECTIVE_
(_British_) to do with the period during
pregnancy before childbirth

antenna _NOUN_
❶ antennae a feeler on the head of an insect
or crustacean ❷ antennas an aerial

ante-room _NOUN_ ante-rooms
a room leading to a more important room

anthem _NOUN_ anthems
a religious or patriotic song, usually sung by a
choir or group of people

anther _NOUN_ anthers
the part of a flower's stamen that contains
pollen

anthill _NOUN_ anthills
a mound of earth over an ants' nest

anthology _NOUN_ anthologies
a collection of poems, stories, songs, etc. in
one book • _an anthology of ghost stories_
WORD ORIGIN from Greek _anthos_ = flower +
-_logia_ = collection

anthrax _NOUN_
a a very serious disease of sheep and cattle
that can also infect people

anthropoid _ADJECTIVE_
looking like a human being • _Gorillas are
anthropoid apes._

anthropology _NOUN_
the study of human beings and their customs
➤ **anthropological** _ADJECTIVE_
➤ **anthropologist** _NOUN_

anti– _PREFIX_
against or preventing something (as in
antifreeze)

anti–aircraft _ADJECTIVE_
used against enemy aircraft

antibiotic _NOUN_ antibiotics
a substance (e.g. penicillin) that destroys
bacteria or prevents them from growing

antibody _NOUN_ antibodies
a protein that forms in the blood as a defence
against certain substances which it then
attacks and destroys

anticipate _VERB_ anticipates, anticipating,
anticipated
❶ to expect something to happen and
be ready for it • _As he had anticipated, it
rained all afternoon._ ❷ to look forward to
something • _We are eagerly anticipating their
arrival._

anticipation _NOUN_
looking forward to something • _A ripple of
anticipation swept through the stadium._
➤ **in anticipation of** expecting something to
happen and being ready for it • _The table had
been set in anticipation of their visit._

anticlimax _NOUN_ anticlimaxes
a disappointing ending or result where
something exciting had been expected

anticlockwise _ADVERB & ADJECTIVE_
(_British_) moving in the opposite direction to
the hands of a clock

antics _PLURAL NOUN_
funny or foolish actions • _She couldn't help
laughing at his antics._

anticyclone _NOUN_ anticyclones
an area where air pressure is high, usually
producing fine settled weather

antidote _NOUN_ antidotes
something that takes away the bad effects of
a poison or disease

antifreeze _NOUN_
a liquid added to water to make it less likely
to freeze

antihistamine _NOUN_ antihistamines
a drug that protects people against
unpleasant effects when they are allergic to
something

antimony _NOUN_
a brittle silvery metal

antipathy (say an-**tip**-ath-ee) _NOUN_
a strong dislike • _He has always had an
antipathy to dogs._

antipodes (say an-**tip**-od-eez) _PLURAL NOUN_
➤ the Antipodes Australia, New Zealand and
the areas near them, in relation to Europe
➤ **Antipodean** _ADJECTIVE_
WORD ORIGIN from Greek, = having the feet
opposite (_podes_ = feet), because you have your
feet on the opposite side of the world from
Europe

antiquarian (say anti-**kwair**-ee-an) ADJECTIVE
to do with the study of antiques

antiquated ADJECTIVE
old-fashioned or out of date

antique (say an-**teek**) NOUN antiques
something that is valuable because it is very
old

antique ADJECTIVE
very old; belonging to the distant past

antiquities PLURAL NOUN
objects that were made in ancient times • *a
collection of Egyptian antiquities*

antiquity (say an-**tik**-wit-ee) NOUN
ancient times • *The statue was brought to
Rome in antiquity.*

anti-Semitic (say anti-sim-**it**-ik) ADJECTIVE
hostile or prejudiced towards Jews
➤ **anti-Semitism** (say anti-**sem**-it-izm) NOUN

antiseptic ADJECTIVE
❶ able to destroy bacteria, especially those
that cause things to become septic or to
decay ❷ thoroughly clean and free from
germs

antiseptic NOUN antiseptics
a substance with an antiseptic effect

antisocial ADJECTIVE
unfriendly or inconsiderate towards other
people • *antisocial behaviour*

antithesis (say an-**tith**-iss-iss) NOUN
antitheses
the antithesis of something is the exact
opposite • *His brother's personality was the
antithesis of his own.*

antivirus ADJECTIVE
designed to find and destroy computer
viruses • *antivirus software*

antivivisectionist NOUN antivivisectionists
a person who is opposed to carrying out
experiments on live animals

antler NOUN antlers
the horn of a deer, which divides into several
branches

antonym (say **ant**-on-im) NOUN antonyms
a word that is opposite in meaning to another
• *'Soft' is an antonym of 'hard'.*

> GRAMMAR
> See also the panel on **synonyms and
> antonyms**.

anus (say **ay**-nus) NOUN anuses
the opening at the lower end of the

alimentary canal, through which solid waste
matter leaves the body

anvil NOUN anvils
a large block of iron on which a blacksmith
hammers metal into shape

anxiety NOUN anxieties
❶ anxiety is a feeling of being worried ❷ an
anxiety is something that you are worried
about

anxious ADJECTIVE
❶ worried and slightly afraid ❷ wanting to
do something very much • *She is anxious to
please us.*
➤ **anxiously** ADVERB

any DETERMINER & PRONOUN
❶ one or some • *Have you any wool?* • *There
isn't any.* ❷ no matter which • *Come any day
you like.* ❸ every • *Any fool knows that!*

any ADVERB
at all; in some degree • *Is it any good?*

anybody PRONOUN
any person

anyhow ADVERB
❶ anyway; in any case • *Anyhow, it doesn't
matter.* ❷ (*informal*) carelessly; in no special
way • *Things had been put on the floor
anyhow.*

anyone PRONOUN
anybody

anything PRONOUN
any thing

anyway ADVERB
whatever happens; whatever the situation
may be • *If it rains, we'll go anyway.*

anywhere ADVERB
in or to any place

anywhere PRONOUN
any place • *Anywhere will do.*

aorta (say ay-**or**-ta) NOUN aortas
the main artery that carries blood away from
the left side of the heart

apace ADVERB
quickly • *The darkness grew apace.*

apart ADVERB
❶ away from each other; separately • *The
trees were planted far apart.* ❷ into pieces
• *It fell apart.* ❸ excluded • *Joking apart,
what do you think of it?*
➤ **apart from** excluding, other than • *Apart
from a banana, he'd eaten nothing all day.*

apartheid (say a-**part**-hayt) *NOUN*
the political policy that used to be practised in South Africa, of keeping people of different races apart

apartment *NOUN* **apartments**
❶ a set of rooms ❷ (*North American*) a flat

apathy (say **ap**-ath-ee) *NOUN*
not having much interest in or caring about something • *There is widespread apathy among the voters.*

ape *NOUN* **apes**
any of the four kinds of monkey (gorillas, chimpanzees, orangutans, gibbons) that do not have a tail

ape *VERB* **apes, aping, aped**
to copy or imitate something, often in a ridiculous way • *She aped his expression of horror.*

aperture *NOUN* **apertures**
an opening

apex (say **ay**-peks) *NOUN* **apexes**
the tip or highest point • *the apex of a triangle*

aphid (say **ay**-fid) *NOUN* **aphids**
a tiny insect (e.g. a greenfly) that sucks the juices from plants

aphis (say **ay**-fiss) *NOUN* **aphides** (say **ay**-fid-eez)
an aphid

apiece *ADVERB*
to, for or by each • *They cost fifty cents apiece.*

aplomb (say a-**plom**) *NOUN*
dignity and confidence • *She handled the crisis with great aplomb.*

apocryphal (say a-**pok**-rif-al) *ADJECTIVE*
not likely to be true; invented • *This account of his travels is apocryphal.*

apologetic *ADJECTIVE*
showing or saying that you are sorry • *She gave him an apologetic smile.*
➤ **apologetically** *ADVERB*

apologize (also **apologise**) *VERB* **apologizes, apologizing, apologized**
to tell someone that you are sorry for something you have done • *I apologize for my behaviour yesterday.*

apology *NOUN* **apologies**
❶ a statement saying that you are sorry for doing something wrong or badly

❷ something very poor • *this feeble apology for a meal*

apoplectic (say ap-o-**plek**-tik) *ADJECTIVE*
violently or fiercely angry

apoplexy (say **ap**-op-lek-see) *NOUN*
❶ sudden loss of the ability to feel and move, caused by the blocking or breaking of a blood vessel in the brain ❷ (*informal*) rage or anger

Apostle *NOUN* **Apostles**
in Christianity, any of the twelve men sent out by Christ to preach the Gospel

apostrophe (say a-**poss**-trof-ee) *NOUN* **apostrophes**
the punctuation mark (') used to show that letters have been missed out (as in *I can't =* I cannot) or to show that something belongs to someone (as in *the boy's book*; *the boys' books*)

> **PUNCTUATION**
>
> **Apostrophes** have two main uses:
>
> to show that letters are missed out of a shortened word, e.g. *didn't* (for *did not*) or *we'd* (for *we would*), or in a time, e.g. *six o'clock* (originally 'of the clock').
>
> to show what someone or something owns or possesses, e.g. *the bat's ears* (= the ears of the bat), or what something is associated with, e.g. *the day's news* (= the news of the day).
>
> Where does the apostrophe for possession go?
>
> For most nouns you add an apostrophe followed by an *s*: *the dragon's claw* (= the claw of the dragon), *the children's shoes* (= the shoes of the children), *the city's cathedral* (= the cathedral in the city), *the boss's desk* (= the desk belonging to the boss), *in a week's time* (= after a week).
>
> When the noun is plural and already ends in *s*, you add an apostrophe by itself: *the dragons' claws* (= the claws of the dragons), *the cities' cathedrals* (= the cathedrals in the cities), *the bosses' desks* (= the desks belonging to the bosses), *in three weeks' time* (= after three weeks).
>
> When a person's name ends in *s*, you add an apostrophe followed by *s* if you normally say an extra *s* in speaking: *Venus's orbit*; *St Thomas's Hospital*. But you just add an apostrophe when you

don't say an extra *s* in speaking: *Achilles' armour.*

There is no apostrophe in ordinary plurals like *bicycles*, *videos* and *Mondays* or in possessive pronouns like *hers* and *its*.

You don't need an apostrophe for plurals of abbreviations, e.g. *CDs* and *DVDs*, or for plurals of decades, e.g. *in the 1990s*.

apothecary (say a-**poth**-ik-er-ee) *NOUN* apothecaries (*old use*)
a chemist who prepares medicines

app *NOUN* apps
a computer program designed to do a particular job, especially one you use on a smartphone

appal *VERB* appals, appalling, appalled
to shock somebody very much • *She stared at him, appalled.* WORD ORIGIN from Old French *apalir* = become pale

appalling *ADJECTIVE*
shocking; very unpleasant • *Some of the children live in appalling conditions.*

apparatus *NOUN*
the equipment for a particular experiment or task

apparel *NOUN*
(*formal*) a person's clothes

apparent *ADJECTIVE*
❶ clear or obvious • *For no apparent reason, everyone was whispering.* ❷ seeming; appearing to be true but not really so • *I could not understand her apparent indifference.*

apparently *ADVERB*
as it seems; so it appears • *The door had apparently been locked.*

apparition *NOUN* apparitions
something that you imagine you can see, especially a ghost • *a ghostly apparition at the window*

appeal *VERB* appeals, appealing, appealed
❶ to ask for something that you badly need • *Police are appealing for information.* ❷ to ask for a decision to be changed • *He appealed against the prison sentence.* ❸ to seem attractive or interesting • *Golf doesn't appeal to me.*

appeal *NOUN* appeals
❶ asking for something you badly need
❷ asking for a decision to be changed

❸ attraction or interest • *I don't understand the appeal of the countryside.*

appear *VERB* appears, appearing, appeared
❶ to come into sight; to begin to exist
❷ to seem • *They appeared very anxious.*
❸ to take part in a play, film or show etc.
SPELLING
There is a double p in **appear**.

appearance *NOUN* appearances
❶ coming into sight ❷ taking part in a play, film or show etc. ❸ what somebody looks like; what something appears to be

appease *VERB* appeases, appeasing, appeased
to calm someone down, often by giving them what they want • *Nothing would appease the goddess.*
➤ appeasement *NOUN*

appendage *NOUN* appendages
something added or attached; a thing that forms a natural part of something larger

appendicitis *NOUN*
inflammation of the appendix

appendix *NOUN*
❶ appendixes a small tube leading off from the intestine ❷ appendices a section added at the end of a book

appetite *NOUN* appetites
❶ desire for food ❷ an enthusiasm for something • *These stories had given her an appetite for adventure.*

appetizer (also **appetiser**) *NOUN* appetizers
a small amount of food eaten before the main meal

appetizing (also **appetising**) *ADJECTIVE*
appetizing food looks and smells good to eat

applaud *VERB* applauds, applauding, applauded
to show that you like something, especially by clapping your hands

applause *NOUN*
clapping by the audience at the end of a performance • *He was given a huge round of applause.*

apple *NOUN* apples
a round fruit with a red, yellow or green skin
➤ the apple of your eye a person or thing that you love and are proud of

appliance *NOUN* appliances
a device or piece of equipment • *electrical appliances*

applicable (say **ap**-lik-a-bul) *ADJECTIVE*
suitable or relevant • *Ignore any questions which are not applicable.*

applicant *NOUN* applicants
a person who applies for a job or position

application *NOUN* applications
❶ a formal written request for something, such as a job ❷ a computer program or piece of software designed for a particular purpose ❸ the practical use of something • *One of the important applications of virtual reality is in medical education.* ❹ hard work or effort

applied *ADJECTIVE*
put to practical use • *applied maths*

apply *VERB* applies, applying, applied
❶ to put or spread one thing on another • *She applied lipstick to her mouth.* ❷ to start using something • *He applied the brakes.* ❸ to ask for something in writing • *Mina applied for a place on the course.* ❹ something applies to a person or thing when it concerns them and they are affected by it • *This rule does not apply to you.*
➤ **apply yourself** to give all your attention to a task or piece of work

appoint *VERB* appoints, appointing, appointed
❶ to choose a person for a job ❷ an appointed time is one officially decided on for a meeting or deadline • *Everyone was assembled at the appointed time.*

appointment *NOUN* appointments
❶ an arrangement to meet or visit somebody at a particular time ❷ choosing somebody for a job ❸ a job or position

apportion *VERB* apportions, apportioning, apportioned
to divide something among people; to give someone a share of something • *Great care was taken in apportioning the parts.*

appraise *VERB* appraises, appraising, appraised
to judge the value or quality of a person or thing • *She stepped back to appraise her workmanship.*
➤ **appraisal** *NOUN*

appreciable *ADJECTIVE*
large enough to be noticed or felt • *The engine showed no appreciable signs of wear.*

appreciate *VERB* appreciates, appreciating, appreciated
❶ to enjoy or value something • *It's nice to be appreciated.* ❷ to be grateful for something • *Thank you, I really appreciate*

your help ❸ to understand something • *I do appreciate the seriousness of the situation.* ❹ to increase in value

appreciation *NOUN*
❶ showing that you enjoy or value something • *She had a keen appreciation of poetry.* ❷ the feeling of being grateful for something • *Please accept this small token of our appreciation.* ❸ understanding of a situation or problem

appreciative *ADJECTIVE*
❶ showing pleasure or admiration • *an appreciative audience* ❷ grateful for something • *He was very appreciative of our efforts to help.*

apprehend *VERB* apprehends, apprehending, apprehended
❶ to seize or arrest someone ❷ to understand something

apprehension *NOUN*
❶ fear or worry • *His mouth was dry with apprehension.* ❷ the arrest of a person

apprehensive *ADJECTIVE*
anxious or worried

apprentice *NOUN* apprentices
a person who is learning a trade or craft by a legal agreement with an employer

apprentice *VERB* apprentices, apprenticing, apprenticed
to give someone a position as an apprentice • *At 13 he was apprenticed to a printer.*

apprenticeship *NOUN* apprenticeships
the time when someone is an apprentice • *He began his apprenticeship as a butcher.*

approach *VERB* approaches, approaching, approached
❶ to come near • *Robin approached the door on tiptoe.* ❷ to go to someone with a request or offer • *They approached me for help.* ❸ to set about doing something or tackling a problem • *What is the best way to approach this problem?*

approach *NOUN* approaches
❶ a way of dealing with something • *He brought a fresh approach to filmmaking.* ❷ coming near • *She did not notice the approach of the two girls.* ❸ a way or road leading up to something • *Two soldiers guarded the approach to the bridge.*

approachable *ADJECTIVE*
friendly and easy to talk to

approbation NOUN
formal or official approval

appropriate (say a-**proh**-pree-at) ADJECTIVE
suitable or right for a particular situation
➤ **appropriately** ADVERB

appropriate (say a-**proh**-pree-ayt) VERB
appropriates, appropriating, appropriated
to take something, usually without permission
and use it as your own • *Someone had
appropriated my locker.*

approval NOUN
❶ thinking well of someone or something
• *Bob was always seeking his father's
approval.* ❷ agreeing to a plan or request
• *The king nodded his approval.*
➤ **on approval** received by a customer to
examine before deciding to buy

approve VERB **approves, approving, approved**
❶ to say or think that a person or thing
is good or suitable ❷ to agree formally to
something • *The committee has approved the
expenditure.*

approximate (say a-**proks**-im-at) ADJECTIVE
almost exact or correct but not completely so
• *All the dates in brackets are approximate.*

approximate (say a-**proks**-im-ayt)
VERB **approximates, approximating,
approximated**
to be almost the same as something • *I
tried on several jackets before finding one
approximating my size.*

approximately ADVERB
roughly; almost exactly • *It's approximately
fifty miles from here.*

approximation NOUN **approximations**
a number or amount that is a rough estimate
and not exact

apricot NOUN **apricots**
a juicy orange-coloured fruit with a stone
in it

April NOUN
the fourth month of the year

apron NOUN **aprons**
❶ a piece of clothing worn over the front
of the body, especially to protect other
clothes ❷ a hard-surfaced area on an airfield
where aircraft are loaded and unloaded
WORD ORIGIN originally *a naperon*, from
French *nappe* = tablecloth

apse NOUN **apses**
a domed semicircular part at the east end of
a church

apt ADJECTIVE
❶ to be apt to do something is to be likely
to do it or to do it a lot • *He is apt to be
careless.* ❷ appropriate or suitable • *an apt
quotation*
➤ **aptly** ADVERB
➤ **aptness** NOUN

aptitude NOUN
to have an aptitude for something is to be
naturally good at it • *She had a natural
aptitude for drama.*

aqualung NOUN **aqualungs**
a diver's portable breathing apparatus, with
cylinders of compressed air connected to a
face mask

aquamarine NOUN **aquamarines**
a bluish-green precious stone
WORD ORIGIN from Latin *aqua marina* = sea
water

aquarium NOUN **aquariums**
a tank or building in which live fish and other
water animals are displayed

aquatic ADJECTIVE
to do with water or living in water • *the
Olympics aquatic centre* • *aquatic plants*

aquatint NOUN **aquatints**
an etching made on copper by using nitric
acid

aqueduct NOUN **aqueducts**
a bridge carrying a water channel across low
ground or a valley

aquiline (say **ak**-wi-lyn) ADJECTIVE
an aquiline nose is hooked like an eagle's beak

Arab NOUN **Arabs**
a member of a Semitic people living in parts
of the Middle East and North Africa
➤ **Arabian** ADJECTIVE

Arabic ADJECTIVE
to do with the Arabs or their language

Arabic NOUN
the language of the Arabs

Arabic numerals PLURAL NOUN
the figures 1, 2, 3, 4, etc. Compare with
Roman numerals.

arable ADJECTIVE
arable land is suitable for ploughing or
growing crops on

arachnid (say a-**rak**-nid) NOUN **arachnids**
a member of the group of animals that
includes spiders and scorpions

a b c d e f g h i j k l m n o p q r s t u v w x y z

arbitrary (say **ar**-bit-rer-ee) *ADJECTIVE*
chosen or done on an impulse, not according
to a rule or law • *an arbitrary decision*

arbour (say **ar**-ber) *NOUN* **arbours**
a shady place among trees

arc *NOUN* **arcs**
❶ a curve; part of the circumference of a
circle ❷ a luminous electric current passing
between two electrodes

arcade *NOUN* **arcades**
a covered passage or area, especially for
shopping **WORD ORIGIN** French or Italian, from
Latin *arcus* = curve (because early arcades had
curved roofs)

arcane *ADJECTIVE*
secret or mysterious **WORD ORIGIN** from Latin
arcere = to shut up, from *arca* = box

arch *NOUN* **arches**
❶ a curved structure that helps to support
a bridge or other building etc. ❷ something
shaped like this

arch *VERB* **arches, arching, arched**
to form something into an arch; to curve
• *The cat arched its back and hissed.*

arch *ADJECTIVE*
pretending to be playful; mischievous • *an
arch smile*
➤ **archly** *ADVERB*

archaeology (say ar-kee-**ol**-oj-ee) *NOUN*
the study of ancient civilizations by digging
for the remains of their buildings, tools, etc.
and examining them
➤ **archaeological** *ADJECTIVE*
➤ **archaeologist** *NOUN*

archaic (say ar-**kay**-ik) *ADJECTIVE*
belonging to former or ancient times

archangel *NOUN* **archangels**
an angel of the highest rank

archbishop *NOUN* **archbishops**
the chief bishop of a region

arch-enemy *NOUN* **arch-enemies**
a person's chief enemy

archer *NOUN* **archers**
a person who shoots with a bow and arrows

archery *NOUN*
the sport of shooting at a target with a bow
and arrows

archipelago (say ark-i-**pel**-ag-oh) *NOUN*
archipelagos
a large group of islands or the sea containing
these

architect (say **ark**-i-tekt) *NOUN* **architects**
a person who designs buildings

architecture *NOUN*
❶ the work of designing buildings
❷ a particular style of building • *Elizabethan
architecture*
➤ **architectural** *ADJECTIVE*

archive (say **ark**-yv) *NOUN*
❶ (also **archives**) a collection of old
documents and records that show the history
of an organization or community
❷ (*in computing*) a set of computer files that
are stored and no longer in active use
SPELLING
The 'k' sound is spelt *ch* in archive.

archivist (say **ar**-kiv-ist) *NOUN* **archivists**
a person trained to deal with archives

archway *NOUN* **archways**
an arched passage or entrance

arc lamp, arc light *NOUN* **arc lamps, arc
lights**
a light using an electric arc

arctic *ADJECTIVE*
very cold • *The weather was arctic.*

ardent *ADJECTIVE*
enthusiastic or passionate • *an ardent
admirer*
➤ **ardently** *ADVERB*

ardour (say **ar**-der) *NOUN*
enthusiasm or passion

arduous *ADJECTIVE*
needing much effort; difficult and tiring • *an
arduous voyage*

area *NOUN* **areas**
❶ the extent or measurement of a surface;
the amount of space a surface covers • *The
area of the room is 20 square metres.* ❷ a
particular region or piece of land ❸ a subject
or activity • *an interesting area of biology*

arena (say a-**reen**-a) *NOUN* **arenas**
an area with seats around it where
sports events or concerts are held
WORD ORIGIN Latin, = sand (because the floors
of Roman arenas were covered with sand)

aren't (*mainly spoken*)
are not

➤ **aren't I?** (*informal*) am I not?

SPELLING

Aren't = are + not. Add an apostrophe between the n and the t.

arguable *ADJECTIVE*
❶ able to be stated as a possibility ❷ open to doubt; not certain

arguably *ADVERB*
used to give your opinion about something, especially when you think others might not agree • *This is arguably his best book.*

argue *VERB* argues, arguing, argued
❶ to say that you disagree; to exchange angry comments ❷ to state that something is true and give reasons • *Some people argue that we are using too many fossil fuels too quickly.*

argument *NOUN* arguments
❶ a disagreement or quarrel ❷ a reason or series of reasons someone puts forward

SPELLING

There is no e after the u in argument.

argumentative *ADJECTIVE*
fond of arguing

aria (say **ar**-ee-a) *NOUN* arias
a solo in an opera or oratorio

arid *ADJECTIVE*
having little or no rain; dry and barren

arise *VERB* arises, arising, arose, arisen
❶ to come into existence; to come to people's notice • *Now a serious problem arose.* ❷ (*old use*) to rise; to stand up • *Arise, Sir Francis.*

aristocracy (say a-ris-**tok**-ra-see) *NOUN*
people of the highest social rank; members of the nobility

aristocrat (say **a**-ris-tok-rat) *NOUN* aristocrats
a member of the aristocracy
➤ **aristocratic** *ADJECTIVE*

arithmetic *NOUN*
the science or study of numbers; calculating with numbers
➤ **arithmetical** *ADJECTIVE*

ark *NOUN* arks
❶ (in the Bible) the ship in which Noah and his family escaped the Flood ❷ a wooden box in which the writings of the Jewish Law were kept

arm *NOUN* arms
❶ either of the two upper limbs of the body,

between the shoulder and the hand ❷ a sleeve ❸ something shaped like an arm or jutting out from a main part ❹ the raised side part of a chair, on which you can rest your arm

arm *VERB* arms, arming, armed
to prepare someone to fight by supplying them with weapons • *We armed ourselves with heavy sticks and waited.*

armada (say ar-**mah**-da) *NOUN* armadas
a fleet of warships
➤ the **Armada** or **Spanish Armada** the warships sent by Spain to invade England in 1588

armadillo *NOUN* armadillos
a small burrowing South American animal whose body is covered with a shell of bony plates **WORD ORIGIN** Spanish, = little armed man

armaments *PLURAL NOUN*
the weapons of an army etc.

armature *NOUN* armatures
the part of a dynamo or electric motor that carries the current

armchair *NOUN* armchairs
a large comfortable chair with arms

armed *ADJECTIVE*
❶ carrying a weapon, especially a gun • *an armed gang* ❷ involving weapons • *armed robbery*

armed forces, armed services *PLURAL NOUN*
a country's army, navy and air force

armful *NOUN* armfuls
the amount you can carry in your arms

armistice *NOUN* armistices
an agreement to stop fighting in a war or battle

armour *NOUN*
❶ metal clothing worn in the past to protect soldiers in battle ❷ a metal covering on a warship, tank or car to protect it from missiles
➤ **armoured** *ADJECTIVE*

armoury *NOUN* armouries
a place where weapons and ammunition are stored

armpit *NOUN* armpits
the hollow underneath the top of the arm, below the shoulder

arms *PLURAL NOUN*
❶ weapons • *The two armies laid down their arms and made peace.* ❷ a coat of arms • *In*

a b c d e f g h i j k l m n o p q r s t u v w x y z

the centre of the shield are the royal arms.
➤ **up in arms** protesting angrily about
something

arms race *NOUN*
competition between nations in building
up supplies of weapons, especially nuclear
weapons

army *NOUN* **armies**
❶ a large number of people trained to fight
on land ❷ a large group of people doing
something together • *There was an army of
servants working in the kitchen.*

aroma (say a-**roh**-ma) *NOUN* **aromas**
a smell, especially a pleasant one

aromatic (say a-ro-**mat**-ik) *ADJECTIVE*
having a pleasant smell • *aromatic herbs*

around *ADVERB & PREPOSITION*
all round; about • *They stood around the
pond.* • *Stop running around.*

arouse *VERB* **arouses, arousing, aroused**
❶ to stir up a feeling in someone • *You've
definitely aroused my curiosity.* ❷ to wake
someone up

arpeggio (say ar-**pej**-ee-oh) *NOUN* **arpeggios**
(*in music*) the notes of a chord played one
after the other instead of together

arrange *VERB* **arranges, arranging, arranged**
❶ to make plans and preparations for
something • *We're arranging a surprise party
for Johnny.* ❷ to put things into a certain
order • *Arrange the chairs in a circle.* ❸ to
prepare music for a particular purpose

arrangement *NOUN* **arrangements**
❶ arrangement is how you arrange or display
something • *a flower arrangement* ❷ an
arrangement is something you agree with
someone else • *We made an arrangement to
meet at the clock tower.*

array *NOUN* **arrays**
a large display or choice of things • *a huge
array of books*

array *VERB* **arrays, arraying, arrayed**
❶ to be arrayed in fine or special clothes is
to be wearing them noticeably • *She was
arrayed in purple and gold robes.* ❷ to
arrange things in a special order • *His pots of
paint were arrayed around his feet.*

arrears *PLURAL NOUN*
❶ money that is owing and ought to have
been paid earlier ❷ a backlog of work etc.
➤ **in arrears** behind with payments

arrest *VERB* **arrests, arresting, arrested**
to seize a person by authority of the law

arrest *NOUN* **arrests**
arresting somebody • *The police made several
arrests.*

arrival *NOUN* **arrivals**
❶ reaching the place to which you were
travelling • *On our arrival we were met by
the mayor.* ❷ a person or thing that has just
arrived • *Have you met the new arrivals?*

arrive *VERB* **arrives, arriving, arrived**
❶ to reach the end of a journey or a point
on it ❷ to come to a decision or agreement
❸ to come or happen • *The great day arrived.*
WORD ORIGIN from Latin *ad-* = to + *ripa* =
shore; the basic meaning is 'come to shore'
SPELLING
There is a double **r** in **arrive**.

arrogant *ADJECTIVE*
behaving in an unpleasantly proud way
because you think you are better than other
people
➤ **arrogantly** *ADVERB*
➤ **arrogance** *NOUN*

arrow *NOUN* **arrows**
❶ a pointed stick to be shot from a bow ❷ a
sign with an outward-pointing V at the end,
used to show direction or position
➤ **arrowhead** *NOUN*

arsenal *NOUN* **arsenals**
a place where weapons and ammunition are
stored or manufactured

arsenic *NOUN*
a strong poison made from a metallic element
WORD ORIGIN originally the name of arsenic
sulphide, which is yellow; from Persian *zar* =
gold

arson *NOUN*
the crime of deliberately setting fire to a
house or building
➤ **arsonist** *NOUN*

art *NOUN* **arts**
❶ producing something beautiful, especially
by painting, drawing or sculpture; things
produced in this way ❷ a skill • *the art of
sailing*

artefact *NOUN* **artefacts**
an object made by humans, especially
one from the past that is studied by
archaeologists

artery *NOUN* **arteries**
❶ one of the tubes that carry blood away

from the heart to all parts of the body. Compare with **vein**. ❷ an important road or route

artesian well *NOUN* artesian wells
a well that is dug straight down into a place where water will rise easily to the surface

artful *ADJECTIVE*
crafty or cunning
➤ **artfully** *ADVERB*

arthritis (say arth-**ry**-tiss) *NOUN*
a disease that makes joints in the body stiff and painful
➤ **arthritic** (say arth-**rit**-ik) *ADJECTIVE*

arthropod *NOUN* arthropods
an animal of the group that includes insects, spiders, crabs and centipedes
WORD ORIGIN from Greek *arthron* = joint + *podes* = feet (because arthropods have jointed limbs)

artichoke *NOUN* artichokes
a kind of plant with a flower head used as a vegetable

article *NOUN* articles
❶ a piece of writing published in a newspaper or magazine ❷ an object or item • *articles of clothing*
➤ **definite article** the word 'the'
➤ **indefinite article** the word 'a' or 'an'

articulate (say ar-**tik**-yoo-lat) *ADJECTIVE*
able to express things clearly and fluently

articulate (say ar-**tik**-yoo-layt) *VERB*
articulates, articulating, articulated
to say or speak clearly • *She articulated the words very carefully.*
➤ **articulation** *NOUN*

articulated *ADJECTIVE*
(British) an articulated vehicle is one in two sections that are connected by a flexible joint • *an articulated lorry*

artifice *NOUN* artifices
a piece of clever trickery • *The clown fell flat on his face, with magnificent artifice.*

artificial *ADJECTIVE*
not natural; made by human beings in imitation of a natural thing
➤ **artificially** *ADVERB*

artificial intelligence *NOUN*
the use of computers to perform tasks normally requiring human intelligence, e.g. decision-making

artificial respiration *NOUN*
helping someone to start breathing again after their breathing has stopped

artillery *NOUN*
❶ large guns ❷ the part of the army that uses large guns

artisan (say art-iz-**an**) *NOUN* artisans
a skilled worker

artist *NOUN* artists
❶ a person who produces works of art, especially a painter ❷ an entertainer

artistic *ADJECTIVE*
❶ to do with art or artists • *Michelangelo's artistic career began at the age of twelve.*
❷ having or showing a talent for art • *She's always been artistic.*
➤ **artistically** *ADVERB*

artistry *NOUN*
the skill of an artist

artless *ADJECTIVE*
simple and natural • *the little girl's artless prattle*
➤ **artlessly** *ADVERB*

arts *PLURAL NOUN*
subjects (e.g. languages, literature, history) in which opinion and interpretation are very important, as opposed to sciences where measurements and calculations are used
➤ **the arts** painting, music and writing etc., considered together

as *ADVERB*
used in making a comparison • *I got dressed as quickly as I could.*

as *PREPOSITION*
in the function or role of • *Use it as a handle.*

as *CONJUNCTION*
❶ when or while • *She slipped as she got off the bus.* ❷ because • *As he was late, we missed the train.* ❸ in a way that • *Leave it as it is.*
➤ **as for** with regard to • *As for you, I despise you.*
➤ **as it were** in a way • *She became, as it were, her own enemy.*
➤ **as well** also

asbestos *NOUN*
a fireproof material made up of fine soft fibres

Asbo (say **az**-boh) *ABBREVIATION*
anti-social behaviour order

ascend *VERB* ascends, ascending, ascended
to go up to a higher point • *He slowly*

a b c d e f g h i j k l m n o p q r s t u v w x y z

ascended a steep staircase. • *The eagle ascended higher and higher.*
➤ **ascend the throne** to become king or queen

ascendancy *NOUN*
being in control over other people • *They gained ascendancy over others.*

ascending *ADJECTIVE*
going up from the lowest to the highest • *Here are the scores for each team, in ascending order.*

ascension *NOUN*
the process of going up

ascent *NOUN* ascents
❶ the process of going up; a climb • *Nobody spoke as the lift began its ascent.* ❷ a way up; an upward path or slope • *The ascent is very steep.*

ascertain (say as-er-**tayn**) *VERB* ascertains, ascertaining, ascertained
to find something out • *We are trying to ascertain the extent of the damage.*

ascetic (say a-**set**-ik) *ADJECTIVE*
not allowing yourself pleasure and luxuries • *an ascetic life*
➤ **asceticism** *NOUN*

ascetic *NOUN* ascetics
a person who leads an ascetic life, often for religious reasons

ascribe *VERB* ascribes, ascribing, ascribed
to ascribe an event or situation to something is to regard that thing as the cause or source • *She ascribes her success to good luck.*

asexual *ADJECTIVE* (*in biology*)
by other than sexual methods • *asexual reproduction*

ash *NOUN* ashes
❶ the powder that is left after something has been burned ❷ a tree with silver-grey bark
➤ **ashy** *ADJECTIVE*

ashamed *ADJECTIVE*
feeling shame • *You ought to be ashamed of yourself.*

ashen *ADJECTIVE*
grey or pale • *Her face was ashen.*

ashore *ADVERB*
to or on the shore • *The girls jumped ashore.*

ashtray *NOUN* ashtrays
a small bowl for putting cigarette ash in

Asian *ADJECTIVE*
to do with Asia or its people

Asian *NOUN* Asians
an Asian person

Asiatic *ADJECTIVE*
to do with Asia

aside *ADVERB*
❶ to or at one side • *He moved aside to let her pass.* ❷ to put something aside is to keep it in case you need it later

aside *NOUN* asides
words spoken so that only certain people will hear

ask *VERB* asks, asking, asked
❶ to speak so as to find out or get something ❷ to ask for something is to say that you want it ❸ to ask someone to something is to invite them • *Ask her to the party.*

askance (say a-**skanss**) *ADVERB*
➤ **look askance at** to regard a person or situation with distrust or disapproval

askew *ADVERB* & *ADJECTIVE*
crooked; not straight or level • *His wig seemed to be slightly askew.*

asleep *ADVERB* & *ADJECTIVE*
sleeping

AS level *NOUN* AS levels
(in the UK except Scotland) an exam in a subject that represents the first part of an A level qualification; short for Advanced Subsidiary Level

asp *NOUN* asps
a small poisonous snake

asparagus *NOUN*
a plant whose young shoots are eaten as a vegetable

aspect *NOUN* aspects
❶ one part of a problem or situation • *The writer covers most aspects of life on a submarine.* ❷ a person's or thing's appearance • *The chief was an elderly man of noble aspect.*

aspen *NOUN* aspens
a tree with leaves that move in the slightest wind

asperity *NOUN*
harshness or severity

aspersions *PLURAL NOUN*
➤ **cast aspersions on somebody** to attack his or her reputation or integrity

WORD ORIGIN from *asperse* = spatter (with water or mud), from Latin *spergere* = sprinkle

asphalt (say **ass**-falt) NOUN
a sticky black substance like tar, often mixed with gravel to make a surface for roads, etc.

asphyxia (say ass-**fiks**-ee-a) NOUN
a condition in which the body does not take in enough oxygen, causing unconsciousness or death

asphyxiate (say ass-**fiks**-ee-ayt) VERB
asphyxiates, asphyxiating, asphyxiated
to suffocate someone

aspic NOUN
a savoury jelly used for coating meats, eggs, etc.

aspidistra NOUN aspidistras
a house plant with broad leaves

aspirant (say **asp**-er-ant) NOUN aspirants
a person who tries to achieve something
• *young aspirants for glory*

aspirate (say **asp**-er-at) NOUN aspirates
the sound of 'h'

aspiration NOUN aspirations
ambition; strong desire • *She had aspirations to become an actress.*

aspire VERB aspires, aspiring, aspired
to have an ambition to achieve something
• *He aspired to be a writer.*

aspirin NOUN aspirins
a medicinal drug used to relieve pain or reduce fever

ass NOUN asses
❶ a donkey ❷ (*informal*) a stupid person

assailant NOUN assailants
a person who attacks someone

assassin NOUN assassins
a person who assassinates someone
WORD ORIGIN from Arabic *hashishi* = hashish-takers, used as a name for a group of Muslims at the time of the Crusades, who were popularly believed to take hashish (= the drug cannabis) before going out on killing missions

assassinate VERB assassinates, assassinating, assassinated
to kill an important person deliberately and violently, especially for political reasons
➤ **assassination** NOUN

assault NOUN assaults
a violent or illegal attack

assault VERB assaults, assaulting, assaulted
to assault someone is to attack them violently

assegai (say **ass**-ig-y) NOUN assegais
an iron-tipped spear used by South African peoples

assemble VERB assembles, assembling, assembled
❶ to assemble something is to fit the separate parts of it together • *The machine is now ready to be assembled.* ❷ to assemble is to come together in one place • *The whole school assembled in the gym.* ❸ to assemble people or things is to bring them together in one place • *The gallery has assembled more than 200 of the painter's finest works.*

assembly NOUN assemblies
❶ an assembly is a regular meeting, such as when everyone in a school meets together • *At the end of assembly, the children streamed out of the hall.* ❷ an assembly is also a group of people who regularly meet for a special purpose; a parliament • *Parliaments are law-making assemblies.* ❸ assembly is putting the parts of something together to make it • *The bookcase is now ready for assembly.*

assembly line NOUN assembly lines
a series of workers and machines along which a product passes to be assembled part by part

assent NOUN
assent is agreement or permission to do something • *There were murmurs of assent.*

assent VERB assents, assenting, assented
If you assent to something, you say you agree or give your permission. • *'All right', he assented*

SPELLING
Do not forget the double s in assent.

assert VERB asserts, asserting, asserted
to state something firmly • *He asserted he was attacked by three men.*
➤ **assert yourself** to behave in a confident and forceful way

assertion NOUN assertions
a statement that you make confidently

assertive ADJECTIVE
acting forcefully and with confidence

assess VERB assesses, assessing, assessed
to decide or estimate the value or quality of a person or thing • *People came out of their houses to assess the damage.*
➤ **assessor** NOUN

a
b
c
d
e
f
g
h
i
j
k
l
m
n
o
p
q
r
s
t
u
v
w
x
y
z

assessment *NOUN* assessments
an opinion about the value or quality of a person or thing • *We have swimming assessment in the evening.*

asset *NOUN* assets
something useful or valuable to someone • *He's a great asset to the team.*

assets *PLURAL NOUN*
a person's or company's property that they could sell to pay debts or raise money

assign *VERB* assigns, assigning, assigned
❶ to give a task or duty to someone • *She assigned each of us a job to do.* ❷ to appoint a person to perform a task • *A guard had been assigned to watch her.*

assignment *NOUN* assignments
a piece of work or task given to someone • *This was his most dangerous assignment yet.*

assimilate *VERB* assimilates, assimilating, assimilated
to take in and absorb something, e.g. nourishment into the body or knowledge into the mind • *Maggie had a gift for assimilating knowledge.*

assist *VERB* assists, assisting, assisted
to help someone, usually in a practical way • *The chefs were assisted by four waitresses.*

assistance *NOUN*
help someone gets when they need information or support • *Fortunately, a passer-by came to her assistance.*

assistant *NOUN* assistants
❶ a person whose job is to help another person in their work ❷ a person who serves customers in a shop

assistant *ADJECTIVE*
helping a person and ranking next below him or her • *the assistant manager*

associate (say a-**soh**-si-ayt) *VERB* associates, associating, associated
❶ to associate one thing with another is to connect them in your mind • *In some countries, black is often associated with bad luck and death.* ❷ to associate with a group of people is to spend time or have dealings with them • *I'm not sure we ought to associate with them.*

associate (say a-**soh**-si-at) *NOUN* associates
a colleague or companion

association *NOUN* associations
❶ an organization for people sharing an interest or doing the same work ❷ a connection or link in your mind • *This place has strange associations for me.* ❸ being friendly with or working with someone • *Depp has had a long association with the film director Tim Burton.*

Association football *NOUN*
(*British*) the game usually known as football, which uses a round ball that may not be handled during play except by the goalkeeper

assonance (say **ass**-on-ans) *NOUN*
a close similarity of the vowel sounds in two or more words, e.g. in **sonnet** and **porridge**

assorted *ADJECTIVE*
of various kinds put together; mixed and different • *assorted sweets*

assortment *NOUN* assortments
a mixed collection of things

assuage (say a-**swayj**) *VERB* assuages, assuaging, assuaged
to assuage a strong or uncomfortable feeling is to reduce it • *She ate some berries to assuage the pangs of hunger.*

assume *VERB* assumes, assuming, assumed
❶ to accept without proof that something is true or sure to happen • *Let's assume you are right.* ❷ to assume a particular manner or expression is to show it or put it on • *Rick assumed an air of wide-eyed innocence.* ❸ to assume a burden or responsibility is to agree to take it on • *This is my fault and I assume full responsibility for it.*
➤ **assumed name** a false name that someone uses for a special purpose

assumption *NOUN* assumptions
something that you accept without proof that it is true or sure to happen

assurance *NOUN* assurances
❶ a promise or guarantee that something is true or will happen • *We gave him our assurances that we would be on time.* ❷ confidence in yourself • *Tom spoke with such assurance that Mr Swift believed him.*

assure *VERB* assures, assuring, assured
❶ to tell someone something confidently • *I haven't mentioned it to anyone, I assure you.* ❷ to make something certain to happen • *Their future was assured.*

aster *NOUN* asters
a garden plant with daisy-like flowers in various colours

asterisk NOUN asterisks
a star-shaped sign * used to draw attention
to something **WORD ORIGIN** from Greek
asteriskos = little star

astern ADVERB
❶ at the back of a ship or aircraft • *The boat
was now directly astern.*

asteroid NOUN asteroids
one of the small planets found mainly
between the orbits of Mars and Jupiter

asthma (say **ass**-ma) NOUN
a disease that makes breathing difficult

asthmatic ADJECTIVE
suffering from asthma

asthmatic NOUN asthmatics
a person who suffers from asthma

astonish VERB astonishes, astonishing,
astonished
to surprise somebody greatly • *They were
astonished to see him at the door.*

astonishment NOUN
a feeling of great surprise • *She looked at him
in astonishment.*

astound VERB astounds, astounding,
astounded
to astonish or shock someone greatly • *What
she saw astounded her.*

astray ADVERB & ADJECTIVE
➤ **go astray** to be lost or mislaid
➤ **lead someone astray** to make someone do
something wrong

astride ADVERB & PREPOSITION
with one leg on each side of something • *The
knight sat astride a black stallion.*

astrology NOUN
the study of the position and movements
of stars and planets in the belief that they
influence people's lives
➤ **astrologer** NOUN
➤ **astrological** ADJECTIVE

astronaut NOUN astronauts
a person who travels in a spacecraft
WORD ORIGIN from Greek *astron* = star +
nautes = sailor

astronomical ADJECTIVE
❶ to do with astronomy • *astronomical
observations* ❷ extremely large • *an
astronomical phone bill*

astronomy NOUN
the study of the stars and planets and their
movements
➤ **astronomer** NOUN

astute ADJECTIVE
clever and good at understanding situations
quickly; shrewd
➤ **astutely** ADVERB
➤ **astuteness** NOUN

asunder ADVERB (*literary*)
apart; into pieces • *He felt his heart had been
torn asunder.*

asylum NOUN asylums
❶ refuge and safety offered by one country
to political refugees from another • *The main
character is a young woman who is seeking
asylum in the UK.* ❷ (*old use*) an institution
for the care of mentally ill people

asymmetrical (say ay-sim-**et**-rik-al) ADJECTIVE
not symmetrical • *The vase has an
asymmetrical shape.*

at PREPOSITION
This word is used to show
❶ position or location (*I was at the hospital.*),
❷ time (*at midnight*), ❸ direction towards
something (*Aim at the target.*), ❹ cost or
level (*Water boils at 100°C.*), ❺ cause (*We
were annoyed at the delay.*)
➤ **at all** in any way
➤ **at it** doing or working at something
➤ **at once** ❶ immediately ❷ at the same
time • *It all came out at once.*

atheist (say **ayth**-ee-ist) NOUN atheists
a person who believes that there is no God
➤ **atheism** NOUN

athlete NOUN athletes
a person who is good at sport, especially
athletics

athletic ADJECTIVE
❶ physically fit and active; good at sports
❷ to do with athletics
➤ **athletically** ADVERB

athletics PLURAL NOUN
physical exercises and sports, e.g. running,
jumping and throwing

atlas NOUN atlases
a book of maps **WORD ORIGIN** named after
Atlas, a giant in Greek mythology, who was
made to support the universe on his shoulders.
His picture was put in the front of early atlases.

atmosphere NOUN atmospheres
❶ the air around the earth ❷ a feeling or
mood given by surroundings • *Suddenly the
atmosphere in the room changed.* ❸ a unit

a
b
c
d
e
f
g
h
i
j
k
l
m
n
o
p
q
r
s
t
u
v
w
x
y
z

of pressure, equal to the pressure of the atmosphere at sea level

atmospheric ADJECTIVE
❶ to do with the earth's atmosphere ❷ having a strong atmosphere • *an atmospheric building*

atoll NOUN atolls
a ring-shaped coral reef

atom NOUN atoms
the smallest particle of a chemical element
WORD ORIGIN from Greek *atomos* = unable to be divided

atom bomb, atomic bomb NOUN atom bombs, atomic bombs
a bomb using atomic energy

atomic ADJECTIVE
❶ to do with an atom or atoms ❷ to do with atomic energy or atom bombs

atomic energy NOUN
energy created by splitting the nuclei of certain atoms

atomic number NOUN atomic numbers
(*in science*) the number of protons in the nucleus of the atom of a chemical element

atomizer (also **atomiser**) NOUN atomizers
a device for making a liquid into a fine spray

atone VERB atones, atoning, atoned
to make amends; to make up for having done something wrong • *He promised to atone for his stupidity.*
➤ **atonement** NOUN
WORD ORIGIN from *at one*, because people who make amends are 'at one' (= on good terms again) with those they have wronged

atrocious (say a-**troh**-shus) ADJECTIVE
extremely bad or wicked • *atrocious weather*
➤ **atrociously** ADVERB

atrocity (say a-**tross**-it-ee) NOUN atrocities
an extremely bad or wicked thing that someone does, such as killing a large number of people

attach VERB attaches, attaching, attached
❶ to fix or join one thing to something else ❷ to attach importance or significance to something is to believe that it is important or worth thinking about • *The newspapers attached great importance to these rumours.*
➤ **attached to** to be attached to someone or something is to be very fond of them

SPELLING
There is no t before the ch in **attach**. Do not forget the double t at the beginning.

attaché (say a-**tash**-ay) NOUN attachés
a special assistant to an ambassador • *our military attaché*

attaché case NOUN attaché cases
a small case in which documents etc. may be carried

attachment NOUN attachments
❶ an extra part to add to a piece if equipment for a special purpose • *The garden hose has an attachment for washing cars.* ❷ a file or piece of software sent with an email ❸ fondness or friendship • *She formed a strong attachment to my sisters.*

attack NOUN attacks
❶ a violent attempt to hurt or overcome someone ❷ a piece of strong criticism ❸ a sudden illness or pain ❹ the players in a team whose job is to score goals; an attempt to score a goal

attack VERB attacks, attacking, attacked
to act violently against someone or to start a fight with them
➤ **attacker** NOUN

attain VERB attains, attaining, attained
to succeed in doing or getting something • *This is the highest speed ever attained on the sea.*

attainment NOUN attainments
something you have achieved

attempt VERB attempts, attempting, attempted
to make an effort to do something

attempt NOUN attempts
an effort to do something; a try

attend VERB attends, attending, attended
❶ to attend something like a meeting or a wedding is to be there ❷ to attend school or college is to be a pupil or student there ❸ to attend to someone is to look after them ❹ to attend to something is to spend time dealing with it • *Excuse me, I have some business to attend to.*

attendance NOUN attendances
❶ attendance is being present at a place • *Attendance at these classes is not compulsory.* ❷ the number of people present at an event • *It was the club's highest attendance of the season.*

attendant NOUN attendants
a person who helps or goes with someone else

attention NOUN
❶ watching, listening to or thinking about someone or something carefully • *Pay attention to what I'm saying* • *She grabbed his arm to get his attention.* ❷ a position in which a soldier stands with feet together and arms straight downwards

attentive ADJECTIVE
giving your attention to something • *She smiled at the circle of attentive faces.*
➤ **attentively** ADVERB
➤ **attentiveness** NOUN

attest VERB attests, attesting, attested
to declare or prove that something is true or genuine • *His skill and bravery during the battle are well attested.*

attic NOUN attics
a room in the roof of a house

attire NOUN (*formal*)
a person's clothes • *She cast a doubtful look at my attire.*

attire VERB attires, attiring, attired (*formal*)
to be attired in particular clothes is to be wearing them • *He was attired in an elegant blue suit.*

attitude NOUN attitudes
❶ the way you think or feel about something and the way you behave ❷ the position of the body or its parts; posture

attorney NOUN attorneys
❶ a person who is appointed to act on behalf of another in business matters ❷ (*North American*) a lawyer

attract VERB attracts, attracting, attracted
❶ to get someone's attention or interest; to seem pleasant to someone • *A slight noise attracted my attention.* ❷ to make something come • *Moths are attracted to light.* ❸ to pull something by means of a physical force • *A magnet attracts many metal objects.*

attraction NOUN attractions
❶ the process of attracting or the ability to attract • *I can't see the attraction of living in the countryside.* ❷ something that attracts visitors • *The Eiffel Tower is one of Paris's main tourist attractions.*

attractive ADJECTIVE
❶ pleasant or good-looking ❷ interesting or appealing • *It was an attractive idea.*
➤ **attractively** ADVERB
➤ **attractiveness** NOUN

attribute (say a-**trib**-yoot) VERB attributes, attributing, attributed
to believe that something belongs to or is caused by a particular person or thing • *She attributes her perfect health to her diet.*

attribute (say **at**-rib-yoot) NOUN attributes
a quality or characteristic • *A sense of compassion is one of his finest attributes.*

attrition (say a-**trish**-on) NOUN
gradually wearing down an enemy by repeatedly attacking them • *a war of attrition*

attuned ADJECTIVE
familiar with and used to something • *My eyes were now attuned to the darkness.*

aubergine (say **oh**-ber-zheen) NOUN aubergines
(*British*) a deep-purple vegetable with thick flesh

auburn ADJECTIVE
auburn hair is reddish-brown

auction NOUN auctions
a public sale where things are sold to the person who offers the most money for them

auction VERB auctions, auctioning, auctioned
to sell something in an auction • *The fan who grabbed the ball auctioned it on a website.*

auctioneer NOUN auctioneers
an official in charge of an auction

audacious (say aw-**day**-shus) ADJECTIVE
bold or daring • *It was an audacious plan.*
➤ **audaciously** ADVERB

audacity NOUN
the confidence to do something daring or shocking • *The sheer audacity of the idea took my breath away.*

audible ADJECTIVE
loud enough to be heard • *Her voice was barely audible now.*
➤ **audibly** ADVERB

audience NOUN audiences
❶ the people who have come to hear or watch a performance ❷ a formal interview with an important person

audio NOUN
reproduced sounds • *You can listen to audio clips on the website.*

audio–visual ADJECTIVE
using both sound and pictures to give information

a b c d e f g h i j k l m n o p q r s t u v w x y z

audit *NOUN* audits
an official examination of a company's financial accounts to see that they are correct

audit *VERB* audits, auditing, audited
to make an audit of accounts
➤ **auditor** *NOUN*

audition *NOUN* auditions
a test to see if an actor or musician is suitable for a job

audition *VERB* audition, auditioning, auditioned
to have or give someone an audition • *I had to audition to get the part.*

auditorium *NOUN* auditoriums
the part of a theatre or hall where the audience sits

augment *VERB* augments, augmenting, augmented
to increase or add to something • *Kathy got a job in a shop to augment the family income.*

augur (say **awg**-er) *VERB* augurs, auguring, augured
to augur well or augur badly is to be a good sign or a bad sign • *He glared at me in a way that did not augur well.*

August *NOUN*
the eighth month of the year
WORD ORIGIN named after *Augustus* Caesar, the first Roman emperor

august (say aw-**gust**) *ADJECTIVE*
majestic or impressive

auk *NOUN* auks
a kind of seabird

aunt *NOUN* aunts
the sister of your father or mother or your uncle's wife

auntie, **aunty** *NOUN* aunties
(*informal*) aunt

au pair (say oh **pair**) *NOUN* au pairs
a person from abroad, usually a young woman, who works for a time in a family's home, helping to look after the children
WORD ORIGIN from a French phrase meaning 'on equal terms'

aura (say **or**-a) *NOUN* auras
a general feeling surrounding a person or thing • *An aura of mystery surrounds her.*

aural (say **or**-al) *ADJECTIVE*
to do with the ear or hearing
WORD ORIGIN from Latin *auris* = ear

SPELLING
Take care not to confuse with **oral**, which means to do with or using your mouth.

au revoir (say oh rev-**wahr**) *EXCLAMATION*
goodbye for the moment
WORD ORIGIN French, literally = to the seeing again

aurora (say aw-**raw**-ra) *NOUN* auroras
bands of coloured light appearing in the sky at night, the **aurora borealis** (say bor-ee-**ay**-liss)
in the northern hemisphere and the **aurora australis** (say aw-**stray**-liss)
in the southern hemisphere

auspices (say **aw**-spiss-eez) *PLURAL NOUN*
➤ **under the auspices of someone** with the help, support or protection of an organization • *The clinic was set up under the auspices of the Red Cross.*
WORD ORIGIN originally = omens; later = influence, protection; same origin as **auspicious**

auspicious (say aw-**spish**-us) *ADJECTIVE*
showing signs that something is likely to be successful in the future • *It was an auspicious start to her acting career.*
WORD ORIGIN from Latin *auspicium* = telling the future from the behaviour of birds, from *avis* = bird

austere (say aw-**steer**) *ADJECTIVE*
❶ very simple and plain; without luxuries
❷ an austere person is very strict and serious

austerity *NOUN*
❶ a plain or simple way of living, without much comfort or luxury ❷ a time when people do not have much money to spend because there are bad economic conditions

authentic *ADJECTIVE*
genuine or true • *an authentic signature*

authenticate *VERB* authenticates, authenticating, authenticated
to confirm something as being authentic
➤ **authentication** *NOUN*

authenticity *NOUN*
authenticity is being genuine or true • *There's no doubt about the authenticity of the letter.*

author *NOUN* authors
the writer of a book, play, poem, etc.
➤ **authorship** *NOUN*

authoritarian *ADJECTIVE*
believing that people should be completely

obedient to those in authority

authoritative *ADJECTIVE*
having proper authority or expert knowledge
• *He sounded quietly authoritative.*

authority *NOUN* **authorities**
❶ authority is the right or power to give orders to other people ❷ an authority is a person or organization with the right to give orders ❸ an authority on a subject is a person or book that gives reliable information about it • *an authority on spiders*

authorize (also **authorise**) *VERB* **authorizes, authorizing, authorized**
to give official permission for something
➤ **authorization** *NOUN*

autistic (say aw-**tist**-ik) *ADJECTIVE*
having a mental condition that makes it difficult for someone to communicate with other people
➤ **autism** *NOUN*

auto *NOUN* **autos** (*informal esp. North American*)
a car • *the auto industry*

autobiography *NOUN* **autobiographies**
the story of a person's life written by himself or herself
➤ **autobiographical** *ADJECTIVE*

autocracy (say aw-**tok**-ra-see) *NOUN* **autocracies**
rule by one person who has total and unlimited power

autocrat *NOUN* **autocrats**
a ruler with total and unlimited power
➤ **autocratic** *ADJECTIVE*

autocue *NOUN* **autocues** (*trade mark*)
(*British*) a device that displays the script for a television presenter or public speaker to read

autograph *NOUN* **autographs**
the signature of a famous person

automate *VERB* **automates, automating, automated**
to make something work by an automatic process • *The assembly system is now fully automated.*

automatic *ADJECTIVE*
❶ working on its own without continuous attention or control by people • *automatic doors* ❷ done without thinking • *After all their rehearsing, their actions were automatic.*

automatically *ADVERB*
❶ by automatic means; without having to use controls all the time • *The door opened*

automatically. ❷ without thinking
• *He automatically reached for his sword.*

automation *NOUN*
making processes automatic; using machines instead of people to do jobs

automaton (say aw-**tom**-at-on) *NOUN* **automatons**
❶ a robot ❷ a person who seems to act mechanically without thinking

automobile *NOUN* **automobiles**
(*North American*) a car

autonomy (say aw-**ton**-om-ee) *NOUN*
❶ self-government ❷ the right to act independently without being told what to do
➤ **autonomous** *ADJECTIVE*

autopsy (say aw-top-see) *NOUN* **autopsies**
an examination of a dead body to find out the cause of death; a post-mortem
WORD ORIGIN from Greek *autopsia* = seeing with your own eyes

autumn *NOUN* **autumns**
the season between summer and winter
SPELLING
There is a silent **n** in **autumn**.

autumnal *ADJECTIVE*
in autumn; to do with autumn • *autumnal colours*

auxiliary *ADJECTIVE*
giving help and support • *auxiliary services*

auxiliary *NOUN* **auxiliaries**
a person who gives help and support

auxiliary verb *NOUN* **auxiliary verbs**
a verb such as *do, have* and *will*, which is used to form parts of other verbs, e.g. *have* in *I have finished.*
GRAMMAR
See also the panels on **be**, **do**, and **have**.

avail *NOUN*
➤ **to** or **of no avail** of no use; without success • *Their pleas for mercy were all to no avail.*

avail *VERB* **avails, availing, availed**
➤ **avail yourself of** to make use of something • *He gladly availed himself of their hospitality.*

available *ADJECTIVE*
able to be found or used • *These sweatshirts are available in a range of colours.*
➤ **availability** *NOUN*

avalanche *NOUN* avalanches
a mass of snow or rock falling down the side
of a mountain

avant-garde (say av-ahn-**gard**) *NOUN*
people who use a very modern style in art or
literature etc.
➤ **avant-garde** *ADJECTIVE*

avarice (say **av**-er-iss) *NOUN*
greed for money or possessions
➤ **avaricious** *ADJECTIVE*

avenge *VERB* avenges, avenging, avenged
to punish someone for something they have
done to harm you or your family • *He vowed
to avenge the death of his father.*
➤ **avenger** *NOUN*

avenue *NOUN* avenues
❶ a wide street ❷ a road with trees along
both sides

average *NOUN* averages
❶ the value obtained by adding several
quantities together and dividing by the
number of quantities ❷ the usual or ordinary
standard

average *ADJECTIVE*
❶ worked out as an average • *Their average
age is ten.* ❷ of the usual or ordinary
standard

average *VERB* averages, averaging, averaged
to work out, produce or amount to as an
average • *The rainfall averages more than
2500mm a year.*

averse (say a-**vers**) *ADJECTIVE*
unwilling to do something or opposed to
something • *I'm not averse to a bit of hard
work.*

aversion *NOUN*
a strong dislike • *She had an aversion to
water and soap.*

avert *VERB* averts, averting, averted
❶ to turn something away • *As he answered,
he blushed and averted his eyes.* ❷ to
prevent something • *We realized we had only
seconds to avert a disaster.*

aviary *NOUN* aviaries
a large cage or building for keeping birds

aviation *NOUN*
the flying of aircraft ⬤**WORD ORIGIN** from Latin
avis = bird

aviator *NOUN* aviators (*old use*)
a person who flies an aircraft

avid (say **av**-id) *ADJECTIVE*
keen or eager • *an avid reader*
➤ **avidly** *ADVERB*

avocado (say av-ok-**ah**-doh) *NOUN* avocados
a pear-shaped tropical fruit

avoid *VERB* avoids, avoiding, avoided
❶ to avoid a person or place is to stay away
from them ❷ to avoid doing something is to
make sure you do not do it • *Emily tried to
avoid getting involved in the argument.*
➤ **avoidance** *NOUN*

avuncular *ADJECTIVE*
kind and friendly towards someone younger,
like an uncle

await *VERB* awaits, awaiting, awaited
to wait for someone to come or something to
happen • *His friends were anxiously awaiting
his return.*

awake *ADJECTIVE*
not asleep • *She lay awake for a long time.*

awake *VERB* awakes, awaking, awoke, awoken
to wake up • *Jack awoke to the sound of
birdsong.*

awaken *VERB* awakens, awakening, awakened
❶ to wake up or to make someone wake up
• *He was awakened by someone shouting.*
❷ to produce a feeling in someone • *The
letter awakened her curiosity.*
➤ **awakening** *NOUN*

award *VERB* awards, awarding, awarded
to give something officially as a prize,
payment or penalty • *De Klerk and Mandela
were awarded the Nobel Peace Prize in 1993.*

award *NOUN* awards
something awarded, such as a prize or a sum
of money

aware *ADJECTIVE*
knowing or realizing something • *Were you
aware of the danger?*
➤ **awareness** *NOUN*

awash *ADJECTIVE*
with waves or water flooding over it • *Her
face was awash with tears.*

away *ADVERB*
❶ to or at a distance; not at the usual place
• *Go away and leave me alone.* ❷ until
disappearing completely • *The noise gradually
died away.* ❸ continuously or persistently
• *We worked away at it for days.*

away *ADJECTIVE*
played on an opponent's ground • *an away
match*

awe *NOUN*
❶ a feeling of great wonder and perhaps slight fear • *I looked up at the starry sky with awe.* ❷ to be in awe of someone is to respect and admire them a lot
➤ **awed** *ADJECTIVE*
➤ **awestricken** *ADJECTIVE*
➤ **awestruck** *ADJECTIVE*

awe-inspiring *ADJECTIVE*
causing a feeling of great wonder and admiration

awesome *ADJECTIVE*
❶ very impressive and perhaps slightly frightening • *The mountains were an awesome sight.* ❷ (*informal*) excellent

awful *ADJECTIVE*
❶ very bad • *an awful accident* ❷ (*informal*) very great • *That's an awful lot of money.*

awfully *ADVERB*
(*informal*) very, extremely • *I'm awfully sorry.*

awhile *ADVERB*
for a short time

awkward *ADJECTIVE*
❶ difficult to use or deal with; not convenient • *The box isn't heavy, but it's awkward to carry.* ❷ embarrassed and not at ease • *I often feel awkward in a group of people.* ❸ clumsy or uncomfortable • *She has been sleeping in an awkward position.*
➤ **awkwardly** *ADVERB*
➤ **awkwardness** *NOUN*

awl *NOUN* awls
a small pointed tool for making holes in leather, wood, etc.

awning *NOUN* awnings
a roof-like shelter made of canvas etc.

awry *ADVERB & ADJECTIVE*
❶ twisted to one side; crooked ❷ wrong; not according to plan, • *Our plans have gone awry.*

axe *NOUN* axes
❶ a tool for chopping things ❷ (*informal*) a person or organization faces the axe when they are about to be made redundant or closed • *A number of workers face the axe.*
➤ **have an axe to grind** to have a personal reason for being involved in something

axe *VERB* axes, axing, axed
to cancel or abolish something

axiom *NOUN* axioms
an established general truth or principle

axis *NOUN* axes
❶ a line through the centre of a spinning object ❷ a line dividing a thing in half ❸ the horizontal or vertical line on a graph

axle *NOUN* axles
the rod through the centre of a wheel, on which the wheel turns

ayatollah (say eye-a-**tol**-a) *NOUN* ayatollahs
a Muslim religious leader in Iran

aye (rhymes with by) *ADVERB*
(*dialect or old use*) yes

azalea (say a-**zay**-lee-a) *NOUN* azaleas
a kind of flowering shrub

azure *ADJECTIVE*
sky-blue

baa *NOUN* baas
the cry of a sheep or lamb

babble *VERB* babbles, babbling, babbled
❶ to talk very quickly without making sense • *What are you babbling on about?* ❷ to make a gentle bubbling sound • *a babbling stream*
➤ **babble** *NOUN*

babe *NOUN* babes
(*old use*) a baby

baboon *NOUN* baboons
a kind of large monkey from Africa and Asia, with a long muzzle and short tail

baby *NOUN* babies
a very young child or animal
WORD ORIGIN probably from the sounds a baby makes when it first tries to speak

babyish *ADJECTIVE*
like a baby or suitable for a baby • *She is too old for such babyish toys.*

babysit *VERB* babysits, babysitting, babysat
to look after a child while its parents are out

babysitter *NOUN* babysitters
someone who looks after a child while its parents are out

bachelor *NOUN* bachelors
a man who has not married

a
b
c
d
e
f
g
h
i
j
k
l
m
n
o
p
q
r
s
t
u
v
w
x
y
z

➤ **Bachelor of Arts** or **Science** a person who has taken a first degree in arts or science

bacillus (say ba-**sil**-us) *NOUN* bacilli
a rod-shaped bacterium

back *NOUN* backs
❶ the part that is furthest from the front ❷ the back part of a person's or animal's body, from the shoulders to the base of the spine ❸ the part of a chair etc. that your back rests against ❹ a defending player near the goal in football, hockey, etc.

back *ADJECTIVE*
❶ placed at or near the back • *Let's sit in the back row.* ❷ to do with the back • *back pain*

back *ADVERB*
❶ to or towards the back ❷ to the place you have come from • *Go back home.* ❸ to an earlier time or position • *Think back to when you were little.*

back *VERB* backs, backing, backed
❶ to move backwards or drive a vehicle backwards ❷ to give someone support or help ❸ to bet on something ❹ to cover the back of something • *Back the rug with canvas.*
➤ **back down** to admit that you were wrong about something
➤ **back out** to refuse to do what you agreed to do
➤ **back someone up** to give someone support or help
➤ **back something up** (*in computing*) to make a spare copy of a file, disk, etc. to be stored in safety separately from the original

backbencher *NOUN* backbenchers
a Member of Parliament who does not hold an important position

backbiting *NOUN*
unkind or nasty things said about someone who is not there

backbone *NOUN* backbones
❶ the column of small bones down the centre of the back; the spine ❷ strength of character; courage • *Show some backbone, girl.*

backdrop *NOUN* backdrops
a large painted cloth that is hung across the back of a stage

backer *NOUN* backers
someone who supports a project or plan by providing money

backfire *VERB* backfires, backfiring, backfired
❶ if a car backfires, it makes a loud noise,

caused by an explosion in the exhaust pipe ❷ if a plan backfires, it goes wrong

backgammon *NOUN*
a game played on a board with draughts and dice

background *NOUN* backgrounds
❶ the back part of a picture, scene or view ❷ all the things that help to explain why an event or situation happened • *I am reading about the background to the American Civil War.* ❸ a person's family, upbringing and education
➤ **in the background** not noticeable or obvious • *I could hear voices in the background.*

backhand *NOUN* backhands
a stroke made in tennis etc. with the back of the hand turned outwards
➤ **backhanded** *ADJECTIVE*

backing *NOUN*
❶ support or help ❷ material that is used to line the back of something ❸ music that is played or sung to support the main singer or tune

backlash *NOUN* backlashes
a strong and angry reaction to an event

backlog *NOUN* backlogs
an amount of work that should have been finished but is still waiting to be done

backpack *NOUN* backpacks
a bag with straps for carrying on your back; a rucksack

backpacking *NOUN*
travelling or hiking with your belongings in a rucksack
➤ **backpacker** *NOUN*

backside *NOUN* backsides (*informal*)
your backside is your bottom

backstage *ADVERB*
in or towards the parts of a theatre behind the stage • *We went backstage to meet the cast.*

backstroke *NOUN*
a way of swimming lying on your back

back-up *NOUN* back-ups
(*in computing*) a spare copy of a file, disk, etc. stored in safety separately from the original

backward *ADJECTIVE*
❶ facing or moving towards the back • *She walked off without a backward glance.*

❷ having not developed at the expected rate
➤ **backwardness** NOUN

backward ADVERB
backwards

USAGE

The adverb **backward** is mainly used in American English.

backwards ADVERB
❶ to or towards the back **❷** with the back end going first **❸** in reverse order • *Count backwards from 10.*
➤ **backwards and forwards** in each direction alternately; to and fro

backwater NOUN backwaters
❶ a branch of a river that comes to a dead end with stagnant water **❷** a quiet place that is not affected by progress or new ideas

backyard NOUN backyards
❶ an open area with a hard surface behind a house **❷** (*North American*) a back garden

bacon NOUN
smoked or salted meat from the back or sides of a pig

bacterium NOUN bacteria
a microscopic organism that can cause disease
➤ **bacterial** ADJECTIVE

USAGE

Take care not to use the plural form **bacteria** as if it were the singular. It is incorrect to say 'a bacteria' or 'this bacteria'; correct usage is *this bacterium* or *these bacteria.*

bad ADJECTIVE worse, worst
❶ of poor quality; not good **❷** not able to do something very well • *I've always been bad at sport.* **❸** serious or unpleasant • *a bad accident* • *I've got some bad news.* **❹** ill or unhealthy **❺** harmful • *Sweets are bad for your teeth.* **❻** decayed or rotten • *This meat has gone bad.* **❼** wicked or evil
➤ **not bad** quite good
➤ **badness** NOUN

baddy NOUN baddies (*informal*)
an evil or wicked character in a story

bade
old past tense of **bid**

badge NOUN badges
a button or sign that you wear to show people who you are, what school or club you belong to or what kind of thing you like

badger NOUN badgers
a grey animal with a black and white head, which lives underground and is active at night

badger VERB badgers, badgering, badgered
to keep asking someone to do something; to pester someone about something • *She's been badgering me to get tickets for the concert.* **WORD ORIGIN** perhaps from **badge** (because of the markings on a badger's head)

badly ADVERB worse, worst
❶ in a bad way; not well • *I did badly in my exams.* **❷** severely; causing serious injury • *He was badly wounded.* **❸** very much • *She badly wanted to win.*

badminton NOUN
a game in which players use rackets to hit a light object called a shuttlecock across a high net

bad-tempered ADJECTIVE
always angry and in a bad mood

baffle VERB baffles, baffling, baffled
to puzzle or confuse someone • *The instructions baffled me completely.*
➤ **baffled** ADJECTIVE
➤ **baffling** ADJECTIVE

bag NOUN bags
a container made of a soft material, for holding or carrying things
➤ **bags of** (*informal*) plenty of • *There's no hurry, we've got bags of time.*

bag VERB bags, bagging, bagged
❶ (*informal*) to catch or claim something • *I bagged the best seat.* **❷** to put something into bags

bagatelle NOUN
a game played on a board in which small balls are struck into holes

bagel NOUN bagels
a ring-shaped bread roll

baggage NOUN
luggage

baggy ADJECTIVE
baggy clothes hang loosely from your body

bagpipes PLURAL NOUN
a musical instrument in which air is squeezed out of a bag into pipes. Bagpipes are played especially in Scotland.

bail NOUN bails
❶ money that is paid or promised as a guarantee that a person who is accused of a crime will return for trial if he or she is released in the meantime **❷** one of the two

a
b
c
d
e
f
g
h
i
j
k
l
m
n
o
p
q
r
s
t
u
v
w
x
y
z

small pieces of wood placed on top of the stumps in cricket

bail *VERB* **bails, bailing, bailed**
❶ to provide bail for a person ❷ to scoop out water that has got into a boat
➤ **bail someone out** to help someone get out of trouble

bailey *NOUN* **baileys**
the courtyard of a castle; the wall round this courtyard

bailiff *NOUN* **bailiffs**
❶ an official who takes people's property when they owe money ❷ a law officer who helps a sheriff by serving writs and carrying out arrests

Bairam (say by-**rahm**) *NOUN*
either of two Muslim festivals, one in the tenth month and one in the twelfth month of the Islamic year

bairn *NOUN* **bairns**
(*Scottish*) a child

Baisakhi *NOUN*
a Sikh festival held in April to commemorate the founding of the Khalsa

bait *NOUN*
❶ food that is put on a hook or in a trap to catch fish or animals ❷ something that is meant to tempt someone

bait *VERB* **baits, baiting, baited**
❶ to put bait on a hook or in a trap ❷ to try to make someone angry by teasing them

baize *NOUN*
the thick green cloth that is used for covering snooker tables

bake *VERB* **bakes, baking, baked**
❶ to cook food in an oven with dry heat; to make bread or cakes ❷ to become very hot, especially in the sun ❸ to make clay hard by heating it

baked beans *PLURAL NOUN*
cooked white beans, usually tinned with tomato sauce

baker *NOUN* **bakers**
a person who bakes or sells bread or cakes

bakery *NOUN* **bakeries**
a place where bread and cakes are baked or a shop where they are sold

baking powder *NOUN*
a powder used to make bread and cakes rise when they are baked

baking soda *NOUN*
sodium bicarbonate

bakkie *NOUN* **bakkies** (*S. African*)
❶ a small pick-up truck with an open back
❷ a small bowl or basin

balaclava, balaclava helmet *NOUN*
balaclavas, balaclava helmets
(*chiefly British*) a hood covering the head and neck and part of the face
WORD ORIGIN named after *Balaclava*, a village in the Crimea (because the helmets were worn by soldiers fighting near there during the Crimean War)

balance *NOUN* **balances**
❶ a steady position, with the weight or amount evenly distributed ❷ a person's feeling of being steady • *She lost her balance and fell to the ground.* ❸ a device for weighing things, with two containers hanging from a bar ❹ the difference between money paid into an account and money taken out of it ❺ the amount of money that someone owes

balance *VERB* **balances, balancing, balanced**
❶ to balance on something is to make yourself steady on it ❷ something is balanced when it is steady with its weight evenly distributed

balcony *NOUN* **balconies**
❶ a platform that sticks out from an outside wall of a building ❷ the upstairs part of a theatre or cinema

bald *ADJECTIVE*
❶ without hair on the top of the head ❷ a bald statement or description is one without any details or explanation
➤ **baldly** *ADVERB*
➤ **baldness** *NOUN*

bale *NOUN* **bales**
a large bundle of hay, straw or cotton, usually tied up tightly

bale *VERB* **bales, baling, baled**
➤ **bale out** (*British*)
to jump out of an aircraft with a parachute in an emergency

baleful *ADJECTIVE*
menacing or harmful • *He gave her a baleful stare.*
➤ **balefully** *ADVERB*

ball *NOUN* **balls**
❶ a round object used in many games
❷ anything that has a round shape • *a ball of string* ❸ a formal party where people dance

➤ **ball of the foot** the rounded part of the foot at the base of the big toe

ballad *NOUN* ballads
❶ a traditional song or poem that tells a story ❷ a slow romantic pop song

ballast (say **bal**-ast) *NOUN*
heavy material that is carried in a ship or hot-air balloon to keep it steady

ball bearings *PLURAL NOUN*
small steel balls rolling in a groove on which machine parts can move easily

ballcock *NOUN* ballcocks
a floating ball that controls the water level in a cistern

ballerina (say bal-er-**een**-a) *NOUN* ballerinas
a female ballet dancer

ballet (say **bal**-ay) *NOUN* ballets
a style of dancing in which a group of dancers perform precise steps and movements to tell a story to music

ballistic (say bal-**ist**-ik) *ADJECTIVE*
to do with objects that are fired through the air, especially bullets and missiles
➤ **go ballistic** (*informal*) to become very angry

ballistic missile *NOUN* ballistic missiles
a missile that is powered and guided when it is launched and then falls under gravity on its target

balloon *NOUN* balloons
❶ a bag made of thin rubber that can be inflated and used as a toy or decoration ❷ a large round bag inflated with hot air or light gases to make it rise in the air, often carrying a basket in which passengers may ride ❸ an outline round spoken words in a cartoon

SPELLING
There is a double l and double o in balloon.

ballot *NOUN* ballots
❶ a secret method of voting, usually by making a mark on a piece of paper and putting it in a box ❷ a piece of paper on which a vote is made **WORD ORIGIN** from Italian *ballotta* = small ball (because one way of voting is by placing a ball in a box; the colour of the ball shows whether you are voting for something or against it)

ballpoint pen *NOUN* ballpoint pens
a pen with a tiny ball round which the ink flows

ballroom *NOUN* ballrooms
a large room where dances are held

balm *NOUN*
❶ a sweet-scented ointment ❷ something that soothes you

balmy *ADJECTIVE*
❶ balmy weather is gentle and warm • *a balmy breeze* ❷ sweet-scented like balm

balsa *NOUN*
a kind of very lightweight wood

balsam *NOUN* balsams
❶ a kind of sweet-smelling oily resin produced by certain trees, used to make perfumes and medicines ❷ a tree producing balsam

balti *NOUN* baltis
a type of Pakistani curry, cooked in a bowl-shaped pan

balustrade *NOUN* balustrades
a row of short posts or pillars that supports a rail or strip of stonework round a balcony or staircase **WORD ORIGIN** from Italian *balustra* = pomegranate flower (because the pillars of a balustrade were the same shape as the flower)

bamboo *NOUN* bamboos
❶ a tall plant with hard hollow stems ❷ a stem of the bamboo plant

bamboozle *VERB* bamboozles, bamboozling, bamboozled (*informal*)
to puzzle or trick someone • *Lucy looked completely bamboozled.*

ban *VERB* bans, banning, banned
to officially forbid someone from doing something • *He has been banned from driving for six months.*

ban *NOUN* bans
an order that bans something

banal (say ban-**ahl**) *ADJECTIVE*
ordinary and uninteresting
➤ **banality** *NOUN*

banana *NOUN* bananas
a long curved fruit with a yellow or green skin

band *NOUN* bands
❶ an organized group of people doing something together • *a band of robbers*
❷ a group of people playing music together ❸ a strip or loop of something ❹ a range of values, wavelengths, etc.

band *VERB* bands, banding, banded
to band together is to form an organized group

a
b
c
d
e
f
g
h
i
j
k
l
m
n
o
p
q
r
s
t
u
v
w
x
y
z

bandage *NOUN* bandages
a strip of material for tying round a wound

bandage *VERB* bandages, bandaging, bandaged
to tie a bandage round a wound

bandit *NOUN* bandits
a member of a gang of robbers who attack travellers

bandstand *NOUN* bandstands
a platform for a band playing music outdoors, usually in a park

bandwagon *NOUN*
➤ **jump on the bandwagon** to join other people in something that has become successful or popular

bandy *ADJECTIVE*
bandy legs curve outwards at the knees

bandy *VERB* bandies, bandying, bandied
if a name, word or story is bandied about, it is mentioned or told by a lot of different people

bane *NOUN*
if something is the bane of your life, it causes you a lot of trouble or worry

bang *NOUN* bangs
❶ a sudden loud noise like that of an explosion ❷ a sharp blow or knock

bang *VERB* bangs, banging, banged
❶ to hit or shut something noisily • *Don't bang the door when you go out.* ❷ to make a sudden loud noise ❸ to bump part of your body against something • *She banged her knee on the desk.*

bang *ADVERB*
(*informal*) exactly • *bang in the middle* • *bang on time*

banger *NOUN* bangers (*British*)
❶ a firework that explodes noisily ❷ (*informal*) a sausage ❸ (*informal*) a noisy old car

bangle *NOUN* bangles
a stiff bracelet

banish *VERB* banishes, banishing, banished
❶ to punish a person by ordering them to leave a place • *He was banished from the kingdom forever.* ❷ to drive away a thought or feeling from your mind • *She struggled to banish these fears.*
➤ **banishment** *NOUN*

banisters *PLURAL NOUN*
a handrail with upright supports beside a staircase

banjo *NOUN* banjos
a musical instrument like a small guitar with a round body

bank *NOUN* banks
❶ a business that looks after people's money ❷ a reserve supply • *a blood bank* ❸ a sloping piece of ground at either side of a river ❹ a long piled-up mass of earth, sand or snow ❺ a long thick mass of cloud or fog ❻ a row of lights or switches

bank *VERB* banks, banking, banked
❶ to put money in a bank ❷ to pile up to form a bank ❸ to tilt sideways while changing direction • *The plane banked as it prepared to land.*
➤ **bank on** to rely or depend on something

banker *NOUN* bankers
a person who runs a bank

bank holiday *NOUN* bank holidays
(*British*) a public holiday, when banks are officially closed

banknote *NOUN* banknotes
a piece of paper money issued by a bank

bankrupt *ADJECTIVE*
not able to pay your debts • *The company must cut its costs or it will go bankrupt.*
➤ **bankruptcy** *NOUN*

banner *NOUN* banners
❶ a strip of cloth with a design or slogan on it, carried on a pole or two poles in a procession or demonstration ❷ a flag

banns *PLURAL NOUN*
an announcement in a church that the two people named are going to marry each other

banquet *NOUN* banquets
a large formal dinner for invited guests which includes several courses
➤ **banqueting** *NOUN*

bantam *NOUN* bantams
a kind of small hen

banter *NOUN*
playful teasing or joking
➤ **banter** *VERB*

Bantu *NOUN* Bantu or Bantus
❶ a member of a group of central and southern African peoples ❷ the group of languages spoken by these peoples

bap *NOUN* baps
(*British*) a soft flat bread roll

baptism *NOUN* baptisms
the ceremony in which a person is formally baptized

Baptist *NOUN* Baptists
a member of a group of Christians who believe that a person should not be baptized until he or she is old enough to understand what baptism means

baptize (also **baptise**) *VERB* baptizes, baptizing, baptized
to receive someone into the Christian Church in a ceremony in which they are sprinkled with or dipped in water and usually given a name or names

bar *NOUN* bars
❶ a long straight piece of metal • *the bars of a prison cell* ❷ a block of something solid • *a bar of soap* ❸ a band of colour or light ❹ a counter or room where refreshments, especially alcoholic drinks, are served ❺ one of the small equal sections into which music is divided • *Can you sing the first few bars?*
➤ **behind bars** in prison

bar *VERB* bars, barring, barred
❶ to fasten something with a bar or bars • *All the windows were barred.* ❷ to bar someone's way or path is to stop them getting past ❸ to forbid or ban someone from doing something

barb *NOUN* barbs
the backward-pointing spike of a spear, arrow or fish hook, which makes it difficult to pull out

barbarian *NOUN* barbarians
an uncivilized or brutal person
WORD ORIGIN from Greek *barbaros* = babbling, not speaking Greek

barbaric, barbarous *ADJECTIVE*
savage and cruel
➤ **barbarity** *NOUN*
➤ **barbarism** *NOUN*

barbecue *NOUN* barbecues
❶ a metal frame for grilling food over an open fire outdoors ❷ a party where food is cooked in this way

barbecue *VERB* barbecues, barbecuing, barbecued
to cook food on a barbecue

barbed *ADJECTIVE*
❶ having a barb or barbs ❷ a barbed comment or remark is deliberately hurtful

barbed wire *NOUN*
wire with small spikes in it, used to make fences

barber *NOUN* barbers
a men's hairdresser **WORD ORIGIN** from Latin *barba* = beard

bar chart *NOUN* bar charts
a diagram that shows amounts as bars of equal width but varying height

bar code *NOUN* bar codes
a set of black lines that are printed on goods, library books, etc. and can be read by a computer to give information about the goods, books, etc.

bard *NOUN* bards (*literary*)
a poet or minstrel

bare *ADJECTIVE*
❶ without clothing or covering • *bare feet* • *a patch of bare ground* ❷ empty • *The cupboard was bare.* ❸ plain and simple, without details • *the bare facts* ❹ only just enough • *the bare necessities of life*
➤ **bareness** *NOUN*
➤ **with your bare hands** without weapons or tools

bare *VERB* bares, baring, bared
to uncover or reveal something • *The dog bared its teeth in a snarl.*

bareback *ADJECTIVE & ADVERB*
riding on a horse without a saddle

barefaced *ADJECTIVE*
a barefaced lie is one that is told boldly without any shame or guilt

barely *ADVERB*
only just; with difficulty • *I was so tired I was barely able to stand.*

bargain *NOUN* bargains
❶ an agreement about doing something in return for something else • *Come on, we've kept our side of the bargain.* ❷ something that you buy cheaply

bargain *VERB* bargains, bargaining, bargained
to argue over the price to be paid or what you will do in return for something
➤ **bargain for** to expect something to happen and be ready for it • *He got more than he bargained for.*

barge *NOUN* barges
a long flat-bottomed boat used on canals

barge *VERB* barges, barging, barged
to barge into someone is to bump clumsily into them or push them out of the way
➤ **barge in** to rush into a room rudely • *My brother suddenly came barging in.*

baritone NOUN baritones
a male singer with a voice between a tenor and a bass

barium (say **bair**-ee-um) NOUN
a soft silvery-white metal

bark NOUN barks
❶ the short harsh sound made by a dog or fox ❷ the outer covering of a tree's branches or trunk

bark VERB barks, barking, barked
❶ to make the sound of a bark ❷ to speak loudly and harshly

barley NOUN
a cereal plant from which malt is made

barley sugar NOUN barley sugars
a sweet made from boiled sugar

bar mitzvah NOUN bar mitzvahs
a religious ceremony for Jewish boys aged 13, when they take on the responsibilities of an adult under Jewish law **WORD ORIGIN** Hebrew, = son of the commandment

barmy ADJECTIVE (*informal*)
(*British*) crazy or mad **WORD ORIGIN** literally full of froth, from *barm* = yeast, froth

barn NOUN barns
a farm building for storing hay or grain

barnacle NOUN barnacles
a shellfish that attaches itself to rocks and the bottoms of ships

barn dance NOUN barn dances
a kind of country dance; an informal gathering for dancing

barnyard NOUN barnyards
a farmyard next to a barn

barometer (say ba-**rom**-it-er) NOUN barometers
an instrument that measures air pressure, used in forecasting the weather

baron NOUN barons
❶ a member of the lowest rank of noblemen ❷ a powerful owner of an industry or business • *a newspaper baron*
➤ **baronial** (say ba-**roh**-nee-al) ADJECTIVE

baroness NOUN baronesses
a female baron or a baron's wife

baronet NOUN baronets
a nobleman with a knighthood inherited from his father

baroque (say ba-**rok**) NOUN
an elaborately decorated style of architecture used in the 17th and 18th centuries

barracks NOUN
a large building or group of buildings for soldiers to live in

barrage (say **ba**-rahzh) NOUN barrages
❶ a dam built across a river ❷ heavy gunfire ❸ a large number of questions or comments that come quickly • *He faced a barrage of questions from reporters.*

barrel NOUN barrels
❶ a large rounded container with flat ends ❷ the metal tube of a gun, through which the shot is fired

barrel organ NOUN barrel organs
a musical instrument which you play by turning a handle

barren ADJECTIVE
❶ barren land is not able to produce crops or has no vegetation ❷ a barren woman is not able to have children ❸ a barren plant or tree is one that cannot bear fruit

barricade NOUN barricades
a barrier, especially one put up hastily across a street or door

barricade VERB barricades, barricading, barricaded
to block a street or door with a barricade • *They had barricaded themselves inside the house.* **WORD ORIGIN** French, from Spanish *barrica* = barrel (because barrels were sometimes used to build barricades)

barrier NOUN barriers
❶ a fence or wall that prevents people from getting past ❷ something that stops you doing something • *Lack of confidence can be a barrier to success.*

barrier reef NOUN barrier reefs
a coral reef close to the shore but separated from it by a channel of deep water

barrister NOUN barristers
a lawyer in England or Wales who represents people in the higher law courts

barrow NOUN barrows
❶ (*British*) a wheelbarrow ❷ (*British*) a small cart that is pushed or pulled by hand ❸ a mound of earth over a prehistoric grave

barter VERB barters, bartering, bartered
to exchange goods for other goods, without using money • *She bartered her jacket for some food.*

barter *NOUN*
the system of bartering

basalt (say **bas**-awlt) *NOUN*
a kind of dark volcanic rock

base *NOUN* bases
❶ the lowest part of something; the part on which a thing stands ❷ a starting point or foundation; a basis ❸ a headquarters ❹ each of the four corners that must be reached by a runner in baseball ❺ a substance that can combine with an acid to form a salt ❻ (*in mathematics*) the number in terms of which other numbers can be expressed in a number system. 10 is the base of the decimal system and 2 is the base of the binary system.

base *VERB* bases, basing, based
❶ to base one thing on another thing is to use the second thing as the starting point for the first • *She based the story on an event in her own childhood.* ❷ to be based somewhere is to live there or work from there

base *ADJECTIVE*
❶ showing no honour or moral principles • *base motives* ❷ a base metal is one that has no great value
➤ **basely** *ADVERB*

baseball *NOUN* baseballs
❶ a game in which runs are scored by hitting a ball and running round a series of four bases, played mainly in North America ❷ the ball used in this game

basement *NOUN* basements
a room or part of a building below ground level

bash *VERB* bashes, bashing, bashed
to hit something or someone hard

bash *NOUN* bashes
❶ a hard hit ❷ (*informal*) a try • *Have a bash at it.*

bashful *ADJECTIVE*
shy and self-conscious
➤ **bashfully** *ADVERB*

basic *ADJECTIVE*
forming an essential part or starting point • *He has a basic knowledge of French.* • *Food is a basic human need.*

basically *ADVERB*
at the simplest or most fundamental level • *She is basically lazy.*

basil *NOUN*
a Mediterranean herb used in cooking

basilica (say ba-**zil**-ik-a) *NOUN* basilicas
a large oblong church with two rows of columns and an apse at one end

basilisk (say **baz**-il-isk) *NOUN* basilisks
a mythical reptile that was said to be able to kill people just by looking at them
WORD ORIGIN from Greek *basilikos* = little king

basin *NOUN* basins
❶ a deep bowl for mixing food in ❷ a washbasin ❸ a sheltered area of water for mooring boats ❹ the area from which water drains into a river • *the Amazon basin*

basis *NOUN* bases
❶ something to start from or add to; the main principle or ingredient • *She used her diaries as the basis for her book.* ❷ the way in which something is done or organized • *They meet on a regular basis.*

bask *VERB* basks, basking, basked
to sit or lie comfortably warming yourself in the sun

basket *NOUN* baskets
a container for holding or carrying things, made of strips of flexible material or wire woven together

basketball *NOUN* basketballs
❶ a game in which goals are scored by putting a ball through high nets ❷ the ball used in this game

bass (say bayss) *ADJECTIVE*
deep-sounding; the bass part of a piece of music is the lowest part

bass (say bayss) *NOUN* basses
❶ a male singer with a very deep voice ❷ a bass instrument or part

bass (say bas) *NOUN* bass
a fish of the perch family

basset *NOUN* bassets
a short-legged dog with drooping ears

bassoon *NOUN* bassoons
a bass woodwind instrument

bastard *NOUN* bastards
❶ (*old use*) an illegitimate child ❷ (*offensive*) an unpleasant or difficult person or thing

baste *VERB* bastes, basting, basted
❶ to moisten meat with fat while it is cooking ❷ to sew fabric together loosely with long stitches

bastion *NOUN* bastions
❶ a part of a fortified building that sticks out

a
b
c
d
e
f
g
h
i
j
k
l
m
n
o
p
q
r
s
t
u
v
w
x
y
z

from the rest ❷ something that protects a belief or way of life

bat *NOUN* bats
❶ a shaped piece of wood used to hit the ball in sports like cricket, baseball and table tennis ❷ a flying mammal that looks like a mouse with wings
➤ **off your own bat** without help from other people

bat *VERB* bats, batting, batted
to have a turn at using a bat in cricket or baseball
➤ **not bat an eyelid** to show no surprise or embarrassment when something unusual happens

batch *NOUN* batches
a set of things or people dealt with together

bated *ADJECTIVE*
➤ **with bated breath** waiting anxiously

bath *NOUN* baths
❶ washing your whole body while sitting in water • *I'm going to have a bath.* ❷ a large container for water in which to wash your whole body; the water in a bath • *Your bath is getting cold.* ❸ a liquid in which something is placed • *an acid bath*

bath *VERB* baths, bathing, bathed (*British*) to give someone a bath • *to bath the baby*

bathe *VERB* bathes, bathing, bathed
❶ (*British*) to go swimming in the sea or a river ❷ to wash something gently ❸ to be bathed in light is to have light shining all over you

bathe *NOUN* bathes (*British*) a swim
➤ **bather** *NOUN*
➤ **bathing suit** *NOUN*

SPELLING

Bathe with an e sounds like b-ay-the.

bathos *NOUN*
a sudden change from a serious subject or tone to a ridiculous or trivial one

bathroom *NOUN* bathrooms
a room containing a bath or shower, a washbasin and often a toilet

baths *PLURAL NOUN*
❶ (*British*) a public swimming pool ❷ a place where people went in the past to wash or have a bath • *Roman baths*

bat mitzvah *NOUN* bat mitzvahs
a religious ceremony for Jewish girls aged 13, when they take on the responsibilities of an

adult under Jewish law WORD ORIGIN Hebrew, = daughter of the commandment

baton *NOUN* batons
a short stick, e.g. one used to conduct an orchestra or in a relay race

batsman *NOUN* batsmen
a player who uses a bat in cricket

battalion *NOUN* battalions
an army unit containing two or more companies

batten *NOUN* battens
a strip of wood or metal that holds something in place

batten *VERB* battens, battening, battened
to fasten something down firmly

batter *VERB* batters, battering, battered
to hit something hard and often • *Huge waves battered the rocks.*

batter *NOUN* batters
❶ a beaten mixture of flour, eggs and milk, used for making pancakes or coating food to be fried ❷ a player who is batting in baseball

battered *ADJECTIVE*
no longer looking new; damaged or out of shape • *a battered leather briefcase*

battering ram *NOUN* battering rams
a heavy pole that is used to break down walls or gates

battery *NOUN* batteries
❶ a device for storing and supplying electricity ❷ a set of pieces of equipment that are used together, especially a group of large guns ❸ a series of cages in which poultry or animals are kept close together • *battery farming*

battle *NOUN* battles
❶ a fight between two armies ❷ a struggle

battle *VERB* battles, battling, battled
to fight or struggle • *She battled to stay afloat.*

battlefield *NOUN* battlefields
a piece of ground on which a battle is or was fought

battlements *PLURAL NOUN*
the top of a castle wall, often with gaps from which the defenders could fire at the enemy

battleship *NOUN* battleships
a heavily armed warship

batty *ADJECTIVE* (*informal*)
(*British*) crazy or eccentric WORD ORIGIN from

the phrase *to have bats in the belfry* = to be crazy

bauble *NOUN* baubles
❶ a bright and showy ornament that has little value ❷ a decorative ball hung on a Christmas tree

bauxite *NOUN*
the clay-like substance from which aluminium is obtained

bawl *VERB* bawls, bawling, bawled
❶ to shout loudly ❷ to cry noisily

bay *NOUN* bays
❶ an area of the sea and coast where the shore curves inwards ❷ an area that is marked out to be used for parking vehicles, storing things, etc. • *a loading bay*
➤ **at bay** cornered but defiantly facing your attackers • *a stag at bay*
➤ **keep something at bay** to prevent something from coming near or threatening you • *He struggled to keep his fears at bay.*

bay *ADJECTIVE*
a bay horse is reddish-brown in colour

bay *VERB* bays, baying, bayed
to howl or cry, like a hunting dog chasing its prey • *a pack of baying hounds*

bayonet *NOUN* bayonets
a blade that can be fixed to the end of a rifle and used for stabbing

bay window *NOUN* bay windows
a window that sticks out from the main wall of a house

bazaar *NOUN* bazaars
❶ a sale held to raise money for charity ❷ a market place in a Middle Eastern country
WORD ORIGIN from Persian *bazar* = market

bazooka *NOUN* bazookas
a tube-shaped portable weapon for firing anti-tank rockets **WORD ORIGIN** the word originally meant a musical instrument rather like a trombone

BC *ABBREVIATION*
before Christ (used with dates counting back from the birth of Jesus Christ)

be *VERB* am, are, is; was, were; being, been
❶ to exist; to occupy a position • *The shop is on the corner.* ❷ to happen; to take place • *When is your birthday?*

be This verb is also used
❶ to describe a person or thing or give more information about them (*He is my teacher.*),
❷ to form parts of other verbs (*It is raining.*)

➤ **have been somewhere** to have gone to a place as a visitor • *We have been to Rome.*

GRAMMAR
Be is a common verb. Its inflections are very different from the infinitive *be* form:

The forms *am*, *are*, and *is* are used for the present tense.

The forms *was* and *were* are used for the past tense.

The present participle is *being*.

The past participle is *been*.

The verb **be** can be used as an auxiliary verb:

to form progressive tenses:

What are you doing?

We were living in London.

to form passive verbs:

The world record was broken in the final.

beach *NOUN* beaches
the part of the seashore nearest to the water

beached *ADJECTIVE*
a beached whale is one that is stranded on a beach

beacon *NOUN* beacons
a light or fire used as a signal or warning

bead *NOUN* beads
❶ a small piece of glass, wood or plastic with a hole through it for threading with others on a string or wire, e.g. to make a necklace ❷ a drop of liquid • *beads of sweat*
WORD ORIGIN from Old English *gebed* = prayer (because people kept count of the prayers they said by moving the beads on a rosary)

beady *ADJECTIVE*
beady eyes are small and bright

beagle *NOUN* beagles
a small hound with long ears, used for hunting hares

beak *NOUN* beaks
the hard horny part of a bird's mouth

beaker *NOUN* beakers (*British*)
❶ a tall drinking mug, often without a handle ❷ a glass container used for pouring liquids in a laboratory

beam *NOUN* beams
❶ a long thick bar of wood or metal ❷ a

a b c d e f g h i j k l m n o p q r s t u v w x y z

ray or stream of light or other radiation ❸ a happy smile

beam VERB beams, beaming, beamed
❶ to smile happily ❷ to send out radio or TV signals • *Live pictures of the ceremony were beamed around the world.* ❸ to send out light and warmth • *The sun beamed down on us.*

bean NOUN beans
❶ a kind of plant with seeds growing in pods ❷ its seed or pod eaten as food ❸ the seed of a coffee plant

bear NOUN bears
a large heavy animal with thick fur and large teeth and claws

bear VERB bears, bearing, bore, born or borne
❶ to carry or support the weight of something ❷ to have or show a mark, signature, etc. • *She still bears the scar.* ❸ to accept something and be able to deal with it; to put up with something • *I can't bear all this noise.* ❹ to produce fruit or give birth to a child • *She bore him two sons.*
➤ **bear something in mind** to remember something and take it into account
➤ **bear something out** to support or confirm the truth of something

bearable ADJECTIVE
that you can accept and deal with; able to be put up with • *The breeze made the heat more bearable.*

beard NOUN beards
hair on a man's chin

bearded ADJECTIVE
with a beard

bearer NOUN
someone who carries or brings something important • *I'm sorry to be the bearer of bad news.*

bearing NOUN bearings
❶ the way that you stand, walk or behave • *a man of aristocratic bearing* ❷ to have a bearing on something is to be relevant to it or to have an effect on it • *Her comments had no bearing on our decision.*
➤ **get your bearings** to work out where you are in a new place or situation
➤ **lose your bearings** to become confused about where you are

beast NOUN beasts
❶ any large four-footed animal ❷ (*informal*) a cruel or vicious person

beastly ADJECTIVE
(*informal*) cruel or unkind

beat VERB beats, beating, beat, beaten
❶ to hit someone repeatedly, especially with a stick ❷ to defeat someone or do better than them ❸ to shape or flatten something by hitting it repeatedly ❹ to stir a cooking mixture quickly so that it becomes thicker ❺ a heart beats when it makes regular movements • *His heart was beating with excitement.* ❻ a bird or insect beats its wings when it flaps them repeatedly
➤ **beat someone up** to attack someone very violently

beat NOUN beats
❶ a regular rhythm or stroke • *the beat of your heart* ❷ emphasis in rhythm; a strong rhythm in pop music ❸ a policeman's regular route

beatific (say bee-a-**tif**-ik) ADJECTIVE
showing great happiness • *a beatific smile*

beautiful ADJECTIVE
attractive to look at; giving pleasure to your senses or your mind

SPELLING
There is a tricky bit in **beautiful**—it has three vowels in a row, **eau**.

beautifully ADVERB
in a beautiful or pleasing way • *She plays the piano beautifully.*

beautify VERB beautifies, beautifying, beautified
to make someone or something beautiful

beauty NOUN beauties
❶ a quality that gives pleasure to your senses or your mind ❷ a beautiful person or thing ❸ an excellent example of something • *The last goal was a beauty.*

beaver NOUN beavers
an animal with soft brown fur and strong teeth; it builds its home in a deep pool which it makes by damming a stream

beaver VERB beavers, beavering, beavered
to beaver away at something is to work hard at it • *He's been beavering away on the computer all morning.*

becalmed ADJECTIVE
a ship that is becalmed is unable to move because there is no wind

because CONJUNCTION
for the reason that
➤ **because of** for the reason of • *He limped*

because of his bad leg.

SPELLING

To spell **because** try remembering: big elephants can always understand small elephants.

beck *NOUN*
➤ **at someone's beck and call** always ready and waiting to do what he or she asks

beckon *VERB* beckons, beckoning, beckoned
to make a sign to someone asking them to come towards you • *She beckoned him inside.*

become *VERB* becomes, becoming, became, become
❶ to begin to be something; to come or grow to be something • *It became dark.* • *She wants to become a pilot.* ❷ to make a person look attractive • *Short hair really becomes you.*
➤ **become of** to happen to someone or something • *Whatever became of Jim?*

bed *NOUN* beds
❶ a piece of furniture that you sleep or rest on, especially one with a mattress and coverings ❷ an area of ground in a garden where plants are grown ❸ the bottom of the sea or of a river ❹ a layer that other things lie or rest on • *chicken served on a bed of rice* ❺ a layer of rock or soil

bedclothes *PLURAL NOUN*
sheets, blankets and duvets for covering a bed

bedding *NOUN*
mattresses, pillows and bedclothes

bedlam *NOUN*
a scene full of noise and confusion • *It was bedlam as the doors opened on the morning of the sale.* **WORD ORIGIN** from *Bedlam*, the popular name of the Hospital of St Mary of Bethlehem, a London mental hospital in the 14th century

Bedouin (say **bed**-oo-in) *NOUN* Bedouin
a member of an Arab people living in tents in the desert regions of Arabia and North Africa

bedpan *NOUN* bedpans
a container used as a toilet by a person who is bedridden

bedraggled (say bid-**rag**-eld) *ADJECTIVE*
looking untidy or messy, especially after getting very wet

bedridden *ADJECTIVE*
too weak or ill to get out of bed

bedrock *NOUN*
❶ solid rock beneath soil ❷ the fundamental facts or principles on which an idea or belief is based

bedroom *NOUN* bedrooms
a room for sleeping in

bedside *NOUN* bedsides
a space beside a bed

bedsitter, bedsit *NOUN* bedsitters, bedsits
a room used for both living and sleeping in

bedspread *NOUN* bedspreads
a covering spread over a bed during the day

bedstead *NOUN* bedsteads
the framework of a bed

bedtime *NOUN* bedtimes
the time for going to bed

bee *NOUN* bees
a stinging insect with four wings that makes honey

beech *NOUN* beeches
a tree with smooth bark and glossy leaves

beef *NOUN*
meat from an ox, bull or cow

beefeater *NOUN* beefeaters
one of the guards at the Tower of London, who wear a uniform based on Tudor dress
WORD ORIGIN originally a scornful word for a fat, lazy servant

beefy *ADJECTIVE*
having a solid muscular body

beehive *NOUN* beehives
a box or other container for bees to live in

beeline *NOUN*
➤ **make a beeline for something** to go straight or quickly towards something
WORD ORIGIN because a bee was believed to fly in a straight line back to its hive

beep *VERB* beeps, beeping, beeped
❶ to give out a short high-pitched sound • *His mobile started beeping.* ❷ to sound a car horn as a signal • *A taxi beeped outside.*

beep *NOUN* beeps
a short high-pitched sound • *Leave your message after the beep.*

beer *NOUN* beers
an alcoholic drink made from malt and hops

beeswax *NOUN*
a yellow substance produced by bees, used for polishing wood and making candles

a b c d e f g h i j k l m n o p q r s t u v w x y z

beet *NOUN* beet or beets
a plant with a thick root used as a vegetable or for making sugar

beetle *NOUN* beetles
an insect with hard shiny wing covers

beetling *ADJECTIVE*
sticking out; overhanging • *beetling brows* • *a beetling cliff*

beetroot *NOUN* beetroot
(*chiefly British*) the dark red root of beet used as a vegetable

befall *VERB* befalls, befalling, befell, befallen
(*formal*)
to happen to someone • *Disaster befell them on the voyage.*

befit *VERB* befits, befitting, befitted
to be suitable or appropriate for someone or something • *She dressed as befitted a woman of her status.*

before *ADVERB*
at an earlier time • *We've seen this film before.*

before *PREPOSITION & CONJUNCTION*
❶ earlier than • *I was here before you!* ❷ in front of • *A vast landscape lay before them.*

> **SPELLING**
> **Before** ends with an e.

beforehand *ADVERB*
earlier or before something else happens • *She had tried to phone me beforehand.*

befriend *VERB* befriends, befriending, befriended
to make friends with someone

beg *VERB* begs, begging, begged
❶ to ask other people for money or food to live on ❷ to ask someone for something something seriously or desperately • *He begged for forgiveness.*
➤ **go begging** to be available because no one else wants it
➤ **I beg your pardon** ❶ I am sorry • *I beg your pardon. I picked up your bag by mistake.* ❷ I did not hear or understand what you said

beget *VERB* begets, begetting, begot, begotten (*old use*)
❶ to be the father of someone ❷ to produce or cause something • *Violence only begets more violence.*

beggar *NOUN* beggars
❶ a person who lives by begging in the street ❷ (*informal*) a person • *You lucky beggar!*

begin *VERB* begins, beginning, began, begun
❶ to do the earliest or first part of something; to start doing something • *He began by thanking everyone for coming.* • *We began the long walk home.* ❷ to start to happen or exist • *What time does the concert begin?* ❸ to have something as its first part • *The word begins with B.*

beginner *NOUN* beginners
a person who is just beginning to learn a subject or skill

beginning *NOUN* beginnings
the first part of something or the time when it starts

> **SPELLING**
> **Begin + ning = beginning.** Don't forget to double the **n** in the middle.

begone *VERB* (*old use*)
go away immediately • *Begone, witch!*

begonia (say big-**oh**-nee-a) *NOUN* begonias
a garden plant with brightly coloured flowers

begot
past tense of **beget**

begrudge *VERB* begrudges, begrudging, begrudged
❶ to resent the fact that someone has something • *I don't begrudge him his success.* ❷ to resent having to do something • *I begrudge paying so much for a ticket.*

beguile (say big-**yl**) *VERB* beguiles, beguiling, beguiled
❶ to amuse or fascinate someone ❷ to deceive someone

behalf *NOUN*
➤ **on behalf of** for the benefit of someone else or as their representative • *We are collecting money on behalf of cancer research.*
➤ **on my behalf** for me • *Will you accept the prize on my behalf?*

> **USAGE**
> Take care not to say *on behalf of* (= for someone else) when you mean *on the part of* (= by someone). For example, do not say *This was a serious mistake on behalf of the government* when you mean *on the part of the government.*

behave *VERB* behaves, behaving, behaved
❶ to act in a particular way • *They behaved badly.* ❷ to show good manners • *Behave yourself!*

behaviour *NOUN*
the way that someone behaves or acts • *I apologize for my behaviour yesterday.*
➤ **behavioural** *ADJECTIVE*

behead *VERB* beheads, beheading, beheaded
to cut the head off a person or thing; to execute a person in this way

behest *NOUN* (*formal*)
➤ **at a person's behest** done because they have asked or commanded you to do it • *At Laura's behest we took the notice down from the window.*

behind *ADVERB*
❶ at or to the back; at a place people have left • *The others are a long way behind.* • *Don't leave your bag behind.* ❷ not making good progress; late • *I'm behind with my work.*

behind *PREPOSITION*
❶ at or to the back of; on the further side of • *She hid behind a tree.* ❷ having made less progress than • *He is behind the rest of the class in French.* ❸ causing or being the reason for something • *What is behind all this trouble?* ❹ supporting or encouraging a person or thing • *We're all behind you.*
➤ **behind a person's back** kept secret from him or her deceitfully
➤ **behind the times** old-fashioned or out of date

behind *NOUN* behinds (*informal*) a person's bottom

behindhand *ADVERB & ADJECTIVE*
late or slow in doing something

behold *VERB* beholds, beholding, beheld (*old use*)
to see something in front of you • *What a sight to behold!*
➤ **beholder** *NOUN*

beige (say bayzh) *NOUN & ADJECTIVE*
a very light brown colour

being *NOUN* beings
❶ the state of existing • *Pakistan came into being in 1947.* ❷ a living creature • *alien beings*

belated *ADJECTIVE*
coming very late or too late • *a belated birthday present*
➤ **belatedly** *ADVERB*

belay *VERB* belays, belaying, belayed
to fasten a rope by winding it round a peg or spike

belch *VERB* belches, belching, belched
❶ to send out wind from your stomach through your mouth noisily ❷ to send out fire or smoke from an opening • *There was a tall chimney belching black smoke.*

belch *NOUN* belches
an act of belching • *He let out a loud belch.*

belfry *NOUN* belfries
a tower or part of a tower in which bells hang

belie *VERB* belies, belying, belied
to give a false idea of something • *His smiling face belied his true feelings.*

belief *NOUN* beliefs
❶ the feeling that something exists or is true • *His belief in UFOs grew stronger.* ❷ something that a person believes • *religious beliefs*

> **SPELLING**
> The 'ee' sound is spelt ie in **belief**.

believable *ADJECTIVE*
able to be believed • *All the characters in the novel are believable.*

believe *VERB* believes, believing, believed
to think that something is true or that someone is telling the truth
➤ **believer** *NOUN*
➤ **believe in** ❶ to think that something exists • *Do you believe in ghosts?* ❷ to think that someone or something is good or can be relied on

> **SPELLING**
> The 'ee' sound is spelt ie in **believe**. Don't forget the e after the v.

belittle *VERB* belittles, belittling, belittled
to talk about something as if it were unimportant or of little value • *Her brother was always belittling her achievements.*

bell *NOUN* bells
❶ a cup-shaped metal instrument that makes a ringing sound when struck by the clapper hanging inside it ❷ any device that makes a ringing or buzzing sound to attract attention ❸ a bell-shaped object

belle *NOUN* belles
a beautiful woman

belligerent (say bil-**ij**-er-ent) *ADJECTIVE*
aggressive; keen to start a fight • *He had a belligerent look in his eye.*
➤ **belligerently** *ADVERB*

bellow *VERB* bellows, bellowing, bellowed
❶ to shout loudly and deeply • *'Sit down!', he*

61

bellowed. ❷ to make a loud deep sound, like a bull does

bellow NOUN bellows
❶ a deep shout • *a bellow of rage* ❷ the loud deep sound made by a bull or other large animal

bellows PLURAL NOUN
a device for pumping air into a fire, organ pipes, etc.

belly NOUN bellies
your stomach or abdomen

belong VERB belongs, belonging, belonged
❶ to belong to someone is to be owned by them • *Who does this phone belong to?* ❷ to belong to a club or group is to be a member of it ❸ to belong somewhere is to have a special place where it goes • *The butter belongs in the fridge.*

belongings PLURAL NOUN
your belongings are the things that you own

beloved ADJECTIVE
dearly loved • *his beloved homeland*

below ADVERB
at or to a lower position; underneath • *I'll have the top bunk and you can sleep below.*

below PREPOSITION
lower than; under • *The temperature was ten degrees below zero.*

belt NOUN belts
❶ a strip of cloth or leather etc. that you wear round your waist ❷ a continuous moving band used in engines and machinery ❸ a long narrow area • *a belt of rain* • *the asteroid belt*

belt VERB belts, belting, belted
❶ (*informal*) to hit someone very hard ❷ (*informal*) to run or travel very fast • *I was belting along on my bike.*

bemused ADJECTIVE
puzzled or confused • *He gave her a bemused look.*

bench NOUN benches
❶ a long seat ❷ a long table for working at in a workshop or laboratory ❸ the seat where judges or magistrates sit; the judges or magistrates hearing a case

bend VERB bends, bending, bent
❶ to make something curved and no longer straight • *It hurts when I bend my knee.* ❷ to be or become curved • *The road bends to the left here.* ❸ to move the top of your body

downwards; to stoop • *She bent down to pick up the cat.*

bend NOUN bends
a place where something bends; a curve or turn • *a bend in the road*

beneath PREPOSITION
❶ under • *The ship disappeared beneath the waves.* ❷ not good enough for someone • *She felt that cleaning for other people was beneath her.*

beneath ADVERB
underneath

benediction NOUN benedictions
a blessing

benefactor NOUN benefactors
a person who gives money or other help

beneficial ADJECTIVE
having a good or helpful effect • *Fresh air is beneficial to health.*

beneficiary (say ben-if-**ish**-er-ee) NOUN
beneficiaries
a person who benefits from another person's will

benefit NOUN benefits
❶ an advantage or good effect that something brings ❷ money that the government pays to help people who are poor, sick or out of work

benefit VERB benefits, benefiting, benefited
❶ to receive an advantage from something • *She would benefit from extra training.* ❷ to give an advantage to someone or something • *The rainforests benefit people all over the world.*

benevolence NOUN
kindness or being helpful • *a face full of benevolence*

benevolent ADJECTIVE
❶ kind and helpful • *a benevolent smile* ❷ formed for charitable purposes • *a benevolent fund*
➤ **benevolently** ADVERB

benign (say bin-**yn**) ADJECTIVE
❶ kind and gentle; not hurting anyone • *Fortunately, he was in a benign mood.* ❷ a benign tumour is not dangerous or likely to cause death
➤ **benignly** ADVERB

bent ADJECTIVE
curved or crooked
➤ **bent on** determined to do something • *He was clearly bent on revenge.*

bent *NOUN*
a liking or talent for something • *She has quite a bent for acting.*

benzene *NOUN*
a substance obtained from coal tar and used as a solvent, motor fuel and in the manufacture of plastics

benzine *NOUN*
a spirit obtained from petroleum and used in dry cleaning

bequeath *VERB* bequeaths, bequeathing, bequeathed
to leave something to a person in a will

bequest *NOUN* bequests
something left to a person in a will

bereaved *ADJECTIVE*
suffering from the recent death of a close relative
➤ **bereavement** *NOUN*

bereft *ADJECTIVE*
deprived of or lacking something • *We felt bereft of all hope.*

beret (say **bair**-ay) *NOUN* berets
a round flat cap with no peak

berg *NOUN* bergs
(*S. African*) a mountain

berry *NOUN* berries
any small round juicy fruit without a stone

berserk (say ber-**zerk**) *ADJECTIVE*
➤ **go berserk** to become extremely angry or violent, often in an uncontrolled way • *He'll go berserk when he finds out.*
WORD ORIGIN from Icelandic *berserkr* = wild warrior, from *ber-* = bear + *serkr* = coat

berth *NOUN* berths
❶ a sleeping place on a ship or train ❷ a place where a ship can moor
➤ **give someone a wide berth** to avoid someone by keeping at a safe distance

berth *VERB* berths, berthing, berthed
to moor in a berth

beryl *NOUN* beryls
a pale-green precious stone

beseech *VERB* beseeches, beseeching, beseeched or besought
to ask or beg someone earnestly to do something; to implore someone • *Let him go, I beseech you!*

beset *VERB* besets, besetting, beset
to be beset by problems or difficulties is to be

badly affected by them • *The team was beset by injuries all season.*

beside *PREPOSITION*
by the side of; near • *a house beside the sea*
➤ **be beside the point** to have nothing to do with the subject you are discussing
➤ **be beside yourself** to be very excited or upset • *She was beside herself with grief.*

besides *PREPOSITION & ADVERB*
in addition to; also • *Who came besides you?* • *And besides, it's the wrong colour.*

besiege *VERB* besieges, besieging, besieged
❶ to surround a place in order to capture it • *The Greeks besieged the city of Troy for ten years.* ❷ to crowd round a person or group • *Fans besieged the singer after the concert.*

besotted *ADJECTIVE*
so much in love with a person or thing that you cannot think or behave normally

besought
past tense of **beseech**

best *ADJECTIVE*
of the most excellent kind; most able to do something • *She's the best swimmer in the class.*

best *ADVERB*
❶ in the best way; most • *Which one do you like best?* ❷ most usefully; most wisely • *We had best go.*

best *NOUN*
❶ the best person or thing; the one that is better than all the others • *He is the best at tennis.* • *We bought the best we could afford.* ❷ to do your best is to do as well as you can

bestial (say **best**-ee-al) *ADJECTIVE*
to do with or like a beast; cruel and disgusting

best man *NOUN*
a man who helps and supports the bridegroom at a wedding

bestow *VERB* bestows, bestowing, bestowed
to give something to someone, especially to show how much they are respected • *It was a title bestowed on him by the king.*

bestseller *NOUN* bestsellers
a book that has sold in large numbers

bet *NOUN* bets
❶ an agreement that you will receive money if you are correct in choosing the winner of a race or game or in saying something will happen and will lose money if you are not correct ❷ the amount of money you risk losing in a bet

bet VERB bets, betting, bet or betted
❶ to make a bet ❷ (informal) to think that something is likely to happen or be true • I bet he will forget.

beta (say beet-a) NOUN
the second letter of the Greek alphabet, equivalent to Roman B, b

betide VERB
➤ woe betide there will be trouble for • Woe betide anyone who gets in her way!

betray VERB betrays, betraying, betrayed
❶ to be disloyal to a person or country; to do harm to someone who trusts you ❷ to reveal something without meaning to • His voice betrayed the anger he was feeling.
➤ betrayer NOUN

betrayal NOUN betrayals
betraying someone or something • a story of love and betrayal

betrothed ADJECTIVE (formal)
engaged to be married
➤ betrothal NOUN

better ADJECTIVE
❶ more excellent; more satisfactory • My sister speaks German better than I do. ❷ no longer ill • I'm feeling better now.
➤ get the better of to defeat or outwit someone

better ADVERB
❶ in a better way; more • Try to do it better next time. ❷ if you had better do something, you should do it or ought to do it • We had better go before it gets dark.
➤ be better off to be more fortunate or have more money

better VERB betters, bettering, bettered
to improve on something • She hopes to better her own record time.

between PREPOSITION & ADVERB
❶ in the space or time that separates two points or limits • The house stood between two large oak trees. • Call me between Tuesday and Friday. ❷ connecting two or more people, places or things • The train runs between London and Glasgow. ❸ shared by • Divide this money between you. ❹ separating; comparing • Can you tell the difference between them?

USAGE
Take care to follow the preposition between with the object form of the pronoun (me, her, him, them or us). For example, you would say between you and me (not 'between you and I').

betwixt PREPOSITION & ADVERB (old use)
between

bevel VERB bevels, bevelling, bevelled
to give a sloping edge to something • a mirror with bevelled edges

beverage NOUN beverages
any kind of drink • hot and cold beverages

bevy NOUN bevies
a large group • a bevy of beauties

bewail VERB bewails, bewailing, bewailed
to express great sorrow about something

beware VERB
to be careful • Beware of pickpockets.

SPELLING
Beware has no other forms; it is only ever used as a command.

bewilder VERB bewilders, bewildering, bewildered
to puzzle or confuse someone completely • He was bewildered by this sudden change of plan.
➤ bewilderment NOUN

bewildering ADJECTIVE
confusing and difficult to understand • It was a bewildering experience.

bewitch VERB bewitches, bewitching, bewitched
❶ to put a magic spell on someone ❷ to delight or fascinate someone very much

beyond PREPOSITION & ADVERB
❶ further than; further on • Don't go beyond the fence. • You can see the next valley and the mountains beyond. ❷ outside the range of; too difficult for • The problem is beyond me.

Bhagavadgita NOUN
a sacred book in Hinduism

bhangra NOUN
a style of music that combines traditional Punjabi music with rock music

biannual ADJECTIVE
happening twice a year
➤ biannually ADVERB

USAGE
Take care not to confuse this word with biennial.

bias *NOUN* biases
 ❶ a strong feeling in favour of one person or side and against another; a prejudice **❷** a tendency to swerve

biased *ADJECTIVE*
 showing that you prefer one person or side over another

bib *NOUN* bibs
 ❶ a cloth or covering put under a baby's chin during meals **❷** the part of an apron above the waist

Bible *NOUN* Bibles
 the sacred book of the Jews (the Old Testament) and of the Christians (the Old and New Testament)

biblical *ADJECTIVE*
 to do with or mentioned in the Bible

bibliography (say bib-lee-**og**-ra-fee) *NOUN* bibliographies
 a list of books about a subject or by a particular author

bicarbonate *NOUN*
 a kind of carbonate

bicentenary (say by-sen-**teen**-er-ee) *NOUN* bicentenaries
 a 200th anniversary

biceps (say **by**-seps) *NOUN* biceps
 the large muscle at the front of the arm above the elbow (**WORD ORIGIN**) Latin, = two-headed (because its end is attached at two points)

bicker *VERB* bickers, bickering, bickered
 to quarrel over unimportant things; to squabble

bicycle *NOUN* bicycles
 a two-wheeled vehicle that you ride by pushing down on pedals with your feet

bid *NOUN* bids
 ❶ the offer of an amount you are willing to pay for something, especially at an auction **❷** an attempt • *a bid to break the world record*

bid *VERB* bids, bidding, bid
 to make a bid • *Someone bid $2 million for the painting.*
 ➤ **bidder** *NOUN*

bid *VERB* bids, bidding, bid (or (*old use*) bade, bid or bidden
 ❶ to say something as a greeting or farewell • *I bid you all good night.* **❷** to command someone to do something • *He bade me come closer.* (**WORD ORIGIN**) from two Old

English words; *biddan* = to ask, and *beodan* = to announce or command

bidding *NOUN*
 if you do someone's bidding, you do what they tell you to do

bide *VERB* bides, biding, bided
 ➤ **bide your time** to wait for the right time to do something

bidet (say **bee**-day) *NOUN* bidets
 a low washbasin to sit on for washing the lower part of the body (**WORD ORIGIN**) from French *bidet* = a pony (because you sit astride it)

biennial (say by-**en**-ee-al) *ADJECTIVE*
 ❶ a biennial plant lives for two years, flowering and dying in the second year **❷** happening once every two years
 ➤ **biennially** *ADVERB*

biennial *NOUN* biennials
 a plant that lives for two years, flowering and dying in the second year

> **USAGE**
> Take care not to confuse this word with **biannual**.

bier (say beer) *NOUN* biers
 a movable stand on which a coffin or a dead body is placed before it is buried

bifocal (say by-**foh**-kal) *ADJECTIVE*
 bifocal lenses for glasses are made in two sections, with the upper part for looking at distant objects and the lower part for reading

bifocals *PLURAL NOUN*
 bifocal glasses

big *ADJECTIVE* bigger, biggest
 ❶ more than the normal size; large **❷** important • *the big match* • *a big decision* **❸** more grown-up; elder • *my big sister*

bigamy (say **big**-a-mee) *NOUN*
 the crime of marrying a person when you are already married to someone else
 ➤ **bigamist** *NOUN*

bigot *NOUN* bigots
 a person who holds strong and unreasonable opinions and is not willing to listen to other people's opinions

bigoted *ADJECTIVE*
 holding strong and unreasonable opinions and not willing to listen to other people's opinions
 ➤ **bigotry** *NOUN*

bike *NOUN* bikes (*informal*)
a bicycle or motorcycle

bikini *NOUN* bikinis
a woman's two-piece swimsuit
WORD ORIGIN named after the island of *Bikini* in the Pacific Ocean, where an atomic bomb test was carried out in 1946, at about the time the bikini was first worn (both caused great excitement)

bilateral *ADJECTIVE*
❶ between two people or groups
• *a bilateral agreement* ❷ affecting both of two sides

bilberry *NOUN* bilberries
a small dark-blue edible berry

bile *NOUN*
a bitter liquid produced by the liver, helping to digest fats

bilge *NOUN* bilges
❶ (the bilges) the bottom of a ship or the water that collects there ❷ (*informal*) nonsense; worthless ideas

bilingual (say by-**ling**-wal) *ADJECTIVE*
❶ able to speak two languages well
❷ written in two languages

bilious *ADJECTIVE*
feeling sick; sickly

bill *NOUN* bills
❶ a piece of paper that shows how much money you owe for goods or services
• *Can we have the bill, please?* • *an electricity bill* ❷ a list of events and performers in a show or concert • *Who's on the bill?* ❸ a poster or notice ❹ the draft of a proposed law to be discussed by parliament
❺ (*North American*) a banknote
❻ a bird's beak

billabong *NOUN* billabongs
(in Australia) a river branch that forms a backwater or a stagnant pool
WORD ORIGIN an Aboriginal word

billboard *NOUN* billboards
a large board near a road where advertisements are displayed

billet *NOUN* billets
a temporary lodging for soldiers, especially in a private house

billet *VERB* billets, billeting, billeted
to house soldiers in a billet

billiards *NOUN*
a game in which three balls are struck with

long sticks (called cues) on a cloth-covered table

billion *NOUN* & *ADJECTIVE* billions
❶ a thousand million (1,000,000,000) ❷ (*old use*) a million million (1,000,000,000,000)
➤ **billionth** *ADJECTIVE* & *NOUN*

USAGE
Although the word originally meant a million million, nowadays it usually means a thousand million.

billow *VERB* billows, billowing, billowed
❶ to fill with air and swell outwards
• *curtains billowing in the breeze* ❷ to move in large clouds through the air • *Smoke billowed from the chimneys.*

billow *NOUN* billows
a large rolling mass of cloud, smoke or steam
• *great billows of black smoke*

billycan *NOUN* billycans
a pot with a lid, used as a kettle or cooking pot when you are camping
WORD ORIGIN from Australian Aboriginal *billa* = water

billy goat *NOUN* billy goats
a male goat. Compare with **nanny goat**.

bin *NOUN* bins
(*British*) a large or deep container, especially one for rubbish or litter

binary (say **by**-ner-ee) *ADJECTIVE*
involving sets of two; consisting of two parts

binary digit *NOUN* binary digits
either of the two digits (0 and 1) used in the binary system

binary number *NOUN* binary numbers
a number expressed in the binary system

binary system, binary notation *NOUN*
a system of expressing numbers by using the digits 0 and 1 only, used in computing

bind *VERB* binds, binding, bound
❶ to tie things together or tie someone up
• *They bound the prisoner's hands behind his back.* ❷ to fasten a strip of material round something ❸ to fasten the pages of a book into a cover ❹ to make people feel that they have a close connection • *They shared a secret which had bound them together.*
❺ to make someone agree to do something

bind *NOUN* (*informal*) something that you find boring or annoying; a nuisance

binder NOUN binders
a cover for holding magazines or loose papers together

binding ADJECTIVE
a binding agreement or promise is one that must be carried out or obeyed

binding NOUN bindings
the covers and glue that hold the pages of a book together

binge NOUN binges (*informal*)
a time spent eating or drinking too much

bingo NOUN
a game using cards on which numbered squares are crossed out as the numbers are called out at random

binoculars PLURAL NOUN
a device with lenses for both eyes, making distant objects seem nearer
WORD ORIGIN from Latin *bini* = two together + *oculus* = eye

biochemistry NOUN
the study of the chemical composition and processes of living things
➤ **biochemical** ADJECTIVE
➤ **biochemist** NOUN

biodegradable ADJECTIVE
able to be broken down by bacteria in the environment • *All our packaging is biodegradable.*

biodiversity NOUN
the existence of a large number of different kinds of animals and plants in an area

biography (say by-**og**-ra-fee) NOUN
biographies
the story of a person's life
➤ **biographical** ADJECTIVE
➤ **biographer** NOUN

biological ADJECTIVE
to do with biology

biology NOUN
the scientific study of the life and structure of living things
➤ **biologist** NOUN

bionic (say by-**on**-ik) ADJECTIVE
a bionic body part is operated by electronic devices

biopsy (say **by**-op-see) NOUN biopsies
an examination of tissue from a living body

biosphere NOUN biospheres
all the parts of the Earth which contain living things

biped (say by-ped) NOUN bipeds
a two-footed animal

biplane NOUN biplanes
an aeroplane with two sets of wings, one above the other

birch NOUN birches
❶ a deciduous tree with slender branches
❷ a bundle of birch twigs used in the past for flogging people

bird NOUN birds
an animal with feathers, two wings and two legs

birdie NOUN birdies
❶ (*informal*) a bird ❷ a score in golf of one stroke under par for a hole

bird of prey NOUN birds of prey
a bird that feeds on animal flesh, such as an eagle or hawk

bird's-eye view NOUN
a view of something from above

Biro NOUN Biros (*British*) (*trademark*)
a kind of ballpoint pen **WORD ORIGIN** named after its Hungarian inventor, László *Biró*

birth NOUN births
❶ birth is when a baby or young animal comes out from its mother's body at the beginning of its life ❷ a person's family origin • *He is of noble birth.* ❸ the beginning of something • *the birth of television*

birth control NOUN
ways of avoiding conceiving a baby

birthday NOUN birthdays
the anniversary of the day you were born

birthmark NOUN birthmarks
a coloured mark that has been on a person's skin since they were born

birthplace NOUN birthplaces
the house or town where someone was born • *We visited Shakespeare's birthplace in Stratford-upon-Avon.*

birth rate NOUN birth rates
the number of children born in one year for every 1,000 people

birthright NOUN
a right or privilege to which a person is entitled through being born into a particular family or country

a b c d e f g h i j k l m n o p q r s t u v w x y z

biscuit NOUN biscuits
a small flat kind of cake that has been baked until it is crisp (WORD ORIGIN) from Latin *bis* = twice + *coctus* = cooked (because originally they were baked and then dried out in a cool oven to make them keep longer)

bisect (say by-**sekt**) VERB bisects, bisecting, bisected
to divide something into two equal parts
➤ **bisector** NOUN

bishop NOUN bishops
❶ a high-ranking member of the Christian clergy in charge of all the churches in a city or district ❷ a chess piece shaped like a bishop's mitre

bishopric NOUN bishoprics
the position or diocese of a bishop

bismuth NOUN
❶ a greyish-white metal ❷ a compound of this used in medicine

bison (say **by**-son) NOUN bison
a wild ox found in North America and Europe, with a large shaggy head

bistro NOUN bistros
a small restaurant

bit NOUN bits
❶ a small piece or amount of something • *Which bit of the film did you like the best?* ❷ the metal part of a horse's bridle that is put into its mouth ❸ the part of a tool that cuts or grips things when twisted ❹ (*in computing*) the smallest unit of information in a computer
➤ **a bit** ❶ a short distance or time • *I'm just going out for a bit.* ❷ slightly • *I'm a bit worried.*
➤ **bit by bit** gradually
➤ **to bits** into small pieces • *She angrily tore the letter to bits.*

bit VERB
past tense of bite

bitch NOUN bitches
❶ a female dog, fox or wolf ❷ (*offensive*) a woman who behaves in a spiteful or nasty way

bitchy ADJECTIVE
talking about other people in a spiteful way • *bitchy remarks*

bite VERB bites, biting, bit, bitten
❶ to cut or take something with your teeth ❷ to pierce skin with a sting or teeth • *I've been bitten all over by midges.* ❸ fish bite when they accept an angler's bait
➤ **bite the dust** to die or be killed

bite NOUN bites
❶ a mouthful cut off by biting • *She took a bite.* ❷ a wound or mark made by biting • *a mosquito bite* ❸ a snack • *Let's grab a quick bite to eat.*

> **SPELLING**
> The past tense of bite is bit; do not add ed.

biting ADJECTIVE
a biting wind is cold and unpleasant

bitter ADJECTIVE
❶ tasting sharp, not sweet ❷ feeling hurt or resentful • *He still feels bitter about the way he was treated.* ❸ causing hurt or sorrow • *a bitter disappointment* ❹ very cold • *a bitter wind*
➤ **bitterness** NOUN

bitterly ADVERB
❶ in an angry and disappointed way • *'I've lost everything,' she said bitterly.* ❷ extremely, unpleasantly • *He was bitterly disappointed.* • *It was a bitterly cold day.*

bittern NOUN bitterns
a marsh bird, the male of which makes a booming cry

bitumen (say **bit**-yoo-min) NOUN
a black sticky substance used for covering roads or roofs

bivalve NOUN bivalves
a shellfish, such as an oyster or mussel, that has a shell with two hinged parts

bivouac (say **biv**-oo-ak) NOUN bivouacs
a temporary camp without tents

bivouac VERB bivouacs, bivouacking, bivouacked
to camp in a bivouac

bizarre (say biz-**ar**) ADJECTIVE
very odd in appearance or effect • *bizarre sea creatures*

blab VERB blabs, blabbing, blabbed
to let out a secret • *Someone must have blabbed to the police.*

black ADJECTIVE
❶ of the very darkest colour, like coal or soot ❷ having dark skin; of African or Australian Aboriginal ancestry ❸ black coffee or tea has no milk added to it ❹ very dirty ❺ dismal; not hopeful • *The outlook is black.* ❻ hostile or angry • *He gave me a black look.*

➤ **blackly** *ADVERB*
➤ **blackness** *NOUN*
black *NOUN* blacks
a black colour • *People often wear black at funerals.*
black *VERB* blacks, blacking, blacked
to make a thing black • *He was busy blacking his boots.*
➤ **black out** to faint or lose consciousness
➤ **black something out** to cover something so that no light can penetrate • *All the windows were blacked out.*

blackberry *NOUN* blackberries
a sweet black berry

blackbird *NOUN* blackbirds
a European songbird, the male of which is black

blackboard *NOUN* blackboards
a dark board for writing on with chalk

black box *NOUN* black boxes
the flight recorder of an aircraft, which records technical information about its flight

blacken *VERB* blackens, blackening, blackened
❶ to make something black or to become black • *The oak beams had been blackened by smoke.* ❷ to blacken someone's name or reputation is to damage it

black eye *NOUN* black eyes
an eye with a bruise round it

blackguard (say **blag**-erd) *NOUN* blackguards (*old use*)
a man who behaves in a wicked or dishonourable way **WORD ORIGIN** originally the *black guard* = the servants who did the dirty jobs

blackhead *NOUN* blackheads
a small black spot in the skin

black hole *NOUN* black holes
a region in outer space with such a strong gravitational field that no matter or radiation can escape from it

black ice *NOUN*
thin transparent ice on roads

blacklist *NOUN* blacklists
a list of people who are disapproved of
➤ **blacklist** *VERB*

black magic *NOUN*
magic used for evil purposes

blackmail *VERB* blackmails, blackmailing, blackmailed
to demand money from someone by threatening to reveal something that they want to keep secret

blackmail *NOUN*
the crime of blackmailing someone
➤ **blackmailer** *NOUN*

black market *NOUN* black markets
illegal trading in goods

blackout *NOUN* blackouts
❶ a period of darkness when no light must be shown ❷ a temporary loss of consciousness

black sheep *NOUN*
a member of a family or other group who is seen as a disgrace to it

blacksmith *NOUN* blacksmiths
a person who makes and repairs iron things, especially one who makes and fits horseshoes
WORD ORIGIN because of the dark colour of iron

black spot *NOUN* black spots
a dangerous place where accidents often happen

bladder *NOUN* bladders
the bag-like part of the body in which urine collects

blade *NOUN* blades
❶ the flat cutting edge of a knife, sword or axe ❷ the flat wide part of an oar, spade or propeller ❸ a long flat narrow leaf of grass ❹ a broad flat bone • *shoulder blade*

blame *VERB* blames, blaming, blamed
❶ to say that somebody or something has caused what is wrong • *My brother broke the window but they blamed me.* ❷ to find fault with someone • *I don't blame you for feeling fed up.*

blame *NOUN*
responsibility for what is wrong • *Why do I always get the blame?*

blameless *ADJECTIVE*
deserving no blame; innocent

blanch *VERB* blanches, blanching, blanched
to turn pale • *He blanched with fear.*

blancmange (say bla-**monj**) *NOUN* blancmanges
(*British*) a jelly-like pudding made with milk
WORD ORIGIN from French *blanc* = white + *mange* = eat

bland *ADJECTIVE*
❶ having a mild flavour rather than a strong one ❷ not having any interesting features or qualities • *a bland style of writing*

a
b
c
d
e
f
g
h
i
j
k
l
m
n
o
p
q
r
s
t
u
v
w
x
y
z

A
B
C
D
E
F
G
H
I
J
K
L
M
N
O
P
Q
R
S
T
U
V
W
X
Y
Z

➤ **blandly** ADVERB
➤ **blandness** NOUN

blank ADJECTIVE
❶ empty, with nothing written, printed or recorded on it • *a blank piece of paper* ❷ showing no interest or expression • *His face looked blank.* ❸ empty of thoughts • *My mind's gone blank.*
➤ **blankness** NOUN

blank NOUN blanks
❶ an empty space ❷ a blank cartridge
(**WORD ORIGIN**) from French *blanc* = white

blank cartridge NOUN blank cartridges
a cartridge for a gun that makes a noise but does not fire a bullet

blank cheque NOUN blank cheques
a cheque with the amount not yet filled in

blanket NOUN blankets
❶ a warm cloth covering for a bed ❷ a thick soft layer covering something completely • *a blanket of snow*

blanket VERB blankets, blanketing, blanketed
to cover something completely with a thick soft layer • *Snow blanketed the ground.*

blanket ADJECTIVE
covering all cases or instances • *a blanket ban*
(**WORD ORIGIN**) originally = woollen cloth which had not been dyed; from French *blanc* = white

blankly ADVERB
without showing any emotion or understanding • *Tom stared at her blankly.*

blank verse NOUN
verse written without rhyme, usually in lines of ten syllables

blare VERB blares, blaring, blared
to make a loud harsh sound • *Car horns blared.*
➤ **blare** NOUN

blasé (say **blah**-zay) ADJECTIVE
not interested in or impressed by something because you are used to it

blaspheme (say blas-**feem**) VERB blasphemes, blaspheming, blasphemed
to talk or write in a rude or disrespectful way about God or religion

blasphemy (say blas-fim-ee) NOUN blasphemies
rude or disrespectful talk about God or religion
➤ **blasphemous** ADJECTIVE

blast NOUN blasts
❶ a strong rush of wind or air ❷ a sharp or

loud noise • *The referee gave a long blast on his whistle.* ❸ an explosion, especially one caused by a bomb

blast VERB blasts, blasting, blasted
❶ to make a hole in something with an explosion; to blow something up • *They had to blast a tunnel through the mountain.* ❷ to hit or kick something with a lot of force • *He blasted the ball over the bar.* ❸ to make a loud noise • *Music was blasting out of the speakers.*
➤ **blast off** to launch by the firing of rockets

blast furnace NOUN blast furnaces
a furnace for smelting ore, which works by having hot air driven into it

blast-off NOUN
the launch of a rocket or spacecraft • *Apollo 11 was ready for blast-off.*

blatant (say **blay**-tant) ADJECTIVE
very obvious • *a blatant lie*
➤ **blatantly** ADVERB
(**WORD ORIGIN**) from an old word meaning 'noisy'

blaze NOUN blazes
a very bright flame, fire or light

blaze VERB blazes, blazing, blazed
❶ to burn or shine brightly ❷ to show great feeling • *He was blazing with anger.*
➤ **blaze a trail** to show the way for others to follow

blazer NOUN blazers
a kind of jacket, often with a badge or in the colours of a school or team
(**WORD ORIGIN**) from **blaze** (because originally blazers were made in very bright colours and were thought of as shining or 'blazing')

bleach NOUN bleaches
a chemical substance used to make clothes white or to clean things and kill germs

bleach VERB bleaches, bleaching, bleached
to make something white or pale by using a chemical or by leaving it in the sun

bleak ADJECTIVE
❶ bare and cold • *a bleak hillside* ❷ dreary or miserable • *The future looks bleak.*
➤ **bleakly** ADVERB

bleary ADJECTIVE
bleary eyes are tired and do not see clearly
➤ **blearily** ADVERB

bleat NOUN bleats
the cry of a lamb, goat or calf

bleat *VERB* bleats, bleating, bleated
to cry with a bleat

bleed *VERB* bleeds, bleeding, bled
to lose blood

bleep *NOUN* bleeps
a short high sound made by a piece of
electronic equipment

bleep *VERB* bleeps, bleeping, bleeped
to make a bleep • *Why is your computer
bleeping?*

bleeper *NOUN* bleepers
(*British*) a small electronic device that bleeps
when the wearer is contacted

blemish *NOUN* blemishes
❶ a mark or flaw that spoils a thing's
appearance ❷ something that spoils a
person's character or reputation
➤ **blemish** *VERB*

blench *VERB* blenches, blenching, blenched
to back away in fear; to flinch

blend *VERB* blends, blending, blended
❶ to mix things together smoothly or easily
• *Blend the flour and the melted butter
together.* ❷ things blend when they combine
well with each other • *The colours blend well.*
➤ **blend in** to fit in well with your
surroundings

blend *NOUN* blends
a mixture • *The book is a blend of action,
history and horror.*

blender *NOUN* blenders
an electric machine used to mix food or turn
it into liquid

bless *VERB* blesses, blessing, blessed
❶ to ask God to protect a person or thing
❷ to make something holy so that it can be
used in a religious ceremony ❸ to be blessed
with something is to be lucky enough to have
it • *She is blessed with good health.*
➤ **bless you** ❶ something you say when
someone has sneezed ❷ something you say
to thank someone

blessing *NOUN* blessings
❶ a prayer that blesses a person or thing
❷ something that you are grateful for • *It's a
blessing no one was hurt.*

blight *NOUN* blights
❶ a disease that withers plants ❷ something
that spoils or damages something
• *Vandalism is a blight on our community.*

blight *VERB* blights, blighting, blighted
❶ to affect a plant with blight ❷ to spoil

or damage something • *Knee injuries have
blighted his career.*

blind *ADJECTIVE*
❶ without the ability to see ❷ without any
thought or understanding • *blind obedience*
❸ a blind bend or corner is one where you
cannot see clearly ahead
➤ **blindness** *NOUN*

blind *VERB* blinds, blinding, blinded
❶ to make someone blind ❷ to dazzle
someone with a bright light

blind *NOUN* blinds
❶ a screen for a window ❷ something used
to hide your real intentions • *His journey was
a blind.*

blind date *NOUN* blind dates
a date between people who have not met
before

blindfold *NOUN* blindfolds
a strip of cloth tied round someone's eyes so
that they cannot see

blindfold *VERB* blindfolds, blindfolding,
blindfolded
to cover someone's eyes with a blindfold

blindfold *ADVERB*
with a blindfold covering your eyes
WORD ORIGIN from Old English *blindfeld* =
struck blind, from **blind** + **fell** *VERB*

blindly *ADVERB*
❶ without being able to see what you are
doing • *He groped blindly for the light switch.*
❷ without thinking about what you are doing
• *They were trained to blindly follow orders.*

blind spot *NOUN* blind spots
a subject that you do not understand or know
much about

bling *NOUN* (*informal*)
showy and expensive jewellery and clothes
WORD ORIGIN perhaps from the sound of
pieces of jewellery clashing together

blink *VERB* blinks, blinking, blinked
❶ to shut and open your eyes rapidly ❷ a
light blinks when it shines unsteadily

blink *NOUN* blinks
when you shut and open your eyes rapidly
➤ **in the blink of an eye** very rapidly

blinkers *PLURAL NOUN*
leather pieces fixed on a bridle to prevent a
horse from seeing sideways
➤ **blinkered** *ADJECTIVE*
WORD ORIGIN originally a person who was
half-blind; from **blink**

a b c d e f g h i j k l m n o p q r s t u v w x y z

bliss NOUN
extreme happiness

blissful ADJECTIVE
feeling or causing extreme happiness • *He gave a blissful sigh.*
➤ **blissfully** ADVERB

blister NOUN blisters
a swelling like a bubble, especially on skin

blister VERB blisters, blistering, blistered
❶ to form blisters ❷ when a surface blisters it swells and cracks • *The paint was starting to blister.*

blistering ADJECTIVE
very intense • *the blistering midday heat*

blithe ADJECTIVE
casual and carefree
➤ **blithely** ADVERB

blitz NOUN blitzes
❶ a sudden violent attack, especially from aircraft ❷ the German bombing of London in 1940 (WORD ORIGIN) short for German *Blitzkrieg* (*Blitz* = lightning, *Krieg* = war)

blizzard NOUN blizzards
a severe snowstorm

bloated ADJECTIVE
swollen by fat, gas or liquid

bloater NOUN bloaters
a salted smoked herring

blob NOUN blobs
a small round lump or drop of something • *blobs of paint*

bloc NOUN blocs
a group of parties or countries who have formed an alliance

block NOUN blocks
❶ a solid piece of something ❷ a large building divided into flats or offices ❸ a group of buildings • *I went for a walk round the block.* ❹ an obstacle or obstruction • *a road block*

block VERB blocks, blocking, blocked
to get in the way of something; to obstruct something • *Tall buildings blocked our view.* • *The pipe is blocked.*

blockade NOUN blockades
the blocking of the entrance to a city or port in order to prevent people and goods from going in or out

blockade VERB blockades, blockading, blockaded
to set up a blockade of a place

blockage NOUN blockages
something that blocks a pipe or passageway

block letters PLURAL NOUN
plain capital letters

blog NOUN blogs
a personal website on which someone writes regularly about their own life or opinions

blog VERB blogs, blogging, blogged
to write on a blog
➤ **blogging** NOUN

blogger NOUN bloggers
someone who keeps a blog or who writes fiction and posts it on the Internet

bloke NOUN blokes (*British*) (*informal*)
a man

blond, blonde ADJECTIVE
fair-haired; fair

blond NOUN blondes
a fair-haired girl or woman

blood NOUN
❶ the red liquid that flows through veins and arteries ❷ family background or ancestry • *Do you have any Irish blood?*
➤ **in cold blood** deliberately and cruelly

blood bank NOUN blood banks
a place where supplies of blood and plasma for transfusions are stored

bloodbath NOUN bloodbaths
a massacre

blood donor NOUN blood donors
a person who gives blood for use in transfusions

blood group NOUN blood groups
any of the classes or types of human blood

bloodhound NOUN bloodhounds
a large dog that was used to track people by their scent

bloodshed NOUN
the killing or wounding of people

bloodshot ADJECTIVE
bloodshot eyes are streaked with red

blood sport NOUN blood sports
a sport that involves wounding or killing animals

bloodstream NOUN
the blood circulating in the body

bloodthirsty ADJECTIVE
enjoying killing and violence

blood vessel *NOUN* blood vessels
a tube carrying blood in the body; an artery, vein or capillary

bloody *ADJECTIVE* bloodier, bloodiest
❶ stained with blood ❷ with much bloodshed • *a bloody battle*

bloom *NOUN* blooms
❶ a flower ❷ the fine powder on fresh ripe grapes etc.
➤ **in bloom** producing flowers • *The cherry trees are in bloom.*

bloom *VERB* blooms, blooming, bloomed
to produce flowers

blossom *NOUN* blossoms
a flower or a mass of flowers, especially on a fruit tree

blossom *VERB* blossoms, blossoming, blossomed
❶ to produce flowers ❷ to develop into something • *She blossomed into a fine singer.*

blot *NOUN* blots
❶ a spot of ink ❷ a flaw or fault; something ugly • *a blot on the landscape*

blot *VERB* blots, blotting, blotted
❶ to make a blot or blots on something ❷ to remove liquid from a surface by pressing paper or cloth on it
➤ **blot something out** ❶ to be in front of something so that it cannot be seen • *Fog blotted out the view.* ❷ to make an effort to forget something unpleasant • *She tried to blot out the memory of what happened.*

blotch *NOUN* blotches
an untidy patch of colour
➤ **blotchy** *ADJECTIVE*

blotter *NOUN* blotters
a pad of blotting paper; a holder for blotting paper

blotting paper *NOUN*
absorbent paper for soaking up ink from writing

blouse *NOUN* blouses
a loose piece of clothing like a shirt, worn by women

blow *VERB* blows, blowing, blew, blown
❶ to send air out of your mouth or nose • *He blew on his hands to warm them up.* ❷ to move in or with a current of air • *The wind was blowing.* • *His hat blew off.* ❸ to form something or make a sound by blowing • *We were blowing bubbles.* • *The referee blew her whistle.* ❹ a fuse or light bulb blows when it melts or breaks because the electric current is too strong
➤ **blow something up** ❶ to destroy something with an explosion ❷ to fill something with air
➤ **blow up** to be destroyed in an explosion

blow *NOUN* blows
❶ a hard knock or hit ❷ a shock or disappointment ❸ the action of blowing

blowlamp, blowtorch *NOUN* blowlamps, blowtorches
a portable device for aiming a very hot flame at a surface, used to remove old paint

blowpipe *NOUN* blowpipes
a tube for sending out a dart or pellet by blowing

blubber *NOUN*
the fat on a whale

bludge *VERB* bludges, bludging, bludged (*Australian/NZ*) (*informal*)
❶ to live off someone else's earnings or on state benefits ❷ to avoid work and responsibilities

bludgeon (say **bluj**-on) *NOUN* bludgeons
a short stick with a thickened end, used as a weapon

bludgeon *VERB* bludgeons, bludgeoning, bludgeoned
to hit someone several times with a heavy stick or other object

blue *NOUN* blues
the colour of a cloudless sky
➤ **out of the blue** unexpectedly

blue *ADJECTIVE*
❶ of the colour blue ❷ unhappy or depressed
➤ **blueness** *NOUN*

> **SPELLING**
> Blue is a colour. Blew is the past tense of blow. *The sky was blue. The wind blew hard.*

bluebell *NOUN* bluebells
a plant with blue bell-shaped flowers

blueberry *NOUN* blueberries
a small, blue-black juicy fruit

blue blood *NOUN*
royal or aristocratic family

bluebottle *NOUN* bluebottles
a large bluish fly

blueprint *NOUN* blueprints
a detailed plan for making or doing

a b c d e f g h i j k l m n o p q r s t u v w x y z

something **WORD ORIGIN** because copies of plans were made on blue paper

blues *NOUN*
a style of music made up of slow sad songs or tunes • *a blues singer*
➤ **the blues** a very sad feeling; depression **WORD ORIGIN** short for *blue devils*, spiteful demons believed to cause depression

bluff *VERB* **bluffs, bluffing, bluffed**
to try to deceive someone, especially by pretending to be someone else or to be able to do something

bluff *NOUN* **bluffs**
❶ bluffing; a threat that you make but do not intend to carry out ❷ a cliff with a broad steep front
➤ **call someone's bluff** to challenge someone to do what they have threatened to do

bluff *ADJECTIVE*
frank and direct, in a good-natured way

bluish *ADJECTIVE*
having a blue tinge

blunder *NOUN* **blunders**
a stupid mistake

blunder *VERB* **blunders, blundering, blundered**
❶ to make a blunder ❷ to move clumsily and uncertainly • *I could hear him blundering about upstairs.*

blunderbuss *NOUN* **blunderbusses**
an old type of gun that fired many balls in one shot **WORD ORIGIN** from Dutch *donderbus* = thunder gun

blunt *ADJECTIVE*
❶ not sharp ❷ saying what you mean without trying to be polite or tactful • *a blunt refusal*
➤ **bluntness** *NOUN*

blunt *VERB* **blunts, blunting, blunted**
to make a point or edge blunt

bluntly *ADVERB*
in plain terms, without trying to be polite • *To put it bluntly, you're not welcome here.*

blur *VERB* **blurs, blurring, blurred**
to make something less clear or distinct

blur *NOUN* **blurs**
something that you cannot see or remember clearly • *Without his glasses on, everything was a blur.*

blurb *NOUN* **blurbs**
a short description of a book that is printed

on the back and meant to make you want to buy it

blurred *ADJECTIVE*
not clear in outline; out of focus

blurt *VERB* **blurts, blurting, blurted**
to say something suddenly or tactlessly • *He blurted it out before he had time to think.*

blush *VERB* **blushes, blushing, blushed**
to become red in the face because you are ashamed or embarrassed

blush *NOUN* **blushes**
reddening in the face

bluster *VERB* **blusters, blustering, blustered**
to talk loudly and aggressively, making empty threats

blustery *ADJECTIVE*
blustery weather is when the wind is blowing strongly in gusts

BMX *ABBREVIATION*
a kind of bicycle for use in racing on a dirt track **WORD ORIGIN** short for *bicycle motocross* (*x* standing for **cross**)

boa (say **boh**-a) (or **boa constrictor**) *NOUN* **boas, boa constrictors**
a large South American snake that squeezes its prey so that it suffocates it

boar *NOUN* **boars**
❶ a wild pig ❷ a male pig

board *NOUN* **boards**
❶ a long flat piece of wood, used in building ❷ a flat piece of stiff material • *a chopping board* • *a chessboard* ❸ a group of people who run a company or organization ❹ daily meals provided in return for payment or work • *board and lodging*
➤ **on board** on or in a boat, ship, train or aircraft

board *VERB* **boards, boarding, boarded**
❶ to get on a boat, ship, train or aircraft ❷ to receive meals and accommodation for payment
➤ **board something up** to block something up with fixed boards • *The windows were all boarded up.*

board game *NOUN* **board games**
a game in which you move pieces around a board

boarder *NOUN* **boarders**
❶ a pupil who lives at a boarding school during the term ❷ a lodger who receives meals

boarding house *NOUN* **boarding houses**
a house where people are provided with rooms and meals for payment

boarding school *NOUN* **boarding schools**
a school where pupils live during the term

boast *VERB* **boasts, boasting, boasted**
❶ to speak with too much pride about yourself and try to impress people ❷ to have something to be proud of • *The city boasts several fine parks.*

boast *NOUN* **boasts**
a boastful statement

boastful *ADJECTIVE*
boasting a lot
➤ **boastfully** *ADVERB*

boat *NOUN* **boats**
a vehicle built to travel on water
➤ **in the same boat** in the same situation; suffering the same difficulties

boater *NOUN* **boaters**
a hard flat straw hat

boating *NOUN*
going out in a boat (especially a rowing boat) for pleasure

boatswain (say **boh**-sun) *NOUN* **boatswains**
a ship's officer in charge of rigging, boats and anchors

bob *VERB* **bobs, bobbing, bobbed**
to move quickly up and down • *Small boats were bobbing around in the water.* • *She bobbed down behind the wall again.*

bobbin *NOUN* **bobbins**
a small spool holding thread or wire in a machine

bobble *NOUN* **bobbles**
a small ball of wool, used to decorate a hat or jumper

bobsleigh, bobsled *NOUN* **bobsleighs, bobsleds**
(*British*) a sledge with two sets of runners

bode *VERB* **bodes, boding, boded**
to bode well (or ill) is to be a sign that something good (or bad) will happen • *His silence over the last few days does not bode well.*

bodice *NOUN* **bodices**
the upper part of a dress

bodily *ADJECTIVE*
to do with your body • *bodily harm*

bodily *ADVERB*
by taking hold of someone's body • *He was picked up bodily and bundled into the car.*

body *NOUN* **bodies**
❶ the whole physical structure of a person or animal; the main part of this apart from the head and limbs ❷ a corpse ❸ the main part of something • *the body of the plane* ❹ an organized group of people • *the school's governing body* ❺ a quantity of something regarded as a unit • *A large body of evidence has built up.* ❻ an object or piece of matter • *Stars and planets are heavenly bodies.*

bodyguard *NOUN* **bodyguards**
a guard whose job is to protect an important person

Boer (say **boh**-er) *NOUN* **Boers**
❶ an Afrikaner ❷ (*historical*) an early Dutch inhabitant of South Africa

boffin *NOUN* **boffins** (*British*) (*informal*)
a person involved in scientific or technical research

bog *NOUN* **bogs**
an area of wet spongy ground
➤ **bogged down** stuck and unable to make any progress

bogeyman *NOUN* **bogeymen**
an imaginary man used in stories to frighten children

boggle *VERB* **boggles, boggling, boggled**
to be amazed or puzzled • *The mind boggles at the idea.*

boggy *ADJECTIVE*
boggy ground is wet and spongy

bogus *ADJECTIVE*
not real or genuine • *He gave a name that turned out to be bogus.*

boil *VERB* **boils, boiling, boiled**
❶ to become hot enough to bubble and give off steam ❷ to heat a liquid so that it boils ❸ to cook something in boiling water ❹ to be very hot

boil *NOUN* **boils**
❶ the point at which a liquid starts to boil • *Bring the milk to the boil.* ❷ an inflamed swelling under the skin

boiler *NOUN* **boilers**
a container for heating water or making steam

boiling point *NOUN* **boiling points**
the temperature at which a liquid boils

a b c d e f g h i j k l m n o p q r s t u v w x y z

boisterous *ADJECTIVE*
noisy and lively

bold *ADJECTIVE*
❶ brave and confident; not afraid to say what you feel or to take risks • *No one felt bold enough to speak up.* ❷ a bold colour or design is strong and vivid ❸ printed in thick black type
➤ **boldly** *ADVERB*
➤ **boldness** *NOUN*

bole *NOUN* **boles**
the trunk of a tree

bollard *NOUN* **bollards**
❶ a short post for keeping vehicles off a road ❷ a short thick post on a quayside to which a ship's rope may be tied

bolster *NOUN* **bolsters**
a long pillow for placing across a bed under other pillows

bolster *VERB* **bolsters, bolstering, bolstered**
to add extra strength or support to something • *Her win last week has really bolstered her confidence.*

bolt *NOUN* **bolts**
❶ a sliding bar for fastening a door or window ❷ a thick metal pin for fastening things together ❸ a sliding bar that opens and closes the breech of a rifle ❹ a shaft of lightning ❺ an arrow shot from a crossbow ❻ the action of bolting • *He saw his chance and made a bolt for freedom.*
➤ **a bolt from the blue** a surprise, usually an unpleasant one
➤ **bolt upright** sitting or standing with your back straight

bolt *VERB* **bolts, bolting, bolted**
❶ to fasten a door or window with a bolt or bolts ❷ to fasten things together with bolts • *A ladder was bolted to the wall.* ❸ to run away or escape • *In a panic, the horse bolted.* ❹ to swallow food quickly • *I just had time to bolt down a pizza.*

bomb *NOUN* **bombs**
an explosive device
➤ **the bomb** the nuclear bomb

bomb *VERB* **bombs, bombing, bombed**
to attack a place with bombs

bombard *VERB* **bombards, bombarding, bombarded**
❶ to attack a place with gunfire or many missiles ❷ to direct a large number of questions or comments at somebody

bombardment *NOUN* **bombardments**
a heavy attack with guns or missiles

bombastic (say bom-**bast**-ik) *ADJECTIVE*
using pompous words **WORD ORIGIN** from *bombast* = material used for padding; later 'padded' language, with long or unnecessary words

bomber *NOUN* **bombers**
❶ someone who plants or sets off a bomb ❷ an aeroplane from which bombs are dropped

bombshell *NOUN* **bombshells**
a great shock

bona fide (say **boh**-na **fy**-dee) *ADJECTIVE*
genuine; without fraud • *Are they bona fide tourists or spies?* **WORD ORIGIN** Latin, = in good faith

bonanza (say bon-**an**-za) *NOUN* **bonanzas**
sudden great wealth or luck
WORD ORIGIN originally an American word; from Spanish, = good weather, prosperity

bond *NOUN* **bonds**
❶ a close friendship or connection between two or more people • *the special bond between mother and daughter* ❷ bonds are ropes or chains used to tie someone up ❸ a document stating an agreement

bond *VERB* **bonds, bonding, bonded**
to become closely linked or connected • *The team has bonded well together.*

bondage *NOUN*
slavery or captivity

bone *NOUN* **bones**
❶ one of the hard whitish parts that make up the skeleton of a person's or animal's body ❷ the substance from which these parts are made • *Antlers are made of bone.*

bone *VERB* **bones, boning, boned**
to remove the bones from meat or fish

bone dry *ADJECTIVE*
completely dry

bonfire *NOUN* **bonfires**
an outdoor fire to burn rubbish or celebrate something **WORD ORIGIN** originally *bone fire* = a fire to dispose of people's or animals' bones

bonnet *NOUN* **bonnets**
❶ the hinged cover over a car engine ❷ a hat with strings that tie under the chin ❸ a flat cap, often with a bobble, worn by Scottish men

bonny *ADJECTIVE* bonnier, bonniest
(*Scottish*) good-looking or pretty

bonus (say **boh**-nus) *NOUN* bonuses
❶ an extra payment in addition to a person's normal wages ❷ an extra benefit
WORD ORIGIN from Latin *bonus* = good

bon voyage (say bawn vwah-**yah** zh)
EXCLAMATION
said to wish someone a good journey
WORD ORIGIN a French phrase = good journey

bony *ADJECTIVE*
❶ so thin that you can see the shape of the bones • *his long bony fingers* ❷ full of bones • *bony fish* ❸ looking or feeling like bone

boo *EXCLAMATION*
❶ shouted out to show that you do not like something ❷ said to take someone by surprise and startle them

boo *VERB* boos, booing, booed
to shout 'boo' in disapproval • *The audience began to boo loudly.*

booby prize *NOUN* booby prizes
a prize given as a joke to someone who comes last in a contest

booby trap *NOUN* booby traps
something designed to hit or injure someone unexpectedly

book *NOUN* books
a set of sheets of paper, usually with printing or writing on them, fastened together inside a cover
➤ **bookseller** *NOUN*
➤ **bookshop** *NOUN*
➤ **bookstall** *NOUN*

book *VERB* books, booking, booked
❶ to reserve a place or ticket in advance ❷ to enter a person in a police record • *The police booked him for speeding.* ❸ to make a note of a player who has committed a foul in a football match

bookcase *NOUN* bookcases
a piece of furniture with shelves for books

bookkeeping *NOUN*
recording details of the money that is spent and received by a business
➤ **bookkeeper** *NOUN*

booklet *NOUN* booklets
a small thin book with paper covers

bookmaker *NOUN* bookmakers
a person whose business is taking bets, especially bets made on horse races

bookmark *NOUN* bookmarks
❶ something to mark a place in a book ❷ a record of the address of a computer file or Internet page so that you can find it again quickly
➤ **bookmark** *VERB*

bookworm *NOUN* bookworms
a person who loves reading

boom *VERB* booms, booming, boomed
❶ to make a deep hollow sound • *Outside, thunder boomed and crashed.* ❷ to speak in a loud deep voice • *A voice boomed out from the darkness.* ❸ to be growing and successful • *Business is booming.*

boom *NOUN* booms
❶ a deep hollow sound • *the boom of distant guns* ❷ a period of increased growth or prosperity • *a boom in car sales* ❸ a long pole at the bottom of a sail to keep it stretched ❹ a long pole carrying a microphone or film camera ❺ a chain or floating barrier that can be placed across a river or a harbour entrance

boomerang *NOUN* boomerangs
a curved piece of wood that can be thrown so that it returns to the thrower, originally used by Australian Aborigines **WORD ORIGIN** an Australian Aboriginal word

boon *NOUN* boons
something that makes life easier

boon companion *NOUN* boon companions
a close friend

boor *NOUN* boors
a rude, bad-mannered person
➤ **boorish** *ADJECTIVE*

boost *VERB* boosts, boosting, boosted
to increase the strength, value or reputation of a person or thing • *Being in the drama group has really boosted his confidence.*

boost *NOUN* boosts
❶ an increase or improvement ❷ something that encourages or helps someone • *Winning that game gave my confidence a great boost.*

booster *NOUN* boosters
❶ a rocket that gives a spacecraft extra power when it leaves the earth ❷ a second dose of a vaccine which renews the effect of an earlier one

boot *NOUN* boots
❶ a shoe that covers the foot and ankle or leg ❷ the compartment for luggage in a car

boot *VERB* boots, booting, booted
❶ to kick something hard ❷ to boot up a

a b c d e f g h i j k l m n o p q r s t u v w x y z

computer is to switch it on and get it ready to use

bootee *NOUN* bootees
a baby's knitted boot

booth *NOUN* booths
an enclosed compartment, e.g. for a public telephone or for voting at elections

booty *NOUN*
valuable goods taken away by soldiers after a battle

booze *VERB* boozes, boozing, boozed (*informal*)
to drink a lot of alcohol

booze *NOUN* (*informal*) alcoholic drink

border *NOUN* borders
❶ the line dividing two countries or other areas ❷ a band or line around the edge of something, often for decoration • *a white tablecloth with a blue border* ❸ a long flower bed

border *VERB* borders, bordering, bordered
to form a border around or along something • *The orchard was bordered by a stone wall.*

borderline *NOUN* borderlines
a boundary

borderline *ADJECTIVE*
only just belonging to a particular group or category • *You're a borderline pass.*

bore *VERB* bores, boring, bored
❶ to make someone feel uninterested by being dull ❷ to drill a hole through something ❸ past tense of **bear** *VERB*

bore *NOUN* bores
❶ a dull and uninteresting person or thing ❷ the width of the inside of a pipe or gun barrel ❸ a tidal wave with a steep front that moves up some estuaries

bored *ADJECTIVE*
weary and uninterested because something is so dull

> **USAGE**
> You can say that you are *bored with* something or *bored by* something: *I'm bored with this game*. It is not acceptable in standard English to say *bored of*.

boredom *NOUN*
a feeling of being bored • *She thought she would die of boredom.*

boring *ADJECTIVE*
dull and uninteresting

born *ADJECTIVE*
❶ to be born is to have come into existence

by birth. (See the note on **borne**.) ❷ having a certain natural quality or ability • *a born leader*

borne
past participle of **bear** *VERB*

> **USAGE**
> The word **borne** is used before **by** or after **have, has** or **had**, e.g. *children borne by Eve*; *she had borne him a son*. The word **born** is used after **be**, e.g. in *a son was born*.

borough (say **bu**rra) *NOUN* boroughs
a town or district that has its own council

borrow *VERB* borrows, borrowing, borrowed
❶ to get something to use for a time, with the intention of giving it back afterwards ❷ to obtain money as a loan ❸ to take something and use it as your own • *Some musical terms are borrowed from Italian.*
➤ **borrower** *NOUN*

> **USAGE**
> Take care not to confuse **borrow**, which means to use something that belongs to someone else for a short time, with **lend**, which means to let someone use something of yours for a short time.

bosom *NOUN* bosoms
a woman's breasts

boss *NOUN* bosses
❶ (*informal*) a person who is in charge of a business or group of workers ❷ a round raised knob or stud

boss *VERB* bosses, bossing, bossed
(*informal*) to order someone about

bossy *ADJECTIVE*
fond of ordering people about
➤ **bossily** *ADVERB*

botany *NOUN*
the study of plants
➤ **botanical** *ADJECTIVE*
➤ **botanist** *NOUN*

botch *VERB* botches, botching, botched
to spoil something by poor or clumsy work

both *DETERMINER & PRONOUN*
the two of them, not only one • *Are both films good?* • *I want them both in the team.*

both *ADVERB*
➤ **both ... and** not only ... but also • *The house is both small and ugly.*

bother *VERB* bothers, bothering, bothered
❶ to cause somebody trouble or worry • *I'm sorry to bother you.* ❷ to take the time or trouble to do something • *Don't bother to reply.*

bother *NOUN*
trouble or worry

bottle *NOUN* bottles
❶ a narrow-necked container for liquids ❷ (*informal*) courage • *She showed a lot of bottle.*

bottle *VERB* bottles, bottling, bottled
to put or store something in bottles
➤ **bottle something up** if you bottle up your feelings, you keep them to yourself

bottle bank *NOUN* bottle banks
(*British*) a large container in which used glass bottles are collected for recycling

bottleneck *NOUN* bottlenecks
a narrow place where something, especially traffic, cannot flow freely

bottom *NOUN* bottoms
❶ the lowest part of something; the base ❷ the part furthest away • *the bottom of the garden* ❸ your buttocks

bottom *ADJECTIVE*
lowest • *the bottom shelf*

bottomless *ADJECTIVE*
extremely deep • *a bottomless pit*

boudoir (say **boo**-dwar) *NOUN* boudoirs
a woman's bedroom or other private room
WORD ORIGIN French, = place to sulk in

bough *NOUN* boughs
a large branch coming from the trunk of a tree

boulder *NOUN* boulders
a very large rock

boulevard (say **bool**-ev-ard) *NOUN* boulevards
a wide street, often with trees on each side

bounce *VERB* bounces, bouncing, bounced
❶ to spring back when thrown against something ❷ to make a ball or other object bounce ❸ to jump up and down repeatedly; to move in a lively manner • *The children were bouncing on their beds.* ❹ a cheque bounces when it is sent back by the bank because there is not enough money in the account

bounce *NOUN* bounces
❶ the action of bouncing • *Rose gave a little bounce of delight.* ❷ a lively confident manner • *full of bounce*

bouncer *NOUN* bouncers
❶ a person who stands at the door of a club and stops unwanted people coming in or makes troublemakers leave ❷ a ball in cricket that bounces high

bouncy *ADJECTIVE*
❶ lively and full of energy ❷ that bounces well or can make things bounce • *a bouncy ball*

bound *VERB* bounds, bounding, bounded
❶ to move or run with large leaps • *She bounded down the stairs.* ❷ to be the boundary of something; to limit something • *Their land is bounded by the river.* ❸ past tense of **bind**

bound *NOUN* bounds
a large leap • *With a couple of bounds he had crossed the room.*

bound *ADJECTIVE*
❶ obstructed or hindered by something • *The airport is fog-bound.* ❷ going towards a place • *We are bound for Spain.*
➤ **bound to** certain or very likely to • *He is bound to fail.*
➤ **bound up with** closely connected with • *Happiness is bound up with success.*

boundary *NOUN* boundaries
❶ a line that marks a limit ❷ a hit to the boundary of a cricket field

SPELLING
There is no e in **boundary**! It ends with **ary**.

boundless *ADJECTIVE*
without limits • *his boundless enthusiasm*

bounds *PLURAL NOUN*
limits • *This was beyond the bounds of possibility.*
➤ **out of bounds** where you are not allowed to go

bountiful *ADJECTIVE*
❶ plentiful; producing a lot • *bountiful harvest* ❷ giving generously

bounty *NOUN* bounties
❶ a reward paid for capturing or killing someone ❷ generosity in giving things

bouquet (say boh-**kay**) *NOUN* bouquets
a bunch of flowers

bout *NOUN* bouts
❶ a boxing or wrestling contest ❷ a period of exercise or work or illness • *a bout of flu*

boutique (say boo-**teek**) *NOUN* boutiques
a small shop selling fashionable clothes

a b c d e f g h i j k l m n o p q r s t u v w x y z

bovine (say **boh**-vyn) *ADJECTIVE*
❶ to do with or like cattle ❷ dull and stupid

bow (rhymes with go) *NOUN* bows
❶ a knot made with two loops and two loose ends ❷ a strip of wood curved by a tight string joining its ends, used for shooting arrows ❸ a wooden rod with horsehair stretched between its ends, used for playing a violin or similar string instrument

bow (rhymes with cow) *VERB* bows, bowing, bowed
❶ to bend your body forwards to show respect or as a greeting ❷ to bend a part of your body downwards • *He bowed his head.*

bow (rhymes with cow) *NOUN* bows
❶ a movement of bowing your body • *The pianist stood up to take a bow.* ❷ the front end of a ship

bowels *PLURAL NOUN*
your intestines (**WORD ORIGIN**) from Latin *botellus* = little sausage

bower *NOUN* bowers
a pleasant shady place under trees

bowl *NOUN* bowls
❶ a round open container for food or liquid ❷ the rounded part of a spoon ❸ a heavy ball used in the game of bowls or in bowling

bowl *VERB* bowls, bowling, bowled
❶ to send a ball to be played by a batsman in cricket ❷ to get a batsman out by hitting the wicket with the ball ❸ to send a ball rolling along the ground

bow-legged *ADJECTIVE*
having legs that curve outwards at the knees

bowler *NOUN* bowlers
❶ a person who bowls ❷ (also **bowler hat**) (*chiefly British*) a man's stiff felt hat with a rounded top

bowling *NOUN*
❶ the game of knocking down skittles with a heavy ball ❷ the game of bowls

bowls *NOUN*
a game played on a smooth piece of grass, in which you roll heavy wooden balls towards a smaller target ball

bow tie *NOUN* bow ties
a tie in the form of a bow, worn by men as part of formal dress

bow window *NOUN* bow windows
a curved window

box *NOUN* boxes
❶ a container made of wood, cardboard, etc., usually with a top or lid ❷ a rectangular space that you fill in on a form or computer screen ❸ a compartment for seating several people in a theatre ❹ an enclosed area for the jury or witnesses in a law court ❺ a small evergreen shrub
➤ **the box** (*informal*) television

box *VERB* boxes, boxing, boxed
❶ to fight with your fists as a sport ❷ to put something into a box
➤ **boxing** *NOUN*

boxer *NOUN* boxers
❶ a person who boxes ❷ a dog that looks like a bulldog

Boxing Day *NOUN*
(*British*) the first weekday after Christmas Day
(**WORD ORIGIN**) from the old custom of giving presents (*Christmas boxes*) to tradesmen and servants on that day

box office *NOUN* box offices
an office for booking seats at a theatre or cinema

boy *NOUN* boys
❶ a male child ❷ a young man

boycott *VERB* boycotts, boycotting, boycotted
to refuse to use or buy something because you do not approve of it • *They boycotted the buses when the fares went up.*
➤ **boycott** *NOUN*
(**WORD ORIGIN**) from the name of Captain *Boycott*, a harsh landlord in Ireland whose tenants in 1880 refused to deal with him

boyfriend *NOUN* boyfriends
a person's regular male friend or lover

boyhood *NOUN*
the time when a man was boy • *He spent his boyhood in India.*

boyish *ADJECTIVE*
like a boy or suitable for a boy • *his boyish enthusiasm*

bra *NOUN* bras
a piece of underwear worn by women to support their breasts

brace *NOUN* braces
❶ a device for holding things in place ❷ a wire device fitted in your mouth to straighten your teeth ❸ a pair of something • *a brace of pheasants*

brace *VERB* braces, bracing, braced
to support something or make it steady • *He braced his back against the wall.*

➤ **brace yourself** to prepare yourself for something unpleasant

bracelet *NOUN* bracelets
a small band or chain you wear round your wrist

braces *PLURAL NOUN*
straps to hold trousers up, which pass over your shoulders

bracing *ADJECTIVE*
making you feel refreshed and healthy • *the bracing sea breeze*

bracken *NOUN*
a type of large fern that grows in open country; a mass of these ferns

bracket *NOUN* brackets
❶ a mark used in pairs to enclose words or figures. There are round brackets ( ) and square brackets [ ]. ❷ a support attached to a wall to hold up a shelf or light fitting ❸ a group or range between certain limits • *a high income bracket*

bracket *VERB* brackets, bracketing, bracketed
❶ to enclose words or figures in brackets ❷ to group things together because they are similar

PUNCTUATION

Brackets are used in pairs to separate off a word or phrase from the main text.

Parentheses (sometimes called **round brackets**) surround a comment or information which is not part of the main flow of the sentence. If you take out the word or phrase between the two brackets, the sentence should still make sense on its own:

Her stomach (which was never very quiet) began to gurgle alarmingly.

Square brackets are sometimes used by someone other than the original writer of a text to add a short note or explanation:

He [the president] said that he would not resign.

brackish *ADJECTIVE*
brackish water tastes slightly salty

brae (say bray) *NOUN* braes (*Scottish*)
a hillside or slope

brag *VERB* brags, bragging, bragged
to boast • *He is always bragging about how brilliant he is at football.*

braggart *NOUN* braggarts
a person who brags

Brahmin *NOUN* Brahmins
a member of the highest Hindu class, originally priests

braid *NOUN* braids
❶ a plait of hair ❷ a strip of cloth with a woven decorative pattern, used as trimming

braid *VERB* braids, braiding, braided
❶ to plait hair • *Her hair was braided down her back.* ❷ to trim something with braid

Braille (rhymes with mail) *NOUN*
a system of representing letters by raised dots which blind people can read by touch
WORD ORIGIN named after Louis *Braille*, a blind French teacher who invented it in about 1830

brain *NOUN* brains
❶ the organ inside the top of the head that controls the body ❷ your mind or intelligence • *He's got a good brain.*

brainwash *VERB* brainwashes, brainwashing, brainwashed
to force a person to give up one set of ideas or beliefs and accept new ones

brainwave *NOUN* brainwaves
a sudden bright idea • *I've just had a brainwave.*

brainy *ADJECTIVE* brainier, brainiest
(*informal*) clever; intelligent

braise *VERB* braises, braising, braised
to cook food slowly in a little liquid in a closed container

brake *NOUN* brakes
a device for slowing down or stopping a moving vehicle

brake *VERB* brakes, braking, braked
to use a brake

SPELLING

Brake is different from **break**, which means to divide something into pieces by hitting or dropping it.

bramble *NOUN* brambles
a blackberry bush or a prickly bush like it

bran *NOUN*
ground-up husks of grain which have been sifted out from flour

branch *NOUN* branches
❶ a woody arm-like part of a tree or shrub ❷ a local shop, bank or office that belongs

to a large organization ❸ a part of a railway, road or river that leads off from the main part ❹ a part of an academic subject • *Calculus is a branch of mathematics.*

branch *VERB* branches, branching, branched
to form a branch or divide into branches • *A footpath branches off from the main track.*
➤ **branch out** to start doing something new • *He has recently branched out into acting.*

brand *NOUN* brands
❶ a particular make of goods • *a cheap brand of tea* ❷ a mark made on cattle or sheep by branding ❸ a piece of burning wood

brand *VERB* brands, branding, branded
❶ to mark cattle or sheep with a piece of hot iron to identify them ❷ to identify or class someone as something bad • *He will be branded forever as a cheat.* ❸ to sell goods under a particular trademark

brandish *VERB* brandishes, brandishing, brandished
to wave something about • *The men leapt out of the boat, brandishing their swords.*

brand name *NOUN* brand names
a name given to a product or range of products

brand new *ADJECTIVE*
completely new

brandy *NOUN* brandies
a strong alcoholic drink, usually made from wine

brash *ADJECTIVE*
too confident in a rude or aggressive way

brass *NOUN* brasses
❶ a metal that is an alloy of copper and zinc ❷ wind instruments made of brass, such as trumpets and trombones
➤ **brass** *ADJECTIVE*
➤ **brassy** *ADJECTIVE*

brass band *NOUN* brass bands
a musical band made up of brass instruments

brassiere (say **bras**-ee-air) *NOUN* brassieres
a bra

brat *NOUN* brats (*informal*)
a badly behaved child

bravado (say brav-**ah**-doh) *NOUN*
a display of boldness to impress people

brave *ADJECTIVE*
having or showing courage
➤ **bravely** *ADVERB*

brave *VERB* braves, braving, braved
to face and endure something dangerous or unpleasant • *They decided to brave the icy winds outside.*

brave *NOUN* braves
a Native American warrior

bravery *NOUN*
brave actions; courage • *a medal for bravery*

bravo (say **brah**-voh) *EXCLAMATION*
well done!

brawl *NOUN* brawls
a noisy quarrel or fight

brawl *VERB* brawls, brawling, brawled
to take part in a brawl

brawn *NOUN*
physical strength • *In this job you need brains as well as brawn.*

brawny *ADJECTIVE*
strong and muscular

bray *VERB* brays, braying, brayed
a donkey brays when it makes a loud harsh cry

bray *NOUN* brays
the loud harsh cry of a donkey

brazen *ADJECTIVE*
❶ bold and shameless • *brazen impudence* ❷ made of brass

brazen *VERB* brazens, brazening, brazened
➤ **brazen it out** to behave, after doing something wrong, as if you have nothing to be ashamed of

brazier (say **bray**-zee-er) *NOUN* braziers
a metal basket in which coals can be burned to keep people warm outdoors

breach *NOUN* breaches
❶ the breaking of an agreement or rule ❷ a gap or broken place in a wall or barrier

breach *VERB* breaches, breaching, breached
to break through something; to make a gap • *They finally breached the castle walls.*

bread *NOUN* breads
a food made by baking flour and water, usually with yeast
➤ **breadcrumbs** *NOUN*

breadth *NOUN*
❶ the distance across something, from one side to another ❷ a wide range • *a breadth of experience*

breadwinner *NOUN* breadwinners
the member of a family who earns money to support the others

break VERB breaks, breaking, broke, broken
❶ to divide something into pieces by hitting or dropping it ❷ to fall into pieces because of being hit ❸ to damage something so that it stops working properly ❹ to fail to keep a promise, rule or law ❺ to stop something for a time; to end something • *She broke her silence.* ❻ weather breaks when it changes suddenly after being hot ❼ a boy's voice breaks when it becomes suddenly deeper at puberty ❽ waves break when they fall in foam on a shore ❾ to go suddenly or with force • *They broke through.* ❿ to appear suddenly • *Dawn had broken.*
➤ **break a record** to do better than anyone else has done before
➤ **break down** ❶ to stop working properly ❷ to collapse
➤ **break off** to stop doing something for a time • *We broke off for lunch.*
➤ **break out** ❶ to begin suddenly, like a disease or fighting ❷ to escape
➤ **break the news** to make something known
➤ **break up** ❶ to break into small parts ❷ a school breaks up when it closes at the end of a term ❸ to end your relationship with someone • *My brother and his girlfriend have broken up.*

break NOUN breaks
❶ a broken place; a gap ❷ an escape; a sudden dash ❸ a short rest from work ❹ a number of points scored continuously in snooker ❺ the winning of a tennis game against the other player's serve ❻ (*informal*) a piece of luck; a fair chance • *Give me a break.*
➤ **break of day** dawn

SPELLING
Break is different from **brake**, which is a device for stopping a vehicle.

breakable ADJECTIVE
easy to break

breakage NOUN breakages
something that is broken • *Breakages must be paid for.*

breakdown NOUN breakdowns
❶ a sudden failure to work properly, especially by a car • *We had a breakdown on the motorway.* ❷ a failure or collapse of something • *There has been a breakdown of communication.* ❸ a period of mental illness caused by anxiety or depression ❹ an analysis of accounts or statistics • *Here's a breakdown of last season's football results.*

breaker NOUN breakers
a large wave breaking on the shore

breakfast NOUN breakfasts
the first meal of the day **(WORD ORIGIN)** from **break** + **fast**, because it is the first meal you eat after fasting overnight

breakneck ADJECTIVE
breakneck speed is dangerously fast

breakthrough NOUN breakthroughs
an important development or discovery • *a major breakthrough in cancer research*

breakwater NOUN breakwaters
a wall built out into the sea to protect a coast from heavy waves

bream NOUN bream
a kind of fish with an arched back

breast NOUN breasts
❶ one of the two fleshy parts on the upper front of a woman's body that produce milk to feed a baby ❷ a person's or animal's chest

breastbone NOUN breastbones
the flat bone down the centre of your chest, joined to your ribs

breastplate NOUN breastplates
a piece of armour covering the chest

breaststroke NOUN
a way of swimming on your front in which you push your arms forward and bring them round and back

breath (say breth) NOUN breaths
❶ air that is drawn into your lungs and sent out again ❷ a gentle blowing • *a breath of wind*
➤ **out of breath** breathing with difficulty after exercise; panting
➤ **take your breath away** to surprise or delight you greatly
➤ **under your breath** in a whisper

SPELLING
Breath is a noun and **breathe** is a verb • *She was out of breath.* • *She found it hard to breathe.*

breathalyser NOUN breathalysers
a device for measuring the amount of alcohol in a person's breath
➤ **breathalyse** VERB

breathe (say breth) VERB breathes, breathing, breathed
❶ to take air into your body and send it out again ❷ to say or speak about something • *Don't breathe a word of this.*

breather (say **bree**-ther) *NOUN* breathers
(*informal*) a pause for rest • *Let's take a
breather.*

breathless *ADJECTIVE*
out of breath
➤ **breathlessly** *ADVERB*

breathtaking *ADJECTIVE*
very impressive or beautiful • *breathtaking
scenery*

breech *NOUN* breeches
the back part of a gun barrel, where the
bullets are put in

breeches (say **brich**-iz) *PLURAL NOUN*
trousers reaching to just below your knees

breed *VERB* breeds, breeding, bred
❶ to produce children or offspring ❷ to
keep animals in order to produce young ones
from them ❸ to create or produce something
• *Poverty breeds illness.* ❹ to be bred in a
particular way is to be brought up or trained
that way • *These people have been bred to
fight.*
➤ **breeder** *NOUN*

breed *NOUN* breeds
a variety of animal that has been specially
developed • *a breed of dog*

breeze *NOUN* breezes
a gentle wind

breeze block *NOUN* breeze blocks
(*British*) a lightweight building block made of
cinders and cement

breezy *ADJECTIVE*
❶ pleasantly windy ❷ relaxed and cheerful
➤ **breezily** *ADVERB*

brethren *PLURAL NOUN* (*old use*)
brothers WORD ORIGIN the old plural of
brother

breve (say breev) *NOUN* breves
a note in music, lasting eight times as long as
a crotchet

brevity *NOUN*
being brief or short • *I was surprised by the
brevity of her answer.*

brew *VERB* brews, brewing, brewed
❶ to make tea or coffee by mixing it with
hot water ❷ to make beer by boiling and
fermentation ❸ something bad is brewing
when it is growing or developing • *Trouble is
brewing.*

brew *NOUN* brews
a brewed drink

brewer *NOUN* brewers
a person who brews beer for sale

brewery *NOUN* breweries
a place where beer is brewed

briar *NOUN* briars
a thorny bush, especially the wild rose

bribe *NOUN* bribes
money or a gift offered to someone to
influence them to do something

bribe *VERB* bribes, bribing, bribed
to persuade someone to do something by
offering them a bribe
➤ **bribery** *NOUN*

brick *NOUN* bricks
❶ a small hard block of baked clay used
to build walls ❷ a rectangular block of
something

brick *VERB* bricks, bricking, bricked
➤ **brick something up** to block an entrance
or window with bricks

bricklayer *NOUN* bricklayers
a worker who builds with bricks

bridal *ADJECTIVE*
to do with a bride or a wedding • *a bridal
gown*

bride *NOUN* brides
a woman on her wedding day

bridegroom *NOUN* bridegrooms
a man on his wedding day

bridesmaid *NOUN* bridesmaids
a woman or girl who accompanies a bride at
her wedding

bridge *NOUN* bridges
❶ a structure built over and across a river,
railway or road to allow people or vehicles to
cross it ❷ a high platform above a ship's deck,
for the officer in charge ❸ the bony upper
part of your nose ❹ a card game rather like
whist

bridge *VERB* bridges, bridging, bridged
to make or form a bridge over something
➤ **bridge a gap** to fill a space between two
things or bring them closer together • *These
novels bridge the gap between children's and
adult fiction.*

bridle *NOUN* bridles
the part of a horse's harness that fits over its
head

bridle *VERB* bridles, bridling, bridled
❶ to put a bridle on a horse ❷ to show you
are angry or offended by something

bridleway, bridle path *NOUN* bridleways, bridle paths
(*British*) a road suitable for horses but not for vehicles

brief *ADJECTIVE*
lasting for a short time or using only a few words
➤ **in brief** in a few words

brief *NOUN* briefs
instructions and information given to someone before they start a piece of work

brief *VERB* briefs, briefing, briefed
to give someone the instructions and information they need before they start a piece of work

briefcase *NOUN* briefcases
a flat case for carrying documents

briefing *NOUN* briefings
a meeting to give someone instructions or information

briefly *ADVERB*
❶ for a short time • *She glanced briefly at the letter.* ❷ using only a few words • *I'll answer that briefly.*

briefs *PLURAL NOUN*
short knickers or underpants

brier *NOUN* briers
a different spelling of **briar**

brigade *NOUN* brigades
❶ a large unit of an army ❷ a group of people organized for a special purpose • *the fire brigade*

brigadier *NOUN* brigadiers
an army officer who commands a brigade, higher in rank than a colonel

brigand *NOUN* brigands
a member of a band of robbers

bright *ADJECTIVE*
❶ giving out a strong light; filled with light or sunlight ❷ a bright colour is strong and vivid ❸ clever ❹ cheerful
➤ **brightly** *ADVERB*
➤ **brightness** *NOUN*

brighten *VERB* brightens, brightening, brightened
to become brighter or more cheerful; to make something brighter • *Her face brightened when she saw him.*

brilliance *NOUN*
❶ bright light ❷ great intelligence or cleverness

brilliant *ADJECTIVE*
❶ very clever or talented ❷ excellent; very enjoyable ❸ shining very brightly
➤ **brilliantly** *ADVERB*

brim *NOUN* brims
❶ the edge round the top of a cup, bowl or other container ❷ the bottom part of a hat that sticks out

brim *VERB* brims, brimming, brimmed
to be full of something • *His eyes were brimming with tears.*
➤ **brim over** a container that is brimming over is overflowing

brimful *ADJECTIVE*
full to the brim

brimstone *NOUN* (*old use*)
sulphur

brine *NOUN*
salt water
➤ **briny** *ADJECTIVE*

bring *VERB* brings, bringing, brought
❶ to carry or take a person or thing with you to a place • *Can I bring a friend to your party?* ❷ to make something come or happen • *Money doesn't always bring happiness.* ❸ to move something somewhere • *She brought the book down off the shelf.*
➤ **bring something about** to make something happen
➤ **bring something off** to achieve something; to do something successfully
➤ **bring someone up** to look after and train children as they grow up
➤ **bring something up** ❶ to mention a subject ❷ to vomit

brinjal *NOUN* brinjals (*Indian & S. African*)
an aubergine or eggplant

brink *NOUN* brinks
❶ the edge of a steep place or of a stretch of water ❷ the point beyond which something will happen • *We were on the brink of war.*

brisk *ADJECTIVE*
❶ quick and lively • *They set off at a brisk pace.* ❷ wanting to get things done quickly and efficiently • *Her voice became brisk and businesslike.*
➤ **briskly** *ADVERB*
➤ **briskness** *NOUN*

bristle *NOUN* bristles
❶ a short stiff hair ❷ one of the stiff pieces of hair, wire or plastic in a brush
➤ **bristly** *ADJECTIVE*

a
b
c
d
e
f
g
h
i
j
k
l
m
n
o
p
q
r
s
t
u
v
w
x
y
z

bristle *VERB* bristles, bristling, bristled
❶ an animal bristles when it raises its bristles in anger or fear ❷ someone bristles when they show indignation
➤ **bristle with** to have a lot of something
• *The room bristled with computer screens.*

Britain *NOUN*
the island made up of England, Scotland and Wales, with the small adjacent islands; Great Britain

> **USAGE**
>
> Note the difference in use between the terms *Britain, Great Britain,* the *United Kingdom* and the *British Isles.* Great Britain (or Britain) is used to refer to the island made up of England, Scotland and Wales. The United Kingdom includes Great Britain and Northern Ireland. The British Isles refers to the whole of the island group which includes Great Britain, Ireland and all the smaller nearby islands.

British Isles *PLURAL NOUN*
the island group which includes Great Britain, Ireland and all the smaller nearby islands

> **USAGE**
>
> See note at **Britain.**

brittle *ADJECTIVE*
hard but easy to break or snap
➤ **brittleness** *NOUN*

broach *VERB* broaches, broaching, broached
❶ to start a discussion of something • *We were unwilling to broach the subject.* ❷ to make a hole in something and draw out liquid

broad *ADJECTIVE*
❶ large across; wide ❷ in general terms; not detailed • *We are in broad agreement.* ❸ strong and unmistakable • *a broad hint* • *a broad accent*
➤ **broad daylight** full daylight; the daytime

broadband *NOUN*
(*in computing*) a system for connecting computers to the Internet at very high speed

broad bean *NOUN* broad beans
a bean with large flat seeds

broadcast *NOUN* broadcasts
a programme sent out on television or the radio

broadcast *VERB* broadcasts, broadcasting, broadcast
to send out a programme on television or the radio
➤ **broadcaster** *NOUN*

WORD ORIGIN originally = to scatter seeds widely: from **broad** + **cast**

broaden *VERB* broadens, broadening, broadened
to become broader; to make something broader • *Her grin broadened.* • *Travel broadens the mind.*

broadly *ADVERB*
❶ generally; on the whole • *They were broadly right.* ❷ widely • *Tom was smiling broadly now*

broad-minded *ADJECTIVE*
tolerant; not easily shocked

broadside *NOUN* broadsides
❶ a round of firing by all the guns on one side of a ship ❷ a strong verbal attack
➤ **broadside on** sideways on

brocade *NOUN*
a rich fabric woven with raised patterns

broccoli *NOUN* broccoli
a kind of cauliflower with greenish flower heads

> **SPELLING**
>
> Double up the **c** in **broccoli** (but the **l** stays single)!

brochure (say **broh**-shoor) *NOUN* brochures
a booklet or pamphlet containing information
WORD ORIGIN from French, = stitching (because originally the pages were roughly stitched together)

brogue (rhymes with rogue) *NOUN* brogues
❶ a strong kind of shoe ❷ a strong regional accent • *He spoke with an Irish brogue.*

broil *VERB* broils, broiling, broiled
❶ to cook food using a direct heat, such as a grill ❷ to be broiling is to be very hot

broke *ADJECTIVE* (*informal*)
having spent all your money

broken-hearted *ADJECTIVE*
feeling great sadness or grief

broken home *NOUN* broken homes
a family in which the parents are divorced or separated

broker *NOUN* brokers
a person who buys and sells things, especially shares, for other people

brolly *NOUN* brollies (*British*) (*informal*)
an umbrella

bromide NOUN
a substance used in medicine to calm the nerves

bronchial (say bronk-ee-al) ADJECTIVE
to do with the tubes that lead from your windpipe to your lungs

bronchitis (say bronk-y-tiss) NOUN
a disease that causes inflammation of the bronchial tubes, which makes you cough a lot

bronze NOUN bronzes
❶ a metal that is an alloy of copper and tin ❷ something made of bronze ❸ a bronze medal, awarded as third prize ❹ a yellowish-brown colour
➤ **bronze** ADJECTIVE

Bronze Age NOUN
the period in human history when tools and weapons were made of bronze

brooch (rhymes with coach) NOUN brooches
an ornament with a hinged pin for fastening it on to clothes

brood NOUN broods
young birds that were hatched together

brood VERB broods, brooding, brooded
❶ to keep thinking and worrying about something • *He was still brooding over his disappointment weeks later.* ❷ to sit on eggs to hatch them

broody ADJECTIVE
❶ a broody hen is ready to sit on her eggs ❷ quietly worried and unhappy about something ❸ a woman who is broody is eager to have children

brook NOUN brooks
a small stream

brook VERB brooks, brooking, brooked
to allow or tolerate something • *She would brook no argument.*

broom NOUN brooms
❶ a brush with a long handle, for sweeping floors ❷ a shrub with yellow, white or pink flowers

broomstick NOUN broomsticks
the handle of a broom, which in stories witches use to ride on

broth NOUN broths
a kind of thin soup

brothel NOUN brothels
a house where men pay to have sex with prostitutes

brother NOUN brothers
❶ a son of the same parents as another person ❷ a member of a Christian religious order of men
➤ **brotherly** ADJECTIVE

brotherhood NOUN brotherhoods
❶ friendliness and companionship between men ❷ a society or association of men

brother-in-law NOUN brothers-in-law
the brother of a married person's husband or wife; the husband of a person's sister or brother

brow NOUN brows
❶ an eyebrow ❷ your forehead ❸ the top of a hill

brown NOUN browns
a colour between orange and black, like the colour of dark wood

brown ADJECTIVE
❶ of the colour brown ❷ having a brown skin; suntanned

brown VERB browns, browning, browned
❶ to make something brown, especially by cooking it ❷ to become brown

brownfield ADJECTIVE
(*British*) a brownfield site is a piece of land that had buildings on it in the past and that may now be cleared for new buildings to be built

Brownie NOUN Brownies
a member of a junior branch of the Guides

brownie NOUN brownies
a flat chocolate cake, served in squares

browse VERB browses, browsing, browsed
❶ to read or look at something casually ❷ to look for information on the Internet ❸ animals browse when they feed on grass or leaves

browser NOUN browsers
(*in computing*) a piece of computer software that allows you to search and look at websites on the Internet

bruise NOUN bruises
a dark mark made on the skin by hitting it

bruise VERB bruises, bruising, bruised
❶ to make a bruise or bruises appear on a person's skin ❷ to develop a bruise • *I bruise easily.*

brunch NOUN (*informal*)
a late-morning meal combining breakfast and lunch (WORD ORIGIN) from **breakfast** and **lunch**

a b c d e f g h i j k l m n o p q r s t u v w x y z

brunette *NOUN* brunettes
a woman with dark-brown hair

brunt *NOUN*
the chief impact of something • *They bore the brunt of the attack.*

brush *NOUN* brushes
❶ an object used for cleaning or painting things or for smoothing the hair, usually with bristles set in a solid base ❷ using a brush • *The floor needs a good brush.* ❸ a fox's bushy tail ❹ an unpleasant experience or encounter • *She told us about her brush with disaster.* ❺ undergrowth, bushes and shrubs that often grow under trees

brush *VERB* brushes, brushing, brushed
❶ to use a brush on something • *I just need to brush my hair.* ❷ to touch something lightly while passing it • *Her hand brushed his arm.*
➤ **brush something aside** to refuse to accept that something is important • *He brushed aside their protests.*
➤ **brush something up** to revise your knowledge of a subject

brusque (say bruusk) *ADJECTIVE*
abrupt and offhand in manner
➤ **brusquely** *ADVERB*

Brussels sprout *NOUN* Brussels sprouts
the edible buds of a kind of cabbage

brutal *ADJECTIVE*
cruel and violent
➤ **brutally** *ADVERB*
➤ **brutality** *NOUN*

brute *NOUN* brutes
❶ a cruel or violent man ❷ an animal

brute *ADJECTIVE*
brute force or strength is purely physical, without using any skill
➤ **brutish** *ADJECTIVE*

BSc *ABBREVIATION*
Bachelor of Science

BSE *ABBREVIATION*
bovine spongiform encephalopathy; a fatal disease of cattle that affects the nervous system and makes the cow stagger about. BSE is sometimes known as 'mad cow disease'

bubble *NOUN* bubbles
❶ a thin transparent ball of liquid filled with air or gas ❷ a small ball of air in something, such as a fizzy drink

bubble *VERB* bubbles, bubbling, bubbled
❶ to send up bubbles or rise to the surface in bubbles • *The kettle was bubbling now.* ❷ to

show great liveliness • *He was bubbling with excitement.*

bubblegum *NOUN*
chewing gum that can be blown into large bubbles

bubbly *ADJECTIVE* bubblier, bubbliest
❶ full of bubbles ❷ cheerful and lively

buccaneer *NOUN* buccaneers
a pirate

buck *NOUN* bucks
❶ a male deer, rabbit or hare ❷ (*North American & Australian/NZ*) a dollar
➤ **pass the buck** (*informal*) to pass the responsibility for something to another person

buck *VERB* bucks, bucking, bucked
a horse bucks when it jumps with its back arched
➤ **buck up** (*informal*)
❶ to cheer up ❷ to hurry up

bucket *NOUN* buckets
a container with a handle, for carrying liquids, sand, etc.
➤ **bucketful** *NOUN*

buckle *NOUN* buckles
a clip at the end of a belt or strap for fastening it

buckle *VERB* buckles, buckling, buckled
❶ to fasten something with a buckle ❷ to bend or give way under a strain • *The arm of the crane was beginning to buckle.*
➤ **buckle down to something** to start working hard at something

buckler *NOUN* bucklers
a small round shield

bud *NOUN* buds
a flower or leaf before it opens

Buddhism (say **buud**-izm) *NOUN*
a religion that started in Asia and follows the teachings of Siddharta Gautama who lived in India in the 5th century BC and became known as 'the Buddha'
➤ **Buddhist** *NOUN*

budding *ADJECTIVE*
beginning to develop • *a budding poet*

buddy *NOUN* buddies (*informal*)
a friend

budge *VERB* budges, budging, budged
if you cannot budge something, you cannot move it at all

budgerigar *NOUN* budgerigars
an Australian bird often kept as a pet in a cage

budget *NOUN* budgets
❶ a plan for spending money wisely ❷ an amount of money set aside for a purpose
➤ **the Budget** the Chancellor of the Exchequer's statement of plans for government spending and taxes

budget *VERB* budgets, budgeting, budgeted
to plan how much you are going to spend

budgie *NOUN* budgies (*informal*)
a budgerigar

buff *NOUN* buffs (*informal*)
a person who is very interested in a subject and knows a lot about it • *a film buff*

buff *ADJECTIVE*
of a dull yellow colour

buff *VERB* buffs, buffing, buffed
to polish something with soft material
WORD ORIGIN noun sense comes from the adjective, originally describing people who went to watch fires, from the buff-coloured uniforms once worn by New York firemen

buffalo *NOUN* buffalo or buffaloes
a large ox. Different kinds are found in Asia, Africa and North America (where they are also called **bison**)

buffer *NOUN* buffers
❶ something that reduces an impact or protects something ❷ (*British*) a device on a railway engine or wagon or at the end of a track, for reducing the shock if there is a collision ❸ (*in computing*) a memory in which text or data can be stored temporarily

buffer state *NOUN* buffer states
a small country between two powerful ones, thought to reduce the chance of these two attacking each other

buffet (say **buu**-fay) *NOUN* buffets
❶ a room or counter selling light meals or snacks ❷ a meal where guests serve themselves

buffet (say **buf**-it) *VERB* buffets, buffeting, buffeted
to hit or knock something repeatedly • *Strong winds buffeted the aircraft.*

buffoon *NOUN* buffoons
a person who acts like a fool

bug *NOUN* bugs
❶ a tiny insect ❷ an error in a computer program that prevents it working properly
❸ (*informal*) a germ or virus ❹ a secret hidden microphone

bug *VERB* bugs, bugging, bugged
❶ to fit a room with a secret hidden microphone ❷ (*informal*) to pester or annoy someone

bugbear *NOUN* bugbears
something you fear or dislike

buggy *NOUN* buggies
❶ a kind of chair on wheels for pushing young children around ❷ a small open-topped vehicle used on beaches or golf courses ❸ a light, horse-drawn carriage

bugle *NOUN* bugles
a brass instrument like a small trumpet, used for sounding military signals
➤ **bugler** *NOUN*

build *VERB* builds, building, built
❶ to make something by putting parts together ❷ to develop or increase something gradually
➤ **build something in** to include something in a structure or plan
➤ **build up** to grow or increase • *The traffic always builds up at this time of the day.*
➤ **build something up** ❶ to establish something gradually • *He has built up a reputation for getting results.* ❷ to increase something or make it stronger • *You need to build up your strength.*

build *NOUN* builds
the shape of someone's body • *She has a slender build.*

builder *NOUN* builders
someone who puts up buildings

building *NOUN* buildings
❶ a structure with walls and a roof, such as a house or office block ❷ the process of constructing houses and other structures

building society *NOUN* building societies
(*British*) an organization that accepts deposits of money and lends to people who want to buy houses

built-in *ADJECTIVE*
made into a permanent part of something
• *The bedroom has a built-in wardrobe.*

built-up *ADJECTIVE*
a built-up area is one with a lot of buildings

bulb *NOUN* bulbs
❶ a glass globe that produces electric light ❷ a thick rounded part of a plant from which a stem grows up and roots grow down ❸ a

a b c d e f g h i j k l m n o p q r s t u v w x y z

rounded part of something • *the bulb of a thermometer* **WORD ORIGIN** from Greek *bolbos* = onion

bulbous *ADJECTIVE*
round and fat in an ugly way • *a bulbous nose*

bulge *NOUN* bulges
a rounded swelling; an outward curve

bulge *VERB* bulges, bulging, bulged
to swell or stick out in a curve • *His eyes bulged with excitement.*

bulimia (say bew-**lim**-ia) *NOUN*
an illness that makes someone alternately overeat and fast, often making themselves vomit after eating
➤ **bulimic** *ADJECTIVE*

bulk *NOUN* bulks
❶ the size of something, especially when it is large ❷ the greater part or the majority • *The bulk of the population voted for it.*
➤ **in bulk** in large amounts

bulk *VERB* bulks, bulking, bulked
➤ **bulk something out** to increase the size or thickness of something

bulky *ADJECTIVE* bulkier, bulkiest
taking up a lot of space

bull *NOUN* bulls
❶ a fully-grown male of the cattle family ❷ a male seal, whale or elephant

bulldog *NOUN* bulldogs
a dog of a powerful breed with a short thick neck **WORD ORIGIN** because it was used for attacking tethered bulls in the sport of 'bull-baiting'

bulldoze *VERB* bulldozes, bulldozing, bulldozed
to clear an area with a bulldozer

bulldozer *NOUN* bulldozers
a powerful tractor with a wide metal blade or scoop in front, used for shifting soil or clearing ground

bullet *NOUN* bullets
a small piece of shaped metal shot from a rifle or revolver

bulletin *NOUN* bulletins
❶ a short announcement of news on radio or television ❷ a regular newsletter or report

bulletin board *NOUN* bulletin boards
(*in computing*) a site on a computer system where people can read or write messages

bullet point *NOUN* bullet points
an important item in a list, printed with a black dot in front of it

bulletproof *ADJECTIVE*
able to keep out bullets

bullfight *NOUN* bullfights
in Spain, a public entertainment in which bulls are fought and usually killed, in an arena
➤ **bullfighter** *NOUN*

bullfinch *NOUN* bullfinches
a bird with a strong beak and a pink breast

bullion *NOUN*
bars of gold or silver

bullock *NOUN* bullocks
a young castrated bull

bullseye *NOUN* bullseyes
❶ the centre of a target ❷ a hard round peppermint sweet

bully *VERB* bullies, bullying, bullied
to use strength or power to hurt or frighten another person

bully *NOUN* bullies
someone who bullies people
➤ **bullying** *NOUN*

bulrush *NOUN* bulrushes
a tall plant which grows in marshes, with a thick velvety head

bulwark *NOUN* bulwarks
a wall of earth built as a defence

bulwarks *PLURAL NOUN*
a ship's side above the level of the deck

bum *NOUN* bums (*British*) (*informal*)
a person's bottom

bumble *VERB* bumbles, bumbling, bumbled
to move or behave or speak clumsily

bumblebee *NOUN* bumblebees
a large bee with a loud hum

bump *VERB* bumps, bumping, bumped
❶ to knock against something ❷ to move along with jolts
➤ **bump into someone** (*informal*) to meet someone by chance
➤ **bump someone off** (*informal*) to kill someone

bump *NOUN* bumps
❶ knocking against something or the sound of this • *He landed with a bump on the floor.*
❷ a swelling or lump • *She had a bump on her forehead.*

bumper NOUN bumpers
a bar along the front or back of a motor vehicle to protect it in collisions

bumper ADJECTIVE
unusually large or plentiful • *a bumper crop of apples*

bumpkin NOUN bumpkins
a country person with awkward manners

bumptious (say **bump**-shus) ADJECTIVE
loud and conceited

bumpy ADJECTIVE bumpier, bumpiest
having a lot of bumps • *a bumpy road*

bun NOUN buns
❶ a small round sweet cake ❷ hair twisted into a round bunch at the back of the head

bunch NOUN bunches
a number of things joined or fastened together • *a bunch of grapes* • *a bunch of keys*

bundle NOUN bundles
a number of things tied or wrapped together

bundle VERB bundles, bundling, bundled
❶ to wrap or tie things into a bundle ❷ to push someone hurriedly or carelessly • *They bundled him into the back of a taxi.*

bung NOUN bungs
a stopper for closing a hole in a barrel or jar

bung VERB bungs, bunging, bunged (British) (informal) to bung something somewhere is to put or throw it there carelessly • *Bung those trousers in the washing machine.*
➤ **bunged up** (informal) blocked • *My nose is all bunged up today.*

bungalow NOUN bungalows
a house without any upstairs rooms
WORD ORIGIN from Hindi *bangla* = of Bengal

bungee jumping NOUN
the sport of jumping from a height with a special elastic rope (called a **bungee**) tied to your legs to stop you from hitting the ground

bungle VERB bungles, bungling, bungled
to make a mess of doing something
➤ **bungler** NOUN

bunion NOUN bunions
a swelling at the side of the joint where your big toe joins your foot

bunk NOUN bunks
❶ a narrow bed built like a shelf ❷ (also **bunk bed**) one of a pair of single beds mounted one above the other
➤ **do a bunk** (British) (informal) to run away

bunk VERB bunks, bunking, bunked
➤ **bunk off** (British) (informal) to sneak away from where you are supposed to be, especially school

bunker NOUN bunkers
❶ a sandy hollow built as an obstacle on a golf course ❷ an underground shelter for use in wartime ❸ an outdoor container for storing coal

bunny NOUN bunnies (informal)
a rabbit

Bunsen burner NOUN Bunsen burners
a small gas burner used in laboratories
WORD ORIGIN named after a German scientist, Robert *Bunsen*, who popularized it

bunting NOUN buntings
❶ a kind of small bird ❷ strips of small flags hung up to decorate streets and buildings

buoy (say boi) NOUN buoys
a floating object anchored to mark a channel or underwater rocks

buoy VERB buoys, buoying, buoyed
❶ to keep something afloat ❷ to encourage someone or keep their spirits up • *They were buoyed up with new hope.*

buoyant (say **boi**-ant) ADJECTIVE
❶ able to float ❷ light-hearted; cheerful • *He was in a buoyant mood.*
➤ **buoyancy** NOUN

bur NOUN burs
a different spelling of **burr** (seed case)

burble VERB burbles, burbling, burbled
❶ to make a gentle murmuring sound ❷ to speak in a confused way • *He burbled an apology.*

burden NOUN burdens
❶ a heavy load that you have to carry ❷ something troublesome that you have to put up with • *He doesn't want to become a burden to his children.*

burden VERB burdens, burdening, burdened
❶ to load someone heavily • *She staggered in, burdened with shopping.* ❷ to cause someone worry or trouble • *I'm sorry to burden you with my troubles.*

bureau (say **bewr**-oh) NOUN bureaux
❶ a writing desk with drawers ❷ an office or department • *They will tell you at the Information Bureau.*

bureaucracy (say bewr-**ok**-ra-see) NOUN
the use of too many rules and forms by officials, especially in government

a b c d e f g h i j k l m n o p q r s t u v w x y

departments
➤ **bureaucratic** (say bewr-ok-**rat**-ik) *ADJECTIVE*

bureaucrat (say **bewr**-ok-rat) *NOUN*
bureaucrats
a person who works in a government
department

burger *NOUN* burgers
a hamburger (**WORD ORIGIN**) short for
hamburger = from *Hamburg*, a city in
Germany; the first syllable was dropped because
people thought it referred to ham

burglar *NOUN* burglars
a person who breaks into a building in order
to steal things

burglary *NOUN* burglaries
the crime of breaking into a building and
stealing things

burgle *VERB* burgles, burgling, burgled
(*British*) to break into a house and steal things
• *Our flat was burgled while we were out.*

burgundy *NOUN* burgundies
a rich red or white wine

burial *NOUN* burials
burying somebody • *an ancient burial mound*

burlesque (say ber-**lesk**) *NOUN* burlesques
a comical imitation that makes fun of
something

burly *ADJECTIVE* burlier, burliest
having a strong heavy body

burn *VERB* burns, burning, burned or burnt
❶ to be on fire; to blaze or glow with fire
• *Firefighters raced to the burning building.*
❷ to damage or destroy something by fire or
heat • *He burnt the letters in the fire.* ❸ to
hurt yourself with fire or heat • *I burnt my
hand on the oven.* ❹ to spoil food by cooking
it for too long • *Sorry, I've burnt the toast
again.* ❺ to feel very hot • *Her face burnt
with embarrassment.*

burn *NOUN* burns
❶ a mark or injury made by burning ❷ the
firing of a spacecraft's rockets ❸ (*Scottish*) a
small stream

USAGE
The word **burnt** (not **burned**) is always
used when an adjective is required, e.g.
in *burnt wood*. As parts of the verb,
either **burned** or **burnt** may be used,
e.g. *the wood had burned* or *had burnt
completely*.

burner *NOUN* burners
the part of a lamp or cooker that gives out
the flame

burning *ADJECTIVE*
❶ a burning desire or ambition is one that is
very intense ❷ a burning issue or question is
one that is very topical and important

burnish *VERB* burnishes, burnishing, burnished
to polish a surface by rubbing

burp *VERB* burps, burping, burped
to make a noise through your mouth by
letting air come up from your stomach

burp *NOUN* burps
the act or sound of burping

burr *NOUN* burrs
❶ a plant's seed case or flower that clings to
hair or clothes ❷ a whirring sound ❸ a strong
pronunciation of the letter 'r', as in some
regional accents

burrow *NOUN* burrows
a hole or tunnel dug by a rabbit or fox as a
place to live

burrow *VERB* burrows, burrowing, burrowed
❶ to dig a burrow ❷ to push your way
through or into something; to search deeply
• *She burrowed in her handbag.*

bursar *NOUN* bursars
(*British*) a person who manages the finances
and other business of a school or college

bursary *NOUN* bursaries
(*British*) a grant given to a student

burst *VERB* bursts, bursting, burst
❶ to come apart or tear open suddenly ❷ to
break or force something apart ❸ to burst
into a room is to go in suddenly in a rush
❹ to start doing something suddenly • *It
burst into flames.* • *They burst out laughing.*
❺ to be very full • *She is bursting with
energy*

burst *NOUN* bursts
❶ a split caused by something bursting
❷ something short and forceful • *a burst of
gunfire*

SPELLING
The past tense of **burst** is also **burst**; don't
add ed.

bury *VERB* buries, burying, buried
❶ to put a dead body in the ground ❷ to
put something underground ❸ to cover
something up or hide it • *The letter was
buried at the bottom of a drawer.*

➤ **bury the hatchet** to agree to stop quarrelling or fighting

bus *NOUN* buses
a large vehicle for passengers to travel in
(**WORD ORIGIN**) short for **omnibus**

busby *NOUN* busbies
a tall fur cap worn by some regiments on ceremonial occasions

bush *NOUN* bushes
❶ a woody plant smaller than a tree; a shrub ❷ wild uncultivated land, especially in Africa and Australia

bushel *NOUN* bushels
a measure for grain and fruit equal to 8 gallons (36.4 litres)

bushman *NOUN* bushmen
a person who lives or travels in the Australian or African bush

bushy *ADJECTIVE* bushier, bushiest
thick and hairy • *bushy eyebrows*

busily *ADVERB*
in a busy way

business (say **biz**-niss) *NOUN* businesses
❶ buying and selling things; trade ❷ a shop or firm ❸ a person's concern or responsibilities • *Mind your own business.* ❹ an affair or subject • *I'm tired of the whole business.*

> **SPELLING**
> Don't forget, the i comes after the s in the middle of bus-i-ness.

businesslike *ADJECTIVE*
dealing with things in a direct and practical way

businessman *NOUN* businessmen
a man or woman who works in business

businesswoman *NOUN* businesswomen
a woman who works in business

busker *NOUN* buskers
a person who plays music in the street for money
➤ **busking** *NOUN*

bust *NOUN* busts
❶ a sculpture of a person's head, shoulders and chest ❷ a woman's breasts or chest

bust *VERB* busts, busting, bust
(*informal*) to break something

bust *ADJECTIVE* (*informal*)
❶ broken or damaged • *My phone is bust.* ❷ bankrupt

bustard *NOUN* bustards
a large bird that can run very fast

bustle *VERB* bustles, bustling, bustled
to hurry in a busy or excited way • *He was bustling about in the kitchen.*

bustle *NOUN* bustles
❶ hurried or excited activity ❷ padding used to puff out the top of a long skirt at the back

busy *ADJECTIVE* busier, busiest
❶ having a lot to do; working on something ❷ full of activity • *The town centre is always busy on Saturdays.* ❸ a busy telephone line or number is one that is engaged
➤ **busyness** *NOUN*

busy *VERB* busies, busying, busied
➤ **busy yourself** to do things to occupy yourself; to keep busy • *Bill busied himself making sandwiches.*

busybody *NOUN* busybodies
a person who meddles or interferes

but *CONJUNCTION*
however; nevertheless • *I wanted to go, but I couldn't.*

but *PREPOSITION*
except • *There is no one here but me.*

but *ADVERB*
only; no more than • *We can but try.*

butcher *NOUN* butchers
❶ a person who cuts up meat and sells it ❷ a person who kills people in a cruel way
➤ **butchery** *NOUN*

butcher *VERB* butchers, butchering, butchered
to kill people in a cruel way

butler *NOUN* butlers
a male servant in charge of other servants in a large private house

butt *NOUN* butts
❶ the thicker end of a weapon or tool ❷ the stub of a cigar or cigarette ❸ a large cask or barrel ❹ someone who is a target for ridicule or teasing • *He was the butt of their jokes.*

butt *VERB* butts, butting, butted
an animal butts something when it pushes or hits it with its head and horns
➤ **butt in** to interrupt or interfere

butter *NOUN*
a soft fatty food made by churning cream

butter *VERB* butters, buttering, buttered
to spread something with butter
➤ **buttery** *ADJECTIVE*

a b c d e f g h i j k l m n o p q r s t u v w x y z

buttercup *NOUN* buttercups
a wild plant with bright yellow cup-shaped flowers

butter-fingers *NOUN*
a clumsy person who often drops things

butterfly *NOUN* butterflies
❶ an insect with large white or brightly coloured wings ❷ a swimming stroke in which both arms are lifted forwards at the same time

buttermilk *NOUN*
the liquid that is left after butter has been made

butterscotch *NOUN*
a kind of hard toffee

buttock *NOUN* buttocks
either of the two fleshy rounded parts of your bottom

button *NOUN* buttons
❶ a knob or disc sewn on clothes as a fastening or ornament ❷ a small knob that you press to work an electric device

button *VERB* buttons, buttoning, buttoned
to fasten a piece of clothing with a button or buttons

buttonhole *NOUN* buttonholes
❶ a slit through which you push a button to fasten clothes ❷ a flower worn on a lapel

buttonhole *VERB* buttonholes, buttonholing, buttonholed
to come up to someone so that you can talk to them

buttress *NOUN* buttresses
a support built against a wall

buy *VERB* buys, buying, bought
to get something by paying for it

buy *NOUN* buys
something that is bought • *That coat was a good buy.*

buyer *NOUN* buyers
a person who buys something

buzz *NOUN* buzzes
a vibrating humming sound
➤ **get a buzz from something** (*informal*) to find something exciting

buzz *VERB* buzzes, buzzing, buzzed
❶ to make a buzz ❷ to be full of excitement or activity • *The whole place was buzzing with excitement.* ❸ to threaten an aircraft by deliberately flying close to it
➤ **buzz off** (*informal*) to go away

buzzard *NOUN* buzzards
a kind of hawk

buzzer *NOUN* buzzers
a device that makes a buzzing sound as a signal

by *PREPOSITION*
This word is used to show
❶ closeness to something (*Sit by me.*)
❷ direction or route (*We got here by a short cut.*) ❸ the time before which something happens (*Try to get there by 6 o'clock.*)
❹ manner or method (*cooking by gas*)
❺ distance or amount (*You missed it by inches.*)
➤ **by the way** used to introduce a new topic
➤ **by yourself** alone; without help

by *ADVERB*
past • *I can't get by.*
➤ **by and by** soon; later on
➤ **by and large** on the whole
➤ **put something by** to keep something in reserve for future use

bye *NOUN* byes
❶ a run scored in cricket when the ball goes past the batsman without being touched
❷ an opportunity to go to the next round of a tournament without having won the current round, because you have no opponent

bye-bye *EXCLAMATION* (*informal*)
goodbye

by-election *NOUN* by-elections
(*British*) an election to replace a Member of Parliament who has died or resigned

bygone *ADJECTIVE*
belonging to the past
➤ **let bygones be bygones** forgive and forget past disagreements

by-law *NOUN* by-laws
a law that applies only to a particular town or district

bypass *NOUN* bypasses
❶ a road taking traffic round the edge of a town or city rather than going through the centre ❷ an operation on the heart to make an alternative passage for the blood so that it does not flow through a part that is damaged or blocked

bypass *VERB* bypasses, bypassing, bypassed
to avoid something by means of a bypass

by-product *NOUN* by-products
something useful produced while something else is being made

byre NOUN byres
(*British*) a cowshed

byroad NOUN byroads
a minor road

bystander NOUN bystanders
a person standing near but taking no part when something happens

byte NOUN bytes
(*in computing*) a unit of information in a computer

> **SPELLING**
> Be careful, this sounds the same as **bite**.

byway NOUN byways
a minor road or path

byword NOUN bywords
a person or thing spoken of as a famous example • *The hotel has become a byword for luxury and comfort.*

cab NOUN cabs
❶ a taxi ❷ a compartment for the driver of a lorry, train, bus or crane

cabaret (say **kab**-er-ay) NOUN cabarets
an entertainment provided for the customers in a restaurant or nightclub

cabbage NOUN cabbages
a vegetable with layers of closely packed green or purple leaves

caber NOUN cabers
a tree trunk used in the Scottish Highland sport of 'tossing the caber'

cabin NOUN cabins
❶ a wooden hut or shelter ❷ a room for sleeping on a ship ❸ the part of an aircraft where the passengers sit ❹ a driver's cab

Cabinet NOUN
the group of chief ministers, chosen by the Prime Minister, who meet to decide government policy

cabinet NOUN cabinets
a cupboard with drawers or shelves for storing things

cable NOUN cables
❶ a thick rope of fibre or wire; a thick chain ❷ a covered group of wires laid underground for transmitting electrical signals ❸ cable television ❹ (*old use*) a telegram sent overseas

cable car NOUN cable cars
a small cabin suspended on a moving cable, used for carrying people up and down a mountainside

cable television NOUN
a broadcasting service with signals transmitted by cable to the sets of people who have paid to receive it

cacao (say ka-**kay**-oh) NOUN cacaos
a tropical tree with a seed from which cocoa and chocolate are made

cache (say kash) NOUN caches
a hidden store of things, especially valuable things

cackle NOUN cackles
❶ a loud unpleasant laugh ❷ noisy chatter ❸ the loud clucking noise a hen makes

cackle VERB cackles, cackling, cackled
❶ to laugh in a loud and unpleasant way ❷ hens cackle when they make loud clucking noises

cacophony (say kak-**off**-on-ee) NOUN cacophonies
a harsh mixture of loud unpleasant sounds • *a cacophony of car alarms*
➤ **cacophonous** ADJECTIVE

cactus NOUN cacti
a fleshy plant, usually with prickles, from a hot dry climate

cad NOUN cads
a dishonourable man

cadaverous (say kad-**av**-er-us) ADJECTIVE
pale and thin, like a dead body

caddie NOUN caddies
a person who carries a golfer's clubs during a game

caddy NOUN caddies
a small box for holding tea

cadence (say **kay**-denss) NOUN cadences
❶ rhythm; the rise and fall of the voice in speaking ❷ the final notes of a musical phrase

cadenza (say ka-**den**-za) NOUN cadenzas
an elaborate passage for a solo instrument or singer, to show the performer's skill

cadet *NOUN* **cadets**
a young person being trained for the armed forces or the police

cadge *VERB* **cadges, cadging, cadged**
(*British*) to get something from someone without paying for it • *I managed to cadge a lift into town.*

cadmium *NOUN*
a metal that looks like tin

Caesarean, Caesarean section (say siz-**air**-ee-an) *NOUN* **Caesareans, Caesarean sections**
a surgical operation for taking a baby out of the mother's womb WORD ORIGIN so called because Julius Caesar is said to have been born in this way

caesura (say siz-**yoor**-a) *NOUN*
a short pause in a line of verse

cafe (say **kaf**-ay) *NOUN* **cafes**
a small restaurant that sells light meals and drinks

cafeteria (say kaf-it-**eer**-ee-a) *NOUN* **cafeterias**
a self-service cafe

caffeine (say **kaf**-een) *NOUN*
the substance found in tea and coffee that makes you feel more awake and full of energy

caftan *NOUN* **caftans**
a long loose coat or dress with wide sleeves

cage *NOUN* **cages**
a container or structure made of bars or wires, in which birds or animals are kept

caged *ADJECTIVE*
kept in a cage • *a caged bird*

cagoule (say kag-**ool**) *NOUN* **cagoules**
(*British*) a lightweight waterproof jacket

cairn *NOUN* **cairns**
a pile of loose stones set up as a landmark or monument

cajole *VERB* **cajoles, cajoling, cajoled**
to persuade someone to do something by saying nice things to them

cake *NOUN* **cakes**
❶ a sweet food made by baking a mixture of flour, fat, eggs, sugar, etc. ❷ something shaped into a lump or block • *a cake of soap* • *fish cakes*

caked *ADJECTIVE*
covered with something that has dried hard • *boots caked in mud*

calamine *NOUN*
a pink powder used to make a soothing lotion for the skin

calamity *NOUN* **calamities**
an event that causes a lot of damage or harm
➤ **calamitous** *ADJECTIVE*

calcium *NOUN*
a chemical substance found in teeth, bones and lime

calculate *VERB* **calculates, calculating, calculated**
❶ to work something out by using mathematics ❷ if something is calculated to have an effect, it is intended or designed to have that effect • *Her remarks were clearly calculated to hurt me.*

calculating *ADJECTIVE*
planning things carefully so that you get what you want

calculation *NOUN* **calculations**
something you work out by using mathematics • *I need to do a quick calculation first.*

calculator *NOUN* **calculators**
a small electronic device for making calculations

calculus *NOUN*
mathematics for working out problems about rates of change WORD ORIGIN from Latin *calculus* = small stone (used on an abacus)

calendar *NOUN* **calendars**
a chart or set of pages showing the dates of the month or year

> SPELLING
> There is a tricky bit in **calendar**—it ends in **ar**.

calf *NOUN* **calves**
❶ a young cow or bull ❷ a young whale, seal or elephant ❸ the fleshy back part of your leg below your knee

calibrate (say **kal**-i-brayt) *VERB* **calibrates, calibrating, calibrated**
to mark a gauge or instrument with a scale of measurements
➤ **calibration** *NOUN*

calibre (say **kal**-ib-er) *NOUN* **calibres**
❶ the diameter of the inside of a tube or gun barrel or of a bullet or shell ❷ ability or quality • *We need more people of your calibre.*

calico *NOUN*
a kind of cotton cloth

caliper *NOUN* **calipers**
a support for a weak or injured leg

calipers *PLURAL NOUN*
compasses for measuring the width of tubes or of round objects

caliph (say **kal**-if or **kay**-lif) *NOUN* **caliphs**
the former title of the ruler in certain Muslim countries

call *VERB* **calls, calling, called**
❶ to name or describe a person or thing • *They've decided to call the baby Alexander.* • *Are you calling me a liar?* ❷ to be called something is to have that as your name • *What is your dog called?* ❸ to shout or speak loudly, e.g. to attract someone's attention ❹ to telephone someone ❺ to tell or ask someone to come to you • *The next day he called everyone in for a meeting.* ❻ to make a short visit

call *NOUN* **calls**
❶ a shout or cry to attract someone's attention ❷ a short visit ❸ telephoning someone ❹ a request for someone to come ➤ **call a person's bluff** to challenge a person to do what they threatened, when you think they are bluffing ➤ **call for something** to require something • *This news calls for a celebration.* ➤ **call something off** to cancel or postpone something ➤ **call someone up** to summon someone to join the armed forces

call box *NOUN* **call boxes**
a telephone box

caller *NOUN* **callers**
a person who telephones or visits someone

calligram *NOUN* **calligrams**
a poem in which the form of the writing relates to the content of the poem, e.g. a poem about growth shown with the letters getting larger

calligraphy (say kal-**ig**-raf-ee) *NOUN*
the art of beautiful handwriting

calling *NOUN* **callings**
❶ a person's profession or trade ❷ a strong feeling that you should follow a particular occupation; a vocation

callous (say **kal**-us) *ADJECTIVE*
hard-hearted; not caring about other people's feelings

➤ **callously** *ADVERB*
➤ **callousness** *NOUN*

callow *ADJECTIVE*
immature and inexperienced • *a callow youth*

callus *NOUN* **calluses**
a small patch of skin that has become thick and hard through being continually pressed or rubbed

calm *ADJECTIVE*
❶ not excited, worried or angry • *Try to keep calm.* ❷ quiet and still; not windy • *a calm sea*
➤ **calmness** *NOUN*

calm *VERB* **calms, calming, calmed**
to become or make someone calm • *Calm down, everyone!* **WORD ORIGIN** from Greek *kauma* = hot time of the day (when people rested)

SPELLING
There is a silent **l** in **calm**.

calmly *ADVERB*
in a calm way • *'I'll call the doctor,' she said calmly.*

calorie *NOUN* **calories**
a unit for measuring an amount of heat or the energy produced by food

calumny (say **kal**-um-nee) *NOUN* **calumnies**
an untrue statement that damages a person's reputation

calve *VERB* **calves, calving, calved**
to give birth to a calf

calypso *NOUN* **calypsos**
a West Indian song about current happenings, made up as the singer goes along

calyx (say **kay**-liks) *NOUN* **calyces**
a ring of leaves (**sepals**) forming the outer case of a bud

camaraderie (say kam-er-**ah**-der-ee) *NOUN*
trust and comradeship between friends

camber *NOUN* **cambers**
a slight curved shape from the middle of a road down to the sides

cambric *NOUN*
thin linen or cotton cloth

camcorder *NOUN* **camcorders**
a combined video camera and sound recorder

camel *NOUN* **camels**
a large animal with a long neck and either one or two humps on its back, used in desert countries for riding and for carrying goods

a b c d e f g h i j k l m n o p q r s t u v w x y z

camellia NOUN camellias
a kind of evergreen flowering shrub
WORD ORIGIN Latin, named after Joseph
Camellus, a botanist

cameo (say **kam**-ee-oh) NOUN cameos
❶ a small hard piece of stone carved with
a raised design in its upper layer ❷ a short
part in a play or film, usually one played by a
well-known actor

camera NOUN cameras
a device for taking photographs, films or
television pictures
➤ **in camera** in a judge's private room; in
private
WORD ORIGIN Latin, = vault, chamber

cameraman, **camerawoman** NOUN
cameramen or camerawomen
a person who operates a film or television
camera

camomile NOUN camomiles
a plant with sweet-smelling daisy-like flowers

camouflage (say **kam**-off-lahzh) NOUN
a way of hiding things by making them look
like part of their surroundings • *An animal's
markings are often used for camouflage.*

camouflage VERB camouflages,
camouflaging, camouflaged
to hide something by camouflage • *The
soldiers camouflaged themselves with leaves.*

camp NOUN camps
a place where people live in tents or huts for
a short time

camp VERB camps, camping, camped
❶ to put up a tent or tents • *Let's camp here
for the night.* ❷ to have a holiday in a tent
➤ **camper** NOUN
➤ **camping** NOUN

campaign NOUN campaigns
❶ a planned series of actions, especially
to get people to support you or become
interested in something • *an advertising
campaign* ❷ a series of battles in one area or
with one purpose

campaign VERB campaigns, campaigning,
campaigned
to take part in a campaign • *They are
campaigning to save the rainforests.*
➤ **campaigner** NOUN

camphor NOUN
a strong-smelling white substance used
in medicine and mothballs and in making
plastics

campsite NOUN campsites
a place for camping

campus NOUN campuses
the grounds and buildings of a university or
college

can AUXILIARY VERB past tense could
❶ to be able to • *He can play the violin.* ❷ to
be allowed to • *Can I go now?*

USAGE
Some people think that **can** should not
be used instead of **may** when asking to
be allowed to do something, e.g. *Can I
go to the bathroom?* However, in most
situations it is acceptable except in formal
or official writing.

can NOUN cans
❶ a sealed tin in which food or drink is
preserved ❷ a metal or plastic container for
liquids

can VERB cans, canning, canned
to preserve food in a sealed can

canal NOUN canals
❶ an artificial water channel cut through
land so that boats can sail along it or for
irrigating land ❷ a tube through which food
or air passes in a plant or animal body • *the
alimentary canal*

canary NOUN canaries
a small yellow bird that sings

cancan NOUN cancans
a lively dance in which the legs are kicked
very high

cancel VERB cancels, cancelling, cancelled
❶ to decide that something planned will
not be done or will not take place • *My train
has been cancelled.* ❷ to stop an order or
instruction for something ❸ to mark a stamp
or ticket etc. so that it cannot be used again
➤ **cancel something out** to have an equal
and opposite effect • *The advantages and
disadvantages cancel each other out.*

cancellation NOUN cancellations
something that has been cancelled • *Bad
weather caused the cancellation of the
parade.*

cancer NOUN cancers
❶ a serious disease in which harmful growths
form in the body ❷ a harmful tumour
➤ **cancerous** ADJECTIVE
WORD ORIGIN Latin, = crab, because the
swollen veins around the area of the tumour
were thought to look like the legs of a crab

candelabrum (say kan-dil-**ab**-rum) *NOUN*
candelabra
a candlestick with several branches for
holding candles

candid *ADJECTIVE*
frank and honest
➤ **candidly** *ADVERB*

candidate *NOUN* candidates
❶ a person who wants to be elected or
chosen for a particular job or position ❷ a
person taking an examination
➤ **candidacy** *NOUN*
WORD ORIGIN from Latin *candidus* = white
(because Roman candidates for office had to
wear a pure white toga)

candied *ADJECTIVE*
coated or preserved in sugar • *candied
cherries*

candle *NOUN* candles
a stick of wax with a wick running through it,
giving light when it is burning

candlelight *NOUN*
the light from a candle • *The hall was lit by
candlelight.*

candlestick *NOUN* candlesticks
a holder for a candle or candles

candour (say **kan**-der) *NOUN*
being candid; frankness and honesty

candy *NOUN* candies
(*North American*) sweets or a sweet

candyfloss *NOUN* candyflosses
(*British*) a fluffy mass of very thin strands of
spun sugar wrapped round a stick

cane *NOUN* canes
❶ the hollow stem of a reed or tall grass ❷ a
long thin stick

cane *VERB* canes, caning, caned
to beat someone with a long thin stick as a
punishment

canine (say **kayn**-yn) *ADJECTIVE*
to do with dogs

canine *NOUN* canines
❶ a dog ❷ a pointed tooth at the front of
the mouth

canister *NOUN* canisters
a round metal container • *a gas canister*

canker *NOUN*
a disease that rots the wood of trees and
plants or causes ulcers and sores on animals

cannabis *NOUN*
hemp smoked as a drug

cannibal *NOUN* cannibals
❶ a person who eats human flesh ❷ an
animal that eats animals of its own kind
➤ **cannibalism** *NOUN*
WORD ORIGIN from Spanish *Canibales*, the
name given to the original inhabitants of the
Caribbean islands, who the Spanish thought ate
people

cannon *NOUN*
❶ cannon a large heavy gun that fires heavy
balls made of metal or stone ❷ cannons
(*chiefly British*) the hitting of two balls in
billiards by the third ball

cannon *VERB* cannons, cannoning, cannoned
(*chiefly British*) to cannon into something is
to collide with it clumsily or heavily • *The two
players cannoned into one another.*
SPELLING
Take care not to confuse with **canon.**

cannon ball *NOUN* cannon balls
a large solid ball fired from a cannon

cannot
can not

canny *ADJECTIVE* cannier, canniest
clever and cautious; shrewd
➤ **cannily** *ADVERB*

canoe *NOUN* canoes
a narrow lightweight boat, moved forwards
with paddles

canoe *VERB* canoes, canoeing, canoed
to travel in a canoe
➤ **canoeist** *NOUN*

canon *NOUN* canons
❶ a general principle; a rule ❷ a clergyman
of a cathedral
SPELLING
Take care not to confuse with **cannon.**

canonize (also **canonise**) *VERB* canonizes,
canonizing, canonized
to declare officially that someone is a saint
➤ **canonization** *NOUN*

canopy *NOUN* canopies
❶ a hanging cover forming a shelter above
a throne or bed ❷ a natural covering, e.g. of
leaves and branches • *The thick jungle canopy
lets very little light through.* ❸ the part of a
parachute that spreads in the air

cant VERB **cants, canting, canted**
to slope or tilt

cant NOUN
insincere talk about moral behaviour

can't (*mainly spoken*)
cannot

> **SPELLING**
> Can't = can + not. Add an **apostrophe** between the **n** and the **t**.

cantaloupe NOUN **cantaloupes**
a small round orange-coloured melon

cantankerous ADJECTIVE
bad-tempered and always complaining • *a cantankerous old man*

cantata (say kant-**ah**-ta) NOUN **cantatas**
a musical composition for singers, usually with a chorus and orchestra

canteen NOUN **canteens**
❶ a restaurant for workers in a factory or office ❷ a case or box containing a set of cutlery ❸ a small water flask carried by a soldier or camper

canter NOUN
a gentle gallop by a horse

canter VERB **canters, cantering, cantered**
to go or ride at a gentle gallop
WORD ORIGIN short for 'Canterbury gallop', the gentle pace at which pilgrims were said to travel to Canterbury in the Middle Ages

cantilever NOUN **cantilevers**
a beam or girder fixed at only one end and used to support a bridge

canton NOUN **cantons**
each of the districts into which a country, especially Switzerland, is divided

canvas NOUN **canvases**
❶ a kind of strong coarse cloth ❷ a piece of canvas for painting on; a painting

canvass VERB **canvasses, canvassing, canvassed**
to visit people to ask them for their support, especially in an election
➤ **canvasser** NOUN

canyon NOUN **canyons**
a deep valley, usually with a river running through it

cap NOUN **caps**
❶ a soft hat without a brim but often with a peak ❷ a special headdress, e.g. that worn by a nurse ❸ a cap awarded to members of

a sports team ❹ a cover or top ❺ something that makes a bang when fired in a toy pistol

cap VERB **caps, capping, capped**
❶ to put a cap or cover on something • *The mountain is always capped with snow.* ❷ to award a sports cap to someone chosen to be in a team ❸ to cap a story or joke is to tell one that is better

capable ADJECTIVE
able to do something • *She is definitely capable of winning this match.*
➤ **capability** NOUN

capacious (say ka-**pay**-shus) ADJECTIVE
roomy; able to hold a large amount • *her capacious handbag*

capacity NOUN **capacities**
❶ the amount that something can hold ❷ ability to do something • *He has a great capacity for work.* ❸ the position that someone occupies • *In my capacity as your guardian I am responsible for you.*

cape NOUN **capes**
❶ a short cloak ❷ a large piece of high land that sticks out into the sea

caper VERB **capers, capering, capered**
to jump about playfully

caper NOUN **capers**
❶ jumping about playfully ❷ (*informal*) an adventure or prank ❸ the pickled bud of a prickly shrub, used in cooking

capillary (say ka-**pil**-er-ee) NOUN **capillaries**
any of the very fine blood vessels that connect veins and arteries

capillary ADJECTIVE
to do with or occurring in a very narrow tube; to do with a capillary

capital NOUN **capitals**
❶ a capital city ❷ a capital letter ❸ money or property that can be used to produce more wealth ❹ the top part of a pillar

capital ADJECTIVE
(*old use*) very good or excellent

capital city NOUN **capital cities**
the most important city in a country, usually where the government is based

capitalism (say **kap**-it-al-izm) NOUN
an economic system in which a country's trade and industry are controlled by private owners for profit and not by the state. Compare with **communism**.

capitalist (say **kap**-it-al-ist) NOUN **capitalists**
❶ a rich person who has a lot of their wealth

invested ❷ a person who is in favour of capitalism

capitalize (also **capitalise**) (say **kap**-it-al-yz) VERB **capitalizes, capitalizing, capitalized**
❶ to write or print a word with a capital letter ❷ to capitalize on something is to use it to your own advantage • *He was able to capitalize on his opponent's mistake.*
➤ **capitalization** NOUN

capital letter NOUN **capital letters**
a large letter of the kind used at the start of a name or sentence

capital punishment NOUN
punishing criminals by putting them to death

capitulate VERB **capitulates, capitulating, capitulated**
to admit that you are defeated and surrender
➤ **capitulation** NOUN

cappuccino NOUN **cappuccinos**
milky coffee made frothy by putting steam through it under pressure
WORD ORIGIN Italian: named after the Capuchin monks who wore coffee-coloured habits

caprice (say ka-**preess**) NOUN **caprices**
a sudden impulsive whim or change of behaviour

capricious (say ka-**prish**-us) ADJECTIVE
deciding or changing your mind in an impulsive way
➤ **capriciously** ADVERB

capsize VERB **capsizes, capsizing, capsized**
a boat or ship capsizes when it overturns in the water

capstan NOUN **capstans**
a thick post that can be turned to wind up a rope or cable

capsule NOUN **capsules**
❶ a hollow pill containing medicine ❷ a plant's seed case that splits open when it is ripe ❸ a compartment of a spacecraft that can be separated from the main part

captain NOUN **captains**
❶ a person in command of a ship or aircraft ❷ the leader of a sports team ❸ an army officer ranking next below a major; a naval officer ranking next below a commodore

captain VERB **captains, captaining, captained**
to be the captain of a sports team

captaincy NOUN **captaincies**
the position of captain of a team • *He had to resign the captaincy.*

caption NOUN **captions**
❶ the words printed next to a picture to describe it ❷ a short title or heading in a newspaper or magazine

captivate VERB **captivates, captivating, captivated**
to charm or delight someone • *The children were captivated by the story.*
➤ **captivating** ADJECTIVE

captive NOUN **captives**
someone who has been taken prisoner

captive ADJECTIVE
taken prisoner; unable to escape • *They were held captive by masked gunmen.*

captivity NOUN
❶ the state of being held prisoner • *He was held in captivity for three years.* ❷ the state of being kept in a zoo or wildlife park rather than living in the wild • *These gorillas were bred in captivity.*

captor NOUN **captors**
someone who has captured a person or animal

capture VERB **captures, capturing, captured**
❶ to catch or imprison a person or animal • *The lion was captured and taken back to the zoo.* ❷ to take control of a place using force • *Rome was captured in 410.* ❸ to make someone interested in something • *The story captured my imagination immediately.* ❹ to succeed in representing or describing something • *A TV cameraman captured the whole scene.* ❺ (*in computing*) to put data in a form that can be stored in a computer

capture NOUN
the act of capturing someone or something • *They evaded capture for three days.*

car NOUN **cars**
❶ a road vehicle with four wheels that can carry a small number of people ❷ a railway carriage • *dining car*

carafe (say ka-**raf**) NOUN **carafes**
a glass bottle holding wine or water for pouring out at the table

caramel NOUN **caramels**
❶ a kind of soft toffee made from sugar and butter ❷ burnt sugar used for colouring and flavouring food

carapace (say **ka**-ra-payss) NOUN **carapaces**
the hard shell on the back of a tortoise or crustacean

a
b
c
d
e
f
g
h
i
j
k
l
m
n
o
p
q
r
s
t
u
v
w
x
y
z

carat *NOUN* carats
❶ a measure of weight for precious stones ❷ a measure of the purity of gold • *Pure gold is 24 carats.*

caravan *NOUN* caravans
❶ a vehicle towed by a car and used for living in, especially by people on holiday ❷ a group of people travelling together across desert country
➤ **caravanning** *NOUN*

caraway *NOUN*
a plant with spicy seeds that are used for flavouring food

carbohydrate *NOUN* carbohydrates
a compound of carbon, oxygen and hydrogen (e.g. sugar or starch), found in food and a source of energy

carbolic *NOUN*
a kind of disinfectant

carbon *NOUN*
❶ an element that is present in all living things and that occurs in its pure form as diamond and graphite ❷ carbon dioxide
• *carbon levels in the atmosphere*

carbonate *NOUN* carbonates
a compound that gives off carbon dioxide when mixed with acid

carbonated *ADJECTIVE*
a carbonated drink has carbon dioxide added to make it fizzy

carbon copy *NOUN* carbon copies
an exact copy of something • *She is a carbon copy of her sister.* **WORD ORIGIN** originally a copy made with carbon paper = thin paper with a coloured coating, placed between sheets of paper to make copies of what is written or typed on the top sheet

carbon dating *NOUN*
the use of a kind of radioactive carbon that decays at a steady rate, to find out how old something

carbon dioxide *NOUN*
a gas formed when things burn or breathed out by humans and animals

carboniferous *ADJECTIVE*
producing coal

carbon monoxide *NOUN*
a poisonous gas found especially in the exhaust fumes of motor vehicles

carbuncle *NOUN* carbuncles
❶ a large boil or abscess in the skin ❷ a bright-red gem

carburettor *NOUN* carburettors
a device for mixing fuel and air in an engine

carcass *NOUN* carcasses
❶ the dead body of an animal ❷ the bony part of a bird's body after the meat has been eaten

carcinogen *NOUN* carcinogens
any substance that can cause cancer

card *NOUN* cards
❶ thick stiff paper or thin cardboard ❷ a small piece of stiff paper for writing or printing on, especially to send messages or greetings or to record information ❸ a small, oblong piece of plastic issued to a customer by a bank or shop for drawing out money and making payments ❹ a playing card
➤ **cards** *PLURAL NOUN*
a game using playing cards
➤ **be on the cards** to be likely or possible

cardboard *NOUN*
a kind of thin board made of layers of paper or wood fibre

cardiac (say **kard**-ee-ak) *ADJECTIVE*
to do with the heart

cardigan *NOUN* cardigans
a knitted jumper fastened with buttons down the front **WORD ORIGIN** named after the Earl of *Cardigan*, a commander in the Crimean War; cardigans were first worn by the troops in that war

cardinal *NOUN* cardinals
a senior priest in the Roman Catholic Church

cardinal *ADJECTIVE*
chief or most important • *This is one of the cardinal rules of scientific research.*

cardinal number *NOUN* cardinal numbers
a number for counting things, e.g. one, two, three, etc. Compare with **ordinal number**.

cardinal point *NOUN* cardinal points
each of the four main points of the compass (North, South, East, West)

cardiology *NOUN*
the study of the heart and its diseases
➤ **cardiological** *ADJECTIVE*
➤ **cardiologist** *NOUN*

care *NOUN* cares
❶ serious attention and thought • *Plan your holiday with care.* ❷ caution to avoid

damage or loss • *Glass - handle with care* ❸ protection or supervision • *You can leave the dog in my care.* ❹ worry or anxiety • *She was free from care.*
➤ **take care** to be especially careful
➤ **take care of someone** to look after someone
➤ **take care of something** to deal with something

care VERB cares, caring, cared
❶ to feel interested or concerned about someone or something • *I'm going and I don't care what anybody says.* ❷ to feel affection • *You really care about her, don't you?*
➤ **care for someone** to look after someone • *He cared for his wife when she was ill.*
➤ **care for something** to be fond of something • *I don't much care for fried food.*

career NOUN careers
the series of jobs that someone has as they make progress in their occupation

career VERB careers, careering, careered
to rush along wildly • *We careered down the hill, faster and faster.*

carefree ADJECTIVE
without worries or responsibilities

careful ADJECTIVE
❶ thinking about what you are doing so that you do not make a mistake, have an accident, etc. • *Be careful crossing the road.* ❷ giving serious thought and attention to something • *This needs careful planning.*
➤ **carefully** ADVERB

> **SPELLING**
> Careful + ly = carefully. Don't forget the double l.

careless ADJECTIVE
not taking enough care to avoid mistakes or harm • *careless work*
➤ **carelessly** ADVERB
➤ **carelessness** NOUN

caress NOUN caresses
a gentle loving touch

caress VERB caresses, caressing, caressed
to touch someone lovingly

caret NOUN carets
a mark (ˆ) showing where something is to be inserted in writing or printing

caretaker NOUN caretakers
a person employed to look after a school, block of flats, etc.

cargo NOUN cargoes
goods carried in a ship or aircraft

Caribbean ADJECTIVE
to do with or from the Caribbean Sea, a part of the Atlantic Ocean east of Central America

caribou (say **ka**-rib-oo) NOUN caribou
a North American reindeer
WORD ORIGIN from a Native American word meaning 'snow-shoveller' (because the caribou scrapes away the snow to feed on the grass underneath)

caricature NOUN caricatures
an amusing or exaggerated picture or description of someone

caries (say **kair**-eez) NOUN caries
decay in teeth or bones

carmine ADJECTIVE & NOUN
deep red

carnage NOUN
the killing of large numbers of people

carnal ADJECTIVE
to do with the body as opposed to the spirit; not spiritual

carnation NOUN carnations
a garden flower with a sweet smell

carnival NOUN carnivals
a festival, often with a procession of people in fancy dress **WORD ORIGIN** from Latin *carnis* = of the flesh (because originally this meant the festivities before Lent, when meat was given up until Easter)

carnivore (say **kar**-niv-or) NOUN carnivores
an animal that feeds on the flesh of other animals. Compare with **herbivore**.

carnivorous (say kar-**niv**-er-us) ADJECTIVE
a carnivorous animal feeds on the flesh of other animals.Compare with **herbivorous**.

carol NOUN carols
a Christmas hymn
➤ **carolling** NOUN

carouse VERB carouses, carousing, caroused
to drink alcohol and enjoy yourself with other people **WORD ORIGIN** from German *gar aus trinken* = drink to the bottom of the glass

carousel (say ka-roo-**sel**) NOUN carousels
❶ a roundabout at a fair ❷ a conveyor belt that goes round in a circle for passengers to collect their baggage at an airport

carp NOUN carp
an edible freshwater fish

a b c d e f g h i j k l m n o p q r s t u v w x y z

carp VERB carps, carping, carped
to keep complaining or finding fault

car park NOUN car parks
(*British*) an area where cars may be parked

carpenter NOUN carpenters
a person who makes things out of wood
➤ **carpentry** NOUN

carpet NOUN carpets
❶ a thick soft covering for a floor ❷ a thick layer of something on the ground • *a carpet of fallen leaves*
➤ **carpeting** NOUN

carpeted ADJECTIVE
❶ covered with a carpet • *carpeted stairs* ❷ covered with a thick layer of something • *The forest floor was carpeted with wild flowers.*

carport NOUN carports
a shelter with a roof and open sides for a car

carriage NOUN carriages
❶ one of the separate parts of a train, where passengers sit ❷ a passenger vehicle pulled by horses ❸ carrying goods from one place to another or the cost of this • *Carriage is extra.* ❹ a moving part carrying or holding something in a machine

carriageway NOUN carriageways
(*British*) the part of a road on which vehicles travel

carrier NOUN carriers
a person or thing that carries something

carrier bag NOUN carrier bags
(*British*) a plastic or paper bag with handles

carrier pigeon NOUN carrier pigeons
a pigeon used to carry messages

carrion NOUN
the decaying flesh of a dead animal

carrot NOUN carrots
a plant with a thick orange-coloured root used as a vegetable

carry VERB carries, carrying, carried
❶ to take something from one place to another ❷ to support the weight of something ❸ to take an amount into the next column when adding figures ❹ to be heard a long way away • *Sound carries in the mountains.* ❺ if a motion is carried, it is approved by most people at the meeting • *The motion was carried by ten votes to six.*
➤ **be carried away** to be very excited
➤ **carry on** to continue or keep doing

something • *They ignored me and carried on chatting.*
➤ **carry something out** to do and complete something • *We need to carry out some tests.*

cart NOUN carts
an open vehicle for carrying loads

cart VERB carts, carting, carted
❶ (*informal*) to carry something heavy or tiring • *I've been carting these books around all morning.* ❷ to carry something in a cart

carthorse NOUN carthorses
a large strong horse used for pulling heavy loads

cartilage NOUN
tough white flexible tissue attached to a bone

cartography NOUN
the art of drawing maps
➤ **cartographer** NOUN

carton NOUN cartons
a light cardboard or plastic container

cartoon NOUN cartoons
❶ an amusing drawing, especially one in a newspaper or magazine ❷ a series of drawings that tell a story ❸ an animated film
➤ **cartoonist** NOUN

cartridge NOUN cartridges
❶ a case containing the explosive for a bullet or shell ❷ a container holding film for a camera, ink for a printer or pen, etc.

cartwheel NOUN cartwheels
❶ a circular movement in which you do a sideways handstand by balancing on each hand in turn with arms and legs spread like spokes of a wheel • *My sister was in the garden doing cartwheels.* ❷ the wheel of a cart

carve VERB carves, carving, carved
❶ to cut wood or stone in order to make something or to put a pattern or writing on it • *The statue is carved out of marble* ❷ to cut cooked meat into slices

carving NOUN carvings
an object or design that has been carved

cascade NOUN cascades
a small waterfall

cascade VERB cascades, cascading, cascaded
to pour down in large amounts • *Water cascaded from the roof.*

case NOUN cases
❶ an instance of something existing or occurring • *In every case we found that*

someone had cheated. ❷ something that the police are investigating or that is being decided in a law trial • *a murder case* ❸ a set of facts or arguments to support something • *She put forward a good case for equality.* ❹ the form of a word that shows how it is related to other words. *Fred's* is the possessive case of *Fred*; *him* is the objective case of *he.* ❺ a container ❻ a suitcase
➤ **in any case** whatever happens; anyway
➤ **in case** because something may happen • *Take an umbrella in case it rains.*

casement NOUN **casements**
a window that opens on hinges at its side

cash NOUN
❶ money in coin or notes ❷ immediate payment for goods

cash VERB **cashes, cashing, cashed**
to cash a cheque is to exchange it for cash

cash card NOUN **cash cards**
(*British*) a plastic card used to draw money from a cash dispenser

cash dispenser NOUN **cash dispensers**
(*British*) a machine, usually outside a bank or building society, from which people can draw out cash by using a cash card

cashew NOUN **cashews**
a kind of small nut

cashier NOUN **cashiers**
a person who takes in and pays out money in a bank or takes payments in a shop

cashmere NOUN
very fine soft wool **WORD ORIGIN** from *Kashmir* in Asia, where it was first produced

cashpoint NOUN **cashpoints**
a cash dispenser

cash register NOUN **cash registers**
a machine that records and stores the money received in a shop

casing NOUN **casings**
a protective case or covering

casino NOUN **casinos**
a public building or room for gambling

cask NOUN **casks**
a large barrel

casket NOUN **caskets**
a small box for jewellery or other valuable objects

cassava NOUN
a tropical plant with starchy roots that are an important source of food in tropical countries

casserole NOUN **casseroles**
❶ a covered dish in which food is cooked and served ❷ a kind of stew cooked in a casserole

cassette NOUN **cassettes**
a small sealed case containing recording tape, film, etc.
➤ **cassette player** NOUN

cassock NOUN **cassocks**
a long piece of clothing worn by clergy and members of a church choir

cast VERB **casts, casting, cast**
❶ to throw something with force ❷ to shed something or throw it off ❸ to make a light or shadow fall on something • *The light from the candle cast her shadow on the wall.* ❹ to direct your eyes or thoughts to something • *Cast your mind back to last Sunday.* ❺ to make a vote in an election ❻ to make something out of metal or plaster in a mould ❼ to choose the performers for a play or film

cast NOUN **casts**
❶ a shape made by pouring liquid metal or plaster into a mould ❷ all the performers in a play or film

castanets PLURAL NOUN
two pieces of wood or ivory held in one hand and clapped together to make a clicking sound, especially in Spanish dancing

castaway NOUN **castaways**
a shipwrecked person

caste NOUN **castes**
(in India) each of the social classes into which Hindus are born

caster sugar NOUN
(*British*) finely ground white sugar

casting vote NOUN **casting votes**
the vote that decides which group wins when the votes on each side are equal

cast iron NOUN
a hard alloy of iron made by casting it in a mould

castle NOUN **castles**
❶ a large fortified building that was built in the past to defend people against attack ❷ a piece in chess, also called a **rook**
➤ **castles in the air** daydreams or wild hopes

castor NOUN **castors**
a small wheel on the leg of a table, chair, etc.

a b c d e f g h i j k l m n o p q r s t u v w x y z

castor oil *NOUN*
oil from the seeds of a tropical plant, used as a laxative

castrate *VERB* castrates, castrating, castrated
to remove the testicles of a male animal. Compare with **spay**.
➤ **castration** *NOUN*

casual *ADJECTIVE*
❶ happening by chance and not planned • *a casual meeting* ❷ not carefully done or thought out • *It was just a casual remark.* ❸ relaxed and not bothered by something • *She tried to sound casual.* ❹ suitable for informal occasions • *casual clothes* ❺ not permanent • *casual work*

casually *ADVERB*
in a casual way • *'What did he say about me?'* *she asked as casually as she could.*

casualty *NOUN* casualties
❶ a person who is killed or injured in war or in an accident ❷ a casualty department in a hospital

casualty department *NOUN* casualty departments
(*British*) the department of a hospital that deals with emergency patients

cat *NOUN* cats
❶ a small furry domestic animal ❷ a wild animal of the same family as a domestic cat, e.g. a lion, tiger or leopard
➤ **let the cat out of the bag** to reveal a secret by mistake

cataclysm (say **kat**-a-klizm) *NOUN* cataclysms
a violent upheaval or disaster, such as a flood or war
➤ **cataclysmic** *ADJECTIVE*

catacombs (say **kat**-a-koomz) *PLURAL NOUN*
underground passages with compartments for tombs

catalogue *NOUN* catalogues
❶ a list of things (e.g. of books in a library), usually arranged in order ❷ a book containing a list of things that can be bought • *our Christmas catalogue*

catalogue *VERB* catalogues, cataloguing, catalogued
to list a collection of things in a catalogue

catalyst (say **kat**-a-list) *NOUN* catalysts
❶ something that starts or speeds up a chemical reaction ❷ something that brings about a change

catalytic converter *NOUN* catalytic converters
a device fitted to a car's exhaust system, with a catalyst for converting the exhaust gases into less harmful ones

catamaran *NOUN* catamarans
a boat with twin parallel hulls

catapult *NOUN* catapults
❶ a forked stick with elastic fastened to each prong, used for shooting small stones ❷ an ancient military weapon for hurling stones

catapult *VERB* catapults, catapulting, catapulted
to hurl something or rush violently • *As the car hit him, he was catapulted into the air.*

cataract *NOUN* cataracts
❶ a large waterfall or rush of water ❷ a cloudy area that forms in the eye and causes blurred vision

catarrh (say ka-**tar**) *NOUN*
inflammation in your nose that makes it drip a watery fluid

catastrophe (say ka-**tass**-trof-ee) *NOUN* catastrophes
a sudden great disaster

catastrophic (say kat-a-**strof**-ik) *ADJECTIVE*
absolutely disastrous • *The earthquake caused catastrophic damage.*
➤ **catastrophically** *ADVERB*

catch *VERB* catches, catching, caught
❶ to take hold of something moving ❷ to capture a person or animal ❸ to reach someone who has been ahead of you ❹ to be in time to get on a bus or train ❺ to become infected with an illness ❻ to hear what someone says • *I didn't catch what he said.* ❼ to discover someone doing something wrong • *She was caught smoking in the playground.* ❽ to get something snagged or entangled • *I caught my dress on a nail.* ❾ to hit or strike something • *The blow caught him on the nose.*
➤ **catch fire** to start burning
➤ **catch it** (*informal*) to be scolded or punished
➤ **catch on** (*informal*)
❶ to become popular ❷ to begin to understand something
➤ **catch someone out** to discover someone in a mistake
➤ **catch up with someone** ❶ to reach someone when they have been ahead of you ❷ to reach the same standard or level as someone else

catch *NOUN* **catches**
❶ catching something, e.g. a ball
❷ something caught or worth catching
• *They had a large catch of fish.* ❸ a hidden difficulty • *It looks like a good offer, but there must be a catch.* ❹ a device for fastening a door or window

> **SPELLING**
> The past tense of catch is **caught**, and the 'or' sound is spelt **augh**.

catching *ADJECTIVE*
a disease is catching when it is infectious

catchment area *NOUN* **catchment areas**
❶ the area from which a hospital takes patients or a school takes pupils ❷ the whole area from which water drains into a river or reservoir

catchphrase *NOUN* **catchphrases**
a well-known phrase, especially one that a famous person has used

catchy *ADJECTIVE*
a catchy tune is pleasant and easy to remember

catechism (say **kat**-ik-izm) *NOUN* **catechisms**
a set of questions and answers that give the basic beliefs of a religion

categorical (say kat-ig-**o**-rik-al) *ADJECTIVE*
completely clear and definite • *a categorical refusal*
➤ **categorically** *ADVERB*

category *NOUN* **categories**
a set of people or things classified as being similar to each other • *This painting won first prize in the junior category.*

cater *VERB* **caters, catering, catered**
❶ to provide food for a lot of people at a social occasion ❷ to provide what is needed
• *The school caters for children of all abilities.*
➤ **caterer** *NOUN*

caterpillar *NOUN* **caterpillars**
the creeping worm-like creature that turns into a butterfly or moth **WORD ORIGIN** from Old French *chatepelose* = hairy cat

cathedral *NOUN* **cathedrals**
the most important church of a district, usually with a bishop in charge of it

Catherine wheel *NOUN* **Catherine wheels**
(*British*) a firework that spins round and throws out sparks **WORD ORIGIN** named after St Catherine of Alexandria, who was martyred on a spiked wheel

cathode *NOUN* **cathodes**
the electrode by which electric current leaves a device. Compare with **anode**.

cathode ray tube *NOUN* **cathode ray tubes**
a tube used in televisions and computers, in which a beam of electrons from a cathode produces an image on a fluorescent screen

Catholic *ADJECTIVE*
belonging to the Roman Catholic Church
➤ **Catholicism** *NOUN*

Catholic *NOUN* **Catholics**
a Roman Catholic

catholic *ADJECTIVE*
including a wide range of things • *She has fairly catholic tastes in music.*

catkin *NOUN* **catkins**
a spike of small soft flowers on trees such as hazel and willow

catnap *NOUN* **catnaps**
a short sleep during the day

Catseye *NOUN* **Catseyes** (*trademark*)
one of a line of reflecting studs that mark the centre or edge of a road

cattle *PLURAL NOUN*
cows and bulls kept by farmers for their milk and beef

catty *ADJECTIVE* **cattier, cattiest**
saying unkind and spiteful things about someone

catwalk *NOUN* **catwalks**
a long narrow platform that models walk along at a fashion show

caucus *NOUN* **caucuses**
a small group within a political party, influencing decisions and policy

cauldron *NOUN* **cauldrons**
a large deep pot for boiling things in

cauliflower *NOUN* **cauliflowers**
a cabbage with a large head of white flowers

cause *NOUN* **causes**
❶ a person or thing that makes something happen or produces an effect • *The cause of the accident is a mystery.* ❷ a good reason
• *There is no cause for worry.* ❸ a purpose for which people work; an organization or charity
• *They were raising money for a good cause.*

cause *VERB* **causes, causing, caused**
to be the cause of something or to make it happen • *Do we know what caused the fire?*

a b c d e f g h i j k l m n o p q r s t u v w x y z

causeway NOUN causeways
a raised road across low or marshy ground

caustic ADJECTIVE
❶ able to burn or wear things away by chemical action ❷ very critical or sarcastic • *caustic comments*
➤ **caustically** ADVERB

cauterize (also **cauterise**) VERB cauterizes, cauterizing, cauterized
to cauterize a wound is to burn the surface of flesh round it to destroy infection or stop any bleeding

caution NOUN cautions
❶ care you take to avoid difficulty or danger
❷ a warning

caution VERB cautions, cautioning, cautioned
to give someone a warning • *He cautioned his sister not to tell anyone.*

cautionary ADJECTIVE
giving a warning • *a cautionary tale*

cautious ADJECTIVE
taking care to avoid difficulty or danger
➤ **cautiously** ADVERB

cavalcade NOUN cavalcades
a procession of vehicles or people on horseback

Cavalier NOUN Cavaliers
a supporter of King Charles I in the English Civil War (1642-9)

cavalry NOUN
soldiers who fight on horseback or in armoured vehicles. Compare with **infantry**.

cave NOUN caves
a large hollow place in the side of a hill or cliff or underground

cave VERB caves, caving, caved
➤ **cave in** ❶ to collapse or fall inwards • *The roof of the tunnel had caved in.* ❷ to give way in an argument • *She finally caved in and agreed that he could go.*

caveat (say **kav**-ee-at) NOUN caveats
a warning (WORD ORIGIN) Latin, = let a person beware

caveman NOUN cavemen
a person living in a cave in prehistoric times

cavern NOUN caverns
a large cave

cavernous ADJECTIVE
a cavernous room or space is huge and often empty or dark • *He looked around the cavernous hall.*

caviare (say **kav**-ee-ar) NOUN
the pickled roe of sturgeon or other large fish

caving NOUN
(*British*) exploring caves

cavity NOUN cavities
a hollow or hole

cavort (say ka-**vort**) VERB cavorts, cavorting, cavorted
to jump or run about excitedly

caw NOUN caws
the harsh cry of a crow or other large bird

CB ABBREVIATION
citizens' band

cc ABBREVIATION
❶ cubic centimetre(s) ❷ used to show that a copy of an email is being sent to another person (WORD ORIGIN) the second meaning is short for 'carbon copy', originally a copy made with carbon paper (= thin paper with a coloured coating) placed between sheets of paper to make copies of what is written or typed on the top sheet

CD ABBREVIATION
compact disc

CD-ROM ABBREVIATION
compact disc read-only memory; a compact disc on which large amounts of data can be stored and then displayed on a computer screen

cease VERB ceases, ceasing, ceased
to stop happening or stop doing something • *You never cease to amaze me!* • *The company ceased trading in June.*

ceasefire NOUN ceasefires
an agreement between the two sides in a conflict for fighting to stop for a time

ceaseless ADJECTIVE
not stopping; going on continuously • *the ceaseless cooing of the pigeons*

cedar NOUN cedars
an evergreen tree with hard fragrant wood
➤ **cedarwood** NOUN

cede (say seed) VERB cedes, ceding, ceded
to give up your rights to something; to surrender something you own • *They had to cede some of their territory.*

cedilla (say sid-**il**-a) NOUN cedillas
a mark under c in certain languages to show that it is pronounced as s, e.g. in *façade*
(WORD ORIGIN) from Spanish, = a little z

ceilidh (say **kay**-lee) *NOUN* **ceilidhs**
an informal gathering for music, singing and dancing, originating from Scotland and Ireland

ceiling *NOUN* **ceilings**
❶ the flat surface at the top of a room ❷ the highest limit that something can reach • *They imposed a ceiling on car imports.*

> **SPELLING**
> In ceiling, e before i is the right way round.

celandine *NOUN* **celandines**
a small wild plant with yellow flowers

celebrate *VERB* **celebrates, celebrating, celebrated**
❶ to do something special or enjoyable to show that a day or event is important ❷ to perform a religious ceremony

celebrated *ADJECTIVE*
famous • *a celebrated author*

celebration *NOUN* **celebrations**
❶ celebrating something • *Her triumph was a cause for celebration.* ❷ a party or other event that celebrates something

celebrity *NOUN* **celebrities**
❶ a celebrity is a famous person ❷ celebrity is fame or being famous • *He never really enjoyed his celebrity.*

celery *NOUN*
a vegetable with crisp white or green stems

celestial (say sil-**est**-ee-al) *ADJECTIVE*
❶ to do with the sky ❷ to do with heaven; divine
➤ **celestial bodies** stars or planets

celibate (say **sel**-ib-at) *ADJECTIVE*
remaining unmarried or not having sex, especially for religious reasons
➤ **celibacy** *NOUN*

cell *NOUN* **cells**
❶ a small room where a prisoner is locked up ❷ a small room in a monastery or convent ❸ a microscopic unit of living matter. All plants and animals are made up of cells. ❹ a compartment of a honeycomb ❺ a device for producing electric current chemically ❻ a small group or unit in an organization

cellar *NOUN* **cellars**
an underground room

cello (say **chel**-oh) *NOUN* **cellos**
a musical instrument like a large violin, played

upright between the knees of a player
➤ **cellist** *NOUN*

Cellophane *NOUN*
(*trademark*) a thin transparent wrapping material

cellular *ADJECTIVE*
❶ to do with or containing cells ❷ with an open mesh • *cellular blankets* ❸ a cellular telephone uses a network of radio stations to allow messages to be sent over a wide area

celluloid *NOUN*
a kind of plastic, used in the past for making cinema films

cellulose *NOUN*
tissue that forms the main part of all plants and trees

Celsius (say **sel**-see-us) *ADJECTIVE*
measuring temperature on a scale using 100 degrees, where water freezes at 0° and boils at 100° **WORD ORIGIN** named after Anders Celsius, a Swedish astronomer, who invented it

Celtic (say **kel**-tik) *ADJECTIVE*
to do with the languages or inhabitants of ancient Britain and France before the Romans came or of their descendants, e.g. Irish, Welsh, Gaelic

cement *NOUN*
❶ a mixture of lime and clay used in building, to join bricks together ❷ a strong glue

cement *VERB* **cements, cementing, cemented**
❶ to build something with cement ❷ to strengthen or join something firmly • *This marriage cemented the relationship between the two countries.*

cemetery (say **sem**-et-ree) *NOUN* **cemeteries**
a place where dead people are buried

cenotaph (say **sen**-o-taf) *NOUN* **cenotaphs**
a monument, especially as a war memorial, to people who are buried in other places

censer *NOUN* **censers**
a container in which incense is burnt

censor *NOUN* **censors**
a person who examines films, books, letters, etc. and removes or bans anything that is thought to be offensive or unacceptable

censor *VERB* **censors, censoring, censored**
to ban or remove parts of a film, book, letter, etc. that are thought to be offensive or unacceptable
➤ **censorship** *NOUN*
WORD ORIGIN Latin, = magistrate with the power to ban unsuitable people from

ceremonies; from *censere* = to judge

> USAGE
>
> Take care not to confuse with **censure**.

censorious (say sen-**sor**-ee-us) *ADJECTIVE*
criticizing something strongly

censure (say **sen**-sher) *NOUN*
strong criticism or disapproval of something

censure *VERB* censures, censuring, censured
to criticize someone severely and openly

> USAGE
>
> Take care not to confuse with **censor**.

census *NOUN* censuses
an official count or survey of the population of a country or area

cent *NOUN* cents
a coin worth one-hundredth of a dollar

centaur (say **sen**-tor) *NOUN* centaurs
(in Greek myths) a creature with the upper body, head and arms of a man and the lower body of a horse

centenarian (say sent-in-**air**-ee-an) *NOUN* centenarians
a person who is 100 years old or more

centenary (say sen-**teen**-er-ee) *NOUN* centenaries
(*British*) a 100th anniversary of an important event
➤ **centennial** (say sen-**ten**-ee-al) *ADJECTIVE*

centigrade *ADJECTIVE*
Celsius

centilitre *NOUN* centilitres
one-hundredth of a litre

> SPELLING
>
> The 's' sound is spelt with a c in **centilitre**. Do not forget the re at the end.

centimetre *NOUN* centimetres
one-hundredth of a metre

> SPELLING
>
> The 's' sound is spelt with a c in **centimetre**. Do not forget the re at the end.

centipede *NOUN* centipedes
a small crawling creature with a long body and many legs

central *ADJECTIVE*
❶ to do with or at the centre • *a map of central Europe* ❷ most important or main • *The film's central character is a fifteen-*

year-old girl.
➤ **centrally** *ADVERB*

central heating *NOUN*
a system of heating a building from one source by circulating hot water or hot air or steam in pipes or by linked radiators

centralize (also **centralise**) *VERB* centralizes, centralizing, centralized
to bring something under the control of a central authority
➤ **centralization** *NOUN*

centre *NOUN* centres
❶ the middle point or part ❷ an important place ❸ a building or place for a special purpose • *shopping centre* • *sports centre*

centre *VERB* centres, centring, centred
to place something at the centre • *Centre the heading at the top of the page.*
➤ **centre on something** or **centre around something** to have something as the main subject of interest or concern • *Our discussions centred on the question of finance.*

centre forward *NOUN* centre forwards
the player in the middle of the forward line in football or hockey

centre of gravity *NOUN* centres of gravity
the point in an object around which its mass is perfectly balanced

centrifugal *ADJECTIVE*
moving away from the centre; using centrifugal force

centrifugal force *NOUN*
a force that makes a thing that is travelling round a central point fly outwards off its circular path

centurion (say sent-**yoor**-ee-on) *NOUN* centurions
an officer in the ancient Roman army, originally commanding a hundred men

century *NOUN* centuries
❶ a period of one hundred years ❷ a hundred runs scored by a batsman in an innings at cricket

cephalopod (say **sef**-al-o-pod) *NOUN* cephalopods
a mollusc (such as an octopus or squid) that has a head with a ring of tentacles round the mouth

ceramic *ADJECTIVE*
to do with or made of pottery

ceramics *PLURAL NOUN*
pottery-making

cereal *NOUN* cereals
❶ a grass producing seeds which are used as food, e.g. wheat, barley or rice ❷ a breakfast food made from these seeds
WORD ORIGIN from *Ceres*, the Roman goddess of farming

SPELLING
Take care not to confuse with **serial**.

cerebral (say se-rib-ral) *ADJECTIVE*
to do with the brain

cerebral palsy *NOUN*
a condition caused by brain damage before birth that makes a person suffer from spasms of the muscles and jerky movements

ceremonial *ADJECTIVE*
to do with or used in a ceremony; formal • *a ceremonial occasion*
➤ **ceremonially** *ADVERB*

ceremonious *ADJECTIVE*
full of ceremony; elaborately performed • *a ceremonious bow*

ceremony *NOUN* ceremonies
❶ a formal religious or public occasion celebrating an important event • *the opening ceremony of the Olympic Games* ❷ the formal actions carried out on an important occasion, e.g. at a wedding or a funeral • *The new hospital was opened with great ceremony.*

certain *ADJECTIVE*
❶ something is certain when it is definitely true or going to happen ❷ you are certain about something when you know it is definitely true
➤ **a certain person** or **thing** a person or thing that is known but not named
➤ **for certain** definitely; for sure
➤ **make certain** to make sure

SPELLING
There is a tricky bit in **certain** – it ends in **ain**.

certainly *ADVERB*
❶ for certain ❷ yes

certainty *NOUN* certainties
❶ something that is sure to happen ❷ being sure

certificate *NOUN* certificates
an official document giving information about a person or event • *a birth certificate*

certify *VERB* certifies, certifying, certified
to declare formally that something is true
➤ **certification** *NOUN*

cervix *NOUN* cervices (say ser-vis-ees)
the entrance to the womb
➤ **cervical** *ADJECTIVE*

cessation *NOUN*
the stopping or ending of something

cesspit, cesspool *NOUN* cesspits, cesspools
a covered pit where liquid waste or sewage is stored temporarily

CFC *ABBREVIATION*
chlorofluorocarbon; a gas containing chlorine and fluorine that is thought to be harmful to the ozone layer in the Earth's atmosphere

chafe *VERB* chafes, chafing, chafed
❶ to make something sore or become sore by rubbing ❷ to become irritated or impatient • *We chafed at the delay.*

chaff *NOUN*
husks of corn, separated from the seed

chaff *VERB* chaffs, chaffing, chaffed
to tease someone

chaffinch *NOUN* chaffinches
a kind of finch

chagrin (say shag-rin) *NOUN*
a feeling of being annoyed or disappointed

chain *NOUN* chains
❶ a row of metal rings fastened together ❷ a connected series of things • *a mountain chain* • *a chain of events* ❸ a number of shops, hotels or other businesses owned by the same company

chain *VERB* chains, chaining, chained
to fasten something with a chain or chains • *He chained his bike up outside.*

chain letter *NOUN* chain letters
a letter that you are asked to copy and send to several other people, who are supposed to do the same

chain reaction *NOUN* chain reactions
a series of happenings in which each causes the next

chain store *NOUN* chain stores
one of a number of similar shops owned by the same firm

chair *NOUN* chairs
❶ a movable seat, with a back, for one person ❷ the person who is in charge of a meeting

chair *VERB* chairs, chairing, chaired
to chair a meeting is to be in charge of it and
run it

chairman, chairwoman *NOUN* chairmen or
chairwomen
the person who is in charge of a meeting
➤ **chairmanship** *NOUN*

> **USAGE**
> The word **chairman** may be used of a man
> or of a woman, but **chairperson** is now
> often used instead.

chairperson *NOUN* chairpersons
a chairman or chairwoman

chalet (say **shal**-ay) *NOUN* chalets
❶ a Swiss hut or cottage ❷ a hut in a holiday
camp etc.

chalice *NOUN* chalices
a large goblet for holding wine, especially one
from which the Communion wine is drunk in
Christian services

chalk *NOUN* chalks
❶ a soft white or coloured stick used for
writing on blackboards or for drawing ❷ soft
white limestone

chalky *ADJECTIVE*
containing chalk or like chalk • *Her face was
chalky white.*

challenge *NOUN* challenges
❶ a task or activity that is new and exciting
but also difficult • *The role will be the biggest
challenge of his acting career.* ❷ a call to
someone to take part in a contest or to show
their ability or strength

challenge *VERB* challenges, challenging,
challenged
❶ to make a challenge to someone • *My
brother challenged me to a game of darts.*
❷ to be a challenge to someone • *This job
doesn't really challenge me.* ❸ to question
whether something is true or correct

challenger *NOUN* challengers
a person who makes a challenge, especially
for a sports title

challenging *ADJECTIVE*
difficult but also interesting and exciting • *a
challenging job*

chamber *NOUN* chambers
❶ (*old use*) a room ❷ a hall used for meetings
of a parliament or council; the members
of the group using it ❸ a compartment in
machinery etc.

chamberlain *NOUN* chamberlains
an official who manages the household of a
sovereign or great noble

chambermaid *NOUN* chambermaids
a woman employed to clean bedrooms at a
hotel etc.

chamber music *NOUN*
classical music for a small group of players

chamber pot *NOUN* chamber pots
a bowl kept in a bedroom and used as a toilet

chameleon (say kam-**ee**-lee-on) *NOUN*
chameleons
a small lizard that can change its colour
to match that of its surroundings
WORD ORIGIN from Greek *khamaileon*, literally
= ground lion

chamois *NOUN* chamois
❶ (say **sham**-wa) a small wild antelope living
in the mountains ❷ (say **sham**-ee) a piece
of soft yellow leather used for washing and
polishing things

champ *VERB* champs, champing, champed
to munch or bite something noisily

champagne (say sham-**payn**) *NOUN*
a bubbly white wine from the region of
Champagne in France

champion *NOUN* champions
❶ a person or thing that has defeated all the
others in a sport or competition ❷ someone
who supports a cause by fighting or speaking
for it • *Martin Luther King was a champion of
human rights.*

champion *VERB* champions, championing,
championed
to support a cause by fighting or speaking
for it

championship *NOUN* championships
a competition to find the best player or team
in a particular sport or game

chance *NOUN* chances
❶ an opportunity or possibility • *This is your
only chance to see them.* ❷ the way things
happen without being planned • *I met her by
chance.*
➤ **take a chance** to take a risk

chance *VERB* chances, chancing, chanced
❶ to happen by chance • *As she was passing,
she chanced to see him come out of the
house.* ❷ to risk something • *I chanced a
quick look behind me.*

chancel *NOUN* chancels
the part of a church nearest to the altar

chancellor *NOUN* chancellors
❶ an important government or legal official
❷ the chief minister of the government in some European countries

Chancellor of the Exchequer *NOUN*
the government minister in charge of a country's finances and taxes

chancy *ADJECTIVE*
risky or uncertain

chandelier (say shand-il-**eer**) *NOUN* chandeliers
a large hanging light with branches for several light bulbs or candles

change *VERB* changes, changing, changed
❶ to make something different or become different • *This town has changed a lot in the last few years.* ❷ to exchange one thing for another • *Could I change this shirt for a larger size?* ❸ to put on different clothes ❹ to go from one train or bus to another • *Change at York for the train to Durham.* ❺ to give smaller units of money or money in another currency, for an amount of money • *Can you change £20?*

change *NOUN* changes
❶ changing; a difference in doing something • *a change in the weather* ❷ coins or notes of small values ❸ money given back to the payer when the price is less than the amount handed over ❹ a fresh set of clothes ❺ something different from what is usual • *Let's walk home for a change.*

changeable *ADJECTIVE*
likely to change; changing frequently • *changeable weather*

changeling *NOUN* changelings
a child who is believed to have been substituted secretly for another, especially by fairies

channel *NOUN* channels
❶ a stretch of water connecting two seas ❷ a broadcasting wavelength ❸ a way for water to flow along ❹ the part of a river or sea that is deep enough for ships

channel *VERB* channels, channelling, channelled
❶ to use something for a particular purpose • *She channelled all her energy into her music.* ❷ to make something move along a particular channel, path or route • *Water is channelled from the river to the fields.*

chant *NOUN* chants
❶ a tune to which words with no regular

rhythm are fitted, especially one used in church music ❷ a rhythmic call or shout

chant *VERB* chants, chanting, chanted
❶ to sing a chant ❷ to call out words in a rhythm

chaos (say **kay**-oss) *NOUN*
great disorder • *Heavy snow has caused chaos on the roads.*

chaotic (say kay-**ot**-ik) *ADJECTIVE*
in a state of complete confusion and disorder
➤ **chaotically** *ADVERB*

chap *NOUN* chaps (*British*) (*informal*)
a man

chapatti *NOUN* chapattis
a flat cake of unleavened bread, used in Indian cookery

chapel *NOUN* chapels
❶ a small building or room used for Christian worship ❷ a section of a large church, with its own altar

chaperone (say **shap**-er-ohn) *NOUN* chaperones
an older woman in charge of a young one on social occasions
➤ **chaperone** *VERB*

chaplain *NOUN* chaplains
a member of the clergy who regularly works in a college, hospital, prison, regiment, etc.

chapped *ADJECTIVE*
with skin split or cracked from cold etc.
• *chapped lips*

chapter *NOUN* chapters
❶ a section or division of a book ❷ the clergy of a cathedral or members of a monastery

char *VERB* chars, charring, charred
to make something black by burning

char *NOUN* chars
(*British*) (*old use*) a charwoman

character *NOUN* characters
❶ a person in a story, film or play ❷ all the qualities that make a person or thing what he, she or it is • *The book gives a fascinating insight into Madonna's character.* ❸ a letter of the alphabet or other written symbol

characteristic *NOUN* characteristics
a quality that forms part of a person's or thing's character

characteristic *ADJECTIVE*
typical of a person or thing • *This style of dancing is characteristic of the region.*
➤ **characteristically** *ADVERB*

characterize (also **characterise**) *VERB*
characterizes, characterizing, characterized
❶ to be a characteristic of something
• *The country's recent history has been characterized by upheaval and conflict.* ❷ to describe a person's character in a certain way
• *His friends characterized him as ambitious.*
➤ **characterization** *NOUN*

charade (say sha-**rahd**) *NOUN* charades
❶ a scene in the game of **charades**, in which people try to guess a word from other people's acting ❷ a pretence • *I'm sorry, I can't keep this charade up any longer.*

charcoal *NOUN*
a black substance made by burning wood slowly. Charcoal can be used for drawing with.

charge *NOUN* charges
❶ the price asked for something ❷ an accusation that someone has committed a crime • *He is facing three charges of burglary.* ❸ a rushing attack ❹ the amount of electricity in something ❺ the amount of explosive needed to fire a gun ❻ a person or thing in someone's care
➤ **in charge** in control; deciding what will happen to a person or thing
➤ **take charge** to take control of something and become responsible for it

charge *VERB* charges, charging, charged
❶ to ask a particular price for something ❷ to accuse someone of committing a crime ❸ to rush forward in an attack • *The bull put its head down and charged.* ❹ to give an electric charge to something • *My phone needs charging.* ❺ to give someone a responsibility or task

charger *NOUN* chargers
❶ a piece of equipment for charging a battery with electricity • *a mobile phone charger* ❷ (*old use*) a cavalry horse

chariot *NOUN* chariots
a horse-drawn vehicle with two wheels, used in ancient times for fighting and racing
➤ **charioteer** *NOUN*

charisma (say ka-**riz**-ma) *NOUN*
the special quality that makes a person attractive or influential

charismatic (say ka-riz-**mat**-ik) *ADJECTIVE*
having charisma • *She was a charismatic leader.*

charitable *ADJECTIVE*
❶ giving money and help to people who need it; to do with a charity • *a charitable*
donation ❷ kind in your attitude to other people • *Let's be charitable and assume she just made a mistake.*
➤ **charitably** *ADVERB*

charity *NOUN* charities
❶ an organization set up to help people who are poor, ill or disabled or have suffered a disaster ❷ giving money or help to people who need it ❸ kindness and sympathy towards others; being unwilling to think badly of people

charlatan (say **shar**-la-tan) *NOUN* charlatans
a person who falsely claims to be an expert

charm *NOUN* charms
❶ the power to please or delight people; attractiveness • *The story has great charm.* ❷ a magic spell ❸ a small object that is believed to bring good luck • *a lucky charm* ❹ an ornament worn on a bracelet

charm *VERB* charms, charming, charmed
❶ to give pleasure or delight to people ❷ to put a spell on someone; bewitch
➤ **charmer** *NOUN*

charming *ADJECTIVE*
pleasant and attractive

chart *NOUN* charts
❶ a map for people sailing ships or flying aircraft ❷ an outline map showing special information • *a weather chart* ❸ a diagram, list or table giving information in an orderly way
➤ **the charts** a list of the CDs and records that have sold the most copies

chart *VERB* charts, charting, charted
to make a chart or map of something • *Cook explored and charted the coast of New Zealand.*

charter *NOUN* charters
❶ an official document stating the rights or aims of an organization or group of people ❷ hiring an aircraft, ship or vehicle

charter *VERB* charters, chartering, chartered
to hire an aircraft, ship or vehicle

chartered accountant *NOUN* chartered accountants
an accountant who is qualified according to the rules of a professional association that has a royal charter

charwoman *NOUN* charwomen (*British*) (*old use*)
a woman employed as a cleaner

chary (say **chair**-ee) *ADJECTIVE*
cautious about doing or giving something

chase *VERB* chases, chasing, chased
to go quickly after a person or thing in order to capture or catch them up or drive them away

chase *NOUN* chases
chasing someone or something • *an exciting car chase*

chasm (say kazm) *NOUN* chasms
a deep opening in the ground

chassis (say **shas**-ee) *NOUN* chassis
the framework under a car etc., on which other parts are mounted

chaste *ADJECTIVE*
not expressing sexual feelings • *a chaste kiss on the cheek*

chasten (say **chay**-sen) *VERB* chastens, chastening, chastened
to make someone realize that they have behaved badly or done something wrong • *He looked chastened and immediately apologized.*

chastise *VERB* chastises, chastising, chastised
to punish or scold someone severely
➤ **chastisement** *NOUN*

chastity (say **chas**-ti-ti) *NOUN*
the state of not having sex with anyone

chat *NOUN* chats
a friendly informal conversation

chat *VERB* chats, chatting, chatted
❶ to have a friendly informal conversation ❷ to exchange messages with other people on the Internet

chateau (say **shat**-oh) *NOUN* chateaux
a castle or large country house in France

chat room *NOUN* chat rooms
an area on the Internet where people can have a conversation by sending messages to each other

chattel *NOUN* chattels
(*old use*) something you own that can be moved from place to place, as distinct from a house or land

chatter *VERB* chatters, chattering, chattered
❶ to talk quickly about unimportant things; to keep on talking ❷ your teeth chatter when they make a rattling sound because you are cold or frightened
➤ **chatterer** *NOUN*

chatter *NOUN*
chattering talk or sound

chatterbox *NOUN* chatterboxes
a talkative person

chatty *ADJECTIVE*
❶ liking to talk a lot in a friendly way ❷ in an informal style • *a chatty letter*

chauffeur (say **shoh**-fer) *NOUN* chauffeurs
a person employed to drive a car

chauvinism (say **shoh**-vin-izm) *NOUN*
❶ prejudiced belief that your own country is superior to any other ❷ the belief of some men that men are superior to women
➤ **chauvinist** *NOUN*
➤ **chauvinistic** *ADJECTIVE*
(**WORD ORIGIN**) from the name of Nicolas *Chauvin*, a French soldier in Napoleon's army, noted for his extreme patriotism

cheap *ADJECTIVE*
❶ low in price; not expensive ❷ of poor quality; of low value
➤ **cheapness** *NOUN*

cheaply *ADVERB*
for a low price

cheat *VERB* cheats, cheating, cheated
❶ to try to do well in an exam or game by breaking the rules ❷ to trick or deceive someone so they lose something • *He had cheated her out of her fortune.*

cheat *NOUN* cheats
a person who cheats

check *VERB* checks, checking, checked
❶ to make sure that something is correct or in good condition ❷ to make something stop or go slower

check *NOUN* checks
❶ checking something ❷ stopping or slowing; a pause ❸ (*North American*) a bill in a restaurant ❹ the situation in chess when a king may be captured ❺ a pattern of squares
(**WORD ORIGIN**) the oldest meaning is the chess meaning, which comes from Persian *shah* = king

checked *ADJECTIVE*
marked with a pattern of squares • *a checked shirt*

checkmate *NOUN*
the winning situation in chess, where one player's king is threatened and cannot be moved out of danger (**WORD ORIGIN**) from Persian *shah mat* = the king is dead

checkout *NOUN* checkouts
a place where goods are paid for in a self-service shop

check-up *NOUN* check-ups
a routine medical or dental examination

Cheddar *NOUN*
a kind of cheese, originally made in Cheddar in Somerset

cheek *NOUN* cheeks
❶ the side of your face below your eye
❷ rude or disrespectful talk or behaviour

cheeky *ADJECTIVE*
rude or disrespectful
➤ **cheekily** *ADVERB*

cheer *NOUN* cheers
❶ a shout of praise or pleasure or encouragement ❷ good cheer is being cheerful and enjoying yourself

cheer *VERB* cheers, cheering, cheered
❶ to give a cheer ❷ to comfort or encourage someone • *They were all cheered by the good news.*
➤ **cheer up** to become more cheerful

cheerful *ADJECTIVE*
❶ looking or sounding happy ❷ pleasantly bright or colourful
➤ **cheerfully** *ADVERB*
➤ **cheerfulness** *NOUN*

cheerio *EXCLAMATION* (*informal*)
goodbye

cheerless *ADJECTIVE*
gloomy or dreary • *a dark and cheerless room*

cheers *EXCLAMATION* (*informal*)
❶ a word that people say to each other as they lift up their glasses to drink ❷ goodbye
❸ thank you

cheery *ADJECTIVE*
bright and cheerful • *a cheery grin*

cheese *NOUN* cheeses
a solid food made from milk

cheesecake *NOUN* cheesecakes
a dessert made of a mixture of sweetened curds on a layer of biscuit

cheetah *NOUN* cheetahs
a large spotted animal of the cat family that can run extremely fast

chef (say shef) *NOUN* chefs
the cook in a hotel or restaurant

chemical *ADJECTIVE*
to do with or produced by chemistry

chemical *NOUN* chemicals
a substance obtained by or used in chemistry

chemist *NOUN* chemists
❶ a person who makes or sells medicines ❷ a shop selling medicines, cosmetics, etc. ❸ an expert in chemistry

chemistry *NOUN*
❶ the way that substances combine and react with one another ❷ the study of substances and their reactions etc.

chemotherapy *NOUN*
the treatment of disease, especially cancer, by the use of chemical substances

cheque *NOUN* cheques
a printed form on which you write instructions to a bank to pay out money from your account

chequered *ADJECTIVE*
marked with a pattern of squares

cherish *VERB* cherishes, cherishing, cherished
❶ to look after a person or thing lovingly
❷ to keep something in your mind for a long time • *He cherished the memory of those days in Paris.*

cherry *NOUN* cherries
a small soft round fruit with a stone

cherub *NOUN* cherubim or cherubs
an angel, often pictured as a chubby child with wings
➤ **cherubic** (say che-**roo**-bik) *ADJECTIVE*

chess *NOUN*
a game for two players with sixteen pieces each (called **chessmen**) on a board of 64 squares (a **chessboard**)

chest *NOUN* chests
❶ the front part of the body between the neck and the waist ❷ a large strong box for storing things in

chestnut *NOUN* chestnuts
❶ a tree that produces hard brown nuts
❷ the nut of this tree ❸ an old joke or story

chest of drawers *NOUN* chests of drawers
a piece of furniture with drawers for storing clothes etc.

chevron (say **shev**-ron) *NOUN* chevrons
a V-shaped stripe

chew *VERB* chews, chewing, chewed
to grind food between your teeth

chewing gum *NOUN*
a sticky flavoured type of sweet for chewing

chewy *ADJECTIVE*
chewy food is tough and needs a lot of chewing

chic (say sheek) *ADJECTIVE*
stylish and elegant

chick *NOUN* chicks
a very young bird

chicken *NOUN* chickens
❶ a young hen **❷** a hen's flesh used as food

chicken *ADJECTIVE* (*informal*) afraid to do something; cowardly

chicken *VERB* chickens, chickening, chickened
➤ **chicken out** (*informal*) to refuse to take part in something because you are afraid

chickenpox *NOUN*
a disease that produces red spots on the skin

chickpea *NOUN* chickpeas
the yellow seed of a plant of the pea family, eaten as a vegetable

chicory *NOUN*
a plant whose leaves are used in salads

chide *VERB* chides, chiding, chided, chidden
to tell someone off

chief *NOUN* chiefs
❶ a leader or ruler of a people, especially of a Native American tribe **❷** a person with the highest rank or authority • *the chief of police*

chief *ADJECTIVE*
❶ most important; main • *Caesar defeated his chief rival, Pompey and took power.*
❷ having the highest rank or authority • *the company's chief executive*

chiefly *ADVERB*
mainly or mostly • *Liam is the one who is chiefly to blame.*

chieftain *NOUN* chieftains
the chief of a tribe or clan

chiffon (say **shif**-on) *NOUN*
a very thin, almost transparent, fabric

chilblain *NOUN* chilblains
a sore swollen place, usually on a hand or foot, caused by cold weather

child *NOUN* children
❶ a young person; a boy or girl **❷** someone's son or daughter

childhood *NOUN* childhoods
the time when a person is a child

childish *ADJECTIVE*
❶ like a child; unsuitable for a grown person

❷ silly and immature • *childish handwriting*
• *Don't be so childish!*
➤ **childishly** *ADVERB*

childless *ADJECTIVE*
having no children

childlike *ADJECTIVE*
having the good qualities that a child has
• *His childlike enthusiasm delighted us all.*

childminder *NOUN* childminders
(*British*) a person who is paid to look after children while their parents are out at work

chill *NOUN* chills
❶ unpleasant coldness • *There's a chill in the air.* **❷** an illness that makes you shiver

chill *VERB* chills, chilling, chilled
❶ to make a person or thing cold
❷ (*informal*) to relax completely • *We've just been chilling in front of the TV.*

chilli *NOUN* chillies
the hot-tasting pod of a red pepper

chilli con carne *NOUN*
a stew of chilli-flavoured minced beef and beans

chilly *ADJECTIVE*
❶ rather cold **❷** unfriendly • *We got a chilly reception.*

chime *NOUN* chimes
a series of ringing sounds made by a set of bells or clock

chime *VERB* chimes, chiming, chimed
to make a chime • *The church clock chimed nine o'clock.*
➤ **chime in** to join in a conversation by saying something

chimney *NOUN* chimneys
a tall pipe or structure that carries smoke away from a fire

chimney pot *NOUN* chimney pots
a pipe fitted to the top of a chimney

chimney sweep *NOUN* chimney sweeps
a person who cleans soot from inside chimneys

chimpanzee *NOUN* chimpanzees
an intelligent African ape, smaller than a gorilla

chin *NOUN* chins
the lower part of the face below the mouth

china *NOUN*
thin delicate pottery

chink *NOUN* **chinks**
❶ a narrow opening that lets light through
• *He looked through a chink in the curtains.*
❷ a chinking sound • *There was a chink of coins as the money changed hands.*

chink *VERB* **chinks, chinking, chinked**
to make a sound like glasses or coins being struck together

chintz *NOUN*
a shiny cotton cloth used for making curtains etc.

chip *NOUN* **chips**
❶ a thin piece cut or broken off something hard ❷ a fried oblong strip of potato ❸ a place where a small piece has been knocked off something ❹ a small counter used in gambling games ❺ a microchip
➤ **a chip off the old block** a child who is very like his or her father or mother
➤ **have a chip on your shoulder** to feel resentful or defensive about something

chip *VERB* **chips, chipping, chipped**
❶ to knock a small piece off something by accident ❷ to cut a potato into chips
➤ **chip in** to make a suggestion or comment during a conversation that other people are having

chipboard *NOUN*
board made from chips of wood pressed and stuck together

chipolata *NOUN* **chipolatas**
(*British*) a small spicy sausage

chiropody (say ki-**rop**-od-ee) *NOUN*
(*chiefly British*) medical treatment of the feet, e.g. corns
➤ **chiropodist** *NOUN*
WORD ORIGIN from Greek *cheir* = hand + *podos* = of the foot (because chiropodists originally treated both hands and feet)

chirp *VERB* **chirps, chirping, chirped**
to make short sharp sounds like a small bird
➤ **chirp** *NOUN*

chirpy *ADJECTIVE*
lively and cheerful

chisel *NOUN* **chisels**
a tool with a sharp end for shaping wood or stone

chisel *VERB* **chisels, chiselling, chiselled**
to shape or cut wood or stone with a chisel

chivalry (say **shiv**-al-ree) *NOUN*
❶ the code of good behaviour and brave fighting that medieval knights used to follow
❷ behaviour that is considerate and helpful,
especially by men towards women
➤ **chivalrous** *ADJECTIVE*

chive *NOUN* **chives**
a small herb with leaves that taste like onions

chivvy *VERB* **chivvies, chivvying, chivvied**
(*British*) to try to make someone hurry
WORD ORIGIN probably from *Chevy Chase*, the scene of a skirmish which was the subject of an old ballad

chlorine (say **klor**-een) *NOUN*
a greenish-yellow gas used to disinfect water etc.

chloroform (say **klo**-ro-form) *NOUN*
a liquid that gives off a vapour that makes people unconscious

chlorophyll (say **klo**-ro-fil) *NOUN*
the substance that makes plants green

choc ice *NOUN* **choc ices**
(*British*) a bar of ice cream covered with chocolate

chock *NOUN* **chocks**
a block or wedge used to prevent an aircraft from moving

chock-a-block *ADJECTIVE*
(*British*) full of people or things crowded or packed together • *The town is always chock-a-block with tourists.*

chock-full *ADJECTIVE*
crammed full of good things • *This issue is chock-full of exciting stories.*

chocolate *NOUN* **chocolates**
❶ a solid brown food or powder made from roasted cacao seeds ❷ a drink made with this powder ❸ a sweet made of or covered with chocolate

SPELLING
There are two tricky bits in **chocolate**—it has an **o** in the middle and it ends in **late**.

choice *NOUN* **choices**
❶ the opportunity to choose between things
• *I'm afraid we have no choice.* ❷ the range of things from which someone can choose
• *There is now a wide choice of TV channels.*
❸ a person or thing that someone has chosen
• *This is my choice.*

choice *ADJECTIVE*
of the best quality • *choice bananas*

choir *NOUN* **choirs**
a group of people trained to sing together, especially in a church
➤ **choirboy** *NOUN* ➤ **choirgirl** *NOUN*

choke *VERB* chokes, choking, choked
  ❶ to be unable to breathe properly because something is blocking your windpipe ❷ to stop someone breathing properly by blocking their windpipe ❸ to block up or clog something • *The roads were choked with traffic.*

choke *NOUN* chokes
  a device controlling the flow of air into the engine of a motor vehicle

cholera (say **kol**-er-a) *NOUN*
  an infectious disease that is often fatal

cholesterol (say kol-**est**-er-ol) *NOUN*
  a fatty substance that can clog the arteries

choose *VERB* chooses, choosing, chose, chosen
  to decide which you want from among a number of people or things

choosy *ADVERB*
  (*informal*) careful or fussy about what you choose

chop *VERB* chops, chopping, chopped
  ❶ to cut something into pieces with a knife • *Chop the carrots up into small pieces.* ❷ to cut or hit something with a heavy blow • *He chopped a branch off the tree.*

chop *NOUN* chops
  ❶ a chopping blow ❷ a small thick slice of meat, usually on a rib

chopper *NOUN* choppers
  ❶ a chopping tool; a small axe ❷ (*informal*) a helicopter

choppy *ADJECTIVE* choppier, choppiest
  the sea is choppy when it is not smooth but full of small waves

chopsticks *PLURAL NOUN*
  a pair of thin sticks used for lifting Chinese and Japanese food to your mouth

chop suey *NOUN* chop sueys
  a Chinese dish of meat fried with bean sprouts and vegetables served with rice

choral *ADJECTIVE*
  to do with or sung by a choir or chorus

chord (say kord) *NOUN* chords
  ❶ a number of musical notes sounded together ❷ a straight line joining two points on a curve

> **SPELLING**
> Chord is different from **cord**, which means a piece of thin rope.

chore (say chor) *NOUN* chores
  a regular or dull task

choreography (say ko-ree-**og**-ra-fee) *NOUN*
  the art of writing the steps for ballets or stage dances
  ➤ **choreographer** *NOUN*

chorister (say **ko**-rist-er) *NOUN* choristers
  a member of a choir

chortle *VERB* chortles, chortling, chortled
  to chuckle loudly

chortle *NOUN* chortles
  a loud chuckle **WORD ORIGIN** a mixture of **chuckle** and **snort**: invented by Lewis Carroll

chorus *NOUN* choruses
  ❶ the words repeated after each verse of a song or poem ❷ a piece of music sung by a group of people ❸ a group singing together

chorus *VERB* choruses, chorusing, chorused
  to all say something at the same time • *'We'll help!' chorused the girls.*

chow mein *NOUN*
  a Chinese dish of fried noodles with shredded meat or shrimps etc. and vegetables

christen *VERB* christens, christening, christened
  ❶ to baptize a child and give them a name ❷ to give a name or nickname to a person or thing

christening *NOUN* christenings
  the church ceremony at which a child is baptized

Christian *NOUN* Christians
  a person who believes in Jesus Christ and his teachings

Christian *ADJECTIVE*
  to do with Christians or their beliefs
  ➤ **Christianity** *NOUN*

Christian name *NOUN* Christian names
  a name given to a person at his or her christening; a person's first name

Christmas *NOUN* Christmases
  the day (25 December) when Christians commemorate the birth of Jesus Christ; the days round it

Christmas pudding *NOUN* Christmas puddings
  (*British*) a dark pudding containing dried fruit etc., eaten at Christmas

Christmas tree *NOUN* Christmas trees
  an evergreen or artificial tree decorated at Christmas

a b c d e f g h i j k l m n o p q r s t u v w x y z

chromatic scale *NOUN* chromatic scales
a musical scale going up or down in semitones

chrome (say krohm) *NOUN*
chromium **WORD ORIGIN** from Greek *chroma* = colour (because its compounds have brilliant colours)

chromium (say **kroh**-mee-um) *NOUN*
a shiny silvery metal

chromosome (say **kroh**-mos-ohm) *NOUN* chromosomes
a tiny thread-like part of an animal cell or plant cell, carrying genes

chronic *ADJECTIVE*
lasting for a long time • *a chronic illness*
➤ **chronically** *ADVERB*

chronicle *NOUN* chronicles
a record of events in the order that they happened

chronological *ADJECTIVE*
arranged in the order that things happened • *Here are the main events of her life in chronological order.*
➤ **chronologically** *ADVERB*

chronology (say kron-**ol**-oj-ee) *NOUN*
the arrangement of events in the order in which they happened, e.g. in history or geology

chronometer (say kron-**om**-it-er) *NOUN* chronometers
a very exact device for measuring time

chrysalis *NOUN* chrysalises
the hard cover a caterpillar makes round itself before it changes into a butterfly or moth

chrysanthemum *NOUN* chrysanthemums
a garden flower that blooms in autumn

chubby *ADJECTIVE* chubbier, chubbiest
plump and healthy

chuck *VERB* chucks, chucking, chucked (*informal*)
to throw something roughly or carelessly • *Someone had chucked a brick through the window.*

chuck *NOUN* chucks
❶ the part of a drill that holds the bit ❷ the gripping part of a lathe

chuckle *NOUN* chuckles
a quiet laugh

chuckle *VERB* chuckles, chuckling, chuckled
to laugh quietly

chug *VERB* chugs, chugging, chugged
to move making the sound of an engine running slowly • *The train chugged out of the station.*

chum *NOUN* chums (*informal*)
a friend
➤ **chummy** *ADJECTIVE*

chunk *NOUN* chunks
a thick piece of something • *a huge chunk of ice*

chunky *ADJECTIVE*
thick and big • *a bike with chunky tyres*

chupatty (say chup-**at**-ee) *NOUN* chupatties
a different spelling of **chapatti**

church *NOUN* churches
❶ a building where Christians go to worship ❷ a religious service in a church • *I will see you after church.* ❸ a particular Christian religion, e.g. the Church of England

churchyard *NOUN* churchyards
the ground round a church, often used as a graveyard

churlish *ADJECTIVE*
rude and bad-tempered

churn *NOUN* churns
❶ a large can in which milk is carried from a farm ❷ a machine in which milk is beaten to make butter

churn *VERB* churns, churning, churned
❶ to stir something or move it around vigorously • *Vast crowds had churned the field into a sea of mud.* ❷ your stomach churns when you feel very nervous or excited ❸ to make butter in a churn
➤ **churn things out** to produce large quantities of something very quickly • *She has been churning out bestsellers for many years.*

chute (say shoot) *NOUN* chutes
a steep channel for people or things to slide down

> **SPELLING**
> **Chute** is different from **shoot** • *Shoot at the target.*

chutney *NOUN* chutneys
a strong-tasting mixture of fruit, peppers, etc., eaten with meat or cheese

CID *ABBREVIATION*
Criminal Investigation Department

cider *NOUN* ciders
an alcoholic drink made from apples

cigar *NOUN* cigars
a roll of compressed tobacco leaves for smoking

cigarette *NOUN* cigarettes
a small roll of shredded tobacco in thin paper for smoking

cinder *NOUN* cinders
a small piece of partly burnt coal or wood

cine camera (say **sin**-ee) *NOUN* cine cameras
a camera used for taking moving pictures

cinema *NOUN* cinemas (*chiefly British*)
❶ a place where films are shown ❷ the business or art of making films • *a classic of Russian cinema*

cinnamon (say **sin**-a-mon) *NOUN*
a yellowish-brown spice

cinquain (say **sin**-kayn) *NOUN* cinquains
a poem of five lines with a total of 22 syllables arranged in the pattern 2, 4, 6, 8, 2

cipher (say **sy**-fer) *NOUN* ciphers
a secret system of writing used for sending messages; a code

circle *NOUN* circles
❶ a perfectly round flat shape or thing ❷ the balcony of a cinema or theatre ❸ a number of people with similar interests • *She's well known in theatrical circles.*

circle *VERB* circles, circling, circled
to move round something in a circle • *The plane circled the town several times before it landed.* • *Vultures circled overhead.*

> **SPELLING**
> There is **le** at the end of **circle**.

circuit (say **ser**-kit) *NOUN* circuits
❶ a circular line or journey ❷ a track for motor racing ❸ the path of an electric current

circuitous (say ser-**kew**-it-us) *ADJECTIVE*
going a long way round, not direct • *a circuitous route*

circular *ADJECTIVE*
❶ shaped like a circle; round ❷ moving round in a circle • *a circular tour of the town*

circular *NOUN* circulars
a letter or advertisement sent to a number of people

circulate *VERB* circulates, circulating, circulated
❶ to go round something continuously • *Blood circulates in the body.* ❷ to spread

or be passed from one person to another • *Rumours about the president's health began to circulate.* ❸ to send something round to a number of people

circulation *NOUN* circulations
❶ the movement of blood around the body ❷ the number of copies of each issue of a newspaper or magazine that are sold or distributed

circumcise *VERB* circumcises, circumcising, circumcised
to cut off the fold of skin at the tip of the penis
➤ **circumcision** *NOUN*

circumference *NOUN* circumferences
the line or distance round something, especially round a circle

> **SPELLING**
> The 's' sound is spelt with a **c** in **circumference**. Do not forget the **ence** at the end.

circumflex accent *NOUN* circumflex accents
a mark (ˆ) over a vowel

circumnavigate *VERB* circumnavigates, circumnavigating, circumnavigated
to sail completely round something • *Francis Drake circumnavigated the globe between 1577 and 1580.*
➤ **circumnavigation** *NOUN*

circumscribe *VERB* circumscribes, circumscribing, circumscribed
to limit or restrict something • *Her powers are circumscribed by many regulations.*

circumspect *ADJECTIVE*
cautious and watchful
➤ **circumspection** *NOUN*

circumstance *NOUN* circumstances
a fact or condition connected with an event or person or action • *She did brilliantly in the circumstances.*

circumstantial (say ser-kum-**stan**-shal) *ADJECTIVE*
circumstantial evidence consists of facts that strongly suggest something but do not actually prove it

circumvent *VERB* circumvents, circumventing, circumvented
to find a way of avoiding something • *We managed to circumvent the rules.*

circus *NOUN* circuses
a travelling show usually performed in a tent,

a b c d e f g h i j k l m n o p q r s t u v w x y z

with clowns, acrobats and sometimes trained animals **WORD ORIGIN** Latin, = ring, because a circus is usually held in a ring-shaped arena in a tent

cirrus (say si-rus) NOUN cirri
cloud made up of light wispy streaks

cistern NOUN cisterns
a tank for storing water

citadel NOUN citadels
a fortress protecting a city

cite (say sight) VERB cites, citing, cited
to quote or name something as an example • *Many reasons have been cited for the rise in these injuries.*
➤ **citation** NOUN

citizen NOUN citizens
a person belonging to a particular city or country

citizenry NOUN
all the citizens

citizens' band NOUN
a range of special radio frequencies on which people can speak to one another over short distances

citizenship NOUN
the rights or duties of a citizen • *She has applied for American citizenship.*

citrus fruit NOUN citrus fruits
a lemon, orange, grapefruit or other sharp-tasting fruit

city NOUN cities
a large important town, often having a cathedral
➤ **the City** the oldest part of London, now a centre of commerce and finance

civic ADJECTIVE
to do with a city or its citizens • *civic leaders* • *civic pride*

civics NOUN
the study of the rights and duties of citizens

civil ADJECTIVE
❶ polite and courteous ❷ to do with citizens ❸ to do with civilians; not military • *civil aviation*
➤ **civilly** ADVERB

civil engineering NOUN
the work of designing or maintaining roads, bridges, dams, etc.
➤ **civil engineer** NOUN

civilian NOUN civilians
a person who is not serving in the armed forces

civility NOUN civilities
polite and courteous behaviour • *I expect to be treated with a little more civility.*

civilization (also **civilisation**) NOUN civilizations
❶ a society or culture at a particular time in history • *ancient civilizations* ❷ a developed or organized way of life • *We were far from civilization.*

civilize (also **civilise**) VERB civilizes, civilizing, civilized
❶ to bring culture and education to a primitive community ❷ to improve a person's behaviour and manners

civil partnership NOUN civil partnerships
(in some countries) a legal union of a couple of the same sex, with rights similar to those of marriage
➤ **civil partner** NOUN

civil rights PLURAL NOUN
the rights of citizens, especially to have freedom, equality and the right to vote

civil service NOUN
all the officials who work for the government to run its affairs
➤ **civil servant** NOUN

civil war NOUN civil wars
war between groups of people of the same country

clack NOUN clacks
a short sharp sound like that of plates struck together

clack VERB clacks, clacking, clacked
to make this sound • *Her heels clacked on the marble floor.*

clad ADJECTIVE
to be clad in something is to be wearing it or covered by it • *He was clad in magnificent robes.*

claim VERB claims, claiming, claimed
❶ to state something without being able to prove it • *They claimed they had been at home all evening.* ❷ to ask for something to which you believe you have a right • *A wallet was handed in yesterday but no one has claimed it yet.*

claim NOUN claims
❶ a statement that something is true, without any proof ❷ a statement that you

have a right to something ❸ a piece of ground claimed by someone for mining etc.

claimant *NOUN* **claimants**
someone who makes a claim for something, especially money

clairvoyant *NOUN* **clairvoyants**
a person who is said to be able to predict future events or know about things that are happening out of sight
➤ **clairvoyance** *NOUN*

clam *NOUN* **clams**
a large shellfish

clamber *VERB* **clambers, clambering, clambered**
to climb with difficulty, using your hands and feet • *We clambered over the slippery rocks.*

clammy *ADJECTIVE*
damp and slimy • *clammy hands*

clamorous *ADJECTIVE*
making a loud confused noise

clamour *NOUN* **clamours**
❶ a loud confused noise • *the clamour of car horns* ❷ a loud protest or demand

clamour *VERB* **clamours, clamouring, clamoured**
to make a loud protest or demand • *The children were clamouring for attention.*

clamp *NOUN* **clamps**
a device for holding things tightly

clamp *VERB* **clamps, clamping, clamped**
❶ to fix something with a clamp ❷ to hold something firmly in position • *She clamped her hand over his mouth.*
➤ **clamp down on something** to become stricter about something or put a stop to it

clan *NOUN* **clans**
a group of families sharing the same ancestor, especially in Scotland

clandestine (say klan-**dest**-in) *ADJECTIVE*
done secretly; kept secret

clang *NOUN* **clangs**
a loud ringing sound

clang *VERB* **clangs, clanging, clanged**
to make a loud ringing sound • *The gate clanged shut behind them.*

clank *NOUN* **clanks**
a sound like heavy pieces of metal banging together

clank *VERB* **clanks, clanking, clanked**
to make a sound like heavy pieces of metal

banging together • *I could hear clanking chains.*

clap *VERB* **claps, clapping, clapped**
❶ to strike the palms of the hands together loudly, especially as applause ❷ to slap someone in a friendly way • *I clapped him on the shoulder.* ❸ to put someone somewhere quickly or with force • *They clapped him into jail.*

clap *NOUN* **claps**
❶ a sudden sharp noise • *a clap of thunder* ❷ a round of clapping • *We all gave the winners a clap.* ❸ a friendly slap

clapper *NOUN* **clappers**
the hanging piece inside a bell that strikes against the bell to make it sound

claptrap *NOUN*
insincere or foolish talk

claret *NOUN* **clarets**
a kind of red wine

clarify *VERB* **clarifies, clarifying, clarified**
to make something clear or easier to understand • *I hope this clarifies the situation.*
➤ **clarification** *NOUN*

clarinet *NOUN* **clarinets**
a woodwind instrument
➤ **clarinettist** *NOUN*

clarion *NOUN* **clarions**
an old type of trumpet

clarity *NOUN*
the quality of being clear or easy to understand • *The report is written with clarity and precision.*

clash *VERB* **clashes, clashing, clashed**
❶ to make a loud sound like that of cymbals banging together ❷ two events clash when they happen inconveniently at the same time ❸ people clash when they have a fight or argument • *Gangs of rival supporters clashed outside the stadium.* ❹ colours clash when they do not go well together

clash *NOUN* **clashes**
❶ a loud sound like that of cymbals banging together • *the clash of swords* ❷ a fight or argument

clasp *NOUN* **clasps**
❶ a device for fastening things, with interlocking parts ❷ a tight grasp

clasp *VERB* **clasps, clasping, clasped**
❶ to grasp or hold someone or something

A B **C** D E F G H I J K L M N O P Q R S T U V W X Y Z

tightly • *She clasped his hand in hers.* ❷ to fasten something with a clasp

class NOUN **classes**
❶ a group of children or students who are taught together ❷ a group of similar people, animals or things ❸ people of the same social or economic level ❹ a level of quality • *first class*

class VERB **classes, classing, classed**
to put something in a particular class or group; to classify something • *These gorillas are classed as an endangered species.*

classic ADJECTIVE
❶ generally agreed to be excellent or important ❷ very typical or common • *a classic case of overconfidence*

classic NOUN **classics**
a book, film or song that is well known and generally agreed to be excellent or important

classical ADJECTIVE
❶ to do with ancient Greek or Roman literature or art ❷ serious or conventional in style and of lasting value • *classical music*

classics NOUN
the study of ancient Greek and Latin languages and literature

classified ADJECTIVE
❶ put into classes or groups ❷ classified information is officially secret and available only to certain people

classify VERB **classifies, classifying, classified**
to arrange things in classes or groups • *The books in the library are classified according to subject.*
➤ **classification** NOUN

classmate NOUN **classmates**
someone in the same class at school

classroom NOUN **classrooms**
a room where a class of children or students is taught

clatter VERB **clatters, clattering, clattered**
to make a sound like hard objects rattling together • *I heard horses' hooves clattering on the cobbles outside.*

clatter NOUN
a clattering noise

clause NOUN **clauses**
❶ a single part of a treaty, law or contract

❷ (*in grammar*) a part of a sentence, with its own verb

> **GRAMMAR**
>
> A **clause** is a part of a sentence that contains a verb. A sentence can contain one or more **main clauses**, linked by a conjunction such as *and, but or* or *yet* or by a semicolon:
>
> *Ladybirds eat aphids.*
>
> *We approached cautiously; the lioness was beginning to stir.*
>
> A **subordinate clause** begins with a conjunction such as *because, if* or *when,* and it can come before or after the main clause. A subordinate clause should not be used without a main clause:
>
> *Because they eat aphids, ladybirds are useful in the garden.*
>
> *I'll never speak to you again if you lose that ring.*
>
> A **relative clause** explains or describes something that has just been mentioned, and is introduced by *that, which, who, whom, whose, when* or *where.* A relative clause can either specify which person or thing you are talking about:
>
> *Of all Tolkien's books, the one which I like best is 'The Hobbit'.*
>
> or can simply add further information, in which case you put a comma before it, and another comma after it if it appears in the middle of a sentence:
>
> *The book, which Tolkien wrote for his children, was an instant success.*
>
> In the first of these two examples, but not the second, you can use *that* instead of *which*; you can also say *the one I like best is* The Hobbit.
>
> See also the panels on **conjunctions and connectives**, **which and that**, and **commas**.

claustrophobia NOUN
an extreme fear of being inside an enclosed space
➤ **claustrophobic** ADJECTIVE

claw NOUN **claws**
❶ a sharp nail on a bird's or animal's foot ❷ a claw-like part or device used for grasping things

claw VERB claws, clawing, clawed
to grasp, pull or scratch something with a claw or hand

clay NOUN
a kind of stiff sticky earth that becomes hard when baked, used for making bricks and pottery
➤ **clayey** ADJECTIVE

clean ADJECTIVE
❶ without any dirt or marks or stains ❷ fresh; not yet used • *Start on a clean page.* ❸ done or played in a fair way according to the rules • *a clean fight* ❹ not rude or indecent • *a clean joke* ❺ a clean catch is one made skilfully with no fumbling

clean VERB cleans, cleaning, cleaned
to make something clean

clean ADVERB (*informal*) completely • *I clean forgot it was your birthday.*

cleaner NOUN cleaners
❶ a person who cleans things, especially rooms etc. ❷ something used for cleaning things

cleanliness (say **klen**-li-nis) NOUN
being clean or keeping things clean

cleanly (say **kleen**-lee) ADVERB
easily or smoothly in one movement; neatly • *The rock split cleanly in two.*

cleanse (say klenz) VERB cleanses, cleansing, cleansed
❶ to clean something ❷ to make something pure
➤ **cleanser** NOUN

clear ADJECTIVE
❶ transparent; not muddy or cloudy ❷ easy to see or hear • *He spoke with a clear voice.* ❸ easy to understand; without doubt • *It was clear to me that he was lying.* ❹ free from obstacles or unwanted things ❺ a clear conscience is one that doesn't make you feel guilty ❻ complete • *Give three clear days' notice.*
➤ **clearness** NOUN

clear ADVERB
❶ in a way that is easy to see or hear; distinctly • *We heard you loud and clear.* ❷ completely • *He got clear away.* ❸ at a distance from something; not too close to something • *Stand clear of the doors.*

clear VERB clears, clearing, cleared
❶ to make something clear or become clear ❷ to show that someone is innocent or reliable ❸ to jump over something

without touching it ❹ to get approval or authorization for something • *The plane was cleared for take-off.*
➤ **clear something away** to remove used plates etc. after a meal
➤ **clear off** or **out** (*informal*) to go away
➤ **clear up** ❶ to make things tidy • *Make sure you clear up before you leave.* ❷ to become better or brighter • *The weather seems to be clearing up.*
➤ **clear something up** to solve something • *Thank you for clearing up that little mystery.*

clearance NOUN clearances
❶ official permission to do something • *Only the staff who have clearance to work there are allowed in.* ❷ getting rid of unwanted goods • *The shoe shop is having a clearance sale.* ❸ the space between one thing and another thing that is passing under or beside it

clearing NOUN clearings
an open space in a forest

clearly ADVERB
❶ in a way that is easy to see, hear or understand • *Please speak clearly after the tone.* ❷ without doubt; obviously • *They were clearly going to win.*

cleavage NOUN
the hollow between a woman's breasts

cleave VERB cleaves, cleaving; past tense cleaved, clove or cleft; past participle cleft or cloven
❶ to divide something by chopping it; to split something • *She cleaved the log in two with an axe.* ❷ to make a way through something • *yachts cleaving through the water*

cleave VERB cleaves, cleaving, cleaved
(*old use*) to cling to something • *Her tongue seemed to cleave to the roof of her mouth.*

cleaver NOUN cleavers
a butcher's chopping tool

clef NOUN clefs
a symbol on a stave in music, showing the pitch of the notes • *treble clef* • *bass clef*

cleft
past tense of **cleave** VERB

cleft NOUN clefts
a split in something • *There was a deep cleft in the mountain side.*

clemency NOUN
gentleness or mildness; mercy

a
b
c
d
e
f
g
h
i
j
k
l
m
n
o
p
q
r
s
t
u
v
w
x
y
z

clench VERB clenches, clenching, clenched
to close your teeth or fingers tightly

clergy NOUN
the people who have been ordained as priests
or ministers of the Christian Church
➤ **clergyman** NOUN
➤ **clergywoman** NOUN

clerical ADJECTIVE
❶ to do with the routine work in an office,
such as filing and writing letters ❷ to do with
the clergy

clerk (say klark) NOUN clerks
a person employed to keep records or
accounts, deal with papers in an office, etc.

clever ADJECTIVE
❶ quick at learning and understanding things
❷ showing intelligence and imagination
• *That's a clever idea.*
➤ **cleverly** ADVERB
➤ **cleverness** NOUN

cliché (say **klee**-shay) NOUN clichés
a phrase or idea that is used so often that it
has little meaning

click NOUN clicks
a short sharp sound

click VERB clicks, clicking, clicked
❶ to make a short sharp sound ❷ to press a
button on a computer mouse

client NOUN clients
a person who gets help or advice from
a professional person such as a lawyer,
accountant, architect, etc.; a customer

clientele (say klee-on-**tel**) NOUN
customers

cliff NOUN cliffs
a steep rock face, especially on a coast

cliffhanger NOUN cliffhangers
a tense and exciting ending to an episode of
a story

climate NOUN climates
the normal weather conditions of an area
• *Palm trees grow best in a hot climate.*
➤ **climatic** (say kly-**mat**-ik) ADJECTIVE

climax NOUN climaxes
the most interesting or important
point of a story, series of events, etc.
WORD ORIGIN from Greek *klimax* = ladder

climb VERB climbs, climbing, climbed
❶ to go up towards the top of something
❷ to move somewhere with difficulty or
effort • *I managed to climb out of the*
window. ❸ to go higher • *The plane climbed*
steadily. ❹ to grow upwards
➤ **climb down** to admit that you have been
wrong

climb NOUN climbs
an act of climbing • *It's a long climb to the*
top of the hill.
SPELLING
Don't forget the silent b at the end of
climb.

climber NOUN climbers
someone who climbs mountains as a sport

clinch VERB clinches, clinching, clinched
❶ to settle something definitely • *We hope to*
clinch the deal today. ❷ boxers clinch when
they clasp each other during a fight
➤ **clinch** NOUN

cling VERB clings, clinging, clung
to hold on tightly • *She clung to the rope*
with all her strength.

cling film NOUN
(*British*) a thin clinging transparent film, used
as a covering for food

clinic NOUN clinics
a place where people see doctors etc. for
treatment or advice

clinical ADJECTIVE
❶ to do with the medical treatment of
patients ❷ cool and unemotional
➤ **clinically** ADVERB

clink NOUN clinks
a thin sharp sound like glasses being struck
together

clink VERB clinks, clinking, clinked
to make a thin sharp sound like glasses being
struck together • *The coins clinked in his*
pocket.

clip NOUN clips
❶ a fastener for keeping things together,
usually worked by a spring ❷ a short piece of
film shown on its own ❸ (*informal*) a hit on
the head

clip VERB clips, clipping, clipped
❶ to fasten something with a clip ❷ to
cut something with shears or scissors
❸ (*informal*) to hit someone or something
• *My front wheel must have clipped the*
pavement.

clipper NOUN clippers
an old type of fast sailing ship

clippers *PLURAL NOUN*
an instrument for cutting hair

clique (say kleek) *NOUN* cliques
a small group of people who stick together and keep others out

clitoris *NOUN* clitorises
the small sensitive piece of flesh near the opening of a woman's vagina

cloak *NOUN* cloaks
a sleeveless piece of outdoor clothing that hangs loosely from the shoulders

cloak *VERB* cloaks, cloaking, cloaked
to cover or conceal something

cloaked *ADJECTIVE*
wearing a cloak • *a cloaked figure*

cloakroom *NOUN* cloakrooms
❶ a place where people can leave coats and bags while visiting a building ❷ a toilet

clobber *VERB* clobbers, clobbering, clobbered (*informal*)
to hit someone hard again and again

cloche (say klosh) *NOUN* cloches
a glass or plastic cover to protect outdoor plants

clock *NOUN* clocks
❶ a device that shows what the time is ❷ a measuring device with a dial or digital display

clock *VERB* clocks, clocking, clocked
(*informal*) to notice or recognize someone • *I clocked her standing at the back of the hall.*
➤ **clock in** or **out** to register the time you arrive at work or leave work
➤ **clock something up** to reach a certain speed or total

clockwise *ADVERB & ADJECTIVE*
moving round a circle in the same direction as a clock's hands

clockwork *NOUN*
a mechanism with a spring that has to be wound up
➤ **like clockwork** or **regular as clockwork** very regularly

clod *NOUN* clods
a lump of earth or clay

clog *NOUN* clogs
a shoe with a wooden sole

clog *VERB* clogs, clogging, clogged
to block something up • *The roads were clogged with traffic.*

cloister *NOUN* cloisters
a covered path along the side of a church or monastery etc., round a courtyard

clone *NOUN* clones
an animal or plant made from the cells of another animal or plant and therefore exactly like it

clone *VERB* clones, cloning, cloned
to produce a clone of an animal or plant

close (say klohss) *ADJECTIVE*
❶ near • *Our hotel is close to the beach.*
❷ detailed or careful • *Now pay close attention.* ❸ that you know well and have a strong friendship with; related to you directly • *She is one of my closest friends.* • *close relatives* ❹ a close fit is tight, with little space to spare ❺ a close contest or fight is one in which competitors are nearly equal ❻ warm and stuffy, without fresh air
➤ **closeness** *NOUN*

close (say klohss) *ADVERB*
at a close distance • *Two men were walking close behind.*

close (say klohss) *NOUN* closes (*British*)
❶ a street that is closed at one end ❷ an enclosed area, especially round a cathedral

close (say klohz) *VERB* closes, closing, closed
❶ to shut something ❷ to be no longer open • *The supermarket closes at 6 o'clock.* ❸ to end a meeting or activity
➤ **close in** ❶ to get nearer someone you are chasing ❷ if the days are closing in, they are getting shorter

close (say klohz) *NOUN*
the close of an activity is when it ends • *The scores were level at the close of play.*

closed *ADJECTIVE*
not open; shut • *Keep your mouth closed.*
• *The supermarket is closed.*

closely *ADVERB*
❶ carefully, with attention • *His friends were watching closely.* ❷ in a way that is very similar or shows a strong connection • *The insect closely resembles a stick.* ❸ so that people or things are close together • *Books were closely packed on the shelves.* • *She climbed out of the window, closely followed by her brother.*

closet *NOUN* closets (*North American*)
a cupboard or storeroom

closet *VERB* closets, closeting, closeted
to shut yourself away in a private room

A
B
C
D
E
F
G
H
I
J
K
L
M
N
O
P
Q
R
S
T
U
V
W
X
Y
Z

close-up NOUN **close-ups**
a photograph or piece of film taken at close range

closure NOUN **closures**
the closing of something permanently • *The local library is threatened with closure.*

clot NOUN **clots**
❶ a small mass of blood, cream, etc. that has become solid ❷ (*informal*) a stupid person

clot VERB **clots, clotting, clotted**
to form clots

cloth NOUN **cloths**
❶ woven material or felt ❷ a piece of this material ❸ a tablecloth

> **SPELLING**
> Do not confuse **cloths**, which are pieces of material, with **clothes**, which are things that you wear.

clothe VERB **clothes, clothing, clothed**
to put clothes on someone • *He was clothed from head to toe in green.*

clothes PLURAL NOUN
things worn to cover the body

> **SPELLING**
> Do not confuse **clothes**, which are things that you wear, with **cloths**, which are pieces of material.

clothing NOUN
clothes

clotted cream NOUN
(*chiefly British*) cream thickened by being scalded

cloud NOUN **clouds**
❶ a mass of condensed water vapour floating in the sky ❷ a mass of smoke, dust, etc., in the air

cloud VERB **clouds, clouding, clouded**
❶ to become difficult to see through • *His eyes clouded with tears.* ❷ if a person's face clouds, their expression becomes more serious, worried or angry
➤ **cloud over** to become full of clouds

cloudburst NOUN **cloudbursts**
a sudden heavy rainstorm

cloudless ADJECTIVE
without clouds

cloudy ADJECTIVE **cloudier, cloudiest**
❶ full of clouds • *a cloudy sky* ❷ a cloudy liquid is not clear or transparent
➤ **cloudiness** NOUN

clout VERB **clouts, clouting, clouted** (*informal*)
to hit someone roughly
➤ **clout** NOUN

clove NOUN **cloves**
❶ the dried bud of a tropical tree, used as a spice ❷ one of the separate sections in a bulb of garlic • *a clove of garlic*

clove VERB
past tense of **cleave**

cloven
past participle of **cleave**
➤ **cloven hoof** a hoof that is divided, like those of cows and sheep

clover NOUN
a small plant usually with three leaves on each stalk
➤ **in clover** in ease and luxury

clown NOUN **clowns**
❶ a performer who does amusing tricks and actions, especially in a circus ❷ a person who does silly things

clown VERB **clowns, clowning, clowned**
to fool about and do silly things

cloying ADJECTIVE
sickeningly sweet

club NOUN **clubs**
❶ a heavy stick used as a weapon ❷ a stick with a shaped head used to hit the ball in golf ❸ a group of people who meet because they are interested in the same thing; the building where they meet ❹ a playing card with black clover leaves on it

club VERB **clubs, clubbing, clubbed**
to hit someone with a heavy stick
➤ **club together** to join with other people in order to pay for something • *They clubbed together to buy a van.*

cluck VERB **clucks, clucking, clucked**
to make a hen's throaty cry
➤ **cluck** NOUN

clue NOUN **clues**
something that helps you to solve a puzzle or a mystery
➤ **not have a clue** (*informal*) to be stupid or helpless
> **WORD ORIGIN** originally a ball of thread: in Greek legend, the warrior Theseus had to go into a maze (the Labyrinth); as he went in he unwound a ball of thread, and found his way out by winding it up again

clump NOUN **clumps**
a cluster or mass of things • *a small clump of trees*

clump *VERB* **clumps, clumping, clumped**
❶ to walk with a heavy tread • *She could hear him clumping around upstairs.* ❷ to form a cluster or mass

clumsy *ADJECTIVE* **clumsier, clumsiest**
❶ careless and likely to knock things over or drop things ❷ not skilful or tactful • *a clumsy apology*
➤ **clumsily** *ADVERB*
➤ **clumsiness** *NOUN*

cluster *NOUN* **clusters**
a group of people or things that stand or grow close together • *a little cluster of buildings*

cluster *VERB* **clusters, clustering, clustered**
to form a cluster • *We all clustered around the computer screen.*

clutch *VERB* **clutches, clutching, clutched**
to grasp something tightly • *He clutched his mother's hand in fear.*

clutch *NOUN* **clutches**
❶ a tight grasp ❷ a device for connecting and disconnecting the engine of a motor vehicle from its gears ❸ a set of eggs laid at the same time

clutter *NOUN*
a lot of things lying about untidily

clutter *VERB* **clutters, cluttering, cluttered**
to fill a place with clutter • *Piles of books and papers cluttered her desk.*

Co. *ABBREVIATION*
Company

c/o *ABBREVIATION*
care of

coach *NOUN* **coaches**
❶ a comfortable bus used for long journeys ❷ a carriage of a railway train ❸ a large horse-drawn carriage with four wheels ❹ an instructor who gives training in sports ❺ a teacher giving private tuition in a subject

coach *VERB* **coaches, coaching, coached**
to instruct or train somebody, especially in sports

coagulate *VERB* **coagulates, coagulating, coagulated**
to change from liquid to semi-solid; to clot
➤ **coagulation** *NOUN*

coal *NOUN*
a hard black mineral substance used for burning to supply heat; a piece of this
➤ **coalfield** *NOUN*

coalesce (say koh-a-**less**) *VERB* **coalesces, coalescing, coalesced**
to combine and form one whole thing

coalition *NOUN* **coalitions**
a temporary alliance, especially of two or more political parties in order to form a government

coarse *ADJECTIVE*
❶ not smooth or delicate; rough • *coarse cloth* ❷ made up of large particles; not fine • *coarse salt* ❸ rude or vulgar
➤ **coarsely** *ADVERB*
➤ **coarseness** *NOUN*

coast *NOUN* **coasts**
the seashore or the land close to it
➤ **the coast is clear** there is no chance of being seen or hindered

coast *VERB* **coasts, coasting, coasted**
to ride downhill without using power

coastal *ADJECTIVE*
by the coast or near the coast • *a coastal resort*

coastguard *NOUN* **coastguards**
a person whose job is to keep watch on the coast, detect or prevent smuggling, etc.

coastline *NOUN* **coastlines**
the shape or outline of a coast

coat *NOUN* **coats**
❶ a piece of clothing with sleeves, worn over other clothes ❷ the hair or fur on an animal's body ❸ a layer of something that covers a surface • *The walls will need two coats of paint.*

coat *VERB* **coats, coating, coated**
to cover a thing with a layer of something • *The furniture was coated with dust.*

coating *NOUN* **coatings**
a thin layer that covers something • *nuts with a coating of chocolate*

coat of arms *NOUN* **coats of arms**
a design on a shield, used as an emblem by a family, city, etc.

coax *VERB* **coaxes, coaxing, coaxed**
to persuade someone gently or patiently to do something • *I managed to coax her into the water.*

cob *NOUN* **cobs**
❶ the central part of an ear of maize, on which the corn grows ❷ (*British*) a round loaf of bread ❸ a sturdy horse for riding ❹ a male swan (The female is a **pen.**)

a b c d e f g h i j k l m n o p q r s t u v w x y z

cobalt *NOUN*
a hard silvery-white metal
WORD ORIGIN from German *Kobalt* = demon (because it was believed to harm the silver ore with which it was found)

cobber *NOUN* cobbers (*informal*)
(*Australian/NZ*) a friend or companion

cobble *NOUN* cobbles
cobbles are a surface of cobblestones on a street

cobble *VERB* cobbles, cobbling, cobbled
to cobble something together is to make it quickly and without much care
➤ **cobbled** *ADJECTIVE*

cobbler *NOUN* cobblers
someone who mends shoes

cobblestone *NOUN* cobblestones
a small smooth rounded stone sometimes used in large numbers to pave roads in towns

cobra (say **koh**-bra) *NOUN* cobras
a poisonous snake that can rear up
WORD ORIGIN from Portuguese *cobra de capello* = snake with a hood

cobweb *NOUN* cobwebs
the thin sticky net made by a spider to trap insects **WORD ORIGIN** from Old English *coppe* = spider, + **web**

cocaine *NOUN*
a drug made from the leaves of a tropical plant called *coca*

cock *NOUN* cocks
❶ a male chicken ❷ a male bird ❸ a lever in a gun

cock *VERB* cocks, cocking, cocked
❶ to make a gun ready to fire by raising the cock ❷ to turn part of your body upwards or in a particular direction • *The dog cocked its ears.* • *She cocked her head to one side and looked at me.*

cockatoo *NOUN* cockatoos
a crested parrot

cocked hat *NOUN* cocked hats
a triangular hat worn with some uniforms

cockerel *NOUN* cockerels
a young male chicken

cocker spaniel *NOUN* cocker spaniels
a kind of small spaniel with long hanging ears

cockle *NOUN* cockles
an edible shellfish

cockney *NOUN* cockneys
❶ a person born in the East End of London ❷ the dialect or accent of cockneys
WORD ORIGIN originally = a small, misshapen egg, believed to be a cock's egg (because country people believed townspeople were feeble)

cockpit *NOUN* cockpits
the compartment where the pilot of an aircraft sits

cockroach *NOUN* cockroaches
a dark brown beetle-like insect, often found in dirty houses

cocksure *ADJECTIVE*
too confident

cocktail *NOUN* cocktails
❶ a mixed alcoholic drink ❷ a dish consisting of small pieces of shellfish or mixed fruit • *a prawn cocktail* **WORD ORIGIN** originally = a racehorse that was not a thoroughbred (because carthorses had their tails cut so that they stood up like a cock's tail)

cocky *ADJECTIVE* cockier, cockiest (*informal*)
too self-confident and cheeky
➤ **cockiness** *NOUN*

cocoa *NOUN* cocoas
❶ a hot drink made from a powder of crushed cacao seeds ❷ this powder

coconut *NOUN* coconuts
❶ a large round nut that grows on a kind of palm tree ❷ its white lining, used in sweets and cookery **WORD ORIGIN** from Spanish *coco* = grinning face (because the base of the nut looks like a monkey's face)

cocoon *NOUN* cocoons
❶ the covering round a chrysalis ❷ a protective wrapping

cocoon *VERB* cocoons, cocooning, cocooned
to protect something by wrapping it up • *He lay in his tent, cocooned in a sleeping bag.*

cod *NOUN* cod
a large edible sea fish

coddle *VERB* coddles, coddling, coddled
to treat someone in a way that protects them too much

code *NOUN* codes
❶ a system of words, letters or numbers used instead of the real letters or words to make a message or information secret • *The message was written in code.* ❷ a set of signals or signs used in sending messages • *Morse code* ❸ a set of numbers used for an area in

making telephone calls • *Do you know the code for Stockholm?* ❹ a set of laws or rules • *the Highway Code* • *a code of behaviour*

code *VERB* **codes, coding, coded**
to put a message into code
➤ **coded** *ADJECTIVE*

codify *VERB* **codifies, codifying, codified**
to arrange laws or rules into a code or system

co-education *NOUN*
educating boys and girls together
➤ **co-educational** *ADJECTIVE*

coefficient *NOUN* **coefficients**
a number by which another number is multiplied; a factor

coerce (say koh-**erss**) *VERB* **coerces, coercing, coerced**
to make someone do something by using threats or force
➤ **coercion** *NOUN*

coexist *VERB* **coexists, coexisting, coexisted**
to exist together or at the same time
➤ **coexistence** *NOUN*

coffee *NOUN* **coffees**
❶ a hot drink made from the roasted ground seeds (**coffee beans**) of a tropical plant
❷ these seeds

coffer *NOUN* **coffers**
a large strong box for holding money and valuables
➤ **coffers** the funds or financial resources of an organization

coffin *NOUN* **coffins**
a long box in which a body is buried or cremated

cog *NOUN* **cogs**
one of a number of tooth-like parts round the edge of a wheel, fitting into and pushing those on another wheel

cogent (say koh-**jent**) *ADJECTIVE*
a cogent argument is strong and convincing

cogitate *VERB* **cogitates, cogitating, cogitated**
to think deeply about something
➤ **cogitation** *NOUN*

cognac (say kon-yak) *NOUN* **cognacs**
brandy, especially from Cognac in France

cogwheel *NOUN* **cogwheels**
a wheel with cogs

cohere *VERB* **coheres, cohering, cohered**
things cohere when they stick to each other

in a mass
➤ **cohesive** *ADJECTIVE*

coherent (say koh-**heer**-ent) *ADJECTIVE*
clear, reasonable and making sense • *a coherent explanation*
➤ **coherently** *ADVERB*

cohesion *NOUN*
the ability to combine or fit together well to form a whole • *There are some good individual players, but the team lacks cohesion.*

coil *NOUN* **coils**
something wound into a spiral or series of loops • *a coil of rope*

coil *VERB* **coils, coiling, coiled**
to wind something into a coil • *The snake coiled itself around his leg.*

coin *NOUN* **coins**
a piece of metal, usually round, used as money

coin *VERB* **coins, coining, coined**
❶ to manufacture coins ❷ to invent a word or phrase

coinage *NOUN* **coinages**
❶ coins; a system of money ❷ a new word or phrase that someone has invented

coincide *VERB* **coincides, coinciding, coincided**
❶ to happen at the same time as something else • *The end of term coincides with my birthday.* ❷ to be the same • *My opinion coincided with hers.*

coincidence *NOUN* **coincidences**
the happening of similar events at the same time by chance

coke *NOUN*
the solid fuel left when gas and tar have been extracted from coal

colander *NOUN* **colanders**
a bowl-shaped container with holes in it, used for straining water from vegetables etc. after cooking

cold *ADJECTIVE*
❶ having or at a low temperature; not warm
❷ not friendly or loving; showing no kindness or understanding • *She gave him a cold, hard look.*
➤ **coldness** *NOUN*
➤ **get cold feet** to have doubts about doing something bold or ambitious
➤ **give someone the cold shoulder** to be deliberately unfriendly

a b c d e f g h i j k l m n o p q r s t u v w x y z

A B **C** D E F G H I J K L M N O P Q R S T U V W X Y Z

cold NOUN **colds**
❶ lack of warmth; low temperature; cold weather ❷ an infectious illness that makes your nose run, your throat sore, etc.

cold-blooded ADJECTIVE
❶ having a body temperature that changes according to the surroundings ❷ showing no feelings or pity for other people • *cold-blooded murder*

coldly ADVERB
in an unfriendly or distant way • *'Nothing's the matter,' she said coldly.*

cold war NOUN
a situation where nations are enemies without actually fighting

colic NOUN
pain in a baby's stomach

collaborate VERB **collaborates, collaborating, collaborated**
to work together on a job • *It is the first time he has collaborated with another songwriter.*
➤ **collaboration** NOUN
➤ **collaborator** NOUN

collage (say kol-**ah** zh) NOUN **collages**
a picture made by fixing small objects to a surface

collapse VERB **collapses, collapsing, collapsed**
❶ to fall down or fall in suddenly, often after breaking apart • *Several buildings collapsed in the earthquake.* ❷ to fall down because of being very weak or ill ❸ to fold up • *The table collapses for easy storage.*

collapse NOUN **collapses**
❶ collapsing • *The walls were strengthened to protect them from collapse.* ❷ a failure or breakdown • *The peace talks were on the verge of collapse.*

collapsible ADJECTIVE
able to be folded up • *a collapsible umbrella*

collar NOUN **collars**
❶ the part of a piece of clothing that goes round your neck ❷ a band that goes round the neck of a dog, cat, horse, etc.

collar VERB **collars, collaring, collared**
(*informal*) to seize or catch someone

collarbone NOUN **collarbones**
the bone joining the breastbone and shoulder blade

collate VERB **collates, collating, collated**
to collect and arrange pieces of information in an organized way • *We collated the results*

in the form of a graph.
➤ **collation** NOUN

collateral ADJECTIVE
additional but less important

collateral NOUN
money or property that is used as a guarantee that a loan will be repaid

colleague NOUN **colleagues**
a person you work with

collect (say kol-**ekt**) VERB **collects, collecting, collected**
❶ to bring people or things together from various places • *We are collecting signatures for a petition.* ❷ to get and keep together examples of things as a hobby • *She collects rare coins.* ❸ to come together • *A crowd collected to see what was going on.* ❹ to ask for money or contributions etc. from people • *We're collecting for charity.* ❺ to go to fetch someone or something • *Don't forget to collect your coat from the cleaners.*

collection NOUN **collections**
❶ a number of things someone has collected • *a coin collection* ❷ collecting something • *What time is the rubbish collection?* ❸ money collected for a charity or some other purpose

collective ADJECTIVE
to do with a group taken as a whole • *It was a collective decision.*

collective noun NOUN **collective nouns**
a noun that is singular in form but refers to many individuals taken as a unit, e.g. *army, herd, choir*

collector NOUN **collectors**
someone who collects things as a hobby or as part of their job • *a stamp collector* • *a ticket collector*

college NOUN **colleges**
a place where people can continue learning something after they have left school

collide VERB **collides, colliding, collided**
to crash into something • *The car collided head-on with the van.*

collie NOUN **collies**
a dog with a long pointed face

colliery NOUN **collieries**
(*British*) a coal mine and its buildings

collision NOUN **collisions**
an accident in which two moving vehicles or people crash into each other • *a collision between two trains*

colloquial (say col-**oh**-kwee-al) ADJECTIVE
suitable for conversation but not for formal
speech or writing

cologne (say kol-**ohn**) NOUN
eau de Cologne or a similar liquid

colon NOUN colons
❶ a punctuation mark (:), often used to
introduce lists or an explanation ❷ the
largest part of the intestine

> **PUNCTUATION**
>
> You use a **colon** to introduce an example
> or explanation within a sentence. The
> part of a sentence after a colon should
> illustrate, explain or expand on what
> comes before it:
>
> *These words were scratched in blood*: 'Do
> *not return without the gold.'*
>
> *It wasn't much of a holiday*: two weeks of
> *constant rain in a leaky tent.*
>
> A colon can also be used to introduce a list
> of people or items, or a range of options:
>
> *The following players are injured*: Messi,
> *Neymar and Suarez.*
>
> *The bags come in four colours*: red, blue,
> *yellow and green.*

colonel (say **ker**-nel) NOUN colonels
an army officer in charge of a regiment

> **SPELLING**
>
> The 'er' sound in **colonel** is spelt **olo**.

colonial ADJECTIVE
to do with a colony

colonialism NOUN
the policy of acquiring and keeping colonies

colonist NOUN colonists
a person who goes to live in a colony abroad

colonize (also **colonise**) VERB colonizes,
colonizing, colonized
to establish a colony in a country • *The
Portuguese colonized Brazil in 1500.*
➤ **colonization** NOUN

colonnade NOUN colonnades
a row of columns

colony NOUN colonies
❶ an area of land that the people of another
country settle in and control ❷ the people of
a colony ❸ a group of people or animals of
the same kind living close together • *a colony
of ants*

coloration NOUN
colouring • *The blue coloration is typical of
the rock of the region.*

colossal ADJECTIVE
extremely large; enormous

colossus NOUN colossi
❶ a huge statue ❷ a person of immense
importance **WORD ORIGIN** from the bronze
statue of Apollo at Rhodes, called the *Colossus
of Rhodes*

colour NOUN colours
❶ the effect produced by waves of light of
a particular wavelength ❷ the use of various
colours, not only black and white • *All the
pictures in the book are in colour.* ❸ the
colour of someone's skin ❹ a substance used
to colour things ❺ the special flag of a ship
or regiment

colour VERB colours, colouring, coloured
❶ to put colour on something, using paint,
crayons, etc. ❷ to blush ❸ to influence what
someone says or believes • *Don't let your
judgement be coloured by personal feelings.*

> **SPELLING**
>
> The 'er' sound is spelt **our** in **colour**.

colour-blind ADJECTIVE
unable to see the difference between certain
colours

coloured ADJECTIVE
having colour

colourful ADJECTIVE
❶ with bright colours ❷ lively; with vivid
details • *The book is full of colourful
characters.*

colouring NOUN
❶ a substance that you add to something,
especially food, to give it a special colour ❷ a
person's colouring is the colour of their skin
and hair

colourless ADJECTIVE
without colour • *a colourless gas*

colt NOUN colts
a young male horse

column NOUN columns
❶ a pillar ❷ something long or tall and
narrow • *a column of smoke* ❸ a vertical
section of a page ❹ a regular article or
feature in a newspaper or magazine

> **SPELLING**
>
> Don't forget the silent **n** at the end of
> **column**.

a b c d e f g h i j k l m n o p q r s t u v w x y z

columnist NOUN columnists
a journalist who writes regularly for one newspaper or magazine

coma (say **koh**-ma) NOUN comas
a state of deep unconsciousness, especially in someone who is ill or injured • *He fell into a deep coma.*

comb NOUN combs
❶ a strip of wood, plastic or metal with a row of teeth, used to tidy hair or hold it in place ❷ something used like this, e.g. to separate strands of wool ❸ the red crest on a fowl's head ❹ a honeycomb

comb VERB combs, combing, combed
❶ to tidy your hair with a comb ❷ to search a place thoroughly • *Police have been combing the beach for clues.*

combat NOUN combats
fighting, especially in a war • *He was killed in combat.*

combat VERB combats, combating, combated
to combat something bad or unpleasant is to fight it and try to get rid of it • *These measures will help police combat crime.*

combatant (say **kom**-ba-tant) NOUN combatants
someone who takes part in a fight

combination NOUN combinations
❶ a number of people or things that have been joined or mixed together • *What an unusual combination of flavours!* ❷ joining or mixing things • *The element silicon is always found in combination with something else.* ❸ a series of numbers or letters used to open a combination lock

combination lock NOUN combination locks
a lock that you can open only by setting a dial or dials to positions shown by numbers or letters

combine (say komb-**yn**) VERB combines, combining, combined
to join or mix things together; to come together to form something • *Now combine all the ingredients in a bowl.* • *Hydrogen and oxygen combine to form water.*

combine harvester NOUN combine harvesters
(*British*) a machine that both reaps and threshes grain

combustible ADJECTIVE
able to be set on fire and burn

combustion NOUN
the process of burning, a chemical process in which substances combine with oxygen in air and produce heat

come VERB comes, coming, came, come
❶ to move or travel to the place where you are • *Come here!* ❷ to arrive at or reach a place or condition or result • *They came to a city.* • *We came to a decision.* ❸ to happen • *How did you come to lose it?* ❹ to occur or be present • *The answer comes on the next page.* ❺ to result • *That's what comes of being careless.*
➤ **come about** to happen
➤ **come across someone** to meet someone by chance
➤ **come by something** to obtain something
➤ **come in for something** to receive a share of something
➤ **come round** or **come to** to become conscious again
➤ **come to pass** to happen
➤ **come to something** to add up to an amount

comedian NOUN comedians
someone who entertains people by making them laugh

comedy NOUN comedies
❶ a play or film etc. that makes people laugh ❷ humour

comely ADJECTIVE
(*old use*) good-looking

comet NOUN comets
an object moving across the sky with a bright tail of light (WORD ORIGIN) from Greek *kometes* = long-haired (star)

comfort NOUN comforts
❶ a feeling of being physically relaxed and satisfied • *These shoes are designed for extra comfort.* ❷ soothing somebody who is worried or unhappy • *She tried to offer a few words of comfort.* ❸ a person or thing that gives comfort • *the comforts of home*

comfort VERB comforts, comforting, comforted
to make a person feel less worried or unhappy

comfortable ADJECTIVE
❶ at ease; free from worry or pain ❷ pleasant to use or wear; making you feel relaxed • *comfortable shoes*
➤ **comfortably** ADVERB

comfy ADJECTIVE (*informal*)
comfortable

comic NOUN comics
❶ a children's magazine full of comic strips
❷ a comedian

comic ADJECTIVE
making people laugh; funny

comical ADJECTIVE
making people laugh; funny
➤ **comically** ADVERB

comic strip NOUN comic strips
a series of drawings telling a story, especially a funny one

comma NOUN commas
a punctuation mark (,) used to mark a pause in a sentence or to separate items in a list

PUNCTUATION

Commas are used:

to mark a pause in a sentence, especially to separate a subordinate clause from the main clause:

When you go out, don't forget to lock the door.

Smiling to herself, she walked out of the room.

before a coordinating conjunction such as *or, and* or *but* to separate the two clauses in a multi-clause sentence:

I like swimming, but I love ice skating.

It's a lovely house, and it's very near the station.

to separate items in a list or series:

Make sure you bring pens, pencils, a ruler and a notebook.

in pairs if a subordinate clause is inserted into the middle of the main clause:

After three weeks, if you have been practising regularly, you should find that your technique has improved.

The robot, who was called Buzz, could speak several languages.

after an adverb or an adverbial if you are using it at the start of a sentence:

Luckily, no one saw her fall over.

To his horror, he saw the ball hit the back of the net.

to separate the name of a person or group of people you are addressing directly from the rest of the sentence:

OK, Sam, what shall we do next?

Ladies and gentlemen, thank you for coming.

command NOUN commands
❶ a statement telling someone to do something; an order ❷ to be in command is to have authority or control over someone ❸ a command of a subject or language is a good knowledge of it and an ability to use it well • *She has a good command of Spanish.*

command VERB commands, commanding, commanded
❶ to give a command to someone; to order someone to do something ❷ to have authority over a group of people ❸ to deserve and get something • *They command our respect.*

GRAMMAR

A **command** is a sentence that gives an order or instruction. A command is usually written in the imperative and the verb is the first word of the sentence. The subject is understood as 'you'. A command can end with a full stop or, if it is an urgent one, an exclamation mark:

Write down your answers.

Come over here.

Don't move!

A single verb can form a command, like *Run!* or *Stop!*

See also the panel on **sentences**.

commandant (say **kom**-an-dant) NOUN commandants
a military officer in charge of a fortress etc.

commandeer VERB commandeers, commandeering, commandeered
to take or seize something for military purposes or for your own use

commander NOUN commanders
a person in command of a group of people

commandment NOUN commandments
a sacred command, especially one of the Ten Commandments given to Moses

commando NOUN commandos
a soldier trained for making dangerous raids

commemorate *VERB* commemorates, commemorating, commemorated
to be a celebration or reminder of some past event or person • *A plaque commemorates the battle.*
➤ **commemoration** *NOUN*
➤ **commemorative** *ADJECTIVE*

commence *VERB* commences, commencing, commenced (*formal*)
to begin • *The ceremony commenced.*
➤ **commencement** *NOUN*

commend *VERB* commends, commending, commended
❶ to praise someone • *He was commended for bravery.* ❷ (*formal*) to entrust a person or thing to someone • *We commend him to your care.*
➤ **commendation** *NOUN*

commendable *ADJECTIVE*
deserving praise

comment *NOUN* comments
an opinion given about something or to explain something

comment *VERB* comments, commenting, commented
to make a comment

commentary *VERB* commentaries
❶ a description of an event by someone who is watching it, especially for radio or television ❷ a set of explanatory comments on a text

commentator *NOUN* commentators
a person who gives a radio or television commentary
➤ **commentate** *VERB*

commerce *NOUN*
the business of buying and selling goods and services; trade

commercial *ADJECTIVE*
❶ to do with commerce ❷ paid for by advertising • *a commercial radio station* ❸ making a profit • *The film was not a commercial success.*
➤ **commercially** *ADVERB*

commercial *NOUN* commercials
a broadcast advertisement

commiserate *VERB* commiserates, commiserating, commiserated
to sympathize with someone
➤ **commiseration** *NOUN*

commission *NOUN* commissions
❶ a task formally given to someone • *a commission to paint a portrait* ❷ an

appointment to be an officer in the armed forces ❸ a group of people given authority to do or investigate something ❹ extra money that a person gets for selling goods
➤ **out of commission** not in working order

commission *VERB* commissions, commissioning, commissioned
to give someone a task or assignment
• *Michelangelo was commissioned to paint the Sistine chapel ceiling in 1508.*

commissionaire *NOUN* commissionaires
(*British*) an attendant in uniform at the entrance to a theatre, large shop, offices, etc.

commissioner *NOUN* commissioners
❶ an official appointed by commission ❷ a member of a commission

commit *VERB* commits, committing, committed
❶ to commit a crime is to do something against the law ❷ to commit yourself to something is to promise to do it or to devote all your energy to doing it • *I can't commit myself to helping you tomorrow.* ❸ to promise that you will make your time etc. available for a particular purpose • *Don't commit all your spare time to helping him.* ❹ to place a person in someone's care or custody • *He was committed to prison.*

commitment *NOUN* commitments
❶ the work, belief and loyalty that a person gives to something because they think it is important • *I admire your commitment to protecting the environment.* ❷ something that regularly takes up some of your time
• *work commitments*

committee *NOUN* committees
a group of people appointed to deal with something

> **SPELLING**
> Committee has a double m, a double t and a double e.

commode *NOUN* commodes
a box or chair into which a chamber pot is fitted

commodious *ADJECTIVE*
having plenty of space; roomy

commodity *NOUN* commodities
a product or material that can be bought and sold

commodore *NOUN* commodores
❶ a naval officer ranking next below a rear admiral ❷ the commander of part of a fleet

common ADJECTIVE
❶ ordinary or usual; occurring frequently • *a common weed* • *Traffic jams are common where we live.* ❷ affecting all or most people • *They worked for the common good.* ❸ shared • *Music is their common interest.* ❹ vulgar; showing a lack of education
➤ **in common** shared by two or more people or things • *We've got a lot in common.*

common NOUN commons
a piece of land that everyone can use

commoner NOUN commoners
a member of the ordinary people, not of the nobility

commonly ADVERB
usually or frequently • *X-rays are commonly used in hospitals.*

commonplace ADJECTIVE
not exciting or unusual; ordinary

common room NOUN common rooms
(*chiefly British*) a room for students or teachers at a school or college to use when they are not involved in lessons

common sense NOUN
normal good sense in thinking or behaviour

commonwealth NOUN
❶ a group of countries cooperating together ❷ a country made up of an association of states • *the Commonwealth of Australia*
➤ **the Commonwealth** ❶ an association of Britain and various other countries that used to be part of the British Empire, including Canada, Australia and New Zealand ❷ the republic set up in Britain by Oliver Cromwell, lasting from 1649 to 1660

commotion NOUN
great noise or excitement; an uproar • *Suddenly he heard a commotion outside.*

communal (say **kom**-yoo-nal) ADJECTIVE
shared by several people • *a communal kitchen*

commune (say **kom**-yoon) NOUN communes
❶ a group of people living together and sharing everything ❷ a district of local government in France and some other countries

commune (say ko-**mewn**) VERB communes, communing, communed
to share your thoughts and feelings with someone or with nature without speaking

communicate VERB communicates, communicating, communicated

❶ to pass news or information to other people ❷ rooms communicate when there is a door leading from one to the other

communication NOUN communications
❶ communicating with other people ❷ a written or spoken message
➤ **communications** PLURAL NOUN
ways of sending messages or information between people and places, e.g. telephones, television and the Internet

communicative ADJECTIVE
willing to talk

communion NOUN
religious fellowship
➤ **Communion** or **Holy Communion** the Christian ceremony in which bread and wine are blessed and given to worshippers

communiqué (say ko-**mew**-nik-ay) NOUN communiqués
an official message giving a report

communism NOUN
a political system in which property is shared by everyone and the state controls the country's industry and resources. Compare with **capitalism**.

communist NOUN communists
a person who believes in communism

community NOUN communities
❶ the people living in one area ❷ a group with similar interests or origins

commute VERB commutes, commuting, commuted
❶ to travel a fairly long way by train, bus or car to and from your daily work ❷ to alter a punishment to something less severe

commuter NOUN commuters
a person who commutes to and from work

compact ADJECTIVE
❶ neat and small • *a compact camera* ❷ closely or neatly packed together

compact NOUN compacts
❶ a small flat container for face powder ❷ an agreement or contract

compact VERB compacts, compacting, compacted
to press something firmly together • *The snow on the pavement soon became compacted.*

compact disc NOUN compact discs
a small plastic disc on which music or information is stored as digital signals and is read by a laser beam

a
b
c
d
e
f
g
h
i
j
k
l
m
n
o
p
q
r
s
t
u
v
w
x
y
z

companion NOUN companions
❶ a person who you spend time with or travel with ❷ a guidebook or reference book • *The Oxford Companion to Music*
WORD ORIGIN literally = someone you eat bread with: from Latin *panis* = bread

companionable ADJECTIVE
friendly and sociable

companionship NOUN
being with someone and enjoying their friendship

company NOUN companies
❶ a business firm ❷ a group of people who perform together • *a theatre company* ❸ having people with you; being with someone • *She was lonely and longed for some company.* • *I enjoy Matt's company.* ❹ visitors • *We've got company.* ❺ a section of a battalion

comparable (say kom-per-a-bul) ADJECTIVE
able to be compared, similar • *These two cases are not really comparable.*

comparative ADJECTIVE
compared with something else • *They live in comparative comfort.*

comparative NOUN comparatives
the form of an adjective or adverb that expresses 'more' • *The comparative of 'big' is 'bigger' and the comparative of 'bad' is 'worse'.*

> **GRAMMAR**
>
> **Comparative** adjectives and adverbs are used to compare and contrast people, things or actions. The comparative shows which of two things is greater or more: *Cheetahs run faster than antelopes.*
>
> For many adjectives, and some adverbs, the comparative is formed by adding -*er* (or -*r* if the word already ends in e). Note that some adjectives double their final letter, and those ending in -*y* change to -*i* before adding -*er*:
>
> *This flower is bigger and paler than the others.*
>
> *His next film was even scarier.*
>
> *The guests arrived sooner than expected.*
>
> For longer adjectives, and for adverbs ending in -*ly*, the comparative is formed with *more*:
>
> *Hot-air balloons are a more interesting*

way to travel.

She started typing more furiously than ever.

However, some common adjectives and adverbs have irregular comparatives which in some cases are different words, e.g. *good / well* (*better*), *bad / badly* (*worse*), and *far* (*farther* or *further*).

You will find guidance in this dictionary on irregular comparatives.

See also the panel on **superlatives**.

comparatively ADVERB
compared to something else or what is usual; relatively • *Fortunately, the disease is comparatively rare nowadays.*

compare VERB compares, comparing, compared
❶ to put or consider things together so that you can see in what ways they are similar or different ❷ to form the comparative and superlative of an adjective or adverb
➤ **compare notes** to share information
➤ **compare with something** ❶ to be similar to something ❷ to be as good as something • *Our art gallery cannot compare with Tate Modern.*

> **USAGE**
>
> When **compare** is used with an object, it can be followed by either **to** or **with**. As a general rule, you use **to** when you are showing the similarity between two things: *She compared me to a pig.* You use **with** when you are looking at the similarities and differences between things: *Just compare this year's exam results with last year's.*

comparison NOUN comparisons
comparing things

compartment NOUN compartments
❶ one of the spaces into which something is divided; a separate room or enclosed space ❷ a division of a railway carriage

compass NOUN compasses
an instrument that shows direction, with a magnetized needle pointing to the north
➤ **compasses** or **pair of compasses** a device for drawing circles, usually with two rods hinged together at one end

compassion NOUN
pity or mercy you show to someone who is

suffering
➤ **compassionate** ADJECTIVE
➤ **compassionately** ADVERB

compatible ADJECTIVE
❶ able to live or exist together without trouble ❷ able to be used together • *This printer is not compatible with my computer.*
➤ **compatibility** NOUN

compatriot (say kom-**pat**-ri-ot) NOUN
a person from the same country as another

compel VERB compels, compelling, compelled
to force someone to do something • *He felt compelled to read on further.*

compelling ADJECTIVE
forcing you to pay attention or believe something • *a compelling story* • *compelling evidence*

compendium NOUN compendiums or compendia
❶ an encyclopedia or handbook in one volume ❷ a set of different board games in one box

compensate VERB compensates, compensating, compensated
❶ to give a person money etc. to make up for a loss or injury ❷ to have a balancing effect • *This victory compensates for our earlier defeats.*

compensation NOUN compensations
❶ money paid to someone to make up for a loss or injury ❷ a thing that reduces the bad effect of something • *It may be a boring job, but there are compensations.*

compère (say **kom**-pair) NOUN compères
(*British*) a person who introduces the performers in a show or broadcast
➤ **compère** VERB

compete VERB competes, competing, competed
❶ to take part in a competition • *She competed in the 1992 Barcelona Olympics.*
❷ to try to be better or more successful than someone else • *These small shops just can't compete with the supermarkets.*

competent ADJECTIVE
having the skill or knowledge to do something in a satisfactory way
➤ **competently** ADVERB
➤ **competence** NOUN

competition NOUN competitions
❶ a game or race or other contest in which people try to win ❷ trying to be better or

more successful than someone else • *There was fierce competition for the job.* ❸ the people who compete with you • *Before the race she tried to size up the competition.*

competitive ADJECTIVE
❶ a competitive person enjoys competing with other people ❷ involving competition between people or firms • *competitive sport*

competitor NOUN competitors
someone who competes; a rival

compile VERB compiles, compiling, compiled
to put together a book, list, etc. by collecting together information from various places
• *He has compiled a collection of children's poems.*
➤ **compiler** NOUN
➤ **compilation** NOUN

complacent ADJECTIVE
smugly satisfied with the way things are and feeling that no change or action is necessary
➤ **complacently** ADVERB
➤ **complacency** NOUN

complain VERB complains, complaining, complained
to say that you are annoyed or unhappy about something

complaint NOUN complaints
❶ a statement complaining about something
❷ a minor illness

complement NOUN complements
❶ the quantity needed to fill or complete something • *The ship had its full complement of sailors.* ❷ the word or words used after verbs such as *be* and *become* to complete the sense. In *She was brave* and *He became king of England*, the complements are *brave* and *king of England*

complement VERB complements, complementing, complemented
one thing complements another when they go well together or when one makes the other complete • *The hat complements the outfit.*

SPELLING
Take care not to confuse with a **compliment**, which is when you tell someone that you approve of something.

complementary ADJECTIVE
going together well or going together to make a whole • *Our skills are different but complementary.*

a b c d e f g h i j k l m n o p q r s t u v w x y z

complementary angle NOUN
complementary angles
either of two angles that add up to 90°

complementary medicine NOUN
(British) medical methods that are not
considered part of ordinary medicine, but
may be used alongside it, e.g. acupuncture
and homoeopathy

complete ADJECTIVE
❶ having all its parts, with nothing missing
❷ finished, with everything done • *The work
should be complete by Friday.* ❸ thorough; in
every way • *a complete stranger*
➤ **completeness** NOUN

complete VERB completes, completing,
completed
❶ to finish something or make it complete
❷ to complete a form is to write on it all the
information you are asked for

completely ADVERB
in every way; totally • *Many buildings were
completely destroyed by the earthquake.*

SPELLING
Complete + ly = completely. Don't forget
to keep the **e** after the **t**.

completion NOUN
making a thing complete; finishing something
• *The new hospital is near to completion.*

complex ADJECTIVE
❶ made up of many different parts • *complex
machinery* ❷ difficult or complicated • *a
complex problem*
➤ **complexity** NOUN

complex NOUN complexes
❶ a set of buildings made up of related parts
• *a sports complex* ❷ a group of feelings
or ideas that influence a person's behaviour
or make them worry about something • *an
inferiority complex*

complexion NOUN complexions
❶ the natural colour and appearance of the
skin of the face ❷ the way things seem • *That
puts a different complexion on the matter.*

compliant ADJECTIVE
willing to obey
➤ **compliance** NOUN

complicate VERB complicates, complicating,
complicated
to make something more difficult to
understand or deal with • *To complicate
matters further, there are no trains today.*

complicated ADJECTIVE
❶ made up of many different parts
❷ difficult to understand or deal with

complication NOUN complications
❶ something that complicates things or adds
difficulties ❷ a new illness that you get when
you are already ill

complicity NOUN
being involved in a crime or something bad

compliment NOUN compliments
something you say or do to show that you
approve of a person or thing • *It was the first
time he had ever paid her a compliment.*
➤ **compliments** PLURAL NOUN
formal greetings given in a message

compliment VERB compliments,
complimenting, complimented
to pay someone a compliment; to
congratulate someone

SPELLING
Take care not to confuse with
complement, which is when things go
well together.

complimentary ADJECTIVE
❶ expressing a compliment ❷ given free of
charge • *complimentary tickets*

comply VERB complies, complying, complied
to obey an order, rule or request • *You must
comply fully with these instructions.*

component NOUN components
each of the parts of which a thing is made up

compose VERB composes, composing,
composed
❶ to write music ❷ to write a letter, speech
or poem ❸ to be composed of several people
or things is to contain or include them • *The
class is composed of 20 students.* ❹ to
compose yourself is to become calm after
being excited or angry

composed ADJECTIVE
calm and in control of your feelings • *a
composed manner*

composer NOUN composers
a person who composes music

composite (say **kom**-poz-it) ADJECTIVE
made up of a number of parts or different
styles

composition NOUN compositions
❶ composing music or poetry ❷ something
composed, especially a piece of music ❸ an
essay or story written as a school exercise

❹ the composition of a substance is the way that it is made up • *the chemical composition of the soil*

compost *NOUN*
❶ decayed leaves and grass etc. used as a fertilizer ❷ a soil-like mixture for growing seedlings, cuttings, etc.

composure *NOUN*
calmness of manner • *He needed a minute to regain his composure.*

compound *ADJECTIVE*
made of two or more parts or ingredients

compound *NOUN* compounds
❶ a compound substance ❷ (*in grammar*) a word or expression made from other words joined together, e.g. 'football' and 'newspaper' ❸ a fenced area containing buildings

compound *VERB* compounds, compounding, compounded
to make something worse • *His irritation was compounded by the fact that she was late.*

comprehend *VERB* comprehends, comprehending, comprehended
to understand something

comprehensible *ADJECTIVE*
able to be understood

comprehension *NOUN* comprehensions
❶ understanding something ❷ an exercise that tests how well you understand something written or spoken in another language

comprehensive *ADJECTIVE*
including all or many kinds of people or things • *a comprehensive list of local restaurants*

comprehensive *NOUN* comprehensives
(*British*) a comprehensive school

comprehensive school *NOUN*
comprehensive schools
(*British*) a secondary school for all or most of the children in an area

compress (say kom-**press**) *VERB* compresses, compressing, compressed
❶ to press or squeeze something together or into a smaller space • *He compressed his lips tightly.* ❷ to alter the form of computer data to reduce the amount of space needed to store it
➤ **compression** *NOUN*
➤ **compressor** *NOUN*

compress (say **kom**-press) *NOUN* compresses
a soft pad or cloth pressed on the body to stop bleeding or cool inflammation etc.

comprise *VERB* comprises, comprising, comprised
to include or consist of • *The pentathlon comprises five events.*

> **USAGE**
> Be careful not to use *comprise of.* The correct usage is: *The country comprises 20 states.*

compromise (say **kom**-prom-yz) *NOUN* compromises
settling a dispute by each side accepting less than it wanted or asked for

compromise *VERB* compromises, compromising, compromised
to accept less than you wanted or asked for in order to settle a dispute

compulsion *NOUN* compulsions
a strong and uncontrollable desire to do something

compulsive *ADJECTIVE*
having or resulting from a strong and uncontrollable desire • *a compulsive liar*

> **USAGE**
> See note at **compulsory**.

compulsory *ADJECTIVE*
something is compulsory when you have to do it and cannot choose • *Wearing seat belts is compulsory.*

> **USAGE**
> Take care not to confuse **compulsory** with **compulsive**. An action is compulsory if a law or rules say that you must do it, but compulsive if you want to do it and cannot resist it.

compunction *NOUN*
a guilty feeling • *She felt no compunction about hitting the burglar.*

compute *VERB* computes, computing, computed
to calculate something
➤ **computation** *NOUN*

computer *NOUN* computers
an electronic machine for making calculations, storing and analysing information put into it or controlling machinery automatically

a b **c** d e f g h i j k l m n o p q r s t u v w x y z

computerize (also **computerise**) *VERB*
computerizes, computerizing, computerized
to use computers to do a job or to store
information • *The library catalogue has now
been computerized.*
➤ **computerization** *NOUN*

computing *NOUN*
the use of computers

comrade *NOUN* comrades
a companion who shares in your activities
➤ **comradeship** *NOUN*

con *VERB* cons, conning, conned (*informal*)
to swindle someone

concave *ADJECTIVE*
curved like the inside of a ball or circle. (The
opposite is **convex**.)

conceal *VERB* conceals, concealing, concealed
to hide something or keep it secret • *She
couldn't conceal her astonishment.*
➤ **concealment** *NOUN*

concede *VERB* concedes, conceding, conceded
❶ to admit that something is true ❷ to admit
that you have been defeated ❸ to give up a
possession or right • *They conceded us the
right to cross their land.*

conceit *NOUN*
too much pride in your abilities and
achievements • *I can't believe the conceit of
the man!*

conceited *ADJECTIVE*
too proud of yourself and your abilities

conceivable *ADJECTIVE*
able to be imagined or believed
➤ **conceivably** *ADVERB*

conceive *VERB* conceives, conceiving,
conceived
❶ to become pregnant; to form a baby in the
womb ❷ to form an idea or plan in your mind
• *I can't conceive what that must feel like.*

concentrate *VERB* concentrates,
concentrating, concentrated
❶ to give your full attention or effort to
something ❷ to bring something together in
one place • *Industry is concentrated in the
north of the country.*

concentrated *ADJECTIVE*
a concentrated liquid has been made stronger
by removing water • *concentrated orange
juice*

concentration *NOUN* concentrations
❶ concentrating on something ❷ the amount
dissolved in each part of a liquid

concentration camp *NOUN* concentration
camps
a prison camp where political prisoners are
kept together, especially one set up by the
Nazis during World War II

concentric *ADJECTIVE*
having the same centre • *concentric circles*

concept *NOUN* concepts
an idea • *It is a difficult concept to grasp.*

conception *NOUN* conceptions
❶ conceiving a baby ❷ forming an idea in
your mind

concern *VERB* concerns, concerning,
concerned
❶ to be important to or affect someone
• *This doesn't concern you, so go away.* ❷ to
worry someone ❸ to be about something;
to have something as its subject • *The story
concerns a group of rabbits.*

concern *NOUN* concerns
❶ something that is important to you or that
affects you; a responsibility ❷ a worry or a
feeling of worry • *My main concern is that
we'll run out of time.* ❸ a business

concerned *ADJECTIVE*
❶ worried or anxious ❷ involved in or
affected by something

concerning *PREPOSITION*
on the subject of; about • *laws concerning
seat belts*

concert *NOUN* concerts
a performance of music

concerted *ADJECTIVE*
done in cooperation with others • *We made a
concerted effort.*

concertina *NOUN* concertinas
a portable musical instrument with bellows,
played by squeezing

concerto (say kon-**chert**-oh) *NOUN* concertos
a piece of music for a solo instrument and an
orchestra

concession *NOUN* concessions
❶ something that you agree to let someone
have or do in order to end an argument or to
be helpful ❷ a reduction in price for a certain
category of person
➤ **concessionary** *ADJECTIVE*

conciliate *VERB* conciliates, conciliating, conciliated
❶ to win over an angry or hostile person by friendliness ❷ to help people who disagree to come to an agreement
➤ **conciliation** *NOUN*

concise *ADJECTIVE*
brief; giving a lot of information in a few words • *clear and concise instructions*
➤ **concisely** *ADVERB*

conclave *NOUN* conclaves
a private meeting

conclude *VERB* concludes, concluding, concluded
❶ to decide about something; to form an opinion by reasoning • *The jury concluded that he was guilty.* ❷ to end or to bring something to an end • *This film concludes the 'Lord of the Rings' trilogy.*

conclusion *NOUN* conclusions
❶ an ending ❷ an opinion formed by reasoning

conclusive *ADJECTIVE*
putting an end to all doubt • *The evidence is conclusive.*
➤ **conclusively** *ADVERB*

concoct *VERB* concocts, concocting, concocted
❶ to make something by putting ingredients together ❷ to invent something or make it up • *We'll have to concoct an excuse.*
➤ **concoction** *NOUN*

concord *NOUN*
friendly agreement or harmony

concourse *NOUN* concourses
an open area through which people pass, e.g. at an airport

concrete *NOUN*
cement mixed with sand and gravel, used in building

concrete *ADJECTIVE*
❶ based on facts, not ideas or guesses • *We need concrete evidence, not theories.* ❷ definite and clear, not general • *I don't have any concrete plans.*

concrete poem *NOUN* concrete poems
a poem printed in a special way, so that the words form a pattern on the page that has something to do with the meaning of the poem

concur *VERB* concurs, concurring, concurred
to agree
➤ **concurrence** *NOUN*

concussion *NOUN*
a temporary injury to the brain caused by a hard knock
➤ **concussed** *ADJECTIVE*

condemn *VERB* condemns, condemning, condemned
❶ to say that you strongly disapprove of something ❷ to convict or sentence a criminal • *He was condemned to death.* ❸ to be condemned to something unpleasant is to have to suffer it • *She was condemned to a lonely life.* ❹ to declare that a building is not fit to be used
➤ **condemnation** *NOUN*

condensation *NOUN*
❶ water from humid air collecting as tiny drops on a cold surface ❷ the process of changing from gas or vapour to liquid

condense *VERB* condenses, condensing, condensed
❶ to make a liquid denser or more compact ❷ to put something into fewer words or less space • *I have condensed the first three chapters into one.* ❸ to change from gas or vapour to liquid • *Steam condenses on windows.*
➤ **condenser** *NOUN*

condescend *VERB* condescends, condescending, condescended
❶ to behave towards someone in a way which shows that you think you are superior to them ❷ to allow yourself to do something that you think is unworthy of you or beneath you
➤ **condescension** *NOUN*

condescending *ADJECTIVE*
behaving towards someone in a way which shows that you think you are superior to them • *a condescending smile*

condiment *NOUN* condiments
a seasoning (e.g. salt or pepper) for food

condition *NOUN* conditions
❶ the state or fitness of a person or thing • *This bike is in good condition.* ❷ the situation or surroundings that affect people • *measures to improve working conditions in factories* ❸ something required as part of an agreement
➤ **on condition that** only if; on the understanding that something will be done

condition *VERB* conditions, conditioning, conditioned
❶ to bring something into a healthy or proper condition ❷ to train someone to behave in a particular way or become used to a particular situation

conditional *ADJECTIVE*
containing a condition; depending on something else

conditioner *NOUN* conditioners
a substance you put on your hair to keep it in good condition

condole *VERB* condoles, condoling, condoled
to express sympathy

condolence *NOUN* condolences
an expression of sympathy, especially for someone who is bereaved • *a letter of condolence*

condom *NOUN* condoms
a rubber sheath worn on the penis during sexual intercourse as a contraceptive and as a protection against sexual disease or infection

condone *VERB* condones, condoning, condoned
to accept or ignore wrongdoing • *I'm sorry, but I can't condone this sort of deception.*

condor *NOUN* condors
a kind of large vulture

conducive *ADJECTIVE*
helping to cause or produce something • *Noisy surroundings are not conducive to work.*

conduct (say kon-**dukt**) *VERB* conducts, conducting, conducted
❶ to manage something or carry it out • *She conducted a series of important experiments.* ❷ to lead or guide someone to a place • *We were conducted around the ruins of the temple.* ❸ to be the conductor of an orchestra or choir ❹ to allow heat, light, sound or electricity to pass along or through something ❺ to behave in a particular way • *They conducted themselves with dignity.*

conduct (say **kon**-dukt) *NOUN*
a person's behaviour

conduction *NOUN*
the conducting of heat or electricity etc

conductor *NOUN* conductors
❶ a person who directs the performance of an orchestra or choir by movements of the arms ❷ something that conducts heat or

electricity etc. ❸ a person who collects the fares on a bus etc.

conduit (say kon-dit) *NOUN* conduits
❶ a pipe or channel for liquid ❷ a tube protecting electric wire

cone *NOUN* cones
❶ an object that is circular at one end and narrows to a point at the other end ❷ an ice cream cornet ❸ the dry cone-shaped fruit of a pine, fir or cedar tree

confection *NOUN* confections
something made of various things, especially sweet ones, put together

confectioner *NOUN* confectioners
someone who makes or sells sweets
➤ **confectionery** *NOUN*

confederacy *NOUN* confederacies
a union of states; a confederation

confederate *ADJECTIVE*
allied; joined by an agreement or treaty

confederate *NOUN* confederates
❶ a member of a confederacy ❷ an ally or accomplice

confederation *NOUN* confederations
❶ the process of joining in an alliance ❷ a group of people, organizations or states joined together by an agreement or treaty

confer *VERB* confers, conferring, conferred
❶ to have a discussion before deciding something ❷ to grant a right or privilege to someone • *Thank you for conferring this honour upon me.*

conference *NOUN* conferences
a meeting at which formal discussions take place

confess *VERB* confesses, confessing, confessed
to state openly that you have done something wrong or have a weakness; to admit something • *I confess that I don't like her very much.*

confession *NOUN* confessions
❶ admitting that you have done wrong • *He made a full confession to the police.* ❷ (in the Roman Catholic Church) an act of telling a priest that you have sinned

confessional *NOUN* confessionals
a small room where a priest hears confessions

confessor *NOUN* confessors
a priest who hears confessions

confetti *NOUN*
tiny pieces of coloured paper thrown by

wedding guests at the bride and bridegroom
WORD ORIGIN Italian, = sweets (which were traditionally thrown at Italian weddings)

confidant NOUN (**confidante** is used of a woman) **confidants, confidantes**
a person you confide in

confide VERB **confides, confiding, confided**
to tell someone a secret • *I decided to confide in my sister.*

confidence NOUN **confidences**
❶ a feeling of being sure that you are right or can do something ❷ firm trust in someone or something ❸ something told as a secret
➤ **in confidence** as a secret or private matter
➤ **in a person's confidence** trusted with his or her secrets

confidence trick NOUN **confidence tricks**
swindling a person after persuading him or her to trust you

confident ADJECTIVE
showing or feeling confidence • *She is confident that she will win.*
➤ **confidently** ADVERB

confidential ADJECTIVE
meant to be kept secret
➤ **confidentially** ADVERB
➤ **confidentiality** NOUN

configuration NOUN **configurations**
the way in which the parts of something or a group of things are arranged. • *the configuration of the continents*

confine VERB **confines, confining, confined**
❶ to keep something within limits; to restrict something • *Please confine your remarks to the subject being discussed.* ❷ to keep someone in a place and not let them leave

confined ADJECTIVE
a confined space is narrow or enclosed

confinement NOUN **confinements**
❶ being forced to stay somewhere • *He spent two weeks in solitary confinement.* ❷ (*old use*) the time of giving birth to a baby

confines (say kon-fynz) PLURAL NOUN
the limits or boundaries of an area

confirm VERB **confirms, confirming, confirmed**
❶ to show definitely that something is true or correct ❷ to make an arrangement definite • *Please write to confirm your order.* ❸ to make a person a full member of the Christian Church

confirmation NOUN **confirmations**
❶ a statement showing that something is

true, correct or definite • *You will receive confirmation of your booking by email.* ❷ a ceremony in which a person is made a full member of the Christian Church

confiscate VERB **confiscates, confiscating, confiscated**
to take something away from someone as a punishment
➤ **confiscation** NOUN

conflagration NOUN **conflagrations**
a great and destructive fire

conflict (say kon-flikt) NOUN **conflicts**
a fight, struggle or disagreement

conflict (say kon-**flikt**) VERB **conflicts, conflicting, conflicted**
two things conflict when they contradict or disagree with one another • *His account of the incident conflicts with hers.*

confluence NOUN **confluences**
the place where two rivers meet

conform VERB **conforms, conforming, conformed**
to keep to accepted rules, customs or ideas
➤ **conformity** NOUN

confound VERB **confounds, confounding, confounded**
to astonish or confuse someone

confront VERB **confronts, confronting, confronted**
❶ to confront someone is to challenge them face to face for a fight or argument ❷ to confront a problem or difficulty is to deal with it rather than ignoring it • *She has learned to confront her fears.* ❸ if a problem or difficulty confronts you, you have to deal with it • *He was confronted with a very difficult decision.*

confrontation NOUN **confrontations**
meeting someone face to face for a fight or argument

confuse VERB **confuses, confusing, confused**
❶ to make a person puzzled or muddled ❷ to mistake one person or thing for another • *I often confuse Ollie with his brother.*
➤ **confused** ADJECTIVE

confusing ADJECTIVE
difficult to understand; not clear

confusion NOUN
❶ not being able to think clearly or not knowing what to do • *He stared in confusion at the exam paper.* ❷ mistaking one thing for

a
b
c
d
e
f
g
h
i
j
k
l
m
n
o
p
q
r
s
t
u
v
w
x
y
z

another • *To avoid confusion, I've written my name on my bag.*

congeal (say kon-**jeel**) VERB congeals, congealing, congealed
to become jelly-like instead of liquid, especially in cooling • *congealed blood*

congenial ADJECTIVE
pleasant through being similar to yourself or suiting your tastes • *a congenial companion*

congenital (say kon-**jen**-it-al) ADJECTIVE
existing in a person from birth • *a congenital heart defect*

congested ADJECTIVE
❶ a congested place is crowded or blocked up with traffic or people • *congested streets*
❷ your breathing or a part of your body are congested when they become blocked with mucus • *congested lungs*

congestion NOUN
❶ when a place is crowded and full of traffic or people ❷ when your nose is blocked with mucus and you cannot breathe properly

conglomerate NOUN conglomerates
a large business group formed by merging several different companies

conglomeration NOUN conglomerations
a mass of different things put together

congratulate VERB congratulates, congratulating, congratulated
to tell a person that you are pleased about what they have achieved or something good that has happened to them
➤ **congratulatory** ADJECTIVE

congratulations PLURAL NOUN
what you say to congratulate someone

congregate VERB congregates, congregating, congregated
to come together in a crowd or group
• *Young people congregate in the square each evening.*

congregation NOUN congregations
a group of people who have come together to take part in religious worship

Congress NOUN
the parliament of the USA

congress NOUN congresses
a large meeting or conference

congruent ADJECTIVE
(*in mathematics*) having exactly the same shape and size • *congruent triangles*
➤ **congruence** NOUN

conical ADJECTIVE
cone-shaped • *a conical hat*

conifer (say **kon**-if-er) NOUN conifers
an evergreen tree with cones
➤ **coniferous** ADJECTIVE

conjecture NOUN conjectures
guesswork or a guess

conjecture VERB conjectures, conjecturing, conjectured
to guess about something

conjoined twins PLURAL NOUN
twins who are born with their bodies joined together

conjugal (say **kon**-jug-al) ADJECTIVE
to do with marriage

conjugate VERB conjugates, conjugating, conjugated
to give all the different forms of a verb
➤ **conjugation** NOUN

conjunction NOUN conjunctions
a word that joins words, phrases or sentences, e.g. *and*, *but* and *because*
➤ **in conjunction with** together with; combined with • *The course book is designed to be used in conjunction with our website.*

GRAMMAR

Conjunctions and other **connectives** are used to link ideas in a piece of writing.

Conjunctions are used to join words, clauses or phrases in a sentence.

Coordinating conjunctions such as *and*, *but* and *or* join words or clauses which are of equal importance:

Would you prefer tea <u>and</u> biscuits, <u>or</u> coffee <u>and</u> cake?

Subordinating conjunctions such as *although, because, if, until, unless* and *when* are used to introduce a subordinate clause:

She felt weak <u>because</u> she was tired and hungry.

The computer won't work <u>unless</u> you switch it on.

Other **connectives** are adverbs or phrases used as adverbials. They often come at the start of a sentence and connect it with a previous sentence or paragraph. Common examples of adverbials used in this way are the adverbs *moreover, nevertheless, finally* and *furthermore*, and the phrases *on the other hand, in addition to this,* and *later that day.*

The goods arrived late. Furthermore, the parcel was damaged.

He left in the morning. Later that day, he was back.

conjure VERB conjures, conjuring, conjured
to perform tricks that look like magic
➤ **conjuror** NOUN
➤ **conjure something up** to produce an image or impression in your mind • *Mention of the Arctic conjures up visions of snow.*

conker NOUN conkers (*British*)
the hard shiny brown nut of the horse chestnut tree
➤ **conkers** a game between players who each have a conker threaded on a string
WORD ORIGIN from a dialect word = snail shell (because conkers was originally played with snail shells)

SPELLING
Be careful, this sounds the same as **conquer.**

connect VERB connects, connecting, connected
❶ to join things together; to link one thing with another • *Have you connected the printer to the computer?* ❷ to think of things or people as being associated with each other • *There was no evidence to connect him with the murder.*

connection NOUN connections
❶ a link or relationship between things • *We all know there is a connection between smoking and cancer.* ❷ a place where two wires, pipes, etc are joined together • *a loose connection* ❸ a train, bus, etc. that leaves a station soon after another arrives, so that passengers can change from one to the other

connective NOUN connectives
a word that joins words, clauses or sentences. Some connectives (e.g. *but*, *and* and *because*) are conjunctions, while some (e.g. *however* and *in addition*) are adverbials.

conning tower NOUN conning towers
the part on top of a submarine, containing the periscope

connive (say kon-**yv**) VERB connives, conniving, connived
➤ **connive at something** to ignore something wrong or quietly approve of it
➤ **connivance** NOUN

connoisseur (say kon-a-**ser**) NOUN connoisseurs
a person with great experience and appreciation of something • *a connoisseur of wine*

conquer VERB conquers, conquering, conquered
❶ to defeat and take control of a country and its people ❷ to succeed in controlling a difficult feeling • *She's trying to conquer her fear of flying.*
➤ **conqueror** NOUN

SPELLING
The 'k' sound is spelt qu in the middle of **conquer.**

conquest NOUN conquests
❶ a victory over someone ❷ conquered territory

conscience (say **kon**-shens) NOUN consciences
knowing what is right and wrong, especially in your own actions

conscientious (say kon-shee-**en**-shus) ADJECTIVE
careful and honest about doing your work properly • *She is a conscientious student.*
➤ **conscientiously** ADVERB

conscientious objector NOUN conscientious objectors
a person who refuses to serve in the armed forces because he or she believes it is morally wrong

conscious (say **kon**-shus) ADJECTIVE
❶ awake and knowing what is happening ❷ aware of something • *I was not conscious of the time.* ❸ done deliberately • *a conscious decision*
➤ **consciously** ADVERB
➤ **consciousness** NOUN

SPELLING
There is a tricky bit in **conscious** – it has sci in the middle.

conscript (say kon-**skript**) VERB conscripts, conscripting, conscripted
to make a person join the armed forces
➤ **conscription** NOUN

conscript (say **kon**-skript) NOUN conscripts
a person who has been conscripted

consecrate VERB consecrates, consecrating, consecrated
to officially say that a thing, especially a building, is holy
➤ **consecration** NOUN

a
b
c
d
e
f
g
h
i
j
k
l
m
n
o
p
q
r
s
t
u
v
w
x
y
z

consecutive ADJECTIVE
following one after another • *Borg won five consecutive Wimbledon titles.*
➤ **consecutively** ADVERB

consensus NOUN **consensuses**
general agreement; the opinion of most people • *There was a growing consensus that the rule should be changed.*

consent NOUN
agreement to what someone wishes; permission • *You can only go on the trip if your parents give their consent.*

consent VERB **consents, consenting, consented**
to say that you are willing to do or allow what someone wishes

consequence NOUN **consequences**
❶ something that happens as the result of an event or action ❷ the importance that something has • *It is of no consequence.*

consequent ADJECTIVE
happening as a result

consequently ADVERB
as a result

conservation NOUN
❶ the preservation of the natural environment ❷ not allowing something valuable from being spoilt or wasted • *the conservation of energy*

conservationist NOUN **conservationists**
a person who believes in preserving the natural environment

Conservative NOUN **Conservatives**
a person who supports the Conservative Party, a British political party that favours private enterprise and freedom from state control
➤ **Conservative** ADJECTIVE

conservative ADJECTIVE
❶ liking traditional ways and disliking changes ❷ lower than what is probably the real amount • *a conservative estimate*
➤ **conservatism** NOUN

conservatory NOUN **conservatories**
a room with a glass roof and large windows, built against an outside wall of a house with a connecting door from the house

conserve VERB **conserves, conserving, conserved**
to prevent something valuable from being changed, spoilt or wasted

consider VERB **considers, considering, considered**
❶ to think carefully about or give attention to something, especially in order to make a decision ❷ to have something as an opinion; to think something • *I consider myself very lucky.*

considerable ADJECTIVE
fairly great or large • *a considerable amount*

considerably ADVERB
very much; a lot • *The new house is considerably larger than our last one.*

considerate ADJECTIVE
always thinking of other people's needs, wishes or feelings
➤ **considerately** ADVERB

consideration NOUN **considerations**
❶ careful thought or attention ❷ considerate behaviour ❸ a fact that must be kept in mind
➤ **take something into consideration** to think carefully about something when you are making a decision or giving an opinion

considering PREPOSITION
taking something into consideration • *The car runs well, considering its age.*

consign VERB **consigns, consigning, consigned**
to put something somewhere in order to get rid of it • *I consigned her letter to the bin.*

consignment NOUN **consignments**
a batch of goods etc. sent to someone

consist VERB **consists, consisting, consisted**
to be made up or formed of • *The band consists of a singer, two guitarists and a drummer.*

consistency NOUN **consistencies**
❶ how thick or smooth a liquid is • *The mixture should have a creamy consistency.*
❷ being consistent • *The team needs to play with more consistency.*

consistent ADJECTIVE
❶ keeping to a regular pattern, style or standard; not changing • *She's our most consistent player.* ❷ agreeing with something else; not contradictory • *These results are consistent with earlier findings.*
➤ **consistently** ADVERB

consolation NOUN **consolations**
❶ consolation is giving comfort or sympathy to someone ❷ a consolation is something that comforts someone who is unhappy or disappointed

consolation prize NOUN consolation prizes
a prize given to a competitor who has just missed winning one of the main prizes

console (say kon-**sohl**) VERB consoles, consoling, consoled
to comfort someone who is unhappy or disappointed

console (say **kon**-sohl) NOUN consoles
a panel or unit containing the controls for electrical or other equipment

consolidate VERB consolidates, consolidating, consolidated
❶ to make something secure and strong • They consolidated their lead with a second goal. ❷ to combine two or more organizations, funds, etc. into one
➤ **consolidation** NOUN

consonant NOUN consonants
a letter that is not a vowel • B, c, d, f, etc. are consonants.

consort (say kon-sort) NOUN consorts
a husband or wife, especially of a monarch

consort (say kon-**sort**) VERB consorts, consorting, consorted
to consort with someone is to be often in their company • He was known to consort with criminals.

consortium NOUN consortia
a group of companies working together

conspicuous ADJECTIVE
easy to see or notice; standing out very clearly • I felt very conspicuous in my new suit.
➤ **conspicuously** ADVERB

conspiracy NOUN conspiracies
a secret plan made by a group of people to do something illegal

conspirator NOUN conspirators
a person who takes part in a conspiracy

conspiratorial ADJECTIVE
showing that you share a secret with someone • He gave her a conspiratorial wink.

conspire VERB conspires, conspiring, conspired
to take part in a conspiracy

constable NOUN constables
a police officer of the lowest rank

constabulary NOUN constabularies
(British) a police force

constancy NOUN
being faithful or loyal

constant ADJECTIVE
❶ not changing; happening all the time
❷ faithful or loyal

constant NOUN constants
❶ a thing that does not vary ❷ (in science and mathematics) a number or value that does not change

constantly ADVERB
all the time; again and again • The situation is constantly changing.

constellation NOUN constellations
a group of stars

constipated ADJECTIVE
unable to empty the bowels easily or regularly
➤ **constipation** NOUN

constituency NOUN constituencies
a district represented by a Member of Parliament elected by the people who live there

constituent NOUN constituents
❶ one of the parts that form a whole thing • Hydrogen and oxygen are the constituents of water. ❷ someone who lives in a particular constituency
➤ **constituent** ADJECTIVE

constitute VERB constitutes, constituting, constituted
❶ to make up or form something • These 50 states constitute the USA. ❷ to be considered to be something • What he did surely constitutes bullying.

constitution NOUN constitutions
❶ the group of laws or principles that state how a country is to be organized and governed ❷ the condition of your body in terms of its general physical health • She has a strong constitution.
➤ **constitutional** ADJECTIVE

constrain VERB constrains, constraining, constrained
to force someone to act in a certain way

constraint NOUN constraints
❶ something that limits you; a restriction
❷ forcing someone to act in a certain way

constrict VERB constricts, constricting, constricted
to become tighter and narrower or to make something do this • She felt her throat constrict with fear.
➤ **constriction** NOUN

construct VERB constructs, constructing, constructed
to make something by placing parts together;

a
b
c
d
e
f
g
h
i
j
k
l
m
n
o
p
q
r
s
t
u
v
w
x
y
z

to build something from parts • *When was the bridge constructed?*
➤ **constructor** *NOUN*

construction *NOUN* **constructions**
❶ constructing something • *Our new school is still under construction.* ❷ something constructed; a building ❸ two or more words put together to form a phrase or clause or sentence

constructive *ADJECTIVE*
helpful and positive • *constructive suggestions*

construe *VERB* **construes, construing, construed**
to interpret or explain something difficult

consul *NOUN* **consuls**
❶ a government official appointed to live in a foreign city to help people from his or her own country who visit there ❷ either of the two chief magistrates in ancient Rome

consulate *NOUN* **consulates**
the building where a consul works

consult *VERB* **consults, consulting, consulted**
❶ to go to a person or book etc. for information or advice ❷ to discuss something with someone before taking a decision

consultant *NOUN* **consultants**
❶ a person who is qualified to give expert advice ❷ a senior hospital doctor who is an expert in one type of medicine

consultation *NOUN* **consultations**
❶ a discussion between people before a decision is taken ❷ meeting someone to get information or advice or looking for it in a book • *a consultation with a doctor*

consume *VERB* **consumes, consuming, consumed**
❶ to eat or drink something ❷ to use something up • *Much time was consumed in waiting.* ❸ to destroy something • *Fire consumed the building.*

consumer *NOUN* **consumers**
a person who buys or uses goods or services

consummate (say kon-**sum**-at) *ADJECTIVE*
perfect; highly skilled • *a consummate artist*

consummate (say **kon**-sum-ayt)
VERB **consummates, consummating, consummated**
to make something complete or perfect
➤ **consummation** *NOUN*

consumption *NOUN*
❶ the using up of something, especially food

or fuel • *Gas consumption increases in cold weather.* ❷ (*old use*) tuberculosis of the lungs

contact *NOUN* **contacts**
❶ communication with someone, by speaking or writing to them regularly • *I've lost contact with my uncle.* ❷ if two things are in contact with one another, they are touching • *Don't let the glue come into contact with your skin.* ❸ a person to communicate with when you need information or help

contact *VERB* **contacts, contacting, contacted**
to get in touch with a person • *You can contact me on this email address.*

contact lens *NOUN* **contact lenses**
a tiny plastic lens worn against the eyeball, instead of glasses

contagion *NOUN* **contagions**
a contagious disease

contagious *ADJECTIVE*
a contagious disease is one that spreads by contact with an infected person

contain *VERB* **contains, containing, contained**
❶ to have something inside • *This book contains a great deal of information.* ❷ to consist of • *A litre contains a hundred centilitres.* ❸ to restrain or hold back a strong feeling • *Try to contain your laughter.*

container *NOUN* **containers**
❶ a box or bottle etc. designed to contain something ❷ a large box-like object of standard design in which goods are transported

contaminate *VERB* **contaminates, contaminating, contaminated**
to make a thing dirty or impure or diseased; to pollute something • *The drinking water may have become contaminated.*
➤ **contamination** *NOUN*

contemplate *VERB* **contemplates, contemplating, contemplated**
❶ to look at something thoughtfully ❷ to consider or think about doing something • *We are contemplating a visit to London.*
➤ **contemplative** *ADJECTIVE*

contemplation *NOUN*
thinking deeply about something • *She sat in quiet contemplation.*

contemporary *ADJECTIVE*
❶ living or happening in the same period • *Dickens was contemporary with Thackeray.* ❷ belonging to the present time; modern • *contemporary art*

contemporary NOUN contemporaries
a person who is about the same age as another or is living at the same time • *She was my contemporary at college.*

contempt NOUN
a feeling of despising a person or thing

contemptible ADJECTIVE
deserving contempt • *Hurting her feelings like that was a contemptible thing to do.*

contemptuous ADJECTIVE
feeling or showing contempt • *She gave me a contemptuous look.*
➤ **contemptuously** ADVERB

contend VERB contends, contending, contended
❶ to contend with a problem or difficulty is to have to deal with it • *The players also had to contend with wind and rain.* ❷ to compete in a contest ❸ to declare or claim that something is true • *We contend that he is innocent.*

contender NOUN contenders
a person who may win a competition • *She is a contender for a gold medal.*

content (say kon-**tent**) ADJECTIVE
happy or satisfied

content (say kon-**tent**) NOUN
a happy or satisfied feeling

content (say **kon**-tent) NOUN
❶ the amount of a substance in something • *milk with a low fat content* ❷ the subject and ideas dealt with in a book, television programme, speech, etc. • *The content of the essay is good, but there are too many spelling mistakes.*

content (say kon-**tent**) VERB contents, contenting, contented
to make a person happy or satisfied

contented ADJECTIVE
happy with what you have; satisfied
➤ **contentedly** ADVERB

contention NOUN contentions
❶ a point of view or opinion that someone puts forward ❷ strong disagreement or arguing

contentment NOUN
a feeling of being happy or satisfied

contents (say **kon**-tents) PLURAL NOUN
❶ the contents of a box or other container are what is inside it ❷ the contents of a book, magazine, etc. are the things you read in it

contest (say **kon**-test) NOUN contests
a competition; a struggle in which rivals try to obtain something or to be the best

contest (say kon-**test**) VERB contests, contesting, contested
❶ to try to win a competition, election, etc. • *The final was fiercely contested.* ❷ to dispute something or argue that it is wrong or not legal • *Several players contested the referee's decision.*

contestant NOUN contestants
a person taking part in a contest; a competitor

context NOUN contexts
❶ the words that come before and after a particular word or phrase and help to fix its meaning ❷ the background to an event that helps to explain it

continent NOUN continents
one of the main masses of land in the world • *The continents are Europe, Asia, Africa, North America, South America, Australia and Antarctica.*
➤ **continental** ADJECTIVE
➤ **the Continent** the mainland of Europe, from the point of view of people living in the British Isles

contingency NOUN contingencies
something that may happen but cannot be known for certain

contingent NOUN contingents
a group that forms part of a larger group or gathering • *The French contingent arrived next.*

contingent ADJECTIVE
one thing is contingent on another when the first depends on the second • *His future is contingent on success in this exam.*

continual ADJECTIVE
happening all the time, usually with breaks in between • *Stop this continual quarrelling!*
➤ **continually** ADVERB

USAGE
Take care not to confuse with **continuous**. You use **continual** to describe something that happens very frequently (*there were continual interruptions*) while you use **continuous** to describe something that happens without a pause (*there is a continuous hum from the fridge*).

a b c d e f g h i j k l m n o p q r s t u v w x y z

A
B
C
D
E
F
G
H
I
J
K
L
M
N
O
P
Q
R
S
T
U
V
W
X
Y
Z

continuance *NOUN*
(*formal*) continuing something

continue *VERB* **continues, continuing, continued**
❶ to do something without stopping ❷ to begin again after stopping • *The game will continue after lunch.*
➤ **continuation** *NOUN*

continuous *ADJECTIVE*
going on and on; without a break
➤ **continuously** *ADVERB*
➤ **continuity** *NOUN*

> **USAGE**
> See note at **continual**.

contort *VERB* **contorts, contorting, contorted**
to twist or force something out of the usual shape • *His face was contorted with pain.*
➤ **contortion** *NOUN*

contortionist *NOUN* **contortionists**
a person who can twist his or her body into unusual positions

contour *NOUN* **contours**
❶ a line on a map joining the points that are the same height above sea level ❷ an outline

contraband *NOUN*
smuggled goods

contraception *NOUN*
the use of contraceptives to prevent pregnancy; birth control

contraceptive *NOUN* **contraceptives**
a substance or device that prevents pregnancy

contract (say **kon**-trakt) *NOUN* **contracts**
❶ a formal agreement to do something ❷ a document stating the terms of an agreement

contract (say kon-**trakt**) *VERB* **contracts, contracting, contracted**
❶ to become smaller or shorter • *Heated metal contracts as it cools.* ❷ to get an illness • *She contracted measles.* ❸ to make a contract

contraction *NOUN* **contractions**
❶ getting smaller or shorter • *the contraction of a muscle* ❷ a shortened form of a word or words. *Can't is a contraction of cannot.*

> **GRAMMAR**
> When a word is made shorter by dropping one or more letters, this is called a **contraction**.
>
> Contractions are used a great deal when

writing direct speech, and also in informal writing.

Contractions are written as a single word and use an apostrophe to show where letters have been left out.

I've finished my homework.

I don't think I can come.

What's the matter?

I'd like to help if I can.

It is fine to use contractions in informal writing, but in most formal writing, including most school work, you should use the full form of the words.

contractor *NOUN* **contractors**
a person or company that has a contract to do work for someone else, especially in the building industry

contradict *VERB* **contradicts, contradicting, contradicted**
❶ to say that something said is not true or that someone is wrong ❷ to say the opposite of something • *These rumours contradict previous ones.*

contradiction *NOUN* **contradictions**
a statement that is opposite to or different from another one • *There were a number of contradictions in what he told the police.*

contradictory *ADJECTIVE*
being opposite to or not matching something else • *Contradictory reports appeared in the newspapers.*

contraflow *NOUN* **contraflows**
(*British*) a special arrangement of traffic when a motorway is being repaired, with traffic going in both directions using the carriageway on the other side

contralto *NOUN* **contraltos**
a female singer with a low voice

contraption *NOUN* **contraptions**
a strange-looking or complicated device or machine

contrary *ADJECTIVE*
❶ (say **kon**-tra-ree) completely different or opposed to something • *Contrary to popular belief, many cats dislike milk.* ❷ (say kon-**trair**-ee) awkward and obstinate

contrary (say **kon**-tra-ree) *NOUN*
the opposite

➤ **on the contrary** the opposite is true; certainly not

contrast (say **kon**-trahst) *NOUN* **contrasts**
❶ a difference clearly seen when things are compared ❷ something showing a clear difference compared with something else

contrast (say kon-**trahst**) *VERB* **contrasts, contrasting, contrasted**
❶ to compare two things in order to show that they are clearly different ❷ to be clearly different when compared

contravene *VERB* **contravenes, contravening, contravened**
to do something that breaks a rule or law
➤ **contravention** *NOUN*

contribute *VERB* **contributes, contributing, contributed**
❶ to give money or help jointly with others ❷ to write something for a newspaper or magazine etc. ❸ to help to cause something • *Fatigue contributed to the accident.*
➤ **contributor** *NOUN*
➤ **contributory** *ADJECTIVE*

contribution *NOUN* **contributions**
money or help that someone gives jointly with others

contrite *ADJECTIVE*
very sorry for having done wrong

contrivance *NOUN* **contrivances**
an ingenious device

contrive *VERB* **contrives, contriving, contrived**
❶ to find a way of doing something although it is difficult • *She contrived to get away without anyone seeing her.* ❷ to plan or make something cleverly

control *VERB* **controls, controlling, controlled**
❶ to have the power to make other people or things do what you want ❷ to operate a machine ❸ to hold something, especially anger, in check
➤ **controller** *NOUN*

control *NOUN*
controlling a person or thing; authority
➤ **in control** having control of something
➤ **out of control** no longer able to be controlled
➤ **under control** being dealt with successfully

controls *PLURAL NOUN*
the switches, buttons, etc. used to control a machine

control tower *NOUN* **control towers**
the building at an airport where people control air traffic by radio

controversial *ADJECTIVE*
likely to cause people to have strong opinions and disagree about it • *a controversial issue*

controversy (say **kon**-tro-ver-see or kon-**trov**-er-see) *NOUN* **controversies**
a long argument or disagreement

contusion *NOUN* **contusions**
a bruise

conundrum *NOUN* **conundrums**
a riddle or difficult question

conurbation *NOUN* **conurbations**
a large urban area where towns have spread into each other

convalesce *VERB* **convalesces, convalescing, convalesced**
to be recovering from an illness
➤ **convalescence** *NOUN*
➤ **convalescent** *ADJECTIVE & NOUN*

convection *NOUN*
the passing on of heat within liquid, air or gas by circulation of the warmed parts

convector *NOUN* **convectors**
a heater that circulates warm air by convection

convene *VERB* **convenes, convening, convened**
to bring people together or come together for a meeting • *An emergency meeting was convened.*

convenience *NOUN* **conveniences**
❶ the quality of being easy to use or of making it easy for you to do something ❷ something that is convenient ❸ a public toilet
➤ **at your convenience** whenever you find it convenient; as it suits you

convenience food *NOUN* **convenience foods**
food sold in a form that is already partly prepared and so is easy to use

convenient *ADJECTIVE*
easy to use or deal with or reach
➤ **conveniently** *ADVERB*

convent *NOUN* **convents**
a place where nuns live and work

convention *NOUN* **conventions**
❶ an accepted way of doing things • *social conventions such as shaking hands* ❷ a large meeting or conference

a b c d e f g h i j k l m n o p q r s t u v w x y z

A

B

C

D

E

F

G

H

I

J

K

L

M

N

O

P

Q

R

S

T

U

V

W

X

Y

Z

conventional *ADJECTIVE*
❶ done or doing things in the normal or accepted way; traditional ❷ conventional weapons are those that are not nuclear
➤ **conventionally** *ADVERB*

converge *VERB* **converges, converging, converged**
to come to or towards the same point from different directions • *The two roads converge at the town square.*

conversant *ADJECTIVE* (*formal*)
familiar with something • *Are you conversant with the rules of this game?*

conversation *NOUN* **conversations**
an informal talk between two or more people

conversational *ADJECTIVE*
informal; as used in conversation • *She has a conversational style of writing.*

converse (say kon-**verss**) *VERB* **converses, conversing, conversed**
to have a conversation • *They conversed in low voices.*

converse (say **kon**-verss) *NOUN*
the opposite of something • *In fact, the converse is true.*
➤ **conversely** *ADVERB*

conversion *NOUN* **conversions**
❶ changing something from one form, system or use to another • *a conversion table for miles and kilometres* ❷ changing your religion

convert (say kon-**vert**) *VERB* **converts, converting, converted**
❶ to change something from one form, system or use to another • *Your body converts food into energy.* ❷ to change to a different religion ❸ to kick a goal after scoring a try at rugby football
➤ **converter** *NOUN*

convert (say **kon**-vert) *NOUN* **converts**
a person who has changed his or her religion

convertible *ADJECTIVE*
able to be converted

convertible *NOUN* **convertibles**
a car with a roof that can be folded down or taken off

convex *ADJECTIVE*
curved like the outside of a ball or circle. (The opposite is **concave**.)

convey *VERB* **conveys, conveying, conveyed**
❶ to communicate a message, idea or feeling • *Please convey my apologies to your mother.*
• *The tone of his voice conveyed his disgust.*
❷ to transport people or goods

conveyance *NOUN* **conveyances**
❶ transporting people or goods ❷ (*formal*) a vehicle for transporting people

conveyancing *NOUN*
transferring the legal ownership of land or property from one person to another

conveyor belt *NOUN* **conveyor belts**
a continuous moving belt for moving objects from one place to another

convict (say kon-**vikt**) *VERB* **convicts, convicting, convicted**
to convict someone of a crime is to decide at their trial that they are guilty of it

convict (say **kon**-vikt) *NOUN* **convicts**
a convicted person who is in prison

conviction *NOUN* **convictions**
❶ being convicted of a crime • *He had several previous convictions for burglary.*
❷ being firmly convinced of something ❸ a firm opinion or belief
➤ **carry conviction** to be convincing

convince *VERB* **convinces, convincing, convinced**
to make someone feel certain that something is true; to persuade someone to do something

convincing *ADJECTIVE*
❶ able to make someone believe that something is true • *a convincing argument*
❷ a convincing victory is a complete and clear one

convivial *ADJECTIVE*
sociable and lively

convoluted *ADJECTIVE*
❶ complicated and difficult to follow • *a convoluted explanation* ❷ having lots of twists and curves

convoy *NOUN* **convoys**
a group of ships or vehicles travelling together

convulse *VERB* **convulses, convulsing, convulsed**
to be convulsed is to have violent movements of the body that you cannot control • *The boys were convulsed with laughter.*
➤ **convulsive** *ADJECTIVE*

convulsion *NOUN* **convulsions**
a violent movement of the body that you cannot control

coo *VERB* coos, cooing, cooed
to make a soft murmuring sound like a dove
➤ **coo** *NOUN*

cook *VERB* cooks, cooking, cooked
to make food ready to eat by heating it
➤ **cook something up** (*informal*) if you cook up a story or plan, you invent it

cook *NOUN* cooks
a person who cooks

cooker *NOUN* cookers
(*British*) a piece of equipment for cooking food

cookery *NOUN*
(*chiefly British*) the skill of cooking food

cookie *NOUN* cookies
(*North American*) a sweet biscuit

cool *ADJECTIVE*
❶ fairly cold; not hot or warm ❷ calm and not easily excited ❸ not friendly or enthusiastic ❹ (*informal*) very good or fashionable • *Hey, cool shoes!*
➤ **coolness** *NOUN*

cool *VERB* cools, cooling, cooled
to become cool or make something cool
➤ **cooler** *NOUN*

coolly *ADVERB*
❶ in a calm way ❷ in a slightly unfriendly way

coop *NOUN* coops
a cage for poultry

cooped up *ADJECTIVE*
having to stay in a place which is small and uncomfortable

cooperate *VERB* cooperates, cooperating, cooperated
❶ to work helpfully with other people ❷ to be helpful by doing what someone asks
➤ **cooperative** *ADJECTIVE*

cooperation *NOUN*
❶ working helpfully with other people ❷ being helpful by doing what someone asks

co-opt *VERB* co-opts, co-opting, co-opted
invite someone to become a member of a committee etc.

coordinate *VERB* coordinates, coordinating, coordinated
to organize people or things to work properly together
➤ **coordinator** *NOUN*

coordinate *NOUN* coordinates
either of the pair of numbers or letters used to fix the position of a point on a graph or map

coordination *NOUN*
❶ organizing people or things to work properly together ❷ the ability to control the movements of your body well

coot *NOUN* coots
a waterbird with a horny white patch on its forehead

cop *VERB* cops, copping, copped
➤ **cop it** to get into trouble or be punished

cop *NOUN* cops (*informal*)
a police officer

cope *VERB* copes, coping, coped
to manage or deal with something successfully • *I really can't cope with this heat.*

copier *NOUN* copiers
a machine for copying pages

co-pilot *NOUN* co-pilots
a second pilot who helps the main pilot in an aircraft

coping *NOUN*
the top row of stones or bricks in a wall, usually slanted so that rainwater will run off

copious *ADJECTIVE*
plentiful; in large amounts • *She made copious notes at the lecture.*
➤ **copiously** *ADVERB*

copper *NOUN* coppers
❶ a reddish-brown metal used to make wire, coins, etc. ❷ a reddish-brown colour ❸ (*British*) coppers are brown coins of low value made of copper or bronze ❹ (*British*) (*informal*) a policeman
➤ **copper** *ADJECTIVE*

copperplate *NOUN*
a style of neat round handwriting
WORD ORIGIN because the books of examples of this writing for learners to copy were printed from copper plates

coppice *NOUN* coppices
a small group of trees

copra *NOUN*
dried coconut kernels

copse *NOUN* copses
a small group of trees

copulate *VERB* copulates, copulating, copulated
to have sexual intercourse
➤ **copulation** *NOUN*

a b c d e f g h i j k l m n o p q r s t u v w x y z

A B C D E F G H I J K L M N O P Q R S T U V W X Y Z

copy *NOUN* **copies**
 ① a thing made to look like another
 ② something written or typed out again from its original form ③ a single book, newspaper, CD, etc. that is one of many produced at the same time

copy *VERB* **copies, copying, copied**
 ① to make a copy of something ② to do the same as someone else; to imitate someone ③ to copy a computer file or program or piece of text is to make another one that is exactly the same, usually one that you store somewhere else

copyright *NOUN*
 the legal right to print a book, reproduce a picture, record a piece of music, etc.

coquette (say ko-**ket**) *NOUN* **coquettes**
 a woman who flirts
 ➤ **coquettish** *ADJECTIVE*

coral *NOUN*
 ① a hard red, pink or white substance formed by the skeletons of tiny sea creatures massed together ② a pink colour

cord *NOUN* **cords**
 ① strong thick string made of twisted threads or strands ② a piece of flex ③ a cord-like structure in the body • *the spinal cord*

SPELLING
 Cord is different from **chord**, which means a number of musical notes sounded together.

cordial *NOUN* **cordials**
 a fruit-flavoured drink

cordial *ADJECTIVE*
 warm and friendly • *We got a cordial welcome.*
 ➤ **cordially** *ADVERB*
 ➤ **cordiality** *NOUN*

cordon *NOUN* **cordons**
 a line of police, soldiers or vehicles placed round an area to guard or enclose it

cordon *VERB* **cordons, cordoning, cordoned**
 ➤ **cordon something off** to stop people entering an area by surrounding it with a ring of police, soldiers or vehicles • *Police have cordoned off the street.*

cordon bleu (say kor-dawn **bler**) *ADJECTIVE*
 of the highest class in cookery

cords *PLURAL NOUN*
 trousers made of corduroy

corduroy *NOUN*
 a thick cotton cloth with velvety ridges

core *NOUN* **cores**
 ① the hard central part of an apple or pear etc., containing the seeds ② the part in the middle of something • *the Earth's core* ③ the most important or basic part of something • *This is the core of the problem.*

corgi *NOUN* **corgis**
 a small dog with short legs and upright ears

cork *NOUN* **corks**
 ① the lightweight bark of a kind of oak tree ② a stopper for a bottle, made of cork or other material

cork *VERB* **corks, corking, corked**
 to close a bottle or other container with a cork

corkscrew *NOUN* **corkscrews**
 ① a device for removing corks from bottles ② a spiral

corm *NOUN* **corms**
 a part of a plant rather like a bulb

cormorant *NOUN* **cormorants**
 a large black seabird

corn *NOUN*
 ① the seed of wheat and similar plants ② a plant, such as wheat, grown for its grain ③ a small hard painful lump on the foot

cornea *NOUN* **corneas**
 the transparent covering over the pupil of the eye

corned beef *NOUN*
 tinned beef preserved with salt

corner *NOUN* **corners**
 ① the angle or area where two lines or sides or walls meet or where two streets join ② a free hit or kick from the corner of a hockey or football field ③ a remote or distant region • *a quiet corner of the world*

corner *VERB* **corners, cornering, cornered**
 ① to drive someone into a corner or other position from which it is difficult to escape • *He finally cornered me in the kitchen.* ② to go round a corner or a bend in the road ③ to corner the market is to get possession of all or most of something that people want

cornerstone *NOUN* **cornerstones**
 ① a stone built into the corner at the base of a building ② a vitally important part that everything else depends on

cornet *NOUN* **cornets**
 ① a cone-shaped wafer for holding ice cream ② a musical instrument rather like a trumpet but shorter and wider

cornflakes *PLURAL NOUN*
toasted maize flakes eaten as a breakfast cereal

cornflour *NOUN*
(*British*) flour made from maize or rice, used in sauces and milk puddings

cornflower *NOUN* **cornflowers**
a plant with blue flowers that grows wild in fields of corn

cornice *NOUN* **cornices**
a band of ornamental moulding on walls just below a ceiling or at the top of a building

cornucopia *NOUN*
❶ a plentiful supply of good things ❷ a horn-shaped container overflowing with fruit and flowers **WORD ORIGIN** from Latin *cornu* = horn + *copiae* = of plenty

corny *ADJECTIVE* **cornier, corniest** (*informal*)
a corny joke or remark is one that is silly or repeated so often that it no longer has much effect

corona (say kor-**oh**-na) *NOUN* **coronas**
a circle of light round something

coronary *NOUN* **coronaries**
short for **coronary thrombosis**, blockage of an artery carrying blood to the heart

coronation *NOUN* **coronations**
the ceremony of crowning a king or queen

coroner *NOUN* **coroners**
an official who holds an inquiry into the cause of a death thought to be from unnatural causes

coronet *NOUN* **coronets**
a small crown

corporal *NOUN* **corporals**
a soldier ranking next below a sergeant

corporal punishment *NOUN*
punishment by hitting or beating someone

corporate *ADJECTIVE*
shared by members of a group, especially in business • *corporate responsibility*

corporation *NOUN* **corporations**
❶ a large business company ❷ a group of people elected to govern a town

corps (say kor) *NOUN* **corps** (say korz)
❶ a special army unit • *the Medical Corps*
❷ a large group of soldiers ❸ a set of people doing the same job • *the diplomatic corps*

corps de ballet (say kor der **bal**-ay) *NOUN*
the whole group of dancers (not the soloists) in a ballet

corpse *NOUN* **corpses**
a dead body

corpulent *ADJECTIVE*
having a bulky body; fat

corpuscle *NOUN* **corpuscles**
one of the red or white cells in blood

corral (say kor-**ahl**) *NOUN* **corrals** (*North American*)
an enclosure for horses or cattle on a farm or ranch

correct *ADJECTIVE*
❶ true or accurate; without any mistakes
❷ correct behaviour is behaving properly or in a way that people approve of
➤ **correctness** *NOUN*

correct *VERB* **corrects, correcting, corrected**
❶ to make a thing correct by altering or adjusting it • *She quickly corrected a couple of spelling mistakes.* ❷ to mark the mistakes in something ❸ to tell someone what mistake they have just made • *'It's Tom, not Tim,' he corrected me.*
➤ **corrective** *ADJECTIVE*

correction *NOUN* **corrections**
❶ a change made in something in order to correct it • *I've made a few small corrections to your letter.* ❷ correcting something • *Some of the punctuation may need correction.*

correctly *ADVERB*
in the right way, without any mistakes • *He guessed my age correctly.*

correspond *VERB* **corresponds, corresponding, corresponded**
❶ to agree or match • *Your story corresponds with his.* ❷ to be similar or equivalent • *Their assembly corresponds to our parliament.*
❸ people correspond when they write letters to each other

correspondence *NOUN*
❶ letters or writing letters ❷ similarity or agreement between things

SPELLING
Don't forget the double r in **correspondence**.

correspondent NOUN **correspondents**
❶ a person who writes letters to someone
else ❷ a person employed to gather news and
send reports to a newspaper or broadcasting
station

corridor NOUN **corridors**
a passage in a building

corroborate VERB **corroborates,
corroborating, corroborated**
to help to confirm a statement etc. • *Can
anyone corroborate your story?*
➤ **corroboration** NOUN

corrode VERB **corrodes, corroding, corroded**
to destroy metal gradually by chemical action
➤ **corrosion** NOUN

corrosive ADJECTIVE
able to corrode something • *corrosive acid*

corrugated ADJECTIVE
shaped into alternate ridges and grooves • *a
roof made of corrugated iron*

corrupt ADJECTIVE
❶ dishonest; willing to accept bribes
❷ wicked or immoral ❸ (*in computing*)
corrupt data is unreliable because of errors
or faults

corrupt VERB **corrupts, corrupting, corrupted**
❶ to cause someone to become dishonest or
wicked ❷ (*in computing*) a bug or other fault
corrupts data when it makes it unreliable or
impossible to read

corruption NOUN
dishonest behaviour by people in authority

corsair NOUN **corsairs**
❶ a pirate ship ❷ a pirate

corset NOUN **corsets**
a close-fitting piece of underwear worn to
shape or support the body

cortège (say kort-**ay** zh) NOUN **cortèges**
a funeral procession

cosh NOUN **coshes**
(*British*) a thick heavy stick used as a weapon

cosine NOUN **cosines**
in a right-angled triangle, the ratio of the
length of a side adjacent to one of the acute
angles to the length of the hypotenuse.
Compare with **sine**.

cosmetic NOUN **cosmetics**
a substance put on the face to make it look
more attractive, e.g. lipstick or face powder

cosmetic surgery NOUN
surgery carried out to make people look more
attractive

cosmic ADJECTIVE
❶ to do with the universe ❷ to do with outer
space • *cosmic rays*

cosmonaut NOUN **cosmonauts**
a Russian astronaut

cosmopolitan ADJECTIVE
from many countries; containing people from
many countries • *a cosmopolitan city*

cosmos (say **koz**-moss) NOUN
the universe

Cossack NOUN **Cossacks**
a member of a people of south Russia,
famous as horsemen

cosset VERB **cossets, cosseting, cosseted**
to pamper someone or treat them very kindly
and lovingly

cost NOUN **costs**
❶ the amount of money needed to buy, do or
make something ❷ the effort or loss needed
to achieve something • *She saved them at
the cost of her own life.*
➤ **at all costs** or **at any cost** no matter what
the cost or difficulty may be

cost VERB **costs, costing, cost**
❶ to have a certain amount as the price or
charge ❷ to cause the loss of something
• *This war has cost many lives.* ❸ past tense
is **costed** to estimate the cost of something

costermonger NOUN **costermongers**
(*British*) (*old use*) a person who sells fruit and
vegetables from a barrow in the street

costly ADJECTIVE **costlier, costliest**
expensive

cost of living NOUN
the average amount each person in a country
spends on food, clothing and housing

costume NOUN **costumes**
❶ a set or style of clothes, especially for a
particular purpose or of a particular place or
period ❷ the clothes worn by an actor

cosy ADJECTIVE **cosier, cosiest**
warm and comfortable
➤ **cosily** ADVERB
➤ **cosiness** NOUN

cosy NOUN **cosies**
a cover placed over a teapot or boiled egg to
keep it hot

cot *NOUN* **cots**
(*British*) a baby's bed with high sides

cottage *NOUN* **cottages**
a small simple house, especially in the country

cottage cheese *NOUN*
soft white cheese made from curds of skimmed milk

cottage pie *NOUN* **cottage pies**
(*British*) a dish of minced meat covered with mashed potato and baked

cottager *NOUN* **cottagers**
a person who lives in a country cottage

cotton *NOUN*
❶ a soft white substance covering the seeds of a tropical plant; the plant itself ❷ thread made from this substance ❸ cloth made from cotton thread

cotton wool *NOUN*
soft fluffy wadding originally made from cotton

couch *NOUN* **couches**
❶ a long soft seat like a sofa but with only one end raised ❷ a sofa or settee

couch *VERB* **couches, couching, couched**
to express something in words of a certain kind • *The request was couched in polite terms.*

cougar (say **koo**-ger) *NOUN* **cougars**
(*North American*) a puma

cough (say kof) *VERB* **coughs, coughing, coughed**
to send out air from the lungs with a sudden sharp sound

cough *NOUN* **coughs**
❶ the act or sound of coughing ❷ an illness that makes you cough

could
past tense of **can** *VERB*

couldn't (*mainly spoken*)
could not

> **SPELLING**
> **Couldn't = could + not.** Add an apostrophe between the n and the t.

council *NOUN* **councils**
a group of people chosen or elected to organize or discuss something, especially those elected to organize the affairs of a town or county

council house *NOUN* **council houses**
(*British*) a house owned and let to tenants by a town council

councillor *NOUN* **councillors**
a member of a town or county council

council tax *NOUN* **council taxes**
a tax paid to a local authority to pay for local services, based on the estimated value of your house or flat

counsel *NOUN* **counsels**
❶ (*formal*) advice given by someone • *Thank you, I will follow your counsel.* ❷ a barrister or group of barristers representing someone in a lawsuit

> **SPELLING**
> **Counsel** is different from **council**, which means a group of people chosen to run something.

counsel *VERB* **counsels, counselling, counselled**
to give advice to someone

counsellor *NOUN* **counsellors**
a person whose job is to give advice

count *VERB* **counts, counting, counted**
❶ to find the total of something by using numbers ❷ to say a sequence of numbers in their proper order ❸ to include something in a total • *There are six of us, counting the dog.* ❹ to be important • *It's what you do that counts.* ❺ to regard or consider something in a particular way • *I should count it an honour to be invited.*
➤ **count on someone** or **something** to rely on a person or thing

count *NOUN* **counts**
❶ a number reached by counting • *On the count of three, let go of the rope.* ❷ each of the points being considered, e.g. in accusing someone of crimes • *He was found guilty on all counts.* ❸ a foreign nobleman

countdown *NOUN* **countdowns**
counting numbers backwards to zero before an event, especially the launching of a space rocket

countenance *NOUN* **countenances**
a person's face or the expression on a person's face

countenance *VERB* **countenances, countenancing, countenanced**
to give approval to or allow something • *Will they countenance this plan?*

a
b
c
d
e
f
g
h
i
j
k
l
m
n
o
p
q
r
s
t
u
v
w
x
y
z

A B C D E F G H I J K L M N O P Q R S T U V W X Y Z

counter NOUN counters
❶ a flat surface over which customers are served in a shop, bank or office ❷ a small round playing piece used in certain board games ❸ a device for counting things

counter VERB counters, countering, countered
❶ to reply to someone by trying to prove that what they said is not true • 'No, I never said that,' Chris countered. ❷ to try to reduce or prevent the bad effects of something

counter ADVERB
contrary to something • This is counter to what we really want.

counteract VERB counteracts, counteracting, counteracted
to act against something and reduce or prevent its effects

counter-attack VERB counter-attacks, counter-attacking, counter-attacked
to attack in response to an enemy's attack
➤ **counter-attack** NOUN

counterbalance NOUN counterbalances
a weight or influence that balances another
➤ **counterbalance** VERB

counterfeit (say **kownt**-er-feet) ADJECTIVE
fake; not genuine • They were using counterfeit money.

counterfeit NOUN counterfeits
a forgery or imitation

counterfeit VERB counterfeits, counterfeiting, counterfeited
to forge or make an imitation of something

counterfoil NOUN counterfoils
(British) a section of a cheque or receipt etc. that is torn off and kept as a record

counterpane NOUN counterpanes
a bedspread

counterpart NOUN counterparts
a person or thing that corresponds to another • Their President is the counterpart of our Prime Minister.

counterpoint NOUN
a method of combining melodies in harmony

countersign VERB countersigns, countersigning, countersigned
to add another signature to a document to give it authority

counterweight NOUN
a counterbalancing weight or influence

countess NOUN countesses
the wife or widow of a count or earl; a female count

countless ADJECTIVE
too many to count • I have told you countless times.

countrified ADJECTIVE
like the countryside

country NOUN countries
❶ the land occupied by a nation ❷ all the people of a country ❸ the countryside

country dance NOUN country dances
a folk dance

countryman NOUN countrymen
❶ a man who lives in the countryside ❷ a man who comes from the same country as you do

countryside NOUN
an area with fields, woods, villages, etc. away from towns

countrywoman NOUN countrywomen
❶ a woman who lives in the countryside ❷ a woman who comes from the same country as you do

county NOUN counties
each of the main areas that a country is divided into for local government

coup (say koo) NOUN coups
❶ the sudden overthrow of a government; a coup d'état ❷ a sudden action taken to win power; a clever victory **WORD ORIGIN** French, = a blow

coup de grâce (say koo der **grahs**) NOUN
a stroke or blow that puts an end to something **WORD ORIGIN** French, = mercy-blow

coup d'état (say koo day-**tah**) NOUN coups d'état
the sudden overthrow of a government
WORD ORIGIN French, = blow of State

couple NOUN couples
two people or things considered together; a pair

couple VERB couples, coupling, coupled
to fasten or link two things together • The fog, coupled with the amount of traffic, made driving very difficult.

couplet NOUN couplets
a pair of lines in rhyming verse

coupon *NOUN* **coupons**
a piece of paper that gives you the right to receive or do something

courage *NOUN*
the ability to face danger or difficulty or pain even when you are afraid; bravery

courageous *ADJECTIVE*
ready to face danger or difficulty or pain even when you are afraid

courgette (say koor-zh **et**) *NOUN* **courgettes**
(*British*) a kind of small vegetable marrow

courier (say **koor**-ee-er) *NOUN* **couriers**
❶ a messenger who takes goods or documents ❷ a person employed to guide and help a group of tourists

course *NOUN* **courses**
❶ the direction followed by something • *The ship's course was to the west.* ❷ a series of events or actions; a way of proceeding • *Your best course is to start again.* ❸ a series of lessons or exercises in learning something ❹ part of a meal • *the meat course* ❺ a racecourse or golf course
➤ **in the course of something** during something • *He mentioned it in the course of the conversation.*
➤ **of course** without a doubt; as we expected

course *VERB* **courses, coursing, coursed**
to move or flow freely • *Tears coursed down his cheeks.*

court *NOUN* **courts**
❶ the royal household ❷ a law court; the judges and lawyers in a law court ❸ an enclosed area for games such as tennis or netball ❹ a courtyard

court *VERB* **courts, courting, courted**
❶ to try to get someone's support ❷ (*old use*) to try to win someone's love

courteous (say **ker**-tee-us) *ADJECTIVE*
polite and helpful
➤ **courteously** *ADVERB*

courtesy (say **ker**-tiss-ee) *NOUN*
polite behaviour towards other people • *She didn't even have the courtesy to say she was sorry.*

courtier *NOUN* **courtiers** (*old use*)
one of a king's or queen's companions at court

courtly *ADJECTIVE*
dignified and polite

court martial *NOUN* **courts martial**
❶ a court for trying members of the armed

services who have broken military law ❷ a trial in this court

court-martial *VERB* **court-martials, court-martialling, court-martialled**
to try a person by a court martial

courtship *NOUN*
❶ (*old use*) a period of courting someone in the hope of marrying them ❷ the mating ritual of some birds and animals • *a courtship display*

courtyard *NOUN* **courtyards**
a space surrounded by walls or buildings

cousin *NOUN* **cousins**
a child of your uncle or aunt

cove *NOUN* **coves**
a small bay

coven (say **kuv**-en) *NOUN* **covens**
a group of witches

covenant (say **kuv**-en-ant) *NOUN* **covenants**
a formal agreement or contract

Coventry *NOUN*
➤ **send a person to Coventry** to refuse to speak to him or her
WORD ORIGIN possibly because, during the English Civil War, Cavalier prisoners were sent to Coventry (a city in the Midlands): the citizens supported the Roundheads, and would not speak to the Cavaliers

cover *VERB* **covers, covering, covered**
❶ to place one thing over or round another; to conceal something ❷ to deal with or include a particular subject • *The book covers all aspects of photography.* ❸ to travel a certain distance • *We covered ten miles a day.* ❹ to aim a gun at or near somebody • *I've got you covered.* ❺ to protect something by insurance or a guarantee • *These goods are covered against fire or theft.* ❻ to be enough money to pay for something • *Do you have enough to cover your fare?*
➤ **cover something up** to conceal an awkward fact or piece of information

cover *NOUN* **covers**
❶ a thing used for covering something else; a lid, wrapper, envelope, etc. ❷ the binding of a book ❸ a place where you can hide or take shelter • *We took cover from the rain under a tree.*

coverage *NOUN*
the amount of time or space given to reporting an event in a newspaper or broadcast

coverlet NOUN coverlets
a bedspread

covert (say **kuv**-ert) NOUN coverts
an area of thick bushes in which birds and animals hide

covert (say koh-**vert**) ADJECTIVE
done secretly • *a covert police operation*

cover-up NOUN cover-ups
an attempt to conceal information about something, especially a crime or mistake

covet (say **kuv**-it) VERB covets, coveting, coveted
to wish to have something that belongs to someone else • *She had always coveted her sister's room.*
➤ **covetous** ADJECTIVE

covey (say **kuv**-ee) NOUN coveys
a group of partridges

cow NOUN cows
❶ the fully-grown female of cattle ❷ the fully-grown female of certain large animals, e.g. the elephant, whale or seal

cow VERB cows, cowing, cowed
to frighten someone into doing what you want them to • *Everyone looked cowed and weary.*

coward NOUN cowards
a person who has no courage and shows fear in a shameful way
➤ **cowardice** NOUN

cowardly ADJECTIVE
behaving like a coward; lacking courage

cowboy NOUN cowboys
a man in charge of grazing cattle on a ranch in the USA

cower VERB cowers, cowering, cowered
to crouch or shrink back in fear

cowl NOUN cowls
❶ a monk's hood ❷ a hood-shaped covering, e.g. on a chimney

cowshed NOUN cowsheds
a shed for cattle

cowslip NOUN cowslips
a wild plant with small yellow flowers in spring

cox NOUN coxes
a person who steers a rowing boat

coxswain (say **kok**-swayn or **kok**-sun) NOUN coxswains
❶ a cox ❷ a sailor with special duties

coy ADJECTIVE
pretending to be shy or modest
➤ **coyly** ADVERB

coyote (say koi-**oh**-ti) NOUN coyotes
a North American mammal, similar to but smaller than a wolf

crab NOUN crabs
a shellfish with ten legs, the first pair being a set of pincers

crab apple NOUN crab apples
a small sour apple

crack NOUN cracks
❶ a line on the surface of something where it has broken but not come completely apart ❷ a narrow gap ❸ a sudden sharp noise • *the crack of a pistol shot* ❹ a hard knock or blow • *a crack on the head* ❺ (*informal*) a joke; a wisecrack ❻ a drug made from cocaine

crack ADJECTIVE (*informal*) first-class • *He is a crack shot.*

crack VERB cracks, cracking, cracked
❶ to make a crack in something ❷ to split without breaking • *The plate has cracked.* ❸ to make a sudden sharp noise ❹ to break down • *He finally cracked under the strain.* ❺ to solve a problem • *Have you cracked the code yet?*
➤ **crack a joke** to tell a joke
➤ **crack down on something** (*informal*) to stop something that is illegal or against rules
➤ **get cracking** (*informal*) to get busy

cracker NOUN crackers
❶ a paper tube that bangs when pulled apart ❷ a thin biscuit

crackle VERB crackles, crackling, crackled
to make small cracking sounds • *The fire crackled in the grate.*
➤ **crackle** NOUN

crackling NOUN
crisp skin on roast pork

cradle NOUN cradles
❶ a small cot for a baby ❷ a supporting framework

cradle VERB cradles, cradling, cradled
to hold someone or something gently and protectively • *She was cradling a kitten in her arms.*

craft NOUN crafts
❶ a job that needs skill, especially with the hands ❷ skill in doing your work • *He is a master of the craft of cooking.* ❸ cunning or trickery ❹ craft a ship or boat; an aircraft or spacecraft

craftsman, craftswoman NOUN craftsmen or craftswomen
a person who is good at a craft
➤ **craftsmanship** NOUN

crafty ADJECTIVE **craftier, craftiest**
cunning or deceitful
➤ **craftily** ADVERB
➤ **craftiness** NOUN

crag NOUN crags
a steep piece of rough rock

craggy ADJECTIVE
❶ steep and rocky • *a craggy coastline* ❷ a craggy face is strong and has deep lines in it • *his craggy features*

cram VERB crams, cramming, crammed
❶ to push many things into something so that it is very full • *I managed to cram all my clothes into one bag.* ❷ to learn as many facts as you can in a short time just before an examination

cramp NOUN cramps
pain caused by a muscle tightening suddenly

cramp VERB cramps, cramping, cramped
to hinder someone's freedom or growth

cramped ADJECTIVE
in a space that is too small or tight • *The four of us felt cramped sleeping in the same room.*

cranberry NOUN cranberries
a small sour red berry used for making jelly and sauce

crane NOUN cranes
❶ a machine for lifting and moving heavy objects ❷ a large wading bird with long legs and a long slender neck

crane VERB cranes, craning, craned
to crane your neck is to stretch it to try to see something

crane fly NOUN crane flies
a flying insect with very long thin legs

cranium NOUN craniums
the skull

crank NOUN cranks
❶ an L-shaped part used for changing the direction of movement in machinery ❷ a person with strange or fanatical ideas

crank VERB cranks, cranking, cranked
to turn or move something using a crank

cranky ADJECTIVE (*informal*)
❶ strange or fanatical • *cranky ideas* ❷ bad-tempered

cranny NOUN crannies
a narrow hole or space; a crevice

crash NOUN crashes
❶ the loud noise of something breaking or colliding ❷ an accident in which a vehicle hits something violently and is badly damaged • *a car crash* ❸ a sudden drop or failure

crash VERB crashes, crashing, crashed
❶ a vehicle crashes when it hits something violently and is badly damage • *We crashed into the car in front.* ❷ to move or fall with a crash • *The tree crashed to the ground.* ❸ a computer system crashes when it stops working suddenly

crash ADJECTIVE
done rapidly and intensively • *a crash course*

crash helmet NOUN crash helmets
a padded helmet worn by cyclists and motorcyclists to protect the head

crash landing NOUN crash landings
an emergency landing of an aircraft, which usually damages it
➤ **crash-land** VERB

crass ADJECTIVE
very stupid or insensitive • *crass remarks*

crate NOUN crates
❶ a packing case made of strips of wood ❷ an open container with compartments for carrying bottles

crater NOUN craters
❶ the mouth of a volcano ❷ a wide hole in the ground caused by an explosion or by something hitting it • *the Moon's craters*

cravat NOUN cravats
a short wide scarf worn by men round the neck and tucked into an open-necked shirt
(WORD ORIGIN) from French *Cravate* = Croatian (because Croatian soldiers wore linen cravats)

crave VERB craves, craving, craved
❶ to want something very strongly
❷ (*formal*) to beg for something • *I humbly crave forgiveness.*

craven ADJECTIVE
cowardly

craving NOUN cravings
a strong desire; a longing

crawl VERB crawls, crawling, crawled
❶ to move with the body close to the ground or other surface or on hands and knees
❷ traffic crawls when it moves slowly ❸ a place is crawling with unpleasant things or

a b c d e f g h i j k l m n o p q r s t u v w x y z

people when there are a lot of them there
• *The floor was crawling with insects.*

crawl NOUN
❶ a crawling movement ❷ a very slow pace
❸ an overarm swimming stroke

crayon NOUN **crayons**
a stick or pencil of coloured wax etc. for
drawing

craze NOUN **crazes**
a brief enthusiasm for something

crazed ADJECTIVE
driven insane

crazy ADJECTIVE **crazier, craziest**
❶ insane ❷ very foolish • *this crazy idea*
➤ **crazily** ADVERB
➤ **craziness** NOUN

crazy paving NOUN
(*British*) paving made of pieces of stone of
different shapes and sizes fitted together

creak NOUN **creaks**
a harsh squeak like that of a stiff door hinge

creak VERB **creaks, creaking, creaked**
to make a creak

creaky ADJECTIVE
making creaks • *creaky floorboards*

cream NOUN **creams**
❶ the fatty part of milk ❷ a yellowish-white
colour ❸ a food containing or looking like
cream • *chocolate cream* ❹ a soft substance
• *face cream* ❺ the best people or things
• *the cream of the world's tennis players*

cream VERB **creams, creaming, creamed**
to make something creamy; to beat a mixture
until it is soft like cream
➤ **cream something off** to remove the best
part of something • *The big clubs cream off
the best young players.*

creamy ADJECTIVE **creamier, creamiest**
❶ smooth and thick like cream ❷ pale
yellowish-white in colour • *creamy skin*

crease NOUN **creases**
❶ a line made in something by folding,
pressing or crushing it ❷ a line on a cricket
pitch marking a batsman's or bowler's
position

crease VERB **creases, creasing, creased**
to make a crease or creases in something

create VERB **creates, creating, created**
❶ to make or produce something, especially
something that no one has made before ❷ to
bring something into existence; to make

something happen • *The bad weather created
huge problems for us.*

creation NOUN **creations**
❶ the act of creating something
❷ something that has been created

creative ADJECTIVE
showing imagination and thought as well as
skill • *his creative use of language*
➤ **creativity** NOUN

creator NOUN **creators**
a person who creates something
➤ **the Creator** a name for God

creature NOUN **creatures**
a living being, especially an animal

crèche (say kresh) NOUN **crèches**
a place where babies and young children are
looked after while their parents are at work

credence NOUN
if you give credence to something, you
believe that it is true • *He gave no credence
to their story.*

credentials PLURAL NOUN
❶ documents showing a person's identity,
qualifications, etc. ❷ a person's past
achievements that make them suitable for
something

credible ADJECTIVE
able to be believed; convincing
➤ **credibly** ADVERB
➤ **credibility** NOUN

> **USAGE**
> Take care not to confuse with **credulous**.

credit NOUN **credits**
❶ a source of pride or honour • *He is a credit
to the school.* ❷ praise or acknowledgement
given for some achievement or good quality
• *I must give you credit for persistence.*
❸ an arrangement allowing a person to buy
something and not pay for it until later on
❹ an amount of money in an account at a
bank etc. or entered in a financial account as
paid in. Compare with **debit**. ❺ belief or trust
• *I put no credit in this rumour.*
➤ **credits** a list of people who have helped to
produce a film or television programme

credit VERB **credits, crediting, credited**
❶ to believe something ❷ to believe or
say that a person has done or achieved
something • *Columbus is credited with the
discovery of America.* ❸ to enter something
as a credit in a financial account. Compare
with **debit**.

creditable *ADJECTIVE*
deserving praise • *That was a very creditable result.*
➤ **creditably** *ADVERB*

credit card *NOUN* **credit cards**
a plastic card that you can use to buy something and pay for it later on

creditor *NOUN* **creditors**
a person to whom money is owed

credulous *ADJECTIVE*
too ready to believe things; gullible

> **USAGE**
> Take care not to confuse with **credible**.

creed *NOUN* **creeds**
a set or formal statement of religious beliefs

creek *NOUN* **creeks**
❶ (*British*) a narrow inlet ❷ (*North American & Australian*) a small stream
➤ **up the creek** (*informal*) in difficulties

creep *VERB* **creeps, creeping, crept**
❶ to move quietly and slowly • *She crept into the room so as not to wake him.* ❷ to move along close to the ground ❸ to appear or increase gradually • *A slight feeling of suspicion crept over me.* ❹ your flesh creeps when it prickles with fear

creep *NOUN* **creeps**
(*informal*) an unpleasant person, especially one who is always trying to get other people's approval
➤ **the creeps** (*informal*) a feeling or fear or disgust • *There's something about him that gives me the creeps.*

> **SPELLING**
> The past tense of **creep** is **crept**. Do not add **ed**.

creeper *NOUN* **creepers**
a plant that grows along the ground or up a wall

creepy *ADJECTIVE* **creepier, creepiest**
(*informal*) slightly frightening and sinister

cremate *VERB* **cremates, cremating, cremated**
to burn a dead body to ashes
➤ **cremation** *NOUN*

crematorium *NOUN* **crematoria**
a place where dead people are cremated

crème de la crème (say krem der la krem) *NOUN*
the very best of something

creosote *NOUN*
an oily brown liquid painted on wood to prevent it from rotting

crêpe (say krayp) *NOUN* **crêpes**
a thin pancake

crêpe paper *NOUN*
paper with a wrinkled surface

crescendo (say krish-**end**-oh) *NOUN* **crescendos**
a gradual increase in loudness

crescent *NOUN* **crescents**
❶ a narrow curved shape coming to a point at each end ❷ a curved street forming an arc
WORD ORIGIN originally = the new moon: from Latin *crescens* = growing

cress *NOUN*
a plant with hot-tasting leaves, used in salads and sandwiches

crest *NOUN* **crests**
❶ a tuft of hair, skin or feathers on an animal's or bird's head ❷ the top of a hill or wave ❸ a design used as the symbol of a family or organization
➤ **crested** *ADJECTIVE*

crestfallen *ADJECTIVE*
disappointed or dejected

cretin (say **kret**-in) *NOUN* **cretins** (*offensive*)
a stupid person

crevasse (say kri-**vass**) *NOUN* **crevasses**
a deep open crack, especially in a glacier

crevice *NOUN* **crevices**
a narrow opening, especially in a rock or wall

crew *NOUN* **crews**
❶ the people working in a ship or aircraft ❷ a group working together • *a film crew*

crew *VERB*
past tense of **crow** *VERB*

crib *NOUN* **cribs**
❶ a baby's cot ❷ a framework holding fodder for animals ❸ a model representing the Nativity of Jesus Christ ❹ a piece of paper with answers to questions on it, used dishonestly by a student in an examination ❺ cribbage

crib *VERB* **cribs, cribbing, cribbed**
to copy someone else's work

cribbage *NOUN*
a card game

crick *NOUN* **cricks**
painful stiffness in the neck or back

cricket *NOUN*
❶ a game played outdoors between teams with a ball, bats and two wickets ❷ a brown insect like a grasshopper
➤ **cricketer** *NOUN*

crime *NOUN* **crimes**
❶ breaking the law • *They say crime does not pay.* ❷ an act that breaks the law • *Arson is a very serious crime.*

criminal *NOUN* **criminals**
a person who has committed a crime or crimes

criminal *ADJECTIVE*
to do with crime or criminals
➤ **criminally** *ADVERB*

criminology *NOUN*
the study of crime

crimp *VERB* **crimps, crimping, crimped**
to press something into small ridges

crimson *ADJECTIVE*
deep red
➤ **crimson** *NOUN*
WORD ORIGIN from Arabic *kirmiz* = an insect which was used to make crimson dye

cringe *VERB* **cringes, cringing, cringed**
❶ to shrink back in fear; to cower ❷ to feel embarrassed • *I cringe when I think of the stories I used to write.*

crinkle *VERB* **crinkles, crinkling, crinkled**
to make something have creases or wrinkles in it • *The boy crinkled his nose.*
➤ **crinkly** *ADJECTIVE*

crinoline *NOUN* **crinolines**
a long skirt worn over a framework that makes it stand out

cripple *NOUN* **cripples**
a person who is permanently lame

cripple *VERB* **cripples, crippling, crippled**
❶ to make a person lame ❷ to weaken or damage something seriously

crisis *NOUN* **crises**
an important and dangerous or difficult situation • *The country was facing a financial crisis.*

crisp *ADJECTIVE*
❶ very dry so that it breaks with a snap ❷ fresh and stiff • *a crisp £10 note* ❸ cold and dry • *a crisp winter morning* ❹ brisk and sharp • *He has a crisp manner.*
➤ **crispness** *NOUN*

crisp *NOUN* **crisps**
a very thin fried slice of potato, usually sold in packets

crisply *ADVERB*
in a brisk and sharp way • *'Take a seat,' she said crisply.*

criss–cross *ADJECTIVE & ADVERB*
with crossing lines

criss–cross *VERB* **criss-crosses, criss-crossing, criss-crossed**
to form a pattern of crossing lines

criterion (say kry-**teer**-ee-on) *NOUN* **criteria**
a standard or principle by which something is judged or decided
USAGE
Note that **criteria** is a plural. You should say *this criterion* and *these criteria*, and not 'this criteria'.

critic *NOUN* **critics**
❶ a person who gives opinions on books, plays, films, music, etc. ❷ a person who criticizes

critical *ADJECTIVE*
❶ pointing out faults or weaknesses in a person or thing • *Why do you always have to be so critical?* ❷ to do with or at a crisis; very serious • *The patient is in a critical condition.* ❸ to do with critics or criticism

critically *ADVERB*
❶ extremely and seriously • *She is critically ill.* ❷ in a critical way

criticism *NOUN* **criticisms**
❶ pointing out faults and weaknesses ❷ the work of a critic

criticize (also **criticise**) *VERB* **criticizes, criticizing, criticized**
to say that a person or thing has faults or weaknesses

croak *NOUN* **croaks**
a deep hoarse sound like that of a frog

croak *VERB* **croaks, croaking, croaked**
to make a croak

crochet (say **kroh**-shay) *NOUN*
a kind of needlework done by using a hooked needle to loop a thread into patterns
➤ **crochet** *VERB* **crochets, crocheting, crocheted**

crock *NOUN* **crocks**
❶ a piece of crockery ❷ (*British*) (*informal*) an old person or an old car in a bad condition

crockery *NOUN*
dishes, plates, cups, etc.

crocodile *NOUN* **crocodiles**
❶ a large tropical reptile with a thick skin, long tail and huge jaws ❷ a long line of schoolchildren walking in pairs
➤ **crocodile tears** sorrow that is not sincere (so called because the crocodile was said to weep while it ate its victim)

crocus *NOUN* **crocuses**
a small plant with yellow, purple or white flowers

croft *NOUN* **crofts**
(*British*) a small rented farm in Scotland
➤ **crofter** *NOUN*

croissant (say **krwah**-sahn) *NOUN* **croissants**
a flaky crescent-shaped bread roll
WORD ORIGIN French, = crescent

crone *NOUN* **crones**
a very old woman

crony *NOUN* **cronies**
a close friend or companion

crook *NOUN* **crooks**
❶ (*informal*) a thief or other criminal ❷ a shepherd's stick with a curved end ❸ a bend at the elbow

crook *VERB* **crooks, crooking, crooked**
to crook a finger is to bend or curl it

crook *ADJECTIVE* (*Australian/NZ*) (*informal*)
bad or unwell

crooked *ADJECTIVE*
❶ bent or twisted; not straight ❷ dishonest or criminal

croon *VERB* **croons, crooning, crooned**
to sing softly and gently

crop *NOUN* **crops**
❶ a plant grown in large quantities for food • *a good crop of wheat* ❷ a very short haircut ❸ a whip with a loop instead of a lash ❹ a pouch in a bird's throat, where it stores food

crop *VERB* **crops, cropping, cropped**
❶ to cut something or bite the top off it • *Sheep were cropping the grass.* ❷ to produce a crop
➤ **crop up** to happen or appear unexpectedly • *His name just cropped up in conversation.*

cropper *NOUN*
➤ **come a cropper** (*informal*)
❶ to have a bad fall ❷ to fail badly

croquet (say **kroh**-kay) *NOUN*
a game played on a lawn with wooden balls and mallets

crore *NOUN* **crore**
(*Indian*) ten million; one hundred lakhs

crosier (say **kroh**-zee-er) *NOUN* **crosiers**
a bishop's staff shaped like a shepherd's crook

cross *NOUN* **crosses**
❶ a mark or shape made like + or x ❷ an upright post with another piece of wood across it, used in ancient times for crucifixion; **the Cross** the cross on which Christ was crucified, used as a symbol of Christianity ❸ a mixture of two different things • *She gave a cross between a groan and a laugh.*

cross *VERB* **crosses, crossing, crossed**
❶ to go across something • *She crossed the room to meet him.* ❷ to cross your arms, legs or fingers is to put one over the other ❸ to draw a line or lines across something ❹ to make the sign or shape of a cross ❺ to cross animals or plants of different kinds is to produce a new animal or plant from them
➤ **cross something out** to draw a line across something because it is unwanted or wrong

cross *ADJECTIVE*
❶ annoyed or bad-tempered ❷ going from one side to another • *There were cross winds on the bridge.*
➤ **crossly** *ADVERB*

crossbar *NOUN* **crossbars**
a horizontal bar between two uprights

crossbow *NOUN* **crossbows**
a powerful bow with a mechanism for pulling and releasing the string

cross-breed *VERB* **cross-breeds, cross-breeding, cross-bred**
to breed by mating an animal with one of a different kind
➤ **cross-breed** *NOUN*
Compare with **hybrid**.

crosse *NOUN* **crosses**
a hooked stick with a net across it, used in lacrosse

cross-examine *VERB* **cross-examines, cross-examining, cross-examined**
to question a witness called by the other side in a law court, to check the evidence they have already given
➤ **cross-examination** *NOUN*

cross-eyed *ADJECTIVE*
with eyes that look or seem to look towards the nose

a
b
c
d
e
f
g
h
i
j
k
l
m
n
o
p
q
r
s
t
u
v
w
x
y
z

crossfire *NOUN*
lines of gunfire that cross each other

cross-hatch *VERB* **cross-hatches, cross-hatching, cross-hatched**
to shade part of a drawing with two sets of parallel lines crossing each other
➤ **cross-hatching** *NOUN*

crossing *NOUN* **crossings**
a place where people can cross a road or railway

cross-legged *ADJECTIVE & ADVERB*
with ankles crossed and knees spread apart

cross-question *VERB* **cross-questions, cross-questioning, cross-questioned**
to question someone carefully in order to test answers they have already given

cross-reference *NOUN* **cross-references**
a note telling readers to look at another part of a book etc. for more information

crossroads *NOUN* **crossroads**
a place where two or more roads cross one another

cross-section *NOUN* **cross-sections**
❶ a drawing of something as if it has been cut through ❷ a typical sample from a larger group

crosswise *ADVERB & ADJECTIVE*
with one thing crossing another

crossword *NOUN* **crosswords**
a puzzle in which words have to be guessed from clues and then written into the blank squares in a diagram

crotch *NOUN* **crotches**
the part between the legs where they join the body; a similar angle in a forked part

crotchet *NOUN* **crotchets**
a note in music, which usually represents one beat (written ♩)

crotchety *ADJECTIVE*
bad-tempered or irritable

crouch *VERB* **crouches, crouching, crouched**
to lower your body, with your arms and legs bent • *He crouched down beside her.*

croup (say kroop) *NOUN*
a disease causing a hard cough and difficulty in breathing

crow *NOUN* **crows**
❶ a large black bird ❷ a shrill cry like that of a cock
➤ **as the crow flies** in a straight line

crow *VERB* **crows, crowing, crowed or crew**
❶ to make a shrill cry as a cock does ❷ to boast or be triumphant • *He's crowing because he beat me at table tennis.*

crowbar *NOUN* **crowbars**
an iron bar used as a lever

crowd *NOUN* **crowds**
a large number of people in one place

crowd *VERB* **crowds, crowding, crowded**
❶ to come together in large numbers; to form a crowd • *Photographers crowded around outside.* ❷ to make a place uncomfortably full of people • *Tourists crowded the streets.* • *Somehow we all crowded into their small living room.*

crowded *ADJECTIVE*
full of people • *a crowded bus*

crown *NOUN* **crowns**
❶ an ornamental headdress worn by a king or queen ❷ (often **Crown**) the king or queen • *This land belongs to the Crown.* ❸ the highest part • *the crown of the road* ❹ a former coin worth 5 shillings (25p)
➤ **Crown Prince** or **Crown Princess** the heir to the throne

crown *VERB* **crowns, crowning, crowned**
❶ to place a crown on someone as a symbol of royal power or victory ❷ to form or cover or decorate the top of something • *The mountain was crowned with snow.* ❸ to reward something; to make a successful end to something • *Our efforts were crowned with victory.* ❹ (*informal*) to hit someone on the head

Crown Court *NOUN* **Crown Courts**
a law court where criminal cases are tried

crow's nest *NOUN* **crow's nests**
a lookout platform high up on a ship's mast

crucial (say **kroo**-shal) *ADJECTIVE*
extremely important because it will affect other things • *a crucial decision* • *It is crucial that we get this right.*

crucible *NOUN* **crucibles**
a melting pot for metals

crucifix *NOUN* **crucifixes**
a model of a cross with a figure of Christ on it

crucify *VERB* **crucifies, crucifying, crucified**
to put a person to death by nailing or tying their hands and feet to a cross
➤ **crucifixion** *NOUN*

crude *ADJECTIVE*
❶ in a natural state; not yet processed or

refined • *crude oil* ❷ not well finished; rough and simple • *a crude carving* ❸ rude or coarse
➤ **crudely** *ADVERB*

cruel *ADJECTIVE* **crueller, cruellest**
deliberately causing pain or suffering to others
➤ **cruelly** *ADVERB*

cruelty *NOUN* **cruelties**
cruel behaviour • *He has campaigned against cruelty to animals.*

cruet *NOUN* **cruets**
a set of small containers for salt, pepper, oil, etc. for use at the table

cruise *NOUN* **cruises**
a voyage on a ship, taken as a holiday

cruise *VERB* **cruises, cruising, cruised**
❶ to sail or travel at a gentle or steady speed ❷ to have a cruise

cruiser *NOUN* **cruisers**
❶ a fast warship ❷ a large motor boat

crumb *NOUN* **crumbs**
a tiny piece of bread, cake or biscuit

crumble *VERB* **crumbles, crumbling, crumbled**
❶ to break something into small pieces • *We crumbled up some bread and threw it to the birds.* ❷ to fall or break into small pieces • *The castle walls were beginning to crumble.*

crumble *NOUN* **crumbles** (*British*) a dessert made with fruit cooked with a crumbly topping • *apple crumble*

crumbly *ADJECTIVE*
that easily breaks into small pieces • *crumbly cheese*

crumpet *NOUN* **crumpets**
a soft flat cake made with yeast, eaten toasted with butter

crumple *VERB* **crumples, crumpling, crumpled**
to crush something or become crushed, into creases or folds • *He crumpled the letter into a ball and threw it away.* • *The front of the car crumpled when it hit the wall.*

crunch *VERB* **crunches, crunching, crunched**
to crush something noisily, for example between your teeth or under your feet • *We crunched through the snow.*

crunch *NOUN* **crunches**
a crunching sound
➤ **the crunch** (*informal*) a crucial event or turning point

crunchy *ADJECTIVE*
crunchy food is firm and crisp and makes a noise when you bite it • *a crunchy apple*

Crusade *NOUN* **Crusades**
a military expedition made by Christians in the Middle Ages to recover the Holy Land from the Muslims who had conquered it
➤ **Crusader** *NOUN*

crusade *NOUN* **crusades**
a campaign against something you believe is wrong or to achieve something you believe is right

crush *VERB* **crushes, crushing, crushed**
❶ to press or squeeze something so that it gets broken or harmed ❷ to break something into very small pieces or powder • *Now crush the garlic.* ❸ to defeat someone completely • *The army soon crushed the rebellion.*

crush *NOUN* **crushes**
❶ a crowd of people pressed together ❷ a drink made with crushed fruit

crust *NOUN* **crusts**
❶ the hard outer layer of something, especially bread ❷ the rocky outer layer of the earth

crustacean (say krust-**ay**-shon) *NOUN* **crustaceans**
an animal with a shell that lives in water, e.g. a crab, lobster or shrimp

crusty *ADJECTIVE* **crustier, crustiest**
❶ having a crisp crust ❷ bad-tempered or irritable

crutch *NOUN* **crutches**
a support like a long walking stick for helping a lame person to walk

cry *NOUN* **cries**
❶ a loud wordless sound expressing pain, grief, joy, etc. ❷ a shout • *No one heard her cries for help.* ❸ the special sound made by a bird or animal ❹ crying • *Have a good cry.*

cry *VERB* **cries, crying, cried**
❶ to shed tears; to weep ❷ to call out loudly
➤ **cry off** to say that you cannot do something that you had promised to do

crypt *NOUN* **crypts**
a room under a church, used as a chapel or burial place

cryptic *ADJECTIVE*
having a hidden meaning that is not easy to understand • *a cryptic remark*
➤ **cryptically** *ADVERB*

a
b
c
d
e
f
g
h
i
j
k
l
m
n
o
p
q
r
s
t
u
v
w
x
y
z

cryptogram *NOUN* **cryptograms**
something written in code

crystal *NOUN* **crystals**
❶ a transparent colourless mineral rather like glass ❷ very clear high-quality glass ❸ a small solid piece of a substance with a symmetrical shape • *ice crystals*

crystalline *ADJECTIVE*
made of crystals or having the structure of crystals

crystallize (also **crystallise**) *VERB* **crystallizes, crystallizing, crystallized**
❶ to form into crystals ❷ to become definite in form • *The solution to the problem began to crystallize.*
➤ **crystallization** *NOUN*

crystallized fruit *NOUN*
fruit preserved in sugar

Cub, Cub Scout *NOUN* **Cubs, Cub Scouts**
a member of the junior branch of the Scout Association

cub *NOUN* **cubs**
a young lion, tiger, fox, bear, etc.

cubbyhole *NOUN* **cubbyholes**
a small compartment or snug place

cube *NOUN* **cubes**
❶ an object that has six equal square sides, like a box or dice ❷ the number you get by multiplying a number by itself twice • *The cube of 3 is 3 x 3 x 3 = 27.*

cube *VERB* **cubes, cubing, cubed**
❶ to multiply a number by itself twice • *4 cubed is 4 x 4 x 4 = 64.* ❷ to cut something into small cubes

cube root *NOUN* **cube roots**
the number that gives a particular number if it is multiplied by itself twice • *The cube root of 27 is 3 (3 x 3 x 3 = 27).*

cubic *ADJECTIVE*
shaped like a cube
➤ **cubic metre, cubic centimetre, etc.,** the volume of a cube with sides one metre, centimetre etc. long, used as a unit of measurement for volume

cubicle *NOUN* **cubicles**
a small room made by separating off part of a larger room

cuboid (say **kew-**boid) *NOUN* **cuboids**
an object with six rectangular sides

cuckoo *NOUN* **cuckoos**
a bird that makes a sound like 'cuck-oo' and lays its eggs in other birds' nests

cucumber *NOUN* **cucumbers**
a long green-skinned vegetable eaten raw or pickled

cud *NOUN*
half-digested food that a cow brings back from its first stomach to chew again

cuddle *VERB* **cuddles, cuddling, cuddled**
to put your arms closely round a person in a loving way

cuddle *NOUN* **cuddles**
to give someone a cuddle is to put your arms closely round them in a loving way

cuddly *ADJECTIVE*
soft and pleasant to cuddle • *a cuddly toy*

cudgel *NOUN* **cudgels**
a short thick stick used as a weapon

cudgel *VERB* **cudgels, cudgelling, cudgelled**
to beat someone with a cudgel

cue *NOUN* **cues**
❶ something said or done that acts as a signal for an actor to say something or come on stage ❷ a long stick for striking the ball in billiards or snooker

cuff *NOUN* **cuffs**
❶ the end of a sleeve that fits round the wrist ❷ a light hit or slap with the hand
➤ **off the cuff** without rehearsal or preparation • *I'm just speaking off the cuff here.*

cuff *VERB* **cuffs, cuffing, cuffed**
to hit someone lightly with your hand

cufflink *NOUN* **cufflinks**
each of a pair of fasteners for shirt cuffs, used instead of buttons

cuisine (say kwiz-**een**) *NOUN* **cuisines**
a style or method of cooking • *French cuisine*

cul-de-sac *NOUN* **culs-de-sac**
a street or passage closed at one end; a dead end (WORD ORIGIN) French, = bottom of a sack

culinary *ADJECTIVE*
to do with cooking

cull *VERB* **culls, culling, culled**
❶ to collect information or ideas from different places • *I've culled lines from several poems.* ❷ to pick out and kill a number of animals from a group to reduce the population

cull *NOUN* culls
the act of culling a group of animals • *a deer cull*

culminate *VERB* culminates, culminating, culminated
to reach its highest point or final result
• *Their long struggle for freedom culminated in victory.*
➤ **culmination** *NOUN*

culprit *NOUN* culprits
the person who has done something wrong

cult *NOUN* cults
❶ a small religious group with special beliefs and practices ❷ a film, TV programme, rock group, etc. that is very popular with a particular group of people

cultivate *VERB* cultivates, cultivating, cultivated
❶ to use land to grow crops ❷ to try to make something grow or develop • *He has made an effort to cultivate a more caring image.*
➤ **cultivation** *NOUN*
➤ **cultivator** *NOUN*

cultivated *ADJECTIVE*
having good manners and education

cultural *ADJECTIVE*
❶ to do with the customs and traditions of a people • *There are cultural differences between the two communities.* ❷ to do with literature, art, music, etc. • *a cultural event*

culture *NOUN* cultures
❶ appreciation and understanding of literature, art, music, etc. ❷ the customs and traditions of a people • *West Indian culture* ❸ (*in science*) a quantity of bacteria or cells grown for study

cultured *ADJECTIVE*
educated to appreciate literature, art, music, etc.

cultured pearl *NOUN* cultured pearls
a pearl formed by an oyster when a speck of grit is put into its shell

culvert *NOUN* culverts
a tunnel taking a stream or drain under a road or railway

cumbersome *ADJECTIVE*
difficult or awkward to carry or use

cumin *NOUN*
a plant with spicy seeds that are used for flavouring foods

cummerbund *NOUN* cummerbunds
a broad sash worn round the waist

cumulative *ADJECTIVE*
increasing by continuous additions

cumulus *NOUN* cumuli
a type of cloud consisting of rounded heaps on a horizontal base

cunning *ADJECTIVE*
❶ clever at deceiving people ❷ cleverly designed or planned • *a cunning trick*

cunning *NOUN*
❶ skill in deceiving people; craftiness ❷ skill or ingenuity

cup *NOUN* cups
❶ a small bowl-shaped container for drinking from ❷ anything shaped like a cup ❸ a trophy shaped like a cup with a stem, given as a prize

cup *VERB* cups, cupping, cupped
to form your hands into the curved shape of a cup • *He cupped his hands to drink from the river.*

cupboard *NOUN* cupboards
a piece of furniture or compartment with a door, for storing things

cupful *NOUN* cupfuls
as much as a cup will hold • *a cupful of water*

cupola (say **kew**-pol-a) *NOUN* cupolas
a small dome on a roof

cur *NOUN* curs
a scruffy or bad-tempered dog

curable *ADJECTIVE*
a curable illness is one that can be cured

curate *NOUN* curates
a member of the clergy who helps a vicar

curator (say kewr-**ay**-ter) *NOUN* curators
a person in charge of a museum or other collection

curb *VERB* curbs, curbing, curbed
to keep something in check; to restrain something • *You need to curb your impatience.*

curb *NOUN* curbs
a limit or restraint on something • *Put a curb on spending.*

> **SPELLING**
> Take care not to confuse with **kerb**, which is the edge of a pavement.

a b c d e f g h i j k l m n o p q r s t u v w x y z

A B **C** D E F G H I J K L M N O P Q R S T U V W X Y Z

curd *NOUN* (or **curds**) *PLURAL NOUN*
a thick substance formed when milk turns sour

curdle *VERB* **curdles, curdling, curdled**
to form into curds or lumps
➤ **make someone's blood curdle** to horrify or terrify someone

cure *VERB* **cures, curing, cured**
❶ to get rid of someone's illness ❷ to stop something bad • *He finally cured the rattling noise in his car.* ❸ to treat meat or fish in order to preserve it • *Fish can be cured in smoke.*

cure *NOUN* **cures**
❶ something that cures a person or thing; a remedy • *They are trying to find a cure for cancer.* ❷ a return to good health; being cured • *We cannot promise a cure.*

curfew *NOUN* **curfews**
a time or signal after which people must remain indoors until the next day
WORD ORIGIN from old French *cuevrefeu*, literally = cover fire (from an old law saying that all fires should be covered or put out by a certain time each evening)

curio *NOUN* **curios**
a rare or unusual object

curiosity *NOUN* **curiosities**
❶ curiosity is being curious ❷ a curiosity is something unusual and interesting

curious *ADJECTIVE*
❶ wanting to find out about things; inquisitive • *She was curious to know what was in the box.* ❷ strange or unusual • *There was a curious silence.*
➤ **curiously** *ADVERB*

curl *NOUN* **curls**
a curve or coil, e.g. of hair

curl *VERB* **curls, curling, curled**
❶ to form into curls ❷ to move in a curve or spiral • *Smoke curled up into the sky.*
➤ **curl up** to pull your arms, legs and head close to your body • *The cat curled up in front of the fire.*

curler *NOUN* **curlers**
a device for curling the hair

curlew *NOUN* **curlews**
a wading bird with a long curved bill

curling *NOUN*
a game played on ice with large flat stones

curly *ADJECTIVE*
full of curls

currant *NOUN* **currants**
❶ a small black dried grape used in cookery ❷ a small round red, black or white berry
WORD ORIGIN from old French *raisins de Courauntz* = grapes from Corinth (a city in Greece)

SPELLING
Take care not to confuse with **current**, which means a flow of water, air or electricity.

currency *NOUN* **currencies**
❶ the money in use in a country ❷ the general use of something • *Some words have no currency now.*

current *ADJECTIVE*
happening or being used now

current *NOUN* **currents**
❶ water or air etc. moving in one direction ❷ the flow of electricity along a wire etc. or through something

SPELLING
Take care not to confuse with **currant**, which means a dried grape.

current affairs *PLURAL NOUN*
political events in the news at the moment

currently *ADVERB*
at present; at the moment • *The road is currently being repaired.*

curriculum *NOUN* **curricula**
the subjects forming a course of study in a school or university

curriculum vitae (say **vee**-ty) *NOUN* **curricula vitae**
a brief account of a person's education, career, etc., which he or she sends when applying for a job

curry *NOUN* **curries**
food cooked with spices that make it taste hot
➤ **curried** *ADJECTIVE*

curry *VERB* **curries, currying, curried**
➤ **curry favour** to try to win someone's approval or support by flattering them

curse *NOUN* **curses**
❶ a call or prayer for a person or thing to be harmed; the evil produced by this ❷ something very unpleasant • *the curse of poverty* ❸ an angry or offensive word or expression

curse *VERB* **curses, cursing, cursed**
❶ to say offensive words; to swear ❷ to use a

curse against a person or thing
➤ **be cursed with something** to suffer from something

cursor NOUN cursors
a movable indicator, usually a flashing light or arrow, on a computer screen, showing where new data will go

cursory ADJECTIVE
hasty and not thorough • *a cursory inspection*

curt ADJECTIVE
brief and hasty or rude • *a curt reply*
➤ **curtly** ADVERB
➤ **curtness** NOUN

curtail VERB curtails, curtailing, curtailed
❶ to cut something short • *The lesson was curtailed.* ❷ to reduce something • *We must curtail our spending.*
➤ **curtailment** NOUN

curtain NOUN curtains
❶ a piece of material hung at a window or door ❷ the large cloth screen hung at the front of a stage

curtsy NOUN curtsies
a movement of respect made by women and girls, putting one foot behind the other and bending the knees

curtsy VERB curtsies, curtsying, curtsied
to make a curtsy

curvature NOUN curvatures
a curving or bending, especially of the earth's horizon • *the curvature of the earth*

curve NOUN curves
a line or shape that bends gradually and smoothly

curve VERB curves, curving, curved
to bend gradually and smoothly; to form a curve
➤ **curvy** ADJECTIVE

curved ADJECTIVE
forming a curve • *a curved blade*

cushion NOUN cushions
❶ a bag, usually of cloth, filled with soft material so that it is comfortable to sit on or lean against ❷ anything soft or springy that protects or supports something • *The hovercraft travels on a cushion of air.*

cushion VERB cushions, cushioning, cushioned
to protect someone from the effects of a knock or shock etc. • *A pile of boxes cushioned his fall.*

cushy ADJECTIVE (*informal*)
pleasant and easy • *a cushy job*

custard NOUN custards
❶ a sweet yellow sauce made with milk ❷ a pudding made with beaten eggs and milk

custodian NOUN custodians
a person who is responsible for looking after something; a keeper

custody NOUN
❶ the legal right or duty to take care of a person or thing ❷ to be in custody is to be in prison awaiting trial
➤ **take someone into custody** to arrest someone

custom NOUN customs
❶ the usual way of behaving or doing something ❷ regular business from customers

customary ADJECTIVE
according to custom; usual
➤ **customarily** ADVERB

custom-built ADJECTIVE
made according to a customer's order

customer NOUN customers
a person who buys goods and services from a shop or business

customs PLURAL NOUN
❶ the place at a port or airport where officials examine your luggage to check that you are not carrying anything illegal ❷ taxes charged on goods brought into a country

cut VERB cuts, cutting, cut
❶ to divide or separate something by using a knife, axe, scissors, etc. ❷ to wound someone with a sharp object or weapon ❸ to make a thing shorter or smaller; to remove part of something • *They are cutting all their prices.* ❹ to divide a pack of playing cards ❺ to hit a ball with a chopping movement ❻ to go through or across something ❼ to switch off electrical power or an engine ❽ in a film, to move from one shot or scene to another ❾ to make a sound recording
➤ **cut a corner** to go across a corner rather than around it
➤ **cut and dried** already decided
➤ **cut and paste** to remove text on a computer screen from one place and put it somewhere else
➤ **cut in** to interrupt someone
➤ **cut something off** to stop the supply of something

➤ **cut something out** to stop doing something

cut *NOUN* cuts
❶ cutting; the result of cutting • *Your hair could do with a cut.* ❷ a small wound ❸ (*informal*) a share of profits
➤ **be a cut above something** to be superior

cute *ADJECTIVE* (*informal*)
pretty or attractive

cuticle (say **kew**-tik-ul) *NOUN* cuticles
the skin round a nail

cutlass *NOUN* cutlasses
a short sword with a broad curved blade

cutlery *NOUN*
knives, forks and spoons used for eating

cutlet *NOUN* cutlets
a thick slice of meat for cooking

cut-out *NOUN* cut-outs
a shape cut out of paper, cardboard, etc.

cut-price *ADJECTIVE*
for sale at a reduced price

cutter *NOUN* cutters
❶ a person or thing that cuts ❷ a small fast sailing ship

cutting *NOUN* cuttings
❶ something cut out of a newspaper or magazine ❷ a piece cut from a plant to form a new plant ❸ a steep-sided passage cut through high ground for a road or railway

cuttlefish *NOUN* cuttlefish
a sea creature with ten arms, which sends out a black liquid when attacked

cyanide *NOUN*
a very poisonous chemical

cycle *NOUN* cycles
❶ a bicycle or motorcycle ❷ a series of events that are regularly repeated in the same order • *Rainfall is part of the water cycle.*

cycle *VERB* cycles, cycling, cycled
to ride a bicycle or tricycle

cyclical, cyclic *ADJECTIVE*
repeated regularly in the same order

cyclist *NOUN* cyclists
a person who rides a bicycle

cyclone *NOUN* cyclones
a violent tropical storm in which strong winds rotate round a calm central area
➤ **cyclonic** *ADJECTIVE*

cygnet (say **sig**-nit) *NOUN* cygnets
a young swan

cylinder *NOUN* cylinders
an object with straight sides and circular ends

cylindrical *ADJECTIVE*
shaped like a cylinder

cymbal *NOUN* cymbals
a percussion instrument consisting of a metal plate that is hit to make a ringing sound

SPELLING
Take care not to confuse with **symbol**.

cynic (say **sin**-ik) *NOUN* cynics
a person who believes that people's reasons for doing things are usually selfish or bad,
➤ **cynicism** *NOUN*

cynical *ADJECTIVE*
believing that people's reasons for doing things are usually selfish or bad

cypress *NOUN* cypresses
an evergreen tree with dark leaves

cyst (say sist) *NOUN* cysts
an abnormal swelling in the body containing fluid or soft matter

czar (say zar) *NOUN* czars
a different spelling of **tsar**

Dd

dab *NOUN* dabs
❶ a quick gentle touch, usually with something wet ❷ a small amount of something put on a surface • *a dab of paint*

dab *VERB* dabs, dabbing, dabbed
to touch something quickly and gently • *I dabbed my eyes with a handkerchief.*

dabble *VERB* dabbles, dabbling, dabbled
❶ to splash something about in water ❷ to do something as a hobby or not very seriously • *I dabble in astronomy.*

dachshund (say **daks**-huund) *NOUN* dachshunds
a small dog with a long body and very short legs **WORD ORIGIN** German = badger-dog (because dachshunds were once used to dig badgers from their sets)

dad, daddy NOUN dads, daddies (*informal*)
father

daddy-long-legs NOUN daddy-long-legs
a crane fly

daffodil NOUN daffodils
a yellow flower that grows from a bulb

daft ADJECTIVE (*British*) (*informal*)
silly or stupid

dag NOUN dags (*informal*)
(*Australian/NZ*) a dirty or untidy person
WORD ORIGIN shortening of *daglock* = a piece
of dung-coated wool on a sheep's hindquarters

dagger NOUN daggers
a pointed knife with two sharp edges, used as
a weapon
➤ **look daggers at someone** to glare angrily
at someone

dahlia (say **day**-lee-a) NOUN dahlias
a garden plant with brightly-coloured flowers
WORD ORIGIN named after Andreas *Dahl*, a
Swedish botanist

daily ADVERB & ADJECTIVE
every day

dainty ADJECTIVE daintier, daintiest
small, delicate and pretty
➤ **daintily** ADVERB
➤ **daintiness** NOUN

dairy NOUN dairies
a place where milk, butter, etc. are produced
or sold

dairy ADJECTIVE
to do with the production of milk; made from
milk • *dairy farming* • *dairy products*

dais (say **day**-iss) NOUN daises
a low platform, especially at the end of a
room

daisy NOUN daisies
a small flower with white petals and a yellow
centre **WORD ORIGIN** from *day's eye* (because
the daisy opens in daylight and closes at night)

dale NOUN dales
a valley

dally VERB dallies, dallying, dallied
to dawdle or waste time

dam NOUN dams
a barrier built across a river to hold water
back

dam VERB dams, damming, dammed
to hold water back with a dam

damage NOUN
harm or injury done to something • *The storm
caused a lot of damage.*

damage VERB damages, damaging, damaged
to harm or spoil something

damages PLURAL NOUN
money paid as compensation for an injury or
loss

Dame NOUN Dames
the title of a woman who has been given the
equivalent of a knighthood

dame NOUN dames
a comic middle-aged woman in a pantomime,
usually played by a man

damn VERB damns, damning, damned
❶ to condemn someone to eternal
punishment in hell ❷ to swear at someone or
curse them

damn EXCLAMATION
(*informal*) said to show you are angry or
annoyed

damnation NOUN
being condemned to hell

damned ADJECTIVE
hateful or annoying

damp ADJECTIVE
slightly wet; not quite dry
➤ **damply** ADVERB
➤ **dampness** NOUN

damp NOUN
moisture in the air or on a surface or all
through something

damp VERB damps, damping, damped
❶ to make something slightly wet ❷ to
reduce the strength of something • *The
defeat damped their enthusiasm.*

damp course NOUN damp courses
(*British*) a layer of material built into a wall to
prevent dampness in the ground from rising

dampen VERB dampens, dampening,
dampened
❶ to make something damp ❷ to reduce
the strength of something • *Even the awful
weather didn't dampen their spirits.*

damper NOUN dampers
❶ a felt pad that presses against a piano
string to stop it vibrating ❷ a metal plate that
can be moved to increase or decrease the
amount of air flowing into a fire or furnace
➤ **put a damper on something** to reduce
people's enthusiasm or enjoyment

damsel *NOUN* damsels (*old use*)
a young woman

damson *NOUN* damsons
a small dark purple plum

dance *VERB* dances, dancing, danced
to move about in time to music

dance *NOUN* dances
❶ a set of movements used in dancing ❷ a piece of music for dancing to ❸ a party or gathering where people dance

dancer *NOUN* dancers
a person who dances

dandelion *NOUN* dandelions
a yellow wild flower with jagged leaves
WORD ORIGIN from French *dent-de-lion* = tooth of a lion (because the jagged edges of the leaves looked like lions' teeth)

dandruff *NOUN*
tiny white flakes of dead skin in a person's hair

D and T *ABBREVIATION*
design and technology

dandy *NOUN* dandies
a man who likes to look very smart

danger *NOUN* dangers
❶ the possibility of suffering harm or death or that something bad might happen • *Are they in any danger?* • *There's a danger they might be sold out.* ❷ a bad effect that happens as a result of doing something • *the dangers of overeating*

dangerous *ADJECTIVE*
likely to kill or harm you
➤ **dangerously** *ADVERB*

dangle *VERB* dangles, dangling, dangled
❶ to swing or hang down loosely • *A single light bulb dangled from the ceiling.* ❷ to hold or carry something so that it swings loosely • *She dangled her legs over the side of the bed.*

dank *ADJECTIVE*
damp and chilly • *a dank dungeon*

dapper *ADJECTIVE*
dressed neatly and smartly

dappled *ADJECTIVE*
marked with patches of a different colour or with patches of shade

dare *VERB* dares, daring, dared
❶ to be brave or bold enough to do something • *He didn't dare look down.* ❷ to challenge a person to do something risky • *I dare you to climb up there.*

dare *NOUN* dares
a challenge to do something risky

daredevil *NOUN* daredevils
a person who enjoys doing dangerous things

daring *ADJECTIVE*
bold or courageous

daring *NOUN*
adventurous courage

dark *ADJECTIVE*
❶ with little or no light ❷ not light in colour • *a dark suit* ❸ having dark hair ❹ sinister or unpleasant • *dark deeds*

dark *NOUN*
❶ absence of light • *Cats can see in the dark.* ❷ the time when it becomes dark • *She went out after dark.*
➤ **be in the dark** to have no information about something

darken *VERB* darkens, darkening, darkened
❶ to become dark or darker • *The sky suddenly darkened.* ❷ to make something dark or darker • *a darkened room*

darkly *ADJECTIVE*
in a threatening or unpleasant way • *He scowled at me darkly.*

darkness *NOUN*
being dark, without any light • *The room was suddenly plunged into total darkness.*

darkroom *NOUN* darkrooms
a room kept dark for developing and printing photographs

darling *NOUN* darlings
someone who is loved very much

darn *VERB* darns, darning, darned
to mend a hole by weaving threads across it

darn *NOUN* darns
a place that has been darned

dart *NOUN* darts
❶ an object with a sharp point, thrown at a target ❷ a sudden swift movement ❸ a tapering tuck stitched in something to make it fit

dart *VERB* darts, darting, darted
❶ to run suddenly and quickly ❷ you dart a look or glance at someone when you look at them suddenly and briefly

darts *NOUN*
a game in which darts are thrown at a circular board (**dartboard**)

dash *VERB* **dashes, dashing, dashed**
❶ to run quickly; to rush ❷ to throw a thing violently against something hard • *The storm dashed the ship against the rocks.* ❸ to destroy a hope or expectation

dash *NOUN* **dashes**
❶ a short quick run; a rush ❷ a small amount of something • *Add a dash of cream.* ❸ a short line (–) used in writing or printing

PUNCTUATION

Dashes are used, especially in informal writing, to mark a break in the flow of a sentence.

They can be used on their own, to add a final comment, question or summary:

I have only two words to say to you— 'Never again'!

Would you like your bagel split, toasted, buttered—or none of the above?

They can be used in pairs before and after an interruption in a narrative or conversation. For example, they can show a change of subject, or a break or hesitation in thought:

Maybe I'll just say—oh, I don't know—that I'm allergic to cats.

or they can be used to elaborate or explain a point:

The creature was vast—over ten feet tall—and was staring at me.

Dashes are quite informal and should be avoided in formal writing.

dashboard *NOUN* **dashboards**
a panel with dials and controls in front of the driver of a vehicle **WORD ORIGIN** originally a board on the front of a carriage to keep out mud, which dashed against it

dashing *ADJECTIVE*
attractive in an exciting and stylish way • *a dashing young officer*

dastardly *ADJECTIVE*
(*old use*) wicked and cruel • *What a dastardly trick!*

data (say **day**-ta) *NOUN*
pieces of information

USAGE

Strictly speaking, this word is a plural noun (the singular is *datum*), so it should be used with a plural verb: *Here are the data.* However, the word is widely used as if it were a singular noun: *Here is the data.*

database *NOUN* **databases**
a store of information held in a computer

date *NOUN* **dates**
❶ the time when something happens or happened, stated as the day, month and year (or any of these) ❷ an appointment to meet someone, especially at the start of a romantic relationship ❸ a small sweet brown fruit that grows on a kind of palm tree

date *VERB* **dates, dating, dated**
❶ to give a date to something • *The letter is dated 3 June 2013.* ❷ to have existed from a particular time • *The church dates from 1684.* ❸ to seem old-fashioned • *Some fashions date very quickly.*

daub *VERB* **daubs, daubing, daubed**
to paint or smear something clumsily
➤ **daub** *NOUN*

daughter *NOUN* **daughters**
a girl or woman who is someone's child

daughter-in-law *NOUN* **daughters-in-law**
a son's wife

daunt *VERB* **daunts, daunting, daunted**
to make someone feel worried and not confident about doing something • *Don't be daunted by the length of the book – it's a good read.*

daunting *ADJECTIVE*
a daunting task makes you feel worried because it seems so difficult

dauntless *ADJECTIVE*
brave and determined

dauphin (say **daw**-fin) *NOUN* **dauphins**
the title of the eldest son of each of the kings of France between 1349 and 1830

dawdle *VERB* **dawdles, dawdling, dawdled**
to walk or do things slowly and lazily

dawn *NOUN* **dawns**
❶ the time when the sun rises ❷ the beginning of something • *the dawn of civilization*

a b c d e f g h i j k l m n o p q r s t u v w x y z

dawn *VERB* dawns, dawning, dawned
❶ to begin to grow light in the morning ❷ to begin to be realized • *The truth dawned on them.*

day *NOUN* days
❶ the 24 hours between midnight and the next midnight ❷ the light part of this time; the daytime ❸ a period of time • *in Queen Victoria's day*

daybreak *NOUN*
the first light of day; dawn

daydream *NOUN* daydreams
pleasant thoughts of something you would like to happen

daydream *VERB* daydreams, daydreaming, daydreamed
to have daydreams

daylight *NOUN*
❶ the light of day; sunlight ❷ dawn

daytime *NOUN*
the time of daylight

day-to-day *ADJECTIVE*
ordinary; happening every day

daze *NOUN*
➤ in a daze unable to think or see clearly

dazed *ADJECTIVE*
unable to think or see clearly

dazzle *VERB* dazzles, dazzling, dazzled
❶ a light dazzles you when it is so bright that you cannot see clearly because of it ❷ to amaze or impress a person by a splendid display

DC *ABBREVIATION*
direct current

deacon *NOUN* deacons
❶ a member of the clergy ranking below a priest in Catholic, Anglican and Orthodox Christian Churches ❷ a church officer who is not a member of the clergy in some Christian Churches
➤ deaconess *NOUN*

dead *ADJECTIVE*
❶ no longer alive ❷ not at all lively • *This town is dead at the weekend.* ❸ no longer working or in use • *The phone went dead.* ❹ exact or complete • *The arrow hit the target in the dead centre.* • *We came to a dead stop.*

deaden *VERB* deadens, deadening, deadened
to make a pain, feeling or sound weaker

dead end *NOUN* dead ends
❶ a road or passage with one end closed ❷ a situation where there is no chance of making progress

dead heat *NOUN* dead heats
a race in which two or more winners finish exactly together

deadline *NOUN* deadlines
a time by which you have to finish something
WORD ORIGIN originally this meant a line round an American military prison; if prisoners went beyond it they could be shot

deadlock *NOUN* deadlocks
a situation in which two sides cannot reach an agreement

deadly *ADJECTIVE* & *ADVERB* deadlier, deadliest
❶ likely to kill ❷ complete or completely • *There was a deadly hush in the room.* • *He was deadly serious.*

deaf *ADJECTIVE*
❶ unable to hear ❷ refusing to listen • *She was deaf to all advice.*
➤ deafness *NOUN*

deafen *VERB* deafens, deafening, deafened
to make someone unable to hear by making a very loud noise • *We were deafened by the roar of the aircraft above.*

deafening *ADJECTIVE*
extremely loud

deal *VERB* deals, dealing, dealt
❶ to hand something out ❷ to give out cards for a card game ❸ to do business; to buy and sell goods • *He deals in scrap metal.* ❹ to deal someone or something a blow is to hit or harm them • *The man dealt Tom a heavy blow on the nose.*
➤ deal with something ❶ to be concerned with something • *This chapter deals with whales and dolphins.* ❷ to do what is needed • *I'll deal with the washing-up.*

deal *NOUN* deals
❶ an agreement or bargain ❷ someone's turn to deal at cards
➤ a good deal or a great deal a large amount

dealer *NOUN* dealers
❶ someone who buys and sells things ❷ the person who deals in a game of cards

dean *NOUN* deans
❶ an important member of the clergy in a cathedral ❷ the head of a university, college or department
➤ deanery *NOUN*

dear ADJECTIVE
❶ loved very much ❷ a polite greeting in letters • *Dear Sir* ❸ expensive

dearly ADVERB
very much; a lot • *She loved her husband dearly.*

dearth (say derth) NOUN dearths
a dearth of something is a lack or shortage of it

death NOUN deaths
dying; the end of life

deathly ADJECTIVE & ADVERB
like death • *There was a deathly silence.*

death trap NOUN death traps
a very dangerous place

debar VERB debars, debarring, debarred
to ban someone from doing or taking part in something • *He was debarred from the contest.*

debase VERB debases, debasing, debased
to reduce the quality or value of something
➤ **debasement** NOUN

debatable ADJECTIVE
not certain; that people might argue about

debate NOUN debates
a formal discussion about a subject

debate VERB debates, debating, debated
❶ to discuss or argue about something ❷ to think about something before deciding what to do • *I was debating whether to go or not.*

debilitating ADJECTIVE
making you very weak • *a debilitating disease*

debit NOUN debits
an entry in an account showing how much money is owed. Compare with **credit**.

debit VERB debits, debiting, debited
to enter an amount as a debit in an account; to remove money from an account

debonair (say deb-on-**air**) ADJECTIVE
fashionable and and confident
WORD ORIGIN from French *de bon air* = of good disposition

debris (say **deb**-ree) NOUN
scattered broken pieces that are left after something has been destroyed

debt (say det) NOUN debts
something, especially money, that you owe someone
➤ **in debt** owing money

➤ **in someone's debt** grateful to someone who has done you a favour

debtor (say **det**-or) NOUN debtors
a person who owes money to someone

debut (say **day**-bew) NOUN debuts
someone's first public appearance as a performer

decade (say **dek**-ayd) NOUN decades
a period of ten years

decadent (say **dek**-a-dent) ADJECTIVE
falling to a lower standard of morality or behaviour, especially in order to enjoy pleasure
➤ **decadence** NOUN

decaffeinated ADJECTIVE
decaffeinated coffee or tea has had caffeine removed from it

decamp VERB decamps, decamping, decamped
to go away suddenly or secretly

decant (say dik-**ant**) VERB decants, decanting, decanted
to pour wine or other liquid gently from one container into another

decanter (say dik-**ant**-er) NOUN decanters
a decorative glass bottle into which wine etc. is poured for serving

decapitate VERB decapitates, decapitating, decapitated
to cut someone's head off; to behead someone
➤ **decapitation** NOUN

decathlon NOUN decathlons
an athletic contest in which each competitor takes part in ten events

decay VERB decays, decaying, decayed
❶ to go bad or rot ❷ to become less good or less strong

decay NOUN
going bad or rotting • *tooth decay*

decease (say dis-**eess**) NOUN (*formal*)
a person's death

deceased ADJECTIVE (*formal*)
dead

deceit (say dis-**eet**) NOUN deceits
making a person believe something that is not true • *I'm tired of his lies and deceit.*

deceitful ADJECTIVE
dishonest; trying to make someone believe

a b c d e f g h i j k l m n o p q r s t u v w x y z

something that is not true
➤ **deceitfully** ADVERB

deceive VERB deceives, deceiving, deceived
to make a person believe something that is
not true

> **SPELLING**
> In deceive, e before i is the right way
> round.

December NOUN
the twelfth month of the year
WORD ORIGIN from Latin *decem* = ten,
because it was the tenth month of the ancient
Roman calendar

decency NOUN
respectable and honest behaviour

decent ADJECTIVE
❶ respectable and honest ❷ of a good
enough standard or quality • *No one can
make a decent living this way.* ❸ (*informal*)
kind or generous
➤ **decently** ADVERB

deception NOUN deceptions
❶ deceiving someone ❷ something that
deceives people

deceptive ADJECTIVE
not what it seems to be; giving a false
impression • *Appearances can be deceptive.*
➤ **deceptively** ADVERB

decibel (say **dess**-ib-el) NOUN decibels
a unit for measuring the loudness of sound

decide VERB decides, deciding, decided
❶ to make up your mind; to make a choice
❷ to settle a contest or argument • *Next
week's match will decide the championship.*
➤ **decider** NOUN

> **SPELLING**
> The 's' sound is spelt with a c in decide.

decided ADJECTIVE
❶ noticeable or definite • *a decided
advantage* ❷ having clear and definite
opinions

decidedly ADVERB
definitely and in an obvious way • *She was
looking decidedly worried.*

deciduous (say dis-**id**-yoo-us) ADJECTIVE
a deciduous tree is one that loses its leaves in
autumn

decimal ADJECTIVE
decimal numbers or fractions are expressed in
tens or tenths

decimal NOUN decimals
a decimal fraction

decimal currency NOUN decimal currencies
a currency in which each unit is ten or one
hundred times the value of the one next
below it

decimal fraction NOUN decimal fractions
a fraction with tenths shown as numbers
after a dot (¼ is 0.25; 1½ is 1.5)

decimalize (also **decimalise**) VERB
decimalizes, decimalizing, decimalized
❶ to express a number as a decimal ❷ to
change something, especially coinage, to a
decimal system
➤ **decimalization** NOUN

decimal point NOUN decimal points
the dot in a decimal fraction

decimate (say **dess**-im-ayt) VERB decimates,
decimating, decimated
to kill or destroy a large part of something
• *The famine decimated the population.*
WORD ORIGIN from Latin *decimare* = kill
every tenth man (this was the ancient Roman
punishment for an army guilty of mutiny or
other serious crime)

decipher (say dis-**y**-fer) VERB deciphers,
deciphering, deciphered
❶ to work out the meaning of a coded
message ❷ to work out the meaning of
something that is hard to read • *I can't
decipher his handwriting.*
➤ **decipherment** NOUN

decision NOUN decisions
❶ a decision is what someone has decided
❷ decision is deciding or making a judgment
about something • *The moment of decision
had arrived.*

decisive (say dis-**y**-siv) ADJECTIVE
❶ that settles or ends something • *a decisive
battle* ❷ able to make decisions quickly and
firmly
➤ **decisively** ADVERB

deck NOUN decks
❶ a floor or level on a ship or bus ❷ a pack of
playing cards ❸ a part of a music system for
playing discs or tapes

deck VERB decks, decking, decked
to decorate a place with something • *The
front of the house was decked with flags and
balloons.*

deckchair NOUN deckchairs
a folding chair with a canvas or plastic seat

WORD ORIGIN because they were first used on the decks of passenger ships

declaim *VERB* declaims, declaiming, declaimed
to speak or say something loudly and dramatically • *She declaimed the famous opening speech of the play.*
➤ **declamation** *NOUN*

declaration *NOUN* declarations
an official or public statement about something

declare *VERB* declares, declaring, declared
❶ to say something clearly or firmly • *He has always declared that he is innocent.* ❷ to tell customs officials that you have goods on which you ought to pay duty ❸ to end a cricket innings before all the batsmen are out
➤ **declare war** to announce that you are starting a war against someone

decline *VERB* declines, declining, declined
❶ to refuse something politely • *She declined his offer of help.* ❷ to become weaker or smaller • *In the last few years his popularity has declined.* ❸ to state the forms of a noun, pronoun or adjective that correspond to particular cases, numbers and genders

decline *NOUN* declines
a gradual decrease or loss of strength • *a decline in the birth rate*

decode *VERB* decodes, decoding, decoded
to work out the meaning of something written in code
➤ **decoder** *NOUN*

decompose *VERB* decomposes, decomposing, decomposed
to decay or rot
➤ **decomposition** *NOUN*

decompression *NOUN*
reducing air pressure

decontamination *NOUN*
getting rid of poisonous chemicals or radioactive material from a place, clothes, etc.

decor (say **day**-kor) *NOUN*
the style of furnishings and decorations used in a room

decorate *VERB* decorates, decorating, decorated
❶ to make something look more beautiful or colourful ❷ to put fresh paint or paper on walls ❸ to give somebody a medal or other award

decoration *NOUN* decorations
❶ something used to decorate a room,

table, etc. on special occasions • *Christmas decorations* ❷ the process of decorating a room or building ❸ a medal or other award given as an honour

decorative *ADJECTIVE*
attractive to look at • *a decorative design*

decorator *NOUN* decorators
a person whose job is to paint and decorate rooms and buildings

decorous (say **dek**-er-us) *ADJECTIVE*
polite and dignified
➤ **decorously** *ADVERB*

decorum (say dik-**or**-um) *NOUN*
polite and dignified behaviour

decoy (say **dee**-koi) *NOUN* decoys
something used to tempt a person or animal into a trap or into danger

decoy (say dik-**oi**) *VERB* decoys, decoying, decoyed
to tempt a person or animal into a trap or danger

decrease *VERB* decreases, decreasing, decreased
❶ to become smaller or fewer ❷ to make something smaller or fewer in number

decrease *NOUN* decreases
decreasing; the amount by which something decreases

decree *NOUN* decrees
an official order or decision

decree *VERB* decrees, decreeing, decreed
to give an official order that something must happen

decrepit (say dik-**rep**-it) *ADJECTIVE*
old and weak

dedicate *VERB* dedicates, dedicating, dedicated
❶ to devote all your time or energy to something • *She dedicated her life to nursing.* ❷ to name a person as a mark of respect or friendship, e.g. at the beginning of a book • *This book is dedicated to my parents.*

dedication *NOUN* dedications
❶ hard work and effort ❷ a message at the beginning of a book, naming a person as a mark of respect or friendship

deduce *VERB* deduces, deducing, deduced
to work something out from facts that you already know are true • *From her name I deduced that she was Polish.*

deduct VERB deducts, deducting, deducted
to subtract an amount from a total • *The examiner may deduct marks for bad spelling.*

deduction NOUN deductions
❶ something you work out from facts that you already know are true • *a brilliant piece of deduction* ❷ an amount taken away from a total

deed NOUN deeds
❶ something that someone has done; an act • *tales of his many brave deeds* ❷ a legal document that shows who owns something

deem VERB deems, deeming, deemed (formal)
to consider something in a certain way • *I should deem it an honour to be invited.*

deep ADJECTIVE
❶ going a long way down or back or in • *a deep well* • *deep cupboards* ❷ measured from top to bottom or front to back • *a hole two metres deep* ❸ a deep feeling is intense or strong • *deep suspicion* ❹ a deep colour is dark and intense • *a deep red* ❺ low-pitched, not shrill • *a deep voice*

deepen VERB deepens, deepening, deepened
to become deeper or more intense • *The darkness deepened.*

deep-freeze NOUN deep-freezes
a freezer

deeply ADVERB
very or very much • *She was deeply upset.* • *I deeply regret what happened.*

deer NOUN deer
a fast-running graceful animal, the male of which usually has antlers

> SPELLING
> Deer is spelt the same in the singular and plural.

deface VERB defaces, defacing, defaced
to spoil the surface of something, e.g. by scribbling on it

defame VERB defames, defaming, defamed
to attack or damage a person's good reputation; to slander or libel someone
➤ **defamation** (say def-a-**may**-shon) NOUN
➤ **defamatory** (say dif-**am**-a-ter-ee) ADJECTIVE

default VERB defaults, defaulting, defaulted
to fail to do what you have agreed to do, especially to pay back a loan
➤ **defaulter** NOUN

default NOUN defaults
❶ failure to do something, especially to

pay back a loan ❷ (*in computing*) what a computer does unless you give it another command
➤ **by default** because something has failed to happen • *The other team didn't arrive in time, so we won by default.*

defeat VERB defeats, defeating, defeated
❶ to win a victory over someone ❷ to baffle someone or be too difficult for them • *The instructions completely defeated me.*

defeat NOUN defeats
❶ being defeated; a lost game or battle • *It's our first defeat of the season.* ❷ defeating someone • *William's defeat of Harold at the Battle of Hastings*

defecate (say **def**-ik-ayt) VERB defecates, defecating, defecated
to get rid of faeces from your body
➤ **defecation** NOUN

defect (say **dee**-fect) NOUN defects
a fault or flaw in something

defect (say dif-**ekt**) VERB defects, defecting, defected
to desert your own country or cause and join the other side
➤ **defection** NOUN
➤ **defector** NOUN

defective ADJECTIVE
having defects; incomplete • *defective goods*

defence NOUN defences
❶ protecting someone or something from an attack or from criticism • *His friends immediately rushed to his defence.* ❷ all the soldiers, weapons, etc. that a country uses to protect itself from attack • *spending on defence* ❸ something that defends or protects you • *High walls were built around the city as a defence against enemy attacks.* ❹ the case put forward by or on behalf of a defendant in a trial; the lawyers who put forward this case ❺ the players in a defending position in a game

defenceless ADJECTIVE
having no defences; not able to defend yourself

defend VERB defends, defending, defended
❶ to protect someone, especially against an attack or accusation ❷ to argue in support of something • *How can you defend such behaviour?* ❸ to try to prove that an accused person is not guilty ❹ to try to stop the other team from scoring
➤ **defender** NOUN

defendant *NOUN* defendants
a person accused of something in a law court

defensible *ADJECTIVE*
able to be defended

defensive *ADJECTIVE*
❶ used or done to defend something;
protective ❷ anxious about being criticized
• *There's no need to be so defensive.*
➤ **defensively** *ADVERB*
➤ **on the defensive** ready to defend yourself
against criticism

defer *VERB* defers, deferring, deferred
❶ to put something off to a later time; to
postpone something • *She deferred her
departure until Saturday.* ❷ to give way to a
person's wishes or authority • *I defer to your
superior knowledge.*

deference (say **def**-er-ens) *NOUN*
polite respect
➤ **deferential** (say def-er-**en**-shal) *ADJECTIVE*
➤ **deferentially** *ADVERB*

defiance *NOUN*
open disobedience • *a look of defiance*

defiant *ADJECTIVE*
openly showing that you refuse to obey
someone • *a defiant laugh*
➤ **defiantly** *ADVERB*

deficiency *NOUN* deficiencies
❶ a lack or shortage • *a vitamin deficiency*
❷ a defect or failing
➤ **deficient** *ADJECTIVE*

deficit (say **def**-iss-it) *NOUN* deficits
❶ the amount by which a total is smaller
than what is required ❷ the amount by which
spending is greater than income

defile *VERB* defiles, defiling, defiled
to make a thing dirty or impure

define *VERB* defines, defining, defined
❶ to explain what a word or phrase means
❷ to show clearly what something is • *We
need to define the problem before we can
solve it.* ❸ to show a thing's outline

definite *ADJECTIVE*
❶ clearly stated; exact • *Let's fix a definite
time.* ❷ certain or settled • *Is it definite that
we are going to move?*

> **SPELLING**
>
> There is a tricky bit in **definite**—it ends
> in ite.

definite article *NOUN* definite articles
the word 'the'. See also the panels at **the** and
at **determiner**

definitely *ADVERB*
without doubt; certainly

> **SPELLING**
>
> There is no a in **definitely**.

definition *NOUN* definitions
❶ a statement of what a word or phrase
means or of what a thing is ❷ being distinct;
clearness of outline (e.g. in a photograph)
• *The face lacks definition.*

definitive (say dif-**in**-it-iv) *ADJECTIVE*
❶ finally settling something; conclusive • *a
definitive victory* ❷ not able to be bettered
• *the definitive history of French cinema*

deflate *VERB* deflates, deflating, deflated
❶ to let out air from a tyre or balloon etc.
❷ to make someone feel less proud or less
confident • *All the criticism left him feeling a
bit deflated.* ❸ to reduce or reverse inflation
➤ **deflation** *NOUN*

deflect *VERB* deflects, deflecting, deflected
to make something turn aside • *He deflected
the blow with his shield.*
➤ **deflection** *NOUN*
➤ **deflector** *NOUN*

deforest *VERB* deforests, deforesting,
deforested
to clear away the trees from an area

deforestation *NOUN*
the cutting down of a lot of trees in an area

deform *VERB* deforms, deforming, deformed
to spoil a thing's shape or appearance
➤ **deformation** *NOUN*

deformed *ADJECTIVE*
not properly shaped because it has grown
wrongly
➤ **deformity** *NOUN*

defraud *VERB* defrauds, defrauding,
defrauded
to get money from someone by fraud

defray *VERB* defrays, defraying, defrayed
to provide money to pay costs or expenses

defrost *VERB* defrosts, defrosting, defrosted
❶ to thaw out frozen food ❷ to remove
the ice and frost from a refrigerator or
windscreen

deft *ADJECTIVE*
skilful and quick • *She painted a fish with a*

a
b
c
d
e
f
g
h
i
j
k
l
m
n
o
p
q
r
s
t
u
v
w
x
y
z

few deft strokes.
➤ **deftly** ADVERB
➤ **deftness** NOUN

defunct ADJECTIVE
no longer in use or existing

defuse VERB **defuses, defusing, defused**
❶ to remove the fuse from a bomb so that it cannot explode ❷ to make a situation less dangerous or tense • *Her joke defused the situation and we all relaxed.*

defy VERB **defies, defying, defied**
❶ to refuse to obey someone or something; to openly resist something • *They defied the law.* ❷ to challenge a person to do something you believe cannot be done • *I defy you to prove this.* ❸ to prevent something being done • *The door defied all efforts to open it.*

degenerate VERB **degenerates, degenerating, degenerated**
to become worse or lower in standard • *The game degenerated into a series of fouls.*
➤ **degeneration** NOUN

degenerate ADJECTIVE
having become immoral or bad
➤ **degeneracy** NOUN

degrade VERB **degrades, degrading, degraded**
❶ to humiliate or dishonour someone ❷ to reduce a chemical substance to a simpler molecular form
➤ **degradation** (say deg-ra-**day**-shon) NOUN

degree NOUN **degrees**
❶ a unit for measuring temperature ❷ a unit for measuring angles ❸ extent or amount • *I agree with you to some degree.* • *a high degree of skill* ❹ an award to someone at a university or college who has successfully finished a course

dehydrated ADJECTIVE
❶ someone who is dehydrated has lost a lot of water from their body ❷ a dehydrated substance has had all its moisture removed
➤ **dehydration** NOUN

de-ice VERB **de-ices, de-icing, de-iced**
to remove ice from a windscreen etc.
➤ **de-icer** NOUN

deign (say dayn) VERB **deigns, deigning, deigned**
to do something that you think is below your dignity • *She did not deign to reply.*

deity (say **dee**-it-ee or **day**-it-ee) NOUN **deities**
a god or goddess • *ancient Egyptian deities*

déjà vu (say day-zha **vew**) NOUN
a feeling that you have already experienced what is happening now (WORD ORIGIN) French = already seen

dejected ADJECTIVE
sad or disappointed
➤ **dejectedly** ADVERB
➤ **dejection** NOUN

delay VERB **delays, delaying, delayed**
❶ to make someone or something late ❷ to postpone something until later ❸ to wait or hesitate before doing something

delay NOUN **delays**
❶ delaying or waiting • *Do it without delay.*
❷ the amount of time by which something is delayed • *a two-hour delay*

delectable ADJECTIVE
delightful or delicious

delegate (say **del**-ig-at) NOUN **delegates**
a person who represents others and acts on their instructions

delegate (say **del**-ig-ayt) VERB **delegates, delegating, delegated**
❶ to choose someone to carry out a task or duty that you are responsible for • *I'm going to delegate this job to my assistant.*
❷ to appoint someone as a delegate • *We delegated Jones to represent us.*

delegation (say del-ig-**ay**-shon) NOUN **delegations**
❶ a group of delegates • *the delegation from South Africa* ❷ delegating

delete (say dil-**eet**) VERB **deletes, deleting, deleted**
to cross out or remove something written or printed or stored on a computer • *He deleted the email without reading it.*
➤ **deletion** NOUN

deliberate (say dil-**ib**-er-at) ADJECTIVE
❶ done on purpose; intentional ❷ slow and careful • *She entered the room with deliberate steps.*

deliberate (say dil-**ib**-er-ayt) VERB **deliberates, deliberating, deliberated**
to think over or discuss something carefully before reaching a decision

deliberately ADVERB
on purpose • *I didn't break it deliberately.*

deliberation NOUN **deliberations**
thinking carefully about something before reaching a decision

delicacy *NOUN* **delicacies**
❶ a delicious food • *Try this – it's a local delicacy.* ❷ being delicate • *We must handle the matter with great delicacy.*

delicate *ADJECTIVE*
❶ fine and graceful • *delicate embroidery* ❷ fragile and easily damaged ❸ pleasant and not strong or intense • *a delicate shade of pink* ❹ becoming ill easily ❺ using or needing great care • *a delicate situation*
➤ **delicately** *ADVERB*

delicatessen *NOUN* **delicatessens**
a shop that sells cooked meats, cheeses, salads, etc. **(WORD ORIGIN)** from German = delicacies to eat

delicious *ADJECTIVE*
tasting or smelling very pleasant
➤ **deliciously** *ADVERB*

delight *VERB* **delights, delighting, delighted**
❶ to please someone greatly ❷ to take great pleasure in something • *He delights in playing tricks on people.*

delight *NOUN* **delights**
great pleasure

delighted *ADJECTIVE*
extremely pleased • *I'd be delighted to come.*

delightful *ADJECTIVE*
giving great pleasure; very pleasant
➤ **delightfully** *ADVERB*

delinquent (say dil-**ing**-kwent) *NOUN* **delinquents**
a young person who breaks the law
➤ **delinquent** *ADJECTIVE*
➤ **delinquency** *NOUN*

delirious (say di-**li**-ri-us) *ADJECTIVE*
❶ in a state of mental confusion and agitation during a feverish illness ❷ extremely excited or enthusiastic
➤ **deliriously** *ADVERB*

delirium (say dil-**irri**-um) *NOUN*
❶ a state of mental confusion and agitation during a feverish illness ❷ wild excitement

deliver *VERB* **delivers, delivering, delivered**
❶ to take letters or goods to the person or place they are addressed to ❷ to give a speech or lecture ❸ to help with the birth of a baby ❹ to aim or strike a blow or an attack ❺ to rescue someone or set them free
➤ **deliverer** *NOUN*

deliverance *NOUN*
being rescued or set free

delivery *NOUN* **deliveries**
❶ delivering letters or goods • *Your order is ready for delivery.* • *We have two deliveries a day.* ❷ the way a person gives a speech or lecture ❸ giving birth to a baby ❹ a ball bowled in cricket

dell *NOUN* **dells**
a small valley with trees

delphinium *NOUN* **delphiniums**
a garden plant with tall spikes of flowers, usually blue

delta *NOUN* **deltas**
a triangular area at the mouth of a river where it spreads into branches
(WORD ORIGIN) shaped like the Greek letter delta (= D), written Δ

delude *VERB* **deludes, deluding, deluded**
to deceive someone into believing something that is not true

deluge *NOUN* **deluges**
❶ a large flood ❷ a heavy fall of rain ❸ something coming in great numbers • *a deluge of questions*

deluge *VERB* **deluges, deluging, deluged**
to be deluged with something is to be overwhelmed by a great number of them • *We have been deluged with replies.*

delusion *NOUN* **delusions**
a false belief

de luxe *ADJECTIVE*
of very high quality

delve *VERB* **delves, delving, delved**
❶ to delve into a subject is to study it closely • *I've been delving into the history of the local area.* ❷ to search for something inside a bag or container

demand *VERB* **demands, demanding, demanded**
❶ to ask for something firmly or forcefully ❷ to need something • *This work demands great skill.*

demand *NOUN* **demands**
❶ a firm or forceful request ❷ a desire to have or buy something • *There was a great demand for tickets.*
➤ **in demand** wanted or needed

demanding *ADJECTIVE*
❶ needing skill or effort • *a demanding job* ❷ needing a lot of attention • *a demanding child*

demarcation (say dee-mar-**kay**-shon) *NOUN*
marking the boundary or limits of something

demean VERB demeans, demeaning, demeaned
to lower a person's dignity • *I wouldn't demean myself to ask for it!*

demeanour (say dim-**een**-er) NOUN demeanours
a person's behaviour or manner • *Suddenly his whole demeanour changed.*

demented ADJECTIVE
driven mad; crazy

demerara (say dem-er-**air**-a) NOUN
light-brown cane sugar

demerit NOUN demerits
a fault or defect

demigod NOUN demigods
a partly divine being

demise (say dim-**yz**) NOUN (*formal*)
❶ a person's death ❷ the end or failure of something

demisemiquaver NOUN demisemiquavers
(*chiefly British*) a note in music, equal in length to one-eighth of a crotchet

demist VERB demists, demisting, demisted
(*British*) to remove misty condensation from a windscreen etc.

demo NOUN demos (*informal*)
a demonstration

democracy NOUN democracies
❶ government of a country by representatives elected by all the people ❷ a country governed in this way

Democrat NOUN Democrats
a member of the Democratic Party in the USA

democrat NOUN democrats
a person who believes in or supports democracy

democratic ADJECTIVE
❶ based on the system of democracy • *democratic elections* ❷ taking account of the views of all people involved • *We've reached a democratic decision.*
➤ **democratically** ADVERB

demolish VERB demolishes, demolishing, demolished
❶ to pull or knock down a building ❷ to destroy something completely • *She demolished his argument in one sentence.*
➤ **demolition** NOUN

demon NOUN demons
❶ a devil or evil spirit ❷ a fierce or forceful person
➤ **demonic** (say dim-**on**-ik) ADJECTIVE

demonstrate VERB demonstrates, demonstrating, demonstrated
❶ to show that something is true; to prove something ❷ to show someone how to do something or how something works ❸ to take part in a demonstration
➤ **demonstrator** NOUN

demonstration NOUN demonstrations
❶ demonstrating; showing how to do or work something ❷ a march or meeting held to show everyone what you think about something

demonstrative (say dim-**on**-strat-iv) ADJECTIVE
❶ showing feelings or affections openly ❷ (*in grammar*) pointing out the person or thing referred to. *This, that, these* and *those* are demonstrative adjectives and pronouns.

demoralize (also **demoralise**) VERB
demoralizes, demoralizing, demoralized
to make someone lose confidence or the courage to continue doing something

demote VERB demotes, demoting, demoted
to move someone to a lower position or rank than they had before
➤ **demotion** NOUN

demur (say dim-**er**) VERB demurs, demurring, demurred
to raise objections to something • *At first he demurred, but finally he agreed.*

demure ADJECTIVE
shy and modest
➤ **demurely** ADVERB

den NOUN dens
❶ a wild animal's lair ❷ a place where something illegal happens • *a gambling den* ❸ a secret place where children go to play

denial NOUN denials
a statement that something is not true

denim NOUN
a kind of strong, usually blue, cotton cloth used to make jeans etc. **WORD ORIGIN** from French *serge de Nim* = serge from Nîmes (a town in southern France)

denizen (say **den**-iz-en) NOUN denizens
an inhabitant • *Monkeys are denizens of the jungle.*

denomination NOUN denominations
❶ a person's name or title ❷ a branch of a Church or religion • *Baptists, Methodists and other denominations* ❸ a unit of money • *coins of small denomination*

denominator NOUN denominators
the number below the line in a fraction, showing how many parts the whole is divided into, e.g. 4 in ¼. Compare with **numerator**.

denote VERB denotes, denoting, denoted
to mean or indicate something • *In road signs, P denotes a car park.*

dénouement (say day-**noo**-mahn) NOUN dénouements
the final outcome of a plot or story, which is revealed at the end (**WORD ORIGIN**) French = unravelling

denounce VERB denounces, denouncing, denounced
to speak strongly against someone or something; to accuse someone of something • *They denounced him as a spy.*
➤ **denunciation** NOUN

dense ADJECTIVE
❶ thick and not easy to see through • *dense fog* ❷ packed closely together • *a dense forest* ❸ (*informal*) stupid

densely ADVERB
thickly; closely together • *a densely populated area*

density NOUN densities
❶ how thick or tightly packed something is ❷ (*in science*) the proportion of mass to volume • *Water has greater density than air.*

dent NOUN dents
a hollow left in a surface where something has pressed or hit it

dent VERB dents, denting, dented
to make a dent in something

dental ADJECTIVE
to do with your teeth or with dentistry

dentist NOUN dentists
a person who is trained to treat people's teeth and gums
➤ **dentistry** NOUN

dentures PLURAL NOUN
a set of false teeth

denunciation NOUN denunciations
denouncing someone or something

deny VERB denies, denying, denied
❶ to say that something is not true • *Do*

you deny it? ❷ to refuse to give or allow something • *She could not deny his request.*
➤ **deny yourself** to go without pleasures

deodorant (say dee-**oh**-der-ant) NOUN deodorants
a substance that removes unpleasant smells

deodorize (also **deodorise**) VERB deodorizes, deodorizing, deodorized
to remove unpleasant smells
➤ **deodorization** NOUN

depart VERB departs, departing, departed
to go away or leave • *The next train to the airport departs from platform 2.*

department NOUN departments
one section of a large organization or shop
➤ **departmental** ADJECTIVE

department store NOUN department stores
a large shop that sells many different kinds of goods

departure NOUN departures
leaving or going away from a place • *He delayed his departure until the following morning.*

depend VERB depends, depending, depended
❶ to rely on someone or something • *We depend on your help.* ❷ to be controlled or decided by something else • *It all depends on the weather.*

dependable ADJECTIVE
that you can depend on; reliable

dependant NOUN dependants
a person who depends on another, especially financially • *She has two dependants, a son and a daughter.*

(**SPELLING**)
Note that the spelling ends **ant** for this noun but **ent** for the adjective **dependent**.

dependence NOUN
being dependent on someone or something • *The country needs to reduce its dependence on imported oil.*

(**SPELLING**)
There is no **a** in **dependence**. Do not forget the **ce** at the end.

dependency NOUN dependencies
a country that is controlled by another

dependent ADJECTIVE
❶ relying on someone else financially • *She has two dependent children.* • *He was*

A
B
C
D
E
F
G
H
I
J
K
L
M
N
O
P
Q
R
S
T
U
V
W
X
Y
Z

dependent on his father. ❷ controlled by or needing something • *Unlike other balloons, an airship is not dependent on the wind.*

SPELLING
Note that the spelling ends **ent** for this adjective but **ant** for the noun **dependant**.

depict *VERB* depicts, depicting, depicted
❶ to show something in a painting or drawing etc. ❷ to describe something in words • *The novel depicts life in the village a century ago.*
➤ **depiction** *NOUN*

deplete (say dip-**leet**) *VERB* depletes, depleting, depleted
to reduce the supply of something by using up large amounts • *Fish stocks have been severely depleted.*
➤ **depletion** *NOUN*

deplorable *ADJECTIVE*
extremely bad or shocking • *Their rudeness was deplorable.*

deplore *VERB* deplores, deploring, deplored
to strongly dislike something because you think it is wrong

deploy *VERB* deploys, deploying, deployed
❶ to place troops or weapons in good positions so that they are ready to be used effectively ❷ to use something effectively • *He deployed his arguments well.*
➤ **deployment** *NOUN*

deport *VERB* deports, deporting, deported
to send an unwanted foreign person out of a country
➤ **deportation** *NOUN*

deportment *NOUN*
a person's way of standing and walking

depose *VERB* deposes, deposing, deposed
to remove a person from power

deposit *NOUN* deposits
❶ an amount of money paid into a bank or other account ❷ a sum of money paid as a first instalment ❸ a layer of solid matter in or on the earth • *New deposits of copper were found.*

deposit *VERB* deposits, depositing, deposited
❶ to put something down • *She deposited the books on the desk.* ❷ to pay money as a deposit
➤ **depositor** *NOUN*

deposition *NOUN* depositions
a written piece of evidence, given under oath

depot (say **dep**-oh) *NOUN* depots
❶ a place where things are stored ❷ a place where buses or trains are kept and repaired

depraved *ADJECTIVE*
behaving wickedly; of bad character
➤ **depravity** *NOUN*

deprecate (say **dep**-rik-ayt) *VERB* deprecates, deprecating, deprecated
to say that you disapprove of something
➤ **deprecation** *NOUN*
➤ **deprecatory** (say dep-rik-**ayt**-er-i) *ADJECTIVE*

depreciate (say dip-**ree**-shee-ayt) *VERB* depreciates, depreciating, depreciated
to become lower in value over a period of time
➤ **depreciation** *NOUN*

depress *VERB* depresses, depressing, depressed
❶ to make someone feel very sad and gloomy ❷ to lower the value of something • *Threat of war depressed prices* ❸ to press something down • *Depress the lever.*
➤ **depressive** *ADJECTIVE*

depressed *ADJECTIVE*
feeling very sad and without hope

depressing *ADJECTIVE*
making you feel sad or gloomy

depression *NOUN* depressions
❶ a feeling of great sadness or hopelessness, often with physical symptoms ❷ a long period when trade is very slack because no one can afford to buy things, with widespread unemployment ❸ a shallow hollow in the ground or on a surface ❹ an area of low air pressure which may bring rain

deprive *VERB* deprives, depriving, deprived
to take or keep something away from someone • *The prisoners were deprived of food.*
➤ **deprivation** *NOUN*

deprived *ADJECTIVE*
not having enough of the things that are essential for a comfortable life, e.g. food, money, etc. • *a deprived area*

depth *NOUN* depths
❶ being deep; how deep something is • *What is the depth of the river here?* ❷ how strong or intense something is • *I was surprised by the depth of his feelings.* ❸ the deepest or lowest part • *the depths of the sea*
➤ **in depth** thoroughly
➤ **out of your depth** ❶ in water that is too

deep to stand in ❷ trying to do something that is too difficult for you

deputation *NOUN* **deputations**
a group of people sent as representatives of others

depute (say dip-**yoot**) *VERB* **deputes, deputing, deputed**
to appoint a person to do something • *We deputed John to take the message.*

deputize (also **deputise**) *VERB* **deputizes, deputizing, deputized**
to act as someone's deputy

deputy *NOUN* **deputies**
a person appointed to help someone else in their job and to take their place when they are away

derail *VERB* **derails, derailing, derailed**
to cause a train to come off the tracks
➤ **derailment** *NOUN*

deranged *ADJECTIVE*
insane; wild and out of control
➤ **derangement** *NOUN*

derby (say **dar**-bi) *NOUN* **derbies**
a sports match between two teams from the same city or area (**WORD ORIGIN**) from the name of the Earl of *Derby*, who in 1780 founded the famous horse race called the Derby which is run at Epsom in Surrey

derelict (say **d**erri-likt) *ADJECTIVE*
abandoned and left to fall into ruin • *an old derelict mill*
➤ **dereliction** *NOUN*

deride *VERB* **derides, deriding, derided**
to laugh at someone or something with contempt or scorn

derision *NOUN*
scorn or ridicule • *She gave a snort of derision.*
➤ **derisive** (say dir-**y**-siv) *ADJECTIVE*
➤ **derisively** *ADVERB*

derisory *ADJECTIVE*
❶ so small that it is ridiculous • *a derisory offer* ❷ scornful

derivation *NOUN* **derivations**
the origin of a word from another language or from another word

derivative *ADJECTIVE*
derived from something; not original
➤ **derivative** *NOUN*

derive *VERB* **derives, deriving, derived**
❶ to obtain something from a source • *She*

derived great enjoyment from music. ❷ to originate from a language or from another word • *Some English words are derived from Latin words.*

dermatology *NOUN*
the study of the skin and its diseases
➤ **dermatologist** *NOUN*

dermis *NOUN*
the layer of skin below the epidermis

derogatory (say di-**rog**-at-er-ee) *ADJECTIVE*
scornful or critical • *derogatory remarks*

derrick *NOUN* **derricks**
❶ a kind of crane for lifting things ❷ a tall framework holding the machinery used in drilling an oil well (**WORD ORIGIN**) originally a gallows; Derrick was the surname of a London hangman

derv *NOUN*
(*British*) diesel fuel for lorries and other heavy vehicles (**WORD ORIGIN**) from the initials of 'diesel-engined road vehicle'

dervish *NOUN* **dervishes**
a member of a Muslim religious group who vowed to live a life of poverty

descant *NOUN* **descants**
a tune sung or played above the main tune

descend *VERB* **descends, descending, descended**
❶ to go or come down • *The plane started to descend.* • *She descended the stairs slowly.*
❷ to surprise someone with a sudden visit • *I hope you don't mind us descending on you like this.*
➤ **be descended from someone** to have someone as an ancestor; to come by birth from a certain person or family

descendant *NOUN* **descendants**
a person who is descended from someone

descending *ADJECTIVE*
going down from the highest to the lowest • *I have listed the scores in descending order.*

descent *NOUN* **descents**
❶ the process of going down; a climb down • *The plane began its descent.* ❷ a way down; a downward path or slope • *The descent is steep.* ❸ a person's family origin • *She is of French descent.*

describe *VERB* **describes, describing, described**
❶ to say what someone or something is like • *How would you describe the painting?* • *Can you describe what happened?* ❷ to move or draw something in a particular pattern or

shape • *The orbit of the Earth around the Sun describes an ellipse.*

description *NOUN* descriptions
❶ describing someone or something ❷ an account or picture in words

descriptive *ADJECTIVE*
giving a description; full of details • *a descriptive poem*

desecrate (say **dess**-ik-rayt) *VERB* desecrates, desecrating, desecrated
to treat a sacred thing without respect
➤ **desecration** *NOUN*

desert (say **dez**-ert) *NOUN* deserts
a large area of dry land, often covered with sand

desert (say diz-**ert**) *VERB* deserts, deserting, deserted
❶ to leave a person or place without intending to return ❷ to run away from the army
➤ **desertion** *NOUN*

> **SPELLING**
> Desert is different from **dessert**, which means food eaten at the end of a meal.

deserted *ADJECTIVE*
empty or abandoned • *The streets were deserted.*

deserter *NOUN* deserters
a soldier who runs away from the army

desert island *NOUN* desert islands
an uninhabited island

deserts (say diz-**erts**) *PLURAL NOUN*
what a person deserves • *He got his deserts.*

deserve *VERB* deserves, deserving, deserved
to have a right to something; to be worthy of something • *Everyone deserves a second chance.*
➤ **deservedly** *ADVERB*

desiccated *ADJECTIVE*
dried, in order to preserve it • *desiccated coconut*

design *NOUN* designs
❶ the way something is made or arranged ❷ a drawing that shows how something is to be made ❸ lines and shapes that form a decoration; a pattern ❹ a plan or scheme in the mind
➤ **have designs on something** to plan to get hold of something

design *VERB* designs, designing, designed
❶ to draw a design for something ❷ to plan

or intend something for a special purpose • *The course is designed for beginners.*

> **SPELLING**
> There is a silent g before the n in **design**.

designate *VERB* designates, designating, designated
❶ to mark or describe a thing as something particular • *They designated the river as the boundary.* • *These arrows designate the emergency exits.* ❷ to appoint someone to a position • *She designated me as her successor.*

designate *ADJECTIVE*
appointed to a job but not yet doing it • *the bishop designate*
➤ **designation** *NOUN*

designer *NOUN* designers
someone who designs things, especially clothes

desirable *ADJECTIVE*
worth having or doing • *It would be desirable to repeat the experiment if possible.*
➤ **desirability** *NOUN*

desire *NOUN* desires
a feeling of wanting something very much
➤ **desirous** *ADJECTIVE*

desire *VERB* desires, desiring, desired
to want something very much

desist (say diz-**ist**) *VERB* desists, desisting, desisted
(*formal*) to stop doing something

desk *NOUN* desks
❶ a piece of furniture with a flat top and often drawers, used when writing or doing work ❷ a counter at which a cashier or receptionist sits

desktop *NOUN* desktops
❶ a screen on a computer that shows the icons of the programs that you can use ❷ a computer that is designed to be used on a desk

desolate *ADJECTIVE*
❶ lonely and sad ❷ uninhabited or barren • *a desolate landscape*
➤ **desolation** *NOUN*

despair *NOUN*
a feeling of hopelessness

despair *VERB* despairs, despairing, despaired
to lose all hope • *She despaired of ever seeing him again.*

despatch *VERB* **despatches, despatching, despatched**
a different spelling of **dispatch**
➤ **despatch** *NOUN*

desperado (say dess-per-**ah**-doh) *NOUN* **desperadoes**
a reckless criminal

desperate *ADJECTIVE*
❶ extremely serious or hopeless • *a desperate situation* ❷ needing or wanting something very much • *She is desperate to get a ticket.* ❸ reckless and ready to do anything
➤ **desperation** *NOUN*

> **SPELLING**
> There is a tricky bit in **desperate**—it has an **e** in the middle.

desperately *ADVERB*
❶ in a desperate way • *She tried desperately to grab the rope.* ❷ very much; extremely
• *He was desperately unlucky not to win.*

despicable *ADJECTIVE*
very unpleasant or evil; deserving to be despised

despise *VERB* **despises, despising, despised**
to hate someone or something or have no respect for them

despite *PREPOSITION*
in spite of • *They went out despite the rain.*

despondent *ADJECTIVE*
sad or gloomy
➤ **despondently** *ADVERB*
➤ **despondency** *NOUN*

despot (say **dess**-pot) *NOUN* **despots**
a tyrant
➤ **despotism** *NOUN*
➤ **despotic** (say dis-**pot**-ik) *ADJECTIVE*

dessert (say diz-**ert**) *NOUN* **desserts**
fruit or a sweet food served as the last course of a meal

> **SPELLING**
> **Dessert** is different from **desert**, which means an area of very dry land.

dessertspoon *NOUN* **dessertspoons**
a medium-sized spoon used for eating puddings etc.

destination *NOUN* **destinations**
the place to which a person or thing is travelling or being sent

destined *ADJECTIVE*
intended by fate; meant to happen • *They felt they were destined to win.*

destiny *NOUN* **destinies**
what will happen or has happened to someone or something, in a way that seems to be beyond human control; fate • *She felt that it was her destiny to be a great singer.*

destitute *ADJECTIVE*
left without anything; living in extreme poverty
➤ **destitution** *NOUN*

destroy *VERB* **destroys, destroying, destroyed**
to damage something so badly that it can no longer be used or no longer exists • *The building was destroyed by fire.*

destroyer *NOUN* **destroyers**
a fast warship

destruction *NOUN*
destroying something or being destroyed
• *The war brought death and destruction to the city.*

destructive *ADJECTIVE*
causing a lot of harm or damage
• *Earthquakes can be very destructive.*

desultory (say **dess**-ul-ter-ee) *ADJECTIVE*
half-hearted, without enthusiasm or a definite plan • *a desultory conversation*
WORD ORIGIN from Latin *desultorius* = like an acrobat (someone who leaps about)

detach *VERB* **detaches, detaching, detached**
to unfasten or separate something • *Detach the coupon from the bottom of the page.*
➤ **detachable** *ADJECTIVE*

detached *ADJECTIVE*
❶ separated; not connected ❷ a detached house is one that is not joined to another ❸ able to stand back from a situation and not get emotionally involved in it • *As a journalist, I need to remain detached.*

detachment *NOUN* **detachments**
❶ the ability to stand back from a situation and not get emotionally involved in it ❷ a small group of soldiers sent away from a larger group for a special duty

detail *NOUN* **details**
❶ a very small part of a design, plan or decoration ❷ a small piece of information
➤ **in detail** describing or dealing with everything fully

detailed *ADJECTIVE*
giving many details • *a detailed description*

a b c d e f g h i j k l m n o p q r s t u v w x y z

A
B
C
D
E
F
G
H
I
J
K
L
M
N
O
P
Q
R
S
T
U
V
W
X
Y
Z

detain VERB detains, detaining, detained
❶ to keep someone waiting • *I'll try not to detain you for long.* ❷ to keep someone at a place

detainee NOUN detainees
a person who is officially detained or kept in custody

detect VERB detects, detecting, detected
to discover or notice something • *A bat's ears can detect sounds that are too high for us to hear.*
➤ **detection** NOUN

detective NOUN detectives
a person, especially a police officer, who investigates crimes

detector NOUN detectors
a device that detects something • *a smoke detector*

detention NOUN detentions
❶ detaining or being detained ❷ being made to stay late in school as a punishment

deter VERB deters, deterring, deterred
to discourage or prevent a person from doing something • *Nothing would deter Will from his plan.*

detergent NOUN detergents
a substance used for cleaning or washing things

deteriorate (say dit-**eer**-ee-er-ayt) VERB
deteriorates, deteriorating, deteriorated
to become worse • *The weather was starting to deteriorate.*
➤ **deterioration** NOUN

determination NOUN
the firm intention to achieve what you have decided to achieve

determine VERB determines, determining, determined
❶ to decide something • *His punishment is still to be determined.* ❷ to cause or influence something • *Where you live can determine your state of health.* ❸ to find out or calculate something • *Can you determine the height of the mountain?*

determined ADJECTIVE
full of determination; with your mind firmly made up

determiner NOUN determiners
(*in grammar*) a word (such as *a, the, many*) that introduces a noun and gives you some

information about it

GRAMMAR

Nouns often have a **determiner** in front of them. Determiners tell you 'which one', 'how many', or 'how much'. The most common determiners are the words *the*, known as the **definite article**, and *a* or *an*, known as the **indefinite article**. The following words are also determiners when they come before a noun:

this, that, these, and *those* (known as **demonstratives**), e.g. *this* weekend, *those* boots;

my, your, his, her, its, our, and *their* (known as **possessives**), e.g. That's *my* idea; It's *your* problem;

what, which, and *whose* (known as **interrogatives**), e.g. *What* flavours do you have? *Which* team won?

Other determiners, such as *all, another, any, both, each, every, few, many, some*, and *several*, are used to express quantity, e.g. *Both* socks are missing; *Few* people have climbed this mountain. Note that *any* and *some* can refer to either a number of separate things (*any* coins, *some* biscuits), or to an amount of something (*any* money, *some* cake).

Numbers can also be determiners when they come before a noun, e.g. *one* slice, *thirty* euros, as can the words *next* and *last*, e.g. *next* season, *last* summer.

See also the panels on **the** and **a** and the panel on **possessives**.

deterrent NOUN deterrents
something that may deter people, e.g. a nuclear weapon that deters countries from making war on the one that has it
➤ **deterrence** NOUN

detest VERB detests, detesting, detested
to strongly dislike a person or thing • *They absolutely detest each other.*
➤ **detestable** ADJECTIVE
➤ **detestation** NOUN

detonate (say **det**-on-ayt) VERB detonates, detonating, detonated
to explode or make a bomb or mine explode
➤ **detonation** NOUN
➤ **detonator** NOUN

detour (say **dee**-toor) NOUN detours
a roundabout route you use instead of the normal one

detract *VERB* **detracts, detracting, detracted**
to make something seem less good or
valuable • *Not even the rain could detract
from our enjoyment.*
➤ **detraction** *NOUN*

detriment (say **det**-rim-ent) *NOUN*
something is to the detriment of a thing if
it is harmful or damaging to it • *She worked
long hours, to the detriment of her health.*

detrimental (say det-rim-**en**-tal) *ADJECTIVE*
harmful or damaging • *The sun can have a
detrimental effect on the skin.*

deuce *NOUN* **deuces**
a score in tennis where both sides have 40
points and must gain two consecutive points
to win

devalue *VERB* **devalues, devaluing, devalued**
❶ to reduce a thing's value ❷ to reduce the
value of a country's currency in relation to
other currencies or to gold
➤ **devaluation** *NOUN*

devastate *VERB* **devastates, devastating,
devastated**
❶ to ruin or cause great destruction to
something • *Floods devastated the region.*
❷ to overwhelm someone with shock or grief
• *The tragedy has devastated the community.*
➤ **devastating** *ADJECTIVE*
➤ **devastation** *NOUN*

develop *VERB* **develops, developing, developed**
❶ to create or improve something gradually
• *Over the years she developed her own
singing style.* ❷ to become bigger or better;
to grow • *Children develop at different rates.*
❸ to come gradually into existence • *A storm
was developing in the distance.* ❹ to begin to
have or use something • *They developed bad
habits.* ❺ to use an area of land for building
houses, shops, factories, etc. ❻ to treat
photographic film with chemicals so that
pictures appear
➤ **developer** *NOUN*

> **SPELLING**
> There is no e at the end of **develop**.

developing country *NOUN* **developing
countries**
a poor country that is building up its industry
and trying to improve its living conditions

development *NOUN* **developments**
❶ developing or being developed ❷ a recent
event that changes a situation • *Have there
been any further developments since I
last saw you?* ❸ an area of land with new

buildings on it

> **SPELLING**
> Be careful: there is only one p and one l in
> **development**.

deviate (say **dee**-vee-ayt) *VERB* **deviates,
deviating, deviated**
to turn aside from a course or from what is
usual or true
➤ **deviation** *NOUN*

device *NOUN* **devices**
a tool or piece of equipment used for a
particular purpose • *a device for opening tins*
➤ **leave someone to their own devices** to
leave someone to do as they wish

devil *NOUN* **devils**
❶ an evil spirit ❷ a wicked, cruel or annoying
person

devilish *ADJECTIVE*
extremely cruel or cunning • *a devilish plan*

devilment *NOUN*
mischief

devious (say **dee**-vee-us) *ADJECTIVE*
❶ cunning and dishonest; underhand • *He
got rich by devious means.* ❷ a devious route
is roundabout and not direct
➤ **deviously** *ADVERB*

devise *VERB* **devises, devising, devised**
to invent a way of doing something • *He
devised a new method of painting.*

devoid *ADJECTIVE*
lacking or without something • *His work is
devoid of merit.*

devolution *NOUN*
handing over power from central government
to local or regional government

devolve *VERB* **devolves, devolving, devolved**
a task or power devolves on a deputy or
successor when it is passed on to them

devote *VERB* **devotes, devoting, devoted**
to devote yourself or your time to something
is to spend all your time doing it • *He devotes
all his free time to music.*

devoted *ADJECTIVE*
very loving or loyal

devotee (say dev-o-**tee**) *NOUN* **devotees**
a person who likes something very much; an
enthusiast • *a devotee of science fiction*

devotion *NOUN*
great love or loyalty

devotions *PLURAL NOUN*
prayers

devour *VERB* **devours, devouring, devoured**
❶ to eat or swallow something hungrily or greedily ❷ to read or look at something eagerly • *She devours two or three books a week.*

devout *ADJECTIVE*
deeply religious
➤ **devoutly** *ADVERB*

dew *NOUN*
tiny drops of water that form during the night on the ground and other surfaces in the open air
➤ **dewdrop** *NOUN*
➤ **dewy** *ADJECTIVE*

> **SPELLING**
> Be careful, this sounds the same as **due**.

dexterity (say deks-**terri**-tee) *NOUN*
skill in handling things **WORD ORIGIN** from Latin *dexter* = on the right-hand side, because the right hand was thought of as the stronger hand

dhal *NOUN*
an Indian dish of cooked lentils

dhoti *NOUN* **dhotis**
a loincloth worn by male Hindus

diabetes (say dy-a-**bee**-teez) *NOUN*
a disease in which there is too much sugar in a person's blood
➤ **diabetic** (say dy-a-**bet**-ik) *ADJECTIVE & NOUN*

diabolical *ADJECTIVE*
❶ like a devil; very wicked ❷ very bad or annoying • *The traffic was diabolical.*

diadem (say **dy**-a-dem) *NOUN* **diadems**
a crown or headband worn by a royal person

diagnose *VERB* **diagnoses, diagnosing, diagnosed**
to find out and say what disease a person has or what is wrong • *My brother was diagnosed with diabetes.*

diagnosis *NOUN* **diagnoses**
saying what is wrong with someone who is ill after examining them • *The doctor made a diagnosis of asthma.*
➤ **diagnostic** *ADJECTIVE*

diagonal (say dy-**ag**-on-al) *NOUN* **diagonals**
a straight line joining opposite corners • *Fold the paper in half along the diagonal.*

diagonal *ADJECTIVE*
slanting; crossing from corner to corner
➤ **diagonally** *ADVERB*

diagram *NOUN* **diagrams**
a kind of drawing or picture that shows the parts of something or how it works

dial *NOUN* **dials**
❶ a circular object with numbers or letters round it, used for measuring something ❷ a round control on a radio, cooker, etc. that you turn to change something

dial *VERB* **dials, dialling, dialled**
to press the numbers on a telephone dial or keypad in order to call a telephone number

dialect *NOUN* **dialects**
the words and pronunciations used by people in one district but not in the rest of a country

dialogue *NOUN* **dialogues**
❶ the words spoken by characters in a play, film or story ❷ a conversation

dialysis (say dy-**al**-iss-iss) *NOUN*
a way of removing harmful substances from a person's blood by letting it flow through a machine

diameter (say dy-**am**-it-er) *NOUN* **diameters**
❶ a line drawn straight across a circle or sphere and passing through its centre ❷ the length of this line

diametrically *ADVERB*
something that is diametrically opposite is completely opposite • *My sister and I took diametrically opposite views about the matter.*

diamond *NOUN* **diamonds**
❶ a very hard precious stone, a form of carbon, that looks like clear glass ❷ a shape with four equal sides and four angles that are not right angles ❸ a playing card with red diamond shapes on it

> **SPELLING**
> There is a tricky bit in **diamond** – there is an **a** after the **i**.

diamond wedding *NOUN* **diamond weddings**
a couple's 60th wedding anniversary

diaper *NOUN* **diapers**
(*North American*) a baby's nappy

diaphanous (say dy-**af**-an-us) *ADJECTIVE*
diaphanous fabric is thin, light and almost transparent

diaphragm (say **dy**-a-fram) *NOUN* **diaphragms**
❶ the muscular layer inside your body that

separates your chest from your abdomen and is used in breathing ❷ a dome-shaped contraceptive device that fits over the neck of the womb

diarist *NOUN* diarists
a person who keeps a diary

diarrhoea (say dy-a-**ree**-a) *NOUN*
too frequent and too watery emptying of the bowels

diary *NOUN* diaries
a book in which someone writes down what happens each day

diatribe *NOUN* diatribes
a strong verbal attack

dice *NOUN* dice
a small cube marked with dots (1 to 6) on its sides, used in games

> **USAGE**
> Dice was originally the plural of the noun die, but now it is often used as a singular, with the plural dice.

dice *VERB* dices, dicing, diced
❶ to cut meat, vegetables, etc. into small cubes ❷ to play gambling games using dice

dictate *VERB* dictates, dictating, dictated
❶ to speak or read something aloud for someone else to write down ❷ to give orders in a bossy way

dictates (say **dik**-tayts) *PLURAL NOUN*
rules or principles that must be obeyed • *the dictates of fashion*

dictation *NOUN* dictations
❶ a test in which students write down what is being read to them, especially in a language lesson ❷ speaking or reading something aloud for someone else to write down

dictator *NOUN* dictators
a ruler who has complete power over the people of a country
➤ **dictatorship** *NOUN*

dictatorial (say dik-ta-**tor**-ee-al) *ADJECTIVE*
always telling people what to do and ignoring their views

diction *NOUN*
❶ a person's way of speaking words • *clear diction* ❷ a writer's choice of words

dictionary *NOUN* dictionaries
a book that contains words in alphabetical order so that you can find out how to spell them and what they mean; a similar product for use on a computer

diddle *VERB* diddles, diddling, diddled (*informal*)
to cheat or swindle someone

didgeridoo *NOUN* didgeridoos
an Australian Aboriginal musical instrument which consists of a long thin pipe that you blow into to make a low humming sound

didn't (*mainly spoken*)
did not

> **SPELLING**
> Didn't = did + not. Add an **apostrophe** between the n and the t.

die *VERB* dies, dying, died
❶ to stop living or existing ❷ to stop working or burning • *The engine sputtered and died.*
➤ **be dying for** or **to** (*informal*) to want to have or do something very much • *We are all dying to see you again.*
➤ **die down** to gradually become less strong • *The wind died down at last.*
➤ **die out** to gradually disappear or become extinct • *The tiger is beginning to die out.*

die *NOUN*
❶ singular of **dice** ❷ dies a device that stamps a design on coins etc. or that cuts or moulds metal

> **SPELLING**
> Change the ie to y and add **ing** to make **dying**.

diehard *NOUN* diehards
a person who obstinately refuses to give up old ideas or policies

diesel (say **dee**-zel) *NOUN* diesels
❶ an engine that works by burning oil in compressed air ❷ fuel for this kind of engine
WORD ORIGIN named after Rudolf *Diesel*, a German engineer, who invented it

diet *NOUN* diets
❶ special meals that someone eats in order to be healthy or to lose weight ❷ the sort of foods usually eaten by a person or animal • *a vegetarian diet* ❸ the parliament of certain countries, such as Japan

diet *VERB* diets, dieting, dieted
to keep to a diet

dietitian (say dy-it-**ish**-an) *NOUN* dietitians
an expert in diet and nutrition

differ *VERB* differs, differing, differed
❶ to be different • *The two accounts differ in some important details.* ❷ to disagree in opinion • *The two writers differ on this point.*

difference *NOUN* **differences**
❶ being different; the way in which things differ • *There's a big difference between reading about China and actually going there.* ❷ the remainder left after one number is subtracted from another • *The difference between 8 and 3 is 5.* ❸ a disagreement

different *ADJECTIVE*
❶ unlike; not the same • *You look completely different with short hair.* ❷ separate or distinct • *I called on three different occasions.*

> **USAGE**
> It is regarded as more acceptable to say *different from* rather than *different to*, which is common in less formal use. The phrase *different than* is used in American English but not in standard British English.

> **SPELLING**
> Remember, there is a silent **er** in the middle of **different** and it ends in **ent**; there is no **a**.

differential *NOUN* **differentials**
❶ a difference in wages between one group of workers and another ❷ a differential gear

differential gear *NOUN* **differential gears**
a system of gears that makes a vehicle's driving wheels revolve at different speeds when going round corners

differentiate *VERB* **differentiates, differentiating, differentiated**
❶ to be a difference between things; to make one thing different from another • *What are the features that differentiate one breed from another?* ❷ to recognize differences between things • *We do not differentiate between them.*
➤ **differentiation** *NOUN*

differently *ADVERB*
in a different way • *You'll feel differently about it tomorrow.*

difficult *ADJECTIVE*
❶ needing a lot of effort or skill; not easy to do or understand ❷ not easy to please or satisfy • *a difficult child*

difficulty *NOUN* **difficulties**
❶ being difficult ❷ something that causes a problem

diffident (say **dif**-id-ent) *ADJECTIVE*
shy and not self-confident; hesitating to put yourself or your ideas forward

➤ **diffidently** *ADVERB*
➤ **diffidence** *NOUN*

diffract *VERB* **diffracts, diffracting, diffracted**
to break up a beam of light
➤ **diffraction** *NOUN*

diffuse (say dif-**yooz**) *VERB* **diffuses, diffusing, diffused**
❶ to spread something widely or thinly • *The Internet is being used to diffuse knowledge.* ❷ if a gas or liquid diffuses in a substance, it becomes slowly mixed with that substance
➤ **diffusion** *NOUN*

diffuse (say dif-**yooss**) *ADJECTIVE*
❶ spread widely; not concentrated • *diffuse light* ❷ using many words; not concise

dig *VERB* **digs, digging, dug**
❶ to break up soil and move it; to make a hole or tunnel by moving soil ❷ to poke or jab something sharply • *Its claws dug into my hand* ❸ to seek or discover something by investigating • *We dug up some facts.*

dig *NOUN* **digs**
❶ a place where archaeologists dig to look for ancient remains ❷ a sharp poke • *She gave me a dig in the ribs.* ❸ an unpleasant remark

digest (say dy-**jest**) *VERB* **digests, digesting, digested**
❶ to soften and break down food in the stomach so that the body can absorb it ❷ to take information into your mind and think it over • *The boy digested this news in silence for a few minutes.*
➤ **digestible** *ADJECTIVE*

digest (say **dy**-jest) *NOUN* **digests**
a summary of news or information

digestion *NOUN*
the process of digesting food

digestive *ADJECTIVE*
to do with digestion • *the digestive system*

digestive biscuit *NOUN* **digestive biscuits**
a wholemeal biscuit

digger *NOUN* **diggers**
❶ a machine for digging ❷ (*informal*) (*Australian/NZ*) a friendly form of address for a man

digit (say **dij**-it) *NOUN* **digits**
❶ any of the numbers from 0 to 9 ❷ a finger or toe

digital *ADJECTIVE*
❶ to do with or using digits ❷ a digital watch or clock shows the time with a row of figures

❸ a digital image or sound is represented as a series of binary digits ❹ a digital camera or recorder records digital sound and images
➤ **digitally** ADVERB

digitize (also **digitise**) VERB digitizes, digitizing, digitized
to convert information to a digital form so that it can be used on a computer

dignified ADJECTIVE
having or showing dignity • *a dignified manner*

dignitary NOUN dignitaries
an important official • *a number of local dignitaries*

dignity NOUN
a calm and serious manner
➤ **beneath your dignity** not considered worthy enough for you to do

digraph NOUN digraphs
a group of two letters forming one sound, e.g. *th* and *ey*

digress VERB digresses, digressing, digressed
to stray from the main subject • *But I digress. Back to the story...*
➤ **digression** NOUN

dike NOUN dikes
a different spelling of **dyke**

dilapidated ADJECTIVE
falling to pieces; in disrepair • *a dilapidated fence*
➤ **dilapidation** NOUN

dilate VERB dilates, dilating, dilated
to become or to make something wider or larger • *His eyes dilated with fear.*
➤ **dilation** NOUN

dilatory (say **dil**-at-er-ee) ADJECTIVE
slow in doing something; not prompt

dilemma (say dil-**em**-a) NOUN dilemmas
a situation where someone has to choose between two or more possible actions, either of which would bring difficulties

> **USAGE**
> Take care not to use **dilemma** to mean simply a problem or difficult situation. There should be some idea of choosing between two (or perhaps more) things.

diligence NOUN
careful and thorough work or effort • *He prepared for the exam with great diligence.*

diligent (say **dil**-ij-ent) ADJECTIVE
careful and hard-working • *a diligent student*
➤ **diligently** ADVERB

dilute VERB dilutes, diluting, diluted
to make a liquid weaker by adding water or other liquid
➤ **dilution** NOUN

dilute ADJECTIVE
diluted • *a dilute acid*

dim ADJECTIVE dimmer, dimmest
❶ not bright or clear; only faintly lit ❷ not distinct or vivid • *I have only a dim memory of the plot.* ❸ (*informal*) stupid
➤ **dimness** NOUN

dim VERB dims, dimming, dimmed
to become or make something dim • *As the curtain rose, the lights dimmed.*
➤ **dimmer** NOUN

dime NOUN dimes
(*North American*) a ten-cent coin

dimension NOUN dimensions
❶ a measurement such as length, width, area or volume • *What are the dimensions of the room?* ❷ the size or extent of something • *a problem of considerable dimensions*
➤ **dimensional** ADJECTIVE

diminish VERB diminishes, diminishing, diminished
❶ to become smaller or less important • *The world's resources are rapidly diminishing.*
❷ to make something smaller or less important • *The bad news did not diminish her enthusiasm.*
➤ **diminution** NOUN

diminutive (say dim-**in**-yoo-tiv) ADJECTIVE
very small

dimly ADVERB
❶ not brightly or clearly • *a dimly lit passage*
❷ not distinctly or vividly • *I was dimly aware of the sound of a car in the distance.*

dimple NOUN dimples
a small hollow or dent, especially in the skin of a person's cheek or chin
➤ **dimpled** ADJECTIVE

din NOUN
a loud annoying noise

dine VERB dines, dining, dined (*formal*)
to have dinner

diner NOUN diners
❶ a person who is dining ❷ (*North American*) a small, inexpensive restaurant

A B C **D** E F G H I J K L M N O P Q R S T U V W X Y Z

dinghy (say **ding**-ee) *NOUN* dinghies
a kind of small boat

dingo *NOUN* dingoes
an Australian wild dog

dingy (say **din**-jee) *ADJECTIVE*
dark and dirty-looking • *a dingy hotel room*

dinkum *ADJECTIVE* (*informal*)
(*Australian/NZ*) genuine, real or honest
➤ **fair dinkum** used for emphasis or to query whether something is true

dinner *NOUN* dinners
❶ the main meal of the day, eaten either in the middle of the day or in the evening
❷ a formal evening meal in honour of something

dinosaur (say **dy**-noss-or) *NOUN* dinosaurs
a prehistoric reptile, often of enormous size
WORD ORIGIN from Greek *deinos* = terrible + *sauros* = lizard

dint *NOUN*
➤ **by dint of** by means of; using • *I got through the exam by dint of a good memory and a lot of luck.*

diocese (say **dy**-oss-iss) *NOUN* dioceses
a district under the care of a bishop in the Christian Church
➤ **diocesan** (say dy-**oss**-iss-an) *ADJECTIVE*

dioxide *NOUN*
an oxide with two atoms of oxygen to one of another element • *carbon dioxide*

dip *VERB* dips, dipping, dipped
❶ to put something into a liquid and then take it out again • *Dip the brush in the paint.*
❷ to go or slope downwards • *The road dips steeply after the hill.* • *The sun dipped below the horizon.* ❸ to move or point something downwards • *The plane dipped its wings.*

dip *NOUN* dips
❶ dipping ❷ a downward slope ❸ a quick swim ❹ a creamy mixture into which you can dip pieces of food

diphtheria (say dif-**theer**-ee-a) *NOUN*
a serious disease that causes inflammation in the throat

diphthong (say **dif**-thong) *NOUN* diphthongs
a compound vowel sound made up of two sounds, e.g. *oi* in *point*, (made up of 'aw' + 'ee') or *ou* in *loud* ('ah' + 'oo')

diploma *NOUN* diplomas
a certificate awarded by a college etc. for skill in a particular subject

diplomacy *NOUN*
❶ the work of making agreements with other countries ❷ skill in dealing with other people without upsetting or offending them; tact

diplomat *NOUN* diplomats
❶ a person who represents their country officially abroad ❷ a tactful person

diplomatic *ADJECTIVE*
❶ to do with diplomats or diplomacy • *a diplomatic career* ❷ tactful; careful not to offend people • *a diplomatic reply*
➤ **diplomatically** *ADVERB*

dipper *NOUN* dippers
❶ a kind of bird that dives for its food
❷ a ladle

dire *ADJECTIVE*
dreadful or serious • *The refugees are in dire need of food and shelter.*

direct *ADJECTIVE*
❶ as straight as possible; not changing direction • *a direct flight to Hong Kong*
❷ with no one or nothing in between • *You should protect your skin from direct sunlight.*
❸ going straight to the point; frank ❹ exact or complete • *the direct opposite*

direct *VERB* directs, directing, directed
❶ to tell or show someone the way ❷ to guide or aim something in a certain direction • *The advert is directed at young people.*
❸ to control or manage someone or something • *She has directed many films.*
❹ to order someone to do something • *He directed his troops to advance.*

direct current *NOUN*
electric current flowing only in one direction

direction *NOUN* directions
❶ the line along which something moves or faces • *She glanced in his direction.*
❷ managing or controlling someone or something • *The mural was painted by the students under the direction of the art teacher.*

directions *PLURAL NOUN*
information on how to use or do something or how to get somewhere

directive *NOUN* directives
an official command

directly *ADVERB*
❶ by a direct route or in a direct line • *The man turned and looked directly at me.*
❷ immediately; without delay • *I want you to come directly.*

directness *NOUN*
being frank and straightforward in what you say • *He replied with his usual directness.*

direct object *NOUN* **direct objects**
(*in grammar*) the word that receives the action of the verb. In *she hit him,* 'him' is the direct object.

director *NOUN* **directors**
❶ a person who is in charge of something, especially one of a group of people managing a company ❷ a person who decides how a film, programme or play should be made or performed

directory *NOUN* **directories**
❶ a book containing a list of people with their telephone numbers, addresses, etc. ❷ (*in computing*) a file containing a group of other files

direct speech *NOUN*
someone's words written down exactly in the way they were said

GRAMMAR

Direct speech shows the exact words that a person or character says. The spoken words—and any punctuation that goes with them, such as full stops, exclamation marks or question marks—are enclosed in quotation marks:

'Wait! Can you at least tell me your name?' I shouted at the retreating figure.

Any description of who is speaking (e.g. *she said, I exclaimed*) is separated from the spoken words by a comma or commas:

'We are planning', said a NASA spokesperson, *'to send a manned expedition to Mars.'*

Reported speech is also called **indirect speech**. It describes or reports what a person or character says without using their exact words. You do not use quotation marks in reported speech and the tense of the verb (*were* in this example) follows that of the reporting verb (*said* in the example):

A NASA spokesperson said that they were planning to send a manned expedition to Mars.

You can also leave out the word *that* at the beginning of the reported speech:

A NASA spokesperson said they were

planning to send a manned expedition to Mars.

See also the panel on **quotation marks**.

dirge *NOUN* **dirges**
a slow sad song

dirk *NOUN* **dirks**
a kind of dagger

dirt *NOUN*
❶ anything that is not clean, such as mud or dust • *His face and hands were covered in dirt.* ❷ loose earth or soil

dirty *ADJECTIVE* **dirtier, dirtiest**
❶ covered with dirt; not clean ❷ unfair or dishonourable • *That was a dirty trick.* ❸ indecent or obscene

disability *NOUN* **disabilities**
a physical or mental condition that restricts someone's movements or senses

disable *VERB* **disables, disabling, disabled**
to stop something from working properly

disabled *ADJECTIVE*
unable to use part of your body properly because of illness or injury

disadvantage *NOUN* **disadvantages**
something that hinders you or is unhelpful
➤ **disadvantageous** *ADJECTIVE*

disadvantaged *ADJECTIVE*
in a bad social or economic situation • *disadvantaged children*

disagree *VERB* **disagrees, disagreeing, disagreed**
❶ to have or express a different opinion from someone ❷ to have a bad effect • *Rich food disagrees with me.*

disagreeable *ADJECTIVE*
unpleasant

disagreement *NOUN* **disagreements**
a situation in which people have different opinions about something and often also argue • *They had a few disagreements with their neighbours.*

disappear *VERB* **disappears, disappearing, disappeared**
❶ to stop being visible; to vanish ❷ to stop happening or existing • *Her nervousness soon disappeared.*
➤ **disappearance** *NOUN*

disappoint *VERB* **disappoints, disappointing, disappointed**

to make you sad by failing to do or be what you hoped for or expected • *I'm sorry to disappoint you, but I can't come after all.*
➤ **disappointed** *ADJECTIVE*

disappointing *ADJECTIVE*
not as good as you hoped or expected • *a disappointing result*

disappointment *NOUN* disappointments
❶ a feeling of being disappointed ❷ a person or thing that disappoints you • *The film was a big disappointment.*

disapproval *NOUN*
a feeling that someone is behaving badly • *She could hear the disapproval in his voice.*

disapprove *VERB* disapproves, disapproving, disapproved
to think that something is wrong or bad, especially the way someone is behaving

disarm *VERB* disarms, disarming, disarmed
❶ to reduce the size of armed forces ❷ to take away someone's weapons ❸ to overcome a person's anger or doubt • *Her friendliness disarmed their suspicions.*
➤ **disarming** *ADJECTIVE*

disarmament *NOUN*
reduction of a country's armed forces or weapons

disarray *NOUN*
disorder or confusion • *Our plans were thrown into disarray by her sudden arrival.*

disassemble *VERB* disassembles, disassembling, disassembled
to take something to pieces

disaster *NOUN* disasters
❶ an event or accident that causes a lot of harm or damage; a very bad misfortune • *earthquakes, floods and other natural disasters* ❷ a complete failure • *The first night of the play was a disaster.*

disastrous *ADJECTIVE*
causing great harm or failing completely • *This mistake had disastrous results.*
➤ **disastrously** *ADVERB*

disband *VERB* disbands, disbanding, disbanded
a group or organization disbands when it breaks up • *The choir disbanded last year.*

disbelief *NOUN*
a feeling of not being able to believe something • *The others stared at him in disbelief.*
➤ **disbelieve** *VERB*

disc *NOUN* discs
❶ any round flat object ❷ a CD or DVD ❸ a layer of cartilage between vertebrae in your spine

discard *VERB* discards, discarding, discarded
to get rid of something because it is useless or unwanted

discern (say dis-**sern**) *VERB* discerns, discerning, discerned
to see or recognize something that is not obvious • *I discerned a note of anger in his voice.*
➤ **discernible** *ADJECTIVE*
➤ **discernment** *NOUN*

discerning *ADJECTIVE*
showing good judgement about the quality of something • *a discerning film-goer*

discharge *VERB* discharges, discharging, discharged
❶ to allow a person to leave a place • *She was discharged from hospital yesterday.*
❷ to send something out • *The engine was discharging black smoke.* ❸ to discharge a debt or promise is to pay it off or do what has been agreed

discharge *NOUN* discharges
❶ an act of discharging someone or something ❷ something that is discharged

disciple *NOUN* disciples
❶ a follower or pupil of a leader or of a religion or philosophy ❷ any of the original followers of Jesus Christ

disciplinarian *NOUN* disciplinarians
a person who believes in strict discipline

discipline *NOUN* disciplines
❶ training people to obey rules and behave well and punishing them if they do not ❷ self-control; the ability to work or behave in a controlled way ❸ a subject for study
➤ **disciplinary** (say **dis**-ip-lin-er-ee) *ADJECTIVE*

discipline *VERB* disciplines, disciplining, disciplined
❶ to train yourself to work or behave in a controlled way • *He disciplined himself to practise the piano every morning.* ❷ to punish someone

disc jockey *NOUN* disc jockeys
a person who introduces and plays records on the radio or at a club

disclaim *VERB* disclaims, disclaiming, disclaimed
to say that you are not responsible for something or have no knowledge of

something • *They disclaimed all responsibility for the bomb.*
➤ **disclaimer** *NOUN*

disclose *VERB* discloses, disclosing, disclosed
you disclose a fact or information when you reveal it or make it known
➤ **disclosure** *NOUN*

disco *NOUN* discos
an event where pop music is played for people to dance to

discolour *VERB* discolours, discolouring, discoloured
to spoil or change the colour of something
➤ **discoloration** *NOUN*

discomfit *VERB* discomfits, discomfiting, discomfited
to make a person feel uneasy or embarrassed

discomfiture *NOUN*
a feeling of unease or embarrassment

discomfort *NOUN*
❶ slight pain ❷ being uneasy or embarrassed • *She was clearly enjoying my discomfort.*

disconcert (say dis-kon-**sert**) *VERB*
disconcerts, disconcerting, disconcerted
to make a person feel uneasy or worried • *His answer disconcerted her.*

disconnect *VERB* disconnects, disconnecting, disconnected
to break a connection; to detach something • *The phone has been disconnected.*
➤ **disconnection** *NOUN*

disconnected *ADJECTIVE*
not joined together in a logical way or order • *a disconnected narrative*

disconsolate (say dis-**kon**-sol-at) *ADJECTIVE*
unhappy and disappointed

discontent *NOUN*
a feeling of being unhappy and not satisfied • *There were a few murmurs of discontent.*
➤ **discontented** *ADJECTIVE*

discontinue *VERB* discontinues, discontinuing, discontinued
to stop doing or producing something

discord *NOUN* discords
❶ disagreement; quarrelling ❷ musical notes sounded together and producing a harsh or unpleasant sound
➤ **discordant** *ADJECTIVE*

discotheque (say **dis**-ko-tek) *NOUN*
discotheques
(*old use*) a disco

discount *NOUN* discounts
an amount by which a price is reduced

discount *VERB* discounts, discounting, discounted
to ignore or disregard something • *We cannot discount the possibility.*

discourage *VERB* discourages, discouraging, discouraged
❶ to take away someone's enthusiasm or confidence • *Don't be discouraged – try again!* ❷ to try to persuade someone not to do something • *His parents tried to discourage him from being an actor.*
➤ **discouragement** *NOUN*

discourse *NOUN* discourses
a formal speech or piece of writing about something

discourse *VERB* discourses, discoursing, discoursed
to speak or write at length about something

discourteous *ADJECTIVE*
not courteous or polite; rude
➤ **discourteously** *ADVERB*
➤ **discourtesy** *NOUN*

discover *VERB* discovers, discovering, discovered
❶ to find or find out something, especially by searching ❷ to be the first person to find something • *Herschel discovered the planet Uranus.*
➤ **discoverer** *NOUN*

discovery *NOUN* discoveries
❶ discovering something or being discovered • *Columbus is famous for the discovery of America.* ❷ something that is discovered • *This drug was an important discovery in the history of medicine.*

discredit *VERB* discredits, discrediting, discredited
❶ to cause an idea or theory to be doubted ❷ to damage someone's reputation

discredit *NOUN*
damage to someone's reputation
➤ **discreditable** *ADJECTIVE*

discreet *ADJECTIVE*
❶ being careful in what you say and not giving away secrets • *I'll make a few discreet enquiries.* ❷ not likely to attract attention
➤ **discreetly** *ADVERB*

> **SPELLING**
> Take care not to confuse with **discrete**.

discrepancy (say dis-**krep**-an-see) *NOUN*
discrepancies
lack of agreement between things which
should be the same • *There are several
discrepancies in the two accounts.*

discrete *ADJECTIVE*
(*formal*) separate; distinct from each other
• *We divided the data into six discrete
categories.*

discretion (say dis-**kresh**-on) *NOUN*
❶ being discreet; keeping secrets • *I hope
I can count on your discretion.* ❷ freedom
to decide things and take action according
to your own judgement • *You can use your
discretion.*

discriminate *VERB* discriminates,
discriminating, discriminated
❶ to notice and understand the differences
between things; to prefer one thing to
another ❷ to treat people differently or
unfairly because of their race, gender or
religion

discrimination *NOUN*
❶ different or unfair treatment of people
because of their race, gender or religion
❷ the ability to notice and understand the
differences between things

discus *NOUN* discuses
a thick heavy disc thrown in athletic contests

discuss *VERB* discusses, discussing, discussed
to talk with other people about a subject or
to write about it in detail

discussion *NOUN* discussions
❶ a conversation about a subject ❷ a piece
of writing in which the writer examines a
subject from different points of view

disdain *NOUN*
scorn or contempt • *She stared at him with
cold disdain.*
➤ **disdainful** *ADJECTIVE*
➤ **disdainfully** *ADVERB*

disdain *VERB* disdains, disdaining, disdained
❶ to regard or treat someone or something
with disdain ❷ to not do something because
of disdain • *She disdained to reply.*

disease *NOUN* diseases
an unhealthy condition; an illness
➤ **diseased** *ADJECTIVE*

disembark *VERB* disembarks, disembarking,
disembarked
to get off a ship or aircraft
➤ **disembarkation** *NOUN*

disembodied *ADJECTIVE*
a disembodied voice comes from an invisible
or unknown source

disembowel *VERB* disembowels,
disembowelling, disembowelled
to take out the bowels or inside parts of
something

disengage *VERB* disengages, disengaging,
disengaged
to disconnect or detach something

disentangle *VERB* disentangles, disentangling,
disentangled
to free something from tangles or confusion
• *I disentangled my coat from the bushes.*

disfavour *NOUN*
disapproval or dislike

disfigure *VERB* disfigures, disfiguring,
disfigured
to spoil a person's or thing's appearance • *His
face was disfigured by a long red scar.*
➤ **disfigurement** *NOUN*

disgorge *VERB* disgorges, disgorging,
disgorged
to pour or send something out • *The pipe
disgorged its contents.*

disgrace *NOUN*
❶ shame; loss of approval or respect
• *You have brought disgrace to your
family.* ❷ something that is shameful or
unacceptable • *The bus service is a disgrace.*

disgrace *VERB* disgraces, disgracing, disgraced
to bring disgrace upon someone

disgraceful *ADJECTIVE*
shameful or unacceptable
➤ **disgracefully** *ADVERB*

disgruntled *ADJECTIVE*
discontented or in a bad mood
WORD ORIGIN from an old word *gruntle* =
grunt softly

disguise *VERB* disguises, disguising, disguised
❶ to make a person or thing look different
so that people will not recognize them ❷ to
conceal your feelings • *She could not disguise
her amazement.*

disguise *NOUN* disguises
something you wear or use to change your
appearance so that nobody recognizes you

disgust *NOUN*
a feeling that something is very unpleasant or
disgraceful

disgust VERB disgusts, disgusting, disgusted
to make someone feel disgust
➤ **disgusted** ADJECTIVE

disgusting ADJECTIVE
making you feel disgust; very unpleasant
• *What a disgusting smell!*

dish NOUN dishes
❶ a plate or bowl for food ❷ food prepared
for eating • *We're having a vegetarian dish
tonight.* ❸ a bowl-shaped aerial for receiving
broadcasting signals transmitted by satellite

dish VERB dishes, dishing, dished (*informal*)
➤ **dish something out** to give out portions
of something to people

dishcloth NOUN dishcloths
a cloth you use for washing dishes

dishearten VERB disheartens, disheartening,
disheartened
to cause a person to lose hope or confidence
➤ **disheartened** ADJECTIVE

dishevelled (say dish-**ev**-eld) ADJECTIVE
untidy in appearance • *He looked tired and
dishevelled.*

dishonest ADJECTIVE
not honest or truthful
➤ **dishonestly** ADVERB
➤ **dishonesty** NOUN

dishonour NOUN
loss of honour or respect; disgrace
➤ **dishonour** VERB
➤ **dishonourable** ADJECTIVE

dishwasher NOUN dishwashers
a machine for washing dishes etc.
automatically

disillusion VERB disillusions, disillusioning,
disillusioned
you disillusion someone if you show them
that something they like to think is true is
wrong or mistaken
➤ **disillusioned** ADJECTIVE
➤ **disillusionment** NOUN

disinclination NOUN
unwillingness to do something

disinclined ADJECTIVE
unwilling to do something • *He was
disinclined to believe anything she said.*

disinfect VERB disinfects, disinfecting,
disinfected
to destroy the germs in something
➤ **disinfection** NOUN

disinfectant NOUN disinfectants
a substance used for disinfecting things

disinherit VERB disinherits, disinheriting,
disinherited
to deprive a person of the right to inherit
something

disintegrate VERB disintegrates,
disintegrating, disintegrated
to break up into small parts or pieces • *The
spacecraft exploded and disintegrated.*
➤ **disintegration** NOUN

disinterested ADJECTIVE
not influenced by the hope of gaining
something yourself; impartial • *She gave us
some disinterested advice.*

USAGE
If you mean 'not interested' or 'bored', use
uninterested.

disjointed ADJECTIVE
disjointed talk or writing is not well joined
together and so is difficult to understand

disk NOUN disks
a flat circular object on which computer data
can be stored

dislike VERB dislikes, disliking, disliked
to not like someone or something

dislike NOUN dislikes
a feeling of not liking someone or something

dislocate VERB dislocates, dislocating,
dislocated
a bone is dislocated when it moves or is
forced from its proper position in one of your
joints
➤ **dislocation** NOUN

dislodge VERB dislodges, dislodging, dislodged
to move or force something from its place
• *The wind dislodged several roof tiles.*

disloyal ADJECTIVE
not loyal
➤ **disloyalty** NOUN

dismal ADJECTIVE
❶ gloomy or dreary • *dismal surroundings*
❷ of poor quality • *a dismal first-half
performance*
➤ **dismally** ADVERB
WORD ORIGIN from Latin *dies mali* = unlucky
days

dismantle VERB dismantles, dismantling,
dismantled
to take something to pieces • *He was busy
dismantling the wardrobe.*

a
b
c
d
e
f
g
h
i
j
k
l
m
n
o
p
q
r
s
t
u
v
w
x
y
z

dismay NOUN
a feeling of strong disappointment and surprise • *I realized to my dismay that we were going to miss our plane.*
➤ **dismayed** ADJECTIVE

dismember VERB dismembers, dismembering, dismembered
to tear or cut the limbs from a body

dismiss VERB dismisses, dismissing, dismissed
❶ to send someone away ❷ to tell someone that you will no longer employ them ❸ to put something out of your thoughts because it is not worth thinking about • *He dismissed the idea as nonsense.*
➤ **dismissal** NOUN

dismissive ADJECTIVE
saying or showing that you think something is not worth taking seriously • *a dismissive gesture*
➤ **dismissively** ADVERB

dismount VERB dismounts, dismounting, dismounted
to get off a horse or bicycle

disobedient ADJECTIVE
not obedient
➤ **disobedience** NOUN

disobey VERB disobeys, disobeying, disobeyed
to refuse to do what you are told to do • *He was punished for disobeying orders.*

disorder NOUN disorders
❶ untidiness or lack of order ❷ an illness • *an eating disorder* ❸ violent behaviour by a large number of people
➤ **disorderly** ADJECTIVE

disorganized (also **disorganised**) ADJECTIVE
muddled and badly organized
➤ **disorganization** NOUN

disown VERB disowns, disowning, disowned
to refuse to acknowledge that a person has any connection with you • *Her family disowned her for marrying a foreigner.*

disparage (say dis-**pa**-rij) VERB disparages, disparaging, disparaged
to criticize something or say that it is unimportant
➤ **disparagement** NOUN

disparity NOUN disparities
difference or inequality • *the wide disparity between rich and poor*

dispassionate ADJECTIVE
calm and impartial; not emotional
➤ **dispassionately** ADVERB

dispatch VERB dispatches, dispatching, dispatched
❶ to send someone or something off to a destination ❷ to kill a person or animal

dispatch NOUN dispatches
❶ dispatching ❷ a report or message sent ❸ to do something with dispatch is to do it promptly and efficiently

dispatch box NOUN dispatch boxes
a container for carrying official documents

dispatch rider NOUN dispatch riders
(*British*) a messenger who travels by motorcycle

dispel VERB dispels, dispelling, dispelled
❶ to drive or clear something away • *Wind dispels fog.* ❷ to get rid of a fear or doubt

dispensary NOUN dispensaries
a place where medicines are dispensed

dispense VERB dispenses, dispensing, dispensed
❶ to distribute something to a number of people ❷ a machine dispenses money or goods when it gives them out to customers ❸ to prepare medicine according to prescriptions
➤ **dispensation** NOUN
➤ **dispense with something** to do without something

dispenser NOUN dispensers
a device that supplies a quantity of something • *a cash dispenser*

disperse VERB disperses, dispersing, dispersed
❶ to separate and go off in different directions; to scatter • *The fog began to disperse.* ❷ to force a crowd to break up • *Police dispersed the protesters.*
➤ **dispersal** NOUN
➤ **dispersion** NOUN

displace VERB displaces, displacing, displaced
❶ to take a person's or thing's place • *Last year she displaced him as captain.* ❷ to force someone or something to move from their usual place • *Thousands of people have been displaced by the fighting.*
➤ **displacement** NOUN

display VERB displays, displaying, displayed
❶ to show or arrange something so that it can be clearly seen ❷ to show a quality or emotion • *They displayed great courage.*

display NOUN displays
❶ the displaying of something ❷ a collection of things displayed in a shop window,

museum, etc. ❸ an electronic device for visually presenting data

displease VERB displeases, displeasing, displeased
to annoy or offend someone
➤ **displeasure** NOUN

disposable ADJECTIVE
made to be thrown away after it has been used • *disposable nappies*

disposal NOUN
getting rid of something • *bomb disposal*
➤ **at your disposal** available for you to use • *The computer is at your disposal all afternoon.*

dispose VERB disposes, disposing, disposed
❶ to dispose of something is to get rid of it • *Please dispose of all your rubbish.* ❷ to be disposed to do something is to be ready or willing to do it • *They were not at all disposed to help us.*
➤ **be well disposed to someone** to be friendly towards someone

disposition NOUN dispositions
a person's nature or qualities • *She has a cheerful disposition.*

disproportionate ADJECTIVE
out of proportion; too large or too small

disprove VERB disproves, disproving, disproved
to show that something is not true • *The theory has now been disproved.*

dispute VERB disputes, disputing, disputed
❶ to argue about something ❷ to question the truth of something • *We dispute their claim.*

dispute NOUN disputes
a disagreement or argument
➤ **in dispute** being argued about • *The cause of the accident is not in dispute.*

disqualify VERB disqualifies, disqualifying, disqualified
to bar someone from a competition because they have broken the rules or are not properly qualified to take part
➤ **disqualification** NOUN

disquiet NOUN
anxiety or worry
➤ **disquieting** ADJECTIVE

disregard VERB disregards, disregarding, disregarded
to take no notice of something; to ignore

something • *Please disregard my earlier instructions.*

disregard NOUN
the act of ignoring something • *He ran into the burning building with complete disregard for his own safety.*

disrepair NOUN
bad condition caused by not doing repairs • *The old mill is in a state of disrepair.*

disreputable ADJECTIVE
not respectable in character

disrepute NOUN
bad reputation • *He has been charged with bringing the game into disrepute.*

disrespect NOUN
lack of respect; rudeness
➤ **disrespectful** ADJECTIVE
➤ **disrespectfully** ADVERB

disrupt VERB disrupts, disrupting, disrupted
to stop something running smoothly; to throw something into confusion • *Fog disrupted traffic.*
➤ **disruption** NOUN

disruptive ADJECTIVE
causing so much disorder that a lesson, meeting, etc. cannot continue

dissatisfied ADJECTIVE
not satisfied or pleased
➤ **dissatisfaction** NOUN

dissect (say dis-**sekt**) VERB dissects, dissecting, dissected
to cut something up so that you can examine it
➤ **dissection** NOUN

disseminate VERB disseminates, disseminating, disseminated
to spread ideas or information widely
➤ **dissemination** NOUN

dissent NOUN
a difference of opinion; disagreement

dissent VERB dissents, dissenting, dissented
to express a difference of opinion about something

dissertation NOUN dissertations
a long essay on an academic subject, written as part of a university degree

disservice NOUN
a harmful action done by someone who was intending to help

dissident NOUN dissidents
a person who disagrees, especially someone

a b c d e f g h i j k l m n o p q r s t u v w x y z

who opposes their government
> **dissident** *ADJECTIVE*
> **dissidence** *NOUN*

dissipate *VERB* dissipates, dissipating, dissipated
❶ to disappear or scatter • *The fog gradually dissipated.* ❷ to waste or squander something
> **dissipation** *NOUN*

dissolute *ADJECTIVE*
having an immoral way of life

dissolution *NOUN* dissolutions
❶ putting an end to a marriage or partnership ❷ formally ending a parliament or assembly

dissolve *VERB* dissolves, dissolving, dissolved
❶ to mix something with a liquid so that it becomes part of the liquid ❷ to break up and become mixed with a liquid • *Wait for the tablet to dissolve.* ❸ to put an end to a marriage or partnership ❹ to formally end a parliament or assembly • *Parliament was dissolved and a general election was held.*

dissuade *VERB* dissuades, dissuading, dissuaded
to persuade someone not to do something • *I tried to dissuade him from going.*

distaff *NOUN* distaffs
a stick holding raw wool for spinning into yarn

distance *NOUN* distances
❶ the amount of space between two places or things ❷ being far away in space or time • *The island looked magical from a distance.*
> **in the distance** far away but visible

distant *ADJECTIVE*
❶ far away • *distant stars* ❷ not closely related • *distant cousins* ❸ not friendly or sociable • *She sounded cold and distant on the phone.*
> **distantly** *ADVERB*

distaste *NOUN*
a feeling of dislike for something • *She looked at his clothes with distaste.*

distasteful *ADJECTIVE*
unpleasant or offensive

distemper *NOUN*
❶ a disease of dogs and certain other animals ❷ a kind of paint

distend *VERB* distends, distending, distended
to make something swell outwards because of pressure from inside
> **distension** *NOUN*

distil *VERB* distils, distilling, distilled
to purify a liquid by boiling it and condensing the vapour
> **distillation** *NOUN*

distillery *NOUN* distilleries
a place where whisky or other alcoholic spirit is made
> **distiller** *NOUN*

distinct *ADJECTIVE*
❶ easily heard or seen; noticeable • *There has been a distinct improvement.* ❷ clearly separate or different • *A rabbit is quite distinct from a hare.*
> **distinctness** *NOUN*

USAGE
See note at **distinctive**.

distinction *NOUN* distinctions
❶ a difference between things ❷ excellence or honour • *She is a writer of distinction.* ❸ an award for excellence; a high mark in an examination

distinctive *ADJECTIVE*
clearly different from others and therefore easy to recognize • *The school has a distinctive uniform.*
> **distinctively** *ADVERB*

USAGE
Take care not to confuse this word with **distinct**. A distinct mark is a clear mark; a distinctive mark is one that is not found anywhere else.

distinctly *ADVERB*
❶ clearly or noticeably • *I can see Mars distinctly through my binoculars.* ❷ particularly; definitely • *His behaviour has been distinctly odd recently.*

distinguish *VERB* distinguishes, distinguishing, distinguished
❶ to make or notice differences between things • *You need to distinguish between facts and opinions.* ❷ to see or hear something clearly • *I was too far away to distinguish what they were saying.* ❸ if you distinguish yourself you do something that brings you honour or respect • *He distinguished himself by his bravery.*
> **distinguishable** *ADJECTIVE*

distinguished *ADJECTIVE*
❶ excellent and famous ❷ dignified in appearance

distort *VERB* distorts, distorting, distorted
❶ to pull or twist something out of its normal

shape • *His face was distorted with anger.*
❷ to give a false account or impression of
something • *The film deliberately distorts the
truth.*
➤ **distortion** NOUN

distract VERB distracts, distracting, distracted
to take a person's attention away from what
they are doing

distracted ADJECTIVE
greatly upset by worry or distress; distraught

distraction NOUN distractions
❶ something that distracts a person's
attention ❷ an amusement or entertainment
❸ great worry or distress

distraught (say dis-**trawt**) ADJECTIVE
greatly upset by worry or distress

distress NOUN distresses
great sorrow, pain or trouble
➤ **in distress** in danger and needing help

distress VERB distresses, distressing,
distressed
to make someone feel very upset or worried
• *It distressed her to see him looking so ill.*

distribute VERB distributes, distributing,
distributed
❶ to give or share something out to
a number of people • *The money was
distributed among all the local schools.* ❷ to
spread or scatter something around • *Make
sure your weight is evenly distributed.*
➤ **distributor** NOUN

distribution NOUN
❶ the way that something is shared out or
spread over an area • *The map shows the
distribution of rainfall in Africa.* ❷ giving or
delivering something to a number of people
or places • *the distribution of food supplies*

district NOUN districts
part of a town or country

distrust NOUN
lack of trust; suspicion
➤ **distrustful** ADJECTIVE

distrust VERB distrusts, distrusting, distrusted
to have no trust in someone or something

disturb VERB disturbs, disturbing, disturbed
❶ to spoil someone's peace or rest • *Sorry,
I didn't mean to disturb you.* ❷ to make
someone feel upset or worried ❸ to move a
thing from its position • *He noticed that the
papers on his desk had been disturbed.*

disturbance NOUN disturbances
❶ something that makes you stop what you

are doing • *We have a lot to do so we don't
want any disturbances.* ❷ fighting or noisy
behaviour in a public place • *There were
several disturbances in the streets.*

disuse NOUN
the state of being no longer used • *The farm
buildings had fallen into disuse.*

disused ADJECTIVE
no longer used • *a disused railway line*

ditch NOUN ditches
a trench dug to hold water or carry it away or
to serve as a boundary

ditch VERB ditches, ditching, ditched
❶ (*informal*) to abandon or get rid of
something • *The thieves ditched the car and
ran off.* ❷ to bring an aircraft down in a
forced landing on the sea

dither VERB dithers, dithering, dithered
to hesitate nervously • *Stop dithering and
make up your mind!*

ditto NOUN
used in a list with the meaning 'the same
again'

ditty NOUN ditties
a short simple song

divan NOUN divans
a bed or couch without a raised back or sides

dive VERB dives, diving, dived
❶ to jump into water with your arms and
head first ❷ to swim under water using
breathing equipment ❸ to move down
quickly • *The engines failed and the plane
dived.*

dive NOUN dives
❶ diving into water ❷ a quick downwards
movement

diver NOUN divers
❶ someone who dives ❷ a person who works
under water in a special suit with an air
supply ❸ a bird that dives for its food

diverge VERB diverges, diverging, diverged
to go aside or in different directions • *The
two paths diverge at this point.*
➤ **divergent** ADJECTIVE
➤ **divergence** NOUN

divers (say **dy**-verz) ADJECTIVE (*old use*)
various or several

diverse (say dy-**verss**) ADJECTIVE
varied; of several different kinds • *people
from diverse backgrounds*

a
b
c
d
e
f
g
h
i
j
k
l
m
n
o
p
q
r
s
t
u
v
w
x
y
z

diversify *VERB* diversifies, diversifying, diversified
to become varied; to involve yourself in different kinds of things
➤ **diversification** *NOUN*

diversion *NOUN* diversions
❶ diverting something from its course ❷ something intended to take people's attention away from something • *You look in the room, while I create a diversion.* ❸ an alternative route for traffic when a road is closed ❹ something amusing or entertaining

diversity *NOUN*
the wide variety of something • *the region's vast diversity of animal species*

divert *VERB* diverts, diverting, diverted
❶ to make something change its direction or path • *All traffic is being diverted while the road is under repair.* ❷ to entertain or amuse someone
➤ **diverting** *ADJECTIVE*

divest *VERB* divests, divesting, divested
to take something away from someone • *They divested him of power.*

divide *VERB* divides, dividing, divided
❶ to separate something into smaller parts; to split something up ❷ to share something out • *We'll divide the money between us.* ❸ to find how many times one number is contained in another • *Divide six by three and you get two (6 ÷ 3 = 2).* ❹ to cause people to disagree • *This issue has divided the party.*

dividend *NOUN* dividends
❶ a share of a business's profit ❷ a number that is to be divided by another. Compare with **divisor**.

dividers *PLURAL NOUN*
a pair of compasses for measuring distances

divine *ADJECTIVE*
❶ belonging to or coming from God ❷ like a god ❸ (*informal*) excellent; extremely beautiful
➤ **divinely** *ADVERB*

divine *VERB* divines, divining, divined
to discover something by guessing or instinct

divinity *NOUN* divinities
❶ being divine ❷ a god or goddess ❸ the study of religion

division *NOUN* divisions
❶ the process of dividing numbers or things ❷ a dividing line or partition ❸ one of the parts into which something is divided ❹ a

difference of opinion within a group of people

divisive (say div-y-siv) *ADJECTIVE*
causing disagreement within a group

divisor *NOUN* divisors
a number by which another is to be divided. Compare **dividend**.

divorce *NOUN* divorces
the legal ending of a marriage

divorce *VERB* divorces, divorcing, divorced
two people divorce when they end their marriage by law

divulge *VERB* divulges, divulging, divulged
to reveal information • *He promised not to divulge the secret formula.*

Diwali (say di-**wah**-lee) *NOUN*
a Hindu religious festival at which lamps are lit, held in October or November
WORD ORIGIN from Sanskrit *dipavali* = row of lights

DIY *ABBREVIATION*
do-it-yourself; the activity of doing your own house repairs and improvements instead of paying someone to do them • *a DIY store*

dizzy *ADJECTIVE* dizzier, dizziest
having or causing the feeling that everything is spinning round; giddy
➤ **dizzily** *ADVERB*
➤ **dizziness** *NOUN*

DJ *ABBREVIATION*
disc jockey

DNA *ABBREVIATION*
deoxyribonucleic acid; a substance in chromosomes that stores genetic information

do *VERB* does, doing, did, done
This word has many different uses, most of which mean performing or dealing with something (*Do your best. I can't do this. She is doing well at school.*) or being suitable or enough (*This will do*). The verb is also used with other verbs:
❶ in questions (*Do you want this?*) ❷ in statements with 'not' (*He does not want it.*) ❸ for emphasis (*I do like nuts.*) ❹ to avoid repeating a verb that has just been used (*We work as hard as they do.*)
➤ **do away with something** to get rid of something
➤ **do something up** ❶ to fasten something • *Do your coat up.* ❷ to repair or redecorate

a room or house • *We're doing up the spare room.*

GRAMMAR

The auxiliary verb **do** is used:

in questions and in short answers:

Do you want to watch this film?

No, I don't, thanks.

Did he pass his exams?

Yes, he did.

in negative statements:

I don't want to watch this film.

He didn't pass his exams.

in negative imperatives:

Do not walk on the grass.

Don't be silly.

for emphasis:

I do want to watch this film.

He did pass his exam!

---

do *NOUN* **dos** (*informal*) a party or other social event

docile (say **doh**-syl) *ADJECTIVE*
quiet, obedient and easy to control • *She was a shy docile child.*
➤ **docility** *NOUN*

dock *NOUN* **docks**
❶ a part of a harbour where ships are loaded, unloaded or repaired ❷ the place in a law court where the prisoner on trial sits or stands ❸ a weed with broad leaves

dock *VERB* **docks, docking, docked**
❶ a ship docks when it comes into a dock ❷ when two spacecraft dock, they join together in space ❸ to cut short an animal's tail ❹ to reduce or take away part of someone's wages or the number of points they have

docker *NOUN* **dockers**
a worker in a port who loads and unloads ships

docket *NOUN* **dockets**
a document or label listing the contents of a package

dockyard *NOUN* **dockyards**
an open area with docks and equipment for building or repairing ships

doctor *NOUN* **doctors**
❶ a person who is trained to treat sick or injured people ❷ a person who holds an advanced degree (a **doctorate**) at a university • *Doctor of Music*

doctrine *NOUN* **doctrines**
a belief held by a religious, political or other group

document *NOUN* **documents**
❶ a written or printed paper giving information or evidence about something ❷ (*in computing*) a computer file that contains text or images and that has a name • *Save the document before logging off.*
➤ **documentation** *NOUN*

documentary *ADJECTIVE*
❶ consisting of documents • *documentary evidence* ❷ showing real events or situations

documentary *NOUN* **documentaries**
a film or television programme giving information about real events

doddery, doddering *ADJECTIVE*
shaking and walking unsteadily because of old age

dodge *VERB* **dodges, dodging, dodged**
❶ to move quickly to avoid someone or something • *He ran across the road, dodging the traffic.* ❷ to avoid doing something • *She tried to dodge the question.*

dodge *NOUN* **dodges**
(*informal*) a trick; a clever way of doing something

dodgem *NOUN* **dodgems**
(*British*) a small electrically driven car at a funfair, in which each driver tries to bump some cars and dodge others
WORD ORIGIN from **dodge** + *'em* (them)

dodgy *ADJECTIVE* (*British*) (*informal*)
❶ awkward or tricky ❷ not working properly ❸ dishonest or unreliable

dodo *NOUN* **dodos**
a large heavy bird that used to live on an island in the Indian Ocean but has been extinct for over 200 years **WORD ORIGIN** from Portuguese *doudo* = fool (because the bird had no fear of people)

doe *NOUN* **does**
a female deer, rabbit or hare

doer *NOUN* **doers**
a person who does things • *He's a doer not a talker.*

doesn't (*mainly spoken*)
does not

> **SPELLING**
> Doesn't = does + not.
> Add an **apostrophe** between the **n** and
> the **t**.

doff *VERB* **doffs, doffing, doffed**
to take off your hat, especially to show
respect for someone **WORD ORIGIN** from *do
off*; compare **don**

dog *NOUN* **dogs**
a four-legged animal that barks, often kept
as a pet

dog *VERB* **dogs, dogging, dogged**
to follow someone closely or persistently
• *Reporters dogged his footsteps.*

doge (say dohj) *NOUN* **doges**
the elected ruler of the former republics of
Venice and Genoa

dog-eared *ADJECTIVE*
a dog-eared book has the corners of its pages
bent from constant use

dogfish *NOUN* **dogfish**
a kind of small shark

dogged (say **dog**-id) *ADJECTIVE*
determined and persistent; not giving up
easily
> **doggedly** *ADVERB*

doggerel *NOUN*
bad or comic verse • *a piece of doggerel*

dogma *NOUN* **dogmas**
a belief or principle that a Church or other
authority declares is true and must be
accepted

dogmatic *ADJECTIVE*
expressing ideas in a very firm authoritative
way
> **dogmatically** *ADVERB*

dogsbody *NOUN* **dogsbodies** (*British*) (*informal*)
a person who is given boring or unimportant
jobs to do

doh *NOUN*
a name for the keynote of a scale in music or
the note C

doily *NOUN* **doilies**
a small ornamental table-mat, made of paper
or lace **WORD ORIGIN** named after a Mr *Doily*
or *Doyley*, who sold household linen in the 17th
century

doldrums *PLURAL NOUN*
the ocean regions near the equator where
there is little or no wind
> **in the doldrums** feeling depressed and
unable to do anything

dole *VERB NOUN* **doles, doling, doled** (*informal*)
money paid by the state to unemployed
people • *He lost his job and had to go on the
dole.*
> **dole something out** to distribute
something among a group of people

doleful *ADJECTIVE*
sad or sorrowful • *a doleful expression*
> **dolefully** *ADVERB*

doll *NOUN* **dolls**
a toy model of a person, especially a baby or
child

dollar *NOUN* **dollars**
a unit of money in the USA and some other
countries

dollop *NOUN* **dollops** (*informal*)
a lump of something soft • *a dollop of cream*

dolly *NOUN* **dollies** (*informal*)
a doll

dolphin *NOUN* **dolphins**
a sea animal like a small whale with a beak-
like snout

domain (say dom-**ayn**) *NOUN* **domains**
❶ a kingdom ❷ an area of knowledge or
interest ❸ a group of Internet addresses that
end with the same letters, such as .com

dome *NOUN* **domes**
a roof shaped like the top half of a ball
> **domed** *ADJECTIVE*

domestic *ADJECTIVE*
❶ to do with your home or household ❷ to
do with your own country; not foreign or
international • *a domestic flight* ❸ domestic
animals are kept by people and are not wild
> **domestically** *ADVERB*

domesticated *ADJECTIVE*
domesticated animals are trained to live with
and be kept by humans

domicile (say dom-iss-syl) *NOUN* **domiciles**
(*formal*)
the place where someone lives; a residence
> **domiciled** *ADJECTIVE*

dominant *ADJECTIVE*
more important or powerful than others
• *Arabic is the dominant language of the*

Middle East.
➤ **dominance** *NOUN*

dominate *VERB* **dominates, dominating, dominated**
❶ to control someone or something by being stronger or more powerful ❷ to be the highest or most noticeable thing in a place • *The mountain dominates the whole landscape.*
➤ **domination** *NOUN*

domineer *VERB* **domineers, domineering, domineered**
to behave in a forceful or arrogant way towards others
➤ **domineering** *ADJECTIVE*

dominion *NOUN* **dominions**
❶ authority to rule others; control ❷ an area over which someone rules

domino *NOUN* **dominoes**
a small flat oblong piece of wood or plastic with dots (1 to 6) or a blank space at each end, used in the game of dominoes

don *VERB* **dons, donning, donned**
(*formal*) to put on a piece of clothing • *Donning his cloak, he went outside.*
WORD ORIGIN from *do on*; compare **doff**

donate *VERB* **donates, donating, donated**
to present money or a gift to a charity or organization
➤ **donation** *NOUN*

donga *NOUN* **dongas** (*S. African*)
❶ a ditch caused by erosion ❷ a dry water channel

donkey *NOUN* **donkeys**
an animal that looks like a small horse with long ears

donor *NOUN* **donors**
someone who gives something • *a blood donor*

don't (*mainly spoken*)
do not

> **SPELLING**
> Don't = do + not. Add an **apostrophe** between the **n** and the **t**.

doodle *VERB* **doodles, doodling, doodled**
to scribble or draw something absent-mindedly

doodle *NOUN* **doodles**
a drawing made by doodling

doom *NOUN*
a grim fate that you cannot avoid, especially

death or destruction • *a sense of impending doom*

doom *VERB* **dooms, dooming, doomed**
to make it certain that someone will suffer a grim fate

doomed *ADJECTIVE*
❶ certain to suffer a grim fate ❷ bound to fail or be destroyed • *The plan was doomed from the start.*

doomsday *NOUN*
the day of the Last Judgement; the end of the world

door *NOUN* **doors**
a movable barrier on hinges (or one that slides or revolves), used to open or close an entrance; the entrance itself
➤ **doorknob** *NOUN*
➤ **doormat** *NOUN*

doorstep *NOUN* **doorsteps**
the step or piece of ground just outside a door

door-to-door *ADJECTIVE*
done at each house in turn

doorway *NOUN* **doorways**
the opening into which a door fits

dope *NOUN* **dopes** (*informal*)
❶ a drug, especially one taken or given illegally ❷ a stupid person

dope *VERB* **dopes, doping, doped** (*informal*) to give a drug to a person or animal

dopey *ADJECTIVE* (*informal*)
❶ stupid or silly ❷ not fully awake

dormant *ADJECTIVE*
❶ sleeping ❷ living or existing but not active; not extinct • *a dormant volcano*

dormitory *NOUN* **dormitories**
a room for several people to sleep in, especially in a school or institution

dormouse *NOUN* **dormice**
an animal like a large mouse that hibernates in winter

dorp *NOUN* **dorps**
(*S. African*) a village or small country town in South Africa

dorsal *ADJECTIVE*
to do with or on the back • *Some fish have a dorsal fin.*

dosage *NOUN* **dosages**
❶ the giving of medicine in doses ❷ the size of a dose

a
b
c
d
e
f
g
h
i
j
k
l
m
n
o
p
q
r
s
t
u
v
w
x
y
z

dose *NOUN* doses
the amount of a medicine that you are meant to take at one time

dose *VERB* doses, dosing, dosed
to give a dose of medicine to a person or animal

dossier (say **doss**-ee-er or **doss**-ee-ay) dossiers
a set of documents containing information about a person or event

dot *NOUN* dots
a small round mark or spot
➤ **on the dot** exactly on time

dot *VERB* dots, dotting, dotted
❶ to mark something with dots ❷ an area is dotted with things when they are scattered all over it • *The hillside was dotted with sheep.*

dotage (say **doh**-tij) *NOUN*
someone is in their dotage when they are old, weak and not able to think clearly

dote *VERB* dotes, doting, doted
➤ **dote on someone** to be very fond of someone

dotty *ADJECTIVE* dottier, dottiest (*British*) (*informal*)
slightly mad or eccentric
➤ **dottiness** *NOUN*

double *ADJECTIVE*
❶ twice as much; twice as many ❷ having two things or parts that form a pair • *a double-barrelled shotgun* ❸ suitable for two people • *a double bed*

double *NOUN* doubles
❶ a double quantity or thing ❷ a person or thing that looks exactly like another • *He's his father's double.*
➤ **doubles** a game of tennis or badminton between two pairs of players

double *VERB* doubles, doubling, doubled
❶ to become twice as much or as many • *The price has doubled in the last two years.* ❷ to make something twice as much or as many • *Think of a number and double it.* ❸ to bend or fold something in two
➤ **double back** to turn and go back the same way you have come • *The fox doubled back on its tracks.*
➤ **double up** to bend over because you are in pain or laughing so much

double bass *NOUN* double basses
a musical instrument with strings, like a large cello

double-click *VERB* double-clicks, double-clicking, double-clicked
to press a button on a computer mouse twice quickly

double-cross *VERB* double-crosses, double-crossing, double-crossed
to deceive or cheat someone who thinks you are working with them

double-decker *NOUN* double-deckers
a bus with two floors, one above the other

doublet *NOUN* doublets
a man's close-fitting jacket worn in the 15th-17th centuries

doubly *ADVERB*
twice as much; more than usual • *It's doubly important that you should go.*

doubt *NOUN* doubts
a feeling of not being sure about something

doubt *VERB* doubts, doubting, doubted
to feel unsure about something; to think that something is unlikely • *I never doubted that she would come.*
➤ **doubter** *NOUN*

> **SPELLING**
> There is a silent **b** before the **t** in **doubt**.

doubtful *ADJECTIVE*
❶ feeling doubt; unsure ❷ not certain to happen • *It is doubtful whether we'll finish on time.*

doubtfully *ADVERB*
in a doubtful way • *'I suppose it'll be all right,' she said doubtfully.*

doubtless *ADVERB*
certainly; without any doubt • *Doubtless she'll have a good excuse for being late.*

dough *NOUN*
❶ a thick mixture of flour and water used for making bread or pastry ❷ (*informal*) money
➤ **doughy** *ADJECTIVE*

> **SPELLING**
> The 'oh' sound is spelt **ough** in **dough**.

doughnut *NOUN* doughnuts
a round or ring-shaped bun that has been fried and covered in sugar

> **SPELLING**
> The 'oh' sound is spelt **ough** in **doughnut**.

doughty (say **dow**-tee) *ADJECTIVE*
brave and determined

dour (say doo-er) *ADJECTIVE*
stern and gloomy-looking
➤ **dourly** *ADVERB*

douse *VERB* douses, dousing, doused
❶ to pour water or other liquid over
something ❷ to put out a light or fire • *She
doused each of the lamps.*

dove *NOUN* doves
a kind of pigeon, often used as a symbol of
peace

dovetail *NOUN* dovetails
a wedge-shaped joint used to join two pieces
of wood

dovetail *VERB* dovetails, dovetailing,
dovetailed
❶ to join pieces of wood with a dovetail ❷ to
fit neatly together • *My plans dovetailed with
hers.* (**WORD ORIGIN**) because the wedge shape
looks like a dove's tail

dowager *NOUN* dowagers
a woman who holds a title or property after
her husband has died • *the dowager duchess*

dowdy *ADJECTIVE* dowdier, dowdiest
shabby and unfashionable; not stylish
➤ **dowdily** *ADVERB*

dowel *NOUN* dowels
a headless wooden or metal pin for holding
together two pieces of wood or stone
➤ **dowelling** *NOUN*

down *ADVERB*
❶ to or in a lower place or position or level
• *It fell down.* • *Can you turn the volume
down?* ❷ in writing • *Take down these
instructions.* ❸ to a source or place • *The
police tracked them down.*

down *PREPOSITION*
downwards through or along or into • *Pour
it down the drain.* • *He walked down the
corridor.*

down *ADJECTIVE*
❶ unhappy or depressed • *He's feeling down
at the moment.* ❷ not connected or working
properly • *All the computers are down.*
➤ **be down to someone** to be someone's
responsibility • *It's down to you to feed the
rabbits.*

down *VERB* downs, downing, downed
to finish a drink

down *NOUN* downs
❶ very fine soft feathers or hair ❷ a grass-
covered hill • *the South Downs*

downcast *ADJECTIVE*
❶ looking downwards • *downcast eyes* ❷ sad
or dejected

downfall *NOUN* downfalls
a person's fall from power or prosperity; the
thing that causes this • *His enemies began to
plot his downfall.* • *Greed was her downfall.*

downgrade *VERB* downgrades, downgrading,
downgraded
to reduce a person or thing to a lower grade
or rank • *She has been downgraded to vice-
captain.*

downhill *ADVERB* & *ADJECTIVE*
down a slope

downland *NOUN*
open countryside of gently rolling hills

download *VERB* downloads, downloading,
downloaded
to transfer data or programs to your
computer from the Internet or a large
computer system

download *NOUN* downloads
a computer program or file that you have
downloaded

downpour *NOUN* downpours
a heavy fall of rain

downright *ADVERB* & *ADJECTIVE*
complete or completely • *a downright lie*
• *That was downright rude.*

Down's syndrome *NOUN*
a medical condition caused by a chromosome
defect that causes intellectual impairment
and physical abnormalities such as short
stature and a broad flattened skull

downstairs *ADVERB* & *ADJECTIVE*
to or on a lower floor

downstream *ADJECTIVE* & *ADVERB*
in the direction in which a stream or river
flows

down-to-earth *ADJECTIVE*
sensible and practical

downward *ADJECTIVE* & *ADVERB*
going towards what is lower • *a downward
movement*
➤ **downwards** *ADVERB*

downy *ADJECTIVE*
covered in very fine soft feathers or hair

dowry *NOUN* dowries
property or money brought by a bride to her
husband when she marries him

a b c d e f g h i j k l m n o p q r s t u v w x y z

A
B
C
D
E
F
G
H
I
J
K
L
M
N
O
P
Q
R
S
T
U
V
W
X
Y
Z

doze *VERB* dozes, dozing, dozed
to sleep lightly

doze *NOUN*
a short light sleep
➤ **dozy** *ADJECTIVE*

dozen *NOUN* dozens
a set of twelve

drab *ADJECTIVE* drabber, drabbest
❶ not colourful ❷ dull or uninteresting • *a drab life*
➤ **drabness** *NOUN*

Draconian (say drak-**oh**-nee-an) *ADJECTIVE*
very harsh or strict • *Draconian laws*
WORD ORIGIN named after *Draco*, who established very severe laws in ancient Athens

draft *NOUN* drafts
❶ a rough plan of a piece of writing, not the final version ❷ a written order for a bank to pay out money

draft *VERB* drafts, drafting, drafted
❶ to make a rough plan of something you are going to write ❷ to select someone for a special duty • *She was drafted to our office in Paris.*

drag *VERB*
❶ to pull something heavy along ❷ to search a river or lake with nets and hooks ❸ to continue slowly in a boring manner • *The morning seemed to drag.*

drag *NOUN*
❶ (*informal*) something that is tedious or a nuisance ❷ women's clothes worn by men

dragon *NOUN* dragons
❶ a mythological monster, usually with wings and able to breathe out fire ❷ a fierce person, especially a woman

dragonfly *NOUN* dragonflies
an insect with a long thin body and two pairs of transparent wings

dragoon *NOUN* dragoons
a member of certain cavalry regiments

dragoon *VERB* dragoons, dragooning, dragooned
to force someone into doing something

drain *NOUN* drains
❶ a pipe or ditch for taking away water or other liquid ❷ something that takes away your strength or resources

drain *VERB* drains, draining, drained
❶ to make an area dry by taking the water away • *The land will have to be drained before it can be used for farming.* ❷ to flow

or trickle away • *The water drained away.* • *All the colour drained from his face.* ❸ to pour off liquid in which something has been cooked • *Drain the pasta thoroughly.* ❹ to take away your strength gradually; to exhaust someone • *I felt drained of energy.*

drainage *NOUN*
a system of drains for taking water away

drainpipe *NOUN* drainpipes
a pipe used for carrying water or sewage from a building

drake *NOUN* drakes
a male duck

drama *NOUN* dramas
❶ a play ❷ writing or performing plays ❸ a series of exciting or emotional events

dramatic *ADJECTIVE*
❶ to do with drama ❷ exciting and impressive • *the film's dramatic opening scene* ❸ sudden and very noticeable • *a dramatic change*
➤ **dramatics** *PLURAL NOUN*
➤ **dramatically** *ADVERB*

dramatis personae (say **dram**-a-tis per-**sohn**-eye) *PLURAL NOUN*
the characters in a play **WORD ORIGIN** Latin = persons of the drama

dramatist *NOUN* dramatists
a person who writes plays

dramatize (also **dramatise**) *VERB* dramatizes, dramatizing, dramatized
❶ to make a story into a play • *The novel has been dramatized for TV.* ❷ to make something seem more exciting than it really is • *The newspaper was accused of dramatizing the facts.*
➤ **dramatization** *NOUN*

drape *VERB* drapes, draping, draped
to arrange cloth or clothing loosely over something • *He draped his coat over the back of the chair.*

draper *NOUN* drapers (*British*) (*old use*)
a shopkeeper who sells cloth or clothes

drapery *NOUN* draperies
cloth arranged in loose folds

drastic *ADJECTIVE*
having a strong or violent effect • *a drastic course of action*
➤ **drastically** *ADVERB*

draught (say drahft) *NOUN* draughts
❶ a current of cold air indoors ❷ a swallow

of liquid

SPELLING
A **draught** is a current of air. A **draft** is a first version of something, and to **draft** something means to make a first version of it.

draughts *NOUN*
(*British*) a game played with 24 round pieces on a chessboard

draughtsman *NOUN* **draughtsmen**
❶ a person who makes drawings or is good at drawing ❷ (*British*) a piece used in the game of draughts

draughty *ADJECTIVE* **draughtier, draughtiest**
a draughty room or building is one that lets in currents of cold air

draw *VERB* **draws, drawing, drew, drawn**
❶ to produce a picture or outline by making marks on a surface ❷ to pull something along • *She drew her chair up to the table.* ❸ to take something out • *A woman was drawing water from the well.* • *He drew his sword.* ❹ to attract people or their attention • *The fair drew large crowds.* ❺ to end a game or contest with the same score on both sides ❻ to move or come gradually • *The ship drew nearer.* ❼ to draw curtains is to open or close them ❽ to get a prize or ticket in a raffle or lottery
➤ **draw a conclusion** to form an opinion about something by thinking about the evidence

draw *NOUN* **draws**
❶ a game or match that ends with the same score on both sides ❷ a raffle or similar competition in which the winner is chosen by picking tickets or numbers at random ❸ an attraction ❹ the drawing out of a gun • *He was quick on the draw.*

SPELLING
The past tense of **draw** is **drew** and the past participle is **drawn**.

drawback *NOUN* **drawbacks**
a disadvantage

drawbridge *NOUN* **drawbridges**
a bridge over a moat, hinged at one end so that it can be raised or lowered

drawer *NOUN* **drawers**
❶ a sliding box-like compartment in a piece of furniture ❷ a person who draws something

drawing *NOUN* **drawings**
❶ a picture drawn with a pencil, pen or

crayon ❷ making pictures in this way • *My brother is good at drawing.*

drawing pin *NOUN* **drawing pins**
(*British*) a short pin with a flat top that you use for fastening paper to a surface

drawing room *NOUN* **drawing rooms** (*old use*)
a sitting room **WORD ORIGIN** short for *withdrawing room* = a private room in a hotel etc., to which guests could withdraw

drawl *VERB* **drawls, drawling, drawled**
to speak very slowly or lazily

drawl *NOUN* **drawls**
a drawling way of speaking

dray *NOUN* **drays**
a strong low flat cart for carrying heavy loads

dread *NOUN*
great fear or worry

dread *VERB* **dreads, dreading, dreaded**
to fear something very much • *I'm dreading the exam results.*
➤ **dreaded** *ADJECTIVE*

dreadful *ADJECTIVE* (*informal*)
very bad or unpleasant • *We've had dreadful weather.*

dreadfully *ADVERB*
(*chiefly British*) extremely; or very badly • *I'm dreadfully sorry.*

dreadlocks *PLURAL NOUN*
hair worn in many ringlets or plaits, especially by Rastafarians

dream *NOUN* **dreams**
❶ a series of pictures or events in your mind while you are asleep ❷ something you imagine; an ambition or ideal • *His dream is to be famous.*

dream *VERB* **dreams, dreaming, dreamt or dreamed**
❶ to have a dream or dreams ❷ to have an ambition • *She dreams of being an astronomer.* ❸ to think something might happen • *I never dreamt she would leave.*
➤ **dream something up** to invent or imagine a plan or idea
➤ **dreamer** *NOUN*

dreamy **dreamier, dreamiest** *ADJECTIVE*
looking as though you are not paying attention but thinking about something pleasant • *a dreamy expression*
➤ **dreamily** *ADVERB*

dreary *ADJECTIVE* **drearier, dreariest**
❶ dull or boring ❷ gloomy or depressing

a b c d e f g h i j k l m n o p q r s t u v w x y z

➤ **drearily** ADVERB
➤ **dreariness** NOUN

dredge VERB dredges, dredging, dredged
to drag something up, especially by scooping at the bottom of a river or the sea
➤ **dredger** NOUN

dregs PLURAL NOUN
the last drops of a liquid at the bottom of a glass, barrel, etc., together with any sediment

drench VERB drenches, drenching, drenched
to make someone or something wet all through; to soak someone or something
• *They got drenched in the rain.*

dress NOUN dresses
❶ a woman's or girl's piece of clothing which has a skirt and also covers the top part of the body ❷ clothes or costume • *fancy dress*

dress VERB dresses, dressing, dressed
❶ to put clothes on someone or yourself
❷ to clean a wound and put a dressing on it
❸ to put a dressing on a salad

dressage (say **dress**-ahzh) NOUN
the training of a horse to perform various manoeuvres in order to show its obedience

dresser NOUN dressers
❶ a sideboard with shelves at the top for displaying plates etc. ❷ a person who dresses in a particular way • *He is a a stylish dresser.*

dressing NOUN dressings
❶ a bandage, plaster or ointment etc. for a wound ❷ a sauce of oil, vinegar, etc. for a salad

dressing gown NOUN dressing gowns
(*British*) a loose light indoor coat you wear when you are not fully dressed

dressmaker NOUN dressmakers
a person who makes women's clothes
➤ **dressmaking** NOUN

dress rehearsal NOUN dress rehearsals
the final rehearsal of a play at which the cast wear their costumes

dribble VERB dribbles, dribbling, dribbled
❶ to let saliva trickle out of your mouth
❷ liquid dribbles when it flows in drops
• *Juice dribbled down his chin.* ❸ to move the ball forward in football or hockey with slight touches of your feet or stick
➤ **dribble** NOUN

drier NOUN driers
a device for drying hair or laundry

drift VERB drifts, drifting, drifted
❶ to be carried gently along by water or air
• *The boat drifted out to sea.* ❷ to move along slowly and casually • *People started to drift out of the hall.* ❸ to live casually with no definite plan or purpose • *He drifted into teaching.*
➤ **drift off** to gradually fall asleep

drift NOUN drifts
❶ a drifting movement ❷ a mass of snow or sand piled up by the wind ❸ the general meaning of what someone says • *I'm afraid I don't get your drift.*

driftwood NOUN
wood floating on the sea or washed ashore by it

drill NOUN drills
❶ a tool for making holes; a machine for boring holes or wells ❷ repeated exercises, e.g. in military training ❸ (*informal*) a set way of doing something • *You should know the drill by now.*

drill VERB drills, drilling, drilled
❶ to make a hole or well with a drill ❷ to teach someone to do something by making them do repeated exercises

drily ADVERB
you speak drily when you say something funny in a clever and sarcastic way • *'I can hardly contain my excitement,' he said drily.*

drink VERB drinks, drinking, drank, drunk
❶ to swallow liquid ❷ to drink a lot of alcoholic drinks
➤ **drinker** NOUN

drink NOUN drinks
❶ a liquid for drinking; an amount of liquid swallowed • *Can I have a drink of water?*
❷ an alcoholic drink

drip VERB drips, dripping, dripped
❶ to fall in drops • *Water dripped from his hair.* ❷ to let liquid fall in drops • *The tap was dripping.*

drip NOUN drips
❶ liquid falling in drops; the sound it makes
❷ a piece of medical equipment for dripping liquid or a drug into the veins of a sick person

drip-dry ADJECTIVE
made of material that dries easily and does not need ironing

dripping NOUN
fat melted from roasted meat and allowed to set

drive *VERB* drives, driving, drove, driven
❶ to operate a motor vehicle or a train; to go or take someone to a place in a car ❷ to make something or someone move • *The dogs drove the sheep into the field.* ❸ to force or compel someone to do something • *Hunger drove them to steal.* ❹ to force someone into a state • *She is driving me crazy.* ❺ to force something into place by hitting it • *He drove a nail into the wall.* ❻ to move or fall rapidly • *The rain was driving down in torrents.*
➤ **driver** *NOUN*

> **SPELLING**
> The past tense of **drive** is **drove** and the past participle is **driven**.

drive *NOUN* drives
❶ a journey in a vehicle ❷ a hard stroke in cricket or golf ❸ a track for vehicles through the grounds of a house ❹ energy or enthusiasm ❺ an organized effort • *a sales drive* ❻ the part of a computer that reads and stores information on disks

drive-in *ADJECTIVE*
that you can use without getting out of your car • *a drive-in restaurant*

drivel *NOUN*
silly talk; nonsense

drizzle *NOUN*
very fine rain

drizzle *VERB* drizzles, drizzling, drizzled
to rain gently

droll *ADJECTIVE*
amusing in an odd way

dromedary *NOUN* dromedaries
a camel with one hump, bred for riding on

drone *VERB* drones, droning, droned
❶ to make a deep humming sound ❷ to talk for a long time in a boring way

drone *NOUN* drones
❶ a droning sound ❷ a male bee

drool *VERB* drools, drooling, drooled
to dribble continuously
➤ **drool over something** to show great pleasure in looking at something you like • *He's been drooling over car catalogues all afternoon.*

droop *VERB* droops, drooping, drooped
to bend or hang down weakly • *The tulips were beginning to droop.*

drop *NOUN* drops
❶ a tiny amount of liquid ❷ a fall or decrease • *There has been a sharp drop in prices.* ❸ a distance down from a high point to a lower point • *a sheer drop of 40 metres to the sea*

drop *VERB* drops, dropping, dropped
❶ to let something fall • *She almost dropped one of the eggs.* ❷ to fall downwards ❸ to become lower or less • *The temperature suddenly dropped.* ❹ to abandon or stop dealing with something • *Let's just drop the subject!* ❺ to leave a passenger, parcel, etc. at a destination • *Can you drop me at the station?*
➤ **drop in** to visit someone casually
➤ **drop off** to fall asleep
➤ **drop out** to stop taking part in something

droplet *NOUN* droplets
a small drop

droppings *PLURAL NOUN*
the dung of animals or birds

drought (say drout) *NOUN* droughts
a long period of dry weather

drove *NOUN* droves
a moving herd or flock
➤ **droves** a large number of people • *Tourists started coming to the village in droves.*

drown *VERB* drowns, drowning, drowned
❶ to die or kill someone by suffocation under water ❷ to make so much noise that another sound cannot be heard • *She turned up the radio to drown out the noise from next door.* ❸ to cover something completely in liquid • *The fruit was drowned in cream.*

drowsy *ADJECTIVE*
sleepy
➤ **drowsily** *ADVERB*
➤ **drowsiness** *NOUN*

drubbing *NOUN* drubbings
a severe defeat

drudge *NOUN* drudges
a person who does hard or boring work
➤ **drudgery** *NOUN*

drug *NOUN* drugs
❶ a substance used in medicine ❷ a substance that affects your senses or your mind, e.g. a narcotic or stimulant, especially one causing addiction • *a drug addict*

drug *VERB* drugs, drugging, drugged
to give a drug to someone, especially to make them unconscious

a b c d e f g h i j k l m n o p q r s t u v w x y z

Druid (say **droo**-id) *NOUN* Druids
a priest of an ancient Celtic religion in Britain and France

drum *NOUN* drums
❶ a musical instrument made of a cylinder with a skin or parchment stretched over one or both ends ❷ a cylindrical object or container • *an oil drum*

drum *VERB* drums, drumming, drummed
❶ to play a drum or drums ❷ to tap repeatedly on something • *He drummed his fingers on the table.* ❸ you drum a lesson or fact into someone when you make them remember it by constant repetition
➤ **drum something up** to try hard to get more support or business

drummer *NOUN* drummers
a person who plays the drums

drumstick *NOUN* drumsticks
❶ a stick for beating a drum ❷ the lower part of a cooked bird's leg

drunk *ADJECTIVE*
not able to control your behaviour because of drinking too much alcohol

drunk *NOUN* drunks
a person who is drunk

drunkard *NOUN* drunkards
a person who is often drunk

drunken *ADJECTIVE*
❶ drunk • *a drunken man* ❷ caused by drinking alcohol • *a drunken brawl*

dry *ADJECTIVE* drier, driest
❶ without water or moisture ❷ thirsty ❸ boring or dull ❹ funny in a clever and not obvious way • *dry wit*
➤ **dryness** *NOUN*

dry *VERB* dries, drying, dried
❶ to make something dry ❷ to become dry

dryad *NOUN* dryads
a wood nymph

dry-cleaning *NOUN*
a method of cleaning clothes using a liquid that evaporates quickly

dry dock *NOUN* dry docks
a dock that can be emptied of water so that ships can float in and then be repaired

DT *ABBREVIATION*
design technology

dual *ADJECTIVE*
having two parts or aspects; double • *This building has a dual purpose.*

> **SPELLING**
> Take care not to confuse this word with **duel**.

dual carriageway *NOUN* dual carriageways
(*British*) a road with a dividing strip between lanes of traffic in opposite directions

dub *VERB* dubs, dubbing, dubbed
❶ to change or add new sound to the soundtrack of a film or to a recording • *It is a Spanish film dubbed into English.* ❷ to give a person or thing a nickname or title ❸ to make a man a knight by touching him on the shoulder with a sword

dubious (say **dew**-bee-us) *ADJECTIVE*
❶ doubtful or suspicious about something • *I'm dubious about our chances of winning.* ❷ not to be relied on; probably not honest • *dubious business dealings*
➤ **dubiously** *ADVERB*

ducal *ADJECTIVE*
to do with a duke

ducat (say **duk**-at) *NOUN* ducats
a former gold coin used in Europe

duchess *NOUN* duchesses
a duke's wife or widow

duchy *NOUN* duchies
the territory of a duke • *the duchy of Cornwall*

duck *NOUN* ducks
❶ a swimming bird with a flat beak; the female of this bird ❷ a batsman's score of nought at cricket

duck *VERB* ducks, ducking, ducked
❶ to bend down quickly to avoid being hit or seen ❷ to push someone's head under water for a short time ❸ to avoid doing something • *He tried to duck out of apologizing.*

duckling *NOUN* ducklings
a young duck

duct *NOUN* ducts
a tube or channel through which liquid, gas, air or cables can pass

ductile *ADJECTIVE*
ductile metal is able to be drawn out into fine strands

dud *NOUN* duds (*informal*)
something that is useless or a fake or fails to work

dudgeon (say **duj**-on) NOUN
➤ **in high dudgeon** very resentful or indignant

due ADJECTIVE
❶ expected; scheduled to do something or to arrive • *The train is due in ten minutes.*
❷ owing; needing to be paid • *Payment for the trip is due next week.* ❸ that ought to be given; rightful • *Treat her with due respect.*
➤ **due to** as a result of; caused by

due ADVERB
exactly or directly • *We sailed due east.*

due NOUN dues
❶ something you deserve or have a right to; proper respect • *Give him his due.* ❷ a fee • *harbour dues*

duel NOUN duels
a fight between two people, especially with pistols or swords
➤ **duelling** NOUN
➤ **duellist** NOUN

> **SPELLING**
> Take care not to confuse this word with **dual**.

duet NOUN duets
a piece of music for two players or singers

duff ADJECTIVE (*British*) (*informal*)
worthless or broken

duffel coat NOUN duffel coats
a thick overcoat with a hood, fastened with toggles

duffer NOUN duffers (*informal*)
a person who is stupid or not good at doing something

dugout NOUN dugouts
❶ an underground shelter ❷ a shelter at the side of a sports field for a team's coaches and substitutes ❸ a canoe made by hollowing out a tree trunk

duke NOUN dukes
a member of the highest rank of noblemen
➤ **dukedom** NOUN

dulcet (say **dul**-sit) ADJECTIVE
sweet-sounding **WORD ORIGIN** from Latin *dulcis* = sweet

dulcimer NOUN dulcimers
a musical instrument with strings that are struck by two small hammers

dull ADJECTIVE
❶ not bright or clear • *dull weather* ❷ not interesting or exciting; boring • *a dull concert*
❸ not sharp • *a dull pain* • *a dull thud*
❹ stupid; slow to understand
➤ **dully** ADVERB
➤ **dullness** NOUN

duly ADVERB
in the due or proper way; as expected • *We duly assembled at 7.30 as agreed.*

dumb ADJECTIVE
❶ without the ability to speak ❷ silent; unable or unwilling to speak • *We were struck dumb with amazement.* ❸ (*informal*) stupid or foolish • *What a dumb thing to do!*
➤ **dumbly** ADVERB
➤ **dumbness** NOUN

dumbfounded ADJECTIVE
unable to say anything because you are so astonished

dummy NOUN dummies
❶ a model of a person used to display clothes ❷ a rubber teat given to a baby to suck ❸ an imitation of something

dump NOUN dumps
❶ a place where rubbish is left or stored ❷ (*informal*) a dull or unattractive place

dump VERB dumps, dumping, dumped
❶ to get rid of something you do not want ❷ to put something down carelessly • *You can dump your bags in the hall.*

dumpling NOUN dumplings
a ball of dough cooked in a stew or baked with fruit inside

dumps PLURAL NOUN (*informal*)
➤ **in the dumps** feeling depressed or unhappy

dumpy ADJECTIVE
short and fat

dunce NOUN dunces
a person who is slow at learning
WORD ORIGIN from John *Duns* Scotus, a Scottish philosopher in the Middle Ages (because his opponents said that his followers could not understand new ideas)

dune NOUN dunes
a mound of loose sand shaped by the wind

dung NOUN
solid waste matter excreted by an animal

dungarees PLURAL NOUN
trousers with a piece in front covering your chest, held up by straps over your shoulders

dungeon (say **dun**-jon) NOUN dungeons
an underground cell for prisoners

a b c d e f g h i j k l m n o p q r s t u v w x y z

dunk *VERB* **dunks, dunking, dunked**
to dip something into liquid

duo (say **dew**-oh) *NOUN* **duos**
a pair of people, especially playing music

duodenum (say dew-o-**deen**-um) *NOUN* **duodenums**
the part of the small intestine that is just below the stomach
➤ **duodenal** *ADJECTIVE*
WORD ORIGIN from Latin *duodecim* = twelve (because its length is about twelve times the breadth of a finger)

dupe *VERB* **dupes, duping, duped**
to deceive or trick someone

duplicate (say **dyoop**-lik-at) *NOUN* **duplicates**
❶ something that is exactly the same as something else ❷ an exact copy • *a duplicate key*

duplicate (say **dyoop**-lik-ayt) *VERB* **duplicates, duplicating, duplicated**
❶ to make an exact copy of something ❷ to do something that has already been done • *There's no point in duplicating the work we did last year.*
➤ **duplication** *NOUN*
➤ **duplicator** *NOUN*

duplicity (say dew-**plis**-it-ee) *NOUN*
deceitful behaviour

durable *ADJECTIVE*
strong and likely to last • *a durable material*
➤ **durability** *NOUN*

duration *NOUN*
the length of time something lasts

duress (say dewr-**ess**) *NOUN*
the use of force or threats to make someone do something against their will • *He signed the confession under duress.*

during *PREPOSITION*
throughout or within a period of time • *During the summer holidays we went swimming every day.* • *He died during the night.*

dusk *NOUN* **dusks**
the darker stage of twilight

dusky *ADJECTIVE*
dark or shadowy

dust *NOUN*
tiny particles of earth or other solid material

dust *VERB* **dusts, dusting, dusted**
❶ to wipe away dust ❷ to sprinkle something with powder • *Dust the cake with sugar.*

dustbin *NOUN* **dustbins**
(*British*) a bin for household rubbish

duster *NOUN* **dusters**
a cloth for dusting things

dustman *NOUN* **dustmen**
(*British*) a person employed to empty dustbins and take away household rubbish

dustpan *NOUN* **dustpans**
a pan into which dust is brushed from a floor

dusty *ADJECTIVE* **dustier, dustiest**
covered with or full of dust

dutiful *ADJECTIVE*
doing your duty; obedient • *a dutiful daughter*
➤ **dutifully** *ADVERB*

duty *NOUN* **duties**
❶ what you ought to do or must do ❷ a task that must be done, often as part of your job ❸ a tax charged on imports and on certain other things
➤ **on** or **off duty** at work (or not at work) • *What time do you go off duty?*

duty-free *ADJECTIVE*
duty-free goods are goods on which duty is not charged

duvet (say **doo**-vay) *NOUN* **duvets**
(*British*) a thick soft quilt used instead of other bedclothes

DVD *ABBREVIATION*
digital video disc; a disc used for storing large amounts of audio or video information, especially films

dwarf *NOUN* **dwarfs** or **dwarves**
❶ a very small person or thing ❷ a creature in stories like a small human being, sometimes with magical powers

dwarf *VERB* **dwarfs, dwarfing, dwarfed**
to make something seem small by contrast • *The ocean liner dwarfed the tugs that were towing it.*

dwell *VERB* **dwells, dwelling, dwelt**
(*formal*) to dwell in a place is to live there
➤ **dweller** *NOUN*
➤ **dwell on something** to think or talk about something for a long time

dwelling *NOUN* **dwellings**
a house or other place to live in

dwindle *VERB* dwindles, dwindling, dwindled
to get smaller or less gradually • *Their savings dwindled away to nothing.*

dye *NOUN* dyes
a substance used to change the colour of something

dye *VERB* dyes, dyeing, dyed
to change the colour of something with dye • *She died her hair green.*

dyke *NOUN* dykes
❶ a long wall or embankment to hold back water and prevent flooding ❷ a ditch for draining water from land

dynamic *ADJECTIVE*
❶ a dynamic person is energetic and forceful ❷ a dynamic force produces motion
➤ **dynamically** *ADVERB*

dynamics *NOUN*
❶ the scientific study of force and motion ❷ (*in music*) the different levels of loudness and softness in a piece of music

dynamite *NOUN*
❶ a powerful explosive ❷ something likely to make people very excited or angry • *This discovery was dynamite.*

dynamo *NOUN* dynamos
(*chiefly British*) a machine that makes electricity

dynasty (say **din**-a-stee) *NOUN* dynasties
a line of rulers or powerful people all from the same family
➤ **dynastic** *ADJECTIVE*

dysentery (say **dis**-en-tree) *NOUN*
a disease causing severe diarrhoea

dyslexia (say dis-**leks**-ee-a) *NOUN*
special difficulty in being able to read and spell, caused by a brain condition
➤ **dyslexic** *ADJECTIVE*

dyspepsia (say dis-**pep**-see-a) *NOUN*
indigestion
➤ **dyspeptic** *ADJECTIVE*

dystrophy (say **dis**-trof-ee) *NOUN*
a disease that weakens the muscles

E. *ABBREVIATION*
east; eastern

each *DETERMINER & PRONOUN*
every one of two or more people or things • *Each player gets seven cards.* • *Each of us wanted to help.*

USAGE

Take care to use the pronoun **each** with a singular verb and singular pronouns: • *Each has chosen her own outfit.*

eager *ADJECTIVE*
wanting very much to do or have something; very keen • *We were all eager to hear his news.*
➤ **eagerly** *ADVERB*
➤ **eagerness** *NOUN*

eagle *NOUN* eagles
a large bird of prey with very strong sight

ear *NOUN* ears
❶ the organ of the body that is used for hearing ❷ the ability to recognize and repeat sounds • *She has a good ear for music.* ❸ the spike of seeds at the top of a stalk of corn

earache *NOUN*
pain inside the ear

eardrum *NOUN* eardrums
a membrane in the ear that vibrates when sounds reach it

earl *NOUN* earls
a British nobleman
➤ **earldom** *NOUN*

early *ADJECTIVE & ADVERB* earlier, earliest
❶ before the usual or expected time • *We arrived ten minutes early.* ❷ near the beginning of something • *The murder happens early in the book.* • *an early goal* ❸ near the beginning of the day • *I have to get up early tomorrow.*
➤ **earliness** *NOUN*

earmark *VERB* earmarks, earmarking, earmarked
to put something aside for a particular purpose WORD ORIGIN from the custom of marking an animal's ear to identify it

a b c d e f g h i j k l m n o p q r s t u v w x y z

A B C D E F G H I J K L M N O P Q R S T U V W X Y Z

earn VERB earns, earning, earned
❶ to get money as an income for doing work
❷ to win or receive something because you deserve it • *Your hard work has earned you a place in the team.*

earnest ADJECTIVE
very serious and sincere • *an earnest young man*
➤ **earnestly** ADVERB
➤ **earnestness** NOUN
➤ **in earnest** ❶ more seriously or with more determination • *The building work will begin in earnest next week.* ❷ meaning what you say

earnings PLURAL NOUN
money earned

earphones PLURAL NOUN
a listening device that fits over or in your ears

earring NOUN earrings
an ornament worn on your ear

earshot NOUN
the distance within which a sound can be heard • *The others were safely out of earshot.*

earth NOUN earths
❶ the planet that we live on ❷ the ground; soil ❸ the hole or burrow where a fox or badger lives ❹ connection to the ground to complete an electrical circuit

earth VERB earths, earthing, earthed
to connect an electrical circuit to the ground

earthenware NOUN
pottery made of coarse baked clay

earthly ADJECTIVE
to do with life on earth rather than with life after death

earthquake NOUN earthquakes
a violent movement of part of the earth's surface

earthworm NOUN earthworms
a worm that lives in the soil

earthy ADJECTIVE
❶ like earth or soil • *a damp earthy smell* ❷ crude and vulgar

earwig NOUN earwigs
a crawling insect with pincers at the end of its body (**WORD ORIGIN**) so named because it was once thought to crawl into people's ears

ease NOUN
❶ a lack of difficulty or trouble • *She climbed the tree with ease.* ❷ to be at ease with

someone is to feel comfortable and relaxed with them

ease VERB eases, easing, eased
❶ to make something less painful or troublesome • *This should ease the pain.* ❷ to move something gently into position • *He eased the key into the lock.* ❸ to become less severe • *The pressure eased.*

easel NOUN easels
a stand for supporting a painting or a blackboard (**WORD ORIGIN**) from Dutch *ezel* = donkey (which carries a load)

easily ADVERB
❶ without difficulty; with ease ❷ by far • *This was easily the best victory of her career.* ❸ very likely • *He could easily be lying.*

east NOUN
❶ the direction where the sun rises ❷ the eastern part of a country, city or other area

east ADJECTIVE & ADVERB
towards or in the east; coming from the east
➤ **easterly** ADJECTIVE
➤ **eastern** ADJECTIVE
➤ **easterner** NOUN
➤ **easternmost** ADJECTIVE

Easter NOUN
the Sunday (in March or April) when Christians commemorate the resurrection of Christ; the days around it

eastward ADJECTIVE & ADVERB
towards the east
➤ **eastwards** ADVERB

easy ADJECTIVE easier, easiest
able to be done or used or understood without trouble

easy ADVERB
➤ **take it easy** to relax or calm down

easy chair NOUN easy chairs
a comfortable armchair

eat VERB eats, eating, ate, eaten
❶ to chew and swallow something as food ❷ to have a meal • *When do we eat?* ❸ to use something up; to destroy something gradually • *Extra expenses ate up our savings.* • *Acid rain will eat away the stonework of buildings.*

eatable ADJECTIVE
fit to be eaten

eau de Cologne (say oh der kol-**ohn**) NOUN
a light perfume first made at Cologne, in Germany

eaves *PLURAL NOUN*
the overhanging edges of a roof

eavesdrop *VERB* eavesdrops, eavesdropping, eavesdropped
to listen secretly to a private conversation
• *They caught her eavesdropping outside the window.*
➤ **eavesdropper** *NOUN*
WORD ORIGIN as if you are listening outside a wall, where water drops from the eaves

ebb *NOUN* ebbs
the movement of the tide when it is going out, away from the land
➤ **at a low ebb** at a low point; in a poor state
• *Our confidence was at a low ebb.*

ebb *VERB* ebbs, ebbing, ebbed
❶ the tide ebbs when it flows away from the land ❷ your strength or courage ebbs when it weakens or fades

ebony *NOUN*
a hard black wood

e-book *NOUN* e-books
a book in electronic form that you can read on a screen

ebullient (say i-**bul**-ient) *ADJECTIVE*
cheerful, full of high spirits
➤ **ebullience** *NOUN*

eccentric (say ik-**sen**-trik) *ADJECTIVE*
behaving strangely
➤ **eccentrically** *ADVERB*
➤ **eccentricity** (say ek-sen-**triss**-it-ee) *NOUN*

ecclesiastical (say ik-lee-zee-**ast**-ik-al) *ADJECTIVE*
to do with the Christian Church or the clergy

echo *NOUN* echoes
a sound that is heard again as it is reflected off something

echo *VERB* echoes, echoing, echoed
❶ to make an echo • *Her footsteps echoed down the corridor.* ❷ to repeat a sound or what someone has said • *'A surprise?' he echoed.*

eclair (say ay-**klair**) *NOUN* eclairs
a finger-shaped cake of pastry with a creamy filling

eclipse *NOUN* eclipses
the blocking of the sun's or moon's light when the moon or the earth is in the way

eclipse *VERB* eclipses, eclipsing, eclipsed
❶ to block the light and cause an eclipse
❷ to seem better or more important than

others • *Her performance eclipsed the rest of the team.*

ecology (say ee-**kol**-o-jee) *NOUN*
the study of living things in relation to each other and to where they live
➤ **ecological** *ADJECTIVE*
➤ **ecologically** *ADVERB*
➤ **ecologist** *NOUN*

economic (say ee-kon-**om**-ik) *ADJECTIVE*
❶ to do with the economy or economics
❷ making enough money; profitable
• *The mine was closed because it was not economic.*

economical *ADJECTIVE*
using money and resources in a careful way that avoids waste • *It would be more economical to buy a bigger pack.*
➤ **economically** *ADVERB*

economics *NOUN*
the study of how money is used and how goods and services are provided and used
➤ **economist** *NOUN*

economize (also **economise**) *VERB* economizes, economizing, economized
to be economical; to use or spend less • *We need to economize on fuel.*

economy *NOUN* economies
❶ the system of trade and industry that a country uses to produce wealth ❷ careful use of money or resources ❸ a way of saving money • *You need to make economies.*

ecosystem (say **ee**-koh-sis-tum) *NOUN* ecosystems
all the plants and animals in a particular area considered in terms of their relationship with their environment

ecstasy (say **ek**-sta-see) *NOUN*
❶ a feeling of great delight ❷ an illegal drug that makes people feel very energetic and can cause hallucinations
SPELLING
Ecstasy ends with asy; not many words end with this pattern.

ecstatic (say ik-**stat**-ik) *ADJECTIVE*
extremely happy
➤ **ecstatically** *ADVERB*

eczema (say **eks**-im-a) *NOUN*
a skin disease that causes rough itching patches

eddy *NOUN* eddies
a swirling patch of water, air or smoke

eddy *VERB* eddies, eddying, eddied
to swirl

edge *NOUN* edges
❶ the part along the side or end of something ❷ the sharp part of a knife or axe or other cutting instrument
➤ **be on edge** to be tense and irritable

edge *VERB* edges, edging, edged
❶ to move gradually and carefully • *We edged closer to get a better view.* ❷ to put something around the edge of something • *The cloth was edged with lace.* ❸ to be the edge or border of something

edgeways *ADVERB*
➤ **not get a word in edgeways** to not be able to say something because someone else is talking a lot

edgy *ADJECTIVE*
tense and irritable
➤ **edginess** *NOUN*

edible *ADJECTIVE*
suitable for eating, not poisonous • *edible fruits*

edict (say **ee**-dikt) *NOUN* edicts
an official command

edifice (say **ed**-if-iss) *NOUN* edifices
a large building

edify *VERB* edifies, edifying, edified
to be an improving influence on a person's mind
➤ **edification** *NOUN*

edit *VERB* edits, editing, edited
❶ to make written material ready for publishing ❷ to make changes to text on a computer screen ❸ to be the editor of a newspaper or other publication ❹ to choose and put the parts of a film or tape recording into order

edition *NOUN* editions
❶ the form in which something is published • *a paperback edition* ❷ all the copies of a book etc. published at the same time • *the first edition* ❸ an individual television or radio programme in a series

editor *NOUN* editors
❶ the person in charge of a newspaper or a section of it ❷ a person who edits something

editorial *ADJECTIVE*
to do with editing or editors

editorial *NOUN* editorials
a newspaper article giving the editor's comments on something

educate *VERB* educates, educating, educated
to provide people with education
➤ **educator** *NOUN*

educated *ADJECTIVE*
showing a high standard of knowledge and culture, as a result of a good education

education *NOUN*
the process of training people's minds and abilities so that they acquire knowledge and develop skills

educational *ADJECTIVE*
to do with education; teaching you something • *an educational toy*
➤ **educationally** *ADVERB*

eel *NOUN* eels
a long fish that looks like a snake

eerie *ADJECTIVE* eerier, eeriest
strange in a frightening or mysterious way
• *an eerie silence*
➤ **eerily** *ADVERB*

efface *VERB* effaces, effacing, effaced
to rub something out or make it disappear
➤ **effacement** *NOUN*

effect *NOUN* effects
❶ a change that is produced by an action or cause; a result • *Some chemicals have a harmful effect on the environment.* ❷ an impression that is produced by something
• *The stage lighting gives the effect of a moonlit scene.*
➤ **come into effect** a law or rule comes into effect when it begins to be used
➤ **take effect** to begin to work or come into operation • *The pills will take effect soon.*

effect *VERB* effects, effecting, effected
to make something happen • *We want to effect a change.*

SPELLING
Effect is different from affect, which is a verb meaning to have an effect on or to harm.

effective *ADJECTIVE*
❶ producing the effect that is wanted
❷ impressive and striking
➤ **effectively** *ADVERB*
➤ **effectiveness** *NOUN*

effectual *ADJECTIVE*
producing the result that is wanted
➤ **effectually** *ADVERB*

effeminate *ADJECTIVE*
an effeminate man looks or behaves like a woman

effervesce (say ef-er-**vess**) *VERB* **effervesces, effervescing, effervesced**
liquid effervesces when it fizzes or gives off bubbles of gas
➤ **effervescent** *ADJECTIVE*
➤ **effervescence** *NOUN*

efficacious (say ef-ik-**ay**-shus) *ADJECTIVE*
able to produce the result that is wanted • *an efficacious remedy*
➤ **efficacy** (say **ef**-ik-a-see) *NOUN*

efficient *ADJECTIVE*
able to work well without making mistakes or wasting time
➤ **efficiently** *ADVERB*
➤ **efficiency** *NOUN*

effigy *NOUN* **effigies**
a model or sculptured figure

effort *NOUN* **efforts**
❶ the use of physical or mental energy; the energy used • *You have all put a lot of effort into this project.* ❷ something difficult or tiring • *It was an effort to stay awake.* ❸ an attempt • *This painting is a good effort.*

effortless *ADJECTIVE*
done with little or no effort
➤ **effortlessly** *ADVERB*

effusive *ADJECTIVE*
showing a great deal of affection or enthusiasm
➤ **effusively** *ADVERB*

e.g. *ABBREVIATION*
for example ◀**WORD ORIGIN**▶ short for Latin *exempli gratia* = for the sake of an example

egg *NOUN* **eggs**
❶ an oval or round object produced by the female of birds, fishes, reptiles and insects, which may develop into a new individual if fertilized ❷ a hen's or duck's egg used as food ❸ an ovum

egg *VERB* **eggs, egging, egged**
➤ **egg someone on** to encourage someone to do something with taunts or dares • *He didn't want to dance but his friends egged him on.*

eggplant *NOUN* **eggplants**
(*North American*) an aubergine

ego (say **eeg**-oh) *NOUN* **egos**
the opinion that you have of yourself and your own importance • *Winning the award really boosted her ego.* ◀**WORD ORIGIN**▶ Latin = I

egotist (say **eg**-oh-tist) *NOUN* **egotists**
a conceited person who is always talking about himself or herself
➤ **egotism** *NOUN*
➤ **egotistic** *ADJECTIVE*

Eid (say eed) *NOUN*
a Muslim festival marking the end of the fast of Ramadan

eiderdown *NOUN* **eiderdowns**
a quilt stuffed with soft material

eight *NOUN & ADJECTIVE* **eights**
the number 8
➤ **eighth** *ADJECTIVE & NOUN*

eighteen *NOUN & ADJECTIVE* **eighteens**
the number 18
➤ **eighteenth** *ADJECTIVE & NOUN*

eighty *NOUN & ADJECTIVE* **eighties**
the number 80
➤ **eightieth** *ADJECTIVE & NOUN*

eisteddfod (say eye-**ste** th-vod) *NOUN* **eisteddfods** or **eisteddfodau**
an annual Welsh gathering of poets and musicians for competitions

either *DETERMINER & PRONOUN*
❶ one or the other of two • *Either team can win.* • *Either of those dates will do.* ❷ both of two • *There are fields on either side of the river.*

either *ADVERB*
also; similarly • *If you won't go, I won't either.*

either *CONJUNCTION*
(used with **or**) the first of two possibilities • *He is either ill or drunk.* • *Either come right in or go away.*

ejaculate *VERB* **ejaculates, ejaculating, ejaculated**
❶ to produce semen from the penis ❷ (*formal*) to suddenly say something
➤ **ejaculation** *NOUN*

eject *VERB* **ejects, ejecting, ejected**
❶ to force someone to leave • *Several protesters were ejected from the hall.* ❷ to send something out forcefully ❸ a pilot ejects when they are deliberately thrown out of an aircraft in a special seat in an emergency ❹ to remove a disk or tape from a machine, usually by pressing a button
➤ **ejection** *NOUN*
➤ **ejector** *NOUN*

eke (say eek) *VERB* **ekes, eking, eked**
➤ **eke something out** to manage to make something last as long as possible by only using small amounts of it

elaborate (say il-**ab**-er-at) *ADJECTIVE*
having many parts or details; complicated
• *an elaborate pattern*
➤ **elaborately** *ADVERB*

elaborate (say il-**ab**-er-ayt) *VERB* **elaborates, elaborating, elaborated**
to explain or work something out in detail
• *Could you elaborate on that idea?*
➤ **elaboration** *NOUN*

elapse *VERB* **elapses, elapsing, elapsed**
an amount of time elapses when it passes
• *Six years elapsed before they met again.*

elastic *NOUN*
cord or material woven with strands of rubber so that it can stretch

elastic *ADJECTIVE*
able to be stretched or squeezed and then go back to its original length or shape
➤ **elasticity** *NOUN*

elated *ADJECTIVE*
feeling very pleased and excited
➤ **elation** *NOUN*

elbow *NOUN* **elbows**
the joint in the middle of your arm, where ir bends

elbow *VERB* **elbows, elbowing, elbowed**
to push or prod someone with your elbow
• *She elbowed me out of the way.*

elder *ADJECTIVE*
older • *my elder brother*

elder *NOUN* **elders**
❶ an older person • *Respect your elders!*
• *a council of village elders* ❷ an official in some Christian Churches ❸ a tree with white flowers and black berries

elderberry *NOUN* **elderberries**
a small black berry, the fruit of the elder tree

elderly *ADJECTIVE*
rather old

eldest *ADJECTIVE*
oldest

elect *VERB* **elects, electing, elected**
❶ to choose someone by voting ❷ to choose or decide to do something

elect *ADJECTIVE*
chosen by a vote but not yet in office • *the president elect*

election *NOUN* **elections**
a time when people choose someone to do a political or official job by voting

elector *NOUN* **electors**
a person who has the right to vote in an election
➤ **electoral** *ADJECTIVE*

electorate *NOUN* **electorates**
all the people who have a right to vote in an election

electric *ADJECTIVE*
❶ to do with or worked by electricity ❷ very tense or exciting • *The atmosphere inside the hall was electric.* **WORD ORIGIN** from Greek *elektron* = amber (which is easily given a charge of static electricity)

electrical *ADJECTIVE*
to do with or worked by electricity • *an electrical fault*
➤ **electrically** *ADVERB*

electric chair *NOUN*
an electrified chair used for capital punishment in the USA

electrician *NOUN* **electricians**
a person whose job is to fit and repair electrical equipment

electricity *NOUN*
a form of energy carried by certain particles of matter (electrons and protons), used for lighting and heating and for making machines work

electrify *VERB* **electrifies, electrifying, electrified**
❶ to supply something with electric power to make it work ❷ to give an electric charge to something • *an electrified fence* ❸ to make someone feel very excited • *Her singing electrified the audience.*
➤ **electrification** *NOUN*

electrocute *VERB* **electrocutes, electrocuting, electrocuted**
to kill someone with electricity that goes through the body
➤ **electrocution** *NOUN*

electrode *NOUN* **electrodes**
a solid conductor through which electricity enters or leaves a battery or other piece of electrical equipment

electromagnet *NOUN* **electromagnets**
a magnet worked by electricity
➤ **electromagnetic** *ADJECTIVE*

electron *NOUN* **electrons**
a particle of matter with a negative electric charge

electronic *ADJECTIVE*
❶ worked by microchips, etc. that control an electric current ❷ done using a computer or the Internet • *electronic banking*
➤ **electronically** *ADVERB*

electronics *NOUN*
the use or study of electronic devices

elegant *ADJECTIVE*
graceful and stylish • *an elegant young woman*
➤ **elegantly** *ADVERB*
➤ **elegance** *NOUN*

elegy (say **el**-ij-ee) *NOUN* **elegies**
a sad or sorrowful poem

element *NOUN* **elements**
❶ each of about 100 substances that cannot be split up into simpler substances, composed of atoms that have the same number of protons ❷ each of the parts that make up a whole thing ❸ a basic or elementary principle • *the elements of algebra* ❹ a wire or coil that gives out heat in an electric fire or cooker ❺ the environment or circumstances that suit you best • *Karen is really in her element at parties.*
➤ **the elements** the forces of weather, such as rain, wind and cold

elementary *ADJECTIVE*
dealing with the simplest stages of something; easy

elephant *NOUN* **elephants**
a very large animal with a trunk, large ears and tusks

elephantine (say el-if-**ant**-yn) *ADJECTIVE*
❶ very large ❷ clumsy and slow-moving

elevate *VERB* **elevates, elevating, elevated**
❶ to lift or raise something to a higher position • *The injured leg should be elevated.* ❷ to give someone a higher position or rank • *He was elevated to the Board of Directors.*

elevation *NOUN* **elevations**
❶ moving to a higher position or rank ❷ the height of a place above sea level ❸ a drawing of a building seen from the side

elevator *NOUN* **elevators**
❶ something that raises things ❷ (*North American*) a lift

eleven *NOUN & ADJECTIVE* **elevens**
the number 11
➤ **eleventh** *ADJECTIVE & NOUN*

elf *NOUN* **elves**
in fairy stories, a small being with pointed ears and magic powers
➤ **elfin** *ADJECTIVE*

elicit (say ill-**iss**-it) *VERB* **elicits, eliciting, elicited**
to manage to get information or a reaction from someone

> **SPELLING**
> Take care not to confuse with **illicit**.

eligible (say **el**-ij-ib-ul) *ADJECTIVE*
qualified or suitable for something • *You have to be under 16 to be eligible for a prize.*
➤ **eligibility** *NOUN*

eliminate *VERB* **eliminates, eliminating, eliminated**
❶ to get rid of someone or something ❷ to defeat someone and stop them going further in a competition • *Our team was eliminated in the first round.*
➤ **elimination** *NOUN*

elision (say il-**li** zh-on) *NOUN*
omitting part of a word in pronouncing it, e.g. in saying *I'm* for *I am*

elite (say ay-**leet**) *NOUN*
a group of people given privileges which are not given to others

elixir (say il-**iks**-er) *NOUN* **elixirs**
a liquid that is believed to have magic powers, such as restoring youth to someone who is old **WORD ORIGIN** from Arabic *al-iksir* = substance that would cure illness and change metals into gold

Elizabethan (say il-iz-a-**beeth**-an) *ADJECTIVE*
from the time of Queen Elizabeth I (1558-1603)
➤ **Elizabethan** *NOUN*

elk *NOUN* **elks**
a large kind of deer

ellipse (say il-**ips**) *NOUN* **ellipses**
an oval shape

> **SPELLING**
> Do not forget to double the **l** in **ellipse**.

ellipsis *NOUN*
omitting a word or words from a sentence, usually so that the sentence can still be understood

elliptical (say il-**ip**-tik-al) *ADJECTIVE*
❶ shaped like an ellipse • *The planets move in an elliptical orbit around the Sun.* ❷ with some words omitted • *an elliptical phrase*
➤ **elliptically** *ADVERB*

elm *NOUN* elms
a tall tree with rough leaves

elocution (say el-o-**kew**-shon) *NOUN*
the art of speaking clearly and correctly

elongated *ADJECTIVE*
made longer; lengthened • *He often paints people with elongated faces and bodies.*

elope *VERB* elopes, eloping, eloped
two people elope if they run away secretly to get married
➤ **elopement** *NOUN*

eloquent *ADJECTIVE*
speaking well and expressing ideas clearly and effectively
➤ **eloquently** *ADVERB*
➤ **eloquence** *NOUN*

else *ADVERB*
❶ besides; other • *Nobody else knows.*
❷ otherwise; if not • *I must run or else I'll be late.*

elsewhere *ADVERB*
somewhere else

elucidate (say il-**oo**-sid-ayt) *VERB* elucidates, elucidating, elucidated
to make something clear by explaining it
➤ **elucidation** *NOUN*

elude (say il-**ood**) *VERB* eludes, eluding, eluded
❶ to avoid being caught by someone • *The fox eluded the hounds.* ❷ to be too difficult for you to remember or understand • *I'm afraid the name eludes me.*

elusive *ADJECTIVE*
difficult to find, catch or remember

emaciated (say im-**ay**-see-ay-tid) *ADJECTIVE*
very thin from illness or starvation
➤ **emaciation** *NOUN*

email *NOUN* emails
❶ a system of sending messages and data from one computer to another by means of a network ❷ a message sent in this way

email *VERB* emails, emailing, emailed
to send an email to someone

emanate (say **em**-an-ayt) *VERB* emanates, emanating, emanated
to come out of a place or thing • *Strange music emanated from the tent.*

emancipate (say im-**an**-sip-ayt) *VERB*
emancipates, emancipating, emancipated
to set someone free from slavery or other restrictions
➤ **emancipation** *NOUN*

embalm *VERB* embalms, embalming, embalmed
to preserve a corpse from decay by using spices or chemicals

embankment *NOUN* embankments
a long bank of earth or stone to hold back water or support a road or railway

embargo *NOUN* embargoes
an official ban, especially on trade with a country

embark *VERB* embarks, embarking, embarked
to go on board a ship or aircraft • *Passengers with cars must embark first.*
➤ **embarkation** *NOUN*
➤ **embark on something** to begin something new or difficult • *They were about to embark on a dangerous mission.*

embarrass *VERB* embarrasses, embarrassing, embarrassed
to make someone feel shy, awkward or ashamed • *Please don't embarrass me in front of my friends again.*

SPELLING
There is a double r and a double s in embarrass.

embarrassed *ADJECTIVE*
feeling shy, awkward or ashamed • *I've never felt so embarrassed in my life!*

embarrassing *ADJECTIVE*
making you feel shy, awkward or ashamed
• *an embarrassing mistake*

embarrassment *NOUN*
the feeling you have when you are embarrassed

embassy *NOUN* embassies
❶ an ambassador and his or her staff ❷ the building where they work

embed *VERB* embeds, embedding, embedded
to fix something firmly in something solid
• *The axe was embedded in the door.*

embellish *VERB* embellishes, embellishing, embellished
to decorate something or add extra details to it • *The story has been embellished over time.*
➤ **embellishment** *NOUN*

embers *PLURAL NOUN*
small pieces of glowing coal or wood in a dying fire

embezzle *VERB* embezzles, embezzling, embezzled
to take money dishonestly that was left in

your care
➤ **embezzlement** *NOUN*

emblazon *VERB* emblazons, emblazoning, emblazoned
❶ to decorate something with a coat of arms ❷ to decorate something with bright or eye-catching designs or words • *The words 'Top Secret' were emblazoned in red on the cover.*

emblem *NOUN* emblems
a symbol that represents something • *The dove is an emblem of peace.*
➤ **emblematic** *ADJECTIVE*

embody *VERB* embodies, embodying, embodied
❶ to express principles or ideas in a visible form • *The marathon embodies the true spirit of the Olympics.* ❷ to include or contain something • *Parts of the old treaty are embodied in the new one.*
➤ **embodiment** *NOUN*

emboss *VERB* embosses, embossing, embossed
to decorate a flat surface with a raised design

embrace *VERB* embraces, embracing, embraced
❶ to hold someone closely in your arms ❷ to accept or adopt a cause or belief • *The country has embraced democracy.* ❸ to include a number of things • *The talks embraced a wide range of issues.*

embrace *NOUN* embraces
a hug • *He held her in a warm embrace.*

embroider *VERB* embroiders, embroidering, embroidered
❶ to decorate cloth by sewing designs or pictures into it ❷ to add made-up details to a story to make it more interesting

embroidery *NOUN*
designs or pictures sewn into cloth; the art of decorating cloth in this way

embroil *VERB* embroils, embroiling, embroiled
to involve someone in an argument or quarrel • *He became embroiled in a dispute with his neighbours.*

embryo (say **em**-bree-oh) *NOUN* embryos
❶ a baby or young animal as it starts to grow in the womb; a young bird growing in an egg ❷ anything in its earliest stages of development
➤ **embryonic** (say em-bree-**on**-ik) *ADJECTIVE*

emerald *NOUN* emeralds
❶ a bright-green precious stone ❷ a bright green colour

emerge *VERB* emerges, emerging, emerged
❶ to come out or appear • *A man emerged from the shadows.* ❷ to become known • *No new evidence has emerged.*
➤ **emergence** *NOUN*

emergency *NOUN* emergencies
a sudden serious happening that needs to be dealt with very quickly

emery paper *NOUN*
paper with a gritty coating like sandpaper

emetic (say im-**et**-ik) *NOUN* emetics
a medicine used to make a person vomit

emigrate *VERB* emigrates, emigrating, emigrated
to leave your own country and go and live in another • *His family emigrated to Canada when he was 14.*
➤ **emigration** *NOUN*
➤ **emigrant** *NOUN*

> **USAGE**
> People are **emigrants** from the country they leave and **immigrants** in the country where they settle.

> **SPELLING**
> There is only one **m** in **emigrate**.

eminent *ADJECTIVE*
famous and respected • *an eminent scientist*
➤ **eminence** *NOUN*

eminently *ADVERB*
(*formal*) very • *She is eminently suitable for the job.*

emir (say em-**eer**) *NOUN* emirs
a Muslim ruler

emission *NOUN* emissions
❶ emitting something ❷ something that is emitted, especially fumes or radiation

emit *VERB* emits, emitting, emitted
to send out light, heat, fumes or sound • *The box began to emit a clicking sound.*

emotion *NOUN* emotions
a strong feeling in the mind, such as love, anger or hate

emotional *ADJECTIVE*
❶ causing strong feelings • *an emotional speech* ❷ expressing your feelings openly • *I didn't mean to get so emotional.* ❸ to do with people's feelings • *emotional problems*
➤ **emotionally** *ADVERB*

a b c d e f g h i j k l m n o p q r s t u v w x y z

emotive *ADJECTIVE*
causing emotion or strong feelings • *It is an emotive issue.*

empathy *NOUN*
the ability to understand and share in someone else's feelings
➤ **empathize** *VERB*

emperor *NOUN* emperors
a man who rules an empire

emphasis (say em-fa-sis) *NOUN* emphases
❶ special importance given to something ❷ stress put on a word or part of a word

emphasize (also **emphasise**) *VERB*
emphasizes, emphasizing, emphasized
to put emphasis on something • *I would like to emphasize the importance of backing up your work.*

emphatic (say im-**fat**-ik) *ADJECTIVE*
using or showing emphasis • *He agreed, with an emphatic nod of the head.*
➤ **emphatically** *ADVERB*

empire *NOUN* empires
❶ a group of countries controlled by one person or government ❷ a large business organization controlled by one person or group

empirical *ADJECTIVE*
based on observation or experiment, not on theory

employ *VERB* employs, employing, employed
❶ to pay a person to work for you ❷ to make use of something • *Our doctor employs the most modern methods.*

employee *NOUN* employees
someone who is employed in a job

employer *NOUN* employers
a person or organization that has people working for them

employment *NOUN*
having a paid job • *He hoped to find employment abroad.*

emporium (say em-**por**-ee-um) *NOUN* emporia or emporiums
a large shop

empower *VERB* empowers, empowering, empowered
to give someone the power or authority to do something

empress *NOUN* empresses
❶ a woman who rules an empire ❷ an emperor's wife

empty *ADJECTIVE*
❶ with nothing in it • *an empty glass* ❷ with nobody in it • *an empty bus* ❸ with no meaning or no effect • *empty promises*
➤ **emptiness** *NOUN*

empty *VERB* empties, emptying, emptied
❶ to remove the contents from something ❷ to become empty • *After the show, the hall quickly emptied.*

emu *NOUN* emus
a large Australian bird rather like an ostrich

emulate *VERB* emulates, emulating, emulated
to try to do as well as someone or something, especially by imitating them • *He hopes to emulate his brother's sporting achievements.*
➤ **emulation** *NOUN*

emulsion *NOUN* emulsions
❶ a creamy or slightly oily liquid ❷ a kind of water-based paint ❸ the coating on photographic film which is sensitive to light

enable *VERB* enables, enabling, enabled
to give someone the means or ability to do something • *The software enables you to create an animated film.*

enact *VERB* enacts, enacting, enacted
❶ to make a law by a formal process • *Parliament enacted new laws against drugs.* ❷ to perform a play or act out a scene • *We enacted scenes from the history of the town.*

enamel *NOUN* enamels
❶ a shiny substance for coating metal ❷ paint that dries hard and shiny ❸ the hard shiny surface of teeth

enamel *VERB* enamels, enamelling, enamelled
to coat or decorate a surface with enamel

encamp *VERB* encamps, encamping, encamped
to settle in a camp

encampment *NOUN* encampments
a camp, especially a military one

encapsulate *VERB* encapsulates, encapsulating, encapsulated
to express an idea or set of ideas concisely

encase *VERB* encases, encasing, encased
to surround or cover something completely • *His leg was encased in a plaster cast.*

enchant *VERB* enchants, enchanting, enchanted
❶ to put someone under a magic spell ❷ to fill someone with intense delight
➤ **enchanter** *NOUN*
➤ **enchantress** *NOUN*

enchanted ADJECTIVE
placed under a magic spell • *an enchanted castle*

enchanting ADJECTIVE
attractive or delightful • *It was an enchanting scene.*

enchantment NOUN
❶ being under a magic spell ❷ a feeling of intense delight

encircle VERB encircles, encircling, encircled
to surround someone or something • *The island is encircled by a coral reef.*

enclave NOUN enclaves
a country's territory lying entirely within the boundaries of another country

enclose VERB encloses, enclosing, enclosed
❶ to put a wall or fence round an area; to shut something in on all sides • *The garden was enclosed by a high wall.* ❷ to put something into an envelope or packet with something else • *She enclosed a couple of photos with her letter.*

enclosure NOUN enclosures
❶ a piece of ground with a wall or fence round it ❷ something enclosed with a letter or packet

encompass VERB encompasses, encompassing, encompassed
❶ to contain or include a number of things • *The course encompasses a range of subjects.* ❷ to surround something

encore (say **on**-kor) NOUN encores
an extra item performed at a concert after previous items have been applauded

encounter VERB encounters, encountering, encountered
❶ to meet someone unexpectedly ❷ to experience something • *We encountered some difficulties.*

encounter NOUN encounters
❶ an unexpected meeting ❷ a battle

encourage VERB encourages, encouraging, encouraged
❶ to give someone confidence or hope ❷ to urge or try to persuade someone to do something ❸ to help something to develop or happen more easily • *The school has launched a poster campaign to encourage healthy eating.*
➤ **encouragement** NOUN

encroach VERB encroaches, encroaching, encroached

to take or use too much of something • *The extra work would encroach on their free time.*
➤ **encroachment** NOUN

encrusted ADJECTIVE
covered with a layer or crust • *a crown encrusted with diamonds*

encrypt VERB encrypts, encrypting, encrypted
to put information into a special code in order to stop people reading it if they are not allowed to
➤ **encryption** NOUN

encumber VERB encumbers, encumbering, encumbered
to be a burden to someone; to hamper someone
➤ **encumbrance** NOUN

encyclopedia NOUN encyclopedias
a book or set of books containing information about many subjects

encyclopedic ADJECTIVE
giving information about many different subjects

end NOUN ends
❶ the last part of something or the point where it stops ❷ the half of a sports pitch or court defended or occupied by one team or player ❸ destruction or death ❹ a person's goal or purpose • *He knew she was just using him for her own ends.*

end VERB ends, ending, ended
❶ to come to an end ❷ to bring something to an end

endanger VERB endangers, endangering, endangered
to cause danger to someone or something • *Smoking seriously endangers your health.*

endangered species NOUN endangered species
a species in danger of extinction

endear VERB endears, endearing, endeared
if you endear yourself to someone, you make them fond of you
➤ **endearing** ADJECTIVE

endearment NOUN endearments
a word or phrase that expresses love or affection

endeavour (say in-**dev**-er) VERB endeavours, endeavouring, endeavoured
to try hard to do something • *I will endeavour to find out what happened.*

endeavour NOUN endeavours
an attempt

ending NOUN endings
the last or final part of something • *I like a story with a happy ending.*

endless ADJECTIVE
❶ never stopping; having no end • *an endless stream of questions* ❷ an endless belt or loop has the ends joined to make a continuous strip for use in machinery
➤ **endlessly** ADVERB

endorse VERB endorses, endorsing, endorsed
❶ to give your approval or support to something ❷ to sign your name on the back of a cheque or document ❸ to make an official entry on a licence about an offence committed by its holder
➤ **endorsement** NOUN

endow VERB endows, endowing, endowed
❶ to provide money to establish something • *She endowed a library in the village where she was born.* ❷ to be endowed with an ability or quality is to possess it • *He was endowed with great talent.*
➤ **endowment** NOUN

endurance NOUN
the ability to put up with difficulty or pain for a long period

endure VERB endures, enduring, endured
❶ to suffer or put up with difficulty or pain • *She could not endure the thought of parting.* ❷ to continue to exist; to last
➤ **endurable** ADJECTIVE

enemy NOUN enemies
❶ a person who hates someone else and wants to harm them ❷ a nation or army that is at war with another

energetic ADJECTIVE
full of or needing energy • *an energetic dance*
➤ **energetically** ADVERB

energy NOUN energies
❶ strength to do things, liveliness ❷ the ability of matter or radiation to do work. Energy is measured in joules ❸ power obtained from fuel and other resources and used for light and heat or to operate machinery

enfold VERB enfolds, enfolding, enfolded
to surround or be wrapped round something • *He enfolded her in his arms.*

enforce VERB enforces, enforcing, enforced
to make people obey a law or rule • *This new law will be hard to enforce.*
➤ **enforcement** NOUN
➤ **enforceable** ADJECTIVE

engage VERB engages, engaging, engaged
❶ to attract and keep a person's interest or attention • *They engaged her in conversation.* ❷ to give someone a job • *They engaged her as a cook.* ❸ to begin a battle against someone • *We engaged the enemy.*

engaged ADJECTIVE
❶ someone who is engaged has promised to marry another person ❷ in use; occupied • *I phoned earlier but the line was engaged.*

engagement NOUN engagements
❶ a promise to marry someone ❷ an arrangement to meet someone or do something ❸ a battle

engaging ADJECTIVE
attractive or charming

engine NOUN engines
❶ a machine that provides power ❷ a vehicle that pulls a railway train; a locomotive

engineer NOUN engineers
an expert in engineering

engineer VERB engineers, engineering, engineered
❶ to arrange for something to happen • *He engineered a meeting between them.* ❷ to plan and construct something • *The car is beautifully engineered.*

engineering NOUN
the design and building or control of machinery or of structures such as roads and bridges

engrave VERB engraves, engraving, engraved
to cut words or a design onto a hard surface such as metal or stone • *His name is engraved on the cup.*
➤ **engraver** NOUN

engraving NOUN engravings
a picture or design that has been cut into metal or stone

engrossed ADJECTIVE
so interested in something that you give it all your attention • *He was engrossed in his book.*

engulf VERB engulfs, engulfing, engulfed
to flow over something and cover it completely • *The vehicle was engulfed in flames.*

enhance VERB enhances, enhancing, enhanced
to improve something or make it more attractive or valuable • *This film is sure to*

enhance her reputation as a director.
➤ **enhancement** NOUN

enigma (say in-**ig**-ma) NOUN enigmas
something very difficult to understand; a puzzle

enigmatic (say en-ig-**mat**-ik) ADJECTIVE
mysterious and puzzling
➤ **enigmatically** ADVERB

enjoy VERB enjoys, enjoying, enjoyed
❶ to get pleasure from something ❷ to enjoy yourself is to have a good time

enjoyable ADJECTIVE
giving pleasure • an enjoyable afternoon

enjoyment NOUN enjoyments
a feeling of pleasure; something that you enjoy doing • She gets a lot of enjoyment from painting.

enlarge VERB enlarges, enlarging, enlarged
to make something bigger • I'm going to have this photo enlarged.
➤ **enlargement** NOUN

enlighten VERB enlightens, enlightening, enlightened
to give someone more knowledge or information about something
➤ **enlightenment** NOUN

enlist VERB enlists, enlisting, enlisted
❶ to join the armed forces ❷ to enlist someone's help or support is to ask for and get it
➤ **enlistment** NOUN

enliven VERB enlivens, enlivening, enlivened
to make something more lively or interesting

en masse (say ahn **mass**) ADVERB
all together; in large numbers • The crowds turned out en masse, despite the weather.

enmity NOUN
the feeling of being someone's enemy; hostility

enormity NOUN enormities
❶ great wickedness • the enormity of this crime ❷ great size; hugeness • We began to realize the enormity of the task.

> **USAGE**
> Some people regard the use in sense 2 as incorrect, though it is very common. Words you can use instead include *extent* and *magnitude*.

enormous ADJECTIVE
very large; huge
➤ **enormousness** NOUN

enormously ADVERB
hugely; a lot • I enjoyed the party enormously.

enough DETERMINER, NOUN & ADVERB
as much or as many as necessary • I've saved enough money for a new bike. • I have had enough. • Are you warm enough?

> **SPELLING**
> The 'uff' sound at the end of **enough** is spelt **ough**.

enquire VERB enquires, enquiring, enquired (*chiefly British*)
❶ to ask for information • He enquired if I was well. ❷ to enquire into something is to find out about it

> **USAGE**
> See the note at **inquire**.

enquiry NOUN enquiries (*chiefly British*)
❶ a question ❷ an investigation

enrage VERB enrages, enraging, enraged
to make someone very angry

enraptured ADJECTIVE
filled with great pleasure

enrich VERB enriches, enriching, enriched
❶ to improve the quality of something • Fertilizer is used to enrich the soil. ❷ to make someone or something richer

enrol VERB enrols, enrolling, enrolled
to arrange for yourself or someone else to join a course or school • You need to enrol before the end of August.
➤ **enrolment** NOUN

en route (say ahn **root**) ADVERB
on the way

ensconce VERB ensconces, ensconcing, ensconced
to be ensconced in a place is to be settled there comfortably • Dad was already ensconced in an armchair.

ensemble (say on-**somb**l) NOUN ensembles
❶ a group of musicians or actors who perform together ❷ a matching outfit of clothes ❸ a group of things that go together

enshrine VERB enshrines, enshrining, enshrined
to preserve an idea or memory with love or

a b c d e f g h i j k l m n o p q r s t u v w x y z

respect • *His memory is enshrined in our hearts.*

ensign *NOUN* ensigns
a military or naval flag

enslave *VERB* enslaves, enslaving, enslaved
to make a slave of someone; to force someone into slavery
➤ **enslavement** *NOUN*

ensue *VERB* ensues, ensuing, ensued
to happen afterwards or as a result • *An argument ensued.*
➤ **ensuing** *ADJECTIVE*

ensure *VERB* ensures, ensuring, ensured
to make sure that something happens or is done • *Please ensure that all lights are switched off.*

> **SPELLING**
>
> Take care not to confuse with **insure**, which means to protect something with insurance.

entail *VERB* entails, entailing, entailed
to involve something or make it necessary • *This job will probably entail a few late nights.*

entangle *VERB* entangles, entangling, entangled
two or more things are entangled when they are tangled together • *A bird was entangled in the net.*
➤ **entanglement** *NOUN*

entente (say on-**tont**) *NOUN* ententes
a friendly understanding between countries

enter *VERB* enters, entering, entered
❶ to come or go into a place ❷ to join an organization • *He entered the army when he was 18.* ❸ to key something into a computer • *Now enter your password.* ❹ to put something into a list or book ❺ to put your name down to take part in a competition or examination

enterprise *NOUN* enterprises
❶ being bold and adventurous ❷ a difficult or important task or project • *Deep-sea diving is still a hazardous enterprise.* ❸ business activity • *private enterprise*

enterprising *ADJECTIVE*
willing to take on new or adventurous projects

entertain *VERB* entertains, entertaining, entertained
❶ to amuse and interest someone ❷ to have

people as guests and give them food and drink ❸ to consider something • *He refused to entertain the idea.*

entertainer *NOUN* entertainers
someone whose job is to amuse and please an audience, such as a singer or comedian

entertainment *NOUN* entertainments
❶ entertaining people; being entertained
❷ something performed in front of an audience to amuse or interest them

enthral (say in-**thrawl**) *VERB* enthrals, enthralling, enthralled
to hold someone's complete attention; to fascinate someone

enthusiasm *NOUN* enthusiasms
a strong liking, interest or excitement
➤ **enthusiast** *NOUN*

enthusiastic *ADJECTIVE*
full of enthusiasm • *You don't sound very enthusiastic about the idea.*
➤ **enthusiastically** *ADVERB*

entice *VERB* entices, enticing, enticed
to persuade someone to do something or go somewhere by offering them something pleasant • *We tried to entice the dog away from the door.*
➤ **enticement** *NOUN*
➤ **enticing** *ADJECTIVE*

entire *ADJECTIVE*
whole or complete • *He read the entire book in two days.*

entirely *ADVERB*
completely; in every way • *I entirely agree with you.*

entirety (say in-**ty**-rit-ee) *NOUN*
the whole of something
➤ **in its entirety** in its complete form

entitle *VERB* entitles, entitling, entitled
to give someone the right to have or do something • *This coupon entitles you to a free ticket.*
➤ **entitlement** *NOUN*

entitled *ADJECTIVE*
having as a title • *a short poem entitled 'Spring'*

entity *NOUN* entities
something that exists as a distinct and separate thing • *A language is a living entity.*

entomb (say in-**toom**) *VERB* entombs, entombing, entombed
to place a body in a tomb
➤ **entombment** *NOUN*

entomology (say en-tom-**ol**-o-jee) *NOUN*
the study of insects
➤ **entomologist** *NOUN*

entourage (say on-toor-**ah** zh) *NOUN*
the people who accompany an important
person

entrails *PLURAL NOUN*
the intestines of a person or animal

entrance (say **en**-trans) *NOUN* **entrances**
❶ the way into a place ❷ coming or going
into a place • *Her entrance is the signal for
applause.*

entrance (say in-**trahns**) *VERB* **entrances,
entrancing, entranced**
to fill someone with delight and wonder

entrant *NOUN* **entrants**
someone who takes part in an examination or
competition

entreat *VERB* **entreats, entreating, entreated**
to beg or plead with someone to do
something

entreaty *NOUN* **entreaties**
a serious and emotional request

entrench *VERB* **entrenches, entrenching,
entrenched**
❶ to fix or establish something firmly so
that it is difficult to change • *These ideas are
deeply entrenched in his mind.* ❷ to settle in
a well-defended position
➤ **entrenchment** *NOUN*

entrepreneur (say **on**-tru-pren-er) *NOUN*
entrepreneurs
a person who starts a new business or sets up
business deals, especially risky ones, in order
to make a profit
➤ **entrepreneurial** *ADJECTIVE*

entrust *VERB* **entrusts, entrusting, entrusted**
to make someone responsible for doing
something or looking after someone • *He
entrusted the task to his nephew.*

entry *NOUN* **entries**
❶ coming or going into a place; the right
to enter a place • *The sign said 'No Entry'.*
❷ something entered in a list, diary or
reference book ❸ something entered in
a competition • *Send your entries to this
address.*

entwine *VERB* **entwines, entwining, entwined**
to twist or wind something round something
else • *They strolled through the park, with
arms entwined.*

enumerate *VERB* **enumerates, enumerating,
enumerated**
to list things one by one

envelop (say en-**vel**-op) *VERB* **envelops,
enveloping, enveloped**
to cover or wrap round something
completely • *The mountain was enveloped
in mist.*

envelope (say **en**-vel-ohp) *NOUN* **envelopes**
a wrapper or covering, especially a folded
cover for a letter

enviable *ADJECTIVE*
likely to be envied

envious *ADJECTIVE*
feeling envy; wanting something that
someone else has
➤ **enviously** *ADVERB*

environment *NOUN* **environments**
❶ your surroundings, especially as they affect
your life • *a happy home environment* ❷ the
natural world of the land, sea and air

> **SPELLING**
> There is a tricky bit in **environment**—it
> has an **n** before the **m** in the middle.

environmental *ADJECTIVE*
to do with the environment • *the
environmental effects of pollution*
➤ **environmentally** *ADVERB*

environmentalist *NOUN* **environmentalists**
a person who wishes to protect or improve
the environment

environmentally–friendly *ADJECTIVE*
not harmful to the environment

environs (say in-**vy**-ronz) *PLURAL NOUN*
the surrounding districts • *They all lived in the
environs of Liverpool.*

envisage (say in-**viz**-ij) *VERB* **envisages,
envisaging, envisaged**
to picture something in the mind; to imagine
something • *It is difficult to envisage such a
change.*

envoy *NOUN* **envoys**
an official representative, especially one sent
by one government to another

envy *NOUN*
❶ a feeling of discontent you have when
someone possesses things that you would
like to have for yourself ❷ something causing

this feeling • *Their car is the envy of all their friends.*

envy *VERB* envies, envying, envied
to feel envy towards someone

enzyme *NOUN* enzymes
a kind of substance that assists chemical processes such as digestion

epaulette (say **ep**-al-et) *NOUN* epaulettes
an ornamental flap on the shoulder of a coat

ephemeral (say if-**em**-er-al) *ADJECTIVE*
lasting only a very short time

epic *NOUN* epics
❶ a long poem or story about heroic deeds or history ❷ a spectacular film

epicentre *NOUN* epicentres
the point where an earthquake reaches the earth's surface

epidemic *NOUN* epidemics
an outbreak of a disease that spreads quickly among the people of an area

epidermis *NOUN*
the outer layer of the skin

epigram *NOUN* epigrams
a short witty saying

epilepsy *NOUN*
a disease of the nervous system which causes convulsions
➤ **epileptic** *ADJECTIVE & NOUN*

epilogue (say **ep**-il-og) *NOUN* epilogues
a short section at the end of a book or play

Epiphany (say ip-**if**-an-ee) *NOUN*
a Christian festival on 6 January, commemorating the showing of the infant Christ to the 'wise men' from the East

episcopal (say ip-**iss**-kop-al) *ADJECTIVE*
❶ to do with a bishop or bishops ❷ an episcopal church is governed by bishops

episode *NOUN* episodes
❶ one event in a series of happenings ❷ one programme in a television or radio serial

epistle *NOUN* epistles
a letter, especially one forming part of the New Testament

epitaph *NOUN* epitaphs
words written on a tomb or describing a person who has died

epithet *NOUN* epithets
a word or phrase used to describe someone

and often forming part of their name, e.g. 'the Great' in *Alfred the Great*

epitome (say ip-**it**-om-ee) *NOUN*
a person or thing that is a perfect example of something • *She is the epitome of kindness.*

epoch (say **ee**-pok) *NOUN* epochs
a period of time in the past during which important events happened
➤ **epoch-making** *ADJECTIVE*
very important in history

eponym (say **ep**-o-nim) *NOUN* eponyms
a word that is derived from the name of a person

equable (say **ek**-wa-bul) *ADJECTIVE*
❶ calm and not likely to get annoyed • *She has an equable manner.* ❷ an equable climate is moderate, neither too hot nor too cold

equal *ADJECTIVE*
❶ the same in amount, size or value ❷ having the necessary strength, courage or ability to do something • *He was equal to the task.*

equal *NOUN* equals
a person or thing that is equal to another • *She has no equal.*

equal *VERB* equals, equalling, equalled
❶ to be the same in amount, size or value ❷ to be as good as someone or something • *No one has yet equalled this score.*

equality *NOUN*
being equal

equalize (also **equalise**) *VERB* equalizes, equalizing, equalized
❶ to make things equal ❷ to score a goal that makes the score equal

equalizer (also **equaliser**) *NOUN* equalizers
a goal or point that makes the score equal

equally *ADVERB*
in the same way or to the same extent • *You are all equally to blame.*

> **SPELLING**
> Don't forget to double the **l** in **equally**.

equanimity (say ekwa-**nim**-it-ee) *NOUN*
calmness of mind or temper

equate *VERB* equates, equating, equated
to think that two things are equal or equivalent

equation *NOUN* equations
(*in mathematics*) a statement that two amounts etc. are equal, e.g. $3 + 4 = 2 + 5$

equator NOUN equators
an imaginary line round the Earth at an equal distance from the North and South Poles

equatorial (say ek-wa-**tor**-ee-al) ADJECTIVE
to do with or near the equator • *equatorial rainforests*

equerry (say **ek**-wer-ee) NOUN equerries
a personal attendant of a member of the British royal family

equestrian (say ik-**wes**-tree-an) ADJECTIVE
to do with horse riding • *equestrian events at the Olympic Games*

equidistant (say ee-kwi-**dis**-tant) ADJECTIVE
at an equal distance

equilateral (say ee-kwi-**lat**-er-al) ADJECTIVE
an equilateral triangle has all its sides equal

equilibrium (say ee-kwi-**lib**-ree-um) NOUN
❶ a balance between different forces or influences ❷ a calm and balanced state of mind

equine (say **ek**-wyn) ADJECTIVE
to do with or like a horse

equinox (say **ek**-win-oks) NOUN equinoxes
the time of year when day and night are equal in length (about 20 March in spring and about 22 September in autumn)

equip VERB equips, equipping, equipped
to supply someone or something with what is needed • *The drama studio is well equipped.*

equipment NOUN
the things needed for a particular purpose

equity (say **ek**-wit-ee) NOUN
fairness
➤ **equitable** ADJECTIVE

equivalent ADJECTIVE
equal in importance, meaning or value • *12km is equivalent to 7.5 miles.*

equivalent NOUN equivalents
a thing that is equivalent to something else • *The Golden Honey Awards are the beekeepers' equivalent of the Oscars.*

equivocal (say ik-**wiv**-ok-al) ADJECTIVE
able to be interpreted in two ways and deliberately vague; ambiguous
➤ **equivocally** ADVERB

era (say **eer**-a) NOUN eras
a period of history • *the era of silent films*

eradicate VERB eradicates, eradicating, eradicated
to get rid of something completely; to remove all traces of something • *Some diseases, like smallpox, have now been eradicated.*
➤ **eradication** NOUN

erase VERB erases, erasing, erased
❶ to rub something out ❷ to wipe out a recording on magnetic tape
➤ **eraser** NOUN

ere (say air) PREPOSITION & CONJUNCTION (*old use*)
before

erect ADJECTIVE
standing straight up

erect VERB erects, erecting, erected
to set up or build something • *Huge TV screens were erected above the stage.*
➤ **erection** NOUN

erection NOUN
❶ the process of erecting something ❷ a building or structure that has been erected ❸ the swelling and hardening of a man's penis when he becomes sexually excited

ermine NOUN ermines
❶ a kind of weasel with brown fur that turns white in winter ❷ this valuable white fur

erode VERB erodes, eroding, eroded
to wear away the surface of something over time • *Water has eroded the rocks.*

erosion NOUN
the wearing away of the earth's surface by the action of water and wind

erotic ADJECTIVE
arousing sexual feelings
➤ **erotically** ADVERB

err (say er) VERB errs, erring, erred
to make a mistake or be incorrect

errand NOUN errands
a short journey to take a message or fetch something • *He used to run errands for his grandmother.*

errant (say **e**-rant) ADJECTIVE
❶ misbehaving ❷ wandering; travelling in search of adventure • *a knight errant*

erratic (say ir-**at**-ik) ADJECTIVE
not regular or reliable • *Most babies have erratic sleep patterns to begin with.*
➤ **erratically** ADVERB

erroneous (say ir-**oh**-nee-us) ADJECTIVE
incorrect; based on wrong information • *an erroneous conclusion*
➤ **erroneously** ADVERB

a b c d e f g h i j k l m n o p q r s t u v w x y z

error NOUN errors
a mistake
➤ **in error** by mistake

erudite (say e-rew-dyt) ADJECTIVE
having great knowledge or learning
➤ **erudition** NOUN

erupt VERB erupts, erupting, erupted
❶ a volcano erupts when it shoots out lava
❷ to start suddenly and powerfully; to break out • *Violence erupted outside the gates.*

eruption NOUN eruptions
❶ when a volcano erupts ❷ a sudden bursting out • *a huge eruption of laughter*

escalate VERB escalates, escalating, escalated
to become greater, more serious or more intense • *The riots escalated into a war.*
➤ **escalation** NOUN

escalator NOUN escalators
a staircase with an endless line of steps moving up or down

escapade (say es-ka-**payd**) NOUN escapades
a reckless adventure

escape VERB escapes, escaping, escaped
❶ to get yourself free; to get out or away • *They managed to escape from the burning building.* ❷ to avoid something unpleasant • *He escaped punishment.* ❸ to be forgotten or not noticed • *Her name escapes me for the moment.*

escape NOUN escapes
❶ escaping from somewhere or something • *an escape of prisoners* ❷ a way to escape • *She knew there was no escape.*

escapism NOUN
escaping from the difficulties of life by thinking about or doing more pleasant things
➤ **escapist** ADJECTIVE

escarpment NOUN escarpments
a steep slope at the edge of some high level ground

escort (say **ess**-kort) NOUN escorts
a person or group accompanying a person or thing, especially to protect or guard them • *an armed escort*

escort (say iss-**kort**) VERB escorts, escorting, escorted
to act as an escort to someone or something

Eskimo NOUN Eskimos or Eskimo
a member of a people living near the Arctic coast of North America, Greenland and Siberia

USAGE
It is becoming less common to refer to these peoples as **Eskimos**. Many people who live in northern Canada and Greenland prefer the term **Inuit**. The name for those who live in Alaska and Asia is *Yupik*.

especial ADJECTIVE
special or particular • *This should be of especial interest to you.*

especially ADVERB
specially; more than anything else • *She loves animals, especially dogs.*

espionage (say **ess**-pee-on-ahzh) NOUN
spying on other countries or organizations

esplanade NOUN esplanades
a flat open area where people can walk, especially by the sea

espresso NOUN espressos
strong black coffee made by forcing steam through ground coffee beans

esprit de corps (say es-pree der **kor**) NOUN
loyalty to your group **WORD ORIGIN** French = spirit of the body

espy VERB espies, espying, espied
to catch sight of someone or something

Esq. ABBREVIATION
(short for **Esquire**)
a title written after a man's surname where no title is used before his name
WORD ORIGIN an *esquire* was originally a knight's attendant; from Latin *scutarius* = shield-bearer

essay (say **ess**-ay) NOUN essays
a short piece of writing on one subject

essay (say ess-**ay**) VERB essays, essaying, essayed (*formal*) to attempt to do something

essence NOUN essences
❶ the most important quality or element of something • *His paintings capture the essence of France.* ❷ a concentrated liquid • *vanilla essence*

essential ADJECTIVE
completely necessary; that you cannot do without • *A car is essential in the country.*

essential NOUN essentials
something that you cannot do without

essentially *ADVERB*
basically; when you consider the basic or most important part of something • *The plots of both films are essentially the same.*

establish *VERB* establishes, establishing, established
❶ to set up a business, government or relationship on a firm basis ❷ to show that something is true; to prove something • *He managed to establish his innocence.*
➤ **the established Church** a country's national Church, officially recognized as such by law

establishment *NOUN* establishments
❶ establishing something ❷ a business firm or other institution
➤ **the Establishment** the people in a country in positions of power and influence

estate *NOUN* estates
❶ an area of land with a set of houses or factories on it ❷ a large area of land owned by one person ❸ all that a person owns when he or she dies

estate agent *NOUN* estate agents
(*British*) a person whose business is selling or letting houses and land

estate car *NOUN* estate cars
(*British*) a car with a door or doors at the back and rear seats that can be removed or folded away

esteem *VERB* esteems, esteeming, esteemed
to respect and admire someone very much • *She is a highly esteemed scientist.*

esteem *NOUN*
respect and admiration • *Please accept this gift as a token of our esteem.*

ester *NOUN* esters
a kind of chemical compound

estimable *ADJECTIVE*
worthy of respect and admiration • *an estimable young man*

estimate (say **ess**-tim-at) *NOUN* estimates
a rough calculation or guess about an amount or value

estimate (say **ess**-tim-ayt) *VERB* estimates, estimating, estimated
to make an estimate • *I estimate that the work will take three weeks.*

estimation *NOUN*
a person's opinion or judgement • *Who is to blame in your estimation?*

estranged *ADJECTIVE*
no longer friendly or in contact with someone who was once close to you • *He became estranged from his family.*
➤ **estrangement** *NOUN*

estuary (say **ess**-tew-er-ee) *NOUN* estuaries
the mouth of a river where it reaches the sea and the tide flows in and out

etc. *ABBREVIATION*
(short for **et cetera**)
and other similar things; and so on
WORD ORIGIN from Latin *et* = and + *cetera* = the other things

etch *VERB* etches, etching, etched
❶ to engrave a picture with acid on a metal plate, especially for printing ❷ if something is etched on your mind or memory, it has made a deep impression and you will never forget it
➤ **etcher** *NOUN*

etching *NOUN* etchings
a picture printed from an etched metal plate

eternal *ADJECTIVE*
lasting for ever; not ending or changing
➤ **eternally** *ADVERB*

eternity *NOUN*
❶ time that goes on for ever ❷ (*informal*) a very long time • *The bus took an eternity to arrive.*

ether (say **ee**-ther) *NOUN*
❶ a colourless liquid that evaporates easily into fumes that are used as an anaesthetic ❷ the upper air

ethereal (say ith-**eer**-ee-al) *ADJECTIVE*
light and delicate • *ethereal music*
➤ **ethereally** *ADVERB*

ethical (say **eth**-ik-al) *ADJECTIVE*
❶ to do with ethics ❷ morally right; honourable
➤ **ethically** *ADVERB*

ethics (say **eth**-iks) *PLURAL NOUN*
standards of right behaviour; moral principles

ethnic *ADJECTIVE*
belonging to a particular national or racial group within a larger set of people • *different ethnic communities*

ethnic cleansing *NOUN*
the mass killing of people from other ethnic or religious groups within a certain area

etiquette (say **et**-ik-et) *NOUN*
the rules of correct behaviour

a b c d e f g h i j k l m n o p q r s t u v w x y z

etymology (say et-im-**ol**-oj-ee) *NOUN* etymologies
❶ a description of the origin and history of a particular word ❷ the study of the origins of words
➤ **etymological** *ADJECTIVE*

EU *ABBREVIATION*
European Union

eucalyptus (say yoo-kal-**ip**-tus) *NOUN* eucalyptuses
❶ a kind of evergreen tree ❷ a strong-smelling oil obtained from its leaves

Eucharist (say **yoo**-ker-ist) *NOUN*
the Christian sacrament in which bread and wine are consecrated and swallowed, commemorating the Last Supper of Christ and his disciples

eulogy (say **yoo**-loj-ee) *NOUN* eulogies
a speech or piece of writing in praise of a person or thing

eunuch (say **yoo**-nuk) *NOUN* eunuchs
a man who has been castrated

euphemism (say **yoo**-fim-izm) *NOUN* euphemisms
a mild word or phrase used instead of an offensive or frank one; *'to pass away'* is a euphemism for *'to die'*
➤ **euphemistic** *ADJECTIVE*
➤ **euphemistically** *ADVERB*

euphonium (say yoof-**oh**-nee-um) *NOUN* euphoniums
a large brass wind instrument

euphoria (say yoo-**for**-ee-a) *NOUN*
a feeling of general happiness

Eurasian *ADJECTIVE*
having European and Asian parents or ancestors
➤ **Eurasian** *NOUN*

eureka (say yoor-**eek**-a) *EXCLAMATION*
a cry of triumph at a great discovery
WORD ORIGIN Greek = 'I have found it', said to have been uttered by the Greek mathematician Archimedes, who was excited by his new idea about the volume and density of matter

euro *NOUN* euros or euro
the single currency introduced in the EU in 1999. Its symbol is €.

European *ADJECTIVE*
to do with Europe or its people
➤ **European** *NOUN*

euthanasia (say yooth-an-**ay**-zee-a) *NOUN*
causing someone to die gently and without pain when they are suffering from a painful incurable disease

evacuate *VERB* evacuates, evacuating, evacuated
to move people away from a dangerous place • *Police evacuated nearby buildings.* • *Thousands of children were evacuated from the war zone.*
➤ **evacuation** *NOUN*

evacuee *NOUN* evacuees
a person who has been evacuated

evade *VERB* evades, evading, evaded
❶ to avoid being caught or meeting someone • *They managed to evade capture for six months.* ❷ to avoid dealing with something • *I asked her directly but she evaded the question.*

evaluate *VERB* evaluates, evaluating, evaluated
to estimate the value or quality of something; to assess something • *We evaluated each of the websites.*
➤ **evaluation** *NOUN*

Evangelist *NOUN* Evangelists
any of the writers (Matthew, Mark, Luke, John) of the four Gospels

evangelist *NOUN* evangelists
a person who preaches the Christian faith enthusiastically
➤ **evangelical** *ADJECTIVE*

evaporate *VERB* evaporates, evaporating, evaporated
❶ to change from liquid into steam or vapour ❷ to disappear completely • *It didn't take long for their enthusiasm to evaporate.*

evaporation *NOUN*
the process of changing from liquid into steam or vapour

evasion *NOUN* evasions
❶ evading someone or something ❷ an evasive answer or excuse

evasive *ADJECTIVE*
trying to avoid answering something; not frank or straightforward
➤ **evasively** *ADVERB*

eve *NOUN* eves
❶ the day or evening before an important day or event • *Christmas Eve* ❷ (*old use*) evening

even *ADJECTIVE*
❶ level and smooth ❷ not changing or varying; regular ❸ calm and not easily upset • *an even temper* ❹ equal or equally balanced • *Our scores were even.* • *an even contest* ❺ able to be divided exactly by two • *Six and fourteen are even numbers.*
Compare with **odd**.
➤ **evenness** *NOUN*
➤ **get even** to take revenge on someone

even *VERB* **evens, evening, evened**
❶ to make something even • *That goal evened the score.* ❷ things **even up** or **even out** when they become even

even *ADVERB*
used to emphasize a word or statement • *She ran even faster.* • *I couldn't even stand, let alone walk.*
➤ **even so** although that is correct

even *NOUN*
(*old use*) evening

even-handed *ADJECTIVE*
fair and impartial

evening *NOUN* **evenings**
the time at the end of the day between the late afternoon and bedtime

evenly *ADVERB*
in a smooth, regular or equal way • *The match was evenly balanced.* • *Spread the cake mixture evenly in the tin.*

event *NOUN* **events**
❶ something that happens, especially something important ❷ a race or competition that forms part of a sports contest

eventful *ADJECTIVE*
full of happenings • *It's been an eventful day.*

eventual *ADJECTIVE*
happening in the end • *his eventual success*

eventuality (say iv-en-tew-**al**-it-ee) *NOUN*
eventualities
something that may happen

eventually *ADVERB*
finally; in the end • *We eventually managed to get the door open.*

ever *ADVERB*
❶ at any time • *It's the best present I've ever had.* ❷ always; at all times • *Scientists are ever hopeful of finding signs of life on other planets.* ❸ (*informal*) used for emphasis • *Why ever didn't you tell me?*

evergreen *ADJECTIVE*
an evergreen tree or shrub has green leaves all through the year

evergreen *NOUN* **evergreens**
an evergreen tree or shrub

everlasting *ADJECTIVE*
lasting for ever or for a very long time

every *DETERMINER*
❶ each without any exceptions • *We enjoyed every minute.* ❷ used for saying how often something happens • *Take one tablet every four hours.*
➤ **every other day** or **week**, etc. each alternate one; every second one • *The magazine is published every other Friday.*

USAGE
Take care to use a singular verb with *every*, e.g. *Every one of the eggs has hatched* (not 'have hatched').

SPELLING
Every has **er** in the middle, ev-**er**-y.

everybody *PRONOUN*
every person; everyone

everyday *ADJECTIVE*
ordinary or usual • *The Internet is now part of everyday life.*

everyone *PRONOUN*
every person; all people • *Everyone likes her.*

SPELLING
Everyone has **er** in the middle, ev-**er**-y-one.

everything *PRONOUN*
❶ all things; all ❷ the only or most important thing • *Winning is not everything.*

everywhere *ADVERB*
in every place

evict *VERB* **evicts, evicting, evicted**
to make people move out from where they are living
➤ **eviction** *NOUN*

evidence *NOUN*
❶ anything that gives people reason to believe something • *There was no evidence of a struggle in the room.* ❷ statements made or objects produced in a law court to prove something

evident *ADJECTIVE*
obvious; clearly seen or understood • *It is evident that he is lying.*

a b c d e f g h i j k l m n o p q r s t u v w x y z

A
B
C
D
E
F
G
H
I
J
K
L
M
N
O
P
Q
R
S
T
U
V
W
X
Y
Z

evidently ADVERB
obviously or clearly • *She had evidently changed her mind.*

evil ADJECTIVE
morally bad; wicked
➤ **evilly** ADVERB

evil NOUN evils
❶ wickedness ❷ something bad or harmful • *the evils of war*

evoke VERB evokes, evoking, evoked
to bring a memory or feeling into your mind • *The photographs evoked happy memories.*
➤ **evocation** NOUN
➤ **evocative** ADJECTIVE

evolution (say ee-vol-**oo**-shon) NOUN
❶ gradual change into something different ❷ the development of animals and plants from earlier or simpler forms of life
➤ **evolutionary** ADJECTIVE

evolve VERB evolves, evolving, evolved
❶ to develop gradually or naturally • *His style of painting evolved over the next 20 years.* ❷ animals and plants evolve when they develop from earlier or simpler forms of life • *Birds evolved from reptiles.*

ewe (say yoo) NOUN ewes
a female sheep

ewer (say **yoo**-er) NOUN ewers
a large water jug

ex– PREFIX
former • *ex-wife* • *ex-president*

exacerbate (say eks-**ass**-er-bayt) VERB
exacerbates, exacerbating, exacerbated
to make a pain or disease or other problem worse

exact ADJECTIVE
❶ completely correct • *I can't tell you the exact number of people who are coming.* ❷ clearly stated; giving all the details • *exact instructions*
➤ **exactness** NOUN

exact VERB exacts, exacting, exacted
❶ to demand and get something from someone • *She was keen to exact a promise from him.* ❷ to exact revenge on someone is to take revenge on them

exacting ADJECTIVE
needing a lot of effort and care • *an exacting task*

exactly ADVERB
❶ in an exact manner; precisely • *Tell me exactly what happened.* ❷ used for agreeing

with someone • *'You mean you've lost all your money?' 'Exactly.'*

exaggerate VERB exaggerates, exaggerating, exaggerated
to make something seem bigger, better or worse than it really is • *Come on, there's no need to exaggerate.*

exaggeration NOUN exaggerations
making something seem bigger, better or worse than it really is • *He has a reputation for exaggeration and making things up.*

exalt (say ig-**zawlt**) VERB exalts, exalting, exalted
❶ to raise someone in rank or status ❷ to praise someone or something highly
➤ **exaltation** NOUN

exam NOUN exams (*informal*)
an examination

examination NOUN examinations
❶ a test of a person's knowledge or skill ❷ examining something; an inspection • *a medical examination*

examine VERB examines, examining, examined
❶ to look at something closely or in detail • *Tom bent down and examined the footprints.* ❷ to test a person's knowledge or skill

examinee NOUN examinees
a person being tested in an examination

examiner NOUN examiners
a person who sets or marks an examination

example NOUN examples
❶ anything that shows what others of the same kind are like or how they work ❷ a person or thing good enough to be worth imitating • *Her courage is an example to us all.*
➤ **for example** as an example

exasperate VERB exasperates, exasperating, exasperated
to annoy someone very much
➤ **exasperation** NOUN

excavate VERB excavates, excavating, excavated
❶ to dig in the ground in order to find things from the past • *Archaeologists excavated the site with great care.* ❷ to uncover something by digging • *The statue was excavated in 1931.*
➤ **excavation** NOUN
➤ **excavator** NOUN

exceed *VERB* **exceeds, exceeding, exceeded**
❶ to be more than a particular number or amount • *The weight should not exceed 20 kilos.* ❷ to go beyond the limit of what is normal or allowed • *He has exceeded his authority.*

> **SPELLING**
> The 's' sound is spelt with a **c** in **exceed**.

exceedingly *ADVERB*
very; extremely • *an exceedingly difficult problem*

excel *VERB* **excels, excelling, excelled**
to be better than others at doing something • *She excels at foreign languages.*

excellence *NOUN*
the quality of being extremely good • *The school has a reputation for academic excellence.*

Excellency *NOUN* **Excellencies**
the title of high officials such as ambassadors and governors

excellent *ADJECTIVE*
extremely good
> **excellently** *ADVERB*

except *PREPOSITION*
not including; apart from • *The museum is open every day except Mondays.* • *I can answer all of the questions except for the last one.*

except *VERB* **excepts, excepting, excepted**
to not include someone or something; to leave someone or something out • *I blame you all, no one is excepted.*

> **SPELLING**
> The 's' sound is spelt with a **c** in **except**. Take care not to confuse with the verb **accept**.

excepting *PREPOSITION*
except for; apart from

exception *NOUN* **exceptions**
a person or thing that is left out or does not follow the general rule
> **take exception to something** to object strongly to something
> **with the exception of** except for; apart from

exceptional *ADJECTIVE*
❶ very unusual ❷ outstandingly good • *He showed exceptional talent for art when he was young.*
> **exceptionally** *ADVERB*

excerpt (say **ek**-serpt) *NOUN* **excerpts**
a passage taken from a book, speech or film

excess *NOUN* **excesses**
too much of something • *Tests showed an excess of alcohol in the driver's blood.*
> **in excess of** more than

excessive *ADJECTIVE*
too much or too great
> **excessively** *ADVERB*

exchange *VERB* **exchanges, exchanging, exchanged**
to give something and receive something else for it

exchange *NOUN* **exchanges**
❶ exchanging things ❷ a place where things (especially stocks and shares) are bought and sold • *a stock exchange* ❸ a place where telephone lines are connected to each other when a call is made

exchequer *NOUN* **exchequers**
a national treasury into which public funds (such as taxes) are paid **WORD ORIGIN** from Latin *scaccarium* = chessboard (because the Norman kings kept their accounts by means of counters placed on a chequered tablecloth)

excise (say **eks**-yz) *NOUN*
a tax charged on certain goods and licences

excitable *ADJECTIVE*
easily excited

excite *VERB* **excites, exciting, excited**
❶ to make someone eager and enthusiastic about something • *The thought of finding the hidden treasure excited them.* ❷ to cause a feeling or reaction • *The invention excited great interest.*

> **SPELLING**
> The 's' sound is spelt with a **c** in **excite**.

excited *ADJECTIVE*
feeling eager and enthusiastic about something
> **excitedly** *ADVERB*

excitement *NOUN* **excitements**
a strong feeling of eagerness or pleasure

exciting *ADJECTIVE*
causing strong feelings or pleasure and interest • *That's very exciting news.*

exclaim *VERB* **exclaims, exclaiming, exclaimed**
to shout or cry out in eagerness or surprise

a b c d e f g h i j k l m n o p q r s t u v w x y z

exclamation NOUN exclamations
❶ exclaiming ❷ a word or words cried out expressing joy, pain or surprise

GRAMMAR

An **exclamation** often expresses a strong feeling such as delight or anger, and can be used as a strong command or warning.

Exclamations do not always have a subject and verb, and may be a single word; they should end with an **exclamation mark**:

What a good a good answer!

Put that down!

Oh, no!

Good!

See also the panels on **exclamation marks** and **sentences**.

exclamation mark NOUN exclamation marks
the punctuation mark (!) placed after an exclamation

PUNCTUATION

You use an **exclamation mark** to indicate shouting, surprise or excitement in direct speech:

'Stop! Don't drink! The goblet is poisoned!'

'Wow! That's a real mammoth's tooth!'

It can also be used to express surprise, alarm or excitement in a story, or in a character's thoughts:

The sun was coming up. She must hurry! Soon the spell would wear off!

Swimming with sharks! That would be something to remember!

An exclamation mark can be used at the end of a sentence to show that it is a command, giving an order or an instruction:

Come in! Sit down!

See also the panel on **exclamations**.

exclude VERB excludes, excluding, excluded
❶ to keep someone or something out of a place ❷ to leave something out • *Do not exclude the possibility of rain.*
➤ **exclusion** NOUN

exclusive ADJECTIVE
❶ allowing only a few people to be involved

• *an exclusive club* ❷ not shared with others
• *This newspaper has an exclusive report.*
➤ **exclusively** ADVERB
➤ **exclusive of** excluding, not including • *This is the price exclusive of meals.*

excommunicate VERB excommunicates, excommunicating, excommunicated
to cut a person off from membership of a Church
➤ **excommunication** NOUN

excrement (say **eks**-krim-ent) NOUN
waste matter excreted from the bowels

excrescence (say iks-**kress**-ens) NOUN
excrescences
❶ a growth or lump on a plant or animal's body ❷ an ugly addition or part

excrete VERB excretes, excreting, excreted
to get rid of waste matter from the body
➤ **excretion** NOUN
➤ **excretory** ADJECTIVE

excruciating (say iks-**kroo**-shee-ayt-ing) ADJECTIVE
extremely painful
➤ **excruciatingly** ADVERB

excursion NOUN excursions
a short journey made for pleasure

excusable ADJECTIVE
able to be excused

excuse (say iks-**kewz**) VERB excuses, excusing, excused
❶ to forgive someone ❷ to allow someone not to do something • *Please may I be excused swimming?* ❸ to allow someone to leave a room, table or meeting

excuse (say iks-**kewss**) NOUN excuses
a reason given to explain why something wrong has been done

execrable (say **eks**-ik-rab-ul) ADJECTIVE
very bad or unpleasant

execute VERB executes, executing, executed
❶ to put someone to death as a punishment ❷ to perform or produce something • *She executed the somersault perfectly.*
➤ **execution** NOUN

executioner NOUN executioners
a person whose job is to execute people

executive (say ig-**zek**-yoo-tiv) NOUN
executives
a senior person with authority in a business or government organization

executive *ADJECTIVE*
having the authority to carry out plans or laws

executor (say ig-**zek**-yoo-ter) *NOUN* executors
a person appointed to carry out the instructions in someone's will

exemplary (say ig-**zem**-pler-ee) *ADJECTIVE*
very good; being a good example to others • *His conduct was exemplary.*

exemplify *VERB* exemplifies, exemplifying, exemplified
to be a typical example of something • *This painting exemplifies the style of his early work.*

exempt *ADJECTIVE*
not having to do something that others have to do • *Charities are exempt from paying tax.*

exempt *VERB* exempts, exempting, exempted
to make someone or something exempt
➤ **exemption** *NOUN*

exercise *NOUN* exercises
❶ using your body to make it strong and healthy ❷ a piece of work done for practice

exercise *VERB* exercises, exercising, exercised
❶ to do exercises ❷ to give exercise to an animal ❸ to use something • *You must exercise more patience.*

exert *VERB* exerts, exerting, exerted
to use power, strength or influence • *The moon exerts a force on the earth that causes the tides.*
➤ **exert yourself** to make an effort

exertion *NOUN* exertions
physical effort or exercise • *He was tired after the exertions of the morning.*

exeunt (say **eks**-ee-unt) *VERB*
a stage direction meaning 'they leave the stage' **WORD ORIGIN** Latin = they go out

exhale *VERB* exhales, exhaling, exhaled
to breathe out • *He took a deep breath and exhaled slowly.*
➤ **exhalation** *NOUN*

exhaust *VERB* exhausts, exhausting, exhausted
❶ to make someone very tired ❷ to use something up completely • *Within three days they had exhausted their supply of food.*

exhaust *NOUN* exhausts
❶ the waste gases or steam from an engine ❷ the pipe through which they are sent out

exhaustion *NOUN*
being very tired

exhaustive *ADJECTIVE*
thorough; including everything possible • *We made an exhaustive search.*

exhibit *VERB* exhibits, exhibiting, exhibited
to show or display something in public
➤ **exhibitor** *NOUN*

exhibit *NOUN* exhibits
something on display in a gallery or museum

exhibition *NOUN* exhibitions
a collection of things put on display for people to look at, for example at a museum or gallery

exhilarate (say ig-**zil**-er-ayt) *VERB* exhilarates, exhilarating, exhilarated
to make someone very happy and excited • *She felt exhilarated by the storm.*
➤ **exhilarating** *ADJECTIVE*
➤ **exhilaration** *NOUN*

exhort (say ig-**zort**) *VERB* exhorts, exhorting, exhorted
to try hard to persuade someone to do something
➤ **exhortation** *NOUN*

exhume (say ig-**zewm**) *VERB* exhumes, exhuming, exhumed
to dig up a body that has been buried
➤ **exhumation** *NOUN*

exile *VERB* exiles, exiling, exiled
to banish someone from a country

exile *NOUN* exiles
❶ to be in exile is to be forced to live away from your own country • *He was in exile for ten years.* ❷ someone who has been banished from their own country

exist *VERB* exists, existing, existed
❶ to be present as part of what is real • *Do ghosts exist?* ❷ to stay alive • *They existed on berries and water.*

existence *NOUN*
❶ existing or being • *This is the oldest human skeleton in existence.* ❷ a way of living • *For several years he led a lonely existence.*

existing *ADJECTIVE*
that is already there or being used • *His time shattered the existing world record.*

exit *NOUN* exits
❶ the way out of a building ❷ going off the stage • *The actress made her exit.*

exit *VERB*
an actor or performer exits when they leave the stage **WORD ORIGIN** Latin = he or she goes out

a
b
c
d
e
f
g
h
i
j
k
l
m
n
o
p
q
r
s
t
u
v
w
x
y
z

A
B
C
D
E
F
G
H
I
J
K
L
M
N
O
P
Q
R
S
T
U
V
W
X
Y
Z

exodus NOUN **exoduses**
the departure of many people

exonerate VERB **exonerates, exonerating, exonerated**
to say or prove that a person is not to blame for something

exorbitant ADJECTIVE
much too great; excessive • *exorbitant prices*

exorcize (also **exorcise**) VERB **exorcizes, exorcizing, exorcized**
to drive out an evil spirit
➤ **exorcism** NOUN
➤ **exorcist** NOUN

exotic ADJECTIVE
❶ very unusual and colourful • *exotic clothes*
❷ from a foreign country, especially a distant or tropical one • *exotic plants*
➤ **exotically** ADVERB

expand VERB **expands, expanding, expanded**
❶ to become larger or fuller • *Metals expand when they are heated.* ❷ to make something larger or fuller

expanse NOUN **expanses**
a wide area of open land, sea or sky

expansion NOUN
becoming larger or making something larger

expansive ADJECTIVE
❶ covering a wide area ❷ friendly and willing to talk a lot • *She was in an expansive mood.*

expatriate (say eks-**pat**-ree-at) NOUN **expatriates**
a person living away from his or her own country

expect VERB **expects, expecting, expected**
❶ to think or believe that something will happen or that someone will come • *I expect that it will rain this afternoon.* ❷ to think that something ought to happen • *She expects obedience.*

expectant ADJECTIVE
❶ expecting something to happen; hopeful
❷ an expectant mother is a woman who is pregnant
➤ **expectantly** ADVERB
➤ **expectancy** NOUN

expectation NOUN **expectations**
❶ expecting something; being hopeful
❷ something you expect to happen or get

expecting ADJECTIVE (*informal*)
a woman who is expecting is pregnant

expedient (say iks-**pee**-dee-ent) ADJECTIVE
❶ suitable or convenient ❷ useful and practical though perhaps unfair
➤ **expediency** NOUN

expedient NOUN **expedients**
a convenient means of achieving something

expedite (say **eks**-pid-dyt) VERB **expedites, expediting, expedited**
to make something happen more quickly
WORD ORIGIN from Latin *expedire* = free someone's feet

expedition NOUN **expeditions**
❶ a journey or voyage made in order to do something • *a climbing expedition* ❷ (*formal*) speed or promptness
➤ **expeditionary** ADJECTIVE

expel VERB **expels, expelling, expelled**
❶ to send or force something out • *This fan expels stale air.* ❷ to make a person leave a school or country
➤ **expulsion** NOUN

expend VERB **expends, expending, expended**
to use or spend time, money or energy doing something • *I have already expended a lot of energy on this show.*

expendable ADJECTIVE
no longer useful or necessary and so not worth keeping or saving

expenditure NOUN **expenditures**
the spending of money or the amount spent

expense NOUN **expenses**
the cost of doing something • *The garden was transformed at great expense.*

expensive ADJECTIVE
costing a lot
➤ **expensively** ADVERB

experience NOUN **experiences**
❶ what you learn from doing or seeing things
❷ something that has happened to you

experience VERB **experiences, experiencing, experienced**
to have something happen to you • *It was the first time she had experienced failure.*

experienced ADJECTIVE
having a lot of skill or knowledge from much experience

experiment NOUN **experiments**
a test made in order to find out what happens or to prove something

experiment VERB **experiments, experimenting, experimented**
❶ to carry out an experiment ❷ to try out

new things
➤ **experimentation** NOUN

experimental ADJECTIVE
to do with experiments or trying out
new ideas • *The machine is still at the
experimental stage.*
➤ **experimentally** ADVERB

expert NOUN experts
a person with great knowledge or skill in
something

expert ADJECTIVE
having great knowledge or skill • *He's an
expert cook.*
➤ **expertly** ADVERB

expertise (say eks-per-**teez**) NOUN
expert ability or knowledge

expire VERB expires, expiring, expired
❶ to come to an end or stop being usable
• *Your season ticket has expired.* ❷ to die
➤ **expiration** NOUN
➤ **expiry** NOUN

explain VERB explains, explaining, explained
❶ to make something clear to someone else;
to show its meaning ❷ to give or be a reason
for something • *That explains his absence.*

explanation NOUN explanations
a statement or fact that explains something
or gives a reason for it

explanatory (say iks-**plan**-at-er-ee) ADJECTIVE
giving an explanation • *an explanatory note*

explicit (say iks-**pliss**-it) ADJECTIVE
stated or stating something openly and
exactly. Compare with **implicit**.
➤ **explicitly** ADVERB

explode VERB explodes, exploding, exploded
❶ to burst or suddenly release energy with a
loud noise ❷ to cause a bomb to go off ❸ to
burst into anger or laughter suddenly • *He
exploded with rage.* ❹ to increase suddenly
or quickly (**WORD ORIGIN**) originally = to drive a
player off the stage by clapping or hissing; from
ex- + Latin *plaudere* = clap

exploit (say **eks**-ploit) NOUN exploits
a brave or exciting deed

exploit (say iks-**ploit**) VERB exploits,
exploiting, exploited
❶ to exploit someone is to treat them
unfairly for your own advantage ❷ to exploit
resources is to use or develop them
➤ **exploitation** NOUN

exploration NOUN
exploring a place • *space exploration*

exploratory (say iks-**plorra**-ter-ee) ADJECTIVE
for the purpose of exploring

explore VERB explores, exploring, explored
❶ to travel through a place in order to
learn about it ❷ to examine a subject or
idea carefully • *We need to explore all the
possibilities before we decide.*

explorer NOUN explorers
someone who explores a remote place to find
out what is there

explosion NOUN explosions
❶ the exploding of a bomb; the noise made
by exploding • *Two people were killed in the
explosion.* ❷ a sudden great increase • *a
population explosion*

explosive ADJECTIVE
able to explode • *Hydrogen is highly
explosive.*

explosive NOUN explosives
a substance that is used for causing
explosions

exponent NOUN exponents
❶ someone who is very good at an activity
• *a major exponent of landscape painting*
❷ a person who puts forward an idea or
theory ❸ (*in mathematics*) the raised number
etc. written to the right of another (e.g. 3 in
2^3) showing how many times the first one is
to be multiplied by itself

export VERB exports, exporting, exported
to send goods abroad to be sold • *Peru
exports copper, lead and zinc.*
➤ **exporter** NOUN

export NOUN exports
❶ exporting goods ❷ something that is
exported

expose VERB exposes, exposing, exposed
❶ to reveal or uncover something ❷ to put
someone in a situation where they could be
harmed • *Some people were exposed to high
levels of radiation.* ❸ to allow light to reach a
photographic film so as to take a picture

expostulate VERB expostulates,
expostulating, expostulated
to argue or protest strongly about something
➤ **expostulation** NOUN

exposure NOUN exposures
❶ the harmful effects of being exposed to
cold weather without enough protection
❷ exposing film to the light so as to take a
picture or a piece of film exposed in this way

expound VERB expounds, expounding, expounded
to describe or explain something in detail

express ADJECTIVE
❶ going or sent quickly ❷ clearly stated • *This was done against my express orders.*

express NOUN expresses
a fast train stopping at only a few stations

express VERB expresses, expressing, expressed
to put ideas or feelings into words; to make your feelings known • *He expressed his opinion on the matter very clearly.*

expression NOUN expressions
❶ the look on a person's face that shows his or her feelings ❷ a word or phrase ❸ a way of speaking or of playing music that shows your feelings ❹ expressing something • *this expression of opinion*

expressive ADJECTIVE
showing your thoughts and feelings • *an expressive gesture*

expressly ADVERB
❶ clearly and plainly • *This was expressly forbidden.* ❷ specially • *The exhibition is designed expressly for children*

expulsion NOUN expulsions
expelling someone or something or being expelled

exquisite (say **eks**-kwiz-it) ADJECTIVE
very beautiful or delicate • *The flowers are painted in exquisite detail.*
➤ **exquisitely** ADVERB

extend VERB extends, extending, extended
❶ to spread or stretch out • *Our land extends as far as the river.* ❷ to make something become longer or larger • *The table can be extended to seat more people.* ❸ to offer or give something • *I would like to extend a warm welcome to our guests.*

extension NOUN extensions
❶ a section added on to a building ❷ an extra period that is allowed for something to be done ❸ one of a set of telephones in an office or house

extensive ADJECTIVE
❶ covering a large area • *extensive gardens* ❷ large in scope; wide-ranging • *an extensive internet search*
➤ **extensively** ADVERB

extent NOUN extents
❶ the area or length over which something extends ❷ the amount, level or scope of something • *We don't yet know the full extent of the damage.*

extenuating ADJECTIVE
making a crime seem less great by providing a partial excuse • *There were extenuating circumstances.*
➤ **extenuation** NOUN

exterior ADJECTIVE
outer • *the exterior walls of the house*

exterior NOUN exteriors
❶ the outside of something ❷ a person's outward appearance

exterminate VERB exterminates, exterminating, exterminated
to kill all the members of a group of people or animals
➤ **extermination** NOUN
➤ **exterminator** NOUN

external ADJECTIVE
on or from the outside of something • *an external fuel tank*
➤ **externally** ADVERB

extinct ADJECTIVE
❶ not existing any more • *The dodo is an extinct bird.* ❷ an extinct volcano is no longer burning or active

extinction NOUN
becoming extinct • *The giant panda is in danger of extinction.*

extinguish VERB extinguishes, extinguishing, extinguished
❶ to put out a fire or light ❷ to put an end to something • *Our hopes of victory were soon extinguished.*

extinguisher NOUN extinguishers
a portable device for sending out water, chemicals or gases to put out a fire

extol VERB extols, extolling, extolled
to praise someone or something enthusiastically

extort VERB extorts, extorting, extorted
to obtain something by force or threats
➤ **extortion** NOUN

extortionate ADJECTIVE
an extortionate price or fee is much too high

extra ADJECTIVE
additional; more than is usual • *There is an extra charge for taking your bike on the train.*

extra ADVERB
more than usually • *extra strong mints*

extra *NOUN* extras
① an extra person or thing **②** a person acting as part of a crowd in a film or play

extract (say iks-**trakt**) *VERB* extracts, extracting, extracted
① to take something out; to remove something **②** to obtain information from someone, usually with difficulty
➤ **extractor** *NOUN*

extract (say **eks**-trakt) *NOUN* extracts
① a passage taken from a book, film, piece of music, etc. **②** a substance separated or obtained from another • *a plant extract*

extraction *NOUN*
① extracting something **②** a person's family history • *He is of Chinese extraction.*

extradite *VERB* extradites, extraditing, extradited
to hand over an accused person to the police of the country where the crime was committed
➤ **extradition** (say eks-tra-**dish**-on) *NOUN*

extraordinary *ADJECTIVE*
very unusual or strange
➤ **extraordinarily** *ADVERB*

extrasensory *ADJECTIVE*
outside the range of the known human senses

extraterrestrial *ADJECTIVE*
from beyond the earth's atmosphere; from outer space

extraterrestrial *NOUN* extraterrestrials
a being from outer space

extravagant *ADJECTIVE*
① spending or using too much of something **②** too much; more than is reasonable
• *extravagant praise*
➤ **extravagantly** *ADVERB*
➤ **extravagance** *NOUN*

extravaganza *NOUN* extravaganzas
a very spectacular show

extreme *ADJECTIVE*
① very great or intense • *extreme cold* **②** furthest away • *the extreme north* **③** going to great lengths in actions or opinions; not moderate • *It seemed a bit extreme to call the police.*

extreme *NOUN* extremes
① something extreme **②** either end of something

extremely *ADVERB*
very • *They are extremely pleased.*

extremist *NOUN* extremists
a person who holds extreme (not moderate) opinions in political or other matters

extremity (say iks-**trem**-it-ee) *NOUN* extremities
① an extreme point; the very end of something **②** your extremities are your hands and feet **③** an extreme need, feeling or danger

extricate (say **eks**-trik-ayt) *VERB* extricates, extricating, extricated
to free someone or something from a difficult position or situation • *He managed to extricate himself from the wreckage.*
➤ **extrication** *NOUN*

extrovert *NOUN* extroverts
a person who is generally lively and confident and likes company. (The opposite is **introvert**.)

extrude *VERB* extrudes, extruding, extruded
to push or squeeze something out
➤ **extrusion** *NOUN*

exuberant (say ig-**zew**-ber-ant) *ADJECTIVE*
very lively and cheerful
➤ **exuberantly** *ADVERB*
➤ **exuberance** *NOUN*

exude *VERB* exudes, exuding, exuded
① to give off moisture or a smell **②** to display a feeling or quality openly • *She exuded confidence.*

exult *VERB* exults, exulting, exulted
to show great pleasure and excitement about something • *'Ha! I win!' exulted Leah.*
➤ **exultation** *NOUN*

exultant *ADJECTIVE*
very pleased and excited about something

eye *NOUN* eyes
① the organ of the body that is used for seeing **②** the power of seeing • *She has sharp eyes.* **③** the small hole in a needle **④** the centre of a storm

eye *VERB* eyes, eyeing, eyed
to look at something with interest

eyeball *NOUN* eyeballs
the ball-shaped part of the eye inside the eyelids

eyebrow *NOUN* eyebrows
the fringe of hair growing on your face above each eye

eye-catching *ADJECTIVE*
striking or attractive

a b c d e f g h i j k l m n o p q r s t u v w x y z

eyelash *NOUN* eyelashes
one of the short hairs that grow on an eyelid

eyelid *NOUN* eyelids
either of the two folds of skin that can close over the eyeball

eyepiece *NOUN* eyepieces
the lens of a telescope or microscope that you put to your eye

eyesight *NOUN*
the ability to see

eyesore *NOUN* eyesores
something that is ugly to look at

eyewitness *NOUN* eyewitnesses
a person who actually saw an accident or crime

eyrie (say **ee**-ree) *NOUN* eyries
the nest of an eagle or other bird of prey

fable *NOUN* fables
a short story that teaches a lesson about how people should behave, often with animals as characters

fabric *NOUN* fabrics
❶ cloth ❷ the basic framework of something, especially the walls, floors and roof of a building

fabricate *VERB* fabricates, fabricating, fabricated
❶ to construct or manufacture something
❷ to invent a story or excuse
➤ **fabrication** *NOUN*

fabulous *ADJECTIVE*
❶ wonderful; really good • *She has a fabulous voice.* ❷ incredibly great • *fabulous wealth* ❸ told of in fables and myths
➤ **fabulously** *ADVERB*

facade (say fas-**ahd**) *NOUN* facades
❶ the front of a building ❷ an outward appearance, especially a deceptive one • *His good humour was just a facade.*

face *NOUN* faces
❶ the front part of the head ❷ the expression on a person's face ❸ the front or upper side of something • *Put the cards face down.* ❹ a flat surface • *A cube has six faces.*

face *VERB* faces, facing, faced
❶ to look or have the front towards something • *Our room faced the sea.* ❷ to have to deal with something difficult or dangerous • *Explorers face many dangers.* ❸ to cover a surface with a layer of different material

facelift *NOUN* facelifts
surgery to remove wrinkles by tightening the skin of the face, done to make someone look younger

facet (say **fas**-it) *NOUN* facets
❶ one of the many sides of a cut stone or jewel ❷ one aspect of a situation or problem • *There are many facets to this argument.*

facetious (say fas-**ee**-shus) *ADJECTIVE*
trying to be funny at an unsuitable time • *facetious remarks*
➤ **facetiously** *ADVERB*

facial (say **fay**-shal) *ADJECTIVE*
to do with the face • *an odd facial expression*

facilitate (say fas-**il**-it-ayt) *VERB* facilitates, facilitating, facilitated
to make something easier to do

facility (say fas-**il**-it-ee) *NOUN* facilities
❶ a building or service that provides you with the means to do things • *The college has excellent sports facilities.* ❷ ease or skill in doing something • *She has a facility for languages.*

facsimile (say fak-**sim**-il-ee) *NOUN* facsimiles
an exact reproduction of a document

fact *NOUN* facts
something that is known to have happened or to be true
➤ **as a matter of fact** or **in fact** really; actually
➤ **the facts of life** information about how babies are conceived

faction *NOUN* factions
a small united group within a larger one, especially in politics

factor *NOUN* factors
❶ something that helps to bring about a result • *Hard work was a big factor in her success.* ❷ a number by which a larger number can be divided exactly • *2 and 3 are factors of 6*

factory *NOUN* **factories**
a large building where machines are used to make things in large quantities

factual *ADJECTIVE*
based on facts; containing facts • *I wrote down a factual account of what happened.*
➤ **factually** *ADVERB*

faculty *NOUN* **faculties**
❶ any of the powers of the body or mind (e.g. sight, speech, understanding) ❷ a department teaching a particular subject in a university or college • *the faculty of music*

fad *NOUN* **fads**
a fashion or interest that only lasts a short time

fade *VERB* **fades, fading, faded**
❶ to lose colour, freshness or strength • *Jeans fade when you wash them.* ❷ to disappear gradually • *The laughter faded away.* ❸ to make a sound etc. become gradually weaker (*fade it out*) or stronger (*fade it in* or *up*)

faeces (say **fee**-seez) *PLURAL NOUN*
solid waste matter passed out of the body

fag *NOUN* **fags** (*British*) (*informal*)
❶ something that is tiring or boring ❷ a cigarette
➤ **fagged out** tired out; exhausted

faggot *NOUN* **faggots**
❶ a meat ball made with chopped liver and baked ❷ a bundle of sticks bound together, used for firewood

Fahrenheit *ADJECTIVE*
measuring temperature on a scale where water freezes at 32° and boils at 212°
WORD ORIGIN named after G. D. *Fahrenheit*, a German scientist, who invented the mercury thermometer

fail *VERB* **fails, failing, failed**
❶ to try to do something but not be able to do it ❷ to become weak or useless; to stop working • *The brakes failed.* ❸ to not do something when you should • *He failed to warn me of the danger.* ❹ to not get enough marks to pass an examination ❺ to judge that someone has not passed an examination

fail *NOUN* **fails**
a mark which does not pass an examination • *Alex got four passes and one fail.*
➤ **without fail** for certain; whatever happens • *I'll be there without fail.*

failing *NOUN* **failings**
a weakness or a fault

failure *NOUN* **failures**
❶ a lack of success; not being able to do something • *All his efforts ended in failure.* ❷ not doing something that you were expected to do • *I was disappointed at his failure to turn up.* ❸ a person or thing that has failed

faint *ADJECTIVE*
❶ pale or dim; not clear or distinct • *a faint sound in the distance* ❷ slight • *a faint hope* ❸ feeling weak and dizzy; nearly unconscious
➤ **faintness** *NOUN*

faint *VERB* **faints, fainting, fainted**
to become unconscious for a short time

SPELLING
Take care not to confuse with **feint**, which means a pretended attack.

faintly *ADVERB*
❶ not in a clear or strong way • *He smiled faintly.* ❷ slightly • *She looked faintly embarrassed.*

fair *ADJECTIVE*
❶ just or reasonable; treating everyone equally • *a fair decision* • *a fair contest* ❷ fair hair or skin is light in colour and a fair person has hair that is light in colour ❸ fair weather is fine and without clouds ❹ of a reasonable size, amount or number • *a fair number of people* ❺ quite good • *We've got a fair chance of winning.* ❻ (*old use*) beautiful
➤ **fairness** *NOUN*

fair *ADVERB*
fairly, according to the rules • *Play fair!*

fair *NOUN* **fairs**
❶ an outdoor entertainment with rides, amusements and stalls ❷ an exhibition or market • *a craft fair*

fairground *NOUN* **fairgrounds**
an open outdoor space where a fair is held

fairly *ADVERB*
❶ justly; according to the rules • *She promised to treat everyone fairly.* ❷ quite or rather • *It is fairly hard.*

fairy *NOUN* **fairies**
an imaginary very small creature with magic powers

fairyland *NOUN*
the imaginary land where fairies live

fairy tale *NOUN* **fairy tales**
a story about fairies or magic

faith *NOUN* **faiths**
❶ strong belief or trust • *We have great faith*

a b c d e f g h i j k l m n o p q r s t u v w x y z

A

in her. ❷ a religion
➤ **in good faith** with honest intentions

B

faithful *ADJECTIVE*
❶ loyal and trustworthy ❷ true to the facts;
accurate • *a faithful account* ❸ sexually loyal
to one partner
➤ **faithfully** *ADVERB*
➤ **faithfulness** *NOUN*
➤ **Yours faithfully** see **yours**

C

D

E

fake *NOUN* fakes
something that looks genuine but is not; a
forgery

F

fake *ADJECTIVE*
not real or genuine • *fake diamonds*

G

fake *VERB* fakes, faking, faked
❶ to make something that looks genuine, in
order to deceive people ❷ to pretend to have
something • *He used to fake illness to miss
games.*

H

I

J

fakir (say **fay**-keer) *NOUN* fakirs
a Muslim or Hindu religious beggar regarded
as a holy man

K

L

falcon *NOUN* falcons
a kind of hawk often used in the sport of
hunting other birds or game
➤ **falconry** *NOUN*

M

N

fall *VERB* falls, falling, fell, fallen
❶ to come or go down without being pushed
or thrown • *Leaves were falling from the
trees.* ❷ to decrease or become lower • *Prices
fell.* ❸ to be captured or overthrown • *The
city fell.* ❹ to die in battle ❺ to happen
• *Silence fell.* ❻ to become • *She fell asleep.*
➤ **fall back** to retreat
➤ **fall back on something** to use something
for support or in an emergency
➤ **fall for someone** to be attracted by a
person
➤ **fall for something** to be taken in by a trick
or deception
➤ **fall in** to collapse • *The roof fell in.*
➤ **fall in love** to begin to love someone
➤ **fall out** to quarrel and stop being friends
➤ **fall through** to fail • *Our plans fell
through.*

O

P

Q

R

S

T

U

V

fall *NOUN* falls
❶ the action of falling ❷ (*North American*)
autumn, when leaves fall

W

X

Y

Z

> **SPELLING**
> The past tense of **fall** is **fell** and the past
> participle is **fallen**.

fallacy (say **fal**-a-see) *NOUN* fallacies
a false or mistaken idea or belief that many
people believe is true

fallible (say **fal**-ib-ul) *ADJECTIVE*
liable to make mistakes; not infallible • *All
people are fallible.*
➤ **fallibility** *NOUN*

Fallopian tube *NOUN* Fallopian tubes
one of the two tubes in a woman's body
along which the eggs travel from the ovaries
to the uterus

fallout *NOUN*
particles of radioactive material carried in the
air after a nuclear explosion

fallow *ADJECTIVE*
fallow land is ploughed but left without
crops in order to make it fertile again
> **WORD ORIGIN** from Old English *falu* = pale
> brown (because of the colour of the bare earth)

fallow deer *NOUN* fallow deer
a kind of light-brown deer

falls *PLURAL NOUN*
a waterfall

false *ADJECTIVE*
❶ untrue or incorrect ❷ not genuine;
artificial • *false teeth* ❸ treacherous or
deceitful
➤ **falsely** *ADVERB*

falsehood *NOUN* falsehoods
❶ a lie ❷ telling lies

falsetto *NOUN* falsettos
a man's voice forced into speaking or singing
higher than is natural

falsify *VERB* falsifies, falsifying, falsified
to alter a document or evidence dishonestly
➤ **falsification** *NOUN*

falter *VERB* falters, faltering, faltered
❶ to hesitate when you move or speak ❷ to
become weaker; to begin to give way • *His
courage began to falter.*

fame *NOUN*
being famous • *His fame spread throughout
Europe.*

famed *ADJECTIVE*
very well known • *The restaurant is famed for
its seafood.*

familiar *ADJECTIVE*
❶ well-known; often seen or experienced
• *His yellow van was a familiar sight in the
village.* ❷ knowing something well • *Are you
familiar with this book?* ❸ very friendly

➤ **familiarly** *ADVERB*
➤ **familiarity** *NOUN*

familiarize (also **familiarise**) *VERB*
familiarizes, familiarizing, familiarized
to make yourself familiar with something

family *NOUN* families
❶ parents and their children, sometimes including grandchildren and other relations
❷ a group of related plants or animals • *Lions belong to the cat family.* ❸ a group of things that are alike in some way • *a family of languages*

family planning *NOUN*
the use of contraceptives to control pregnancies; birth control

family tree *NOUN* family trees
a diagram showing how people in a family are related

famine *NOUN* famines
a very bad shortage of food in an area

famished *ADJECTIVE*
very hungry

famous *ADJECTIVE*
known to very many people

famously *ADVERB* (*informal*)
very well • *They get on famously.*

fan *NOUN* fans
❶ a device or machine for making air move about in order to cool people or things ❷ an enthusiastic admirer or supporter

fan *VERB* fans, fanning, fanned
to send a current of air on something
➤ **fan out** to spread out in the shape of a fan
• *The police fanned out across the field.*

fanatic *NOUN* fanatics
a person who is very enthusiastic or too enthusiastic about something
➤ **fanaticism** *NOUN*

fanatical *ADJECTIVE*
very enthusiastic or too enthusiastic about something • *He's fanatical about keeping things tidy.*
➤ **fanatically** *ADVERB*

fanciful *ADJECTIVE*
❶ imagined; not based on reality or reason
• *What a fanciful idea!* ❷ imagining things
• *a fanciful child*

fancy *NOUN* fancies
❶ a liking or desire for something
❷ something that you imagine

fancy *ADJECTIVE*
decorated or elaborate; not plain • *fancy stitching*

fancy *VERB* fancies, fancying, fancied
❶ to have a liking or desire for something
• *Do you fancy getting a bite to eat?* ❷ to imagine something ❸ to believe or suppose something • *I fancy it's raining.*

fancy dress *NOUN*
unusual costume worn for a party, often to make you look like a famous person

fanfare *NOUN* fanfares
a short piece of loud music played on trumpets, especially as part of a ceremony

fang *NOUN* fangs
a long sharp tooth

fanlight *NOUN* fanlights
a window above a door

fantasia (say fan-**tay**-zee-a) *NOUN* fantasias
an imaginative piece of music or writing

fantasize (also **fantasise**) *VERB* fantasizes, fantasizing, fantasized
to imagine something pleasant or strange that you would like to happen

fantastic *ADJECTIVE*
❶ (*informal*) excellent ❷ strange or unusual; showing a lot of imagination • *a story full of fantastic creatures*
➤ **fantastically** *ADVERB*

fantasy *NOUN* fantasies
❶ something pleasant that you imagine but is not likely to happen; imagining things ❷ a very imaginative story that is not based on real life

far *ADVERB*
❶ at or to a great distance • *We didn't go far.* ❷ much; by a great amount • *This is far better.*
➤ **by far** by a great amount

far *ADJECTIVE*
❶ distant or remote • *We could see the hills in the far distance.* ❷ the far side or end of something is the side or end facing you or furthest away • *A boy was standing on the far side of the river.*

farce *NOUN* farces
❶ a comedy in which the humour is exaggerated ❷ a situation or series of events that is ridiculous or a pretence • *The trial was a complete farce.*
➤ **farcical** *ADJECTIVE*
WORD ORIGIN French, literally = stuffing (the

name given to a comic interlude between acts of a play)

fare NOUN fares
❶ the price charged for a passenger to travel
❷ food and drink • *There was only very plain fare.*

fare VERB fares, faring, fared
to get on or make progress • *How did they fare?*

farewell EXCLAMATION & NOUN farewells
goodbye

far-fetched ADJECTIVE
unlikely to be true, difficult to believe • *It all sounds rather far-fetched to me.*

farm NOUN farms
❶ an area of land and its buildings used for growing crops or keeping animals for food or other use ❷ a farmhouse

farm VERB farms, farming, farmed
❶ to grow crops or keep animals for food etc.
❷ to use land for growing crops

farmer NOUN farmers
a person who owns or manages a farm

farmhouse NOUN farmhouses
the main house on a farm, where the farmer lives

farmyard NOUN farmyards
the yard or area round farm buildings

farrier (say **fa**-ree-er) NOUN farriers
a smith who shoes horses

farther ADVERB & ADJECTIVE
at or to a greater distance; more distant

> **USAGE**
> Farther and farthest are used only if you are talking about distance (e.g. *She lives farther from the school than I do*), but even in such cases many people prefer to use **further**. Only **further** can be used to mean 'additional', e.g. in *Phone this number for further details.* If you are not sure which is right, use **further**.

farthest ADVERB & ADJECTIVE
at or to the greatest distance; most distant

> **USAGE**
> See the note at **farther**.

farthing NOUN farthings
a former British coin worth one-quarter of a penny

fascinate VERB fascinates, fascinating, fascinated
to be very attractive or interesting to someone • *Ancient Egypt has always fascinated me.*
➤ **fascinating** ADJECTIVE

> **SPELLING**
> There is a tricky bit in **fascinate**—the 's' sound is spelt **sc**.

fascination NOUN
great interest in something • *She watched him with increasing fascination.*

Fascist (say **fash**-ist) NOUN Fascists
a person who supports a type of government in which a country is ruled by a powerful dictator and people are not allowed to hold opposing political views
➤ **Fascism** NOUN

> **WORD ORIGIN** from Latin *fasces*, the bundle of rods with an axe through it, carried before a magistrate in ancient Rome as a symbol of his power to punish people

fashion NOUN fashions
❶ the style of clothes or other things that most people like at a particular time ❷ a way of doing something • *He's been behaving in a very strange fashion.*

fashion VERB fashions, fashioning, fashioned
to make something in a particular shape or style • *She fashioned a pot from the clay.*

fashionable ADJECTIVE
following the fashion of the time; popular
➤ **fashionably** ADVERB

fast ADJECTIVE faster, fastest
❶ moving or done quickly • *She's a fast runner.* • *Thank you for your fast response.*
❷ allowing fast movement • *a fast road*
❸ showing a time later than the correct time • *Your watch is fast.* ❹ firmly fixed or attached • *He made the boat fast before he got out.* ❺ a fast colour or dye is not likely to fade or run

fast ADVERB
❶ quickly • *How fast can you run?* ❷ firmly
• *His leg was stuck fast in the mud.*
➤ **fast asleep** in a deep sleep

fast VERB fasts, fasting, fasted
to go without food, especially for religious or medical reasons

fast NOUN fasts
a period of fasting

fasten VERB fastens, fastening, fastened
❶ to fix one thing firmly to another ❷ to close or lock something firmly

fastener, fastening NOUN fasteners or fastenings
a device used to fasten something

fast food NOUN
restaurant food that is quickly prepared and served

fastidious ADJECTIVE
❶ fussy and hard to please ❷ very careful about small details of dress or cleanliness
➤ **fastidiously** ADVERB
➤ **fastidiousness** NOUN

fat NOUN fats
❶ the white greasy part of meat ❷ oil or grease used in cooking

fat ADJECTIVE fatter, fattest
❶ having a very thick round body ❷ thick • *a fat book*
➤ **fatness** NOUN

fatal ADJECTIVE
❶ causing or ending in death • *a fatal accident* ❷ likely to have bad results • *He then made a fatal mistake.*
➤ **fatally** ADVERB

fatalist NOUN fatalists
a person who accepts whatever happens and thinks it could not have been avoided
➤ **fatalism** NOUN
➤ **fatalistic** ADJECTIVE

fatality (say fa-**tal**-it-ee) NOUN fatalities
a death caused by an accident, war or other disaster

fate NOUN fates
❶ a person's fate is what will happen or has happened to them • *She sat outside, waiting to find out her fate.* ❷ a power that is thought to make things happen • *It was fate that brought them together again after 20 years.*

fated ADJECTIVE
destined by fate; doomed

fateful ADJECTIVE
bringing events that are important and often disastrous • *How well she remembered that fateful day.*
➤ **fatefully** ADVERB

father NOUN fathers
❶ a male parent ❷ the title of certain priests

father VERB fathers, fathering, fathered
to become a father • *He fathered six children.*

father-in-law NOUN fathers-in-law
the father of a married person's husband or wife

fatherly ADJECTIVE
typical of a father • *a piece of fatherly advice*

fathom NOUN fathoms
a unit used to measure the depth of water, equal to 1.83 metres or 6 feet

fathom VERB fathoms, fathoming, fathomed
to understand something difficult; to work something out • *I can't fathom how you did it.*

fatigue NOUN
❶ extreme tiredness ❷ weakness in metals, caused by stress
➤ **fatigued** ADJECTIVE

fatten VERB fattens, fattening, fattened
to feed a person or animal to make them fatter

fatty ADJECTIVE
fatty meat or food contains a lot of fat

fatuous ADJECTIVE
a fatuous remark is pointless and silly
➤ **fatuously** ADVERB

fatwa NOUN fatwas
a ruling on a religious matter given by an Islamic authority

faucet NOUN faucets
(*North American*) a tap

fault NOUN faults
❶ anything that makes a person or thing imperfect; a flaw or mistake ❷ the responsibility for something wrong • *It wasn't your fault.* ❸ a break in a layer of rock, caused by movement of the earth's crust ❹ an incorrect serve in tennis
➤ **at fault** responsible for a mistake or failure

fault VERB faults, faulting, faulted
to find faults in something • *I cannot fault this book – it's brilliant.*

faultless ADJECTIVE
without a fault; perfect
➤ **faultlessly** ADVERB

faulty ADJECTIVE
having a fault or faults; not working or made properly • *a faulty light switch*

faun NOUN fauns
an ancient Roman god with a man's goat's legs, horns and tail
the name of *Faunus* a
god (see **fauna**

fauna *NOUN*
the animals of a certain area or period of time. Compare with **flora**. • *the flora and fauna of South America* **WORD ORIGIN** from the name of *Fauna*, an ancient Roman country goddess, sister of Faunus (see **faun**)

favour *NOUN* favours
❶ something kind or helpful that you do for someone ❷ approval or liking • *The idea found favour with most people.*
➤ **be in favour of** to agree with or support something • *I'm in favour of longer holidays!*

favour *VERB* favours, favouring, favoured
❶ to approve of or prefer something • *I favour the second explanation.* ❷ to help or support one person or group more than others • *Fortune seemed to favour him.*

favourable *ADJECTIVE*
❶ helpful or advantageous • *Conditions are favourable for skiing.* ❷ showing or earning approval • *favourable comments* • *I hope I made a favourable impression on them.*
➤ **favourably** *ADVERB*

favourite *ADJECTIVE*
liked more than others

favourite *NOUN* favourites
❶ a person or thing that you like most ❷ a competitor that is generally expected to win

SPELLING
The 'er' sound is spelt **our** in the middle of **favourite**.

favouritism *NOUN*
unfairly being kinder to one person than to others

fawn *NOUN* fawns
❶ a young deer ❷ a light-brown colour

fawn *VERB* fawns, fawning, fawned
to get someone to like you by flattering or praising them too much

fa... at sends an exact copy of a ...nically ❷ a copy produced

...red
...nt using a fax

...mal)
...hocked,
...She

fear *NOUN* fears
a feeling that you are in danger or that something unpleasant may happen

fear *VERB* fears, fearing, feared
❶ to feel fear; to be afraid of someone or something ❷ to be anxious or sad about something • *I fear we may be late.*

fearful *ADJECTIVE*
❶ afraid or worried • *He was fearful of going out alone.* ❷ causing fear or horror • *It was a fearful sight.* ❸ (*informal*) very great or bad • *We made a fearful mess.*
➤ **fearfully** *ADVERB*

fearless *ADJECTIVE*
without fear
➤ **fearlessly** *ADVERB*
➤ **fearlessness** *NOUN*

fearsome *ADJECTIVE*
frightening or dreadful

feasible *ADJECTIVE*
❶ able to be done; possible • *a feasible plan* ❷ likely or probable • *a feasible explanation*
➤ **feasibly** *ADVERB*
➤ **feasibility** *NOUN*

feast *NOUN* feasts
❶ a large splendid meal for a lot of people ❷ a religious festival

feast *VERB* feasts, feasting, feasted
to eat a feast or a large amount
➤ **feast your eyes on something** to gaze at something with great pleasure

feat *NOUN* feats
a deed or achievement that shows a lot of skill, strength or courage • *a remarkable feat of endurance*

feather *NOUN* feathers
one of the very light coverings that grow from a bird's skin

feathered *ADJECTIVE*
covered with or having feathers • *a feathered headdress*

featherweight *NOUN* featherweights
a boxer weighing between 54 and 57 kg

feathery *ADJECTIVE*
light and soft; like a feather • *feathery green leaves*

feature *NOUN* features
❶ any part of the face (e.g. mouth, nose, eyes) • *He has rugged features.* ❷ an important or noticeable part of something; a characteristic ❸ a special newspaper article or programme that deals with a particular

subject ❹ the main film in a cinema programme

feature VERB **features, featuring, featured**
❶ to include something as an important part • *The film features an all-star cast.* ❷ to play an important part in something • *Elves feature in many of his books.*

February NOUN
the second month of the year
WORD ORIGIN named after *februa*, the ancient Roman feast of purification held in this month

SPELLING
February can be difficult to spell—the letter r appears twice.

feckless ADJECTIVE
not having the determination to achieve anything in life

fed
past tense of **feed**
➤ **fed up** (*informal*) depressed, unhappy or bored

federal ADJECTIVE
to do with a system in which several states are ruled by a central government but have the power to make some of their own laws

federation NOUN **federations**
a group of states that have joined together under a central government

fee NOUN **fees**
a charge for something

feeble ADJECTIVE
weak; without strength or force • *a feeble excuse*
➤ **feebly** ADVERB
➤ **feebleness** NOUN

feed VERB **feeds, feeding, fed**
❶ to give food to a person or animal ❷ to take and eat food • *Sheep feed on grass.* ❸ to put something into a machine • *We fed all the figures into the database.*
➤ **feeder** NOUN

feed NOUN
food for animals or babies

feedback NOUN
❶ the response you get from people to something you have done ❷ the harsh noise produced when some of the sound from an amplifier goes back into it

feel VERB **feels, feeling, felt**
❶ to touch something to find out what it is like ❷ to think or have something as an

opinion • *I feel that she was badly treated.* ❸ to experience an emotion • *I feel a lot happier now.* ❹ to be affected by something • *Suddenly he felt very cold.* ❺ to give a certain sensation • *It feels damp in here.*
➤ **feel like something** to want something • *I don't feel like going out.*

feel NOUN
what something is like when you touch it • *I like the feel of silk.*

SPELLING
The past tense of **feel** is **felt**.

feeler NOUN **feelers**
❶ either of the two long thin parts that stick out from an insect's or crustacean's body, used for feeling ❷ a cautious question or suggestion to test people's reactions

feeling NOUN **feelings**
❶ the ability to feel things; the sense of touch • *She lost the feeling in her right hand.* ❷ what a person feels in the mind; emotion • *I didn't mean to hurt your feelings.* ❸ what you think about something • *I have a feeling that we are going to win.*

feign (say fayn) VERB **feigns, feigning, feigned**
to pretend to have a feeling or to be ill • *He feigned surprise when she walked in.*

feint (say faynt) NOUN **feints**
a pretended attack or punch meant to deceive an opponent

feint VERB **feints, feinting, feinted**
to pretend to attack or hit someone

SPELLING
Take care not to confuse with **faint**, which means pale, slight or dizzy.

felicity NOUN
❶ great happiness ❷ a pleasing manner or style • *He expressed himself with great felicity.*
➤ **felicitous** ADJECTIVE

feline (say **feel**-yn) ADJECTIVE
to do with cats; cat-like

fell
past tense of **fall**

fell VERB **fells, felling, felled**
❶ to cut down a tree ❷ to knock someone down with a hard blow

fell NOUN **fells**
a piece of wild hilly country, especially in the north of England

a
b
c
d
e
f
g
h
i
j
k
l
m
n
o
p
q
r
s
t
u
v
w
x
y
z

A
B
C
D
E
F
G
H
I
J
K
L
M
N
O
P
Q
R
S
T
U
V
W
X
Y
Z

fellow *NOUN* **fellows**
❶ a friend or companion; one who belongs to the same group ❷ a man or boy ❸ a member of a learned society

fellow *ADJECTIVE*
of the same group or kind • *Her fellow students supported her.*

fellowship *NOUN* **fellowships**
❶ friendship between people ❷ a group of friends; a society

felon (say **fel**-on) *NOUN* **felons**
a criminal

felony (say **fel**-on-ee) *NOUN* **felonies**
a serious crime

felt
past tense of **feel**

felt *NOUN*
a thick fabric made of wool fibres pressed together

female *ADJECTIVE*
of the sex that can bear offspring or produce eggs or fruit

female *NOUN* **females**
a female person, animal or plant

feminine *ADJECTIVE*
❶ to do with or like women; thought to be suitable for a woman ❷ belonging to the class of words (in some languages) which includes the words referring to women
➤ **femininity** *NOUN*

feminist *NOUN* **feminists**
a person who believes that women should have the same rights and opportunities as men
➤ **feminism** *NOUN*

femur (say **fee**-mer) *NOUN* **femurs**
the thigh bone

fen *NOUN* **fens**
an area of low-lying marshy or flooded ground

fence *NOUN* **fences**
❶ a barrier made of wood or wire etc. round an area ❷ a structure for a horse to jump over ❸ a person who buys stolen goods and sells them again

fence *VERB* **fences, fencing, fenced**
❶ to put a fence round or along something ❷ to fight with long narrow swords (called foils) as a sport
➤ **fencer** *NOUN*
➤ **fencing** *NOUN*

fend *VERB* **fends, fending, fended**
➤ **fend for yourself** to take care of yourself
➤ **fend someone** or **something off** to defend yourself from a person or thing that is attacking you • *She managed to fend off all their awkward questions.*

fender *NOUN* **fenders**
❶ something placed round a fireplace to stop coals from falling into the room ❷ something hung over the side of a boat to protect it from knocks

fennel *NOUN*
a herb with yellow flowers whose seeds and root are used for flavouring

feral *ADJECTIVE*
wild and untamed • *feral cats*

ferment (say fer-**ment**) *VERB* **ferments, fermenting, fermented**
to bubble and change chemically by the action of a substance such as yeast • *The wine is starting to ferment.*
➤ **fermentation** *NOUN*

> **SPELLING**
> Take care not to confuse **ferment** with **foment**, which means to stir up trouble.

ferment (say **fer**-ment) *NOUN*
a state of great excitement or agitation • *The crowd was in a ferment.*

fern *NOUN* **ferns**
a plant with feathery leaves and no flowers

ferocious *ADJECTIVE*
fierce or savage • *a ferocious beast*
➤ **ferociously** *ADVERB*

ferocity *NOUN*
violence or fierceness • *He hadn't expected the ferocity of the attack.*

ferret *NOUN* **ferrets**
a small weasel-like animal used for catching rabbits and rats
➤ **ferrety** *ADJECTIVE*

ferret *VERB* **ferrets, ferreting, ferreted**
❶ to hunt with a ferret ❷ to search or rummage about for something • *She ferreted around in her bag for her phone.*

ferric, ferrous *ADJECTIVE*
containing iron

ferry *NOUN* **ferries**
a boat or ship used for carrying people or things across a short stretch of water

ferry *VERB* ferries, ferrying, ferried
to carry people or things across water or for a short distance • *The fisherman agreed to ferry us across to the island.*

fertile *ADJECTIVE*
❶ fertile soil is rich and produces good crops ❷ people or animals that are fertile can produce babies or young animals ❸ a fertile brain or imagination is able to produce ideas

fertility *NOUN*
being fertile • *a goddess of fertility*

fertilize (also **fertilise**) *VERB* fertilizes, fertilizing, fertilized
❶ to add substances to the soil to make it more fertile ❷ to put pollen into a plant or sperm into an egg or female animal so that it develops seed or young
➤ **fertilization** *NOUN*

fertilizer (also **fertiliser**) *NOUN* fertilizers
chemicals or manure added to the soil to make it more fertile

fervent *ADJECTIVE*
showing warm or strong feelings about something • *She is one of his most fervent admirers.*
➤ **fervently** *ADVERB*
➤ **fervour** *NOUN*

fester *VERB* festers, festering, festered
❶ a wound festers if it becomes septic and fills with pus ❷ to cause resentment for a long time • *The hatred between them has been festering for years.*

festival *NOUN* festivals
❶ a time of celebration, especially for religious reasons ❷ an organized series of concerts, films, performances, etc., especially one held every year

festive *ADJECTIVE*
❶ to do with a festival ❷ suitable for a festival; joyful • *We were all in a festive mood.*

festivity *NOUN* festivities
❶ festivities are the parties and other events that are held to celebrate something • *The festivities went on until dawn.* ❷ festivity is being happy and celebrating something • *There was an air of festivity in the village.*

festoon *VERB* festoons, festooning, festooned
to hang decorations, such as chains of flowers or paper, across something • *The streets were festooned with coloured flags.*

fetch *VERB* fetches, fetching, fetched
❶ to go for something and bring it back • *Can you fetch a cloth from the kitchen?* • *There was no time to fetch a doctor.* ❷ to be sold for a particular price • *The painting is expected to fetch $20,000.*

fete (say fayt) *NOUN* fetes
an outdoor event with stalls, games and things for sale, often held to raise money • *a school fete*

fete *VERB* fetes, feting, feted
to honour a person with celebrations

> **SPELLING**
> A **fete** is an outdoor entertainment with stalls. **Fate** is a power that is thought to make things happen.

fetlock *NOUN* fetlocks
the part of a horse's leg above and behind the hoof

fetter *NOUN* fetters
a chain or shackle put round a prisoner's ankle

fetter *VERB* fetters, fettering, fettered
to put fetters on a prisoner

fettle *NOUN*
➤ **in fine fettle** in good health

feud (say fewd) *NOUN* feuds
a long-lasting quarrel, especially between two families

feud *VERB* feuds, feuding, feuded
to keep up a quarrel for a long time • *feuding families*

feudal (say **few**-dal) *ADJECTIVE*
to do with the system used in the Middle Ages in which people could farm land in exchange for work done for the owner
➤ **feudalism** *NOUN*

fever *NOUN* fevers
❶ an abnormally high body temperature, usually with an illness ❷ excitement or agitation
➤ **fevered** *ADJECTIVE*

feverish *ADJECTIVE*
❶ having a fever or high temperature ❷ showing great excitement or agitation • *months of feverish activity*
➤ **feverishly** *ADVERB*

a b c d e f g h i j k l m n o p q r s t u v w x y z

few *DETERMINER*
not many

> **USAGE**
>
> Take care not to confuse **fewer** and **less**. You should use **fewer** when you mean 'not so many', and **less** when you mean 'not so much':• *Venus has fewer craters than the Earth and also less water.*

few *PRONOUN*
a small number of people or things
➤ **quite a few** or **a good few** a fairly large number

fez *NOUN* fezzes
a high flat-topped red hat with a tassel, worn by men in some Muslim countries
WORD ORIGIN named after *Fez*, a town in Morocco, where fezzes were made

fiancé (say fee-**ahn**-say) *NOUN* fiancés
a woman's fiancé is the man who she is engaged to be married to

fiancée (say fee-**ahn**-say) *NOUN* fiancées
a man's fiancée is the woman who he is engaged to be married to

fiasco (say fee-**as**-koh) *NOUN* fiascos
a complete and embarrassing failure

fib *NOUN* fibs
a lie about something unimportant

fib *VERB* fibs, fibbing, fibbed
to tell a lie about something unimportant
➤ **fibber** *NOUN*

fibre *NOUN* fibres
❶ a very thin thread ❷ a substance made of thin threads ❸ parts of certain foods that your body cannot digest but that move the rest of the food quickly through your body
• *Wholemeal bread is high in fibre.*

fibreglass *NOUN*
❶ fabric made from glass fibres ❷ plastic containing glass fibres

fibrous *ADJECTIVE*
made up of lots of fibres • *fibrous roots*

fickle *ADJECTIVE*
constantly changing your mind; not staying loyal to one person or group
➤ **fickleness** *NOUN*

fiction *NOUN* fictions
❶ writings about events that have not really happened; stories and novels ❷ something made up or untrue

fictional *ADJECTIVE*
existing only in a story, not in real life • *a fictional character*

fictitious *ADJECTIVE*
made up by someone and not true or real
• *This friend she kept talking about turned out to be completely fictitious.*

fiddle *NOUN* fiddles
❶ (*informal*) a violin ❷ (*informal*) a swindle

fiddle *VERB* fiddles, fiddling, fiddled
❶ (*informal*) to play the violin ❷ to keep touching or playing with something, using your fingers • *Stop fiddling with your keys.* ❸ (*informal*) to alter accounts or records dishonestly
➤ **fiddler** *NOUN*

fiddly *ADJECTIVE*
(*British*) small and awkward to use or do • *The buttons on my coat are quite fiddly.*

fidelity *NOUN*
❶ faithfulness or loyalty ❷ accuracy; the exactness with which sound is reproduced

fidget *VERB* fidgets, fidgeting, fidgeted
to make small restless movements because you are bored or nervous
➤ **fidgety** *ADJECTIVE*

fidget *NOUN* fidgets
a person who fidgets

field *NOUN* fields
❶ a piece of land with grass or crops growing on it ❷ an area of interest or study • *recent advances in the field of genetics* ❸ those who are taking part in a race or outdoor game ❹ (*in computing*) one area of a database, where one particular type of information is stored

field *VERB* fields, fielding, fielded
❶ to stop or catch the ball in cricket or other ball games ❷ to be on the side not batting in cricket ❸ to put a team into a match • *They fielded their best players.*
➤ **fielder** *NOUN*

> **SPELLING**
>
> The 'ee' sound in **field** is spelt ie.

field events *PLURAL NOUN*
athletic sports other than track races, such as jumping and throwing events

Field Marshal *NOUN* Field Marshals
an army officer of the highest rank

fieldwork *NOUN*
practical work or research done in various places outside, not in a school, college or

laboratory • *We went to the coast to do some geography fieldwork.*

fiend (say feend) *NOUN* fiends
❶ an evil spirit or devil **❷** a very wicked or cruel person **❸** a person who is enthusiastic about doing or having something • *She is a fresh-air fiend.*

fiendish *ADJECTIVE*
❶ very wicked or cruel **❷** extremely difficult or complicated • *a fiendish puzzle*
➤ **fiendishly** *ADVERB*

fierce *ADJECTIVE*
❶ angry and violent and likely to attack you • *a fierce dog* **❷** strong or intense • *fierce heat*
➤ **fierceness** *NOUN*

fiercely *ADVERB*
❶ in a fierce way • *The man glared fiercely at us.* **❷** strongly or intensely • *The fire was now burning fiercely.*

fiery *ADJECTIVE*
❶ full of flames or heat **❷** easily made angry • *His sister had a fiery temper.* **❸** full of emotion and passion

fife *NOUN* fifes
a small shrill flute

fifteen *NOUN & ADJECTIVE* fifteens
the number 15
➤ **fifteenth** *ADJECTIVE & NOUN*

fifth *ADJECTIVE & NOUN* fifths
next after the fourth
➤ **fifthly** *ADVERB*

fifty *NOUN & ADJECTIVE* fifties
the number 50
➤ **fiftieth** *ADJECTIVE & NOUN*

fifty-fifty *ADJECTIVE & ADVERB*
❶ shared equally between two people or groups • *We'll split the money fifty-fifty.*
❷ evenly balanced • *a fifty-fifty chance*

fig *NOUN* figs
a soft fruit full of small seeds

fight *NOUN* fights
❶ a struggle against someone using hands or weapons **❷** an attempt to achieve or overcome something • *the fight against crime*

fight *VERB* fights, fighting, fought
❶ to have a fight **❷** to try to achieve or overcome something • *He has spent the last ten years fighting for justice.* • *They fought the fire all night.*

SPELLING
The past tense of **fight** is **fought**.

fighter *NOUN* fighters
❶ someone who fights **❷** a fast military plane that attacks other aircraft

figment *NOUN* figments
➤ **a figment of your imagination** something that you only imagine and is not real

figurative *ADJECTIVE*
figurative language uses words or phrases for special effect and not in their literal meanings
➤ **figuratively** *ADVERB*

figure *NOUN* figures
❶ the symbol of a number **❷** an amount or value **❸** a diagram or illustration **❹** a shape • *a five-sided figure* **❺** the shape of a person's, especially a woman's, body **❻** a person • *a leading figure in the music industry* **❼** a representation of a person or animal in painting, sculpture, etc.

figure *VERB* figures, figuring, figured
❶ to appear or take part in something • *She figures in some of the stories about King Arthur.* **❷** (*informal, chiefly North American*) to think that something is probably true • *I figured that the best thing to do was to wait.*
➤ **figure something out** to work something out • *Can you figure out the answer?*

figurehead *NOUN* figureheads
❶ a carved figure decorating the prow of a sailing ship **❷** a person who is head of a country or organization but has no real power

figure of speech *NOUN* figures of speech
a word or phrase used for special effect and not intended literally, e.g. 'flood' in *a flood of emails*

filament *NOUN* filaments
a thread or thin wire, especially one in a light bulb

filch *VERB* filches, filching, filched
to steal something slyly

file *NOUN* files
❶ a folder or box for keeping papers in order **❷** a collection of data stored under one name in a computer **❸** a line of people one behind the other **❹** a metal tool with a rough surface that is rubbed on things to shape them or make them smooth

file *VERB* files, filing, filed
❶ to put something into a file **❷** to walk in a line one behind the other • *They filed out of the classroom.* **❸** to shape or smooth

something with a file • *She sat there, filing her nails.*

filial (say **fil**-ee-al) *ADJECTIVE*
(*formal*) to do with a son or daughter

filigree *NOUN*
delicate lace-like decoration made from twisted metal wire

filings *PLURAL NOUN*
tiny pieces of metal rubbed off by a metal file • *iron filings*

fill *VERB* fills, filling, filled
❶ to make something full or to become full • *I'll just fill the kettle.* • *The room was filling quickly.* ❷ to block up a hole or cavity ❸ to appoint a person to a vacant post
➤ **fill someone in** to give someone the information they need
➤ **fill something in** to put answers or other information in a form or document

fill *NOUN*
enough to make you full • *We ate our fill.*

filler *NOUN* fillers
a substance used to fill holes or cracks in wood or plaster

fillet *NOUN* fillets
a piece of fish or meat without bones

fillet *VERB* fillets, filleting, filleted
remove the bones from fish or meat

filling *NOUN* fillings
❶ something used to fill a hole or gap, e.g. in a tooth ❷ something put in pastry to make a pie or between layers of bread to make a sandwich

filling station *NOUN* filling stations
a place where petrol is sold from pumps

filly *NOUN* fillies
a young female horse

film *NOUN* films
❶ a story or event recorded by a camera as a series of moving pictures and shown in cinemas, on television, etc. ❷ a rolled strip or sheet of thin plastic coated with material that is sensitive to light, used, especially in the past, for taking photographs or cinema images ❸ a very thin layer of something • *a film of grease*

film *VERB* films, filming, filmed
to record moving pictures using a camera; to make a film of a story • *She was put in charge of filming the school play.*

filmy *ADJECTIVE* filmier, filmiest
thin and almost transparent

filter *NOUN* filters
a device for holding back dirt or other unwanted material from a liquid or gas that passes through it

filter *VERB* filters, filtering, filtered
❶ to pass something through a filter ❷ to move gradually • *They filtered into the hall.* • *News began to filter out.*

filth *NOUN*
disgusting dirt

filthy *ADJECTIVE* filthier, filthiest
❶ extremely dirty ❷ obscene or offensive

fin *NOUN* fins
❶ a thin flat part sticking out from a fish's body, that helps it to swim ❷ a flat part that sticks out from an aircraft or rocket and helps it to balance

final *ADJECTIVE*
❶ coming at the end; last ❷ that cannot be argued with or changed • *The judge's decision is final.* • *You must go and that's final!*

final *NOUN* finals
the last in a series of contests, that decides the overall winner

finale (say fin-**ah**-lee) *NOUN* finales
the final section of a piece of music or entertainment

finalist *NOUN* finalists
a person or team taking part in a final

finality *NOUN*
the quality of being final and impossible to change • *There was a note of finality in his voice.*

finalize (also **finalise**) *VERB* finalizes, finalizing, finalized
to put something into its final form

finally *ADVERB*
❶ after a long time; at last • *We finally got there around midnight.* ❷ as the last thing • *Finally, I would like to thank my parents.*

SPELLING
Finally = final + ly. Don't forget to double the l.

finance *NOUN*
❶ the use or management of money ❷ the money used to pay for something
➤ **finances** *PLURAL NOUN*
someone's finances are the money and other funds they have

finance *VERB* finances, financing, financed
to provide the money for something
➤ **financier** *NOUN*

financial *ADJECTIVE*
to do with finance
➤ **financially** *ADVERB*

finch *NOUN* finches
a small bird with a short stubby bill

find *VERB* finds, finding, found
❶ to get or see something by looking for
it or by chance ❷ to learn something by
experience • *He found that digging was hard
work.* ❸ something is found in a particular
place when it lives, grows or exists there
• *This species is found only in Australia.* ❹ to
decide and give a verdict • *The jury found him
guilty.*
➤ **find something out** to get or discover
some information

find *NOUN* finds
something interesting or valuable that has
been found

findings *PLURAL NOUN*
the conclusions reached from an investigation

fine *ADJECTIVE*
❶ of high quality; excellent ❷ dry and clear;
sunny • *fine weather* ❸ very thin or delicate
• *The curtains were made of fine material.*
❹ consisting of small particles ❺ in good
health; well • *I'm fine.*
➤ **fineness** *NOUN*

fine *ADVERB*
❶ finely • *a bunch of parsley, chopped fine*
❷ (*informal*) very well • *That will suit me fine.*

fine *NOUN* fines
money which has to be paid as a punishment

fine *VERB* fines, fining, fined
to make someone pay a fine

fine arts *PLURAL NOUN*
painting, sculpture and music

finely *ADVERB*
❶ into very small grains or pieces • *Slice the
tomato finely.* ❷ carefully and delicately • *a
finely embroidered shirt*

finery *NOUN*
fine clothes or decorations

finesse (say fin-**ess**) *NOUN*
skill and elegance in doing something

finger *NOUN* fingers
❶ one of the long thin parts sticking out
from the hand ❷ something shaped like a
finger • *chocolate fingers*

finger *VERB* fingers, fingering, fingered
to touch or feel something with your fingers
• *He fingered his watch chain nervously.*

fingernail *NOUN* fingernails
the hard covering at the end of a finger

fingerprint *NOUN* fingerprints
a mark made by the tiny ridges on your
fingertip, used as a way of identifying
someone

fingertip *NOUN* fingertips
the tip of a finger
➤ **have something at your fingertips** to be
very familiar with a subject and ready to talk
about it

finicky *ADJECTIVE*
fussy about details; hard to please

finish *VERB* finishes, finishing, finished
❶ to complete something or reach the end of
it • *Have you finished your essay yet?* ❷ to
come to an end • *What time does the film
finish?*

finish *NOUN* finishes
❶ the last stage of something; the end ❷ the
surface or coating on woodwork etc.

finite (say **fy**-nyt) *ADJECTIVE*
limited; not infinite • *We have only a finite
supply of coal.*

finite verb *NOUN* finite verbs
a verb that agrees with its subject in person
and number; 'was', 'went' and 'says' are finite
verbs; 'going' and 'to say' are not

fiord (say fee-**ord**) *NOUN* fiords
a different spelling of **fjord**

fir *NOUN* firs
an evergreen tree with needle-like leaves,
that produces cones

fire *NOUN* fires
❶ the flames, heat and light produced when
something burns ❷ coal and wood etc.
burning in a grate or furnace to give heat ❸ a
device using electricity or gas to heat a room
❹ the shooting of guns • *Hold your fire!*
➤ **on fire** burning
➤ **set fire to something** to set something
alight and start it burning

fire *VERB* fires, firing, fired
❶ to set fire to something ❷ to bake pottery
or bricks in a kiln ❸ to shoot a gun; to send
out a bullet or missile ❹ to tell someone that
you will no longer employ them ❺ to produce
a strong feeling in someone • *The talk had
fired her with enthusiasm.*

a b c d e f g h i j k l m n o p q r s t u v w x y z

firearm *NOUN* firearms
a gun that you can carry; a rifle, pistol or revolver

firebrand *NOUN* firebrands
a person who stirs up trouble

fire brigade *NOUN* fire brigades
(*British*) a team of people organized to fight fires

fire drill *NOUN* fire drills
a rehearsal of the procedure that needs to be followed in case of a fire

fire engine *NOUN* fire engines
a large vehicle that carries firefighters and equipment to put out large fires

fire escape *NOUN* fire escapes
a special staircase by which people may escape from a burning building

fire extinguisher *NOUN* fire extinguishers
a metal cylinder from which water or foam can be sprayed to put out a fire

firefighter *NOUN* firefighters
a member of a fire brigade

firefly *NOUN* fireflies
a kind of beetle that gives off a glowing light

fireman *NOUN* firemen
a man who is a member of a fire brigade

fireplace *NOUN* fireplaces
an opening in the wall of a room for holding a fire

fireproof *ADJECTIVE*
able to stand fire or great heat without burning • *a fireproof door*

fireside *NOUN* firesides
the part of the room near a fireplace

firewood *NOUN*
wood for use as fuel

firework *NOUN* fireworks
a device containing chemicals that burn or explode attractively and noisily

firing squad *NOUN* firing squads
a group of soldiers given the duty of shooting a condemned person

firm *NOUN* firms
a business organization

firm *ADJECTIVE*
❶ not giving way when pressed; hard or solid ❷ steady; not shaking or moving ❸ definite and not likely to change • *a firm belief*
➤ **firmness** *NOUN*

firm *ADVERB*
firmly • *They are standing firm on their decision.*

firm *VERB* firms, firming, firmed
to make something firm or definite • *We'll firm up the date later.*

firmament *NOUN* (*poetical use*)
the sky with its clouds and stars

firmly *ADVERB*
❶ in a strong or definite way • *'No, you can't come,' he said firmly.* ❷ in a fixed or steady way • *She kept her eyes firmly on the road ahead.*

first *ADJECTIVE*
coming before all others in time or order or importance

first *ADVERB*
before everything else • *We should have read the instructions first.*

first *NOUN* firsts
a person or thing that is first
➤ **at first** at the beginning; to start with

first aid *NOUN*
treatment given to an injured person before a doctor comes

first-class *ADJECTIVE*
❶ using the best class of a service • *first-class post* ❷ excellent

first-hand *ADJECTIVE & ADVERB*
obtained directly, rather than from other people or from books • *first-hand experience* • *She had experienced poverty first-hand.*

firstly *ADVERB*
as the first thing • *Firstly, let me introduce myself.*

firth *NOUN* firths
an estuary or inlet of the sea on the coast of Scotland

fish *NOUN* fish or fishes
an animal with gills and fins that always lives and breathes in water

fish *VERB* fishes, fishing, fished
❶ to try to catch fish ❷ to search for something; to try to get something • *He is only fishing for compliments.*
➤ **fish something out** to pull something out of a place after searching for it

fisherman *NOUN* fishermen
a person who catches fish either as a job or as a sport

fishery *NOUN* fisheries
❶ the part of the sea where fishing is carried on ❷ the business of fishing

fishmonger *NOUN* fishmongers
a shopkeeper who sells fish

fishy *ADJECTIVE* fishier, fishiest
❶ smelling or tasting of fish ❷ (*informal*) causing doubt or suspicion • *Parts of his story sound fishy to me.*

fission *NOUN*
❶ splitting something ❷ splitting the nucleus of an atom so as to release energy

fissure (say **fish**-er) *NOUN* fissures
a narrow opening made where something splits

fist *NOUN* fists
a tightly closed hand with the fingers bent into the palm

fit *ADJECTIVE* fitter, fittest
❶ suitable or good enough • *a meal fit for a king* ❷ healthy, in good physical condition • *Dancing is a good way to keep fit.* ❸ ready or likely • *They worked till they were fit to collapse.*
➤ **see** or **think fit** to decide or choose to do something

fit *VERB* fits, fitting, fitted
❶ to be the right size and shape for something ❷ to be suitable for something • *Her speech fitted the occasion perfectly.* ❸ to put something into place • *We need to fit a new lock on the door.* ❹ to alter something to make it the right size and shape ❺ to make someone suitable for something • *His training fits him for the job.*
➤ **fitter** *NOUN*

fit *NOUN* fits
❶ the way something fits • *These trousers are a good fit.* ❷ a sudden illness, especially one that makes you move violently or become unconscious ❸ a sudden outburst • *a fit of rage*

fitful *ADJECTIVE*
happening in short periods, not steadily • *a fitful sleep*
➤ **fitfully** *ADVERB*

fitness *NOUN*
❶ being healthy and in good physical condition • *Fitness is important in most sports.* ❷ being suitable for something • *No one doubts her fitness for the job.*

fitting *ADJECTIVE*
proper or appropriate • *This statue is a fitting memorial to an extraordinary woman.*

fitting *NOUN* fittings
having a piece of clothing fitted • *I needed several fittings.*

fittings *PLURAL NOUN*
pieces of furniture or equipment in a room or building

five *NOUN & ADJECTIVE* fives
the number 5

fiver *NOUN* fivers (*informal*)
a five-pound note; £5

fix *VERB* fixes, fixing, fixed
❶ to fasten or place something firmly ❷ to make something permanent and unable to change ❸ to decide or arrange something • *We fixed a date for the party.* ❹ to repair something that is broken • *I need to get my bike fixed.*
➤ **fix something up** to arrange or organize something

fix *NOUN* fixes
❶ (*informal*) an awkward situation • *I'm in a fix.* ❷ finding the position of something, by using a compass, radar, etc.

fixation *NOUN* fixations
a strong interest or a concentration on one idea; an obsession
➤ **fixated** *ADJECTIVE*

fixative *NOUN* fixatives
a substance used to keep something in position or make it permanent

fixed *ADJECTIVE*
not changing • *fixed prices* • *a fixed expression*

fixedly *ADVERB*
with a fixed expression • *She looked at me fixedly but said nothing.*

fixture *NOUN* fixtures
❶ something fixed in its place, such as a cupboard or washbasin ❷ a sports event planned for a particular day

fizz *VERB* fizzes, fizzing, fizzed
to make a hissing or spluttering sound; to produce a lot of small bubbles

fizzle *VERB* fizzles, fizzling, fizzled
to make a slight fizzing sound
➤ **fizzle out** to come to a disappointing end • *The game fizzled out in the second half.*

a b c d e **f** g h i j k l m n o p q r s t u v w x y z

fizzy *ADJECTIVE*
a fizzy drink has a lot of small bubbles

fjord (say fee-**ord**) *NOUN* fjords
an inlet of the sea between high cliffs, as in Norway

flabbergasted *ADJECTIVE*
greatly astonished

flabby *ADJECTIVE*
fat and soft, not firm
➤ **flabbiness** *NOUN*

flag *NOUN* flags
❶ a piece of cloth with a coloured pattern or shape on it, used as the symbol of a country or organization or as a signal ❷ a small piece of paper or plastic that looks like a flag ❸ a flagstone

flag *VERB* flags, flagging, flagged
to become weak or droop because of tiredness
➤ **flag someone down** to signal a driver to stop by waving

flagon *NOUN* flagons
a large bottle or container for drink, especially wine

flagpole, flagstaff *NOUN* flagpoles, flagstaffs
a pole used for flying a flag

flagrant (say **flay**-grant) *ADJECTIVE*
very bad and noticeable • *flagrant disobedience*
➤ **flagrantly** *ADVERB*
➤ **flagrancy** *NOUN*
WORD ORIGIN from Latin *flagrans* = blazing

flagship *NOUN* flagships
❶ a main ship in a navy's fleet, which has the fleet's admiral on board ❷ a company's best or most important product or store

flagstone *NOUN* flagstones
a flat slab of stone used for paving

flail *NOUN* flails
an old-fashioned tool for threshing grain

flail *VERB* flails, flailing, flailed
to flail your arms or legs is to wave them about wildly

flair *NOUN*
a natural ability or talent • *Ian has a flair for languages.*

SPELLING
Take care not to confuse **flair** with **flare**, which means a bright flame.

flak *NOUN*
❶ shells fired by anti-aircraft guns ❷ strong criticism **WORD ORIGIN** short for German *Fliegerabwehrkanone* = aircraft defence cannon

flake *NOUN* flakes
❶ a very light thin piece of something ❷ a small flat piece of falling snow
➤ **flaky** *ADJECTIVE*

flake *VERB* flakes, flaking, flaked
to come off in flakes • *The paint is beginning to flake.*

flamboyant *ADJECTIVE*
very showy in appearance or manner • *a flamboyant costume* **WORD ORIGIN** from French, meaning 'flaming, blazing'

flame *NOUN* flames
a tongue-shaped portion of fire or burning gas

flame *VERB* flames, flaming, flamed
❶ to produce flames ❷ to become bright red • *Her cheeks flamed with rage.*

flamenco (say fla-**menk**-oh) *NOUN* flamencos
a lively Spanish style of guitar playing and dance **WORD ORIGIN** from Spanish, = Flemish, 'like a gypsy'

flaming *ADJECTIVE*
❶ burning brightly • *flaming torches*
❷ bright red or orange • *a flaming sunset*

flamingo *NOUN* flamingoes
a wading bird with long legs, a long neck and pinkish feathers

flammable *ADJECTIVE*
able to be set on fire

USAGE
See the note at **inflammable**.

flan *NOUN* flans
a pastry or sponge shell with no cover over the filling

flank *NOUN* flanks
the side of something, especially an animal's body or an army

flank *VERB* flanks, flanking, flanked
to be positioned at the side of something • *He stepped off the boat, flanked by two guards.*

flannel *NOUN* flannels
❶ a soft cloth for washing your face ❷ a soft woollen material

flap *VERB* flaps, flapping, flapped
❶ to move loosely back and forth in the wind or air • *The sails were flapping in the breeze.*

❷ to make something move back and forth in the air • *The parrot flapped her wings and flew to her perch.* ❸ (*informal*) to panic or fuss about something

flap NOUN **flaps**
  ❶ a part that is fixed at one edge onto something else, often to cover an opening ❷ the action or sound of flapping ❸ (*informal*) a panic or fuss • *Don't get in a flap.*

flapjack NOUN
a cake made from oats and golden syrup

flare VERB **flares, flaring, flared**
  ❶ to blaze with a sudden bright flame ❷ to become angry suddenly ❸ to become gradually wider • *The bull flared its nostrils.*
➤ **flare up** to start suddenly or to suddenly get worse • *Her asthma flared up over the weekend.*

flare NOUN **flares**
  ❶ a sudden bright flame or light, especially one fired into the sky as a signal ❷ a gradual widening, especially in skirts or trousers

> **SPELLING**
> Take care not to confuse **flare** with **flair**, which means a talent for something.

flash NOUN **flashes**
  ❶ a sudden bright flame or light ❷ a device for making a sudden bright light for taking photographs ❸ a sudden display of anger, wit, etc. ❹ a short item of news
➤ **in a flash** immediately or very quickly • *The idea came to him in a flash.*

flash VERB **flashes, flashing, flashed**
  ❶ to make a flash of light ❷ to appear or move suddenly and quickly • *The train flashed past us.*

flashback NOUN **flashbacks**
going back in a film or story to something that happened earlier • *The hero's childhood was shown in flashbacks.*

flashy ADJECTIVE
showy and expensive • *a flashy car*

flask NOUN **flasks**
  ❶ a bottle with a narrow neck ❷ a vacuum flask

flat ADJECTIVE **flatter, flattest**
  ❶ with no curves or bumps; smooth and level ❷ spread out; lying at full length • *Lie flat on the ground.* ❸ a flat tyre has no air inside ❹ flat feet do not have the normal arch underneath ❺ firm and absolute • *a flat refusal* ❻ dull; showing no interest or

emotion • *She spoke in a flat voice.* ❼ a drink that is flat is no longer fizzy ❽ (*British*) a flat battery is unable to produce any more electric current ❾ (*in music*) one semitone lower than the natural note • *E flat*
➤ **flatness** NOUN

flat ADVERB
  ❶ so as to be flat • *Press it flat.* ❷ (*informal*) exactly and no more • *He won the race in ten seconds flat.* ❸ (*in music*) below the correct pitch
➤ **flat out** as fast as possible

flat NOUN **flats**
  ❶ (*chiefly British*) a set of rooms for living in, usually on one floor of a building ❷ (*in music*) a note one semitone lower than the natural note; the sign (♭) that indicates this ❸ a punctured tyre

flatly ADVERB
  ❶ in a definite way, leaving no room for doubt • *They flatly refused to go.* ❷ in a way that shows no interest or emotion

flatten VERB **flattens, flattening, flattened**
  ❶ to make something flat ❷ to become flat

flatter VERB **flatters, flattering, flattered**
  ❶ to praise someone more than they deserve ❷ to make a person or thing seem better or more attractive than they really are • *The portrait flatters him, don't you think?*
➤ **flatterer** NOUN

flattery NOUN
flattering someone • *I don't think flattery will work on her.*

flaunt VERB **flaunts, flaunting, flaunted**
to display something proudly in a way that annoys people; to show something off • *He liked to flaunt his expensive clothes and cars.*

flavour NOUN **flavours**
the taste of something

flavour VERB **flavours, flavouring, flavoured**
to give something a flavour; to season food
➤ **flavouring** NOUN

flaw NOUN **flaws**
something that makes a person or thing imperfect
➤ **flawed** ADJECTIVE

flawless ADJECTIVE
without a flaw; perfect
➤ **flawlessly** ADVERB

flax NOUN
a plant that produces fibres from which linen is made and seeds from which linseed oil is obtained

a b c d e f g h i j k l m n o p q r s t u v w x y z

flaxen *ADJECTIVE*
pale yellow like flax fibres • *flaxen hair*

flay *VERB* flays, flaying, flayed
❶ to strip the skin from an animal ❷ to whip or beat someone

flea *NOUN* fleas
a small jumping insect that sucks blood

flea market *NOUN* flea markets
a street market that sells cheap or second-hand goods

fleck *NOUN* flecks
❶ a very small patch of colour • *His hair was dark, with flecks of grey.* ❷ a very small piece of something • *flecks of dirt*

flecked *ADJECTIVE*
with small spots of colour • *green eyes flecked with brown*

fledged *ADJECTIVE*
young birds are fledged when they have grown feathers and are able to fly

fledgeling *NOUN* fledgelings
a young bird that is just fledged

flee *VERB* flees, fleeing, fled
to run or hurry away from something • *As the fire approached, people fled their homes.*

fleece *NOUN* fleeces
❶ the woolly hair of a sheep or similar animal ❷ a warm piece of clothing made from a soft fabric

fleece *VERB* fleeces, fleecing, fleeced
❶ to shear the fleece from a sheep ❷ to swindle a person out of some money

fleecy *ADJECTIVE*
made of soft material like fleece; soft and light • *fleecy clouds*

fleet *NOUN* fleets
a number of ships, aircraft or vehicles owned by one country or company

fleet *ADJECTIVE*
able to run or move swiftly

fleeting *ADJECTIVE*
passing quickly; brief • *I caught a fleeting glimpse of him.*

Flemish *ADJECTIVE*
to do with Flanders in Belgium or its people or language
➤ **Flemish** *NOUN*

flesh *NOUN*
❶ the soft substance of the bodies of people and animals, consisting of muscle and fat

❷ the body as opposed to the mind or soul
❸ the pulpy part of fruits and vegetables
➤ **fleshy** *ADJECTIVE*

flex *VERB* flexes, flexing, flexed
to bend or stretch a limb or muscle

flex *NOUN* flexes (*British*) flexible insulated wire for carrying electric current

flexible *ADJECTIVE*
❶ easy to bend or stretch without breaking ❷ able to be changed or adapted • *Our plans are flexible.*
➤ **flexibility** *NOUN*

flick *NOUN* flicks
a quick light hit or movement

flick *VERB* flicks, flicking, flicked
❶ to hit or move something with a flick ❷ to flick through a book or magazine etc. is to turn its pages quickly, without reading carefully

flicker *VERB* flickers, flickering, flickered
❶ to burn or shine unsteadily ❷ to move quickly to and fro

flicker *NOUN* flickers
a flickering light or movement

flick knife *NOUN* flick knives
(*British*) a knife with a blade that springs out when a button is pressed

flier *NOUN* fliers
a different spelling of **flyer**

flight *NOUN* flights
❶ flying • *The picture shows an owl in flight.* ❷ a journey in an aircraft ❸ a series of stairs ❹ a group of flying birds or aircraft ❺ the feathers or fins on a dart or arrow ❻ fleeing; an escape

flight recorder *NOUN* flight recorders
an electronic device in an aircraft that records technical information about its flight. It may be used after an accident to help find the cause.

flighty *ADJECTIVE* flightier, flightiest
silly and frivolous

flimsy *ADJECTIVE* flimsier, flimsiest
❶ made of something thin or weak; fragile • *a flimsy bookcase* ❷ not convincing • *a flimsy excuse*

flinch *VERB* flinches, flinching, flinched
to make a sudden movement backwards because you are afraid or in pain

fling VERB flings, flinging, flung
to throw something violently or carelessly
• *He flung his shoes under the bed.*

fling NOUN flings
❶ a short time of enjoyment • *a final fling
before the exams* ❷ a brief romantic affair
❸ a vigorous dance • *the Highland fling*

flint NOUN flints
❶ a very hard kind of stone ❷ a piece of flint
or hard metal used to produce sparks
➤ **flinty** ADJECTIVE

flip VERB flips, flipping, flipped
❶ to turn something over with a quick
movement • *She flipped open her sketchbook.*
❷ (*informal*) to become crazy or very angry

flip NOUN flips
a flipping movement

flippant ADJECTIVE
not being serious when you should be • *a
flippant comment*
➤ **flippantly** ADVERB
➤ **flippancy** NOUN

flipper NOUN flippers
❶ a limb that water animals use for
swimming ❷ a kind of flat rubber shoe,
shaped like a duck's foot, that you wear on
your feet to help you to swim

flirt VERB flirts, flirting, flirted
❶ to behave as though you are attracted to
someone, in a playful rather than a serious
way ❷ to take an interest in an idea without
being too serious about it
➤ **flirt with danger** or **death** to risk danger
➤ **flirtation** NOUN

flirt NOUN flirts
a person who flirts
➤ **flirtatious** ADJECTIVE
➤ **flirtatiously** ADVERB

flit VERB flits, flitting, flitted
to fly or move lightly and quickly • *A moth
flitted across the room.*

flitter VERB flitters, flittering, flittered
to flit about

float VERB floats, floating, floated
❶ to stay or move on the surface of a liquid
or in air ❷ to make something move on the
surface of a liquid ❸ to launch a business
by getting financial support from the sale of
shares

float NOUN floats
❶ a device designed to float ❷ a vehicle with
a platform used for delivering milk or for
carrying a display in a parade or carnival ❸ a

small amount of money kept for paying small
bills or giving change

floating voter NOUN floating voters
(*British*) a person who has not yet decided
who to vote for in an election

flock NOUN flocks
❶ a number of birds flying or resting
together ❷ a number of sheep or goats kept
together ❸ a tuft of wool or cotton

flock VERB flocks, flocking, flocked
to gather or move in a crowd or in large
numbers • *People flocked to hear him sing.*

floe NOUN floes
a sheet of floating ice

flog VERB flogs, flogging, flogged
❶ to beat a person or animal hard with a
whip or stick as a punishment ❷ (*British*)
(*informal*) to sell something
➤ **flogging** NOUN

flood NOUN floods
❶ a large amount of water spreading over a
place that is usually dry ❷ a large number of
things • *a flood of requests* ❸ the movement
of the tide when it is coming in towards the
land

flood VERB floods, flooding, flooded
❶ to cover an area with a flood ❷ a river
floods when its waters flow over the banks
❸ to come in large quantities • *Letters
flooded in.*

floodlight NOUN floodlights
a lamp that makes a broad bright beam to
light up a stadium or a public building
➤ **floodlit** ADJECTIVE

floor NOUN floors
❶ the part of a room that people walk on
❷ a storey of a building; all the rooms at the
same level

> **USAGE**
>
> In Britain, the *ground floor* of a building is
> the one at street level, and the one above
> it is the *first floor*. In the USA, the *first
> floor* is the one at street level, and the one
> above it is the *second floor*.

floor VERB floors, flooring, floored
❶ to knock a person down ❷ to baffle
someone

floorboard NOUN floorboards
one of the boards forming the floor of a room

flop VERB flops, flopping, flopped
❶ to fall or sit down clumsily ❷ to hang or

sway heavily and loosely • *Her hair flopped over her eyes.* ❸ (*informal*) to be a failure

flop *NOUN* flops
❶ a flopping movement or sound
❷ (*informal*) a failure or disappointment

floppy *ADJECTIVE*
hanging loosely; not firm or rigid • *Our dog has huge floppy ears.*

flora *NOUN*
the plants of a particular area or period. Compare with **fauna**. **WORD ORIGIN** from the name of *Flora*, the ancient Roman goddess of flowers; her name comes from Latin *flores* = flowers

floral *ADJECTIVE*
decorated with a pattern of flowers or made of flowers • *a floral dress*

florid (say **flo**-rid) *ADJECTIVE*
❶ red and flushed • *a florid complexion*
❷ elaborate and ornate • *florid language*

florin *NOUN* florins
a former British coin worth two shillings (10p) **WORD ORIGIN** from Italian *fiore* = flower; the name was originally given to an Italian coin which had a lily on one side

florist *NOUN* florists
a person who sells flowers

floss *NOUN*
❶ silky thread or fibres ❷ a soft medicated thread pulled between the teeth to clean them
➤ **flossy** *ADJECTIVE*

flotation *NOUN* flotations
floating something

flotilla (say flot-**il**-a) *NOUN* flotillas
a fleet of boats or small ships

flotsam *NOUN*
wreckage or cargo found floating after a shipwreck
➤ **flotsam and jetsam** odds and ends

flounce *VERB* flounces, flouncing, flounced
to go in an impatient or annoyed manner • *She flounced out of the room.*

flounce *NOUN* flounces
❶ a flouncing movement ❷ a wide frill on a skirt or dress

flounder *VERB* flounders, floundering, floundered
❶ to move clumsily and with difficulty • *He was floundering around in the water.* ❷ to

make mistakes or become confused when trying to do something

flounder *NOUN* flounder
a small flat edible sea fish

flour *NOUN*
a fine powder of wheat or other grain, used in cooking
➤ **floury** *ADJECTIVE*

flourish *VERB* flourishes, flourishing, flourished
❶ to grow or develop strongly • *These plants flourish in a damp climate.* ❷ to be successful; to prosper • *Over the next few years the town flourished.* ❸ to wave something about dramatically • *She proudly flourished two tickets for the concert.*

flourish *NOUN* flourishes
a showy or dramatic sweeping movement, curve or passage of music • *He took out his pen with a flourish.*

flout *VERB* flouts, flouting, flouted
to disobey a rule or instruction openly and scornfully • *She shaved her head one day, just because she loved to flout convention.*

flow *VERB* flows, flowing, flowed
❶ to move along smoothly or continuously
❷ to gush out • *Water flowed from the tap.*
❸ to hang loosely • *flowing hair* ❹ the tide flows when it comes in towards the land

flow *NOUN* flows
❶ a flowing movement or mass ❷ a steady continuous stream of something • *a flow of ideas* ❸ the movement of the tide when it is coming in towards the land • *the ebb and flow of the tide*

flow chart *NOUN* flow charts
a diagram that shows how the different stages of a process or parts of a system are connected

flower *NOUN* flowers
❶ the part of a plant from which seed and fruit develops ❷ a blossom and its stem used for decoration, usually in groups

flower *VERB* flowers, flowering, flowered
to produce flowers

flowerpot *NOUN* flowerpots
a pot in which a plant may be grown

flowery *ADJECTIVE*
❶ full of flowers ❷ flowery language is elaborate and fully of fancy phrases • *a flowery style of writing*

flu *NOUN*
influenza

fluctuate *VERB* fluctuates, fluctuating, fluctuated
to keep changing, especially by rising and falling • *Prices fluctuated.*
➤ **fluctuation** *NOUN*

flue *NOUN* flues
a pipe or tube that takes smoke and fumes away from a stove or boiler

fluent (say **floo**-ent) *ADJECTIVE*
❶ skilful at speaking clearly and without hesitating ❷ able to speak a foreign language easily and well
➤ **fluently** *ADVERB*
➤ **fluency** *NOUN*

fluff *NOUN*
the small soft pieces that come off wool and cloth

fluff *VERB* fluffs, fluffing, fluffed (*informal*) to make a mistake
➤ **fluff something up** to make a pillow or cushion softer and rounder by patting it

fluffy *ADJECTIVE*
having a mass of soft fur or fibres

fluid *NOUN* fluids
a substance that is able to flow freely as liquids and gases do

fluid *ADJECTIVE*
❶ able to flow freely and smoothly • *He drew his sword in a single fluid movement.* ❷ not fixed and able to be changed • *My plans for Christmas are fluid.*
➤ **fluidity** *NOUN*

fluke *NOUN* flukes
a success that you achieve by unexpected good luck

flummox *VERB* flummoxes, flummoxing, flummoxed (*informal*)
to baffle someone

fluorescent (say floo-er-**ess**-ent) *ADJECTIVE*
❶ creating light from radiation • *a fluorescent lamp* ❷ very bright and shining in the dark • *a fluorescent yellow armband*
➤ **fluorescence** *NOUN*

fluoridation *NOUN*
adding fluoride to drinking water in order to help prevent tooth decay

fluoride *NOUN*
a chemical substance that is thought to prevent tooth decay

flurry *NOUN* flurries
❶ a sudden whirling gust of wind, rain or snow ❷ a short period of activity or excitement

flush *VERB* flushes, flushing, flushed
❶ to become red in the face; to blush ❷ to clean or remove something with a fast flow of water

flush *NOUN* flushes
❶ a slight blush ❷ a fast flow of water ❸ a hand of playing cards of the same suit

flush *ADJECTIVE*
❶ level with the surrounding surface • *The doors are flush with the walls.* ❷ (*informal*) having plenty of money

fluster *NOUN*
➤ **in a fluster** nervous and confused

flustered *ADJECTIVE*
nervous and confused • *She was looking hot and flustered.*

flute *NOUN* flutes
a musical instrument consisting of a long pipe with holes that are stopped by fingers or keys, which you play by blowing across a hole at one end

flutter *VERB* flutters, fluttering, fluttered
❶ to flap wings quickly • *A butterfly fluttered in through the window.* ❷ to move or flap quickly and lightly • *Flags fluttered in the breeze.*

flutter *NOUN* flutters
a fluttering movement
➤ **in a flutter** nervous and excited

flux *NOUN* fluxes
continual change or flow

fly *VERB* flies, flying, flew, flown
❶ to move through the air by means of wings or in an aircraft ❷ to move quickly or suddenly, especially through the air • *A large stone came flying through the window.* • *The door flew open.* ❸ to wave in the air • *Flags were flying.* ❹ to make something fly • *They were flying model aircraft.* ❺ a period of time flies when it passes quickly • *The weekend has just flown by.*

fly *NOUN* flies
❶ a small flying insect with two wings ❷ a real or artificial fly used as bait in fishing ❸ the front opening of a pair of trousers

flyer *NOUN* flyers
❶ a person or vehicle that flies ❷ a small poster advertising an event

a
b
c
d
e
f
g
h
i
j
k
l
m
n
o
p
q
r
s
t
u
v
w
x
y
z

flying saucer *NOUN* flying saucers
a mysterious saucer-shaped object that some people say they have seen in the sky and believe to be an alien spacecraft

flying squad *NOUN* flying squads
(*British*) a team of police officers organized so that they can move rapidly

flyleaf *NOUN* flyleaves
a blank page at the beginning or end of a book

flyover *NOUN* flyovers
a bridge that carries one road over another

flywheel *NOUN* flywheels
a heavy wheel in a machine that helps it to run smoothly and at a steady speed

foal *NOUN* foals
a young horse

foal *VERB* foals, foaling, foaled
to give birth to a foal

foam *NOUN*
❶ a white mass of tiny bubbles on a liquid; froth ❷ a spongy kind of rubber or plastic
➤ **foamy** *ADJECTIVE*

foam *VERB* foams, foaming, foamed
to form a white mass of tiny bubbles; to froth • *Water foamed around the rocks.*

fob *NOUN* fobs
❶ a chain for a pocket watch ❷ a tab on a key ring

fob *VERB* fobs, fobbing, fobbed
➤ **fob someone off** to get rid of someone by an excuse or a trick

focal *ADJECTIVE*
to do with or at a focus

focal point *NOUN* focal points
❶ the point on a lens at which rays seem to meet ❷ something that is a centre of interest or attention

focus *NOUN* focuses or foci
❶ the distance from an eye or lens at which an object appears clearest ❷ the point at which rays seem to meet ❸ something that is a centre of interest or attention
➤ **in focus** appearing clearly
➤ **out of focus** not appearing clearly; blurred

focus *VERB* focuses, focusing, focused
❶ to adjust the focus of your eye or a lens so that objects appear clearly ❷ to concentrate on something • *She focused her attention on the problem.* **WORD ORIGIN** Latin, = hearth (the central point of a household)

fodder *NOUN*
food for horses and farm animals

foe *NOUN* foes (*old use*)
an enemy

foetus (say **fee**-tus) *NOUN* foetuses
a developing embryo, especially an unborn human baby
➤ **foetal** *ADJECTIVE*

fog *NOUN*
thick mist

fogey *NOUN* fogeys
➤ **old fogey** a person with old-fashioned ideas

foggy *ADJECTIVE*
full of fog • *It was a foggy night.*

foghorn *NOUN* foghorns
a loud horn for warning ships in fog

foible (say **foy**-bel) *NOUN* foibles
a slight peculiarity in someone's character or tastes

foil *NOUN* foils
❶ a very thin sheet of metal ❷ a person or thing that makes another look better in contrast ❸ a long narrow sword used in the sport of fencing

foil *VERB* foils, foiling, foiled
to prevent something from being successful • *We foiled his evil plan.*

foist *VERB* foists, foisting, foisted
to force a person to accept something that they do not want • *They foisted the job on me at the last minute.*

fold *VERB* folds, folding, folded
❶ to bend or wrap one part of something over another part • *He folder the letter and put it in the envelope.* ❷ to bend or move in this way • *The table folds up flat.* ❸ you fold your arms when you put one of your arms over the other one and hold them against your chest

fold *NOUN* folds
❶ a line where something is folded ❷ an enclosure for sheep

folder *NOUN* folders
❶ a folding cover for loose papers ❷ a place where a set of files are grouped together in a computer

foliage *NOUN*
the leaves of a tree or plant

folk *PLURAL NOUN*
people

folk dance *NOUN* folk dances
a dance in the traditional style of a country

folklore *NOUN*
old beliefs and legends

folk music *NOUN*
the traditional music of a country

folk song *NOUN* folk songs
a song in the traditional style of a country

follow *VERB* follows, following, followed
❶ to go or come after someone or something
❷ to do a thing after something else ❸ to act
according to someone's instructions, advice
or example • *I followed the instructions
carefully.* ❹ to go along a road or path
• *Follow this road for a mile.* ❺ to take an
interest in the progress of events or a sport or
team ❻ to understand someone or something
• *Did you follow what he said?* ❼ to result
from something ❽ to receive the messages
that a particular person sends on social
networking websites such as Twitter

follower *NOUN* followers
a person who follows or supports someone or
something

following *PREPOSITION*
after, as a result of • *Following the burglary,
we had new locks fitted.*

folly *NOUN* follies
foolishness; a foolish action • *It would be
folly to ignore their warnings.*

foment (say fo-**ment**) *VERB* foments,
fomenting, fomented
to stir up trouble or difficulty deliberately

fond *ADJECTIVE*
❶ loving or liking a person or thing • *She's
fond of reading.* ❷ pleasant and affectionate
• *I have fond memories of my grandmother.*
➤ **fondly** *ADVERB*
➤ **fondness** *NOUN*

fondle *VERB* fondles, fondling, fondled
to touch or stroke someone or something
lovingly

font *NOUN* fonts
❶ a basin (often of carved stone) in a
Christian church, to hold water for baptism
❷ a set of characters used in printing and
computer documents

food *NOUN* foods
any substance that a plant or animal can take
into its body to help it to grow and be healthy

food chain *NOUN* food chains
a series of plants and animals each of which
serves as food for the one above it in the
series

foodstuff *NOUN* foodstuffs
something that can be used as food

food technology *NOUN*
the study of foods, what they are made of
and how they are prepared

fool *NOUN* fools
❶ a stupid person; someone who acts
unwisely ❷ a jester or clown ❸ (*British*)
a creamy pudding with crushed fruit in it
• *gooseberry fool*
➤ **fool's errand** a useless errand
➤ **fool's paradise** happiness that comes only
from being mistaken about something

fool *VERB* fools, fooling, fooled
to trick or deceive someone
➤ **fool about** or **around** to behave in a silly
or stupid way

foolhardy *ADJECTIVE*
bold but foolish; reckless
➤ **foolhardiness** *NOUN*

foolish *ADJECTIVE*
without good sense or judgement; unwise
➤ **foolishly** *ADVERB*
➤ **foolishness** *NOUN*

foolproof *ADJECTIVE*
easy to use or do without anything going
wrong • *My plan is foolproof.*

foot *NOUN* feet
❶ the lower part of your leg below the ankle
❷ any similar part, e.g. one used by certain
animals to move or attach themselves to
things ❸ the lowest part or end of something
• *the foot of the hill* ❹ a measure of length,
12 inches (30.48 centimetres) • *a ten-foot
pole* • *It is ten feet long.* ❺ a unit of rhythm
in a line of poetry, e.g. each of the four
divisions in *Jack / and Jill / went up / the hill*
➤ **on foot** walking • *We came back on foot.*

footage *NOUN*
an amount of film showing something
• *footage of the first moon landing*

foot-and-mouth disease *NOUN*
a serious contagious disease that affects
cattle, sheep and other animals

football *NOUN* footballs
❶ a game played by two teams of eleven
players who try to kick a ball into their
opponents' goal ❷ the round ball used in this
game

a b c d e f g h i j k l m n o p q r s t u v w x y z

A B C D E **F** G H I J K L M N O P Q R S T U V W X Y Z

footballer NOUN footballers
a person who plays football

foothill NOUN foothills
a low hill near the bottom of a mountain or range of mountains

foothold NOUN footholds
❶ a place to put your foot when climbing ❷ a small but firm position from which further progress can be made

footing NOUN
❶ having your feet firmly placed on something • *He lost his footing and slipped.* ❷ the status or nature of a relationship • *We must try to get on a more friendly footing with our neighbours.*

footlights PLURAL NOUN
a row of lights along the front of the floor of a stage

footman NOUN footmen
a male servant who opens doors, serves at table, etc.

footnote NOUN footnotes
a note printed at the bottom of the page

footpath NOUN footpaths
a path for people to walk along, especially one in the countryside

footprint NOUN footprints
a mark made by a foot or shoe

footsore ADJECTIVE
having feet that are painful or sore from walking

footstep NOUN footsteps
❶ a step taken in walking or running ❷ the sound of a step being taken

footstool NOUN footstools
a stool for resting your feet on when you are sitting

footwear NOUN
shoes, boots and other coverings for the feet

for PREPOSITION
This word is used to show
❶ purpose or direction (*This letter is for you; We set out for home.*) ❷ distance or time (*They walked for three miles; We've been waiting for hours.*) ❸ price or exchange (*We bought it for £5; New lamps for old.*) ❹ cause or reason (*She was fined for speeding.*) ❺ defence or support (*He fought for his country; Are you for us or against us?*) ❻ what something refers to or relates to (*She has a good ear for music; What's*

the Russian for 'goodbye'?) ❼ similarity or correspondence (*We took him for a fool.*)
➤ **for ever** for all time; always

for CONJUNCTION
because • *They hesitated, for they were afraid.*

forage VERB forages, foraging, foraged
to go searching for something, especially food or fuel

foray NOUN forays
a sudden attack or raid

forbear VERB forbears, forbearing, forbore, forborne
❶ to avoid or refrain from doing something something • *We forbore to mention it.* ❷ to be patient or tolerant
➤ **forbearance** NOUN

forbid VERB forbids, forbidding, forbade, forbidden
❶ to order someone not to do something ❷ to refuse to allow something • *Smoking is forbidden in this station.*

forbidding ADJECTIVE
looking stern or unfriendly

force NOUN forces
❶ strength or power ❷ (*in science*) an influence, which can be measured, that causes something to move ❸ an organized group of police, soldiers or workers
➤ **in** or **into force** being used; having effect • *The new law comes into force next week.*
➤ **the forces** a country's armed forces

force VERB forces, forcing, forced
❶ to get someone to do something by using force or power ❷ to break something open by force

forceful ADJECTIVE
strong and vigorous
➤ **forcefully** ADVERB

forceps NOUN forceps
pincers or tongs used by dentists or surgeons

forcible ADJECTIVE
done by force; forceful
➤ **forcibly** ADVERB

ford NOUN fords
a shallow place where you can walk across a river

ford VERB fords, fording, forded
to cross a river at a ford

fore ADJECTIVE & ADVERB
at or towards the front

fore *NOUN*
the front part
➤ **to the fore** to or at the front; in a leading position • *This latest incident has brought the issue to the fore.*

forearm *NOUN* forearms
the arm from the elbow to the wrist or fingertips

forearm *VERB* forearms, forearming, forearmed
to be forearmed is to be prepared in advance against possible danger

forebears *PLURAL NOUN*
your forebears are your ancestors

foreboding *NOUN*
a feeling that trouble is coming • *He was filled with a sense of foreboding.*

forecast *NOUN* forecasts
a statement that tells in advance what is likely to happen • *a weather forecast*

forecast *VERB* forecasts, forecasting, forecast
to say in advance what is likely to happen • *The weather report forecasts snow for tomorrow.*
➤ **forecaster** *NOUN*

forecastle (say **foh**-ksul) *NOUN* forecastles
the forward part of certain ships

forecourt *NOUN* forecourts
an open area in front of a large building or petrol station

forefathers *PLURAL NOUN*
your forefathers are your ancestors (both male and female)

forefinger *NOUN* forefingers
the finger next to your thumb

forefoot *NOUN* forefeet
an animal's front foot

forefront *NOUN*
the leading position; the position at the front • *They were at the forefront of the Green movement.*

foregoing *ADJECTIVE*
preceding; previously mentioned • *the foregoing discussion*

> **SPELLING**
> Note the spelling of this word. It has an 'e' in it, whereas **forgo**, meaning 'give up', does not.

foregone conclusion *NOUN* foregone conclusions
a result that is certain to happen

foreground *NOUN*
the part of a scene, picture or view that is nearest to you

forehand *NOUN* forehands
a stroke made in tennis etc. with the palm of the hand turned forwards

forehead (say **forr**id or **for**-hed) *NOUN* foreheads
the part of your face above your eyes

foreign *ADJECTIVE*
❶ belonging to or in another country
❷ not belonging naturally to a place or to someone's nature • *Lying is foreign to her nature.*

foreigner *NOUN* foreigners
a person from another country

foreleg *NOUN* forelegs
an animal's front leg

foreman *NOUN* foremen
❶ a worker in charge of a group of other workers ❷ a member of a jury who is in charge of the jury's discussions and who speaks on its behalf

foremost *ADJECTIVE* & *ADVERB*
first in position or rank; most important • *Athens became the foremost naval power in the Greek world.* • *First and foremost, thank you for coming.*

forensic (say fer-**en**-sik) *ADJECTIVE*
❶ to do with or used in law courts ❷ using scientific tests to find out about a crime

forensic medicine *NOUN*
medical knowledge needed in legal matters or in solving crimes

forerunner *NOUN* forerunners
a person or thing that comes before another; a sign of what is to come

foresee *VERB* foresees, foreseeing, foresaw, foreseen
to realize that something is likely to happen • *She could foresee many difficulties ahead.*

foreseeable *ADJECTIVE*
a foreseeable event is one that you should realize is likely to happen
➤ **for the foreseeable future** for as long as can be seen or planned at the moment

a b c d e f g h i j k l m n o p q r s t u v w x y z

foreshadow VERB foreshadows, foreshadowing, foreshadowed
to be a sign of something that is to come

foreshorten VERB foreshortens, foreshortening, foreshortened
to draw or paint an object with some lines shortened to give an effect of distance or depth

foresight NOUN
the ability to realize what is likely to happen in the future and be prepared for it

foreskin NOUN foreskins
the fold of skin covering the end of a penis

forest NOUN forests
trees and undergrowth covering a large area
➤ **forested** ADJECTIVE

forestall VERB forestalls, forestalling, forestalled
to prevent something from happening or someone from doing something by taking action first

forestry NOUN
planting forests and looking after them
➤ **forester** NOUN

foretaste NOUN foretastes
an experience of something that is to come in the future

foretell VERB foretells, foretelling, foretold
to know or say what will happen in the future; to predict something • *Everything happened as the witch had foretold.*

forethought NOUN
careful thought and planning for the future

forever ADVERB
❶ for all time or for a long time
❷ continually or constantly • *He is forever complaining.*

forewarn VERB forewarns, forewarning, forewarned
to warn someone beforehand

forewoman NOUN forewomen
❶ a female worker in charge of other workers
❷ a female member of a jury who is in charge of the jury's discussions and who speaks on its behalf

foreword NOUN forewords
a short introduction at the beginning of a book

forfeit (say **for**-fit) VERB forfeits, forfeiting, forfeited
to pay or give up something as a penalty • *If*

you cancel your flight, you will forfeit your deposit.
➤ **forfeiture** NOUN

forfeit NOUN forfeits
something forfeited

forge NOUN forges
a place where metal is heated and shaped; a blacksmith's workshop

forge VERB forges, forging, forged
❶ to shape metal by heating and hammering it ❷ to copy a banknote, document or painting in order to deceive people
➤ **forger** NOUN
➤ **forge ahead** to move forward with a strong effort

forgery NOUN forgeries
❶ the crime of copying something in order to deceive people ❷ a copy of something made to deceive people • *The painting was proved to be a forgery.*

forget VERB forgets, forgetting, forgot, forgotten
❶ to fail to remember something • *I've forgotten what I was going to say.* ❷ to stop thinking or worrying about something • *Try to forget about your troubles for a while.*
➤ **forget yourself** to behave rudely or thoughtlessly

forgetful ADJECTIVE
frequently forgetting things
➤ **forgetfulness** NOUN

forget-me-not NOUN forget-me-nots
a plant with small blue flowers
WORD ORIGIN because in the Middle Ages the flower was worn by lovers

forgive VERB forgives, forgiving, forgave, forgiven
to stop feeling angry towards someone for something they have done

forgiveness NOUN
forgiving someone • *He begged for forgiveness for what he had done.*

forgo VERB forgoes, forgoing, forwent, forgone
to decide to give something up; to go without something • *We may have to forgo lunch.*

SPELLING
Note the spelling of this word. It does not have an 'e' in it, whereas **foregoing**, meaning 'preceding', does.

fork NOUN forks
❶ a small device with prongs for lifting food

to your mouth ❷ a large device with prongs used for digging or lifting things ❸ a place where a road or river separates into two or more parts • *a fork in the road*

fork *VERB* forks, forking, forked
❶ to lift or dig something with a fork ❷ a road or river forks when it separates into two or more branches ❸ to follow one fork of a road or river • *Fork left.*
➤ **fork out for something** (*informal*) to pay out money for something

forklift truck *NOUN* forklift trucks
a truck with two metal bars at the front for lifting and moving heavy loads

forlorn *ADJECTIVE*
left alone and unhappy
➤ **forlornly** *ADVERB*
➤ **forlorn hope** the only faint hope left

form *NOUN* forms
❶ the shape, appearance or condition of something • *They could see a shadowy form in front of them.* • *The letters have been published in book form.* ❷ a kind or type of something • *Swimming is a good form of exercise.* ❸ a class in school ❹ a piece of paper with spaces to be filled in

form *VERB* forms, forming, formed
❶ to shape or construct something; to create something • *We have formed a book club.* ❷ to come into existence or develop • *Icicles formed on the window.*

formal *ADJECTIVE*
❶ strictly following the accepted rules or customs; not casual • *a formal occasion* • *formal dress* ❷ rather serious and stiff in your manner ❸ official or ceremonial • *The formal opening of the bridge takes place tomorrow.*

formality *NOUN* formalities
❶ formal behaviour ❷ something done to obey a rule or custom

formally *ADVERB*
in a formal way • *They bowed formally.*

format *NOUN* formats
❶ the shape and size of something ❷ the way something is arranged or organized ❸ (*in computing*) the way data is organized for processing or storage by a computer

format *VERB* formats, formatting, formatted
(*in computing*) to organize data in a particular format

formation *NOUN* formations
❶ the act of forming something • *This*

chapter is about the formation of ice crystals. ❷ something that has been formed • *a rock formation* ❸ a special arrangement or pattern • *The aircraft were flying in formation.*

formative *ADJECTIVE*
having an important and lasting influence on how a person develops • *His formative years were spent in Australia.*

former *ADJECTIVE*
of an earlier time • *In former times the house had been an inn.* • *Bill Clinton, the former US President*
Compare with **latter**.
➤ **the former** the first of two people or things just mentioned

formerly *ADVERB*
at an earlier time; previously

formidable (say **for**-mid-a-bul) *ADJECTIVE*
❶ difficult to deal with or do • *a formidable task* ❷ impressive and frightening • *a formidable opponent*
➤ **formidably** *ADVERB*

formula *NOUN* formulae or formulas
❶ a set of chemical symbols showing what a substance consists of ❷ a rule or statement expressed in symbols or numbers ❸ a list of the ingredients you need to make something ❹ a fixed wording for a speech or ceremony ❺ one of the groups into which racing cars are placed according to the size of their engines • *Formula One*

formulate *VERB* formulates, formulating, formulated
to express an idea or plan clearly and exactly

forsake *VERB* forsakes, forsaking, forsook, forsaken
❶ to give something up; to leave a place ❷ to abandon someone

fort *NOUN* forts
a building that has been strongly built against attack

forth *ADVERB*
❶ out; into view • *They set forth at dawn.* ❷ onwards or forwards • *from this day forth*
➤ **and so forth** and so on

forthcoming *ADJECTIVE*
❶ due to happen soon • *forthcoming events* ❷ made available when needed • *Money for the trip was not forthcoming.* ❸ willing to talk or give information

forthright *ADJECTIVE*
frank and outspoken

a b c d e f g h i j k l m n o p q r s t u v w x y z

forthwith ADVERB
immediately

fortification NOUN **fortifications**
❶ fortifying something ❷ a wall or building constructed to make a place strong against attack

fortify VERB **fortifies, fortifying, fortified**
❶ to make a place strong against attack, especially by building fortifications ❷ to make someone feel stronger • *He fortified himself against the cold with hot soup.*

fortissimo ADVERB
(*in music*) to be played very loudly

fortitude NOUN
courage in bearing pain or trouble

fortnight NOUN **fortnights**
a period of two weeks
➤ **fortnightly** ADVERB & ADJECTIVE
WORD ORIGIN from Old English *feowertene niht* = fourteen nights

fortress NOUN **fortresses**
a castle or town that has been strongly built against attack

fortuitous (say for-**tew**-it-us) ADJECTIVE
happening by chance; accidental • *The timing of his return was entirely fortuitous.*
➤ **fortuitously** ADVERB

USAGE
Note that **fortuitous** does not mean the same as **fortunate**.

fortunate ADJECTIVE
having or caused by good luck; lucky

fortunately ADVERB
by good luck • *Fortunately the train hadn't left when we got to the station.*

fortune NOUN **fortunes**
❶ luck, especially good luck ❷ a large amount of money
➤ **tell someone's fortune** to predict what will happen to someone in the future

forty NOUN & ADJECTIVE **forties**
the number 40
➤ **fortieth** ADJECTIVE & NOUN
➤ **forty winks** a short sleep; a nap

forum NOUN **forums**
❶ the public square in an ancient Roman city ❷ a place or meeting where people can exchange and discuss ideas • *The website provides a forum for young musicians to share their experiences.*

forward ADJECTIVE
❶ going forwards ❷ placed in the front ❸ too eager or bold

forward ADVERB
forwards or ahead

forward NOUN **forwards**
a player in the front line of a team in football, hockey, etc.

forward VERB **forwards, forwarding, forwarded**
to send on a letter, parcel or email to a new address

forwards ADVERB
❶ to or towards the front ❷ in the direction you are facing

fossick VERB **fossicks, fossicking, fossicked** (*Australian/NZ*)
❶ to turn things over or move them about while looking for something ❷ to search for gold or precious stones in streams or old mines

fossil NOUN **fossils**
the remains or traces of a prehistoric animal or plant that has been buried in the ground for a very long time and become hardened in rock

fossil fuel NOUN **fossil fuels**
a natural fuel such as coal or gas formed in the geological past

fossilized (also **fossilised**) ADJECTIVE
formed into a fossil • *fossilized dinosaur bones*

foster VERB **fosters, fostering, fostered**
❶ to take care of and bring up a child who is not your own ❷ to help something to grow or develop • *Reading to young children can foster a long-lasting love of books.*
➤ **foster child** NOUN
➤ **foster parent** NOUN
➤ **foster family** NOUN

foul ADJECTIVE
❶ disgusting; tasting or smelling unpleasant ❷ foul weather is wet and stormy ❸ unfair; breaking the rules of a game • *That was a foul shot.*
➤ **foulness** NOUN

foul NOUN **fouls**
an action that breaks the rules of a game

foul VERB **fouls, fouling, fouled**
❶ to commit a foul against a player in a game ❷ to make something foul or unpleasant • *Smoke had fouled the air.*

foul play *NOUN*
a violent crime, especially murder

found
past tense of **find**

found *VERB* founds, founding, founded
❶ to start or set up an organization or institution, especially by providing money • *The museum was founded in 1683.* ❷ to be founded on something is to be based on it • *This novel is founded on fact.*

foundation *NOUN* foundations
❶ a building's foundations are the solid base under the ground on which it is built ❷ the basis for something ❸ the founding of an organization or institution ❹ a fund of money set aside for a charitable purpose

founder *NOUN* founders
a person who founds something • *the founder of the hospital*

founder *VERB* founders, foundering, foundered
❶ to fill with water and sink • *The ship foundered on the rocks.* ❷ to fail completely • *Their plans foundered.*

foundling *NOUN* foundlings
a child found abandoned, whose parents are not known

foundry *NOUN* foundries
a factory or workshop where metal or glass is made

fount *NOUN* founts (*poetical use*)
a fountain

fountain *NOUN* fountains
an ornamental structure in which a jet of water shoots up into the air

fountain pen *NOUN* fountain pens
a pen that can be filled with a supply of ink

four *NOUN & ADJECTIVE* fours
the number 4
➤ **on all fours** on your hands and knees

fourteen *NOUN & ADJECTIVE* fourteens
the number 14
➤ **fourteenth** *ADJECTIVE & NOUN*

fourth *ADJECTIVE*
next after the third
➤ **fourthly** *ADVERB*

fourth *NOUN* fourths
❶ the fourth person or thing ❷ one of four equal parts; a quarter

fowl *NOUN* fowls
a bird, especially one kept on a farm for its eggs or meat

fox *NOUN* foxes
a wild animal that looks like a dog with a long furry tail
➤ **foxy** *ADJECTIVE*

fox *VERB* foxes, foxing, foxed
to deceive or puzzle someone • *The last question really foxed me.*

foxglove *NOUN* foxgloves
a tall plant with flowers like the fingers of gloves

foyer (say **foy**-ay) *NOUN* foyers
the entrance hall of a theatre, cinema or hotel

fraction *NOUN* fractions
❶ a number that is not a whole number, e.g. ½ or 0.5 ❷ a tiny part or amount of something • *It took me a fraction of a second to realize my mistake.*

fractionally *ADVERB*
by a small amount; very slightly • *The ball was fractionally over the line.*

fractious (say **frak**-shus) *ADJECTIVE*
irritable or bad-tempered • *a fractious toddler*

fracture *NOUN* fractures
the breaking of something, especially of a bone

fracture *VERB* fractures, fracturing, fractured
to break something, especially a bone

fragile *ADJECTIVE*
easy to break or damage • *Be careful, this bowl is fragile.*
➤ **fragility** *NOUN*

fragment *NOUN* fragments
❶ a small piece broken off ❷ a small part of something • *He overheard fragments of their conversation.*
➤ **fragmentary** *ADJECTIVE*
➤ **fragmented** *ADJECTIVE*

fragrance *NOUN* fragrances
a pleasant smell or perfume

fragrant *ADJECTIVE*
having a pleasant smell

frail *ADJECTIVE*
not strong or healthy; physically weak • *a frail old man*

frailty *NOUN* frailties
weakness in someone's body or character

a b c d e f g h i j k l m n o p q r s t u v w x y z

frame *NOUN* frames
❶ a holder that fits round the outside of a picture or mirror ❷ a rigid structure that supports something • *the frame of a bicycle* ❸ a human or animal body • *He has a small frame.* ❹ each of the single photographs that a cinema film or video is made from
➤ **frame of mind** the way you think or feel for a while

frame *VERB* frames, framing, framed
❶ to put a frame on or round something ❷ to express something in a particular way • *They framed the question badly.* ❸ to make an innocent person seem guilty by arranging false evidence

framework *NOUN* frameworks
❶ a frame supporting something ❷ a basic plan or system

franc *NOUN* francs
a unit of money in Switzerland and formerly in France, Belgium and some other countries (until replaced by the euro)

franchise *NOUN* franchises
❶ the right to vote in elections ❷ a licence to sell a firm's goods or services in a certain area

frank *ADJECTIVE*
honest and saying exactly what you think • *I'll be frank with you.*
➤ **frankness** *NOUN*

frank *VERB* franks, franking, franked
to mark a letter or parcel automatically in a machine to show that postage has been paid

frankincense *NOUN*
a sweet-smelling gum burnt as incense

frankly *ADVERB*
in an honest and direct way • *Please tell me frankly what you think.*

frantic *ADJECTIVE*
❶ wildly anxious or frightened • *She was frantic with worry.* ❷ done in a hurried and urgent way • *a frantic search for survivors*
➤ **frantically** *ADVERB*

fraternal (say fra-**tern**-al) *ADJECTIVE*
to do with brothers; brotherly

fraternity *NOUN* fraternities
❶ a brotherly feeling ❷ a group of people who have the same interests or occupation • *the medical fraternity*

fraternize (also **fraternise**) *VERB* fraternizes, fraternizing, fraternized
to be friendly towards a group of people and spend time with them • *She was accused of fraternizing with the enemy.*

fraud *NOUN* frauds
❶ the crime of getting money by tricking people ❷ a dishonest trick ❸ a person who is not what they pretend to be

fraudulent (say **fraw**-dew-lent) *ADJECTIVE*
involving fraud; deceitful or dishonest
➤ **fraudulently** *ADVERB*

fraught *ADJECTIVE*
❶ filled with problems or difficulties • *The situation is fraught with danger.* ❷ tense or upset • *I'm feeling rather fraught this morning.*

fray *VERB* frays, fraying, frayed
❶ material frays or becomes frayed when some of the threads become loose and start to come apart • *Your shirt collar is frayed.* ❷ a person's temper or nerves fray when they become strained or upset

fray *NOUN*
a fight or conflict • *They were ready for the fray.*

freak *NOUN* freaks
❶ a very strange or abnormal person, animal or thing ❷ a person with a very strong interest in something • *She is a fitness freak.*

freakish *ADJECTIVE*
very unusual or strange • *freakish weather*

freckle *NOUN* freckles
a small brown spot on the skin
➤ **freckled** *ADJECTIVE*

free *ADJECTIVE* freer, freest
❶ able to do what you want to do or go where you want to go ❷ not costing anything ❸ not fixed • *Leave one end free.* ❹ not having or being affected by something • *The main roads are still free of snow.* ❺ available; not being used or occupied ❻ not already having things to do • *Are you free next Saturday?* ❼ generous • *She is very free with her money.*

free *VERB* frees, freeing, freed
to set someone or something free

freedom *NOUN* freedoms
❶ the right to do or say what you like • *freedom of speech* ❷ being free; not being a prisoner • *He was finally given his freedom after 25 years in jail.*

freehand *ADJECTIVE* & *ADVERB*
a freehand drawing is done without a ruler

or compasses or without tracing it • *Draw a circle freehand.*

freehold *NOUN*
(*chiefly British*) possessing land or a house as its absolute owner, not as a tenant renting from a landlord

freely *ADVERB*
❶ without being controlled or limited • *the country's first freely elected president* • *I freely admit that I made a mistake.* ❷ without anything stopping the movement or flow of something • *The wheel can now turn freely.*

free-range *ADJECTIVE*
❶ free-range hens are not kept in small cages but are allowed to move about freely ❷ free-range eggs are ones laid by these hens

free verse *NOUN*
poetry that does not rhyme or have a regular rhythm

freeway *NOUN* freeways
(*North American*) a dual-carriageway main road

freewheel *VERB* freewheels, freewheeling, freewheeled
to ride a bicycle without pedalling

freeze *VERB* freezes, freezing, froze, frozen
❶ to turn into ice or to become covered with ice • *The pond froze last night.* ❷ to feel very cold ❸ to freeze food is to store it at a low temperature to preserve it ❹ to suddenly stand completely still ❺ to keep wages or prices at a fixed level

freeze *NOUN* freezes
❶ a period of freezing weather ❷ the freezing of wages or prices

freezer *NOUN* freezers
a refrigerator in which food can be frozen quickly and stored

freezing *ADJECTIVE*
very cold • *I'm freezing.* • *It's freezing outside.*

freezing point *NOUN* freezing points
the temperature at which a liquid freezes

freight (say frayt) *NOUN*
goods carried by road or in a ship or aircraft

freighter (say **fray**-ter) *NOUN* freighters
a ship or aircraft used for carrying goods

French window *NOUN* French windows
a long window that serves as a door on an outside wall

frenzied *ADJECTIVE*
wildly excited or angry • *a frenzied attack*
➤ **frenziedly** *ADVERB*

frenzy *NOUN*
wild and uncontrolled excitement or anger • *He had worked the crowd up into a frenzy.*

frequency *NOUN* frequencies
❶ being frequent; happening often ❷ how often something happens ❸ the number of vibrations made each second by a wave of sound, radio or light

frequent (say **freek**-went) *ADJECTIVE*
happening often

frequent (say frik-**went**) *VERB* frequents, frequenting, frequented
to visit a place or be seen there, often • *They frequented the club.*

frequently *ADVERB*
often • *I frequently forget my keys.*

fresco *NOUN* frescoes or frescos
a picture painted on a wall or ceiling before the plaster is dry **WORD ORIGIN** from Italian *affresco* = on the fresh (plaster)

fresh *ADJECTIVE*
❶ newly made or produced or arrived; not stale • *fresh bread* ❷ not tinned or preserved • *fresh fruit* ❸ fresh air is cool and refreshing ❹ fresh water is not salty ❺ full of energy and not tired
➤ **freshness** *NOUN*

freshen *VERB* freshens, freshening, freshened
❶ to make something fresh ❷ to become fresh

freshly *ADVERB*
newly or recently • *freshly baked bread*

freshwater *ADJECTIVE*
living in rivers or lakes, not the sea • *freshwater fish*

fret *VERB* frets, fretting, fretted
to worry or be upset about something
➤ **fretful** *ADJECTIVE*
➤ **fretfully** *ADVERB*

fret *NOUN* frets
a bar or ridge on the fingerboard of a guitar etc.

fretsaw *NOUN* fretsaws
a very narrow saw used for cutting patterns in thin wood

fretwork *NOUN*
cutting decorative patterns in wood; wood cut in this way

a b c d e f g h i j k l m n o p q r s t u v w x y z

friar *NOUN* friars
a man who is a member of a Roman Catholic religious order and has vowed to live a life of poverty

friary *NOUN* friaries
a building where friars live

friction *NOUN*
❶ the rubbing of one thing against another ❷ (*in science*) the resistance that one surface or object meets when it moves against another ❸ bad feeling between people; quarrelling

Friday *NOUN*
the day of the week following Thursday
WORD ORIGIN from Old English *Frigedaeg* = day of Frigga, a Norse goddess

fridge *NOUN* fridges
(*British*) a refrigerator

friend *NOUN* friends
❶ a person you like and who likes you ❷ a person you send messages to on a social networking site ❸ a helpful or kind person

SPELLING
There is a silent i before the e in **friend**.

friendless *ADJECTIVE*
without any friends

friendly *ADJECTIVE* friendlier, friendliest
❶ behaving like a friend; kind and pleasant ❷ helpful and easy to use; not harmful
• *environmentally-friendly farming methods*
➤ **friendliness** *NOUN*

friendly *NOUN* friendlies
(*British*) a sports match that is not part of a formal competition

friendship *NOUN* friendships
friendly feelings between people; being friends

frieze (say freez) *NOUN* friezes
a strip of designs or pictures round the top of a wall or building

frigate *NOUN* frigates
a small warship

fright *NOUN* frights
❶ sudden great fear ❷ (*informal*) a person or thing that looks ridiculous

frighten *VERB* frightens, frightening, frightened
to make someone afraid
➤ **be frightened of** to be afraid of someone or something • *When I was young I was frightened of spiders.*
➤ **frightening** *ADJECTIVE*

frightful *ADJECTIVE*
(*British*) awful; very great or bad
➤ **frightfully** *ADVERB*

frigid *ADJECTIVE*
❶ extremely cold ❷ unfriendly; not affectionate
➤ **frigidly** *ADVERB*

frill *NOUN* frills
❶ a decorative gathered or pleated trimming on a dress, shirt, curtain, etc. ❷ something extra that is pleasant but unnecessary • *a simple hotel with no frills*
➤ **frilled** *ADJECTIVE*
➤ **frilly** *ADJECTIVE*

fringe *NOUN* fringes
❶ a decorative edging with many threads hanging down loosely ❷ a straight line of hair hanging down over your forehead ❸ the edge of something • *These hills mark the northern fringe of the desert.*

fringe *VERB*
➤ **be fringed with something** to have something as a border or around the edge
• *The lake was fringed with pine trees.*

frisk *VERB* frisks, frisking, frisked
❶ to jump or run about playfully ❷ to search someone by running your hands over his or her clothes

frisky *ADJECTIVE*
playful or lively

fritter *NOUN* fritters
a slice of meat, potato or fruit coated in batter and fried

fritter *VERB* fritters, frittering, frittered
if you fritter away your time or money, you waste it on trivial things

frivolous *ADJECTIVE*
without a serious purpose; light-hearted when you should be serious
➤ **frivolity** *NOUN*

frizzy *ADJECTIVE*
frizzy hair is in tight stiff curls

fro *ADVERB*
➤ **to and fro** backwards and forwards

frock *NOUN* frocks
(*British*) a girl's or woman's dress

frog *NOUN* frogs
a small jumping animal that can live both in water and on land
➤ **have a frog in your throat** to be hoarse and unable to speak clearly

frogman NOUN frogmen
a swimmer equipped with a rubber suit, flippers and breathing apparatus for swimming and working underwater

frolic NOUN frolics
a lively cheerful game or entertainment
➤ **frolicsome** ADJECTIVE

frolic VERB frolics, frolicking, frolicked
to play about in a lively cheerful way

from PREPOSITION
This word is used to show
❶ a starting point in space or time or order (*We flew from London to Paris. We work from 9 to 5 o'clock. Count from one to ten.*)
❷ distance (*We are a mile from home.*)
❸ source or origin (*Get water from the tap.*)
❹ separation or release (*Take the gun from him. She was freed from prison.*) ❺ difference (*How do you tell one twin from the other?*)
❻ cause (*We were all suffering from exhaustion.*)

frond NOUN fronds
a leaf-like part of a fern, palm tree, etc.

front NOUN fronts
❶ the part or side that comes first or is the most important or furthest forward ❷ a road or promenade along the seashore ❸ the place where fighting is happening in a war ❹ in weather systems, the forward edge of an approaching mass of air
➤ **in front** at or near the front

front ADJECTIVE
of the front; in front • *We sat in the front row.*

frontage NOUN frontages
the front of a building; the land beside this

frontier NOUN frontiers
the boundary between two countries or regions

frontispiece NOUN frontispieces
an illustration opposite the title page of a book

frost NOUN frosts
❶ powdery ice that forms on things in freezing weather ❷ weather with a temperature below freezing point

frost VERB frosts, frosting, frosted
➤ **frost up** or **over** to become covered with frost

frostbite NOUN
harm done to the body by very cold weather
➤ **frostbitten** ADJECTIVE

frosted glass NOUN
glass made cloudy so that you cannot see clearly through it

frosting NOUN
sugar icing for cakes

frosty ADJECTIVE frostier, frostiest
❶ so cold that there is frost • *It was a frosty morning.* ❷ unfriendly and unwelcoming • *She gave us a frosty look.*
➤ **frostily** ADVERB

froth NOUN
a white mass of tiny bubbles on a liquid

froth VERB froths, frothing, frothed
to form a froth • *The dog was frothing at the mouth.*
➤ **frothy** ADJECTIVE

frown VERB frowns, frowning, frowned
to wrinkle your forehead because you are angry or worried

frown NOUN frowns
a frowning movement or look

frozen ADJECTIVE
❶ frozen food is stored at a low temperature in order to preserve it ❷ very cold • *My feet are frozen!* ❸ with a layer of ice on the surface • *a frozen pond*

frugal (say **froo-gal**) ADJECTIVE
❶ spending very little money ❷ small and meagre; costing very little money • *a frugal meal*
➤ **frugally** ADVERB
➤ **frugality** NOUN

fruit NOUN fruits or fruit
❶ the seed container that grows on a tree or plant and is often used as food ❷ the result of doing something • *It will be years before we see the fruits of all this work.*

fruit VERB fruits, fruiting, fruited
a tree or plant fruits when it produces fruit

> **SPELLING**
> The 'oo' sound is spelt **ui** in fruit.

fruitful ADJECTIVE
producing good results • *fruitful discussions*
➤ **fruitfully** ADVERB

fruition (say froo-**ish**-on) NOUN
the achievement of what was hoped or worked for • *Our plans never came to fruition.*

fruitless ADJECTIVE
producing no results • *a fruitless search*
➤ **fruitlessly** ADVERB

a b c d e f g h i j k l m n o p q r s t u v w x y z

fruit machine *NOUN* **fruit machines**
(*British*) a gambling machine worked by
putting a coin in a slot

fruity *ADJECTIVE*
❶ like or containing fruit ❷ a fruity voice is
deep and rich

frustrate *VERB* **frustrates, frustrating,
frustrated**
❶ to make someone annoyed and upset
because they are prevented from doing
something • *The delay was beginning to
frustrate me.* ❷ to prevent something from
being successful • *All our plans have been
frustrated.*

frustrating *ADJECTIVE*
making you annoyed or upset because you
cannot do what you want • *It's been a very
frustrating day.*

frustration *NOUN*
a feeling of annoyance when you have been
prevented from doing something

fry *VERB* **fries, frying, fried**
to cook food in very hot fat
➤ **fryer** *NOUN*

fry *PLURAL NOUN*
very young fishes

frying pan *NOUN* **frying pans**
a shallow pan for frying things

fuchsia (say **few**-sha) *NOUN* **fuchsias**
an ornamental plant with flowers that hang
down (WORD ORIGIN) named after Leonard
Fuchs, a German botanist

fudge *NOUN*
a soft sugary sweet

fudge *VERB* **fudges, fudging, fudged**
to avoid giving clear and accurate
information or a clear answer • *People accuse
us of fudging the issue.*

fuel *NOUN* **fuels**
something that is burnt to produce heat or
power

fuel *VERB* **fuels, fuelling, fuelled**
❶ to supply something with fuel ❷ to
strengthen a feeling or belief • *His answers
only fuelled my suspicions.*

fug *NOUN* (*British*) (*informal*)
a stuffy or smoky atmosphere in a room
➤ **fuggy** *ADJECTIVE*

fugitive (say **few**-jit-iv) *NOUN* **fugitives**
a person who is running away from
something, especially from the police

fugue (say fewg) *NOUN* **fugues**
a piece of music in which tunes are repeated
in a complicated pattern

fulcrum *NOUN* **fulcrums** or **fulcra**
the point on which something balances or
turns

fulfil *VERB* **fulfils, fulfilling, fulfilled**
❶ to do what is required; to carry something
out • *You must fulfil your promises.* ❷ to
make something come true • *It fulfilled an
ancient prophecy.* ❸ to give you a feeling of
satisfaction

fulfilment *NOUN*
the feeling of satisfaction you have when you
have achieved something

full *ADJECTIVE*
❶ containing as much or as many as possible
• *The cinema was full.* ❷ having many people
or things • *She's full of ideas.* ❸ complete
• *Tell me the full story.* ❹ the greatest
possible • *at full speed* ❺ fitting loosely; with
many folds • *a full skirt*
➤ **fullness** *NOUN*
➤ **in full** with nothing left out • *We have
paid in full.*
➤ **to the full** completely or thoroughly

full *ADVERB*
completely and directly • *It hit him full in the
face.*

full-blown *ADJECTIVE*
fully developed

full moon *NOUN* **full moons**
the moon when you can see the whole of it as
a bright disc

full stop *NOUN* **full stops**
(*British*) the dot (.) used as a punctuation
mark at the end of a sentence or an
abbreviation or after an initial

(PUNCTUATION)

A **full stop** (called a **period** in American
English) is used to show where a sentence
ends, when the sentence is neither a
question nor an exclamation:

I am the tallest in my class.

You can text me later.

It can also be used to indicate a complete
break between single words or phrases
that are not complete sentences:

*There was nothing left of the cake. Not a
crumb. Not a particle. Nothing.*

Full stops go within quotation marks in direct speech:

He said, 'I'll meet you outside the cinema.'

A full stop is also used after an initial or to mark an abbreviation (e.g. *Mon.* = Monday). This is no longer necessary for common abbreviations, like *Mr, Mrs,* and *Dr.*

full-time *ADJECTIVE & ADVERB*
for all the normal working hours of the day • *a full-time job* • *She works full-time.*

fully *ADVERB*
completely • *He has fully recovered from his illness.*

fully-fledged *ADJECTIVE*
fully trained or developed • *a fully-fledged engineer*

fumble *VERB* fumbles, fumbling, fumbled
to handle or feel for something something clumsily • *I fumbled in the dark for the light switch.*

fume *VERB* fumes, fuming, fumed
❶ to give off fumes ❷ to be very angry

fumes *PLURAL NOUN*
strong-smelling smoke or gas

fun *NOUN*
amusement or enjoyment
➤ **make fun of someone** to laugh at someone in an unkind way or make other people do this

function *NOUN* functions
❶ what someone or something is there to do • *The function of the heart is to pump blood round the body.* ❷ an important event or party ❸ a basic operation in a computer or calculator ❹ (*in mathematics*) a variable quantity whose value depends on the value of other variable quantities • *X is a function of Y and Z.*

function *VERB* functions, functioning, functioned
to perform a function; to work properly • *Only one engine was still functioning.*

functional *ADJECTIVE*
❶ working properly ❷ practical and useful without being decorative or luxurious

fund *NOUN* funds
❶ an amount of money collected or kept for a special purpose ❷ a stock or supply • *He has a fund of stories and jokes.*

fund *VERB* funds, funding, funded
to supply someone or something with money

fundamental *ADJECTIVE*
basic; involving the central and most important part of something
➤ **fundamentally** *ADVERB*

funeral *NOUN* funerals
the ceremony when a dead person is buried or cremated

funereal (say few-**neer**-ee-al) *ADJECTIVE*
gloomy or depressing

funfair *NOUN* funfairs
(*British*) a fair consisting of amusements and sideshows

fungus *NOUN* fungi (say **fung**-eye)
a plant without leaves or flowers that grows on other plants or on decayed material, such as mushrooms and toadstools

funk *VERB* funks, funking, funked
(*British*) (*old-fashioned use*) to be afraid of doing something and avoid it

funk *NOUN*
a style of popular music with a strong rhythm, based on jazz and blues

funnel *NOUN* funnels
❶ a metal chimney on a ship or steam engine ❷ a tube that is wide at the top and narrow at the bottom to help you pour things into a narrow opening

funny *ADJECTIVE* funnier, funniest
❶ that makes you laugh or smile ❷ strange or odd • *a funny smell*
➤ **funnily** *ADVERB*

funny bone *NOUN* funny bones
part of your elbow which produces a tingling feeling if you knock it

fur *NOUN* furs
❶ the soft hair that covers some animals ❷ animal skin with the fur on it, used for clothing; fabric that looks like animal fur

furious *ADJECTIVE*
❶ very angry ❷ violent or intense • *They were travelling at a furious speed.*

furiously *ADVERB*
❶ angrily ❷ with great energy or speed • *We worked furiously to get it finished on time.*

furl *VERB* furls, furling, furled
to roll up a sail, flag or umbrella

furlong *NOUN* furlongs
one-eighth of a mile, 220 yards (201 metres)

a b c d e f g h i j k l m n o p q r s t u v w x y z

WORD ORIGIN from Old English *furlang* = 'furrow long'; the length of a furrow in a common field

furnace *NOUN* furnaces
a type of large oven that produces great heat for making glass or melting metals

furnish *VERB*
❶ to put furniture in a room or building ❷ to provide someone with something • *She furnished him with all the facts he needed.*

furnishings *PLURAL NOUN*
furniture, curtains and fittings for a room or house

furniture *NOUN*
tables, chairs and other movable things that you need in a house, school or office

furore (say few-**ror**-ee) *NOUN*
an excited or angry uproar

furrow *NOUN* furrows
❶ a long cut in the ground made by a plough ❷ a deep wrinkle in the skin

furrow *VERB* furrows, furrowing, furrowed
to make furrows in something • *Tom furrowed his brow.*

furry *ADJECTIVE*
like fur; covered with fur

further *ADVERB & ADJECTIVE*
❶ at or to a greater distance; more distant ❷ more; additional • *We made further enquiries.*
USAGE
See the note at **farther.**

further *VERB* furthers, furthering, furthered
to help something to progress • *It was a chance for her to further her career.*

further education *NOUN*
(*British*) education for people above school age

furthermore *ADVERB*
also; moreover

furthest *ADVERB & ADJECTIVE*
at or to the greatest distance; most distant
USAGE
See the note at **farther.**

furtive *ADJECTIVE*
stealthy; trying not to be seen • *He gave a furtive glance over his shoulder.*
➤ **furtively** *ADVERB*

fury *NOUN* furies
wild anger; rage • *She was speechless with fury.*

furze *NOUN*
gorse shrubs

fuse *NOUN* fuses
❶ a safety device containing a short piece of wire that melts if too much electricity is passed through it ❷ a length of material that burns easily, used for setting off an explosive

fuse *VERB* fuses, fusing, fused
❶ an electrical device fuses when it stops working because a fuse has melted ❷ to fuse things is to blend them together, especially through melting

fuselage (say **few**-zel-ahzh) *NOUN* fuselages
the main body of an aircraft

fusillade (say few-zil-**ayd**) *NOUN* fusillades
❶ an outburst of rapid gunfire ❷ a rapid series of questions

fusion *NOUN*
❶ the action of blending or uniting things ❷ the uniting of atomic nuclei, usually releasing energy

fuss *NOUN* fusses
❶ unnecessary excitement or worry about something • *What's all the fuss about?* ❷ angry complaints about something
➤ **make a fuss of someone** to treat someone with great kindness and attention

fuss *VERB* fusses, fussing, fussed
to be too anxious about something that is not important • *She fusses when I go out on my bike.*

fussy *ADJECTIVE* fussier, fussiest
❶ worrying too much about something that is not important ❷ choosing very carefully; hard to please • *My brother is a fussy eater.* ❸ full of unnecessary details or decorations • *a fussy design*
➤ **fussily** *ADVERB*

fusty *ADJECTIVE* fustier, fustiest
smelling stale or stuffy

futile (say **few**-tyl) *ADJECTIVE*
useless or pointless; having no chance of success • *He knew it was futile to argue with her.*
➤ **futility** *NOUN*

futon (say **foo**-ton) *NOUN* futons
a seat with a mattress that rolls out to form a bed

future *NOUN*
❶ the time that will come • *Who knows what will happen in the future?* ❷ what is going to happen to someone or something in the time to come • *She has a bright future.* ❸ (*in grammar*) the use of verbs and phrases such as 'will', 'shall', 'be going to', or 'be about to' to talk about something happening in the future

> **GRAMMAR**
> See also the panel at **tense**.

future *ADJECTIVE*
belonging or referring to the future

futuristic *ADJECTIVE*
very modern, as if belonging to the future rather than the present • *futuristic buildings*

fuzz *NOUN*
something soft and fluffy like soft hair

fuzzy *ADJECTIVE*
❶ a fuzzy picture or image is blurred and not clear ❷ covered with short soft hair or fur
➤ **fuzziness** *NOUN*

Gg

gabble *VERB* gabbles, gabbling, gabbled
to talk so quickly that it is difficult to hear the words • *She was nervous and started to gabble.*

gable *NOUN* gables
the pointed triangular part at the top of an outside wall, between two sloping roofs
➤ **gabled** *ADJECTIVE*

gad *VERB* gads, gadding, gadded
➤ **gad about** (*informal*)
to have a lot of fun in different places

gadget *NOUN* gadgets
any small useful tool or device
➤ **gadgetry** *NOUN*

Gaelic (say **gay**-lik) *NOUN*
the Celtic languages of Scotland and Ireland

gaffe *NOUN* gaffes
an obvious and embarrassing mistake

gag *NOUN* gags
❶ something put into a person's mouth or tied over it to prevent them speaking ❷ a joke

gag *VERB* gags, gagging, gagged
❶ to put a gag on a person ❷ to prevent someone from making comments • *We cannot gag the press.* ❸ to retch

gaggle *NOUN* gaggles
❶ a flock of geese ❷ a group of noisy people • *a gaggle of tourists*

gaiety *NOUN*
being cheerful and having fun

gaily *ADVERB*
in a cheerful way

gain *VERB* gains, gaining, gained
❶ to get something that you did not have before ❷ a clock or watch gains when it shows a time later than the correct time ❸ (*literary*) to reach or arrive at a place • *At last we gained the shore.*
➤ **gain on someone** to come closer to someone when you are chasing them or in a race

gain *NOUN* gains
something that you gain; a profit or improvement

gait *NOUN* gaits
a way of walking or running • *He walked with a shuffling gait.*

gaiter *NOUN* gaiters
a leather or cloth covering for the lower part of the leg

gala (say **gah**-la) *NOUN* galas
❶ a festival or celebration ❷ a set of sports contests, especially in swimming

galaxy *NOUN* galaxies
a very large group of stars
➤ **galactic** (say ga-**lak**-tik) *ADJECTIVE*
WORD ORIGIN originally = the Milky Way: from Greek *galaxias* = milky

gale *NOUN* gales
a very strong wind

gall (say gawl) *NOUN*
being bold or cheeky enough to do something • *I don't know how he had the gall to say it was his idea.*

gall *VERB* galls, galling, galled
to annoy or upset someone, especially because something is unfair • *It galls me that I ended up getting the blame.*

gallant (say **gal**-lant) *ADJECTIVE*
❶ brave or heroic • *a gallant effort*
❷ courteous towards women
➤ **gallantly** *ADVERB*
➤ **gallantry** *NOUN*

gallant

. NOUN **gall bladders**
..ached to the liver, in which bile

. OUN **galleons**
Spanish sailing ship used in the 16th
/th centuries

gallery NOUN **galleries**
❶ a room or building for showing works
of art ❷ the highest balcony in a cinema
or theatre ❸ a long room or passage ❹ a
platform jutting out from the wall in a church
or hall

galley NOUN **galleys**
❶ an ancient type of ship driven by oars
❷ the kitchen in a ship or aircraft

galling (say **gawl**-ing) ADJECTIVE
annoying and upsetting because of being
unfair

gallivant VERB **gallivants, gallivanting,
gallivanted**
to go about in search of pleasure

gallon NOUN **gallons**
a unit used to measure liquids, 8 pints or
4.546 litres

gallop NOUN **gallops**
❶ the fastest pace that a horse can go ❷ a
fast ride on a horse

gallop VERB **gallops, galloping, galloped**
to go or ride at a gallop

gallows NOUN **gallows**
a framework with a noose for hanging
criminals

galore ADVERB
in great numbers; in a large amount • _There
will be bargains galore._

galoshes PLURAL NOUN
a pair of waterproof shoes worn over ordinary
shoes

galvanize (also **galvanise**) VERB **galvanizes,
galvanizing, galvanized**
❶ to shock or stimulate someone into sudden
activity • _The urgency of his voice galvanized
them into action._ ❷ to coat iron with zinc
to protect it from rust **WORD ORIGIN** named
after an Italian scientist, Luigi _Galvani_, who
discovered that muscles move because of
electricity in the body

gambit NOUN **gambits**
❶ a kind of opening move in chess ❷ an
action or remark intended to gain an
advantage

gamble VERB **gambles, gambling, gambled**
❶ to bet on the result of a game, race or
other event ❷ to take risks in the hope of
gaining something • _I wouldn't gamble on the
weather staying fine._
➤ **gambler** NOUN

gamble NOUN **gambles**
❶ a bet or chance • _a gamble on the lottery_
❷ something you do that is a risk • _He knew
that playing when he had an injury was a
gamble._

gambol VERB **gambols, gambolling, gambolled**
to jump or skip about in play

game NOUN **games**
❶ something that you can play, usually with
rules • _a game of football_ • _a computer game_
❷ a section of a long game such as tennis or
whist ❸ a scheme or plan; a trick • _Whatever
his game is, he won't succeed._ ❹ wild animals
or birds hunted for sport or food
➤ **give the game away** to reveal a secret

game ADJECTIVE
willing to do or try something • _Are you game
for a swim?_
➤ **gamely** ADVERB

gamekeeper NOUN **gamekeepers**
a person employed to protect game birds and
animals, especially from poachers

gameplay NOUN
the design of a computer game and how it is
played

games PLURAL NOUN
❶ a meeting for sporting contests • _the
Olympic Games_ ❷ athletics or sports as a
subject taught at school

gaming NOUN
❶ gambling ❷ playing computer games

gamma NOUN
the third letter of the Greek alphabet,
equivalent to Roman G, g

gamma rays PLURAL NOUN
very short X-rays emitted by radioactive
substances

gammon NOUN
(_British_) a kind of ham

gamut (say **gam**-ut) NOUN
the whole range or scope of anything • _He
ran the whole gamut of emotions from joy to
despair._

gander NOUN **ganders**
a male goose

gang NOUN gangs
❶ a group of people who do things together
❷ a group of young people who cause trouble and fight other groups ❸ a group of criminals

gang VERB gangs, ganging, ganged
➤ **gang up on someone** to form a group to fight or oppose someone

gangling ADJECTIVE
tall, thin and awkward-looking

gangplank NOUN gangplanks
a plank placed so that people can walk on or off a boat

gangrene (say **gang**-green) NOUN
decay of body tissue in a living person

gangster NOUN gangsters
a member of a gang of violent criminals

gangway NOUN gangways
❶ a gap left for people to pass between rows of seats, e.g. in a theatre or aircraft ❷ a movable bridge placed so that people can walk onto or off a ship

gannet NOUN gannets
a large seabird which catches fish by flying above the sea and then diving in

gaol (say jayl) NOUN gaols
(*British*) a different spelling of **jail**
➤ **gaol** VERB
➤ **gaoler** NOUN

gap NOUN gaps
❶ a break or opening in something continuous such as a hedge or fence ❷ an interval or break ❸ a wide difference in ideas

gape VERB gapes, gaping, gaped
❶ to stare in amazement with your mouth open ❷ to be wide open • *a gaping wound*

garage (say **ga**-rahzh or **ga**-rij) NOUN garages
❶ a building for keeping a motor vehicle or vehicles ❷ a place where petrol is sold and vehicles are repaired and serviced

garb NOUN
special clothing • *a man dressed in prison garb*

garbage NOUN
(*esp. North American*) rubbish, especially household rubbish

garbed ADJECTIVE
(*old use*) or (*poetical use*) dressed in a particular way • *They were garbed in robes of pure white.*

garbled ADJECTIVE
a garbled message or story is mixed up so that it is difficult to understand
WORD ORIGIN from Arabic *garbala* = sift, select (because the real facts are 'sifted out')

garden NOUN gardens
a piece of ground where flowers, fruit or vegetables are grown
➤ **gardener** NOUN
➤ **gardening** NOUN

gargantuan (say gar-**gan**-tew-an) ADJECTIVE
gigantic **WORD ORIGIN** from *Gargantua*, the name of a giant in a book by the French writer Rabelais

gargle VERB gargles, gargling, gargled
to hold a liquid at the back of the mouth and push air through it to wash the inside of the throat
➤ **gargle** NOUN

gargoyle NOUN gargoyles
an ugly or comical face or figure carved on a building, especially on a waterspout
WORD ORIGIN from French *gargouille* = throat (because the water passes through the throat of the figure)

garish (say **gair**-ish) ADJECTIVE
too bright or highly coloured; gaudy
➤ **garishly** ADVERB

garland NOUN garlands
a wreath of flowers worn or hung as a decoration

garland VERB garlands, garlanding, garlanded
to decorate something with a garland

garlic NOUN
a plant with a bulb divided into smaller bulbs (called cloves), which have a strong smell and taste and are used for flavouring food

garment NOUN garments
a piece of clothing

garner VERB garners, garnering, garnered
(*formal*)
to gather or collect something • *He managed to garner plenty of information.*

garnet NOUN garnets
a dark red stone used as a gem

garnish VERB garnishes, garnishing, garnished
to decorate something, especially food
• *Garnish the fish with slices of lemon.*

garnish NOUN
something used to decorate food or give it extra flavour

a b c d e f g h i j k l m n o p q r s t u v w x y z

garret *NOUN* **garrets**
a dingy attic room

garrison *NOUN* **garrisons**
❶ troops who stay in a town or fort to defend it ❷ the building they live in
➤ **garrison** *VERB*

garrulous (say **ga**-rool-us) *ADJECTIVE*
extremely talkative

garter *NOUN* **garters**
a band of elastic to hold up a sock or stocking

gas *NOUN* **gases**
❶ a substance, such as oxygen, that can move freely and is not liquid or solid at ordinary temperatures ❷ a gas that can be burned, used for lighting, heating or cooking ❸ (*North American*) (*informal*) short for gasoline

gas *VERB* **gasses, gassing, gassed**
❶ to kill or injure someone with gas ❷ (*informal*) to chatter idly

gas chamber *NOUN* **gas chambers**
a room that can be filled with poisonous gas to kill people or animals

gaseous (say **gas**-ee-us) *ADJECTIVE*
in the form of a gas

gash *NOUN* **gashes**
a long deep cut or wound

gash *VERB* **gashes, gashing, gashed**
to make a gash in something

gasket *NOUN* **gaskets**
a flat ring or strip of soft material for sealing a joint between metal surfaces in machinery

gasoline *NOUN*
(*North American*) petrol

gasometer (say gas-**om**-it-er) *NOUN* **gasometers**
a large round tank in which gas is stored

gasp *VERB* **gasps, gasping, gasped**
❶ to breathe in suddenly when you are shocked or surprised ❷ to struggle to breathe with your mouth open when you are tired or ill ❸ to speak in a breathless way

gasp *NOUN* **gasps**
a sudden deep breath, especially one caused by shock or surprise

gassy *ADJECTIVE*
fizzy

gastric *ADJECTIVE*
to do with the stomach

gastronomy (say gas-**tron**-om-ee) *NOUN*
the art or practice of good eating
➤ **gastronomic** *ADJECTIVE*

gastropod *NOUN* **gastropods**
an animal (e.g. a snail or slug) that moves by means of a fleshy 'foot' on its stomach
WORD ORIGIN from Greek *gaster* = stomach + *podos* = of the foot

gate *NOUN* **gates**
❶ a movable barrier, usually on hinges, used as a door in a wall or fence ❷ a barrier for controlling the flow of water in a dam or lock ❸ a place where you wait before you board an aircraft ❹ the number of people attending a football match or other sports event

gateau (say **gat**-oh) *NOUN* **gateaus** or **gateaux**
a large rich cream cake

gatecrash *VERB* **gatecrashes, gatecrashing, gatecrashed**
to go to a private party without being invited
➤ **gatecrasher** *NOUN*

gateway *NOUN* **gateways**
❶ an opening containing a gate ❷ a way to reach something • *the gateway to success*

gather *VERB* **gathers, gathering, gathered**
❶ to come together • *A crowd soon gathered round.* ❷ to bring people or things together • *He gathered up all his papers.* ❸ to collect something; to obtain something gradually • *We've been gathering information.* ❹ to collect crops as harvest; to pick plants or fruit • *Gather the corn when it is ripe.* • *She was out gathering mushrooms.* ❺ to understand or learn something • *I gather you've been on holiday.* ❻ to pull cloth into folds by running a thread through it
➤ **gather speed** to move gradually faster

gathering *NOUN* **gatherings**
an assembly or meeting of people; a party

gaudy *ADJECTIVE*
very showy and bright • *gaudy jewellery*
➤ **gaudily** *ADVERB*

gauge (say gayj) *NOUN* **gauges**
❶ a measuring instrument • *a fuel gauge* ❷ a standard measurement ❸ the distance between the rails on a railway track

gauge *VERB* **gauges, gauging, gauged**
❶ to measure something ❷ to estimate or form a judgement about something • *It was difficult to gauge the mood of the audience.*

gaunt *ADJECTIVE*
lean and haggard • *His face was gaunt and unshaven.*

gauntlet *NOUN* **gauntlets**
a glove with a wide cuff covering the wrist
➤ **run the gauntlet** to have to face criticism or hostility from a lot of people
➤ **throw down the gauntlet** to offer a challenge
WORD ORIGIN 'Running the gauntlet' was once a former military and naval punishment in which the victim was made to pass between two rows of men who struck him as he passed

gauze *NOUN*
❶ thin transparent woven material ❷ fine wire mesh
➤ **gauzy** *ADJECTIVE*

gay *ADJECTIVE*
❶ homosexual ❷ cheerful ❸ brightly coloured
➤ **gayness** *NOUN*

USAGE

Nowadays the most common meaning of *gay* is 'homosexual'. The other two meanings are older and are becoming less and less common in everyday use. *Gayness* is the noun from meaning 1 of *gay*. The noun that relates to the other two meanings is **gaiety**.

gaze *VERB* **gazes, gazing, gazed**
to look at something steadily for a long time
• *She gazed at him in amazement.*

gaze *NOUN* **gazes**
a long steady look

gazelle *NOUN* **gazelles** or **gazelle**
a small antelope, usually fawn and white, from Africa or Asia

gazette *NOUN* **gazettes**
❶ a newspaper ❷ an official journal of an organization **WORD ORIGIN** from Italian *gazetta de la novità* = a halfpenny worth of news (a *gazetta* was a Venetian coin of small value)

gazetteer (say gaz-it-**eer**) *NOUN* **gazetteers**
a dictionary or list of place names
WORD ORIGIN originally = journalist; the first list of this kind was called *The Gazetteer's or Newsman's Interpreter*, and was intended to help journalists

GCSE *ABBREVIATION*
(*British*) General Certificate of Secondary Education

gear *NOUN* **gears**
❶ a set of toothed wheels in a motor vehicle that turn power from the engine into movement of the wheels ❷ equipment or apparatus • *camping gear* ❸ (*informal*) clothing

gear *VERB* **gears, gearing, geared**
to gear one thing to another is to make it match or be suitable for the other thing
• *Health care should be geared to people's needs, not to whether they can pay.*
➤ **be geared up** to be fully prepared or equipped for something • *We were all geared up to play cricket, but then it rained.*

gearbox *NOUN* **gearboxes**
a set of gears in a casing

Geiger counter (say **gy**-ger) *NOUN* **Geiger counters**
an instrument that detects and measures radioactivity **WORD ORIGIN** named after a German scientist, H. W. *Geiger*

gel *NOUN* **gels**
a jelly-like substance, especially one used to give a style to hair

gelatin, gelatine *NOUN*
a clear jelly-like substance made by boiling animal tissue and used to make jellies and other foods and in photographic film
➤ **gelatinous** (say jil-**at**-in-us) *ADJECTIVE*

geld *VERB* **gelds, gelding, gelded**
to castrate a male animal

gelding *NOUN* **geldings**
a castrated horse or other male animal

gelignite (say **jel**-ig-nyt) *NOUN*
a kind of explosive

gem *NOUN* **gems**
❶ a precious stone ❷ an excellent person or thing

gender *NOUN* **genders**
❶ the group in which a noun is classed in the grammar of some languages, e.g. masculine, feminine or neuter ❷ a person's sex • *Jobs should be open to all, regardless of race or gender.*

gene (say jeen) *NOUN* **genes**
the part of a living cell that controls which characteristics (such as the colour of hair or eyes) are inherited from parents

genealogy (say jeen-ee-**al**-o-jee) *NOUN* **genealogies**
❶ a list or diagram showing how people are descended from an ancestor ❷ the study of family history and ancestors

genera (say **jen**-e-ra) *PLURAL NOUN*
plural of **genus**

a b c d e f g h i j k l m n o p q r s t u v w x y z

general ADJECTIVE
❶ to do with or involving most people or things • *This drug is now in general use.*
❷ not detailed; broad • *I've got the general idea.* ❸ chief or head • *the general manager*
➤ **in general** in most cases; usually

general NOUN **generals**
a senior army officer

general election NOUN **general elections**
an election of Members of Parliament for the whole country

generalize (also **generalise**) VERB
generalizes, generalizing, generalized
to make a statement that is true in most cases
➤ **generalization** NOUN

generally ADVERB
❶ by or to most people • *He is generally considered to be the greatest player ever.*
❷ usually • *She generally cycles to school.*
❸ in a general sense; without regard to details • *I was speaking generally.*

general practitioner NOUN **general practitioners**
a doctor who treats all kinds of diseases and is the first doctor that people see when they are ill

generate VERB **generates, generating, generated**
to produce or create something • *There are various ways of generating electricity.*

generation NOUN **generations**
❶ generating something ❷ a single stage in a family • *Three generations were included: children, parents and grandparents.* ❸ all the people born at about the same time • *our parents' generation*

generator NOUN **generators**
a machine for converting mechanical energy into electricity

generic (say jin-**e**-rik) ADJECTIVE
belonging to a whole class, group or genus

generosity NOUN
the quality of being generous • *He was known for his generosity.*

generous ADJECTIVE
❶ willing to give things or share them
❷ given freely; larger than usual • *a generous helping*
➤ **generously** ADVERB

genesis NOUN
the beginning or origin of something

genetic (say jin-**et**-ik) ADJECTIVE
❶ to do with genes ❷ to do with characteristics inherited from parents or ancestors
➤ **genetically** ADVERB

genetics NOUN
the study of genes and genetic behaviour

genial (say **jee**-nee-al) ADJECTIVE
friendly and cheerful • *a genial manner*
➤ **genially** ADVERB
➤ **geniality** (say jee-nee-**al**-it-ee) NOUN

genie (say **jee**-nee) NOUN **genii** (say **jee**-nee-y)
in Arabian tales, a spirit with strange powers, especially one who can grant wishes

genital (say **jen**-it-al) ADJECTIVE
to do with the reproductive organs of a person or animal

genitals (say **jen**-it-alz) PLURAL NOUN
external reproductive organs

genius NOUN **geniuses**
❶ an unusually clever person; a person with very great creativity or natural ability
❷ unusual cleverness; very great creativity or natural ability • *He has a real genius for music.*

genocide (say **jen**-o-syd) NOUN
the deliberate killing of large numbers of people from a particular nation or ethnic group

genome (say **jen**-ohm) NOUN **genomes**
(*in science*) the complete set of genes in one cell of a living thing • *the human genome*

genre (say zhahnr) NOUN **genres**
a particular kind or style of art or literature, e.g. epic, romance or western

gent NOUN **gents** (*informal*)
a gentleman; a man

genteel (say jen-**teel**) ADJECTIVE
trying to seem polite and refined
➤ **gentility** (say jen-**til**-it-ee) NOUN

gentile NOUN **gentiles**
a person who is not Jewish

gentle ADJECTIVE
❶ mild or kind; not rough ❷ not harsh or severe • *a gentle breeze*
➤ **gentleness** NOUN

gentleman NOUN **gentlemen**
❶ a well-mannered or honourable man ❷ a man of good social position ❸ (*in polite use*) a man

gently *ADVERB*
in a gentle way • *She kissed him gently on the forehead.* • *'We have to go now,' he said gently.*

gentry *PLURAL NOUN (old use)*
upper-class people

genuine *ADJECTIVE*
❶ real; not faked or pretending ❷ sincere and honest
➤ **genuinely** *ADVERB*
➤ **genuineness** *NOUN*
WORD ORIGIN from Latin *genu* = knee (because a father would take a baby onto his knee to show that he accepted it as his)

genus (say **jee**-nus) *NOUN* **genera** (say **jen**-er-a)
a group of similar animals or plants • *Lions and tigers belong to the same genus.*

geo- *PREFIX*
earth **WORD ORIGIN** from Greek *ge* = earth

geographical *ADJECTIVE*
to do with geography or where something is • *The Roman empire covered a vast geographical area.*
➤ **geographically** *ADVERB*

geography (say jee-**og**-ra-fee) *NOUN*
the study of the earth's surface and of its climate, peoples and products
➤ **geographer** *NOUN*

geology (say jee-**ol**-o-jee) *NOUN*
the study of the structure of the earth's crust and its layers
➤ **geological** *ADJECTIVE*
➤ **geologically** *ADVERB*
➤ **geologist** *NOUN*

geometric, geometrical *ADJECTIVE*
consisting of regular shapes and lines • *a geometric pattern*

geometry (say jee-**om**-it-ree) *NOUN*
the study of lines, angles, surfaces and solids in mathematics

Georgian *ADJECTIVE*
belonging to the time of the British kings George I-IV (1714-1830) or George V-VI (1910-52)

geranium *NOUN* **geraniums**
a garden plant with red, pink or white flowers

gerbil (say **jer**-bil) *NOUN* **gerbils**
a small brown rodent with long hind legs, often kept as a pet

geriatric (say je-ree-**at**-rik) *ADJECTIVE*
to do with the care of old people and their health

germ *NOUN* **germs**
❶ a micro-organism, especially one that can cause disease ❷ a tiny living structure from which a plant or animal may develop ❸ part of the seed of a cereal plant ❹ a first stage from which something might develop • *Rick had the germ of an idea.*

Germanic *NOUN*
❶ a group of languages spoken in northern Europe and Scandinavia ❷ an unrecorded language believed to be the ancestor of this group

German measles *NOUN*
rubella

German shepherd dog *NOUN* **German shepherd dogs**
a large strong dog, often used by the police

germicide *NOUN* **germicides**
a substance that kills germs

germinate *VERB* **germinates, germinating, germinated**
when a seed germinates, it begins to develop and roots and shoots grow from it
➤ **germination** *NOUN*

gerund (say **je**-rund) *NOUN* **gerunds**
(*in grammar*) a form of a verb (in English ending in *-ing*) that functions as a noun, e.g. *telling* in *do you mind my telling her?*

gestation (say jes-**tay**-shun) *NOUN*
the process of carrying a foetus in the womb between conception and birth; the time this takes

gesticulate (say jes-**tik**-yoo-layt) *VERB* **gesticulates, gesticulating, gesticulated**
to make movements with your hands and arms in order to express something • *The farmer began gesticulating wildly and shouting.*
➤ **gesticulation** *NOUN*

gesture (say **jes**-cher) *NOUN* **gestures**
❶ a movement that expresses what a person feels ❷ an action that shows goodwill • *It would be a nice gesture to send her some flowers.*

gesture *VERB* **gestures, gesturing, gestured**
to tell a person something by making a gesture • *She gestured me to be quiet.*

get *VERB* **gets, getting, got**
❶ to obtain or receive something • *She*

got first prize. ❷ to become • *Don't get angry!* ❸ to reach a place • *We got there by midnight.* ❹ to put or move something into position • *I can't get my shoe on.* ❺ to make or prepare something • *Will you get the tea?* ❻ to persuade or order someone to do something • *How did you get her to say yes?* ❼ to catch or suffer from an illness ❽ (*informal*) to understand something • *I don't get that joke.*
➤ **get away with something** ❶ to escape with something ❷ to avoid being punished for what you have done
➤ **get by** (*informal*) to manage
➤ **get on** ❶ to make progress ❷ to be friendly with someone
➤ **get out of something** to avoid having to do something
➤ **get over something** to recover from an illness or shock
➤ **get up** ❶ to stand up ❷ to get out of bed in the morning
➤ **get your own back** (*informal*) to have your revenge
➤ **have got to** must • *We have got to go now.*

getaway NOUN getaways
an escape after committing a crime • *They made their getaway in a stolen car.*

geyser (say **gee**-zer or **gy**-zer) NOUN geysers
❶ a natural spring that shoots up columns of hot water ❷ a kind of water heater

ghastly ADJECTIVE
❶ very unpleasant or bad • *It's all been a ghastly mistake.* ❷ looking pale and ill

gherkin (say **ger**-kin) NOUN gherkins
a small cucumber used for pickling

ghetto (say **get**-oh) NOUN ghettos
an area of a city, often a slum area, where a group of people live who are treated unfairly in comparison with others

ghost NOUN ghosts
the spirit of a dead person that a living person believes they can see or hear

> **SPELLING**
> There is a silent h after the g in ghost.

ghostly ADJECTIVE
looking or sounding like a ghost • *ghostly shadows*

ghoul (say gool) NOUN ghouls
an evil spirit in stories that eats dead bodies
WORD ORIGIN from Arabic *gul* = a demon that eats dead bodies

ghoulish (say **gool**-ish) ADJECTIVE
enjoying watching ot thinking about things to do with death, murder and suffering
➤ **ghoulishly** ADVERB

giant NOUN giants
❶ (in myths or fairy tales) a creature like a huge man ❷ a man, animal or plant that is much larger than the usual size
giant ADJECTIVE
much larger than the usual size

gibber (say **jib**-er) VERB gibbers, gibbering, gibbered
to speak very quickly without making sense, especially when shocked or terrified

gibberish (say **jib**-er-ish) NOUN
meaningless speech; nonsense • *You were talking gibberish in your sleep.*

gibbet (say **jib**-it) NOUN gibbets
❶ a gallows ❷ an upright post with an arm from which a criminal's body was hung after execution, as a warning to others

gibbon NOUN gibbons
a small ape from south-east Asia. Gibbons have very long arms to help them swing through the trees where they live

giblets (say **jib**-lits) PLURAL NOUN
the parts of the inside of a bird, such as the heart, liver, etc., that are taken out before it is cooked

giddy ADJECTIVE
❶ feeling that everything is spinning round and that you might fall ❷ causing this feeling • *We looked down from the giddy height of the cliff.*
➤ **giddily** ADVERB
➤ **giddiness** NOUN

gift NOUN gifts
❶ a present ❷ a natural talent • *She has a gift for music.*

gifted ADJECTIVE
having a special talent or ability • *a gifted songwriter*

gig NOUN gigs (*informal*)
a live performance by a musician, comedian, etc.

gigabyte (say **gi**-ga-byt) NOUN gigabytes
(*in computing*) a unit of information equal to one thousand million bytes or (more precisely) 230 bytes

gigantic (say jy-**gan**-tik) ADJECTIVE
extremely large; huge

giggle *VERB* giggles, giggling, giggled
to laugh in a silly way

giggle *NOUN* giggles
❶ a silly laugh ❷ (*informal*) something amusing; a bit of fun

gild *VERB* gilds, gilding, gilded
to cover something with a thin layer of gold or gold paint

gills *PLURAL NOUN*
the part of the body through which fish and certain other water animals breathe

gilt *NOUN*
a thin covering of gold or gold paint

gilt *ADJECTIVE*
gilded; gold-coloured

gimlet *NOUN* gimlets
a small tool with a screw-like tip for boring holes

gimmick *NOUN* gimmicks
something unusual or silly done or used just to attract people's attention

gin *NOUN* gins
❶ a clear alcoholic drink flavoured with juniper berries ❷ a machine for separating the fibres of the cotton plant from its seeds

ginger *NOUN*
❶ the hot-tasting root of a tropical plant or a flavouring made from this root, used especially in drinks and Eastern cooking ❷ a reddish-yellow colour

ginger *ADJECTIVE*
reddish-yellow • *ginger hair*

ginger *VERB* gingers, gingering, gingered
to make something more lively or exciting
• *This will ginger things up!*

gingerbread *NOUN*
a ginger-flavoured cake or biscuit

gingerly *ADVERB*
in a cautious or careful way • *He gingerly tiptoed towards the door.*

gipsy *NOUN* gipsies
a different spelling of **gypsy**

giraffe *NOUN* giraffe or giraffes
an African animal with long legs and a very long neck, the world's tallest mammal

gird (say gerd) *VERB* girds, girding, girded
❶ to fasten something with a belt or band
• *He girded on his sword.* ❷ to prepare for an effort • *It is time to gird yourself for action.*

girder *NOUN* girders
a metal beam supporting part of a building or a bridge

girdle *NOUN* girdles
❶ a belt or cord worn round the waist ❷ a woman's elastic corset covering from the waist to the thigh

girl *NOUN* girls
❶ a female child ❷ a young woman

girlfriend *NOUN* girlfriends
a person's regular female friend or lover

girlhood *NOUN*
the time when a woman was a girl • *She used to tell us stories of her girlhood.*

girlish *ADJECTIVE*
like a girl or suitable for a girl • *a girlish giggle*

giro (say **jy**-roh) *NOUN*
a system of sending money directly from one bank account or post office account to another

girth *NOUN* girths
❶ the measurement round something, especially a person's waist • *a man of enormous girth* ❷ a band passing under a horse's body to hold the saddle in place

gist (say jist) *NOUN*
the essential points or general sense of what someone says

give *VERB* gives, giving, gave, given
❶ to let someone have something ❷ to make or do something • *He gave a little laugh.*
❸ to present or perform something • *They gave a concert to raise money.* ❹ be flexible or springy; to bend or collapse when pressed
• *The branch began to give under my weight.*
➤ **giver** *NOUN*
➤ **give in** to accept that you have been defeated
➤ **give up** ❶ to stop trying ❷ to end a habit
➤ **give something up** to stop doing or using something

given *ADJECTIVE*
named or stated in advance • *Work out how much you can do in a given time.*

gizzard *NOUN* gizzards
a bird's second stomach, in which food is ground up

glacé (say **glas**-ay) *ADJECTIVE*
iced with sugar; crystallized

glacial (say **glay**-shal) *ADJECTIVE*
❶ made of ice or formed by glaciers • *a*

a b c d e f g h i j k l m n o p q r s t u v w x y z

glacial landscape ❷ icy or very cold • *glacial winds*

glaciation (say glay-see-**ay**-shun) *NOUN*
the process or state of being covered with glaciers or ice sheets
➤ **glaciated** *ADJECTIVE*

glacier (say **glas**-ee-er) *NOUN* **glaciers**
a mass of ice that moves very slowly down a mountain valley

glad *ADJECTIVE*
❶ pleased or happy; expressing joy ❷ giving pleasure or happiness • *We've heard the glad news.* ❸ to be glad of something is to be grateful for it or pleased with it
➤ **gladness** *NOUN*

gladden *VERB* **gladdens, gladdening, gladdened**
to make a person glad

glade *NOUN* **glades**
an open space in a forest

gladiator (say **glad**-ee-ay-ter) *NOUN* **gladiators**
a man trained to fight for public entertainment in ancient Rome
➤ **gladiatorial** (say glad-ee-at-**or**-ee-al) *ADJECTIVE*

gladly *ADVERB*
with pleasure or willingly • *I gladly accept your invitation.*

glamorize (also **glamorise**) *VERB* **glamorizes, glamorizing, glamorized**
to make something seem glamorous or romantic

glamorous *ADJECTIVE*
excitingly attractive • *glamorous movie stars*

glamour *NOUN*
exciting attractiveness or romantic charm • *the glamour of Hollywood*

glance *VERB* **glances, glancing, glanced**
❶ to look at something briefly ❷ to strike something at an angle and slide off it • *The ball glanced off his bat.*

glance *NOUN* **glances**
a quick look • *The sisters exchanged glances.*

gland *NOUN* **glands**
an organ of the body that separates substances from the blood so that they can be used or passed out of the body
➤ **glandular** *ADJECTIVE*

glare *VERB* **glares, glaring, glared**
❶ to stare angrily or fiercely at someone ❷ to shine with a bright or dazzling light

glare *NOUN* **glares**
❶ an angry stare ❷ a strong light

glaring *ADJECTIVE*
very obvious • *a glaring error*

glass *NOUN* **glasses**
❶ a hard brittle substance that is usually transparent ❷ a container made of glass for drinking from ❸ (*old use*) a mirror

glasses *PLURAL NOUN*
a pair of lenses in a frame, worn over the eyes to help improve eyesight

glassy *ADJECTIVE*
❶ like glass; smooth and shiny • *a glassy lake* ❷ dull; without liveliness or expression • *He gave a glassy stare.*

glaze *VERB* **glazes, glazing, glazed**
❶ to fit a window or building with glass ❷ to give a shiny surface to pottery or food ❸ your eyes glaze when they lose expression or interest

glaze *NOUN* **glazes**
a shiny surface or coating, especially on pottery or food

glazier (say **glay**-zee-er) *NOUN* **glaziers**
a person whose job is to fit glass in windows

gleam *NOUN* **gleams**
❶ a beam of soft light, especially one that comes and goes ❷ a small amount of hope, humour, etc.

gleam *VERB* **gleams, gleaming, gleamed**
to shine brightly, especially after cleaning or polishing

glean *VERB* **gleans, gleaning, gleaned**
❶ to gather information bit by bit • *I gleaned as much information as I could from the Internet.* ❷ to pick up grain left by harvesters

glee *NOUN*
great delight • *He rubbed his hands in glee.*
➤ **gleeful** *ADJECTIVE*
➤ **gleefully** *ADVERB*

glen *NOUN* **glens**
a narrow valley, especially in Scotland

glib *ADJECTIVE*
speaking or writing fluently but not sincerely or thoughtfully
➤ **glibly** *ADVERB*

glide *VERB* **glides, gliding, glided**
❶ to move along smoothly • *The dancers glided across the floor.* ❷ to fly without using an engine ❸ birds glide when they fly without

beating their wings
➤ **glide** NOUN

glider NOUN gliders
an aircraft without an engine that flies by
floating on warm air currents called thermals

glimmer NOUN glimmers
❶ a faint light that flickers ❷ a small sign or
trace of something • *a glimmer of hope*

glimmer VERB glimmers, glimmering,
glimmered
to shine with a faint, flickering light • *The
candle glimmered in the corner.*

glimpse NOUN glimpses
a brief view of something • *He caught a
glimpse of her in the crowd.*

glimpse VERB glimpses, glimpsing, glimpsed
to see something briefly

glint NOUN glints
a very brief flash of light

glint VERB glints, glinting, glinted
to shine with small flashes of light • *His sword
glinted in the moonlight.*

glisten (say **glis**-en) VERB glistens, glistening,
glistened
to shine like something wet or oily • *Her eyes
glistened with tears.*

glitter VERB glitters, glittering, glittered
to shine with tiny flashes of light; to sparkle
• *The river glittered in the sunlight.*

glitter NOUN
tiny sparkling pieces used for decoration

gloaming NOUN
(*Scottish*) the evening twilight

gloat VERB gloats, gloating, gloated
to be pleased in an unkind way that you have
succeeded or that someone else has failed or
had problems

global ADJECTIVE
❶ to do with the whole world; worldwide
❷ to do with the whole of a system
➤ **globally** ADVERB

globalization (also **globalisation**) NOUN
the fact that different economies and
cultures around the world are becoming
connected and similar to each other because
of improved communication and the
influence of very large companies

global warming NOUN
the increase in the temperature of the earth's
atmosphere, caused by the greenhouse effect

globe NOUN globes
❶ something shaped like a ball, especially one
with a map of the whole world on it ❷ the
world • *She has travelled all over the globe.*
❸ a hollow round glass object

globular (say **glob**-yoo-ler) ADJECTIVE
shaped like a globe

globule (say **glob**-yool) NOUN globules
a small rounded drop

gloom NOUN
❶ darkness • *He peered into the gathering
gloom.* ❷ sadness or despair

gloomy ADJECTIVE gloomier, gloomiest
❶ almost dark; not well lit • *a gloomy
corridor* ❷ depressed or depressing
➤ **gloomily** ADVERB
➤ **gloominess** NOUN

glorify VERB glorifies, glorifying, glorified
❶ to give great praise or great honour to
someone ❷ to make a thing seem more
splendid or attractive than it really is • *It is a
film that glorifies war.*

glorious ADJECTIVE
splendid or magnificent
➤ **gloriously** ADVERB

glory NOUN glories
❶ fame and honour you get for achieving
something • *The team was welcomed home
in a blaze of glory.* ❷ praise and worship of
God ❸ beauty or magnificence

glory VERB glories, glorying, gloried
to rejoice over an achievement and take great
pride in it • *They gloried in victory.*

gloss NOUN glosses
the shine on a smooth surface

gloss VERB glosses, glossing, glossed
➤ **gloss over something** to mention a fault
or mistake only briefly to make it seem less
serious than it really is

glossary NOUN glossaries
a list of difficult words with their meanings
explained • *There is a glossary at the back of
the book.*

gloss paint NOUN gloss paints
a paint with a glossy finish

glossy ADJECTIVE glossier, glossiest
smooth and shiny • *glossy hair*

glove NOUN gloves
a covering for the hand, usually with separate
divisions for each finger and thumb
➤ **gloved** ADJECTIVE

a b c d e f g h i j k l m n o p q r s t u v w x y z

glow *NOUN*
❶ brightness and warmth without flames ❷ a warm or cheerful feeling • *We felt a glow of pride.*

glow *VERB* glows, glowing, glowed
to shine with a soft, warm light • *Her watch glows in the dark.*

glower (rhymes with flower) *VERB* glowers, glowering, glowered
to stare with an angry look; to scowl

glowing *ADJECTIVE*
very enthusiastic or favourable • *a glowing report*

glow-worm *NOUN* glow-worms
a kind of beetle whose tail gives out a green light

glucose *NOUN*
a form of sugar found in fruit juice and honey

glue *NOUN* glues
a sticky substance used for joining things together
➤ **gluey** *ADJECTIVE*

glue *VERB* glues, gluing, glued
❶ to stick something with glue ❷ to be glued to something is to pay close attention to it for a long period • *Our eyes were glued to the screen all evening.*

glum *ADJECTIVE*
miserable or depressed • *Hey, don't look so glum.*
➤ **glumly** *ADVERB*

glut *NOUN* gluts
more of something than is needed • *a glut of action films in cinemas*

gluten (say **gloo**-ten) *NOUN*
a sticky protein substance in flour

glutinous (say **gloo**-tin-us) *ADJECTIVE*
glue-like or sticky

glutton *NOUN* gluttons
a person who eats too much
➤ **gluttonous** *ADJECTIVE*
➤ **a glutton for punishment** a person who seems to enjoy doing something difficult or unpleasant

gluttony *NOUN*
eating too much

glycerine (say **glis**-er-een) *NOUN*
a thick sweet colourless liquid used in ointments and medicines and in explosives

gm *ABBREVIATION*
gram

GMT *ABBREVIATION*
Greenwich Mean Time

gnarled (say narld) *ADJECTIVE*
twisted and knobbly, like an old tree • *the old man's gnarled hands*

SPELLING
There is a silent **g** in **gnarled**, **gnash**, **gnat**, **gnaw**, **gnome** and **gnu**.

gnash (say nash) *VERB* gnashes, gnashing, gnashed
to grind your teeth together, especially because you are angry

gnat (say nat) *NOUN* gnats
a tiny fly that bites

gnaw (say naw) *VERB* gnaws, gnawing, gnawed
to keep on biting something hard so that it wears away

gnome (say nohm) *NOUN* gnomes
a kind of dwarf in fairy tales, usually living underground

gnu (say noo) *NOUN* gnu or gnus
a large ox-like antelope

go *VERB* goes, going, went, gone
This word has many uses, including
❶ to move or travel from one place to another • *Where are you going?* ❷ to leave • *I must go.* ❸ to disappear or be used up • *Has your headache gone yet?* • *Most of their money went on rent.* ❹ to lead from one place to another • *This road goes to the coast.* ❺ to become • *The milk has gone sour.* ❻ to make a sound • *The gun went bang.* ❼ to work properly • *This clock doesn't go.* ❽ to belong in some place or position • *Plates go on that shelf.* ❾ to be sold • *The house went very cheaply.*
➤ **go off** ❶ to explode ❷ to become stale
➤ **go off something** to stop liking something
➤ **go on** to continue or happen
➤ **go out** to stop burning or shining
➤ **go through** to experience something unpleasant or difficult

go *NOUN* goes
❶ a turn or try • *May I have a go?*
❷ (*informal*) energy or liveliness • *She is full of go.*
➤ **make a go of something** to be successful at something
➤ **on the go** active; always working or moving

goad *NOUN* goads
a stick with a pointed end for prodding cattle to move onwards

goad VERB goads, goading, goaded
to stir someone into action by being annoying
• *He goaded me into fighting.*

go-ahead NOUN
permission to do something • *We have been given the go-ahead to paint a mural in the gym.*

goal NOUN goals
❶ the area between two posts where a ball must go to score a point in football, hockey, etc. ❷ a successful shot at goal, scoring a point ❸ something that you are trying to reach or achieve

goalkeeper NOUN goalkeepers
the player in football or hockey who stands in the goal and tries to keep the ball out

goat NOUN goats
a mammal with horns and a beard, closely related to the sheep. Domestic goats are kept for their milk.

gobble VERB gobbles, gobbling, gobbled
to eat something quickly and greedily • *We soon gobbled up all the sandwiches.*

gobbledegook NOUN (informal)
pompous and technical language that is difficult to understand, especially in official documents

go-between NOUN go-betweens
a person who acts as a messenger or negotiator between others

goblet NOUN goblets
a drinking glass with a long stem and a base

goblin NOUN goblins
a mischievous ugly elf in stories

God NOUN
the creator of the universe in many religions

god NOUN gods
a male being that is worshipped • *Mars was a Roman god.*

godchild NOUN godchildren
a child that a godparent promises to see brought up as a Christian
➤ **god-daughter** NOUN
➤ **godson** NOUN

goddess NOUN goddesses
a female being that is worshipped

SPELLING
There is a double **d** and double **s** in **goddess**.

godly ADJECTIVE godlier, godliest
sincerely religious
➤ **godliness** NOUN

godparent NOUN godparents
a person at a child's christening who promises to see that it is brought up as a Christian
➤ **godfather** NOUN
➤ **godmother** NOUN

godsend NOUN godsends
a piece of unexpected good luck

gogga NOUN goggas (informal)
(*S. African*) an insect or any small flying or crawling creature

goggle VERB goggles, goggling, goggled
to stare with wide-open eyes

goggles PLURAL NOUN
large glasses that you wear to protect your eyes from wind, water, dust, etc.

going
present participle of **go**
➤ **be going to do something** to be ready or likely to do it

going NOUN
➤ **good going** quick progress • *It was good going to get home before dark.*

go-kart NOUN go-karts
a kind of small lightweight racing car

gold NOUN golds
❶ a precious yellow metal ❷ a deep yellow colour ❸ a gold medal, awarded as first prize

gold ADJECTIVE
❶ made of gold ❷ deep yellow in colour

golden ADJECTIVE
❶ made of gold ❷ coloured like gold ❸ precious or excellent • *It was a golden opportunity.*

golden wedding NOUN golden weddings
a couple's fiftieth wedding anniversary

goldfinch NOUN goldfinches
a bird with yellow feathers in its wings

goldfish NOUN goldfish
a small red or orange fish, often kept as a pet

gold leaf NOUN
gold that has been beaten into a very thin sheet

goldsmith NOUN goldsmiths
a person who makes things in gold

golf NOUN
an outdoor game played by hitting a small white ball with a club into a series of holes on

a b c d e f g h i j k l m n o p q r s t u v w x y z

a specially prepared ground (a **golf course**) and taking as few strokes as possible
➤ **golfing** NOUN

golfer NOUN golfers
a person who plays golf

gondola (say **gond**-ol-a) NOUN gondolas
a boat with high pointed ends used on the canals in Venice

gondolier NOUN gondoliers
the person who moves a gondola along with a pole

gone
past participle of **go**

gone ADJECTIVE
not present any longer; completely used or finished • She stood at the gate for a moment and then she was gone. • The milk's all gone.

gong NOUN gongs
a large metal disc that makes an echoing sound when it is hit

good ADJECTIVE **better, best**
❶ having the right qualities; of the kind that people like • a good book ❷ kind • It was good of you to help us. ❸ well-behaved • Be a good boy. ❹ skilled or talented • a good pianist ❺ healthy; giving benefit • Exercise is good for you. ❻ thorough • Give it a good clean. ❼ large; considerable • It's a good distance from the shops.

good NOUN
❶ something good • They tried to do good to others. ❷ benefit or advantage • It's for your own good.
➤ **for good** for ever
➤ **no good** useless

> **USAGE**
> In standard English, **good** cannot be used as an adverb. You can say She's a good player but not She played good. The adverb that goes with **good** is well.

goodbye EXCLAMATION
a word used when you leave someone or at the end of a phone call

Good Friday NOUN
the Friday before Easter, when Christians commemorate the Crucifixion of Christ

good-looking ADJECTIVE
attractive or handsome

goodness NOUN
❶ being good ❷ the good part of something

goods PLURAL NOUN
❶ things that are bought and sold ❷ things that are carried on trains or lorries

goodwill NOUN
a kindly or helpful feeling towards another person

goody NOUN goodies (informal)
❶ something good or attractive, especially to eat ❷ a good person, especially one of the heroes in a story

gooey ADJECTIVE
sticky or slimy

goose NOUN geese
a long-necked water bird with webbed feet, larger than a duck

gooseberry NOUN gooseberries
❶ a small green fruit that grows on a prickly bush ❷ (informal) an unwanted extra person when two people want to be alone together

goose pimples, goosebumps PLURAL NOUN
skin that has turned rough with small bumps on it because a person is cold or afraid
WORD ORIGIN because it looks like the skin of a plucked goose

gore VERB gores, goring, gored
to wound a person or animal by piercing them with a horn or tusk • He was gored to death by a bull.

gore NOUN
thickened blood from a cut or wound

gorge NOUN gorges
a narrow valley with steep sides

gorge VERB gorges, gorging, gorged
to eat something greedily; to stuff yourself with food • We gorged ourselves on cakes.

gorgeous ADJECTIVE
very attractive or beautiful
➤ **gorgeously** ADVERB

gorilla NOUN gorillas
a large powerful African ape, the largest of all the apes

> **SPELLING**
> Take care not to confuse with **guerrilla**, which is a person in an unofficial army.

gorse NOUN
a prickly bush with small yellow flowers

gory ADJECTIVE
❶ involving a lot of violence and bloodshed • a gory film ❷ covered with blood

gosh *EXCLAMATION*
an exclamation of surprise

gosling *NOUN* **goslings**
a young goose

gospel *NOUN*
❶ the teachings of Jesus Christ ❷ something you can safely believe to be true • *You can take what she says as gospel.*
➤ **the Gospels** the first four books of the New Testament, telling of the life and teachings of Jesus Christ
(WORD ORIGIN) from Old English *god* = good + *spel* = news

gospel music *NOUN*
a style of black American religious singing

gossamer *NOUN*
❶ fine cobwebs made by small spiders ❷ any fine delicate material **(WORD ORIGIN)** from *goose summer*, a period of fine weather in the autumn (when geese were eaten), when gossamer is very common

gossip *VERB* **gossips, gossiping, gossiped**
to talk a lot about other people

gossip *NOUN* **gossips**
❶ talk, especially rumours, about other people ❷ a person who enjoys gossiping
➤ **gossipy** *ADJECTIVE*
(WORD ORIGIN) from Old English *godsibb* = close friend (literally = god-brother or sister), someone to gossip with

got
past tense of **get**
➤ **have got something** to possess or be carrying something • *Have you got a pen?*
➤ **have got to** must

Gothic *NOUN*
the style of building common in the 12th-16th centuries, with pointed arches and much decorative carving

gouge (say gowj) *VERB* **gouges, gouging, gouged**
to scoop or force something out by pressing • *Glaciers gouged out valleys from the hills.*

goulash (say **goo**-lash) *NOUN*
a Hungarian meat stew seasoned with paprika

gourd (say goord) *NOUN* **gourds**
the rounded hard-skinned fruit of a climbing plant

gourmet (say **goor**-may) *NOUN* **gourmets**
a person who knows about and enjoys good food and drink

gout *NOUN*
a disease that causes painful swelling in the legs and feet
➤ **gouty** *ADJECTIVE*

govern *VERB* **governs, governing, governed**
to be in charge of the public affairs of a country or region

governess *NOUN* **governesses**
a woman employed to teach children in a private household

government *NOUN* **governments**
❶ the group of people who are in charge of the public affairs of a country ❷ the process of governing

governor *NOUN* **governors**
❶ a person who governs a state or a colony etc. ❷ a member of the group of people who manage a school or other institution ❸ the person in charge of a prison

gown *NOUN* **gowns**
❶ a woman's long dress ❷ a loose robe worn by lawyers, members of a university, etc.

GP *ABBREVIATION*
general practitioner (a doctor who treats all kinds of diseases and is the first doctor that people see when they are ill)

grab *VERB* **grabs, grabbing, grabbed**
to take hold of something firmly or suddenly

grace *NOUN*
❶ beauty, especially of movement ❷ dignity or good manners • *At least he had the grace to apologize.* ❸ extra time that is allowed for something • *His teacher gave him a week's grace to finish his project.* ❹ a short prayer of thanks before or after a meal ❺ the title of a duke, duchess or archbishop • *His Grace the Duke of Kent*

grace *VERB* **graces, gracing, graced**
to bring honour or dignity to something • *The mayor himself graced the occasion with his presence.*

graceful *ADJECTIVE*
beautiful and elegant in movement or shape • *a graceful dancer*
➤ **gracefully** *ADVERB*
➤ **gracefulness** *NOUN*

gracious *ADJECTIVE*
generous and pleasant • *I am pleased to accept your gracious offer.*
➤ **graciously** *ADVERB*
➤ **graciousness** *NOUN*

a b c d e f g h i j k l m n o p q r s t u v w x y z

grade *NOUN* **grades**
❶ a mark showing the quality of a student's work ❷ a step in a scale of quality or value or rank

grade *VERB* **grades, grading, graded**
to sort or divide things into grades • *The eggs are then graded by size.*

gradient (say **gray**-dee-ent) *NOUN* **gradients**
a slope or the steepness of a slope

gradual *ADJECTIVE*
happening slowly but steadily

gradually *ADVERB*
slowly but steadily; bit by bit • *The weather gradually improved.*

graduate (say **grad**-yoo-ayt) *VERB* **graduates, graduating, graduated**
❶ to get a university or college degree ❷ to divide something into graded sections; to mark something with units of measurement • *The jug is graduated in millimetres.*

graduate (say **grad**-yoo-at) *NOUN* **graduates**
a person who has a university or college degree

graduation *NOUN*
graduating from a university or college; a ceremony at which degrees are given out • *It was her first job after graduation.*

graffiti *NOUN*
words or drawings scribbled or sprayed on a wall **WORD ORIGIN** Italian, = scratchings

USAGE
Strictly speaking, this word is a plural noun and should be used with a plural verb: *There are graffiti all over the wall.* However, the word is widely used nowadays as if it were a singular noun and most people do not regard this as wrong: *There is graffiti all over the wall.*

graft *NOUN* **grafts**
❶ a shoot from one plant or tree fixed into another to form a new growth ❷ a piece of living tissue transplanted by a surgeon to replace what is diseased or damaged • *a skin graft* ❸ (*British*) (*informal*) hard work

graft *VERB* **grafts, grafting, grafted**
to insert or transplant something as a graft

grain *NOUN* **grains**
❶ a small hard seed or similar particle ❷ cereal plants when they are growing or after being harvested ❸ a very small amount • *There is a grain of truth in the story.* ❹ the

pattern of lines made by the fibres in a piece of wood or paper

grainy *ADJECTIVE*
❶ a grainy photograph or film is not clear because the image looks like it is made up of small spots • *The film is shot in grainy black and white.* ❷ with grains in it • *grainy mustard*

gram *NOUN* **grams**
a unit of mass or weight in the metric system

grammar *NOUN* **grammars**
❶ the rules for putting words together to form sentences ❷ a book about these rules

SPELLING
The 'er' sound at the end of **grammar** is spelt **ar**.

grammar school *NOUN* **grammar schools**
a secondary school for children with high academic ability

grammatical *ADJECTIVE*
following the rules of grammar
➤ **grammatically** *ADVERB*

gramophone *NOUN* **gramophones**
(*old use*) a record player

granary *NOUN* **granaries**
a storehouse for grain

grand *ADJECTIVE*
❶ large and impressive ❷ most important or highest-ranking ❸ (*informal*) very good or pleasant • *You've done a grand job!*
➤ **grandly** *ADVERB*

grandad *NOUN* **grandads** (*informal*)
grandfather

grandchild *NOUN* **grandchildren**
the child of a person's son or daughter
➤ **granddaughter** *NOUN*
➤ **grandson** *NOUN*

grandeur (say **grand**-yer) *NOUN*
impressive beauty; splendour • *the grandeur of the Rocky Mountains*

grandfather *NOUN* **grandfathers**
the father of a person's father or mother

grandfather clock *NOUN* **grandfather clocks**
a clock in a tall wooden case

grandiose (say **grand**-ee-ohss) *ADJECTIVE*
larger or more complicated than is necessary; trying to seem impressive • *a grandiose palace*

grandma NOUN (*informal*)
grandmother

grandmother NOUN grandmothers
the mother of a person's father or mother

grandpa NOUN (*informal*)
grandfather

grandparent NOUN grandparents
a grandfather or grandmother

grand piano NOUN grand pianos
a large piano with the strings fixed
horizontally

grandstand NOUN grandstands
a building with a roof and rows of seats for
spectators at a racecourse or sports ground

grand total NOUN
the sum of other totals

grange NOUN granges
a large country house

granite NOUN
a very hard kind of rock used for building

granny NOUN grannies (*informal*)
grandmother

granny knot NOUN granny knots
a reef knot with the strings crossed the
wrong way and therefore likely to slip

grant VERB grants, granting, granted
❶ to give or allow someone what they have
asked for • *We have decided to grant your
request.* ❷ to admit something or agree that
it is true • *They are a bit odd, I grant you.*
➤ **take for granted** ❶ to assume that
something is true or will happen ❷ to be so
used to having something that you no longer
appreciate it

grant NOUN grants
a sum of money awarded for a special
purpose

Granth (say grunt) NOUN
the sacred scriptures of the Sikhs

granulated sugar NOUN
white sugar in the form of small grains

granule NOUN granules
a small grain; a small hard piece of something

grape NOUN grapes
a small green or purple berry that grows in
bunches on a vine. Grapes are used to make
wine

grapefruit NOUN grapefruit
a large round yellow citrus fruit

grapevine NOUN grapevines
❶ a vine on which grapes grow ❷ a way by
which news spreads unofficially, with people
passing it on from one to another • *I heard on
the grapevine that you are getting married.*

graph NOUN graphs
a diagram showing how two quantities or
variables are related

grapheme NOUN graphemes
a letter or combination of letters which can
be used to represent a sound, for example *f*
and *ph* to represent the same sound at the
beginning of the words *face* and *phase*

graphic ADJECTIVE
❶ to do with drawing or painting • *a graphic
artist* ❷ very detailed and lively • *a graphic
description of the battle*
➤ **graphically** ADVERB

graphics PLURAL NOUN
diagrams, lettering and drawings, especially
pictures that are produced by a computer

graphite NOUN
a soft black form of carbon used for the
lead in pencils, as a lubricant and in nuclear
reactors

graph paper NOUN
paper printed with small squares, used for
drawing graphs

grapnel NOUN grapnels
a heavy metal device with claws for hooking
things

grapple VERB grapples, grappling, grappled
❶ to struggle or wrestle with someone ❷ to
seize or hold something firmly ❸ to try to
deal with a problem • *I've been grappling
with this essay all day.*

grasp VERB grasps, grasping, grasped
❶ to seize something and hold it firmly ❷ to
understand something

grasp NOUN
❶ a person's understanding of something • *a
good grasp of electronics* ❷ a firm hold • *The
sword slipped from his grasp and fell to the
floor.*

grasping ADJECTIVE
greedy for money or possessions

grass NOUN grasses
❶ a plant with green blades and stalks that
are eaten by animals ❷ ground covered with
grass; lawn

a b c d e f g h i j k l m n o p q r s t u v w x y z

grasshopper NOUN **grasshoppers**
a jumping insect that makes a shrill noise

grassland NOUN **grasslands**
a wide area covered in grass with few trees

grass roots PLURAL NOUN
the ordinary people in a political party or other group

grassy ADJECTIVE
covered with grass • *grassy slopes*

grate NOUN **grates**
❶ a metal framework that keeps fuel in a fireplace ❷ a fireplace

grate VERB **grates, grating, grated**
❶ to shred something into small pieces by rubbing it on a rough surface ❷ to make a harsh sound by rubbing on something • *Her nails grated against the window.*
➤ **grate on someone** to have an irritating effect on someone • *His voice really grates on me.*

grateful ADJECTIVE
feeling or showing that you want to thank someone for what they have done for you
➤ **gratefully** ADVERB

grater NOUN **graters**
a device with a jagged surface for grating food

gratify VERB **gratifies, gratifying, gratified**
❶ to give pleasure to someone ❷ to satisfy a feeling or desire • *Please gratify our curiosity.*
➤ **gratifying** ADJECTIVE
➤ **gratification** NOUN

grating NOUN **gratings**
a framework of metal bars placed across an opening

gratis (say **grah**-tiss) ADVERB & ADJECTIVE
free of charge • *You can have the leaflet gratis.* (WORD ORIGIN) Latin, = out of kindness

gratitude NOUN
a feeling of being grateful • *I would like to express my gratitude.*

gratuitous (say gra-**tew**-it-us) ADJECTIVE
done without good reason; uncalled for
➤ **gratuitously** ADVERB

grave NOUN **graves**
the place where a dead person is buried

grave ADJECTIVE
serious or solemn • *She told him he was in grave danger.*

grave accent (rhymes with starve) NOUN
grave accents
a backward-sloping mark over a vowel, as in *vis-à-vis*

gravel NOUN
small stones mixed with coarse sand, used to make paths
➤ **gravelled** ADJECTIVE

gravelly ADJECTIVE
❶ a gravelly voice is deep and rough-sounding ❷ containing many small stones • *gravelly soil*

gravely ADVERB
seriously or solemnly • *He is gravely ill.* • *She nodded gravely.*

gravestone NOUN **gravestones**
a stone monument put over a grave

graveyard NOUN **graveyards**
a burial ground

gravitate VERB **gravitates, gravitating, gravitated**
to move or be attracted towards something

gravitation NOUN
the force of gravity
➤ **gravitational** ADJECTIVE

gravity NOUN
❶ the force that pulls all objects in the universe towards each other ❷ the force that pulls everything towards the earth ❸ the seriousness or importance of something • *I don't think you understand the gravity of the situation.*

gravy NOUN
a hot brown sauce made from meat juices

graze VERB **grazes, grazing, grazed**
❶ animals graze when they feed on growing grass ❷ to scrape your skin slightly • *I grazed my elbow on the wall.* ❸ to touch something lightly in passing

graze NOUN **grazes**
a raw place where skin has been scraped

grease NOUN
❶ any thick oily substance ❷ melted fat

grease VERB **greases, greasing, greased**
to put grease on something

greasy ADJECTIVE **greasier, greasiest**
oily like grease • *greasy hair*

great ADJECTIVE
❶ very large; much above average • *The party was a great success.* ❷ very important or talented • *a great composer* ❸ (*informal*) very good or enjoyable • *It's great to see you again.* ❹ older or younger by one generation

• *great-grandfather*
➤ **greatness** *NOUN*

Great Britain *NOUN*
the island made up of England, Scotland and Wales, with the small islands close to it

USAGE
See the note at **Britain**.

greatly *ADVERB*
very much • *I am greatly relieved to see you.*

grebe (say greeb) *NOUN* **grebes**
a kind of diving bird

greed *NOUN*
being greedy • *Nothing would satisfy his greed for power.*

greedy *ADJECTIVE* **greedier, greediest**
wanting more food, money or other things than you need
➤ **greedily** *ADVERB*

green *NOUN* **greens**
❶ the colour of grass, leaves, etc. ❷ an area of grassy land • *the village green* • *a putting green*

green *ADJECTIVE*
❶ of the colour green ❷ concerned with protecting the natural environment ❸ inexperienced and likely to make mistakes
➤ **greenness** *NOUN*

green belt *NOUN* **green belts**
an area kept as open land round a city

greenery *NOUN*
green leaves or plants

greenfield *ADJECTIVE*
(*British*) a greenfield site is a piece of land that has not yet had buildings on it, though there may be plans to build on it. Compare with **brownfield**.

greenfly *NOUN* **greenfly**
a small green insect that feeds on and damages plants

greengrocer *NOUN* **greengrocers**
(*British*) a person who keeps a shop that sells fruit and vegetables
➤ **greengrocery** *NOUN*

greenhouse *NOUN* **greenhouses**
a glass building where plants are protected from cold

greenhouse effect *NOUN*
the warming up of the earth's surface when heat from the sun is trapped in the earth's atmosphere by gases such as carbon dioxide and methane

greenhouse gas *NOUN* **greenhouse gases**
any of the gases, especially carbon dioxide and methane, that are found in the earth's atmosphere and contribute to the greenhouse effect

greens *PLURAL NOUN*
green vegetables, such as cabbage and spinach

Greenwich Mean Time (say **gren**-ich) *NOUN*
the time on the line of longitude which passes through Greenwich in London, used as a basis for calculating time throughout the world

greet *VERB* **greets, greeting, greeted**
❶ to say hello to someone or to welcome them when they arrive ❷ to receive something in a certain way • *They greeted the song with applause.* ❸ to be the first thing that you notice • *A strange sight greeted our eyes.*

greeting *NOUN* **greetings**
words or actions used to greet someone

greetings *PLURAL NOUN*
good wishes • *a greetings card*

gregarious (say grig-**air**-ee-us) *ADJECTIVE*
❶ fond of company ❷ living in flocks or communities **WORD ORIGIN** from Latin *gregis* = of a herd

grenade (say grin-**ayd**) *NOUN* **grenades**
a small bomb thrown by hand
WORD ORIGIN from old French *pome grenate* = pomegranate (because of the shape of the grenade)

grey *NOUN* **greys**
the colour between black and white, like ashes or dark clouds

grey *ADJECTIVE*
of the colour grey
➤ **greyness** *NOUN*

greyhound *NOUN* **greyhounds**
a slender dog with smooth hair and long legs, used in racing

grid *NOUN* **grids**
❶ a framework or pattern of bars or lines crossing each other ❷ a network of cables or wires for carrying electricity over a large area

griddle *NOUN* **griddles**
a round iron plate for cooking things on

gridiron *NOUN* **gridirons**
a framework of bars for cooking on

a b c d e f g h i j k l m n o p q r s t u v w x y z

A B C D E F G H I J K L M N O P Q R S T U V W X Y Z

grid reference NOUN grid references
a set of numbers that allows you to describe the exact position of something on a map

grief NOUN
deep sorrow, especially because a close relative or friend has died
➤ **come to grief** to suffer a disaster

grievance NOUN grievances
something that people are unhappy or angry about

grieve VERB grieves, grieving, grieved
❶ to feel deep sorrow, especially because a close relative or friend has died ❷ to make a person feel very sad • *It grieves me to have to tell you this.*

grievous (say **gree**-vus) ADJECTIVE
very serious • *a grievous error*
➤ **grievously** ADVERB

griffin NOUN griffins
a creature in fables, with an eagle's head and wings on a lion's body

grill NOUN grills
❶ (*British*) a heated element on a cooker, for sending heat downwards ❷ food cooked under this ❸ a grille

grill VERB grills, grilling, grilled
❶ (*British*) to cook food under a grill ❷ to question someone closely and severely • *The police grilled him for an hour.*

grille NOUN grilles
a metal grating covering a window or similar opening

grim ADJECTIVE grimmer, grimmest
❶ stern or severe • *She looked grim.*
❷ unpleasant or unattractive • *a grim prospect*
➤ **grimly** ADVERB
➤ **grimness** NOUN

grimace (say grim-**ayss** or **grim**-as) NOUN grimaces
a twisted expression on the face made in pain or disgust

grimace VERB grimaces, grimacing, grimaced
to make a grimace

grime NOUN
dirt in a layer on a surface or on the skin

grimy ADJECTIVE
very dirty • *grimy windows*

grin NOUN grins
a broad smile showing your teeth

grin VERB grins, grinning, grinned
to smile broadly showing your teeth

grind VERB grinds, grinding, ground
❶ to crush something into tiny pieces or powder ❷ to sharpen or smooth something by rubbing it on a rough surface ❸ to grind your teeth is to rub the upper and lower teeth harshly together, often as sign of anger or impatience
➤ **grinder** NOUN
➤ **grind to a halt** to stop suddenly with a loud noise

grindstone NOUN grindstones
a thick round rough revolving stone for sharpening or grinding things
➤ **keep your nose to the grindstone** to keep working hard

grip VERB grips, gripping, gripped
❶ to hold something firmly ❷ to hold a person's attention • *The opening chapter really gripped me.*

grip NOUN grips
❶ a firm hold ❷ a handle, especially on a sports racket or bat ❸ a travelling bag ❹ control or power • *The country was in the grip of revolution.*
➤ **get to grips with something** to begin to deal with something successfully

gripe VERB gripes, griping, griped (*informal*)
to grumble or complain

gripe NOUN gripes (*informal*) a complaint

gripping ADJECTIVE
very interesting and exciting in a way that holds your attention • *This book is a gripping read.*

grisly ADJECTIVE grislier, grisliest
causing horror or disgust; gruesome • *a grisly murder*

grist NOUN
corn for grinding
➤ **grist to the mill** experience or knowledge that you can make use of

gristle NOUN
tough rubbery tissue in meat
➤ **gristly** ADJECTIVE

grit NOUN
❶ tiny pieces of stone or sand ❷ courage and determination to do something difficult
➤ **gritty** ADJECTIVE

grit VERB grits, gritting, gritted
to spread a road or path with grit
➤ **grit your teeth** ❶ to clench your teeth when in pain or trouble ❷ to use your

courage or determination to continue in the face of difficulty

grizzle *VERB* **grizzles, grizzling, grizzled**
(*British*) (*informal*) a baby or young child grizzles when it cries or whimpers

grizzled *ADJECTIVE*
streaked with grey hairs • *his grizzled beard*

grizzly *ADJECTIVE*
grey-haired

grizzly bear *NOUN* **grizzly bears**
a large fierce bear of North America

groan *VERB* **groans, groaning, groaned**
❶ to make a long deep sound in pain, distress or disapproval ❷ to creak loudly under a heavy load

groan *NOUN* **groans**
the sound of groaning

grocer *NOUN* **grocers**
a person who keeps a shop that sells food and household goods (**WORD ORIGIN**) originally = wholesaler; from Latin *grossus* = gross (because a wholesaler buys goods *in the gross* = in large quantities)

groceries *PLURAL NOUN*
goods sold by a grocer

grocery *NOUN* **groceries**
a grocer's shop

groggy *ADJECTIVE* **groggier, groggiest**
dizzy and unsteady, especially after illness or injury
➤ **groggily** *ADVERB*

groin *NOUN*
the hollow between your thigh and the trunk of the body

groom *NOUN* **grooms**
❶ a person whose job is to look after horses ❷ a bridegroom

groom *VERB* **grooms, grooming, groomed**
❶ to clean and brush a horse or other animal ❷ to make something, especially hair or a beard, neat and trim ❸ to prepare or train a person for a certain job or position • *Evans is being groomed for the captaincy.*

groove *NOUN* **grooves**
a long narrow furrow or channel cut in the surface of something
➤ **grooved** *ADJECTIVE*

grope *VERB* **gropes, groping, groped**
to feel about for something you cannot see • *He groped around for the light switch.*

gross (say grohss) *ADJECTIVE*
❶ fat and ugly ❷ very obvious or shocking • *gross stupidity* ❸ having bad manners; crude or vulgar ❹ (*informal*) disgusting ❺ total; without anything being deducted • *our gross income*
Compare with **net**.

gross *NOUN* **gross**
twelve dozen (144) of something • *ten gross*

grossly *ADVERB*
to an extremely bad degree • *That is grossly unfair.*

grotesque (say groh-**tesk**) *ADJECTIVE*
very strange and ugly • *The dancers wore grotesque masks.*
➤ **grotesquely** *ADVERB*

grotto *NOUN* **grottoes**
❶ an attractive cave ❷ an artificial cave, especially one that is brightly decorated

ground *NOUN* **grounds**
❶ the solid surface of the earth ❷ a sports field ❸ land of a certain kind • *marshy ground* ❹ the amount of a subject that is dealt with • *The course covers a lot of ground.*

ground *VERB* **grounds, grounding, grounded**
❶ to prevent a plane from flying • *All aircraft are grounded because of the fog.* ❷ to stop a child from going out, as a punishment • *You're grounded for a week!* ❸ an idea or story is grounded on something when it is based on it • *This theory is grounded on reliable evidence.*

ground past tense of **grind**

ground control *NOUN*
the people and machinery that control and monitor an aircraft or spacecraft from the ground

grounding *NOUN*
basic training or instruction

groundless *ADJECTIVE*
having no good reason or cause • *Your fears are groundless.*

grounds *PLURAL NOUN*
❶ the gardens of a large house ❷ small solid pieces that sink to the bottom of a drink • *coffee grounds* ❸ good reasons • *There are grounds for suspicion.*

groundsheet *NOUN* **groundsheets**
(*British*) a piece of waterproof material for spreading on the ground inside a tent

a b c d e f g h i j k l m n o p q r s t u v w x y z

groundsman *NOUN* **groundsmen**
(*chiefly British*) a person whose job is to look after a sports ground

groundwork *NOUN*
work that lays the basis for something

group *NOUN* **groups**
❶ a number of people, animals or things that come together or belong together in some way ❷ a band of musicians

group *VERB* **groups, grouping, grouped**
to put people or things together in a group or groups; to gather into a group • *Scientists group together living things that share certain features.*

grouse *NOUN* **grouse**
a bird with feathered feet, hunted as game

grouse *VERB* **grouses, grousing, groused**
(*informal*)
to grumble or complain

grove *NOUN* **groves**
a small wood or group of trees

grovel *VERB* **grovels, grovelling, grovelled**
❶ to crawl on the ground, especially in a show of fear or humility ❷ to act in an excessively humble way, for example by apologizing a lot

grow *VERB* **grows, growing, grew, grown**
❶ to become bigger or greater ❷ a plant or seed grows when it develops in the ground ❸ to put a plant in the ground or a pot and look after it • *She grows roses.* ❹ to become • *He grew rich.* • *By now it was growing dark.*
➤ **grow on someone** something grows on you when you gradually start to like it • *This music is definitely growing on me.*
➤ **grow up** to become an adult

grower *NOUN* **growers**
a person who grows plants or fruit for sale • *orange growers*

growl *VERB* **growls, growling, growled**
to make a deep angry sound in the throat

growl *NOUN* **growls**
the sound of growling

grown-up *NOUN* **grown-ups**
an adult person
➤ **grown-up** *ADJECTIVE*

growth *NOUN* **growths**
❶ growing or developing ❷ something that has grown ❸ a lump that has grown on or inside a person's body; a tumour

grub *NOUN* **grubs**
❶ a tiny worm-like creature that will become an insect; a larva ❷ (*informal*) food

grub *VERB* **grubs, grubbing, grubbed**
❶ to turn things over or move them about while looking for something • *The dog was grubbing around under a bush.* ❷ to dig something up by the roots

grubby *ADJECTIVE* **grubbier, grubbiest**
rather dirty

grudge *NOUN* **grudges**
unfriendly feelings towards someone because you are angry about what has happened in the past • *She isn't the sort of person who bears a grudge.*

grudge *VERB* **grudges, grudging, grudged**
to be unhappy that someone has something or that you have to do something • *I don't grudge him his success – he deserves it.*

grudging *ADJECTIVE*
given or done although you do not want to • *grudging thanks*
➤ **grudgingly** *ADVERB*

gruelling *ADJECTIVE*
difficult and exhausting • *It was a gruelling race.*

gruesome *ADJECTIVE*
horrible or shocking • *He told me the gruesome story of how she died.*

gruff *ADJECTIVE*
having a rough unfriendly voice or manner
➤ **gruffly** *ADVERB*
➤ **gruffness** *NOUN*

grumble *VERB* **grumbles, grumbling, grumbled**
to complain in a bad-tempered way

grumble *NOUN* **grumbles**
a bad-tempered complaint

grumpy *ADJECTIVE*
bad-tempered
➤ **grumpily** *ADVERB*
➤ **grumpiness** *NOUN*

grunt *VERB* **grunts, grunting, grunted**
to make a gruff snorting sound like a pig

grunt *NOUN* **grunts**
the sound of grunting

guarantee *NOUN* **guarantees**
a formal promise to do something or to repair something you have sold if it breaks or goes wrong

guarantee *VERB* **guarantees, guaranteeing, guaranteed**
❶ to give a guarantee; to make a formal

promise ❷ to make it certain that something will happen • *Money cannot guarantee happiness.*

guard *VERB* **guards, guarding, guarded**
❶ to protect a place or thing from danger; to keep something safe ❷ to watch over a prisoner and prevent them from escaping
➤ **guard against something** to try to prevent something happening

guard *NOUN* **guards**
❶ guarding or protecting people or things • *Keep the prisoners under close guard.* ❷ someone who guards a person or place ❸ a group of soldiers or police officers etc. acting as a guard ❹ a railway official in charge of a train ❺ a protecting device or screen • *a fireguard*
➤ **on guard** alert for possible danger or difficulty

> **SPELLING**
> There is a silent **u** in **guard**.

guardian *NOUN* **guardians**
❶ someone who guards or protects something ❷ a person who is legally in charge of a child whose parents cannot look after him or her
➤ **guardianship** *NOUN*

guerrilla (say ger-**il**-a) *NOUN* **guerrillas**
a member of a small unofficial army who fights by making surprise attacks

> **SPELLING**
> Take care not to confuse with **gorilla,** which is an ape.

guess *NOUN* **guesses**
an opinion or answer that you give without making careful calculations or without being certain

guess *VERB* **guesses, guessing, guessed**
to make a guess
➤ **guesser** *NOUN*

guesswork *NOUN*
something you do or think by guessing • *The police had a few facts but the rest was guesswork.*

guest *NOUN* **guests**
❶ a person who is invited to your house for a meal or a visit or to a special event • *We have guests staying this weekend.* • *wedding guests* ❷ a person staying at a hotel ❸ a person who takes part in another's show as a visiting performer

guest house *NOUN* **guest houses**
a kind of small hotel

guffaw *VERB* **guffaws, guffawing, guffawed**
to laugh noisily

guffaw *NOUN* **guffaws**
a noisy laugh

guidance *NOUN*
help and advice • *He learned to cook under the guidance of the head chef.*

Guide *NOUN* **Guides**
a member of the Guide Association, an organization for girls

guide *NOUN* **guides**
❶ a person who shows others the way or points out interesting sights ❷ a book giving information about a place or subject

guide *VERB* **guides, guiding, guided**
to show someone the way or how to do something

guidebook *NOUN* **guidebooks**
a book of information about a place, for travellers or visitors

guided missile *NOUN* **guided missiles**
an explosive rocket that is guided to its target by remote control or by equipment inside it

guide dog *NOUN* **guide dogs**
a dog trained to lead a blind person

guidelines *PLURAL NOUN*
statements that give general advice about how something should be done

guild (say gild) *NOUN* **guilds**
a society of people with similar skills or interests

guilder (say **gild**-er) *NOUN* **guilders**
a unit of money used in the Netherlands before the introduction of the euro

guile (rhymes with mile) *NOUN*
craftiness and deceit
➤ **guileless** *ADJECTIVE*

guillotine (say **gil**-ot-een) *NOUN* **guillotines**
❶ a machine with a heavy blade for beheading criminals, used in the past in France ❷ a machine with a long sharp blade for cutting paper

guillotine *VERB* **guillotines, guillotining, guillotined**
to cut off someone's head with a guillotine
WORD ORIGIN named after Dr *Guillotin,* who suggested its use in France during the Revolution in 1789

a b c d e f g h i j k l m n o p q r s t u v w x y z

guilt NOUN
❶ an unpleasant feeling you have when you have done wrong or are to blame for something bad that has happened **❷** the fact that you have committed a crime or done wrong • *Everyone was convinced of her guilt.*

guilty ADJECTIVE
❶ having done wrong • *He was found guilty of murder.* **❷** feeling or showing guilt • *a guilty conscience* • *a guilty look*
➤ **guiltily** ADVERB

guinea (say gin-ee) NOUN guineas
❶ a former British gold coin worth 21 shillings (£1.05) **❷** this amount of money
WORD ORIGIN originally = a coin used by British traders in Africa: named after *Guinea* in west Africa

guinea pig NOUN guinea pigs
❶ a small furry animal without a tail, kept as a pet **❷** a person who is used to try out something new **WORD ORIGIN** from *Guinea* in west Africa, probably by mistake for Guiana, in South America, where the guinea pig comes from

guise (say guys) NOUN guises
an outward disguise or pretence • *He returned to his father's kingdom in the guise of a servant.*

guitar NOUN guitars
a musical instrument played by plucking its strings
➤ **guitarist** NOUN

gulf NOUN gulfs
❶ a large area of the sea that is partly surrounded by land **❷** a wide gap; a great difference • *the gulf between rich and poor*

gull NOUN gulls
a seagull

gullet NOUN gullets
the tube from the throat to the stomach

gullible ADJECTIVE
easily deceived or persuaded to believe something

gully NOUN gullies
a narrow channel that carries water

gulp VERB gulps, gulping, gulped
❶ to swallow something hastily or greedily **❷** to make a loud swallowing noise, especially because of fear

gulp NOUN gulps
❶ the act of gulping food or drink **❷** a large mouthful of liquid

gum NOUN gums
❶ the firm flesh in which your teeth are rooted **❷** a sticky substance produced by some trees and shrubs, used as glue **❸** a sweet made with gum or gelatin • *a fruit gum* **❹** chewing gum **❺** a gum tree

gum VERB gums, gumming, gummed
to cover or stick something with gum

gummy ADJECTIVE
sticky like gum

gumption NOUN (informal)
common sense

gum tree NOUN gum trees
a eucalyptus

gun NOUN guns
❶ a weapon that fires shells or bullets from a metal tube **❷** a starting pistol **❸** a device that forces a substance out of a tube • *a grease gun*

gun VERB guns, gunning, gunned
➤ **gun someone down** to shoot and kill someone with a gun **WORD ORIGIN** probably from the Swedish girl's name *Gunnhildr*, from *gunnr* = war

gunboat NOUN gunboats
a small warship

gunfire NOUN
the rapid firing of guns

gunman NOUN gunmen
a criminal with a gun

gunner NOUN gunners
a person in the armed forces who operates a large gun

gunnery NOUN
the making or use of large guns

gunpowder NOUN
an explosive made from a powdered mixture of potassium nitrate, charcoal and sulphur

gunshot NOUN gunshots
the sound of a gun being fired

gunwale (say gun-al) NOUN gunwales
the upper edge of the side of a boat

gurdwara NOUN gurdwaras
a Sikh temple

gurgle VERB gurgles, gurgling, gurgled
to make a low bubbling sound • *Water gurgled through the pipes.*

gurgle NOUN gurgles
a low bubbling sound

guru *NOUN* **gurus**
❶ a spiritual teacher in Hinduism and Sikhism
❷ an influential teacher; an expert on a subject whose ideas people follow

gush *VERB* **gushes, gushing, gushed**
❶ to flow out suddenly or quickly ❷ to talk too enthusiastically or emotionally
➤ **gush** *NOUN*

gust *NOUN* **gusts**
a short sudden rush of wind

gust *VERB* **gusts, gusting, gusted**
to blow in gusts

gusto *NOUN*
great enjoyment and enthusiasm

gusty *ADJECTIVE*
with the wind blowing in gusts • *a gusty breeze*

gut *NOUN* **guts**
the lower part of the digestive system; the intestine

gut *VERB* **guts, gutting, gutted**
❶ to remove the guts from a dead fish or other animal ❷ to remove or destroy the inside of something • *The fire completely gutted the factory.*

guts *PLURAL NOUN*
❶ the digestive system; the insides of a person or thing ❷ (*informal*) courage and determination

gutted *ADJECTIVE* (*British*) (*informal*)
extremely disappointed or upset

gutter *NOUN* **gutters**
a long narrow channel at the side of a street or along the edge of a roof, for carrying away rainwater

gutter *VERB* **gutters, guttering, guttered**
a candle gutters when it burns unsteadily so that melted wax runs down

guttural (say **gut**-er-al) *ADJECTIVE*
a guttural voice is throaty and harsh-sounding

guy *NOUN* **guys**
❶ a figure representing Guy Fawkes, burnt on 5 November in memory of the Gunpowder Plot which planned to blow up Parliament on that day in 1605 ❷ (*informal*) a man ❸ (also **guy-rope**) a rope used to hold something in place, especially a tent

guzzle *VERB* **guzzles, guzzling, guzzled**
to eat or drink greedily
➤ **guzzler** *NOUN*

gym (say jim) *NOUN* **gyms** (*informal*)
❶ a gymnasium ❷ gymnastics

gymkhana (say jim-**kah**-na) *NOUN* **gymkhanas**
a series of horse-riding contests and other sports events

gymnasium *NOUN* **gymnasiums**
a large room or building with equipment for doing physical exercise **WORD ORIGIN** from Greek *gymnos* = naked (because in ancient Greece men exercised naked)

gymnast *NOUN* **gymnasts**
a person trained in gymnastics

gymnastics *PLURAL NOUN*
exercises performed to develop the muscles or to show the performer's agility
➤ **gymnastic** *ADJECTIVE*

gynaecology (say guy-ni-**kol**-o-ji) *NOUN*
the branch of medicine concerned with the female reproductive system

gypsy *NOUN* **gypsies**
a member of a community of people, also called travellers, who live in caravans or similar vehicles and travel from place to place **WORD ORIGIN** from *Egyptian*, because gypsies were originally thought to have come from Egypt

gyrate (say jy-**rayt**) *VERB* **gyrates, gyrating, gyrated**
to move round in circles or spirals • *They began gyrating to the music.*
➤ **gyration** *NOUN*

gyroscope (say **jy**-ro-skohp) *NOUN* **gyroscopes**
a device used in navigation, that keeps steady because of a heavy wheel spinning inside it

habit *NOUN* **habits**
❶ something that you do regularly or often; a settled way of behaving ❷ something that is hard to give up • *a smoking habit* ❸ a piece of clothing like a long dress worn by a monk or nun

habitat *NOUN* **habitats**
where an animal or plant lives or grows naturally • *We were taken to see elephants in their natural habitat.*

a b c d e f g h i j k l m n o p q r s t u v w x y z

habitation *NOUN* habitations
❶ a place to live in ❷ living in a place • *There was no sign of human habitation.*

habitual *ADJECTIVE*
done regularly; usual or typical of someone
• *her habitual afternoon walk*
➤ **habitually** *ADVERB*

hack *VERB* hacks, hacking, hacked
❶ to chop or cut something roughly • *They began hacking their way through the dense forest.* ❷ (*informal*) to break into a computer system

hacker *NOUN* hackers
a person who breaks into a computer system, especially that of a company or government

hackles *PLURAL NOUN*
➤ **make someone's hackles rise** to make someone angry or indignant
WORD ORIGIN *hackles* are the long feathers on some birds' necks, which the bird raises when alarmed

hackneyed *ADJECTIVE*
used so often that it is no longer interesting

hacksaw *NOUN* hacksaws
a saw for cutting metal

haddock *NOUN* haddock
a sea fish like cod but smaller, used as food

hadn't (*mainly spoken*)
had not

SPELLING
Hadn't = had + not. Add an **apostrophe** between the n and the t.

haemoglobin (say heem-a-**gloh**-bin) *NOUN*
the red substance that carries oxygen in the blood

haemophilia (say heem-o-**fil**-ee-a) *NOUN*
a disease that causes people to bleed dangerously from even a slight cut
➤ **haemophiliac** *NOUN*

haemorrhage (say **hem**-er-ij) *NOUN*
severe bleeding, especially inside a person's body

hag *NOUN* hags
an ugly old woman

haggard *ADJECTIVE*
looking ill or very tired

haggis *NOUN* haggises
a Scottish food made from sheep's offal

haggle *VERB* haggles, haggling, haggled
to argue about a price or agreement

haiku (say **hy**-koo) *NOUN* haiku
a Japanese form of poem, written in three lines of five, seven and five syllables

hail *NOUN*
❶ frozen drops of rain ❷ a hail of bullets or arrows is a large number of them coming quickly

hail *VERB* hails, hailing, hailed
❶ it is hailing when rain is falling in frozen drops ❷ to call out or wave to someone to get their attention
➤ **hail from somewhere** to come from a particular place • *He hails from Ireland.*

hail *EXCLAMATION* (*old use*)
an exclamation of greeting • *Hail, Caesar!*

hailstone *NOUN* hailstones
a frozen drop of rain

hair *NOUN* hairs
❶ a soft covering that grows on the heads and bodies of people and animals ❷ one of the threads that make up this covering
➤ **keep your hair on** (*informal*) stay calm and do not lose your temper
➤ **split hairs** to make petty or unimportant distinctions of meaning

hairbrush *NOUN* hairbrushes
a brush for tidying your hair

haircut *NOUN* haircuts
❶ cutting a person's hair when it gets too long ❷ the style in which someone's hair is cut

hairdresser *NOUN* hairdressers
a person whose job is to cut and arrange people's hair

hairdryer *NOUN*
an electrical device for drying the hair with warm air

hairpin *NOUN* hairpins
a U-shaped pin for keeping hair in place

hair-raising *ADJECTIVE*
terrifying but also exciting • *a hair-raising chase across the rooftops*

hairstyle *NOUN* hairstyles
a way or style of arranging your hair

hairy *ADJECTIVE*
❶ with a lot of hair ❷ (*informal*) dangerous and frightening • *a hairy experience*

hajj *NOUN*
the pilgrimage to Mecca which all Muslims are expected to make at least once

hake *NOUN* hake
a sea fish used as food

halal *ADJECTIVE*
halal meat is prepared according to Muslim law

halcyon (say **hal**-see-on) *ADJECTIVE*
halcyon days are happy and peaceful days that you long for from the past
WORD ORIGIN from Greek *alkyon* = a bird which was once believed to build its nest on the sea, which magically stayed calm

hale *ADJECTIVE*
➤ **hale and hearty** strong and healthy

half *NOUN* halves
one of the two equal parts or amounts into which something is or can be divided

half *ADVERB*
partly; not completely • *This meat is only half cooked.*
➤ **not half** (*informal*) extremely • *Was she cross? Not half!*

half-baked *ADJECTIVE* (*informal*)
not properly planned or thought out

half-brother *NOUN* half-brothers
a brother to whom you are related by one parent but not by both parents

half-hearted *ADJECTIVE*
not very keen or enthusiastic
➤ **half-heartedly** *ADVERB*

half-life *NOUN* half-lives
the time taken for the radioactivity of a substance to fall to half its original value

half mast *NOUN*
a point about halfway up a flagpole, to which a flag is lowered as a mark of respect for a person who has died

halfpenny (say **hayp**-nee) *NOUN* halfpennies
for individual coins or **halfpence** for a sum of money, a former British coin worth half a penny

half-sister *NOUN* half-sisters
a sister to whom you are related by one parent but not by both parents

half-term *NOUN* half-terms
(in British schools) a short holiday in the middle of a school term

half-time *NOUN*
the point or interval halfway through a game

halfway *ADJECTIVE* & *ADVERB*
at a point half the distance or amount

between two places or times • *He stopped halfway up the stairs.*

half-witted *ADJECTIVE*
(*informal*) stupid
➤ **half-wit** *NOUN*

halibut *NOUN* halibut
a large flat fish used as food
WORD ORIGIN from **holy** + *butt*, a dialect word = flatfish (because it was eaten on Christian holy days, when meat was forbidden)

hall *NOUN* halls
❶ a space or passage just inside the front entrance of a house ❷ a large room or building used for meetings, concerts or social events ❸ a large country house

hallelujah *EXCLAMATION* & *NOUN* hallelujahs
alleluia

hallmark *NOUN* hallmarks
❶ an official mark made on gold, silver and platinum to show its quality ❷ a typical quality or feature by which you can recognize a person or thing • *The book has all the hallmarks of a classic.*

hallo *EXCLAMATION*
a different spelling of **hello**

hallowed *ADJECTIVE*
honoured as being holy

Hallowe'en *NOUN*
31 October, traditionally a time when ghosts and witches are believed to appear
WORD ORIGIN from *All Hallow Even*, the evening before the Christian festival honouring all the *hallows* = saints

hallucination *NOUN* hallucinations
something you think you can see or hear that is not really there, usually because of illness or drugs
➤ **hallucinate** *VERB*

halo *NOUN* haloes
a circle of light round something, especially round the head of a saint or other holy person in paintings

halt *VERB* halts, halting, halted
to stop or to make something stop • *The parade halted briefly at the square.* • *The judge decided to halt the trial.*

halt *NOUN* halts
❶ a stop or standstill • *Work came to a halt when the digger broke down.* ❷ a small stopping place on a railway

a
b
c
d
e
f
g
h
i
j
k
l
m
n
o
p
q
r
s
t
u
v
w
x
y
z

halter *NOUN* **halters**
a rope or strap put round a horse's head so that it can be led or fastened to something

halting *ADJECTIVE*
slow and uncertain • *He has a halting walk.*
➤ **haltingly** *ADVERB*

halve *VERB* **halves, halving, halved**
❶ to reduce something to half its size or amount • *We need to halve our expenses.*
❷ to divide something into halves • *Halve the peach and remove the stone.*

ham *NOUN* **hams**
❶ meat from a pig's leg ❷ (*informal*) an actor who acts in a very exaggerated way ❸ (*informal*) someone who operates a radio to send and receive messages as a hobby

hamburger *NOUN* **hamburgers**
a flat round cake of minced beef served fried, often in a bread roll **WORD ORIGIN** named after Hamburg in Germany (not after **ham**)

hamlet *NOUN* **hamlets**
a small village

hammer *NOUN* **hammers**
a tool with a heavy metal head used for hitting nails into things

hammer *VERB* **hammers, hammering, hammered**
❶ to hit something with a hammer ❷ to knock loudly • *Someone was hammering on the door.* ❸ (*informal*) to criticize or defeat someone

hammock *NOUN* **hammocks**
a bed made of a strong net or piece of cloth hung up above the ground or floor

hamper *NOUN* **hampers**
a large box-shaped basket with a lid

hamper *VERB* **hampers, hampering, hampered**
to hinder someone or prevent them from moving or working freely • *Later in the match he was hampered by his shoulder injury.*

hamster *NOUN* **hamsters**
a small furry animal with cheek pouches for carrying grain

hamstring *NOUN* **hamstrings**
any of the five tendons at the back of a person's knee

hand *NOUN* **hands**
❶ the end part of the arm below the wrist ❷ a pointer on a clock or dial ❸ a worker; a member of a ship's crew • *All hands on deck!* ❹ the cards held by one player in a card game ❺ side or direction • *the right-hand side* • *on*

the other hand ❻ help or assistance • *Give me a hand with these boxes.*
➤ **at hand** nearby
➤ **by hand** using your hand or hands
➤ **give someone** or **receive a big hand** to applaud someone or be applauded
➤ **hands down** winning easily
➤ **in good hands** in the care or control of someone who can be trusted
➤ **in hand** being dealt with
➤ **on hand** available; ready to help
➤ **out of hand** out of control

hand *VERB* **hands, handing, handed**
to give or pass something to someone • *Hand it over.*
➤ **hand something down** to pass something from one generation to the next

handbag *NOUN* **handbags**
a small bag for holding a purse and other personal items

handbook *NOUN* **handbooks**
a small book that gives useful facts about something

handcuff *NOUN* **handcuffs**
one of a pair of metal rings linked by a chain, for fastening wrists together

handcuff *VERB* **handcuffs, handcuffing, handcuffed**
to put handcuffs on someone

handful *NOUN* **handfuls**
❶ as much as you can hold in one hand ❷ a few people or things • *There were only a handful of people in the audience.* ❸ (*informal*) a difficult or awkward person or task

handicap *NOUN* **handicaps**
❶ a disadvantage ❷ (*offensive*) a physical or mental disability
➤ **handicapped** *ADJECTIVE*

USAGE
Do not use *handicapped* to describe people with disabilities as this is offensive.

handicraft *NOUN* **handicrafts**
artistic work done with your hands, e.g. woodwork or needlework

handily *ADVERB*
in a handy way

handiwork *NOUN*
❶ something made by hand ❷ something done • *Is this mess your handiwork?*

handkerchief *NOUN* handkerchiefs
a small square of cloth for wiping your nose
or face

handle *NOUN* handles
the part of a thing by which you can hold,
carry or control it

handle *VERB* handles, handling, handled
❶ to touch or feel something with your
hands ❷ to deal with or manage something
• *I thought you handled the situation very
well.*
➤ **handler** *NOUN*

handlebar *NOUN* (or **handlebars**) *PLURAL NOUN*
the bar, with a handle at each end, that steers
a bicycle or motorcycle

handout *NOUN* handouts
❶ money given to a needy person ❷ a sheet
of information given out in a lesson, lecture,
etc.

handrail *NOUN* handrails
a narrow rail for people to hold as a support

handset *NOUN* handsets
❶ the part of a telephone that you hold up
to speak into and listen to ❷ a hand-held
control device for a piece of electronic
equipment

handshake *NOUN* handshakes
shaking hands with someone as a greeting or
to show you agree to something

handsome *ADJECTIVE*
❶ attractive or good-looking ❷ large and
generous • *a handsome offer*
➤ **handsomely** *ADVERB*

hands-on *ADJECTIVE*
involving actual experience of using
equipment or doing something • *The science
museum has many hands-on activities you
can try.*

handstand *NOUN* handstands
balancing on your hands with your feet in
the air

handwriting *NOUN*
writing done by hand; a person's style of
writing

handwritten *ADJECTIVE*
written by hand, not typed or printed • *a
handwritten sign*

handy *ADJECTIVE* handier, handiest
❶ convenient or useful; within easy reach • *a
handy little tool* • *Have you got a pen handy?*
❷ good at using the hands

handyman *NOUN* handymen
a person who does household repairs or odd
jobs

hang *VERB* hangs, hanging, hung
❶ to fix the top part of something to a hook
or nail etc. so that the lower part is free; to
be supported in this way • *Coats hung from
pegs along one wall.* ❷ to stick wallpaper to a
wall ❸ to decorate something with drapery or
hanging ornaments etc. • *The tree was hung
with lights.* ❹ to lean or lie over something
• *Her clothes hung over a chair.* ❺ to remain
in the air or as something unpleasant
• *Smoke hung over the city.* • *The threat is
still hanging over him.* ❻ with past tense &
past participle **hanged** to execute someone
by hanging them from a rope that tightens
round the neck • *He was hanged in 1950.*
➤ **hang about** to wait around doing nothing
➤ **hang back** to hesitate to go forward or to
do something
➤ **hang on** (*informal*) to wait • *Hang on! I'm
not ready yet.*
➤ **hang on to something** to hold something
tightly
➤ **hang up** to end a telephone conversation

hang *NOUN*
➤ **get the hang of** (*informal*) to learn how to
do or use something

hangar *NOUN* hangars
a large shed where aircraft are kept

hanger *NOUN* hangers
a curved piece of wood, plastic or wire with
a hook at the top, for hanging clothes from
a rail

hang-glider *NOUN* hang-gliders
a framework like a large kite from which a
person can hang and glide through the air
➤ **hang-gliding** *NOUN*

hangman *NOUN* hangmen
a man whose job it is to hang people
condemned to death

hangover *NOUN* hangovers
a headache and sick feeling after drinking too
much alcohol

hank *NOUN* hanks
a coil or piece of wool or thread

hanker *VERB* hankers, hankering, hankered
to hanker after something is to feel a longing
for it

hanky *NOUN* hankies (*informal*)
a handkerchief

a b c d e f g h i j k l m n o p q r s t u v w x y z

Hanukkah (say hah-noo-ka) *NOUN*
the eight-day Jewish festival of lights
beginning in December

haphazard *ADJECTIVE*
done or chosen at random, with no particular
order or plan • *The books were piled on the
shelf in a haphazard fashion.*
➤ **haphazardly** *ADVERB*

hapless *ADJECTIVE*
having no luck

happen *VERB* happens, happening, happened
❶ to take place; to occur ❷ to do something
by chance • *I happened to see him in the
street.*

happening *NOUN* happenings
something that happens; an event

happily *ADVERB*
❶ in a happy way • *The children were playing
happily outside.* ❷ it is lucky that • *Happily,
no one was hurt.*

happy *ADJECTIVE* happier, happiest
❶ pleased or contented ❷ willing to do
something • *I'd be happy to help.* ❸ fortunate
• *a happy coincidence*
➤ **happiness** *NOUN*

harangue (say ha-**rang**) *VERB* harangues,
haranguing, harangued
to speak to someone at length in a loud
aggressive way, often to criticize them

harangue *NOUN*
a long aggressive speech criticizing someone

harass (say **ha**-ras) *VERB* harasses, harassing,
harassed
to trouble or annoy someone continually
➤ **harassment** (say **ha**-ras-ment) *NOUN*

harassed *ADJECTIVE*
tired and anxious because you have too much
to do • *a harassed-looking waiter*

harbour *NOUN* harbours
a place where ships can shelter or unload

harbour *VERB* harbours, harbouring,
harboured
❶ to keep something in your mind for a long
time • *I think she still harbours a grudge
against them.* ❷ to give shelter to someone,
especially a criminal

hard *ADJECTIVE*
❶ firm or solid; not soft ❷ strong and
violent • *a hard punch* ❸ difficult to do or
understand • *These questions are too hard.*
❹ severe or harsh ❺ causing suffering • *hard
luck* ❻ using or needing great effort • *a*

hard worker • *a hard climb* ❼ hard drugs are
strong and addictive ❽ hard water contains
minerals that prevent soap from making
much lather
➤ **hardness** *NOUN*
➤ **hard of hearing** slightly deaf
➤ **hard up** (*informal*) short of money

hard *ADVERB*
❶ so as to be hard • *The ground froze hard.*
❷ with great effort or force • *We worked
hard.* • *It is raining hard.* ❸ with difficulty
• *hard-earned cash*

hardback *NOUN* hardbacks
a book bound in stiff covers

hardboard *NOUN*
stiff board made of compressed wood pulp

hard disk *NOUN* hard disks
a disk fixed inside a computer, able to store
large amounts of data

harden *VERB* hardens, hardening, hardened
❶ to make something hard or to become
hard • *Wait for the varnish to harden.* ❷ to
become more serious and unfriendly • *Her
face hardened immediately.*
➤ **hardener** *NOUN*

hard-hearted *ADJECTIVE*
unkind or unsympathetic

hardly *ADVERB*
only just; only with difficulty • *She can hardly
walk.*

hardship *NOUN* hardships
difficult conditions that cause discomfort or
suffering • *a life of hardship*

hard shoulder *NOUN* hard shoulders
(*British*) a strip at the edge of a motorway
where vehicles can stop in an emergency

hardware *NOUN*
❶ tools and other pieces of equipment
that you use in the house and garden
• *a hardware shop* ❷ the machinery of
a computer as opposed to the software.
Compare with **software**.

hard-wearing *ADJECTIVE*
able to stand a lot of wear

hardwood *NOUN* hardwoods
hard heavy wood from deciduous trees, e.g.
oak and teak

hardy *ADJECTIVE* hardier, hardiest
able to endure cold or difficult conditions • *a
hardy plant*

hare *NOUN* hares
a fast-running animal like a large rabbit

hare *VERB* hares, haring, hared
(*British*) to hare about or hare off is to rush
away at great speed

harem (say **har**-eem) *NOUN* harems
the part of a Muslim palace or house where
the women live; the women living there

hark *VERB* harks, harking, harked
(*old use*) to listen
➤ **hark back to something** to return to an
earlier subject

harm *VERB* harms, harming, harmed
to damage or injure someone or something

harm *NOUN*
damage or injury

harmful *ADJECTIVE*
causing harm or likely to cause harm
• *harmful rays from the sun*

harmless *ADJECTIVE*
not able or likely to cause harm • *These
spiders are completely harmless.*
➤ **harmlessly** *ADVERB*

harmonic *ADJECTIVE*
to do with harmony in music

harmonica *NOUN* harmonicas
a mouth organ

harmonious *ADJECTIVE*
❶ combining together in a pleasant,
attractive or effective way ❷ sounding
pleasant ❸ peaceful and friendly

harmonize (also **harmonise**) *VERB*
harmonizes, harmonizing, harmonized
❶ to combine together in a pleasant,
attractive or effective way • *He believed
that buildings should harmonize with
their environment.* ❷ musicians or singers
harmonize when they play or sing together
with notes that combine in a pleasant way
with the main tune

harmony *NOUN* harmonies
❶ a pleasant combination of musical notes
played or sung at the same time ❷ being
friendly to each other and not quarrelling

harness *NOUN* harnesses
the straps put round a horse's head and neck
for controlling it

harness *VERB* harnesses, harnessing,
harnessed
❶ to put a harness on a horse ❷ to control
and use something • *Could we harness the
power of the wind?*

harp *NOUN* harps
a musical instrument made of strings
stretched across a frame and plucked with
the fingers
➤ **harpist** *NOUN*

harp *VERB* harps, harping, harped
to harp on about something is to keep on
talking about it in a tiresome way • *He keeps
harping on about all the work he has to do.*

harpoon *NOUN NOUN* harpoons
a spear attached to a rope, used for catching
whales or large fish

harpoon *VERB* harpoons, harpooning,
harpooned
to spear a whale or fish with a harpoon

harpsichord *NOUN* harpsichords
an instrument like a piano but with strings
that are plucked (not struck) when keys are
pressed

harrow *NOUN* harrows
a heavy device pulled over the ground to
break up the soil

harrowing *ADJECTIVE*
very upsetting or distressing

harry *VERB* harries, harrying, harried
to keep bothering or harassing someone
• *She has been harried by reporters all week.*

harsh *ADJECTIVE*
❶ rough and unpleasant ❷ severe or cruel
➤ **harshly** *ADVERB*
➤ **harshness** *NOUN*

hart *NOUN* harts
a male deer. Compare with **hind**.

harvest *NOUN* harvests
❶ the time when farmers gather in the corn,
fruit or vegetables that they have grown
❷ the crop that is gathered in

harvest *VERB* harvests, harvesting,
harvested
to gather in a crop
➤ **harvester** *NOUN*

hash *NOUN*
❶ a mixture of small pieces of meat and
vegetables, usually fried ❷ (*chiefly British*)
the symbol #
➤ **make a hash of something** (*informal*) to
make a mess of something or bungle it

hashtag *NOUN* hashtags
a word or phrase with the symbol # in front
of it, used on websites such as Twitter to
identify the subject of a message

a b c d e f g h i j k l m n o p q r s t u v w x y z

hasn't (*mainly spoken*)
has not

> **SPELLING**
>
> Hasn't = has + not. Add an **apostrophe** between the **n** and the **t**.

hassle (*informal*) NOUN
something that is difficult or troublesome

hassle VERB hassles, hassling, hassled
to annoy or pester someone

haste NOUN
doing something in a short time or too quickly • *The letter had clearly been written in haste.*
➤ **make haste** to move or act quickly

hasten VERB hastens, hastening, hastened
❶ to be quick to do or say something • *She hastened to apologize.* ❷ to make something happen or be done earlier or more quickly

hasty ADJECTIVE
hurried; done too quickly • *a hasty decision*
➤ **hastily** ADVERB

hat NOUN hats
a covering for the head, worn out of doors
➤ **keep something under your hat** to keep something a secret

hatch NOUN hatches
an opening in a floor, wall or door, usually with a covering

hatch VERB hatches, hatching, hatched
❶ to break out of an egg ❷ to keep an egg warm until a baby bird comes out ❸ to plan something • *They hatched a plot.* ❹ to shade part of a drawing with close parallel lines

hatchback NOUN hatchbacks
a car with a sloping back hinged at the top

hatchet NOUN hatchets
a small axe

hate VERB hates, hating, hated
to dislike someone or something very strongly

hate NOUN hates
❶ extreme dislike ❷ something you dislike very much

hateful ADJECTIVE
extremely unkind or unpleasant; horrible • *It was a hateful thing to say.*

hatred NOUN
extreme dislike

hatter NOUN hatters
a person who makes hats

hat-trick NOUN hat-tricks
getting three goals, wickets or victories one after the other

haughty ADJECTIVE haughtier, haughtiest
proud of yourself and looking down on other people
➤ **haughtily** ADVERB
➤ **haughtiness** NOUN

haul VERB hauls, hauling, hauled
to pull or drag something with great effort

haul NOUN hauls
❶ an amount taken or obtained by an effort • *Police recovered a large haul of weapons.* ❷ a distance to be covered • *It was a long haul to the summit.*

haulage NOUN (*British*)
❶ transporting goods by road ❷ a charge for this

haunches PLURAL NOUN
the buttocks and top part of the thighs

haunt VERB haunts, haunting, haunted
❶ a ghost haunts a place or person when it appears often ❷ to visit a place often ❸ to stay for a long time in your mind • *The memory haunts me still.*

haunt NOUN haunts
a place that you often visit

haunted ADJECTIVE
a haunted place is one that people think is visited by ghosts

haunting ADJECTIVE
so beautiful and sad that it stays in your mind • *a haunting tune*

have VERB has, having, had
This word has many uses, including
❶ to possess or own something • *We have two dogs.* ❷ to contain something • *This tin has sweets in it.* ❸ to experience something • *He had a shock.* ❹ to be obliged or forced to do something • *We have to go now.* ❺ to allow something to happen • *I won't have him bullied.* ❻ to receive or accept something • *Will you have a sweet?* ❼ to get something done; to organize something • *I'm having my phone mended.* • *We're having a party next week.* ❽ (*informal*) to be had is to be cheated or deceived
➤ **have someone on** (*informal*) to fool someone

have *AUXILIARY VERB*
used to form the past tense of verbs, e.g. *He has gone*

> **GRAMMAR**
>
> The auxiliary verb **have** is used in perfect tenses (**have** + **past participle** of the main verb):
>
> *Have you watched this film before?*
>
> *He had already arrived.*
>
> *It has rained all night.*
>
> *The sea had swept everything away.*
>
> In writing, take care to follow modal verbs like *could, might* and *would* with *have,* not *of:*
>
> *If I'd got there in time, I could have helped.*
>
> *It might have been Jack who scored, but I'm not sure.*

haven *NOUN* havens
a safe place for people or animals • *The river banks are a haven for wildlife.*

haven't (*mainly spoken*)
have not

> **SPELLING**
>
> Have + not = haven't.
> Add an **apostrophe** between the n and the t.

haversack *NOUN* haversacks
a strong bag carried on your back or over your shoulder

havoc *NOUN*
great destruction or disorder • *The floods caused havoc throughout the country.*
➤ **play havoc with something** to disrupt something completely

hawk *NOUN* hawks
a bird of prey with very strong eyesight

hawk *VERB* hawks, hawking, hawked
to carry goods about and try to sell them
➤ **hawker** *NOUN*

hawthorn *NOUN* hawthorns
a thorny tree with small red berries (called *haws*)

hay *NOUN*
dried grass for feeding to animals

hay fever *NOUN*
an allergy to pollen that causes irritation of the nose, throat and eyes

haystack *NOUN* haystacks
a large neat pile of hay packed for storing

haywire *ADJECTIVE* (*informal*)
out of control • *My computer's gone haywire.*
WORD ORIGIN because wire for tying up hay bales was often used for makeshift repairs

hazard *NOUN* hazards
❶ a danger or risk ❷ an obstacle on a golf course

hazard *VERB* hazards, hazarding, hazarded
to put something at risk
➤ **hazard a guess** to make a guess
WORD ORIGIN from Persian or Turkish *zar* = dice

hazardous *ADJECTIVE*
dangerous or risky • *a hazardous expedition*

haze *NOUN*
thin mist

hazel *NOUN* hazels
❶ a bush with small nuts ❷ a light brown colour
➤ **hazelnut** *NOUN*

hazy *ADJECTIVE*
❶ misty • *hazy sunshine* ❷ vague or uncertain • *I have a hazy memory of the party.*
➤ **hazily** *ADVERB*
➤ **haziness** *NOUN*

H-bomb *NOUN* H-bombs
a hydrogen bomb

he *PRONOUN*
❶ the male person or animal being talked about ❷ a person (male or female) • *He who hesitates is lost.*

head *NOUN* heads
❶ the part of the body containing the brains, eyes and mouth ❷ your brains or mind; intelligence • *Use your head!* ❸ a talent or ability • *She has a good head for figures.* ❹ heads is the side of a coin on which someone's head is shown • *Heads or tails?* ❺ a person • *It costs £5 a head.* ❻ the top or front of something • *a pinhead* • *at the head of the procession* ❼ the person in charge of an organization or group of people ❽ a headteacher
➤ **come to a head** to reach a crisis point
➤ **keep your head** to stay calm and not panic
➤ **off the top of your head** without preparation or thinking carefully

head *VERB* heads, heading, headed
❶ to be at the top or front of something
• *Spain heads the table after two games.*
❷ to be in charge of or lead something **❸** to
hit a ball with your head **❹** to start to go in
a particular direction • *We headed for the
coast.*
➤ **head someone off** to force someone to
turn aside by getting in front of them

headache *NOUN* headaches
❶ a pain in the head **❷** (*informal*) a worrying
problem

headdress *NOUN* headdresses
a covering or decoration for the head

header *NOUN* headers
a shot or pass made with the head in football

heading *NOUN* headings
a word or words put at the top of a piece of
printing or writing

headland *NOUN* headlands
a large piece of high land that sticks out into
the sea

headlight *NOUN* headlights
a powerful light at the front of a car, engine,
etc.

headline *NOUN* headlines
a heading in a newspaper, printed in large
type
➤ **the headlines** the main items of news

headlong *ADVERB & ADJECTIVE*
❶ falling head first **❷** in a hasty or
thoughtless way • *He's always rushing
headlong into trouble.*

headmaster *NOUN* headmasters
(*chiefly British*) a male headteacher

headmistress *NOUN* headmistresses
(*chiefly British*) a female headteacher

head-on *ADVERB & ADJECTIVE*
with the front parts hitting each other • *a
head-on collision*

headphones *PLURAL NOUN*
a pair of earphones on a band that fits over
the head

headquarters *NOUN & PLURAL NOUN*
the place from which an organization is
controlled

headstone *NOUN* headstones
a stone set up on a grave, with the name of
the person buried there

headstrong *ADJECTIVE*
determined to do what you want

headteacher *NOUN* headteachers
the person in charge of a school

headway *NOUN*
➤ **make headway** to make good progress

heal *VERB* heals, healing, healed
❶ a wound or injury heals when it gets better
• *The cut should heal up in a few days.* **❷** to
make a wound or injury better **❸** (*old use*) to
cure someone who is ill
➤ **healer** *NOUN*

health *NOUN*
❶ the condition of a person's body or mind
• *His health is bad.* **❷** being healthy and not
ill • *in sickness and in health*

health food *NOUN* health foods
food that contains only natural substances
and is thought to be good for your health

healthy *ADJECTIVE* healthier, healthiest
❶ being well; free from illness **❷** producing
good health • *Fresh air is healthy.*
➤ **healthily** *ADVERB*

heap *NOUN* heaps
a pile, especially an untidy one
➤ **heaps** *PLURAL NOUN*
(*informal*) a great amount; plenty • *There's
heaps of time.*

heap *VERB* heaps, heaping, heaped
❶ to put things in a pile • *Heap all the leaves
up over there.* **❷** to put large amounts on
something • *She heaped his plate with food.*
❸ to give a lot of something, such as praise or
criticism, to someone • *The press heaped the
team with praise.*

hear *VERB* hears, hearing, heard
❶ to take in sounds through the ears **❷** to
receive news or information **❸** to listen to
and try a case in a law court **❹** to hear from
someone is to get a phone call, letter or email
from them
➤ **hearer** *NOUN*
➤ **hear! hear!** (in a debate) I agree
➤ **not hear of** to refuse to allow something
• *He wouldn't hear of my paying for it.*

SPELLING
The past tense of **hear** is **heard**.

hearing *NOUN* hearings
❶ the ability to hear **❷** a chance to give your
opinion or to defend yourself • *Please give
me a fair hearing.* **❸** a trial in a law court

hearing aid *NOUN* hearing aids
a device to help a partially deaf person to
hear

hearsay *NOUN*
something you have heard from another
person or as a rumour, which may or may not
be true

hearse *NOUN* hearses
a vehicle for taking the coffin to a funeral

heart *NOUN* hearts
❶ the organ in your chest that pumps the
blood around your body ❷ a person's feelings
or emotions; sympathy ❸ enthusiasm or
courage • *We must take heart.* ❹ the middle
or most important part of something • *Let's
get to the heart of the problem.* ❺ a curved
shape representing a heart ❻ a playing card
with red heart shapes on it
➤ **break a person's heart** to make someone
very unhappy
➤ **by heart** by using only your memory • *She
knows the whole speech by heart.*

heart attack *NOUN* heart attacks
a sudden failure of the heart to work
properly, which results in great pain or
sometimes death

heartbroken *ADJECTIVE*
very unhappy

hearten *VERB* heartens, heartening,
heartened
to make a person feel encouraged • *He was
heartened by her words of support.*
➤ **heartening** *ADJECTIVE*

heart failure *NOUN*
gradual failure of the heart to work properly,
especially as a cause of death

heartfelt *ADJECTIVE*
felt deeply and sincerely • *my heartfelt
thanks*

hearth *NOUN* hearths
the floor of a fireplace or the area in front
of it

heartily *ADVERB*
❶ in an enthusiastic way • *The boy laughed
heartily.* ❷ completely • *I am heartily sick of
this place.*

heartland *NOUN*
the central or most important region

heartless *ADJECTIVE*
cruel or without pity

hearty *ADJECTIVE*
❶ strong and healthy ❷ enthusiastic
and sincere • *He offered his hearty
congratulations.* ❸ a hearty meal is large and
filling
➤ **heartiness** *NOUN*

heat *NOUN* heats
❶ hotness or (in scientific use) the form of
energy that causes things to be hot ❷ hot
weather ❸ strong feeling, especially anger
❹ a race or contest to decide who will take
part in the final
➤ **on heat** a female mammal is on heat when
it is ready for mating

heat *VERB* heats, heating, heated
❶ to make something hot ❷ to become hot

heater *NOUN* heaters
a device for heating a room or vehicle

heath *NOUN* heaths
an area of flat open land with low shrubs

heathen *NOUN* heathens
a person who does not believe in any of the
world's chief religions

heather *NOUN*
an evergreen plant with small purple, pink or
white flowers

heatwave *NOUN* heatwaves
a long period of hot weather

heave *VERB* heaves, heaving, heaved (when
used of ships hove)
❶ to lift or move something heavy
❷ (*informal*) to throw something ❸ to rise
and fall • *Her shoulders heaved with laughter.*
❹ if your stomach heaves, you feel like
vomiting
➤ **heave into view** a ship heaves into view
when appears on the horizon
➤ **heave a sigh** to utter a deep sigh
➤ **heave to** a ship heaves to when it stops
without mooring or anchoring

heave *NOUN* heaves
an act of heaving; a strong pull or shove
• *With a mighty heave, he lifted the sack
onto the truck.*

heaven *NOUN* heavens
❶ the place where, in some religions, good
people are thought to go when they die and
where God and angels are thought to live ❷ a
very pleasant place or state
➤ **the heavens** the sky

heavenly *ADJECTIVE*
❶ to do with heaven ❷ a heavenly body is

A
B
C
D
E
F
G
H
I
J
K
L
M
N
O
P
Q
R
S
T
U
V
W
X
Y
Z

a star or planet in the sky ➌ (*informal*) very pleasing

heavily *ADVERB*
➊ to a great degree; in large amounts • *It was raining heavily.* ➋ with a lot of force or effort • *She fell heavily to the ground.* ➌ in a slow and sad way • *He sighed heavily.*

heavy *ADJECTIVE* **heavier, heaviest**
➊ weighing a lot; difficult to lift or carry ➋ used to ask or say how much something weighs • *How heavy is that bag?* ➌ great in amount or force • *heavy rain* • *a heavy penalty* ➍ needing much effort • *heavy work* ➎ full of sadness or worry • *with a heavy heart*
➤ **heaviness** *NOUN*

heavy industry *NOUN* **heavy industries**
industry producing metal, large machines, etc.

heavyweight *NOUN* **heavyweights**
➊ a heavy person ➋ a boxer of the heaviest weight
➤ **heavyweight** *ADJECTIVE*

Hebrew *NOUN*
the language of the Jews in ancient Palestine and modern Israel

heckle *VERB* **heckles, heckling, heckled**
to interrupt a speaker with awkward questions
➤ **heckler** *NOUN*

hectare (say **hek**-tar) *NOUN* **hectares**
a unit of area equal to 10,000 square metres or nearly 2.5 acres

hectic *ADJECTIVE*
full of frantic activity • *It's been a hectic morning.*

hector *VERB* **hectors, hectoring, hectored**
to talk to someone in a bullying way
WORD ORIGIN from a gang of young bullies in London in the 17th century who named themselves after Hector, a hero in Greek legend

hedge *NOUN* **hedges**
a row of bushes forming a barrier or boundary

hedge *VERB* **hedges, hedging, hedged**
➊ to surround a field or other area with a hedge ➋ to avoid giving a definite answer
➤ **hedge your bets** to avoid committing yourself when you are faced with a difficult choice

hedgehog *NOUN* **hedgehogs**
a small animal covered with long prickles

hedgerow *NOUN* **hedgerows**
a hedge of bushes bordering a field

heed *VERB* **heeds, heeding, heeded**
to pay attention to someone or something

heed *NOUN*
➤ **take** or **pay heed** to give your attention to something

heedless *ADJECTIVE*
taking no notice of something • *Heedless of the danger, she started climbing up the rocks.*

hee-haw *NOUN* **hee-haws**
a donkey's bray

heel *NOUN* **heels**
➊ the back part of the foot ➋ the part of a sock or shoe round or under your heel
➤ **take to your heels** to run away

heel *VERB* **heels, heeling, heeled**
➊ to repair the heel of a shoe ➋ a ship heels when it leans over to one side

hefty *ADJECTIVE* **heftier, heftiest**
large and strong
➤ **heftily** *ADVERB*

Hegira (say **hej**-ir-a) *NOUN*
the flight of Muhammad from Mecca in AD 622. The Muslim era is reckoned from this date.

heifer (say **hef**-er) *NOUN* **heifers**
a young cow

height *NOUN* **heights**
➊ how high something is; the distance from the base to the top or from head to foot ➋ a high place • *My brother is afraid of heights.* ➌ the highest or most intense part • *at the height of the holiday season*

SPELLING
There is a tricky bit in **height**—it begins with **hei**.

heighten *VERB* **heightens, heightening, heightened**
➊ to become or make something more intense • *Their excitement heightened as the kick-off approached.* ➋ to make something higher

heinous (say **hay**-nus or **hee**-nus) *ADJECTIVE*
very bad or wicked • *a heinous crime*

heir (say air) *NOUN* **heirs**
a person who inherits money or a title

heir apparent *NOUN* **heirs apparent**
an heir whose right to inherit cannot be set

aside even if someone with a stronger right is born

heiress (say **air**-ess) *NOUN* **heiresses**
a female heir, especially to great wealth

heirloom (say **air**-loom) *NOUN* **heirlooms**
a valued possession that has been handed down in a family for several generations

heir presumptive *NOUN* **heirs presumptive**
an heir whose right to inherit may be set aside if someone with a stronger right is born

helicopter *NOUN* **helicopters**
a kind of aircraft with a large horizontal propeller or rotor

heliotrope *NOUN* **heliotropes**
a plant with small fragrant purple flowers

helium (say **hee**-lee-um) *NOUN*
a light colourless gas that does not burn and is sometimes used to fill balloons

helix (say **hee**-liks) *NOUN* **helices** (say **hee**-liss-eez)
a spiral

hell *NOUN*
❶ a place where, in some religions, wicked people are thought to be punished after they die ❷ a very unpleasant place or situation ❸ (*informal*) an exclamation of anger
➤ **hell for leather** (*informal*) at high speed

hellish *ADJECTIVE* (*informal*)
very difficult or unpleasant

hello *EXCLAMATION*
a word used to greet someone or to attract their attention

helm *NOUN* **helms**
the handle or wheel used to steer a ship
➤ **helmsman** *NOUN*

helmet *NOUN* **helmets**
a strong hat or covering worn to protect the head

help *VERB* **helps, helping, helped**
❶ to do something useful for someone ❷ to make something better or easier • *This will help you to sleep.* ❸ if you cannot help doing something, you cannot avoid doing it • *I can't help coughing.* ❹ to serve food or drink to someone
➤ **helper** *NOUN*

help *NOUN*
❶ helping someone • *I need your help.* ❷ a person or thing that helps • *Thank you, you've been a great help.*

helpful *ADJECTIVE*
giving help; useful
➤ **helpfully** *ADVERB*

helping *NOUN* **helpings**
a portion of food at a meal

helpless *ADJECTIVE*
not able to do things or look after yourself
➤ **helplessly** *ADVERB*
➤ **helplessness** *NOUN*

helpline *NOUN* **helplines**
a telephone service giving advice on problems

helter-skelter *ADVERB*
in great haste

helter-skelter *NOUN* **helter-skelters**
a tall spiral slide at a fair

hem *NOUN* **hems**
the edge of a piece of cloth that is folded over and sewn down

hem *VERB* **hems, hemming, hemmed**
to put a hem on something
➤ **hem someone in** to surround someone and prevent them from leaving

hemisphere *NOUN* **hemispheres**
❶ half a sphere ❷ half the earth, divided into north and south • *Australia is in the southern hemisphere.*
➤ **hemispherical** *ADJECTIVE*

hemlock *NOUN*
a poisonous plant or poison made from it

hemp *NOUN*
❶ a plant that produces coarse fibres from which cloth and ropes are made ❷ the drug cannabis, made from this plant
➤ **hempen** *ADJECTIVE*

hen *NOUN* **hens**
❶ a female bird ❷ a female fowl

hence *ADVERB*
❶ as a result; therefore ❷ from now on ❸ (*old use*) from here

henceforth *ADVERB*
from now on

henchman *NOUN* **henchmen**
a trusty supporter

henna *NOUN*
a reddish-brown dye, especially used for colouring hair

hepatitis *NOUN*
a disease causing inflammation of the liver

heptagon *NOUN* **heptagons**
a flat shape with seven sides and seven angles

heptathlon *NOUN* **heptathlons**
an athletic contest in which each competitor takes part in seven events

her *PRONOUN*
the form of **she** used as the object of a verb or after a preposition • *He took the books from her.*

her *DETERMINER*
belonging to her • *That is her book.*

herald *NOUN* **heralds**
❶ an official in former times who made announcements and carried messages for a king or queen ❷ a person or thing that is a sign of something to come • *Spring is the herald of summer.*

herald *VERB* **heralds, heralding, heralded**
to show that something is coming • *Voices outside heralded their arrival.*

heraldry *NOUN*
the study of coats of arms
➤ **heraldic** (say hir-**al**-dik) *ADJECTIVE*

herb *NOUN* **herbs**
a plant used for flavouring or for making medicine

herbaceous (say her-**bay**-shus) *ADJECTIVE*
containing many flowering plants • *a herbaceous border*

herbal *ADJECTIVE*
made of or using herbs • *a herbal remedy*

herbivore (say **her**-biv-or) *NOUN* **herbivores**
an animal that feeds on plants and not on the flesh of other animals. Compare with **carnivore**.

herbivorous (say her-**biv**-er-us) *ADJECTIVE*
a herbivorous animal feeds on plants and not on the flesh of other animals. Compare with **carnivorous**.

Herculean (say her-kew-**lee**-an) *ADJECTIVE*
needing great strength or effort • *a Herculean task* **WORD ORIGIN** from *Hercules*, a hero in ancient Greek legend

herd *NOUN* **herds**
❶ a group of cattle or other animals that feed together ❷ a mass of people; a mob

herd *VERB* **herds, herding, herded**
❶ to gather or move in a large group • *We all herded onto the bus.* ❷ to move people or animals together in a large group • *The visitors were herded into two large halls.* ❸ to look after a herd of animals • *a shepherd herding his flock*

herdsman *NOUN* **herdsmen**
a person who looks after a herd of animals

here *ADVERB*
in or to this place
➤ **here and there** in various places or directions

hereafter *ADVERB*
from now on; in future

hereby *ADVERB*
as a result of this act or statement. • *I hereby swear to tell the truth.*

hereditary *ADJECTIVE*
passed down to a child from a parent • *a hereditary disease*

heredity (say hir-**ed**-it-ee) *NOUN*
the process of inheriting physical or mental characteristics from parents or ancestors

heresy (say **herri**-see) *NOUN* **heresies**
an opinion or belief that disagrees with those that are generally accepted, especially in Christianity

heretic (say **herri**-tik) *NOUN* **heretics**
a person who supports a heresy
➤ **heretical** (say hi-**ret**-ik-al) *ADJECTIVE*

heritage *NOUN*
things that have been passed from one generation to another; a country's history and traditions • *Music is part of our cultural heritage.*

hermetically *ADVERB*
so as to be airtight • *The tin is hermetically sealed.*

hermit *NOUN* **hermits**
a person who lives alone and keeps away from people, often for religious reasons

hermitage *NOUN* **hermitages**
a hermit's home

hernia *NOUN* **hernias**
a condition in which an internal part of the body pushes through a weak point in another part

hero *NOUN* **heroes**
❶ a man or boy who is admired for doing something very brave or great ❷ the chief male character in a story, play or film

heroic *ADJECTIVE*
showing great courage or determination • *a heroic effort*
➤ **heroically** *ADVERB*

heroin *NOUN*
a very strong drug, made from morphine

heroine *NOUN* heroines
❶ a woman or girl who is admired for doing something very brave or great ❷ the chief female character in a story, play or film

heroism *NOUN*
great courage

heron *NOUN* herons
a wading bird with long legs and a long neck

herring *NOUN* herring or herrings
a sea fish used as food

hers *POSSESSIVE PRONOUN*
belonging to her • *Those books are hers.*
> **SPELLING**
There is never an apostrophe in **hers**.

herself *PRONOUN*
she or her and nobody else. The word is used to refer back to the subject of a sentence (e.g. *She cut herself.*) or for emphasis (e.g. *She herself has said it.*)
➤ **by herself** alone; on her own

hertz *NOUN* hertz
a unit of frequency of electromagnetic waves, equal to one cycle per second
WORD ORIGIN named after a German scientist, H. R. *Hertz*, who discovered radio waves

hesitant *ADJECTIVE*
slow to speak or do something because you are not sure if you should or not
➤ **hesitantly** *ADVERB*
➤ **hesitancy** *NOUN*

hesitate *VERB* hesitates, hesitating, hesitated
to pause before doing or saying something, because you are uncertain or worried

hesitation *NOUN* hesitations
a pause before doing or saying something, because you are uncertain or worried • *She agreed without a moment's hesitation.*

hessian *NOUN*
(*chiefly British*) a type of strong coarse cloth, used for making sacks

heterogeneous (say het-er-o-**jeen**-ee-us) *ADJECTIVE*
consisting of people or things of different kinds

heterosexual *ADJECTIVE*
attracted to people of the opposite sex; not homosexual
➤ **heterosexual** *NOUN*

hew *VERB* hews, hewing, hewn
to chop or cut wood or stone with an axe or other tool

hexagon *NOUN* hexagons
a flat shape with six sides and six angles
➤ **hexagonal** *ADJECTIVE*

hey *EXCLAMATION*
an exclamation used to attract attention or to express surprise or interest

heyday *NOUN*
the time of a person's or thing's greatest success or popularity

hi *EXCLAMATION*
an exclamation used as a friendly greeting

hiatus (say hy-**ay**-tus) *NOUN* hiatuses
a gap in something that is otherwise continuous

hibernate *VERB* hibernates, hibernating, hibernated
an animal hibernates when it spends the winter in a state like deep sleep
➤ **hibernation** *NOUN*

hiccup *NOUN* hiccups
❶ a high gulping sound made when your breath is briefly interrupted ❷ a brief hitch or setback

hiccup *VERB* hiccups, hiccuping, hiccuped
to make a sound of hiccups
> **SPELLING**
There is a double **c** in **hiccups**.

hickory *NOUN* hickories
a tree rather like the walnut tree

hide *VERB* hides, hiding, hid, hidden
❶ to get into a place where you cannot be seen ❷ to keep a person or thing from being seen ❸ to keep a thing secret

hide *NOUN* hides
❶ an animal's skin ❷ (*British*) a camouflaged shelter used to observe wildlife at close quarters

hide-and-seek *NOUN*
a game in which one person looks for others who are hiding

hidebound *ADJECTIVE*
narrow-minded; having old-fashioned attitudes and ideas **WORD ORIGIN** originally used of underfed cattle, with skin stretched tight over their bones, later of a tree whose bark was so tight it could not grow

a
b
c
d
e
f
g
h
i
j
k
l
m
n
o
p
q
r
s
t
u
v
w
x
y
z

hideous *ADJECTIVE*
very ugly or unpleasant
➤ **hideously** *ADVERB*

hideout *NOUN* hideouts
a place where someone hides

hiding *NOUN* hidings
❶ being hidden • *She went into hiding.* ❷ a thrashing or beating

hierarchy (say **hyr**-ark-ee) *NOUN* hierarchies
an organization that ranks people one above another according to the power or authority that they hold

hieroglyphics (say hyr-o-**glif**-iks) *PLURAL NOUN*
pictures or symbols used in ancient Egypt to represent words

hi-fi *NOUN* hi-fis (*informal*)
equipment for playing CDs or other recorded music

higgledy-piggledy *ADVERB & ADJECTIVE*
completely mixed up; not in any order
• *Books were piled higgledy-piggledy on the table.*

high *ADJECTIVE* higher, highest
❶ reaching a long way upwards • *high hills* ❷ far above the ground or above sea level • *high clouds* ❸ measuring from top to bottom • *The post is two metres high.* ❹ above average level in importance, quality or amount • *high rank* • *high prices* ❺ a high note is one at the top end of a musical scale ❻ meat is high when it is beginning to go bad ❼ (*informal*) affected by a drug
➤ **it is high time** it is past the time when something should have happened • *It's high time we left.*

high *ADVERB*
❶ far above the ground or a long way up
• *They flew high above us.* ❷ at or to a high level • *The temperature is going to rise even higher this week.*

highbrow *ADJECTIVE*
having serious or intellectual tastes
(**WORD ORIGIN**) from *highbrowed* = having a high forehead (thought to be a sign of intelligence)

Higher *NOUN* Highers
the advanced level of the Scottish Certificate of Education

higher education *NOUN*
education at a university or college

high explosive *NOUN* high explosives
a powerful explosive

high fidelity *NOUN*
reproducing recorded sound with very little distortion

high jump *NOUN*
an athletic contest in which competitors try to jump over a high bar

highlands *PLURAL NOUN*
mountainous country • *the Scottish Highlands*
➤ **highland** *ADJECTIVE*
➤ **highlander** *NOUN*

highlight *NOUN* highlights
❶ the most interesting part of something
• *The highlight of the holiday was the trip to Pompeii.* ❷ a light area in a painting or photograph ❸ highlights are light-coloured streaks in a person's hair

highlight *VERB* highlights, highlighting, highlighted
❶ to draw special attention to something
• *The test was designed to highlight students' strengths and weaknesses.* ❷ to mark part of a text with a different colour so that people give it more attention • *Click on the highlighted word to go to the section you want.*

highlighter *NOUN* highlighters
a felt-tip pen that you use to spread bright colour over lines of text to draw attention to them

highly *ADVERB*
❶ extremely; to a high degree • *He is highly intelligent.* • *a highly paid job* ❷ very well or favourably • *We think highly of her.*

highly-strung *ADJECTIVE*
nervous and easily upset

Highness *NOUN* Highnesses
the title of a prince or princess

high-pitched *ADJECTIVE*
high in sound

high-rise *ADJECTIVE*
a high-rise building is tall with many storeys

high school *NOUN* high schools
a secondary school

high spirits *PLURAL NOUN*
cheerful and lively behaviour
➤ **high-spirited** *ADJECTIVE*

high street *NOUN* high streets
(*British*) a town's main street

high-tech *ADJECTIVE*
using the most advanced technology, especially electronic devices and computers

highway *NOUN* highways
a main road or route for vehicles

highwayman *NOUN* highwaymen
a man who robbed travellers on highways in former times

hijab *NOUN* hijabs
a head covering worn in public by some Muslim women

hijack *VERB* hijacks, hijacking, hijacked
to seize control of an aircraft or vehicle by force during a journey
➤ **hijack** *NOUN*
➤ **hijacker** *NOUN*

hike *NOUN* hikes
a long walk in the countryside

hike *VERB* hikes, hiking, hiked
to go on a hike
➤ **hiker** *NOUN*

hilarious *ADJECTIVE*
very funny
➤ **hilariously** *ADVERB*

hilarity *NOUN*
great amusement and laughter • *My new hairstyle was the cause of much hilarity.*

hill *NOUN* hills
a piece of land that is higher than the ground around it

hillock *NOUN* hillocks
a small hill or mound

hillside *NOUN* hillsides
a piece of land forming the side of a hill

hilly *ADJECTIVE*
having a lot of hills • *The country's very hilly around here.*

hilt *NOUN* hilts
the handle of a sword, dagger or knife
➤ **to the hilt** to a high degree; completely • *I'll defend you to the hilt.*

him *PRONOUN*
the form of **he** used as the object of a verb or after a preposition

himself *PRONOUN*
he or him and nobody else. The word is used to refer back to the subject of a sentence (e.g. *He has hurt himself*) or for emphasis (e.g. *He himself has told us*)
➤ **by himself** alone; on his own

hind *ADJECTIVE*
at the back • *the hind legs*

hind *NOUN* hinds
a female deer. Compare with **hart**.

hinder *VERB* hinders, hindering, hindered
to get in your way or make things difficult for you • *Bad weather hindered our journey.*

Hindi *NOUN*
one of the languages of India

hindmost *ADJECTIVE*
furthest behind

hindquarters *PLURAL NOUN*
an animal's hind legs and rear parts

hindrance *NOUN*
a person or thing that gets in your way or makes it difficult for you to do something • *She was more of a hindrance than a help.*

hindsight *NOUN*
looking back on an event with knowledge or understanding that you did not have at the time

Hindu *NOUN* Hindus
a person who believes in Hinduism, which is one of the religions of India

hinge *NOUN* hinges
a joining device on which a lid or door etc. turns when it opens

hinge *VERB* hinges, hinging, hinged
❶ to be hinged is to be fixed with a hinge
❷ to hinge on something is to depend on it • *Everything hinges on this meeting.*

hint *NOUN* hints
❶ a slight indication or suggestion • *Give me a hint of what you want.* ❷ a useful idea or piece of advice • *household hints*

hint *VERB* hints, hinting, hinted
to suggest something without actually saying it • *She hinted at the plot of her next book.*

hinterland *NOUN* hinterlands
the district lying inland beyond a coast or port

hip *NOUN* hips
❶ your hips are the bony parts at the side of your body between your waist and your thighs ❷ the fruit of the wild rose

hip hop *NOUN*
a type of popular dance music with spoken words and a steady beat, played on electronic instruments

hippie *NOUN* hippies (*informal*)
a young person who joins with others to live in an unconventional way, often based on ideas of peace and love. Hippies first appeared in the 1960s.

hippo *NOUN* hippos (*informal*)
a hippopotamus

hippopotamus *NOUN* hippopotamuses
a very large African animal that lives near water **WORD ORIGIN** from Greek *hippos ho potamios* = horse of the river

hire *VERB* hires, hiring, hired
❶ to pay to have use of something for a time • *We hired a boat for the afternoon.* ❷ to lend something in return for payment • *He hires out bicycles.* ❸ to pay someone to do a job for you

hire *NOUN*
➤ **for hire** available for people to hire • *Do you have bicycles for hire?*

hire purchase *NOUN*
(*British*) buying something by paying for it in instalments

his *DETERMINER & POSSESSIVE PRONOUN*
belonging to him • *That is his book.* • *That book is his.*

hiss *VERB* hisses, hissing, hissed
❶ to make a sound like a continuous *s* • *The cat hissed at me.* ❷ to say something in a quiet angry voice • *'Stay away from me!' she hissed.*

hiss *NOUN* hisses
the sound of hissing • *There were boos and hisses from the audience.*

histogram *NOUN* histograms
a chart showing amounts as rectangles of varying sizes

historian *NOUN* historians
a person who writes or studies history

historic *ADJECTIVE*
famous or important in history; likely to be remembered • *a historic town* • *a historic meeting*

USAGE
Take care not to confuse with **historical**.

historical *ADJECTIVE*
❶ to do with history ❷ that actually existed or took place in the past • *The novel is based*
on historical events.
➤ **historically** *ADVERB*

USAGE
Take care not to confuse with **historic**.

history *NOUN* histories
❶ what happened in the past • *an important moment in history* ❷ the study of past events ❸ a description of important events

hit *VERB* hits, hitting, hit
❶ to come forcefully against a person or thing. or to give them a blow ❷ to have a bad effect on a place or group of people • *Famine has hit the poorer countries.* ❸ something hits you when you suddenly realize or feel it • *Then it hit me where I'd seen him before.* ❹ to reach something • *I can't hit that high note.*
➤ **hit it off** to get on well with someone
➤ **hit on something** to discover something suddenly or by chance

hit *NOUN* hits
❶ hitting; a knock or stroke ❷ a shot that hits the target ❸ a success ❹ a successful song or show ❺ a result of a search on a computer, especially on the Internet • *How many hits did you get?*

hit-and-run *ADJECTIVE*
a hit-and-run driver is one who injures someone in an accident and drives off without stopping

hitch *VERB* hitches, hitching, hitched
❶ to raise or pull something with a slight jerk • *She hitched up her skirt and waded into the river.* ❷ to fasten something with a loop or hook ❸ to hitch-hike

hitch *NOUN* hitches
❶ a slight difficulty causing delay ❷ a knot

hitch-hike *VERB* hitch-hikes, hitch-hiking, hitch-hiked
to travel by getting lifts from passing vehicles
➤ **hitch-hiker** *NOUN*

hi-tech *ADJECTIVE*
a different spelling of **high-tech**

hither *ADVERB*
(*old use*) to or towards this place

hitherto *ADVERB*
until this time

HIV *ABBREVIATION*
human immunodeficiency virus; a virus that causes Aids

hive *NOUN* hives
❶ a beehive ❷ the bees living in a beehive
➤ **a hive of activity** or **industry** a place full of people working busily

hoard *NOUN* hoards
a carefully saved store of money, treasure, food, etc.

hoard *VERB* hoards, hoarding, hoarded
to collect and store away large quantities of something
➤ **hoarder** *NOUN*

> **SPELLING**
> **Hoard** is different from **horde**, which means a large group or crowd.

hoarding *NOUN* hoardings
(*British*) a tall fence covered with advertisements

hoar frost *NOUN*
the white frost that forms on the ground in the morning after a cold night

hoarse *ADJECTIVE*
having a rough or croaking voice • *He was hoarse from shouting.*
➤ **hoarsely** *ADVERB*
➤ **hoarseness** *NOUN*

hoary *ADJECTIVE*
❶ white or grey from age • *hoary hair* ❷ old and overused • *hoary jokes*

hoax *NOUN* hoaxes
a trick played on someone in which they are told about something that is not true
➤ **hoax** *VERB*
➤ **hoaxer** *NOUN*

hob *NOUN* hobs
a flat surface on the top of a cooker, for cooking or heating food

hobble *VERB* hobbles, hobbling, hobbled
to walk with difficulty because your feet or legs hurt

hobby *NOUN* hobbies
something you enjoy doing in your spare time

hobby horse *NOUN* hobby horses
❶ a stick with a horse's head, used as a toy ❷ a subject that a person likes to talk about whenever they get the chance

hobgoblin *NOUN* hobgoblins
a mischievous or evil spirit

hobnob *VERB* hobnobs, hobnobbing, hobnobbed
to spend a lot of time with someone famous or important • *She's been hobnobbing with rock stars.*

hock *NOUN* hocks
the middle joint of an animal's hind leg

hockey *NOUN*
a game played by two teams with curved sticks and a hard ball

hoe *NOUN* hoes
a gardening tool with a long handle and a metal blade, used for scraping up weeds and making soil loose

hoe *VERB* hoes, hoeing, hoed
to scrape or dig the ground with a hoe

hog *NOUN* hogs
❶ a male pig ❷ (*informal*) a greedy person
➤ **go the whole hog** (*informal*) to do something completely or thoroughly

hog *VERB* hogs, hogging, hogged (*informal*) to take more than your fair share of something

Hogmanay *NOUN*
New Year's Eve in Scotland

hoi polloi *NOUN*
the ordinary people; the masses
> **WORD ORIGIN** Greek, = the many

hoist *VERB* hoists, hoisting, hoisted
to lift something up, especially by using ropes or pulleys • *The crew soon hoisted the sails.* • *He hoisted the boy onto his shoulders.*

hold *VERB* holds, holding, held
❶ to have something in your hands ❷ to keep something in a certain position • *Hold your head up straight.* ❸ to contain or have room for a certain amount • *The jug holds two pints.* ❹ to support something • *This plank won't hold my weight.* ❺ to stay the same; to continue • *Will the fine weather hold?* ❻ to have or possess something • *She holds the world high jump record.* ❼ to believe or consider something • *We shall hold you responsible.* ❽ to arrange something or cause it to take place • *The 2012 Olympics were held in London.* ❾ to keep someone somewhere or stop them getting away • *The police are holding three men for the robbery.*
➤ **hold forth** to make a long speech
➤ **hold it** stop; wait a minute
➤ **hold out** ❶ to refuse to give in ❷ to last or continue
➤ **hold someone up** ❶ to hinder or delay someone ❷ to stop and rob someone by threats or force
➤ **hold with something** to approve of something • *We don't hold with bullying.*

➤ **hold your tongue** (*informal*) to stop talking

hold *NOUN* **holds**
❶ holding something; a grasp • *Don't lose hold of the rope.* ❷ a place where you can put your hand or foot when climbing ❸ the part of a ship where cargo is stored, below the deck
➤ **get hold of someone** to make contact with a person
➤ **get hold of something** ❶ to grasp something ❷ to obtain something

holdall *NOUN* **holdalls**
(*British*) a large portable bag or case

holder *NOUN* **holders**
a person or thing that holds something • *the world record holder*

hold–up *NOUN* **hold-ups**
❶ a brief delay ❷ a robbery with threats or force

hole *NOUN* **holes**
❶ a hollow place; a gap or opening made in something ❷ an animal's burrow ❸ one of the small holes into which you have to hit the ball in golf ❹ (*informal*) an unpleasant place
➤ **holey** *ADJECTIVE*
➤ **in a hole** in an awkward situation

hole *VERB* **holes, holing, holed**
❶ to make a hole or holes in something, especially a boat or ship ❷ to hit a golf ball into one of the holes

SPELLING

Hole is different from whole, which means all of something.

Holi *NOUN*
a Hindu festival held in the spring

holiday *NOUN* **holidays** (*chiefly British*)
❶ a day or time when people do not go to work or to school ❷ a time when you go away to enjoy yourself **WORD ORIGIN** from **holy** + **day** (because holidays were originally religious festivals)

holiness *NOUN*
being holy or sacred
➤ **His Holiness** the title of the pope

hollow *ADJECTIVE*
❶ with an empty space inside; not solid ❷ loud and echoing • *hollow footsteps* ❸ not sincere • *a hollow promise*
➤ **hollowly** *ADVERB*

hollow *NOUN* **hollows**
a hollow or sunken place

hollow *VERB* **hollows, hollowing, hollowed**
to make a thing hollow • *We always hollow out a pumpkin at Halloween.*

holly *NOUN*
an evergreen bush with shiny prickly leaves and red berries

hollyhock *NOUN* **hollyhocks**
a plant with large flowers on a very tall stem

holocaust *NOUN* **holocausts**
large-scale destruction, especially by fire or in a war • *the nuclear holocaust*
➤ **the Holocaust** the mass murder of Jews by the Nazis from 1939 to 1945
WORD ORIGIN from Greek *holos* + *kaustos* = completely burnt

hologram *NOUN* **holograms**
a type of photograph made by laser beams that produces a three-dimensional image

holster *NOUN* **holsters**
a leather case in which a pistol or revolver is carried

holy *ADJECTIVE* **holier, holiest**
❶ to do with God or a particular religion • *the holy city of Mecca* ❷ a holy person is religious and leads a pure life

homage *NOUN* **homages**
an act or expression of respect or honour • *We paid homage to his achievements.*

home *NOUN* **homes**
❶ the place where you live ❷ the place where you were born or where you feel you belong ❸ a place where those who need help are looked after • *an old people's home* ❹ the place to be reached in a race or in certain games

home *ADJECTIVE*
❶ to do with your own home or country • *home industries* ❷ played on a team's own ground • *a home match*

home *ADVERB*
❶ to or at home • *Is she home yet?* ❷ to the point aimed at • *Push the bolt home.*
➤ **bring something home to someone** to make a person realize something

home *VERB* **homes, homing, homed**
➤ **home in on something** to aim at something and move straight towards it • *The missile homed in on its target.*

home economics *NOUN*
the study of cookery and how to run a home

homeland *NOUN* **homelands**
a person's native country

homeless *ADJECTIVE*
having no home
➤ **homelessness** *NOUN*

homely *ADJECTIVE*
simple and ordinary • *a homely meal*

home-made *ADJECTIVE*
made at home, not bought from a shop

homeopath *NOUN* **homeopaths**
a person who practises homeopathy

homeopathy *NOUN*
the treatment of disease by tiny doses of
drugs that in a healthy person would produce
symptoms of the disease
➤ **homeopathic** *ADJECTIVE*

home page *NOUN* **home pages**
an introductory page on a website

homesick *ADJECTIVE*
sad or upset because you are away from
home
➤ **homesickness** *NOUN*

homestead *NOUN* **homesteads**
a farmhouse, usually with the land and
buildings round it

homeward *ADJECTIVE & ADVERB*
going towards home • *the long homeward
journey*
➤ **homewards** *ADVERB*

homework *NOUN*
school work that you have to do at home

homicide *NOUN* **homicides**
the crime of killing another person
➤ **homicidal** *ADJECTIVE*

homily *NOUN* **homilies**
a lecture about behaviour

homing *ADJECTIVE*
❶ trained or having the natural ability, to
find its way home from a long distance away
• *a homing pigeon* ❷ programmed to find
and hit its target • *a missile fitted with a
homing device*

homogeneous (say hom-o-**jeen**-ee-us)
ADJECTIVE
formed of people or things of the same kind

homograph *NOUN* **homographs**
a word that is spelt like another but has a
different meaning or origin, e.g. *bat* (a flying
animal) and *bat* (for hitting a ball)

homonym (say **hom**-o-nim) *NOUN* **homonyms**
a homograph or homophone

homophone *NOUN* **homophones**
a word with the same sound as another but a
different spelling and meaning, e.g. *son, sun*

Homo sapiens *NOUN*
human beings regarded as a species of animal

homosexual *ADJECTIVE*
attracted to people of the same sex; not
heterosexual
➤ **homosexual** *NOUN*
➤ **homosexuality** *NOUN*

honest *ADJECTIVE*
not stealing or cheating or telling lies;
truthful

honestly *ADVERB*
❶ in an honest way • *I can't believe he got
that money honestly.* ❷ speaking truthfully
• *I honestly don't mind.*

honesty *NOUN*
being honest and truthful • *I appreciate your
honesty.*

honey *NOUN*
a sweet sticky food made by bees

honeycomb *NOUN* **honeycombs**
a wax structure of small six-sided sections
made by bees to hold their honey and eggs

honeycombed *ADJECTIVE*
with many holes or tunnels

honeymoon *NOUN* **honeymoons**
a holiday spent together by a newly-married
couple

honeysuckle *NOUN*
a climbing plant with fragrant yellow or pink
flowers

honk *NOUN* **honks**
a loud sound like that made by a goose or an
old-fashioned car horn

honk *VERB* **honks, honking, honked**
to make a honking sound

honorary *ADJECTIVE*
❶ given or received as an honour • *an
honorary degree* ❷ unpaid • *the honorary
treasurer of the club*

USAGE
Take care not to confuse with
honourable.

honour *NOUN* **honours**
❶ great respect or reputation ❷ a person
or thing that brings honour ❸ something
a person is proud to do • *It is an honour to
meet you.* ❹ honesty and loyalty • *a man*

a
b
c
d
e
f
g
h
i
j
k
l
m
n
o
p
q
r
s
t
u
v
w
x
y
z

of honour ❺ an award given as a mark of respect
➤ **in honour of** out of respect for • *A banquet was held in honour of her visit.*

honour *VERB* honours, honouring, honoured
❶ to feel or show honour for a person ❷ to keep to the terms of an agreement or promise

honourable *ADJECTIVE*
able to be trusted and always trying to do the right thing; deserving honour and respect
➤ **honourably** *ADVERB*

USAGE
Take care not to confuse with **honorary**.

hood *NOUN* hoods
❶ a covering of soft material for the head and neck ❷ a folding roof or cover
➤ **hooded** *ADJECTIVE*

hoodie *NOUN* hoodies
❶ a jacket or sweatshirt with a hood that goes over the head ❷ a person who wears a hoodie

hoodwink *VERB* hoodwinks, hoodwinking, hoodwinked
to deceive someone **WORD ORIGIN** originally = to blindfold with a hood: from **hood** + an old sense of *wink* = close the eyes

hoof *NOUN* hoofs or hooves
the hard horny part of the feet of horses and some other animals

hook *NOUN* hooks
a bent or curved piece of metal or plastic for hanging things on or for catching hold of something
➤ **be let off the hook** (*informal*) to escape punishment

hook *VERB* hooks, hooking, hooked
❶ to fasten something with or on a hook ❷ to catch a fish with a hook ❸ to hit a ball in a curving path
➤ **be hooked on something** (*informal*) to be addicted to something

hookah *NOUN* hookahs
an oriental tobacco pipe with a long tube passing through a jar of water

hooked *ADJECTIVE*
hook-shaped • *a hooked nose*

hooligan *NOUN* hooligans
a rough and violent young person
➤ **hooliganism** *NOUN*

hoop *NOUN* hoops
a large ring made of metal, wood or plastic

hoopla *NOUN*
a game in which people try to throw hoops round an object, which they then win as a prize

hooray *EXCLAMATION*
a different spelling of **hurray**

hoot *NOUN* hoots
❶ the sound made by an owl or a vehicle's horn or a steam whistle ❷ a cry of scorn or disapproval ❸ a loud laugh ❹ something funny

hoot *VERB* hoots, hooting, hooted
❶ to make the sound of a hoot ❷ to laugh loudly
➤ **hooter** *NOUN*

Hoover *NOUN* Hoovers (*trademark*) (*British*)
a vacuum cleaner

hoover *VERB* hoovers, hoovering, hoovered
to clean a carpet with a vacuum cleaner

hop *VERB* hops, hopping, hopped
❶ to jump on one foot ❷ an animal hops when it springs from all its feet at once ❸ (*informal*) to move quickly • *Hop in and I'll give you a lift.*
➤ **hop it** (*informal*) to go away

hop *NOUN* hops
❶ a hopping movement ❷ a climbing plant used to give beer its flavour

hope *NOUN* hopes
❶ the feeling of wanting something to happen and thinking that it will happen ❷ a person or thing that gives hope • *You are our only hope.*

hope *VERB* hopes, hoping, hoped
to feel hope; to want and expect something • *I hope that you feel better soon.*

hopeful *ADJECTIVE*
❶ feeling hope ❷ likely to be good or successful • *The future did not seem very hopeful.*

hopefully *ADVERB*
❶ in a hopeful way • *'Can I come too?' she asked hopefully.* ❷ it is to be hoped; I hope that • *Hopefully we will be there by lunchtime.*

hopeless *ADJECTIVE*
❶ without hope ❷ very bad at something
➤ **hopelessly** *ADVERB*
➤ **hopelessness** *NOUN*

hopper *NOUN* hoppers
a large funnel-shaped container for grain or sand

hopscotch *NOUN*
a game of hopping into squares drawn on the ground

horde *NOUN* **hordes**
a large group or crowd • *hordes of tourists*

> **SPELLING**
> **Horde** is different from **hoard**, which means a hidden store of something.

horizon *NOUN* **horizons**
the line where the earth and the sky seem to meet

horizontal *ADJECTIVE*
level or flat; going across from side to side, not up and down. (The opposite is **vertical**.)
➤ **horizontally** *ADVERB*

hormone *NOUN* **hormones**
a substance produced by glands in the body and carried by the blood to stimulate other organs in the body
➤ **hormonal** *ADJECTIVE*

horn *NOUN* **horns**
❶ a hard substance that grows into a point on the head of a bull, cow, ram, etc. ❷ a brass musical instrument played by blowing ❸ a device for making a warning sound

horned *ADJECTIVE*
having horns • *a horned helmet*

hornet *NOUN* **hornets**
a large kind of wasp

hornpipe *NOUN* **hornpipes**
a sailors' lively dance or the music for this

horny *ADJECTIVE*
hard like horn • *a horny beak*

horoscope *NOUN* **horoscopes**
an astrologer's forecast of what is going to happen to someone in the future

horrendous *ADJECTIVE*
extremely unpleasant **WORD ORIGIN** from Latin *horrendus* = making your hair stand on end

horrible *ADJECTIVE*
❶ shocking or horrifying • *a horrible murder* ❷ very unpleasant or nasty • *Don't be so horrible!*
➤ **horribly** *ADVERB*

horrid *ADJECTIVE*
nasty or unkind; horrible

horrific *ADJECTIVE*
shocking or horrifying • *a horrific accident*
➤ **horrifically** *ADVERB*

horrify *VERB* **horrifies, horrifying, horrified**
to make someone feel shocked or disgusted • *He was horrified when he discovered the truth.*

horror *NOUN* **horrors**
❶ great fear or disgust ❷ a person or thing causing horror ❸ (*informal*) a badly behaved child

hors-d'oeuvre (say or-**dervr**) *NOUN* **hors-d'oeuvres**
food served as an appetizer at the start of a meal

horse *NOUN* **horses**
❶ a large four-legged animal used for riding on and for pulling carts etc. ❷ a padded wooden block for vaulting over in gymnastics

horseback *NOUN*
➤ **on horseback** riding on a horse

horse chestnut *NOUN* **horse chestnuts**
a large tree that produces dark-brown nuts (conkers)

horseman *NOUN* **horsemen**
a man who rides a horse, especially a skilled rider

horsemanship *NOUN*
skill in riding horses

horseplay *NOUN*
rough play

horsepower *NOUN*
a unit for measuring the power of an engine, equal to 746 watts **WORD ORIGIN** because the unit was based on the amount of work a horse could do

horseshoe *NOUN* **horseshoes**
a U-shaped piece of metal nailed to a horse's hoof

horsewoman *NOUN* **horsewomen**
a woman who rides a horse, especially a skilled rider

horticulture *NOUN*
the art of planning and looking after gardens
➤ **horticultural** *ADJECTIVE*

hose *NOUN* **hoses**
❶ a flexible tube for taking water to something ❷ (*old use*) men's breeches • *doublet and hose*

hose *VERB* **hoses, hosing, hosed**
to water or spray something with a hose

hosiery *NOUN*
socks, stockings and tights sold in shops

a b c d e f g h i j k l m n o p q r s t u v w x y z

hospice (say **hosp**-iss) *NOUN* hospices
a nursing home for people who are very ill or dying

hospitable *ADJECTIVE*
welcoming and friendly to guests and visitors
➤ **hospitably** *ADVERB*

hospital *NOUN* hospitals
a place where ill or injured people are given medical treatment

hospitality *NOUN*
welcoming guests and visitors and giving them food and entertainment

host *NOUN* hosts
❶ a person who has guests and looks after them ❷ the presenter of a television or radio programme ❸ a large number of people or things ❹ in the Christian Church, the bread consecrated at Communion

host *VERB* hosts, hosting, hosted
to organize a party, event, etc. and look after the people who come • *London hosted the 2012 Olympic Games.*

hostage *NOUN* hostages
a person who is held prisoner until the people who are holding them get what they want • *The hijackers took the crew hostage.*

hostel *NOUN* hostels
a building where travellers, students or other groups can stay or live

hostess *NOUN* hostesses
a woman who has guests and looks after them

hostile *ADJECTIVE*
❶ unfriendly and angry • *a hostile glance* ❷ opposed to something ❸ to do with an enemy • *hostile aircraft*

hostility *NOUN*
unfriendliness and strong dislike • *She did not speak but I could sense her hostility.*

hot *ADJECTIVE* hotter, hottest
❶ having great heat or a high temperature ❷ giving a burning sensation in the mouth; spicy ❸ passionate or excitable • *He has a hot temper.*
➤ **hotness** *NOUN*
➤ **be in hot water** (*informal*) to be in trouble or disgrace

hot *VERB* hots, hotting, hotted
➤ **hot up** (*British*) (*informal*) to become hotter or more exciting

hot cross bun *NOUN* hot cross buns
a spicy bun marked with a cross, eaten at Easter

hot dog *NOUN* hot dogs
a hot sausage in a long bread roll

hotel *NOUN* hotels
a building where people pay to stay for the night when they are travelling or on holiday

hotfoot *ADVERB*
in eager haste • *She had just arrived hotfoot from Madrid.*

hothead *NOUN* hotheads
an impetuous person
➤ **hot-headed** *ADJECTIVE*

hothouse *NOUN* hothouses
a heated greenhouse

hotly *ADVERB*
strongly or forcefully • *He hotly denied that he'd done it.*

hotplate *NOUN* hotplates
a heated surface for cooking food or keeping it hot

hotpot *NOUN* hotpots
(*British*) a kind of stew

hot-water bottle *NOUN* hot-water bottles
a container that is filled with hot water and used to warm a bed

hound *NOUN* hounds
a dog used in hunting or racing

hound *VERB* hounds, hounding, hounded
to keep on chasing and bothering someone

hour *NOUN* hours
❶ one of the twenty four parts into which a day is divided; sixty minutes ❷ a particular time • *Why are you up at this hour?*
➤ **hours** *PLURAL NOUN*
a fixed period for work • *Office hours are 9 a.m. to 5 p.m.*

> **SPELLING**
> Be careful, this sounds the same as **our** which means 'belonging to us'.

hourglass *NOUN* hourglasses
a glass container with a very narrow part in the middle through which sand runs from the top half to the bottom half, taking one hour

hourly *ADVERB* & *ADJECTIVE*
every hour • *Trains run hourly.* • *an hourly bus service*

house (say howss) *NOUN* **houses**
❶ a building made for people to live in, usually designed for one family ❷ a building or establishment for a special purpose • *the opera house* ❸ a building for a government assembly; the assembly itself • *the House of Commons* ❹ one of the divisions in some schools for sports competitions and other events ❺ a family or dynasty • *the royal house of Tudor*

house (say howz) *VERB* **houses, housing, housed**
to provide a place for someone to live or a place where something can be kept • *The hangar was big enough to house two large aircraft.*

houseboat *NOUN* **houseboats**
a barge-like boat for living in

household *NOUN* **households**
all the people who live together in the same house

householder *NOUN* **householders**
a person who owns or rents a house

housekeeper *NOUN* **housekeepers**
a person employed to look after a household

housekeeping *NOUN*
❶ looking after a household ❷ the money for food and the other things that you need at home

housemaid *NOUN* **housemaids**
a woman servant in a house, especially one who cleans rooms

house plant *NOUN* **house plants**
a plant grown indoors

house-proud *ADJECTIVE*
very careful to keep a house clean and tidy

house-trained *ADJECTIVE*
an animal that is house-trained is trained to be clean in the house

house-warming *NOUN* **house-warmings**
a party to celebrate moving into a new home

housewife *NOUN* **housewives**
a woman who does the housekeeping for her family and does not have a paid job

housework *NOUN*
the regular work that has to be done in a house, such as cleaning and cooking

housing *NOUN* **housings**
❶ buildings in which people live ❷ a stiff cover or guard for a piece of machinery

housing estate *NOUN* **housing estates**
(*British*) a set of houses planned and built together in one area

hove
past tense of **heave** (when used of ships)

hovel *NOUN* **hovels**
a small shabby house

hover *VERB* **hovers, hovering, hovered**
❶ to stay in one place in the air ❷ to wait about near someone or something • *He hovered nervously outside the door.*

hovercraft *NOUN* **hovercraft**
a vehicle that travels just above the surface of land or water, supported by a strong current of air sent downwards from its engines

how *ADVERB*
❶ in what way; by what means • *How did you do it?* ❷ to what extent or amount etc. • *How high can you jump?* ❸ in what condition • *How are you?* ❹ used for emphasis • *How odd!*
➤ **how about** would you like • *How about a game of football?*
➤ **how do you do?** a formal greeting

however *ADVERB*
❶ in whatever way; to whatever extent • *You will never catch him, however hard you try.* ❷ all the same; nevertheless • *Later, however, he decided to go.*

however *CONJUNCTION*
in any way • *You can do it however you like.*

howl *NOUN* **howls**
a long loud sad-sounding cry or sound, such as that made by a dog or wolf

howl *VERB* **howls, howling, howled**
❶ to make a howl ❷ to weep loudly

howler *NOUN* **howlers**
(*informal*) a silly and embarrassing mistake

HQ *ABBREVIATION*
headquarters

hub *NOUN* **hubs**
❶ the central part of a wheel ❷ the central point of interest or activity

hubbub *NOUN*
a loud confused noise of voices

huddle *VERB* **huddles, huddling, huddled**
❶ people huddle when they crowd together, often for warmth • *We huddled together round the fire.* ❷ to curl up your body closely

huddle *NOUN* **huddles**
a small group of people crowded together

a b c d e f g h i j k l m n o p q r s t u v w x y z

hue *NOUN* hues
a colour or tint
➤ **hue and cry** a public outcry of alarm or protest

huff *VERB* huffs, huffing, huffed
to breathe out noisily • *He climbed up the hill, huffing and puffing.*
➤ **in a huff** offended or sulking about something • *She went away in a huff.*
➤ **huffy** *ADJECTIVE*

hug *VERB* hugs, hugging, hugged
❶ to clasp someone tightly in your arms ❷ to keep close to something • *The little boat hugged the shore.*

hug *NOUN* hugs
clasping someone tightly in your arms

huge *ADJECTIVE*
extremely large; enormous
➤ **hugeness** *NOUN*

hugely *ADVERB*
extremely; very much • *The singer is hugely popular.*

hulk *NOUN* hulks
❶ the body or wreck of an old ship ❷ a large clumsy person or thing

hulking *ADJECTIVE*
large and heavy in appearance

hull *NOUN* hulls
the main framework of a ship

hullabaloo *NOUN* hullabaloos
an uproar or commotion

hullo *EXCLAMATION*
a different spelling of **hello**

hum *VERB* hums, humming, hummed
❶ to sing a tune with your lips closed ❷ to make a low continuous sound like that of a bee

hum *NOUN* hums
a humming sound • *the hum of distant traffic*

human *ADJECTIVE*
to do with human beings

human *NOUN* humans
a human being

human being *NOUN* human beings
a person; a man, woman or child

humane (say hew-**mayn**) *ADJECTIVE*
showing kindness and a wish to cause as little suffering or pain as possible
➤ **humanely** *ADVERB*

humanist *NOUN* humanists
a person who believes that people can live using reason and understanding of others, rather than using religious belief
➤ **humanism** *NOUN*

humanitarian *ADJECTIVE*
concerned with people's welfare and the reduction of suffering
➤ **humanitarian** *NOUN*

humanity *NOUN*
❶ human beings as a whole; people ❷ being human ❸ compassion and understanding
➤ **humanities** *PLURAL NOUN*
arts subjects such as history, literature and music, not sciences

humble *ADJECTIVE*
❶ modest; not proud or showy ❷ not special or important • *He comes from a humble background.*
➤ **humbly** *ADVERB*

humble *VERB* humbles, humbling, humbled
to make someone feel humble or humiliated

humbug *NOUN* humbugs
❶ insincere or dishonest talk or behaviour ❷ a hard peppermint sweet

humdrum *ADJECTIVE*
dull and boring; commonplace • *a humdrum existence.*

humid (say **hew**-mid) *ADJECTIVE*
humid air is warm and damp
➤ **humidity** *NOUN*

humiliate *VERB* humiliates, humiliating, humiliated
to make a person feel ashamed or foolish in front of other people
➤ **humiliation** *NOUN*

humility *NOUN*
being humble

hummingbird *NOUN* hummingbirds
a small tropical bird that makes a humming sound by beating its wings rapidly

humorist *NOUN* humorists
a humorous writer

humorous *ADJECTIVE*
amusing or funny

humour *NOUN*
❶ being amusing; what makes people laugh ❷ the ability to enjoy things that are funny • *a sense of humour* ❸ a person's mood • *She is in a good humour today.*

humour *VERB* **humours, humouring, humoured**
to keep a person happy by doing what they want or agreeing with them

hump *NOUN* **humps**
❶ a rounded lump or mound ❷ an abnormal outward curve at the top of a person's back

hump *VERB* **humps, humping, humped**
to carry something heavy with difficulty • *We've been humping furniture around all day.*

humpback bridge *NOUN* **humpback bridges**
(*British*) a small bridge that steeply curves upwards in the middle

humus (say **hew**-mus) *NOUN*
rich earth made by decayed plants

hunch *NOUN* **hunches**
a feeling that you can guess what is going to happen • *I have a hunch that she won't come.*

hunch *VERB* **hunches, hunching, hunched**
to hunch your shoulders is to raise them so that your back is rounded

hunchback *NOUN* **hunchbacks**
(*old use*) someone with a hump on their back
➤ **hunchbacked** *ADJECTIVE*

hundred *NOUN* & *ADJECTIVE* **hundreds**
the number 100
➤ **hundredth** *ADJECTIVE* & *NOUN*

hundredweight *NOUN* **hundredweight**
a unit of weight equal to 112 pounds (about 50.8 kilograms)

hunger *NOUN*
❶ the feeling that you have when you need to eat ❷ a strong desire for something • *a hunger for knowledge*

hunger *VERB* **hungers, hungering, hungered**
to hunger for something is to want it very much

hunger strike *NOUN* **hunger strikes**
refusing to eat, as a way of making a protest

hungry *ADJECTIVE* **hungrier, hungriest**
❶ wanting or needing to eat ❷ wanting something very much • *He was hungry for power.*
➤ **hungrily** *ADVERB*

hunk *NOUN* **hunks**
❶ a large piece of something • *a hunk of bread* ❷ (*informal*) a muscular, good-looking man

hunt *VERB* **hunts, hunting, hunted**
❶ to chase and kill animals for food or as a sport • *Owls hunt at night.* ❷ to search for something • *I've hunted everywhere, but I can't find it.*

hunt *NOUN* **hunts**
❶ hunting or searching • *The hunt for clues has begun.* ❷ a group of hunters

hunter, huntsman *NOUN* **hunters** or **huntsmen**
someone who hunts for sport

hurdle *NOUN* **hurdles**
❶ an upright frame that runners jump over in hurdling ❷ a difficulty or problem that you need to overcome

hurdling *NOUN*
racing in which the runners jump over hurdles
➤ **hurdler** *NOUN*

hurl *VERB* **hurls, hurling, hurled**
to throw something with great force

hurly-burly *NOUN*
a rough bustle of activity

hurray, hurrah *EXCLAMATION*
a shout of joy or approval; a cheer

hurricane *NOUN* **hurricanes**
a storm with violent wind

hurriedly *ADVERB*
in a hurry • *We hurriedly got dressed.*

hurry *VERB* **hurries, hurrying, hurried**
❶ to move or do something quickly ❷ to try to make someone be quick
➤ **hurried** *ADJECTIVE*

hurry *NOUN*
hurrying; a need to hurry • *She got up late and left in a hurry.* • *It's all right, there's no hurry.*

hurt *VERB* **hurts, hurting, hurt**
❶ to cause pain or injury to someone ❷ to feel painful • *My leg hurts.* ❸ to upset or offend someone • *I'm sorry if I hurt your feelings.*

hurt *NOUN*
physical or mental pain or injury

hurtful *ADJECTIVE*
upsetting and unkind • *a hurtful remark*

hurtle *VERB* **hurtles, hurtling, hurtled**
to move rapidly, sometimes in an uncontrolled way • *The train hurtled along.*

husband *NOUN* **husbands**
the man someone is married to

a b c d e f g h i j k l m n o p q r s t u v w x y z

husbandry *NOUN*
farming • *animal husbandry*

hush *VERB* hushes, hushing, hushed
to become silent or quiet or to make someone
do this • *Hush now and try to sleep.*
➤ **hush something up** to prevent something
from becoming generally known

hush *NOUN*
silence or quiet • *A hush descended over the
crowd.*

hush-hush *ADJECTIVE* (*informal*)
highly secret or confidential

husk *NOUN* husks
the dry outer covering of some seeds and
fruits

husky *ADJECTIVE* huskier, huskiest
a husky voice is low-pitched and slightly
hoarse
➤ **huskily** *ADVERB*
➤ **huskiness** *NOUN*

husky *NOUN* huskies
a large powerful dog used in the Arctic for
pulling sledges

hustle *VERB* hustles, hustling, hustled
❶ to push or shove someone roughly • *He
grabbed her arm and hustled her out of the
room.* ❷ to hurry

hut *NOUN* huts
a small roughly-made house or shelter

hutch *NOUN* hutches
a box or cage for a rabbit or other pet animal

hyacinth *NOUN* hyacinths
a sweet-smelling flower that grows from
a bulb **WORD ORIGIN** because, in Greek
legend, the flower sprang from the blood of
Hyacinthus, a youth who was accidentally killed
by Apollo

hybrid *NOUN* hybrids
❶ a plant or animal produced by
combining two different species or varieties
❷ something that combines parts or
characteristics of two different things

hydra *NOUN* hydras
a microscopic freshwater animal with a
tubular body

hydrangea (say hy-**drayn**-ja) *NOUN*
hydrangeas
a shrub with pink, blue or white flowers
growing in large clusters

hydrant *NOUN* hydrants
an outdoor water tap with a nozzle that a fire
hose can be attached to

hydraulic *ADJECTIVE*
worked by the force of water or other fluid
• *hydraulic brakes*

hydrochloric acid *NOUN*
a strong colourless acid containing hydrogen
and chlorine

hydroelectric *ADJECTIVE*
using water power to produce electricity
➤ **hydroelectricity** *NOUN*

hydrofoil *NOUN* hydrofoils
a boat designed to skim over the surface of
water

hydrogen *NOUN*
a lightweight gas that combines with oxygen
to form water

hydrogen bomb *NOUN* hydrogen bombs
a very powerful bomb using energy created
by the fusion of hydrogen nuclei

hydrophobia *NOUN*
abnormal fear of water, as in someone
suffering from rabies

hyena *NOUN* hyenas
a wild animal that looks like a wolf and makes
a shrieking howl

hygiene (say **hy**-jeen) *NOUN*
keeping things clean in order to remain
healthy and prevent disease

hygienic *ADJECTIVE*
clean and healthy and free of germs
➤ **hygienically** *ADVERB*

hymn *NOUN* hymns
a Christian religious song, usually one praising
God
➤ **hymn book** *NOUN*

hype *NOUN* (*informal*)
extravagant publicity or advertising

hyperactive *ADJECTIVE*
unable to relax and always moving about or
doing things

hyperbola (say hy-**per**-bol-a) *NOUN*
hyperbolas
(*in mathematics*) a kind of curve

hyperbole (say hy-**per**-bol-ee) *NOUN*
hyperboles
a dramatic exaggeration that is not meant to
be taken literally, e.g. 'I've got a stack of work
a mile high.'

hyperlink *NOUN* **hyperlinks**
a place in a computer document that is linked to another computer document • *Click on the hyperlink.*

hypermarket *NOUN* **hypermarkets**
(*British*) a very large supermarket, usually outside a town

hypertext *NOUN* **hypertexts**
a computer document that contains links that allow the user to move from one document to another

hyphen *NOUN* **hyphens**
a short dash (-) used to join words or parts of words together (e.g. in *hitch-hiker*)

> **PUNCTUATION**
>
> A **hyphen** is used to join two or more words which make up a compound noun or adjective. A hyphen is shorter than a dash and does not have a space on either side of it. Sometimes, the hyphen is part of a fixed compound, like *close-up*, *free-range* or *great-aunt*, but hyphens can join any pair or group of words to form a new compound: an *ultra-squidgy sandwich*; *that morning-after-the-night-before feeling.*
>
> A hyphen is sometimes used to join prefixes to words, especially where there would be a confusing combination of letters without it, as in *co-education* and *re-enter.*
>
> Hyphens are often useful to make things clearer. Note, for example, the difference between *a cross-section of the audience* (= a typical sample) and *a cross section of the audience* (= an annoyed group). You do not need a hyphen for compound adjectives when they follow a noun (*an out-of-date hairstyle* but *a hairstyle which looks out of date*).
>
> Hyphens are also used in compound numbers and fractions, such as *thirty-two* and *four-fifths.*
>
> A hyphen is also used to divide the two parts of a word that is split between the end of one line and the beginning of the next line.

hyphenate *VERB* **hyphenates, hyphenating, hyphenated**
to write a word or group of words with a hyphen

hypnosis (say hip-**noh**-sis) *NOUN*
a condition like a deep sleep in which a person can be made to follow the commands of someone else

hypnotic *ADJECTIVE*
❶ having a regular, repeated sound or movement which makes you feel sleepy • *the hypnotic ticking of the clock* ❷ to do with hypnosis

hypnotize (also **hypnotise**) *VERB* **hypnotizes, hypnotizing, hypnotized**
to put someone in a state of hypnosis
> ➤ **hypnotism** *NOUN*
> ➤ **hypnotist** *NOUN*

hypochondriac (say hy-po-**kon**-dree-ak) *NOUN* **hypochondriacs**
a person who constantly imagines that they are ill even though there is nothing wrong with them
> ➤ **hypochondria** *NOUN*
>
> **WORD ORIGIN** from Greek *hypochondrios* = under the breastbone (because the organs there were once thought to be the source of depression and anxiety)

hypocrite (say **hip**-o-krit) *NOUN* **hypocrites**
someone who pretends to be a better person than they really are
> ➤ **hypocrisy** (say hip-**ok**-riss-ee) *NOUN*
> ➤ **hypocritical** *ADJECTIVE*

hypodermic *ADJECTIVE*
a hypodermic needle or syringe is one used to inject something under the skin

hypotenuse (say hy-**pot**-i-newz) *NOUN* **hypotenuses**
the side opposite the right angle in a right-angled triangle

hypothermia *NOUN*
the condition of having a body temperature well below normal

hypothesis (say hy-**poth**-i-sis) *NOUN* **hypotheses**
a suggestion or guess that tries to explain something but has not yet been proved to be true or correct

hypothetical (say hy-po-**thet**-ikal) *ADJECTIVE*
based on a theory or possibility, not on proven facts • *a hypothetical example*

hysteria *NOUN*
wild uncontrollable excitement or emotion • *There was mass hysteria when the band came on stage.* **WORD ORIGIN** from Greek *hystera* = womb (because people used to

believe that the womb was the source of
hysteria, and that only women suffered from it)

hysterical *ADJECTIVE*
❶ in a state of hysteria ❷ (*informal*)
extremely funny
➤ **hysterically** *ADVERB*

hysterics (say hiss-**te**-riks) *PLURAL NOUN*
a fit of hysteria
➤ **in hysterics** (*informal*) laughing a lot

Ii

I *PRONOUN*
a word used by a person to refer to himself
or herself

ice *NOUN* **ices**
❶ solid frozen water ❷ an ice cream

ice *VERB* **ices, icing, iced**
❶ to become covered with ice • *The pond has
iced over.* ❷ to put icing on a cake

ice age *NOUN* **ice ages**
a period in the past when most of the earth's
surface was covered with ice

iceberg *NOUN* **icebergs**
a large mass of ice floating in the sea with
most of it under water

ice cap *NOUN* **ice caps**
a permanent covering of ice and snow at the
North or South Pole

ice cream *NOUN* **ice creams**
a sweet creamy frozen food

ice hockey *NOUN*
a form of hockey played on ice

ice lolly *NOUN* **ice lollies**
(*British*) frozen juice on a small stick

ice rink *NOUN* **ice rinks**
a place made for skating

icicle *NOUN* **icicles**
a pointed hanging piece of ice formed when
dripping water freezes

icily *ADVERB*
in a very unfriendly way • *'I don't care what
you think,' he said icily.*

icing *NOUN*
a sugary liquid mixture for decorating cakes

icon (say **eye**-kon) *NOUN* **icons**
❶ a small symbol or picture on a computer
screen, representing a program, window, etc.
that you can select ❷ a sacred painting or
mosaic of a holy person

ICT *ABBREVIATION*
information and communication technology

icy *ADJECTIVE* **icier, iciest**
❶ covered with ice ❷ very cold • *an icy wind*
❸ very unfriendly • *an icy stare*

Id *NOUN*
a different spelling of **Eid**

idea *NOUN* **ideas**
❶ a plan or thought that you form in your
mind ❷ an opinion or belief ❸ what you
know about something • *I have no idea what
you are talking about.*

ideal *ADJECTIVE*
perfect; completely suitable

ideal *NOUN* **ideals**
❶ a person or thing that seems to be a
perfect example of something ❷ a high
standard or principle that people try to follow

idealist *NOUN* **idealists**
a person who has high ideals and wishes to
achieve them
➤ **idealism** *NOUN*
➤ **idealistic** *ADJECTIVE*

ideally *ADVERB*
if things were perfect • *Ideally, I would train
every day.*

identical *ADJECTIVE*
exactly the same • *All the desks were
identical.* • *identical twins*
➤ **identically** *ADVERB*

identification *NOUN*
❶ any document, such as a passport or
driving licence, that proves who you are
❷ identifying someone or something

identify *VERB* **identifies, identifying,
identified**
❶ to recognize a person or thing as being
who or what they are • *The police have
identified the car used in the robbery.*
❷ to treat something as being identical to
something else • *Don't identify wealth with
happiness.* ❸ to think of yourself as sharing
someone else's feelings or experiences • *We
can identify with the hero of this play.*
➤ **identifiable** *ADJECTIVE*

identity *NOUN* **identities**
who or what a person or thing is • *Can you guess the identity of our mystery guest?*

ideology (say eye-dee-**ol**-o-jee) *NOUN* **ideologies**
a set of beliefs and aims, especially in politics • *a socialist ideology*
➤ **ideological** *ADJECTIVE*

idiocy *NOUN*
stupid behaviour

idiom *NOUN* **idioms**
a phrase that means something different from the meanings of the words in it, e.g. *in hot water* (= in trouble) or *hell for leather* (= at great speed)

idiosyncrasy (say id-ee-o-**sink**-ra-see) *NOUN* **idiosyncrasies**
one person's own way of behaving or doing something
➤ **idiosyncratic** *ADJECTIVE*

idiot *NOUN* **idiots**
a stupid or foolish person

idiotic *ADJECTIVE*
stupid or foolish • *That was an idiotic thing to say.*
➤ **idiotically** *ADVERB*

idle *ADJECTIVE*
❶ doing no work; lazy ❷ not being used • *The machines were idle.* ❸ useless; with no real purpose • *idle gossip* • *an idle threat*
➤ **idly** *ADVERB*
➤ **idleness** *NOUN*

idle *VERB* **idles, idling, idled**
❶ to be idle or lazy • *We idled away the afternoon.* ❷ an engine idles when it is working slowly
➤ **idler** *NOUN*

idol *NOUN* **idols**
❶ a statue or image that is worshipped as a god ❷ a famous person who is widely admired

idolatry *NOUN*
❶ worship of idols ❷ great admiration for someone
➤ **idolatrous** *ADJECTIVE*

idolize (also **idolise**) *VERB* **idolizes, idolizing, idolized**
to admire or love someone very much • *She idolized her older brother.*

idyll (say **id**-il) *NOUN* **idylls**
❶ a beautiful or peaceful scene or situation

❷ a poem describing a peaceful or romantic scene

idyllic (say id-**il**-ik) *ADJECTIVE*
beautiful and peaceful • *an idyllic scene*

i.e. *ABBREVIATION*
that is • *The world's highest mountain (i.e. Mount Everest) is in the Himalayas.*
WORD ORIGIN short for Latin *id est* = that is

if *CONJUNCTION*
❶ on condition that; supposing that • *I'll tell you if you promise to keep it a secret.* ❷ even though • *I'll finish this job if it kills me.* ❸ whether • *Do you know if lunch is ready?*
➤ **if only** I wish • *If only I were taller!*

igloo *NOUN* **igloos**
an Inuit round house built of blocks of hard snow

igneous *ADJECTIVE*
igneous rock is formed when hot liquid rock from a volcano cools and becomes hard

ignite *VERB* **ignites, igniting, ignited**
❶ to set fire to something ❷ to catch fire • *The petrol suddenly ignited and there was an explosion.*

ignition *NOUN* **ignitions**
❶ igniting ❷ the part of a motor engine that starts the fuel burning

ignoble *ADJECTIVE*
not noble; shameful

ignominious *ADJECTIVE*
humiliating; bringing disgrace or shame • *an ignominious defeat*
➤ **ignominy** *NOUN*

ignoramus *NOUN* **ignoramuses**
an ignorant person

ignorance *NOUN*
a lack of information or knowledge • *They were kept in ignorance of her plans.*

ignorant *ADJECTIVE*
❶ not knowing about something ❷ knowing very little
➤ **ignorantly** *ADVERB*

ignore *VERB* **ignores, ignoring, ignored**
to take no notice of a person or thing • *She ignored him and carried on reading.*

iguana (say ig-**wah**-na) *NOUN* **iguanas**
a large tree-climbing tropical lizard

ilk *NOUN*
➤ **of that ilk** (*informal*) of that kind

a b c d e f g h i j k l m n o p q r s t u v w x y z

ill *ADJECTIVE*
❶ unwell; in bad health ❷ bad or harmful
• *There were no ill effects.*

ill *ADVERB*
badly • *The animals had been ill-treated.*
➤ **ill at ease** uncomfortable or embarrassed

illegal *ADJECTIVE*
not legal; against the law
➤ **illegally** *ADVERB*

illegible *ADJECTIVE*
illegible writing is not clear enough to read
➤ **illegibly** *ADVERB*

illegitimate *ADJECTIVE*
(*old use*) an illegitimate child is born of
parents who are not married to each other
➤ **illegitimacy** *NOUN*

ill-fated *ADJECTIVE*
bound to fail or have bad luck • *an ill-fated
expedition*

illicit *ADJECTIVE*
done in a way that is against the law; not
allowed
➤ **illicitly** *ADVERB*

SPELLING
Take care not to confuse with **elicit**.

illiterate *ADJECTIVE*
unable to read or write
➤ **illiteracy** *NOUN*

illness *NOUN* illnesses
❶ being ill • *He missed two weeks of school
through illness.* ❷ a particular form of bad
health; a disease

illogical *ADJECTIVE*
not logical; not reasoning correctly
➤ **illogically** *ADVERB*

ills *PLURAL NOUN*
problems and difficulties • *the ills of the
modern world*

illuminate *VERB* illuminates, illuminating,
illuminated
❶ to light something up ❷ to decorate
streets or buildings with lights ❸ to decorate
a manuscript with coloured designs ❹ to help
to explain something or make it clearer
➤ **illumination** *NOUN*

illusion *NOUN* illusions
❶ something that seems to be real or actually
happening but is not, especially something
that deceives the eye • *an optical illusion*
❷ a false idea or belief • *He had no illusions
about the danger he was in.*

illusionist *NOUN* illusionists
an entertainer who performs tricks that
deceive the eye

illustrate *VERB* illustrates, illustrating,
illustrated
❶ to show or explain something by pictures
or examples • *To illustrate my point, let me
tell you a little story.* ❷ to illustrate a book is
to put illustrations in it

illustration *NOUN* illustrations
❶ a picture in a book etc. ❷ an example that
helps to explain something ❸ illustrating
something

illustrator *NOUN* illustrators
a person who produces the illustrations in a
book

illustrious *ADJECTIVE*
famous and respected

ill will *NOUN*
unkind feelings towards a person

image *NOUN* images
❶ a picture or statue of a person or thing
❷ what you see in a mirror or through a lens
❸ a person or thing that looks very much
like another • *He is the image of his father.*
❹ a word or phrase that describes something
in an imaginative way ❺ a person's or
company's public reputation

imagery *NOUN*
a writer's or speaker's use of words to produce
pictures in the mind of the reader or hearer

imaginable *ADJECTIVE*
able to be imagined • *It was the worst smell
imaginable.*

imaginary *ADJECTIVE*
existing only in your mind; not real • *When
she was a little girl she had an imaginary
friend.*

imagination *NOUN* imaginations
the ability to imagine things, especially in a
creative or inventive way • *He has a lively
imagination.*

imaginative *ADJECTIVE*
having or showing imagination • *Her stories
are full of imaginative ideas.*

imagine *VERB* imagines, imagining, imagined
❶ to form pictures or ideas in your mind
• *Close your eyes and imagine you are on a
beach.* ❷ to suppose or think something • *I
don't imagine there'll be any tickets left.*

imam NOUN imams
a Muslim religious leader

imbalance NOUN
a lack of balance

imbecile (say **imb**-i-seel) NOUN imbeciles
a very stupid person
➤ **imbecility** NOUN

imbibe VERB imbibes, imbibing, imbibed
(formal)
❶ to drink alcohol ❷ to absorb information
or ideas

imitate VERB imitates, imitating, imitated
to copy or mimic something
➤ **imitator** NOUN
➤ **imitative** ADJECTIVE

imitation NOUN imitations
❶ a copy of something else • He does a good
imitation of his father. ❷ copying something
• A child learns to talk by imitation.

immaculate ADJECTIVE
❶ perfectly clean; spotless • an immaculate
white shirt ❷ without any faults or mistakes
• an immaculate performance
➤ **immaculately** ADVERB

immaterial ADJECTIVE
not important; not mattering at all • It is
immaterial whether he goes or stays.

immature ADJECTIVE
❶ not fully grown or developed ❷ behaving
in a silly or childish way
➤ **immaturity** NOUN

immediate ADJECTIVE
❶ happening or done without any delay
❷ nearest; with nothing or no one between
• our immediate neighbours

immediately ADVERB
at once; without any delay • You must come
immediately.

immemorial ADJECTIVE
➤ **from time immemorial** further back in
time than anyone can remember

immense ADJECTIVE
extremely large or great; huge
➤ **immensity** NOUN

immensely ADVERB
extremely; very much • I am immensely
grateful.

immerse VERB immerses, immersing,
immersed
❶ to put something completely into a liquid
❷ to be immersed in something is to be

concentrating fully on it • She was immersed
in her work.
➤ **immersion** NOUN

immersion heater NOUN immersion heaters
a device that heats up water by means of an
electric element immersed in the water in a
tank

immigrant NOUN immigrants
a person who has come into a country to live
there

> **USAGE**
>
> If you mean someone who has left a
> country to live somewhere else, use
> **emigrant**.

immigration NOUN
the process by which people come into a
country to live there
➤ **immigrate** VERB

imminent ADJECTIVE
likely to happen at any moment • an
imminent storm
➤ **imminence** NOUN

immobile ADJECTIVE
not moving or not able to move • He stood
immobile by the door.
➤ **immobility** NOUN

immobilize (also **immobilise**) VERB
immobilizes, immobilizing, immobilized
to stop a thing from moving or working

immodest ADJECTIVE
❶ not behaving or dressing decently or
modestly ❷ conceited

immoral ADJECTIVE
morally wrong; wicked
➤ **immorality** NOUN

immortal ADJECTIVE
❶ living for ever; not mortal ❷ famous for
all time
➤ **immortal** NOUN
➤ **immortality** NOUN

immortalize (also **immortalise**) VERB
immortalizes, immortalizing, immortalized
to make someone famous for all time

immovable ADJECTIVE
unable to be moved

immune ADJECTIVE
❶ not able to catch a disease ❷ not affected
by something • I'm immune to flattery.
❸ protected from something and able to
avoid it • No one should be immune from

a b c d e f g h i j k l m n o p q r s t u v w x y z

prosecution.
➤ **immunity** *NOUN*

immune system *NOUN* **immune systems**
the body's means of resisting infection

immunize (also **immunise**) *VERB* **immunizes,
immunizing, immunized**
to make a person immune from a disease etc.,
e.g. by vaccination
➤ **immunization** *NOUN*

immutable (say i-**mewt**-a-bul) *ADJECTIVE*
that cannot be changed

imp *NOUN* **imps**
❶ a small devil ❷ a mischievous child

impact *NOUN* **impacts**
❶ the force of one thing hitting another
❷ an influence or effect • *the impact of the
Internet on our lives*

impair *VERB* **impairs, impairing, impaired**
to damage or weaken something • *Ear
infections can impair hearing.*
➤ **impairment** *NOUN*

impala (say im-**pah**-la) *NOUN* **impala**
a small African antelope

impale *VERB* **impales, impaling, impaled**
to pierce or fix something on a sharp pointed
object

impart *VERB* **imparts, imparting, imparted**
❶ to impart news or information is to tell it
to someone • *She imparted the good news
to her brother.* ❷ to give something a certain
taste, smell or quality • *The lamp imparted a
warm glow to the room.*

impartial *ADJECTIVE*
not favouring one side more than the other;
treating everyone equally
➤ **impartially** *ADVERB*
➤ **impartiality** *NOUN*

impassable *ADJECTIVE*
not able to be travelled along or over • *The
road is impassable because of flooding.*

impasse (say **am**-pahss) *NOUN* **impasses**
a situation in which no progress can be made;
a deadlock

impassive *ADJECTIVE*
not showing any emotion • *His face remained
impassive as the charges were read out.*
➤ **impassively** *ADVERB*

impasto (say im-**past**-oh) *NOUN*
(*in art*) the technique of applying paint so
thickly that it stands out from the surface of
the picture

impatient *ADJECTIVE*
❶ not able to wait for something without
getting annoyed • *The passengers were
getting impatient at the delay.* ❷ eager to do
something and not wanting to wait • *She was
impatient to get home.*
➤ **impatiently** *ADVERB*
➤ **impatience** *NOUN*

impeach *VERB* **impeaches, impeaching,
impeached**
to bring an important person to trial for a
serious crime against their country
➤ **impeachment** *NOUN*

impeccable *ADJECTIVE*
without any mistakes or faults; perfect • *He
has impeccable manners.*
➤ **impeccably** *ADVERB*

impede *VERB* **impedes, impeding, impeded**
to hinder someone or get in their way
WORD ORIGIN from Latin *impedire* = shackle
the feet

impediment *NOUN* **impediments**
❶ a hindrance ❷ a fault or defect • *He has a
slight speech impediment.*

impel *VERB* **impels, impelling, impelled**
to urge or drive someone to do something
• *Curiosity impelled her to investigate.*

impending *ADJECTIVE*
about to happen; imminent • *a feeling of
impending disaster*

impenetrable *ADJECTIVE*
❶ impossible to get through or see through
• *impenetrable darkness* ❷ impossible to
understand

imperative *ADJECTIVE*
❶ (*in grammar*) expressing a command or
instruction ❷ essential • *Speed is imperative.*

imperative *NOUN* **imperatives** (*in grammar*)
the form of a verb used in making commands
(e.g. 'come' in *Come here!*)

imperceptible *ADJECTIVE*
too small or gradual to be noticed
➤ **imperceptibly** *ADVERB*

imperfect *ADJECTIVE*
❶ with faults or problems; not perfect • *She
speaks imperfect English.* ❷ the imperfect
tense of a verb shows a continuous action in
the past, e.g. *She was singing.*
➤ **imperfectly** *ADVERB*
➤ **imperfection** *NOUN*

imperial *ADJECTIVE*
❶ to do with an empire or its rulers

❷ imperial weights and measures are the non-metric ones formerly in use in Britain and still used for some purposes • *an imperial gallon*

imperious ADJECTIVE
haughty and bossy • *an imperious command*

impermeable ADJECTIVE
not allowing liquid or gas to pass through it • *impermeable rock*

impersonal ADJECTIVE
❶ not showing friendly human feelings • *Her manner was cold and impersonal.* ❷ not referring to any particular person

impersonate VERB impersonates, impersonating, impersonated
to pretend to be another person
➤ **impersonation** NOUN
➤ **impersonator** NOUN

impertinent ADJECTIVE
rude to someone and not showing them proper respect • *impertinent questions*
➤ **impertinently** ADVERB
➤ **impertinence** NOUN

imperturbable ADJECTIVE
always calm and not easily worried
➤ **imperturbably** ADVERB

impervious ADJECTIVE
❶ not affected by something and not noticing it • *He seems impervious to criticism.* ❷ not allowing water, heat, etc. to pass through • *The rock is impervious to water.*

impetuous ADJECTIVE
acting hastily without thinking

impetus NOUN
❶ the force that makes an object start moving and that keeps it moving ❷ the influence that causes something to develop more quickly • *The ceasefire gave an impetus to peace talks.*

impinge VERB impinges, impinging, impinged
to have an effect or influence on something • *The economic recession impinged on all aspects of our lives.*

impish ADJECTIVE
mischievous • *an impish grin*

implacable ADJECTIVE
not able to be calmed; relentless • *an implacable enemy*
➤ **implacably** ADVERB

implant VERB implants, implanting, implanted
to fix something into a person's body by means of an operation

implant NOUN implants
an organ or piece of tissue implanted into a person's body

implement NOUN implements
a tool or device you use for something

implement VERB implements, implementing, implemented
to put a plan or idea into action • *We shall implement these plans next month.*

implicate VERB implicates, implicating, implicated
to involve a person in a crime etc. or to show that a person is involved • *His evidence implicates his sister.*

implication NOUN implications
❶ something that someone suggests without actually saying it ❷ a possible effect or result of something

implicit (say im-**pliss**-it) ADJECTIVE
❶ suggested but not stated openly. Compare with **explicit**. • *implicit criticism* ❷ absolute or unquestioning • *She expects implicit obedience.*
➤ **implicitly** ADVERB

implode VERB implodes, imploding, imploded
to burst or explode inwards
➤ **implosion** NOUN

implore VERB implores, imploring, implored
to beg someone to do something • *She implored him to stay.*

imply VERB implies, implying, implied
to suggest something without actually saying it • *Are you implying that I'm lazy?*

USAGE
If you mean to work something out from what someone says or does, use **infer**.

impolite ADJECTIVE
not polite; having bad manners

import VERB imports, importing, imported
to bring in goods from another country

import NOUN imports
❶ importing goods ❷ something that is imported ❸ (*formal*) meaning or importance • *The message was of great import.*

importance NOUN
being important • *She explained the importance of training properly.*

important ADJECTIVE
❶ having a great effect or value ❷ having great authority or influence
➤ **importantly** ADVERB

impose VERB imposes, imposing, imposed
❶ to make someone have to put up with or accept something • *The building plans were imposed on the village against everyone's wishes.* ❷ to make people have to pay something • *A new tax was imposed on fuel.*
➤ **impose on someone** to take unfair advantage of someone • *I hate to impose on you, but can you lend me some money?*

imposing ADJECTIVE
grand and impressive • *The embassy is an imposing building.*

imposition NOUN impositions
❶ an unfair burden or inconvenience • *I'd like to stay if it's not too much of an imposition.* ❷ imposing something

impossible ADJECTIVE
❶ not possible ❷ (*informal*) very annoying; unbearable • *He really is impossible!*
➤ **impossibly** ADVERB
➤ **impossibility** NOUN

impostor NOUN impostors
a person who dishonestly pretends to be someone else

impotent ADJECTIVE
❶ powerless; unable to take action • *She blazed with impotent rage.* ❷ a man is impotent when he is unable to have an erection
➤ **impotently** ADVERB
➤ **impotence** NOUN

impound VERB impounds, impounding, impounded
to confiscate something or take possession of it

impoverished ADJECTIVE
❶ poor • *impoverished students* ❷ poor in quality • *impoverished soil*

impracticable ADJECTIVE
not able to be done in practice

impractical ADJECTIVE
not practical or sensible • *Many of his ideas are impractical.*

imprecise ADJECTIVE
not precise

impregnable ADJECTIVE
strong enough to be safe against attack • *an impregnable fortress*

impregnated ADJECTIVE
something is impregnated with a substance when the substance has spread all the way through it • *The air was impregnated with the scent.*

impresario NOUN impresarios
a person who organizes concerts, shows, etc.

impress VERB impresses, impressing, impressed
❶ to make a person admire something or think it is very good ❷ to impress something on someone is to make them realize its importance • *He impressed on them the need for secrecy.* ❸ to press a mark into something

impression NOUN impressions
❶ an effect produced on the mind • *The book made a big impression on me.* ❷ a vague idea that you have about something • *I got the impression that she didn't like me.* ❸ an imitation of a person or a sound ❹ a reprint of a book

impressionable ADJECTIVE
easily influenced or affected

Impressionism NOUN
a style of painting that gives the general effect of a scene but without details

impressionist NOUN impressionists
an entertainer who does impressions of famous people
➤ **Impressionist** a painter in the style of Impressionism

impressive ADJECTIVE
making a strong impression; seeming to be very good
➤ **impressively** ADVERB

imprint NOUN imprints
a mark pressed into or on something

imprison VERB imprisons, imprisoning, imprisoned
to put someone in prison; to shut someone up in a place
➤ **imprisonment** NOUN

improbable ADJECTIVE
unlikely
➤ **improbably** ADVERB
➤ **improbability** NOUN

impromptu ADJECTIVE
done without any rehearsal or preparation • *We ended up having an impromptu party in the garden.*

improper ADJECTIVE
❶ unsuitable or wrong ❷ rude or indecent

➤ **improperly** *ADVERB*
➤ **impropriety** (say im-pro-**pry**-it-ee) *NOUN*

improper fraction *NOUN* improper fractions
a fraction that is greater than 1, with the numerator greater than the denominator, e.g. ⁵⁄₄

improve *VERB* improves, improving, improved
to make something better or to become better

improvement *NOUN* improvements
making something better or becoming better
• *There is still room for improvement.*

improvise *VERB* improvises, improvising, improvised
❶ to perform something by making it up as you go along, rather than following a score or script ❷ to make something quickly with whatever is available • *We managed to improvise some shelves out of planks of wood and bricks.*
➤ **improvisation** *NOUN*

imprudent *ADJECTIVE*
unwise or rash

impudent *ADJECTIVE*
cheeky or disrespectful
➤ **impudently** *ADVERB*
➤ **impudence** *NOUN*

impulse *NOUN* impulses
❶ a sudden desire or urge to do something
• *I did it on impulse.* ❷ (*in science*) a force acting on something for a very short time
• *electrical impulses*

impulsive *ADJECTIVE*
done or acting on impulse, not after careful thought
➤ **impulsively** *ADVERB*

impunity (say im-**pewn**-it-ee) *NOUN*
freedom from any risk of being punished

impure *ADJECTIVE*
not pure

impurity *NOUN* impurities
a small amount of something in a substance that makes it not pure • *The filter removes impurities from the water.*

impute *VERB* imputes, imputing, imputed
(*formal*) to claim that someone has something or is responsible for something
➤ **imputation** *NOUN*

in *PREPOSITION*
This word is used to show position or condition, e.g.

❶ at or inside something (*I was in the kitchen; He fell in a puddle.*) ❷ within the limits of something (*I will see you in an hour.*) ❸ arranged as; consisting of (*a serial in four parts*) ❹ a member of (*He is in the army.*) ❺ by means of (*We paid in cash.*)
➤ **in all** in total number; altogether

in *ADVERB*
❶ so as to be in something or inside (*Get in.*) ❷ inwards (*The top caved in.*) ❸ at home; indoors (*Is anybody in?*) ❹ having arrived (*The train will be in soon.*)
➤ **be in for something** to be likely to get something • *You're in for a shock.*
➤ **be in on something** (*informal*) to be aware of or sharing in something • *We were all in on the secret.*

inability *NOUN*
being unable to do something • *His main problem is his inability to concentrate.*

inaccessible *ADJECTIVE*
not able to be reached • *The beach is inaccessible by car.*

inaccurate *ADJECTIVE*
not accurate
➤ **inaccuracy** *NOUN*

inactive *ADJECTIVE*
not active or working
➤ **inaction** *NOUN*
➤ **inactivity** *NOUN*

inadequate *ADJECTIVE*
❶ not enough; not good enough ❷ not able to cope or deal with something
➤ **inadequately** *ADVERB*
➤ **inadequacy** *NOUN*

inadvertently *ADVERB*
by accident; without intending to • *He inadvertently picked up her phone when he left.*
➤ **inadvertent** *ADJECTIVE*

inadvisable *ADJECTIVE*
not advisable; unwise

inalienable *ADJECTIVE*
that cannot be taken away • *an inalienable right*

inane *ADJECTIVE*
silly; without sense • *an inane grin*
➤ **inanely** *ADVERB*
➤ **inanity** *NOUN*

inanimate *ADJECTIVE*
❶ not living • *inanimate objects* ❷ showing no sign of life

a b c d e f g h i j k l m n o p q r s t u v w x y z

inappropriate *ADJECTIVE*
not appropriate or suitable

inarticulate *ADJECTIVE*
❶ not able to speak or express yourself clearly • *He was inarticulate with rage.* ❷ not expressed in words • *an inarticulate cry*

inattentive *ADJECTIVE*
not listening or paying attention
➤ **inattention** *NOUN*

inaudible *ADJECTIVE*
not loud enough to be heard • *Her voice was almost inaudible.*
➤ **inaudibly** *ADVERB*

inaugurate *VERB* inaugurates, inaugurating, inaugurated
❶ to start or introduce something new and important ❷ to formally establish a person in office • *The new President will be inaugurated next month.*
➤ **inaugural** *ADJECTIVE*
➤ **inauguration** *NOUN*

inauspicious *ADJECTIVE*
not auspicious; unlikely to be successful

inborn *ADJECTIVE*
present in a person or animal from birth • *an inborn ability*

inbox *NOUN* inboxes
the place on a computer where new email messages are shown

inbred *ADJECTIVE*
❶ inborn ❷ produced by inbreeding

inbreeding *NOUN*
breeding from closely related individuals over many generations

incalculable *ADJECTIVE*
not able to be calculated or predicted

in camera *ADVERB*
in a judge's private room, not in public
WORD ORIGIN Latin, = in the room

incandescent *ADJECTIVE*
❶ giving out a bright light when heated; shining ❷ very angry • *She was incandescent with rage.*
➤ **incandescence** *NOUN*

incantation *NOUN* incantations
a set of words spoken as a spell or charm

incapable *ADJECTIVE*
not able to do something • *They seem incapable of understanding how serious the situation is.*

incapacitate *VERB* incapacitates, incapacitating, incapacitated
to make a person too ill or weak to be able to do things normally

incapacity *NOUN*
inability; lack of sufficient strength or power

incarcerate *VERB* incarcerates, incarcerating, incarcerated
to shut in or imprison a person
➤ **incarceration** *NOUN*

incarnate *ADJECTIVE*
having a body or human form • *She looked at him as if he were the devil incarnate.*

incarnation *NOUN* incarnations
❶ a period of life in a particular form • *one of the incarnations of the god Vishnu* ❷ a perfect example of a certain quality • *She is the incarnation of style.*
➤ **the Incarnation** in Christian teaching, God's taking a human form as Jesus Christ

incendiary *ADJECTIVE*
an incendiary bomb or device is one that is designed to start a fire

incense (say **in**-sens) *NOUN*
a substance making a spicy smell when it is burnt

incense (say in-**sens**) *VERB* incenses, incensing, incensed
to make a person very angry • *They were incensed by the decision.*

incentive *NOUN* incentives
something that encourages a person to do something or to work harder

inception *NOUN*
the beginning of something

incessant *ADJECTIVE*
continuing for a long time without a pause • *He kept up an incessant stream of chatter.*
➤ **incessantly** *ADVERB*

incest *NOUN*
sexual intercourse between two people who are so closely related that they cannot marry each other
➤ **incestuous** *ADJECTIVE*

inch *NOUN* inches
a measure of length, one-twelfth of a foot (about 2½ centimetres)

inch *VERB* inches, inching, inched
to move slowly and gradually • *I inched along the ledge.*

incidence NOUN
the extent or frequency of something • *What is the incidence of heart disease in the population?*

incident NOUN incidents
an event, especially an unusual or unpleasant one • *One particular incident sticks in my mind.*

incidental ADJECTIVE
happening as a minor part of something else • *incidental expenses*

incidentally ADVERB
by the way • *Incidentally, we're out of printer paper.*

incinerate VERB incinerates, incinerating, incinerated
to destroy something by burning it
➤ **incineration** NOUN

incinerator NOUN incinerators
a device for burning rubbish

incipient (say in-**sip**-ee-ent) ADJECTIVE
just beginning • *incipient decay*

incise VERB incises, incising, incised
to cut or engrave something into a surface • *A floral design is incised along the edge of the bowl.*

incision NOUN incisions
a cut, especially one made in a surgical operation

incisive ADJECTIVE
clear and sharp • *incisive comments*

incisor (say in-**sy**-zer) NOUN incisors
each of the sharp-edged front teeth in the upper and lower jaws

incite VERB incites, inciting, incited
to urge a person to do something; to stir people up • *They were accused of inciting a riot.*
➤ **incitement** NOUN

incivility NOUN
rudeness or discourtesy

inclement ADJECTIVE (*formal*)
cold, wet or stormy • *inclement weather*

inclination NOUN inclinations
❶ a feeling that makes you want to do something • *He did not show the slightest inclination to help.* ❷ a tendency to do something ❸ a slope or the angle of a slope

incline (say in-**klyn**) VERB inclines, inclining, inclined

❶ to lean or slope ❷ to bend the head or body forward, as in a nod or bow ❸ to influence someone to act or think in a certain way • *Her frank manner inclines me to believe her.*
➤ **be inclined** to have a tendency or willingness to do something • *The door is inclined to bang.* • *I'm inclined to agree with you.*

incline (say **in**-klyn) NOUN inclines
a slope

include VERB includes, including, included
to make or consider something as part of a group of things • *The tour of the castle includes a visit to the dungeon.*
➤ **inclusion** NOUN

inclusive ADJECTIVE
including everything; including all the things mentioned • *Read pages 20 to 28 inclusive.*

incognito (say in-kog-**neet**-oh or in-**kog**-nit-oh) ADJECTIVE & ADVERB
with your name or identity concealed • *The film star was travelling incognito.*

incoherent ADJECTIVE
not speaking or reasoning in a way that can be understood

income NOUN incomes
money received regularly from doing work or from investments

income tax NOUN
tax charged on income

incoming ADJECTIVE
❶ arriving or being received • *an incoming flight* • *incoming texts* ❷ about to take over from someone else • *the incoming chairman*

incomparable (say in-**komp**-er-abul) ADJECTIVE
so good or great that it does not have an equal • *incomparable beauty*

incompatible ADJECTIVE
not able to exist or be used together

incompetent ADJECTIVE
not able or skilled enough to do something properly
➤ **incompetence** NOUN

incomplete ADJECTIVE
not complete

incomprehensible ADJECTIVE
not able to be understood • *The instructions are incomprehensible.*
➤ **incomprehension** NOUN

a b c d e f g h i j k l m n o p q r s t u v w x y z

inconceivable *ADJECTIVE*
not able to be imagined; most unlikely

inconclusive *ADJECTIVE*
not leading to a definite decision or result
• *inconclusive evidence*

incongruous *ADJECTIVE*
out of place or unsuitable
➤ **incongruously** *ADVERB*
➤ **incongruity** *NOUN*

inconsiderable *ADJECTIVE*
small or unimportant • *a not inconsiderable sum of money*

inconsiderate *ADJECTIVE*
not considerate towards other people

inconsistent *ADJECTIVE*
not consistent • *The witnesses' accounts of what happened are inconsistent.*
➤ **inconsistently** *ADVERB*
➤ **inconsistency** *NOUN*

inconsolable *ADJECTIVE*
not able to be consoled; overcome with sadness

inconspicuous *ADJECTIVE*
not attracting attention or clearly visible • *I tried to make myself as inconspicuous as possible.*
➤ **inconspicuously** *ADVERB*

incontinent *ADJECTIVE*
not able to control the bladder or bowels
➤ **incontinence** *NOUN*

incontrovertible *ADJECTIVE*
not able to be denied or disputed

inconvenience *NOUN* inconveniences
difficulty or problems caused by something
• *We are sorry for the inconvenience.*

inconvenience *VERB* inconveniences, inconveniencing, inconvenienced
to cause slight difficulty for someone

inconvenient *ADJECTIVE*
not convenient; awkward • *Have I come at an inconvenient time?*

incorporate *VERB* incorporates, incorporating, incorporated
to include something as a part of something larger • *He incorporated several of her ideas into his story.*
➤ **incorporation** *NOUN*

incorrect *ADJECTIVE*
not correct; wrong
➤ **incorrectly** *ADVERB*

incorrigible *ADJECTIVE*
not able to be reformed or changed • *an incorrigible liar*

incorruptible *ADJECTIVE*
❶ not able to decay ❷ not able to be bribed

increase *VERB* increases, increasing, increased
❶ to become larger or more • *His excitement increased.* ❷ to make something larger or more • *We increased our speed.*

increase *NOUN* increases
increasing; the amount by which a thing increases

increasingly *ADVERB*
more and more • *He was becoming increasingly anxious.*

incredible *ADJECTIVE*
❶ very difficult to believe • *an incredible story* ❷ (*informal*) extremely good or big

incredibly *ADVERB*
❶ extremely • *I felt incredibly nervous.*
❷ in a way that is very difficult to believe
• *Incredibly, no one was hurt.*

incredulous *ADJECTIVE*
finding it difficult to believe someone; doubtful that something is true • *She was incredulous when I told her that I had won the lottery.*
➤ **incredulously** *ADVERB*
➤ **incredulity** *NOUN*

increment (say in-krim-ent) *NOUN* increments
an increase; an added amount

incriminate *VERB* incriminates, incriminating, incriminated
to make it seem as if a person is guilty of a crime or doing something wrong • *Her evidence appears to incriminate her brother.*
➤ **incriminating** *ADJECTIVE*

incrustation *NOUN* incrustations
a crust or deposit that forms on a surface

incubate *VERB* incubates, incubating, incubated
❶ to hatch eggs by keeping them warm ❷ to cause bacteria or a disease to develop
➤ **incubation** *NOUN*

incubation period *NOUN* incubation periods
the time it takes for symptoms of a disease to be seen in an infected person

incubator *NOUN* incubators
❶ a device in which a baby born prematurely can be kept warm and supplied with oxygen
❷ a device for incubating eggs

incumbent *ADJECTIVE*
if it is incumbent on you to do something, it is your duty to do it • *It is incumbent on you to warn people of the danger.*

incumbent *NOUN* **incumbents**
a person who holds a particular office or position

incur *VERB* **incurs, incurring, incurred**
to bring something upon yourself • *I hope you don't incur too much expense.*

incurable *ADJECTIVE*
not able to be cured
➤ **incurably** *ADVERB*

incurious *ADJECTIVE*
feeling or showing no curiosity about something

incursion *NOUN* **incursions**
a raid or brief invasion

indebted *ADJECTIVE*
owing money or gratitude to someone

indecent *ADJECTIVE*
something that is indecent is rude or shocking because it involves sex or the body
➤ **indecently** *ADVERB*
➤ **indecency** *NOUN*

indecipherable *ADJECTIVE*
not able to be deciphered

indecision *NOUN*
being unable to make up your mind; hesitation

indecisive *ADJECTIVE*
not able to make decisions easily

indeed *ADVERB*
❶ used to strengthen a meaning • *It's very cold indeed.* ❷ really and truly; in fact • *I am indeed surprised.*

indefinable *ADJECTIVE*
not able to be defined or described clearly

indefinite *ADJECTIVE*
not definite or fixed • *He's gone away for an indefinite period.*

indefinite article *NOUN* **indefinite articles**
the word 'a' or 'an'. See also the panels on **a** and on **determiners**.

indefinitely *ADVERB*
for an indefinite or unlimited time

indelible *ADJECTIVE*
impossible to rub out or remove
➤ **indelibly** *ADVERB*

indelicate *ADJECTIVE*
❶ slightly indecent ❷ tactless
➤ **indelicacy** *NOUN*

indent *VERB* **indents, indenting, indented**
to start a line of writing or printing further in from the margin than other lines • *Always indent the first line of a new paragraph.*

indentation *NOUN* **indentations**
a dent or notch made in something

independence *NOUN*
❶ the freedom to live your life without being dependent on someone else ❷ the freedom of a country from foreign rule and the ability to govern itself

independent *ADJECTIVE*
❶ not dependent on any other person or thing for help, money or support ❷ an independent country is one that governs itself ❸ not connected or involved with something
➤ **independently** *ADVERB*

indescribable *ADJECTIVE*
unable to be described
➤ **indescribably** *ADVERB*

indestructible *ADJECTIVE*
unable to be destroyed
➤ **indestructibility** *NOUN*

indeterminate *ADJECTIVE*
not fixed or decided exactly; left vague

index *NOUN*
❶ indexes an alphabetical list of things, especially at the end of a book ❷ a number showing how prices or wages have changed from a previous level ❸ (*in mathematics*) indices the raised number etc. written to the right of another (e.g. 3 in 2^3) showing how many times the first one is to be multiplied by itself

index *VERB* **indexes, indexing, indexed**
to make an index to a book etc.; to put something into an index

index finger *NOUN* **index fingers**
the finger next to your thumb; the forefinger

Indian *ADJECTIVE*
❶ to do with India or its people ❷ to do with Native Americans
➤ **Indian** *NOUN*

> **USAGE**
> The preferred term for the descendants of the original inhabitants of North and South America is *Native American*. *American Indian* is usually acceptable but the term *Red Indian* is offensive and should not be used.

a
b
c
d
e
f
g
h
i
j
k
l
m
n
o
p
q
r
s
t
u
v
w
x
y
z

Indian summer NOUN Indian summers
a period of warm weather in autumn

indicate VERB indicates, indicating, indicated
❶ to point something out or make it known
❷ to be a sign of something ❸ when drivers
indicate, they signal which direction they are
turning by using their indicators

indication NOUN indications
a sign of something • *He gave no indication
that he was thinking of quitting.*

indicative ADJECTIVE
being a sign of something • *Her remarks were
indicative of the change in her attitude.*

indicative NOUN
the form of a verb used in making a
statement (e.g. 'he said' or 'He is coming.'),
not in a command, question or wish

indicator NOUN indicators
❶ a thing that indicates or points to
something ❷ a flashing light used to signal
that a motor vehicle is turning ❸ (*in science*)
a chemical compound (such as litmus) that
changes colour in the presence of a particular
substance or condition

indict (say ind-**yt**) VERB indicts, indicting,
indicted
to charge a person with having committed a
serious crime
➤ **indictment** NOUN

indie ADJECTIVE
used to describe popular music that is
produced by small independent companies
• *indie bands*

indifferent ADJECTIVE
❶ not caring about something; not interested
in something at all ❷ not very good
• *indifferent weather*
➤ **indifferently** ADVERB
➤ **indifference** NOUN

indigenous (say in-**dij**-in-us) ADJECTIVE
growing or originating in a particular country;
native • *The koala bear is indigenous to
Australia.*

indigent (say **in**-dij-ent) ADJECTIVE
poor or needy

indigestible ADJECTIVE
difficult or impossible to digest

indigestion NOUN
pain or discomfort caused by difficulty in
digesting food

indignant ADJECTIVE
angry at something you think is wrong or
unfair
➤ **indignantly** ADVERB

indignation NOUN
anger about something you think is wrong or
unfair

indignity NOUN indignities
treatment that makes a person feel
undignified or humiliated; an insult

indigo NOUN
a deep-blue colour

indirect ADJECTIVE
not direct or straight
➤ **indirectly** ADVERB

indirect speech NOUN
a speaker's words given in a changed form
reported by someone else, as in *He said that
he would come.* (reporting the words 'I will
come.')

indiscreet ADJECTIVE
❶ not discreet; revealing secrets or too much
information ❷ not cautious; rash
➤ **indiscreetly** ADVERB
➤ **indiscretion** NOUN

indiscriminate ADJECTIVE
showing no discrimination; not making a
careful choice
➤ **indiscriminately** ADVERB

indispensable ADJECTIVE
that you cannot do without; essential • *A
good waterproof jacket is indispensable here.*
➤ **indispensability** NOUN

indisposed ADJECTIVE
slightly unwell so that you are unable to do
something
➤ **indisposition** NOUN

indisputable ADJECTIVE
definitely true; that cannot be shown to be
wrong

indistinct ADJECTIVE
not distinct or clear • *indistinct shapes in the
darkness*
➤ **indistinctly** ADVERB
➤ **indistinctness** NOUN

indistinguishable ADJECTIVE
not able to be told apart • *From a distance
the two colours are indistinguishable.*

individual ADJECTIVE
❶ of or for one person ❷ single or separate
• *Count each individual word.*

individual *NOUN* **individuals**
one person, animal or plant

individuality *NOUN*
the things that make one person or thing different from another; distinctive identity

individually *ADVERB*
separately; one by one • *The coach talked to each of us individually.*

indivisible *ADJECTIVE*
not able to be divided or separated

indoctrinate *VERB* **indoctrinates, indoctrinating, indoctrinated**
to fill a person's mind with particular ideas or beliefs, so that they come to accept them without thinking
➤ **indoctrination** *NOUN*

indolent *ADJECTIVE*
lazy
➤ **indolently** *ADVERB*
➤ **indolence** *NOUN*

indomitable *ADJECTIVE*
not able to be overcome or conquered • *She was a woman of indomitable courage.*

indoor *ADJECTIVE*
used, placed or done inside a building
• *indoor games*

indoors *ADVERB*
inside a building

indubitable (say in-**dew**-bit-a-bul) *ADJECTIVE*
not able to be doubted; certain
➤ **indubitably** *ADVERB*

induce *VERB* **induces, inducing, induced**
❶ to persuade someone to do something
• *Nothing could induce him to change his mind.* ❷ to produce or cause something
• *Some substances induce sleep.* ❸ if a pregnant woman is induced, the birth is brought on artificially with the use of drugs
➤ **induction** *NOUN*

inducement *NOUN* **inducements**
something that is offered to someone to persuade them to do something

indulge *VERB* **indulges, indulging, indulged**
to allow a person to have or do whatever they want
➤ **indulge in something** to allow yourself to have or do something that you enjoy • *On the journey we indulged in jokes and bad puns.*

indulgent *ADJECTIVE*
allowing someone to have or do whatever

they want; kind and lenient
➤ **indulgence** *NOUN*

industrial *ADJECTIVE*
to do with industry; working or used in industry

industrial action *NOUN*
(*chiefly British*) ways for workers to protest, such as striking or working to rule

industrialist *NOUN* **industrialists**
a person who owns or manages an industrial business

industrialized (also **industrialised**) *ADJECTIVE*
an industrialized country or district has many industries
➤ **industrialization** *NOUN*

Industrial Revolution *NOUN*
the expansion of British industry by the use of machines in the late 18th and early 19th century

industrious *ADJECTIVE*
working hard
➤ **industriously** *ADVERB*

industry *NOUN* **industries**
❶ making or producing goods, especially in factories ❷ a particular branch of this or any business activity • *the motor industry* • *the tourist industry* ❸ hard work and effort • *We were impressed by his industry.*

inebriated *ADJECTIVE*
drunk

inedible *ADJECTIVE*
not suitable for eating

ineffective *ADJECTIVE*
not producing the effect or result that you want
➤ **ineffectively** *ADVERB*

ineffectual *ADJECTIVE*
not achieving anything

inefficient *ADJECTIVE*
not working well and wasting time or energy
➤ **inefficiently** *ADVERB*
➤ **inefficiency** *NOUN*

inelegant *ADJECTIVE*
not elegant

ineligible *ADJECTIVE*
not eligible

inept *ADJECTIVE*
lacking any skill • *an inept wizard*
➤ **ineptly** *ADVERB*
➤ **ineptitude** *NOUN*

inequality NOUN inequalities
not being equal

inert ADJECTIVE
not moving or reacting • *He lay inert on the ground.*

inert gas NOUN inert gases
a gas that almost never combines with other substances

inertia (say in-**er**-sha) NOUN
❶ being unwilling to move or take action
❷ (*in science*) the tendency for a moving thing to keep moving in a straight line

inescapable ADJECTIVE
unavoidable • *an inescapable conclusion*

inestimable ADJECTIVE
too great or precious to be able to be estimated • *His advice was of inestimable value.*

inevitable ADJECTIVE
something is inevitable when it cannot be avoided and is sure to happen • *War seemed to be inevitable.*
➤ **inevitably** ADVERB
➤ **inevitability** NOUN

inexcusable ADJECTIVE
not able to be excused or justified

inexhaustible ADJECTIVE
so great that it cannot be used up completely • *Ben has an inexhaustible supply of jokes.*

inexorable (say in-**eks**-er-a-bul) ADJECTIVE
not able to be stopped; relentless
➤ **inexorably** ADVERB

inexpensive ADJECTIVE
not expensive; cheap
➤ **inexpensively** ADVERB

inexperience NOUN
lack of experience
➤ **inexperienced** ADJECTIVE

inexplicable ADJECTIVE
impossible to explain
➤ **inexplicably** ADVERB

in extremis (say eks-**treem**-iss) ADVERB
at the point of death; in very great difficulties

infallible ADJECTIVE
❶ never wrong ❷ never failing • *an infallible remedy*
➤ **infallibly** ADVERB
➤ **infallibility** NOUN

infamous (say **in**-fam-us) ADJECTIVE
famous for being bad or wicked • *an*
infamous bank robber
➤ **infamy** NOUN

infancy NOUN
❶ the time when you are a baby or young child ❷ an early stage of development • *Cinema was still in its infancy.*

infant NOUN infants
a baby or young child

infantile ADJECTIVE
❶ very childish and silly ❷ to do with babies or young children

infantry NOUN
soldiers who fight on foot. Compare with **cavalry**.

infatuated ADJECTIVE
filled with an unreasonably strong feeling of love that does not last long
➤ **infatuation** NOUN

infect VERB infects, infecting, infected
to pass on a disease or bacteria to a person, animal or plant • *We must clean the wound before it becomes infected.*

infection NOUN infections
❶ infecting someone or something • *A dirty water supply can be a source of infection.*
❷ an infectious disease or condition

infectious ADJECTIVE
❶ an infectious disease is able to be spread by air, water, etc. Compare with **contagious**.
❷ quickly spreading to others • *His enthusiasm is infectious.*

infer VERB infers, inferring, inferred
to form an opinion or work something out from what someone says or does, even though they do not actually say it • *I infer from your passport that you are going on holiday.*
➤ **inference** NOUN

> **USAGE**
> If you mean to suggest something without actually saying it, use **imply**.

inferior ADJECTIVE
less good or less important; low or lower in position, quality, etc.
➤ **inferiority** NOUN

inferior NOUN inferiors
a person who is lower in position or rank than someone else

infernal ADJECTIVE
❶ (*informal*) awful; very annoying • *Stop that*

infernal noise. ❷ to do with or like hell • *the infernal regions*

inferno *NOUN* infernos
a raging fire

infertile *ADJECTIVE*
not fertile • *infertile soil*
➤ **infertility** *NOUN*

infest *VERB* infests, infesting, infested
insects or other pests infest a place when they are numerous and troublesome there
➤ **infestation** *NOUN*
➤ **infested** *ADJECTIVE*

infidel (say in-fid-el) *NOUN* infidels (*old use*)
a person who does not believe in a religion

infidelity *NOUN*
being unfaithful to your husband, wife or partner

infiltrate *VERB* infiltrates, infiltrating, infiltrated
to get into a place or organization gradually and without being noticed
➤ **infiltration** *NOUN*
➤ **infiltrator** *NOUN*

infinite *ADJECTIVE*
❶ endless; without a limit ❷ too great to be measured

infinitely *ADVERB*
very much; with no limit • *This book is infinitely better than any of his others.*

infinitesimal *ADJECTIVE*
extremely small
➤ **infinitesimally** *ADVERB*

infinitive *NOUN* infinitives
(*in grammar*) the form of a verb that does not change to indicate a particular tense, number or person, in English used with or without *to*, e.g. *go* in 'Let him go.' or 'Allow him to go.'

infinity *NOUN*
an infinite number, distance or time • *The landscape seemed to stretch into infinity.*

infirm *ADJECTIVE*
weak, especially from old age or illness
➤ **infirmity** *NOUN*

infirmary *NOUN* infirmaries
❶ a hospital ❷ a place where sick people are cared for in a school, monastery, etc.

inflame *VERB* inflames, inflaming, inflamed
❶ to produce strong feelings or anger in people ❷ a part of the body is inflamed when it becomes painfully red and swollen

inflammable *ADJECTIVE*
able to be set on fire

USAGE

This word means the same as **flammable**. If you want to say that something is not able to be set on fire, use **non-flammable**.

inflammation *NOUN*
painful redness or swelling in a part of the body

inflammatory *ADJECTIVE*
likely to make people angry • *inflammatory remarks*

inflatable *ADJECTIVE*
able to be inflated • *an inflatable mattress*

inflate *VERB* inflates, inflating, inflated
❶ to fill something with air or gas so that it expands ❷ to increase something too much

inflation *NOUN*
a general rise in prices and fall in the purchasing power of money

inflect *VERB* inflects, inflecting, inflected
❶ (*in grammar*) to change the ending or form of a word to show its tense or its grammatical relation to other words, e.g. *sing* changes to *sang* or *sung, child* changes to *children* ❷ to alter the voice in speaking

inflection *NOUN* inflections
❶ (*in grammar*) an ending or form of a word used to inflect it, e.g. *-ed* in *killed* and *-es* in *bunches* ❷ the rise and fall in your voice when you are speaking

inflexible *ADJECTIVE*
not able to be bent, changed or persuaded
➤ **inflexibly** *ADVERB*
➤ **inflexibility** *NOUN*

inflict *VERB* inflicts, inflicting, inflicted
to make someone suffer something • *They inflicted a heavy defeat on us last season.*

influence *NOUN* influences
❶ the power to affect other people or things • *He had a huge influence on landscape painting.* ❷ a person or thing with this power • *She is a good influence on her brother.*

influence *VERB* influences, influencing, influenced
to have an influence on a person or thing • *The tides are influenced by the moon.*

influential *ADJECTIVE*
having great influence • *a hugely influential writer*

influenza *NOUN*
an infectious disease that causes fever, catarrh and pain

influx *NOUN*
a flowing in, especially of people or things coming in • *the summer influx of tourists*

inform *VERB* informs, informing, informed
to tell someone something or give them information about it • *Please inform us of any change of address.*

informal *ADJECTIVE*
not formal; casual and relaxed • *The restaurant has an informal atmosphere.*
➤ **informally** *ADVERB*
➤ **informality** *NOUN*

USAGE

In this dictionary, words marked *informal* are used in everyday speaking but not when you are writing or speaking formally.

informant *NOUN* informants
a person who gives information

information *NOUN*
facts or knowledge about something • *The website has lots of information on the history of aircraft.*

information technology *NOUN*
the study or use of ways of storing, arranging and giving out information, especially computers and telecommunications

informative *ADJECTIVE*
giving a lot of useful information • *an entertaining and informative programme*

informed *ADJECTIVE*
knowing about something

informer *NOUN* informers
a person who gives information against someone, especially to the police

infra-red *ADJECTIVE*
below or beyond red in the spectrum

infrastructure *NOUN* infrastructures
the basic services and systems that a country needs in order for its society and economy to work properly, such as buildings, roads, transport and power supplies

infrequent *ADJECTIVE*
not happening often
➤ **infrequently** *ADVERB*

infringe *VERB* infringes, infringing, infringed
❶ to break a rule, law or agreement ❷ to reduce or limit a person's rights
➤ **infringement** *NOUN*

infuriate *VERB* infuriates, infuriating, infuriated
to make a person very angry

infuse *VERB* infuses, infusing, infused
❶ to fill someone or something with a feeling or quality • *His novels are infused with sadness.* ❷ to soak or steep tea, herbs, etc. in a liquid to extract the flavour
➤ **infusion** *NOUN*

ingenious *ADJECTIVE*
❶ cleverly made or done • *an ingenious plan*
❷ clever at inventing things
➤ **ingeniously** *ADVERB*

ingenuity *NOUN*
cleverness in inventing things or solving problems

ingenuous *ADJECTIVE*
without cunning; innocent
➤ **ingenuously** *ADVERB*

ingot *NOUN* ingots
a lump of gold or silver that is cast in a brick shape

ingrained *ADJECTIVE*
❶ ingrained feelings or habits are deeply fixed in people's minds ❷ ingrained dirt marks a surface deeply

ingratiate *VERB* ingratiates, ingratiating, ingratiated
➤ **ingratiate yourself** to get yourself into favour with someone, especially by flattering them or always agreeing with them

ingratitude *NOUN*
lack of gratitude

ingredient *NOUN* ingredients
one of the parts of a mixture; one of the things used in a recipe

inhabit *VERB* inhabits, inhabiting, inhabited
to live in a place • *Many rare species inhabit the island.*

inhabitant *NOUN* inhabitants
a person or animal that lives in a place • *the oldest inhabitant of the village*

inhale *VERB* inhales, inhaling, inhaled
to breathe in • *He opened a window and inhaled deeply.*
➤ **inhalation** *NOUN*

inhaler *NOUN* inhalers
a device used for relieving asthma by inhaling medicine into your mouth

inherent (say in-**heer**-ent) *ADJECTIVE*
existing in something as one of its natural
or permanent qualities • *I pointed out the
inherent stupidity of this idea.*
➤ **inherently** *ADVERB*

inherit *VERB* inherits, inheriting, inherited
❶ to receive money, property or a title when
its previous owner dies ❷ to get certain
qualities or characteristics from your parents
or predecessors • *She has inherited her
father's love of music.*
➤ **inheritor** *NOUN*

inheritance *NOUN*
inheriting something; the money, property,
etc. that you inherit

inhibit *VERB* inhibits, inhibiting, inhibited
to hinder or restrain something

inhibition *NOUN* inhibitions
a feeling of embarrassment or worry that
prevents you from doing something or
expressing your emotions
➤ **inhibited** *ADJECTIVE*

inhospitable *ADJECTIVE*
❶ unfriendly to visitors ❷ an inhospitable
place is difficult to live in because it gives no
shelter from the weather

inhuman *ADJECTIVE*
cruel; without pity or kindness
➤ **inhumanity** *NOUN*

inhumane *ADJECTIVE*
not humane

inimitable *ADJECTIVE*
impossible to imitate

iniquitous *ADJECTIVE*
very unjust
➤ **iniquity** *NOUN*

initial *NOUN* initials
the first letter of a word or name

initial *VERB* initials, initialling, initialled
to mark or sign something with the initials of
your names

initial *ADJECTIVE*
at the beginning • *the initial stages*

initially *ADVERB*
at the beginning; at first • *Initially, everything
went well.*

initiate *VERB* initiates, initiating, initiated
❶ to start something • *He pressed the button
to initiate the launch sequence.* ❷ to admit
a person as a member of a society or group,

often with special ceremonies
➤ **initiation** *NOUN*

initiative (say in-**ish**-a-tiv) *NOUN*
❶ the power or right to get something
started ❷ the ability to make decisions and
take action on your own without being told
what to do
➤ **take the initiative** to take action yourself
to start something happening

inject *VERB* injects, injecting, injected
❶ to put a medicine or drug into the body
by means of a hollow needle ❷ to put liquid
into something by means of a syringe etc.
❸ to add a new quality • *Try to inject some
humour into the story.*
➤ **injection** *NOUN*

injunction *NOUN* injunctions
a command given with authority, e.g. by a
law court

injure *VERB* injures, injuring, injured
to harm or hurt someone • *He injured his
knee playing football.*
➤ **injured** *ADJECTIVE*

injury *NOUN* injuries
harm or damage done to someone • *They
escaped with only minor injuries.*
➤ **injurious** (say in-**joor**-ee-us) *ADJECTIVE*

injustice *NOUN* injustices
lack of justice; unjust treatment
➤ **do someone an injustice** to judge
someone unfairly

ink *NOUN* inks
a black or coloured liquid used in writing and
printing

inkling *NOUN* inklings
a slight idea or suspicion • *I had no inkling of
what was going to happen.*

inky *ADJECTIVE*
❶ stained with ink ❷ black like ink • *inky
darkness*

inland *ADJECTIVE & ADVERB*
in or towards the middle part of a country,
away from the coast • *The village lies twenty
kilometres inland.*

Inland Revenue *NOUN*
(formerly in the UK) the government
department responsible for collecting income
tax and some other taxes

in-laws *PLURAL NOUN* (*informal*)
relatives by marriage, especially the parents
of your husband or wife

a b c d e f g h i j k l m n o p q r s t u v w x y z

inlay *VERB* inlays, inlaying, inlaid
to set pieces of wood or metal into a surface to form a design • *The lid of the box was inlaid with silver.*

inlay *NOUN* inlays
a design formed by inlaying

inlet *NOUN* inlets
a strip of water reaching into the land from a sea or lake

inmate *NOUN* inmates
one of the people kept in a prison or mental hospital

in memoriam *PREPOSITION*
in memory of

inmost *ADJECTIVE*
most inward

inn *NOUN* inns
a hotel or public house, especially in the country
➤ **innkeeper** *NOUN*

innards *PLURAL NOUN* (*informal*)
the internal organs of a person or animal; the inner parts of a machine

innate *ADJECTIVE*
an innate ability or quality is one that you were born with

inner *ADJECTIVE*
inside; nearer to the centre • *an inner courtyard*

innermost *ADJECTIVE*
❶ nearest to the centre; furthest inside
❷ most secret or private • *She could not talk about her innermost feelings to anyone.*

innings *NOUN* innings
the time when a cricket team or player is batting

innocence *NOUN*
❶ not being guilty of doing something wrong
❷ lack of experience of the world, especially of bad things

innocent *ADJECTIVE*
❶ not guilty of doing something wrong
❷ lacking experience of the world, especially of bad things ❸ harmless • *an innocent remark*
➤ **innocently** *ADVERB*

innocuous *ADJECTIVE*
harmless

innovation *NOUN* innovations
❶ introducing new things or new methods

❷ a completely new process or way of doing things that has just been introduced
➤ **innovator** *NOUN*

innovative *ADJECTIVE*
an innovative design or way of doing something is new and clever

innuendo *NOUN* innuendoes
indirect reference to something insulting or rude

innumerable *ADJECTIVE*
too many to be counted

inoculate *VERB* inoculates, inoculating, inoculated
to inject or treat someone with a vaccine or serum as a protection against a disease
➤ **inoculation** *NOUN*

inoffensive *ADJECTIVE*
not likely to upset or offend anyone • *a shy, inoffensive young man*

inordinate *ADJECTIVE*
excessive • *He spends an inordinate amount of time watching TV.*
➤ **inordinately** *ADVERB*

inorganic *ADJECTIVE*
not of living organisms; of mineral origin

in-patient *NOUN* in-patients
a patient who stays at a hospital for treatment

input *NOUN*
what you put into something, especially data put into a computer

input *VERB* inputs, inputting, input or inputted
to put data into a computer

inquest *NOUN* inquests
an official inquiry to find out how a person died

inquire *VERB* inquires, inquiring, inquired
❶ to investigate something carefully ❷ to ask for information

> **USAGE**
> You can spell this word **inquire** or **enquire** in either of its meanings. It is probably more common for **inquire** to be used for 'investigate' and **enquire** to be used for 'ask for information', but there is no real need to follow this distinction.

inquiry *NOUN* inquiries
❶ an official investigation ❷ a question

inquisition *NOUN* inquisitions
a detailed questioning or investigation

➤ **inquisitor** *NOUN*
➤ **the Inquisition** a council of the Roman Catholic Church in the Middle Ages, especially the very severe one in Spain, set up to discover and punish heretics

inquisitive *ADJECTIVE*
always asking questions or trying to find out things • *Don't be so inquisitive – it's none of your business.*
➤ **inquisitively** *ADVERB*

inroads *PLURAL NOUN*
➤ **make inroads on** or **into something** to take away or use up large quantities of something

inrush *NOUN* **inrushes**
a sudden rushing in

insane *ADJECTIVE*
not sane; mad
➤ **insanely** *ADVERB*
➤ **insanity** *NOUN*

insanitary *ADJECTIVE*
unclean and likely to be harmful to health

insatiable (say in-**say**-sha-bul) *ADJECTIVE*
impossible to satisfy • *an insatiable appetite*

inscribe *VERB* **inscribes, inscribing, inscribed**
to write or carve words or symbols on something • *The names of the previous winners are inscribed on the trophy.*

inscription *NOUN* **inscriptions**
words written or carved on a monument, coin, stone, etc. or written in the front of a book

inscrutable *ADJECTIVE*
mysterious; impossible to interpret • *an inscrutable smile*

insect *NOUN* **insects**
a small animal with six legs, no backbone and a body divided into three parts (head, thorax, abdomen)

insecticide *NOUN* **insecticides**
a substance for killing insects

insectivorous *ADJECTIVE*
feeding on insects and other small invertebrate creatures
➤ **insectivore** *NOUN*

insecure *ADJECTIVE*
❶ not secure or safe ❷ lacking confidence about yourself
➤ **insecurely** *ADVERB*
➤ **insecurity** *NOUN*

insensible *ADJECTIVE*
❶ unconscious ❷ unaware of something • *He was insensible of her needs.*

insensitive *ADJECTIVE*
not sensitive or thinking about other people's feelings
➤ **insensitively** *ADVERB*
➤ **insensitivity** *NOUN*

inseparable *ADJECTIVE*
❶ liking to be constantly together • *inseparable friends* ❷ not able to be separated

insert *VERB* **inserts, inserting, inserted**
to put a thing into something else or between two things • *He inserted a coin into the slot.* • *Where do you want to insert that paragraph?*
➤ **insertion** *NOUN*

inshore *ADVERB & ADJECTIVE*
near or nearer to the shore • *The boat came inshore.*

inside *NOUN* **insides**
the inner side, surface or part
➤ **inside out** with the inside turned to face outwards
➤ **insides** (*informal*) a person's stomach and bowels

inside *ADJECTIVE*
on or coming from the inside; in or nearest to the middle • *an inside pocket*

inside *ADVERB & PREPOSITION*
on or to the inside of something; in • *Come inside.* • *It's inside that box.*

insidious *ADJECTIVE*
causing harm gradually, without being noticed
➤ **insidiously** *ADVERB*

insight *NOUN* **insights**
❶ the ability to see the truth about things • *With a flash of insight, she realized what had really happened that day.* ❷ an understanding of something • *The book gives us a good insight into life as a pirate.*

insignia *SINGULAR NOUN & PLURAL NOUN*
a badge or symbol that shows that you belong to something or hold a particular office

insignificant *ADJECTIVE*
not important or influential • *She felt small and insignificant.*
➤ **insignificance** *NOUN*

a
b
c
d
e
f
g
h
i
j
k
l
m
n
o
p
q
r
s
t
u
v
w
x
y
z

insincere *ADJECTIVE*
not sincere
➤ **insincerely** *ADVERB*
➤ **insincerity** *NOUN*

insinuate *VERB* insinuates, insinuating, insinuated
❶ to hint something unpleasant • *What are you insinuating?* ❷ to introduce a thing or yourself gradually or craftily into a place

insinuation *NOUN* insinuations
an unpleasant hint or suggestion that someone makes

insipid *ADJECTIVE*
❶ lacking flavour ❷ not lively or interesting
➤ **insipidity** *NOUN*

insist *VERB* insists, insisting, insisted
to be very firm in saying or asking for something • *He insisted that he was innocent.* • *I insist on seeing the manager.*

insistent *ADJECTIVE*
❶ insisting on doing or having something ❷ continuing for a long time in a way that you cannot ignore • *an insistent tapping on the window*
➤ **insistence** *NOUN*

insolent *ADJECTIVE*
very rude and disrespectful • *an insolent stare*
➤ **insolently** *ADVERB*
➤ **insolence** *NOUN*

insoluble *ADJECTIVE*
❶ impossible to solve • *an insoluble problem* ❷ impossible to dissolve

insolvent *ADJECTIVE*
unable to pay your debts
➤ **insolvency** *NOUN*

insomnia *NOUN*
being unable to sleep • *Do you ever suffer from insomnia?*
➤ **insomniac** *NOUN*

inspect *VERB* inspects, inspecting, inspected
to examine something carefully to check that everything is as it should be • *The teacher walked around inspecting their work.*
➤ **inspection** *NOUN*

inspector *NOUN* inspectors
❶ a person whose job is to inspect or supervise things ❷ a police officer ranking next above a sergeant

inspiration *NOUN* inspirations
❶ a sudden brilliant idea ❷ a person or thing that fills you with ideas or enthusiasm

inspire *VERB* inspires, inspiring, inspired
to fill a person with ideas, enthusiasm or creative feeling • *The applause inspired us with confidence.*

instability *NOUN*
lack of stability

install *VERB* installs, installing, installed
❶ to put something in position and ready to use • *They have installed a new computer system.* ❷ to put a person into an important position with a ceremony • *He was installed as pope.*
➤ **installation** *NOUN*

instalment *NOUN* instalments
❶ each of a series of payments made for something over a period of time • *You can pay by monthly instalments.* ❷ each part of a television serial or or of a series of publications

instance *NOUN* instances
an example
➤ **for instance** for example

instant *ADJECTIVE*
❶ happening immediately • *It was an instant success.* ❷ instant food or drink is designed to be prepared quickly and easily • *instant coffee*

instant *NOUN* instants
a moment • *I don't believe it for an instant.*
➤ **this instant** at once • *Come here this instant!*

instantaneous *ADJECTIVE*
happening immediately • *The effect was instantaneous.*
➤ **instantaneously** *ADVERB*

instantly *ADVERB*
without delay; immediately

instead *ADVERB*
in place of something else

instep *NOUN* insteps
the top of the foot between the toes and the ankle

instigate *VERB* instigates, instigating, instigated
to make something start to happen; to stir something up • *The were accused of instigating the rebellion.*
➤ **instigation** *NOUN*
➤ **instigator** *NOUN*

instil *VERB* instils, instilling, instilled
to put ideas into a person's mind gradually

instinct *NOUN* **instincts**
a natural tendency or ability • *Birds learn to fly by instinct.* • *I didn't have time to think – I just acted on instinct.*

instinctive *ADJECTIVE*
following instinct, not thought • *His instinctive reaction was to run.*
➤ **instinctively** *ADVERB*

institute *NOUN* **institutes**
a society or organization; the building used by this

institute *VERB* **institutes, instituting, instituted**
to establish or introduce something • *The new head instituted many innovations and changes.*

institution *NOUN* **institutions**
❶ an institute; a public organization, e.g. a hospital or university ❷ an established habit or custom • *Going out for a walk on Sunday was a family institution.* ❸ instituting something

instruct *VERB* **instructs, instructing, instructed**
❶ to teach a person a subject or skill ❷ to tell a person what they must do

instruction *NOUN* **instructions**
❶ teaching a subject or skill ❷ an order or piece of information • *Follow the instructions carefully.*
➤ **instructional** *ADJECTIVE*

instructive *ADJECTIVE*
giving useful information or knowledge

instructor *NOUN* **instructors**
a person who teaches a practical skill or sport • *a driving instructor*

instrument *NOUN* **instruments**
❶ a device for producing musical sounds ❷ a tool used for delicate or scientific work ❸ a measuring device

instrumental *ADJECTIVE*
❶ performed on musical instruments, without singing ❷ to be instrumental in doing something is to play an important part in it • *She was instrumental in getting me a job.*

instrumentalist *NOUN* **instrumentalists**
a person who plays a musical instrument

insubordinate *ADJECTIVE*
disobedient or rebellious
➤ **insubordination** *NOUN*

insufferable *ADJECTIVE*
annoying and difficult to bear • *an insufferable bore*

insufficient *ADJECTIVE*
not enough • *There is insufficient evidence.*

insular *ADJECTIVE*
❶ to do with or like an island ❷ narrow-minded

insulate *VERB* **insulates, insulating, insulated**
to cover or protect something to prevent heat, cold or electricity from passing in or out
➤ **insulation** *NOUN*
➤ **insulator** *NOUN*

insulin *NOUN*
a substance that controls the amount of sugar in the blood. The lack of insulin causes diabetes.

insult (say in-**sult**) *VERB* **insults, insulting, insulted**
to speak to or treat someone in a rude way that offends them

insult (say **in**-sult) *NOUN* **insults**
an insulting remark or action

insuperable *ADJECTIVE*
unable to be overcome • *an insuperable difficulty*

insurance *NOUN*
an agreement to compensate someone for a loss, damage or injury etc., in return for a payment (called a **premium**) made in advance

insure *VERB* **insures, insuring, insured**
to protect something with insurance • *Is your jewellery insured?*

> **SPELLING**
> Take care not to confuse with **ensure**, which means to make sure that something happens.

insurgent *NOUN* **insurgents**
someone who rebels against a ruler or government
➤ **insurgent** *ADJECTIVE*

insurmountable *ADJECTIVE*
unable to be overcome • *insurmountable difficulties*

insurrection *NOUN* **insurrections**
a rebellion

intact *ADJECTIVE*
not damaged; complete • *Only a few buildings remained intact after the earthquake.*

a b c d e f g h i j k l m n o p q r s t u v w x y z

intake *NOUN* intakes
❶ taking something in • *a sharp intake of breath* ❷ the number of people or things taken in • *We have a high intake of students this year.*

intangible *ADJECTIVE*
difficult to describe or measure; not able to be touched • *intangible benefits*

integer *NOUN* integers
a whole number (e.g. 0, 3, 19), not a fraction

integral (say in-tig-ral) *ADJECTIVE*
that is an essential part of a whole thing • *An engine is an integral part of a car.*

integrate *VERB* integrates, integrating, integrated
❶ to make parts into a whole; to combine things ❷ to bring people together harmoniously into a single community
➤ **integration** *NOUN*

integrity (say in-**teg**-rit-ee) *NOUN*
being honest and behaving well • *a person of great integrity*

intellect *NOUN* intellects
the ability to think and work things out with your mind

intellectual *ADJECTIVE*
❶ to do with or using the intellect ❷ having a good intellect and a liking for knowledge
➤ **intellectually** *ADVERB*

intellectual *NOUN* intellectuals
an intellectual person

intelligence *NOUN*
❶ being intelligent ❷ information, especially of military value; the people who collect and study this information

intelligent *ADJECTIVE*
able to learn and understand things; having great mental ability
➤ **intelligently** *ADVERB*

SPELLING
There is a double l in **intelligent**.

intelligible *ADJECTIVE*
able to be understood • *The message was barely intelligible.*

intend *VERB* intends, intending, intended
❶ to have something in mind as what you want to do • *We finished later than we intended.* ❷ to plan that something should have a particular meaning or purpose • *It was intended to be a joke.*

intense *ADJECTIVE*
❶ very strong or great • *The heat was intense.* ❷ feeling things very strongly and seriously • *He's a very intense young man.*
➤ **intensely** *ADVERB*

intensify *VERB* intensifies, intensifying, intensified
to make something more intense or to become more intense • *The fighting intensified.*

intensity *NOUN*
the intensity of something is how strong or great it is • *The storm increased in intensity with every passing second.*

intensive *ADJECTIVE*
concentrated; using a lot of effort over a short time • *two weeks of intensive training*
➤ **intensively** *ADVERB*

intensive care *NOUN*
medical treatment of a patient who is dangerously ill, with constant supervision

intent *NOUN* intents
what someone intends; an intention

intent *ADJECTIVE*
showing great attention and interest • *She was so intent upon her work that she didn't hear me come in.*
➤ **intent on something** eager or determined to do something

intention *NOUN* intentions
what someone intends; a purpose or plan

intentional *ADJECTIVE*
deliberate, not accidental
➤ **intentionally** *ADVERB*

intently *ADVERB*
with great attention and interest • *The boys listened intently.*

inter *VERB* inters, interring, interred
to bury a corpse

interact *VERB* interacts, interacting, interacted
❶ to talk to or mix with other people • *It is interesting to watch how young children interact.* ❷ to have an effect upon one another • *In a chemical reaction, two or more chemicals interact with each other.*
➤ **interaction** *NOUN*

interactive *ADJECTIVE*
(*in computing*) allowing information to be sent immediately in either direction between a computer system and its user

interbreed *VERB* interbreeds, interbreeding, interbred
animals interbreed when they breed with each other

intercede *VERB* intercedes, interceding, interceded
to speak or act on behalf of another person or as a peacemaker
➤ **intercession** *NOUN*

intercept *VERB* intercepts, intercepting, intercepted
to stop or catch a person or thing that is going from one place to another • *Police intercepted him on the way to the airport.*
➤ **interception** *NOUN*

interchange *VERB* interchanges, interchanging, interchanged
❶ to put each of two things into the other's place ❷ to exchange things

interchange *NOUN* interchanges
❶ interchanging • *a lively interchange of ideas* ❷ a road junction where vehicles can move from one motorway etc. to another

interchangeable *ADJECTIVE*
things are interchangeable when they can be changed or swapped around

intercom *NOUN* intercoms
a system of communication between rooms or compartments, operating rather like a telephone

intercourse *NOUN*
❶ communication or dealings between people ❷ sexual intercourse

interdependent *ADJECTIVE*
dependent upon each other

interest *NOUN* interests
❶ a feeling of wanting to know about or be involved with something ❷ a thing that interests someone • *Science fiction is one of my interests.* ❸ an advantage or benefit • *She looks after her own interests.* ❹ money paid regularly in return for money lent or deposited

interest *VERB* interests, interesting, interested
to attract a person's interest • *Sport doesn't interest me very much.*
➤ **interested** *ADJECTIVE*

> **SPELLING**
> There is a tricky bit in **interest**—there is an e after the first t.

interesting *ADJECTIVE*
catching and holding your attention • *That's*

an interesting idea.
➤ **interestingly** *ADVERB*

interface *NOUN* interfaces
a connection between two parts of a computer system

interfere *VERB* interferes, interfering, interfered
❶ to take part in something that has nothing to do with you ❷ to get in the way of something • *She never allowed her personal feelings to interfere with her work.*

interference *NOUN*
❶ interfering in something ❷ a crackling or distorting of a radio or television signal

interim *NOUN*
an interval of time between two events

interim *ADJECTIVE*
in use for the time being until something more permanent is arranged • *an interim report*

interior *NOUN* interiors
the inside of something; the central or inland part of a country • *the interior of the cave*

interior *ADJECTIVE*
inner • *interior walls*

interject *VERB* interjects, interjecting, interjected
to break in with a remark while someone is speaking

interjection *NOUN* interjections
a word or words exclaimed expressing joy or pain or surprise, such as *oh!* or *wow!* or *good heavens!*

interlock *VERB* interlocks, interlocking, interlocked
things interlock when they fit into each other

interloper *NOUN* interlopers
an intruder

interlude *NOUN* interludes
❶ an interval ❷ something happening in an interval or between other events

intermediary *NOUN* intermediaries
someone who tries to settle a dispute by negotiating with both sides; a mediator

intermediate *ADJECTIVE*
coming between two things in time, place or order • *an intermediate stage* • *intermediate students*

interminable *ADJECTIVE*
seeming to go on for ever; long and boring

a b c d e f g h i j k l m n o p q r s t u v w x y z

A

• *an interminable speech*
➤ **interminably** *ADVERB*

B

intermission *NOUN* **intermissions**
an interval between parts of a film or show

C

intermittent *ADJECTIVE*
happening at intervals; not continuous
• *intermittent showers*
➤ **intermittently** *ADVERB*

D

intern *VERB* **interns, interning, interned**
to imprison someone in a special camp or
area, usually in wartime

E

F

internal *ADJECTIVE*
inside; within something • *internal injuries*
➤ **internally** *ADVERB*

G

H

internal-combustion engine *NOUN*
internal-combustion engines
an engine that produces power by burning
fuel inside the engine itself

I

J

international *ADJECTIVE*
to do with or belonging to more than one
country; agreed between nations • *an
international trade organization*
➤ **internationally** *ADVERB*

K

L

international *NOUN* **internationals**
❶ a sports contest between teams
representing different countries ❷ a sports
player who plays for his or her country

M

N

Internet *NOUN*
a computer network that allows users all over
the world to communicate and exchange
information

O

P

internment *NOUN*
being interned in wartime

Q

interplanetary *ADJECTIVE*
between planets

R

S

interpolate *VERB* **interpolates, interpolating,
interpolated**
to add a remark during a conversation
➤ **interpolation** *NOUN*

T

U

interpose *VERB* **interposes, interposing,
interposed**
❶ to add a question or remark into a
conversation • *'Just a minute,' Kerry
interposed. 'How do you know?'* ❷ to place
something between two things

V

W

X

interpret *VERB* **interprets, interpreting,
interpreted**
❶ to explain what something means ❷ to
translate what someone says into another
language as they are speaking ❸ to perform
music, a part in a play, etc. in a way that

Y

Z

shows your feelings about its meaning
➤ **interpretation** *NOUN*

interpreter *NOUN* **interpreters**
a person whose job is to translate what
someone is saying immediately into another
language

interregnum *NOUN* **interregnums** or
interregna
an interval between the reign of one ruler
and that of his or her successor

interrogate *VERB* **interrogates, interrogating,
interrogated**
to question someone closely or aggressively
• *The prisoner was interrogated for six hours.*
➤ **interrogation** *NOUN*
➤ **interrogator** *NOUN*

interrogative *ADJECTIVE*
questioning; expressing a question

interrupt *VERB* **interrupts, interrupting,
interrupted**
❶ to stop someone while they are in the
middle of speaking or concentrating by saying
something to them • *They kept interrupting
me with silly questions.* ❷ to stop something
continuing for a short time • *The match was
interrupted several times by rain.*

interruption *NOUN* **interruptions**
interrupting someone or something • *It was
the only quiet place where he could work
without interruption.*

intersect *VERB* **intersects, intersecting,
intersected**
❶ lines or roads intersect when they cross
each other • *The lines intersect at right
angles.* ❷ to divide a thing by passing or lying
across it

intersection *NOUN* **intersections**
a place where lines or roads cross each other

intersperse *VERB* **intersperses, interspersing,
interspersed**
to be interspersed with things is to have them
mixed in here and there • *Her speech was
interspersed with jokes.*

interval *NOUN* **intervals**
❶ a time between two events or parts of
a play or show ❷ (*in music*) the musical
difference between the pitches of two notes
➤ **at intervals** with some time or distance
between each one

intervene *VERB* **intervenes, intervening,
intervened**
❶ to come between two events • *in the*

intervening years ❷ to interrupt a discussion or fight to try and stop it or change its result
➤ **intervention** *NOUN*

interview *NOUN* interviews
a meeting with someone to ask him or her questions or to obtain information

interview *VERB* interviews, interviewing, interviewed
to have an interview with someone
➤ **interviewer** *NOUN*

intestine *NOUN* intestines
the long tube along which food passes while being absorbed by the body, between the stomach and the anus
➤ **intestinal** *ADJECTIVE*

intimacy *NOUN*
having a very close friendship or relationship with someone

intimate (say **in**-tim-at) *ADJECTIVE*
❶ very friendly with someone ❷ private and personal • *intimate thoughts* ❸ detailed • *He has an intimate knowledge of the country.*
➤ **intimately** *ADVERB*

intimate (say **in**-tim-ayt) *VERB* intimates, intimating, intimated
to hint at something • *She has not yet intimated what her plans are.*
➤ **intimation** *NOUN*

intimidate *VERB* intimidates, intimidating, intimidated
to frighten a person into doing something by using threats
➤ **intimidation** *NOUN*

into *PREPOSITION*
❶ used to express movement to the inside of something (*Go into the house.*) ❷ used to express a change of condition or state (*It broke into pieces. She went into politics.*) ❸ used to show division (*4 into 20 = 20 divided by 4*)

intolerable *ADJECTIVE*
too much to bear • *The heat was intolerable.*
➤ **intolerably** *ADVERB*

intolerant *ADJECTIVE*
not tolerant or willing to put up with people
➤ **intolerantly** *ADVERB*
➤ **intolerance** *NOUN*

intonation *NOUN* intonations
the tone or pitch of the voice in speaking

intone *VERB* intones, intoning, intoned
to recite something in a chanting voice

intoxicate *VERB* intoxicates, intoxicating, intoxicated
❶ to make someone very drunk ❷ to make someone wildly excited
➤ **intoxicated** *ADJECTIVE*
➤ **intoxication** *NOUN*

intransitive *ADJECTIVE*
an intransitive verb is one that is used without a direct object after it, e.g. *hear* in *We can hear.* (but not in *We can hear you.*) Compare with **transitive**.
➤ **intransitively** *ADVERB*

intravenous (say in-tra-**veen**-us) *ADJECTIVE*
an intravenous injection is made directly into a vein

intrepid *ADJECTIVE*
fearless and brave • *an intrepid explorer*
➤ **intrepidly** *ADVERB*
➤ **intrepidity** *NOUN*

intricate *ADJECTIVE*
very complicated, with a lot of fine details • *an intricate pattern*
➤ **intricately** *ADVERB*
➤ **intricacy** *NOUN*

intrigue (say in-**treeg**) *VERB* intrigues, intriguing, intrigued
to interest someone very much and make them curious • *The subject intrigues me.*
➤ **intriguing** *ADJECTIVE*

intrigue (say **in**-treeg) *NOUN* intrigues
❶ plotting; an underhand plot ❷ (*old use*) a secret love affair

intrinsic *ADJECTIVE*
being part of the essential nature or character of something • *The coin has little intrinsic value.*

introduce *VERB* introduces, introducing, introduced
❶ to bring an idea or practice into use • *The new law was introduced in 2011.* ❷ to make a person known to other people • *Come with me and I'll introduce you to my brother.* ❸ to announce a broadcast, speaker, etc.

introduction *NOUN* introductions
❶ introducing someone or something • *the introduction of computers into the classroom* ❷ an explanation put at the beginning of a book, speech, etc.
➤ **introductory** *ADJECTIVE*

introspective *ADJECTIVE*
examining your own thoughts and feelings
➤ **introspection** *NOUN*

introvert NOUN **introverts**
a shy person who does not like to talk about their own thoughts and feelings with other people. (The opposite is **extrovert**.)
➤ **introverted** ADJECTIVE

intrude VERB **intrudes, intruding, intruded**
to come in or join in without being wanted • *I hope I am not intruding.*
➤ **intrusion** NOUN
➤ **intrusive** ADJECTIVE

intruder NOUN **intruders**
someone who forces their way into a place where they are not supposed to be

intuition NOUN
the power to know or understand things without having to think hard or without being taught
➤ **intuitive** ADJECTIVE
➤ **intuitively** ADVERB

Inuit (say **in**-yoo-it) NOUN **Inuit**
❶ a member of a people living in northern Canada and Greenland; an Eskimo ❷ the language of the Inuit

USAGE
See the note at **Eskimo**.

inundate VERB **inundates, inundating, inundated**
to send someone so many things that they cannot deal with them all • *We've been inundated with letters about the programme.*

inure (say in-**yoor**) VERB **inures, inuring, inured**
to accustom someone to something unpleasant • *I've become inured to criticism by now.*

invade VERB **invades, invading, invaded**
❶ to attack and enter a country ❷ to crowd into a place • *Tourists invade Oxford in summer.*
➤ **invader** NOUN

invalid (say **in**-va-leed) NOUN **invalids**
a person who is ill or who is weakened by illness

invalid (say in-**val**-id) ADJECTIVE
not valid; not able to be used legally • *This passport is invalid.*
➤ **invalidity** NOUN

invalidate VERB **invalidates, invalidating, invalidated**
to make a thing invalid
➤ **invalidation** NOUN

invaluable ADJECTIVE
having a value that is too great to be

measured; extremely valuable • *invaluable information*

invariable ADJECTIVE
not variable; never changing

invariably ADVERB
without exception; always • *She invariably arrives late.*

invasion NOUN **invasions**
❶ attacking and entering a country
❷ crowding into a place • *an invasion of ants*

invective NOUN
abusive words

inveigle (say in-**vay**-gul) VERB **inveigles, inveigling, inveigled**
to coax or entice someone to do something

invent VERB **invents, inventing, invented**
❶ to be the first person to make or think of a particular thing ❷ to make up a false story • *She had to invent an excuse quickly.*

invention NOUN **inventions**
❶ a thing that has been made or designed by someone for the first time ❷ inventing something • *The invention of the telephone changed the world.*

inventive ADJECTIVE
having clever new ideas • *She has an inventive mind.*

inventor NOUN **inventors**
a person who has invented something

inventory (say **in**-ven-ter-ee) NOUN **inventories**
a detailed list of goods or furniture

inverse ADJECTIVE
opposite or reverse
➤ **inversely** ADVERB

invert VERB **inverts, inverting, inverted**
to turn something upside down
➤ **inversion** NOUN

invertebrate NOUN **invertebrates**
an animal without a backbone
➤ **invertebrate** ADJECTIVE

inverted commas PLURAL NOUN
punctuation marks (" " or ' ') which are put round quotations and spoken words

PUNCTUATION
Inverted commas (also known as **quotation marks** or **speech marks**) are used in pairs and can surround a single word or phrase or a longer piece of text. The punctuation always goes inside the

inverted commas. They are used:

in direct speech to show which words are being spoken:

'Look!' said a voice behind me. 'Look at the sky!'

to highlight a word to which you are referring:

The words 'turn back' were scratched on the door.

to show that a word is being used in a slightly odd way, for example because it is a slang word:

Disneyland wasn't my idea of a place to 'chill' on holiday.

to show that something is the title of a poem, story, piece of music, etc.

She stood up and recited Kipling's poem 'If'.

to enclose direct quotations from a speech, book, play or film:

Which film contains the famous line, 'Toto, I've a feeling we're not in Kansas anymore'?

Pairs of inverted commas can be single (' ') or double (" "), but are never mixed. You can, however, use a pair of double inverted commas within a pair of single inverted commas:

'When I say, "Action", start the gladiator scene again.'

See also the panel on **direct and reported speech**.

invest *VERB* **invests, investing, invested**
❶ to use money to make a profit, e.g. by lending it in return for interest to be paid or by buying stocks and shares or property ❷ to give someone an honour, medal or special title in a formal ceremony
➤ **investor** *NOUN*

investigate *VERB* **investigates, investigating, investigated**
to find out as much as you can about something • *Police are investigating the robbery.*
➤ **investigator** *NOUN*
➤ **investigative** *ADJECTIVE*

investigation *NOUN* **investigations**
a careful search for information about something • *a murder investigation*

investiture *NOUN* **investitures**
the ceremony of investing someone with an honour etc.

investment *NOUN* **investments**
❶ an amount of money invested ❷ something in which money is invested • *Property is a good investment.*

inveterate *ADJECTIVE*
always doing something and not likely to stop • *an inveterate gambler*

invigilate *VERB* **invigilates, invigilating, invigilated**
(*British*) to supervise the people taking an examination
➤ **invigilation** *NOUN*
➤ **invigilator** *NOUN*

invigorate *VERB* **invigorates, invigorating, invigorated**
to make someone feel healthy and full of energy • *He felt invigorated after his swim.*
➤ **invigorating** *ADJECTIVE*

invincible *ADJECTIVE*
not able to be defeated
➤ **invincibility** *NOUN*

invisible *ADJECTIVE*
not visible; not able to be seen • *These creatures are so tiny that they are invisible to the human eye.*
➤ **invisibly** *ADVERB*
➤ **invisibility** *NOUN*

invitation *NOUN* **invitations**
a request for a person to do or come to something

invite *VERB* **invites, inviting, invited**
❶ to ask a person to come or do something ❷ to be likely to cause something unpleasant to happen • *You are inviting disaster.*

inviting *ADJECTIVE*
attractive or tempting
➤ **invitingly** *ADVERB*

invoice *NOUN* **invoices**
a list of goods sent or work done, with the prices charged

invoke *VERB* **invokes, invoking, invoked**
❶ to mention a law or someone's authority to support what you are doing ❷ to call upon a god in prayer asking for help etc.
➤ **invocation** *NOUN*

a b c d e f g h i j k l m n o p q r s t u v w x y z

involuntary *ADJECTIVE*
not deliberate; done without thinking • *an involuntary shudder*
➤ **involuntarily** *ADVERB*

involve *VERB* involves, involving, involved
❶ to have or include something as a necessary part • *The job involved a lot of effort.* ❷ to make or let someone share or take part in something • *We want to involve everybody in the celebrations.*
➤ **involvement** *NOUN*

involved *ADJECTIVE*
❶ taking part in something; closely connected with something • *I didn't want to get involved in their argument.* ❷ long and complicated • *The book has an involved plot.*

invulnerable *ADJECTIVE*
not able to be harmed

inward *ADJECTIVE*
❶ on the inside ❷ going or facing inwards

inward *ADVERB*
inwards

inwardly *ADVERB*
in your thoughts; privately • *He groaned inwardly.*

inwards *ADVERB*
towards the inside • *A concave lens curves inwards.*

iodine *NOUN*
a chemical substance used as an antiseptic

ion *NOUN* ions
an electrically charged particle

ionosphere (say eye-**on**-os-feer) *NOUN*
a region of the upper atmosphere, containing ions

iota *NOUN* iotas
a tiny amount of something • *There's not an iota of truth in what she says.*
WORD ORIGIN the name of *i*, the ninth and smallest letter of the Greek alphabet

IOU *NOUN* IOUs
a signed note acknowledging that you owe someone some money **WORD ORIGIN** short for 'I owe you'

IQ *ABBREVIATION*
intelligence quotient; a number showing how a person's intelligence compares with that of an average person

irascible (say ir-**as**-ib-ul) *ADJECTIVE*
easily becoming angry; irritable

irate (say eye-**rayt**) *ADJECTIVE*
angry • *irate customers*

iridescent *ADJECTIVE*
showing rainbow-like colours
➤ **iridescence** *NOUN*

iris *NOUN* irises
❶ the coloured part of your eyeball ❷ a plant with long pointed leaves and large flowers

irk *VERB* irks, irking, irked
to annoy someone

irksome *ADJECTIVE*
annoying or tiresome

iron *NOUN* irons
❶ a hard grey metal ❷ a device with a flat base that is heated for smoothing clothes or cloth ❸ a tool made of iron • *a branding iron*
➤ **iron** *ADJECTIVE*

iron *VERB* irons, ironing, ironed
to smooth clothes or cloth with an iron
➤ **iron something out** to sort out a difficulty or problem

Iron Age *NOUN*
the time when tools and weapons were made of iron

ironic (say eye-**ron**-ik) *ADJECTIVE*
❶ an ironic situation is strange because the opposite happens to what you might expect ❷ you are being ironic when you say the opposite of what you mean
➤ **ironical** *ADJECTIVE*
➤ **ironically** *ADVERB*

ironmonger *NOUN* ironmongers
(*British*) a shopkeeper who sells tools and other metal objects
➤ **ironmongery** *NOUN*

irons *PLURAL NOUN*
shackles or fetters

irony (say **eye**-ron-ee) *NOUN* ironies
❶ saying the opposite of what you mean in order to emphasize it or as a joke, e.g. saying 'What a lovely day.' when it is pouring with rain ❷ a situation that is the opposite of what you might have expected • *The irony of it is that I tripped while telling someone else to be careful.*

irrational *ADJECTIVE*
not rational; illogical • *an irrational fear*
➤ **irrationally** *ADVERB*

irrefutable (say ir-**ef**-yoo-ta-bul) *ADJECTIVE*
unable to be proven wrong • *The evidence is irrefutable.*

irregular *ADJECTIVE*
❶ not regular; uneven • *His visits became more and more irregular.* • *an irregular shape*
❷ not following the normal rules or usual custom
➤ **irregularly** *ADVERB*
➤ **irregularity** *NOUN*

irrelevant (say ir-**el**-iv-ant) *ADJECTIVE*
not relevant; not having anything to do with what is being discussed
➤ **irrelevantly** *ADVERB*
➤ **irrelevance** *NOUN*

irreparable (say ir-**ep**-er-a-bul) *ADJECTIVE*
unable to be repaired • *irreparable damage*
➤ **irreparably** *ADVERB*

irreplaceable *ADJECTIVE*
unable to be replaced

irrepressible *ADJECTIVE*
unable to be repressed; always lively and cheerful
➤ **irrepressibly** *ADVERB*

irreproachable *ADJECTIVE*
blameless or faultless
➤ **irreproachably** *ADVERB*

irresistible *ADJECTIVE*
too strong or attractive or tempting to resist
• *I had an irresistible urge to laugh.*
➤ **irresistibly** *ADVERB*

irresolute *ADJECTIVE*
feeling uncertain; hesitant
➤ **irresolutely** *ADVERB*

irrespective *ADJECTIVE*
not taking something into account • *Prizes are awarded to winners, irrespective of age.*

irresponsible *ADJECTIVE*
not thinking enough about the effects of your actions
➤ **irresponsibly** *ADVERB*
➤ **irresponsibility** *NOUN*

irretrievable *ADJECTIVE*
not able to be retrieved
➤ **irretrievably** *ADVERB*

irreverent *ADJECTIVE*
not reverent or respectful
➤ **irreverently** *ADVERB*
➤ **irreverence** *NOUN*

irrevocable (say ir-**ev**-ok-a-bul) *ADJECTIVE*
unable to be changed • *an irrevocable decision*
➤ **irrevocably** *ADVERB*

irrigate *VERB* irrigates, irrigating, irrigated
to supply land with water so that crops can grow
➤ **irrigation** *NOUN*

irritable *ADJECTIVE*
easily annoyed; bad-tempered
➤ **irritably** *ADVERB*
➤ **irritability** *NOUN*

irritate *VERB* irritates, irritating, irritated
❶ to annoy someone ❷ to make a part of your body itch or feel sore • *This soap irritates my skin.*
➤ **irritating** *ADJECTIVE*
➤ **irritant** *NOUN*

irritation *NOUN* irritations
❶ being annoyed • *There was a hint of irritation in her voice.* ❷ something that annoys you

Islam *NOUN*
the religion of Muslims
➤ **Islamic** *ADJECTIVE*

island *NOUN* islands
❶ a piece of land surrounded by water
❷ something that resembles an island because it is isolated or detached • *a traffic island*

islander *NOUN* islanders
someone who lives on an island

isle (rhymes with mile) *NOUN* isles (*poetic & in names*)
an island

isn't (*mainly spoken*)
is not

> **SPELLING**
> **Isn't** = **is** + **not**. Add an **apostrophe** between the **n** and the **t**.

isobar (say **eye**-so-bar) *NOUN* isobars
a line on a map connecting places that have the same atmospheric pressure

isolate *VERB* isolates, isolating, isolated
to place or keep a person or thing apart from other people or things • *Patients with the disease need to be isolated.*
➤ **isolated** *ADJECTIVE*

isolation *NOUN*
being separate or alone • *He lived in complete isolation from the outside world.*

isosceles (say eye-**soss**-il-eez) *ADJECTIVE*
an isosceles triangle has two sides of equal length

a b c d e f g h i j k l m n o p q r s t u v w x y z

isotope *NOUN* **isotopes**
(*in science*) a form of an element that differs from other forms in the structure of its nucleus but has the same chemical properties as the other forms **WORD ORIGIN** from Greek *isos* = same + *topos* = place (because they appear in the same place in the table of chemical elements)

ISP *ABBREVIATION*
Internet service provider, a company providing individual users with a connection to the Internet

issue *VERB* **issues, issuing, issued**
❶ to supply something or give it out to people • *We issued one blanket to each refugee.* ❷ to send something out • *They issued a gale warning.* ❸ to put something out for sale; to publish something ❹ to come or go out; to flow out • *Black smoke issued from the chimneys.*

issue *NOUN* **issues**
❶ a subject for discussion or concern • *There were two main issues the jury had to consider.* ❷ a particular edition of a newspaper or magazine • *Look out for the free poster in next week's issue.* ❸ issuing something • *The issue of passports has been held up.* ❹ (*formal*) the birth of children • *He died without issue.*
➤ **take issue with someone** to disagree with someone

isthmus (say **iss**-mus) *NOUN* **isthmuses**
a narrow strip of land connecting two larger pieces of land

IT *ABBREVIATION*
information technology

it *PRONOUN*
❶ the thing being talked about ❷ used in statements about the weather, the time or a distance • *It is raining.* • *It is six miles to York.* ❸ used to refer to a phrase • *It is a pity that she was so tired.* ❹ used as an indefinite object • *Run for it!*

italic (say it-**al**-ik) *ADJECTIVE*
printed with sloping letters (called **italics**) *like this*

itch *VERB* **itches, itching, itched**
❶ to have or feel a tickling sensation in the skin that makes you want to scratch it ❷ to long to do something • *I am itching to get started.*

itch *NOUN* **itches**
❶ an itching feeling ❷ a longing

itchy *ADJECTIVE* **itchier, itchiest**
making you want to scratch your skin
• *My nose is itchy.*
➤ **itchiness** *NOUN*

item *NOUN* **items**
❶ one thing in a list or group of things
❷ one piece of news, article, etc., in a newspaper or bulletin

itinerant (say it-**in**-er-ant) *ADJECTIVE*
travelling from place to place • *itinerant musicians*

itinerary (say eye-**tin**-er-er-ee) *NOUN* **itineraries**
a list of places to be visited on a journey; a route

its *DETERMINER*
belonging to it • *The cat was licking its paw.*
SPELLING
Take care not to confuse this word **its**, meaning 'belonging to it', with the word **it's**, meaning 'it is' or 'it has'.

it's (*mainly spoken*)
❶ it is • *It's very hot.* ❷ it has • *It's broken all records.*
SPELLING
Take care not to confuse this word **it's**, meaning 'it is' or 'it has', with the word **its**, meaning 'belonging to it'.

itself *PRONOUN*
it and nothing else. The word is used to refer back to the subject of a sentence (e.g. *The cat has hurt itself.*) or for emphasis (e.g. *The house itself is quite small.*).
➤ **by itself** on its own; alone

ivory *NOUN*
❶ the hard creamy-white substance that forms elephants' tusks ❷ a creamy-white colour

ivy *NOUN* **ivies**
a climbing evergreen plant with shiny leaves

jab *VERB* jabs, jabbing, jabbed
❶ to poke someone roughly with your finger or something pointed • *She jabbed me in the ribs with her elbow.* ❷ to push a thing roughly into something else • *He jabbed his gun into my back.*

jab *NOUN* jabs
❶ a rough push or hit with something pointed or a fist ❷ (*informal*) an injection

jabber *VERB* jabbers, jabbering, jabbered
to speak quickly and not clearly; to chatter • *They were all jabbering excitedly.*
➤ **jabber** *NOUN*

jack *NOUN* jacks
❶ a device for lifting something heavy off the ground, especially a car ❷ a playing card with a picture of a young man ❸ a small white ball that players aim at in the game of bowls
➤ **jack of all trades** someone who can do many different kinds of work

jack *VERB* jacks, jacking, jacked
to lift something with a jack
➤ **jack it in** (*informal*) to give up or abandon something
(**WORD ORIGIN**) the name *Jack* was given to various sorts of tool (as though it was a person helping you)

jackal *NOUN* jackals
a wild animal rather like a dog

jackaroo *NOUN* jackaroos (*informal*)
(*Australian*) a young male trainee worker on a sheep or cattle station

jackass *NOUN* jackasses
❶ a male donkey ❷ (*informal*) a stupid person

jackdaw *NOUN* jackdaws
a kind of small crow

jacket *NOUN* jackets
❶ a short coat, usually reaching to your hips ❷ a cover to keep the heat in a water tank or boiler ❸ a paper wrapper for a book ❹ the skin of a potato that is baked without being peeled

jack-in-the-box *NOUN* jack-in-the-boxes
a toy figure that springs out of a box when the lid is lifted

jackknife *VERB* jackknifes, jackknifing, jackknifed
an articulated lorry jackknifes if it folds against itself in an accidental skidding movement

jackpot *NOUN* jackpots
an amount of prize money that increases until someone wins it
➤ **hit the jackpot** ❶ to win a large prize ❷ to have remarkable luck or success
(**WORD ORIGIN**) originally = a kitty which could be won only by playing a pair of jacks or cards of higher value

Jacobean *ADJECTIVE*
from the reign of James I of England (1603-25)

Jacobite *NOUN* Jacobites
a supporter of the exiled Stuarts after the abdication of James II of England (1688)

Jacuzzi (say ja-**koo**-zi) *NOUN* Jacuzzis (*trademark*)
a large bath in which underwater jets of water massage your body
(**WORD ORIGIN**) named after its inventor Candido *Jacuzzi*

jade *NOUN*
a hard green stone that is carved to make ornaments and jewellery

jaded *ADJECTIVE*
tired and bored after doing the same thing for too long (**WORD ORIGIN**) from an old word *jade* = a worn-out horse

jagged (say **jag**-id) *ADJECTIVE*
a jagged line or outline has an uneven edge with sharp points

jaguar *NOUN* jaguars
a large fierce South American animal of the cat family rather like a leopard

jail *NOUN* jails
a prison

jail *VERB* jails, jailing, jailed
to put someone in prison

jailer *NOUN* jailers
a person in charge of a jail

Jain (say Jane) *NOUN* Jains
a follower of Jainism

a b c d e f g h i j k l m n o p q r s t u v w x y z

Jainism (say **jayn**-izm) NOUN
an ancient philosophy originating in India and closely linked to Hinduism

jam NOUN jams
❶ a sweet food made of fruit boiled with sugar until it is thick ❷ a lot of people, cars or logs etc. crowded together so that movement is difficult
➤ **in a jam** (informal)
in a difficult situation

jam VERB jams, jamming, jammed
❶ to become or make something fixed and difficult to move • The paper keeps jamming in the printer. ❷ to squeeze something into a space where there is not much room • Six of us were jammed into one small car. ❸ to push something with a lot of force • He jammed his fingers in his ears. • I jammed the brakes on. ❹ to block a broadcast by causing interference with the transmission

jamb (say jam) NOUN jambs
a side post of a doorway or window frame

jamboree NOUN jamborees
a large party or celebration

jangle VERB jangles, jangling, jangled
❶ to make a loud harsh ringing sound • His keys jangled in his pocket. ❷ your nerves are jangling when you feel anxious
➤ **jangle** NOUN

janitor NOUN janitors
a caretaker

January NOUN
the first month of the year
WORD ORIGIN named after *Janus*, a Roman god of gates and beginnings, usually shown with two faces that look in opposite directions

jar NOUN jars
a container made of glass or pottery

jar VERB jars, jarring, jarred
❶ to cause an unpleasant jolt or shock • I jarred my neck when I fell. ❷ to make a harsh sound, especially in an annoying way • Her voice really jars on me.

jargon NOUN
words or expressions used by a profession or group that are difficult for other people to understand • The guide is full of computer jargon.

jasmine NOUN
a shrub with yellow or white flowers

jaundice NOUN
a disease in which the skin becomes yellow

jaunt NOUN jaunts
a short trip for fun

jaunty ADJECTIVE jauntier, jauntiest
lively and cheerful • She gave them a jaunty little wave as she left.
➤ **jauntily** ADVERB

javelin NOUN javelins
a lightweight spear used for throwing in athletics competitions

jaw NOUN jaws
❶ either of the two bones that form the framework of the mouth ❷ the lower part of the face; the mouth and teeth of a person or animal ❸ the part of a tool that grips something

jay NOUN jays
a noisy brightly-coloured bird

jaywalker NOUN jaywalkers
a person who dangerously walks across a road without looking out for traffic
➤ **jaywalking** NOUN

jazz NOUN
a kind of music with strong rhythm, often improvised
➤ **jazz something up** to make something more lively or interesting

jealous ADJECTIVE
❶ angry or upset because someone you love seems to be showing interest in someone else ❷ unhappy or resentful because you feel that someone is more successful or luckier than you or has something that you would like to have ❸ careful in keeping something • He is very jealous of his privacy.
➤ **jealously** ADVERB

SPELLING
There is a tricky bit in **jealous**—it begins with **jea**.

jealousy NOUN jealousies
a jealous feeling • I felt sick with jealousy.

jeans PLURAL NOUN
trousers made of denim or another strong cotton fabric

Jeep NOUN Jeeps (trademark)
a small sturdy motor vehicle with four-wheel drive, especially one used in the army
WORD ORIGIN from G.P., short for 'general purpose'

jeer VERB jeers, jeering, jeered
to laugh rudely at someone and shout insults at them

jeer *VERB* jeers
a rude or scornful remark

jelly *NOUN* jellies
❶ a soft transparent food with a fruit flavour
❷ any soft slippery substance
➤ **jellied** *ADJECTIVE*

jellyfish *NOUN* jellyfish
a sea animal with a body like jelly and stinging tentacles

jemmy *NOUN* jemmies
a burglar's crowbar

jeopardize (also **jeopardise**) (say **jep**-er-dyz) *VERB* jeopardizes, jeopardizing, jeopardized
to put something at risk • *This could jeopardize the whole mission.*

jeopardy (say **jep**-er-dee) *NOUN*
danger of harm or failure • *The future of the factory is now in jeopardy.*

jerk *VERB* jerks, jerking, jerked
❶ to make a sudden sharp movement • *The train jerked forwards.* ❷ to pull something suddenly

jerk *NOUN* jerks
❶ a sudden sharp movement ❷ (*informal*) a stupid person

jerkin *NOUN* jerkins
a sleeveless jacket

jerky *ADJECTIVE*
moving with sudden sharp movements
➤ **jerkily** *ADVERB*

jersey *NOUN* jerseys
❶ a pullover with sleeves ❷ a plain machine-knitted material used for making clothes
WORD ORIGIN originally = a woollen cloth made in *Jersey*, one of the Channel Islands

jest *NOUN* jests
a joke
➤ **in jest** as a joke

jest *VERB* jests, jesting, jested
to make jokes

jester *NOUN* jesters
a professional entertainer at a royal court in the Middle Ages

jet *NOUN* jets
❶ a stream of water, gas, flame, etc. shot out from a narrow opening ❷ a spout or nozzle from which a jet comes ❸ an aircraft driven by engines that send out a high-speed jet of hot gases at the back ❹ a hard black mineral substance ❺ a deep glossy black colour

jet *VERB* jets, jetting, jetted
❶ to come out or send something out in a strong stream ❷ (*informal*) to travel in a jet aircraft

jet lag *NOUN*
extreme tiredness that a person feels after a long flight between different time zones

jetsam *NOUN*
goods thrown overboard from a ship in difficulty and washed ashore
WORD ORIGIN from **jettison**

jettison *VERB* jettisons, jettisoning, jettisoned
❶ to throw something overboard ❷ to release or drop something from an aircraft or spacecraft in flight ❸ to get rid of something that you no longer want

jetty *NOUN* jetties
a small landing stage for boats

Jew *NOUN* Jews
❶ a member of a people descended from the ancient tribes of Israel ❷ someone who believes in Judaism
➤ **Jewish** *ADJECTIVE*

jewel *NOUN* jewels
❶ a precious stone ❷ an ornament containing precious stones
➤ **jewelled** *ADJECTIVE*

jeweller *NOUN* jewellers
a person who sells or makes jewellery

jewellery *NOUN*
jewels and similar ornaments for wearing

jib *NOUN* jibs
❶ a triangular sail stretching forward from a ship's front mast ❷ the arm of a crane

jib *VERB* jibs, jibbing, jibbed
to be unwilling to do or accept something

jibe *NOUN* jibes
a remark that is meant to hurt someone's feelings or make them look silly

jibe *VERB* jibes, jibing, jibed
to make hurtful remarks; to mock someone

jiffy *NOUN* (*informal*)
a brief moment • *I'll be ready in a jiffy.*

jig *NOUN* jigs
❶ a lively jumping dance ❷ a device that holds something in place while you work on it with tools

jig *VERB* jigs, jigging, jigged
to move up and down quickly and jerkily

jiggle VERB jiggles, jiggling, jiggled
to move around with short quick movements
• *Stop jiggling around!*

jigsaw NOUN jigsaws
❶ a puzzle made of differently shaped pieces that you have to fit together to make a picture ❷ a saw that can cut curved shapes

jihad NOUN jihads
(among Muslims) a war or struggle against unbelievers or a spiritual struggle

jilt VERB jilts, jilting, jilted
to abandon a boyfriend or girlfriend, especially after promising to marry them

jingle VERB jingles, jingling, jingled
❶ metal objects jingle when they make a tinkling sound like small bells ❷ to shake metal objects together so that they make a tinkling sound like small bells • *She jingled the coins in her pocket.*

jingle NOUN jingles
❶ a jingling sound ❷ a catchy verse or tune, especially one used in advertising

jingoism NOUN
an extremely strong and unreasonable belief that your country is superior to others
➤ **jingoistic** ADJECTIVE
WORD ORIGIN from the saying *by jingo!*, used in a patriotic song in the 19th century

jinx NOUN jinxes
a person or thing that is thought to bring bad luck **WORD ORIGIN** probably a variation of *jynx* = wryneck, a bird used in witchcraft

jitters PLURAL NOUN (*informal*)
a feeling of extreme nervousness

jittery ADJECTIVE (*informal*)
extremely nervous and anxious • *The horses were getting jittery.*

job NOUN jobs
❶ work that someone does regularly to earn a living ❷ a piece of work that needs to be done ❸ (*informal*) a difficult task • *You'll have a job to lift that box.* ❹ (*informal*) a thing; a state of affairs • *It's a good job you're here.*
➤ **just the job** (*informal*) exactly what you want

jobcentre NOUN jobcentres
a government office with information about available jobs

jockey NOUN jockeys
a person who rides horses in races

jocular ADJECTIVE
joking or humorous
➤ **jocularly** ADVERB
➤ **jocularity** NOUN

jodhpurs (say **jod**-perz) PLURAL NOUN
trousers for horse riding, fitting closely from the knee to the ankle **WORD ORIGIN** named after *Jodhpur*, a city in India, where similar trousers are worn

joey NOUN joeys
(*Australian*) a young animal, especially a kangaroo, still young enough to be carried in its mother's pouch

jog VERB jogs, jogging, jogged
❶ to run or trot slowly, especially for exercise ❷ to give something a slight knock or push
➤ **jogger** NOUN
➤ **jog someone's memory** to help someone to remember something

jog NOUN jogs
a slow run or trot

joggle VERB joggles, joggling, joggled
to shake slightly or move jerkily

joie de vivre (say zhwah der **veevr**) NOUN
a feeling of great enjoyment of life
WORD ORIGIN French, = joy of life

join VERB joins, joining, joined
❶ two things join when they come together ❷ to put things together; to fasten or connect things ❸ to take part with others in doing something or going somewhere • *Do you mind if I join you?* ❹ to become a member of a group or organization • *Join the Navy.*
➤ **join in** to take part in something
➤ **join up** to become a member of the armed forces

join NOUN joins
a place where things join

joiner NOUN joiners
a person whose job is to make doors, window frames, etc. and furniture out of wood
➤ **joinery** NOUN

joint NOUN joints
❶ a place where two things are joined ❷ the place where two bones fit together ❸ a large piece of meat cut ready for cooking ❹ (*informal*) a cannabis cigarette

joint ADJECTIVE
shared or done by two or more people, groups or countries • *The song was a joint effort.*
➤ **jointly** ADVERB

joist *NOUN* joists
any of the long beams supporting a floor or ceiling

joke *NOUN* jokes
❶ something said or done to make people laugh ❷ a ridiculous person or thing

joke *VERB* jokes, joking, joked
❶ to make jokes ❷ to tease someone or not be serious • *I'm only joking.*

joker *NOUN* jokers
❶ someone who likes making jokes ❷ an extra playing card with a picture of a jester on it

jolly *ADJECTIVE* jollier, jolliest
cheerful and good-humoured
➤ **jollity** *NOUN*

jolly *ADVERB* (*British*) (*informal*) very • *jolly good*

jolly *VERB* jollies, jollying, jollied (*British*) (*informal*)
➤ **jolly someone along** to keep someone in a cheerful mood

jolt *VERB* jolts, jolting, jolted
❶ to shake or dislodge something with a sudden sharp movement ❷ to move along jerkily, e.g. on a rough road ❸ to give someone a shock

jolt *NOUN* jolts
❶ a jolting movement ❷ a shock

jostle *VERB* jostles, jostling, jostled
to push someone roughly, especially in a crowd • *People jostled to get a better view.*

jot *VERB* jots, jotting, jotted
to jot something down is to write it down quickly

jot *NOUN* jots
a tiny amount • *He doesn't care a jot about other people.*

jotter *NOUN* jotters
(*British*) a notepad or notebook

joule (say jool) *NOUN* joules
(*in science*) a unit of work or energy
WORD ORIGIN named after an English scientist, James *Joule*

journal *NOUN* journals
❶ a newspaper or magazine ❷ a diary

journalist *NOUN* journalists
a person who writes for a newspaper or magazine or who prepares news broadcasts on television or radio
➤ **journalism** *NOUN*
➤ **journalistic** *ADJECTIVE*

journey *NOUN* journeys
❶ going from one place to another ❷ the distance or time taken to travel somewhere • *The town was two days' journey away.*

journey *VERB* journeys, journeying, journeyed
to make a journey • *They journeyed for seven long months.*

joust (say jowst) *VERB* jousts, jousting, jousted
to fight on horseback with lances, as knights did in medieval times
➤ **joust** *NOUN*

jovial *ADJECTIVE*
cheerful and good-humoured
➤ **jovially** *ADVERB*
➤ **joviality** *NOUN*
WORD ORIGIN from Latin *jovialis* = to do with Jupiter (because people born under the planet's influence were said to be cheerful)

jowl *NOUN* jowls
❶ the jaw or cheek ❷ loose skin on the neck

joy *NOUN* joys
❶ a feeling of great pleasure or happiness ❷ a thing that causes joy ❸ satisfaction or success • *Any joy with the crossword?*

joyful *ADJECTIVE*
very happy • *a joyful occasion*
➤ **joyfully** *ADVERB*
➤ **joyfulness** *NOUN*

joyous *ADJECTIVE*
full of joy; causing joy
➤ **joyously** *ADVERB*

joyride *NOUN* joyrides
a drive in a stolen car for amusement
➤ **joyrider** *NOUN*
➤ **joyriding** *NOUN*

joystick *NOUN* joysticks
❶ the control lever of an aircraft ❷ a device for moving a cursor or image on a computer screen, especially in computer games

jubilant *ADJECTIVE*
very happy because you have won or succeeded
➤ **jubilantly** *ADVERB*
➤ **jubilation** *NOUN*

jubilee (say **joo**-bil-ee) *NOUN* jubilees
a special anniversary of an important event

USAGE
A *silver jubilee* is the 25th anniversary, a *golden jubilee* is the 50th anniversary, and a *diamond jubilee* is a 60th anniversary.

WORD ORIGIN from Hebrew *yobel* = a year when slaves were freed and property returned

a b c d e f g h i j k l m n o p q r s t u v w x y z

to its owners, held in ancient Israel every 50 years

Judaism (say **joo**-day-izm) *NOUN*
the religion of the Jewish people

judder *VERB* judders, juddering, juddered
(*British*) to shake noisily or violently • *The van juddered to a halt.*

judge *NOUN* judges
❶ a person appointed to hear cases in a law court and decide what should be done ❷ a person who decides the winner of a contest or competition ❸ someone who is good at forming opinions or making decisions about things • *She's a good judge of character.*

judge *VERB* judges, judging, judged
❶ to act as a judge ❷ to form and give an opinion ❸ to estimate something • *He judged the distance carefully.*

judgement *NOUN* judgements
❶ judging ❷ the decision made by a law court ❸ someone's opinion • *In my judgement, you're making a big mistake.*
❹ the ability to make decisions wisely
❺ something considered as a punishment from God • *It's a judgement on you!*

> **SPELLING**
> There is a tricky bit in **judgement** – there is an e after the g.

judicial *ADJECTIVE*
to do with law courts, judges or legal judgements • *the British judicial system*

> **USAGE**
> Take care not to confuse with **judicious**.

judiciary (say joo-**dish**-er-ee) *NOUN* judiciaries
all the judges in a country

judicious (say joo-**dish**-us) *ADJECTIVE*
having or showing good sense or good judgement
> **judiciously** *ADVERB*

> **USAGE**
> Take care not to confuse with **judicial**.

judo *NOUN*
a Japanese method of self-defence without using weapons **WORD ORIGIN** from Japanese *ju* = gentle + *do* = way

jug *NOUN* jugs
a container for holding and pouring liquids, with a handle and a lip

juggernaut *NOUN* juggernauts
(*British*) a huge lorry **WORD ORIGIN** named

after a huge wagon bearing the image of the Hindu god *Jagannatha*, dragged through the streets at an annual festival

juggle *VERB* juggles, juggling, juggled
❶ to toss and catch a number of objects skilfully for entertainment, keeping one or more in the air at any time ❷ to try to deal with several jobs or activities at the same time
> **juggler** *NOUN*

jugular *ADJECTIVE*
to do with your throat or neck • *the jugular veins*

juice *NOUN* juices
❶ the liquid from fruit, vegetables or other food ❷ a liquid produced by the body • *the digestive juices*

> **SPELLING**
> **Juice** is a tricky word to spell: the 'oo' sound is spelt **ui** and the 's' sound is spelt with a **c**.

juicy *ADJECTIVE* juicier, juiciest
full of juice

jukebox *NOUN* jukeboxes
a machine that automatically plays a record you have selected when you put a coin in

July *NOUN*
the seventh month of the year
WORD ORIGIN named after *Julius* Caesar, who was born in this month

jumble *VERB* jumbles, jumbling, jumbled
to mix things up in a confused and untidy way

jumble *NOUN*
a confused mixture of things; a muddle • *a jumble of books and paper*

jumble sale *NOUN* jumble sales
(*British*) a sale of second-hand goods to raise money

jumbo *NOUN* jumbos
❶ something very large ❷ a jumbo jet
WORD ORIGIN the name of a very large elephant in London Zoo

jumbo jet *NOUN* jumbo jets
a very large jet aircraft

jump *VERB* jumps, jumping, jumped
❶ to move up suddenly from the ground into the air ❷ to go over something by jumping
• *The horse jumped the fence.* ❸ to move suddenly in surprise • *Oh, it's only you – you made me jump.* ❹ to get into or out of a

vehicle quickly • *A taxi stopped and we jumped in.* ❺ to pass over something; to miss out part of a book etc. ❻ to pass quickly to a higher level
➤ **jump at something** to accept something eagerly
➤ **jump on someone** to start criticizing someone
➤ **jump the gun** to start before you should
➤ **jump the queue** to go in front of people before it is your turn

jump *NOUN* jumps
❶ a jumping movement ❷ an obstacle to jump over ❸ a sudden rise or change

jumper *NOUN* jumpers
a pullover with sleeves

jumpy *ADJECTIVE*
nervous and edgy

junction *NOUN* junctions
a place where roads or railway lines meet

juncture *NOUN* junctures
a point of time while something is happening • *At this juncture there was a knock on the door.*

June *NOUN*
the sixth month of the year
WORD ORIGIN named after the Roman goddess *Juno*

jungle *NOUN* jungles
a thick tangled forest, especially in the tropics

junior *ADJECTIVE*
❶ younger ❷ for young children • *a junior school* ❸ lower in rank or importance • *junior officers*

junior *NOUN* juniors
a junior person

juniper *NOUN* junipers
an evergreen shrub

junk *NOUN* junks
❶ old worthless things that should be thrown away • *The attic is full of junk.* ❷ a Chinese sailing boat

junk food *NOUN*
food that is not nourishing

junkie *NOUN* junkies (*informal*)
a drug addict

junk mail *NOUN*
unwanted advertising material sent by post or email

jurisdiction *NOUN*
authority; official power, especially to interpret and apply the law

juror *NOUN* jurors
a member of a jury

jury *NOUN* juries
❶ a group of people (usually twelve) appointed to give a verdict about a case in a law court ❷ a group of people chosen to judge a competition

just *ADJECTIVE*
❶ fair and right; giving proper consideration to everyone's claims • *a just decision* ❷ deserved; right in amount etc. • *a just reward*
➤ **justly** *ADVERB*

just *ADVERB*
❶ exactly • *It's just what I wanted.* ❷ only; simply • *I just wanted to see him.* ❸ barely; by only a small amount • *The ball hit her just below the knee.* ❹ at this moment or only a little while ago • *She has just gone.*

justice *NOUN* justices
❶ being just; fair treatment • *a struggle for justice* ❷ the system by which courts deal with people who break the law • *a court of justice* ❸ a judge or magistrate

justifiable *ADJECTIVE*
that you can accept because there is good reason for it • *Her actions were entirely justifiable.*

justify *VERB* justifies, justifying, justified
❶ to show that something is fair, just or reasonable • *Can you justify your decision?* ❷ to arrange lines of printed text so that one or both edges are straight
➤ **justification** *NOUN*

jut *VERB* juts, jutting, jutted
to stick out • *Rocky cliffs jutted out into the sea.*

jute *NOUN*
fibre from tropical plants, used for making sacks etc.

juvenile *ADJECTIVE*
❶ to do with or for young people ❷ childish

juvenile *NOUN* juveniles
a young person, not old enough to be legally considered an adult

juvenile delinquent *NOUN* juvenile delinquents
a young person who has broken the law

a b c d e f g h i j k l m n o p q r s t u v w x y z

juxtapose *VERB* **juxtaposes, juxtaposing, juxtaposed**
to juxtapose two or more things is to put them next to each other to show how they are different
➤ **juxtaposition** *NOUN*

kale *NOUN*
a kind of cabbage with curly leaves

kaleidoscope (say kal-**y**-dos-kohp) *NOUN* **kaleidoscopes**
❶ a tube that you look through to see brightly coloured patterns which change as you turn the end of the tube ❷ something full of colour and variety
➤ **kaleidoscopic** *ADJECTIVE*
WORD ORIGIN from Greek *kalos* = beautiful + *eidos* = form + *skopein* = look at

kangaroo *NOUN* **kangaroos**
an Australian animal that jumps along on its strong hind legs. (See **marsupial**.)

kaolin *NOUN*
fine white clay used in making porcelain and in medicine **WORD ORIGIN** from Chinese *gao ling* = high hill (because it was first found on a hill in northern China)

karaoke *NOUN*
a form of entertainment in which people sing well-known songs against a pre-recorded backing **WORD ORIGIN** Japanese = empty orchestra

karate (say ka-**rah**-tee) *NOUN*
a Japanese method of self-defence in which the hands and feet are used as weapons **WORD ORIGIN** from Japanese *kara* = empty + *te* = hand

karoo *NOUN* **karoos**
(*S. African*) a dry plateau in southern Africa

kayak *NOUN* **kayaks**
a small canoe with a covering that fits round the canoeist's waist

KB, Kb *ABBREVIATION*
kilobytes

kebab *NOUN* **kebabs**
small pieces of meat or vegetables cooked on a skewer

keel *NOUN* **keels**
the long piece of wood or metal along the bottom of a boat
➤ **on an even keel** well balanced and steady

keel *VERB* **keels, keeling, keeled**
➤ **keel over** to fall down or overturn • *The ship keeled over.*

keen *ADJECTIVE*
❶ enthusiastic or eager • *a keen swimmer* ❷ to be keen on a person or thing is to like or be interested in them ❸ very sharp • *a keen edge* ❹ piercingly cold • *a keen wind*
➤ **keenly** *ADVERB*
➤ **keenness** *NOUN*

keen *VERB* **keens, keening, keened**
to wail in grief for a dead person

keep *VERB* **keeps, keeping, kept**
❶ to have something and look after it or not get rid of it ❷ to stay or cause something to stay in the same condition etc. • *Keep still.* • *I'll keep it hot.* ❸ to do something continually or repeatedly • *They kept laughing at her.* ❹ food or drink keeps when it lasts without going bad • *How long will this milk keep?* ❺ to keep a promise or your word is to respect and not break it ❻ to keep a diary is to make regular entries in it
➤ **keep up** to make the same progress as others
➤ **keep something up** to continue doing something • *Keep up the good work!*

keep *NOUN* **keeps**
❶ the food, clothes, etc. that a person needs to live • *She earns her keep.* ❷ a strong tower in a castle
➤ **for keeps** (*informal*) to keep for always • *Is this football mine for keeps?*

SPELLING
The past tense of **keep** is **kept**.

keeper *NOUN* **keepers**
❶ a person who looks after an animal, building, etc. • *the park keeper* ❷ a goalkeeper or wicketkeeper

keeping *NOUN*
something is in your keeping when you are looking after it • *The diaries are in safe keeping.*
➤ **be in keeping with something** to fit in with something or be suitable • *Modern furniture is not in keeping with such an old house.*

keepsake *NOUN* **keepsakes**
a gift to be kept in memory of the person who gave it

keg *NOUN* **kegs**
a small barrel

kelp *NOUN*
a large type of seaweed

kelvin *NOUN* **kelvins**
the SI unit of thermodynamic temperature
WORD ORIGIN named after a British scientist, Lord *Kelvin*, who invented it

kennel *NOUN* **kennels**
a shelter for a dog

kennels *NOUN*
a place where dogs are bred or where they can be looked after while their owners are away

kenning *NOUN* **kennings**
a type of expression or riddle from Anglo-Saxon times, in which something is described without using its name, e.g. *oar-steed* meaning 'ship'

kerb *NOUN* **kerbs**
the edge of a pavement
> **SPELLING**
> Take care not to confuse with **curb**, which is a verb meaning to put a limit on something.

kerchief *NOUN* **kerchiefs** (*old use*)
❶ a square scarf worn on the head ❷ a handkerchief

kernel *NOUN* **kernels**
the part inside the shell of a nut
> **SPELLING**
> Do not confuse this word with **colonel**.

kerosene (say **ke**-ro-seen) *NOUN*
paraffin

kestrel *NOUN* **kestrels**
a small falcon

ketchup *NOUN*
a thick sauce made from tomatoes and vinegar

kettle *NOUN* **kettles**
a container with a spout and handle, for boiling water

kettledrum *NOUN* **kettledrums**
a drum consisting of a large metal bowl with skin or plastic over the top

key *NOUN* **keys**
❶ a piece of metal shaped so that it will open a lock ❷ a device for winding up a clock or clockwork toy ❸ a small lever or button to be pressed by a finger, e.g. on a piano, typewriter or computer ❹ a system of notes in music • *the key of C major* ❺ a fact or clue that explains or solves something • *the key to the mystery* ❻ a list of symbols used in a map or table

key *VERB* **keys, keying, keyed**
➤ **key something in** to type information into a computer using a keyboard • *Now key in your password.*

keyboard *NOUN* **keyboards**
the set of keys on a piano, computer, etc.

keyhole *NOUN* **keyholes**
the hole through which a key is put into a lock

keyhole surgery *NOUN*
surgery carried out through a very small cut in the patient's body, using special instruments

keynote *NOUN* **keynotes**
❶ the note on which a key in music is based • *The keynote of C major is C.* ❷ the main idea or theme in something that is said, written or done

keypad *NOUN* **keypads**
a small keyboard or set of buttons used to operate a telephone, television, etc.

keystone *NOUN* **keystones**
the central wedge-shaped stone in an arch, locking the others together

keyword *NOUN* **keywords**
a word that you type into a computer search engine so that it will search for that word on the Internet

kg *ABBREVIATION*
kilogram

khaki *NOUN*
a dull yellowish-brown colour, used for military uniforms **WORD ORIGIN** from Urdu *khaki* = dust-coloured

Khalsa *NOUN*
members of the Sikh religion who vow to wear five signs of their faith known as the five Ks

kibbutz *NOUN* **kibbutzim**
a farming commune in Israel

a
b
c
d
e
f
g
h
i
j
k
l
m
n
o
p
q
r
s
t
u
v
w
x
y
z

kick *VERB* **kicks, kicking, kicked**
❶ to hit or move a person or thing with your foot ❷ to move your legs about vigorously ❸ a gun kicks if it moves back sharply when it is fired
➤ **kick off** ❶ to start a football match ❷ (*informal*) to start doing something
➤ **kick someone out** to get rid of someone
➤ **kick up a fuss** (*informal*) to protest strongly about something
➤ **kick yourself** to be annoyed with yourself

kick *NOUN* **kicks**
❶ a kicking movement ❷ the sudden backwards movement a gun makes when it is fired ❸ (*informal*) a feeling of great excitement or pleasure • *She gets a real kick out of climbing.* ❹ (*informal*) an interest or activity • *He's on a health kick.*

kick-off *NOUN* **kick-offs**
the start of a football match

kid *NOUN* **kids**
❶ (*informal*) a child ❷ a young goat ❸ fine leather made from goatskin

kid *VERB* **kids, kidding, kidded** (*informal*) to tease or fool someone in fun • *Don't worry, I'm only kidding.*

kiddie *NOUN* **kiddies** (*informal*)
a child

kidnap *VERB* **kidnaps, kidnapping, kidnapped**
to take someone away by force, especially in order to obtain a ransom
➤ **kidnapper** *NOUN*

kidney *NOUN* **kidneys**
either of the two organs in the body that remove waste products from the blood and turn them into urine

kidney bean *NOUN* **kidney beans**
a dark red bean with a curved shape like a kidney

kill *VERB* **kills, killing, killed**
❶ to make a person or animal die ❷ to destroy or put an end to something ❸ (*informal*) to cause a person pain or mental suffering • *My feet are killing me.*
➤ **kill time** to spend time idly while waiting

kill *NOUN* **kills**
❶ killing an animal • *Lions often make a kill in the evening.* ❷ an animal that has been hunted and killed

killer *NOUN* **killers**
a person, animal or thing that kills

killing *NOUN* **killings**
an act causing death; a murder
➤ **make a killing** to make a lot of money

kiln *NOUN* **kilns**
an oven for hardening pottery or bricks, or for drying hops

kilo *NOUN* **kilos**
a kilogram

kilobyte *NOUN* **kilobytes**
(*in computing*) a unit of memory or data equal to 1,024 bytes

kilogram *NOUN* **kilograms**
a unit of mass or weight equal to 1,000 grams (about 2.2 pounds)

> **SPELLING**
> There is only one **m** in **kilogram**.

kilometre (say **kil**-o-meet-er or kil-**om**-it-er) *NOUN* **kilometres**
a unit of length equal to 1,000 metres (about ⅔ of a mile)

> **SPELLING**
> There is a tricky bit in **kilometre** – it is spelt **re** at the end and not **er**.

kilowatt *NOUN* **kilowatts**
a unit of electrical power equal to 1,000 watts

kilt *NOUN* **kilts**
a kind of pleated skirt worn by men as part of traditional Scottish dress
➤ **kilted** *ADJECTIVE*

kimono *NOUN* **kimonos**
a long loose Japanese robe with wide sleeves
WORD ORIGIN from Japanese *ki* = wearing + *mono* = thing

kin *NOUN*
a person's relatives
➤ **kinsman** *NOUN*
➤ **kinswoman** *NOUN*
➤ **next of kin** a person's closest relative

kind *NOUN* **kinds**
a class of similar things or animals; a sort or type • *What kind of music do you like?*

kind *ADJECTIVE*
friendly and helpful; considerate
➤ **kindness** *NOUN*
➤ **in kind** ❶ in the same way • *She repaid his insults in kind.* ❷ payment in kind is given in the form of goods or services, not in money
➤ **kind of** (*informal*) in a way; to some extent • *I felt kind of sorry for him.*

kindergarten *NOUN* kindergartens
a school or class for very young children

kind-hearted *ADJECTIVE*
kind and sympathetic

kindle *VERB* kindles, kindling, kindled
❶ to start a flame; to set light to something
❷ to begin burning

kindling *NOUN*
small pieces of wood used for lighting fires

kindly *ADVERB*
❶ in a kind manner ❷ please • *Kindly close the door.*

kindly *ADJECTIVE* kindlier, kindliest
kind or friendly • *a kindly smile*
➤ **kindliness** *NOUN*

kindred *NOUN*
a person's family and relatives

kindred *ADJECTIVE*
related or similar • *chemistry and kindred subjects*
➤ **kindred spirit** someone whose tastes or attitudes are similar to your own

kinetic *ADJECTIVE*
to do with or produced by movement
• *kinetic energy*

king *NOUN* kings
❶ a man who is the ruler of a country through inheriting the position ❷ a person or thing regarded as supreme • *The lion is the king of beasts.* ❸ the most important piece in chess ❹ a playing card with a picture of a king
➤ **kingly** *ADJECTIVE*
➤ **kingship** *NOUN*

kingdom *NOUN* kingdoms
❶ a country ruled by a king or queen ❷ a division of the natural world • *the animal kingdom*

kingfisher *NOUN* kingfishers
a small bird with blue feathers that dives to catch fish

king-size, king-sized *ADJECTIVE*
extra large

kink *NOUN* kinks
❶ a short twist in a rope, wire or length of hair ❷ a peculiarity

kiosk *NOUN* kiosks
❶ a telephone booth ❷ a small hut or stall where newspapers, sweets, etc. are sold

kip *NOUN* kips (*British informal*)
a sleep • *I need to get some kip.*
➤ **kip** *VERB*

kipper *NOUN* kippers
a smoked herring

kirk *NOUN* kirks (*Scottish*)
a church

kiss *NOUN* kisses
touching someone with your lips as a sign of affection or greeting

kiss *VERB* kisses, kissing, kissed
to give someone a kiss

kiss of life *NOUN*
blowing air from your mouth into someone else's to help them start breathing again, especially after an accident

kit *NOUN* kits
❶ equipment or clothes that you need to do a sport, a job or some other activity • *a drum kit* ❷ a set of parts sold ready to be fitted together • *a model aircraft kit*

kitchen *NOUN* kitchens
a room in which meals are prepared and cooked

kitchenette *NOUN* kitchenettes
a small kitchen

kite *NOUN* kites
❶ a light framework covered with cloth or paper that you fly in the wind on the end of a long piece of string ❷ a large hawk

kith and kin *PLURAL NOUN*
friends and relatives

kitten *NOUN* kittens
a very young cat

kitty *NOUN* kitties
❶ a fund of money for use by several people ❷ an amount of money that you can win in a card game

kiwi (say **kee**-wee) *NOUN* kiwis
❶ a New Zealand bird that cannot fly
❷ (*informal*) (**Kiwi**) someone who comes from or lives in New Zealand

kiwi fruit *NOUN* kiwi fruits
a fruit with thin hairy skin, green flesh and black seeds **WORD ORIGIN** named after the kiwi, because the fruit was exported from New Zealand

kleptomania *NOUN*
an uncontrollable urge to steal things
➤ **kleptomaniac** *NOUN*

a b c d e f g h i j k l m n o p q r s t u v w x y z

A B C D E F G H I J **K** L M N O P Q R S T U V W X Y Z

kloof *NOUN* kloofs
(*S. African*) a narrow valley or mountain pass, usually wooded

km *ABBREVIATION*
kilometre

knack *NOUN*
a special skill or talent • *There's a knack to putting up a deckchair.*

knapsack *NOUN* knapsacks
a bag carried on the back by soldiers, hikers, etc.

knave *NOUN* knaves
❶ (*old use*) a dishonest man; a rogue ❷ a jack in a pack of playing cards

knead *VERB* kneads, kneading, kneaded
to press and stretch something soft (especially dough) with your hands

knee *NOUN* knees
the joint in the middle of your leg

kneecap *NOUN* kneecaps
the small bone covering the front of your knee joint

kneel *VERB* kneels, kneeling, knelt
to be or get yourself in a position where you are resting on your knees

knell *NOUN* knells
the sound of a bell rung solemnly after a death or at a funeral

knickerbockers *PLURAL NOUN*
loose-fitting short trousers gathered in at the knees **WORD ORIGIN** from D. *Knickerbocker*, the imaginary author of a book in which people were shown wearing these kinds of trousers

knickers *PLURAL NOUN*
underpants worn by women and girls

knick-knack *NOUN* knick-knacks
a small ornament

knife *NOUN* knives
a cutting instrument or weapon consisting of a sharp blade set in a handle

knife *VERB* knifes, knifing, knifed
to stab someone with a knife

> **SPELLING**
> There is a silent **k** at the beginning of **knife**.

knight *NOUN* knights
❶ a man who has been given the rank that allows him to put 'Sir' before his name ❷ a warrior of high social rank in the Middle Ages, usually mounted and in armour ❸ a piece in

chess, with a horse's head
➤ **knighthood** *NOUN*

knight *VERB* knights, knighting, knighted
to make someone a knight

> **SPELLING**
> **Knight** is different from **night**, which is the time when it is dark.

knit *VERB* knits, knitting, knitted or knit
❶ to make something by looping together wool or other yarn, using long needles or a machine ❷ broken bones knit together when they join back together and heal
➤ **knit your brow** to frown

knitting *NOUN*
❶ the activity of making things by knitting ❷ something that is being knitted

knitting needle *NOUN* knitting needles
a long thick needle used in knitting

knob *NOUN* knobs
❶ the round handle of a door or drawer ❷ a round lump on something ❸ a round button or switch on a dial or machine ❹ a small round piece of something • *a knob of butter*

knobbly *ADJECTIVE*
having many small hard lumps or bumps • *knobbly knees*

knock *VERB* knocks, knocking, knocked
❶ to make a noise by hitting a thing hard • *Someone's knocking at the door.* ❷ to hit something hard or bump into it, especially by accident • *Sorry, I knocked the vase over.* ❸ to produce something by hitting • *We need to knock a hole in the wall.* ❹ (*informal*) to criticize someone or something • *People are always knocking this country.*
➤ **knock off** (*informal*) to stop working
➤ **knock something off** ❶ to deduct something from a price ❷ (*informal*) to steal something
➤ **knock someone out** to make a person unconscious, especially by a blow to the head

knock *NOUN* knocks
the act or sound of knocking

> **SPELLING**
> There is a silent **k** at the beginning of **knock**.

knocker *NOUN* knockers
a hinged metal device for knocking on a door

knockout *NOUN* knockouts
❶ knocking someone out ❷ a contest in which the loser in each round has to drop

out ❸ (*informal*) an extremely attractive or outstanding person or thing

knoll *NOUN* knolls
a small round hill; a mound

knot *NOUN* knots
❶ a fastening made by tying or looping two ends of string, rope or cloth together ❷ a lump where hair or threads have become tangled together ❸ a round spot on a piece of wood where a branch once joined it ❹ a small group of people standing close together ❺ a unit for measuring the speed of ships and aircraft, equal to 2,025 yards (1,852 metres or 1 nautical mile) per hour

knot *VERB* knots, knotting, knotted
❶ to tie or fasten something with a knot
❷ to become tangled up

> **SPELLING**
> There is a silent **k** at the start of **knot**.
> A **knot** is a place where a piece of string or rope is twisted round. **Not** is used to show that something is negative, e.g. *Samir was not happy.*

knotty *ADJECTIVE* knottier, knottiest
❶ full of knots ❷ difficult or puzzling • *a knotty problem*

know *VERB* knows, knowing, knew, known
❶ to have something in your mind that you have learned or discovered ❷ to recognize or be familiar with a person or place • *I've known him for years.* ❸ to understand or realize something • *She knows how to please people.*
> **be known as something** to be called or named something

> **SPELLING**
> There is a silent **k** at the start of **know**.

know-all *NOUN* know-alls
(*British*) a person who behaves as if they know everything

know-how *NOUN*
practical knowledge or skill for a particular job

knowing *ADJECTIVE*
showing that you know or are aware of something • *a knowing look*

knowingly *ADVERB*
❶ in a knowing way • *He winked at me knowingly.* ❷ deliberately • *She would never have done such a thing knowingly.*

knowledge *NOUN*
❶ information and skills you have through experience and education ❷ knowing about a particular thing • *She did it without my knowledge.* ❸ all that is known
> **to my knowledge** as far as I know

knowledgeable *ADJECTIVE*
knowing a lot about something; well-informed
> **knowledgeably** *ADVERB*

knuckle *NOUN* knuckles
a joint in your finger

knuckle *VERB* knuckles, knuckling, knuckled
> **knuckle down** to begin to work hard
> **knuckle under** to accept someone else's authority

koala (say koh-**ah**-la) *NOUN* koalas
a furry Australian animal that looks like a small bear

koppie (say **kop**-i) *NOUN* koppies
(*S. African*) a small hill

Koran, Qur'an (say kor-**ahn**) *NOUN*
the sacred book of Islam **WORD ORIGIN** from Arabic *kur'an* = reading

kosher (say koh-sher) *ADJECTIVE*
keeping to Jewish laws about the preparation of food • *kosher meat*

kraal (say krahl) *NOUN* kraals (*S. African*)
❶ a traditional African village of huts ❷ an enclosure for sheep and cattle

krill *NOUN*
a mass of tiny shrimp-like creatures, the chief food of certain whales

krypton *NOUN*
an inert gas that is present in the earth's atmosphere and is used in fluorescent lamps

kudos (say **kew**-doss) *NOUN*
honour and glory

kung fu *NOUN*
a Chinese method of self-defence, similar to karate

kW *ABBREVIATION*
kilowatt

a
b
c
d
e
f
g
h
i
j
k
l
m
n
o
p
q
r
s
t
u
v
w
x
y
z

Ll

L *ABBREVIATION*
learner, a person learning to drive a car

lab *NOUN* **labs** (*informal*)
a laboratory

label *NOUN* **labels**
a small piece of paper, cloth or metal fixed on or beside something to show what it is or what it costs or its owner, destination, etc.

label *VERB* **labels, labelling, labelled**
❶ to put a label on something ❷ to describe something in a particular way • *He was soon labelled as a troublemaker.*

laboratory *NOUN* **laboratories**
a room or building equipped for scientific experiments

laborious *ADJECTIVE*
❶ needing or using a lot of hard work
❷ explaining something at great length and with obvious effort
➤ **laboriously** *ADVERB*

Labour *NOUN*
the Labour Party, a British political party formed to represent the interests of working people and believing in social equality and socialism

labour *NOUN* **labours**
❶ hard work ❷ a task ❸ workers ❹ the contractions of the womb when a baby is being born

labour *VERB* **labours, labouring, laboured**
❶ to work hard at something ❷ to explain or discuss something at great length and with obvious effort • *I will not labour the point.*

labourer *NOUN* **labourers**
a person who does hard manual work, especially outdoors

Labrador *NOUN* **Labradors**
a large black or light-brown dog
WORD ORIGIN named after Labrador, a district in Canada, where it was bred

laburnum *NOUN* **laburnums**
a tree with hanging yellow flowers

labyrinth *NOUN* **labyrinths**
a complicated arrangement of passages or paths; a maze • *a labyrinth of tunnels*

WORD ORIGIN from Greek, originally referring to the maze in Greek mythology that the Minotaur lived in

lace *NOUN* **laces**
❶ net-like material with decorative patterns of holes in it ❷ a piece of thin cord or leather for fastening a shoe, etc.

lace *VERB* **laces, lacing, laced**
❶ to fasten something with a lace ❷ to thread a cord through something ❸ to add spirits to a drink

lacerate *VERB* **lacerates, lacerating, lacerated**
to injure flesh by cutting or tearing it
➤ **laceration** *NOUN*

lack *NOUN*
being without something or not having enough of it • *The trip was cancelled because of lack of interest.*

lack *VERB* **lacks, lacking, lacked**
to be without something • *He lacks courage.*

lackadaisical *ADJECTIVE*
lacking energy or determination; careless
WORD ORIGIN from *lack-a-day*, an old phrase expressing grief or surprise

lackey *NOUN* **lackeys**
a servant; a person who behaves or is treated like a servant

lacking *ADJECTIVE*
not having any or enough of something • *The story is lacking in humour.*

laconic *ADJECTIVE*
using few words; terse • *a laconic reply*
➤ **laconically** *ADVERB*
WORD ORIGIN from Greek *Lakon* = a native of Laconia, an area in Greece (because the Laconians were famous for their terse speech)

lacquer *NOUN*
a hard glossy varnish
➤ **lacquered** *ADJECTIVE*

lacrosse *NOUN*
a game using a stick with a net on it (called a *crosse*) to catch and throw a ball

lactate *VERB* **lactates, lactating, lactated**
female mammals lactate when they produce milk

lacy *ADJECTIVE*
made of lace or like lace • *lacy wings*

lad *NOUN* **lads**
a boy or young man

ladder *NOUN* **ladders**
❶ two upright pieces of wood or metal and

crosspieces (**rungs**), used for climbing up or down ➋ (*British*) a vertical ladder-like flaw in a pair of tights or stockings where a stitch has become undone

ladder *VERB* **ladders, laddering, laddered**
(*British*) to get a ladder in a pair of tights or stockings

laden *ADJECTIVE*
carrying something heavy or a lot of something • *She appeared at the door, laden with bags.* • *The trees were laden with apples.*

ladle *NOUN* **ladles**
a large deep spoon with a long handle, used for lifting and pouring liquids

ladle *VERB* **ladles, ladling, ladled**
to lift and pour a liquid with a ladle

lady *NOUN* **ladies**
➊ a polite word for a woman ➋ a well-mannered woman ➌ a woman of good social position
➤ **Lady** *NOUN*
the title of a noblewoman

ladybird *NOUN* **ladybirds**
(*British*) a small flying beetle, usually red with black spots

lady-in-waiting *NOUN* **ladies-in-waiting**
a woman of good social position who attends a queen or princess

ladylike *ADJECTIVE*
behaving in a well mannered and refined way that was traditionally thought to be suitable for a woman

ladyship *NOUN*
a title used in speaking to or about a woman of the rank of 'Lady'

lag *VERB* **lags, lagging, lagged**
➊ to go too slowly and fail to keep up with others • *The little boy was lagging behind.*
➋ (*British*) to wrap a pipe or boiler in insulating material (*lagging*) to prevent loss of heat

lag *NOUN* **lags**
a delay

lager (say **lah**-ger) *NOUN* **lagers**
a light beer

laggard *NOUN* **laggards**
a person who lags behind

lagoon *NOUN* **lagoons**
a salt-water lake separated from the sea by sandbanks or reefs

laid
past tense of **lay**

laid-back *ADJECTIVE* (*informal*)
relaxed and easy-going

lain
past participle of **lie**

lair *NOUN* **lairs**
a sheltered place where a wild animal lives

laity (say **lay**-it-ee) *NOUN*
lay people, not the clergy

lake *NOUN* **lakes**
a large area of water entirely surrounded by land

lakh (say **lak**) *NOUN* **lakh**
(*Indian*) a hundred thousand (rupees etc.)

lama *NOUN* **lamas**
a Buddhist priest or monk in Tibet and Mongolia

lamb *NOUN* **lambs**
➊ a young sheep ➋ meat from a lamb
➤ **lambswool** *NOUN*

lame *ADJECTIVE*
➊ not able to walk normally because of an injury to the leg or foot ➋ weak and not very convincing • *a lame excuse*
➤ **lameness** *NOUN*

lamely *ADVERB*
in a weak and unconvincing way • *'I must have made a mistake,' I said lamely.*

lament *VERB* **laments, lamenting, lamented**
to express grief or disappointment about something • *She lamented the loss of her local library.*

lament *NOUN* **laments**
a statement, song or poem expressing grief or regret
➤ **lamentation** *NOUN*

lamentable (say **lam**-in-ta-bul) *ADJECTIVE*
disappointing or regrettable

laminated *ADJECTIVE*
made of thin layers or sheets joined one upon the other • *laminated plastic*

lamp *NOUN* **lamps**
a device for producing light from electricity, gas or oil
➤ **lamplight** *NOUN*

lamp post *NOUN* **lamp posts**
a tall post in a street or path, with a lamp at the top

a
b
c
d
e
f
g
h
i
j
k
l
m
n
o
p
q
r
s
t
u
v
w
x
y
z

lamprey *NOUN* lampreys
a small eel-like water animal

lampshade *NOUN* lampshades
a cover for the bulb of an electric lamp, to soften the light

lance *NOUN* lances
a long spear

lance *VERB* lances, lancing, lanced
to cut open a boil on someone's skin with a surgical knife

lance corporal *NOUN* lance corporals
a soldier ranking between a private and a corporal

lancet *NOUN* lancets
❶ a pointed two-edged knife used by surgeons ❷ a tall narrow pointed window or arch

land *NOUN* lands
❶ the part of the earth's surface not covered by sea ❷ the ground or soil; an area of country • *forest land* ❸ the area occupied by a nation; a country

land *VERB* lands, landing, landed
❶ to arrive on land from a ship or aircraft ❷ to reach the ground after jumping or falling • *Where did the arrow land?* ❸ to come down through the air and settle on something • *A fly landed on his arm.* ❹ to bring a fish out of the water ❺ to succeed in getting something • *She landed an excellent job.* ❻ to give someone something unpleasant to do • *I got landed with all the boring jobs.*
➤ **land up** to finish in a certain place or position • *They landed up in jail.*

landed *ADJECTIVE*
❶ owning land ❷ consisting of land • *landed estates*

landing *NOUN* landings
❶ the level area at the top of a flight of stairs ❷ bringing an aircraft to the ground • *The pilot made a smooth landing.* ❸ a place where people can get on and off a boat

landing stage *NOUN* landing stages
(*British*) a platform on which people and goods are taken on and off a boat

landlady *NOUN* landladies
❶ a woman who lets rooms to lodgers ❷ a woman who runs a pub

landline *NOUN* landlines
a telephone connection that uses wires carried on poles or under the ground • *I'll call you later on the landline.*

landlocked *ADJECTIVE*
almost or entirely surrounded by land
• *Switzerland is completely landlocked.*

landlord *NOUN* landlords
❶ a person who lets a house, room or land to a tenant ❷ a person who runs a pub

landlubber *NOUN* landlubbers (*informal*)
a person who is not used to travelling on the sea (**WORD ORIGIN**) from an old word *lubber* = an awkward, clumsy person

landmark *NOUN* landmarks
❶ an object that is easily seen in a landscape ❷ an important event in the history or development of something

landmine *NOUN* landmines
an explosive mine laid on or just under the surface of the ground

landowner *NOUN* landowners
a person who owns a large amount of land

landscape *NOUN* landscapes
❶ a view of a particular area of countryside or town ❷ a picture of a scene in the countryside

landscape gardening *NOUN*
laying out a garden to imitate natural scenery

landslide *NOUN* landslides
❶ a landslip ❷ an overwhelming victory in an election • *She won the General Election by a landslide.*

landslip *NOUN* landslips
(*chiefly British*) a huge mass of soil and rocks sliding down a slope

landward *ADJECTIVE* & *ADVERB*
towards the land
➤ **landwards** *ADVERB*

lane *NOUN* lanes
❶ a narrow road, especially in the country ❷ a strip of road for a single line of traffic ❸ a strip of track or water for one athlete or swimmer in a race

language *NOUN* languages
❶ the words we speak and write ❷ the words used in a particular country or by a particular group of people ❸ a system of signs or symbols giving information, especially in computing (**WORD ORIGIN**) from Latin *lingua* = tongue

language laboratory *NOUN* language laboratories
a room equipped with audio equipment for learning a foreign language

languid *ADJECTIVE*
lacking energy and moving slowly, sometimes in an elegant way • *a languid wave of the hand*
➤ **languidly** *ADVERB*
➤ **languor** *NOUN*

languish *VERB* languishes, languishing, languished
❶ to be forced to suffer miserable conditions for a long time • *He has been languishing in prison for three years.* ❷ to become weaker

lank *ADJECTIVE*
lank hair is long and limp

lanky *ADJECTIVE* lankier, lankiest
a lanky person is awkwardly thin and tall

lanolin *NOUN*
a kind of ointment, made of fat from sheep's wool

lantern *NOUN* lanterns
a transparent case for holding a light and shielding it from the wind

lanyard *NOUN* lanyards
a short cord for fastening or holding something

lap *NOUN* laps
❶ the level place formed by the top of your legs when you are sitting down with your knees together ❷ going once round a racetrack ❸ one section of a journey • *the last lap*

lap *VERB* laps, lapping, lapped
❶ to overtake another competitor in a race to go one or more laps ahead ❷ a cat or other animal laps a liquid when it drinks it by scooping it up in its tongue ❸ waves lap when they make a gentle splash on rocks or the shore

lapel (say la-**pel**) *NOUN* lapels
a flap folded back at the front edge of a coat or jacket

lapse *NOUN* lapses
❶ a slight mistake or failure • *a lapse of concentration* ❷ an amount of time that has passed • *After a lapse of six months work began again.*

lapse *VERB* lapses, lapsing, lapsed
❶ to pass or slip gradually into a state • *He lapsed into unconsciousness.* ❷ to be no longer valid, through not being renewed • *My insurance policy has lapsed.*

laptop *NOUN* laptops
a portable computer for use while travelling

lapwing *NOUN* lapwings
a black and white bird with a crested head and a shrill cry

larceny *NOUN*
the crime of stealing other people's possessions

larch *NOUN* larches
a tall deciduous tree that bears small cones

lard *NOUN*
a white greasy substance prepared from pig fat and used in cooking

larder *NOUN* larders
a cupboard or small room for storing food

large *ADJECTIVE*
of more than the ordinary or average size; big
➤ **largeness** *NOUN*
➤ **at large** ❶ free to roam about, not captured • *The escaped prisoners are still at large.* ❷ in general, as a whole • *She is respected by the country at large.*

largely *ADVERB*
to a great extent; mostly • *You are largely responsible for the accident.*

largesse (say lar-**jess**) *NOUN*
money or gifts generously given

lark *NOUN* larks
❶ a small sandy-brown bird; the skylark
❷ (*informal*) something amusing; a bit of fun • *We did it for a lark.*

lark *VERB* larks, larking, larked
➤ **lark about** (*British*) (*informal*) to have fun playing jokes or tricks

larrikin *NOUN* larrikins
(*Australian/NZ*) a young person who behaves in a wild and mischievous way

larva *NOUN* larvae
an insect in the first stage of its life, after it comes out of the egg
➤ **larval** *ADJECTIVE*
WORD ORIGIN Latin, = ghost or mask

laryngitis *NOUN*
inflammation of the larynx, causing hoarseness

larynx (say **la**-rinks) *NOUN* larynxes
the part of your throat that contains the vocal cords

lasagne (say laz-**an**-ya) *NOUN*
pasta in the form of flat sheets, usually cooked with minced meat and cheese sauce

a b c d e f g h i j k l m n o p q r s t u v w x y z

laser *NOUN* lasers
a device that makes a very strong narrow beam of light or other electromagnetic radiation **WORD ORIGIN** from the initials of 'light amplification (by) stimulated emission (of) radiation', which is a technical description of what a laser does

lash *NOUN* lashes
❶ a stroke with a whip or stick ❷ the cord or cord-like part of a whip ❸ an eyelash

lash *VERB* lashes, lashing, lashed
❶ to strike a person or animal with a whip or stick ❷ to hit something with great force • *Wind and rain lashed the windows.* ❸ to tie something tightly with a rope or cord • *During the storm they lashed the boxes to the mast.*
➤ **lash down** rain lashes down when it is raining heavily
➤ **lash out** to speak or hit out angrily at someone

lashings *PLURAL NOUN*
(*British*) (*informal*) plenty of food or drink • *lashings of custard*

lass *NOUN* lasses
a girl or young woman
➤ **lassie** *NOUN*

lassitude *NOUN*
tiredness; lack of energy

lasso *NOUN* lassoes or lassos
a rope with a sliding noose at the end, used for catching cattle

lasso *VERB* lassoes, lassoing, lassoed
to catch an animal with a lasso

last *ADJECTIVE*
❶ coming after all others; final • *We caught the last bus home.* ❷ latest; most recent • *Where were you last night?* ❸ least likely • *She is the last person I'd have chosen.*
➤ **the last straw** a final thing that makes a problem unbearable

last *ADVERB*
at the end; after everything or everyone else • *He came last in the race.*

last *VERB* lasts, lasting, lasted
❶ to continue; to go on existing or living or being usable • *The good weather lasted until September.* • *Those shoes didn't last very long.* ❷ to be enough for your needs • *The food will last us for three days.*

last *NOUN*
❶ a person or thing that is last • *I was the last to arrive.* ❷ lasts
a block of wood or metal shaped like a foot, used in making and repairing shoes
➤ **at last** or **at long last** finally; after much delay
➤ **to the last** to the end • *He was brave to the last.*

lasting *ADJECTIVE*
able to last for a long time • *a lasting peace*

lastly *ADVERB*
in the last place; finally • *Lastly, I would like to thank my parents.*

last post *NOUN*
a military bugle call sounded at sunset and at military funerals

last rites *PLURAL NOUN*
a Christian ceremony given to a person who is close to death

latch *NOUN* latches
a small bar fastening a door or gate, lifted by a lever or spring
➤ **latchkey** *NOUN*

latch *VERB* latches, latching, latched
to fasten a door or gate with a latch
➤ **latch on to someone** to meet someone and follow them around all the time
➤ **latch on to something** to understand something • *It took them a while to latch on to what she was talking about.*

late *ADJECTIVE & ADVERB*
❶ after the usual or expected time • *Sorry I'm late.* ❷ near the end • *late in the afternoon* ❸ who has died recently • *the late king*
➤ **of late** recently

lately *ADVERB*
recently • *She has been very busy lately.*

latent (say **lay**-tent) *ADJECTIVE*
existing but not yet developed, active or visible • *her latent talent*

latent heat *NOUN*
the heat needed to change a solid into a liquid or vapour, or a liquid into a vapour, without a change in temperature

later *ADVERB*
after in time; afterwards • *Two days later we set off again.*

lateral *ADJECTIVE*
❶ to do with the side or sides of something • *the lateral branches of a tree* ❷ sideways • *lateral movement*
➤ **laterally** *ADVERB*

lateral thinking *NOUN*
solving problems by thinking about them

in an unusual and creative (and apparently illogical) way

latest *ADJECTIVE*
very recent or new • *Have you heard the latest news?*

latest *NOUN*
the most recent or the newest thing or piece of news • *This is the very latest in smartphone technology.*
➤ **at the latest** no later than the time mentioned • *I'll ring you on Friday at the latest.*

latex *NOUN*
the milky juice of various plants and trees, especially the rubber tree

lath *NOUN* **laths**
a narrow thin strip of wood

lathe (say layth) *NOUN* **lathes**
a machine for holding and turning pieces of wood while they are being shaped

lather *NOUN*
the thick foam you get when you mix soap with water

lather *VERB* **lathers, lathering, lathered**
❶ to cover something with lather ❷ to form a lather

Latin *NOUN*
the language of the ancient Romans

Latin America *NOUN*
the parts of Central and South America where the main language is Spanish or Portuguese **WORD ORIGIN** because these languages developed from Latin

latitude *NOUN* **latitudes**
❶ the distance of a place from the equator, measured in degrees ❷ freedom to choose what you do or the way that you do it

latrine (say la-**treen**) *NOUN* **latrines**
a toilet in a camp or barracks

latter *ADJECTIVE*
later or more recent • *the latter part of the year*
Compare with **former**.
➤ **the latter** the second of two people or things just mentioned

latterly *ADVERB*
recently; not long ago

lattice *NOUN* **lattices**
a framework of crossed strips or bars with spaces between

laud (rhymes with ford) *VERB* **lauds, lauding, lauded** (*formal*)
to praise someone or something

laudable *ADJECTIVE*
deserving praise • *a laudable aim*

laugh *VERB* **laughs, laughing, laughed**
to make the sounds that show you are happy or think something is funny

laugh *NOUN* **laughs**
❶ the sound of laughing ❷ (*informal*) something that is fun or amusing

laughable *ADJECTIVE*
deserving to be laughed at

laughing stock *NOUN* **laughing stocks**
a person or thing that is the object of ridicule and scorn

laughter *NOUN*
laughing or the sound of laughing

launch *VERB* **launches, launching, launched**
❶ to send a ship from the land into the water ❷ to send a rocket or spacecraft into space ❸ to set a thing moving by throwing or pushing it ❹ to make a new product available for the first time • *Our new model will be launched in April.* ❺ to start something off • *They planned to launch an attack the next day.*

launch *NOUN* **launches**
❶ the launching of a ship or spacecraft ❷ a large motor boat

launch pad *NOUN* **launch pads**
a platform from which a rocket is launched

launder *VERB* **launders, laundering, laundered**
to wash and iron clothes etc.

launderette *NOUN* **launderettes**
(*British*) a place fitted with washing machines that people pay to use

laundry *NOUN* **laundries**
❶ a place where clothes, sheets, etc. are washed and ironed for customers ❷ clothes, sheets, etc. to be washed or sent to a laundry

laureate (say **lorri**-at) *ADJECTIVE*
➤ **Poet Laureate** a person appointed to write poems for national occasions
WORD ORIGIN from **laurel**, because a laurel wreath was worn in ancient times as a sign of victory

laurel *NOUN* **laurels**
an evergreen shrub with smooth shiny leaves

a b c d e f g h i j k l m n o p q r s t u v w x y z

lava *NOUN*
molten rock that flows from a volcano; the solid rock formed when it cools

lavatory *NOUN* **lavatories**
❶ a toilet ❷ a room containing a toilet
WORD ORIGIN from Latin *lavatorium* = a basin or bath for washing

lavender *NOUN*
❶ a shrub with sweet-smelling purple flowers ❷ a light-purple colour

lavish *ADJECTIVE*
❶ generous ❷ plentiful
➤ **lavishly** *ADVERB*

lavish *VERB* **lavishes, lavishing, lavished**
to give large or generous amounts of something • *They lavished praise upon him.*

law *NOUN* **laws**
❶ a rule or set of rules that everyone must obey ❷ the profession of being a lawyer ❸ (*informal*) the police ❹ a scientific statement of something that always happens • *the law of gravity*

law-abiding *ADJECTIVE*
obeying the law

law court *NOUN* **law courts**
a room or building in which a judge or magistrate hears evidence and decides whether someone has broken the law

lawful *ADJECTIVE*
allowed or accepted by the law • *She was the lawful heiress.*
➤ **lawfully** *ADVERB*

lawless *ADJECTIVE*
❶ without proper laws • *a lawless country* ❷ not obeying the law
➤ **lawlessness** *NOUN*

lawn *NOUN* **lawns**
❶ an area of closely-cut grass in a garden or park ❷ very fine cotton material

lawnmower *NOUN* **lawnmowers**
a machine for cutting the grass of lawns

lawn tennis *NOUN*
tennis played on an outdoor grass or hard court

lawsuit *NOUN* **lawsuits**
a dispute or claim that is brought to a law court to be settled

lawyer *NOUN* **lawyers**
a person who is qualified to give advice in matters of law

lax *ADJECTIVE*
slack; not strict enough • *Discipline was lax.*

laxative *NOUN* **laxatives**
a medicine that you take to empty your bowels

lay *VERB* **lays, laying, laid**
❶ to put something down in a particular place or way ❷ to lay a table is to arrange things on it for a meal ❸ to place blame or responsibility on someone • *He laid the blame on his sister.* ❹ to form or prepare something • *We laid our plans.* ❺ to lay an egg is to produce it
➤ **lay off** (*informal*) to stop doing something
➤ **lay someone off** to stop employing someone for a while
➤ **lay something on** to supply or provide something
➤ **lay someone out** ❶ to knock a person unconscious ❷ to prepare a corpse for burial
➤ **lay something out** to arrange or prepare something

lay *VERB*
past tense of **lie**

USAGE
Lay is different from **lie**, which means to be in a flat position. However, the past tense of **lie** is **lay**: *Go and lie down. I lay down. Lay the parcel by the floor. I laid it on the floor.*

lay *ADJECTIVE*
❶ not belonging to the clergy • *a lay preacher* ❷ not professionally qualified • *lay opinion*

lay *NOUN* **lays**
(*old use*) a poem meant to be sung; a ballad

layabout *NOUN* **layabouts**
(*British*) (*informal*) a person who lazily avoids working for a living

lay-by *NOUN* **lay-bys**
a place where vehicles can stop beside a main road

layer *NOUN* **layers**
a single thickness or coating

layman, layperson *NOUN* **laymen** or **laypeople**
❶ a person who does not have specialized knowledge or training (e.g. as a doctor or lawyer) ❷ a person who is not ordained as a member of the clergy

layout *NOUN* **layouts**
the way in which the parts of something are

arranged • *The home page of his website has a new layout.*

laywoman *NOUN* laywomen
❶ a woman who does not have specialized knowledge or training (e.g. as a doctor or lawyer) ❷ a woman who is not ordained as a member of the clergy

laze *VERB* lazes, lazing, lazed
to spend time in a lazy way

lazy *ADJECTIVE* lazier, laziest
not wanting to work; doing little work
➤ **lazily** *ADVERB*
➤ **laziness** *NOUN*

lea *NOUN* leas (*poetical use*)
a meadow

leach *VERB* leaches, leaching, leached
to remove a soluble substance from soil or rock by making water percolate through it

lead (say leed) *VERB* leads, leading, led
❶ to take or guide someone, especially by going in front ❷ to be winning in a race or contest; to be ahead ❸ to be in charge of a group of people ❹ to be a way or route • *This path leads to the beach.* ❺ to play the first card in a card game ❻ to live or experience a particular kind of life • *He leads a dull life.*
➤ **lead to something** to result in or cause something • *Their carelessness led to the accident.*

lead (say leed) *NOUN* leads
❶ a leading place, part or position • *She took the lead on the final bend.* ❷ a good example or guidance for others to follow • *We should be taking a lead on this issue.* ❸ a clue to be followed ❹ a strap or cord for leading a dog or other animal ❺ an electrical wire attached to something

lead (say leed) *ADJECTIVE*
the most important of a number or group
• *the lead singer*

lead (say led) *NOUN* leads
❶ a soft heavy grey metal ❷ the writing substance (graphite) in a pencil

lead (say led) *ADJECTIVE*
made of or like lead

> **SPELLING**
> The past tense of **lead** is **led**.

leaden (say **led**-en) *ADJECTIVE*
❶ made of lead ❷ heavy and slow ❸ lead-coloured; dark grey • *leaden skies*

leader *NOUN* leaders
❶ the person in charge of a group of people;

a chief ❷ the person who is winning ❸ a newspaper article giving the editor's opinion

leadership *NOUN*
being a leader; the ability to be a good leader

leaf *NOUN* leaves
❶ a flat, usually green, part of a plant, growing out from its stem, branch or root ❷ the paper forming one page of a book ❸ a very thin sheet of metal • *gold leaf* ❹ a flap that makes a table larger
➤ **leafless** *ADJECTIVE*
➤ **turn over a new leaf** to make a fresh start and improve your behaviour

leaf *VERB* leafs, leafing, leafed
➤ **leaf through something** to turn the pages of a book, etc. quickly one by one

leaflet *NOUN* leaflets
a piece of paper printed with information

leafy *ADJECTIVE*
having a lot of leaves or trees • *a leafy bush*
• *leafy streets*

league *NOUN* leagues
❶ a group of teams who compete against each other for a championship ❷ a group of people or nations who agree to work together ❸ an old measure of distance, about 3 miles
➤ **in league with someone** working or plotting together

leak *NOUN* leaks
❶ a hole or crack through which liquid or gas accidentally escapes ❷ the revealing of secret information

leak *VERB* leaks, leaking, leaked
❶ to get out or let something out through a leak • *The roof is leaking.* ❷ to reveal secret information
➤ **leakage** *NOUN*

leaky *ADJECTIVE*
a leaky pipe or tap has a leak

lean *VERB* leans, leaning, leaned or leant
❶ to bend your body towards or over something • *She leaned out of the window and waved.* ❷ to put something or be in a sloping position • *Don't lean your bike against the window.* ❸ to rest against something ❹ to lean on someone is to rely or depend on them for help

lean *ADJECTIVE*
❶ lean meat has little or no fat ❷ a lean person or body is thin with little or no body fat

a b c d e f g h i j k l m n o p q r s t u v w x y z

leaning *NOUN* **leanings**
a tendency or preference • *He has a leaning towards the sciences.*

leap *VERB* **leaps, leaping, leaped** or **leapt**
❶ to jump high or a long way ❷ to increase sharply in amount or value

leap *NOUN* **leaps**
❶ a high or long jump ❷ a sudden increase in amount or value

> **SPELLING**
> The past tense of **leap** is **leapt** or **leaped**.

leapfrog *NOUN*
a game in which each player jumps with legs apart over another who is bending down

leap year *NOUN* **leap years**
a year with an extra day in it (29 February)
WORD ORIGIN probably because the dates from March onwards 'leap' a day of the week; a date which would fall on a Monday in an ordinary year will be on Tuesday in a leap year

learn *VERB* **learns, learning, learned** or **learnt**
❶ to get knowledge or skill through study or training • *She's learning to play the guitar.*
❷ to find out about something • *I was sorry to learn that he was ill.*

> **USAGE**
> Take care not to use **learn** to mean 'to teach'.

learned (say **ler**-nid) *ADJECTIVE*
a learned person has gained a lot of knowledge through study

learner *NOUN* **learners**
a person who is learning something, especially how to drive a car

learning *NOUN*
knowledge you get by studying

lease *NOUN* **leases**
an agreement to allow someone to use a building or land for a fixed period in return for payment
➤ **leaseholder** *NOUN*
➤ **a new lease of life** a chance to be healthy, active or usable again

lease *VERB* **leases, leasing, leased**
to allow or obtain the use of something by lease

leash *NOUN* **leashes**
a dog's lead

least *DETERMINER & ADVERB*
smallest in amount or degree; less than all the others • *the least amount of time* • *the least expensive bike*
➤ **at least** ❶ not less than what is mentioned • *It will take at least two weeks to do.*
❷ anyway • *He's at home or at least I think he is.*

least *PRONOUN*
the smallest amount or degree • *The least I could do was to offer to pay for his ticket.*

leather *NOUN*
material made from animal skins

leathery *ADJECTIVE*
tough like leather • *leathery skin*

leave *VERB* **leaves, leaving, left**
❶ to go away from a person or place ❷ to stop belonging to a group or working somewhere ❸ to allow something to stay where it is or as it is • *You left the door open.*
❹ to go away without taking something • *I left my phone at home.* ❺ to let someone deal with something • *Leave the washing-up to me.* ❻ to put something somewhere so that it can be collected or passed on later • *Would you like to leave a message?*
➤ **leave off** to stop doing something
➤ **leave something out** to omit something or not include it
➤ **be left over** to remain when other things have been used

leave *NOUN*
❶ permission ❷ official permission to be away from work; the time for which this permission lasts • *three days' leave*

> **SPELLING**
> The past tense of **leave** is **left**.

leaven (say **lev**-en) *NOUN*
a substance, especially yeast, used to make dough rise

leaven *VERB* **leavens, leavening, leavened**
to add leaven to dough

lectern *NOUN* **lecterns**
a stand to hold a Bible or other large book or notes for reading

lecture *NOUN* **lectures**
❶ a talk about a subject to an audience or a class ❷ a long serious talk to someone that warns them about something or tells them off

lecture *VERB* **lectures, lecturing, lectured**
to give a lecture
➤ **lecturer** *NOUN*

led
past tense of **lead**

ledge NOUN ledges
a narrow shelf • *a window ledge* • *a mountain ledge*

ledger NOUN ledgers
an account book

lee NOUN lees
the sheltered side or part of something, away from the wind

leech NOUN leeches
a small blood-sucking worm that lives in water

leek NOUN leeks
a long green and white vegetable of the onion family

leer VERB leers, leering, leered
to look at someone in a lustful or unpleasant way
➤ **leer** NOUN

leeward ADJECTIVE
on the lee side

leeway NOUN
extra space or time available
➤ **make up leeway** to make up lost time or to regain a lost position

left ADJECTIVE & ADVERB
❶ on or towards the west if you think of yourself as facing north ❷ in favour of socialist or radical views

left NOUN
the left-hand side or part of something

left VERB
past tense of **leave**

left-hand ADJECTIVE
on the left side of something • *the top left-hand corner of the page*

left-handed ADJECTIVE
using the left hand in preference to the right hand

leftovers PLURAL NOUN
food not eaten at a meal

leg NOUN legs
❶ one of the limbs on a person's or animal's body on which they stand or move ❷ one of the parts of a pair of trousers that cover your leg ❸ each of the supports of a chair or other piece of furniture ❹ one part of a journey ❺ one of a pair of matches played between the same teams in a round of a competition

legacy NOUN legacies
❶ something left to a person in a will ❷ a thing received from someone who did

something before you or because of earlier events • *The conflict has left a legacy of distrust.*

legal ADJECTIVE
❶ allowed by the law ❷ to do with the law or lawyers
➤ **legally** ADVERB
➤ **legality** NOUN

legalize (also **legalise**) VERB legalizes, legalizing, legalized
to make a thing legal

legate NOUN legates
an official representative, especially of the Pope

legend NOUN legends
❶ an old story handed down from the past, which may or may not be true. Compare with **myth.** ❷ a very famous person

legendary ADJECTIVE
❶ to do with legends or happening in legends • *legendary heroes* ❷ very famous or well known for a long time • *Her temper is legendary.*

leggings PLURAL NOUN
❶ tight-fitting stretchy trousers, worn by women ❷ protective outer coverings for each leg from knee to ankle

legible ADJECTIVE
legible writing is clear enough to read
➤ **legibly** ADVERB
➤ **legibility** NOUN

legion NOUN legions
❶ a division of the ancient Roman army ❷ a group of soldiers or former soldiers

legionnaire NOUN legionnaires
a member of an association of former soldiers

legionnaires' disease NOUN
a serious form of pneumonia caused by bacteria **WORD ORIGIN** so-called because of an outbreak at a meeting of the American Legion of ex-servicemen in 1976

legislate VERB legislates, legislating, legislated
to make laws
➤ **legislator** NOUN

legislation NOUN
making laws; a set of laws passed by a parliament

legislative ADJECTIVE
having the authority to make laws • *a legislative assembly*

legislature *NOUN* **legislatures**
a country's parliament or law-making assembly

legitimate *ADJECTIVE*
❶ allowed by a law or rule ❷ (*old use*) a legitimate child is born of parents who are married to each other
➤ **legitimately** *ADVERB*
➤ **legitimacy** *NOUN*

leisure *NOUN*
time that is free from work, when you can do what you like • *His busy life leaves little time for leisure.*
➤ **at leisure** having leisure; not hurried
➤ **at your leisure** when you have time

leisurely *ADJECTIVE*
done with plenty of time; unhurried • *We took a leisurely stroll by the river.*

lemming *NOUN* **lemmings**
a small mouse-like animal of Arctic regions that migrates in large numbers and is said to run headlong into the sea and drown

lemon *NOUN* **lemons**
❶ an oval yellow citrus fruit with a sour taste ❷ a pale yellow colour

lemonade *NOUN*
a lemon-flavoured drink

lemur (say **lee**-mer) *NOUN* **lemurs**
a monkey-like animal

lend *VERB* **lends, lending, lent**
❶ to allow a person to use something of yours for a short time ❷ to provide someone with money that they must repay over time, usually in return for payments (called **interest**) ❸ to give or add a quality • *She lent dignity to the occasion.*
➤ **lender** *NOUN*
➤ **lend a hand** to give help or assistance

USAGE

Take care not to confuse **lend**, which means to let someone use something of yours for a short time, with **borrow**, which means to use something that belongs to someone else for a short time.

length *NOUN* **lengths**
❶ how long something is ❷ a piece of cloth, rope or wire cut from a larger piece ❸ the distance of a swimming pool from one end to the other
➤ **at length** ❶ after a long time ❷ taking a long time; in detail • *We discussed the matter at length.*

➤ **go to great lengths** to take a lot of trouble or effort over something

SPELLING

There is a silent **g** in **length**.

lengthen *VERB* **lengthens, lengthening, lengthened**
❶ to make something longer • *He started to lengthen his stride.* ❷ to become longer • *The shadows were lengthening.*

lengthways, lengthwise *ADVERB*
from end to end; along the longest part • *Slice the carrots lengthways.*

lengthy *ADJECTIVE*
going on for a long time • *He gave a lengthy speech.*

lenient (say **lee**-nee-ent) *ADJECTIVE*
not as strict as expected, especially when punishing someone
➤ **leniently** *ADVERB*
➤ **leniency** *NOUN*

lens *NOUN* **lenses**
❶ a curved piece of glass or plastic used to focus things ❷ the transparent part of the eye, immediately behind the pupil
WORD ORIGIN Latin, = lentil (because a lens has a shape like a lentil)

Lent *NOUN*
a period of about six weeks before Easter when some Christians give up something they enjoy

lent
past tense of **lend**

lentil *NOUN* **lentils**
a kind of small bean

leopard (say **lep**-erd) *NOUN* **leopards**
a large spotted mammal of the cat family, also called a panther

leotard (say **lee**-o-tard) *NOUN* **leotards**
a close-fitting piece of clothing worn for dance, exercise and gymnastics
WORD ORIGIN named after a French trapeze artist, J. *Leotard*, who designed it

leper *NOUN* **lepers**
a person who has leprosy

lepidopterous *ADJECTIVE*
to do with the group of insects that includes butterflies and moths

leprechaun (say **lep**-rek-awn) *NOUN* **leprechauns**
in Irish folklore, an elf who looks like a little

old man (**WORD ORIGIN**) from Irish, = a small
body

leprosy NOUN
an infectious disease that makes parts of the
body waste away
➤ **leprous** ADJECTIVE
(**WORD ORIGIN**) from Greek *lepros* = scaly
(because white scales form on the skin)

lesbian NOUN lesbians
a homosexual woman (**WORD ORIGIN**) named
after the Greek island of *Lesbos* (because
Sappho, a poetess who lived there about 600 BC,
was said to be homosexual)

less DETERMINER & ADVERB
smaller in amount; not so much • *My new
computer makes less noise than the old one.*
• *It is less important.*

> **USAGE**
>
> Take care not to confuse less and fewer.
> You should use fewer when you mean
> 'not so many', and less when you mean
> 'not so much': • *Venus has fewer craters
> than the Earth and also less water.*

less PRONOUN
a smaller amount • *I have less than you.*

less PREPOSITION
minus; deducting • *She earned $20,000, less
tax.*

lessen VERB lessens, lessening, lessened
to make something less or to become less
• *Her fear gradually lessened.*

lesser ADJECTIVE
not so great as the other • *the lesser evil*

lesson NOUN lessons
❶ an amount of teaching given at one time
❷ something to be learnt by a pupil or
student ❸ an example or experience from
which you should learn • *Let this be a lesson
to you!* ❹ a passage from the Bible read
aloud as part of a Christian church service

lest CONJUNCTION (*old use*)
so that something should not happen
• *Remind us, lest we forget.*

let VERB lets, letting, let
❶ to allow someone to do something • *Let
me see it.* ❷ to allow something to happen
and not prevent it • *Don't let the paper get
wet.* ❸ used to make a suggestion • *Let's
go for a walk.* ❹ to allow or cause a person
or thing to come or go or pass • *Let me
out!* ❺ to allow someone to use a house or
building in return for payment (**rent**)

➤ **let someone down** to disappoint someone
or fail to do what you said you would
➤ **let something down** to let down a tyre or
balloon is to let the air out of it
➤ **let someone off** to excuse someone from
a duty or punishment
➤ **let something off** to make something
explode
➤ **let on** (*informal*) to reveal a secret
➤ **let up** (*informal*)
❶ to relax or do less work ❷ to become less
intense • *The rain didn't let up.*

lethal (say **lee**-thal) ADJECTIVE
deadly; causing death • *a lethal blow*

lethargy (say **leth**-er-jee) NOUN
extreme lack of energy or interest in doing
anything
➤ **lethargic** (say lith-**ar**-jik) ADJECTIVE

letter NOUN letters
❶ a symbol representing a sound used in
speech ❷ a written message, usually sent by
post
➤ **to the letter** paying strict attention to
every detail

letter box NOUN letter boxes
❶ a slot in a door, through which letters are
delivered ❷ a postbox

lettering NOUN
letters drawn or painted • *The inscription was
in gold lettering.*

lettuce NOUN lettuces
a garden plant with broad crisp leaves used
in salads

leukaemia (say lew-**kee**-mee-a) NOUN
a disease in which there are too many white
corpuscles in the blood

level ADJECTIVE
❶ flat or horizontal • *Put the tent up on level
ground.* ❷ at the same height or position as
something else • *Are these pictures level?*

level NOUN levels
❶ height, depth or position • *Fix the shelves
at eye level.* ❷ a standard or grade of
achievement • *a high level of skill* ❸ a stage
of a computer game that you reach • *What
level are you on?* ❹ a level surface ❺ a device
that shows whether something is level
➤ **on the level** (*informal*) honest; telling the
truth

level VERB levels, levelling, levelled
❶ to make something level or to become
level • *United levelled the score with a late*

a b c d e f g h i j k l m n o p q r s t u v w x y z

goal. ② to aim a gun or missile ③ to direct an accusation at a person

level crossing *NOUN* **level crossings**
(*British*) a place where a road crosses a railway at the same level

lever *NOUN* **levers**
① a bar that turns on a fixed point (the **fulcrum**) in order to lift something or force something open ② a bar used as a handle to operate machinery • *a gear lever*

lever *VERB* **levers, levering, levered**
to lift or move something by means of a lever

leverage *NOUN*
① the force you need when you use a lever ② influence over people

leveret *NOUN* **leverets**
a young hare

levitation *NOUN*
rising into the air and floating there
➤ **levitate** *VERB*

levity *NOUN*
being humorous, especially at an unsuitable time • *He was shocked at her levity.*

levy *VERB* **levies, levying, levied**
to collect a tax or other payment by the use of authority or force

levy *NOUN* **levies**
an amount of money paid in tax

lewd *ADJECTIVE*
indecent or crude

lexicography *NOUN*
the writing of dictionaries
➤ **lexicographer** *NOUN*

liability *NOUN* **liabilities**
① being legally responsible for something ② a debt or obligation ③ a disadvantage or handicap • *Our goalkeeper has become a liability.*

liable *ADJECTIVE*
① likely to do or suffer something • *She is liable to colds.* • *The cliff is liable to crumble.* ② legally responsible for something

liaise (say lee-**ayz**) *VERB* **liaises, liaising, liaised**
to work closely with someone and keep them informed

liaison (say lee-**ay**-zon) *NOUN* **liaisons**
① communication and cooperation between people or groups ② a person who is a link or go-between ③ a romantic affair

liar *NOUN* **liars**
a person who tells lies

libel (say **ly**-bel) *NOUN* **libels**
an untrue written, printed or broadcast statement that damages a person's reputation. Compare with **slander**.
➤ **libellous** *ADJECTIVE*

libel *VERB* **libels, libelling, libelled**
to make a libel against someone

liberal *ADJECTIVE*
① tolerant of other people's point of view or behaviour • *Your parents are more liberal than mine.* ② supporting individual freedom and gradual political and social change ③ giving or given freely and generously • *a liberal sprinkling of sugar*
➤ **liberality** *NOUN*

liberal *NOUN* **liberals**
a person with liberal views

Liberal Democrat *NOUN* **Liberal Democrats**
a member of the Liberal Democrat party in the UK, a political party favouring moderate reforms

liberally *ADVERB*
in large amounts or generously • *Pour the cream on liberally.*

liberate *VERB* **liberates, liberating, liberated**
to liberate a person or animal is to set them free
➤ **liberation** *NOUN*
➤ **liberator** *NOUN*

liberty *NOUN* **liberties**
the freedom to go where you want or do what you want
➤ **take liberties** to behave too casually or in too familiar a way
➤ **take the liberty** to do something without asking permission • *I took the liberty of helping myself to a drink.*

librarian *NOUN* **librarians**
a person in charge of or working in a library
➤ **librarianship** *NOUN*

library (say **ly**-bra-ree) *NOUN* **libraries**
① a place where books are kept for people to use or borrow ② a collection of books, records, films, etc.

libretto *NOUN* **librettos**
the words of an opera or other long musical work

lice
plural of **louse**

licence *NOUN* **licences**
❶ an official document allowing someone to do or use or own something • *a driving licence* ❷ special freedom to avoid the usual rules or customs

> **SPELLING**
> **Licence** is a noun and **license** is a verb • *a TV licence* • *The ship is licensed to carry passengers.*

license *VERB* **licenses, licensing, licensed**
to give a licence to a person; to authorize someone to do something • *The restaurant is not licensed to sell alcohol.*

lichen (say **ly**-ken) *NOUN* **lichens**
a dry-looking plant that grows on rocks, walls or trees

lick *VERB* **licks, licking, licked**
❶ to move your tongue over something ❷ a wave or flame licks a surface when it touches it lightly ❸ (*informal*) to defeat someone

lick *NOUN* **licks**
❶ licking something • *Can I have a lick of your ice cream?* ❷ a small amount of paint • *The kitchen could do with a lick of paint.*
➤ **at a lick** (*informal*) at a fast pace

lid *NOUN* **lids**
❶ a cover for a box, pot or jar ❷ an eyelid

lido (say **leed**-oh) *NOUN* **lidos**
(*British*) a public open-air swimming pool or pleasure beach **WORD ORIGIN** from Lido, the name of a beach near Venice

lie *VERB* **lies, lying, lay, lain**
❶ to be or get in a flat or resting position • *He lay on the grass.* • *The cat has lain here all night.* ❷ to be or remain a certain way • *The island lies near the coast.* • *The machinery lay idle.*
➤ **lie low** to keep yourself hidden

> **USAGE**
> See the note at **lay**.

lie *VERB* **lies, lying, lied**
to say something that you know is untrue

lie *NOUN* **lies**
something you say that you know is not true
➤ **the lie of the land** ❶ the features of an area ❷ the way a situation is developing

liege, liege lord (say leej) *NOUN* **lieges** or **liege lords** (*old use*)
a person who is entitled to receive feudal service or allegiance

lieu (say lew) *NOUN*
➤ **in lieu** instead • *He accepted a cheque in lieu of cash.*

lieutenant (say lef-**ten**-ant) *NOUN* **lieutenants**
❶ an officer in the army or navy ❷ a deputy or chief assistant

life *NOUN* **lives**
❶ the period between birth and death or the period that a person has been alive ❷ being alive and able to function and grow ❸ living things • *Is there life on Mars?* ❹ liveliness • *She is full of life.* ❺ a biography ❻ the length of time that something exists or functions • *The battery has a life of two years.*

lifebelt *NOUN* **lifebelts**
a ring of material that will float, used to support someone's body in water

lifeboat *NOUN* **lifeboats**
a boat for rescuing people at sea

lifebuoy *NOUN* **lifebuoys**
a device to support someone's body in water

life cycle *NOUN* **life cycles**
the series of changes in the life of a living thing • *The diagram shows the life cycle of a frog.*

life form *NOUN* **life forms**
any living thing • *an alien life form*

lifeguard *NOUN* **lifeguards**
someone whose job is to rescue swimmers who are in difficulty

life jacket *NOUN* **life jackets**
a jacket of material that will float, used to support someone's body in water

lifeless *ADJECTIVE*
❶ dead or appearing to be dead • *his lifeless body* ❷ with no signs of life or living things • *The place seemed lifeless.*
➤ **lifelessly** *ADVERB*

lifelike *ADJECTIVE*
looking exactly like a real person or thing

lifelong *ADJECTIVE*
continuing for the whole of someone's life • *a lifelong love of reading*

lifespan *NOUN* **lifespans**
the length of someone's life

lifestyle *NOUN* **lifestyles**
the way of life of a person or a group of people

a
b
c
d
e
f
g
h
i
j
k
l
m
n
o
p
q
r
s
t
u
v
w
x
y
z

lifetime *NOUN* lifetimes
the time for which someone is alive • *His diary was not published during his lifetime.*

lift *VERB* lifts, lifting, lifted
❶ to pick something up or move it to a higher position • *The box is too heavy to lift.* ❷ to rise or go upwards • *The balloon lifted off the ground.* ❸ to remove or abolish something • *The ban has been lifted.* ❹ (*informal*) to steal something

lift *NOUN* lifts
❶ a device in a building for taking people or goods from one floor or level to another ❷ a ride in someone else's vehicle • *Can you give me a lift to the station?* ❸ a movement upwards

lift-off *NOUN* lift-offs
the vertical take-off of a rocket or spacecraft

ligament *NOUN* ligaments
a piece of the tough flexible tissue that holds your bones together

light *NOUN* lights
❶ radiation that stimulates the sense of sight and makes things visible ❷ something that provides light, especially an electric lamp • *Can you switch on the light?* ❸ a flame
➤ **bring something to light** to make something known
➤ **come to light** to become known
➤ **in the light of something** taking something into consideration

light *ADJECTIVE*
❶ full of light; not dark ❷ pale • *light blue* ❸ having little weight; not heavy ❹ small in amount or force; not severe • *light rain* • *a light punishment* ❺ needing little effort • *light work* ❻ cheerful, not sad • *with a light heart* ❼ not serious or profound • *light music*
➤ **lightness** *NOUN*

light *ADVERB*
➤ **travel light** to travel without much luggage

light *VERB* lights, lighting, lit or lighted
❶ to start a thing burning or to begin to burn • *The fire won't light.* ❷ to provide light for something • *The stage was lit by a bright spotlight.*
➤ **light on** or **upon something** to see or find something by accident • *His eyes lit upon a small boat on the horizon.*
➤ **light up** ❶ to become bright with lights ❷ if a person's face lights up, it becomes bright with happiness or excitement
➤ **light something up** to make something bright with lights

USAGE
Say *He lit the lamps; the lamps were lit* (not 'lighted'), but *She carried a lighted candle* (not 'a lit candle').

lighten *VERB* lightens, lightening, lightened
❶ to make something lighter in weight or less heavy; to become less heavy ❷ to make something brighter or less dark; to become less dark

lighter *NOUN* lighters
a device for lighting cigarettes etc.

light-hearted *ADJECTIVE*
❶ cheerful and free from worry ❷ not serious

lighthouse *NOUN* lighthouses
a tower with a bright light at the top to guide or warn ships

lighting *NOUN*
lights or the way that a place is lit • *street lighting*

lightly *ADVERB*
❶ gently, with very little force • *He touched her lightly on the arm.* ❷ only a little; not much • *It began to snow lightly.* ❸ not seriously; without serious thought • *We do not take our customers' complaints lightly.*

lightning *NOUN*
a flash of bright light produced by natural electricity during a thunderstorm
➤ **like lightning** with very great speed

SPELLING
Lightning can be tricky to spell – there is no e in the middle.

lightning conductor *NOUN* lightning conductors
(*British*) a metal rod or wire fixed on a building to divert lightning into the earth

lightweight *ADJECTIVE*
less than average weight • *a bicycle with a lightweight frame*

lightweight *NOUN* lightweights
❶ a person who is not heavy ❷ a boxer weighing between 57.1 and 59 kg

light year *NOUN* light years
a unit of distance equal to the distance that light travels in one year (about 9.5 million million km)

like *VERB* likes, liking, liked
❶ to think a person or thing is pleasant or satisfactory; to enjoy doing something ❷ to

A B C D E F G H I J K L M N O P Q R S T U V W X Y Z

wish to do something • *I'd like to come.* ❸ to click a button to show that you agree with or like something on a social media website

like *PREPOSITION*
❶ similar to; in the manner of • *He swims like a fish.* ❷ in a suitable state for • *It looks like rain.* • *I feel like a cup of tea.* ❸ such as • *She's good at things like art and music.*

like *ADJECTIVE*
similar; having some or all of the qualities of another person or thing • *We are of like mind about it.*

like *NOUN* likes
❶ a similar person or thing • *We shall not see his like again.* ❷ a symbol on a social media website that shows that someone agrees with or likes something

likeable *ADJECTIVE*
pleasant and easy to like

likelihood *NOUN*
the chance of something happening; how likely something is to happen • *There's not much likelihood of finding anything.*

likely *ADJECTIVE* likelier, likeliest
❶ probable; expected to happen or be true • *Rain is likely.* ❷ expected to be suitable or successful • *This is the most likely spot for our picnic.*

liken *VERB* likens, likening, likened
to compare one person or thing to another • *He likened the human heart to a pump.*

likeness *NOUN* likenesses
❶ a similarity in appearance; a resemblance ❷ a portrait

likewise *ADVERB*
similarly; in the same way • *I intend to apologize and suggest you do likewise.*

liking *NOUN*
a feeling that you like something • *She has a liking for large earrings.*

lilac *NOUN*
❶ a bush with fragrant purple or white flowers ❷ pale purple

lilt *NOUN* lilts
a light pleasant rhythm in a voice or tune
➤ **lilting** *ADJECTIVE*

lily *NOUN* lilies
a garden plant with trumpet-shaped flowers, growing from a bulb

limb *NOUN* limbs
❶ a leg, arm or wing ❷ a large branch of a tree

➤ **out on a limb** isolated; without any support

limber *VERB* limbers, limbering, limbered
➤ **limber up** to do exercises in preparation for a sport or athletic activity

limbo *NOUN*
a West Indian dance in which you bend backwards to pass under a low bar
➤ **in limbo** in an uncertain situation where you are waiting for something to happen • *Lack of money has left our plans in limbo.*
WORD ORIGIN The phrase 'in limbo' comes from the name of a place formerly believed by Christians to exist on the borders of hell, where the souls of people who were not baptized waited for God's judgement.

lime *NOUN* limes
❶ a green fruit like a small round lemon ❷ a drink made from lime juice ❸ a tree with yellow flowers ❹ a white chalky substance (calcium oxide) used in making cement and as a fertilizer

limelight *NOUN*
➤ **in the limelight** receiving a lot of publicity and attention **WORD ORIGIN** from **lime** (calcium oxide) which gives a bright light when heated and was formerly used to light up the stage of a theatre

limerick *NOUN* limericks
a type of amusing poem with five lines
WORD ORIGIN named after *Limerick*, a town in Ireland

limestone *NOUN*
a kind of rock from which lime (calcium oxide) is obtained

limit *NOUN* limits
❶ the greatest amount allowed • *the speed limit* ❷ a line, point or level where something ends • *She had reached the limit of her patience.* • *the city limits*

limit *VERB* limits, limiting, limited
to keep something within a limit • *You are limited to one choice each.* • *We did all we could to limit the damage.*

limitation *NOUN* limitations
a thing that stops someone or something from going beyond a certain point • *There are no limitations on what we can do.*

limited *ADJECTIVE*
kept within limits; not great • *a limited choice* • *limited experience*

limited company *NOUN* limited companies
(*British*) a business company whose

a b c d e f g h i j k l m n o p q r s t u v w x y z

shareholders would have to pay only some of its debts

limousine (say lim-oo-**zeen**) *NOUN* **limousines**
a large luxurious car (WORD ORIGIN) originally, a hooded cape worn in *Limousin*, a district in France; the name was given to the cars because early ones had a canvas roof to shelter the driver

limp *VERB* **limps, limping, limped**
to walk with difficulty because of an injury to your leg or foot

limp *NOUN* **limps**
a limping walk

limp *ADJECTIVE*
❶ not stiff or firm • *limp celery* ❷ without strength or energy • *a limp handshake*
➤ **limply** *ADVERB*

limpet *NOUN* **limpets**
a small shellfish that attaches itself firmly to rocks

limpid *ADJECTIVE*
a liquid is limpid if it is clear or transparent

linchpin *NOUN* **linchpins**
the person or thing that is vital to the success of something

line *NOUN* **lines**
❶ a long thin mark on paper or another surface ❷ a row or series of people or things; a row of words ❸ a length of rope, string or wire used for a special purpose • *a fishing line* ❹ a railway; a railway track ❺ a company operating a transport service of ships, aircraft or buses ❻ a way of doing things or behaving; a type of business • *What line are you in?* ❼ a telephone connection ❽ several generations of a family • *He comes from a long line of musicians.*
➤ **in line** ❶ forming a straight line ❷ under control

line *VERB* **lines, lining, lined**
❶ to mark something with lines • *Use lined paper.* ❷ to form something into a line or lines; to form a line along something • *Line them up.* • *Crowds lined the streets to watch the race.* ❸ to cover the inside of something with a different material

lineage (say **lin**-ee-ij) *NOUN* **lineages**
ancestry; a line of descendants from an ancestor

linear (say **lin**-ee-er) *ADJECTIVE*
❶ arranged in a line ❷ to do with a line or length

linen *NOUN*
❶ cloth made from flax ❷ shirts, sheets and tablecloths etc. (which were formerly made of linen)

liner *NOUN* **liners**
a large passenger ship

linger *VERB* **lingers, lingering, lingered**
to stay for a long time, as if unwilling to leave; to be slow to leave • *The smell of her perfume lingered in the room.*

lingerie (say **lan**-zher-ee) *NOUN*
women's underwear

lingo *NOUN* **lingos** or **lingoes** (*informal*)
a foreign language

linguist *NOUN* **linguists**
an expert in languages or someone who can speak several languages well

linguistics *NOUN*
the study of languages
➤ **linguistic** *ADJECTIVE*

liniment *NOUN*
a lotion for rubbing on parts of the body that ache

lining *NOUN* **linings**
a layer of material that covers the inside of something

link *NOUN* **links**
❶ one of the rings or loops of a chain ❷ a connection or relationship ❸ a connection between documents on the Internet • *Click on the link at the bottom of the page.*

link *VERB* **links, linking, linked**
❶ to join things together; to connect people or things • *The new bridge will link the island to the mainland.* ❷ to link up is to become connected • *The two spacecraft linked up in orbit.*

links *NOUN & PLURAL NOUN*
a golf course, especially one near the sea
(WORD ORIGIN) from Old English *hlinc* = sandy ground near the seashore

linnet *NOUN* **linnets**
a kind of finch

lino *NOUN*
(*British*) (*informal*) linoleum

linocut *NOUN* **linocuts**
a print made from a design cut into a block of thick linoleum

linoleum *NOUN*
a stiff shiny floor covering

linseed *NOUN*
the seed of flax, from which oil is obtained

lint *NOUN*
a soft material for covering wounds

lintel *NOUN* **lintels**
a horizontal piece of wood or stone above a door or other opening

lion *NOUN* **lions**
a large strong flesh-eating animal of the cat family found in Africa and India

lioness *NOUN* **lionesses**
a female lion

lip *NOUN* **lips**
❶ either of the two fleshy edges of the mouth ❷ the edge of something hollow, such as a cup or crater ❸ the pointed part at the top of a jug or saucepan from which you pour things

lip-read *VERB* **lip-reads, lip-reading, lip-read**
to understand what a person says by watching the movements of their lips, not by hearing their voice

lipstick *NOUN* **lipsticks**
a stick of a waxy substance for colouring the lips

liquefy *VERB* **liquefies, liquefying, liquefied**
to make something liquid or to become liquid
➤ **liquefaction** *NOUN*

liqueur (say lik-**yoor**) *NOUN* **liqueurs**
a strong sweet alcoholic drink

liquid *NOUN* **liquids**
a substance like water or oil that flows freely but (unlike a gas) has a constant volume

liquid *ADJECTIVE*
in the form of a liquid; flowing freely

liquidate *VERB* **liquidates, liquidating, liquidated**
to close down a business and divide its value between its creditors
➤ **liquidation** *NOUN*
➤ **liquidator** *NOUN*

liquidize (also **liquidise**) *VERB* **liquidizes, liquidizing, liquidized**
(*British*) to make something, especially food, into a liquid or pulp
➤ **liquidizer** *NOUN*

liquor *NOUN*
❶ alcoholic drink ❷ juice produced in cooking; liquid in which food has been cooked

liquorice (say **lick**-er-iss) *NOUN*
❶ a black substance used in medicine and as a sweet ❷ the plant from whose root this substance is obtained

lisp *NOUN* **lisps**
a fault in speech in which *s* and *z* are pronounced like *th*

lisp *VERB* **lisps, lisping, lisped**
to speak with a lisp

list *NOUN* **lists**
❶ a number of names, items or figures written or printed one after another ❷ leaning over to one side

list *VERB* **lists, listing, listed**
❶ to make a list of people or things ❷ a boat or ship lists when it leans over to one side

listen *VERB* **listens, listening, listened**
to pay attention in order to hear something • *Listen to me.* • *I like listening to music.*
➤ **listener** *NOUN*

listless *ADJECTIVE*
too tired to be active or enthusiastic
➤ **listlessly** *ADVERB*

lit
past tense of **light** *VERB*

litany *NOUN* **litanies**
a formal prayer with fixed responses

literacy *NOUN*
the ability to read and write

literal *ADJECTIVE*
❶ meaning exactly what is said, not metaphorical or exaggerated ❷ word for word • *a literal translation*

literally *ADVERB*
really; exactly as stated • *The noise made me literally jump out of my seat.*

literary (say **lit**-er-er-i) *ADJECTIVE*
to do with literature; interested in literature

literate *ADJECTIVE*
able to read and write

literature *NOUN*
books and other writings, especially those that are widely read and thought to be well written

lithe *ADJECTIVE*
flexible and supple • *He was tall and lithe.*

litigation *NOUN* **litigations**
a lawsuit; the process of carrying on a lawsuit

litmus *NOUN*
a blue substance that is turned red by acids and can be turned back to blue by alkalis

litmus paper *NOUN*
paper stained with litmus

litre *NOUN* litres
a measure of liquid, about 1¾ pints

> **SPELLING**
> There is a tricky bit in litre – it is spelt re at the end and not er.

litter *NOUN* litters
❶ rubbish or untidy things left lying about ❷ the young animals born to one mother at one time ❸ absorbent material put down on a tray for a cat to urinate and defecate in indoors ❹ a kind of stretcher

litter *VERB* litters, littering, littered
to be scattered all over a place, making it untidy • *The floor was littered with books and papers.*

little *ADJECTIVE*
❶ small in size or amount; not great or big • *a little house* ❷ short in time or distance • *A little while later the phone rang.*

little *DETERMINER & PRONOUN* less, least
not much • *I have very little money left.* • *I understood little of what he said.*
➤ **a little** ❶ a small amount • *Could I have a little milk, please?* ❷ slightly • *I'm feeling a little tired.*
➤ **little by little** gradually; by a small amount at a time

little *ADVERB* less, least
not much; only slightly • *I eat very little.*

liturgy *NOUN* liturgies
a fixed form of public worship used in Christian churches
➤ **liturgical** *ADJECTIVE*

live (rhymes with give) *VERB* lives, living, lived
❶ to have life; to be alive ❷ to have your home somewhere • *She lives in Glasgow.* ❸ to pass your life in a certain way • *He lived as a hermit.*
➤ **live something down** if you cannot live down a mistake or embarrassment, you cannot make people forget it
➤ **live on something** to use something as food; to depend on something for your living • *The islanders lived mainly on fish.*

live (rhymes with hive) *ADJECTIVE*
❶ alive ❷ a live wire or connection is connected to a source of electric current ❸ a live television programme is broadcast while it is actually happening, not from a recording ❹ a live coal is still burning

livelihood *NOUN* livelihoods
a way of earning money or providing enough food to support yourself

lively *ADJECTIVE* livelier, liveliest
full of life, energy and excitement • *The town is quite lively at night.*
➤ **liveliness** *NOUN*

liven *VERB* livens, livening, livened
to make something lively or to become lively • *The match livened up in the second half.*

liver *NOUN* livers
❶ a large organ of the body, found in your abdomen, that processes digested food and purifies the blood ❷ an animal's liver used as food

livery *NOUN* liveries
❶ a uniform worn by male servants in a household ❷ the distinctive colours used by a railway, bus company or airline

livery stable *NOUN* livery stables
a place where horses are kept for their owner or where horses may be hired

livestock *NOUN*
farm animals

live wire *NOUN* live wires
a person who is lively and full of energy

livid *ADJECTIVE*
❶ bluish-grey • *a livid bruise* ❷ furiously angry

living *ADJECTIVE*
alive now • *her only living relative*

living *NOUN*
❶ the way that a person lives • *a good standard of living* ❷ a way of earning money or providing enough food to support yourself • *What do you do for a living?*

living room *NOUN* living rooms
a room for general use during the day

lizard *NOUN* lizards
a reptile with a rough or scaly skin, four legs and a long tail

llama (say **lah**-ma) *NOUN* llamas
a South American animal with woolly fur, like a camel but with no hump

lo *EXCLAMATION* (old use)
see; behold

load *NOUN* loads
❶ something that is being carried ❷ the

quantity that can be carried ❸ the total amount of electric current supplied ❹ (*informal*) a large amount • *It's a load of nonsense.*
➤ **loads** (*informal*) a lot; plenty • *We've got loads of time.*

load *VERB* loads, loading, loaded
❶ to put a load in or on something • *I'll go and load the back of the car.* ❷ to load someone with something is to give them large amounts of it • *They loaded him with gifts.* ❸ to load dice is to put a weight into them to make them land in a certain way ❹ to load a gun is to put a bullet or shell into it ❺ to load a camera is to put a film into it ❻ to enter programs or data into a computer

loaf *NOUN* loaves
a shaped mass of bread baked in one piece
➤ **use your loaf** to think or use your common sense

loaf *VERB* loafs, loafing, loafed
to spend time idly; to loiter or stand about
➤ **loafer** *NOUN*

loam *NOUN*
rich soil containing clay, sand and decayed leaves
➤ **loamy** *ADJECTIVE*

loan *NOUN* loans
something lent, especially money
➤ **on loan** being lent • *This painting is on loan from the National Gallery.*

loan *VERB* loans, loaning, loaned
to lend something

loath (rhymes with both) *ADJECTIVE*
unwilling to do something • *I was loath to go.*

loathe (rhymes with clothe) *VERB* loathes, loathing, loathed
to feel great hatred and disgust for someone or something • *They loathe each other.*
➤ **loathing** *NOUN*

loathsome *ADJECTIVE*
making you feel great hatred and disgust; repulsive

lob *VERB* lobs, lobbing, lobbed
to throw, hit or kick a ball high into the air, especially in a high arc

lob *NOUN* lobs
a lobbed ball in tennis or football

lobby *NOUN* lobbies
❶ an entrance hall ❷ a group of people who try to influence politicians or officials or persuade them of something • *the anti-hunting lobby*

lobby *VERB* lobbies, lobbying, lobbied
to try to persuade a politician or other person to support your cause, by speaking to them in person or writing letters **WORD ORIGIN** the lobby of the Houses of Parliament is where members of the public can meet MPs

lobe *NOUN* lobes
❶ a rounded fairly flat part of a leaf or an organ of the body ❷ the rounded soft part at the bottom of your ear
➤ **lobed** *ADJECTIVE*

lobster *NOUN* lobsters
a large shellfish with eight legs and two long claws

local *ADJECTIVE*
belonging to a particular place or a small area
• *Where is your local library?*
➤ **locally** *ADVERB*

local *NOUN* locals (*informal*)
❶ someone who lives in a particular district ❷ the pub nearest to a person's home

local anaesthetic *NOUN* local anaesthetics
an anaesthetic affecting only the part of the body where it is applied

local government *NOUN*
the system of administration of a town or county by people elected by those who live there

locality *NOUN* localities
a place and the area that surrounds it • *There is no airport in the locality.*

localized (also **localised**) *ADJECTIVE*
restricted to a particular place • *localized showers*

locate *VERB* locates, locating, located
to discover where something is • *I have located the fault.*
➤ **be located** to be situated in a particular place • *The cinema is located in the High Street.*

location *NOUN* locations
the place where something is situated • *What is the exact location of the submarine?*
➤ **on location** filmed in natural surroundings, not in a studio

loch *NOUN* lochs
a lake in Scotland

lock *NOUN* locks
❶ a fastening that is opened with a key or other device ❷ a section of a canal or river fitted with gates and sluices so that boats can be raised or lowered to the level beyond

a
b
c
d
e
f
g
h
i
j
k
l
m
n
o
p
q
r
s
t
u
v
w
x
y
z

each gate ❸ the distance that a vehicle's front wheels can turn ❹ a wrestling hold that keeps an opponent's arm or leg from moving ❺ a clump of hair
➤ **lock, stock, and barrel** completely

lock *VERB* **locks, locking, locked**
❶ to fasten something by means of a lock • *Have you locked the door?* ❷ to put or keep something in a safe place that can be fastened with a lock • *The diamonds are locked away in a safe.* ❸ to become fixed in one place; to jam • *The brakes locked and the car skidded.*

locker *NOUN* **lockers**
a small cupboard for keeping things safe, often in a changing room

locket *NOUN* **lockets**
a small ornamental case for holding a portrait or lock of hair, worn on a chain round the neck

locks *PLURAL NOUN*
the hair on a person's head

locksmith *NOUN* **locksmiths**
a person whose job is to make and mend locks

locomotion *NOUN*
movement or the ability to move

locomotive *NOUN* **locomotives**
a railway engine

locum *NOUN* **locums**
(*British*) a doctor or member of the clergy who takes the place of another who is temporarily away

locus (say **loh**-kus) *NOUN* **loci** (say **loh**-ky)
(*in mathematics*) the path traced by a moving point or made by points placed in a certain way

locust *NOUN* **locusts**
a kind of grasshopper that travels in large swarms which eat all the plants in an area

lodestone *NOUN* **lodestones**
a kind of stone that can be used as a magnet

lodge *NOUN* **lodges**
❶ a small house, especially at the gates of a park ❷ a porter's room at the entrance to a college or other building ❸ a beaver's or otter's lair

lodge *VERB* **lodges, lodging, lodged**
❶ to stay somewhere as a lodger ❷ to provide a person with somewhere to live temporarily ❸ to become stuck or caught somewhere • *The ball lodged in the tree.*

➤ **lodge a complaint** to make an official complaint

lodger *NOUN* **lodgers**
(*chiefly British*) a person who pays to live in another person's house

lodgings *PLURAL NOUN*
a room or rooms, not in a hotel, rented for living in

loft *NOUN* **lofts**
a room or storage space under the roof of a house or barn

lofty *ADJECTIVE*
❶ high or tall • *lofty towers* ❷ a lofty aim or ambition is a noble one that deserves praise ❸ a lofty attitude or manner is a very arrogant one • *her lofty disdain for other people*
➤ **loftily** *ADVERB*

log *NOUN* **logs**
❶ a large piece of a tree that has fallen or been cut down; a piece cut off this ❷ a detailed record kept of a voyage or flight

log *VERB* **logs, logging, logged**
to enter facts in a log
➤ **log in** or **on** to gain access to a computer system
➤ **log out** or **off** to finish using a computer system

loganberry *NOUN* **loganberries**
a dark-red fruit like a blackberry
(**WORD ORIGIN**) named after an American lawyer H. R. *Logan*, who first grew it

logarithm *NOUN* **logarithms**
one of a series of numbers set out in tables which make it possible to do sums by adding and subtracting instead of multiplying and dividing

logbook *NOUN* **logbooks**
❶ a book in which a log of a voyage is kept ❷ the registration document of a motor vehicle

log cabin *NOUN* **log cabins**
a hut built of logs

loggerheads *PLURAL NOUN*
➤ **at loggerheads** disagreeing or quarrelling

logic *NOUN*
❶ reasoning; a system or method of reasoning • *I don't see the logic of your argument.* ❷ the principles used in designing a computer

logical *ADJECTIVE*
using logic or worked out by logic; reasonable

or sensible • *That was the logical thing to do.*
➤ **logically** *ADVERB*

login *NOUN* **logins**
the process of starting to use a computer system; the name or password you use to do this • *Enter your login name.*

logo (say **loh**-goh or **log**-oh) *NOUN* **logos**
a printed symbol used by a business company as its emblem

loin *NOUN* **loins**
the side and back of the body between the ribs and the hip bone

loincloth *NOUN* **loincloths**
a piece of cloth wrapped round the hips, worn by men in some hot countries as their only piece of clothing

loiter *VERB* **loiters, loitering, loitered**
to stand about idly for no obvious reason
➤ **loiterer** *NOUN*

loll *VERB* **lolls, lolling, lolled**
❶ to lean lazily against something • *He lolled back in his chair by the fire.* ❷ to hang loosely • *The dog's tongue lolled from its mouth.*

lollipop *NOUN* **lollipops**
a large round hard sweet on a stick

lollipop woman, lollipop man *NOUN*
lollipop women, lollipop men
an official who uses a circular sign on a stick to signal traffic to stop so that children can cross a road

lolly *NOUN* **lollies** (*informal*)
❶ a lollipop or an ice lolly ❷ money

lone *ADJECTIVE*
solitary; on its own • *a lone rider*

lonely *ADJECTIVE* **lonelier, loneliest**
❶ sad because you are on your own or have no friends ❷ far from inhabited places; not often visited or used • *a lonely road*
➤ **loneliness** *NOUN*

lonesome *ADJECTIVE*
lonely

long *ADJECTIVE*
❶ measuring a lot from one end to the other ❷ taking a lot of time • *a long holiday* ❸ having a certain length • *The river is 10 miles long.*

long *ADVERB*
❶ for a long time • *Have you been waiting long?* ❷ at a long time before or after • *They left long ago.* ❸ throughout a time • *all night*

long
➤ **as long as** or **so long as** provided that; on condition that • *I'll come as long as I can bring my dog.*
➤ **before long** soon
➤ **no longer** not any more

long *VERB* **longs, longing, longed**
to want something very much • *She had always longed for a brother.*

long-distance *ADJECTIVE*
travelling or covering a long distance • *a long-distance runner*

long division *NOUN*
dividing one number by another and writing down all the calculations

longevity (say lon-**jev**-it-ee) *NOUN*
long life

longhand *NOUN*
ordinary writing, contrasted with shorthand or typing

longing *NOUN* **longings**
a strong desire for something or someone

longitude *NOUN* **longitudes**
the distance east or west, measured in degrees, from the Greenwich meridian

longitudinal *ADJECTIVE*
❶ to do with longitude ❷ to do with length; measured lengthways

long jump *NOUN*
an athletic contest in which competitors jump as far as possible along the ground in one leap

long-range *ADJECTIVE*
covering a long distance or period of time • *a long-range missile* • *a long-range weather forecast*

longship *NOUN* **longships**
a long narrow warship, with oars and a sail, used by the Vikings

long-sighted *ADJECTIVE*
(*chiefly British*) able to see distant things clearly but not things close to you

long-suffering *ADJECTIVE*
putting up with things patiently

long-term *ADJECTIVE*
to do with or happening over a long period of time

long wave *NOUN*
a radio wave of a wavelength above one

a b c d e f g h i j k l m n o p q r s t u v w x y z

kilometre and a frequency less than 300 kilohertz

long-winded *ADJECTIVE*
talking or writing at too great a length and therefore boring

loo *NOUN* loos (*British*) (*informal*)
a toilet

loofah *NOUN* loofahs
a rough sponge made from a dried gourd

look *VERB* looks, looking, looked
❶ to use your eyes; to turn your eyes in a particular direction ❷ to face in a particular direction ❸ to have a certain appearance; to seem a certain way • *You look sad.*
➤ **look after someone** to protect or take care of someone
➤ **look after something** to be in charge of something
➤ **look down on someone** to regard someone with contempt
➤ **look for something** to try to find something
➤ **look forward to something** to be waiting eagerly for something to happen
➤ **look into something** to investigate something
➤ **look out** to be careful
➤ **look something up** to search for information about something
➤ **look up** to improve in prospects • *Things are looking up.*
➤ **look up to someone** to admire or respect someone

look *NOUN* looks
❶ the act of looking; a gaze or glance • *Take a look at this.* ❷ the expression on a person's face • *She gave me a surprised look.* ❸ an appearance or general impression • *I don't like the look of this place.*

look-alike *NOUN* look-alikes
someone who looks very like a famous person

looking glass *NOUN* looking glasses (*old use*)
a glass mirror

lookout *NOUN* lookouts
❶ looking out or watching for something • *Keep a lookout for snakes.* ❷ a place from which you can keep watch ❸ a person whose job is to keep watch ❹ (*informal*) a person's own fault or concern • *If he wastes his money, that's his lookout.*

loom *VERB* looms, looming, loomed
to appear suddenly; to seem large or close and threatening • *An iceberg loomed up through the fog.*

loom *NOUN* looms
a machine for weaving cloth

loony *ADJECTIVE* loonier, looniest (*informal*)
mad or crazy

loop *NOUN* loops
the shape made by a curve crossing itself; a piece of string, ribbon or wire made into this shape

loop *VERB* loops, looping, looped
❶ to make string etc. into a loop ❷ to enclose something in a loop

loophole *NOUN* loopholes
❶ a way of avoiding a law, rule or promise without actually breaking it ❷ a narrow opening in the wall of a castle, for shooting arrows through

loose *ADJECTIVE* looser, loosest
❶ not tight or firmly fixed • *a loose tooth* ❷ not tied up or shut in • *The dog got loose.* ❸ not packed in a box or packet ❹ not exact • *a loose translation*
➤ **at a loose end** with nothing to do
➤ **on the loose** free after escaping

> **SPELLING**
> Loose is different from lose. Loose is when something is not tight and lose is when you misplace something.

loose *VERB* looses, loosing, loosed
❶ to fire an arrow, bullet, etc. • *He rapidly loosed a second arrow.* ❷ to loosen something ❸ to untie or release someone or something

loose-leaf *ADJECTIVE*
with each sheet of paper separate and able to be removed • *a loose-leaf folder*

loosely *ADVERB*
not tightly or firmly • *She tied the scarf loosely round her waist.*

loosen *VERB* loosens, loosening, loosened
❶ to make something loose or looser • *He loosened his grip on the rope.* ❷ to become loose

loot *NOUN*
stolen things; goods taken from an enemy

loot *VERB* loots, looting, looted
❶ to rob a place violently, especially during a war or riot ❷ to take something as loot
➤ **looter** *NOUN*

lop *VERB* lops, lopping, lopped
to lop a branch or twig is to cut it off from a tree or bush

lope _VERB_ lopes, loping, loped
to run with a long bounding stride
➤ **lope** _NOUN_

lopsided _ADJECTIVE_
with one side lower or smaller than the other
• _She had a lopsided smile._

loquacious (say lok-**way**-shus) _ADJECTIVE_
talkative
➤ **loquacity** (say lok-**wass**-it-ee) _NOUN_

lord _NOUN_ lords
❶ a nobleman, especially one who is allowed to use the title 'Lord' in front of his name ❷ a master or ruler
➤ **Our Lord** in Christianity, Jesus Christ
➤ **the Lord** God

lord _VERB_ lords, lording, lorded
➤ **lord it over someone** to behave in a superior or domineering way towards someone • _At school Liam always used to lord it over the rest of us._

lordly _ADJECTIVE_ lordlier, lordliest
❶ to do with a lord ❷ proud or haughty

Lord Mayor _NOUN_ Lord Mayors
the title of the mayor of some large cities

lordship _NOUN_
a title used in speaking to or about a man of the rank of 'Lord'

lore _NOUN_
a set of traditional facts or beliefs about something • _forest lore and legends_

lorgnette (say lorn-**yet**) _NOUN_ lorgnettes
a pair of spectacles held on a long handle
WORD ORIGIN French, from _lorgner_ = to squint

lorry _NOUN_ lorries
(_British_) a large strong motor vehicle for carrying heavy goods or troops

lose _VERB_ loses, losing, lost
❶ to be without something that you once had, especially because you cannot find it ❷ to fail to keep or obtain something • _We lost control._ ❸ to be defeated in a contest or argument ❹ to cause the loss of something • _That one mistake lost us the game._ ❺ a clock or watch loses time if it shows a time that is earlier than the correct one
➤ **lose your life** to be killed
➤ **lose your way** to not know where you are or which is the right path

loser _NOUN_ losers
❶ a person who is defeated ❷ (_informal_) a person who is never successful

loss _NOUN_ losses
❶ losing something ❷ something that has been lost
➤ **be at a loss** to not know what to do or say

lost
past tense and past participle of **lose**

lost _ADJECTIVE_
❶ not knowing where you are or not able to find your way • _I think we're lost._ ❷ missing or strayed • _a lost dog_
➤ **lost cause** an idea or policy that is failing
➤ **be lost in something** to be engrossed in a task or activity • _She was lost in thought._

lot _NOUN_ lots
❶ a large number or amount • _You have a lot of friends._ • _There's lots of time._ ❷ something for sale at an auction ❸ a piece of land ❹ a person's fate or situation in life • _She was unhappy with her lot._
➤ **a lot** very much • _I feel a lot better._
➤ **draw lots** to draw cards or other objects from a set in turn in order to choose or decide something by chance • _We drew lots to see who should go first._
➤ **the lot** or **the whole lot** everything; all

SPELLING
A lot is two words, not one.

loth _ADJECTIVE_
a different spelling of **loath**

lotion _NOUN_ lotions
a liquid for putting on the skin

lottery _NOUN_ lotteries
a way of raising money by selling numbered tickets and giving prizes to people who hold winning numbers, which are chosen by a method depending on chance

lotto _NOUN_
a game like bingo

lotus _NOUN_ lotuses
a kind of tropical water lily

loud _ADJECTIVE_
❶ easily heard; producing a lot of noise ❷ unpleasantly bright; gaudy • _The room was painted in loud colours._
➤ **loudly** _ADVERB_
➤ **loudness** _NOUN_

loudspeaker _NOUN_ loudspeakers
a device that changes electrical signals into sound, for reproducing music or voices

lounge _NOUN_ lounges
a sitting room

a b c d e f g h i j k l m n o p q r s t u v w x y z

lounge *VERB* lounges, lounging, lounged
to sit or stand in a lazy and relaxed way • *He was lounging in an armchair by the fire.*

louse *NOUN* lice
a small insect that lives as a parasite on animals or plants

lousy *ADJECTIVE* lousier, lousiest
❶ full of lice ❷ (*informal*) very bad or unpleasant

lout *NOUN* louts
a bad-mannered man

lovable *ADJECTIVE*
easy to love • *a lovable little dog*

love *NOUN* loves
❶ great liking or affection ❷ sexual affection or passion ❸ a loved person; a sweetheart ❹ a score of nil in tennis
➤ **in love** feeling strong love for someone
➤ **make love** to have sexual intercourse

love *VERB* loves, loving, loved
❶ to feel love for a person ❷ to like something very much

love affair *NOUN* love affairs
a romantic or sexual relationship between two people in love

loveless *ADJECTIVE*
without love

lovelorn *ADJECTIVE*
pining with love, especially when abandoned by a lover

lovely *ADJECTIVE* lovelier, loveliest
❶ beautiful ❷ very pleasant or enjoyable
➤ **loveliness** *NOUN*

lover *NOUN* lovers
❶ someone who loves something • *an art lover* ❷ a person who someone is having a sexual relationship with but is not married to

lovesick *ADJECTIVE*
longing for someone you love, especially someone who does not love you

loving *ADJECTIVE*
feeling or showing love or affection • *a loving family*
➤ **lovingly** *ADVERB*

low *ADJECTIVE*
❶ only reaching a short way up; not high ❷ below average in importance, quality or amount • *low prices* • *people of low rank* ❸ unhappy • *I'm feeling low.* ❹ not high-pitched; not loud • *low notes* • *a low voice*
➤ **lowness** *NOUN*

low *ADVERB*
at or to a low level or position • *The plane was flying low.*

low *VERB* lows, lowing, lowed
to moo like a cow

low-down *NOUN*
the true facts or relevant information • *Go to our website for the low-down on disability sport in your area.*

lower *ADJECTIVE & ADVERB*
less high

lower *VERB* lowers, lowering, lowered
to make something lower or move it down • *They lowered the boat into the water.*

lower case *NOUN*
small letters, not capitals

lowlands *PLURAL NOUN*
low-lying country
➤ **lowland** *ADJECTIVE*
➤ **lowlander** *NOUN*

lowly *ADJECTIVE* lowlier, lowliest
low in importance or rank; humble • *a lowly peasant*

loyal *ADJECTIVE*
always firmly supporting your friends, group or country
➤ **loyally** *ADVERB*

loyalist *NOUN* loyalists
a person who is loyal to the government during a revolt

loyalty *NOUN* loyalties
❶ being loyal • *She showed great loyalty to her friends.* ❷ a strong feeling that you want to be loyal to someone • *You have got to decide where your loyalties lie.*

lozenge *NOUN* lozenges
❶ a small flavoured tablet, especially one containing medicine ❷ a diamond-shaped design

Ltd. *ABBREVIATION*
limited (used after the name of a company)

lubricant *NOUN* lubricants
oil or grease for lubricating machinery

lubricate *VERB* lubricates, lubricating, lubricated
to oil or grease something so that it moves smoothly
➤ **lubrication** *NOUN*

lucid *ADJECTIVE*
❶ clear and easy to understand • *a lucid explanation* ❷ thinking clearly; not confused

in your mind
➤ **lucidly** *ADVERB*
➤ **lucidity** *NOUN*

luck *NOUN*
❶ the way things happen by chance without being planned • *There's no skill in this game – it's all a matter of luck.* ❷ good fortune • *She phoned to wish me luck.*

luckily *ADVERB*
by a lucky chance; fortunately • *Luckily it stayed warm all day.*

luckless *ADJECTIVE*
unlucky

lucky *ADJECTIVE* **luckier, luckiest**
having, bringing or resulting from good luck
• *He was lucky to be alive.* • *a lucky escape*

lucrative (say **loo**-kra-tiv) *ADJECTIVE*
profitable; earning you a lot of money

ludicrous *ADJECTIVE*
ridiculous or laughable
➤ **ludicrously** *ADVERB*

ludo *NOUN*
(*British*) a game played with dice and counters on a board **WORD ORIGIN** Latin, = I play

lug *VERB* **lugs, lugging, lugged**
to drag or carry something heavy • *I had to lug my suitcase up all those stairs.*

lug *NOUN* **lugs**
❶ an ear-like part on an object, by which it may be carried or fixed ❷ (*informal*) an ear

luggage *NOUN*
suitcases and bags for holding things to take on a journey

lugubrious (say lug-**oo**-bree-us) *ADJECTIVE*
gloomy or mournful
➤ **lugubriously** *ADVERB*

lukewarm *ADJECTIVE*
❶ only slightly warm; tepid ❷ not very enthusiastic • *lukewarm applause*

lull *VERB* **lulls, lulling, lulled**
❶ to soothe or calm someone; to send someone to sleep ❷ to give someone a false feeling of being safe

lull *NOUN* **lulls**
a short period of quiet or inactivity • *There was a lull in the fighting.*

lullaby *NOUN* **lullabies**
a song that you sing to send a baby to sleep

lumbago *NOUN*
pain in the muscles of the lower back

lumbar *ADJECTIVE*
to do with the lower back area

lumber *NOUN*
❶ unwanted furniture or other goods; junk
❷ (*North American*) timber

lumber *VERB* **lumbers, lumbering, lumbered**
❶ to move in a heavy clumsy way • *We could hear someone lumbering about upstairs.*
❷ to leave someone with an unwanted or unpleasant task • *I'm sorry you got lumbered with all the washing-up.*

lumberjack *NOUN* **lumberjacks**
a person whose job is to cut or carry timber

luminescent *ADJECTIVE*
giving out light
➤ **luminescence** *NOUN*

luminous *ADJECTIVE*
glowing in the dark • *luminous green eyes*
➤ **luminosity** *NOUN*

lump *NOUN* **lumps**
❶ a solid piece of something ❷ a swelling

lump *VERB* **lumps, lumping, lumped**
to lump things together is to put or treat them in a group because you regard them as alike in some way
➤ **lump it** (*informal*) to put up with something you dislike

lump sum *NOUN* **lump sums**
a single payment, especially one covering a number of items

lumpy *ADJECTIVE* **lumpier, lumpiest**
full of lumps or covered in lumps • *This bed is very lumpy.*

lunacy *NOUN* **lunacies**
insanity or great foolishness

lunar *ADJECTIVE*
to do with the moon **WORD ORIGIN** from Latin *luna* = moon

lunar month *NOUN* **lunar months**
the period between new moons; four weeks

lunatic *NOUN* **lunatics**
an insane person
➤ **lunatic** *ADJECTIVE*
WORD ORIGIN from Latin *luna* = moon (because it was once thought that people could be affected by changes of the moon)

lunch *NOUN* **lunches**
a meal eaten in the middle of the day
➤ **lunch** *VERB*

luncheon *NOUN* **luncheons** (*formal*)
lunch

a b c d e f g h i j k l m n o p q r s t u v w x y z

lung *NOUN* lungs
either of the two parts of the body, in your chest, used in breathing

lunge *VERB* lunges, lunging, lunged
to thrust your body forward suddenly

lunge *NOUN* lunges
a sudden forward movement • *He made a lunge for the phone.*

lupin *NOUN* lupins
a garden plant with tall spikes of flowers

lurch *VERB* lurches, lurching, lurched
❶ to stagger; to lean suddenly to one side ❷ if you heart or stomach lurches, you have a sudden feeling of fear or excitement

lurch *NOUN* lurches
a sudden staggering or leaning movement • *The train moved forward with a lurch.*
➤ **leave someone in the lurch** to desert someone when they are in difficulty

lure *VERB* lures, luring, lured
to tempt a person or animal into a trap; to entice someone

lure *NOUN* lures
the attractive qualities of something • *the lure of adventure*

lurid (say **lewr**-id) *ADJECTIVE*
❶ in very bright colours; gaudy ❷ sensational and shocking • *the lurid details of the murder*
➤ **luridly** *ADVERB*

lurk *VERB* lurks, lurking, lurked
to wait where you cannot be seen

luscious (say **lush**-us) *ADJECTIVE*
tasting delicious • *luscious fruit*

lush *ADJECTIVE*
growing thickly and strongly • *lush grass*

lust *NOUN* lusts
powerful desire, especially sexual desire
➤ **lustful** *ADJECTIVE*

lust *VERB* lusts, lusting, lusted
to have a powerful desire for a person or thing • *people who lust after power*

lustre *NOUN*
brightness or brilliance • *Her eyes had lost their lustre.*
➤ **lustrous** *ADJECTIVE*

lusty *ADJECTIVE* lustier, lustiest
strong and vigorous • *a lusty cheer*
➤ **lustily** *ADVERB*

lute *NOUN* lutes
a stringed musical instrument with a pear-shaped body, popular in the 14th-17th centuries

luxuriant *ADJECTIVE*
growing thickly and strongly • *luxuriant vegetation*

luxuriate *VERB* luxuriates, luxuriating, luxuriated
to luxuriate in something is to enjoy it as a luxury • *We've been luxuriating in the warm sunshine.*

luxurious *ADJECTIVE*
full of luxury; expensive and comfortable • *a luxurious hotel*
➤ **luxuriously** *ADVERB*

luxury *NOUN* luxuries
❶ something expensive that you enjoy but do not really need ❷ expensive and comfortable surroundings • *a life of luxury*

lychgate *NOUN* lychgates
a churchyard gate with a roof over it
WORD ORIGIN from Old English *lic* = corpse (because the coffin-bearers would shelter there until it was time to enter the church)

Lycra *NOUN* (*trademark*)
a thin stretchy material used especially for sports clothing

lying
present participle of **lie**

lymph (say **limf**) *NOUN*
a colourless fluid from the flesh or organs of the body, containing white blood cells
➤ **lymphatic** *ADJECTIVE*

lynch *VERB* lynches, lynching, lynched
to join together to execute someone without a proper trial, especially by hanging them
WORD ORIGIN named after William *Lynch*, an American judge who allowed this kind of punishment in about 1780

lynx *NOUN* lynxes
a wild animal like a very large cat with thick fur and very sharp sight

lyre *NOUN* lyres
an ancient musical instrument like a small harp

lyric (say **li**-rik) *NOUN* lyrics
❶ a short poem that expresses the poet's feelings ❷ lyrics are the words of a popular song

lyrical *ADJECTIVE*
❶ like a song ❷ expressing poetic feelings ❸ expressing yourself enthusiastically

MA *ABBREVIATION*
Master of Arts

ma *NOUN* (*informal*)
mother

ma'am (say mam) *NOUN*
a word used when speaking politely
to a woman (especially the Queen)
WORD ORIGIN short for **madam**

mac *NOUN* macs (*British*) (*informal*)
a raincoat

macabre (say mak-**ah**br) *ADJECTIVE*
gruesome; strange and horrible

macadam *NOUN*
layers of broken stone rolled flat to make a
firm road surface **WORD ORIGIN** named after
a Scottish engineer, J. *McAdam*, who first laid
such roads

macaroni *NOUN*
pasta in the form of short narrow tubes

macaroon *NOUN* macaroons
a small sweet cake or biscuit made with
ground almonds

macaw (say ma-**kaw**) *NOUN* macaws
a brightly coloured parrot from Central and
South America

mace *NOUN* maces
an ornamental staff carried or placed in front
of an official

Mach (say mahk) *NOUN*
➤ **Mach number** the ratio of the speed of a
moving object to the speed of sound. Mach
one is the speed of sound, Mach two is twice
the speed of sound and so on.
WORD ORIGIN named after the Austrian
scientist Ernst *Mach* (1838-1916)

machete (say mash-**et**-ee) *NOUN* machetes
a broad heavy knife used as a tool or weapon

machinations (say mash-in-**ay**-shonz) *PLURAL
NOUN*
clever schemes or plots

machine *NOUN* machines
a piece of equipment made of moving parts
that work together to do a job

machine gun *NOUN* machine guns
a gun that can keep firing bullets quickly one
after another

machine-readable *ADJECTIVE*
machine-readable data is in a form that a
computer can process

machinery *NOUN*
❶ machines • *farm machinery* ❷ the moving
parts of a machine • *He was tinkering with
the machinery of the motor.* ❸ an organized
system for doing something • *the machinery
of local government*

macho (say **mach**-oh) *ADJECTIVE*
showing off masculine strength

mackerel *NOUN* mackerel
a sea fish used as food

mackintosh *NOUN* mackintoshes (*British*) (*old
use*)
a raincoat **WORD ORIGIN** named after the
Scottish inventor of a waterproof material, C.
Macintosh

mad *ADJECTIVE* madder, maddest
❶ having something wrong with the mind;
insane ❷ extremely foolish ❸ very keen • *She
is mad about football.* ❹ (*informal*) very
excited or annoyed
➤ **madness** *NOUN*
➤ **madman** *NOUN*
➤ **like mad** (*informal*) with great speed,
energy or enthusiasm

madam *NOUN*
a word used when speaking politely to a
woman • *Can I help you, madam?*

madcap *ADJECTIVE*
foolish and rash • *a madcap scheme*

mad cow disease *NOUN*
BSE

madden *VERB* maddens, maddening,
maddened
to make a person mad or angry

maddening *ADJECTIVE*
annoying • *She has some really maddening
habits.*

madly *ADVERB*
extremely; very much • *They are madly in
love.*

madonna *NOUN* madonnas
a picture or statue of the Virgin Mary

madrigal *NOUN* madrigals
a song for several voices singing different
parts together

maelstrom (say **mayl**-strom) *NOUN* maelstroms
❶ a great whirlpool ❷ a state of great confusion (**WORD ORIGIN**) originally the name of a whirlpool off the Norwegian coast: from Dutch *malen* = whirl + *stroom* = stream

maestro (say **my**-stroh) *NOUN* maestros
a master, especially a musician

mafia *NOUN*
❶ a large organization of criminals in Italy, Sicily and the United States of America ❷ any group of people who act together in a sinister way

magazine *NOUN* magazines
❶ a paper-covered publication that comes out regularly, with articles, stories or features by several writers ❷ the part of a gun that holds the cartridges ❸ a store for weapons and ammunition or for explosives ❹ a device that holds film for a camera or slides for a projector (**WORD ORIGIN**) from Arabic *makhazin* = storehouses, the original meaning in English. The word then came to be used for a store for weapons and ammunition, and later the part of a gun.

magenta (say ma-**jen**-ta) *NOUN*
a colour between bright red and purple (**WORD ORIGIN**) named after *Magenta*, a town in north Italy, where Napoleon III won a battle in the year when the dye was first developed (1859)

maggot *NOUN* maggots
the larva of some kinds of fly
➤ **maggoty** *ADJECTIVE*

Magi (say **mayj**-eye) *PLURAL NOUN*
the 'wise men' from the East who brought offerings to the infant Jesus at Bethlehem (**WORD ORIGIN**) from old Persian *magus* = priest; later = astrologer or wizard

magic *NOUN*
❶ the art of making impossible things happen by a mysterious or supernatural power ❷ mysterious tricks performed for entertainment ❸ a mysterious and enchanting quality • *the magic of Greece*
magic *ADJECTIVE*
❶ used in or using magic • *a magic potion* ❷ having a special or mysterious quality. • *It was a magic moment.*

magical
❶ to do with magic or using magic ❷ wonderful or marvellous • *a magical evening*
➤ **magically** *ADVERB*

magician *NOUN* magicians
❶ a person who does magic tricks ❷ a wizard

magistrate *NOUN* magistrates
an official who hears and judges minor cases in a local court

magma *NOUN*
a molten substance beneath the earth's crust

magnanimous (say mag-**nan**-im-us) *ADJECTIVE*
generous and forgiving, not petty-minded
➤ **magnanimously** *ADVERB*
➤ **magnanimity** *NOUN*

magnate *NOUN* magnates
a wealthy influential person, especially in business

magnesia *NOUN*
a white powder that is a compound of magnesium, used in medicine

magnesium *NOUN*
a silvery-white metal that burns with a very bright flame

magnet *NOUN* magnets
a piece of iron or steel that can attract iron and that points north and south when it is hung up

magnetic *ADJECTIVE*
❶ having or using the powers of a magnet ❷ having the power to attract people • *a magnetic personality*
➤ **magnetically** *ADVERB*

magnetic tape *NOUN* magnetic tapes
a plastic strip coated with a magnetic substance, for recording sound or pictures or storing computer data

magnetism *NOUN*
❶ the properties and effects of magnetic substances ❷ great personal charm and attraction

magnetize (also **magnetise**) *VERB*
magnetizes, magnetizing, magnetized
to make something into a magnet
➤ **magnetization** *NOUN*

magneto (say mag-**neet**-oh) *NOUN* magnetos
a small electric generator using magnets

magnificent *ADJECTIVE*
❶ looking grand or splendid • *She rode a magnificent black horse.* ❷ very good; excellent
➤ **magnificently** *ADVERB*
➤ **magnificence** *NOUN*

magnify *VERB* magnifies, magnifying, magnified

❶ to make something look bigger than it really is, as a lens or microscope does ❷ to exaggerate something
➤ **magnification** NOUN
➤ **magnifier** NOUN

magnifying glass NOUN magnifying glasses
a lens that magnifies things

magnitude NOUN magnitudes
the magnitude of something is how large or important it is • *At first we didn't realize the magnitude of the problem.*

magnolia NOUN magnolias
a tree with large white or pale-pink flowers
(**WORD ORIGIN**) named after a French botanist, P. *Magnol*

magpie NOUN magpies
a noisy bird with black and white feathers, related to the crow

maharajah NOUN maharajahs
the title of certain Indian princes

mah-jong NOUN
a Chinese game for four people, played with pieces called tiles

mahogany NOUN
a hard brown wood

maid NOUN maids
❶ a female servant ❷ (*old use*) a girl

maiden NOUN maidens (*old use*)
a girl
➤ **maidenhood** NOUN

maiden ADJECTIVE
❶ a maiden aunt is one who is not married
❷ a ship's maiden voyage is its first voyage after being built

maiden name NOUN maiden names
a woman's family name before she marries

maiden over NOUN maiden overs
a cricket over in which no runs are scored

mail NOUN mails
❶ letters and parcels sent by post ❷ email; an email • *I had a mail from Danny this morning.*
❸ armour made of metal rings joined together • *a suit of chain mail*

mail VERB mails, mailing, mailed
to send something by post or by email

mailing list NOUN mailing lists
a list of names and addresses of people to whom an organization sends information from time to time

mail order NOUN
a system for buying and selling goods by post

maim VERB maims, maiming, maimed
to injure a person so badly that part of their body is damaged for life

main ADJECTIVE
largest or most important

main NOUN
❶ the main pipe or cable in a public system carrying water, gas, or (usually called **mains**) electricity to a building ❷ (*old use*) the seas
• *Drake sailed the Spanish main.*
➤ **in the main** for the most part; on the whole

main clause NOUN main clauses
a clause that can be used as a complete sentence. Compare with **subordinate clause**.

mainframe NOUN mainframes
a large powerful computer that a lot of people can use at the same time

mainland NOUN
the main part of a country or continent, not the islands round it

mainly ADVERB
chiefly or mostly • *They eat mainly fruit and nuts.*

mainmast NOUN mainmasts
the tallest and most important mast on a ship

mainstay NOUN
the chief support or main part • *Cocoa is the mainstay of the country's economy.*

mainstream NOUN
the most widely accepted ideas or opinions about something • *Music should be part of the mainstream of education.*

maintain VERB maintains, maintaining, maintained
❶ to make something continue at the same standard or level • *The pilot maintained a constant flying speed.* ❷ to keep a thing in good condition • *Wind turbines can be costly to maintain.* ❸ to keep saying that something is true • *I still maintain that I did the right thing.* ❹ to provide money for a person to live on

maintenance NOUN
❶ maintaining or keeping something in good condition ❷ money for food and clothing
❸ money to be paid by a husband or wife to the other partner after a divorce

a b c d e f g h i j k l m n o p q r s t u v w x y z

maize NOUN
(*British*) a tall kind of corn with large seeds on cobs

majestic ADJECTIVE
❶ stately and dignified ❷ very impressive
➤ **majestically** ADVERB

majesty NOUN majesties
❶ the title of a king or queen • *Her Majesty the Queen* ❷ being majestic

major ADJECTIVE
❶ greater; very important or serious • *major roads* • *a major operation* ❷ of the musical scale that has a semitone after the 3rd and 7th notes. Compare with **minor**.

major NOUN majors
an army officer ranking next above a captain

major VERB majors, majoring, majored (*North American & Australian/NZ*) to specialize in a particular subject at college or university • *He's majoring in psychology.*

majority NOUN majorities
❶ the greatest part of a group of people or things. Compare with **minority**. • *The vast majority of the people who live in China speak Chinese.* ❷ the amount by which the winner in an election beats the loser • *She had a majority of 25 over her opponent.* ❸ the age at which a person becomes an adult according to the law, now usually 18 • *He attained his majority.*

make VERB makes, making, made
❶ to bring something into existence, especially by putting things together ❷ to cause something to happen • *You made me jump!* • *Make him repeat it.* ❸ to gain or earn an amount of money • *She makes £30,000 a year.* ❹ to achieve or reach something • *He made 25 runs.* • *The swimmer just made the shore.* ❺ to estimate or reckon something • *What do you make the time?* ❻ to result in or add up to something • *4 and 6 make 10* ❼ to perform an action • *Can I make a suggestion?* ❽ to arrange something for use • *I'll just make the beds.* ❾ to cause someone to be successful or happy • *Her visit made my day.*
➤ **make do** to manage with something that is not what you really want
➤ **make for somewhere** to go towards a place
➤ **make love** ❶ to have sexual intercourse ❷ (*old use*) to try to win someone's love
➤ **make off** to go away quickly
➤ **make out** to claim or pretend that something is true

➤ **make something out** to manage to see, hear or understand something
➤ **make up** ❶ to be friendly again after a disagreement ❷ to put on make-up
➤ **make something up** ❶ to build something or put it together • *Elements are made up of atoms.* ❷ to invent a story or excuse
➤ **make up for something** to compensate for something
➤ **make up your mind** to decide about something

make NOUN makes
a brand of goods; something made by a particular firm

> SPELLING
> The past tense of **make** is **made**.

make-believe NOUN
pretending or imagining things

make-over NOUN make-overs
changes in your make-up, hairstyle and the way you dress to make you look and feel more attractive

maker NOUN makers
the person or firm that has made something

makeshift ADJECTIVE
used for the time being because you have nothing better • *We used a box as a makeshift table.*

make-up NOUN
❶ creams and powders put on your face to make it look more attractive or different ❷ the way something is made up ❸ a person's character

maladjusted ADJECTIVE
unable to fit in or cope with other people or your own circumstances

malady NOUN maladies
an illness or disease

malapropism NOUN malapropisms
a comical confusion of words, e.g. using *hooligan* instead of *hurricane*
WORD ORIGIN named after Mrs *Malaprop* in Sheridan's play *The Rivals*, who made mistakes of this kind

malaria NOUN
a feverish disease spread by mosquitoes
➤ **malarial** ADJECTIVE
WORD ORIGIN from Italian *mala aria* = bad air, which was once thought to cause the disease

male ADJECTIVE
of the sex that reproduces by fertilizing egg cells produced by the female

male *NOUN* males
a male person, animal or plant

male chauvinist *NOUN* male chauvinists
a man who thinks that women are not as
good as men

malefactor (say **mal**-if-ak-ter) *NOUN*
malefactors
a criminal or wrongdoer

malevolent (say ma-**lev**-ol-ent) *ADJECTIVE*
showing a desire to harm other people
➤ **malevolently** *ADVERB*
➤ **malevolence** *NOUN*

malformed *ADJECTIVE*
faultily formed

malfunction *NOUN* malfunctions
faulty functioning • *a computer malfunction*

malfunction *VERB* malfunctions,
malfunctioning, malfunctioned
to fail to work properly

malice *NOUN*
a desire to harm other people; spite • *His eyes
glinted with malice.*

malicious *ADJECTIVE*
intending to do harm • *malicious gossip*
➤ **maliciously** *ADVERB*

malign (say mal-**y**'n) *ADJECTIVE*
❶ harmful and sinister • *a malign influence*
❷ showing malice
➤ **malignity** (say mal-**ig**-nit-ee) *NOUN*

malign *VERB* maligns, maligning, maligned
to say unpleasant and untrue things about
someone

malignant *ADJECTIVE*
❶ a malignant tumour is one that is growing
uncontrollably ❷ full of malice
➤ **malignantly** *ADVERB*
➤ **malignancy** *NOUN*

malinger *VERB* malingers, malingering,
malingered
to pretend to be ill in order to avoid work
➤ **malingerer** *NOUN*

mall (say mal or mawl) *NOUN* malls
a large covered shopping centre

mallard *NOUN* mallard or mallards
a kind of wild duck of North America, Europe
and parts of Asia

malleable *ADJECTIVE*
❶ able to be pressed or hammered into shape
❷ easy to influence
➤ **malleability** *NOUN*

mallet *NOUN* mallets
❶ a large hammer, usually made of wood
❷ an implement with a long handle, used in
croquet or polo for striking the ball

malnutrition *NOUN*
bad health because you do not have enough
food or the right kind of food
➤ **malnourished** *ADJECTIVE*

malt *NOUN*
dried barley used in brewing, making vinegar,
etc.
➤ **malted** *ADJECTIVE*

maltreat *VERB* maltreats, maltreating,
maltreated
to ill-treat a person or animal
➤ **maltreatment** *NOUN*

mama, mamma *NOUN* (old use)
mother

mammal *NOUN* mammals
any animal of which the female gives birth to
live babies which are fed with milk from her
own body
➤ **mammalian** (say mam-**ay**-lee-an) *ADJECTIVE*

mammoth *NOUN* mammoths
an extinct elephant with a hairy skin and
curved tusks

mammoth *ADJECTIVE*
huge • *a mammoth effort*

man *NOUN* men
❶ a grown-up male human being ❷ an
individual person ❸ people in general;
mankind • *Early man lived by hunting.* ❹ a
piece used in chess or some other board game

man *VERB* mans, manning, manned
to provide a place or machine with the people
to run or work it • *Man the pumps!*

manacle *NOUN* manacles
a fetter or handcuff

manacle *VERB* manacles, manacling,
manacled
to put manacles on someone

manage *VERB* manages, managing, managed
❶ to succeed in doing or dealing with
something difficult • *She finally managed
to open the door.* ❷ to be in charge of a
business or part of it or a group of people

manageable *ADJECTIVE*
not too big or too difficult to deal with

management *NOUN*
❶ managing something ❷ managers; the
people in charge of a business

a
b
c
d
e
f
g
h
i
j
k
l
m
n
o
p
q
r
s
t
u
v
w
x
y
z

manager *NOUN* **managers**
a person who manages something
➤ **managerial** (say man-a-**jeer**-ee-al)
ADJECTIVE

manageress *NOUN* **manageresses**
(*British*) a woman manager, especially of a shop or hotel

mandarin *NOUN* **mandarins**
❶ an important official ❷ a kind of small orange

mandate *NOUN* **mandates**
authority given to someone to carry out a certain task or policy • *An elected government has a mandate to govern the country.*

mandatory *ADJECTIVE*
obligatory or compulsory

mandible *NOUN* **mandibles**
❶ a jaw, especially the lower one ❷ either part of a bird's beak or the similar part in insects etc. Compare with **maxilla**.

mandolin *NOUN* **mandolins**
a musical instrument rather like a guitar

mane *NOUN* **manes**
the long hair on a horse's or lion's neck

manfully *ADVERB*
using a lot of effort in a brave or determined way

manganese *NOUN*
a hard brittle metal

mange *NOUN*
a skin disease of dogs etc.

manger *NOUN* **mangers**
a trough in a stable for horses or cattle to feed from

mangle *VERB* **mangles, mangling, mangled**
to damage something by crushing or cutting it roughly • *The motorway was covered with the mangled wreckage of cars.*

mango *NOUN* **mangoes**
a tropical fruit with yellow pulp

mangrove *NOUN* **mangroves**
a tropical tree growing in mud and swamps, with many tangled roots above the ground

mangy *ADJECTIVE*
❶ having mange ❷ scruffy or dirty

manhandle *VERB* **manhandles, manhandling, manhandled**
to handle or push a person or thing roughly

• *Two burly men manhandled him out of the door.*

manhole *NOUN* **manholes**
a space or opening, usually with a cover, by which a person can get into a sewer or boiler etc. to inspect or repair it

manhood *NOUN*
❶ the condition of being a man • *When he reached manhood he moved away from the village.* ❷ manly qualities

mania *NOUN* **manias**
❶ violent madness ❷ a great enthusiasm for something • *a mania for fast cars*

maniac *NOUN* **maniacs**
a person who acts in a wild or violent way

manic *ADJECTIVE*
❶ to do with or suffering from mania ❷ (*informal*) full of excited activity or nervous energy • *Things are a bit manic here at the moment.*

manicure *NOUN* **manicures**
care and treatment of the hands and nails
➤ **manicured** *ADJECTIVE*
➤ **manicurist** *NOUN*

manifest *ADJECTIVE*
clear and obvious
➤ **manifestly** *ADVERB*

manifest *VERB* **manifests, manifesting, manifested**
to manifest a feeling or sign is to show it clearly

manifestation *NOUN* **manifestations**
a sign that something is happening

manifesto *NOUN* **manifestos**
a public statement of a group's or person's policy or principles

manifold *ADJECTIVE*
of many kinds; very varied

manipulate *VERB* **manipulates, manipulating, manipulated**
❶ to handle or arrange something skilfully • *He began to manipulate the controls and levers.* ❷ to get someone to do what you want by treating them cleverly • *She uses her charm to manipulate people.*
➤ **manipulation** *NOUN*
➤ **manipulator** *NOUN*

mankind *NOUN*
human beings in general

manly *ADJECTIVE*
❶ suitable for a man ❷ brave and strong
➤ **manliness** *NOUN*

manner *NOUN*
❶ the way something happens or is done ❷ a person's way of behaving
➤ **all manner of** many different kinds of
• *They asked me all manner of strange questions.*

mannerism *NOUN* **mannerisms**
a person's own particular gesture or way of speaking

manners *PLURAL NOUN*
how a person behaves with other people; politeness

mannish *ADJECTIVE*
a woman is mannish when she is like a man

manoeuvre (say man-**oo**-ver) *NOUN* **manoeuvres**
a difficult or skilful or cunning action
• *Parking the car in that small space was a tricky manoeuvre.*

manoeuvre *VERB* **manoeuvres, manoeuvring, manoeuvred**
❶ to move something skilfully into position
• *She manoeuvred the boat through the gap in the rocks.* ❷ to move carefully and skilfully
➤ **manoeuvrable** *ADJECTIVE*

man-of-war *NOUN* **men-of-war**
a warship

manor *NOUN* **manors** (*British*)
❶ a manor house ❷ the land belonging to a manor house

manor house *NOUN* **manor houses**
(*British*) a large important house in the country

manpower *NOUN*
the number of people who are working or needed or available for work on something

manse *NOUN* **manses**
a church minister's house, especially in Scotland

mansion *NOUN* **mansions**
a large stately house

manslaughter *NOUN*
the crime of killing a person unlawfully but without meaning to

mantelpiece *NOUN* **mantelpieces**
a shelf above a fireplace

mantilla *NOUN* **mantillas**
a lace veil worn by Spanish women over the hair and shoulders

mantle *NOUN* **mantles**
❶ a cloak ❷ a covering • *There was a mantle of snow on the hills.*

mantra *NOUN* **mantras**
a word or phrase that is constantly repeated to help people meditate, originally in Hinduism and Buddhism

manual *ADJECTIVE*
worked by or done with the hands • *a manual typewriter* • *manual work*
➤ **manually** *ADVERB*

manual *NOUN* **manuals**
a handbook or book of instructions

manufacture *VERB* **manufactures, manufacturing, manufactured**
to make things in large quantities using machines

manufacture *NOUN*
the process of making things in large quantities using machines

manufacturer *NOUN* **manufacturers**
a business that manufactures things

manure *NOUN*
animal dung added to the soil as fertilizer

manuscript *NOUN* **manuscripts**
something written or typed but not printed
WORD ORIGIN from Latin *manu* = by hand + *scriptum* = written

Manx *ADJECTIVE*
to do with the Isle of Man

many *DETERMINER* **more, most**
❶ great in number; numerous • *Many people are afraid of spiders.* ❷ used to talk about the size of a number • *How many tickets do you want?*

many *PRONOUN*
a large number of people or things • *Many were found.*

Maori (rhymes with flowery) *NOUN* **Maoris**
❶ a member of the people who were living in New Zealand before European settlers arrived ❷ their language

map *NOUN* **maps**
a diagram of part or all of the earth's surface or of the sky

map *VERB* **maps, mapping, mapped**
to make a map of an area

a b c d e f g h i j k l m n o p q r s t u v w x y z

➤ **map something out** to plan the details of something

maple *NOUN* maples
a tree with broad leaves

maple syrup *NOUN*
a sweet substance made from the sap of some kinds of maple

mar *VERB* mars, marring, marred
to spoil something • *The game was marred by crowd trouble.*

marathon *NOUN* marathons
a long-distance running race, especially one covering 26 miles 385 yards (42.195 km) **WORD ORIGIN** named after *Marathon* in Greece, from which a messenger is said to have run to Athens (about 40 kilometres) to announce that the Greeks had defeated the Persian army

marauding *ADJECTIVE*
a marauding army or pack of animals goes about attacking people or stealing things
➤ **marauder** *NOUN*

marble *NOUN* marbles
❶ a small glass ball used in games ❷ a kind of limestone polished and used in sculpture or building

March *NOUN*
the third month of the year
WORD ORIGIN named after *Mars*, the Roman god of war

march *VERB* marches, marching, marched
❶ to walk with regular steps ❷ to make someone walk somewhere • *He marched them up the hill.*
➤ **marcher** *NOUN*

march *NOUN* marches
❶ a large group of people marching, sometimes to protest about something ❷ a journey by marching ❸ music suitable for marching to

marchioness *NOUN* marchionesses
the wife or widow of a marquis

mare *NOUN* mares
a female horse or donkey

margarine (say mar-ja-**reen**) *NOUN*
a substance used like butter, made from animal or vegetable fats

marge *NOUN* (*British*) (*informal*)
margarine

margin *NOUN* margins
❶ an edge or border ❷ the blank space between the edge of a page and the writing or pictures on it ❸ the difference between two scores or prices etc. • *She won by a narrow margin.*

marginal *ADJECTIVE*
❶ very slight • *a marginal difference* ❷ in a margin • *marginal notes*

marginally *ADVERB*
very slightly; by a small amount • *I did marginally better this time.*

marginal seat *NOUN* marginal seats
a constituency where an MP was elected with only a small majority and may be defeated in the next election

marigold *NOUN* marigolds
a yellow or orange garden flower

marijuana (say ma-ri-**hwah**-na) *NOUN*
a drug made from hemp

marina *NOUN* marinas
a harbour for yachts, motor boats, etc.

marinade *NOUN* marinades
a flavoured liquid in which meat or fish is soaked before being cooked

marinate *VERB* marinates, marinating, marinated
to soak meat or fish in a marinade

marine (say ma-**reen**) *ADJECTIVE*
to do with the sea; living in the sea • *marine life*

marine *NOUN* marines
a member of the troops who are trained to serve at sea as well as on land

mariner (say **ma**-rin-er) *NOUN* mariners
a sailor

marionette *NOUN* marionettes
a puppet that you work by strings or wires
WORD ORIGIN French, = little Mary

marital *ADJECTIVE*
to do with marriage

maritime *ADJECTIVE*
❶ to do with the sea or ships ❷ found near the sea

marjoram *NOUN*
a herb with a mild flavour, used in cooking

mark *NOUN* marks
❶ a spot, dot, line or stain on something ❷ a number or letter put on a piece of work to show how good it is ❸ a distinguishing feature ❹ a sign or symbol • *They all stood as a mark of respect.* ❺ a target ❻ a unit

of money used in Germany before the introduction of the euro
➤ **on your marks!** a command to runners to get ready to begin a race
➤ **be up to the mark** to reach the normal or expected standard

mark *VERB* **marks, marking, marked**
❶ to put a mark on something ❷ to give a mark to a piece of work ❸ to keep close to an opposing player in football etc. ❹ to pay attention to something • *Mark my words!*
➤ **mark time** ❶ to march on the spot without moving forward ❷ to occupy your time without making any progress

marked *ADJECTIVE*
clear or noticeable • *a marked improvement*
➤ **markedly** *ADVERB*

marker *NOUN* **markers**
a thing that shows the position of something
• *a boundary marker*

market *NOUN* **markets**
❶ a place where things are bought and sold, usually from stalls in the open air ❷ a demand for goods • *There is hardly any market for typewriters now.*
➤ **on the market** offered for sale

market *VERB* **markets, marketing, marketed**
to offer things for sale

marketing *NOUN*
the branch of business concerned with advertising and selling the product

marketplace *NOUN* **marketplaces**
the place in a town where a market is held or used to be held

market research *NOUN*
the study of what people need or want to buy

marksman, markswoman *NOUN* **marksmen** or **markswomen**
an expert in shooting at a target
➤ **marksmanship** *NOUN*

marmalade *NOUN*
jam made from oranges, lemons or other citrus fruit

marmoset *NOUN* **marmosets**
a kind of small monkey

maroon *VERB* **maroons, marooning, marooned**
to abandon someone in a deserted place that they cannot leave • *The sailors were marooned on a little island.*

maroon *NOUN*
dark red

marquee (say mar-**kee**) *NOUN* **marquees**
a large tent used for a party or exhibition

marquis *NOUN* **marquises**
a nobleman ranking next above an earl

marriage *NOUN* **marriages**
❶ the legal relationship between a husband and wife or a similar legal relationship between any couple ❷ a wedding

marrow *NOUN* **marrows**
❶ a large gourd eaten as a vegetable ❷ the soft substance inside bones

marry *VERB* **marries, marrying, married**
❶ to marry someone is to be legally joined in marriage with them ❷ to marry two people is to perform a marriage ceremony
➤ **married** *ADJECTIVE*

marsh *NOUN* **marshes**
a low-lying area of very wet ground
➤ **marshy** *ADJECTIVE*

marshal *NOUN* **marshals**
❶ an official who helps to organize or control a large public event ❷ an army officer of very high rank • *a Field Marshal* ❸ a police official in the USA

marshal *VERB* **marshals, marshalling, marshalled**
❶ to gather things together and arrange them neatly • *He spent some time marshalling his thoughts.* ❷ to control or organize a large group of people

marshmallow *NOUN* **marshmallows**
a soft spongy sweet, usually pink or white

marsupial (say mar-**soo**-pee-al) *NOUN* **marsupials**
an animal such as a kangaroo, wallaby or koala. The female has a pouch on the front of its body in which its babies are carried.

martial *ADJECTIVE*
to do with war; warlike **WORD ORIGIN** Latin, = belonging to Mars, the Roman god of war

martial arts *PLURAL NOUN*
fighting sports, such as judo and karate

martial law *NOUN*
government of a country by the armed forces during a crisis

martin *NOUN* **martins**
a bird rather like a swallow
WORD ORIGIN probably after St *Martin* of Tours, who gave half his cloak to a beggar (because of the bird's markings, which look like a torn cloak)

a
b
c
d
e
f
g
h
i
j
k
l
m
n
o
p
q
r
s
t
u
v
w
x
y
z

martinet *NOUN* martinets
a very strict person (WORD ORIGIN) named after a French army officer, J. *Martinet*, who imposed harsh discipline on his troops

martyr *NOUN* martyrs
a person who is killed or made to suffer because of their beliefs, especially religious beliefs
➤ **martyrdom** *NOUN*

martyr *VERB* martyrs, martyring, martyred
to kill someone or make them suffer as a martyr

marvel *NOUN* marvels
a wonderful thing

marvel *VERB* marvels, marvelling, marvelled
to be filled with wonder or astonishment by something • *The whole town marvelled at her bravery.*

marvellous *ADJECTIVE*
extremely good; wonderful
➤ **marvellously** *ADVERB*

Marxism *NOUN*
the Communist theories of the German writer Karl Marx (1818-83)
➤ **Marxist** *NOUN* & *ADJECTIVE*

marzipan *NOUN*
a soft sweet food made of ground almonds, eggs and sugar

mascara *NOUN*
a cosmetic for darkening the eyelashes

mascot *NOUN* mascots
a person, animal or object that is believed to bring good luck

masculine *ADJECTIVE*
❶ to do with or like men; thought to be suitable for a man ❷ belonging to the class of words (in some languages) which includes the words referring to men
➤ **masculinity** *NOUN*

mash *VERB* mashes, mashing, mashed
to crush something into a soft mass

mash *NOUN* mashes
❶ a soft mixture of cooked grain or bran etc. ❷ (*informal*) mashed potatoes

mask *NOUN* masks
a covering that you wear over your face to disguise or protect it

mask *VERB* masks, masking, masked
❶ to cover your face with a mask ❷ to disguise or conceal something • *She masked her anger with a smile.*

mason *NOUN* masons
a person who builds or works with stone

masonry *NOUN*
❶ the parts of a building that are made of stone • *He was injured by falling masonry.* ❷ a mason's work

masquerade *NOUN* masquerades
a pretence

masquerade *VERB* masquerades, masquerading, masqueraded
to pretend to be something • *He masqueraded as a police officer.*

Mass *NOUN* Masses
the Communion service in a Roman Catholic church

mass *NOUN* masses
❶ a large amount of something • *They had gathered a mass of evidence.* ❷ a heap or other collection of matter • *A huge mass of snow and rocks blocked the path.* ❸ (*in science*) the quantity of physical matter that a thing contains
➤ **the masses** the ordinary people

mass *ADJECTIVE*
involving a large number of people • *mass murder*

mass *VERB* masses, massing, massed
to collect into a mass • *People were massing in the square.*

massacre *NOUN* massacres
the deliberate and brutal killing of a large number of people

massacre *VERB* massacres, massacring, massacred
to kill a large number of people deliberately

massage (say **mas**-ahzh) *VERB* massages, massaging, massaged
to rub and press the body to make it less stiff or less painful

massage *NOUN* massages
massaging someone's body

massive *ADJECTIVE*
large and heavy; huge
➤ **massively** *ADVERB*

mass media *PLURAL NOUN*
the main media of news information, especially newspapers and broadcasting

mass production *NOUN*
manufacturing goods in large quantities
➤ **mass-produced** *ADJECTIVE*

mast *NOUN* masts
a tall pole that holds up a ship's sails or a flag or an aerial

master *NOUN* masters
❶ a man who is in charge of something ❷ a person who is extremely skilled at doing something, such as a great artist or composer ❸ (*old use*) a male teacher ❹ something from which copies are made ❺ (*old use*) a title put before a boy's name

master *VERB* masters, mastering, mastered
❶ to master a subject or a skill is to learn it thoroughly ❷ to master a fear or difficulty is to control it • *She succeeded in mastering her fear of heights.* ❸ to overcome someone

masterful *ADJECTIVE*
having control; domineering
➤ **masterfully** *ADVERB*

master key *NOUN* master keys
a key that will open several different locks

masterly *ADJECTIVE*
very skilful • *a masterly performance*

mastermind *NOUN* masterminds
❶ a very clever person ❷ the person who plans and organizes a scheme or crime

mastermind *VERB* masterminds, masterminding, masterminded
to plan and organize a scheme or crime

Master of Arts *NOUN* Masters of Arts
a person who has taken the next degree after Bachelor of Arts

master of ceremonies *NOUN* masters of ceremonies
a person who introduces the speakers at a formal event or the entertainers at a variety show

Master of Science *NOUN* Masters of Science
a person who has taken the next degree after Bachelor of Science

masterpiece *NOUN* masterpieces
❶ an excellent piece of work ❷ a person's best piece of work

mastery *NOUN*
complete control or thorough knowledge or skill in something • *The battle was fought for mastery of the seas.*

masticate *VERB* masticates, masticating, masticated (*formal*)
to chew food
➤ **mastication** *NOUN*

mastiff *NOUN* mastiffs
a large kind of dog

masturbate *VERB* masturbates, masturbating, masturbated
to get sexual pleasure by touching the genitals
➤ **masturbation** *NOUN*

mat *NOUN* mats
❶ a small carpet ❷ a doormat ❸ a small piece of material put on a table to protect the surface

matador *NOUN* matadors
a bullfighter who fights on foot

match *NOUN* matches
❶ a small thin stick with a head made of a substance that gives a flame when rubbed on something rough ❷ a game or contest between two teams or players ❸ one person or thing that is equal to or similar to another • *Can you find a match for this sock?* ❹ a marriage

match *VERB* matches, matching, matched
❶ to be equal or similar to another person or thing • *This book doesn't match the standard of her earlier ones.* ❷ to go well with something so that they look good together • *That shirt matches your jacket.* ❸ to find something that is similar or corresponding ❹ to put teams or players together to compete against each other

matchbox *NOUN* matchboxes
a small box for matches

matchstick *NOUN* matchsticks
the thin wooden part of a match

mate *NOUN* mates
❶ a friend or companion ❷ each of a pair of birds or animals that produce young together ❸ an officer on a merchant ship ❹ checkmate in chess

mate *VERB* mates, mating, mated
❶ a pair of animals or birds mate when they come together in order to breed ❷ to mate a pair of animals is to bring them together in order to breed

material *NOUN* materials
❶ anything used for making something else ❷ cloth or fabric

material *ADJECTIVE*
❶ to do with possessions, money, etc. • *material comforts* ❷ important or relevant • *The changes made little material difference.*

materialism *NOUN*
the belief that possessions are very important

➤ **materialist** *NOUN*
➤ **materialistic** *ADJECTIVE*

materialize (also **materialise**) *VERB*
materializes, materializing, materialized
❶ to become visible; to appear • *The ghost didn't materialize.* ❷ to become a fact; to happen • *The trip he had been promised failed to materialize.*

maternal *ADJECTIVE*
❶ to do with a mother ❷ motherly

maternity *NOUN*
motherhood

maternity *ADJECTIVE*
to do with having a baby • *maternity ward*

matey *ADJECTIVE*
(*British*) (*informal*) friendly and sociable

mathematical *ADJECTIVE*
to do with or using mathematics
• *mathematical calculations*
➤ **mathematically** *ADVERB*

mathematician (say math-em-a-**tish**-an)
NOUN mathematicians
an expert in mathematics

mathematics *NOUN*
the study of numbers, measurements and shapes

maths *NOUN* (*British*) (*informal*)
mathematics

matinee *NOUN* matinees
an afternoon performance at a theatre or cinema **WORD ORIGIN** French *matinée*, literally = morning, because the performances used to be in the morning as well as the afternoon

matins *NOUN*
the church service of morning prayer

matriarch (say **may**-tree-ark) *NOUN*
matriarchs
a woman who is head of a family or tribe. Compare with **patriarch**.
➤ **matriarchal** *ADJECTIVE*

matrimony *NOUN*
marriage
➤ **matrimonial** *ADJECTIVE*

matrix (say **may**-triks) *NOUN* matrices, (say **may**-tri-seez)
❶ (*in mathematics*) a set of quantities arranged in rows and columns ❷ a mould or framework in which something is made or allowed to develop

matron *NOUN* matrons
❶ an older married woman ❷ a woman in charge of nursing in a school etc. or (formerly) of the nursing staff in a hospital
➤ **matronly** *ADJECTIVE*

matt *ADJECTIVE*
not shiny • *matt paint*

matted *ADJECTIVE*
matted hair or fur is tangled into a mass

matter *NOUN* matters
❶ something you can touch or see, not the spirit or mind or qualities etc. ❷ a substance • *Peat consists mainly of vegetable matter.* ❸ things of a certain kind • *printed matter* ❹ something you can think about or do • *It's a serious matter.* ❺ a quantity • *in a matter of minutes*
➤ **as a matter of course** as the natural or expected thing • *I always lock my bike up, as a matter of course*
➤ **as a matter of fact** in fact
➤ **no matter** it is not important
➤ **what is the matter?** what is wrong?

matter *VERB* matters, mattering, mattered
to be important • *Nobody's hurt and that's all that matters.*

matter-of-fact *ADJECTIVE*
keeping to facts; not imaginative or emotional • *She talked about death in a very matter-of-fact way.*

matting *NOUN*
rough material for covering floors

mattress *NOUN* mattresses
soft or springy material in a fabric covering, used on or as a bed

mature *ADJECTIVE*
❶ fully grown or developed ❷ behaving in a sensible adult manner
➤ **maturely** *ADVERB*

mature *VERB* matures, maturing, matured
to become fully grown or developed • *It takes a few years for the wine to mature.*

maturity *NOUN*
❶ being fully grown or developed • *The forest will take 100 years to reach maturity.* ❷ behaving in a sensible adult manner

maudlin *ADJECTIVE*
sentimental in a silly or tearful way
WORD ORIGIN from an old pronunciation of St Mary Magdalen (because pictures usually show her weeping)

maul *VERB* **mauls, mauling, mauled**
to injure someone by violent handling or clawing • *He was mauled by a lion.*

mausoleum (say maw-sol-**ee**-um) *NOUN* **mausoleums**
a magnificent tomb **WORD ORIGIN** named after the tomb of *Mausolus,* a king in the 4th century BC in what is now Turkey

mauve (say mohv) *NOUN*
pale purple

maverick *NOUN* **mavericks**
a person who belongs to a group but often disagrees with its beliefs or acts on his or her own **WORD ORIGIN** originally = an unbranded calf: named after an American rancher, S. A. *Maverick,* who did not brand his cattle

maw *NOUN* **maws**
the jaws, mouth or stomach of a hungry or fierce animal

maxilla *NOUN* **maxillae,** (say **mak**-si-lee)
the upper jaw; a similar part in a bird or insect etc. Compare with **mandible.**

maxim *NOUN* **maxims**
a short saying giving a general truth or rule of behaviour, e.g. 'Waste not, want not'

maximize (also **maximise**) *VERB* **maximizes, maximizing, maximized**
to make something as great, large or effective as possible

maximum *NOUN* **maxima** or **maximums**
the greatest possible number or amount. (The opposite is **minimum.**) • *The bus can carry a maximum of 40 people.*

maximum *ADJECTIVE*
the greatest possible • *The maximum speed is 50 km per hour.*

May *NOUN*
the fifth month of the year
WORD ORIGIN named after *Maia,* a Roman goddess

may *AUXILIARY VERB* **may, might**
used to express
❶ permission (*You may go now*) ❷ possibility (*It may be true*) ❸ wish (*Long may she reign*) ❹ uncertainty (*whoever it may be*)

maybe *ADVERB*
perhaps; possibly

Mayday *NOUN* **Maydays**
an international radio signal calling for help
WORD ORIGIN from French *m'aider* = help me

mayfly *NOUN* **mayflies**
an insect that lives for only a short time, in spring

mayhem *NOUN*
violent confusion or damage • *The mob caused mayhem.*

mayonnaise *NOUN*
a creamy sauce made from eggs, oil, vinegar, etc., eaten with salad

mayor *NOUN* **mayors**
the person in charge of the council in a town or city
➤ **mayoress** *NOUN*

maypole *NOUN* **maypoles**
a decorated pole round which people dance on 1 May

maze *NOUN* **mazes**
a network of paths, especially one designed as a puzzle in which to try and find your way

Mb *ABBREVIATION*
megabyte(s)

MC *ABBREVIATION*
master of ceremonies

MD *ABBREVIATION*
Doctor of Medicine

ME *NOUN*
(*British*) long-lasting fever, weakness and pain in the muscles following a viral infection
WORD ORIGIN abbreviation of the scientific name, *myalgic encephalomyelitis*

me *PRONOUN*
the form of I used as the object of a verb or after a preposition

mead *NOUN*
an alcoholic drink made from honey and water

meadow (say **med**-oh) *NOUN* **meadows**
a field of grass

meagre *ADJECTIVE*
scanty in amount; barely enough • *a meagre diet of bread and water*

meal *NOUN* **meals**
❶ food served and eaten at one sitting
❷ coarsely-ground grain

mealie *NOUN* **mealies**
(*S. African*) a maize plant or cob

mealtime *NOUN* **mealtimes**
a regular time for having a meal

mealy-mouthed *ADJECTIVE*
too polite or timid to say what you really mean

mean *VERB* **means, meaning, meant** (say ment)
❶ to have something as an equivalent or explanation; have a certain meaning • *I'm not sure what this word means.* ❷ to intend to do something • *I meant to tell you, but I forgot.* ❸ to be serious • *Don't open that door – I mean it!* ❹ to show that something is likely • *Dark clouds mean rain.* ❺ to have something as a result • *It means I'll have to get the early train.*

mean *ADJECTIVE* **meaner, meanest**
❶ not generous; miserly ❷ unkind or spiteful • *That was a mean trick.* ❸ poor in quality or appearance • *They lived in a mean little hovel.*
➤ **meanly** *ADVERB*
➤ **meanness** *NOUN*

mean *NOUN* **means**
a point or number midway between two extremes; the average of a set of numbers

mean *ADJECTIVE*
midway between two points; average • *We worked out the mean temperature.*

meander (say mee-**an**-der) *VERB* **meanders, meandering, meandered**
❶ a river or road that meanders has a lot of bends in it ❷ to walk or travel slowly or without any definite direction
➤ **meander** *NOUN*
WORD ORIGIN named after the *Meander*, a river in Turkey (now Mendere or Menderes)

meaning *NOUN* **meanings**
what something means

meaningful *ADJECTIVE*
expressing an important meaning • *He gave her a meaningful look.*

meaningless *ADJECTIVE*
with no meaning or purpose • *a meaningless phrase*

means *NOUN*
a way of achieving something or producing a result • *a means of transport*
➤ **by all means** certainly; of course
➤ **by means of** by this method; using this
➤ **by no means** not at all

means *PLURAL NOUN*
money or other wealth
➤ **live beyond your means** to spend more than you can afford

meantime *NOUN*
➤ **in the meantime** in the time between two events or while something else is happening

meanwhile *ADVERB*
in the time between two events or while something else is happening

measles *NOUN*
an infectious disease that causes small red spots on the skin

measly *ADJECTIVE* (*informal*)
not adequate or generous • *I only got a measly three points.*

measure *VERB* **measures, measuring, measured**
❶ to find the size, amount or extent of something by comparing it with a fixed unit or with an object of known size ❷ to be a certain size • *The room measures 4 metres by 5.*

measure *NOUN* **measures**
❶ a unit used for measuring • *A kilometre is a measure of length.* ❷ a device used in measuring ❸ the size or quantity of something ❹ something done for a particular purpose • *We took measures to stop vandalism.*

measurement *NOUN* **measurements**
❶ the process of measuring something ❷ a size or amount found by measuring • *She took some measurements with a ruler.*

meat *NOUN*
animal flesh used as food
➤ **meaty** *ADJECTIVE*

mecca *NOUN*
a place which attracts people with a particular interest • *Wimbledon is a mecca for tennis fans.* **WORD ORIGIN** from *Mecca* in Saudi Arabia, a holy city and place of pilgrimage for Muslims

mechanic *NOUN* **mechanics**
a person who maintains or repairs machinery

mechanical *ADJECTIVE*
❶ to do with machines ❷ produced or worked by machines ❸ done or doing something without thinking about it

mechanically *ADVERB*
without thinking about it • *'That's good,' she replied mechanically.*

mechanics *NOUN*
❶ the study of movement and force ❷ the study or use of machines

mechanism *NOUN* mechanisms
❶ the moving parts of a machine ❷ the way a machine works ❸ the process by which something is done

mechanized (also **mechanised**) *ADJECTIVE* equipped with machines
➤ **mechanization** *NOUN*

medal *NOUN* medals
a piece of metal shaped like a coin, star or cross, given to a person for bravery or for achieving something • *She won two Olympic gold medals.*

medallion *NOUN* medallions
a large medal, usually worn round the neck as an ornament

medallist *NOUN* medallists
a winner of a medal

meddle *VERB* meddles, meddling, meddled
❶ to interfere in something without being asked ❷ to tinker with something • *Don't meddle with it.*
➤ **meddlesome** *ADJECTIVE*

media
plural of **medium noun**
➤ **the media** newspapers, radio and television, which convey information and ideas to the public. (see **medium**)

median *ADJECTIVE*
in the middle

median *NOUN* medians
❶ a median point or line ❷ (*in mathematics*) the middle number in a set of numbers that have been arranged in order. The median of 2, 3, 5, 8, 9, 14 and 15 is 8 ❸ a straight line passing from a point of a triangle to the centre of the opposite side

mediate *VERB* mediates, mediating, mediated
to negotiate between the opposing sides in a dispute
➤ **mediation** *NOUN*
➤ **mediator** *NOUN*

medical *ADJECTIVE*
to do with the treatment of disease
➤ **medically** *ADVERB*

medicated *ADJECTIVE*
treated with a medicinal substance • *medicated shampoo*

medication *NOUN*
❶ a medicine ❷ treatment using medicine

medicinal (say med-**iss**-in-al) *ADJECTIVE*
helping to cure an illness • *medicinal plants*
➤ **medicinally** *ADVERB*

medicine *NOUN* medicines
❶ a substance, usually swallowed, used to try to cure a disease ❷ the study and treatment of diseases

medieval (say med-ee-**ee**-val) *ADJECTIVE*
belonging to or to do with the Middle Ages

> **SPELLING**
> There is a tricky bit in **medieval** – it is spelt **al** at the end and not **il**.

mediocre (say mee-dee-**oh**-ker) *ADJECTIVE*
not very good; of only medium quality
➤ **mediocrity** *NOUN*

meditate *VERB* meditates, meditating, meditated
❶ to think deeply or seriously about something ❷ to think deeply in silence for religious reasons or to make your mind calm
➤ **meditation** *NOUN*
➤ **meditative** *ADJECTIVE*

Mediterranean *ADJECTIVE*
to do with the Mediterranean Sea (which lies between Europe and Africa) or the countries round it **WORD ORIGIN** from Latin *Mare Mediterraneum* = sea in the middle of land, from *medius* = middle + *terra* = land

medium *ADJECTIVE*
neither large nor small; average

medium *NOUN*
❶ media a thing in which something exists, moves or is expressed • *Air is the medium in which sound travels.* • *Television is used as a medium for advertising.*
(see **media**) ❷ mediums a person who claims to be able to communicate with the dead

medium wave *NOUN*
(*chiefly British*) a radio wave of a frequency between 300 kilohertz and 3 megahertz

medley *NOUN* medleys
❶ an assortment or mixture of things • *a medley of flavours* ❷ a collection of songs or tunes played as a continuous piece

meek *ADJECTIVE* meeker, meekest
quiet and obedient
➤ **meekly** *ADVERB*
➤ **meekness** *NOUN*

meet *VERB* meets, meeting, met
❶ to come together from different places • *We all met in London.* ❷ to see someone for the first time and get to know them • *I*

met her at a party. ❸ to go to a place and wait there for someone to arrive • *I'll meet you off the train.* ❹ to touch, join or come into contact • *They came to a spot where two rivers met.* ❺ to meet the cost of something is to pay it ❻ to satisfy or fulfil something • *I hope this meets your needs.*
➤ **meet with something** to get a particular reaction or result • *My suggestion was met with howls of protest.*

meet *NOUN* meets
a gathering of riders and hounds for a hunt

meeting *NOUN* meetings
❶ a time when a number of people come together in order to discuss or decide something ❷ coming together

megabyte *NOUN* megabytes
(*in computing*) a unit of information roughly equal to one million bytes

megalomaniac *NOUN* megalomaniacs
a person who has an exaggerated idea of their own importance
➤ **megalomania** *NOUN*

megaphone *NOUN* megaphones
a funnel-shaped device for amplifying a person's voice

melancholy *ADJECTIVE*
sad and gloomy

melancholy *NOUN*
sadness or depression • *There was an air of melancholy about her.*

melee (say **mel**-ay) *NOUN* melees
a situation in which a lot of people are rushing or pushing each other in a confused way

mellow *ADJECTIVE* mellower, mellowest
❶ not harsh; soft and rich in flavour, colour or sound ❷ having become kinder and more sympathetic with age

mellow *VERB* mellows, mellowing, mellowed
❶ to make something softer or less harsh or to become this ❷ a person mellows when they become kinder and more sympathetic with age

melodic *ADJECTIVE*
to do with melody; pleasant to listen to

melodious *ADJECTIVE*
like a melody; pleasant to listen to • *a melodious voice*

melodrama *NOUN* melodramas
a play full of dramatic excitement and strong emotion

melodramatic *ADJECTIVE*
behaving in an exaggerated way that is full of emotion • *Don't be so melodramatic – of course you're not going to die!*

melody *NOUN* melodies
a tune, especially one that is pleasant to listen to

melon *NOUN* melons
a large sweet fruit with a yellow or green skin

melt *VERB* melts, melting, melted
❶ to make something liquid by heating it • *Melt the butter in a saucepan.* ❷ to become liquid by heating • *The snow has melted.* ❸ to disappear slowly • *The crowd just melted away.* ❹ to become softer • *Her heart melted at these words.*

melting pot *NOUN* melting pots
a place where people of many different races and cultures live and influence each other

member *NOUN* members
❶ a person or thing that belongs to a particular society or group ❷ a part of something

Member of Parliament *NOUN* Members of Parliament
a person elected to represent the people of an area in Parliament

membership *NOUN*
being a member of a particular society or group • *Visit our website to apply for membership.*

membrane *NOUN* membranes
a thin skin or similar covering

memento *NOUN* mementoes
a souvenir

memo (say **mem**-oh) *NOUN* memos
a note from one person to another in the same firm

memoir (say **mem**-wahr) *NOUN* memoirs
a biography, especially one written by someone who knew the person

memoirs *PLURAL NOUN*
an autobiography

memorable *ADJECTIVE*
❶ worth remembering • *It was a memorable holiday.* ❷ easy to remember • *He has a memorable name.*
➤ **memorably** *ADVERB*

memorandum *NOUN* memoranda or memorandums
(*formal*) a memo

memorial *NOUN* memorials
something set up to remind people of a person or event • *a war memorial*
➤ **memorial** *ADJECTIVE*

memorize (also **memorise**) *VERB* memorizes, memorizing, memorized
to learn something so that you can remember it exactly

memory *NOUN* memories
❶ the ability to remember things
❷ something that you remember from the past ❸ the part of a computer where information is stored
➤ **in memory of someone** in order to remind people of someone who has died

menace *NOUN* menaces
❶ a threat or danger ❷ a troublesome person or thing

menace *VERB* menaces, menacing, menaced
to threaten someone with harm or danger

menacing *ADJECTIVE*
threatening to cause harm or danger • *There was something menacing in the tone of his voice.*

menagerie *NOUN* menageries
a small zoo

mend *VERB* mends, mending, mended
❶ to repair something broken ❷ to make something better • *He promised he would mend his ways.*
➤ **mender** *NOUN*

mend *NOUN*
➤ **on the mend** getting better after an illness

meneer *NOUN*
(*S. African*) a title in Afrikaans meaning 'Mr' or 'sir'

menial (say **meen**-ee-al) *ADJECTIVE*
needing little or no skill or thought • *menial tasks*

menial *NOUN* menials
a person who does menial work; a servant

meningitis *NOUN*
a disease causing inflammation of the membranes (*meninges*) round the brain and spinal cord

menopause *NOUN*
the time of life when a woman gradually stops menstruating

menstruate *VERB* menstruates, menstruating, menstruated
to bleed from the womb about once a month, as girls and women normally do from their

teens until middle age
➤ **menstruation** *NOUN*
➤ **menstrual** *ADJECTIVE*

mental *ADJECTIVE*
❶ to do with or in the mind • *mental arithmetic* ❷ (*informal*) mad

mentality *NOUN* mentalities
a person's mental ability or attitude

mentally *ADVERB*
in your mind; to do with the mind • *She mentally added up how much she had spent.*

menthol *NOUN*
a solid white peppermint-flavoured substance

mention *VERB* mentions, mentioning, mentioned
to speak or write about a person or thing briefly; to refer to a person or thing

mention *NOUN* mentions
an example of mentioning someone or something • *Our school got a mention in the local paper.*

mentor *NOUN* mentors
an experienced and trusted adviser
WORD ORIGIN named after *Mentor* in Greek legend, who advised Odysseus' son

menu (say **men**-yoo) *NOUN* menus
❶ a list of the food available in a restaurant or served at a meal ❷ (*in computing*) a list of possible actions, shown on a screen, from which you choose what you want a computer to do

MEP *ABBREVIATION*
Member of the European Parliament

mercantile *ADJECTIVE*
to do with trade or trading

mercenary *ADJECTIVE*
interested only in the money you can get for the work you do

mercenary *NOUN* mercenaries
a soldier who fights for any army or country that will pay them

merchandise *NOUN*
goods for sale

merchant *NOUN* merchants
a person involved in trade

merchant bank *NOUN* merchant banks
(*British*) a bank that gives loans and advice to businesses

a b c d e f g h i j k l m n o p q r s t u v w x y z

merchant navy *NOUN*
(*British*) the ships and sailors that carry goods for trade

merciful *ADJECTIVE*
showing mercy
➤ **mercifully** *ADVERB*

merciless *ADJECTIVE*
showing no mercy; cruel
➤ **mercilessly** *ADVERB*

mercurial *ADJECTIVE*
❶ having sudden changes of mood ❷ to do with mercury

mercury *NOUN*
a heavy silvery metal that is usually liquid, used in thermometers

mercy *NOUN* mercies
❶ kindness or pity shown towards someone instead of harming them or punishing them ❷ something to be thankful for
➤ **at the mercy of someone** or **something** having no power against someone or something • *We were at the mercy of the weather.*

mere *ADJECTIVE*
not more than • *He's a mere child.*

mere *NOUN* meres
(*British*) (*poetical use*) a lake

merely *ADVERB*
only; simply • *He merely smiled and walked away.*

merest *ADJECTIVE*
very small or slight • *the merest trace of colour*

merge *VERB* merges, merging, merged
when two or more things merge they combine together to form a single thing • *The sea and the sky seemed to merge.*

merger *NOUN* mergers
the combining of two business companies into one

meridian *NOUN* meridians
a line on a map or globe from the North Pole to the South Pole. The meridian that passes through Greenwich is shown on maps as 0° longitude.

meringue (say mer-**ang**) *NOUN* meringues
a crisp cake made from egg white and sugar

merino *NOUN* merinos
a kind of sheep with fine soft wool

merit *NOUN* merits
❶ a quality that deserves praise • *I can see the merits of this argument.* ❷ excellence
➤ **meritorious** *ADJECTIVE*

merit *VERB* merits, meriting, merited
to deserve something • *This suggestion merits further discussion.*

mermaid *NOUN* mermaids
a mythical sea creature with a woman's body but with a fish's tail instead of legs
➤ **merman** *NOUN*

merriment *NOUN*
happy talk, enjoyment and the sound of people laughing

merry *ADJECTIVE* merrier, merriest
cheerful and lively
➤ **merrily** *ADVERB*

merry-go-round *NOUN* merry-go-rounds
a roundabout at a fair

mesh *NOUN* meshes
❶ the open spaces in a net, sieve or other criss-cross structure ❷ material made like a net

mesh *VERB* meshes, meshing, meshed
gears mesh when they fit together as they move

mesmerize (also **mesmerise**) *VERB*
mesmerizes, mesmerizing, mesmerized
❶ (*old use*) to hypnotize someone ❷ to fascinate or hold a person's attention completely • *The audience were mesmerized by his performance.*
➤ **mesmeric** *ADJECTIVE*
WORD ORIGIN named after an Austrian doctor, F. A. *Mesmer,* who made hypnosis famous

mess *NOUN* messes
❶ a dirty or untidy condition or thing ❷ a difficult or confused situation ❸ in the armed forces, a dining room
➤ **make a mess of something** to do something very badly

mess *VERB* messes, messing, messed
➤ **mess about** to behave stupidly or idly
➤ **mess something up** ❶ to make a thing dirty or untidy ❷ to bungle or ruin something • *They messed up our plans.*
➤ **mess with something** to interfere or tinker with something

message *NOUN* messages
❶ a piece of information sent from one person to another • *I left a message on her voicemail.* ❷ the main theme or moral of a

book, film, etc. • *It is a funny film but it also has a serious message.*

messenger *NOUN* **messengers**
a person who carries a message

Messiah (say mis-**y**-a) *NOUN* **Messiahs**
❶ the saviour expected by the Jews ❷ Jesus Christ, who Christians believe was this saviour

Messrs (plural of **Mr**)

messy *ADJECTIVE* **messier, messiest**
❶ dirty and untidy ❷ difficult and complicated • *I'm afraid it's a messy situation.*
➤ **messily** *ADVERB*
➤ **messiness** *NOUN*

metabolism (say mit-**ab**-ol-izm) *NOUN*
the process by which food is built up into living material in a plant or animal or used to supply it with energy
➤ **metabolic** *ADJECTIVE*

metal *NOUN* **metals**
a chemical substance, usually hard, that conducts heat and electricity and melts when it is heated. Gold, silver, copper, iron and uranium are metals.

metallic *ADJECTIVE*
made of or like metal • *a metallic sound*

metallurgy (say mit-**al**-er-jee) *NOUN*
❶ the study of metals ❷ the craft of making and using metals
➤ **metallurgist** *NOUN*

metamorphic *ADJECTIVE*
formed or changed by heat or pressure • *Marble is a metamorphic rock.*

metamorphosis (say met-a-**mor**-fo-sis) *NOUN*
metamorphoses (say met-a-**mor**- fo-seez)
❶ a complete change made by some living things, such as a caterpillar changing into a butterfly ❷ a change of form or character
➤ **metamorphose** *VERB*

metaphor *NOUN* **metaphors**
using a word or phrase in a way that describes one thing as if it were something else, e.g. 'He was a little monkey' and 'Her heart leapt for joy'

SPELLING
The 'f' sound is spelt **ph** in **metaphor**.

metaphorical *ADJECTIVE*
to do with or using metaphors • *metaphorical language*
➤ **metaphorically** *ADVERB*

mete *VERB* **metes, meting, meted**
➤ **mete something out** to give someone a punishment or bad treatment • *Severe penalties were meted out.*

meteor (say **meet**-ee-er) *NOUN* **meteors**
a piece of rock or metal that moves through space and burns up when it enters the earth's atmosphere

meteoric (say meet-ee-o-rik) *ADJECTIVE*
❶ to do with meteors ❷ becoming very successful very rapidly • *They have had a meteoric rise to fame.*

meteorite *NOUN* **meteorites**
the remains of a meteor that has landed on the earth

meteorology *NOUN*
the study of the conditions of the atmosphere, especially in order to forecast the weather
➤ **meteorological** *ADJECTIVE*
➤ **meteorologist** *NOUN*

meter *NOUN* **meters**
a device for measuring something, especially the amount of something used • *a gas meter*
➤ **meter** *VERB*

SPELLING
Meter is different from **metre**: • *an electricity meter* • *The table measures two metres.*

methane (say **mee**-thayn) *NOUN*
an inflammable gas produced by decaying matter

method *NOUN* **methods**
❶ a procedure or way of doing something ❷ good organization or orderly behaviour

methodical *ADJECTIVE*
doing things in a careful and well-organized way • *He is a methodical worker.*
➤ **methodically** *ADVERB*

Methodist *NOUN* **Methodists**
a member of a Christian religious group started by John and Charles Wesley in the 18th century
➤ **Methodism** *NOUN*

methodology *NOUN* **methodologies**
the methods and main principles that you use when you are studying a particular subject or doing a particular kind of work

meths *NOUN* (*British*) (*informal*)
methylated spirit

methylated spirit, **spirits** *NOUN*
a liquid fuel made from alcohol

meticulous *ADJECTIVE*
very careful and precise • *She keeps
meticulous records.*
➤ **meticulously** *ADVERB*

metre *NOUN* **metres**
❶ a unit of length in the metric system,
about 39½ inches ❷ rhythm in poetry

> SPELLING
> **Metre** is different from **meter:** • *The
> table measures two metres.* • *an
> electricity meter*

metric *ADJECTIVE*
❶ to do with the metric system ❷ to do with
metre in poetry
➤ **metrically** *ADVERB*

metrical *ADJECTIVE*
in, or to do with, rhythmic metre, not prose
• *metrical psalms*

metric system *NOUN*
a measuring system based on decimal units
(the metre, litre and gram)

metric ton *NOUN* **metric tons**
1,000 kilograms

metronome *NOUN* **metronomes**
a device that makes a regular clicking noise to
help you keep in time when practising music

metropolis *NOUN* **metropolises**
the chief city of a country or region

metropolitan *ADJECTIVE*
❶ to do with a metropolis ❷ to do with a city
and its suburbs

mettle *NOUN*
courage or strength of character • *The next
game will be a real test of their mettle.*
➤ **be on your mettle** to be ready to show
your courage or ability

mew *VERB* **mews, mewing, mewed**
to make a cat's cry

mew *NOUN* **mews**
a cat's cry

mews *NOUN* **mews**
(*British*) a row of houses in a small street
or square, converted from former stables
WORD ORIGIN first used of royal stables in
London, built on the site of hawks' cages (called
mews)

miaow (say mee-**ow**) *VERB* **miaows, miaowing,
miaowed**
to make a cat's cry

miaow *NOUN* **miaows**
a cat's cry

miasma (say mee-**az**-ma) *NOUN* **miasmas**
unpleasant or unhealthy air

mica *NOUN*
a mineral substance used to make electrical
insulators

mice
plural of **mouse**

microbe *NOUN* **microbes**
a tiny organism that can only be seen with a
microscope; a microorganism

microchip *NOUN* **microchips**
a very small piece of silicon etc. made to work
like a complex wired electric circuit

microcomputer *NOUN* **microcomputers**
a small computer with a microprocessor as its
central processing unit

microcosm *NOUN* **microcosms**
a world in miniature; something regarded as
resembling something else on a very small
scale

microfiche *NOUN* **microfiches**
a piece of film on which pages of information
are photographed in greatly reduced size

microfilm *NOUN*
a length of film on which written or printed
material is photographed in greatly reduced
size

micron *NOUN* **microns**
a unit of measurement equal to one millionth
of a metre

microorganism *NOUN* **microorganisms**
a microscopic creature, e.g. a bacterium or
virus

microphone *NOUN* **microphones**
an electrical device that picks up sound waves
for recording them or making them louder

microprocessor *NOUN* **microprocessors**
the central processing unit of a computer,
consisting of one or more microchips

microscope *NOUN* **microscopes**
an instrument with lenses that magnify tiny
objects or details

microscopic *ADJECTIVE*
❶ extremely small; too small to be seen

without the aid of a microscope • *microscopic creatures* ❷ to do with a microscope

microwave *NOUN* microwaves
❶ a very short electromagnetic wave ❷ a microwave oven

microwave *VERB* microwaves, microwaving, microwaved
to cook food in a microwave oven

microwave oven *NOUN* microwave ovens
an oven that uses microwaves to heat or cook food very quickly

mid *ADJECTIVE*
❶ in the middle of • *mid-July* ❷ middle • *He's in his mid thirties.*

mid-air *NOUN*
the area above the ground; the open sky • *The bird caught the insects in mid-air.*

midday *NOUN*
the middle of the day; noon

middle *NOUN* middles
❶ the place or part of something that is at the same distance from all its sides or edges or from both its ends ❷ someone's waist
➤ **in the middle of something** during or halfway through a process or activity • *I'm just in the middle of cooking.*

middle *ADJECTIVE*
❶ placed or happening in the middle ❷ moderate in size or rank etc.

middle-aged *ADJECTIVE*
aged between about 45 and 65
➤ **middle age** *NOUN*

Middle Ages *NOUN*
the period in history from about AD 1000 to 1400

middle class, classes *NOUN*
the class of people between the upper class and the working class, including business and professional people such as teachers, doctors and lawyers
➤ **middle-class** *ADJECTIVE*

Middle East *NOUN*
the countries from Egypt to Iran inclusive

Middle English *NOUN*
the English language from about 1150 to 1500

middleman *NOUN* middlemen
❶ a trader who buys from a producer and sells to a consumer ❷ a go-between or intermediary

middle school *NOUN* middle schools
a school for children aged from about 9 to 13

middling *ADJECTIVE*
of medium size or quality

midge *NOUN* midges
a small insect like a gnat

midget *NOUN* midgets
an extremely small person or thing
➤ **midget** *ADJECTIVE*

midland *ADJECTIVE*
❶ to do with the middle part of a country
❷ to do with the Midlands

Midlands *PLURAL NOUN*
the central part of a country, especially the central counties of England

midnight *NOUN*
twelve o'clock at night

midriff *NOUN* midriffs
the front part of the body just above the waist

midshipman *NOUN* midshipmen
a sailor ranking next above a cadet

midst *NOUN*
➤ **in the midst of** in the middle of or surrounded by • *The country is in the midst of a recession.*
➤ **in our midst** among us • *There is a traitor in our midst.*

midsummer *NOUN*
the middle part of summer

Midsummer's Day *NOUN*
24 June

midway *ADVERB*
halfway between two points

midwife *NOUN* midwives
a person trained to look after a woman who is giving birth to a baby
➤ **midwifery** (say **mid**-wif-ri) *NOUN*

midwinter *NOUN*
the middle part of winter

mien (say meen) *NOUN* (*old or poetical use*)
a person's manner and expression • *a tall youth of noble mien*

might *NOUN*
great strength or power
➤ **with all your might** using all your strength and determination

might *AUXILIARY VERB*
❶ the past tense of **may** (*We told her she*

might go.) ❷ used to express possibility (*It might be true.*)

mightily *ADVERB*
❶ very; very much • *We were mightily impressed.* ❷ with great strength or effort • *They fought mightily.*

mighty *ADJECTIVE*
very strong or powerful • *a mighty blow*

migraine (say **mee**-grayn or **my**-grayn) *NOUN* migraines
a severe kind of headache

migrant *NOUN* migrants
a person or animal that migrates or has migrated

migrate *VERB* migrates, migrating, migrated
❶ to leave one place or country and settle in another ❷ birds and animals migrate when they move periodically from one area to another
➤ **migratory** *ADJECTIVE*

migration *NOUN* migrations
moving in large numbers from one area to another • *seasonal migration of birds*

mike *NOUN* mikes (*informal*)
a microphone

mild *ADJECTIVE* milder, mildest
❶ not harsh or severe • *a mild infection* ❷ not great or extreme; slight • *a look of mild surprise* ❸ gentle and kind ❹ not strongly flavoured • *a mild curry* ❺ mild weather is quite warm and pleasant
➤ **mildness** *NOUN*

mildew *NOUN*
a tiny fungus that forms a white coating on things kept in damp conditions
➤ **mildewed** *ADJECTIVE*

mildly *ADVERB*
❶ slightly • *She was mildly irritated by this.* ❷ in a gentle manner

mile *NOUN* miles
a measure of distance equal to 1,760 yards (about 1.6 kilometres)

mileage *NOUN* mileages
the number of miles you have travelled

milestone *NOUN* milestones
❶ a stone of a kind that used to be fixed beside a road to mark the distance between towns ❷ an important stage or event in history or in a person's life

militant *ADJECTIVE*
❶ eager to fight ❷ forceful or aggressive • *a*

militant protest
➤ **militant** *NOUN*
➤ **militancy** *NOUN*

military *ADJECTIVE*
to do with soldiers or the armed forces
➤ **the military** a country's armed forces

militate *VERB* militates, militating, militated
to be a strong influence against something; to make something difficult or unlikely • *The weather militated against the success of our plans.*

militia (say mil-**ish**-a) *NOUN* militias
a military force, especially one raised from civilians

milk *NOUN*
❶ a white liquid that female mammals produce in their bodies to feed their babies ❷ the milk of cows, used as food by human beings ❸ a milky liquid, e.g. that in a coconut

milk *VERB* milks, milking, milked
to get the milk from a cow or other animal

milkman *NOUN* milkmen
a man who delivers milk to customers' houses

milkshake *NOUN* milkshakes
a cold frothy drink made from milk whisked with sweet fruit flavouring

milk tooth *NOUN* milk teeth
one of the first set of teeth of a child or animal, which will be replaced by adult teeth

milky *ADJECTIVE* milkier, milkiest
❶ like milk; white • *milky white skin* ❷ made with a lot of milk • *milky coffee*

Milky Way *NOUN*
the broad band of stars formed by our galaxy

mill *NOUN* mills
❶ machinery for grinding corn to make flour; a building containing this machinery ❷ a grinding machine • *a coffee mill* ❸ a factory for processing certain materials • *a paper mill*

mill *VERB* mills, milling, milled
❶ to grind or crush something in a mill ❷ to cut markings round the edge of a coin
➤ **mill about** or **around** to move in a confused crowd • *There were a lot of people milling about outside.*

millennium *NOUN* millenniums
a period of 1,000 years

miller *NOUN* millers
a person who runs a flour mill

millet *NOUN*
a kind of cereal with tiny seeds

milligram *NOUN* milligrams
one-thousandth of a gram

millilitre *NOUN* millilitres
one-thousandth of a litre

> **SPELLING**
>
> Take care: **millilitre** is spelt **re** at the end and not **er**.

millimetre *NOUN* millimetres
one-thousandth of a metre

> **SPELLING**
>
> Take care: **millimetre** is spelt **re** at the end and not **er**.

milliner *NOUN* milliners
a person who makes or sells women's hats
➤ **millinery** *NOUN*
WORD ORIGIN originally = a person from *Milan*, an Italian city where fashionable accessories and hats were made

million *NOUN & ADJECTIVE* millions
one thousand thousand (1,000,000)
➤ **millionth** *ADJECTIVE & NOUN*

millionaire *NOUN* millionaires
a person who has at least a million pounds or dollars; an extremely rich person

> **SPELLING**
>
> Double up the **l** in **millionaire** (but the **n** stays single).

millipede *NOUN* millipedes
a small crawling creature like a centipede, with many legs **WORD ORIGIN** from Latin *mille* = thousand + *pedes* = feet

millstone *NOUN* millstones
either of a pair of large circular stones between which corn is ground
➤ **a millstone around someone's neck** a heavy responsibility or burden

milometer *NOUN* milometers
(*British*) an instrument for measuring how far a vehicle has travelled

mime *NOUN* mimes
acting with movements of the body, not using words

mime *VERB* mimes, miming, mimed
to use mime to act or express something
• *She mimed washing her hands.*

mimic *VERB* mimics, mimicking, mimicked
to imitate someone, especially to amuse people
➤ **mimicry** *NOUN*

mimic *NOUN* mimics
a person who is good at imitating others

mimosa *NOUN* mimosas
a tropical tree or shrub with small ball-shaped flowers

minaret *NOUN* minarets
the tall tower of a mosque

mince *VERB* minces, mincing, minced
❶ to cut meat or other food into very small pieces in a machine ❷ to walk in an affected way with short quick steps
➤ **mincer** *NOUN*
➤ **not to mince words** or **matters** to speak bluntly

mince *NOUN* (*British*) minced meat

mincemeat *NOUN*
(*chiefly British*) a sweet mixture of currants, raisins, apple, etc. used in pies

mince pie *NOUN* mince pies
(*chiefly British*) a pie containing mincemeat

mind *NOUN* minds
❶ the ability to think, feel, understand and remember, originating in the brain • *He has a brilliant mind.* ❷ a person's thoughts, opinion or intention • *Have you made your mind up?* • *I changed my mind.*
➤ **in two minds** not able to decide
➤ **out of your mind** insane or very foolish

mind *VERB* minds, minding, minded
❶ to look after a person or animal for a while • *He was minding the baby.* ❷ to be careful about something • *Mind the step.* ❸ to be sad or upset about something; to object to something • *We don't mind waiting.*
➤ **minder** *NOUN*

mindful *ADJECTIVE*
taking thought or care • *He was mindful of his reputation.*

mindless *ADJECTIVE*
done without thinking; stupid or pointless

mine *POSSESSIVE PRONOUN*
belonging to me • *He is a friend of mine.*

mine *NOUN* mines
❶ a place where coal, metal or precious stones are dug out of the ground ❷ an explosive placed in or on the ground or in the sea to destroy people or things that come close to it

mine *VERB* mines, mining, mined
❶ to dig something from a mine ❷ to lay explosive mines in a place

minefield *NOUN* minefields
❶ an area where explosive mines have been laid ❷ something with hidden dangers or problems

miner *NOUN* miners
a person who works in a mine

mineral *NOUN* minerals
❶ a substance that is formed naturally in rocks and in the ground, such as iron, salt and coal ❷ a cold fizzy non-alcoholic drink

mineralogy (say min-er-**al**-o-jee) *NOUN*
the study of minerals
➤ **mineralogist** *NOUN*

mineral water *NOUN*
water from a natural spring, containing mineral salts or gases

minestrone (say mini-**stroh**-nee) *NOUN*
an Italian soup containing vegetables and pasta

mingle *VERB* mingles, mingling, mingled
to mix or blend with other things • *Tears ran down her face, mingling with the seawater.* • *The sounds of laughter and singing mingled in the evening air.*

mingy *ADJECTIVE* mingier, mingiest (*informal*)
not generous; mean

miniature *ADJECTIVE*
❶ very small ❷ copying something on a very small scale • *a miniature railway*

miniature *NOUN* miniatures
❶ a very small portrait ❷ a small-scale model

SPELLING
Take care with this word—there is an **a** after **mini**.

minibus *NOUN* minibuses
a small bus, seating about ten people

minim *NOUN* minims
a note in music, lasting twice as long as a crotchet (written ♩)

minimal *ADJECTIVE*
very little; as little as possible • *The damage to the car was minimal.*

minimize (also **minimise**) *VERB* minimizes, minimizing, minimized
to make something as small as possible • *Good hygiene helps to minimize the risk of infection.*

minimum *NOUN* minima or minimums
the lowest possible number or amount. (The opposite is **maximum**.) • *Keep the noise to a minimum.*

minimum *ADJECTIVE*
least or smallest • *What is the minimum amount of sleep you need?*

minion *NOUN* minions
a very humble or obedient assistant or servant

minister *NOUN* ministers
❶ a person in charge of a government department ❷ a member of the clergy
➤ **ministerial** *ADJECTIVE*

minister *VERB* ministers, ministering, ministered
to attend to people's needs

ministry *NOUN* ministries
❶ a government department • *the Ministry of Defence* ❷ the work of the clergy

mink *NOUN* mink or minks
❶ an animal rather like a stoat ❷ this animal's valuable brown fur or a coat made from it

minnow *NOUN* minnows
a tiny freshwater fish

minor *ADJECTIVE*
❶ not very important, especially when compared to something else • *a minor problem* ❷ of the musical scale that has a semitone after the second note. Compare with **major**.

minor *NOUN* minors
a person under the age of legal responsibility

minority *NOUN* minorities
❶ the smallest part of a group of people or things • *There was a minority who wanted to leave.* ❷ a small group that is different from others. Compare with **majority**.

minstrel *NOUN* minstrels
a travelling singer and musician in the Middle Ages

mint *NOUN* mints
❶ a plant with fragrant leaves that are used for flavouring things ❷ a sweet flavoured with peppermint ❸ the place where a country's coins are made
➤ **in mint condition** in perfect condition, as though it had never been used

mint *VERB* mints, minting, minted
to make coins by stamping metal

minuet *NOUN* minuets
a slow stately dance

minus *PREPOSITION*
with the next number or thing subtracted
• *Ten minus four equals six (10 - 4 = 6).*

minus *ADJECTIVE*
less than zero • *temperatures of minus ten degrees (-10°)*

minuscule *ADJECTIVE*
extremely small

minute (say **min**-it) *NOUN* **minutes**
❶ one-sixtieth of an hour ❷ a very short time; a moment • *I'll be ready in a minute.* ❸ one-sixtieth of a degree (used in measuring angles)

minute (say my-**newt**) *ADJECTIVE*
❶ very small • *a minute insect* ❷ very detailed • *a minute examination*

minutely *ADVERB*
in a very detailed way • *He examined the envelope minutely.*

minutes *PLURAL NOUN*
a written summary of what was said at a meeting

minx *NOUN* **minxes** (*old use*)
a cheeky or mischievous girl

miracle *NOUN* **miracles**
❶ a wonderful event that seems to be impossible and is believed to have a supernatural or divine cause ❷ something fortunate and surprising • *It's a miracle that no one was killed in the crash.*

miraculous *ADJECTIVE*
completely unexpected and very lucky • *She made a miraculous recovery.*
➤ **miraculously** *ADVERB*

mirage (say mi-**rahzh**) *NOUN* **mirages**
an illusion; something that seems to be there but is not, especially when a lake seems to appear in a desert

mire *NOUN*
❶ a swamp ❷ deep mud

mirror *NOUN* **mirrors**
a device or surface of reflecting material, usually glass

mirror *VERB* **mirrors, mirroring, mirrored**
to reflect something in or like a mirror • *She saw herself mirrored in the window.*

mirth *NOUN*
merriment or laughter • *His eyes twinkled with mirth.*
➤ **mirthful** *ADJECTIVE*
➤ **mirthless** *ADJECTIVE*

misadventure *NOUN* **misadventures**
a piece of bad luck

misapprehension *NOUN* **misapprehensions**
a wrong idea or impression of something

misbehave *VERB* **misbehaves, misbehaving, misbehaved**
to behave badly
➤ **misbehaviour** *NOUN*

miscalculate *VERB* **miscalculates, miscalculating, miscalculated**
to calculate something incorrectly • *I had miscalculated how long it would take.*
➤ **miscalculation** *NOUN*

miscarriage *NOUN* **miscarriages**
❶ a woman has a miscarriage when she gives birth to a baby before it has developed enough to survive ❷ failure to achieve the right result • *a miscarriage of justice*
➤ **miscarry** *VERB*

miscellaneous (say mis-el-**ay**-nee-us) *ADJECTIVE*
of various kinds; mixed • *miscellaneous musical instruments*

miscellany (say mis-**el**-an-ee) *NOUN* **miscellanies**
a collection or mixture of different things

mischance *NOUN*
misfortune; bad luck

mischief *NOUN*
❶ naughty or troublesome behaviour
❷ trouble caused by this

mischievous *ADJECTIVE*
liking to behave badly or cause trouble • *a mischievous grin*
➤ **mischievously** *ADVERB*

misconception *NOUN* **misconceptions**
a wrong or mistaken idea

misconduct *NOUN*
bad behaviour by someone in a responsible position • *professional misconduct*

misconstrue *VERB* **misconstrues, misconstruing, misconstrued**
to understand or interpret something wrongly

miscreant (say **mis**-kree-ant) *NOUN* **miscreants**
a wrongdoer or criminal

misdeed *NOUN* **misdeeds**
a wrong or wicked act

a
b
c
d
e
f
g
h
i
j
k
l
m
n
o
p
q
r
s
t
u
v
w
x
y
z

misdemeanour *NOUN* **misdemeanours**
an action which is wrong or illegal, but not very serious; a petty crime

miser *NOUN* **misers**
a person who hoards money and spends as little as possible
➤ **miserly** *ADJECTIVE*
➤ **miserliness** *NOUN*

miserable *ADJECTIVE*
❶ full of misery; very unhappy or uncomfortable ❷ unpleasant; making you feel depressed • *What miserable weather!*
➤ **miserably** *ADVERB*

misery *NOUN* **miseries**
❶ great unhappiness or discomfort or suffering, especially lasting for a long time ❷ (*informal*) a person who is always unhappy or complaining

misfire *VERB* **misfires, misfiring, misfired**
❶ a gun or engine misfires when it fails to fire or start ❷ a plan or idea or joke misfires when it goes wrong or has the wrong effect

misfit *NOUN* **misfits**
a person who does not fit in well with other people or with their surroundings

misfortune *NOUN* **misfortunes**
❶ bad luck ❷ an unlucky event or accident

misgiving *NOUN* **misgivings**
a feeling of doubt, or slight fear or mistrust • *I had serious misgivings about leaving him on his own.*

misguided *ADJECTIVE*
guided by mistaken ideas or beliefs

mishap (say **mis**-hap) *NOUN* **mishaps**
an unlucky accident

misinterpret *VERB* **misinterprets, misinterpreting, misinterpreted**
to interpret something incorrectly
➤ **misinterpretation** *NOUN*

misjudge *VERB* **misjudges, misjudging, misjudged**
to judge something wrongly; to form a wrong idea or opinion about someone or something • *I think I may have misjudged him.*
➤ **misjudgement** *NOUN*

mislay *VERB* **mislays, mislaying, mislaid**
to lose something for a short time because you cannot remember where you put it

mislead *VERB* **misleads, misleading, misled**
to give someone a wrong idea or impression deliberately

mismanagement *NOUN*
bad management

misplaced *ADJECTIVE*
❶ put in the wrong place ❷ inappropriate or unjustified • *misplaced loyalty*

misprint *NOUN* **misprints**
a mistake in printing, such as a spelling mistake

mispronounce *VERB* **mispronounces, mispronouncing, mispronounced**
to pronounce a word or name incorrectly
➤ **mispronunciation** *NOUN*

misquote *VERB* **misquotes, misquoting, misquoted**
to quote someone or something incorrectly
➤ **misquotation** *NOUN*

misread *VERB* **misreads, misreading, misread**
(say mis-**red**)
to read or interpret something incorrectly • *She had completely misread the situation.*

misrepresent *VERB* **misrepresents, misrepresenting, misrepresented**
to represent someone or something in a false or misleading way
➤ **misrepresentation** *NOUN*

misrule *NOUN*
bad government

Miss *NOUN* **Misses**
a title put before a girl's or unmarried woman's name

miss *VERB* **misses, missing, missed**
❶ to fail to hit, reach, catch, see, hear or find something ❷ to be sad because someone or something is not with you ❸ to miss a train, bus or plane is to arrive too late to catch it ❹ to miss a lesson or other activity is to fail to attend it • *How many classes have you missed?* ❺ to notice that something is not where it should be
➤ **miss something out** to leave something out
➤ **miss out on something** to not get the benefit or enjoyment from something that others have had

miss *NOUN* **misses**
missing something • *Was that shot a hit or a miss?*
➤ **give something a miss** to decide not to do or have something

misshapen *ADJECTIVE*
distorted or badly shaped

missile *NOUN* missiles
❶ a weapon that is fired a long distance and explodes when it hits its target ❷ an object that is thrown at someone in order to hurt them

missing *ADJECTIVE*
❶ lost; not in the proper place ❷ absent

mission *NOUN* missions
❶ an important job that someone is sent to do or feels they must do ❷ a place or building where missionaries work ❸ a military or scientific expedition • *a space mission*

missionary *NOUN* missionaries
a person who is sent to another country to spread a religious faith

misspell *VERB* misspells, misspelling, misspelt or misspelled
to spell a word wrongly

mist *NOUN* mists
❶ damp cloudy air near the ground ❷ condensed water vapour on a window, mirror, etc.

mist *VERB* mists, misting, misted
to become covered with mist • *My goggles kept misting up.*

mistake *NOUN* mistakes
❶ something done wrongly ❷ an incorrect opinion
➤ **by mistake** by accident; without intending to • *I picked up your bag by mistake.*

mistake *VERB* mistakes, mistaking, mistook, mistaken
❶ to choose or identify a person or thing wrongly • *We mistook her for her sister.* ❷ to misunderstand something • *Don't mistake my meaning.*

mistaken *ADJECTIVE*
❶ incorrect • *a case of mistaken identity* ❷ having an incorrect opinion • *You are mistaken if you believe that.*
➤ **mistakenly** *ADVERB*

mister *NOUN* (*informal*)
a form of address to a man

mistime *VERB* mistimes, mistiming, mistimed
to do or say something at a wrong time

mistletoe *NOUN*
a plant with white berries that grows as a parasite on trees

mistreat *VERB* mistreats, mistreating, mistreated
to treat a person or thing in a cruel or unkind

way • *He was accused of mistreating his horse.*

mistress *NOUN* mistresses
❶ a woman who is in charge of something ❷ a woman teacher ❸ the woman owner of a dog or other animal ❹ a woman who is a man's lover but not his wife

mistrust *VERB* mistrusts, mistrusting, mistrusted
to feel no trust in someone or something
➤ **mistrust** *NOUN*

misty *ADJECTIVE* mistier, mistiest
❶ full of mist • *a misty morning* ❷ not clear or distinct • *misty memories* ❸ misty eyes are full of tears
➤ **mistily** *ADVERB*
➤ **mistiness** *NOUN*

misunderstand *VERB* misunderstands, misunderstanding, misunderstood
to get a wrong idea or impression of something • *You misunderstand what I said.*

misunderstanding *NOUN* misunderstandings
a situation in which someone gets a wrong idea or impression of something • *I think there's been a misunderstanding.*

misuse (say mis-**yooz**) *VERB* misuses, misusing, misused
❶ to use something incorrectly ❷ to treat someone badly

misuse (say mis-**yooss**) *NOUN*
using something incorrectly • *the misuse of power*

mite *NOUN* mites
❶ a tiny spider-like creature that lives on plants, animals, carpets, etc. ❷ a small child

mitigate *VERB* mitigates, mitigating, mitigated
to make a thing less intense or less severe • *These measures are designed to mitigate the effects of air pollution.*
➤ **mitigation** *NOUN*

mitigating circumstances *PLURAL NOUN*
facts that may partially excuse wrongdoing

mitre *NOUN* mitres
❶ the tall tapering hat that a bishop wears ❷ a joint of two pieces of wood or cloth with their ends tapered so that together they form a right angle

mitten *NOUN* mittens
a kind of glove without separate parts for the fingers

mix *VERB* mixes, mixing, mixed
① to put different things together so that they make a single substance or thing; to blend or combine things • *Mix all the ingredients together in a bowl.* **②** to get together with other people
➤ **mix things up ①** to mix things together thoroughly **②** to confuse two things in your mind

mix *NOUN* mixes
a mixture

mixed *ADJECTIVE*
① containing two or more kinds of things or people • *I have mixed feelings about what happened.* **②** for both sexes • *mixed doubles*

mixed farming *NOUN*
farming of both crops and animals

mixer *NOUN* mixers
a machine used for mixing something • *a food mixer*

mixture *NOUN* mixtures
something made of different things mixed together

mix-up *NOUN*
a confusion or misunderstanding

mnemonic (say nim-**on**-ik) *NOUN* mnemonics
a verse or saying that helps you to remember something **WORD ORIGIN** from Greek *mnemonikos* = for the memory

> **SPELLING**
> There is a silent **m** at the beginning of mnemonic.

moan *VERB* moans, moaning, moaned
① to make a long low sound of pain or suffering **②** to complain or grumble

moan *NOUN* moans
① a long low sound of pain or suffering **②** a complaint or grumble

moat *NOUN* moats
a deep wide ditch round a castle, usually filled with water

mob *NOUN* mobs
a large disorderly crowd

mob *VERB* mobs, mobbing, mobbed
people mob someone when they crowd round them • *The band was mobbed by fans as they left the hotel.* **WORD ORIGIN** from Latin *mobile vulgus* = excitable crowd

mobile *ADJECTIVE*
able to move or be moved or carried easily
➤ **mobility** *NOUN*

mobile *NOUN* mobiles
① a mobile phone **②** a decoration for hanging up so that its parts move in currents of air

mobile phone *NOUN* mobile phones
a phone you can carry around with you

mobilize (also **mobilise**) *VERB* mobilizes, mobilizing, mobilized
to assemble people or things for a particular purpose, especially for war
➤ **mobilization** *NOUN*

moccasin *NOUN* moccasins
a soft leather shoe

mock *VERB* mocks, mocking, mocked
① to make fun of a person or thing **②** to imitate someone or something to make people laugh

mock *ADJECTIVE*
① imitation, not real • *He held up his hands in mock surprise.* **②** a mock exam is one done as a practice before the real one

mockery *NOUN*
① ridicule or contempt **②** a ridiculous imitation

mock-up *NOUN* mock-ups
a model of something, made in order to test or study it

modal verb *NOUN*
a verb such as *can, may* or *will* that is used with another verb to express possibility, permission, intention, etc.

mode *NOUN* modes
① the way a thing is done; a type of something • *different modes of transport* **②** one of the ways in which a machine can work • *The game has a two-player mode.* **③** what is fashionable

model *NOUN* models
① a copy of an object, usually on a smaller scale **②** a particular design **③** a person who poses for an artist or displays clothes by wearing them **④** a person or thing that is worth copying

model *VERB* models, modelling, modelled
① to make a model of something; to make something out of wood or clay **②** to design or plan something using another thing as an example • *The building is modelled on a Roman villa.* **③** to work as an artist's model or a fashion model

modem (say **moh**-dem) NOUN modems
a device that links a computer to a telephone line for transmitting data

moderate (say **mod**-er-at) ADJECTIVE
❶ medium; not too little and not too much • *a moderate climate* ❷ not extreme or unreasonable • *moderate opinions*
➤ **moderately** ADVERB

moderate (say **mod**-er-ayt) VERB moderates, moderating, moderated
to become or make something less strong or extreme

moderation NOUN
being moderate
➤ **in moderation** in moderate amounts

modern ADJECTIVE
❶ belonging to the present or recent times ❷ in fashion now

modernize (also **modernise**) VERB modernizes, modernizing, modernized
to make a thing more modern
➤ **modernization** NOUN

modest ADJECTIVE
❶ not boasting about how good you are ❷ quite small in size or amount • *a modest income* ❸ dressing or behaving in a decent or shy way
➤ **modestly** ADVERB
➤ **modesty** NOUN

modicum NOUN
a small amount

modification NOUN modifications
a slight change in something

modify VERB modifies, modifying, modified
❶ to change something slightly ❷ to describe a word or limit its meaning • *Adjectives modify nouns.*

modulate VERB modulates, modulating, modulated
❶ to vary the pitch or tone of your voice or a sound ❷ to alter an electronic wave to allow signals to be sent
➤ **modulation** NOUN

module NOUN modules
❶ a separate section or part of something larger, such as a spacecraft or building ❷ a unit or section of a course of study

modus operandi (say moh-dus op-er-**and**-ee) NOUN
a particular method of working

mogul (say **moh**-gul) NOUN moguls (*informal*)
an important or influential person
WORD ORIGIN the *Moguls* were the ruling family in northern India in the 16th-19th centuries

mohair NOUN
fine silky wool from an angora goat

moist ADJECTIVE
slightly wet • *Her eyes were moist with tears.*

moisten VERB moistens, moistening, moistened
to make something moist • *He moistened his lips before he spoke.*

moisture NOUN
water in tiny drops in the air or on a surface

moisturizer (also **moisturiser**) NOUN
a cream used to make the skin less dry

molar NOUN molars
any of the wide teeth at the back of the jaw, used in chewing

molasses NOUN
dark syrup from raw sugar

mole NOUN moles
❶ a small furry animal that burrows under the ground ❷ a spy working within an organization and passing information to another organization or country ❸ a small dark spot on skin

molecular (say mo-**lek**-yoo-ler) ADJECTIVE
to do with molecules • *the molecular structure of penicillin*

molecule NOUN molecules
the smallest part into which a substance can be divided without changing its chemical nature; a group of atoms

molehill NOUN molehills
a small pile of earth thrown up by a burrowing mole

molest VERB molests, molesting, molested
❶ to annoy or pester someone ❷ to illegally touch or attack someone in a sexual way
➤ **molestation** NOUN

mollify VERB mollifies, mollifying, mollified
to make a person feel less angry or upset • *She seemed slightly mollified by his apology.*

mollusc NOUN molluscs
any of a group of animals including snails, slugs and mussels, with soft bodies, no backbones, and, in some cases, external shells

molten *ADJECTIVE*
melted; made liquid by great heat • *Molten lava flowed down the side of the volcano.*

moment *NOUN* **moments**
❶ a very short time • *Wait a moment.* ❷ a particular time • *I'll call you the moment she arrives.*
➤ **at the moment** now

momentary *ADJECTIVE*
lasting for only a moment • *There was a momentary pause.*
➤ **momentarily** *ADVERB*

momentous (say mo-**ment**-us) *ADJECTIVE*
very important • *a momentous occasion*

momentum *NOUN*
❶ the ability something has to keep developing or increasing • *The protests gathered momentum.* ❷ the ability an object has to keep moving as a result of the speed it already has • *The stone gathered momentum as it rolled downhill.* ❸ (*in science*) the quantity of motion of a moving object, measured as its mass multiplied by its velocity

monarch *NOUN* **monarchs**
a king, queen, emperor or empress ruling a country

monarchy *NOUN* **monarchies**
❶ a country ruled by a monarch
❷ government by a monarch
➤ **monarchist** *NOUN*

monastery *NOUN* **monasteries**
a building where monks live and work

monastic *ADJECTIVE*
to do with monks or monasteries

Monday *NOUN*
the day of the week following Sunday
WORD ORIGIN from Old English *monandaeg* = day of the moon

monetary *ADJECTIVE*
to do with money

money *NOUN*
❶ coins and banknotes ❷ wealth or riches

mongoose *NOUN* **mongooses**
a small tropical animal rather like a stoat, that can kill snakes

mongrel (say **mung**-rel) *NOUN* **mongrels**
a dog of mixed breeds

monitor *NOUN* **monitors**
❶ a device for watching or testing how something is working ❷ a screen that displays data and images produced by a computer ❸ a pupil who is given a special responsibility in a school

monitor *VERB* **monitors, monitoring, monitored**
to regularly watch or test what is happening with something • *Pollution levels in the lake are closely monitored.*

monk *NOUN* **monks**
a member of a community of men who live according to the rules of a religious organization. Compare with **nun**.

monkey *NOUN* **monkeys**
❶ an animal with long arms, hands with thumbs and often a tail ❷ a mischievous person, especially a child

monochrome *ADJECTIVE*
done in one colour or in black and white

monocle *NOUN* **monocles**
a lens worn over one eye, like half of a pair of glasses

monogram *NOUN* **monograms**
a design made up of a letter or letters, especially a person's initials
➤ **monogrammed** *ADJECTIVE*

monograph *NOUN* **monographs**
a scholarly book or article on one particular subject

monolith *NOUN* **monoliths**
a large single upright block of stone

monolithic *ADJECTIVE*
❶ to do with or like a monolith ❷ huge and difficult to move or change

monologue *NOUN* **monologues**
a long speech by one person

monoplane *NOUN* **monoplanes**
a type of aeroplane with only one set of wings

monopolize (also **monopolise**) *VERB* **monopolizes, monopolizing, monopolized**
to take the whole of something for yourself • *One girl monopolized my attention.*

monopoly *NOUN* **monopolies**
❶ complete control by a single company over selling a product or supplying a service ❷ complete possession, control or use of something by one group

monorail *NOUN* **monorails**
a railway that uses a single rail, not a pair of rails

monosyllable *NOUN* monosyllables
a word with only one syllable
➤ **monosyllabic** *ADJECTIVE*

monotone *NOUN*
a level unchanging tone of voice in speaking
or singing • *He spoke in a flat monotone.*

monotonous *ADJECTIVE*
boring because it does not change
• *monotonous work*
➤ **monotonously** *ADVERB*

monotony *NOUN*
being always the same and therefore dull
and boring • *the monotony of his job in the
factory*

monoxide *NOUN* monoxides
an oxide with one atom of oxygen

monsoon *NOUN* monsoons
❶ a strong wind in and near the Indian
Ocean, bringing heavy rain in summer ❷ the
rainy season brought by this wind

monster *NOUN* monsters
❶ a large frightening creature ❷ a huge
thing ❸ a wicked or cruel person

monster *ADJECTIVE*
very large; huge

monstrosity *NOUN* monstrosities
a monstrous thing

monstrous *ADJECTIVE*
❶ like a monster; huge ❷ very shocking or
outrageous • *a monstrous crime*

montage (say mon-tahzh) *NOUN*
a picture, film, or other work of art made by
putting together separate pieces or pieces
from different works

month *NOUN* months
each of the twelve parts into which a year is
divided **WORD ORIGIN** from Old English; related
to **moon** (because time was measured by the
changes in the moon's appearance)

monthly *ADJECTIVE & ADVERB*
happening or done once a month

monument *NOUN* monuments
a statue, building or column put up to remind
people of some person or event

monumental *ADJECTIVE*
❶ built as a monument ❷ very large
or important • *It was a monumental
achievement.*

moo *VERB* moos, mooing, mooed
to make the low deep sound of a cow

moo *NOUN* moos
the low deep sound a cow makes

mood *NOUN* moods
the way someone feels • *She is in a cheerful
mood.*

moody *ADJECTIVE* moodier, moodiest
❶ gloomy or sullen • *He lapsed into a moody
silence.* ❷ having sudden changes of mood
for no apparent reason
➤ **moodily** *ADVERB*
➤ **moodiness** *NOUN*

moon *NOUN* moons
❶ the natural satellite of the earth that can
be seen in the sky at night ❷ a satellite of any
planet • *the moons of Jupiter*

moon *VERB* moons, mooning, mooned
to go about in a dreamy way, often because
you are in love

moonbeam *NOUN* moonbeams
a ray of moonlight

moonlight *NOUN*
the light from the moon
➤ **moonlit** *ADJECTIVE*

Moor *NOUN* Moors
a member of a Muslim people of north-
west Africa who controlled southern Spain
between the 8th and 15th centuries
➤ **Moorish** *ADJECTIVE*

moor *NOUN* moors
(*chiefly British*) an area of rough land covered
with heather, bracken and bushes

moor *VERB* moors, mooring, moored
to fasten a boat to a fixed object with a rope
or cable

moorhen *NOUN* moorhens
a small waterbird

mooring *NOUN* moorings
a place where a boat can be moored

moorland *NOUN* moorlands
(*chiefly British*) land that consists of moors

moose *NOUN* moose
a North American elk

moot *ADJECTIVE*
➤ **a moot point** a question that is undecided
or debatable

mop *NOUN* mops
❶ a bunch or pad of soft material fastened
on the end of a stick, used for cleaning floors
etc. ❷ a thick mass of hair

mop *VERB* mops, mopping, mopped
to clean or wipe something with a mop or

sponge
➤ **mop something up ❶** to wipe or soak up liquid **❷** to deal with the last parts of something • *The army is mopping up the last of the rebels.*

mope *VERB* mopes, moping, moped
to be miserable and not interested in doing anything • *She's been moping about in the house all day.*

moped (say **moh**-ped) *NOUN* mopeds
a kind of small motorcycle that can be pedalled

moraine *NOUN* moraines
a mass of stones and earth carried down by a glacier

moral *ADJECTIVE*
❶ to do with what is right and wrong in behaviour **❷** good or virtuous
➤ **morally** *ADVERB*
➤ **morality** *NOUN*
➤ **moral support** help in the form of encouragement

moral *NOUN* morals
a lesson in right behaviour taught by a story or event

morale (say mor-**ahl**) *NOUN*
the level of confidence and good spirits in a person or group of people • *Morale was high after the victory.*

moralize (also **moralise**) *VERB* moralizes, moralizing, moralized
to talk or write about right and wrong behaviour
➤ **moralist** *NOUN*

morals *PLURAL NOUN*
standards of behaviour

morass (say mo-**rass**) *NOUN* morasses
❶ a marsh or bog **❷** a confused mass

morbid *ADJECTIVE*
❶ thinking about gloomy or unpleasant things such as death • *She has a morbid interest in funerals.* **❷** (*in medicine*) unhealthy • *a morbid growth*
➤ **morbidly** *ADVERB*

more *DETERMINER* (comparative of **much** and **many**)
greater in amount or degree • *We need more money.*

more *PRONOUN*
a greater amount • *I want more.*

more *ADVERB*
❶ to a greater extent • *This is more*

important. • *You must work more.* **❷** again • *I don't want to do it any more.*
➤ **more or less ❶** approximately **❷** nearly or practically

moreover *ADVERB*
besides; in addition to what has been said

Mormon *NOUN* Mormons
a member of a religious group founded in the USA

morn *NOUN* (*poetical use*)
morning

morning *NOUN* mornings
the early part of the day, before noon or before lunchtime

morocco *NOUN*
a kind of leather originally made in Morocco from goatskins

moron *NOUN* morons (*informal*)
a very stupid person
➤ **moronic** *ADJECTIVE*

morose (say mo-**rohss**) *ADJECTIVE*
bad-tempered and miserable
➤ **morosely** *ADVERB*
➤ **moroseness** *NOUN*

morpheme *NOUN* morphemes
the smallest unit of meaning that a word can be divided into, e.g. *go* and *-ing* in the word *going*

morphine (say **mor**-feen) *NOUN*
a drug made from opium, used to lessen pain
WORD ORIGIN named after *Morpheus*, the Roman god of dreams

morris dance *NOUN* morris dances
a traditional English dance performed in costume by men with ribbons and bells
WORD ORIGIN originally *Moorish dance* (because it was thought to have come from the Moors)

morrow *NOUN* (*poetical use*)
the following day

Morse code *NOUN*
a signalling code using short and long sounds or flashes of light (dots and dashes) to represent letters **WORD ORIGIN** named after its American inventor, S. F. B. *Morse*

morsel *NOUN* morsels
a small piece of food

mortal *ADJECTIVE*
❶ not living for ever • *All of us are mortal.*
❷ causing death; fatal • *a mortal wound*

❸ deadly or extreme • *mortal enemies*
➤ **mortally** ADVERB

mortal NOUN mortals
a human being, as compared to a god or immortal spirit

mortality NOUN
❶ the state of being mortal and bound to die ❷ the number of people who die over a period of time • *a low rate of infant mortality*

mortar NOUN mortars
❶ a mixture of sand, cement and water used in building to stick bricks together ❷ a hard bowl in which substances are pounded with a pestle ❸ a short cannon for firing shells at a high angle

mortar board NOUN mortar boards
an academic cap with a stiff square top
(**WORD ORIGIN**) because it looks like the board used by workmen to hold mortar

mortgage (say **mor**-gij) NOUN mortgages
an arrangement to borrow money to buy a house, with the house as security for the loan

mortgage VERB mortgages, mortgaging, mortgaged
to take out a loan, with your house as security

mortify VERB mortifies, mortifying, mortified
to humiliate someone or make them feel very ashamed • *I was mortified to realize she had heard every word I said.*
➤ **mortification** NOUN

mortise NOUN mortises
a slot made in a piece of wood for another piece to be joined to it. Compare with **tenon**.

mortise lock NOUN mortise locks
a lock set into a door

mortuary NOUN mortuaries
a place where dead bodies are kept before being buried or cremated

mosaic (say mo-**zay**-ik) NOUN mosaics
a picture or design made from small coloured pieces of stone or glass

mosque (say mosk) NOUN mosques
a building where Muslims worship

mosquito NOUN mosquitoes
a kind of gnat that sucks blood

moss NOUN mosses
a plant that grows in damp places and has no flowers

mossy ADJECTIVE
covered in moss

most DETERMINER
(superlative of **much** and **many**)

most PRONOUN
the greatest amount • *Most of the food was eaten.*

most ADVERB
❶ to the greatest extent; more than any other • *It seemed the most natural thing in the world.* • *I liked this book most.* ❷ very or extremely • *It was most amusing.*

mostly ADVERB
mainly; in most ways • *The Sun is mostly made of hydrogen gas.*

motel NOUN motels
a hotel for people who are travelling by car, with space for parking cars near the rooms

moth NOUN moths
an insect rather like a butterfly, that usually flies at night

mother NOUN mothers
a female parent
➤ **motherhood** NOUN

mother VERB mothers, mothering, mothered
to look after someone in a motherly way

Mothering Sunday NOUN
(*British*) Mother's Day

mother-in-law NOUN mothers-in-law
the mother of a married person's husband or wife

motherly ADJECTIVE
kind and gentle like a mother

mother-of-pearl NOUN
a pearly substance lining the shells of mussels etc.

Mother's Day NOUN
the fourth Sunday in Lent, when many people give cards or presents to their mothers

motif (say moh-**teef**) NOUN motifs
a repeated design or theme

motion NOUN motions
❶ a way of moving; movement • *The motion of the boat made me feel sick.* ❷ a formal suggestion at a meeting that people discuss and vote on
➤ **go through the motions** to do or say something because you have to, without much interest

motion VERB motions, motioning, motioned
to signal to someone with a gesture • *She motioned him to sit beside her.*

A

motionless *ADJECTIVE*
not moving

B

motivate *VERB* motivates, motivating, motivated
❶ to give a person a motive or reason to do something • *She seems to be motivated by a sense of duty.* ❷ to make a person determined to achieve something • *He is good at motivating his players.*
➤ **motivation** *NOUN*

motive *NOUN* motives
what makes a person do something • *The police couldn't discover a motive for the murder.*

motive *ADJECTIVE*
producing movement • *The engine provides motive power.*

motley *ADJECTIVE*
made up of various sorts of things or people that do not seem to belong together • *They were a motley bunch.*

motor *NOUN* motors
a machine providing power to drive machinery etc.; an engine

motor *ADJECTIVE*
having a motor; to do with vehicles that have motors • *motor vehicles* • *the motor industry*

motor *VERB* motors, motoring, motored
to travel by car

motorbike *NOUN* motorbikes
a motorcycle

motorcade *NOUN* motorcades
a procession of cars

motorcycle *NOUN* motorcycles
a two-wheeled road vehicle with an engine
➤ **motorcyclist** *NOUN*

motorist *NOUN* motorists
a person who drives a car

motorized (also **motorised**) *ADJECTIVE*
equipped with a motor or with motor vehicles

motor neuron disease *NOUN*
a disease of the nerves that control movement, so that the muscles get weaker and weaker until the person dies

motorway *NOUN* motorways
a wide road for fast long-distance traffic

mottled *ADJECTIVE*
marked with spots or patches of colour

motto *NOUN* mottoes
❶ a short saying used as a guide for behaviour • *'Better safe than sorry' is my*

motto. ❷ a short verse or riddle found inside a cracker

mould *NOUN* moulds
❶ a hollow container of a particular shape, in which a liquid or soft substance is put to set into this shape ❷ a fine furry growth of very small fungi

mould *VERB* moulds, moulding, moulded
❶ to make something have a particular shape • *First, mould the clay into a ball.* ❷ to strongly influence how someone develops • *He moulded them into a superb team.*

moulder *VERB* moulders, mouldering, mouldered
to rot away or decay into dust

mouldy *ADJECTIVE*
covered with mould • *The cheese has gone mouldy.*

moult *VERB* moults, moulting, moulted
to shed feathers, hair or skin while a new growth forms

mound *NOUN* mounds
❶ a pile of earth or stones etc. ❷ a small hill

mount *VERB* mounts, mounting, mounted
❶ to go up something • *She slowly mounted the stairs.* ❷ to get on a horse or bicycle ❸ to increase in amount • *Our costs are mounting.* ❹ to mount a picture or photograph is to put it in a frame or album in order to display it ❺ to organize something • *The gallery is to mount an exhibition of young British artists.*

mount *NOUN* mounts
❶ a mountain • *Mount Everest* ❷ something on which an object is mounted ❸ a horse for riding

mountain *NOUN* mountains
❶ a very high hill ❷ a large heap, pile, or quantity • *We have a mountain of work to do.*

mountaineer *NOUN* mountaineers
a person who climbs mountains
➤ **mountaineering** *NOUN*

mountainous *ADJECTIVE*
❶ having many mountains • *a mountainous region* ❷ huge • *mountainous waves*

mounted *ADJECTIVE*
on horseback • *mounted police*

mourn *VERB* mourns, mourning, mourned
to be sad, especially because someone has died • *When he died, he was mourned all over the world.*

mourner *NOUN* **mourners**
mourners are the people who go to a funeral, especially the family and friends of the person who has died

mournful *ADJECTIVE*
sad and sorrowful • *a mournful song*
➤ **mournfully** *ADVERB*

mouse *NOUN* **mice**
❶ a small animal with a long thin tail and a pointed nose ❷ (*in computing*) **mouses** or **mice** a small device which you move around on a mat to control the movements of a cursor on a computer screen

mousetrap *NOUN* **mousetraps**
a trap for catching and killing mice

moussaka *NOUN*
a dish of minced meat, aubergine, etc., with a cheese sauce

mousse (say mooss) *NOUN* **mousses**
❶ a creamy pudding flavoured with fruit or chocolate ❷ a frothy creamy substance put on the hair so that it can be styled more easily

moustache (say mus-**tahsh**) *NOUN* **moustaches**
a strip of hair that a man grows above his upper lip

mousy *ADJECTIVE* **mousier, mousiest**
❶ mousy hair is a dull light brown in colour ❷ a mousy person is timid and feeble

mouth *NOUN* **mouths**
❶ the opening in your face that you use for eating and speaking ❷ the place where a river enters the sea ❸ an opening or outlet

mouth *VERB* **mouths, mouthing, mouthed**
to form words carefully with your lips, especially without saying them aloud • *'Time to go,' she mouthed.*

mouthful *NOUN* **mouthfuls**
an amount of food you put in your mouth

mouth organ *NOUN* **mouth organs**
(*British*) a small musical instrument that you play by blowing and sucking while passing it along your lips

mouthpiece *NOUN* **mouthpieces**
the part of a musical instrument or other device that you put to your mouth

movable *ADJECTIVE*
able to be moved • *model soldiers with movable arms and legs*

move *VERB* **moves, moving, moved**
❶ to go or take something from one place to another; to change a person's or thing's position ❷ to affect a person's feelings • *Their sad story moved us deeply.* ❸ to put forward a formal suggestion (a **motion**) to be discussed and voted on at a meeting
➤ **mover** *NOUN*

move *NOUN* **moves**
❶ a movement or action ❷ a player's turn to move a piece in a game such as chess
➤ **get a move on** (*informal*) to hurry up
➤ **on the move** moving or making progress

movement *NOUN* **movements**
❶ moving or being moved ❷ a group of people working together to achieve something ❸ (*in music*) one of the main divisions of a symphony or other long musical work

movie *NOUN* **movies** (*North American*) (*informal*)
a cinema film **WORD ORIGIN** short for *moving picture*

moving *ADJECTIVE*
making someone feel strong emotion, especially sorrow or pity • *It was a very moving story.*

mow *VERB* **mows, mowing, mowed, mown**
to cut down grass or cereal crops
➤ **mower** *NOUN*
➤ **mow someone down** to kill someone with a car or gun

mozzarella *NOUN*
a kind of Italian cheese used in cooking, originally made from buffalo's milk

MP *ABBREVIATION*
Member of Parliament

Mr (say **mist**-er) *NOUN* **Messrs**
a title put before a man's name

Mrs (say **mis**-iz) *NOUN* **Mrs**
a title put before a married woman's name

MS *ABBREVIATION*
multiple sclerosis

Ms (say miz) *NOUN*
a title put before a woman's name, regardless of whether she is married or not

MSc *ABBREVIATION*
Master of Science

MSP *ABBREVIATION*
Member of the Scottish Parliament

Mt *ABBREVIATION*
mount or mountain

much *ADJECTIVE* more, most
existing in a large amount • *There is much work to do.*

much *PRONOUN*
a large amount of something • *That's not very much.*

much *ADVERB*
❶ greatly or considerably • *I feel much better today.* • *He came, much to my surprise.*
❷ approximately • *These are much the same.*

muck *NOUN*
❶ farmyard manure ❷ (*informal*) dirt or filth

muck *VERB*
➤ **muck about** (*informal*) to mess about
➤ **muck something out** to clean out the place where an animal is kept
➤ **muck something up** (*informal*)
❶ to make something dirty ❷ to spoil or make a mess of something

mucky *ADJECTIVE* muckier, muckiest
dirty or filthy

mucous (say **mew**-kus) *ADJECTIVE*
❶ like mucus ❷ covered with mucus • *a mucous membrane*

mucus (say **mew**-kus) *NOUN*
the moist sticky substance on the inner surface of the throat etc.

mud *NOUN*
wet soft earth

muddle *VERB* muddles, muddling, muddled
❶ to jumble or mix things up ❷ to confuse things in your mind • *I always get those two names muddled up.*

muddle *NOUN* muddles
confusion or disorder • *My papers are all in a muddle.*

muddy *ADJECTIVE* muddier, muddiest
full of or covered with mud • *muddy boots*

mudguard *NOUN* mudguards
a curved cover over the top part of a bicycle wheel to protect the rider from the mud and water thrown up by the wheel

muesli (say **mooz**-lee) *NOUN*
(*chiefly British*) a breakfast food made of mixed cereals, dried fruit and nuts

muezzin (say moo-**ez**-in) *NOUN* muezzins
a Muslim crier who calls the hours of prayer from a minaret

muff *NOUN* muffs
a short tube-shaped piece of warm material into which the hands are pushed from opposite ends

muff *VERB* muffs, muffing, muffed
(*informal*) to bungle something

muffin *NOUN* muffins
❶ a flat bun eaten toasted and buttered ❷ a small sponge cake, usually containing fruit, chocolate chips, etc.

muffle *VERB* muffles, muffling, muffled
❶ to cover or wrap something to protect it or keep it warm ❷ to deaden the sound of something • *a muffled scream*

muffler *NOUN* mufflers
a warm scarf

mug *NOUN* mugs
❶ a kind of large straight-sided cup
❷ (*British*) (*informal*) a fool; a person who is easily fooled or cheated ❸ (*informal*) a person's face

mug *VERB* mugs, mugging, mugged
to attack and rob someone in the street
➤ **mugger** *NOUN*

muggy *ADJECTIVE* muggier, muggiest
muggy weather is unpleasantly warm and damp

mulberry *NOUN* mulberries
a purple or white fruit rather like a blackberry

mule *NOUN* mules
an animal that is the offspring of a donkey and a mare, known for being stubborn
➤ **mulish** *ADJECTIVE*

mull *VERB* mulls, mulling, mulled
➤ **mull something over** to think about something carefully • *I'll have to mull it over before making a decision.*

mulled *ADJECTIVE*
mulled wine is heated with sugar and spices

mullet *NOUN* mullet
a kind of fish used as food

multi– *PREFIX*
many (as in *multicoloured* = with many colours)

multicultural *ADJECTIVE*
made up of people of many different races, religions and cultures

multifarious (say multi-**fair**-ee-us) *ADJECTIVE*
of many kinds; very varied

multilateral *ADJECTIVE*
a multilateral agreement or treaty is made between three or more people, organizations, or countries

multimedia *ADJECTIVE*
using more than one medium of communication • *a multimedia show with pictures, lights and music*

multimedia *NOUN*
a computer program with sound and still and moving pictures linked to the text

multimillionaire *NOUN* multimillionaires
a person with a fortune of several million pounds or dollars

multinational *NOUN* multinationals
a large business company which works in several countries

multiple *ADJECTIVE*
having many parts or elements • *a monster with multiple heads*

multiple *NOUN* multiples
a number that contains another number (a **factor**) an exact amount of times with no remainder • *8 and 12 are multiples of 4.*

multiple sclerosis *NOUN*
a disease of the nervous system which makes a person unable to control their movements and may affect their sight

multiplex *NOUN* multiplexes
a large cinema complex that has many screens

multiplication *NOUN*
the process of multiplying one number by another

multiplicity *NOUN*
a great variety or large number

multiply *VERB* multiplies, multiplying, multiplied
❶ to add a number to itself a given quantity of times • *Five multiplied by four equals twenty* (5 x 4 = 20). ❷ to make things many or to become many; to increase • *His doubts started to multiply.*

multiracial *ADJECTIVE*
consisting of people of many different races

multitude *NOUN* multitudes
a very large number of people or things • *a multitude of birds*
➤ **multitudinous** *ADJECTIVE*

mum *NOUN* mums (*British*) (*informal*)
mother

mum *ADJECTIVE* (*informal*)
saying nothing • *He promised to keep mum.*

mumble *VERB* mumbles, mumbling, mumbled
to speak indistinctly so that you are not easy to hear • *Stop mumbling and speak up!*
➤ **mumble** *NOUN*
➤ **mumbler** *NOUN*

mumbo-jumbo *NOUN*
(*informal*) talk or ceremony that has no real meaning

mummify *VERB* mummifies, mummifying, mummified
in ancient Egypt, to preserve a corpse as a mummy

mummy *NOUN* mummies
❶ (*British*) (*informal*) mother ❷ in ancient Egypt, a corpse wrapped in cloth and treated with oils etc. before being buried so that it does not decay

mumps *NOUN*
an infectious disease that makes the neck swell painfully

munch *VERB* munches, munching, munched
to chew food steadily and often noisily • *He sat there munching his toast.*

mundane *ADJECTIVE*
ordinary, not exciting

municipal (say mew-**nis**-ip-al) *ADJECTIVE*
to do with a town or city that has its own local government • *municipal buildings*

munificent *ADJECTIVE* (*formal*)
extremely generous
➤ **munificently** *ADVERB*
➤ **munificence** *NOUN*

munitions *PLURAL NOUN*
military weapons, ammunition and equipment

mural *NOUN* murals
a large picture painted on a wall

murder *VERB* murders, murdering, murdered
to kill a person unlawfully and deliberately
➤ **murderer** *NOUN*
➤ **murderess** *NOUN*

murder *NOUN* murders
the murdering of someone • *They were found guilty of murder.*

murderous *ADJECTIVE*
likely to murder someone or looking as though you might • *There was a murderous look in his eyes.*

murky ADJECTIVE murkier, murkiest
dark and gloomy • *He peered into the murky water.*
➤ **murk** NOUN

murmur VERB murmurs, murmuring, murmured
❶ to speak in a soft voice • *She murmured something in her sleep.* ❷ to make a low continuous sound • *The wind murmured in the trees.*

murmur NOUN murmurs
a sound of soft voices

muscle NOUN muscles
❶ a band or bundle of fibrous tissue that can contract and relax and so produce movement in parts of the body ❷ the power of muscles; strength **WORD ORIGIN** from Latin *musculus* = little mouse (because a flexed muscle was thought to have the shape of a mouse hiding under a mat)

SPELLING
Take care: the s sound is spelt **sc.**

muscular ADJECTIVE
❶ to do with the muscles ❷ having well-developed muscles

muse VERB muses, musing, mused
❶ to think deeply about something; to ponder ❷ to say something to yourself in a thoughtful way • *'I wonder where he's gone?' mused Lisa.*

museum NOUN museums
a place where interesting, old or valuable objects are displayed for people to see **WORD ORIGIN** from Greek *mouseion* = place of Muses (goddesses of the arts and sciences)

mush NOUN
a soft thick mass • *The vegetables had turned to mush.*

mushroom NOUN mushrooms
an edible fungus with a stem and a dome-shaped top

mushroom VERB mushrooms, mushrooming, mushroomed
to grow or appear suddenly in large numbers • *Blocks of flats mushroomed in the city*

mushy ADJECTIVE
❶ soft and thick, like mush ❷ too emotional or sentimental • *a mushy film*

music NOUN
❶ a pattern of pleasant or interesting sounds made by instruments or by the voice ❷ printed or written symbols which stand for musical sounds

musical ADJECTIVE
❶ to do with music ❷ producing music ❸ good at music or interested in it
➤ **musically** ADVERB

musical NOUN musicals
a play or film containing a lot of songs

musician NOUN musicians
someone who plays a musical instrument

musk NOUN
a strong-smelling substance used in perfumes
➤ **musky** ADJECTIVE

musket NOUN muskets
a kind of gun with a long barrel, used in the past by soldiers

musketeer NOUN musketeers
a soldier armed with a musket

Muslim NOUN Muslims
someone who follows the religion of Islam

muslin NOUN
very thin cotton cloth **WORD ORIGIN** named after *Mosul*, a city in Iraq, where it was first made

mussel NOUN mussels
a black shellfish

must AUXILIARY VERB
used to show
❶ that someone has to do something or that it is necessary that something happens (*I must go home soon.*) ❷ that something is certain (*You must be joking!*)

mustang NOUN mustangs
a wild horse of the United States of America and Mexico

mustard NOUN
a yellow paste or powder used to give food a hot taste

muster VERB musters, mustering, mustered
❶ to find as much of something as you can • *He was trying to muster up the courage to speak to her.* ❷ to gather people together in one place; to assemble

muster NOUN musters
an assembly of people or things
➤ **pass muster** to be up to the required standard

mustn't (*mainly spoken*)
must not

musty *ADJECTIVE* **mustier, mustiest**
smelling or tasting mouldy or stale
➤ **mustiness** *NOUN*

mutant *NOUN* **mutants**
a living creature that is different from others
of the same type because of changes in its
genes
➤ **mutant** *ADJECTIVE*

mutation *NOUN* **mutations**
a change in the form of a living creature
because of changes in its genes
➤ **mutate** *VERB*

mute *ADJECTIVE*
❶ silent; not speaking or able to speak ❷ not
pronounced • *The g in 'gnat' is mute.*

mute *NOUN* **mutes**
❶ a person who cannot speak ❷ a device
fitted to a musical instrument to deaden its
sound

muted *ADJECTIVE*
quiet; not strongly expressed • *muted
applause*

mutely *ADVERB*
without speaking • *I shook my head mutely.*

mutilate *VERB* **mutilates, mutilating,
mutilated**
to damage something by breaking or cutting
off part of it
➤ **mutilation** *NOUN*

mutineer *NOUN* **mutineers**
a person who takes part in a mutiny

mutinous *ADJECTIVE*
taking part in a mutiny; refusing to obey
orders • *The crew became mutinous.*
➤ **mutinously** *ADVERB*

mutiny *NOUN* **mutinies**
rebellion against authority, especially refusal
by soldiers or sailors to obey orders

mutiny *VERB* **mutinies, mutinying, mutinied**
to take part in a mutiny

mutter *VERB* **mutters, muttering, muttered**
❶ to speak in a low voice ❷ to grumble
➤ **mutter** *NOUN*

mutton *NOUN*
meat from a sheep

mutual (say **mew**-tew-al) *ADJECTIVE*
❶ given or done to each other • *They have
mutual respect for one another.* ❷ shared by
two or more people • *a mutual friend*
➤ **mutually** *ADVERB*

muzzle *NOUN* **muzzles**
❶ an animal's nose and mouth ❷ a cover put
over an animal's nose and mouth so that it
cannot bite ❸ the open end of a gun

muzzle *VERB* **muzzles, muzzling, muzzled**
❶ to put a muzzle on an animal ❷ to
silence someone; to prevent a person from
expressing opinions

my *DETERMINER*
belonging to me

myriad (say **mi**rri-ad) *ADJECTIVE*
very many; countless • *She gazed at the
myriad stars in the sky above.*

myriad *NOUN*
a huge number of people or things • *a myriad
of colours*

myrrh (say mer) *NOUN*
a substance used in perfumes, incense, and
medicine

myrtle *NOUN* **myrtles**
an evergreen shrub with dark leaves and
white flowers

myself *PRONOUN*
I or me and nobody else. The word is used to
refer back to the subject of a sentence (e.g.
I have hurt myself.) or for emphasis (e.g. *I
myself will not be coming.*).
➤ **by myself** alone; on my own

mysterious *ADJECTIVE*
full of mystery; puzzling • *her mysterious
disappearance*
➤ **mysteriously** *ADVERB*

mystery *NOUN* **mysteries**
something that cannot be explained or
understood; something puzzling • *Exactly
why the ship sank is a mystery.*

mystic *NOUN* **mystics**
a person who seeks to obtain spiritual contact
with God by deep religious meditation

mystic *ADJECTIVE*
mystical

mystical *ADJECTIVE*
having spiritual powers or qualities that are
difficult to understand or explain • *Watching
the sun set over the island was an almost
mystical experience.*
➤ **mystically** *ADVERB*

mystify *VERB* **mystifies, mystifying, mystified**
to puzzle or bewilder someone • *I'm
completely mystified about how this
happened.*
➤ **mystification** *NOUN*

a b c d e f g h i j k l m n o p q r s t u v w x y z

mystique (say mis-**teek**) *NOUN*
an air of mystery or secret power

myth (say mith) *NOUN* **myths**
❶ an old story containing ideas about ancient times or about supernatural beings. Compare with **legend**. ❷ an untrue story or belief

mythical *ADJECTIVE*
❶ imaginary; found only in myths • *a mythical animal* ❷ to do with myths

mythological *ADJECTIVE*
to do with myths • *mythological stories*

mythology *NOUN*
myths or the study of myths

myxomatosis (say miks-om-at-**oh**-sis) *NOUN*
a disease that kills rabbits

N. *ABBREVIATION*
❶ north ❷ northern

nab *VERB* **nabs, nabbing, nabbed** (*informal*)
to catch or arrest someone; to seize or grab something

nag *VERB* **nags, nagging, nagged**
❶ to pester a person by keeping on criticizing, complaining or asking for things ❷ to keep on hurting or bothering you • *a nagging pain*

nag *NOUN* **nags**
(*informal*) a horse

nail *NOUN* **nails**
❶ the hard covering over the end of a finger or toe ❷ a small sharp piece of metal hammered in to fasten pieces of wood together

nail *VERB* **nails, nailing, nailed**
❶ to fasten something with a nail or nails ❷ (*informal*) to catch or arrest someone

naive (say nah-**eev**) *ADJECTIVE*
showing a lack of experience or good judgement; innocent and trusting
➤ **naively** *ADVERB*
➤ **naivety** *NOUN*

naked *ADJECTIVE*
❶ without any clothes or coverings on ❷ obvious; not hidden • *the naked truth*
➤ **nakedness** *NOUN*

naked eye *NOUN*
the eye when it is not helped by a telescope, binoculars or microscope • *These creatures are too tiny to see with the naked eye.*

name *NOUN* **names**
❶ the word or words by which a person, animal, place or thing is known ❷ a person's reputation

name *VERB* **names, naming, named**
❶ to give a name to a person or thing • *Braille is named after its inventor, Louis Braille.* ❷ to say what someone or something is called • *Can you name all the planets?* ❸ to say what you want something to be • *Name your price.*
➤ **name the day** to decide when something, especially a wedding, is to take place or happen • *Have you two named the day yet?*

nameless *ADJECTIVE*
❶ without a name • *a nameless grave* ❷ not named or identified • *The culprit shall remain nameless.*

namely *ADVERB*
that is to say • *My two favourite subjects are sciences, namely chemistry and biology.*

namesake *NOUN* **namesakes**
a person or thing with the same name as another

nanny *NOUN* **nannies**
❶ a person, usually a woman, who looks after young children ❷ (*informal*) grandmother

nanny goat *NOUN* **nanny goats**
a female goat. Compare with **billy goat**.

nap *NOUN* **naps**
a short sleep
➤ **catch a person napping** to catch a person unprepared for something or not alert

napalm (say **nay**-pahm) *NOUN*
a substance made of petrol, used in some incendiary bombs

nape *NOUN* **napes**
the back part of your neck

napkin *NOUN* **napkins**
❶ a piece of cloth or paper used at meals to protect your clothes or for wiping your lips or fingers ❷ (*old use*) a nappy

nappy *NOUN* **nappies**
(*British*) a piece of cloth or other fabric put round a baby's bottom

narcissistic *ADJECTIVE*
extremely vain **WORD ORIGIN** from *Narcissus,*

a youth in Greek legend who fell in love with his own reflection and was turned into a flower

narcissus NOUN narcissi
a garden flower like a daffodil

narcotic NOUN narcotics
a drug that makes a person sleepy or unconscious
➤ **narcotic** ADJECTIVE

narrate VERB narrates, narrating, narrated
to tell a story or give an account of something • *Each chapter is narrated by a different character.*
➤ **narration** NOUN

narrative NOUN narratives
a spoken or written account of something

narrator NOUN narrators
the person who is telling a story

narrow ADJECTIVE
❶ not wide or broad ❷ uncomfortably close; with only a small margin of error or safety • *We all had a narrow escape.*

narrow VERB narrows, narrowing, narrowed
to make something narrower or to become narrower • *He narrowed his eyes.* • *As they drove on, the road narrowed.*

narrowly ADVERB
only by a small amount • *The car narrowly missed a cyclist.*

narrow-minded ADJECTIVE
not willing to accept other people's beliefs and ways

nasal ADJECTIVE
❶ to do with the nose ❷ sounding as if the breath comes out through the nose • *a nasal voice*
➤ **nasally** ADVERB

nasturtium (say na-**ster**-shum) NOUN
nasturtiums
a garden plant with round leaves and red, yellow or orange flowers (WORD ORIGIN) from Latin *nasus* = nose + *torquere* = to twist (because of its sharp smell)

nasty ADJECTIVE nastier, nastiest
❶ horrid or unpleasant • *a nasty smell*
❷ cruel or unkind • *a nasty remark*
➤ **nastily** ADVERB
➤ **nastiness** NOUN

nation NOUN nations
a large community of people most of whom have the same ancestors, language, history and customs and who usually live in the same part of the world under one government

national ADJECTIVE
to do with or belonging to a nation or country • *national dress* • *a national newspaper*
➤ **nationally** ADVERB

national NOUN nationals
a citizen of a particular country

national anthem NOUN national anthems
a nation's official song, which is played or sung on important occasions

national curriculum NOUN
the subjects that must be taught by state schools in England and Wales

nationalist NOUN nationalists
❶ a person who is very patriotic ❷ a person who wants their country to be independent and not to form part of another country
• *Scottish Nationalists*
➤ **nationalism** NOUN
➤ **nationalistic** ADJECTIVE

nationality NOUN nationalities
the condition of belonging to a particular nation • *What is your nationality?*

nationalize (also **nationalise**) VERB
nationalizes, nationalizing, nationalized
to put an industry or business under the ownership or control of the state
➤ **nationalization** NOUN

national park NOUN national parks
an area of natural beauty which is protected by the government and which the public may visit

nationwide ADJECTIVE & ADVERB
over the whole of a country • *a nationwide campaign*

native NOUN natives
a person born in a particular place • *He is a native of Sweden.*

native ADJECTIVE
❶ your native country or city is the place where you were born ❷ your native language is the language that you first learned to speak ❸ grown or originating in a particular place • *a plant native to China* ❹ that you have naturally without having to learn it • *native cunning*

Native American NOUN Native Americans
one of the original inhabitants of North and South America

nativity *NOUN* **nativities**
a person's birth
➤ **the Nativity** the birth of Jesus Christ

natter *VERB* **natters, nattering, nattered**
(*informal*) to chat informally

natty *ADJECTIVE* **nattier, nattiest** (*informal*)
neat in appearance
➤ **nattily** *ADVERB*

natural *ADJECTIVE*
❶ produced or done by nature, not by people or machines ❷ normal; not surprising • *It's only natural to be nervous before an exam.* ❸ having a quality or ability that you were born with • *a natural leader* ❹ a natural note is neither sharp nor flat
➤ **naturalness** *NOUN*

natural *NOUN* **naturals**
❶ a person who is naturally good at something ❷ a natural note in music; a sign (♮) that shows this

natural gas *NOUN*
gas found underground or under the sea, not made from coal

natural history *NOUN*
the study of plants and animals

naturalist *NOUN* **naturalists**
an expert in natural history

naturalize (also **naturalise**) *VERB* **naturalizes, naturalizing, naturalized**
❶ to give a person full rights as a citizen of a country although they were not born there ❷ to cause a plant or animal to grow or live naturally in a country that is not its own
➤ **naturalization** *NOUN*

naturally *ADVERB*
❶ in a natural way • *The gas is produced naturally.* ❷ as you would expect • *We were naturally disappointed to lose.*

natural science *NOUN*
the study of physics, chemistry and biology

natural selection *NOUN*
Charles Darwin's theory that only the plants and animals best suited to their surroundings will survive and breed

nature *NOUN* **natures**
❶ everything in the world that was not made by people, such as plants and animals ❷ the qualities and characteristics of a person or thing • *She has a loving nature.* ❸ a kind or sort of thing • *He likes things of that nature.*

nature reserve *NOUN* **nature reserves**
an area of land which is managed in a way that preserves the wild animals and plants that live there

nature trail *NOUN* **nature trails**
a path in a country area with signs telling you about the plants and animals that live there

naught *NOUN* (*old use*)
nothing

naughty *ADJECTIVE* **naughtier, naughtiest**
❶ badly behaved or disobedient ❷ slightly rude or indecent • *naughty pictures*
➤ **naughtily** *ADVERB*
➤ **naughtiness** *NOUN*

nausea (say **naw-zee-a**) *NOUN*
a feeling of sickness or disgust
➤ **nauseating** *ADJECTIVE*

nauseous *ADJECTIVE*
feeling that you are going to be sick; sickening

nautical *ADJECTIVE*
to do with ships or sailors • *a nautical term*

nautical mile *NOUN* **nautical miles**
a measure of distance used at sea, equal to 2,025 yards (1.852 kilometres)

naval *ADJECTIVE*
to do with a navy • *a naval officer*

nave *NOUN* **naves**
the main central part of a church (the other parts are the chancel, aisles and transepts)

navel *NOUN* **navels**
the small hollow in the centre of the abdomen, where the umbilical cord was attached

navigable *ADJECTIVE*
suitable for ships and boats to sail in • *a navigable river*

navigate *VERB* **navigates, navigating, navigated**
❶ to sail in or through a river or sea etc. • *The ship navigated the Suez Canal.* ❷ to make sure that a ship, aircraft or vehicle is going in the right direction ❸ to find your way around a website

➤ **navigation** *NOUN*
➤ **navigator** *NOUN*

navvy *NOUN* **navvies**
(*British*) a labourer digging a road, railway or canal (**WORD ORIGIN**) short for 'navigator', a person who constructs a 'navigation' (= canal)

navy *NOUN* **navies**
❶ a country's warships and the people trained to use them ❷ (also **navy blue**) a very dark blue, the colour of naval uniform

nay *ADVERB* (*old use*)
no

Nazi (say **nah**-tsee) *NOUN* **Nazis**
a member of the National Socialist Party in Germany in Hitler's time, with Fascist beliefs
➤ **Nazism** *NOUN*

NB *ABBREVIATION*
take note that (**WORD ORIGIN**) Latin *nota bene* = note well

NE *ABBREVIATION*
❶ north-east ❷ north-eastern

Neanderthal (say nee-**an**-der-tahl) *NOUN* **Neanderthals**
an early type of human who lived in Europe during the Stone Age

near *ADVERB* & *ADJECTIVE*
not far away
➤ **near by** not far away • *They live near by.*
near *PREPOSITION*
not far away from • *The bus stops near our house.*
near *VERB* **nears, nearing, neared**
to come close to something • *The ship neared the harbour.*

nearby *ADJECTIVE*
near; not far away • *a nearby house*

nearly *ADVERB*
almost; not quite • *We have nearly finished.*

neat *ADJECTIVE* **neater, neatest**
❶ arranged carefully; tidy and in order • *a neat desk* ❷ clever or skilful • *a neat trick* ❸ drunk without anything added • *neat whisky* ❹ (*North American*) (*informal*) excellent
➤ **neatness** *NOUN*

neaten *VERB* **neatens, neatening, neatened**
to make something neat

neatly *ADVERB*
❶ in a tidy or carefully arranged way • *neatly folded clothes* ❷ in a clever or skilful way • *She neatly avoided answering the question.*

nebula *NOUN* **nebulae**
a bright or dark patch in the sky, caused by a distant galaxy or a cloud of dust or gas

nebulous *ADJECTIVE*
unclear or vague • *nebulous ideas*

necessarily *ADVERB*
in a way that cannot be avoided • *The number of tickets available is necessarily limited.*
➤ **not necessarily** not always or not definitely • *Expensive restaurants are not necessarily better than cheaper ones.*

necessary *ADJECTIVE*
needed for something; essential

SPELLING
Double up the s in **necessary** (but the c stays single).

necessitate *VERB* **necessitates, necessitating, necessitated**
to make a thing necessary • *This route up the mountain necessitated a tricky climb.*

necessity *NOUN* **necessities**
❶ need; great importance • *the necessity of buying food and clothing* ❷ something necessary

neck *NOUN* **necks**
❶ the part of the body that joins the head to the shoulders ❷ the part of a piece of clothing round your neck ❸ a narrow part of something, especially of a bottle
➤ **neck and neck** almost exactly together in a race or contest

necklace *NOUN* **necklaces**
a piece of jewellery worn round the neck

necktie *NOUN* **neckties**
a strip of material worn passing under the collar of a shirt and knotted in front

nectar *NOUN*
❶ a sweet liquid collected by bees from flowers ❷ a delicious drink
(**WORD ORIGIN**) from Greek *nektar* = the drink of the gods

nectarine *NOUN* **nectarines**
a kind of peach with a thin smooth skin

nectary *NOUN* **nectaries**
the nectar-producing part of a plant

née (say nay) *ADJECTIVE*
born, used to give a married woman's maiden name • *Mrs Smith, née Jones*
(**WORD ORIGIN**) French = born

a b c d e f g h i j k l m n o p q r s t u v w x y z

need *VERB* needs, needing, needed
❶ to be without something you should have; to require something • *We need two more chairs.* ❷ (as an auxiliary verb) to have to do something • *You need not answer.*

need *NOUN* needs
❶ something needed; a necessary thing ❷ a situation where something is necessary • *There is no need to shout.* ❸ great poverty or hardship

needle *NOUN* needles
❶ a very thin pointed piece of steel used in sewing ❷ either of a pair of metal, plastic or bamboo rods used in knitting ❸ a thin spike on a tree or plant • *pine needles* ❹ the pointer of a meter or compass

needless *ADJECTIVE*
not necessary because it could have been avoided • *It was a needless waste of time.*
➤ **needlessly** *ADVERB*

needlework *NOUN*
sewing or embroidery

needy *ADJECTIVE* needier, neediest
very poor; lacking things necessary for life
➤ **neediness** *NOUN*

ne'er *ADVERB* (*poetical use*)
never

nefarious (say nif-**air**-ee-us) *ADJECTIVE*
wicked or criminal • *his nefarious plans*

negate *VERB* negates, negating, negated
❶ to make something ineffective ❷ to disprove or deny something
➤ **negation** *NOUN*

negative *ADJECTIVE*
❶ that says 'no' • *a negative answer* ❷ looking only at the bad aspects of a situation • *Don't be so negative.* ❸ showing no sign of what is being tested for • *Her pregnancy test was negative.* ❹ less than zero; minus ❺ to do with the kind of electric charge carried by electrons
➤ **negatively** *ADVERB*

USAGE
The opposite of meaning 1 is affirmative; the opposite of the other meanings is positive.

negative *NOUN* negatives
❶ a negative statement ❷ a photograph or film with the dark parts light and the light parts dark, from which a positive print (with the dark and light or colours correct) can be made

neglect *VERB* neglects, neglecting, neglected
❶ to fail to look after or pay attention to a person or thing • *The buildings have been neglected for many years.* ❷ to fail or forget to do something • *He neglected to shut the door.*

neglect *NOUN*
neglecting or being neglected
➤ **neglectful** *ADJECTIVE*

negligence *NOUN*
lack of proper care or attention; carelessness
➤ **negligent** *ADJECTIVE*
➤ **negligently** *ADVERB*

negligible *ADJECTIVE*
not big enough or important enough to be worth bothering about • *Fortunately, the damage was negligible.*

negotiable *ADJECTIVE*
able to be changed after being discussed • *The salary is negotiable.*

negotiate *VERB* negotiates, negotiating, negotiated
❶ to bargain or discuss something with others in order to reach an agreement ❷ to arrange something after discussion • *They negotiated a treaty.* ❸ to get over or past an obstacle or difficulty • *We first had to negotiate a five-metre wall.*
➤ **negotiator** *NOUN*

negotiation *NOUN* negotiations
negotiations are discussions people have to reach an agreement about something

neigh *VERB* neighs, neighing, neighed
to make the high-pitched cry of a horse

neigh *NOUN* neighs
the high-pitched cry of a horse

neighbour *NOUN* neighbours
someone who lives next door or near to you

SPELLING
The 'ay' sound is spelt eigh at the start of neighbour, and the 'er' sound at the end is spelt our.

neighbourhood *NOUN* neighbourhoods
❶ the surrounding district or area ❷ a part of a town where people live • *a quiet neighbourhood*

neighbouring *ADJECTIVE*
near each other • *neighbouring villages*

neighbourly *ADVERB*
friendly and helpful to people who live near you

neither (say **ny**-ther or **nee**-ther) *DETERMINER &*
PRONOUN
not either • *Neither parent was there.*
• *Neither of them likes cabbage.*

neither *ADVERB CONJUNCTION*
➤ **neither ... nor** not one thing and not the
other • *She neither knew nor cared.*

> **USAGE**
>
> Correct use is *Neither of them likes it.*
> *Neither he nor his children like it.* Use a
> singular verb (e.g. *likes*) unless one of its
> subjects is plural (e.g. *children*).

nemesis (say **nem**-i-sis) *NOUN*
a punishment that is deserved and cannot be
avoided **WORD ORIGIN** named after *Nemesis*,
goddess of retribution in Greek mythology

Neolithic (say nee-o-**lith**-ik) *ADJECTIVE*
belonging to the later part of the Stone Age

neon *NOUN*
a gas that glows when electricity passes
through it, used in glass tubes to make
illuminated signs

nephew *NOUN* nephews
the son of a person's brother or sister

nepotism (say **nep**-ot-izm) *NOUN*
showing favouritism to relatives in appointing
them to jobs **WORD ORIGIN** from Latin *nepos*
= nephew

nerve *NOUN* nerves
❶ any of the fibres in your body that carry
messages to and from your brain, so that
parts of your body can feel and move
❷ courage and calmness in a dangerous
situation • *Don't lose your nerve.* ❸ cheek or
impudence • *You've got a nerve!*
➤ **get on someone's nerves** to irritate
someone
➤ **nerves** nervousness or anxiety • *I always
suffer from nerves before exams.*

nerve *VERB* nerves, nerving, nerved
to give someone the courage to do something
• *He nerved himself to look down.*

nerve centre *NOUN* nerve centres
the place from which a system or
organization is controlled

nerve-racking *ADJECTIVE*
making you feel anxious or stressed

nervous *ADJECTIVE*
❶ anxious about something or afraid of
something • *I always get nervous just before
a match.* ❷ easily worried or frightened
• *She's quite a nervous girl.* ❸ to do with the

nerves • *a nervous illness*
➤ **nervousness** *NOUN*

nervous breakdown *NOUN* nervous
breakdowns
a state of severe depression and anxiety,
making it difficult to cope with life

nervously *ADVERB*
in a way that shows you are nervous • *He
smiled nervously.*

nervous system *NOUN* nervous systems
the system, consisting of the brain, spinal
cord and nerves, which sends electrical
messages from one part of your body to
another

nervy *ADJECTIVE* nervier, nerviest
nervous or anxious

nest *NOUN* nests
❶ a structure or place in which a bird lays
its eggs and feeds its young ❷ a place where
some small creatures, especially mice and
wasps, live ❸ a set of similar things that fit
inside each other • *a nest of tables*

nest *VERB* nests, nesting, nested
❶ to have or make a nest • *Gulls were nesting
on the cliffs.* ❷ to fit inside something

nest egg *NOUN* nest eggs
a sum of money saved up for future use
WORD ORIGIN originally = an egg left in the
nest to encourage a hen to lay more

nestle *VERB* nestles, nestling, nestled
❶ to curl up comfortably or put something
in a comfortable position • *She nestled her
head on his shoulder.* ❷ to be in a sheltered
position • *A little village nestled at the foot
of the hill.*

nestling *NOUN* nestlings
a bird that is too young to leave the nest

net *NOUN* nets
❶ material made of pieces of thread, cord or
wire joined together in a criss-cross pattern
with holes between ❷ something made of
this • *a fishing net*
➤ **the Net** the Internet

net *ADJECTIVE*
remaining when nothing more is to be
deducted. Compare with **gross**. • *The net
weight, without the box, is 100 grams.*

net *VERB* nets, netting, netted
❶ to catch something with a net; to kick
a ball into a net ❷ to gain or produce an
amount as a net profit

a b c d e f g h i j k l m **n** o p q r s t u v w x y z

netball *NOUN*
a game in which two teams try to throw a ball into a high net hanging from a ring

nether *ADJECTIVE*
lower • *the nether regions*

netting *NOUN*
a piece of net

nettle *NOUN* nettles
a wild plant with leaves that sting when they are touched

nettle *VERB* nettles, nettling, nettled
to annoy someone • *Her remarks clearly nettled him.*

network *NOUN* networks
❶ a net-like arrangement or pattern of intersecting lines or parts • *the railway network* ❷ an organization with many connecting parts that work together • *a spy network* ❸ a group of radio or television stations which broadcast the same programmes ❹ a set of computers which are linked to each other

neuralgia (say newr-al-ja) *NOUN*
pain along a nerve, especially in your face or head

neurology *NOUN*
the study of nerves and their diseases
➤ **neurological** *ADJECTIVE*
➤ **neurologist** *NOUN*

neuron, neurone *NOUN* neurons or neurones
a cell that is part of the nervous system and sends messages to and from your brain

neurotic (say newr-ot-ik) *ADJECTIVE*
always very worried about something

neuter *ADJECTIVE*
in some languages, belonging to the class of words which are neither masculine nor feminine, such as *Fenster* in German

neuter *VERB* neuters, neutering, neutered
to remove an animal's sex organs so that it cannot breed

neutral *ADJECTIVE*
❶ not supporting either side in a war or quarrel ❷ not very distinctive • *a neutral colour such as grey* ❸ neither acid nor alkaline
➤ **neutrality** *NOUN*

neutral *NOUN* neutrals
❶ a neutral person or country ❷ a gear that is not connected to the driving parts of an engine

neutralize (also **neutralise**) *VERB* neutralizes, neutralizing, neutralized
❶ to stop something from having any effect ❷ to make a substance chemically neutral
➤ **neutralization** *NOUN*

neutron *NOUN* neutrons
a particle of matter with no electric charge

never *ADVERB*
❶ at no time; not ever ❷ not at all • *I never realized she was so unhappy.*

nevertheless *ADVERB*
in spite of this; although this is a fact

new *ADJECTIVE*
❶ not existing before; just made, invented, discovered or received ❷ fresh; not used before • *Start on a new page.* ❸ different or changed • *We've just moved to a new house.*
➤ **newness** *NOUN*

new *ADVERB*
recently • *new-laid eggs*

New Age *ADJECTIVE*
to do with a way of living and thinking that includes belief in astrology and alternative medicine and concern for environmental and spiritual matters rather than possessions

newborn *ADJECTIVE*
recently born • *a newborn baby*

newcomer *NOUN* newcomers
a person who has arrived recently

newfangled *ADJECTIVE*
disliked because it is new in method or style

newly *ADVERB*
recently • *a newly discovered comet*

new moon *NOUN* new moons
the moon at the beginning of its cycle, when only a thin crescent can be seen

news *NOUN*
❶ information about recent events or a broadcast report of this ❷ a piece of new information • *That's news to me.*

newsagent *NOUN* newsagents
(*British*) a shopkeeper who sells newspapers

newsflash *NOUN* newsflashes
a short news broadcast which interrupts a programme because something important has happened

newsgroup *NOUN* newsgroups
a place on the Internet where people discuss a particular subject and exchange information about it

newsletter *NOUN* newsletters
a short, informal report sent regularly to members of an organization

newspaper *NOUN* newspapers
❶ a daily or weekly publication on large sheets of paper, containing news reports, reviews and articles ❷ the sheets of paper forming a newspaper • *Wrap it in newspaper.*

newsy *ADJECTIVE* (*informal*)
full of news • *a newsy email*

newt *NOUN* newts
a small animal rather like a lizard, that lives near or in water (WORD ORIGIN) from Old English: originally *an ewt*

newton *NOUN* newtons
a unit for measuring force
(WORD ORIGIN) named after the English scientist, Isaac *Newton*

New Year's Day *NOUN*
the first day of the year, which in the modern Western calendar is 1 January

next *ADJECTIVE*
nearest; coming immediately after • *on the next day* • *When does the next bus leave?*

next *ADVERB*
❶ after this; then • *What happened next?* ❷ in the next place in order • *Jo was the next oldest after Ali.*
➤ **next to** close beside someone or something • *He sat down next to me.*

next door *ADVERB & ADJECTIVE*
in the next house or building • *Who lives next door?*

NGO *ABBREVIATION*
non-governmental organization (a charity or association that is independent of government or business)

nib *NOUN* nibs
the pointed metal part of a pen

nibble *VERB* nibbles, nibbling, nibbled
to eat something by taking small, quick or gentle bites • *He sat at the table nibbling a biscuit.*

nice *ADJECTIVE* nicer, nicest
❶ kind and friendly ❷ pleasant or enjoyable ❸ precise or careful • *Dictionaries make nice distinctions between meanings of words.*
➤ **nicely** *ADVERB*
➤ **niceness** *NOUN*
(WORD ORIGIN) originally = stupid: from Latin *nescius* = ignorant

nicety (say **ny**-sit-ee) *NOUN* niceties
❶ a small detail or difference pointed out ❷ precision or accuracy

niche (say nich or neesh) *NOUN* niches
❶ a small recess, especially in a wall • *The vase stood in a niche.* ❷ a suitable place or position • *She found her niche in the drama club.*

nick *NOUN* nicks
❶ a small cut or notch ❷ (*informal*) a police station or prison
➤ **in good nick** (*informal*) in good condition
➤ **in the nick of time** only just in time

nick *VERB* nicks, nicking, nicked
❶ to make a nick in something ❷ (*informal*) to steal something ❸ (*informal*) to arrest someone

nickel *NOUN* nickels
❶ a silvery-white metal ❷ (*North American*) a 5-cent coin

nickname *NOUN* nicknames
an informal name given to a person instead of his or her real name (WORD ORIGIN) originally *an eke-name*: from Middle English *eke* = addition + **name**

nicotine *NOUN*
a poisonous substance found in tobacco
(WORD ORIGIN) from the name of J. *Nicot*, who introduced tobacco into France in 1560

niece *NOUN* nieces
the daughter of a person's brother or sister

niggardly *ADJECTIVE*
mean or stingy

niggle *VERB* niggles, niggling, niggled
to be a small but constant worry • *The question niggled away at the back of his mind.*
➤ **niggling** *ADJECTIVE*

nigh *ADVERB & PREPOSITION* (*poetical use*)
near or nearly

night *NOUN* nights
❶ the dark hours between sunset and sunrise ❷ a particular night or evening • *the first night of the play*

SPELLING

Night is different from **knight**, which is a noble warrior.

nightcap *NOUN* nightcaps
❶ (*old use*) a knitted cap worn in bed ❷ a drink, especially an alcoholic one, which you have before going to bed

nightclub *NOUN* nightclubs
a place that is open at night where people go to drink and dance

nightdress *NOUN* nightdresses
a loose dress that girls or women wear in bed

nightfall *NOUN*
the coming of darkness at the end of the day

nightie *NOUN* nighties (*informal*)
a nightdress

nightingale *NOUN* nightingales
a small brown bird that sings sweetly

nightlife *NOUN*
the places of entertainment that you can go to at night • *a popular resort with plenty of nightlife*

nightly *ADJECTIVE & ADVERB*
happening every night • *nightly patrols*

nightmare *NOUN* nightmares
❶ a frightening dream ❷ an unpleasant experience • *The journey was a nightmare.*
➤ **nightmarish** *ADJECTIVE*
WORD ORIGIN from **night** + Middle English *mare* = an evil spirit

nil *NOUN*
nothing or nought • *We lost three-nil.*
WORD ORIGIN from Latin *nihil* = nothing

nimble *ADJECTIVE*
able to move quickly and easily; agile • *You need nimble fingers for that job.*
➤ **nimbly** *ADVERB*

nine *NOUN & ADJECTIVE* nines
the number 9

ninepins *NOUN*
the game of skittles played with nine objects

nineteen *NOUN & ADJECTIVE* nineteens
the number 19
➤ **nineteenth** *ADJECTIVE & NOUN*

ninety *NOUN & ADJECTIVE* nineties
the number 90
➤ **ninetieth** *ADJECTIVE & NOUN*

ninth *ADJECTIVE & NOUN* ninths
❶ next after eighth ❷ one of nine equal parts of a thing

nip *VERB* nips, nipping, nipped
❶ to pinch or bite someone quickly
❷ (*informal*) to go somewhere quickly • *I'm just nipping out to the shops.*

nip *NOUN* nips
❶ a quick pinch or bite ❷ sharp coldness

• *There's a nip in the air.* ❸ a small drink of a spirit • *a nip of brandy*

nipper *NOUN* nippers (*informal*)
a young child

nipple *NOUN* nipples
the small part that sticks out at the front of a person's breast, from which babies suck milk

nippy *ADJECTIVE* nippier, nippiest (*informal*)
❶ quick or nimble ❷ rather cold

nirvana *NOUN*
in Buddhism and Hinduism, the highest state of knowledge and understanding, achieved by meditation

nit *NOUN* nits
a parasitic insect or its egg, found in people's hair

nit-picking *NOUN*
pointing out very small faults or mistakes

nitrate *NOUN* nitrates
❶ a chemical compound containing nitrogen
❷ potassium or sodium nitrate, used as a fertilizer

nitric acid (say **ny**-trik) *NOUN*
a very strong colourless acid containing nitrogen

nitrogen (say **ny**-tro-jen) *NOUN*
a gas that makes up about four-fifths of the air

nitwit *NOUN* nitwits (*informal*)
a stupid person

no *DETERMINER*
not any • *We have no money.*

no *EXCLAMATION*
used to deny or refuse something • *'Will you come?' 'No.'*

no *ADVERB*
not at all • *She is no better.*

No., no. *ABBREVIATION* Nos. or nos.
number

nobility *NOUN*
❶ being noble ❷ the aristocracy

noble *ADJECTIVE* nobler, noblest
❶ of high social rank; aristocratic ❷ having a very good character or qualities • *a noble king* ❸ stately or impressive • *a noble building*
➤ **nobly** *ADVERB*

noble *NOUN* nobles
a person of high social rank

nobleman, noblewoman NOUN noblemen, noblewomen
a man or woman of high social rank

nobody PRONOUN
no person; no one

nobody NOUN nobodies (*informal*) an unimportant person

nocturnal ADJECTIVE
❶ happening at night ❷ active at night
• *Badgers are nocturnal animals.*

nocturne NOUN nocturnes
a piece of music with the quiet dreamy feeling of night

nod VERB nods, nodding, nodded
to move your head up and down, especially as a way of agreeing with someone or as a greeting
➤ **nod off** to fall asleep

nod NOUN nods
a movement of your head up and down

node NOUN nodes
a small round swelling

nodule NOUN nodules
a small node

noise NOUN noises
a sound, especially one that is loud or unpleasant

noiseless ADJECTIVE
making no noise • *She moved with noiseless steps.*
➤ **noiselessly** ADVERB

noisome (say **noi**-sum) ADJECTIVE
smelling unpleasant; harmful • *a noisome dungeon*

noisy ADJECTIVE noisier, noisiest
making a lot of noise or full of noise • *a noisy classroom*
➤ **noisily** ADVERB

nomad NOUN nomads
a member of a tribe that moves from place to place looking for pasture for their animals

nomadic ADJECTIVE
moving from place to place • *a nomadic tribe*

no man's land NOUN
an area that does not belong to anybody, especially the land between opposing armies

nom de plume NOUN noms de plume
a name used by a writer instead of their real name; a pseudonym **WORD ORIGIN** French, = pen-name (this phrase is not used in French)

nominal ADJECTIVE
❶ in name only • *He is the nominal ruler, but the real power is held by the generals.*
❷ small or insignificant • *We charged them only a nominal fee.*
➤ **nominally** ADVERB

nominate VERB nominates, nominating, nominated
to formally suggest that someone should be a candidate in an election or should be given a job or award • *His latest novel has been nominated for several book prizes.*
➤ **nomination** NOUN

nominee NOUN nominees
a person who is nominated

non- PREFIX
not (as in *non-stop*) • *non-existent*

nonagenarian NOUN nonagenarians
a person aged between 90 and 99

nonchalant (say **non**-shal-ant) ADJECTIVE
calm and casual; showing no anxiety or excitement • *He tried to sound nonchalant.*
➤ **nonchalantly** ADVERB
➤ **nonchalance** NOUN

non-committal ADJECTIVE
not saying what you think or what you plan to do • *a non-committal reply*

Nonconformist NOUN Nonconformists
a member of a Protestant Church (e.g. Baptist, Methodist) that does not conform to all the customs of the Church of England

nondescript ADJECTIVE
having no special or distinctive qualities and therefore difficult to describe

none PRONOUN
❶ not any • *Sorry, we've got none left.* ❷ no one • *None can tell.*

none ADVERB
not at all • *He is none too bright.* • *She seemed none the worse for the experience.*

nonentity (say non-**en**-tit-ee) NOUN nonentities
an unimportant person

nonetheless ADVERB
in spite of this; although this is a fact

non-existent ADJECTIVE
not existing or unreal

non-fiction NOUN
writings that are not fiction; books about real people and things and true events

non-flammable *ADJECTIVE*
not able to be set on fire

> **USAGE**
> See note at **inflammable**.

nonplussed *ADJECTIVE*
puzzled or confused

nonsense *NOUN*
❶ words put together in a way that does not mean anything ❷ stupid ideas or behaviour
➤ **nonsensical** (say non-**sens**-ik-al) *ADJECTIVE*

non sequitur (say non **sek**-wit-er) *NOUN* **non sequiturs**
a conclusion that does not follow from the evidence given

non-stop *ADJECTIVE & ADVERB*
❶ not stopping • *They talked non-stop for hours.* ❷ not stopping between two main stations • *a non-stop train*

noodles *PLURAL NOUN*
pasta made in narrow strips, used in soups and stir-fries

nook *NOUN* **nooks**
a small sheltered place or corner
➤ **every nook and cranny** every part of a place

noon *NOUN*
twelve o'clock midday

no one *PRONOUN*
no person; nobody

> **SPELLING**
> **No one** is two separate words.

noose *NOUN* **nooses**
a loop in a rope that gets smaller when the rope is pulled

nor *CONJUNCTION*
and not • *She cannot do it; nor can I.*

norm *NOUN* **norms**
❶ a standard or average type, amount or level ❷ normal or expected behaviour • *social norms*

normal *ADJECTIVE*
❶ usual or ordinary ❷ natural and healthy; not suffering from an illness
➤ **normality** *NOUN*

normally *ADVERB*
❶ usually • *The journey normally takes an hour.* ❷ in the usual way • *Just breathe normally.*

Norman *NOUN* **Normans**
a member of the people of Normandy in northern France, who conquered England in 1066
➤ **Norman** *ADJECTIVE*
> **WORD ORIGIN** from Old Norse *northmathr* = man from the north (because the Normans were partly descended from the Vikings)

north *NOUN*
❶ the direction to the left of a person who faces east ❷ the northern part of a country, city or other area

north *ADJECTIVE & ADVERB*
towards or in the north; coming from the north
➤ **northerly** *ADJECTIVE*
➤ **northern** *ADJECTIVE*
➤ **northerner** *NOUN*
➤ **northernmost** *ADJECTIVE*

north-east *NOUN, ADJECTIVE & ADVERB*
midway between north and east
➤ **north-easterly** *ADJECTIVE*
➤ **north-eastern** *ADJECTIVE*

northward *ADJECTIVE & ADVERB*
towards the north
➤ **northwards** *ADVERB*

north-west *NOUN, ADJECTIVE & ADVERB*
midway between north and west
➤ **north-westerly** *ADJECTIVE*
➤ **north-western** *ADJECTIVE*

Nos., nos.
plural of **No.** or **no**

nose *NOUN* **noses**
❶ the part of the face that is used for breathing and for smelling things ❷ the front end or part of something

nose *VERB* **noses, nosing, nosed**
to go forward cautiously • *Ships nosed through the ice.*
➤ **nose about** or **around** (*informal*) to look for private information about someone; to pry

nosebag *NOUN* **nosebags**
a bag containing fodder, for hanging on a horse's head

nosedive *NOUN* **nosedives**
a steep downward dive, especially by an aircraft
➤ **nosedive** *VERB*

nosegay *NOUN* **nosegays**
a small bunch of flowers

nostalgia (say nos-**tal**-ja) *NOUN*
a feeling of pleasure, mixed with sadness,
when you remember happy times in the past
➤ **nostalgic** *ADJECTIVE*
➤ **nostalgically** *ADVERB*
WORD ORIGIN originally = homesickness: from
Greek *nostos* = return home + *algos* = pain

nostril *NOUN* **nostrils**
either of the two openings in the nose
WORD ORIGIN from Old English *nosthryl* =
nose-hole

nosy *ADJECTIVE* **nosier, nosiest** (*informal*)
always wanting to know other people's
business
➤ **nosiness** *NOUN*
WORD ORIGIN from *sticking your nose in* =
being inquisitive

not *ADVERB*
used to change the meaning of something to
its opposite or absence

notable *ADJECTIVE*
worth noticing; remarkable or famous • *It
was a notable achievement.* • *The area is
notable for its wildlife.*

notably *ADVERB*
especially or remarkably • *Many important
people, most notably the Prime Minister, have
given their support.*

notation *NOUN* **notations**
a system of symbols representing numbers,
quantities or musical notes

notch *NOUN* **notches**
a small V-shape cut into a surface

notch *VERB* **notches, notching, notched**
to cut a notch or notches in a surface
➤ **notch something up** to score or achieve
a certain score or figure • *He has already
notched up 20 goals this season.*

note *NOUN* **notes**
❶ something written down as a reminder
or as a comment or explanation ❷ a short
letter ❸ a banknote ❹ a single sound in
music ❺ any of the keys on a piano or other
keyboard instrument ❻ a sound or quality
that indicates something • *There was a note
of warning in his voice.*
➤ **take note of something** to pay attention
to something and be sure to remember it

note *VERB* **notes, noting, noted**
❶ to make a note about something; to write
something down ❷ to notice or pay attention
to something • *Note the instructions on the
label.*

notebook *NOUN* **notebooks**
❶ a book with blank pages on which to write
notes ❷ a small computer that you can carry
around with you

noted *ADJECTIVE*
famous, especially for a particular reason • *an
area noted for its mild climate*

notepaper *NOUN*
paper for writing letters

nothing *PRONOUN*
❶ no thing; not anything • *There was nothing
to do.* ❷ no amount; nought
➤ **for nothing** ❶ without payment; free
❷ without a result • *His hard work was all for
nothing.*

nothing *ADVERB*
not at all; in no way • *It's nothing like as good
as her first book.*

notice *NOUN* **notices**
❶ something written or printed and displayed
for people to see ❷ attention • *It escaped my
notice.* ❸ warning that something is going to
happen ❹ a formal announcement that you
are about to end an agreement or leave a job
at a specified time • *You will need to give a
month's notice.*

notice *VERB* **notices, noticing, noticed**
to see or become aware of something • *Did
you notice the tattoo on his arm?*

noticeable *ADJECTIVE*
easily seen or noticed • *The scar is barely
noticeable now.*
➤ **noticeably** *ADVERB*

noticeboard *NOUN* **noticeboards**
(*British*) a board on which notices may be
displayed

notify *VERB* **notifies, notifying, notified**
to tell someone about something formally or
officially • *We had better notify the police.*
➤ **notification** *NOUN*

notion *NOUN* **notions**
an idea, especially one that is vague or
incorrect

notorious *ADJECTIVE*
well known for something bad • *a notorious
criminal*
➤ **notoriously** *ADVERB*
➤ **notoriety** (say noh-ter-**y**-it-ee) *NOUN*

notwithstanding *PREPOSITION*
in spite of

a
b
c
d
e
f
g
h
i
j
k
l
m
n
o
p
q
r
s
t
u
v
w
x
y
z

nougat (say **noo**-gah) NOUN
a chewy sweet made from nuts, sugar or honey and egg white

nought (say nawt) NOUN
(*British*) the figure 0

noun NOUN nouns
a word that stands for a person, place or thing. **Common nouns** are words such as *boy, dog, river, sport, table*, which are used of a whole kind of people or things; **proper nouns** are words such as *Jennifer, Thames* and *London* which name a particular person or thing.

> **GRAMMAR**
>
> Nouns are used to name people, places or things and tell you who or what a sentence is about.
>
> **Common nouns** describe a whole group or category of people or things: for example, *footballer, lizard, picture, television, day*. They can be divided into
>
> **concrete nouns**, which are used to talk about things which can be physically seen or touched (e.g. *baby, penguin, telescope*), and **abstract nouns**, which are used to talk about things which cannot be physically touched or seen, such as a state, idea, process or feeling (e.g. *beauty, horror, mystery*).
>
> **Proper nouns** give the name of a specific person, place or thing. They include personal names and titles (e.g. *Alexander, Shakespeare, the Queen*), place names and names of geographical features (e.g. *Rome, Antarctica, Saturn, the Grand Canyon*), the names of organizations and religions (e.g. *the United Nations, Buddhism*), the days of the week, months of the year and festivals (e.g. *Tuesday, July, Diwali, Hallowe'en*). Proper nouns always begin with a capital letter; common nouns only begin with a capital when they start a sentence: *Penguins are non-flying birds that live in Antarctica.*
>
> Nouns that can be made plural are called **countable nouns**. Most common nouns are countable.
>
> Nouns that cannot be made plural are called **uncountable nouns** (e.g. *rice, music, anger* and *information*).

nourish VERB nourishes, nourishing, nourished
to keep a person, animal or plant alive and well by means of food
> **nourishing** ADJECTIVE

nourishment NOUN
food that a person, animal or plant needs to stay alive and well

nova (say **noh**-va) NOUN novae (say **noh**-vee) or novas
a star that suddenly becomes much brighter for a short time

novel NOUN novels
a story that fills a whole book

novel ADJECTIVE
of a new and unusual kind • *a novel experience*

novelist NOUN novelists
a person who writes novels

novelty NOUN novelties
❶ the quality of being new, different and interesting • *The novelty of living in a cave soon wore off.* ❷ something new and unusual ❸ a cheap toy or ornament

November NOUN
the eleventh month of the year
> **WORD ORIGIN** from Latin *novem* = nine, because it was the ninth month of the ancient Roman calendar

novice NOUN novices
❶ a beginner ❷ a person preparing to be a monk or nun

now ADVERB
❶ at the present time; this moment • *They will be at home by now.* ❷ by this time ❸ immediately • *You must go now.* ❹ I wonder or I am telling you • *Now why didn't I think of that?*
> **for now** until a later time
> **now and again** or **now and then** sometimes; occasionally

now CONJUNCTION
as a result of or at the same time as something • *Now that you have come, we'll start.*

nowadays ADVERB
at the present time, as contrasted with years ago

nowhere ADVERB
not anywhere; in or to no place • *There's nowhere to sit.*

noxious ADJECTIVE
unpleasant and harmful • *noxious fumes*

nozzle *NOUN* nozzles
the spout of a hose, pipe or tube

nuance (say **new**-ahns) *NOUN* nuances
a slight difference or shade of meaning

nub *NOUN* nubs
❶ a small knob or lump ❷ the central point
of a problem

nuclear *ADJECTIVE*
❶ to do with a nucleus, especially of an
atom ❷ using the energy that is created by
reactions in the nuclei of atoms • *nuclear
power* • *nuclear weapons*

nucleus *NOUN* nuclei
❶ the central part of an atom or biological
cell ❷ the part in the centre of something,
round which other things are grouped • *The
queen bee is the nucleus of the hive.*

nude *ADJECTIVE*
not wearing any clothes; naked
➤ **nudity** *NOUN*

nude *NOUN* nudes
a painting or sculpture of a naked human
figure
➤ **in the nude** not wearing any clothes

nudge *VERB* nudges, nudging, nudged
❶ to poke a person gently with your elbow
❷ to push something slightly or gradually

nudge *NOUN* nudges
a slight push or poke

nugget *NOUN* nuggets
❶ a rough lump of something, especially
gold, found in the earth ❷ a small but
valuable fact

nuisance *NOUN* nuisances
a person or thing that is annoying or causes
trouble

null *ADJECTIVE*
➤ **null and void** not legally valid • *The
agreement is null and void.*

nullify *VERB* nullifies, nullifying, nullified
to make a thing no longer valid; to cancel an
agreement or arrangement
➤ **nullification** *NOUN*

numb *ADJECTIVE*
not able to feel anything • *My fingers were
numb with cold.*
➤ **numbly** *ADVERB*
➤ **numbness** *NOUN*

numb *VERB* numbs, numbing, numbed
to make you unable to feel anything • *We
were all numbed by the dreadful news.*

number *NOUN* numbers
❶ a symbol or word that tells you how many
of something there are; a numeral or figure
❷ a series of numbers given to a thing to
identify it • *a telephone number* ❸ a quantity
of people or things • *He found a large
number of people waiting outside.* ❹ one
issue of a magazine or newspaper ❺ a song
or piece of music

USAGE
Note that *a number of*, meaning 'a
quantity of' or 'several', should be
followed by a plural verb • *A number of
problems remain.*

number *VERB* numbers, numbering, numbered
❶ to give something a number or mark it
with a number • *The houses are numbered
from 1 to 34.* ❷ to amount to a certain figure
• *The crowd numbered 10,000.*

GRAMMAR
Numbers tell you how many of something
there are.

A **cardinal number** is a number that
expresses a quantity and is used for
counting things, e.g. *one, two, three,* etc.

An **ordinal number** is a number that
shows a thing's position in a series, e.g.
first, fifth, twentieth, etc.

numberless *ADJECTIVE*
too many to count

numeracy *NOUN*
a good basic knowledge of mathematics
➤ **numerate** *ADJECTIVE*

numeral *NOUN* numerals
a symbol that represents a certain number;
a figure

numerator *NOUN* numerators
the number above the line in a fraction,
showing how many parts are to be taken, e.g.
2 in ⅖. Compare with **denominator**.

numerical (say new-**merri**-kal) *ADJECTIVE*
to do with or consisting of numbers • *The
pages are not in numerical order.*
➤ **numerically** *ADVERB*

numerous *ADJECTIVE*
many; lots of • *There are numerous websites
on the subject.*

numismatics (say new-miz-**mat**-iks) *NOUN*
the study of coins
➤ **numismatist** *NOUN*

nun *NOUN* nuns
a member of a community of women who live according to the rules of a religious organization. Compare with **monk**.

nunnery *NOUN* nunneries
a convent

nuptial *ADJECTIVE*
to do with marriage or a wedding

nuptials *PLURAL NOUN*
a wedding

nurse *NOUN* nurses
❶ a person trained to look after people who are ill or injured ❷ a woman employed to look after young children

nurse *VERB* nurses, nursing, nursed
❶ to look after someone who is ill or injured ❷ to take care of an injury or illness • *I got up slowly, nursing my bruised shoulder.* ❸ to feed a baby at the breast ❹ to have a feeling for a long time • *She's been nursing a grudge against him for years* ❺ to hold something carefully in your hands • *He sat nursing his mug of coffee.*

nursemaid *NOUN* nursemaids
a young woman employed to look after young children

nursery *NOUN* nurseries
❶ a place where young children are looked after or play ❷ a place where young plants are grown and usually for sale

nursery rhyme *NOUN* nursery rhymes
a simple rhyme or song of the kind that young children like

nursery school *NOUN* nursery schools
a school for children below primary school age

nursing home *NOUN* nursing homes
a small hospital or home for invalids

nurture *VERB* nurtures, nurturing, nurtured
❶ to take care of and educate a young child while he or she is growing ❷ to help something to grow or develop • *He has nurtured the talent of many young footballers.* ❸ to cherish an idea or hope • *She nurtured a hope of becoming famous.*

nurture *NOUN*
a child's upbringing and education

nut *NOUN* nuts
❶ a fruit with a hard shell ❷ a kernel ❸ a small piece of metal with a hole in the middle, for screwing onto a bolt ❹ (*informal*) the head ❺ (*informal*) a mad or eccentric person

nutcrackers *PLURAL NOUN*
pincers for cracking nuts

nutmeg *NOUN*
the hard seed of a tropical tree, grated and used in cooking

nutrient (say **new**-tree-ent) *NOUN* nutrients
a substance that is needed to keep a plant or animal alive and to help it grow • *Plants take minerals and other nutrients from the soil.*

nutriment (say **new**-trim-ent) *NOUN*
nourishing food

nutrition (say new-**trish**-on) *NOUN*
the food that you eat and the way that it affects your health; nourishment
➤ **nutritional** *ADJECTIVE*
➤ **nutritionally** *ADVERB*

nutritious (say new-**trish**-us) *ADJECTIVE*
nutritious food has substances in it that help you to stay healthy • *a nutritious meal*

nuts *ADJECTIVE*
(*informal*) mad or eccentric

nutshell *NOUN* nutshells
the shell of a nut
➤ **in a nutshell** stated very briefly

nutty *ADJECTIVE*
❶ tasting of nuts or full of nuts ❷ (*informal*) slightly crazy

nuzzle *VERB* nuzzles, nuzzling, nuzzled
to rub gently against someone with the nose or face • *The dog began nuzzling my hand.*

NW *ABBREVIATION*
❶ north-west ❷ north-western

nylon *NOUN*
a synthetic, strong, lightweight cloth or fibre

nymph (say nimf) *NOUN* nymphs
❶ in myths, a young goddess living in the sea or woods etc. ❷ the immature form of insects such as the dragonfly

NZ *ABBREVIATION*
New Zealand

O EXCLAMATION
oh

oaf NOUN oafs
a stupid or clumsy man

oak NOUN oaks
a large deciduous tree with seeds called acorns
➤ **oaken** ADJECTIVE

oar NOUN oars
a pole with a flat blade at one end, used for rowing a boat
➤ **oarsman** NOUN

oasis (say oh-**ay**-sis) NOUN oases
a fertile place in a desert, with a spring or well of water

oath NOUN oaths
❶ a solemn promise to do something or that something is true, sometimes appealing to God as witness ❷ a swear word
➤ **on** or **under oath** having sworn to tell the truth in a law court

oatmeal NOUN
ground oats, used to make porridge or in baking

oats PLURAL NOUN
a cereal used to make food for animals and for people

obedient ADJECTIVE
doing what you are told; willing to obey
➤ **obediently** ADVERB
➤ **obedience** NOUN

obeisance (say o-**bay**-sans) NOUN obeisances
a deep bow or curtsy showing respect

obelisk NOUN obelisks
a tall pillar set up as a monument

obese (say o-**beess**) ADJECTIVE
very fat; overweight

obesity (say o-**beess**-it-ee) NOUN
being too fat in a way that is unhealthy • *the problem of obesity in children*

obey VERB obeys, obeying, obeyed
to do what you are told to do • *Soldiers are trained to obey orders.*

obituary NOUN obituaries
an announcement in a newspaper of a person's death, often with a short account of their life

object (say ob-jikt) NOUN objects
❶ something solid that can be seen or touched ❷ a purpose or intention • *Making money is his sole object in life.* ❸ a person or thing to which some action or feeling is directed • *She has become an object of pity.* ❹ (*in grammar*) the word or words naming the person or thing that is affected by the action of a verb or preposition, e.g. *him* in *The dog bit him.* and *I threw the ball to him.*

object (say ob-**jekt**) VERB objects, objecting, objected
to say that you are not in favour of something or do not agree • *I'd like to come too, if you don't object.*
➤ **objector** NOUN

objection NOUN objections
❶ objecting to something ❷ a reason for objecting • *I have a couple of objections to your plan.*

objectionable ADJECTIVE
unpleasant or nasty

objective NOUN objectives
what you are trying to reach or do; an aim • *My main objective is to tell a good story.*

objective ADJECTIVE
❶ not influenced by personal feelings or opinions • *He tried to give an objective account of what happened.*
Compare with **subjective.** ❷ having real existence outside someone's mind • *Is there any objective evidence to prove his claims?*
➤ **objectively** ADVERB
➤ **objectivity** NOUN

objet d'art (say ob-zhay **dar**) NOUN objets d'art
a small artistic object

obligation NOUN obligations
❶ being obliged to do something ❷ what you are obliged to do; a duty
➤ **under an obligation** owing gratitude to someone who has helped you

obligatory (say ob-**lig**-a-ter-ee) ADJECTIVE
something is obligatory when you must do it because of a law or rule

oblige VERB obliges, obliging, obliged
❶ to force someone to do something • *I felt obliged to invite her to the party.* ❷ to help someone by doing what they ask • *Can you*

oblige me with a loan?
➤ **be obliged to someone** to feel gratitude to a person who has helped you

obliging *ADJECTIVE*
polite and helpful

oblique (say ob-**leek**) *ADJECTIVE*
❶ slanting ❷ not saying something straightforwardly • *an oblique reply*
➤ **obliquely** *ADVERB*

obliterate *VERB* obliterates, obliterating, obliterated
to remove all traces of something by destroying it completely or covering it up
• *The snow had obliterated their footprints.*
➤ **obliteration** *NOUN*
WORD ORIGIN from Latin *obliterare* = cross out, from *littera* = letter

oblivion *NOUN*
❶ being forgotten ❷ being unconscious

oblivious *ADJECTIVE*
completely unaware of what is happening around you • *She seemed oblivious to the danger.*

oblong *ADJECTIVE*
rectangular in shape and longer than it is wide

oblong *NOUN* oblongs
a rectangular shape that is longer than it is wide

obnoxious *ADJECTIVE*
very unpleasant or offensive

oboe *NOUN* oboes
a high-pitched woodwind instrument
➤ **oboist** *NOUN*

obscene (say ob-**seen**) *ADJECTIVE*
indecent in a very offensive way
➤ **obscenity** *NOUN*

obscure *ADJECTIVE*
❶ difficult to see or to understand; not clear ❷ not well known
➤ **obscurely** *ADVERB*

obscure *VERB* obscures, obscuring, obscured
to make a thing difficult to see or to understand • *Clouds obscured the sun.*

obscurity *NOUN*
❶ being not well known • *He spent most of his life working in obscurity.* ❷ the quality of being difficult to understand

obsequious (say ob-**seek**-wee-us) *ADJECTIVE*
showing too much respect or too willing to obey or serve someone

➤ **obsequiously** *ADVERB*
➤ **obsequiousness** *NOUN*

observance *NOUN*
obeying or keeping a law, custom or religious festival

observant *ADJECTIVE*
quick at observing or noticing things
➤ **observantly** *ADVERB*

observation *NOUN* observations
❶ noticing or watching something carefully ❷ a comment or remark • *She made a few observations about the weather.*

observatory *NOUN* observatories
a building with telescopes and other instruments for observing the stars or weather

observe *VERB* observes, observing, observed
❶ to see and notice something • *I observed her putting the letter into her bag.* ❷ to watch something carefully • *The puffins were observed throughout the breeding season.* ❸ to obey a law or rule ❹ to keep or celebrate a custom or religious festival ❺ to make a remark
➤ **observer** *NOUN*

obsessed *ADJECTIVE*
to be obsessed with something is to be continually thinking about it • *He is obsessed with dinosaurs.*

obsession *NOUN* obsessions
something you cannot stop thinking about
• *She seems to have an obsession with aliens.*

obsessive *ADJECTIVE*
showing that a person thinks too much about something in a way that is not normal • *his obsessive cleanliness*

obsolete *ADJECTIVE*
not used any more; out of date

obstacle *NOUN* obstacles
something that stands in the way or makes it difficult to do something

obstetrics *NOUN*
the branch of medicine and surgery that deals with the birth of babies

obstinate *ADJECTIVE*
❶ refusing to change your ideas or ways, even though they may be wrong ❷ difficult to overcome or remove • *an obstinate problem*
➤ **obstinately** *ADVERB*
➤ **obstinacy** *NOUN*

obstreperous (say ob-**strep**-er-us) *ADJECTIVE*
noisy and unruly

obstruct *VERB* obstructs, obstructing, obstructed
to stop a person or thing from getting past; to hinder the progress of something • *A fallen tree was obstructing the road.*
➤ **obstructive** *ADJECTIVE*

obstruction *NOUN* obstructions
❶ obstructing something ❷ something that obstructs or hinders progress

obtain *VERB* obtains, obtaining, obtained
to get or be given something • *You need to obtain permission to take photos there.*
➤ **obtainable** *ADJECTIVE*

obtrude *VERB* obtrudes, obtruding, obtruded
to force yourself or your ideas on someone; to be obtrusive
➤ **obtrusion** *NOUN*

obtrusive *ADJECTIVE*
unpleasantly noticeable

obtuse *ADJECTIVE*
slow to understand something
➤ **obtuseness** *NOUN*

obtuse angle *NOUN* obtuse angles
an angle of more than 90° but less than 180°. Compare with **acute angle**.

obverse *NOUN*
the side of a coin or medal showing the head or chief design (the other side is the **reverse**)

obvious *ADJECTIVE*
easy to see or understand

obviously *ADVERB*
it is obvious that; clearly • *There has obviously been a mistake.*

occasion *NOUN* occasions
❶ the time when something happens ❷ a special event ❸ a suitable time or opportunity • *I will speak to him about it if the occasion arises.*
➤ **on occasion** from time to time

occasion *VERB* occasions, occasioning, occasioned (*formal*) to cause something to happen

occasional *ADJECTIVE*
❶ happening from time to time but not regularly or frequently ❷ for special occasions • *occasional music*

occasionally *ADVERB*
sometimes, but not often • *We text each other occasionally.*

occult *ADJECTIVE*
to do with the supernatural or magic • *occult powers*

occupant *NOUN* occupants
someone who is in a place or building • *The other occupants of the car got out.*
➤ **occupancy** *NOUN*

occupation *NOUN* occupations
❶ a person's job or profession ❷ something you do to pass your time ❸ capturing a country by military force

occupational *ADJECTIVE*
caused by an occupation • *an occupational disease*

occupational therapy *NOUN*
creative work designed to help people to recover from certain illnesses
➤ **occupational therapist** *NOUN*

occupy *VERB* occupies, occupying, occupied
❶ to live or work in a place or building; to inhabit somewhere ❷ to fill a space or position • *A large table occupied most of the room.* ❸ to keep someone busy or interested • *This game should occupy them for a few hours.* ❹ to capture a country by force and place troops there
➤ **occupier** *NOUN*

occur *VERB* occurs, occurring, occurred
❶ to happen or take place • *An earthquake occurred on the island in 1953.* ❷ to exist or be found somewhere • *These plants occur in ponds.* ❸ to come into a person's mind • *Just then an idea occurred to me.*

occurrence *NOUN* occurrences
❶ something that happens; an incident or event ❷ occurring

ocean *NOUN* oceans
the seas that surround the continents of the earth, especially one of the large named areas of this • *the Pacific Ocean*
➤ **oceanic** *ADJECTIVE*
WORD ORIGIN from *Oceanus*, the river that the ancient Greeks thought surrounded the world

ocelot (say **oss**-il-ot) *NOUN* ocelots
a leopard-like animal of Central and South America

ochre (say **oh**-ker) *NOUN*
❶ a yellow, red or brownish mineral used as a pigment ❷ pale brownish-yellow

o'clock *ADVERB*
used after the number of the hour when you

a
b
c
d
e
f
g
h
i
j
k
l
m
n
o
p
q
r
s
t
u
v
w
x
y
z

are saying what time it is • *Lunch is at one o'clock.* **WORD ORIGIN** short for *of the clock*

octagon *NOUN* **octagons**
a flat shape with eight sides and eight angles
➤ **octagonal** *ADJECTIVE*

octave *NOUN* **octaves**
the interval of eight steps between one musical note and the next note of the same name above or below it

octet *NOUN* **octets**
a group of eight instruments or singers

October *NOUN*
the tenth month of the year
WORD ORIGIN from Latin *octo* = eight, because it was the eighth month of the ancient Roman calendar

octogenarian *NOUN* **octogenarians**
a person aged between 80 and 89

octopus *NOUN* **octopuses**
a sea creature with eight long tentacles
WORD ORIGIN from Greek *okto* = eight + *pous* = foot

ocular *ADJECTIVE*
to do with your eyes or vision

oculist *NOUN* **oculists**
a doctor who treats diseases of the eye

odd *ADJECTIVE*
❶ strange or unusual ❷ an odd number is one that cannot be divided exactly by two Compare with **even**. ❸ left over from a pair or set • *I've got one odd sock.* ❹ of various kinds; not regular • *odd jobs*
➤ **oddness** *NOUN*

oddity *NOUN* **oddities**
a strange person or thing

oddly *ADVERB*
❶ strangely • *She's been behaving very oddly recently.* ❷ surprisingly • *Oddly enough, the most expensive tickets sold fastest.*

oddments *PLURAL NOUN*
scraps or pieces left over from a larger piece or set

odds *PLURAL NOUN*
❶ the chances that a certain thing will happen ❷ the proportion of money that you will win if a bet is successful • *When the odds are 10 to 1, you will win £10 if you bet £1.*
➤ **be at odds with someone** or **something** to disagree or conflict with someone or something

➤ **odds and ends** small things of various kinds

ode *NOUN* **odes**
a poem addressed to a person or thing

odious (say **oh**-dee-us) *ADJECTIVE*
extremely unpleasant; hateful

odour *NOUN* **odours**
a smell, especially an unpleasant one
➤ **odorous** *ADJECTIVE*
➤ **odourless** *ADJECTIVE*

odyssey (say **od**-iss-ee) *NOUN* **odysseys**
a long adventurous journey
WORD ORIGIN named after the *Odyssey*, a Greek poem telling of the wanderings of Odysseus

o'er *PREPOSITION & ADVERB* (*poetical use*)
over; above

oesophagus (say ee-**sof**-a-gus) *NOUN* **oesophagi**
the tube leading from the throat to the stomach; the gullet

oestrogen (say **ees**-tro-jen) *NOUN*
a hormone which develops and maintains female sexual and physical characteristics

of *PREPOSITION*
❶ belonging to • *the mother of the child*
❷ concerning; about • *news of the disaster*
❸ made from • *built of stone* ❹ from • *north of the town*

SPELLING
Of is different from **off** • *I've never heard of it.* • *He fell off his bike.*

off *PREPOSITION*
❶ not on; away or down from • *He fell off the ladder.* ❷ not taking or wanting • *She is off her food.* ❸ deducted from • *£5 off the price*

off *ADVERB*
❶ away or down from something • *His hat blew off.* ❷ not working or happening • *The heating is off.* • *The match is off because of snow.* ❸ to the end; completely • *I'll finish it off tonight.* ❹ as regards money or supplies • *How are you off for cash?* ❺ food that is off is beginning to go bad ❻ behind or at the side of a stage • *There were noises off.*

offal *NOUN*
the organs of an animal, such as liver and kidneys, sold as food

off-colour *ADJECTIVE*
slightly unwell

offence *NOUN* offences
① a crime or something illegal ② a feeling of annoyance or resentment
➤ **give offence** to hurt someone's feelings
➤ **take offence** to be upset by what someone has said or done

offend *VERB* offends, offending, offended
① to cause offence to someone; to hurt a person's feelings ② to commit a crime or do something wrong
➤ **offender** *NOUN*

offensive *ADJECTIVE*
① causing offence; insulting ② disgusting • *an offensive smell* ③ used for attacking • *offensive weapons*
➤ **offensively** *ADVERB*

offensive *NOUN* offensives
a forceful attack or campaign
➤ **be on the offensive** to be ready to attack or criticize someone first

offer *VERB* offers, offering, offered
① to hold something out or present it so that people can accept it if they want to ② to say that you are willing to do or give something or to pay a certain amount

offer *NOUN* offers
① offering something • *Thank you for your offer of help.* ② an amount of money offered ③ a specially reduced price

offering *NOUN* offerings
something that is offered

offhand *ADJECTIVE*
rather casual and rude, without thought or consideration • *an offhand manner*

offhand *ADVERB*
without previous thought or preparation • *I don't know offhand how much it cost.*

office *NOUN* offices
① a room or building where people work, usually sitting at desks ② a place where people can go for tickets, information or some other service • *a lost property office* ③ a government department • *the Foreign and Commonwealth Office* ④ an important job or position
➤ **be in office** to hold an official position

officer *NOUN* officers
① a person who is in charge of others, especially in the armed forces ② a member of the police force ③ an official

official *ADJECTIVE*
① approved or done by someone with authority • *an official announcement* ② done as part of your job or position • *official duties*

official *NOUN* officials
a person who holds a position of authority

officially *ADVERB*
① publicly and by someone in a position of authority • *The new school will be officially opened next month.* ② according to a set of rules • *I'm not officially supposed to be here.*

officiate *VERB* officiates, officiating, officiated
to be in charge of a meeting or event

officious *ADJECTIVE*
too ready to give orders; bossy
➤ **officiously** *ADVERB*

> **USAGE**
>
> Take care not to confuse with **official**, which means approved of or done by someone in authority.

offing *NOUN*
➤ **in the offing** likely to happen soon

off-licence *NOUN* off-licences
(*British*) a shop with a licence to sell alcoholic drinks to be drunk away from the shop

off-putting *ADJECTIVE*
making you less keen on something • *There was a rather off-putting smell coming from the kitchen.*

offset *VERB* offsets, offsetting, offset
to cancel out or make up for something • *The failures were offset by some successes.*

offshoot *NOUN* offshoots
① a side shoot on a plant ② a by-product

offshore *ADJECTIVE*
① in the sea some distance from the shore • *an offshore island* ② from the land towards the sea • *an offshore breeze*

offside *ADJECTIVE & ADVERB*
a player in football or other sports is offside when they are in a position where the rules do not allow them to play the ball

offspring *NOUN* offspring
a person's child or children; the young of an animal

oft *ADVERB* (*old use*)
often

often *ADVERB*
many times; in many cases

ogle *VERB* ogles, ogling, ogled
to stare at someone whom you find attractive

ogre NOUN ogres
❶ a cruel giant in fairy tales and legends ❷ a terrifying person

oh EXCLAMATION
❶ a cry of pain, surprise or delight ❷ used for emphasis • *Oh yes I will!*

ohm NOUN ohms
a unit of electrical resistance
(**WORD ORIGIN**) named after a German scientist, G. S. *Ohm*, who studied electric currents

oil NOUN oils
❶ a thick slippery liquid that will not dissolve in water ❷ a kind of petroleum used as fuel ❸ oil paint

oil VERB oils, oiling, oiled
to put oil on something, especially to make it work smoothly • *I need to oil the chain on my bike.*

oilfield NOUN oilfields
an area where oil is found in the ground or under the sea

oil paint NOUN oil paints
paint made with oil

oil painting NOUN oil paintings
a painting done with oil paints

oil rig NOUN oil rigs
a structure set up to support the equipment for drilling for oil

oilskin NOUN oilskins
cloth made waterproof by treatment with oil

oil well NOUN oil wells
a hole drilled in the ground or under the sea to get oil

oily ADJECTIVE
❶ containing or like oil; covered or soaked with oil ❷ behaving in an insincerely polite way
➤ **oiliness** NOUN

ointment NOUN ointments
a cream or slippery paste for putting on sore skin and cuts

OK, okay ADVERB & ADJECTIVE (*informal*)
all right (**WORD ORIGIN**) perhaps from the initials of *oll* (or *orl*) *korrect*, a humorous spelling of *all correct*, first used in the USA in 1839

old ADJECTIVE
❶ having lived for a long time ❷ made or existing from a long time ago • *an old tradition* ❸ of a particular age • *I'm ten years old.* ❹ former or original • *I liked my old*

school better than the one I go to now.
➤ of old long ago; in the distant past

old age NOUN
the time when a person is old

olden ADJECTIVE
of former times

Old English NOUN
the English language from about 700 to 1150, also called *Anglo-Saxon*

old-fashioned ADJECTIVE
of the kind that was usual a long time ago; no longer fashionable

Old Norse NOUN
the language spoken by the Vikings, the ancestor of modern Scandinavian languages

olfactory ADJECTIVE
to do with your sense of smell

oligarchy NOUN oligarchies
a country ruled by a small group of people
➤ **oligarch** NOUN

olive NOUN olives
❶ an evergreen tree with a small bitter fruit ❷ this fruit, from which an oil (*olive oil*) is made ❸ a shade of green like an unripe olive

olive branch NOUN olive branches
something you do or offer that shows you want to make peace (**WORD ORIGIN**) from a story in the Bible, where the dove brings Noah an olive branch as a sign that God is no longer angry with mankind

Olympic Games, Olympics PLURAL NOUN
a series of international sports contests held every four years in a different part of the world
➤ **Olympic** ADJECTIVE
(**WORD ORIGIN**) from the name of *Olympia*, a city in Greece where they were held in ancient times

ombudsman NOUN ombudsmen
an official whose job is to investigate complaints against government organizations

omega (say **oh**-meg-a) NOUN
the last letter of the Greek alphabet, equivalent to Roman *o* (**WORD ORIGIN**) from Greek *o mega* = big O

omelette NOUN omelettes
eggs beaten together and cooked in a pan, often with a filling

omen NOUN omens
an event regarded as a sign of what is going to happen

ominous *ADJECTIVE*
suggesting that trouble is coming • *There was another ominous rumble of thunder.*
➤ **ominously** *ADVERB*

omission *NOUN* omissions
❶ something that has been missed out or not done ❷ missing something out or failing to do it

omit *VERB* omits, omitting, omitted
❶ to miss something out • *We can omit the last two verses.* ❷ to fail to do something • *He omitted to mention that they were staying the night.*

omnibus *NOUN* omnibuses
❶ a book containing several stories or books that were previously published separately ❷ a single edition of several radio or television programmes previously broadcast separately ❸ (*old use*) a bus **WORD ORIGIN** Latin, = for everybody

omnipotent *ADJECTIVE*
having unlimited power or very great power

omniscient (say om-**niss**-ee-ent) *ADJECTIVE*
knowing everything
➤ **omniscience** *NOUN*

omnivore (say **om**-niv-or) *NOUN* omnivores
an animal that feeds on both plants and the flesh of other animals. Compare with **carnivore**, **herbivore**.

omnivorous (say om-**niv**-er-us) *ADJECTIVE*
an omnivorous animal feeds on both plants and the flesh of other animals. Compare with **carnivorous**, **herbivorous**.

on *PREPOSITION*
❶ supported by, covering or attached to something • *There was no sign on the door.* • *We sat on the floor.* ❷ during; at the time of • *I'll see you on Monday.* ❸ close to; towards • *The army advanced on Paris.* ❹ by reason of • *Two men were arrested on suspicion of murder.* ❺ concerning; about • *a book on butterflies* ❻ in a state of; using or showing • *The house was on fire.*

on *ADVERB*
❶ so that it is on something • *Put the lid on.* ❷ further forward • *Move on.* ❸ working; in action • *Is the central heating on?*
➤ **on and off** occasionally; not all the time

once *ADVERB*
❶ for one time or on one occasion only • *They came only once.* ❷ at an earlier time; formerly • *They once lived here.*

once *CONJUNCTION*
as soon as • *You can go once I have taken your names.*

oncoming *ADJECTIVE*
approaching or coming towards you • *oncoming traffic*

one *ADJECTIVE*
❶ single; only • *This was my one chance.* ❷ identical; the same • *We are all of one mind.* ❸ a certain • *You must come for lunch one day.*

one *NOUN*
❶ the smallest whole number, 1 ❷ a person or thing alone
➤ **one another** each other

one *PRONOUN*
❶ a person or thing previously mentioned • *There are lots of films on but I can't find one I want to see.* ❷ a person; any person • *One likes to help.*
➤ **oneself** *PRONOUN*

onerous (say **ohn**-er-us or **on**-er-us) *ADJECTIVE*
difficult to bear or do • *an onerous task*

one-sided *ADJECTIVE*
❶ with one side or person in a contest or conversation being much stronger or doing a lot more than the other • *a one-sided match* ❷ showing only one point of view in an unfair way • *This is a very one-sided account of the conflict.*

one-way *ADJECTIVE*
where traffic is allowed to travel in one direction only • *a one-way street*

ongoing *ADJECTIVE*
continuing to exist or be in progress • *It's an ongoing project.*

onion *NOUN* onions
a round vegetable with a strong flavour

online *ADJECTIVE & ADVERB*
connected to a computer or to the Internet

onlooker *NOUN* onlookers
a spectator

only *ADJECTIVE*
being the one person or thing of a kind; sole • *She's the only person we can trust.*
➤ **only child** a child who has no brothers or sisters

only *ADVERB*
❶ no more than; and that is all • *There are only three cakes left.* ❷ nothing other than • *I only eat pizza.*

only *CONJUNCTION*
but then; however • *He makes promises, only he never keeps them.*

onomatopoeia (say on-om-at-o-**pee**-a) *NOUN*
forming or using words that sound like the thing they stand for, e.g. *cuckoo, plop, sizzle*
➤ **onomatopoeic** *ADJECTIVE*

onrush *NOUN*
a surging rush forward

onset *NOUN*
❶ the beginning of something • *the onset of winter* ❷ the first part of a syllable, e.g. *d* in *dog*

onshore *ADJECTIVE*
from the sea towards the land • *an onshore breeze*

onslaught *NOUN* onslaughts
a fierce attack

onto, on to *PREPOSITION*
to a position on

onus (say **oh**-nus) *NOUN*
the duty or responsibility of doing something • *The onus is on the prosecution to prove he did it.*

onward *ADVERB & ADJECTIVE*
going forward; further on
➤ **onwards** *ADVERB*

onyx *NOUN*
a stone rather like marble, with different colours in layers

ooze *VERB* oozes, oozing, oozed
❶ to flow or trickle out of something slowly ❷ a wound, crack or other opening oozes when liquid flows out of it slowly • *The wound oozed blood.*

ooze *NOUN*
mud at the bottom of a river or sea

opal *NOUN* opals
a kind of stone with a rainbow sheen
➤ **opalescent** *ADJECTIVE*

opaque (say o-**payk**) *ADJECTIVE*
not able to be seen through; not transparent or translucent • *opaque glass*

open *ADJECTIVE*
❶ allowing people or things to go in and out; not closed or fastened ❷ not covered or blocked up ❸ spread out; unfolded • *She greeted us with open arms.* ❹ not limited or restricted • *an open championship* ❺ letting in visitors or customers ❻ with wide empty spaces • *open country* ❼ honest and frank;

not secret or secretive • *Be open about the danger.* ❽ not decided • *an open mind* ❾ willing or likely to receive something • *I'm open to suggestions.*
➤ **openness** *NOUN*
➤ **in the open** ❶ outside ❷ not secret
➤ **in the open air** not inside a house or building
➤ **open-air** *ADJECTIVE*

open *VERB* opens, opening, opened
❶ to make something open or more open ❷ to become open or more open ❸ to begin; to start something • *I'd like to open the meeting by welcoming everybody.* ❹ a shop or office opens when it starts business for the day • *What time do you open?*

opencast *ADJECTIVE*
(*British*) an opencast mine is worked by removing layers of earth from the surface, not underground

opener *NOUN* openers
a device for opening a bottle or can

opening *NOUN* openings
❶ a space or gap; a place where something opens ❷ the beginning of something ❸ an opportunity, especially for a job

openly *ADVERB*
without trying to hide anything • *No one dared to criticize him openly.*

open-minded *ADJECTIVE*
ready to listen to other people's ideas and opinions; not having fixed ideas

opera *NOUN*
❶ operas
a play in which all or most of the words are sung to music; works of this kind ❷ plural of **opus**

operate *VERB* operates, operating, operated
❶ to make a machine work ❷ to work or be in action • *How does this machine operate?* ❸ to perform a surgical operation on someone

operatic *ADJECTIVE*
to do with opera • *an operatic composer*

operating system *NOUN* operating systems
the software that controls a computer's basic functions

operation *NOUN* operations
❶ something done to the body by a surgeon to take away or repair a part of it ❷ a carefully planned activity involving a lot of people • *a rescue operation* ❸ a piece of work performed by a machine • *The computer*

can perform this operation in a fraction of a second.
➤ **in operation** working or in use • *When does the new system come into operation?*
➤ **operational** *ADJECTIVE*

operative *ADJECTIVE*
❶ working or functioning ❷ to do with surgical operations

operator *NOUN* **operators**
a person who works something, especially a telephone switchboard or exchange

operetta *NOUN* **operettas**
a short opera on a light or humorous theme

ophthalmic (say off-**thal**-mik) *ADJECTIVE*
to do with or for your eyes

ophthalmic optician *NOUN* **ophthalmic opticians**
(*British*) a person who is qualified to test people's eyesight and prescribe glasses and contact lenses

opinion *NOUN* **opinions**
what you think of something; a belief or judgement • *I have recently changed my opinion of her.*

opinionated *ADJECTIVE*
having strong opinions and holding them whatever anybody says

opinion poll *NOUN* **opinion polls**
an estimate of what people think, made by questioning a sample of them

opium *NOUN*
a powerful drug made from the juice of certain poppies, used in the past in medicine

opossum *NOUN* **opossums**
a small furry marsupial that lives in trees, with different kinds in America and Australia

opponent *NOUN* **opponents**
a person or group opposing another in a contest or war

opportune *ADJECTIVE*
❶ an opportune time is convenient or suitable for a purpose ❷ done or happening at a suitable time
➤ **opportunely** *ADVERB*
WORD ORIGIN from Latin *ob* = towards, against + *portus* = harbour (originally used of wind blowing a ship towards a harbour)

opportunity *NOUN* **opportunities**
a good chance to do a particular thing • *I'd like to take this opportunity to thank everyone for coming.*

oppose *VERB* **opposes, opposing, opposed**
to argue or fight against someone or something; to resist something
➤ **as opposed to** in contrast with; rather than • *This game relies on skill as opposed to luck.*
➤ **be opposed to something** to be strongly against something • *We are opposed to parking in the town centre.*

opposite *ADJECTIVE*
❶ placed on the other or further side; facing • *on the opposite side of the road* ❷ moving away from or towards each other • *The trains were travelling in opposite directions.*
❸ completely different • *My efforts to calm him down had the opposite effect.*

opposite *NOUN* **opposites**
an opposite person or thing • *'Happy' is the opposite of 'sad'.*

opposite *ADVERB*
in an opposite position or direction • *I'll sit opposite.*

opposite *PREPOSITION*
opposite to • *They live opposite the school.*

opposition *NOUN*
❶ opposing something; resistance ❷ the people who oppose something
➤ **the Opposition** the chief political party opposing the one that is in power

oppress *VERB* **oppresses, oppressing, oppressed**
❶ to govern or treat someone cruelly or unjustly ❷ to weigh someone down with worry or sadness • *The gloomy atmosphere at home oppressed him.*
➤ **oppressed** *ADJECTIVE*
➤ **oppressor** *NOUN*

oppression *NOUN*
governing or treating people cruelly or unjustly • *a struggle against oppression*

oppressive *ADJECTIVE*
❶ cruel or harsh • *an oppressive regime* ❷ worrying and difficult to bear • *an oppressive silence* ❸ oppressive weather is unpleasantly hot and humid

opt *VERB* **opts, opting, opted**
to choose something • *I opted for the chicken salad.*
➤ **opt out** to decide not to take part in something

optic *ADJECTIVE*
to do with your eyes or sight • *the optic nerve*

a b c d e f g h i j k l m n o p q r s t u v w x y z

optical ADJECTIVE
to do with sight; aiding sight • *optical instruments*
➤ **optically** ADVERB

optical illusion NOUN optical illusions
a deceptive appearance that makes you think you see something that is not really there

optician NOUN opticians
a person who tests people's eyesight and makes or sells glasses and contact lenses

optics NOUN
the study of sight and of light as connected with this

optimist NOUN optimists
a person who expects that things will turn out well. Compare with **pessimist**.
➤ **optimism** NOUN

optimistic ADJECTIVE
expecting things to turn out well • *I'm not very optimistic about our chances.*
➤ **optimistically** ADVERB

optimum ADJECTIVE
best; most favourable
➤ **optimum** NOUN
➤ **optimal** ADJECTIVE

option NOUN options
❶ the right or power to choose something
• *You have the option of staying.*
❷ something chosen or that may be chosen
• *Your options are to travel by bus or by train.*

optional ADJECTIVE
that you can choose, not compulsory
➤ **optionally** ADVERB

opulent ADJECTIVE
wealthy or luxurious
➤ **opulence** NOUN

opus (say oh-pus) NOUN opuses or opera
a numbered musical composition • *Beethoven opus 15*

or CONJUNCTION
used to show that there is a choice or an alternative • *Do you want a cake or a biscuit?*

oracle NOUN oracles
❶ a shrine where the ancient Greeks consulted one of their gods for advice or a prophecy ❷ a wise or knowledgeable adviser
➤ **oracular** (say or-**ak**-yoo-ler) ADJECTIVE

oral ADJECTIVE
❶ spoken, not written ❷ to do with or using your mouth
➤ **orally** ADVERB

oral NOUN orals
a spoken examination or test
WORD ORIGIN from Latin *oris* = of the mouth

SPELLING
Take care not to confuse with **aural**, which means to do with the ear or hearing.

orange NOUN oranges
❶ a round juicy citrus fruit with reddish-yellow peel ❷ a reddish-yellow colour

orange ADJECTIVE
reddish-yellow in colour

orangutan NOUN orangutans
a large ape of Borneo and Sumatra
WORD ORIGIN from Malay *orang hutan* = man of the forest (Malay is spoken in Malaysia)

oration NOUN orations
a long formal speech

orator NOUN orators
a person who is good at making speeches in public
➤ **oratorical** ADJECTIVE

oratorio NOUN oratorios
a piece of music for voices and an orchestra, usually on a religious subject

oratory NOUN
❶ the art of making speeches in public
❷ eloquent speech

orb NOUN orbs
a sphere or globe

orbit NOUN orbits
❶ the curved path taken by something moving round a planet, moon or star ❷ the range of someone's influence or control
➤ **orbital** ADJECTIVE

orbit VERB orbits, orbiting, orbited
to move in an orbit round something • *The satellite has been orbiting the earth since 1986.*

orchard NOUN orchards
a piece of ground planted with fruit trees

orchestra NOUN orchestras
a large group of people playing various musical instruments together
➤ **orchestral** ADJECTIVE

orchestrate VERB orchestrates, orchestrating, orchestrated
❶ to compose or arrange music for an orchestra ❷ to coordinate things deliberately
• *a carefully orchestrated campaign*
➤ **orchestration** NOUN

orchid *NOUN* orchids
a kind of plant with brightly coloured, often unevenly shaped, flowers

ordain *VERB* ordains, ordaining, ordained
❶ to make a person a member of the clergy in the Christian Church • *He was ordained in 1981.* **❷** to declare or order something by law

ordeal *NOUN* ordeals
a difficult or horrific experience

order *NOUN* orders
❶ a command to do something **❷** a request for something to be supplied • *The waiter came to take our order.* **❸** the way things are arranged • *in alphabetical order* **❹** a neat arrangement, with everything in the right place • *We were busy getting the house in order.* **❺** a situation in which people are behaving properly and obeying the rules • *The police managed to restore order.* **❻** a kind or sort of thing • *She showed courage of the highest order.* **❼** a group of monks or nuns who live by certain religious rules
➤ **in order that** or **in order to** for the purpose of
➤ **out of order** broken or not working

order *VERB* orders, ordering, ordered
❶ to command someone to do something **❷** to ask for something to be supplied to you **❸** to put something into order; to arrange things neatly • *He needed a few minutes to order his thoughts.*

orderly *ADJECTIVE*
❶ arranged neatly or well • *an orderly desk* **❷** well-behaved and obedient • *an orderly demonstration*
➤ **orderliness** *NOUN*

orderly *NOUN* orderlies
❶ an assistant in a hospital **❷** a soldier whose job is to assist an officer

ordinal number *NOUN* ordinal numbers
a number that shows a thing's position in a series, e.g. first, fifth, twentieth, etc. Compare with **cardinal number**.

ordinance *NOUN* ordinances
a command or decree

ordinarily *ADVERB*
usually or normally • *Ordinarily, I wouldn't have minded.*

ordinary *ADJECTIVE*
normal or usual; not special
➤ **out of the ordinary** unusual

ordination *NOUN* ordinations
ordaining someone or being ordained, as a member of the Christian clergy

ordnance *NOUN*
weapons and other military equipment

Ordnance Survey *NOUN*
an official survey organization that makes detailed maps of the British Isles
WORD ORIGIN because the maps were originally made for the army

ore *NOUN* ores
rock with metal or other useful substances in it • *iron ore*

oregano (say o-ri-**gah**-noh) *NOUN*
the dried leaves of wild marjoram used as a herb in cooking

organ *NOUN* organs
❶ a musical instrument from which sounds are produced by air forced through pipes, played by keys and pedals **❷** a part of the body with a particular function • *the digestive organs*

organdie *NOUN*
a kind of thin fabric, usually stiffened

organic *ADJECTIVE*
❶ to do with or formed from living things • *organic matter* **❷** organic food is grown or produced without using chemical fertilizers or pesticides • *organic farming* **❸** to do with the organs of the body • *organic diseases*
➤ **organically** *ADVERB*

organism *NOUN* organisms
a living thing; an individual animal or plant

organist *NOUN* organists
a person who plays the organ

organization (also **organisation**) *NOUN* organizations
❶ an organized group of people, such as a business, charity or government department **❷** the organizing of something
➤ **organizational** *ADJECTIVE*

organize (also **organise**) *VERB* organizes, organizing, organized
❶ to plan and prepare something • *We organized a picnic.* **❷** to put things in order • *I'm trying to organize all my notebooks.* **❸** to form people into a group to work together

organizer (also **organiser**) *NOUN* organizers
❶ a person who arranges an event or activity **❷** a thing used for organizing

a b c d e f g h i j k l m n o p q r s t u v w x y z

orgasm NOUN orgasms
the moment during sexual activity when feelings of sexual pleasure are at their strongest

Orient NOUN
the countries of the East, especially east Asia

orient VERB orients, orienting, oriented
to orientate something

oriental ADJECTIVE
(old use) to do with the countries east of the Mediterranean Sea, especially China and Japan

orientate VERB orientates, orientating, orientated (chiefly British)
❶ to place something or face in a certain direction ❷ to get your bearings • I'm just trying to orientate myself.
➤ orientation NOUN
(WORD ORIGIN) originally = turn to face the east

orienteering NOUN
the sport of finding your way across rough country with a map and compass

orifice (say o-rif-iss) NOUN orifices
an opening in your body

origami (say o-rig-**ah**-mee) NOUN
the art of folding paper into decorative shapes (WORD ORIGIN) from Japanese ori = fold + kami = paper

origin NOUN origins
❶ the start of something; the point or cause from which something began • a book about the origins of life on earth ❷ a person's family background • a man of humble origins ❸ the point where two or more axes on a graph meet

original ADJECTIVE
❶ existing from the start; earliest • the original inhabitants ❷ new and interesting; different from others of its type • an original idea ❸ producing new ideas; inventive • an original thinker ❹ made or created first, before copies • an original painting by a local artist

original NOUN originals
a document, painting or other work which was the first one made and is not a copy

originality NOUN
the quality of being new and interesting • His stories show great originality.

originally ADVERB
at first, before anything changed • My family originally came from Pakistan.

originate VERB originates, originating, originated
❶ to have its origin; to begin to happen or appear • Buddhism originated in India. ❷ to create something • Who originated this theory?
➤ originator NOUN

ornament NOUN ornaments
an object you display or wear as a decoration

ornament VERB ornaments, ornamenting, ornamented
to decorate something with beautiful things • The tree was ornamented with coloured glass balls and tiny flags.
➤ ornamentation NOUN

ornamental ADJECTIVE
used as an ornament; decorative rather than useful • an ornamental fountain

ornate ADJECTIVE
elaborately decorated • an ornate box
➤ ornately ADVERB

ornithology NOUN
the study of birds
➤ ornithologist NOUN
➤ ornithological ADJECTIVE

orphan NOUN orphans
a child whose parents are dead
➤ orphaned ADJECTIVE

orphanage NOUN orphanages
a home for orphans

orthodox ADJECTIVE
❶ holding beliefs that are correct or generally accepted ❷ conventional or normal
➤ orthodoxy NOUN

Orthodox Church NOUN
the Christian Churches of eastern Europe

orthopaedics (say orth-o-**pee**-diks) NOUN
the treatment of deformities and injuries to bones and muscles
➤ orthopaedic ADJECTIVE

oscillate VERB oscillates, oscillating, oscillated
to keep moving to and fro; to vibrate • The needle on the dial began to oscillate.
➤ oscillation NOUN

osier (say **oh**-zee-er) NOUN osiers
a willow with flexible twigs used in making baskets

osmosis NOUN
the passing of fluid through a porous partition into another more concentrated fluid

ostensible *ADJECTIVE*
apparently true, but actually concealing the
true reason • *Their ostensible reason for
travelling was to visit friends.*
➤ **ostensibly** *ADVERB*

ostentatious *ADJECTIVE*
making a showy display of something to
impress people • *ostentatious gold jewellery*
➤ **ostentatiously** *ADVERB*
➤ **ostentation** *NOUN*

osteopath *NOUN* **osteopaths**
a person who treats certain diseases by
pressing and moving a patient's bones and
muscles
➤ **osteopathy** *NOUN*
➤ **osteopathic** *ADJECTIVE*

ostracize (also **ostracise**) *VERB* **ostracizes,
ostracizing, ostracized**
to exclude someone from your group and
completely ignore them
➤ **ostracism** *NOUN*
WORD ORIGIN from Greek *ostrakon* = piece
of pottery (because people voted to banish
someone by writing their name on this)

ostrich *NOUN* **ostriches**
a large long-legged African bird that can run
very fast but cannot fly. It is said to bury its
head in the sand when pursued, in the belief
that it then cannot be seen.

other *ADJECTIVE*
❶ different; not the same • *Play some other
tune.* ❷ remaining • *Try the other shoe.*
❸ additional • *my other friends* ❹ just recent
or past • *I saw him the other day.*
➤ **other than** apart from; except

other *PRONOUN* **others**
the other person or thing • *Where are the
others?*

otherwise *ADVERB*
❶ if things happen differently; if you do not
• *Write it down, otherwise you'll forget.* ❷ in
other ways • *It rained, but otherwise the
holiday was good.* ❸ differently • *We could
not do otherwise.*

otter *NOUN* **otters**
a fish-eating animal with webbed feet, a flat
tail and thick brown fur, living near water

ottoman *NOUN* **ottomans**
❶ a long padded seat ❷ a storage box with a
padded top

ought *AUXILIARY VERB*
used with other words to show
❶ what you should or must do • *We ought to*

feed them. • *You ought to take more exercise.*
❷ what is likely to happen • *At this speed, we
ought to be there by noon.*

oughtn't (*mainly spoken*)
ought not

ounce *NOUN* **ounces**
❶ a unit of weight equal to ¹⁄₁₆ of a pound
(about 28 grams) ❷ a tiny amount • *There
was not an ounce of strength left in him.*

our *DETERMINER*
belonging to us
SPELLING
Be careful, this sounds the same as **hour**
which means 'sixty minutes'.

ours *POSSESSIVE PRONOUN*
belonging to us • *These seats are ours.*
SPELLING
There is never an apostrophe in *ours*.

ourselves *PRONOUN*
we or us and nobody else. The word is used to
refer back to the subject of a sentence (e.g.
We blame ourselves.) or for emphasis (e.g. *We
made all the costumes ourselves.*).
➤ **by ourselves** alone; on our own

oust *VERB* **ousts, ousting, ousted**
to drive someone out from a position or
office • *The rebels ousted the government
from power.*

out *ADVERB*
❶ away from or not in a particular place or
position or state; not at home • *She phoned
while you were out.* ❷ into the open; into
existence or sight • *The sun came out.* ❸ no
longer burning or shining • *The fire has gone
out.* ❹ in error • *Your estimate was 10% out.*
❺ to or at an end; completely • *The concert
is sold out.* • *I'm worn out.* ❻ loudly or boldly
• *He cried out.* ❼ no longer batting in cricket
➤ **be out to do something** to be seeking or
wanting to do something • *They are out to
make trouble.*
➤ **be out of something** to have no more of
something left
➤ **out of date** ❶ old-fashioned ❷ no longer
valid
➤ **out of doors** in the open air
➤ **out of the way** remote or distant

out-and-out *ADJECTIVE*
thorough or complete • *He is an out-and-out
villain.*

a b c d e f g h i j k l m n o p q r s t u v w x y z

outback *NOUN*
the remote inland districts of Australia

outboard motor *NOUN* outboard motors
a motor fitted to the outside of a boat's stern

outbreak *NOUN* outbreaks
the start of something unpleasant, such as a disease or war

outburst *NOUN* outbursts
a sudden bursting out of anger or laughter

outcast *NOUN* outcasts
a person who has been rejected by family, friends or society

outcome *NOUN* outcomes
the result of what happens or has happened

outcrop *NOUN* outcrops
a large piece of rock from a lower level that sticks out on the surface of the ground

outcry *NOUN* outcries
a strong protest • *There was an outcry over the rise in rail fares.*

outdated *ADJECTIVE*
out of date • *outdated ideas*

outdistance *VERB* outdistances, outdistancing, outdistanced
to get far ahead of someone in a race

outdo *VERB* outdoes, outdoing, outdid, outdone
to do better than another person • *They tried to outdo each other in making up silly words.*

outdoor *ADJECTIVE*
done or used outdoors

outdoors *ADVERB*
in the open air

outer *ADJECTIVE*
outside or external; nearer to the outside • *the outer walls*

outermost *ADJECTIVE*
nearest to the outside; furthest from the centre

outer space *NOUN*
the universe beyond the earth's atmosphere

outfit *NOUN* outfits
❶ a set of clothes worn together ❷ a set of equipment ❸ (*informal*) a team or organization

outflow *NOUN* outflows
❶ flowing out; what flows out ❷ a pipe for liquid flowing out

outgoing *ADJECTIVE*
❶ soon to leave or retire from office • *the outgoing chairman* ❷ sociable and friendly • *Vicky is cheerful and outgoing.*

outgoings *PLURAL NOUN*
what you have to spend; expenditure

outgrow *VERB* outgrows, outgrowing, outgrew, outgrown
❶ to grow out of clothes or habits • *She has outgrown those red shoes.* ❷ to grow faster or larger than another person or thing

outgrowth *NOUN* outgrowths
something that grows out of another thing • *Feathers are outgrowths on a bird's skin.*

outhouse *NOUN* outhouses
a small building, such as a shed or barn, that belongs to a house but is separate from it

outing *NOUN* outings
a journey for pleasure

outlandish *ADJECTIVE*
looking or sounding strange or foreign • *an outlandish costume*

outlast *VERB* outlasts, outlasting, outlasted
to last longer than something else

outlaw *NOUN* outlaws
a robber or bandit who is hiding to avoid being caught and is not protected by the law

outlaw *VERB* outlaws, outlawing, outlawed
to make something illegal

outlay *NOUN* outlays
the amount of money spent on something

outlet *NOUN* outlets
❶ a way for something to get out • *The tank has an outlet at the bottom.* ❷ a way of expressing strong feelings ❸ a place from which goods are sold or distributed

outline *NOUN* outlines
❶ a line round the outside of something, showing its boundary or shape ❷ a summary

outline *VERB* outlines, outlining, outlined
❶ to make an outline of something ❷ to summarize something

outlive *VERB* outlives, outliving, outlived
to live or last longer than another person or thing • *He outlived his wife by three years.*

outlook *NOUN* outlooks
❶ a view on which people look out • *a pleasant outlook over the lake* ❷ a person's mental attitude to something • *She has an optimistic outlook on life.* ❸ what seems

likely to happen in the future • *The outlook is bleak.*

outlying *ADJECTIVE*
far from the centre; remote • *the outlying districts*

outmanoeuvre *VERB* outmanoeuvres, outmanoeuvring, outmanoeuvred
to use skill or cunning to gain an advantage over someone

outmoded *ADJECTIVE*
out of date

outnumber *VERB* outnumbers, outnumbering, outnumbered
to be greater in number than another group • *The girls outnumber the boys in our team.*

outpatient *NOUN* outpatients
a person who visits a hospital for treatment but does not stay there

outpost *NOUN* outposts
a small town or camp that is in a remote place

output *NOUN* outputs
❶ the amount produced, especially by a factory or business ❷ the information or results produced by a computer

outrage *NOUN* outrages
❶ a strong feeling of shock and anger ❷ something that shocks people by being very wicked or cruel

outrage *VERB* outrages, outraging, outraged
to shock and anger people greatly • *He was outraged at the way he had been treated.*

outrageous *ADJECTIVE*
making people feel very angry or shocked • *outrageous behaviour*
➤ **outrageously** *ADVERB*

outrider *NOUN* outriders
a person riding on a motorcycle as an escort or guard

outrigger *NOUN* outriggers
a framework attached to the side of a boat, e.g. to prevent a canoe from capsizing

outright *ADVERB*
❶ completely; not gradually • *This drug should be banned outright.* ❷ frankly • *We told him outright what we thought about it.*

outright *ADJECTIVE*
thorough or complete • *an outright victory*

outrun *VERB* outruns, outrunning, outran, outrun
to run faster or further than someone else

outset *NOUN*
➤ **at** or **from the outset** at or from the beginning of something • *It was clear from the outset that it was a bad idea.*

outside *NOUN* outsides
the outer side, surface or part of something
➤ **at the outside** at the most • *a mile at the outside*

outside *ADJECTIVE*
❶ on or coming from the outside • *the outside edge* ❷ remote or slight • *There is an outside chance that he will come.*

outside *ADVERB*
on or to the outside; outdoors • *Leave your trainers outside.* • *It's cold outside.*

outside *PREPOSITION*
on or to the outside of • *He poked his head outside the tent.*

outside broadcast *NOUN* outside broadcasts
(*British*) a broadcast made where something is happening and not in a studio

outsider *NOUN* outsiders
❶ a person who does not belong to a certain group ❷ a horse or person that people think has no chance of winning a race or competition

outsize *ADJECTIVE*
much larger than average

outskirts *PLURAL NOUN*
the parts of a town or city on its outside edge, furthest from the centre

outspoken *ADJECTIVE*
speaking or spoken very frankly

outspread *ADJECTIVE*
spread out • *a bird with outspread wings*

outstanding *ADJECTIVE*
❶ extremely good or distinguished • *She is an outstanding athlete.* ❷ an outstanding debt or bill is not yet paid or dealt with

outstretched *ADJECTIVE*
reaching out as far as possible • *He ran towards her with outstretched arms.*

outstrip *VERB* outstrips, outstripping, outstripped
❶ to run faster or further than someone else ❷ to achieve more or be more successful, than someone else

outvote *VERB* outvotes, outvoting, outvoted
to defeat someone by a majority of votes

outward *ADJECTIVE*
❶ going outwards ❷ on the outside

a b c d e f g h i j k l m n o p q r s t u v w x y z

outwardly *ADVERB*
on the surface; for people to see • *She remained outwardly calm.*

outwards *ADVERB*
(*British*) towards the outside • *That door opens outwards.*

outweigh *VERB* outweighs, outweighing, outweighed
to be greater in weight or importance than something else • *The advantages outweigh the disadvantages.*

outwit *VERB* outwits, outwitting, outwitted
to deceive or defeat someone by being clever or crafty

ova
plural of **ovum**

oval *ADJECTIVE*
shaped like an O, rounded and longer than it is broad

oval *NOUN* ovals
an oval shape **(WORD ORIGIN)** from Latin *ovum* = egg

ovary *NOUN* ovaries
❶ either of the two organs in which ova or egg-cells are produced in a woman's or female animal's body ❷ part of the pistil in a plant, from which fruit is formed

ovation *NOUN* ovations
enthusiastic applause • *She received a huge ovation.*

oven *NOUN* ovens
a closed space in which things are cooked or heated

over *PREPOSITION*
❶ above; higher than • *There's a light over the door.* ❷ more than • *It's over a mile away.* ❸ concerning; about • *They quarrelled over money.* ❹ across the top of; on or to the other side of • *They rowed the boat over the lake.* ❺ during • *We can talk over dinner.* ❻ being better than • *their victory over United*

over *ADVERB*
❶ out and down from the top or edge; from an upright position • *He fell over.* ❷ so that a different side shows • *Turn it over.* ❸ at or to a place; across • *Walk over to our house.* ❹ remaining; still available • *There is nothing left over.* ❺ all through; thoroughly • *Think it over.* ❻ at an end • *The lesson is over.*
➤ **over and over** many times; repeatedly

over *NOUN* overs
a series of six balls bowled in cricket

over- *PREFIX*
too much; too (as in *over-anxious*)

overact *VERB* overacts, overacting, overacted
an actor overacts when they act their part in an exaggerated manner

overall *ADJECTIVE*
including everything; total • *What is the overall cost?*

overall *ADVERB*
taken as a whole • *Overall, this is a very useful book.*

overall *NOUN* overalls
a type of coat worn over other clothes to protect them when working

overalls *PLURAL NOUN*
a piece of clothing, like a shirt and trousers combined, worn over other clothes to protect them

overarm *ADJECTIVE & ADVERB*
(*chiefly British*) with your arm lifted above shoulder level and coming down in front of your body • *bowling overarm*

overawed *ADJECTIVE*
so impressed by something that you feel nervous or frightened

overbalance *VERB* overbalances, overbalancing, overbalanced
(*chiefly British*) to lose balance and fall over

overbearing *ADJECTIVE*
trying to control other people in an unpleasant way • *an overbearing manner*

overboard *ADVERB*
over the side of a ship into the water • *She jumped overboard.*

overcast *ADJECTIVE*
covered with cloud • *The sky was grey and overcast.*

overcoat *NOUN* overcoats
a warm outdoor coat

overcome *VERB* overcomes, overcoming, overcame, overcome
❶ to find a way of dealing with a problem or difficulty • *She managed to overcome her fear of flying.* ❷ to win a victory over someone; to defeat someone
➤ **be overcome by something** to be strongly affected by something and made helpless • *He was overcome by the fumes.*

overcrowded *ADJECTIVE*
an overcrowded place or vehicle has too

many people crammed into it
➤ **overcrowding** NOUN

overdo VERB overdoes, overdoing, overdid, overdone
❶ to do something too much ❷ to cook food for too long
➤ **overdo it** to work too hard, exhausting yourself

overdose NOUN overdoses
too large a dose of a drug

overdose VERB overdoses, overdosing, overdosed
to take an overdose

overdraft NOUN overdrafts
the amount by which a bank account is overdrawn

overdraw VERB overdraws, overdrawing, overdrew, overdrawn
to draw more money from a bank account than the amount you have in it
➤ **overdrawn** ADJECTIVE

overdrive NOUN
➤ **go into overdrive** to start being very active

overdue ADJECTIVE
late; not paid or arrived by the proper time
• *Her baby is a week overdue.*

overestimate VERB overestimates, overestimating, overestimated
to estimate something too highly

overflow VERB overflows, overflowing, overflowed
to flow over the edge or limits of something
• *The tap was left on and the bath overflowed.*

overflow NOUN overflows
❶ an amount of something that overflows
❷ an outlet for excess liquid

overgrown ADJECTIVE
covered with weeds or unwanted plants

overhang VERB overhangs, overhanging, overhung
to jut out over something

overhang NOUN overhangs
a part of a building that juts out

overhaul VERB overhauls, overhauling, overhauled
❶ to examine something thoroughly and repair it if necessary ❷ to overtake someone or something

overhaul NOUN
an examination and repair of something

overhead ADJECTIVE & ADVERB
❶ above the level of your head • *an overhead light* ❷ in the sky • *A helicopter flew overhead.*

overheads PLURAL NOUN
the expenses of running a business

overhear VERB overhears, overhearing, overheard
to hear something accidentally or without the speaker intending you to hear it • *I overheard them having an argument yesterday.*

overjoyed ADJECTIVE
filled with great joy

overland ADJECTIVE & ADVERB
travelling over the land, not by sea or air • *an overland expedition* • *We travelled overland to Moscow.*

overlap VERB overlaps, overlapping, overlapped
❶ two things overlap when one lies across part of the other • *The roof tiles overlap.*
❷ events overlap when they happen partly at the same time
➤ **overlap** NOUN

overlay VERB overlays, overlaying, overlaid
to cover something with a layer; to lie on top of something • *The surface of the table is overlaid with gold.*

overlay NOUN overlays
a thing laid over another

overleaf ADVERB
on the other side of the page • *See the diagram overleaf.*

overlie VERB overlies, overlying, overlay, overlain
to lie over something

overload VERB overloads, overloading, overloaded
to put too great a load on someone or something • *The boat was overloaded with people.*

overlook VERB overlooks, overlooking, overlooked
❶ to fail to notice or consider something
• *You have overlooked one important fact.*
❷ to overlook a mistake or offence is to ignore it or decide not to punish it ❸ to have a view of a place from above • *The hotel overlooks a lake.*

a b c d e f g h i j k l m n o p q r s t u v w x y z

overlord *NOUN* overlords
a supreme lord

overly *ADVERB*
too; excessively • *an overly optimistic view*

overnight *ADJECTIVE & ADVERB*
of or during a night • *an overnight stop in Rome* • *We stayed overnight in a hotel.*

overpower *VERB* overpowers, overpowering, overpowered
❶ to defeat someone by being stronger than they are ❷ to affect someone very strongly • *Terror overpowered him.*

overpowering *ADJECTIVE*
very strong or powerful • *an overpowering smell of fish*

overrate *VERB* overrates, overrating, overrated
to have too high an opinion of something

overreach *VERB* overreaches, overreaching, overreached
➤ **overreach yourself** to fail through being too ambitious

override *VERB* overrides, overriding, overrode, overridden
❶ to be more important than something • *Safety overrides all other considerations.* ❷ to stop an automatic process and control it yourself • *This code lets you override the security system.* ❸ to overrule someone or something

overriding *ADJECTIVE*
more important than anything else • *My overriding feeling was relief.*

overripe *ADJECTIVE*
too ripe

overrule *VERB* overrules, overruling, overruled
to reject a suggestion or decision by using your authority • *We voted for having a disco but the head teacher overruled the idea.*

overrun *VERB* overruns, overrunning, overran, overrun
❶ to spread all over a place in large numbers • *The attic is overrun with mice.* ❷ to go on for longer than it should • *The programme overran by ten minutes*

overseas *ADVERB*
across or beyond the sea; abroad • *He lived overseas for a while.*

overseas *ADJECTIVE*
from abroad; foreign • *overseas students*

oversee *VERB* oversees, overseeing, oversaw, overseen
to watch over people working to make sure things are done properly
➤ **overseer** *NOUN*

overshadow *VERB* overshadows, overshadowing, overshadowed
❶ to cast a shadow over something ❷ to make a person or thing seem unimportant in comparison • *He always felt overshadowed by his older brother.*

overshoot *VERB* overshoots, overshooting, overshot
to go beyond a target or limit • *The plane overshot the runway.*

oversight *NOUN* oversights
a mistake you make by not noticing something

oversleep *VERB* oversleeps, oversleeping, overslept
to sleep for longer than you intended

overspill *NOUN* overspills
❶ what spills over ❷ the extra population of a town, who take homes in nearby districts

overstate *VERB* overstates, overstating, overstated
to exaggerate how important something is

overstep *VERB* oversteps, overstepping, overstepped
to go beyond a limit

overt *ADJECTIVE*
done or shown openly • *overt hostility*
➤ **overtly** *ADVERB*

overtake *VERB* overtakes, overtaking, overtook, overtaken
❶ to pass a moving vehicle or person ❷ to affect you without warning • *She was suddenly overtaken by remorse.*

overtax *VERB* overtaxes, overtaxing, overtaxed
❶ to tax people too heavily ❷ to put too heavy a burden or strain on someone

overthrow *VERB* overthrows, overthrowing, overthrew, overthrown
to remove a ruler or government from power by force • *The rebels planned to overthrow the president.*

overthrow *NOUN* overthrows
❶ overthrowing a ruler or government ❷ throwing a ball too far

overtime *NOUN*
time spent working outside the normal hours; payment for this

overtone *NOUN* overtones
a feeling or quality that is suggested but not expressed directly • *There were overtones of envy in his speech.*

overture *NOUN* overtures
❶ a piece of music written as an introduction to an opera or ballet ❷ a friendly attempt to start a discussion or relationship • *They made overtures of peace.*

overturn *VERB* overturns, overturning, overturned
❶ to turn over or upside down or to make something do this • *One of the boats overturned in the storm.* ❷ to reverse a legal decision

overview *NOUN* overviews
a general outline of a subject or situation that gives the main ideas without explaining all the details • *The first paragraph gives a quick overview of the topic.*

overweight *ADJECTIVE*
too heavy or fat

overwhelm *VERB* overwhelms, overwhelming, overwhelmed
❶ to have a strong emotional effect on someone • *I was overwhelmed by everyone's kindness.* ❷ to defeat someone completely ❸ to come in such large numbers that you cannot deal with them • *They were overwhelmed by complaints.*

overwhelming *ADJECTIVE*
extremely great or strong • *I had an overwhelming desire to see him again.*

overwork *VERB* overworks, overworking, overworked
❶ to work too hard or to make someone work too hard ❷ to use something too often • *'Nice' is an overworked word.*

overwork *NOUN*
working too hard

overwrought *ADJECTIVE*
very upset and nervous or worried

ovoid *ADJECTIVE*
egg-shaped

ovulate *VERB* ovulates, ovulating, ovulated
to produce an ovum from an ovary

ovum (say **oh**-vum) *NOUN* ova
a female cell that can develop into a new individual when it is fertilized

owe *VERB* owes, owing, owed
❶ to have a duty to pay or give something to someone, especially money • *I still owe you for the cinema ticket.* • *You owe him an apology.* ❷ to have something because of the action of another person or thing • *They owed their lives to the pilot's skill.*

owing to *PREPOSITION*
because of; caused by • *It was a difficult journey owing to the heavy snow.*

owl *NOUN* owls
a bird of prey with large eyes and a short beak, usually flying at night

own *ADJECTIVE*
belonging to yourself or itself • *I saw it with my own eyes.*
➤ **get your own back** (*informal*) to get revenge
➤ **on your own** by yourself; alone • *I did it all on my own.* • *I sat on my own in the empty room.*

own *VERB* owns, owning, owned
to have something as your property
➤ **own up** to admit that you did something wrong or stupid

owner *NOUN* owners
the person who owns something
➤ **ownership** *NOUN*

own goal *NOUN* own goals
a goal scored by a member of a team against their own side

ox *NOUN* oxen
a male animal of the cattle family kept for its meat and for pulling carts

oxide *NOUN* oxides
a compound of oxygen and one other element

oxidize (also **oxidise**) *VERB* oxidizes, oxidizing, oxidized
❶ to combine or to cause a substance to combine, with oxygen ❷ to coat something with an oxide
➤ **oxidation** *NOUN*

oxtail *NOUN*
meat from the tail of a cow, used to make soup or stew

oxygen *NOUN*
a colourless odourless tasteless gas that exists in the air and is essential for living things

a b c d e f g h i j k l m n o p q r s t u v w x y z

oxymoron (say oksi-**mor**-on) *NOUN*
oxymorons
putting together words which seem to contradict one another, e.g. *bitter-sweet, living death* (**WORD ORIGIN**) from Greek *oxumoros* = pointedly foolish

oyster *NOUN* **oysters**
a kind of shellfish whose shell sometimes contains a pearl

ozone *NOUN*
a form of oxygen with a sharp smell
(**WORD ORIGIN**) from Greek *ozein* = to smell

ozone layer *NOUN*
a layer of ozone high in the atmosphere, which protects the earth from harmful amounts of the sun's radiation

p *ABBREVIATION*
penny or pence

p. *ABBREVIATION* **pp.**
page

pa *NOUN* (*informal*)
father

pace *NOUN* **paces**
❶ one step in walking or running • *Now take two paces forward.* ❷ the speed at which someone moves or something happens • *He set a fast pace.*

pace *VERB* **paces, pacing, paced**
❶ to walk with slow or regular steps • *She was nervously pacing up and down.* ❷ to measure a distance in paces • *I paced out the length of the stage.*

pacemaker *NOUN* **pacemakers**
❶ a person who sets the pace for someone else in a race ❷ an electrical device for keeping the heart beating

pacific (say pa-**sif**-ik) *ADJECTIVE*
peaceful; making or loving peace
➤ **pacifically** *ADVERB*

pacifist (say **pas**-if-ist) *NOUN* **pacifists**
a person who believes that war is always wrong
➤ **pacifism** *NOUN*

pacify *VERB* **pacifies, pacifying, pacified**
to calm a person down

pack *NOUN* **packs**
❶ a bundle or collection of things wrapped or tied together ❷ a set of playing cards (usually 52) ❸ a bag carried on your back ❹ a large amount • *a pack of lies* ❺ a group of hounds, wolves or other animals that hunt together ❻ a group of Brownies or Cub Scouts

pack *VERB* **packs, packing, packed**
❶ to put things into a suitcase, bag or box in order to move or store them ❷ to crowd together and fill a place • *Hundreds of fans packed the hall.*
➤ **pack someone off** to send a person away
➤ **send someone packing** to dismiss someone angrily

package *NOUN* **packages**
❶ a parcel or packet ❷ a number of things offered or accepted together

package holiday *NOUN* **package holidays**
a holiday with all the travel and accommodation arranged and included in the price

packaging *NOUN*
the container and wrapping in which something is sold

packed *ADJECTIVE*
❶ a room or space is packed when it is crowded with people • *The train was packed.* ❷ full of something • *The website is packed with useful information.*

packet *NOUN* **packets**
a small box or bag in which something is sold • *a packet of crisps*

pack ice *NOUN*
a mass of pieces of ice floating in the sea

pact *NOUN* **pacts**
an agreement or treaty

pad *NOUN* **pads**
❶ a set of sheets of paper fastened together at one edge ❷ a soft thick mass of material, used to protect or stuff something ❸ a piece of soft material worn to protect your leg in cricket and other games ❹ the soft fleshy part under an animal's foot or the end of a finger or toe ❺ a flat surface from which rockets are launched or where helicopters take off and land

pad *VERB* **pads, padding, padded**
❶ to walk softly • *He padded across the landing.* ❷ to put a pad on or in something

➤ **pad something out** to make a book, speech, etc. longer than it needs to be

padding NOUN
material used to pad things

paddle NOUN paddles
❶ a short oar with a broad blade; something shaped like this ❷ (*British*) walking about with bare feet in shallow water • *Let's go for a paddle.*

paddle VERB paddles, paddling, paddled
❶ (*British*) to walk about with bare feet in shallow water ❷ to move a boat along with a paddle or paddles; to row gently

paddock NOUN paddocks
a small field where horses are kept

paddy NOUN paddies
a field where rice is grown
➤ **paddy field** NOUN

padkos NOUN
(*S. African*) food that is packed for and eaten on a journey (**WORD ORIGIN**) from Afrikaans *pad* = road, + *kos* = food

padlock NOUN padlocks
a lock with a metal loop that passes through a ring or chain

padlock VERB padlocks, padlocking, padlocked
to lock something with a padlock

padre (say **pah**-dray) NOUN padres (*informal*)
a chaplain in the armed forces

paean (say **pee**-an) NOUN paeans
a song of praise or triumph

paediatrics (say peed-ee-**at**-riks) NOUN
the study of children's diseases
➤ **paediatric** ADJECTIVE
➤ **paediatrician** NOUN

pagan (say **pay**-gan) NOUN pagans
❶ a person who believes in a religion which is not one of the chief religions of the world ❷ a follower of a modern religion based on reverence for nature
➤ **pagan** ADJECTIVE
➤ **paganism** NOUN

page NOUN pages
❶ a piece of paper that is part of a book, magazine or newspaper; one side of this ❷ the information that you can see on a computer screen at any one time • *Click here to go back to the previous page.* ❸ a boy or man employed to go on errands or be an attendant ❹ a young boy attending a bride at a wedding

pageant NOUN pageants
❶ a play or entertainment about historical events and people ❷ a procession of people in costume as an entertainment
➤ **pageantry** NOUN

pagoda (say pag-**oh**-da) NOUN pagodas
a Buddhist tower or a Hindu temple shaped like a pyramid, in India and the Far East

paid
past tense of **pay**
➤ **put paid to something** (*informal*) to put an end to what someone is doing or hoping for

pail NOUN pails
a bucket

pain NOUN pains
❶ an unpleasant feeling caused by injury or disease ❷ suffering in the mind
➤ **on** or **under pain of** with the threat of
➤ **take pains** to make a careful effort or take trouble over something

pain VERB pains, paining, pained
to cause suffering or distress to someone • *It pains me to see you like this.*

painful ADJECTIVE
causing pain • *My ankle is very painful.* • *a painful memory*

painfully ADVERB
❶ extremely • *The dog was painfully thin.* ❷ in a way that causes pain • *He banged his knee painfully against the table.*

painkiller NOUN painkillers
a medicine or drug that reduces pain

painless ADJECTIVE
not causing any pain

painstaking ADJECTIVE
very careful and thorough • *Making an animated film is painstaking work.*

paint NOUN paints
a liquid substance put on something to colour it

paint VERB paints, painting, painted
❶ to put paint on something • *We painted the fence.* ❷ to make a picture with paints • *She painted some fish on the wall.*

paintbox NOUN paintboxes
a box of paints for painting pictures

paintbrush NOUN paintbrushes
a brush you use for painting with

painter NOUN painters
a person who paints

a b c d e f g h i j k l m n o p q r s t u v w x y z

painting *NOUN* paintings
① a painted picture ② using paints to make a picture • *He likes painting.*

pair *NOUN* pairs
① a set of two things or people • *a pair of shoes* ② something made of two joined parts • *a pair of scissors*

pair *VERB* pairs, pairing, paired
to put two things together as a pair
➤ **pair off** or **up** to form a couple

pal *NOUN* pals (*informal*)
a friend **WORD ORIGIN** Romany, = brother

palace *NOUN* palaces
a grand building where a king, queen or other important person lives

Palaeolithic (say pal-ee-o-**lith**-ik) *ADJECTIVE*
belonging to the early part of the Stone Age

palaeontology (say pal-ee-on-**tol**-o-jee)
NOUN
the study of fossils

palatable *ADJECTIVE*
tasting pleasant

palate *NOUN* palates
① the roof of your mouth ② a person's sense of taste • *She has a refined palate.*

> **SPELLING**
> Take care not to confuse with **palette** and **pallet**, which have different meanings.

palatial (say pa-**lay**-shal) *ADJECTIVE*
like a palace; large and splendid

pale *ADJECTIVE* paler, palest
① almost white • *a pale face* ② without much colour or brightness • *pale green* • *the pale moonlight*
➤ **palely** *ADVERB*
➤ **paleness** *NOUN*
➤ **beyond the pale** beyond the limits of acceptable behaviour
WORD ORIGIN *beyond the pale* comes from an old word 'pale' = a boundary, from Latin *palus* = a stake or fence post

palette *NOUN* palettes
a board on which an artist mixes colours ready for use

> **SPELLING**
> Take care not to confuse with **palate** and **pallet**, which have different meanings.

palindrome *NOUN* palindromes
a word or phrase that reads the same

backwards as forwards, e.g. *radar* or *Madam, I'm Adam*

paling *NOUN* palings
a fence made of wooden posts or railings; one of its posts

palisade *NOUN* palisades
a fence of pointed sticks or boards

pall (say pawl) *NOUN* palls
① a cloth spread over a coffin ② a thick dark cloud of something • *A pall of smoke lay over the town.*

pall *VERB* palls, palling, palled
to become uninteresting or boring after a time • *The novelty of the new computer game soon began to pall.*

pallbearer *NOUN* pallbearers
a person helping to carry the coffin at a funeral

pallet *NOUN* pallets
① a mattress stuffed with straw ② a hard narrow bed ③ a large platform for carrying goods that are being stacked, especially one that can be lifted by a forklift truck

> **SPELLING**
> Take care not to confuse with **palate** and **palette**, which have different meanings.

palliative *NOUN* palliatives
something that lessens pain or suffering
➤ **palliative** *ADJECTIVE*

pallid *ADJECTIVE*
pale, especially because of illness

pallor *NOUN*
paleness in a person's face, especially because of illness

palm *NOUN* palms
① the inner part of the hand, between the fingers and the wrist ② a palm tree

palm *VERB* palms, palming, palmed
to pick something up secretly and hide it in the palm of your hand
➤ **palm something off on someone** to fool a person into accepting something they do not want

palmistry *NOUN*
fortune-telling by looking at the creases in the palm of a person's hand

Palm Sunday *NOUN*
the Sunday before Easter, when Christians commemorate Jesus Christ's entry into Jerusalem when the people spread palm leaves in his path

palm tree *NOUN* palm trees
a tropical tree with large leaves and no
branches

palpable *ADJECTIVE*
❶ able to be touched or felt ❷ obvious • *a
palpable lie*
➤ **palpably** *ADVERB*

palpitate *VERB* palpitates, palpitating,
palpitated
❶ the heart palpitates when it beats hard
and quickly ❷ a person palpitates when they
quiver with fear or excitement
➤ **palpitation** *NOUN*

palsy (say **pawl**-zee) *NOUN* (*old use*)
paralysis with tremors

paltry (say **pol**-tree) *ADJECTIVE*
very small and almost worthless • *a paltry
amount*

pampas *NOUN*
wide grassy plains in South America

pampas grass *NOUN*
a tall grass with long feathery flowers

pamper *VERB* pampers, pampering, pampered
to take care of someone very well and make
them feel as comfortable as possible

pamphlet *NOUN* pamphlets
a leaflet or booklet giving information on a
subject

pan *NOUN* pans
❶ a wide container with a flat base, used for
cooking ❷ something shaped like this ❸ the
bowl of a lavatory

panacea (say pan-a-**see**-a) *NOUN* panaceas
a cure for all kinds of diseases or troubles

panache (say pan-**ash**) *NOUN*
a confident stylish manner
WORD ORIGIN originally referring to a plume of
feathers on a helmet or headdress, via French
and Italian from Latin *pinnaculum* = little
feather

panama *NOUN* panamas
a hat made of a fine straw-like material
WORD ORIGIN from *Panama* in Central
America (because the hats were originally made
from the leaves of a plant which grows there)

pancake *NOUN* pancakes
a thin round cake of batter fried on both sides

Pancake Day *NOUN*
Shrove Tuesday, when people often eat
pancakes

pancreas (say **pan**-kree-as) *NOUN*
a gland near the stomach, producing insulin
and digestive juices

panda *NOUN* pandas
a large bear-like black-and-white animal
found in China

pandemonium *NOUN*
uproar and complete confusion
• *Pandemonium broke out in the courtroom.*

pander *VERB* panders, pandering, pandered
➤ **pander to someone** to let someone have
whatever they want even though you know
it is not right • *You shouldn't pander to his
taste for gossip.*

pane *NOUN* panes
a sheet of glass in a window

panegyric (say pan-i-**jirrik**) *NOUN* panegyrics
a speech or piece of writing praising a person
or thing

panel *NOUN* panels
❶ a long flat piece of wood, metal, etc. that
is part of a door, wall or piece of furniture
❷ a flat board with controls or instruments
on it ❸ a group of people chosen to discuss
or decide something • *The winner will be
decided by a panel of judges.*
➤ **panelled** *ADJECTIVE*
➤ **panelling** *NOUN*

pang *NOUN* pangs
a sudden sharp feeling of pain or emotion • *a
pang of guilt*

panic *NOUN*
sudden uncontrollable fear that stops you
from thinking clearly • *People fled in panic as
the fire spread.*

panic *VERB* panics, panicking, panicked
to be filled with panic • *Stay calm and don't
panic.* **WORD ORIGIN** from the name of *Pan*, an
ancient Greek god thought to be able to cause
sudden fear

panicky *ADJECTIVE*
(*informal*) feeling or showing panic

panic-stricken *ADJECTIVE*
very frightened in a way that stops you from
thinking clearly

pannier *NOUN* panniers
a large bag or basket hung on one side of a
bicycle, motorcycle or horse

panoply *NOUN* panoplies
a splendid display or collection of things

A

panorama *NOUN* panoramas
a view or picture of a wide area
➤ **panoramic** *ADJECTIVE*

B

pansy *NOUN* pansies
a small brightly coloured garden flower with
velvety petals

C

pant *VERB* pants, panting, panted
to take short quick breaths, usually after
running or working hard

D

E

pantaloons *PLURAL NOUN*
wide trousers, gathered at the ankle
WORD ORIGIN from *Pantalone*, a character in
old Italian comedies who wore these

F

G

pantechnicon (say pan-**tek**-nik-on) *NOUN*
pantechnicons
(*British*) a kind of large lorry, used for
carrying furniture **WORD ORIGIN** originally the
name of a large art and craft gallery in London,
which was later used for storing furniture: from
Greek *pan* = all + *techne* = art

H

I

J

panther *NOUN* panthers
a leopard, especially a black one

K

panties *PLURAL NOUN* (*informal*)
short knickers

L

pantomime *NOUN* pantomimes
a Christmas entertainment, usually based on
a fairy tale

M

N

pantry *NOUN* pantries
a small room for storing food and crockery

O

P

pants *PLURAL NOUN*
❶ (*informal*) underpants or knickers ❷ (*North
American*) trousers

Q

pap *NOUN*
❶ soft food suitable for babies ❷ trivial
entertainment; nonsense

R

papa *NOUN* (*old use*)
father

S

papacy (say **pay**-pa-see) *NOUN* papacies
the position of pope

T

papal (say **pay**-pal) *ADJECTIVE*
to do with the pope

U

V

paparazzi (say **pap**-a-rat-si) *PLURAL NOUN*
photographers who pursue famous people to
get photographs of them

W

X

paper *NOUN* papers
❶ a substance made in thin sheets from
wood, rags, etc. and used for writing,
printing, or drawing on or for wrapping
things ❷ a newspaper ❸ wallpaper ❹ a set

Y

Z

of examination questions • *the history paper*
❺ papers are official documents

paper *VERB* papers, papering, papered
to cover a wall or room with wallpaper

paperback *NOUN* paperbacks
a book with a thin flexible cover

paperweight *NOUN* paperweights
a small heavy object used for holding down
loose papers

paperwork *NOUN*
all the writing of reports and keeping of
records that someone has to do as part of
their job

papier mâché (say pap-yay **mash**-ay) *NOUN*
paper made into pulp and moulded to make
models, ornaments, etc.

paprika (say **pap**-rik-a) *NOUN*
a powdered spice made from red pepper

papyrus (say pap-**y**-rus) *NOUN* papyri
❶ a kind of paper made from the stems of a
plant like a reed, used in ancient Egypt ❷ a
document written on this paper

par *NOUN*
the number of strokes in golf that a good
player should normally take for a particular
hole or course
➤ **below par** not as good or as well as usual
➤ **on a par with** equal to in amount or
quality

parable *NOUN* parables
a story told to teach people something,
especially one of those told by Jesus Christ

parabola (say pa-**rab**-ol-a) *NOUN* parabolas
a curve like the path of an object thrown into
the air and falling down again
➤ **parabolic** *ADJECTIVE*

parachute *NOUN* parachutes
an umbrella-like device on which people or
things can fall slowly to the ground from an
aircraft

parachute *VERB* parachutes, parachuting,
parachuted
to fall or drop something by means of a
parachute
➤ **parachutist** *NOUN*

parade *NOUN* parades
❶ a line of people or vehicles moving forward
through a place as a celebration ❷ an
assembly of soldiers for inspection or drill ❸ a
public square or row of shops

parade *VERB* parades, parading, paraded
❶ to move forward through a place as a

celebration ❷ soldiers parade when they assemble for inspection or drill

paradise *NOUN*
❶ heaven or, in the Bible, the Garden of Eden
❷ a place that seems perfect • *a tropical paradise*

paradox *NOUN* **paradoxes**
a statement that seems to contradict itself but which contains a truth, e.g. 'More haste, less speed'
➤ **paradoxical** *ADJECTIVE*
➤ **paradoxically** *ADVERB*

paraffin *NOUN*
a kind of oil used as fuel

paragliding *NOUN*
the sport of gliding through the air while being supported by a wide parachute

paragon *NOUN* **paragons**
a person or thing that seems to be perfect

paragraph *NOUN* **paragraphs**
one or more sentences on a single subject, forming a section of a piece of writing and beginning on a new line, usually slightly in from the margin of the page

parakeet *NOUN* **parakeets**
a kind of small parrot

parallax *NOUN*
what seems to be a change in the position of something when you look at it from a different place

parallel *ADJECTIVE*
❶ parallel lines run side by side and the same distance apart from each other for their whole length, like railway lines ❷ similar or corresponding • *When petrol prices rise there is a parallel rise in bus fares.*

parallel *NOUN* **parallels**
❶ something similar or corresponding
❷ a comparison • *You can draw a parallel between the two situations.* ❸ a line that is parallel to another ❹ a line of latitude

parallel *VERB* **parallels, paralleling, paralleled**
to find or be a parallel to something

> **SPELLING**
> Double up the first l in **parallel** (but the last l stays single).

parallelogram *NOUN* **parallelograms**
a four-sided figure with its opposite sides equal and parallel

paralyse *VERB* **paralyses, paralysing, paralysed**
❶ to cause paralysis in a person or part of the

body ❷ to be paralysed with fear or emotion is to be so affected by it that you cannot move or do anything

paralysis *NOUN*
being unable to move, especially because of a disease or an injury to the nerves
➤ **paralytic** (say pa-ra-**lit**-ik) *ADJECTIVE*

paramedic *NOUN* **paramedics**
a person who is trained to do medical work, especially emergency first aid, but is not a fully qualified doctor

parameter (say pa-**ram**-it-er) *NOUN* **parameters**
one of the factors or limits which affect the way something is done • *We have to work within the parameters of time and money.*

paramilitary *ADJECTIVE*
organized like a military force but not part of the armed services

paramount *ADJECTIVE*
more important than anything else • *Secrecy is paramount.*

paranoia *NOUN*
❶ a mental illness in which a person has delusions or suspects and distrusts people ❷ an unjustified suspicion and mistrust of others

paranoid *ADJECTIVE*
suffering from paranoia

paranormal *ADJECTIVE*
beyond what is normal and can be rationally explained; supernatural

parapet *NOUN* **parapets**
a low wall along the edge of a balcony, bridge or roof

paraphernalia *NOUN*
numerous pieces of equipment or belongings
WORD ORIGIN originally = the personal belongings a woman could keep after her marriage (as opposed to her dowry, which went to her husband)

paraphrase *VERB* **paraphrases, paraphrasing, paraphrased**
to give the meaning of something by using different words
➤ **paraphrase** *NOUN*

paraplegia *NOUN*
paralysis of the lower half of the body
➤ **paraplegic** *NOUN & ADJECTIVE*

parasite *NOUN* **parasites**
an animal or plant that lives in or on another,

from which it gets its food
➤ **parasitic** *ADJECTIVE*
WORD ORIGIN from Greek *parasitos* = guest at a meal

parasol *NOUN* **parasols**
a lightweight umbrella used to shade yourself from the sun

paratroops *PLURAL NOUN*
troops trained to be dropped from aircraft by parachute
➤ **paratrooper** *NOUN*

parboil *VERB* **parboils, parboiling, parboiled**
to boil food until it is partly cooked

parcel *NOUN* **parcels**
something wrapped up to be sent by post or carried

parcel *VERB* **parcels, parcelling, parcelled**
❶ to wrap something up as a parcel ❷ to divide something into portions • *We'll need to parcel out the work.*

parched *ADJECTIVE*
very dry or thirsty

parchment *NOUN* **parchments**
a kind of heavy paper, originally made from animal skins **WORD ORIGIN** from the city of Pergamum, now in Turkey, where parchment was made in ancient times

pardon *NOUN*
❶ forgiveness ❷ the cancelling of a punishment • *a free pardon*

pardon *VERB* **pardons, pardoning, pardoned**
❶ to forgive or excuse someone ❷ to cancel a person's punishment

pardon *EXCLAMATION*
(also **I beg your pardon** or **pardon me**) used to mean 'I didn't hear or understand what you said.' or 'I apologize.'

pardonable *ADJECTIVE*
a pardonable mistake is one that can be forgiven

pare (say pair) *VERB* **pares, paring, pared**
❶ to trim something by cutting away the edges ❷ to reduce something gradually • *We had to pare down our expenses.*

parent *NOUN* **parents**
❶ a father or mother; an animal or plant that has produced others of its kind ❷ something that produces others of the same type • *the parent company*
➤ **parenting** *NOUN*

parentage *NOUN*
who your parents are

parental (say pa-**rent**-al) *ADJECTIVE*
to do with parents • *parental advice*

parenthesis (say pa-**ren**-thi-sis) *NOUN* **parentheses**
❶ something extra that is put into a sentence, usually between brackets or dashes ❷ either of the pair of brackets (like these) used to mark off words from the rest of a sentence
➤ **parenthetical** *ADJECTIVE*

parenthood *NOUN*
being a parent

par excellence (say par eks-el-**ahns**) *ADVERB*
more than all the others; to the greatest degree **WORD ORIGIN** French, = because of special excellence

pariah (say pa-**ry**-a) *NOUN* **pariahs**
an outcast

parish *NOUN* **parishes**
in the Christian Church, a district with its own church
➤ **parishioner** *NOUN*

park *NOUN* **parks**
❶ a large open area with grass and trees for public use ❷ an area of grassland or woodland belonging to a country house

park *VERB* **parks, parking, parked**
to leave a vehicle somewhere for a time

parka *NOUN* **parkas**
a warm jacket with a hood attached

Parkinson's disease *NOUN*
a disease that makes a person's arms and legs shake and the muscles become stiff **WORD ORIGIN** named after an English doctor, James *Parkinson*

parley *VERB* **parleys, parleying, parleyed**
to hold a discussion with an opponent or enemy in order to reach an agreement
➤ **parley** *NOUN*

parliament *NOUN* **parliaments**
the assembly that makes a country's laws
➤ **parliamentary** *ADJECTIVE*

parlour *NOUN* **parlours** (old use)
a sitting room **WORD ORIGIN** originally = a room in a monastery where the monks were allowed to talk: from French *parler* = speak

parochial (say per-**oh**-kee-al) *ADJECTIVE*
❶ to do with a church parish ❷ having a narrow point of view; interested only in your own local area

parody *NOUN* **parodies**
an amusing imitation of the style of a writer, composer, literary work, etc.

parody *VERB* **parodies, parodying, parodied**
to make or be a parody of a person or thing

parole *NOUN*
the release of a prisoner before the end of their sentence on the condition that they behave well • *He was on parole.*

paroxysm (say pa-roks-izm) *NOUN* **paroxysms**
a sudden outburst of laughter, crying or strong feeling • *He was driven into a paroxysm of rage.*

parquet (say par-kay) *NOUN*
wooden blocks arranged in a pattern to make a floor

parrot *NOUN* **parrots**
a brightly-coloured tropical bird with a curved beak that can learn to repeat words or sounds

parry *VERB* **parries, parrying, parried**
❶ to turn aside an opponent's weapon or blow by using your own to block it ❷ to avoid an awkward question skilfully

parse *VERB* **parses, parsing, parsed**
to state what is the grammatical form and function of a word or words in a sentence

parsimonious *ADJECTIVE*
stingy; very sparing in the use of something
➤ **parsimony** *NOUN*

parsley *NOUN*
a plant with crinkled green leaves used to flavour and decorate food

parsnip *NOUN* **parsnips**
a plant with a pointed pale-yellow root used as a vegetable

parson *NOUN* **parsons**
a member of the Church of England clergy, especially a rector or vicar

parsonage *NOUN* **parsonages**
a parson's house

part *NOUN* **parts**
❶ some but not all of a thing or number of things; anything that belongs to something bigger ❷ the character played by an actor or actress ❸ the words spoken by a character in a play ❹ how much a person or thing is involved in something • *She played a huge part in her daughter's success.* ❺ one side in an agreement or in a dispute or quarrel
➤ **take something in good part** to accept

something without being upset or offended
➤ **take part** to join in an activity

part *VERB* **parts, parting, parted**
❶ two people part when they leave each other • *I hope we can part friends.* ❷ to move apart or to make people or things move apart • *At last the clouds parted.*
➤ **part with something** to give something away or get rid of it

partake *VERB* **partakes, partaking, partook, partaken**
❶ to eat or drink something • *We all partook of the food* ❷ to take part in something

part exchange *NOUN*
(*British*) giving something that you own as part of the price of what you are buying

partial *ADJECTIVE*
❶ not complete or total • *a partial eclipse*
❷ favouring one side more than the other; biased or unfair
➤ **be partial to something** to be fond of something

partiality *NOUN*
❶ unfair support for one side over another
❷ a fondness for something

partially *ADVERB*
partly; not completely • *He was partially to blame.*

participant *NOUN* **participants**
a person who takes part in something

participate *VERB* **participates, participating, participated**
to take part in something or have a share in it • *The whole class participated in the discussion.*
➤ **participation** *NOUN*

participle *NOUN* **participles**
a word formed from a verb (e.g. *gone, going; guided, guiding*) and used with an auxiliary verb to form certain tenses (e.g. *It has gone. It is going.*) or the passive (e.g. *We were guided to our seats.*) or as an adjective (e.g. *a guided missile; a guiding light*). The **past participle** (e.g. *gone, guided*) describes a completed action or past condition. The **present participle** (which ends in -*ing*) describes a continuing action or condition.

particle *NOUN* **particles**
a very small piece or amount of something
• *dust particles*

particular *ADJECTIVE*
❶ only this one and no other; individual
• *This particular stamp is very rare.* ❷ special

or exceptional • *Take particular care of it.*
❸ wanting something to be exactly right; difficult to please • *He is very particular about his clothes.*

particular *NOUN* **particulars**
a detail or single fact • *Can you give me the particulars of the case?*
➤ **in particular** ❶ especially • *We liked this one in particular.* ❷ special • *We did nothing in particular.*

particularly *ADVERB*
especially; more than usual or more than the rest • *I enjoyed the film, particularly the second half.*

parting *NOUN* **partings**
❶ leaving or separation ❷ a line where hair is combed away in different directions

parting shot *NOUN* **parting shots**
a sharp remark made by a person who is just leaving

> **USAGE**
>
> This is also sometimes called a *Parthian shot*, after the horsemen of Parthia (an ancient kingdom in what is now Iran), who, while retreating, would shoot arrows back at the enemy.

partisan *NOUN* **partisans**
❶ a strong supporter of a party or group ❷ a member of an armed group fighting secretly against an army that has taken control of its country

partisan *ADJECTIVE*
strongly supporting a particular cause

partition *NOUN* **partitions**
❶ a thin wall that divides a room or space ❷ dividing a country or territory into separate parts

partition *VERB* **partitions, partitioning, partitioned**
❶ to divide something into separate parts ❷ to divide a room or space with a partition

partly *ADVERB*
to some extent but not completely • *It was partly my fault.*

partner *NOUN* **partners**
❶ one of a pair of people who do something together, such as dancing or playing a game ❷ a person who jointly owns a business with one or more other people ❸ the person that someone is married to, in a civil partnership with or is having a sexual relationship with

partner *VERB* **partners, partnering, partnered**
to be a person's partner

partnership *NOUN* **partnerships**
❶ being a partner with someone, especially in business • *The two engineers decided to go into partnership.* ❷ a business owned by two or more people

part of speech *NOUN* **parts of speech**
any of the groups into which words are divided in grammar (noun, pronoun, determiner, adjective, verb, adverb, preposition, conjunction, exclamation)

> **GRAMMAR**
>
> See also **word class**.

partook
past tense of **partake**

partridge *NOUN* **partridges**
a game bird with brown feathers

part-time *ADJECTIVE & ADVERB*
working for only some of the normal hours • *a part-time job* • *She works part-time on a farm.*

party *NOUN* **parties**
❶ a gathering of people to enjoy themselves • *a birthday party* ❷ a group working or travelling together • *a search party* ❸ an organized group of people with similar political beliefs • *the Labour Party* ❹ a person who is involved in a legal agreement or dispute • *the guilty party*

pas de deux (say pah der **der**) *NOUN* **pas de deux**
a dance for two people, usually in a ballet
WORD ORIGIN French, = step of two

pass *VERB* **passes, passing, passed**
❶ to go or move in a certain direction • *They passed over the bridge.* ❷ to go past something • *He passed me in the street but didn't see me.* ❸ to move something in a certain direction • *Pass the cord through the ring.* ❹ to give or transfer something to another person • *Could you pass the butter?* ❺ in ball games, to kick or throw the ball to another player of your own side ❻ to be successful in a test or examination ❼ to approve or accept something • *They passed a law.* ❽ to spend time doing something • *How did you pass the time in hospital?* ❾ to happen or go by • *We heard what passed when they met.* • *Time passed very quickly.* ❿ to come to an end or no longer be there • *Her opportunity passed.* ⓫ to pass a remark or comment is to make it ⓬ in a game, quiz, etc., to let your turn go by or choose not to answer
➤ **pass away** to die
➤ **pass out** to faint

pass *NOUN* passes
❶ passing something ❷ a success in an examination ❸ in ball games, kicking or throwing the ball to another player on the same side ❹ a permit to go in or out of a place ❺ a route through a gap in a range of mountains
➤ **come to a pretty pass** to reach a bad state of affairs

> SPELLING
>
> **Passed** is the past tense of **pass**; if you go **past** something, you go near it and then continue moving until it is behind you, e.g. *We passed the house. Carry on past the supermarket then turn right.*

passable *ADJECTIVE*
❶ satisfactory but not especially good ❷ able to be passed
➤ **passably** *ADVERB*

passage *NOUN* passages
❶ a way through something; a corridor ❷ a journey by sea or air ❸ a section of a piece of writing or music ❹ going by or passing • *the passage of time*

passageway *NOUN* passageways
a passage or way through, especially between buildings

passé (say **pas**-say) *ADJECTIVE*
no longer fashionable

passenger *NOUN* passengers
a person who is driven or carried in a car, train, ship or aircraft

passer-by *NOUN* passers-by
a person who happens to be going past something

passion *NOUN* passions
❶ strong emotion ❷ a great enthusiasm for something • *She has a passion for reading.*
➤ **the Passion** the sufferings of Jesus Christ at the Crucifixion

passionate *ADJECTIVE*
full of passion or strong feeling
➤ **passionately** *ADVERB*

passive *ADJECTIVE*
❶ not resisting or fighting against something ❷ acted upon and not active ❸ (*in grammar*) describing the form of a verb when the subject of the verb receives the action, e.g. *was hit* in 'She was hit on the head'. talk about something happening in the future

> GRAMMAR
>
> See also the panel at **active**.

➤ **passively** *ADVERB*

passive smoking *NOUN*
breathing in other people's cigarette smoke, thought of as a health risk

Passover *NOUN*
a Jewish religious festival commemorating the freeing of the Jews from slavery in Egypt

passport *NOUN* passports
an official document that allows you to travel abroad

password *NOUN* passwords
❶ a secret word or phrase that you need to know in order to be allowed into a place ❷ a word you need to key in to gain access to a computer system or interface

past *ADJECTIVE*
of the time gone by • *during the past week*

past *NOUN*
❶ the time gone by • *Writing letters was more common in the past.* ❷ (*in grammar*) the tense of a verb used to describe an action that happened at a time before now, e.g. *took* is the past tense of *take*

> GRAMMAR
>
> See also the panel at **tense**.

past *PREPOSITION*
❶ beyond a certain place • *Go past the school and turn right.* ❷ after a certain time • *It is past midnight.*
➤ **past it** (*informal*) too old to be able to do something

> SPELLING
>
> **Past** is different from **passed**, which is a form of the verb **pass**: • *Police cars rushed past us.* • *We passed three police cars.*

pasta *NOUN*
an Italian food consisting of a dried paste made from flour and shaped into macaroni, spaghetti, lasagne, etc.

paste *NOUN* pastes
❶ a soft, moist and sticky substance ❷ a glue, especially for paper ❸ a soft edible mixture • *tomato paste*

paste *VERB* pastes, pasting, pasted
❶ to stick something onto a surface by using paste ❷ to coat something with paste

pastel *NOUN* pastels
❶ a crayon that is like chalk ❷ a light delicate colour

a b c d e f g h i j k l m n o p q r s t u v w x y z

pasteurize (also **pasteurise**) *VERB*
pasteurizes, pasteurizing, pasteurized
to purify milk by heating and then cooling it
WORD ORIGIN named after a French scientist,
Louis *Pasteur*, who invented the process

pastille *NOUN* pastilles
a small flavoured sweet that you suck

pastime *NOUN* pastimes
something you do to make time pass
pleasantly; a hobby or game

pastor *NOUN* pastors
a member of the clergy who is in charge of a
church or congregation

pastoral *ADJECTIVE*
❶ to do with country life • *a pastoral scene*
❷ to do with a pastor or a pastor's duties

pastry *NOUN* pastries
❶ dough made with flour, fat and water,
rolled flat and baked ❷ something made of
pastry

pasture *NOUN* pastures
land covered with grass that cattle, sheep or
horses can eat

pasture *VERB* pastures, pasturing, pastured
to put animals to graze in a pasture

pasty (say **pas**-tee) *NOUN* pasties
(*British*) a folded pastry case with a filling of
meat and vegetables

pasty (say **pay**-stee) *ADJECTIVE*
looking pale and unhealthy

pat *VERB* pats, patting, patted
to tap something gently with the open hand
or with something flat

pat *NOUN* pats
❶ a patting movement or sound ❷ a small
piece of butter
➤ **a pat on the back** praise for doing
something good • *She deserves a pat on the
back for all her hard work.*

patch *NOUN* patches
❶ a piece of material put over a hole or
damaged place ❷ an area that is different
from its surroundings • *a black cat with a
white patch on its chest* ❸ a piece of ground
• *a vegetable patch* ❹ a small area or piece of
something • *There were patches of fog on the
motorway.*
➤ **not a patch on** (*informal*) not nearly as
good as

patch *VERB* patches, patching, patched
to put a patch on something

➤ **patch something up** ❶ to repair
something roughly ❷ to settle a quarrel

patchwork *NOUN*
❶ needlework in which small pieces of
different cloth are sewn edge to edge ❷ a
collection of different things making up a
whole • *From the plane, the landscape below
was a patchwork of fields.*

patchy *ADJECTIVE*
occurring in some areas but not others;
uneven • *There may be some patchy rain.*

pate *NOUN* pates (*old use*)
the top of a person's head • *his bald pate*

pâté (say **pat**-ay) *NOUN* pâtés
paste made of meat or fish

patent (say **pat**-ent or **pay**-tent) *NOUN* patents
the official right given to an inventor to make
or sell their invention and to prevent other
people from copying it

patent (say **pay**-tent) *ADJECTIVE*
❶ protected by a patent • *patent medicines*
❷ very clear or obvious • *It's a patent lie.*

patent *VERB* patents, patenting, patented
to get a patent for an idea or invention

patentee (say pay-ten-**tee** or pat-en-**tee**)
NOUN patentees
a person who holds a patent

patent leather *NOUN*
glossy leather

patently *ADVERB*
clearly or obviously • *This is patently untrue.*

paternal *ADJECTIVE*
❶ to do with a father ❷ fatherly
➤ **paternally** *ADVERB*

paternity *NOUN*
❶ fatherhood ❷ being the father of a
particular baby

path *NOUN* paths
❶ a narrow way along which people or
animals can walk ❷ a line along which
a person or thing moves • *The tornado
destroyed everything in its path.* ❸ a course
of action • *the path to success*

pathetic *ADJECTIVE*
❶ making you feel pity or sympathy ❷ poor,
weak or useless • *He made a pathetic attempt
to climb the tree.*
➤ **pathetically** *ADVERB*

pathological *ADJECTIVE*
❶ to do with pathology or disease

❷ (*informal*) compulsive or uncontrollable • *a pathological liar*

pathology *NOUN*
the study of diseases of the body
➤ **pathologist** *NOUN*

pathos (say **pay**-thoss) *NOUN*
a quality of making people feel pity or sympathy

patience *NOUN*
❶ being patient **❷** a card game for one person

patient *ADJECTIVE*
able to wait for a long time or put up with trouble or inconvenience without getting anxious or angry

patient *NOUN* patients
a person who is receiving treatment from a doctor or dentist

patiently *ADVERB*
in a patient way • *He waited patiently for his turn.*

patio *NOUN* patios
a paved area beside a house

patriarch (say **pay**-tree-ark) *NOUN* patriarchs
❶ a man who is head of a family or tribe. Compare with **matriarch**. **❷** a bishop of high rank in the Orthodox Christian churches
➤ **patriarchal** *ADJECTIVE*

patriot (say **pay**-tree-ot or **pat**-ree-ot) *NOUN* patriots
a person who loves their country and supports it loyally
➤ **patriotism** *NOUN*

patriotic *ADJECTIVE*
loving your country and supporting it loyally
➤ **patriotically** *ADVERB*

patrol *VERB* patrols, patrolling, patrolled
to walk or travel regularly over an area in order to guard it and see that all is well

patrol *NOUN* patrols
❶ a patrolling group of people, ships, aircraft, etc. **❷** a group of Scouts or Guides
➤ **on patrol** patrolling an area

patron (say **pay**-tron) *NOUN* patrons
❶ someone who supports a person or cause with money or encouragement **❷** a regular customer

patronage (say **pat**-ron-ij) *NOUN*
support given by a patron

patronize (also **patronise**) (say **pat**-ron-yz)
VERB patronizes, patronizing, patronized

❶ to be a regular customer of a particular shop, restaurant, etc. **❷** to talk to someone in a way that shows you think they are stupid or inferior to you

patron saint *NOUN* patron saints
a saint who is thought to protect a particular place or activity

patter *NOUN*
❶ a series of light tapping sounds • *the patter of rain on the roof* **❷** the quick talk of a comedian, conjuror, salesperson, etc.

patter *VERB* patters, pattering, pattered
to make light tapping sounds • *Rain pattered on the window panes.*

pattern *NOUN* patterns
❶ a repeated arrangement of lines, shapes or colours • *a shirt with a floral pattern on it* **❷** a thing to be copied in order to make something • *a dress pattern* **❸** the regular way in which something happens • *James Bond films follow a set pattern.*
➤ **patterned** *ADJECTIVE*

paunch *NOUN* paunches
a large belly

pauper *NOUN* paupers
a person who is very poor

pause *NOUN* pauses
a temporary stop in speaking or doing something • *There was a long pause before she answered.*

pause *VERB* pauses, pausing, paused
❶ to stop speaking or doing something for a short time before starting again **❷** to temporarily interrupt the playing of a piece of music, film, computer game, etc.

pave *VERB* paves, paving, paved
to lay a hard surface on a road or path
➤ **pave the way** to prepare for something

pavement *NOUN* pavements
(*British*) a paved path along the side of a street

pavilion *NOUN* pavilions
❶ a building at a sports ground for players and spectators to use **❷** an ornamental building or shelter used for dances, concerts or exhibitions

paving stone *NOUN* paving stones
a flat piece of stone used for covering the ground

paw *NOUN* paws
the foot of an animal that has claws

a
b
c
d
e
f
g
h
i
j
k
l
m
n
o
p
q
r
s
t
u
v
w
x
y
z

paw *VERB* paws, pawing, pawed
to touch or scrape something with a hand or foot • *The horse pawed the ground nervously.*

pawn *NOUN* pawns
❶ the least valuable piece in chess ❷ a person whose actions are controlled by someone else

pawn *VERB* pawns, pawning, pawned
to leave something with a pawnbroker in exchange for money • *He had to pawn his watch.*

pawnbroker *NOUN* pawnbrokers
a shopkeeper who lends money to people in return for objects that they leave and which are sold if the money is not paid back
➤ **pawnshop** *NOUN*

pawpaw *NOUN* pawpaws
an orange-coloured tropical fruit used as food

pay *VERB* pays, paying, paid
❶ to give money in return for goods or services • *I'll just pay for this comic.* ❷ to give what is owed • *They could no longer pay the rent.* ❸ to be profitable or worthwhile • *It pays to advertise.* ❹ to give or express something • *Now pay attention.* • *It's time we paid them a visit.* • *He doesn't often pay her compliments.* ❺ to suffer a penalty for something you have done • *I'll make you pay for this.* ❻ to let out a rope by loosening it gradually
➤ **pay someone back** ❶ to pay money that you owe someone ❷ to get revenge on someone
➤ **pay off** to be worthwhile or have good results • *All the preparation she did really paid off.*
➤ **pay something off** to pay in full what you owe
➤ **pay up** to pay the full amount you owe

pay *NOUN*
salary or wages

> **SPELLING**
> The past tense of **pay** is **paid**.

payable *ADJECTIVE*
that must be paid • *A small deposit is payable in advance.*

payment *NOUN* payments
❶ paying someone or being paid for something • *You can't expect him to do the work without payment.* ❷ an amount of money paid

payphone *NOUN* payphones
a public telephone operated by coins or a card

PC *ABBREVIATION*
❶ personal computer ❷ police constable

PE *ABBREVIATION*
physical education

pea *NOUN* peas
the small round green seed of a climbing plant, growing inside a pod and used as a vegetable; the plant bearing these pods

peace *NOUN*
❶ a time when there is no war, violence or disorder ❷ quietness and calm

peaceable *ADJECTIVE*
fond of peace; not quarrelsome or warlike
➤ **peaceably** *ADVERB*

peaceful *ADJECTIVE*
❶ quiet and calm ❷ not involving violence
• *a peaceful protest*
➤ **peacefully** *ADVERB*
➤ **peacefulness** *NOUN*

peach *NOUN* peaches
❶ a round soft juicy fruit with a pinkish or yellowish skin and a large stone ❷ (*informal*) a thing of great quality • *a peach of a shot*

peacock *NOUN* peacocks
a large male bird with a long brightly coloured tail that it can spread out like a fan
➤ **peahen** *NOUN*

peak *NOUN* peaks
❶ a pointed top of a mountain ❷ the highest or most intense part of something • *Traffic reaches its peak at 5 p.m.* ❸ the part of a cap that sticks out in front

peak *VERB* peaks, peaking, peaked
to reach the highest point or value • *Sales peak just before Christmas.*

peaked *ADJECTIVE*
a peaked hat or cap is one with a peak

peaky *ADJECTIVE*
(*British*) looking pale and ill

peal *NOUN* peals
❶ the loud ringing of a bell or set of bells ❷ a loud burst of thunder or laughter • *The girls burst into peals of laughter.*

peal *VERB* peals, pealing, pealed
bells peal when they ring loudly

peanut *NOUN* peanuts
a small round nut that grows in a pod in the ground

peanut butter *NOUN*
roasted peanuts crushed into a paste

pear *NOUN* pears
a juicy fruit that gets narrower near the stalk

pearl *NOUN* pearls
a small shiny white ball found in the shells of some oysters and used as a jewel

pearl barley *NOUN*
grains of barley made small by grinding

pearly *ADJECTIVE*
like a pearl; white and shiny • *pearly white teeth*

peasant *NOUN* peasants
a person who belongs to a farming community, especially in poor areas of the world

peasantry *NOUN*
the peasants of a region or country

peat *NOUN*
rotted plant material that can be dug out of the ground and used as fuel or in gardening
➤ **peaty** *ADJECTIVE*

pebble *NOUN* pebbles
a small round stone found on a beach or in a river

pebbly *ADJECTIVE*
covered with pebbles • *a pebbly beach*

peck *VERB* pecks, pecking, pecked
❶ to bite at something quickly with the beak • *Birds were pecking at crumbs on the ground.* ❷ to kiss someone lightly on the cheek

peck *NOUN* pecks
❶ a quick bite by a bird ❷ a light kiss on the cheek

peckish *ADJECTIVE* (*British*) (*informal*)
hungry

pectoral *ADJECTIVE*
to do with the chest or breast • *pectoral muscles*

peculiar *ADJECTIVE*
❶ strange or unusual • *There's a peculiar smell in here.* ❷ belonging to a particular person, place or thing; restricted • *The custom is peculiar to this tribe.* ❸ special • *This point is of peculiar interest.*

peculiarity *NOUN* peculiarities
a strange or distinctive feature or habit • *It took a while to get used to his teacher's peculiarities.*

peculiarly *ADVERB*
❶ especially; more than usual • *She has a peculiarly annoying laugh.* ❷ strangely

pecuniary *ADJECTIVE* (*formal*)
to do with money • *pecuniary aid*
WORD ORIGIN from Latin *pecunia* = money (from *pecu* = cattle, because in early times a person's wealth was measured by how many cattle or sheep they owned)

pedagogue (say **ped**-a-gog) *NOUN* pedagogues
a teacher, especially one who teaches in a strict or exact way **WORD ORIGIN** from Greek *paidagogos* = a slave who took a boy to school

pedal *NOUN* pedals
a lever that you press with your foot to operate a bicycle, car or machine or to play certain musical instruments

pedal *VERB* pedals, pedalling, pedalled
to use a pedal; to move or work something, especially a bicycle, by means of pedals

pedant *NOUN* pedants
a pedantic person

pedantic *ADJECTIVE*
too concerned with minor details or with sticking strictly to formal rules
➤ **pedantically** *ADVERB*

peddle *VERB* peddles, peddling, peddled
❶ to go from house to house selling goods ❷ to sell illegal drugs ❸ to try to get people to accept an idea or way of life

pedestal *NOUN* pedestals
the raised base on which a statue or pillar stands
➤ **put someone on a pedestal** to admire someone greatly or too much

pedestrian *NOUN* pedestrians
a person who is walking

pedestrian *ADJECTIVE*
ordinary and dull

pedestrian crossing *NOUN* pedestrian crossings
(*British*) a place where pedestrians can cross the road safely

pedigree *NOUN* pedigrees
a list of a person's or animal's ancestors, especially to show how well an animal has been bred **WORD ORIGIN** from old French *pé de grue* = crane's foot (from the shape made by the lines on a family tree)

a
b
c
d
e
f
g
h
i
j
k
l
m
n
o
p
q
r
s
t
u
v
w
x
y
z

A
B
C
D
E
F
G
H
I
J
K
L
M
N
O
P
Q
R
S
T
U
V
W
X
Y
Z

pediment *NOUN* pediments
a wide triangular part decorating the top of a building

pedlar *NOUN* pedlars
(*chiefly British*) a person who goes from house to house selling small things

peek *VERB* peeks, peeking, peeked
to have a quick or sly look at something • *He peeked over the wall.*

peek *NOUN* peeks
a quick or sly look • *I risked a peek around the corner.*

peel *NOUN* peels
the skin of certain fruits and vegetables

peel *VERB* peels, peeling, peeled
❶ to remove the peel or covering from something ❷ to come off in strips or layers • *Paint was peeling off the walls.* ❸ to lose a covering or skin

peelings *PLURAL NOUN*
strips of skin peeled from potatoes etc.

peep *VERB* peeps, peeping, peeped
❶ to look quickly or secretly ❷ to look through a narrow opening ❸ to come slowly or briefly into view • *The moon peeped out from behind the clouds.*

peep *NOUN* peeps
a quick look

peephole *NOUN* peepholes
a small hole in a door or wall that you can look through

peer *VERB* peers, peering, peered
to look at something closely or with difficulty • *I peered into the darkness.*

peer *NOUN* peers
❶ your peers are the people who are the same age or status as you ❷ a member of the nobility

peerage *NOUN* peerages
❶ peers ❷ the rank of peer • *He was raised to the peerage.*

peer group *NOUN* peer groups
a group of people of roughly the same age or status

peerless *ADJECTIVE*
without an equal; better than the others

peer pressure *NOUN*
the pressure to do what others in your peer group do

peeved *ADJECTIVE* (*informal*)
annoyed or irritated

peevish *ADJECTIVE*
irritable or bad-tempered

peewit *NOUN* peewits
(*British*) a lapwing

peg *NOUN* pegs
a piece of wood or metal or plastic for fastening things together or for hanging things on

peg *VERB* pegs, pegging, pegged to fix something with pegs • *We pegged out the tent.*
➤ **peg away** to keep working hard at something in a determined way
➤ **peg it** (*informal*) to die

pejorative (say pij-**o**rra-tiv) *ADJECTIVE*
showing disapproval; derogatory

peke *NOUN* pekes (*informal*)
a Pekinese

Pekinese, Pekingese *NOUN* Pekinese or Pekingese
a small kind of dog with short legs, a flat face and long silky hair **WORD ORIGIN** from *Peking*, the old name of Beijing, the capital of China (where the breed came from)

pelican *NOUN* pelicans
a large bird with a pouch in its long beak for storing fish

pelican crossing *NOUN* pelican crossings
(*British*) a place where pedestrians can cross a street safely by operating lights that signal traffic to stop **WORD ORIGIN** from *pe(destrian) li(ght) con(trolled)*

pellet *NOUN* pellets
a tiny ball of metal, food, paper, etc.

pell-mell *ADVERB & ADJECTIVE*
in a hasty uncontrolled way

pelmet *NOUN* pelmets
an ornamental strip of wood or material above a window, used to conceal a curtain rail

pelt *VERB* pelts, pelting, pelted
❶ to throw a lot of things at someone • *We pelted him with snowballs.* ❷ to run fast ❸ to rain very hard • *It's pelting down outside.*

pelt *NOUN* pelts
an animal skin, especially with the fur still on it
➤ **at full pelt** as fast as possible

pelvis *NOUN* pelvises
the round framework of bones at the lower

end of the spine
➤ **pelvic** *ADJECTIVE*

pen *NOUN* pens
❶ an instrument with a point for writing
with ink ❷ an enclosure for sheep, cattle,
pigs or other farm animals ❸ a female swan.
Compare with **cob**.

pen *VERB* pens, penning, penned
❶ to shut animals into a pen or other
enclosed space ❷ to write something

penal (say **peen**-al) *ADJECTIVE*
to do with the punishment of criminals,
especially in prisons

penalize (also **penalise**) *VERB* penalizes,
penalizing, penalized
to punish someone or make them suffer a
disadvantage

penalty *NOUN* penalties
❶ a punishment for breaking a rule or law
❷ a point or advantage given to one side
in a game when a member of the other side
has broken a rule, e.g. a free kick at goal in
football

penance *NOUN*
a punishment that you willingly suffer to
show that you regret something wrong that
you have done

pence *PLURAL NOUN*
see **penny**

penchant (say **pahn**-shahn) *NOUN*
a special liking for something • *She has a
penchant for old films.*

pencil *NOUN* pencils
an instrument for drawing or writing, made
of a thin stick of graphite or coloured chalk
enclosed in a cylinder of wood or metal

pencil *VERB* pencils, pencilling, pencilled
to write or mark something with a pencil

pendant *NOUN* pendants
an ornament worn hanging on a cord or chain
round the neck

pending *ADJECTIVE*
❶ waiting to be decided or settled ❷ about
to happen

pending *PREPOSITION*
while waiting for; until • *Please take charge,
pending his return.*

pendulum *NOUN* pendulums
a weight hung so that it can swing from side
to side, especially in the works of a clock

penetrate *VERB* penetrates, penetrating,
penetrated
to make or find a way through or into
something • *The knife had penetrated his
chest.* • *Our eyes could not penetrate the
gloom.*
➤ **penetration** *NOUN*

penetrating *ADJECTIVE*
❶ showing great insight or understanding
• *She gave him a penetrating look.* ❷ clearly
heard above other sounds

penfriend *NOUN* penfriends
a friend, usually in another country, who you
write to without meeting

penguin *NOUN* penguins
an Antarctic seabird that cannot fly but uses
its wings as flippers for swimming

penicillin *NOUN*
an antibiotic obtained from mould

peninsula *NOUN* peninsulas
a piece of land that is almost surrounded by
water
➤ **peninsular** *ADJECTIVE*

penis (say **peen**-iss) *NOUN* penises
the part of the body with which a male
urinates and has sexual intercourse

penitent *ADJECTIVE*
sorry for having done something wrong
➤ **penitence** *NOUN*
➤ **penitently** *ADVERB*

penknife *NOUN* penknives
a small folding knife **WORD ORIGIN** originally
used for sharpening quill pens

pen name *NOUN* pen names
a name used by an author instead of their
real name

pennant *NOUN* pennants
a long pointed flag

penniless *ADJECTIVE*
having no money; very poor

penny *NOUN* pennies for separate coins, pence
for a sum of money
❶ a British coin worth $\frac{1}{100}$ of a pound ❷ a
former coin worth $\frac{1}{12}$ of a shilling

pension *NOUN* pensions
an income consisting of regular payments
made to someone who is retired, widowed or
disabled

pension *VERB* pensions, pensioning, pensioned
to pension someone off is to make them
retire and pay them a pension

a
b
c
d
e
f
g
h
i
j
k
l
m
n
o
p
q
r
s
t
u
v
w
x
y
z

pensioner *NOUN* pensioners
a person who receives a pension

pensive *ADJECTIVE*
deep in thought
➤ **pensively** *ADVERB*

pentagon *NOUN* pentagons
a flat shape with five sides and five angles
➤ **pentagonal** (say pent-**ag**-on-al) *ADJECTIVE*
➤ **the Pentagon** a five-sided building in Washington, headquarters of the leaders of the American armed forces

pentameter *NOUN* pentameters
a line of verse with five rhythmic beats

pentathlon *NOUN* pentathlons
an athletic contest consisting of five events

Pentecost *NOUN*
❶ the Jewish harvest festival, fifty days after Passover ❷ Whit Sunday

penthouse *NOUN* penthouses
an expensive flat at the top of a tall building

pent-up *ADJECTIVE*
pent-up feelings are ones that you hold inside and do not express • *pent-up anger*

penultimate *ADJECTIVE*
last but one

penumbra *NOUN* penumbras or penumbrae
an area that is partly but not fully shaded, e.g. during an eclipse

penury (say **pen**-yoor-ee) *NOUN* (*formal*)
great poverty

peony *NOUN* peonies
a plant with large round red, pink or white flowers

people *PLURAL NOUN*
human beings; persons

people *NOUN* peoples
a community or nation • *They are a peaceful people.* • *the English-speaking peoples*

people *VERB* peoples, peopling, peopled
to fill a place with people; to populate a place • *He lived in an imaginary world peopled by heroes, giants and wizards.*

people carrier *NOUN* people carriers
(*British*) a large car which carries up to eight people

pep *NOUN* (*informal*)
vigour or energy

pepper *NOUN* peppers
❶ a hot-tasting powder used to flavour food

❷ a bright green, red or yellow vegetable
➤ **peppery** *ADJECTIVE*

pepper *VERB* peppers, peppering, peppered
❶ to sprinkle something with pepper ❷ to pelt an area with many small objects • *The walls had been peppered with bullets.*

peppercorn *NOUN* peppercorns
the dried black berry from which pepper is made

peppermint *NOUN* peppermints
❶ a kind of mint used for flavouring ❷ a sweet flavoured with this mint

pepperoni *NOUN*
beef and pork sausage seasoned with pepper

pep talk *NOUN* pep talks (*informal*)
a talk given to someone to encourage them

per *PREPOSITION*
for each • *The charge is €5 per person.*

perambulator *NOUN* perambulators (*old use*)
a baby's pram

per annum *ADVERB*
for each year; yearly

per capita (say **kap**-it-a) *ADVERB & ADJECTIVE*
for each person

perceive *VERB* perceives, perceiving, perceived
to see, notice or understand something • *She perceived that she was no longer welcome.*

per cent *ADVERB*
for or in every hundred • *three per cent (3%)*

percentage *NOUN* percentages
an amount or rate expressed as a proportion of 100

perceptible *ADJECTIVE*
able to be seen or noticed • *There was no perceptible difference between them.*
➤ **perceptibly** *ADVERB*

perception *NOUN* perceptions
❶ the ability to notice or understand something ❷ receiving information through the senses, especially the sense of sight

perceptive *ADJECTIVE*
quick to notice or understand things

perch *NOUN* perches
❶ a place where a bird sits or rests ❷ a seat high up ❸ an edible freshwater fish

perch *VERB* perches, perching, perched
❶ to rest on a perch or place something on a perch ❷ to sit on the edge of something

or somewhere high or narrow • *She perched herself on the arm of the sofa.*

percolate *VERB* percolates, percolating, percolated
to flow through small holes or spaces
➤ **percolation** *NOUN*

percolator *NOUN* percolators
a pot for making coffee, in which boiling water percolates through coffee grounds

percussion *NOUN*
❶ musical instruments that you play by hitting them or shaking them, such as drums and cymbals ❷ the striking of one thing against another
➤ **percussive** *ADJECTIVE*

peregrine *NOUN* peregrines
a kind of falcon

peremptory *ADJECTIVE*
giving commands and expecting to be obeyed at once

perennial *ADJECTIVE*
lasting for a long time; happening again and again • *It is a perennial problem.*

perennial *NOUN* perennials
a plant that lives for many years

perfect (say **per**-fikt) *ADJECTIVE*
❶ so good that it cannot be made any better ❷ complete • *He is a perfect stranger.* ❸ the perfect tense of a verb shows a completed action, e.g. *He has arrived.*

perfect (say per-**fekt**) *VERB* perfects, perfecting, perfected
to make a thing perfect • *He spent hours perfecting some new magic tricks.*

perfection *NOUN*
being perfect
➤ **to perfection** perfectly • *The fish was cooked to perfection.*

perfectionist *NOUN* perfectionists
a person who is only satisfied if something is done perfectly

perfectly *ADVERB*
❶ completely • *She stood perfectly still.* ❷ without any faults • *The TV works perfectly now.*

perforate *VERB* perforates, perforating, perforated
❶ to make tiny holes in something, especially so that it can be torn off easily ❷ to pierce a surface
➤ **perforated** *ADJECTIVE*

perforation *NOUN* perforations
perforations are the tiny holes made in something so that it can be torn off easily

perforce *ADVERB* (*old use*)
by necessity; unavoidably

perform *VERB* performs, performing, performed
❶ to do something in front of an audience • *They performed the play in the school hall.* ❷ to do or carry out something • *Surgeons had to perform an emergency operation.*

performance *NOUN* performances
❶ a form of entertainment presented to an audience • *What time does the performance start?* ❷ the way in which someone does something or the standard they reach • *It was the striker's best performance of the season.*

performer *NOUN* performers
a person who performs an entertainment in front of an audience

perfume *NOUN* perfumes
❶ a pleasant smell ❷ a pleasant-smelling liquid that you put on your skin

perfume *VERB* perfumes, perfuming, perfumed
to give a sweet smell to something
WORD ORIGIN originally used of pleasant-smelling smoke from something burning: via French from old Italian *parfumare* = to smoke through

perfunctory *ADJECTIVE*
done without much care or interest • *a perfunctory glance*
➤ **perfunctorily** *ADVERB*

pergola *NOUN* pergolas
an arch formed by climbing plants growing over trellis-work

perhaps *ADVERB*
it may be; possibly

peril *NOUN* perils
great danger
➤ **at your peril** at your own risk

perilous *ADJECTIVE*
very dangerous • *a perilous journey*
➤ **perilously** *ADVERB*

perimeter *NOUN* perimeters
❶ the outer edge or boundary of something • *A fence marks the perimeter of the airfield.* ❷ the distance round the edge

period *NOUN* periods
❶ a length of time ❷ the time allowed for a

a b c d e f g h i j k l m n o p q r s t u v w x y z

lesson in school ❸ the time when a woman or girl menstruates ❹ a full stop

periodic *ADJECTIVE*
occurring at regular intervals • *periodic checks*
➤ **periodically** *ADVERB*

periodical *NOUN* periodicals
a magazine published at regular intervals (e.g. monthly)

periodic table *NOUN*
a table in which the chemical elements are arranged in order of increasing atomic number

peripatetic *ADJECTIVE*
going from place to place

peripheral *ADJECTIVE*
❶ of minor importance ❷ at the edge or boundary

periphery (say per-**if**-er-ee) *NOUN* peripheries
the part at the edge or boundary

periscope *NOUN* periscopes
a device with a tube and mirrors with which a person in a trench or submarine etc. can see things that are otherwise out of sight

perish *VERB* perishes, perishing, perished
❶ to die or be destroyed • *Many sailors perished in the shipwreck.* ❷ to rot • *The rubber ring has perished.*

perishable *ADJECTIVE*
perishable food is likely to go off quickly

perished *ADJECTIVE* (*informal*)
feeling very cold

perishing *ADJECTIVE* (*British*) (*informal*)
freezing cold • *It's perishing outside!*

periwinkle *NOUN* periwinkles
❶ a trailing plant with blue or white flowers ❷ a winkle (a kind of edible shellfish)

perjure *VERB* perjures, perjuring, perjured
➤ **perjure yourself** to commit perjury

perjury *NOUN*
telling a lie while you are on oath to speak the truth in a law court

perk *VERB* perks, perking, perked
➤ **perk up** to become more cheerful or lively • *She perked up at the mention of lunch.*

perk *NOUN* perks (*informal*)
something extra given to a worker • *Free bus travel is one of the perks of the job.*

perky *ADJECTIVE* perkier, perkiest
lively and cheerful

perm *NOUN* perms
treatment of the hair to give it long-lasting waves or curls
➤ **perm** *VERB*

permafrost *NOUN*
a permanently frozen layer of soil in polar regions

permanent *ADJECTIVE*
lasting for always or for a very long time • *Fortunately the damage was not permanent.*
➤ **permanently** *ADVERB*
➤ **permanence** *NOUN*

permeable *ADJECTIVE*
allowing liquid or gas to pass through it
• *permeable rock*
➤ **permeability** *NOUN*

permeate *VERB* permeates, permeating, permeated
to spread into every part of a thing or place
• *A sweet smell permeated the air.*

permissible *ADJECTIVE*
permitted or allowable

permission *NOUN*
the right to do something, given by someone else • *He took the car without permission.*

permissive *ADJECTIVE*
letting people do what they wish; tolerant or liberal

permit (say per-**mit**) *VERB* permits, permitting, permitted
to allow someone to do something or allow something to be done • *Mobile phones are not permitted in the classroom.*

permit (say **per**-mit) *NOUN* permits
written or printed permission to do something or go somewhere

permutation *NOUN* permutations
❶ changing the order of a set of things ❷ a changed order • *3, 1, 2 is a permutation of 1, 2, 3.*

pernicious *ADJECTIVE*
very harmful

peroxide *NOUN*
a chemical used for bleaching hair

perpendicular *ADJECTIVE*
upright; at a right angle (90°) to a line or surface

perpetrate *VERB* perpetrates, perpetrating, perpetrated
to commit a crime or serious error
➤ **perpetrator** *NOUN*

perpetual *ADJECTIVE*
lasting for a long time; continual • *She was in a perpetual state of panic.*
➤ **perpetually** *ADVERB*

perpetuate *VERB* perpetuates, perpetuating, perpetuated
to cause something to continue or be remembered for a long time • *The statue will perpetuate his memory.*
➤ **perpetuation** *NOUN*

perpetuity *NOUN*
➤ **in perpetuity** for ever

perplex *VERB* perplexes, perplexing, perplexed
to bewilder or puzzle someone
➤ **perplexing** *ADJECTIVE*

perplexed *ADJECTIVE*
confused because you cannot understand something • *She looked utterly perplexed.*

perplexity *NOUN*
a puzzled and confused state of mind • *They stared at him in perplexity.*

persecute *VERB* persecutes, persecuting, persecuted
to be continually cruel to someone, especially because you disagree with their beliefs
➤ **persecution** *NOUN*
➤ **persecutor** *NOUN*

persevere *VERB* perseveres, persevering, persevered
to go on doing something even though it is difficult
➤ **perseverance** *NOUN*

Persian *ADJECTIVE*
to do with Persia, a country in the Middle East now called Iran, or its people or language

Persian *NOUN*
the language of Persia. The modern form of the Persian language is called Farsi.

persist *VERB* persists, persisting, persisted
❶ to continue to do something firmly or obstinately • *She persists in breaking the rules.* ❷ to continue to exist for a long time • *The custom persists in some countries.*

persistent *ADJECTIVE*
❶ continuing or constant • *The rain was persistent.* ❷ determined to continue doing something and refusing to give up

➤ **persistently** *ADVERB*
➤ **persistence** *NOUN*

person *NOUN* people or persons
❶ a human being; a man, woman, or child ❷ (*in grammar*) any of the three groups of personal pronouns and forms taken by verbs. The **first person** (= *I, me, we, us*) refers to the person or people speaking; the **second person** (= *you*) refers to the person or people spoken to; the **third person** (= *he, him, she, her, it, they, them*) refers to the person or thing or the people or things spoken about.
➤ **in person** being actually present yourself • *She hopes to be there in person.*
WORD ORIGIN from Latin *persona* = mask used by an actor

personage *NOUN* personages
an important or well-known person

personal *ADJECTIVE*
❶ to do with, belonging to or done by a particular person • *personal belongings* ❷ private • *We have personal business to discuss.* ❸ criticizing a person's appearance, character or private affairs • *There's no need to make personal remarks.*

personal computer *NOUN* personal computers
a small computer designed to be used by one person at a time

personality *NOUN* personalities
❶ a person's character • *She has a cheerful personality.* ❷ a well-known person • *a TV personality*

personally *ADVERB*
❶ in person; being actually there • *The head thanked me personally.* ❷ as far as I am concerned • *Personally, I'd rather stay here.*

personify *VERB* personifies, personifying, personified
❶ to represent a quality or idea as if it were a person ❷ to be a perfect example of something • *She is courage personified.*
➤ **personification** *NOUN*

personnel *NOUN*
the people employed by a firm or other large organization

perspective *NOUN* perspectives
❶ the impression of depth and space in a picture or scene ❷ a person's point of view
➤ **in perspective** giving a well-balanced view of things • *Try to see the problem in perspective.*

a b c d e f g h i j k l m n o p q r s t u v w x y z

Perspex *NOUN* (*trademark*)
a tough transparent plastic used instead of glass

perspiration *NOUN*
moisture given off by the body through the pores of the skin; sweat

perspire *VERB* perspires, perspiring, perspired
to sweat

persuade *VERB* persuades, persuading, persuaded
to make someone believe or agree to do something • *I managed to persuade him to stay.*

persuasion *NOUN*
persuading someone to believe or agree to do something • *It took a lot of persuasion to get her to come.*

persuasive *ADJECTIVE*
able to make someone believe or agree to do something • *a persuasive argument*
➤ **persuasively** *ADVERB*

pert *ADJECTIVE*
cheeky
➤ **pertly** *ADVERB*

pertain *VERB* pertains, pertaining, pertained
to be relevant to something • *The police looked again at all the evidence pertaining to the murder.*

pertinent *ADJECTIVE*
relevant to what you are talking about • *a pertinent question*

perturbed *ADJECTIVE*
worried or anxious • *She didn't seem at all perturbed.*
➤ **perturbation** *NOUN*

peruse (say per-**ooz**) *VERB* peruses, perusing, perused
to read something carefully
➤ **perusal** *NOUN*

pervade *VERB* pervades, pervading, pervaded
to spread all through something • *The smell of herbs pervades the kitchen.*
➤ **pervasive** *ADJECTIVE*

perverse *ADJECTIVE*
obstinately doing something different from what is reasonable or expected
➤ **perversely** *ADVERB*
➤ **perversity** *NOUN*

pervert (say per-**vert**) *VERB* perverts, perverting, perverted
❶ to turn something from the right course of action • *By false evidence they perverted the course of justice.* ❷ to make a person behave in a wrong or unacceptable way
➤ **perversion** *NOUN*

pervert (say **per**-vert) *NOUN* perverts
a person whose sexual behaviour is thought to be unnatural or unacceptable

Pesach (say **pay**-sahk) *NOUN*
the Passover festival

pessimist *NOUN* pessimists
a person who expects that things will turn out badly. Compare with **optimist**.
➤ **pessimism** *NOUN*

pessimistic *ADJECTIVE*
expecting things to turn out badly
➤ **pessimistically** *ADVERB*

pest *NOUN* pests
❶ a destructive insect or animal, such as a locust or a mouse ❷ an annoying person or thing

pester *VERB* pesters, pestering, pestered
to keep annoying someone by frequent questions or requests

pesticide *NOUN* pesticides
a substance for killing harmful insects and other pests

pestilence *NOUN* pestilences
a deadly epidemic

pestle *NOUN* pestles
a tool with a heavy rounded end for pounding substances in a mortar

pet *NOUN* pets
❶ a tame animal kept at home for companionship and pleasure ❷ a person treated as a favourite • *teacher's pet*

pet *ADJECTIVE*
favourite or particular • *Natural history is my pet subject.*

pet *VERB* pets, petting, petted
to stroke a person or animal affectionately • *He bent down to pet one of the dogs.*

petal *NOUN* petals
one of the separate coloured outer parts of a flower

peter *VERB* peters, petering, petered
➤ **peter out** to become gradually less and come to an end • *The footprints soon petered out.*

petition *NOUN* petitions
a formal request for something, especially a written one signed by many people

petition *VERB* petitions, petitioning, petitioned
to request something by a petition
➤ **petitioner** *NOUN*

petrel *NOUN* petrels
a kind of seabird (**WORD ORIGIN**) perhaps named after St *Peter*, who tried to walk on the water (because the bird flies just over the waves with its legs dangling)

petrify *VERB* petrifies, petrifying, petrified
❶ to make someone so terrified that they cannot move ❷ to turn something to stone
➤ **petrified** *ADJECTIVE*

petrochemical *NOUN* petrochemicals
a chemical substance obtained from petroleum or natural gas

petrol *NOUN*
(*British*) a liquid made from petroleum, used as fuel for engines

petroleum *NOUN*
an oil found underground that is refined to make fuel (e.g. petrol or paraffin) or for use in dry-cleaning etc.

petticoat *NOUN* petticoats
a woman's or girl's dress-length piece of underwear worn under a skirt or dress

petting *NOUN*
affectionate touching or fondling

pettish *ADJECTIVE*
irritable or bad-tempered

petty *ADJECTIVE* pettier, pettiest
❶ unimportant or trivial • *petty regulations*
❷ mean and small-minded
➤ **pettiness** *NOUN*

petty cash *NOUN*
cash kept by an office for small payments

petty officer *NOUN* petty officers
a non-commissioned officer in the navy

petulant *ADJECTIVE*
irritable or bad-tempered, especially in a childish way
➤ **petulantly** *ADVERB*
➤ **petulance** *NOUN*

petunia *NOUN* petunias
a garden plant with funnel-shaped flowers

pew *NOUN* pews
a long wooden seat, usually fixed in rows, in a church

pewter *NOUN*
a grey alloy of tin and lead

pH *NOUN*
a measure of the acidity or alkalinity of a solution. Pure water has a pH of 7, acids have a pH between 0 and 7 and alkalis have a pH between 7 and 14. (**WORD ORIGIN**) from the initial letter of German *Potenz* = power, + H, the symbol for hydrogen

phalanx *NOUN* phalanxes
a number of people or soldiers in a close formation • *a phalanx of armed guards*

phantasm *NOUN* phantasms
a phantom

phantom *NOUN* phantoms
❶ a ghost ❷ something that does not really exist

Pharaoh (say **fair**-oh) *NOUN* Pharaohs
the title of the king of ancient Egypt

pharmaceutical (say farm-as-**yoot**-ik-al) *ADJECTIVE*
to do with medicinal drugs or with pharmacy
• *the pharmaceutical industry*

pharmacist *NOUN* pharmacists
a person who is trained to prepare and sell medicines

pharmacology *NOUN*
the study of medicinal drugs
➤ **pharmacological** *ADJECTIVE*
➤ **pharmacologist** *NOUN*

pharmacy *NOUN* pharmacies
❶ a shop where medicines are prepared and sold ❷ the job of preparing medicines

phase *NOUN* phases
a stage in the progress or development of something

phase *VERB* phases, phasing, phased
to do something in stages, not all at once • *a phased withdrawal*
➤ **phase something out** to stop something gradually

PhD *ABBREVIATION*
Doctor of Philosophy; a university degree awarded to someone who has done advanced research in their subject

pheasant (say **fez**-ant) *NOUN* pheasants
a game bird with a long tail

phenomenal *ADJECTIVE*
amazing or remarkable • *She has a phenomenal memory.*
➤ **phenomenally** *ADVERB*

phenomenon *NOUN* phenomena
an event or fact, especially one that is

remarkable or interesting • *A solar eclipse is an extraordinary natural phenomenon.*

> **USAGE**
> The word **phenomena** is a plural. If you mean a single event, use **phenomenon**.

phial *NOUN* **phials**
a small glass bottle

philanderer *NOUN* **philanderers**
a man who has many casual affairs with women
➤ **philandering** *NOUN*

philanthropist *NOUN* **philanthropists**
a rich person who generously gives money to people who need it

philanthropy *NOUN*
concern for your fellow human beings, especially as shown by kind and generous acts that benefit large numbers of people
➤ **philanthropic** *ADJECTIVE*

philately (say fil-**at**-il-ee) *NOUN*
collecting postage stamps
➤ **philatelist** *NOUN*

philistine (say **fil**-ist-yn) *NOUN* **philistines**
a person who does not like or understand art, literature, music, etc. **WORD ORIGIN** from the *Philistines* in the Bible, who were enemies of the Israelites

philosopher *NOUN* **philosophers**
an expert in philosophy

philosophical *ADJECTIVE*
❶ to do with philosophy ❷ calm and not upset after a misfortune or disappointment • *He seems to be philosophical about losing.*
➤ **philosophically** *ADVERB*

philosophy *NOUN* **philosophies**
❶ the study of truths about life, knowledge, morals, etc. ❷ a set of ideas or principles or beliefs

phlegm (say flem) *NOUN*
thick mucus that forms in the throat and lungs when you have a bad cold

phlegmatic (say fleg-**mat**-ik) *ADJECTIVE*
not easily excited or worried
WORD ORIGIN same origin as **phlegm** (because too much phlegm in the body was believed to make you sluggish)

phobia (say **foh**-bee-a) *NOUN* **phobias**
a great or abnormal fear of something • *He has a phobia about flying.*

phoenix (say **feen**-iks) *NOUN* **phoenixes**
a mythical bird that was said to burn itself to death in a fire and be born again from the ashes

phone *NOUN* **phones**
a telephone

phone *VERB* **phones, phoning, phoned**
to telephone someone

phone-in *NOUN* **phone-ins**
(*British*) a radio or television programme in which people telephone the studio and take part in a discussion

phoneme *NOUN* **phonemes**
a distinct unit of sound that distinguishes one word from another, e.g. *p, b, d* and *t* in *pad, pat, bad* and *bat*

phonetic (say fon-**et**-ik) *ADJECTIVE*
❶ to do with speech sounds ❷ representing speech sounds
➤ **phonetically** *ADVERB*

phoney *ADJECTIVE* (*informal*)
sham; not genuine

phonic *ADJECTIVE*
to do with speech sounds

phonics *NOUN*
a method of teaching reading by relating sounds to letters of the alphabet

phosphate *NOUN* **phosphates**
a substance containing phosphorus, especially an artificial fertilizer

phosphorescent (say fos-fer-**ess**-ent) *ADJECTIVE*
glowing in the dark; luminous
➤ **phosphorescence** *NOUN*

phosphorus *NOUN*
a chemical substance that glows in the dark

photo *NOUN* **photos** (*informal*)
a photograph

photocopier *NOUN* **photocopiers**
a machine that makes photocopies

photocopy *NOUN* **photocopies**
a copy of a document or page made by photographing it on special paper

photocopy *VERB* **photocopies, photocopying, photocopied**
to make a photocopy of a document or page

photoelectric *ADJECTIVE*
using the electrical effects of light

photogenic *ADJECTIVE*
looking attractive in photographs

photograph *NOUN* **photographs**
a picture made using a camera

photograph *VERB* **photographs, photographing, photographed**
to take a photograph of a person or thing

photographer *NOUN* **photographers**
a person who takes photographs

photography *NOUN*
taking photographs
➤ **photographic** *ADJECTIVE*

photosynthesis *NOUN*
the process by which green plants use sunlight to turn carbon dioxide and water into complex substances, giving off oxygen

phrase *NOUN* **phrases**
❶ a group of words that form a unit in a sentence or clause, e.g. *in the garden* in 'The Queen was in the garden.' ❷ a short section of a tune

phrase *VERB* **phrases, phrasing, phrased**
❶ to put something into words • *He wanted to phrase the question just right.* ❷ to divide music into phrases

---

GRAMMAR

A **phrase** is a group of words that can be understood as a unit.

A **noun phrase** is a group of words that has a noun as its head or key word.

In the sentence *The teacher over there is my form tutor*, the words *the teacher over there* and *my form tutor* are noun phrases.

An **adjective phrase** is a group of words that has an adjective as its head:

She is a <u>very good</u> teacher.

He is <u>as thin as a rake</u>.

An **adverb phrase** is a group of words that has an adverb as its head:

Please get here <u>as quickly as possible</u>.

She was old, and walked <u>very slowly</u>.

A **preposition phrase** is a group of words that has a preposition as its head:

The mouse ran <u>along the windowsill</u>.

See also the panel on **clauses**.

---

phrase book *NOUN* **phrase books**
a book which lists useful words and expressions in a foreign language, with their translations

phraseology (say fray-zee-**ol**-o-jee) *NOUN* **phraseologies**
the way something is worded or expressed

physical *ADJECTIVE*
❶ to do with the body rather than the mind or feelings ❷ to do with things that you can touch or see ❸ to do with physics ❹ physical geography is the study of natural features of the Earth's surface, such as mountains and volcanoes

physical education, physical training *NOUN*
exercises and sports done to keep the body healthy

physically *ADVERB*
in a way that is connected with the body rather than the mind or feelings • *I was exhausted, both physically and mentally.*

physician *NOUN* **physicians**
a doctor, especially one who is not a surgeon

physicist (say **fiz**-i-sist) *NOUN* **physicists**
an expert in physics

physics (say **fiz**-iks) *NOUN*
the study of the properties of matter and energy (e.g. heat, light, sound and movement)

physiognomy (say fiz-ee-**on**-o-mee) *NOUN* **physiognomies**
the features of a person's face

physiology (say fiz-ee-**ol**-o-jee) *NOUN*
the study of the body and its parts and how they function
➤ **physiological** *ADJECTIVE*
➤ **physiologist** *NOUN*

physiotherapy (say fiz-ee-o-th'**erra**-pee) *NOUN*
(*British*) the treatment of a disease or injury by physical methods such as massage and exercise
➤ **physiotherapist** *NOUN*

physique (say fiz-**eek**) *NOUN* **physiques**
a person's build • *He had the physique of a heavyweight boxer.*

pi *NOUN*
the symbol (π) of the ratio of the circumference of a circle to its diameter. The value of pi is approximately 3.14159.

pianist *NOUN* **pianists**
a person who plays the piano

piano *NOUN* pianos
a large musical instrument with a row
of black and white keys on a keyboard
WORD ORIGIN short for **pianoforte**, from
Italian *piano* = soft + *forte* = loud (because it
can produce soft notes and loud notes)

piccolo *NOUN* piccolos
a small high-pitched flute

pick *VERB* picks, picking, picked
❶ to pull a flower or fruit away from its plant
• *We picked apples.* ❷ to choose something
from a group • *Pick a number from one to
twenty.* ❸ to pull bits off or out of something
❹ to open a lock by using something pointed,
not with a key
➤ **pick a fight** or **quarrel** to deliberately
start a fight or quarrel with someone
➤ **pick holes in something** to find fault with
something
➤ **pick on someone** to single someone out
for criticism or unkind treatment
➤ **pick someone's pocket** to steal from
someone's pocket
➤ **pick up** to recover or improve
➤ **pick someone up** to give someone a lift in
a vehicle
➤ **pick something up** ❶ to lift something
or take it up ❷ to collect something from
somewhere ❸ to learn or acquire something
❹ to manage to hear something

pick *NOUN* picks
❶ a choice • *Take your pick.* ❷ the best of a
group ❸ a pickaxe ❹ a plectrum

pickaxe *NOUN* pickaxes
a heavy pointed tool with a long handle, used
for breaking up hard ground or concrete
WORD ORIGIN from old French *picois*, later
confused with **axe**

picket *NOUN* pickets
❶ a striker or group of strikers who try to
persuade other people not to go into a place
of work during a strike ❷ a pointed post as
part of a fence

picket *VERB* pickets, picketing, picketed
to stand outside a place of work to try to
persuade other people not to go in during a
strike

pickle *NOUN* pickles
❶ a strong-tasting food made of pickled
vegetables ❷ (*informal*) a difficulty or mess

pickle *VERB* pickles, pickling, pickled
to preserve food in vinegar or salt water

pickpocket *NOUN* pickpockets
a thief who steals from people's pockets or
bags

pick-up *NOUN* pick-ups
an open truck for carrying small loads

picnic *NOUN* picnics
a meal eaten in the open air away from home

picnic *VERB* picnics, picnicking, picnicked
to have a picnic
➤ **picnicker** *NOUN*

Pict *NOUN* Picts
a member of an ancient people of north
Britain
➤ **Pictish** *ADJECTIVE*

pictogram *NOUN* pictograms
a picture or symbol that stands for a word or
phrase

pictorial *ADJECTIVE*
with or using pictures
➤ **pictorially** *ADVERB*

picture *NOUN* pictures
❶ a representation of a person or thing made
by painting, drawing or photography ❷ a film
at the cinema ❸ how something seems; an
impression
➤ **be in the picture** to be fully informed
about something

picture *VERB* pictures, picturing, pictured
❶ to show someone or something in a picture
• *She is pictured here with her two brothers.*
❷ to imagine a person or thing • *He pictured
himself holding up the trophy.*

picturesque *ADJECTIVE*
❶ forming an attractive scene • *a
picturesque village* ❷ vivid and expressive
• *picturesque language*
➤ **picturesquely** *ADVERB*

pidgin *NOUN* pidgins
a simplified form of a language, especially
English, Dutch or Portuguese, including
words from a local language, used by
people who do not speak the same language
WORD ORIGIN from the Chinese pronunciation
of **business** (because it was used by traders)

pie *NOUN* pies
a baked dish of meat, fish or fruit covered
with pastry

piebald *ADJECTIVE*
with patches of black and white • *a piebald
pony*

piece *NOUN* pieces
❶ a part or portion of something; a fragment

❷ a separate thing or example • *a fine piece of work* ❸ something written, composed or painted • *a piece of music* ❹ one of the objects used to play a game on a board • *a chess piece* ❺ a coin • *a 50p piece*
➤ **in one piece** not harmed or damaged
➤ **piece by piece** gradually; one bit at a time

piece *VERB* pieces, piecing, pieced
to put different parts together to make something • *We began to piece together the whole story.*

> SPELLING
> Remember you can have a piece of pie.

pièce de résistance (say pee-ess der ray-zees-**tahns**) *NOUN* pièces de résistance
the most important item

piecemeal *ADJECTIVE & ADVERB*
done or made one piece at a time

pie chart *NOUN* pie charts
a diagram in the form of a circle divided into sectors to represent the way in which a quantity is divided up

pier *NOUN* piers
❶ a long structure built out into the sea for people to walk on ❷ a pillar supporting a bridge or arch

pierce *VERB* pierces, piercing, pierced
❶ to make a hole through something • *The arrow pierced his shoulder.* ❷ to be suddenly seen or heard • *A flash of lightning pierced the darkness.*

piercing *ADJECTIVE*
❶ very loud and high-pitched • *The dog let out a piercing howl.* ❷ penetrating; very strong • *a piercing wind*

piety *NOUN*
being very religious and devout

piffle *NOUN* (*informal*)
nonsense

pig *NOUN* pigs
❶ a fat animal with short legs and a blunt snout, kept for its meat ❷ (*informal*) someone greedy, dirty or unpleasant
➤ **piggy** *ADJECTIVE & NOUN*

pigeon *NOUN* pigeons
❶ a bird with a fat body and a small head ❷ (*informal*) a person's business or responsibility • *That's your pigeon.*

pigeon-hole *NOUN* pigeon-holes
a small compartment for holding letters, messages or papers for someone to collect

pigeon-hole *VERB* pigeon-holes, pigeon-holing, pigeon-holed
to decide that a person belongs to a particular category • *She doesn't want to be pigeon-holed simply as a pop singer.*

piggyback *NOUN* piggybacks
a ride on someone else's back or shoulders

piggy bank *NOUN* piggy banks
a money box made in the shape of a hollow pig

pig-headed *ADJECTIVE*
stubborn or obstinate

pig iron *NOUN*
iron that has been processed in a smelting furnace **(WORD ORIGIN)** because the blocks of iron reminded people of pigs

piglet *NOUN* piglets
a young pig

pigment *NOUN* pigments
❶ a substance that colours skin or other tissue in animals and plants ❷ a substance that gives colour to paint, inks and dyes
➤ **pigmentation** *NOUN*

pigsty *NOUN* pigsties
❶ a partly covered pen for pigs ❷ a filthy room or house

pigtail *NOUN* pigtails
a plait of hair worn hanging at the back of the head

pike *NOUN* pikes
❶ a heavy spear ❷ pike a large freshwater fish

pilau (say pi-**low**) *NOUN*
an Indian dish of spiced rice with meat and vegetables

pilchard *NOUN* pilchards
a small sea fish

pile *NOUN* piles
❶ a number of things on top of one another ❷ (*informal*) a large quantity; a lot of money ❸ a large impressive building ❹ a heavy beam made of metal, concrete or timber driven into the ground to support something ❺ a raised surface on fabric, made of upright threads • *a carpet with a thick pile*

pile *VERB* piles, piling, piled
to put things into a pile; to make a pile • *He started piling food onto his plate.*
➤ **pile up** to increase in quantity • *The work was piling up.*

pile–up *NOUN* pile-ups
a road accident that involves a number of vehicles

pilfer *VERB* pilfers, pilfering, pilfered
to steal things of little value
➤ **pilferer** *NOUN*

pilgrim *NOUN* pilgrims
a person who travels to a holy place for religious reasons

pilgrimage *NOUN* pilgrimages
a journey to a holy place

pill *NOUN* pills
a small solid piece of medicine for swallowing
➤ **the pill** a contraceptive pill

pillage *VERB* pillages, pillaging, pillaged
to carry off goods using force, especially in a war; to plunder a place
➤ **pillage** *NOUN*

pillar *NOUN* pillars
a tall stone or wooden post

pillar box *NOUN* pillar boxes
a postbox standing in a street

pillion *NOUN* pillions
a seat behind the driver on a motorcycle

pillory *NOUN* pillories
a wooden framework with holes for a person's head and hands, in which offenders were formerly made to stand and be ridiculed by the public as a punishment

pillory *VERB* pillories, pillorying, pilloried
to expose a person to public ridicule and scorn • *Football managers get used to being pilloried in the newspapers.*

pillow *NOUN* pillows
a cushion for a person's head to rest on, especially in bed

pillow *VERB* pillows, pillowing, pillowed
to rest the head on something soft • *He pillowed his head on his arms.*

pillowcase *NOUN* pillowcases
a cloth cover for a pillow

pilot *NOUN* pilots
❶ a person who works the controls for flying an aircraft ❷ a person qualified to steer a ship in and out of a port or through a difficult stretch of water

pilot *VERB* pilots, piloting, piloted
❶ to be pilot of an aircraft or ship ❷ to guide or steer someone

pilot *ADJECTIVE*
testing on a small scale how something will work • *a pilot scheme*

pilot light *NOUN* pilot lights
a small flame that lights a larger burner on a gas cooker or boiler

pimp *NOUN* pimps
a man who gets clients for prostitutes and lives off their earnings

pimpernel (say **pimp**-er-nel) *NOUN* pimpernels
a plant with small red, blue or white flowers that close in cloudy weather

pimple *NOUN* pimples
a small round raised spot on the skin
➤ **pimply** *ADJECTIVE*

PIN *ABBREVIATION*
personal identification number; a number that you need to key in when you use a cash machine or bank card

pin *NOUN* pins
❶ a short thin piece of metal with a sharp point and a rounded head, used to fasten pieces of material or paper together ❷ a pointed device for fixing or marking something
➤ **pins and needles** a tingling feeling in the skin

pin *VERB* pins, pinning, pinned
❶ to fasten something with a pin or pins
❷ to hold someone firmly so that they cannot move • *He was pinned under the wreckage for hours.* ❸ to fix blame or responsibility on someone • *They pinned the blame for the mix-up on her.*

pinafore *NOUN* pinafores
an apron like a dress without sleeves, worn over clothes to keep them clean

pinball *NOUN*
a game in which you shoot small metal balls across a special table and score points when they strike special pins

pincer *NOUN* pincers
the claw of a shellfish such as a lobster

pincers *PLURAL NOUN*
a tool with two parts that are pressed together for gripping and holding things

pinch *VERB* pinches, pinching, pinched
❶ to squeeze something tightly or painfully between two things, especially between the finger and thumb ❷ (*informal*) to steal something

pinch *NOUN* pinches
❶ a pinching movement ❷ the amount that can be held between the tips of your thumb and forefinger • *a pinch of salt*
➤ **at a pinch** if it is really necessary • *The canoe could seat three people – four at a pinch.*
➤ **feel the pinch** to be short of money

pincushion *NOUN* pincushions
a small pad into which you stick pins to keep them ready for use

pine *NOUN* pines
an evergreen tree with needle-shaped leaves

pine *VERB* pines, pining, pined
❶ to feel an intense longing for someone or something • *She was pining for the sight of the sea again.* ❷ to become weak through longing for someone or something • *After his wife died, he just pined away.*

pineapple *NOUN* pineapples
a large tropical fruit with a tough prickly skin and yellow flesh

ping *NOUN* pings
a short sharp ringing sound

ping *VERB* pings, pinging, pinged
to make a sharp ringing sound • *The microwave pinged.*

ping–pong *NOUN*
table tennis **WORD ORIGIN** from the sound of the bats hitting the ball

pinion *NOUN* pinions
❶ a bird's wing, especially the outer end ❷ a small cogwheel that fits into another or into a rod (called a **rack**)

pinion *VERB* pinions, pinioning, pinioned
❶ to clip a bird's wings to prevent it from flying ❷ to hold or fasten someone's arms or legs in order to prevent them from moving • *His arms were pinioned behind his back.*
WORD ORIGIN the 'bird's wing' sense comes from Latin *pinna* = arrow or feather; the 'cogwheel' sense comes from Latin *pinus* = pine tree (because the wheel's teeth reminded people of a pine cone)

pink *ADJECTIVE*
pale red

pink *NOUN* pinks
❶ a pink colour ❷ a garden plant with fragrant flowers, often pink or white

pinnacle *NOUN* pinnacles
❶ a pointed ornament on a roof ❷ a high pointed piece of rock ❸ the highest point of something • *Winning the gold medal was the pinnacle of her career.*

pinpoint *ADJECTIVE*
exact or precise • *He can pass the ball with pinpoint accuracy.*

pinpoint *VERB* pinpoints, pinpointing, pinpointed
to find or identify something precisely

pinprick *NOUN* pinpricks
❶ a tiny round spot of something • *pinpricks of light* ❷ a small annoyance

pinstripe *NOUN* pinstripes
one of the very narrow stripes that form a pattern in cloth
➤ **pinstriped** *ADJECTIVE*

pint *NOUN* pints
a measure for liquids, equal to one-eighth of a gallon (or 0.57 of a litre)

pin-up *NOUN* pin-ups (*informal*)
a picture of an attractive or famous person for pinning on a wall

pioneer *NOUN* pioneers
one of the first people to go to a place or do or study something • *He was one of the pioneers of early photography.*

pioneer *VERB* pioneers, pioneering, pioneered
to be one of the first people to go to a place or do something **WORD ORIGIN** from French *pionnier* = foot soldier, later = one of the troops who went ahead of the army to prepare roads

pious *ADJECTIVE*
very religious or devout
➤ **piously** *ADVERB*

pip *NOUN* pips
❶ a small hard seed of an apple, pear, orange or other fruit ❷ (*British*) one of the stars on the shoulder of an army officer's uniform ❸ (*British*) a short high-pitched sound • *She heard the six pips of the time signal on the radio.*

pip *VERB* pips, pipping, pipped (*British*) (*informal*) to defeat someone by a small amount

pipe *NOUN* pipes
❶ a tube through which water, gas or oil can flow from one place to another ❷ a short narrow tube with a bowl at one end for burning tobacco for smoking ❸ a tube forming a musical instrument or part of one
➤ **the pipes** bagpipes

pipe *VERB* pipes, piping, piped
❶ to send something along pipes ❷ to

transmit music or other sound by wire or cable ❸ to play music on a pipe or the bagpipes ❹ to decorate a cake with thin lines of icing, cream, etc.
➤ **pipe down** (*informal*) to be quiet
➤ **pipe up** to begin to say something

pipe dream *NOUN* **pipe dreams**
an impossible wish

pipeline *NOUN* **pipelines**
a pipe for carrying oil, water or gas over a long distance
➤ **in the pipeline** planned and ready to happen soon

piper *NOUN* **pipers**
a person who plays a pipe or bagpipes

pipette *NOUN* **pipettes**
a small glass tube used in a laboratory, usually filled by suction

piping *NOUN*
❶ pipes; a length of pipe ❷ a decorative line of icing, cream, etc. on a cake or other dish ❸ a long, narrow pipe-like fold decorating clothing, upholstery, etc.

piping *ADJECTIVE*
shrill • *a piping voice*
➤ **piping hot** very hot and ready to eat

pipit *NOUN* **pipits**
a small songbird

pippin *NOUN* **pippins**
a kind of apple

piquant (say **pee**-kant) *ADJECTIVE*
❶ pleasantly sharp and appetizing • *a piquant smell* ❷ pleasantly stimulating
➤ **piquancy** *NOUN*

pique (say peek) *NOUN*
a feeling of hurt pride

pique *VERB* **piques, piquing, piqued**
to be piqued is to feel irritated or annoyed
➤ **pique someone's interest** or **curiosity** to make someone want to know more

piracy *NOUN*
❶ the crime of attacking ships in order to steal from them ❷ the crime of illegally making and selling copies of books, DVDs, computer programs, etc.

piranha *NOUN* **piranhas**
a South American freshwater fish that has sharp teeth and eats flesh

pirate *NOUN* **pirates**
❶ a person on a ship who attacks and robs other ships at sea ❷ someone who copies

books, DVDs, computer programs, etc. in order to sell them illegally
➤ **piratical** *ADJECTIVE*

pirouette (say pir-oo-**et**) *NOUN* **pirouettes**
a spinning movement of the body made while balanced on the point of the toe or on one foot

pirouette *VERB* **pirouettes, pirouetting, pirouetted**
to perform a pirouette

pistachio *NOUN* **pistachios**
a nut with an edible green kernel

pistil *NOUN* **pistils**
the part of a flower that produces the seed, consisting of the ovary, style and stigma

pistol *NOUN* **pistols**
a small handgun

piston *NOUN* **pistons**
a disc or cylinder that fits inside a tube in which it moves up and down as part of an engine or pump

pit *NOUN* **pits**
❶ a deep hole ❷ a hollow ❸ a coal mine ❹ the part of a race circuit where racing cars are refuelled and repaired during a race

pit *VERB* **pits, pitting, pitted**
❶ to make holes or hollows in something • *The surface of the planet was pitted with craters.* ❷ to put someone in competition with someone else • *He was pitted against the champion in the final.*
➤ **pitted** *ADJECTIVE*

pit bull terrier *NOUN* **pit bull terriers**
a small strong and fierce breed of dog

pitch *NOUN* **pitches**
❶ a piece of ground marked out for cricket, football or another game ❷ how high or low a voice or a musical note is ❸ intensity or strength • *Excitement was at fever pitch.* ❹ the steepness of a slope • *the pitch of the roof* ❺ a black sticky substance rather like tar

pitch *VERB* **pitches, pitching, pitched**
❶ to throw or fling something • *She pitched his hat over the wall.* ❷ to set up a tent or camp ❸ to fall heavily forward • *He pitched forward as the bus braked suddenly.* ❹ a ship pitches when it moves up and down on a rough sea ❺ to set something at a particular level • *They have pitched their prices too high.* ❻ a bowled ball in cricket pitches when it strikes the ground
➤ **pitch in** (*informal*) to join in and help with something • *Everyone pitched in with ideas.*

pitch–black, pitch–dark *ADJECTIVE*
completely black or dark

pitchblende *NOUN*
a mineral ore (uranium oxide) from which radium is obtained

pitched battle *NOUN* pitched battles
a battle between armies in prepared positions

pitcher *NOUN* pitchers
a large jug

pitchfork *NOUN* pitchforks
a large fork with two prongs, used for lifting hay

piteous *ADJECTIVE*
making you feel pity • *It was a piteous sight.*
➤ **piteously** *ADVERB*

pitfall *NOUN* pitfalls
a hidden danger or difficulty

pith *NOUN*
the spongy substance in the stems of certain plants or lining the rind of oranges or other fruits

pithy *ADJECTIVE*
❶ like pith; containing much pith ❷ short and full of meaning • *pithy comments*

pitiable *ADJECTIVE*
making you feel pity

pitiful *ADJECTIVE*
making you feel pity • *He let out a pitiful moan.*
➤ **pitifully** *ADVERB*

pitiless *ADJECTIVE*
showing no pity; harsh or cruel
➤ **pitilessly** *ADVERB*

pitta *NOUN*
a kind of flat thick bread with a hollow inside

pittance *NOUN*
a very small allowance of money

pity *NOUN*
❶ the feeling of being sorry because someone is in pain or trouble ❷ a cause for regret • *It's a pity that you can't come.*
➤ **take pity on someone** to feel sorry for someone and try to help them

pity *VERB* pities, pitying, pitied
to feel pity for someone

pivot *NOUN* pivots
a point or part on which something turns or balances

pivot *VERB* pivots, pivoting, pivoted
to turn or balance on a pivot

pivotal *ADJECTIVE*
of great importance, because other things depend on it • *He plays a pivotal role in the story.*

pixel (say **piks**-el) *NOUN* pixels
one of the tiny dots on a computer display screen from which the image is formed
WORD ORIGIN short for *picture element*

pixie *NOUN* pixies
a small fairy or elf

pizza (say **peets**-a) *NOUN* pizzas
an Italian food that consists of a layer of dough baked with a savoury topping

pizzicato (say pits-i-**kah**-toh) *ADJECTIVE* & *ADVERB*
(*in music*) plucking the strings of a musical instrument such as a violin

placard *NOUN* placards
a poster or notice, especially one carried at a demonstration

placate *VERB* placates, placating, placated
to make someone feel calmer and less angry
➤ **placatory** *ADJECTIVE*

place *NOUN* places
❶ a particular part of space, especially where something belongs; an area or position ❷ a city, town or village ❸ a position in a race or competition • *She finished in second place.* ❹ a seat • *Save me a place.* ❺ a job; employment ❻ a building; a home • *Come round to our place* ❼ a role or function • *It's not my place to interfere.* ❽ a point in a series of things • *In the first place, the date is wrong.*
➤ **in place** in the correct position
➤ **in place of** instead of
➤ **out of place** ❶ in the wrong position ❷ not appropriate or suitable
➤ **take place** to happen • *The wedding will take place early next year.*

place *VERB* places, placing, placed
to put something in a particular place • *He carefully placed the bowl on the table.*

placebo (say plas-**ee**-boh) *NOUN* placebos
a harmless substance given as if it were a medicine, usually to reassure a patient
WORD ORIGIN Latin, = I shall be pleasing

placement *NOUN* placements
placing something in a position

placenta *NOUN*
a piece of body tissue that forms in the womb during pregnancy and supplies the foetus with nourishment

A B C D E F G H I J K L M N O P Q R S T U V W X Y Z

placid *ADJECTIVE*
calm and peaceful; not easily made anxious or upset • *a placid horse*
➤ **placidly** *ADVERB*
➤ **placidity** *NOUN*

plagiarize (also **plagiarise**) (say **play**-jeer-yz) *VERB* **plagiarizes, plagiarizing, plagiarized**
to take someone else's writings or ideas and use them as if they were your own
➤ **plagiarism** *NOUN*

plague *NOUN* **plagues**
❶ a dangerous illness that spreads very quickly ❷ a large number of pests • *a plague of locusts*

plague *VERB* **plagues, plaguing, plagued**
to keep causing someone trouble • *The project was plagued with problems from the start.*

plaice *NOUN* **plaice**
a flat edible sea fish

plaid (say plad) *NOUN*
cloth with a tartan or similar pattern

plain *ADJECTIVE*
❶ simple; not decorated or elaborate ❷ not pretty or beautiful ❸ easy to see or hear or understand ❹ frank and straightforward • *I'll be quite plain with you.*
➤ **plainness** *NOUN*

plain *NOUN* **plains**
a large area of flat country

SPELLING
Take care not to confuse with **plane**, which means an aeroplane.

plain clothes *NOUN*
civilian clothes worn instead of a uniform, e.g. by police

plainly *ADVERB*
❶ clearly or obviously • *He was plainly very upset.* ❷ simply • *She was plainly dressed.*

plaintiff *NOUN* **plaintiffs**
the person who brings a complaint against someone else to a law court. Compare with **defendant**.

plaintive *ADJECTIVE*
sounding sad • *a plaintive cry*
➤ **plaintively** *ADVERB*

plait (say plat) *VERB* **plaits, plaiting, plaited**
to weave three or more strands of hair or rope to form one length

plait *NOUN* **plaits**
a length of hair or rope that has been plaited

plan *NOUN* **plans**
❶ a way of doing something that you think out in advance ❷ a drawing showing how the parts of something are arranged ❸ a map of a town or district

plan *VERB* **plans, planning, planned**
❶ to think out in advance how you are going to do something ❷ to intend or expect to do something • *We plan to arrive there at lunchtime.*
➤ **planner** *NOUN*

plane *NOUN* **planes**
❶ an aeroplane ❷ a tool for making wood smooth by scraping its surface ❸ a flat or level surface ❹ a tall tree with broad leaves

plane *VERB* **planes, planing, planed**
to smooth wood with a plane

plane *ADJECTIVE*
flat or level • *a plane surface*

SPELLING
Take care not to confuse with **plain**, which means simple or straightforward.

planet *NOUN* **planets**
one of the large bodies in space that move in an orbit round the sun or another star
WORD ORIGIN from Greek *planetes* = wanderer (because planets seem to move in relation to the stars)

planetary *ADJECTIVE*
to do with planets • *planetary exploration*

plank *NOUN* **planks**
a long flat piece of wood

plankton *NOUN*
microscopic plants and animals that float in the sea and lakes

plant *NOUN* **plants**
❶ a living thing that cannot move, makes its food from chemical substances and usually has a stem, leaves and roots. Flowers, trees and shrubs are plants. ❷ a small plant, not a tree or shrub ❸ a factory or its equipment ❹ (*informal*) something deliberately placed for other people to find, usually to mislead people or cause trouble

plant *VERB* **plants, planting, planted**
❶ to put something in soil for growing ❷ to put something firmly in place • *He planted his feet on the ground and took hold of the rope.* ❸ to place something where it will be found, usually to mislead people or cause trouble

plantain (say **plan**-tin) *NOUN* **plantains**
❶ a tropical tree and fruit resembling the banana ❷ a wild plant with broad flat leaves,

bearing seeds that are used as food for cage birds

plantation *NOUN* **plantations**
❶ a large area of land where a crop such as cotton, tobacco or tea is planted ❷ a group of planted trees

planter *NOUN* **planters**
someone who owns a plantation • *a tea planter*

plaque (say plak) *NOUN* **plaques**
❶ a flat piece of metal or porcelain fixed on a wall as an ornament or memorial ❷ a filmy substance that forms on teeth and gums, where bacteria can live

plasma *NOUN*
the colourless liquid part of blood, carrying the corpuscles

plaster *NOUN* **plasters**
❶ a small covering put over the skin around a cut or wound to protect it ❷ a mixture of lime, sand and water etc. for covering walls and ceilings ❸ plaster of Paris or a cast made of this to hold broken bones in place

plaster *VERB* **plasters, plastering, plastered**
❶ to cover a wall or other surface with plaster ❷ to cover something thickly • *His clothes were plastered with mud.*

plaster of Paris *NOUN*
a white paste used for making moulds or for casts round a broken leg or arm

plastic *NOUN* **plastics**
a strong, light synthetic substance that can be moulded into a permanent shape

plastic *ADJECTIVE*
❶ made of plastic • *a plastic bag* ❷ soft and easy to mould • *Clay is a plastic substance.*

plastic surgery *NOUN*
surgery to repair or replace damaged skin or to improve the appearance of someone's face or body
➤ **plastic surgeon** *NOUN*

plate *NOUN* **plates**
❶ an almost flat usually circular object from which food is eaten or served ❷ a thin flat sheet of metal, glass or other hard material ❸ an illustration on special paper in a book

plate *VERB* **plates, plating, plated**
❶ to coat metal with a thin layer of gold, silver, tin, etc. ❷ to cover something with sheets of metal

plateau (say **plat**-oh) *NOUN* **plateaux** or **plateaus** (say **plat**-ohz)
a flat area of high land

plateful *NOUN* **platefuls**
the amount of food that a plate can hold

platform *NOUN* **platforms**
❶ a flat raised area along the side of a line at a railway station, where passengers get on and off trains ❷ a flat surface that is above the level of the ground or floor, especially one from which someone speaks to an audience

platinum *NOUN*
a valuable silver-coloured metal that does not tarnish

platitude *NOUN* **platitudes**
a trite or insincere remark that people often use

platoon *NOUN* **platoons**
a small group of soldiers

platter *NOUN* **platters**
a flat dish or plate

platypus *NOUN* **platypuses**
an Australian animal with a beak like that of a duck, that lays eggs like a bird but is a mammal and suckles its young

plaudits *PLURAL NOUN*
applause; expressions of approval

plausible *ADJECTIVE*
seeming likely to be true; reasonable • *a plausible explanation*
➤ **plausibly** *ADVERB*
➤ **plausibility** *NOUN*

play *VERB* **plays, playing, played**
❶ to take part in a game, sport or other amusement ❷ to make music with a musical instrument ❸ to put a CD, DVD, etc. into a machine and listen to it or watch it ❹ to perform a part in a play or film
➤ **play about** or **around** to have fun or be mischievous
➤ **play something down** to give people the impression that something is not important
➤ **play up** (*informal*) to tease or annoy someone

play *NOUN* **plays**
❶ a story acted on a stage or on radio or television ❷ doing things for fun or amusement • *Young children learn through play.* ❸ the playing of a game or sport • *Rain stopped play.*
➤ **a play on words** a pun

a b c d e f g h i j k l m n o p q r s t u v w x y z

playback *NOUN* **playbacks**
playing back something that has been recorded

player *NOUN* **players**
❶ a person who plays a game or sport • *a tennis player* ❷ a person who plays a musical instrument • *a trumpet player* ❸ a machine for playing recorded sound or pictures • *a DVD player*

playful *ADJECTIVE*
❶ wanting to play; full of fun ❷ done in fun; not serious
➤ **playfully** *ADVERB*
➤ **playfulness** *NOUN*

playground *NOUN* **playgrounds**
a piece of ground for children to play on

playgroup *NOUN* **playgroups**
(*British*) a group of very young children who play together regularly, supervised by adults

playing card *NOUN* **playing cards**
each of a set of cards (usually 52) used for playing games

playing field *NOUN* **playing fields**
a field used for outdoor games

playmate *NOUN* **playmates**
a person you play games with

play-off *NOUN* **play-offs**
an extra match that is played between teams with equal scores to decide who the winner is

plaything *NOUN* **playthings**
❶ a toy ❷ a person that someone has fun with and treats as unimportant

playtime *NOUN*
the time when young schoolchildren go out to play

playwright *NOUN* **playwrights**
a person who writes plays; a dramatist

PLC, plc *ABBREVIATION*
(*British*) public limited company

plea *NOUN* **pleas**
❶ a request or appeal • *a plea for mercy* ❷ a formal statement of 'guilty' or 'not guilty' made in a law court by someone accused of a crime

plead *VERB* **pleads, pleading, pleaded**
❶ to beg someone to do something ❷ to state formally in a law court that you are guilty or not guilty of a crime ❸ to give something as an excuse • *She didn't come on holiday with us, pleading poverty.*

pleasant *ADJECTIVE*
pleasing; giving pleasure
➤ **pleasantness** *NOUN*

pleasantly *ADVERB*
in a pleasant way • *I was pleasantly surprised.*

pleasantry *NOUN* **pleasantries**
a friendly or good-humoured remark • *They exchanged a few pleasantries.*

please *VERB* **pleases, pleasing, pleased**
❶ to make a person feel satisfied or glad ❷ used to make a request or an order polite • *Please ring the bell.*
➤ **as you please** in whatever way you think is suitable

pleased *ADJECTIVE*
happy or satisfied about something • *I'm very pleased to meet you.*

pleasurable *ADJECTIVE*
causing pleasure; enjoyable

pleasure *NOUN* **pleasures**
❶ a feeling of satisfaction or gladness; enjoyment ❷ something that pleases you • *It's been a pleasure talking to you.*

pleat *NOUN* **pleats**
a flat fold made by doubling cloth upon itself
➤ **pleated** *ADJECTIVE*

plectrum *NOUN* **plectra**
a small piece of metal, plastic or bone for plucking the strings of a musical instrument

plentiful *ADJECTIVE*
available in large amounts • *a plentiful supply of food*
➤ **plentifully** *ADVERB*

plenty *NOUN*
quite enough; as much as is needed or wanted

plenty *ADVERB* (*informal*) quite or fully • *It's plenty big enough.*

plethora *NOUN*
too large a quantity of something

pleurisy (say **ploor**-i-see) *NOUN*
inflammation of the membrane round the lungs

pliable *ADJECTIVE*
❶ easy to bend; flexible ❷ easy to influence or control

pliant *ADJECTIVE*
flexible or pliable

pliers *PLURAL NOUN*
pincers that have jaws with flat surfaces for gripping things

plight *NOUN* plights
a dangerous or difficult situation • *the plight of the homeless*

plight *VERB* plights, plighting, plighted (*old use*)
to pledge devotion or loyalty

plimsoll *NOUN* plimsolls
(*British*) a canvas sports shoe with a rubber sole **WORD ORIGIN** from **Plimsoll line** (because the thin sole reminded people of a Plimsoll line)

Plimsoll line *NOUN* Plimsoll lines
a mark on a ship's side showing how deeply it may legally go down in the water when loaded **WORD ORIGIN** named after an English politician, S. *Plimsoll*, who in the 1870s protested about ships being overloaded

plinth *NOUN* plinths
a block or slab forming the base of a column or a support for a statue or vase

plod *VERB* plods, plodding, plodded
❶ to walk slowly and heavily • *We plodded back through the rain.* ❷ to work slowly but steadily
➤ **plodder** *NOUN*

plonk *NOUN* (*British*) (*informal*)
cheap wine **WORD ORIGIN** originally Australian; probably from French *blanc* = white, in *vin blanc* = white wine

plonk *VERB* plonks, plonking, plonked
(*informal, chiefly British*) to put something down carelessly or heavily • *Just plonk your bag down anywhere.*

plop *NOUN* plops
the sound of something dropping into water

plop *VERB* plops, plopping, plopped
to fall into liquid with a plop

plot *NOUN* plots
❶ a secret plan by a group of people to do something illegal or wrong ❷ the story in a play, novel or film ❸ a small piece of land

plot *VERB* plots, plotting, plotted
❶ to make a secret plan to do something ❷ to make a chart or graph of something • *We plotted the ship's route on our map.*

plotter *NOUN* plotters
someone who takes part in a plot

plough *NOUN* ploughs
a farming implement for turning the soil over, in preparation for planting seeds

plough *VERB* ploughs, ploughing, ploughed
❶ to turn over soil with a plough ❷ to plough through something is to read all of it

with great effort or difficulty • *He ploughed through the book over the weekend.*
➤ **ploughman** *NOUN*

ploughshare *NOUN* ploughshares
the cutting blade of a plough

plover (say **pluv**-er) *NOUN* plovers
a kind of wading bird

ploy *NOUN* ploys
a cunning trick or deception you use to get what you want

pluck *VERB* plucks, plucking, plucked
❶ to pick a flower or fruit ❷ to pull the feathers off a bird ❸ to pull something up or out • *She plucked the letter out of his hand.* ❹ to pull a string (e.g. on a guitar) and let it go again
➤ **pluck up courage** to try to get enough courage to do something

pluck *NOUN*
courage or spirit

plucky *ADJECTIVE* pluckier, pluckiest
brave or spirited
➤ **pluckily** *ADVERB*

plug *NOUN* plugs
❶ something used to stop up a hole • *a bath plug* ❷ a device that fits into a socket to connect a piece of electrical equipment to a supply of electricity ❸ (*informal*) a piece of publicity for something

plug *VERB* plugs, plugging, plugged
❶ to stop up a hole ❷ (*informal*) to publicize something
➤ **plug something in** to connect something to an electrical socket by means of a plug

plum *NOUN* plums
❶ a soft juicy fruit with a pointed stone in the middle ❷ a reddish purple colour

plum *ADJECTIVE*
(*informal*) that is the best of its kind • *a plum job*

plumage (say **ploom**-ij) *NOUN* plumages
a bird's feathers

plumb *VERB* plumbs, plumbing, plumbed
❶ to investigate something mysterious in order to understand it • *Scientists are trying to plumb the mysteries of the universe.* ❷ (*British*) to fit a room or building with a plumbing system

plumb *ADJECTIVE*
exactly upright or vertical • *The wall was plumb.*

a b c d e f g h i j k l m n o **p** q r s t u v w x y z

plumb *ADVERB* (*informal*) exactly or precisely
• *It fell plumb in the middle.*

plumber *NOUN* **plumbers**
a person who fits and mends plumbing

plumbing *NOUN*
❶ the water pipes, water tanks and drainage pipes in a building ❷ the work of a plumber
WORD ORIGIN from Latin *plumbum* = lead (because water pipes used to be made of lead)

plumb line *NOUN* **plumb lines**
a cord with a weight on the end, used to find how deep something is or whether a wall etc. is vertical

plume *NOUN* **plumes**
❶ a large feather ❷ a thin column of something that rises in the air • *a plume of smoke*

plumed *ADJECTIVE*
decorated with plumes • *a plumed helmet*

plummet *VERB* **plummets, plummeting, plummeted**
❶ to drop downwards quickly • *The plane plummeted towards the ground.* ❷ to decrease rapidly in value • *Prices have plummeted.*

plump *ADJECTIVE*
having a full, rounded shape; slightly fat
• *plump cheeks*
➤ **plumpness** *NOUN*

plump *VERB* **plumps, plumping, plumped**
to plump up a cushion or pillow is to shake it to give it a rounded shape
➤ **plump for something** (*informal*) to choose something

plunder *VERB* **plunders, plundering, plundered**
to rob a person or place using force, especially during a war • *The invading army plundered many of the churches and monasteries.*
➤ **plunderer** *NOUN*

plunder *NOUN*
❶ plundering a person or place ❷ goods that have been plundered

plunge *VERB* **plunges, plunging, plunged**
❶ to jump or dive into water with force ❷ to push something forcefully into something
• *She plunged the knife into his chest.* ❸ to fall or go downwards suddenly • *The car plunged off the cliff.* ❹ to force someone or something into an unpleasant situation • *They plunged the world into war.* • *The room was suddenly plunged into darkness.*

plunge *NOUN* **plunges**
a sudden fall or dive
➤ **take the plunge** to start a bold course of action

plunger *NOUN* **plungers**
a rubber cup on a handle used for clearing blocked pipes

plural *NOUN* **plurals**
the form of a noun or verb used when it stands for more than one person or thing
• *The plural of 'child' is 'children'.*
Compare with **singular**.

plural *ADJECTIVE*
in the plural; meaning more than one
• *'Mice' is a plural noun.*

GRAMMAR

Most words in English form their **plurals** by adding -s or -es (*ants, branches*). However, some types of words have more unusual plurals:

words which are the same in the singular and plural, e.g. *aircraft, deer, fish, sheep, series* and *species.*

words which have irregular plurals: *child, children; goose, geese; louse, lice; mouse, mice; ox, oxen; tooth, teeth.*

words of Greek and Latin origin which keep a Greek or Latin plural form:

-a, -ae, e.g. *antenna, antennae; formula, formulae*

-ex, -ices, e.g. *index, indices; vortex, vortices*

-is, -es, e.g. *axis, axes; basis, bases; thesis, theses*

-ix, -ices, e.g. *appendix, appendices*

-on, -a, e.g. *phenomenon, phenomena*

-um, -a, e.g. *medium, media*

-us, -i, e.g. *radius, radii; sarcophagus, sarcophagi*

Sometimes the use of a Latin or Greek plural is optional, e.g. *plectrums* or *plectra, radiuses* or *radii*; it can also depend on meaning, e.g. the form *appendixes* is used for parts of the body, but *appendices* for sections of a book.

Words from other languages which keep their original plurals, e.g. *gateau, gateaux.*

plus *PREPOSITION*
with the next number or thing added • *2 plus 2 equals four (2 + 2 = 4).*

plus *ADJECTIVE*
❶ being a grade slightly higher • *B plus*
❷ more than zero • *a temperature between minus ten and plus ten degrees*

plush *NOUN*
a thick velvety cloth used in furnishings

plush *ADJECTIVE*
smart and expensive • *a plush hotel*

plutonium *NOUN*
a radioactive substance used in nuclear weapons and reactors (**WORD ORIGIN**) named after the planet *Pluto*

ply *VERB* plies, plying, plied
❶ to keep offering something to someone
• *They plied her with food from the moment she arrived.* ❷ to ply a trade is to work at it as your regular job ❸ to go regularly back and forth • *The boat plies between the two harbours.*

ply *NOUN* plies
❶ a thickness or layer of wood or cloth etc.
❷ a strand in yarn • *4-ply wool*

plywood *NOUN*
strong thin board made of layers of wood glued together

PM *ABBREVIATION*
Prime Minister

p.m. *ABBREVIATION*
after 12 o'clock midday (**WORD ORIGIN**) short for Latin *post meridiem* = after noon

pneumatic (say new-**mat**-ik) *ADJECTIVE*
filled with or worked by compressed air • *a pneumatic drill*

pneumonia (say new-**moh**-nee-a) *NOUN*
a serious illness caused by inflammation of one or both lungs

poach *VERB* poaches, poaching, poached
❶ to cook an egg (removed from its shell) in or over boiling water ❷ to cook fish or fruit in a small amount of liquid ❸ to steal game or fish from someone else's land or water
❹ to take something unfairly • *One club was poaching members from another.*

poacher *NOUN* poachers
a person who steals game or fish from someone else's land or water

pocket *NOUN* pockets
❶ a small bag-shaped part of a piece of clothing, for carrying things in ❷ a person's

supply of money • *The cost is well beyond my pocket.* ❸ a small isolated area of something
• *There will be pockets of rain in the south.*
➤ **pocketful** *NOUN*
➤ **be out of pocket** to have spent more money than you have gained

pocket *ADJECTIVE*
small enough to carry in your pocket
• *a pocket calculator*

pocket *VERB* pockets, pocketing, pocketed
to put something into a pocket • *He pocketed the money and walked out.*

pocket money *NOUN*
(*British*) money given to a child to spend

pockmark *NOUN* pockmarks
a scar or mark left on the skin by a disease
➤ **pockmarked** *ADJECTIVE*

pod *NOUN* pods
a long seed container of the kind found on a pea or bean plant

podcast *NOUN* podcasts
a digital recording, especially of a radio programme, that you can download from the Internet to a computer or portable media player

podgy *ADJECTIVE* podgier, podgiest
(*British*) (*informal*) short and fat • *podgy fingers*

podium (say **poh**-dee-um) *NOUN* podiums or podia
a small platform on which a music conductor or someone making a speech stands

poem *NOUN* poems
a piece of writing arranged in short lines, usually with a particular rhythm and sometimes with rhymes

poet *NOUN* poets
a person who writes poetry

poetic *ADJECTIVE*
to do with poetry or like poetry • *poetic language*
➤ **poetical** *ADJECTIVE*
➤ **poetically** *ADVERB*

poetry *NOUN*
poems or the writing of poems • *Do you like poetry?*

poignant (say **poin**-yant) *ADJECTIVE*
having a strong effect on your feelings and making you feel sad • *poignant memories*
➤ **poignancy** *NOUN*

point *NOUN* points

❶ the narrow or sharp end of something ❷ a dot • *the decimal point* ❸ a single mark in a game or quiz • *How many points did I get?* ❹ a particular place or time • *At this point she was winning.* ❺ something that someone says during a discussion • *That's a very good point.* ❻ a detail or characteristic • *He has his good points.* ❼ the important or essential idea • *Keep to the point!* ❽ purpose or value • *There is no point in hurrying.* ❾ an electrical socket ❿ a device for changing a train from one track to another

point *VERB* points, pointing, pointed

❶ to show where something is, especially by holding out your finger towards it ❷ to aim or direct something at a person or thing • *She pointed a gun at me.* ❸ to fill in the parts between bricks with mortar or cement
➤ **point something out** to draw attention to something

point-blank *ADJECTIVE*

❶ aimed or fired from close to the target ❷ direct and straightforward • *a point-blank refusal*

point-blank *ADVERB*

in a point-blank manner • *He refused point-blank to let us in.*

point duty *NOUN*

(*British*) the duties of a police officer stationed at a road junction to control the movement of traffic

pointed *ADJECTIVE*

❶ with a point at the end ❷ clearly directed at a particular person, especially to criticize them • *a pointed remark*

pointedly *ADVERB*

in a way that clearly shows what you mean • *She yawned and looked pointedly at her watch.*

pointer *NOUN* pointers

❶ a stick, rod or mark used to point at something ❷ a dog that points with its muzzle towards birds that it scents ❸ an indication or hint

pointless *ADJECTIVE*

without a point; with no purpose • *It's pointless arguing with him.*
➤ **pointlessly** *ADVERB*

point of view *NOUN* points of view

❶ a way of looking at something or thinking about it ❷ the way that a writer chooses to tell a story, e.g. by telling it through the experiences of one of the characters

poise *NOUN*

a dignified self-confident manner • *She handled the situation with great poise.*

poise *VERB* poises, poising, poised

to balance something or keep it steady • *He poised the javelin in his hand.*

poised *ADJECTIVE*

❶ not moving but ready to move • *He had a pen poised in his hand.* ❷ dignified and self-confident
➤ **be poised to do something** or **for something** to be ready to do something • *The snake was poised to strike.* • *She was poised for revenge.*

poison *NOUN* poisons

a substance that can harm or kill a living thing if swallowed or absorbed into the body

poison *VERB* poisons, poisoning, poisoned

❶ to give poison to someone; to kill someone with poison ❷ to put poison in something ❸ to spoil or have a bad effect on something • *He poisoned their minds.*
➤ **poisoner** *NOUN*

poisonous *ADJECTIVE*

❶ causing death or illness if swallowed or absorbed into the body ❷ producing poison • *a poisonous snake*

poke *VERB* pokes, poking, poked

❶ to prod or jab something with your finger or a pointed object ❷ to push something out or forward; to stick out • *He poked his head out of the window.* ❸ to search in a casual way • *I was poking about in the attic.*
➤ **poke fun at someone** to ridicule someone

poke *NOUN* pokes

a poking movement; a prod
➤ **buy a pig in a poke** to buy something without seeing it first

poker *NOUN* pokers

❶ a stiff metal rod for poking a fire ❷ a card game in which players bet on who has the best cards

poky *ADJECTIVE* pokier, pokiest

small and cramped • *poky little rooms*

polar *ADJECTIVE*

to do with or near the North Pole or South Pole • *the polar regions*

polar bear *NOUN* polar bears

a white bear living in Arctic regions

Polaroid *NOUN* (*trademark*)

a type of plastic, used in sunglasses, which reduces the brightness of light passing through it

Polaroid camera *NOUN* **Polaroid cameras**
(*trademark*)
a camera that takes a picture and produces
the finished photograph a few seconds later

pole *NOUN* **poles**
❶ a long slender rounded piece of wood or
metal ❷ a point on the earth's surface that
is as far north (**North Pole**) or as far south
(**South Pole**) as possible ❸ either of the ends
of a magnet ❹ either terminal of an electric
cell or battery

polecat *NOUN* **polecats**
an animal of the weasel family with an
unpleasant smell

pole star *NOUN*
the star above the North Pole

pole vault *NOUN*
an athletic contest in which competitors
jump over a high bar with the help of a long
flexible pole

police *NOUN*
the people whose job is to catch criminals and
make sure that people obey the law

police *VERB* **polices, policing, policed**
to keep order in a place by means of police

policeman *NOUN* **policemen**
a male police officer

police officer *NOUN* **police officers**
a member of the police

policewoman *NOUN* **policewomen**
a female police officer

policy *NOUN* **policies**
❶ the aims or plan of action of a person
or group • *the country's foreign policy* ❷ a
document stating the terms of a contract of
insurance

polio *NOUN*
a disease that can cause paralysis

polish *VERB* **polishes, polishing, polished**
❶ to make a thing smooth and shiny by
rubbing ❷ to make a thing better by making
corrections and alterations
➤ **polish something off** to finish something
quickly • *We soon polished off all the
sandwiches.*

polish *NOUN* **polishes**
❶ a substance used in polishing ❷ polishing
a surface • *He gave his shoes a good polish.*
❸ elegance of manner

polite *ADJECTIVE*
having good manners; showing respect to

other people • *She gave me a polite smile.*
➤ **politely** *ADVERB*
➤ **politeness** *NOUN*

political *ADJECTIVE*
connected with the governing of a country or
region • *a political party*
➤ **politically** *ADVERB*

politician *NOUN* **politicians**
a person who is involved in politics

politics *NOUN*
political matters; the business of governing a
country or region

polka *NOUN* **polkas**
a lively dance for couples

poll (say pole) *NOUN* **polls**
❶ voting at an election or the votes cast
❷ an opinion poll

poll *VERB* **polls, polling, polled**
❶ to receive a certain number of votes in an
election ❷ to ask members of the public their
opinion on a subject **WORD ORIGIN** from an
old meaning of *poll* = head. In some polls those
voting yes stand apart from those voting no,
and the decision is reached by counting the
heads in the two groups.

pollarded *ADJECTIVE*
a tree is pollarded when its top and branches
are trimmed so that young shoots start to
grow thickly there

pollen *NOUN*
a fine yellow powder produced by the anthers
of flowers, containing male cells for fertilizing
other flowers

pollen count *NOUN* **pollen counts**
a measurement of the amount of pollen in
the air, given as a warning for people who are
allergic to pollen

pollinate *VERB* **pollinates, pollinating,
pollinated**
to fertilize a plant with pollen
➤ **pollination** *NOUN*

polling station *NOUN* **polling stations**
a place where people go to vote in an election

pollutant *NOUN* **pollutants**
something that pollutes

pollute *VERB* **pollutes, polluting, polluted**
to make the air, rivers, etc. dirty or impure

pollution *NOUN*
making the air, rivers, etc. dirty or impure
• *Using less fuel helps to reduce pollution.*

a
b
c
d
e
f
g
h
i
j
k
l
m
n
o
p
q
r
s
t
u
v
w
x
y
z

polo *NOUN*
a game rather like hockey, with players on horseback using long mallets

polo neck *NOUN* polo necks
(*British*) a high round turned-over collar

poltergeist *NOUN* poltergeists
a ghost or spirit that throws things about noisily (**WORD ORIGIN**) from German *poltern* = make a disturbance + *Geist* = ghost

polychrome *ADJECTIVE*
having many colours

polyester *NOUN*
a synthetic material, used to make clothing

polygamy (say pol-**ig**-a-mee) *NOUN*
having more than one wife at a time
➤ **polygamous** *ADJECTIVE*

polyglot *ADJECTIVE*
knowing or using several languages

polygon *NOUN* polygons
a flat shape with many sides. Hexagons and octagons are polygons.
➤ **polygonal** *ADJECTIVE*

polyhedron *NOUN* polyhedrons
a solid shape with many sides

polymer *NOUN* polymers
a substance with a molecule structure consisting of a large number of simple molecules combined

polyp (say **pol**-ip) *NOUN* polyps
❶ a tiny creature with a tube-shaped body ❷ a small abnormal growth

polystyrene *NOUN*
a kind of plastic used for insulating or packing things

polytechnic *NOUN* polytechnics
a name used before 1992 for a college teaching subjects at degree level or below

polythene *NOUN*
(*British*) a lightweight plastic used to make bags or wrappings

pomegranate *NOUN* pomegranates
a tropical fruit with many seeds

pommel *NOUN* pommels
❶ a knob on the handle of a sword ❷ the raised part at the front of a saddle

pomp *NOUN*
the ceremonial splendour that is traditional on important public occasions

pompom *NOUN* pompoms
a ball of coloured threads used as a decoration

pompous *ADJECTIVE*
speaking or behaving in a grand way that shows you think too much of your own importance
➤ **pompously** *ADVERB*
➤ **pomposity** *NOUN*

pond *NOUN* ponds
a small lake

ponder *VERB* ponders, pondering, pondered
to think deeply and seriously about something • *I pondered his words before replying.*

ponderous *ADJECTIVE*
❶ heavy and awkward ❷ slow, dull and too serious • *He writes in a ponderous style.*
➤ **ponderously** *ADVERB*

pong (*British*) (*informal*) *NOUN*
an unpleasant smell

pong *VERB* pongs, ponging, ponged
to have an unpleasant smell

pontiff *NOUN* pontiffs
the Pope

pontoon *NOUN* pontoons
❶ a boat or float used to support a bridge (a **pontoon bridge**) over a river ❷ (*British*) a card game in which players try to get cards whose value totals 21

pony *NOUN* ponies
a small horse

ponytail *NOUN* ponytails
a bunch of long hair tied at the back of the head

pony-trekking *NOUN*
(*British*) travelling across country on a pony for pleasure

poodle *NOUN* poodles
a dog with thick curly hair

pooh *EXCLAMATION*
a word used to express disgust or contempt

pool *NOUN* pools
❶ a pond ❷ a puddle ❸ a swimming pool ❹ a group of things shared by several people ❺ a game similar to snooker but played on a smaller table
➤ **the pools** a form of gambling based on the results of football matches

pool *VERB* pools, pooling, pooled
to put money or things together for sharing
• *We need to pool our resources.*

poop *NOUN* poops
the stern of a ship

poor *ADJECTIVE*
❶ with very little money ❷ not good;
inadequate • *a poor piece of work*
❸ unfortunate; deserving pity • *Poor fellow!*

poorly *ADVERB*
in a poor way • *We've played poorly this
season.*

poorly *ADJECTIVE*
(*British*) rather ill • *I've felt poorly all week.*

pop *NOUN* pops
❶ modern popular music ❷ a small explosive
sound ❸ a fizzy drink

pop *VERB* pops, popping, popped
❶ (*informal*) to go quickly or put something
somewhere quickly • *Can you pop down to
the shop for me?* • *I'll just pop this pie into
the microwave.* ❷ to make a pop

popcorn *NOUN*
maize heated to burst and form fluffy balls

Pope *NOUN* Popes
the leader of the Roman Catholic Church

pop-eyed *ADJECTIVE*
with bulging eyes

popgun *NOUN* popguns
a toy gun that shoots a cork or pellet with a
popping sound

poplar *NOUN* poplars
a tall slender tree

poplin *NOUN*
a plain woven cotton material

poppadam, poppadom *NOUN* poppadams or
poppadoms
a thin crisp biscuit made of lentil flour, eaten
with Indian food

poppy *NOUN* poppies
a plant with large red flowers

populace *NOUN*
the general public

popular *ADJECTIVE*
❶ liked or enjoyed by many people ❷ held
or believed by many people • *popular
superstitions* ❸ intended for the general
public

popularity *NOUN*
being liked or enjoyed by a lot of people • *The
sport is growing in popularity.*

popularize (also **popularise**) *VERB*
popularizes, popularizing, popularized
to make a thing known and liked by a lot
of people • *His TV programmes helped to
popularize archaeology.*

popularly *ADVERB*
by many people; generally • *Edward Teach,
popularly known as Blackbeard, was a
notorious pirate.*

populate *VERB* populates, populating,
populated
to fill a place with people; to inhabit a
country • *The region is sparsely populated.*

population *NOUN* populations
the people who live in a district or country;
the total number of these people • *What's
the population of New York?*

porcelain *NOUN*
the finest kind of china

porch *NOUN* porches
a shelter outside the entrance to a building

porcupine *NOUN* porcupines
a small animal covered with long prickles
WORD ORIGIN from old French *porc espin* =
spiny pig

pore *NOUN* pores
a tiny opening on your skin through which
moisture can pass in or out

pore *VERB* pores, poring, pored
➤ **pore over something** to study something
with close attention • *He was poring over his
books.*
SPELLING
Take care not to confuse with **pour**,
which means to make a liquid flow out of
something.

pork *NOUN*
meat from a pig

pornography (say porn-**og**-ra-fee) *NOUN*
pictures, magazines and films that show
naked people and sexual acts in a way that
is intended to be sexually exciting and that
many people find offensive
➤ **pornographic** *ADJECTIVE*

porous *ADJECTIVE*
allowing liquid or air to pass through • *porous
rock*

porphyry (say por-fir-ee) *NOUN*
a kind of rock containing crystals of minerals

porpoise (say por-pus) *NOUN* porpoises
a sea animal rather like a small whale
WORD ORIGIN from Latin *porcus* = pig + *piscis* = fish

porridge *NOUN*
a food made by boiling oatmeal to a thick paste

port *NOUN* ports
❶ a harbour ❷ a city or town with a harbour ❸ the left-hand side of a ship or aircraft when you are facing forward. Compare with **starboard**. ❹ a strong red Portuguese wine

portable *ADJECTIVE*
able to be carried easily • *a portable TV*

portal *NOUN* portals
❶ a doorway or gateway ❷ a website with information on a particular subject and links to other websites • *a literacy portal*

portcullis *NOUN* portcullises
a strong heavy vertical grating that can be lowered to block the gateway to a castle

portend *VERB* portends, portending, portended
to be a sign or warning that something bad will happen • *Dark clouds portend a storm.*

portent *NOUN* portents
an omen; a sign that something will happen
➤ **portentous** *ADJECTIVE*

porter *NOUN* porters
❶ a person whose job is to carry luggage or other goods ❷ (*British*) a person whose job is to look after the entrance to a large building

portfolio *NOUN* portfolios
❶ a case for holding documents or drawings ❷ a government minister's special responsibility ❸ a collection of examples of art or photography work that you have done

porthole *NOUN* portholes
a small window in the side of a ship or aircraft

portico *NOUN* porticoes
a roof supported on columns, usually forming a porch to a building

portion *NOUN* portions
a part or share given to someone

portion *VERB* portions, portioning, portioned
to divide something into portions • *The food was portioned out.*

portly *ADJECTIVE* portlier, portliest
rather fat

portmanteau (say port-**mant**-oh) *NOUN* portmanteaus
a large travelling bag that opens into two equal parts

portmanteau word *NOUN* portmanteau words
a word made from the sounds and meanings of two others, e.g. *motel* (from *mo*tor + ho*tel*)

portrait *NOUN* portraits
❶ a picture of a person ❷ a description in words or on film

portray *VERB* portrays, portraying, portrayed
❶ to make a picture of a person or scene ❷ to describe or show a person or thing in a certain way • *The play portrays the king as a kindly man.*
➤ **portrayal** *NOUN*

pose *NOUN* poses
❶ a position in which someone stands or sits for a portrait or photograph ❷ a way of behaving that someone adopts to give a particular impression

pose *VERB* poses, posing, posed
❶ to take up a pose • *We all posed for a photograph.* ❷ to put someone into a pose ❸ to pretend to be someone • *The thieves posed as police officers.* ❹ to pose a question or problem is to present it • *The bad weather poses several problems for us.*

poser *NOUN* posers
❶ a puzzling question or problem ❷ a person who behaves in a showy or unnatural way in order to impress other people

posh *ADJECTIVE* (*informal*)
❶ very smart; high-class • *a posh restaurant* ❷ upper-class • *a posh accent*

position *NOUN* positions
❶ the place where something is or should be ❷ the way a person or thing is placed or arranged • *He pushed himself up into a sitting position.* ❸ a person's place in a race or competition ❹ a situation or condition • *I am in no position to help you.* ❺ paid employment; a job

position *VERB* positions, positioning, positioned
to place a person or thing in a certain position • *She positioned herself at the top of the stairs.*

positive *ADJECTIVE*
❶ definite or certain • *Are you positive you*

saw him? • *We have positive proof that he is guilty.* ❷ agreeing or saying 'yes' • *We received a positive reply.* ❸ looking at the best or most hopeful aspects of a situation ❹ showing signs of what is being tested for • *Her pregnancy test was positive.* ❺ greater than zero ❻ to do with the kind of electric charge that lacks electrons ❼ the positive form of an adjective or adverb is its simplest form, not the comparative or superlative • *The positive form is 'big', the comparative is 'bigger', the superlative is 'biggest'.*

positive *NOUN* **positives**
a photograph or film in which the light and dark parts or colours appear as in the thing photographed or filmed. Compare with **negative**.

positively *ADVERB*
❶ really; extremely • *She wasn't just annoyed – she was positively furious!* ❷ in a positive way • *You need to think positively.*

positron *NOUN* **positrons**
a particle of matter with a positive electric charge

posse (say **poss**-ee) *NOUN* **posses**
a group of people, especially one put together to help a sheriff

possess *VERB* **possesses, possessing, possessed**
❶ to have or own something ❷ to control someone's thoughts or behaviour • *I don't know what possessed you to do such a thing!*
➤ **possessor** *NOUN*

possessed *ADJECTIVE*
seeming to be controlled by strong emotion or an evil spirit • *He fought like a man possessed.*

possession *NOUN* **possessions**
❶ something you own ❷ having or owning something • *I am now in possession of all the facts.*

possessive *ADJECTIVE*
❶ wanting to possess and keep things for yourself ❷ (*in grammar*) showing what or whom something belongs to • *'His' and 'ours' are possessive pronouns.*

GRAMMAR

Possessive **determiners** and **possessive pronouns** show to whom or to what, something belongs or is connected. The **possessive determiners** are *my, your, his, her, its, our* and *their*:

Is it okay to wear my trainers?

All of the students had done their homework.

The **possessive pronouns** are: *mine, yours, his, hers, ours* and *theirs*:

Is that last slice of pizza mine or yours?

Ours was the best score.

Possessive pronouns can also be used after *of*:

That song is an old favourite of mine.

Note that there is no apostrophe in the possessive pronouns *hers, ours, yours* and *theirs* or in the possessive determiner *its*:
The shark opened its jaws.

possibility *NOUN* **possibilities**
❶ being possible • *Is there any possibility you will change your mind?* ❷ something that may happen or be the case • *There are many possibilities.*

SPELLING

There is no **a** in **possibility**. Do not forget to double the **s**.

possible *ADJECTIVE*
that can exist, happen, be done or be used • *It's possible we may be late.*

possibly *ADVERB*
❶ in any way • *I can't possibly do it.*
❷ perhaps • *I'll get there at 6 o'clock or possibly earlier.*

possum *NOUN* **possums**
an opossum

post *NOUN* **posts**
❶ an upright piece of wood, concrete or metal fixed in the ground ❷ the starting point or finishing point of a race • *He was left at the post.* ❸ the collecting and delivering of letters and parcels ❹ letters and parcels sent or delivered ❺ a message sent to an Internet site; a piece of writing on a blog ❻ a position of paid employment; a job ❼ the place where someone is on duty • *a sentry post*

post *VERB* **posts, posting, posted**
❶ to put up a notice or poster to announce something ❷ to send a message to an Internet site; to display information online ❸ to put a letter or parcel into a postbox for collection ❹ to send someone to go and work somewhere; to place someone on duty • *She*

was posted to Washington for two years.
• We posted sentries.
➤ **keep someone posted** to keep someone informed

post- *PREFIX*
after (as in *post-war*)

postage *NOUN*
the charge for sending something by post

postage stamp *NOUN* **postage stamps**
a stamp for sticking on letters and parcels to be posted, showing the amount paid

postal *ADJECTIVE*
to do with or by the post • *the postal service*

postal order *NOUN* **postal orders**
(*British*) a document bought from a post office which can be sent by post and exchanged for money by the person receiving it

postbox *NOUN* **postboxes**
a box into which letters are put for collection

postcard *NOUN* **postcards**
a card for sending messages by post without an envelope

postcode *NOUN* **postcodes**
(*British*) a group of letters and numbers included in an address to help in sorting the post

poster *NOUN* **posters**
a large sheet of paper announcing or advertising something, for display in a public place

posterior *NOUN* **posteriors**
a person's bottom

posterity *NOUN*
future generations of people • *These letters and diaries should be preserved for posterity.*

postern *NOUN* **posterns**
a small entrance at the back or side of a fortress etc.

postgraduate *ADJECTIVE*
to do with studies carried on after taking a first university degree

postgraduate *NOUN* **postgraduates**
a person who continues studying or doing research after taking a first university degree

post-haste *ADVERB*
with great speed or haste • *He returned post-haste to France.*

posthumous (say **poss**-tew-mus) *ADJECTIVE*
coming or happening after a person's death

• *a posthumous award for bravery*
➤ **posthumously** *ADVERB*

postilion (say poss-**til**-yon) *NOUN* **postilions**
a person riding one of the horses pulling a carriage

postman *NOUN* **postmen**
(*British*) a person who delivers or collects post

postmark *NOUN* **postmarks**
an official mark put on something sent by post to show where and when it was posted

post-mortem *NOUN* **post-mortems**
an examination of a dead body to discover the cause of death **WORD ORIGIN** Latin, = after death

post office *NOUN* **post offices**
❶ a building or room where postal business is carried on ❷ the national organization responsible for postal services

postpone *VERB* **postpones, postponing, postponed**
to arrange for something to take place later than was originally planned • *They had to postpone their wedding.*
➤ **postponement** *NOUN*

postscript *NOUN* **postscripts**
something extra added at the end of a letter (after the writer's signature) or at the end of a book

postulate *VERB* **postulates, postulating, postulated**
to assume that something is true and use it in reasoning

posture *NOUN* **postures**
the position in which you hold your body when you stand, sit or walk • *Suddenly he relaxed his stiff posture and smiled.*

post-war *ADJECTIVE*
happening in the period after a war

posy *NOUN* **posies**
a small bunch of flowers

pot *NOUN* **pots**
❶ a deep round container ❷ a flowerpot
❸ (*informal*) the drug cannabis
➤ **go to pot** (*informal*) to lose quality or be ruined
➤ **pots of money** (*informal*) a lot of money
➤ **take pot luck** (*informal*) to take whatever happens to be available

pot *VERB* **pots, potting, potted**
❶ to pot a plant is to plant it in a flowerpot
❷ to pot a ball in a game such as snooker or pool is to knock it into a pocket

potash NOUN
potassium carbonate

potassium NOUN
a soft silvery-white metal substance that is essential for living things

potato NOUN potatoes
a round white vegetable with a brown or red skin that grows underground

potent (say **poh**-tent) ADJECTIVE
having great power or effect • *a potent drug*
➤ **potency** NOUN

potentate (say **poh**-ten-tayt) NOUN potentates
a powerful monarch or ruler

potential (say po-**ten**-shal) ADJECTIVE
capable of happening or being used or developed • *a potential winner*

potential NOUN
❶ the ability of a person or thing to develop or succeed in the future • *She has great potential as a sprinter.* ❷ the voltage between two points

potentially ADVERB
as a possibility in the future • *He is potentially one of our best players.*

pothole NOUN potholes
❶ a deep natural hole in the ground ❷ a hole in a road

potholing NOUN
exploring underground caves by climbing down potholes
➤ **potholer** NOUN

potion NOUN potions
a drink containing medicine or poison or having magical powers • *a love potion*

potpourri (say **poh**-poor-ee) NOUN potpourris
a scented mixture of dried petals and spices

pot shot NOUN pot shots
a shot aimed casually at something

potted ADJECTIVE
❶ shortened or abridged • *a potted account of the story* ❷ preserved in a pot • *potted shrimps*

potter NOUN potters
a person who makes pottery

potter VERB potters, pottering, pottered
to spend time doing little jobs in a relaxed or leisurely way • *I spent the afternoon pottering around in the garden.*

pottery NOUN potteries
❶ cups, plates, ornaments, etc. made of baked clay ❷ the craft of making these things ❸ a place where a potter works

potty ADJECTIVE (*British*) (*informal*)
mad or foolish

potty NOUN potties (*informal*)
a small bowl used by a young child instead of a toilet

pouch NOUN pouches
❶ a small bag ❷ a fold of skin in which a kangaroo etc. keeps its young ❸ something shaped like a bag

poultice NOUN poultices
a soft hot dressing put on a sore or inflamed place

poultry NOUN
chickens, geese, turkeys and other birds kept for their eggs and meat

pounce VERB pounces, pouncing, pounced
to jump or swoop down quickly on something and grab it • *The lion crouched, ready to pounce.*
➤ **pounce** NOUN

pound NOUN pounds
❶ a unit of money, in Britain equal to 100 pence ❷ a unit of weight equal to 16 ounces or about 454 grams ❸ a place where stray animals are taken ❹ a public enclosure for vehicles officially removed

pound VERB pounds, pounding, pounded
❶ to hit something repeatedly • *Waves pounded the rocks.* ❷ to run or go heavily • *He pounded down the stairs.* ❸ your heart pounds when it beats very fast and hard • *My heart was pounding with excitement.*

pour VERB pours, pouring, poured
❶ to make a liquid flow steadily out of a container ❷ to flow in a large amount • *Tears were pouring down her cheeks.* ❸ to rain heavily • *It poured all day.* ❹ to come or go in large amounts • *Letters of complaint poured in.*

> **SPELLING**
>
> Take care not to confuse with **pore over**, which means to study something with close attention.

pout VERB pouts, pouting, pouted
to push out your lips when you are annoyed or sulking
➤ **pout** NOUN

a b c d e f g h i j k l m n o p q r s t u v w x y z

poverty *NOUN*
❶ being poor ❷ a lack or scarcity • *a poverty of ideas*

POW *ABBREVIATION*
prisoner of war

powder *NOUN* powders
❶ a mass of fine dry particles of something ❷ make-up in the form of powder ❸ gunpowder • *Keep your powder dry.*

powder *VERB* powders, powdering, powdered
to put powder on something • *She powdered her face.*

powdered *ADJECTIVE*
dried and made into a powder • *powdered milk*

powder room *NOUN* powder rooms
a women's toilet in a public building

powdery *ADJECTIVE*
like powder • *powdery snow*

power *NOUN* powers
❶ strength or energy • *The power of the storm was frightening.* ❷ the ability to do something • *the power of speech* ❸ control over other people • *She seemed to have a strange power over him.* ❹ political control of a country • *The party has been in power for three years.* ❺ a powerful country, person or organization ❻ mechanical or electrical energy; the electricity supply • *There was a power failure after the storm.* ❼ (*in science*) the rate of doing work, measured in watts or horsepower ❽ (*in mathematics*) the product of a number multiplied by itself a given number of times • *The third power of 2 = 2 x 2 x 2 = 8.*

power *VERB* powers, powering, powered
to supply power to a vehicle or machine • *The aircraft is powered by a jet engine.* • *a solar-powered calculator*

powerboat *NOUN* powerboats
a powerful motor boat

powerful *ADJECTIVE*
❶ having great power, strength or influence • *one of the most powerful nations in the world* • *a powerful computer* ❷ having a strong effect • *a powerful speech*
➤ **powerfully** *ADVERB*

powerhouse *NOUN* powerhouses
a person or thing with great strength and energy

powerless *ADJECTIVE*
not able to act or control things • *He was powerless to stop them.*

power station *NOUN* power stations
a building where electricity is produced

pp. *ABBREVIATION*
pages

practicable *ADJECTIVE*
able to be done • *Your plan is simply not practicable.*

practical *ADJECTIVE*
❶ able to do or make useful things • *She is a very practical person.* ❷ likely to be useful or effective • *a practical invention* ❸ actually doing something, rather than just learning or thinking about it • *She has had practical experience.*
➤ **practicality** *NOUN*

practical *NOUN* practicals (*British*) a lesson or examination in which you actually do or make something rather than reading or writing about it • *a chemistry practical*

practical joke *NOUN* practical jokes
a trick played on someone

practically *ADVERB*
❶ almost • *I've practically finished.* ❷ in a practical way

practice *NOUN* practices
❶ doing something repeatedly in order to become better at it • *I must do my piano practice.* ❷ actually doing something rather than thinking or talking about it • *It's time to put this theory into practice.* ❸ the professional business of a doctor, dentist, lawyer, etc. ❹ a habit or custom • *It is his practice to work until midnight.*
➤ **out of practice** no longer skilful because you have not practised recently

> **SPELLING**
> Practice is a noun and practise is a verb:
> • *music practice* • *I need to practise more.*

practise *VERB* practises, practising, practised
❶ to do something repeatedly in order to become better at it ❷ to practise an activity or custom is to do it regularly • *She was accused of practising witchcraft.* ❸ to work as a doctor, lawyer or other professional person

> **SPELLING**
> Practise is a verb and practice is a noun:
> • *I need to practise more.* • *music practice*

practised *ADJECTIVE*
experienced or expert

practitioner *NOUN* **practitioners**
a professional worker, especially a doctor

prairie *NOUN* **prairies**
a large area of flat grass-covered land in North America

praise *VERB* **praises, praising, praised**
❶ to say that someone or something is very good or has done well ❷ to honour God in words

praise *NOUN*
words that praise someone or something

praiseworthy *ADJECTIVE*
deserving praise

pram *NOUN* **prams**
(*British*) a four-wheeled carriage for a baby, pushed by a person walking

prance *VERB* **prances, prancing, pranced**
to move about in a lively or happy way • *The lead singer was prancing around the stage.*

prank *NOUN* **pranks**
a trick played on someone for mischief; a practical joke
➤ **prankster** *NOUN*

prattle *VERB* **prattles, prattling, prattled**
to chatter like a young child
➤ **prattle** *NOUN*

prawn *NOUN* **prawns**
an edible shellfish like a large shrimp

pray *VERB* **prays, praying, prayed**
❶ to talk to God to give thanks or ask for help ❷ to hope very strongly for something • *We are praying for good weather.*

pray *ADVERB*
(*formal*) please • *Pray be seated.*

> **SPELLING**
> Be careful, this sounds the same as **prey**, which means an animal that is hunted or killed by another for food.

prayer *NOUN* **prayers**
praying; words used in praying

pre– *PREFIX*
before (as in *pre-war*)

preach *VERB* **preaches, preaching, preached**
to give a talk about religion or about right and wrong

preacher *NOUN* **preachers**
a person who preaches

preamble *NOUN* **preambles**
the introduction to a speech or book or document

pre–arranged *ADJECTIVE*
arranged beforehand

precarious (say pri-**kair**-ee-us) *ADJECTIVE*
not very safe or secure • *She was in a precarious position on the ledge.*
➤ **precariously** *ADVERB*

precaution *NOUN* **precautions**
something you do to prevent future trouble or danger
➤ **precautionary** *ADJECTIVE*

precede *VERB* **precedes, preceding, preceded**
to come or go before something else • *The film was preceded by a short cartoon.*

> **SPELLING**
> Take care not to confuse with **proceed**, which means to go forward or continue.

precedence (say **press**-i-dens) *NOUN*
the right of something to be put first because it is more important
➤ **take precedence** to be dealt with first because it is the most important thing

precedent (say **press**-i-dent) *NOUN* **precedents**
a previous case that is taken as an example or guide to be followed

precept (say **pree**-sept) *NOUN* **precepts**
a rule about how to behave or what to think; an instruction

precinct (say **pree**-sinkt) *NOUN* **precincts**
❶ a part of a town where traffic is not allowed • *a shopping precinct* ❷ the precincts of a place are the buildings and land around it

precious *ADJECTIVE*
❶ very valuable ❷ greatly loved

precious *ADVERB* (*informal*) very • *We have precious little time.*

precipice *NOUN* **precipices**
a very steep place, such as the face of a cliff

precipitate *VERB* **precipitates, precipitating, precipitated**
❶ to make something happen suddenly or soon • *The insult precipitated a quarrel.*
❷ to throw or send something down; to make something fall • *A shove in the back precipitated him into the room.*

precipitate *NOUN* **precipitates**
a solid substance that has been separated chemically from a solution

precipitate *ADJECTIVE*
hurried or hasty • *a precipitate departure*
➤ **precipitately** *ADVERB*

precipitation *NOUN*
the amount of rain, snow or hail that falls
during a period of time

precipitous *ADJECTIVE*
like a precipice; steep • *precipitous cliffs*
➤ **precipitously** *ADVERB*

precis (say **pray**-see) *NOUN* precis (say **pray**-seez)
a summary

precise *ADJECTIVE*
❶ clear and accurate • *I gave them precise
instructions.* ❷ exact • *At that precise
moment, the doorbell rang.*

precisely *ADVERB*
exactly • *She arrived at 10 o'clock precisely.*
• *What precisely do you mean?*

precision *NOUN*
being exact and accurate • *He drew the map
with great precision.*

preclude *VERB* precludes, precluding,
precluded
to prevent something from happening

precocious (say prik-**oh**-shus) *ADJECTIVE*
a precocious child is very advanced or
developed for their age (**WORD ORIGIN**) from
Latin *praecox* = ripe very early

preconceived *ADJECTIVE*
a preconceived idea is one you have before
you know all the facts that might affect it
➤ **preconception** *NOUN*

precursor *NOUN* precursors
something that was an earlier form of
something that came later; a forerunner

predator (say **pred**-a-ter) *NOUN* predators
an animal that hunts or preys upon others
➤ **predatory** *ADJECTIVE*

predecessor (say **pree**-dis-ess-er) *NOUN*
predecessors
an earlier person or thing, e.g. an ancestor or
the former holder of a job

predestined *ADJECTIVE*
certain to happen because it has been
decided by fate
➤ **predestination** *NOUN*

predicament (say prid-**ik**-a-ment) *NOUN*
predicaments
a difficult or unpleasant situation • *He was in
a dreadful predicament.*

predicate *NOUN* predicates
the part of a sentence that says something
about the subject, e.g. 'is short' in *Life is short.*

predict *VERB* predicts, predicting, predicted
to say what will happen in the future;
to foretell or prophesy a future event
• *Scientists try to predict when earthquakes
will happen.*

predictable *ADJECTIVE*
❶ able to be predicted • *a predictable result*
❷ always behaving in the same way • *I knew
you would say that – you're so predictable.*
➤ **predictably** *ADJECTIVE*

prediction *NOUN* predictions
saying what will happen; what someone
thinks will happen • *Her predictions kept
coming true.*

predominant *ADJECTIVE*
greatest in size or most noticeable or most
important • *The predominant colour was
blue.*
➤ **predominance** *NOUN*
➤ **predominantly** *ADVERB*

predominate *VERB* predominates,
predominating, predominated
to be the greatest in number or the most
important • *Girls predominate in our class.*

pre-eminent *ADJECTIVE*
better than all the others; outstanding
➤ **pre-eminently** *ADVERB*
➤ **pre-eminence** *NOUN*

pre-empt *VERB* pre-empts, pre-empting,
pre-empted
to take action to prevent or block something
➤ **pre-emptive** *ADJECTIVE*

preen *VERB* preens, preening, preened
a bird preens its feathers when it smooths
them with its beak
➤ **preen yourself** ❶ to smarten your
appearance ❷ to congratulate yourself

prefab *NOUN* prefabs (*informal*)
a prefabricated building

prefabricated *ADJECTIVE*
made in sections ready to be assembled on
a site

preface (say **pref**-as) *NOUN* prefaces
an introduction at the beginning of a book
or speech
➤ **preface** *VERB*

prefect *NOUN* prefects
❶ a senior pupil in a school, given authority

to help to keep order ❷ a regional official in France, Japan and other countries

prefer *VERB* **prefers, preferring, preferred**
to like one person or thing more than another
• *Would you prefer rice or pasta?*

preferable (say **pref**-er-a-bul) *ADJECTIVE*
something is preferable to something else when it is better or you like it more
➤ **preferably** *ADVERB*

preference *NOUN* **preferences**
a liking for one thing rather than another; something you prefer • *I have a slight preference for the red one.*

preferential (say pref-er-**en**-shal) *ADJECTIVE*
better than other people get • *preferential treatment*

preferment *NOUN*
promotion

prefix *NOUN* **prefixes**
a word or syllable joined to the front of a word to change or add to its meaning, as in *dis*order, *out*stretched, *un*happy

---
GRAMMAR

A **prefix** is a group of letters that can be added to the beginning of the base or root form of a word to change its meaning and form a new word (e.g. *anti*clockwise, *in*definite, *re*birth).

Some prefixes make words that are closely related to the original word. For example, *in-* and *un-* often make words opposite in meaning (e.g. *ineffective, unnatural*); *re-* often indicates a repeated action (e.g. *rebuild, remake*). *In-* sometimes changes to *il-* (e.g. *illegible*), *im-* (e.g. *impossible*) or *ir-* (e.g. *irresponsible*), depending on the letter that follows. Other prefixes (many of them based on Greek or Latin words) contain their own meaning, which they combine with that of the words they join; for example, *ecosystem, interface, multicultural, supermarket, transatlantic, ultraviolet*.

You sometimes need a hyphen after a prefix to make a special meaning clear (e.g. to *re-mark* an exam, to distinguish it from the word *remark*) or when the word after the prefix begins with a capital letter (e.g. *anti-British, pre-Victorian*).

---

pregnancy *NOUN* **pregnancies**
being pregnant

pregnant *ADJECTIVE*
❶ a woman is pregnant when she has a baby developing in the womb ❷ a pregnant pause or silence is one full of meaning or significance

prehensile *ADJECTIVE*
an animal's foot or tail is called prehensile when it is able to grasp things

prehistoric *ADJECTIVE*
belonging to very ancient times, before written records of events were made
➤ **prehistory** *NOUN*

prejudice *NOUN* **prejudices**
a strong unreasonable feeling of not liking or trusting someone
➤ **prejudiced** *ADJECTIVE*

prelate (say **prel**-at) *NOUN* **prelates**
an important member of the clergy

preliminary *ADJECTIVE*
coming before something and preparing for it
• *I'd like to make a few preliminary remarks.*

prelude *NOUN* **preludes**
❶ a thing that introduces or leads up to something else ❷ a short piece of music, especially one that introduces a longer piece

premature *ADJECTIVE*
too early; coming before the usual or proper time • *a premature baby*
➤ **prematurely** *ADVERB*

premeditated *ADJECTIVE*
planned beforehand • *a premeditated crime*

premier (say **prem**-ee-er) *ADJECTIVE*
best or most important

premier *NOUN* **premiers**
a prime minister or other head of government

premiere (say prem-**yair**) *NOUN* **premieres**
the first public performance of a play or film

premise (say **prem**-iss) *NOUN* **premises**
a statement used as the basis for a piece of reasoning

premises *PLURAL NOUN*
a building and its grounds

premium *NOUN* **premiums**
❶ an amount of money paid regularly to an insurance company ❷ an extra charge or payment
➤ **at a premium** ❶ above the normal price ❷ in demand but scarce

Premium Bond *NOUN* Premium Bonds
a savings certificate that gives the person
who holds it a chance to win a prize of money

premonition *NOUN* premonitions
a feeling that something bad is about to
happen

preoccupation *NOUN* preoccupations
something you think or worry about all the
time

preoccupied *ADJECTIVE*
thinking or worrying about something so
much that you cannot pay attention to
anything else

preparation *NOUN* preparations
❶ getting something ready • *She packed
her bags in preparation for the journey.*
❷ something done in order to get ready for
an event or activity • *We were making last-
minute preparations.* ❸ a mixture to be used
as a medicine or cosmetic

preparatory *ADJECTIVE*
preparing for something • *preparatory
sketches*

preparatory school *NOUN* preparatory
schools
a school that prepares pupils for a higher
school

prepare *VERB* prepares, preparing, prepared
to get ready or to make something ready
• *They are preparing to launch the rocket.*
• *He was in the kitchen preparing lunch.*

prepared *ADJECTIVE*
ready and able to deal with something • *She
felt well prepared for the task ahead.*
➤ **be prepared to do something** to be ready
and willing to do something

preposition *NOUN* prepositions
a word used with a noun or pronoun to show
place, position, time or means, e.g. *at* home,
in the hall, *on* Sunday, *by* train

GRAMMAR

Prepositions show how a noun, pronoun
or noun phrase relates to the other words
in a sentence or clause. They can show:

**the position or direction of a person or
thing:**

*The spider scurried <u>along</u> the wall, <u>across</u>
the carpet, <u>through</u> the doorway, <u>down</u>
the stairs, <u>past</u> the cat, up the curtain,
<u>out</u> of the window, and <u>into</u> the garden.*

the time something happens or lasts:

*Can you come <u>to</u> my house <u>on</u> Tuesday
<u>around</u> five o'clock?*

*We were <u>in</u> Athens <u>in</u> August, <u>during</u> the
Olympics.*

**the connection between people or
things:**

*My sister is always grumbling <u>about</u>
something.*

*Does this jacket go better <u>with</u> the red
shirt or the blue one?*

You also use prepositions with verbs to
form special meanings, e.g. *deal <u>with</u>, look
<u>after</u>,* and *run <u>into</u>.*

Some words can be either prepositions or
adverbs, depending on how they are used.
In the sentence *We could hear giggling
<u>outside</u> the classroom* the word *<u>outside</u>* is
a preposition as it is used before the noun
phrase *<u>the classroom</u>.* In the sentence *We
ran outside* the word *<u>outside</u>* is an adverb
as it is not followed by a noun, pronoun or
noun phrase.

prepossessing *ADJECTIVE*
attractive • *Its appearance is not very
prepossessing.*

preposterous *ADJECTIVE*
completely absurd or ridiculous • *What a
preposterous idea!* **WORD ORIGIN** from Latin
praeposterus = back to front, from *prae* =
before + *posterus* = behind

prerogative *NOUN* prerogatives
a right or privilege that belongs to one person
or group

Presbyterian (say prez-bit-**eer**-ee-an) *NOUN*
Presbyterians
a member of a Christian Church governed by
elders who are all of equal rank, especially the
national Church of Scotland

pre-school *ADJECTIVE*
to do with the time before a child is old
enough to go to school

prescribe *VERB* prescribes, prescribing,
prescribed
❶ to advise a person to use a particular
medicine or treatment ❷ to say what should
be done

SPELLING

Take care not to confuse with **proscribe**,
which means to forbid something by law.

prescription *NOUN* prescriptions
a doctor's written order for a medicine or the medicine itself

presence *NOUN*
❶ being present in a place • *Your presence is required.* ❷ a person's impressive appearance or manner
➤ **in someone's presence** with someone, in the same place as they are • *You must sign the document in the presence of two witnesses.*

presence of mind *NOUN*
the ability to act quickly and sensibly in an emergency

present (say **prez**-ent) *ADJECTIVE*
❶ in a particular place • *No one else was present.* ❷ belonging or referring to what is happening now; existing now • *the present Queen*

present (say **prez**-ent) *NOUN* presents
❶ the time now • *The head is away at present.* ❷ (*in grammar*) the tense of a verb used to describe an action that is happening now, e.g. *likes* in *He likes swimming.* ❸ something you give or receive as a gift

present (say pri-**zent**) *VERB* presents, presenting, presented
❶ to give something, especially with a ceremony • *Who is going to present the prizes?* ❷ to introduce someone to another person; to introduce a radio or television programme to an audience ❸ to put on a play or other entertainment ❹ to show or reveal something ❺ to cause or provide something • *Translating a poem presents a number of problems.*

presentable *ADJECTIVE*
fit to be presented to other people; looking good

presentation *NOUN* presentations
❶ a talk showing or demonstrating something ❷ a ceremony in which someone is given a gift or prize ❸ the way in which work is written or set out

presenter *NOUN* presenters
(*British*) someone who introduces the different parts of a radio or television programme

presentiment *NOUN* presentiments
a feeling that something bad is about to happen

presently *ADVERB*
❶ soon; after a short time • *I shall be with*

you presently. ❷ now • *the person who is presently in charge*

preservative *NOUN* preservatives
a substance added to food to preserve it

preserve *VERB* preserves, preserving, preserved
to keep something safe or in good condition • *The wall paintings have been beautifully preserved.*
➤ **preserver** *NOUN*
➤ **preservation** *NOUN*

preserve *NOUN* preserves
❶ jam made with preserved fruit ❷ an activity that belongs to a particular person or group • *Football is no longer the preserve of men.*

preside *VERB* presides, presiding, presided
to be in charge of a meeting or other occasion • *The mayor presided over the opening ceremony.*

presidency *NOUN* presidencies
the job of being president or the period of time that someone is president

president *NOUN* presidents
❶ the person in charge of a club, society or council etc. ❷ the head of a country that is a republic
➤ **presidential** *ADJECTIVE*

press *VERB* presses, pressing, pressed
❶ to put weight or force steadily on something; to squeeze something ❷ to make clothes smooth by ironing them ❸ to urge someone or make demands of them • *We need to press them for an answer.*

press *NOUN* presses
❶ pushing something firmly • *Give the bell another press.* ❷ a device for pressing things • *a trouser press* ❸ a machine for printing things ❹ a firm that prints or publishes books or magazines • *Oxford University Press* ❺ newspapers and journalists • *The story has been reported in the press.*

press conference *NOUN* press conferences
a meeting when a famous or important person answers questions from a group of journalists

press-gang *NOUN* press-gangs (*historical*)
a group of men whose job was to force people to serve in the army or navy

pressing *ADJECTIVE*
needing immediate action; urgent • *We have a pressing need for volunteers.*

press–up *NOUN* **press-ups**
(*British*) an exercise in which you lie face downwards and press down with your hands to lift your body

pressure *NOUN* **pressures**
❶ continuous pressing • *Apply pressure to the cut to stop it bleeding.* ❷ the force with which something presses ❸ the force of the atmosphere on the earth's surface • *a band of high pressure* ❹ an influence that persuades or forces you to do something • *The press is putting pressure on her to resign.*

pressure cooker *NOUN* **pressure cookers**
a large air-tight pan used for cooking food quickly under steam pressure

pressure group *NOUN* **pressure groups**
an organized group that tries to influence public policy on a particular issue

pressurize (also **pressurise**) *VERB* **pressurizes, pressurizing, pressurized**
❶ to keep a compartment at the same air pressure all the time ❷ to try to force a person to do something
➤ **pressurization** *NOUN*

prestige (say pres-**teej**) *NOUN*
great respect that something has gained for being important, successful or of high quality

prestigious *ADJECTIVE*
respected for being important, successful or of high quality • *a prestigious prize*

presumably *ADVERB*
I imagine; I suppose • *Presumably the library will have a copy of the book.*

presume *VERB* **presumes, presuming, presumed**
❶ to suppose something or assume that it is true • *I presumed that she was dead.* ❷ to dare to do something which you have no right to do • *I wouldn't presume to advise you.*
➤ **presumption** *NOUN*

presumptuous *ADJECTIVE*
too bold or confident

pretence *NOUN* **pretences**
an attempt to pretend that something is true • *Their friendliness was just a pretence.*
➤ **false pretences** pretending to be something that you are not, in order to deceive people • *You've invited me here under false pretences.*

pretend *VERB* **pretends, pretending, pretended**
❶ to behave as if something is true or real when you know that it is not, in order to deceive people • *She pretended not to notice me.* ❷ to imagine that something is true as part of a game • *The children were under the bed pretending to be snakes.* ❸ to claim that something is the case • *I cannot pretend that this is going to be easy.*

pretender *NOUN* **pretenders**
a person who claims a throne or title • *The son of King James II was known as the Old Pretender.*

pretension *NOUN* **pretensions**
❶ a doubtful claim • *I have no pretensions to be a great singer.* ❷ pretentious or showy behaviour

pretentious *ADJECTIVE*
trying to impress people by appearing more serious or important than you really are
➤ **pretentiously** *ADVERB*
➤ **pretentiousness** *NOUN*

pretext *NOUN* **pretexts**
a reason put forward to conceal the true reason

pretty *ADJECTIVE* **prettier, prettiest**
attractive in a delicate way
➤ **prettily** *ADVERB*
➤ **prettiness** *NOUN*

pretty *ADVERB*
quite; fairly • *It's pretty cold outside.*

prevail *VERB* **prevails, prevailing, prevailed**
❶ to be the most frequent or general • *The prevailing view is that we were wrong.* ❷ to be successful or victorious

prevalent (say **prev**-a-lent) *ADJECTIVE*
most frequent or common; widespread
➤ **prevalence** *NOUN*

prevaricate *VERB* **prevaricates, prevaricating, prevaricated**
to say something that is not actually a lie but is evasive or misleading
➤ **prevarication** *NOUN*

prevent *VERB* **prevents, preventing, prevented**
❶ to stop something from happening • *The accident could not have been prevented.* ❷ to stop a person from doing something • *You cannot prevent me from going.*
➤ **preventable** *ADJECTIVE*
➤ **prevention** *NOUN*

preventive, preventative *ADJECTIVE*
intended to help prevent something
• *preventive medicine*

preview *NOUN* previews
a showing of a film or play before it is shown to the general public

previous *ADJECTIVE*
coming before this; preceding • *There had been a storm the previous night.*

previously *ADVERB*
before the present time; earlier • *The building had previously been used as a hotel.*

prey (say pray) *NOUN*
an animal that is hunted or killed by another for food

prey *VERB* preys, preying, preyed
➤ **prey on something** to hunt and kill an animal for food • *Owls prey on mice and other small animals.*
➤ **prey on your mind** to worry you constantly • *The accident has been preying on his mind.*

SPELLING
Be careful, this sounds the same as **pray**, which means to talk to God or to wish very strongly for something.

price *NOUN* prices
❶ the amount of money for which something is bought or sold ❷ what you have to give or do in order to achieve something • *An apology seemed a small price to pay for ending the quarrel.*

price *VERB* prices, pricing, priced
to decide the price of something

priceless *ADJECTIVE*
❶ very valuable ❷ (*informal*) very amusing

prick *VERB* pricks, pricking, pricked
❶ to make a tiny hole in something ❷ to hurt someone with a pin or needle etc.
➤ **prick up your ears** to start listening suddenly

prick *NOUN* pricks
a pricking feeling

prickle *NOUN* prickles
❶ a small thorn ❷ a sharp spine on a hedgehog or cactus etc. ❸ a feeling that a lot of small sharp points are sticking into your skin

prickle *VERB* prickles, prickling, prickled
to feel as though a lot of small sharp points are sticking into your skin; to cause this feeling • *She felt her skin prickle with fear.*

prickly *ADJECTIVE*
❶ covered in prickles or feeling like prickles ❷ irritable or bad-tempered

pride *NOUN* prides
❶ a feeling of deep pleasure or satisfaction when you have done something well • *My heart swelled with pride.* ❷ something that makes you feel proud • *This autograph is the pride of my collection.* ❸ dignity or self-respect ❹ too high an opinion of yourself ❺ a group of lions
➤ **pride of place** the most important or most honoured position

pride *VERB* prides, priding, prided
➤ **pride yourself on something** to be proud of something • *He prided himself on his logical mind.*

priest *NOUN* priests
❶ a member of the clergy in certain Christian Churches ❷ a person who performs religious ceremonies in a non-Christian religion
➤ **priesthood** *NOUN*
➤ **priestly** *ADJECTIVE*

priestess *NOUN* priestesses
a female priest in a non-Christian religion

prig *NOUN* prigs
a self-righteous person
➤ **priggish** *ADJECTIVE*

prim *ADJECTIVE* primmer, primmest
always behaving in a formal and correct manner and easily shocked by anything rude
➤ **primly** *ADVERB*
➤ **primness** *NOUN*

prima donna (say **preem**-a) *NOUN* prima donnas
the chief female singer in an opera company

primarily (say **pry**-mer-il-ee or pry-**me**-ril-ee) *ADVERB*
more than anything else; mainly • *The programme is aimed primarily at teenagers.*

primary *ADJECTIVE*
first or most important. Compare with **secondary**.

primary colour *NOUN* primary colours
one of the colours from which all others can be made by mixing (red, yellow and blue for paint; red, green and violet for light)

primary school *NOUN* primary schools
(*British*) a school for the first stage of a child's education

primate (say **pry**-mat) *NOUN* primates
❶ an animal of the group that includes human beings, apes and monkeys ❷ an archbishop

a b c d e f g h i j k l m n o p q r s t u v w x y z

prime *ADJECTIVE*
❶ chief or most important • *The weather was the prime cause of the accident.* ❷ of the best quality • *prime beef*

prime *NOUN*
the best time or stage of something • *He was in the prime of his life.*

prime *VERB* **primes, priming, primed**
❶ to prepare something for use or action • *The cannon was primed and loaded.* ❷ to put a coat of liquid on something to prepare it for painting ❸ to give someone information in order to prepare them for something

prime minister *NOUN* **prime ministers**
the leader of a government

prime number *NOUN* **prime numbers**
a number (e.g. 2, 3, 5, 7, 11) that can be divided exactly only by itself and one

primer *NOUN* **primers**
❶ a liquid for priming a surface ❷ a textbook dealing with the first or simplest stages of a subject

primeval (say pry-**mee**-val) *ADJECTIVE*
belonging to the earliest times of the world • *a primeval forest*

primitive *ADJECTIVE*
❶ at an early stage of civilization • *Primitive humans were hunters rather than farmers.* ❷ at an early stage of development; not complicated or sophisticated • *primitive technology*

primordial *ADJECTIVE*
belonging to the earliest times of the world; primeval

primrose *NOUN* **primroses**
a pale-yellow flower that blooms in spring

prince *NOUN* **princes**
❶ the son of a king or queen ❷ a man or boy in a royal family

princely *ADJECTIVE*
❶ to do with or like a prince ❷ large, generous or splendid • *a princely gift*

princess *NOUN* **princesses**
❶ the daughter of a king or queen ❷ a woman or girl in a royal family ❸ the wife of a prince

principal *ADJECTIVE*
chief or most important • *the principal towns of the region*

principal *NOUN* **principals**
the head of a college or school

SPELLING
Take care not to confuse with **principle**, which means a general truth, belief or rule.

principality *NOUN* **principalities**
a country ruled by a prince
➤ the Principality Wales

principally *ADVERB*
chiefly or mainly • *The book is aimed principally at beginners.*

principle *NOUN* **principles**
❶ a general truth, belief or rule • *She taught me the principles of geometry.* ❷ a rule of conduct based on what a person believes is right • *Cheating is against his principles.*
➤ **in principle** in general, not in details • *I agree with your plan in principle.*
➤ **on principle** because of your principles of behaviour

SPELLING
Take care not to confuse with **principal**, which means chief or most important.

print *VERB* **prints, printing, printed**
❶ to put words or pictures on paper by using a machine ❷ to write with letters that are not joined together • *Print your name clearly at the top of the page.* ❸ to press a mark or design on a surface ❹ to make a picture from the negative of a photograph

print *NOUN* **prints**
❶ printed lettering or words ❷ a mark made by something pressing on a surface • *Her thumb left a print on the glass.* ❸ a printed picture, photograph or design
➤ **in print** a book is in print when it is available from the publisher
➤ **out of print** a book is out of print when it is no longer available from the publisher

printed circuit *NOUN* **printed circuits**
an electric circuit made by pressing thin metal strips onto a board

printer *NOUN* **printers**
❶ a machine that prints on paper from data in a computer ❷ someone who prints books or newspapers

printout *NOUN* **printouts**
information produced in printed form by a computer

prior *ADJECTIVE*
coming before or earlier • *a prior*

arrangement
➤ **prior to** before • *She made a phone call just prior to her departure.*

prior *NOUN* **priors**
a monk who is the head of a religious house or order
➤ **prioress** *NOUN*

prioritize (also **prioritise**) *VERB* **prioritizes, prioritizing, prioritized**
to put tasks in order of importance, so that you can deal with the most important first

priority *NOUN* **priorities**
❶ something that is more urgent or important than other things and needs to be dealt with first • *Safety is a priority.* ❷ the right to go first or be dealt with before other things • *Emergency cases take priority over other patients in hospital.*

priory *NOUN* **priories**
a religious house governed by a prior or prioress

prise *VERB* **prises, prising, prised**
to force or lever something out or open • *He prised open the lid with a screwdriver.*

prism (say prizm) *NOUN* **prisms**
❶ (*in mathematics*) a solid shape with ends that are triangles or polygons which are equal and parallel ❷ a glass prism that breaks up light into the colours of the rainbow
➤ **prismatic** *ADJECTIVE*

prison *NOUN* **prisons**
a place where criminals are kept as a punishment

prisoner *NOUN* **prisoners**
❶ a person kept in prison ❷ a person who has been captured and kept somewhere

prisoner of war *NOUN* **prisoners of war**
a person captured and imprisoned by the enemy in a war

pristine *ADJECTIVE*
in its original condition; unspoilt • *a pristine white shirt*

privacy (say **priv**-a-see) *NOUN*
being able to be alone without other people watching you or knowing what you are doing • *Our new garden fence will give us more privacy.*

private *ADJECTIVE*
❶ belonging to a particular person or group • *private property* ❷ meant to be kept secret; confidential • *private talks* ❸ quiet and secluded ❹ not holding public office • *a*

private citizen ❺ independent or commercial; not run by the government • *private medicine* • *a private detective*
➤ **privately** *ADVERB*
➤ **in private** where only particular people can see or hear; not in public

private *NOUN* **privates**
a soldier of the lowest rank

privation *NOUN* **privations**
loss or lack of something; lack of necessities

privatize (also **privatise**) *VERB* **privatizes, privatizing, privatized**
to transfer the running of a business or industry from the state to private owners
➤ **privatization** *NOUN*

privet *NOUN* **privets**
an evergreen shrub with small leaves, used to make hedges

privilege *NOUN* **privileges**
a special right, advantage or opportunity given to one person or group • *It was a great privilege to hear her sing.*

privileged *ADJECTIVE*
having an advantage or opportunity that most people do not have • *I feel privileged to be a member of this team.*

privy *ADJECTIVE*
➤ **be privy to something** to be allowed to know about something secret • *She was not privy to their plans.*

privy *NOUN* **privies** (*old use*) an outside toilet

Privy Council *NOUN*
(in the UK) a group of distinguished people who advise the sovereign

prize *NOUN* **prizes**
❶ an award given to someone who wins a game or competition or who does very good work ❷ something of great value that is worth trying to obtain

prize *VERB* **prizes, prizing, prized**
to value something greatly • *These horses were highly prized.*

SPELLING
Choose the right word! A **prize** (noun) is something that you win in a competition. To **prize** (verb) something means to value it highly. To **prise** (verb) something open means to open it using force.

pro *NOUN* **pros**
(*informal*) a professional
➤ **pros and cons** reasons for and against something

a b c d e f g h i j k l m n o **p** q r s t u v w x y z

pro- *PREFIX*
in favour of or supporting something (as in *pro-British*)

probability *NOUN* **probabilities**
❶ how likely it is that something will happen • *There is a high probability of more snow.*
❷ something that is likely to happen

probable *ADJECTIVE*
likely to happen or be true

probably *ADVERB*
almost certainly • *You're probably right.*

probation *NOUN*
a period of time at the start of a new job when a person is tested to see if they are suitable
➤ **probationary** *ADJECTIVE*
➤ **on probation** being supervised by a probation officer instead of being sent to prison

probation officer *NOUN* **probation officers**
an official who supervises the behaviour of a convicted criminal who is not in prison

probe *NOUN* **probes**
❶ a long thin instrument used to look closely at something such as a wound ❷ an unmanned spacecraft used for exploring ❸ an investigation

probe *VERB* **probes, probing, probed**
❶ to ask questions in order to find out hidden information ❷ to explore or look closely at something, especially with a probe

probity (say **proh**-bit-ee) *NOUN*
honesty or integrity

problem *NOUN* **problems**
❶ something that causes trouble or is difficult to deal with ❷ a question that you have to solve by thinking about it
➤ **problematic** ➤ **problematical** *ADJECTIVE*

proboscis (say pro-**boss**-iss) *NOUN* **proboscises**
❶ a long flexible snout ❷ an insect's long mouthpart

procedure *NOUN* **procedures**
a fixed or special way of doing something • *Printing out the file is a simple procedure.*

proceed *VERB* **proceeds, proceeding, proceeded**
❶ to go forward or onward ❷ to continue; to go on to do something • *She proceeded to explain the plan.*

> SPELLING
>
> Take care not to confuse with **precede**, which means to come before something else.

proceedings *PLURAL NOUN*
❶ things that happen, especially at a formal meeting or ceremony ❷ a lawsuit

proceeds *PLURAL NOUN*
the money made from a sale or event

process (say proh-sess) *NOUN* **processes**
a series of actions for making or doing something
➤ **in the process of** in the course of doing something

process (say proh-sess) *VERB* **processes, processing, processed**
to put something through a manufacturing or other process • *processed cheese*

process (say pro-**sess**) *VERB* **processes, processing, processed**
to go in procession

procession *NOUN* **processions**
a number of people or vehicles moving steadily forward following each other

processor *NOUN* **processors**
❶ a machine that processes things ❷ the part of a computer that controls all its operations

proclaim *VERB* **proclaims, proclaiming, proclaimed**
to announce something officially or publicly

proclamation *NOUN* **proclamations**
a public or official announcement

procrastinate *VERB* **procrastinates, procrastinating, procrastinated**
to put off doing something
➤ **procrastination** *NOUN*
➤ **procrastinator** *NOUN*

procreate *VERB* **procreates, procreating, procreated**
to produce offspring by the natural process of reproduction
➤ **procreation** *NOUN*

procure *VERB* **procures, procuring, procured**
to obtain or acquire something
➤ **procurement** *NOUN*

prod *VERB* **prods, prodding, prodded**
❶ to poke something or someone with your finger or a pointed object ❷ to encourage or remind someone to do something
➤ **prod** *NOUN*

prodigal *ADJECTIVE*
wasteful or extravagant
➤ **prodigality** *NOUN*

prodigious *ADJECTIVE*
remarkably large or impressive • *a prodigious*

achievement
➤ **prodigiously** *ADVERB*

prodigy *NOUN* **prodigies**
❶ a child or young person with wonderful abilities ❷ a wonderful thing

produce (say pro-**dewss**) *VERB* **produces, producing, produced**
❶ to make or create something; to bring something into existence ❷ to bring something out so that it can be seen ❸ to organize the performance of a play, making of a film, etc. ❹ to extend a line further • *Produce the base of the triangle.*

produce (say **prod**-yewss) *NOUN*
things that have been produced or grown, especially by farmers

producer *NOUN* **producers**
❶ a person, company or country that makes or grows something ❷ someone who produces a play, film, etc.

product *NOUN* **products**
❶ something made or produced for sale ❷ the result of multiplying two numbers. Compare with **quotient**.

production *NOUN* **productions**
❶ the process of making or creating something, especially in large quantities ❷ the amount produced • *Oil production increased last year.* ❸ a version of a play, opera or other show

productive *ADJECTIVE*
❶ producing a lot of things • *a productive factory* ❷ producing good results; useful • *a productive discussion*
➤ **productivity** *NOUN*

profane *ADJECTIVE*
showing disrespect for religion; blasphemous

profane *VERB* **profanes, profaning, profaned**
to treat something, especially religion, with disrespect

profanity *NOUN* **profanities**
words or language that show disrespect for religion

profess *VERB* **professes, professing, professed**
❶ to claim to have or do something • *I don't profess to be an expert on the subject.* ❷ to declare or express something • *He professed his admiration for their work.*

profession *NOUN* **professions**
❶ an occupation that needs special education and training, such as medicine or law ❷ a

declaration • *They made professions of loyalty.*

professional *ADJECTIVE*
❶ to do with a profession ❷ doing a certain kind of work as a full-time job for payment, not as an amateur • *a professional footballer* ❸ done with a high standard of skill
➤ **professionally** *ADVERB*

professional *NOUN* **professionals**
❶ a person who has been trained in a profession ❷ a person who does something to earn money, not as an amateur

professor *NOUN* **professors**
a university teacher of the highest rank

> **SPELLING**
> There is one f and a double s in **professor**.

proffer *VERB* **proffers, proffering, proffered**
to offer something • *'How are you?' he said, proffering his hand.*

proficient *ADJECTIVE*
able to do something well because of training or practice; skilled • *She is proficient in French.*
➤ **proficiency** *NOUN*

profile *NOUN* **profiles**
❶ a side view of a person's face ❷ a short description of a person's character or career
➤ **keep a low profile** to try to avoid being noticed

profit *NOUN* **profits**
❶ the extra money obtained by selling something for more than it cost to buy or make ❷ an advantage gained by doing something

profit *VERB* **profits, profiting, profited**
to gain an advantage or benefit from something

profitable *ADJECTIVE*
making a profit
➤ **profitably** *ADVERB*

profligate *ADJECTIVE*
wasteful and extravagant
➤ **profligacy** *NOUN*

profound *ADJECTIVE*
❶ very deep or intense • *His death had a profound effect on them all.* ❷ showing or needing great knowledge, understanding or thought • *The poem she wrote was quite profound.*
➤ **profoundly** *ADVERB*

a b c d e f g h i j k l m n o **p** q r s t u v w x y z

profuse *ADJECTIVE*
given or produced in large amounts • *profuse apologies*
➤ **profusely** *ADVERB*

profusion *NOUN*
a very large quantity of something • *Wild flowers grew in profusion in the fields.*

progeny (say **proj**-in-ee) *NOUN*
offspring or descendants

prognosis (say prog-**noh**-sis) *NOUN* **prognoses**
a forecast or prediction, especially about how a disease will develop

program *NOUN* **programs**
a series of coded instructions for a computer to carry out

program *VERB* **programs, programming, programmed**
to put instructions into a computer by means of a program **(WORD ORIGIN)** the American spelling of **programme**, used when you are talking about computers

programme *NOUN* **programmes**
❶ a show, play or talk on radio or television ❷ a list of planned events ❸ a leaflet or pamphlet giving details of a play, concert, football match, etc.

programmer *NOUN* **programmers**
a person whose job is to write computer programs

progress (say **proh**-gress) *NOUN*
❶ forward movement • *The procession made slow progress.* ❷ development or improvement • *He was making progress in his research.*
➤ **in progress** taking place • *There seemed to be a feast in progress.*

progress (say pro-**gress**) *VERB* **progresses, progressing, progressed**
❶ to move forward or continue • *She became more and more tired as the evening progressed.* ❷ to develop or improve • *Medical knowledge has progressed steadily in the last twenty years.*
➤ **progression** *NOUN*

progressive *ADJECTIVE*
❶ moving forward or developing steadily ❷ in favour of political or social reforms ❸ a progressive disease is one that becomes gradually more severe
➤ **progressively** *ADVERB*

prohibit *VERB* **prohibits, prohibiting, prohibited**
to forbid or ban something • *Smoking is prohibited.*
➤ **prohibition** *NOUN*

prohibitive *ADJECTIVE*
prices and costs are prohibitive when they are too high for most people to be able to afford
➤ **prohibitively** *ADVERB*

project (say **proj**-ekt) *NOUN* **projects**
❶ the task of finding out as much as you can about something and writing about it ❷ a plan or scheme • *a building project*

project (say pro-**jekt**) *VERB* **projects, projecting, projected**
❶ to stick out • *Oars projected from the sides of the ship.* ❷ to show a film or picture on a screen ❸ to project your voice is to speak loudly and clearly so that it carries a long way ❹ to give people a particular impression • *He likes to project an image of absent-minded brilliance.*

projectile *NOUN* **projectiles**
something fired from a gun or thrown; a missile

projection *NOUN* **projections**
❶ a part of something that sticks out ❷ showing a film or picture on a screen with a projector

projectionist *NOUN* **projectionists**
a person who works a projector

projector *NOUN* **projectors**
a machine for showing films or photographs on a screen

proletariat (say proh-lit-**air**-ee-at) *NOUN*
working people

prolific *ADJECTIVE*
producing a lot • *a prolific author*

prologue (say **proh**-log) *NOUN* **prologues**
an introduction to a poem, play or story

prolong *VERB* **prolongs, prolonging, prolonged**
to make something last longer • *They decided to prolong their visit by a few more days.*

prolonged *ADJECTIVE*
continuing for a long time • *a prolonged silence*

prom *NOUN* **proms** (*informal*)
❶ a formal dance for secondary school students ❷ a promenade ❸ a promenade concert

promenade (say prom-in-**ahd**) *NOUN* **promenades**
❶ a place suitable for walking, especially beside the seashore ❷ a leisurely walk

promenade *VERB* promenades, promenading, promenaded
to take a leisurely walk

promenade concert promenade concerts
a concert where part of the audience stands in an area without seating

prominence *NOUN*
being important or well known • *He first came to prominence two years ago.*

prominent *ADJECTIVE*
❶ easy to see or notice • *The house stood in a prominent position.* ❷ sticking out • *She had a long nose and prominent teeth.* ❸ important • *He plays a prominent part in the story.*
➤ **prominently** *ADVERB*

promiscuous *ADJECTIVE*
❶ having many casual sexual relationships ❷ indiscriminate or casual
➤ **promiscuously** *ADVERB*
➤ **promiscuity** *NOUN*

promise *NOUN* promises
❶ a statement that you will definitely do or not do something ❷ signs of future success or good results • *His work shows promise.*

promise *VERB* promises, promising, promised
to make a promise

promising *ADJECTIVE*
likely to be good or successful • *a promising pianist*

promontory *NOUN* promontories
a piece of high land that sticks out into a sea or lake

promote *VERB* promotes, promoting, promoted
❶ to move a person to a more senior or more important job or position ❷ a sports team is promoted when it moves to a higher division or league ❸ to help the progress of something • *He has done much to promote the cause of peace.* ❹ to publicize or advertise a product in order to sell it
➤ **promoter** *NOUN*

promotion *NOUN* promotions
❶ a move to a higher position or more important job ❷ when a sports team moves to a higher division or league ❸ a piece of publicity or advertising ❹ helping the progress of something

prompt *ADJECTIVE*
❶ without delay • *a prompt reply* ❷ punctual
➤ **promptness** *NOUN*

prompt *ADVERB* (*British*) exactly at that time
• *I'll pick you up at 7.20 prompt.*

prompt *VERB* prompts, prompting, prompted
❶ to cause or encourage a person to do something • *What prompted you to start writing the blog?* ❷ to remind an actor or speaker of words when they have forgotten them

promptly *ADVERB*
❶ without delay; immediately • *When I told her she promptly burst into tears.* ❷ punctually • *They arrived promptly at 8 o'clock.*

prone *ADJECTIVE*
lying face downwards
➤ **be prone to something** to be likely to do or suffer from something • *He is prone to jealousy.*

prong *NOUN* prongs
one of the spikes on a fork
➤ **pronged** *ADJECTIVE*

pronoun *NOUN* pronouns
a word used instead of a noun: **demonstrative pronouns** are *this, that, these, those*; **interrogative pronouns** are *who?, what?, which?*, etc.; **personal pronouns** are *I, me, we, us, you, he, him, she, her, it, they, them*, etc.; **possessive pronouns** are *mine, yours, theirs*, etc.; **reflexive pronouns** are *myself, yourself*, etc.; **relative pronouns** are *who, what, which, that*, etc.

GRAMMAR

Pronouns replace a noun or noun phrase in a sentence or clause, and help to avoid having to repeat words. There are several types of pronoun:

Personal pronouns replace the name of a person or thing. *I, you, he, she, it, we* and *they* are used when the pronoun is the subject of the clause; *me, you, him, her, it, us,* and *them*, are used when the pronoun is the object: *Zoe and Bill are coming to the concert. She's got a ticket, but he hasn't. The guards were following us and we were unable to shake them off.*

Reflexive pronouns (*myself, yourself, himself, herself, itself, ourselves, yourselves* and *themselves*) are used when the object of the verb is the same as the subject of the verb: *Most baby birds are unable to feed themselves.* They are also used after a preposition: *I wanted to see for myself what all the fuss was about.*

A
B
C
D
E
F
G
H
I
J
K
L
M
N
O
P
Q
R
S
T
U
V
W
X
Y
Z

Relative pronouns (*what, who, whom, whose, which* and *that*) introduce a clause which gives more information about a noun, e.g. *the artist who painted this portrait; the song that I love.*

Interrogative pronouns (*what?, who?, whom?, whose?*) are used to form questions e.g. *What is happening? Who wants some ice cream?*

Demonstrative pronouns (*this, that, these* and *those*) are used to identify or indicate a particular person or thing, or a particular time or situation, e.g. *These are my glasses, and those are yours; This has been a hectic week.*

pronounce *VERB* pronounces, pronouncing, pronounced
❶ to say a sound or word in a particular way • *'Two' and 'too' are pronounced the same* ❷ to declare something formally • *I now pronounce you man and wife.*

pronounced *ADJECTIVE*
very noticeable • *This street has a pronounced slope.*

pronouncement *NOUN* pronouncements
a formal public statement

pronunciation *NOUN* pronunciations
the way a word is pronounced

SPELLING
Note the spelling of this word; it should not be written or spoken as 'pronounciation'.

proof *NOUN* proofs
❶ a fact or thing that shows something is true • *There is no proof that he stole the money.* ❷ a printed copy of a book or photograph made for checking before other copies are printed

proof *ADJECTIVE*
able to resist something or not be affected by it • *a bullet-proof jacket*

prop *NOUN* props
❶ a support, especially one made of a long piece of wood or metal ❷ an object or piece of furniture used on a theatre stage or in a film

prop *VERB* props, propping, propped
to support something by leaning it against something else • *The ladder was propped up against the wall.*

propaganda *NOUN*
false or exaggerated information that is spread around to make people believe something

propagate *VERB* propagates, propagating, propagated
❶ to grow new plants from an original plant ❷ to spread an idea or belief to a lot of people
➤ **propagation** *NOUN*

propel *VERB* propels, propelling, propelled
to push something forward • *They grabbed me and propelled me through the door.*

propellant *NOUN* propellants
a fuel or other substance that propels things

propeller *NOUN* propellers
a device with blades that spin round to drive an aircraft or ship

propensity *NOUN* propensities
a tendency to behave in a particular way

proper *ADJECTIVE*
❶ suitable or right • *This is the proper way to hold a tennis racket.* ❷ respectable or socially acceptable • *He raised his hat, thinking it was the proper thing to do.* ❸ (*informal*) complete or thorough • *You're a proper nuisance!*

proper fraction *NOUN* proper fractions
a fraction that is less than 1, with the numerator less than the denominator, e.g.⅓

properly *ADVERB*
in a correct or suitable way • *The lid won't close properly.*

proper noun *NOUN* proper nouns
the name of an individual person or thing, e.g. *Mary, London, Spain*, usually written with a capital first letter

property *NOUN* properties
❶ a thing or things that a person owns ❷ a building with the land belonging to it ❸ a quality or characteristic • *It has the property of becoming soft when heated.*

prophecy *NOUN* prophecies
❶ a statement that says what will happen in the future ❷ the power to say what will happen in the future • *She was believed to have the gift of prophecy.*

prophesy *VERB* prophesies, prophesying, prophesied
to say what you think will happen in the future • *Many people have been prophesying disaster.*

prophet *NOUN* **prophets**
❶ a person who makes prophecies ❷ a religious teacher who is believed to be inspired by God
➤ **prophetess** *NOUN*
➤ **the Prophet** a name for Muhammad, the founder of the Muslim faith

SPELLING
Be careful, this sounds the same as **profit**.

prophetic *ADJECTIVE*
saying or showing what will happen in the future • *a prophetic dream*

propitiate (say pro-**pish**-ee-ayt) *VERB* **propitiates, propitiating, propitiated**
to win a person's favour or forgiveness
➤ **propitiatory** *ADJECTIVE*

propitious (say pro-**pish**-us) *ADJECTIVE*
favourable; likely to bring good results • *a propitious moment*

proponent (say prop-**oh**-nent) *NOUN* **proponents**
a person who supports a proposal or idea

proportion *NOUN* **proportions**
❶ a part or share of a whole thing • *A large proportion of the earth's surface is covered by sea.* ❷ the proportion of one thing to another is how much there is of one compared to the other • *What is the proportion of girls to boys in the class?* ❸ the correct relationship in size, amount or importance between two things • *You've drawn his head out of proportion.*
➤ **proportions** *PLURAL NOUN*
size or scale • *a ship of gigantic proportions*

proportional, proportionate *ADJECTIVE*
in proportion; according to a ratio
➤ **proportionally** *ADVERB*
➤ **proportionately** *ADVERB*

proportional representation *NOUN*
a system in which each political party has a number of Members of Parliament in proportion to the number of votes for all its candidates

proposal *NOUN* **proposals**
❶ a plan that has been suggested ❷ when someone asks another person to marry them

propose *VERB* **proposes, proposing, proposed**
❶ to suggest an idea or plan ❷ to plan or intend to do something • *What do you propose to do now?* ❸ to ask a person to marry you

proposition *NOUN* **propositions**
❶ a suggestion or offer • *I have a proposition for you.* ❷ a statement ❸ a problem or task • *Climbing over that wall is a tricky proposition.*

propound *VERB* **propounds, propounding, propounded**
to put forward an idea for consideration

proprietary (say pro-**pry**-it-er-ee) *ADJECTIVE*
❶ made or sold by one firm; branded • *proprietary medicines* ❷ to do with an owner or ownership

proprietor *NOUN* **proprietors**
the owner of a shop or business
➤ **proprietress** *NOUN*

propriety (say pro-**pry**-it-ee) *NOUN* **proprieties**
correctness of social or moral behaviour

propulsion *NOUN*
propelling something or driving it forward

prosaic *ADJECTIVE*
plain or dull and ordinary
➤ **prosaically** *ADVERB*

proscribe *VERB* **proscribes, proscribing, proscribed**
to forbid something by law

SPELLING
Take care not to confuse with **prescribe**, which means to advise someone to use medicine or treatment.

prose *NOUN*
writing that is not in verse

prosecute *VERB* **prosecutes, prosecuting, prosecuted**
❶ to make someone go to a law court to be tried for a crime ❷ (*formal*) to continue doing something • *They had overwhelming support to prosecute the war.*
➤ **prosecutor** *NOUN*

prosecution *NOUN* **prosecutions**
❶ the process of prosecuting someone ❷ the lawyers who try to show that someone is guilty of a crime in a court of law

prospect *NOUN* **prospects**
❶ a possibility or expectation of something • *There is little prospect of success.* ❷ a wide view

prospect (say pro-**spekt**) *VERB* **prospects, prospecting, prospected**
to explore an area in search of gold or some other mineral
➤ **prospector** *NOUN*

a b c d e f g h i j k l m n o **p** q r s t u v w x y z

prospective *ADJECTIVE*
expected to be or to happen; possible
• *prospective customers*

prospectus *NOUN* **prospectuses**
a booklet describing and advertising a school, business company, etc.

prosper *VERB* **prospers, prospering, prospered**
to be successful or do well • *The business continued to prosper.*

prosperity *NOUN*
being successful or rich • *a time of peace and prosperity*

prosperous *ADJECTIVE*
successful or rich • *a prosperous town*

prostitute *NOUN* **prostitutes**
a person who takes part in sexual acts for payment
➤ **prostitution** *NOUN*

prostrate *ADJECTIVE*
lying face downwards

prostrate *VERB* **prostrates, prostrating, prostrated**
➤ **prostrate yourself** to lie flat on the ground face down, usually in submission
➤ **prostration** *NOUN*

protagonist *NOUN* **protagonists**
❶ the main character in a play ❷ one of the main people involved in a situation

protect *VERB* **protects, protecting, protected**
to keep someone or something safe from harm or damage
➤ **protector** *NOUN*

protection *NOUN*
keeping someone or something safe from harm or damage • *Vaccination gives protection against diseases.*

protective *ADJECTIVE*
❶ that prevents a person or thing from being harmed or damaged • *protective clothing*
❷ wanting to keep someone or something safe • *Her parents were very protective of her.*

protectorate *NOUN* **protectorates**
a country that is under the official protection of a stronger country

protégé (say **prot**-ezh-ay) *NOUN* **protégés**
someone who is helped and supported by an older or more experienced person

protein *NOUN* **proteins**
a substance that is found in all living things and is an essential part of the food of animals

protest (say **proh**-test) *NOUN* **protests**
a statement or action showing that you disapprove of something • *He cried out in protest.*

protest (say pro-**test**) *VERB* **protests, protesting, protested**
❶ to make a protest ❷ to declare something firmly • *They protested their innocence.*
➤ **protestation** *NOUN*

Protestant *NOUN* **Protestants**
a member of any of the western Christian Churches separated from the Roman Catholic Church (**WORD ORIGIN**) because in the 16th century many people protested (= declared firmly) their opposition to the Catholic Church

protester *NOUN* **protesters**
someone who protests about something, especially publicly

protocol *NOUN*
the correct or official procedure for behaving in certain formal situations

proton *NOUN* **protons**
a particle of matter with a positive electric charge

prototype *NOUN* **prototypes**
the first model of something, from which others are copied or developed

protracted *ADJECTIVE*
lasting longer than usual or expected • *a protracted stay in hospital*

protractor *NOUN* **protractors**
a device for measuring angles, usually a semicircle marked off in degrees

protrude *VERB* **protrudes, protruding, protruded**
to stick out from somewhere • *His tongue protruded from his lips.*
➤ **protrusion** *NOUN*

protuberance *NOUN* **protuberances**
a part that bulges out from a surface

protuberant *ADJECTIVE*
bulging out from a surface

proud *ADJECTIVE*
❶ very pleased with yourself or with someone else who has done well • *I am so proud of my sister.* ❷ causing pride • *This is a proud moment for us.* ❸ full of self-respect and independence • *They were too proud to ask for help.* ❹ having too high an opinion of yourself
➤ **proudly** *ADVERB*

prove *VERB* proves, proving, proved
❶ to show that something is true • *I can prove that I am innocent.* ❷ to turn out a certain way • *The forecast proved to be correct.*

proven (say **proh**-ven) *ADJECTIVE*
that has been shown to be true • *a man of proven ability*

proverb *NOUN* proverbs
a short well-known saying that states a truth, e.g. 'Many hands make light work.'

proverbial *ADJECTIVE*
❶ referred to in a proverb ❷ familiar or well known

provide *VERB* provides, providing, provided
❶ to make something available; to supply something • *Our website should provide you with all the information you need.* ❷ to prepare for something that might happen • *They have tried to provide for emergencies.*

provided *CONJUNCTION*
on condition that; only if • *You can stay provided you help.*

providence *NOUN*
❶ being careful and providing for the future ❷ God's or nature's care and protection

provident *ADJECTIVE*
wisely providing for the future; thrifty

providential *ADJECTIVE*
happening very luckily
➤ **providentially** *ADVERB*

provider *NOUN* providers
a person or thing that provides something • *an Internet service provider*

providing *CONJUNCTION*
on condition that; only if • *You can look around, providing you don't touch anything.*

province *NOUN* provinces
❶ a section of a country ❷ the area of a person's special knowledge or responsibility • *I'm afraid carpentry is not my province.*
➤ **the provinces** the parts of a country outside its capital city

provincial (say pro-**vin**-shul) *ADJECTIVE*
❶ to do with the provinces • *a provincial town* ❷ culturally limited or narrow-minded • *provincial attitudes*

provision *NOUN* provisions
❶ providing something • *the provision of free meals for old people* ❷ a statement in a legal document • *the provisions of the treaty*

provisional *ADJECTIVE*
arranged or agreed on for the time being but possibly to be changed later • *a provisional driving licence*
➤ **provisionally** *ADVERB*

provisions *PLURAL NOUN*
supplies of food and drink

proviso (say prov-**y**-zoh) *NOUN* provisos
a condition that is insisted on in advance

provocation *NOUN*
something done or said deliberately to annoy someone • *He hit me without the slightest provocation.*

provocative *ADJECTIVE*
❶ likely to make someone angry • *a provocative remark* ❷ intended to make someone feel sexual desire
➤ **provocatively** *ADVERB*

provoke *VERB* provokes, provoking, provoked
❶ to deliberately make a person angry ❷ to cause or give rise to something • *The joke provoked laughter.*

provost *NOUN* provosts
a Scottish official with authority similar to a mayor in England and Wales

prow *NOUN* prows
the front end of a ship

prowess *NOUN*
great ability or skill • *sporting prowess*

prowl *VERB* prowls, prowling, prowled
to move about quietly or cautiously, like a hunter

prowl *NOUN*
➤ **on the prowl** moving about quietly or cautiously, hunting or looking for something • *There was a fox on the prowl.*
➤ **prowler** *NOUN*

proximity *NOUN*
nearness • *Their house is in close proximity to the school.*

proxy *NOUN* proxies
a person authorized to represent or act for another person • *I will be abroad, so I have arranged to vote by proxy.*

prude *NOUN* prudes
a person who is easily shocked
➤ **prudish** *ADJECTIVE*

prudent *ADJECTIVE*
sensible and careful; not taking risks • *It may be prudent to get some advice first.*

a
b
c
d
e
f
g
h
i
j
k
l
m
n
o
p
q
r
s
t
u
v
w
x
y
z

> **prudently** *ADVERB*
> **prudence** *NOUN*

prune *NOUN* prunes
a dried plum

prune *VERB* prunes, pruning, pruned
to cut off unwanted parts of a tree or bush

pry *VERB* pries, prying, pried
to look into or ask about someone else's
private business • *I'm sorry, I didn't mean to
pry.*

PS *ABBREVIATION*
postscript (used when you add something at
the end of a letter)

psalm (say sahm) *NOUN* psalms
a religious song, especially one from the Book
of Psalms in the Bible

pseudonym *NOUN* pseudonyms
a name used by a writer instead of their real
name

PSHE *ABBREVIATION*
personal, social and health education (as a
school subject)

psychedelic *ADJECTIVE*
having vivid colours and patterns • *a
psychedelic design*

psychiatrist (say sy-**ky**-a-trist) *NOUN*
psychiatrists
a doctor who treats mental illnesses
> **psychiatry** *NOUN*
> **psychiatric** *ADJECTIVE*

psychic (say **sy**-kik) *ADJECTIVE*
❶ appearing to have supernatural powers,
especially being able to predict the future or
read people's minds ❷ supernatural

psychoanalysis *NOUN*
investigation of a person's mental processes,
especially in psychotherapy
> **psychoanalyst** *NOUN*

psychological *ADJECTIVE*
❶ to do with the mind or how it works ❷ to
do with psychology

psychology *NOUN*
the study of the mind and how it works
> **psychologist** *NOUN*

psychotherapy *NOUN*
treatment of mental illness by psychological
methods
> **psychotherapist** *NOUN*

PT *ABBREVIATION*
(*British*) physical training

PTA *ABBREVIATION*
parent-teacher association; an organization
that arranges discussions between teachers
and parents about school business and raises
money for the school

ptarmigan (say **tar**-mig-an) *NOUN* ptarmigans
a bird of the grouse family

pterodactyl (say te-ro-**dak**-til) *NOUN*
pterodactyls
an extinct flying reptile **WORD ORIGIN** from
Greek *pteron* = wing + *daktylos* = finger
(because one of the 'fingers' on its front leg was
enlarged to support its wing)

PTO *ABBREVIATION*
please turn over (put at the end of a page of
writing when there is more writing on the
next page)

pub *NOUN* pubs
(*British*) a building licensed to serve alcoholic
drinks to the public **WORD ORIGIN** short for
public house

puberty (say **pew**-ber-tee) *NOUN*
the time when a young person is developing
physically into an adult

pubic (say **pew**-bik) *ADJECTIVE*
to do with the lower front part of the
abdomen

public *ADJECTIVE*
❶ belonging to everyone or able to be used
by everyone • *public transport* ❷ to do with
people in general • *There was some public
support for the idea.*
> **publicly** *ADVERB*

public *NOUN*
people in general • *The police have asked for
help from members of the public.*
> **in public** openly, not in private

publican *NOUN* publicans
(*British*) the person in charge of a pub

publication *NOUN* publications
❶ publishing • *She became famous after the
publication of her first novel.* ❷ a published
book, newspaper or magazine

public house *NOUN* public houses
(*British*) (*formal*) a pub

publicity *NOUN*
information or advertising that makes people
know about something

publicize (also **publicise**) *VERB* publicizes,
publicizing, publicized

to bring something to people's attention; to advertise something

public school *NOUN* public schools
❶ in England, a private secondary school that charges fees ❷ in Scotland and the USA, a school run by a local authority or by the state

publish *VERB* publishes, publishing, published
❶ to produce a book, magazine, etc. and sell it to the public ❷ to make something available for people to read online • *The winning poems will be published on our website.* ❸ to make something known publicly

publisher *NOUN* publishers
a person or company that publishes books, magazines, etc.

puce *NOUN*
a dark red or brownish-purple colour
(WORD ORIGIN) from French *couleur puce* = the colour of a flea

puck *NOUN* pucks
a hard rubber disc used in ice hockey

pucker *VERB* puckers, puckering, puckered
to form into wrinkles or to make something do this • *His brow puckered into a frown.*

pudding *NOUN* puddings (*chiefly British*)
❶ the sweet course of a meal ❷ a food made in a soft mass, especially in a mixture of flour and other ingredients

puddle *NOUN* puddles
a shallow patch of liquid, especially of rainwater on a road

pudgy *ADJECTIVE*
short and fat • *pudgy fingers*

puerile (say **pew**-er-yl) *ADJECTIVE*
silly and childish

puff *NOUN* puffs
❶ a short blowing of breath, wind, smoke or steam • *He vanished in a puff of smoke.* ❷ a soft pad for putting powder on the skin ❸ a cake of very light pastry filled with cream

puff *VERB* puffs, puffing, puffed
❶ to blow out puffs of smoke or steam ❷ to pant or breathe with difficulty • *She was puffing when she got to the top of the hill.* ❸ to inflate or swell something • *He puffed out his chest.*

puffin *NOUN* puffins
a seabird with a large striped beak

puffy *ADJECTIVE*
puffed out or swollen • *His eyes were puffy*

and red.
➤ **puffiness** *NOUN*

pug *NOUN* pugs
a small dog with a flat face like a bulldog

pugilist (say **pew**-jil-ist) *NOUN* pugilists
a boxer

pugnacious *ADJECTIVE*
wanting to fight; aggressive
➤ **pugnaciously** *ADVERB*
➤ **pugnacity** *NOUN*

puke *VERB* pukes, puking, puked (*informal*)
to vomit

pull *VERB* pulls, pulling, pulled
❶ to hold something and make it come towards you • *I pulled the door open.* ❷ to move something along behind you • *The train is pulled by a powerful engine.* ❸ to move with an effort • *She tried to grab the boy but he pulled away.*
➤ **pull a face** to make a strange face
➤ **pull in** ❶ a vehicle pulls in when it moves to the side of the road and stops ❷ a train pulls in when it comes to a station and stops
➤ **pull someone's leg** to tease someone
➤ **pull something off** to achieve something
➤ **pull out** ❶ to decide to stop taking part in something • *He had to pull out of the race after twisting his ankle.* ❷ a vehicle pulls out when it moves out into the road from the side ❸ a train pulls out when it leaves a station
➤ **pull through** to recover from an illness
➤ **pull up** a vehicle pulls up when it stops abruptly
➤ **pull yourself together** to become calm again after being upset

pull *NOUN* pulls
a pulling movement • *Give the handle a good pull.*

pullet *NOUN* pullets
a young hen

pulley *NOUN* pulleys
a wheel with a rope, chain or belt over it, used for lifting or moving heavy things

pullover *NOUN* pullovers
a knitted piece of clothing for the top half of the body

pulmonary (say **pul**-mon-er-ee) *ADJECTIVE*
to do with the lungs

pulp *NOUN*
❶ the soft moist part of fruit ❷ any soft moist mass • *Wood pulp is used to make paper.*
➤ **pulpy** *ADJECTIVE*

a b c d e f g h i j k l m n o p q r s t u v w x y z

pulpit *NOUN* pulpits
a small enclosed platform for the preacher in a church or chapel

pulsate *VERB* pulsates, pulsating, pulsated
to move or shake with strong regular movements • *a pulsating rhythm*
➤ **pulsation** *NOUN*

pulse *NOUN* pulses
❶ the rhythmical movement of the arteries as blood is pumped through them by the beating of the heart • *The pulse can be felt in a person's wrists.* ❷ a throb ❸ the edible seed of peas, beans, lentils, etc.

pulse *VERB* pulses, pulsing, pulsed
to move or flow with strong regular movements; to throb • *He could feel the blood pulsing through his body.*

pulverize (also **pulverise**) *VERB* pulverizes, pulverizing, pulverized
to crush something into powder

puma (say **pew**-ma) *NOUN* pumas
a large brown cat of western America, also called a cougar or mountain lion

pumice *NOUN*
a kind of porous stone used for rubbing stains from the skin or as powder for polishing things

pummel *VERB* pummels, pummelling, pummelled
to keep on hitting something

pump *NOUN* pumps
❶ a device that pushes air or liquid into or out of something or along pipes ❷ a canvas sports shoe with a rubber sole

pump *VERB* pumps, pumping, pumped
❶ to move air or liquid into or out of something with a pump ❷ (*informal*) to question a person to obtain information
➤ **pump something up** to fill something with air using a pump

pumpkin *NOUN* pumpkins
a very large round fruit with a hard orange skin

pun *NOUN* puns
a joking use of a word sounding the same as another or having more than one meaning, e.g. 'Deciding where to bury him was a *grave* decision.'

punch *VERB* punches, punching, punched
❶ to hit someone with your fist ❷ to make a hole in something • *The guard came to punch our tickets.* • *She punched a few holes in the side of the box.*

punch *NOUN* punches
❶ a hit with a fist ❷ a device for making holes in paper, metal, leather, etc. ❸ a drink made by mixing wine or spirits and fruit juice in a bowl (**WORD ORIGIN**) The 'drink' meaning comes from Sanskrit *pañca* = five (the number of ingredients in the traditional recipe: spirits, fruit juice, water, sugar, and spice)

punchline *NOUN* punchlines
words that give the climax of a joke or story

punch-up *NOUN* punch-ups (*British*) (*informal*)
a fight

punctilious *ADJECTIVE*
very careful about correct behaviour and detail
➤ **punctiliously** *ADVERB*
➤ **punctiliousness** *NOUN*

punctual *ADJECTIVE*
arriving exactly on time; not late
➤ **punctually** *ADVERB*
➤ **punctuality** *NOUN*

punctuate *VERB* punctuates, punctuating, punctuated
❶ to put punctuation marks into a piece of writing ❷ to be punctuated by something is to be frequently interrupted by it • *His speech was punctuated by bursts of applause.*
(**WORD ORIGIN**) from Latin *punctuare* = mark with points or dots

punctuation *NOUN*
marks such as commas, full stops and brackets put into a piece of writing to make it easier to read

---
PUNCTUATION

Punctuation marks show divisions and connections between sentences, clauses or individual words: for example, a *full stop* (.) marks the end of a sentence; a *comma* (,) separates clauses or items in a list; a *question mark* (?) indicates a question; and *quotation marks* (' ' or " ") show direct speech (the actual words someone speaks). Other types of punctuation are the use of *capital letters* at the start of a sentence or proper noun, and the use of an *apostrophe* to show possession (*the cat's bowl*) or to indicate a missing letter (*don't, I've*).

Punctuation can completely change the meaning of a piece of writing.

Compare, for example, the meaning of these two sentences:

Let's eat Granny!

Let's eat, Granny!

puncture *NOUN* punctures
a small hole made by something sharp, especially in a tyre

puncture *VERB* punctures, puncturing, punctured
to make a small hole in something

pundit *NOUN* pundits
a person who is an expert on a subject and is asked for their opinions

pungent (say pun-jent) *ADJECTIVE*
❶ having a strong taste or smell ❷ pungent remarks are sharp and effective
➤ **pungently** *ADVERB*
➤ **pungency** *NOUN*

punish *VERB* punishes, punishing, punished
to make a person suffer because they have done something wrong • *He will be punished for disobeying orders.*
➤ **punishable** *ADJECTIVE*

punishment *NOUN* punishments
something a person suffers because they have done something wrong

punk *NOUN* punks
❶ (also **punk rock**) a loud aggressive style of rock music ❷ a person who likes this music

punnet *NOUN* punnets
(*British*) a small container for soft fruit such as strawberries

punt *NOUN* punts
a flat-bottomed boat moved by pushing a pole against the bottom of a river while standing in the punt

punt *VERB* punts, punting, punted
❶ to move a punt along with a pole ❷ to kick a football after dropping it from your hands and before it touches the ground

punter *NOUN* punters
❶ a person who lays a bet ❷ (*informal*) a customer

puny (say pew-nee) *ADJECTIVE*
very small and weak

pup *NOUN* pups
❶ a puppy ❷ a young seal

pupa (say pew-pa) *NOUN* pupae
an insect at the stage of development

between a larva and an adult insect; a chrysalis

pupate (say pew-**payt**) *VERB* pupates, pupating, pupated
to become a pupa
➤ **pupation** *NOUN*

pupil *NOUN* pupils
❶ someone who is being taught by a teacher, especially at school ❷ the opening in the centre of the eye (**WORD ORIGIN**) from Latin *pupilla* = little girl or doll (the use in meaning 2 refers to the tiny images of people and things that can be seen in the eye)

puppet *NOUN* puppets
❶ a kind of doll that can be made to move by fitting it over your hand or working it by strings or wires ❷ a person whose actions are controlled by someone else
➤ **puppetry** *NOUN*

puppy *NOUN* puppies
a young dog

purchase *VERB* purchases, purchasing, purchased
to buy something
➤ **purchaser** *NOUN*

purchase *NOUN* purchases
❶ something you have bought ❷ buying something • *Keep the receipt as proof of purchase.* ❸ a firm hold or grip • *It was hard to get a purchase on the slippery rock.*

purdah *NOUN*
the practice in some Muslim and Hindu societies of keeping women from the sight of men or strangers (**WORD ORIGIN**) from Persian or Urdu *parda* = veil or curtain

pure *ADJECTIVE*
❶ not mixed with anything else • *pure olive oil* ❷ clean and clear • *pure spring water* ❸ free from evil or sin ❹ mere; nothing but • *What he said was pure nonsense.*

purée (say **pewr**-ay) *NOUN* purées
fruit or vegetables made into pulp

purely *ADVERB*
only or simply • *They did it purely for the money.*

purgatory *NOUN*
❶ a state of temporary suffering ❷ in Roman Catholic belief, a place in which souls are purified by punishment before they can enter heaven

A B C D E F G H I J K L M N O **P** Q R S T U V W X Y Z

purge *VERB* purges, purging, purged
to get rid of unwanted people or things • *He vowed to purge the oceans of pirates.*

purge *NOUN* purges
an act of purging

purify *VERB* purifies, purifying, purified
to make something pure, especially by removing dirty or harmful substances from it
➤ **purification** *NOUN*
➤ **purifier** *NOUN*

purist *NOUN* purists
a person who likes things to be exactly right, especially in people's use of words

Puritan *NOUN* Puritans
a Protestant in the 16th and 17th centuries who wanted simpler religious ceremonies and strict moral behaviour

puritan *NOUN* puritans
a person with very strict morals
➤ **puritanical** *ADJECTIVE*

purity *NOUN*
being pure • *White often symbolizes purity.*

purl *NOUN* purls
a knitting stitch that makes a ridge towards the knitter

purl *VERB* purls, purling, purled (*poetical use*)
a stream purls when it ripples with a murmuring sound

purloin *VERB* purloins, purloining, purloined (*formal*)
to take something without permission

purple *NOUN*
a deep reddish-blue colour

purport (say per-**port**) *VERB* purports, purporting, purported
to claim to be something or someone • *The letter purports to be from the council.*
➤ **purportedly** *ADVERB*

purport (say per-**port**) *NOUN*
the general meaning of something • *The purport of the letter could not be clearer.*

purpose *NOUN* purposes
❶ what you intend to do; a plan or aim
❷ determination • *Her strength of purpose was to be put to the test.*
➤ **on purpose** deliberately, not by accident

purposeful *ADJECTIVE*
determined and having a definite plan or aim
• *He strode off in a purposeful manner.*
➤ **purposefully** *ADVERB*

purposely *ADVERB*
on purpose • *She was purposely avoiding him.*

purr *VERB* purrs, purring, purred
❶ a cat purrs when it makes a low murmuring sound to show it is pleased ❷ to make a low continuous sound • *The limousine purred away.* ❸ to speak in a low and gentle voice
• *He was purring with satisfaction.*

purr *NOUN* purrs
a purring sound

purse *NOUN* purses
a small pouch for carrying money

purse *VERB* purses, pursing, pursed
to draw your lips tightly together, especially to show disapproval • *She frowned and pursed up her lips.*

purser *NOUN* pursers
a ship's officer in charge of accounts

pursuance *NOUN* (*formal*)
the performance or carrying out of something • *in pursuance of my duties*

pursue *VERB* pursues, pursuing, pursued
❶ to chase someone in order to catch them
❷ to continue with something; to work at something • *She pursued her studies at college.*
➤ **pursuer** *NOUN*

pursuit *NOUN* pursuits
❶ chasing someone • *We set off in pursuit of the thief.* ❷ a regular activity

purveyor *NOUN* purveyors
a person or company that sells or supplies something

pus *NOUN*
a thick yellowish substance produced in boils or other sore or infected places on your body

push *VERB* pushes, pushing, pushed
❶ to make a thing go away from you by using force on it ❷ to press something • *Push the red button.* ❸ to move yourself by using force • *He pushed in front of me.* ❹ to try to force someone to do or use something; to urge someone
➤ **push off** (*informal*) to go away

push *NOUN* pushes
a pushing movement or effort
➤ **at a push** if necessary but only with difficulty
➤ **get the push** (*informal*) to be dismissed from a job

pushchair NOUN pushchairs
(*British*) a folding chair on wheels, for pushing a child along

pusher NOUN pushers
a person who sells illegal drugs

pushy ADJECTIVE
determined to get what you want, in an unpleasant way

puss NOUN (*informal, chiefly British*)
a cat

pussy NOUN pussies (*informal*)
a cat

pussyfoot VERB pussyfoots, pussyfooting, pussyfooted
to act too cautiously and timidly

pussy willow NOUN pussy willows
a willow with furry catkins

pustule NOUN pustules
a pimple containing pus

put VERB puts, putting, put
❶ to move a person or thing to a place or position • *She put the phone down.* ❷ to make a person or thing do or experience something or be in a certain condition • *I'll put the light on.* • *That put me in a good mood.* ❸ to express something in words • *She put it tactfully.*
➤ **be hard put to do something** to have difficulty in doing something
➤ **put someone off** to make someone less keen on something • *The smell puts me off.*
➤ **put something off** to postpone something to a later time
➤ **put someone out** to annoy or inconvenience someone • *Our lateness has put her out.*
➤ **put something out** to stop a fire from burning or a light from shining
➤ **put someone up** to give someone a place to sleep • *Can you put me up for the night?*
➤ **put something up** ❶ to construct or build something ❷ to raise the price of something ❸ to provide something • *Who will put up the money?*
➤ **put up with something** to be willing to accept something without complaining

SPELLING
To **put** something somewhere is to place it there. To **putt** a ball is to tap it gently.

putrefy (say **pew**-trif-eye) VERB putrefies, putrefying, putrefied
to decay or rot
➤ **putrefaction** NOUN

putrid (say **pew**-trid) ADJECTIVE
❶ decaying or rotting ❷ smelling bad

putt VERB putts, putting, putted
to hit a golf ball gently towards the hole

putt NOUN putts
hitting a golf ball gently towards the hole
➤ **putting green** NOUN

putter NOUN putters
a golf club used to putt the ball

putty NOUN
a soft paste that sets hard, used for fitting the glass into a window frame

puzzle NOUN puzzles
❶ a difficult question or problem ❷ a game or toy that sets a problem to solve or a difficult task to complete

puzzle VERB puzzles, puzzling, puzzled
❶ to give someone a problem that is hard to understand • *'There is one thing that puzzles me,' she said.* ❷ to think hard about something in order to understand or explain it • *We were puzzling over the map.*

puzzled ADJECTIVE
not able to understand or explain something • *a puzzled expression*

puzzlement NOUN
a feeling of being confused because you do not understand something • *He frowned in puzzlement.*

PVC ABBREVIATION
polyvinyl chloride, a plastic used to make clothing, pipes, flooring, etc.
WORD ORIGIN the initial letters of *polyvinyl chloride*, a polymer of vinyl, from which it is made

pygmy (say **pig**-mee) NOUN pygmies
❶ a very small person or thing ❷ a member of certain unusually short peoples of equatorial Africa

pyjamas PLURAL NOUN
a loose jacket and trousers that you wear in bed **WORD ORIGIN** from Persian or Urdu *pay* = leg + *jamah* = clothing: the word originally meant long loose trousers

pylon NOUN pylons
a tall framework made of strips of steel, supporting electric cables

pyramid NOUN pyramids
❶ a structure with a square base and with

a b c d e f g h i j k l m n o **p** q r s t u v w x y z

sloping sides that meet in a point at the top
❷ an ancient Egyptian royal tomb shaped
like this
➤ **pyramidal** (say pir-**am**-id-al) *ADJECTIVE*

pyre *NOUN* pyres
a pile of wood for burning a dead body as
part of a funeral ceremony

python *NOUN* pythons
a large snake that kills its prey by coiling
round and crushing it **WORD ORIGIN** the name
of a huge serpent in Greek legend, killed by
Apollo

QED *ABBREVIATION*
quod erat demonstrandum (Latin, = which
was the thing that had to be proved)

quack *VERB* quacks, quacking, quacked
to make the harsh cry of a duck

quack *NOUN* quacks
❶ the harsh cry made by a duck ❷ a person
who falsely claims to have medical skill or
have remedies to cure diseases

quad (say kwod) *NOUN* quads
❶ a quadrangle ❷ a quadruplet

quadrangle *NOUN* quadrangles
a rectangular courtyard with large buildings
round it

quadrant *NOUN* quadrants
a quarter of a circle

quadratic equation *NOUN* quadratic
equations
an equation that involves quantities or
variables raised to the power of two, but no
higher than two

quadriceps *NOUN* quadriceps
the large muscle at the front of the thigh
WORD ORIGIN Latin, = four-headed (because
the muscle is attached at four points)

quadrilateral *NOUN* quadrilaterals
a flat geometric shape with four sides

quadruped *NOUN* quadrupeds
an animal with four feet

quadruple *ADJECTIVE*
❶ four times as much or as many ❷ having
four parts

quadruple *VERB* quadruples, quadrupling,
quadrupled
to become or make something, four times as
much or as many

quadruplet *NOUN* quadruplets
each of four children born to the same
mother at one time

quaff (say kwof) *VERB* quaffs, quaffing,
quaffed
to drink a lot of something

quagmire *NOUN* quagmires
a bog or marsh

quail *NOUN* quail or quails
a bird related to the partridge

quail *VERB* quails, quailing, quailed
to feel or show fear • *He quailed at the sight
of the tiger.*

quaint *ADJECTIVE*
attractively odd or old-fashioned • *a quaint
old custom*
➤ **quaintly** *ADVERB*

quake *VERB* quakes, quaking, quaked
to tremble or shake because you are afraid
• *Quaking with fear, she opened the door.*

quake *NOUN* quakes
an earthquake

Quaker *NOUN* Quakers
a member of a religious group called the
Society of Friends, founded by George Fox in
the 17th century **WORD ORIGIN** originally an
insult, probably from George Fox's saying that
people should 'tremble at the name of the Lord'

qualification *NOUN* qualifications
❶ a skill or ability that makes someone
suitable for a job ❷ an exam that you have
passed or a course of study that you have
completed ❸ something that limits the
meaning of a remark or statement or makes it
less extreme

qualify *VERB* qualifies, qualifying, qualified
❶ to become able to do something through
having certain qualities or training or by
passing an exam or to make someone able to
do this • *She qualified as a doctor last year.*
❷ to qualify for a competition is to reach a
high enough standard to take part in it • *It
is the first time the country has qualified for
the World Cup Finals.* ❸ to make a remark or
statement less extreme or to limit its meaning
❹ an adjective qualifies a noun when it

describes it or adds meaning to it
➤ **qualified** *ADJECTIVE*

quality *NOUN* qualities
❶ how good or bad something is • *a performance of the highest quality* ❷ a characteristic; something that is special in a person or thing • *The paper has a shiny quality.*

qualm (say kwahm) *NOUN* qualms
a feeling of worry that what you are doing may not be right • *She had no qualms about accepting the money.*

quandary *NOUN* quandaries
a difficult situation where you are uncertain what to do

quantity *NOUN* quantities
❶ how much of something there is or the number of things there are ❷ a large amount • *It's usually cheaper to buy goods in quantity.*

quantum leap, quantum jump *NOUN*
quantum leaps or **quantum jumps**
a sudden large increase or advance

quarantine *NOUN*
keeping a person or animal isolated in case they have a disease which could spread to others (**WORD ORIGIN**) from Italian *quaranta* = forty (because the original period of isolation was 40 days)

quarrel *NOUN* quarrels
an angry argument

quarrel *VERB* quarrels, quarrelling, quarrelled
to argue fiercely with someone

quarrelsome *ADJECTIVE*
often quarrelling with people

quarry *NOUN* quarries
❶ an open place where stone or slate is dug or cut out of the ground ❷ an animal or person that is being hunted or pursued

quarry *VERB* quarries, quarrying, quarried
to dig or cut stone or slate from a quarry

quart *NOUN* quarts
a measure for liquids, equal to two pints (or 1.136 litres)

quarter *NOUN* quarters
❶ each of four equal parts into which a thing is or can be divided ❷ three months, one-fourth of a year ❸ a district or region • *People came from every quarter.*
➤ **at close quarters** very close together • *They fought at close quarters.*
➤ **give no quarter** to show no mercy

quarter *VERB* quarters, quartering, quartered
❶ to divide something into quarters ❷ to put soldiers into lodgings

quarterdeck *NOUN* quarterdecks
the part of a ship's upper deck nearest the stern, usually reserved for the officers

quarter-final *NOUN* quarter-finals
each of the matches or rounds before a semi-final, in which there are eight contestants or teams
➤ **quarter-finalist** *NOUN*

quarterly *ADJECTIVE & ADVERB*
happening or produced once in every three months

quarterly *NOUN* quarterlies
a quarterly magazine

quarters *PLURAL NOUN*
rooms where soldiers or servants live; lodgings

quartet *NOUN* quartets
❶ a group of four musicians ❷ a piece of music for four musicians ❸ a set of four people or things

quartz *NOUN*
a hard mineral, often in crystal form

quash *VERB* quashes, quashing, quashed
to cancel or annul a decision or verdict • *The judges quashed his conviction.*

quatrain *NOUN* quatrains
a stanza with four lines

quaver *VERB* quavers, quavering, quavered
to speak unsteadily because you are afraid or nervous • *'What do you want?' he asked in a quavering voice.*

quaver *NOUN* quavers
❶ a quavering sound ❷ a note in music (♪) lasting half as long as a crotchet

quay (say kee) *NOUN* quays
a landing place where ships can be tied up for loading and unloading; a wharf

quayside *NOUN* quaysides
the area around a quay

queasy *ADJECTIVE*
feeling slightly sick
➤ **queasily** *ADVERB*
➤ **queasiness** *NOUN*

queen *NOUN* queens
❶ a woman who is the ruler of a country through inheriting the position ❷ the wife of a king ❸ a female bee or ant that produces eggs ❹ the most powerful piece in chess ❺ a

playing card with a picture of a queen on it
➤ **queenly** ADJECTIVE

queen mother NOUN queen mothers
a title given to the widow of a king who has died and who is the mother of the present king or queen

queer ADJECTIVE
❶ strange or odd ❷ slightly ill or faint
➤ **queerly** ADVERB
➤ **queerness** NOUN

quell VERB quells, quelling, quelled
❶ to crush a rebellion by force ❷ to stop yourself from feeling fear, anger etc. • *I tried to quell my feelings of dread.*

quench VERB quenches, quenching, quenched
❶ to satisfy your thirst by drinking ❷ to put out a fire or flame

querulous (say **kwe**-rew-lus) ADJECTIVE
complaining all the time
➤ **querulously** ADVERB

query (say **kweer**-ee) NOUN queries
a question asking for information or expressing doubt about something

query VERB queries, querying, queried
to question whether something is true or correct • *No one queried his explanation.*

quest NOUN quests
a long search for something • *the quest for gold*

question NOUN questions
❶ a sentence asking something ❷ a problem or subject that needs to be discussed or dealt with • *There is also the question of cost.*
❸ doubt about something • *Whether we shall win is open to question.*
➤ **in question** being discussed or disputed
• *His honesty is not in question.*
➤ **out of the question** impossible or not worth considering

question VERB questions, questioning, questioned
❶ to ask someone questions ❷ to say that you are doubtful about something • *A few people questioned the wisdom of that decision.*
➤ **questioner** NOUN

> **GRAMMAR**
>
> A **question** is a sentence which asks something and ends with a question mark:
>
> *Have you all written down your answers?*

> *Where are you?*
>
> *What was that noise?*
>
> *Could you give me a hand?*
>
> Questions are often introduced by an **interrogative pronoun** such as *how?, what?, when?, where?, who?, whose?* or *why?*
>
> Questions are also often introduced by a form of the auxiliary verb *do:*
>
> *Do you want to watch this film?*
>
> *Did she pass her exams?*

questionable ADJECTIVE
causing doubt; not certainly true or honest or advisable

question mark NOUN question marks
the punctuation mark (?) placed after a question

> **PUNCTUATION**
>
> A **question mark** is used at the end of a sentence to show that it is a question:
>
> *What time is it?*
>
> *Are there wild animals in this wood?*
>
> You also use them to indicate a query in direct speech or in the thought of a character or narrator:
>
> *'Mr Green? Are you there?'*
>
> *Did the label say one spoonful or ten? If only she could remember.*
>
> Question marks are not needed in reported speech:
>
> *The patient opened his eyes and asked me what day of the week it was.*

questionnaire NOUN questionnaires
a written set of questions asked to provide information for a survey

queue (say kew) NOUN queues
a line of people or vehicles waiting for something

queue VERB queues, queueing, queued
to wait in a queue • *We have been queuing for over an hour.*

> **SPELLING**
>
> Queue can be tricky to spell—the letter u appears twice.

quibble *NOUN* quibbles
a trivial complaint or objection

quibble *VERB* quibbles, quibbling, quibbled
to make trivial complaints or objections
WORD ORIGIN probably from Latin *quibus* =
what?, for which, for whom (because *quibus*
often appeared in legal documents)

quiche (say keesh) *NOUN* quiches
an open tart with a savoury filling

quick *ADJECTIVE*
❶ taking only a short time to do something
• *I'll be as quick as I can.* ❷ done in a short
time • *a quick meal* ❸ able to notice or learn
or think quickly

quick *ADVERB*
quickly • *Quick! She's coming!*
➤ **quickness** *NOUN*

quicken *VERB* quickens, quickening, quickened
❶ to make something quicker • *He quickened
his pace.* ❷ to become quicker • *She felt her
heartbeat quicken.*

quickly *ADVERB*
fast; in a short time • *I quickly got dressed.*

quicksand *NOUN* quicksands
an area of loose wet deep sand that sucks in
anything resting or falling on top of it

quicksilver *NOUN*
(*old use*) mercury

quick-witted *ADJECTIVE*
able to think quickly

quid *NOUN* quid (*British*) (*informal*)
£1

quid pro quo (say kwoh) *NOUN* quid pro quos
something given or done in return for
something **WORD ORIGIN** Latin, = something
for something

quiet *ADJECTIVE*
❶ silent; not saying anything • *Be quiet!*
❷ with little sound; not loud or noisy • *He
spoke in a quiet voice.* ❸ calm and peaceful;
without disturbance • *They lead a quiet life.*
❹ quiet colours are soft and not bright
➤ **quietness** *NOUN*

quiet *NOUN*
a time when it is calm and there is no noise • *I
was glad of the peace and quiet.*

quieten *VERB* quietens, quietening, quietened
(*chiefly British*) to become quiet or to make a
person or thing quiet • *The crowd gradually
quietened down.*

quietly *ADVERB*
❶ without making much noise • *I closed the
door quietly.* ❷ in a quiet voice • *'I want to go
home,' he said quietly.* ❸ without attracting
much attention • *She lived quietly in Ireland
until her death in 1960.*

quiff *NOUN* quiffs
(*chiefly British*) an upright tuft of hair

quill *NOUN* quills
❶ a large feather ❷ a pen made from a large
feather ❸ one of the spines on a porcupine or
hedgehog

quilt *NOUN* quilts
a cover for a bed filled with soft padding

quilt *VERB* quilts, quilting, quilted
to line material with padding and fix it with
lines of stitching

quin *NOUN* quins
(*British*) (*informal*) a quintuplet

quince *NOUN* quinces
a hard pear-shaped fruit used for making jam

quinine (say kwin-**een**) *NOUN*
a bitter-tasting medicine used to cure malaria

quintessence *NOUN*
❶ the most essential part of something ❷ a
perfect example of a quality
➤ **quintessential** *ADJECTIVE*
WORD ORIGIN from Latin *quinta essentia*
= the fifth essence (after earth, air, fire and
water, which the alchemists thought everything
contained)

quintet *NOUN* quintets
❶ a group of five musicians ❷ a piece of
music for five musicians

quintuplet *NOUN* quintuplets
each of five children born to the same mother
at one time

quip *NOUN* quips
a witty remark

quip *VERB* quips, quipping, quipped
to make a witty remark

quirk *NOUN* quirks
❶ a peculiarity of a person's behaviour ❷ a
trick of fate
➤ **quirky** *ADJECTIVE*

quit *VERB* quits, quitting, quitted or quit
❶ to leave or abandon a place or job
❷ (*informal*) to stop doing something • *Quit
teasing him!*
➤ **quitter** *NOUN*

a
b
c
d
e
f
g
h
i
j
k
l
m
n
o
p
q
r
s
t
u
v
w
x
y
z

A
B
C
D
E
F
G
H
I
J
K
L
M
N
O
P
Q
R
S
T
U
V
W
X
Y
Z

quite *ADVERB*
❶ completely or entirely • *I am quite all right.*
❷ rather or fairly; to some extent • *It is quite cold today.*
➤ **quite a** used to show that something is unusual or important • *The news was quite a surprise.*

quits *ADJECTIVE*
people are quits when they are even or equal again and neither owes the other anything or has an advantage over them • *I think you and I are quits now.*

quiver *VERB* quivers, quivering, quivered
to tremble • *He was quivering with excitement.*

quiver *NOUN* quivers
❶ a container for arrows ❷ a trembling movement

quixotic (say kwiks-**ot**-ik) *ADJECTIVE*
having imaginative or idealistic ideas that are not practical
➤ **quixotically** *ADVERB*
WORD ORIGIN named after Don *Quixote*, hero of a 17th-century Spanish story by Cervantes

quiz *NOUN* quizzes
a series of questions, especially as an entertainment or competition

quiz *VERB* quizzes, quizzing, quizzed
to ask someone a lot of questions

quizzical *ADJECTIVE*
seeming to be asking a question, especially in an amused way • *She gave him a quizzical look.*
➤ **quizzically** *ADVERB*

quoit (say koit) *NOUN* quoits
a ring thrown at a peg in the game of **quoits**

quota *NOUN* quotas
a fixed or limited amount or share that is allowed or expected • *We are given a quota of work to get through each week.*

quotation *NOUN* quotations
❶ something quoted • *It is a quotation from Shakespeare.* ❷ a statement of how much a piece of work will cost

GRAMMAR

Direct speech shows the exact words that a person or character says. The spoken words—and any punctuation that goes with them, such as full stops, exclamation marks or question marks—go inside the quotation marks:

'Wait! Can you at least tell me your

name?' I shouted at the retreating figure.

Any description of who is speaking (e.g. *she said, I exclaimed*) is separated from the spoken words by a comma or commas:

'We are planning', said a NASA spokesperson, 'to send a manned expedition to Mars.'

Reported speech is also called **indirect speech**. It describes or reports what a person or character says without using their exact words. You do not use quotation marks and the tense of the verb (*were* in this example) follows that of the reporting verb (*said* in the example):

A NASA spokesperson <u>said</u> that they <u>were</u> planning to send a manned expedition to Mars.

You can also leave out the word *that* at the beginning of the reported speech:

A NASA spokesperson <u>said</u> they <u>were</u> planning to send a manned expedition to Mars.

quotation marks *PLURAL NOUN*
inverted commas (" " or ' ') used to mark direct speech or a quotation

PUNCTUATION

Quotation marks (also known as **inverted commas** or **speech marks**) are used in pairs and can surround a single word or phrase, or a longer piece of text. They are used:

in direct speech to show which words are being spoken:

'Look!' said a voice behind me. 'Look at the sky!'

to highlight a word to which you are referring:

The words 'turn back' were scratched on the door.

to show that word is being used in a slightly odd way, for example because it is a slang word:

Disneyland wasn't my idea of a place to 'chill' on holiday.

to show that something is the title of a poem, story, piece of music, etc.

She stood up and recited Kipling's poem 'If'.

to enclose direct quotations from a speech, book, play or film:

Which film contains the famous line, 'Toto, I've a feeling we're not in Kansas anymore'?

Pairs of quotation marks can be single (' ') or double (" "), but are never mixed. You can, however, use a pair of double quotation marks within a pair of single quotation marks:

'When I say, "Action", start the gladiator scene again.'

quote *VERB* **quotes, quoting, quoted**
❶ to repeat words that were first written or spoken by someone else ❷ to mention an example of something to support what you are saying ❸ to state the price of goods or services that you can supply

quote *NOUN* **quotes**
a quotation

quoth *VERB* (*old use*)
said • *'My lord,' quoth he.*

quotient (say **kwoh**-shent) *NOUN* **quotients**
the result of dividing one number by another. Compare with **product**.

Qur'an *NOUN*
another spelling of **Koran**

rabbi (say **rab**-eye) *NOUN* **rabbis**
a Jewish religious leader
WORD ORIGIN Hebrew, = my master

rabbit *NOUN* **rabbits**
a furry animal with long ears that digs burrows

rabble *NOUN* **rabbles**
a noisy or disorderly crowd or mob

rabid (say **rab**-id) *ADJECTIVE*
❶ extreme or fanatical • *a rabid fascist*
❷ suffering from rabies

rabies (say **ray**-beez) *NOUN*
a fatal disease that affects dogs and other mammals and can be passed to humans by the bite of an infected animal

raccoon *NOUN* **raccoons** or **raccoon**
a North American animal with a bushy, striped tail and greyish-brown fur

race *NOUN* **races**
❶ a sports contest in which the fastest competitor wins ❷ a competition to be the first to reach a particular place or to do something • *the race to land people on the Moon* ❸ a very large group of people thought to have the same ancestors and with physical characteristics (e.g. colour of skin and hair, shape of eyes and nose) that differ from those of other groups ❹ racial origin • *discrimination on grounds of race*

race *VERB* **races, racing, raced**
❶ to compete in a race • *I'll race you home.*
❷ to move very fast • *She raced up the stairs.*

racecourse *NOUN* **racecourses**
a place where horse races are run

racehorse *NOUN* **racehorses**
a horse bred or kept for racing

racer *NOUN* **racers**
a competitor in a race • *a wheelchair racer*

race relations *NOUN*
relationships between people of different races in the same country

racetrack *NOUN* **racetracks**
a track for horse or vehicle races

racial (say **ray**-shul) *ADJECTIVE*
to do with a particular race or based on race
• *different racial groups*
➤ **racially** *ADVERB*

racism (say **ray**-sizm) *NOUN*
❶ discrimination against or hostility towards people of other races ❷ belief that a particular race of people is better than others
➤ **racist** *NOUN* & *ADJECTIVE*

rack *NOUN* **racks**
❶ a framework used as a shelf or container
• *a plate rack* ❷ an ancient device for torturing people by stretching them ❸ a bar or rail with cogs into which the cogs of a gear or wheel fit
➤ **go to rack and ruin** to gradually become worse in condition due to neglect

rack *VERB* **racks, racking, racked**
to be racked with physical or mental pain is to be tormented by it • *He was racked with*

guilt.

➤ **rack your brains** to think hard in trying to remember something or solve a problem

racket *NOUN* **rackets**
❶ a bat with strings stretched across a frame, used in tennis, badminton and squash ❷ a loud noise or din ❸ a dishonest or illegal business • *a drugs racket*

racketeer *NOUN* **racketeers**
a person involved in a dishonest or illegal business
➤ **racketeering** *NOUN*

racoon *NOUN* **racoons** or **racoon**
a different spelling of **raccoon**

racquet *NOUN* **racquets**
a different spelling of **racket**

racy *ADJECTIVE* **racier, raciest**
lively and slightly shocking in style • *She gave a racy account of her travels.*

radar *NOUN*
a system or apparatus that uses radio waves to show on a screen the position of ships, planes, etc. that cannot be seen because of distance or poor visibility
➤ **be on someone's radar** to have come to someone's attention
WORD ORIGIN from the initial letters of *radio detection and ranging*

radial *ADJECTIVE*
❶ to do with rays or radii ❷ having spokes or lines that radiate from a central point
➤ **radially** *ADVERB*

radiant *ADJECTIVE*
❶ radiating light or heat • *the radiant sun*
❷ transmitted by radiation • *radiant heat*
❸ looking very bright and happy • *a radiant smile*
➤ **radiantly** *ADVERB*
➤ **radiance** *NOUN*

radiate *VERB* **radiates, radiating, radiated**
❶ to send out light, heat or other energy in rays ❷ to give out a strong feeling or quality • *She radiated confidence.* ❸ to spread out from a central point like the spokes of a wheel • *The city's streets radiate from the central square.*

radiation *NOUN*
❶ light, heat or other energy given out by something ❷ the energy or particles sent out by a radioactive substance ❸ the process of radiating light, heat or other energy

radiator *NOUN* **radiators**
❶ a device that gives out heat, especially a metal case that is heated electrically or through which steam or hot water flows
❷ a device that cools the engine of a motor vehicle

radical *ADJECTIVE*
❶ basic and thorough; going right to the root of something • *Radical changes are needed.*
❷ wanting to make great social or political reforms • *a radical politician*
➤ **radically** *ADVERB*

radical *NOUN* **radicals**
a person who wants to make great social or political reforms **WORD ORIGIN** from Latin *radicis* = of a root

radicchio (say ra-**dee**-ki-oh) *NOUN*
a kind of chicory with dark red leaves

radio *NOUN* **radios**
❶ the process of sending and receiving sound or pictures by means of electromagnetic waves ❷ an apparatus for receiving radio programmes or for sending or receiving radio messages ❸ sound broadcasting

radio *VERB* **radios, radioing, radioed**
to send a message to someone by radio

radioactive *ADJECTIVE*
having atoms that break up spontaneously and send out radiation which produces electrical and chemical effects and penetrates things
➤ **radioactivity** *NOUN*

radio beacon *NOUN* **radio beacons**
an instrument that sends out radio signals, which aircraft use to find their way

radiocarbon dating *NOUN*
carbon dating

radiography *NOUN*
the production of X-ray photographs
➤ **radiographer** *NOUN*

radiology *NOUN*
the study of X-rays and similar radiation, especially in treating diseases
➤ **radiologist** *NOUN*

radio telescope *NOUN* **radio telescopes**
an instrument that can detect radio waves from space

radiotherapy *NOUN*
the use of radioactive substances in treating diseases such as cancer

radish *NOUN* **radishes**
a small hard round red vegetable with a hot taste, eaten raw in salads

radium *NOUN*
a radioactive substance found in pitchblende, often used in radiotherapy

radius *NOUN* **radii** or **radiuses**
❶ a straight line from the centre of a circle to the circumference; the length of this line ❷ a range or distance from a central point • *The school takes pupils living within a radius of ten kilometres.*

radon *NOUN*
a radioactive gas used in radiotherapy

RAF *ABBREVIATION*
Royal Air Force

raffia *NOUN*
soft fibre from the leaves of a kind of palm tree, used for making mats and baskets

raffle *NOUN* **raffles**
a way of raising money, usually for a charity, by selling numbered tickets, some of which win prizes

raffle *VERB* **raffles, raffling, raffled**
to offer something as a prize in a raffle

raft *NOUN* **rafts**
❶ a flat floating structure made of wood etc., used as a boat ❷ a large number or amount of things • *a raft of new proposals*

rafter *NOUN* **rafters**
any of the long sloping pieces of wood that hold up a roof

rag *NOUN* **rags**
❶ an old or torn piece of cloth ❷ a piece of ragtime music ❸ (*British*) a series of entertainments and activities held by students to collect money for charity
➤ **dressed in rags** wearing old and torn clothes

rag *VERB* **rags, ragging, ragged**
(*informal*) to tease someone

rage *NOUN* **rages**
great or violent anger
➤ **all the rage** very popular or fashionable for a time

rage *VERB* **rages, raging, raged**
❶ to be very angry ❷ to continue violently or with great force • *The storm was still raging outside.*

ragged (say **rag**-id) *ADJECTIVE*
❶ torn or frayed ❷ wearing torn clothes

❸ not smooth or controlled • *a ragged performance*

ragtime *NOUN*
a kind of jazz music played on the piano

raid *NOUN* **raids**
❶ a sudden attack ❷ a surprise visit by police to arrest people or seize illegal goods

raid *VERB* **raids, raiding, raided**
to make a raid on a place
➤ **raider** *NOUN*

rail *NOUN* **rails**
❶ a level or sloping bar for hanging things on or forming part of a fence or banisters ❷ a long metal bar forming part of a railway track
➤ **by rail** on a train

rail *VERB* **rails, railing, railed**
to complain angrily or bitterly about something • *She railed against the injustice of it all.*

railings *PLURAL NOUN*
a fence made of metal bars

railroad *NOUN* **railroads**
(*North American*) a railway

railway *NOUN* (*British*)
❶ the parallel metal bars that trains travel on ❷ a system of transport using rails

raiment *NOUN* (*old use*)
clothing

rain *NOUN*
drops of water that fall from the sky

rain *VERB* **rains, raining, rained**
❶ it is raining when rain is falling • *It was raining heavily.* ❷ to come down in large amounts • *Bombs rained down on the city.* ❸ to send something down in large amounts • *They rained blows on him.*

rainbow *NOUN* **rainbows**
an arch of all the colours of the spectrum formed in the sky when the sun shines through rain

raincoat *NOUN* **raincoats**
a waterproof coat

raindrop *NOUN* **raindrops**
a single drop of rain

rainfall *NOUN*
the amount of rain that falls in a particular place or time

rainforest *NOUN* **rainforests**
a dense tropical forest in an area of very heavy rainfall

a b c d e f g h i j k l m n o p q r s t u v w x y z

rainy *ADJECTIVE*
having a lot of rainfall • *the rainy season*

raise *VERB* **raises, raising, raised**
❶ to move something to a higher place or an upright position ❷ to increase the amount or level of something • *We are trying to raise standards.* ❸ to succeed in collecting an amount of money • *The event raised €2000 for the earthquake appeal.* ❹ to bring up young children or animals • *She had to raise her family alone.* ❺ to mention or put something forward for people to think about • *We raised several objections.* ❻ to raise a laugh or smile is to make people laugh or smile ❼ to raise your voice is to speak more loudly

raisin *NOUN* **raisins**
a dried grape

raison d'être (say ray-zawn **detr**) *NOUN*
raisons d'être
the reason or purpose for a thing's existence
WORD ORIGIN French, = reason for being

Raj (say rahj) *NOUN*
the period of Indian history when the country was ruled by Britain

raja, rajah *NOUN* **rajas, rajahs**
an Indian king or prince. Compare with **ranee**.

rake *NOUN* **rakes**
❶ a gardening tool with a row of short spikes fixed to a long handle ❷ (*old use*) a man who lives an irresponsible and immoral life

rake *VERB* **rakes, raking, raked**
❶ to gather or smooth something with a rake • *He was in the garden raking up leaves.* ❷ to search through something • *I raked around in my desk for the letter.*
➤ **rake it in** (*informal*) to make a lot of money
➤ **rake something up** to start talking about something that it would be better to forget • *Don't rake all that up again.*

rakish (say **ray**-kish) *ADJECTIVE*
jaunty and dashing in appearance • *His hat was tilted at a rakish angle.*
➤ **rakishly** *ADVERB*

rally *NOUN* **rallies**
❶ a large meeting to support something or share an interest ❷ a competition to test skill in driving • *the Monte Carlo Rally* ❸ an exchange of strokes in tennis, squash, etc. before a point is won

rally *VERB* **rallies, rallying, rallied**
❶ to bring people together for a united effort
• *They rallied support for the campaign.* ❷ to come together to help or support someone • *My family all rallied round.* ❸ to improve or become stronger after an illness or setback • *She came fourth in the 800m, but rallied to win the 400m.*

RAM *ABBREVIATION*
(*in computing*) random-access memory, with contents that can be retrieved or stored directly without having to read through items already stored

ram *NOUN* **rams**
❶ a male sheep ❷ a part of a machine that is used for hitting something very hard

ram *VERB* **rams, ramming, rammed**
❶ to push one thing hard against another • *He quickly rammed the gun into his pocket.* ❷ to crash into another vehicle

Ramadan *NOUN*
the ninth month of the Muslim year, when Muslims do not eat or drink between sunrise and sunset

ramble *NOUN* **rambles**
a long walk in the countryside

ramble *VERB* **rambles, rambling, rambled**
❶ to go for a ramble; to wander ❷ to talk a lot without keeping to the subject • *Halfway through the speech he began to ramble.*
➤ **rambler** *NOUN*

rambling *ADJECTIVE*
❶ confused and wandering from one subject to another • *a rambling speech* ❷ growing or spreading in many directions • *a rambling old house*

ramifications *PLURAL NOUN*
the many effects of a plan or action • *The decision had far-reaching ramifications.*

ramp *NOUN* **ramps**
a slope joining two different levels

rampage *VERB* **rampages, rampaging, rampaged**
to rush about wildly or destructively • *a herd of rampaging elephants*
➤ **on the rampage** rushing about wildly

rampant *ADJECTIVE*
❶ growing or spreading uncontrollably • *Disease was rampant in the poorer districts.* ❷ (said about an animal on coats of arms) standing upright on a hind leg • *a lion rampant*

rampart *NOUN* **ramparts**
a wide bank of earth built as a fortification or a wall on top of this

ramrod *NOUN* **ramrods**
a straight rod formerly used for ramming an explosive into a gun
➤ **like a ramrod** very stiff and straight

ramshackle *ADJECTIVE*
badly made and rickety • *a ramshackle hut*

ranch *NOUN* **ranches**
a large cattle farm in North America

rancid *ADJECTIVE*
smelling or tasting unpleasant like stale fat

rancour (say **rank**-er) *NOUN*
bitter resentment or ill will
➤ **rancorous** *ADJECTIVE*

random *NOUN*
➤ **at random** using no particular order or method • *The numbers were chosen at random.*

random *ADJECTIVE*
done or taken at random • *a random sample*
➤ **randomly** *ADVERB*

ranee (say **rah**-nee) *NOUN* **ranees**
a raja's wife or widow

range *NOUN* **ranges**
❶ a set of different things of the same type • *a wide range of backgrounds* • *a lovely range of colours* ❷ the limits between which something varies • *the age range 15 to 18* ❸ the distance that a gun can shoot, an aircraft can travel or a sound can be heard ❹ a place with targets for shooting practice ❺ a line or series of mountains or hills ❻ a kitchen fireplace with ovens

range *VERB* **ranges, ranging, ranged**
❶ to exist or vary between two limits • *Prices ranged from £1 to £50.* ❷ to arrange things in a certain way • *The desks were ranged in straight lines.* ❸ to wander or move over a wide area • *Hens ranged all over the farm.*

Ranger *NOUN* **Rangers**
a senior Guide

ranger *NOUN* **rangers**
someone who looks after or patrols a park or forest

rank *NOUN* **ranks**
❶ a position in a series of different levels • *He holds the rank of sergeant.* ❷ a line of people or things • *ranks of marching soldiers* ❸ a place where taxis stand to wait for customers

rank *VERB* **ranks, ranking, ranked**
❶ to have a certain rank or place • *She ranks among the greatest novelists.* ❷ to put things in order according to their rank • *The puzzles are ranked in order of difficulty.*

rank *ADJECTIVE* **ranker, rankest**
❶ smelling very unpleasant ❷ unmistakably bad; complete • *rank stupidity* ❸ growing too thickly and coarsely

rank and file *NOUN*
the ordinary people or soldiers, not the leaders

rankle *VERB* **rankles, rankling, rankled**
to cause lasting annoyance or resentment • *What she said that night still rankled with him.*

ransack *VERB* **ransacks, ransacking, ransacked**
❶ to search a place thoroughly or roughly ❷ to rob or pillage a place

ransom *NOUN* **ransoms**
money that has to be paid for a prisoner to be set free
➤ **hold someone to ransom** to keep someone a prisoner and demand a ransom

ransom *VERB* **ransoms, ransoming, ransomed**
❶ to free someone by paying a ransom ❷ to get a ransom for someone

rant *VERB* **rants, ranting, ranted**
to speak or shout loudly and angrily

rant *NOUN* **rants**
a spell of ranting

rap *VERB* **raps, rapping, rapped**
❶ to knock quickly and loudly • *He rapped at the door with his stick.* ❷ to speak words rapidly in rhythm to a strong musical beat ❸ (*informal*) to criticize someone strongly

rap *NOUN* **raps**
❶ a rapping movement or sound • *There was a rap at the door.* ❷ a type of pop music in which you speak words rapidly in rhythm to a strong musical beat
➤ **take the rap** (*informal*) to take the blame or punishment for something

rapacious (say ra-**pay**-shus) *ADJECTIVE*
greedy and grasping, especially for money
➤ **rapacity** *NOUN*

rape *NOUN* **rapes**
❶ the crime of forcing someone to have sexual intercourse when they do not want to ❷ a plant with bright yellow flowers, grown as food for sheep and for its seed from which oil is obtained

a
b
c
d
e
f
g
h
i
j
k
l
m
n
o
p
q
r
s
t
u
v
w
x
y
z

rape *VERB* rapes, raping, raped
to force someone to have sexual intercourse
➤ **rapist** *NOUN*

rapid *ADJECTIVE*
moving or happening very quickly; swift • *She is making rapid progress.*
➤ **rapidly** *ADVERB*
➤ **rapidity** *NOUN*

rapids *PLURAL NOUN*
part of a river where the water flows very quickly

rapier *NOUN* rapiers
a thin lightweight sword

rapport (say rap-**or**) *NOUN*
a friendly and understanding relationship between people

rapt *ADJECTIVE*
so interested and absorbed in something that you do not notice anything else • *She listened with rapt attention.*

rapture *NOUN*
very great joy or delight
➤ **rapturous** *ADJECTIVE*
➤ **rapturously** *ADVERB*

rare *ADJECTIVE* rarer, rarest
❶ unusual; not often found or happening • *a rare species of butterfly* ❷ meat is rare when it is lightly cooked so that the inside is still red

rarefied *ADJECTIVE*
❶ rarefied air is thin and below normal pressure ❷ remote from everyday life • *the rarefied atmosphere of the university*

rarely *ADVERB*
not very often • *She is rarely seen in public.*

rarity *NOUN* rarities
❶ rareness ❷ something uncommon; a thing valued because it is rare

rascal *NOUN* rascals
a dishonest or mischievous person
➤ **rascally** *ADJECTIVE*

rash *ADJECTIVE*
doing something or done without thinking of the possible risks or effects • *It was a rash decision.*
➤ **rashly** *ADVERB*
➤ **rashness** *NOUN*

rash *NOUN* rashes
❶ an outbreak of red spots or patches on the skin ❷ a number of unwelcome events happening in a short time • *a rash of accidents*

rasher *NOUN* rashers
a slice of bacon

rasp *NOUN* rasps
❶ a file with sharp points on its surface ❷ a rough grating sound

rasp *VERB* rasps, rasping, rasped
❶ to say something in a rough unpleasant voice • *'Come with me,' he rasped.* ❷ to make a rough grating sound or effect • *a rasping cough* ❸ to scrape something roughly

raspberry *NOUN* raspberries
a small soft red fruit

Rastafarian *NOUN* Rastafarians
a member of a religious group that started in Jamaica **WORD ORIGIN** from *Ras Tafari* (*ras* = chief), the title of a former Ethiopian king whom the group reveres

rat *NOUN* rats
❶ an animal like a large mouse ❷ an unpleasant or treacherous person

ratchet *NOUN* ratchets
a row of notches on a bar or wheel in which a device catches to prevent it running backwards

rate *NOUN* rates
❶ how fast or how often something happens • *Crime was increasing at a great rate.* ❷ a charge, cost or value • *Postage rates went up.* ❸ quality or standard • *first-rate*
➤ **at any rate** anyway; whatever else is true
➤ **at this rate** if this is typical or true

rate *VERB* rates, rating, rated
❶ to say how good you think something is • *Drivers rate the new car very highly.* ❷ to regard something in a certain way • *I rated the show as a success.*

rates *PLURAL NOUN*
a local tax paid by owners of commercial land and buildings

rather *ADVERB*
❶ slightly or quite • *It's rather dark in there.* ❷ you would rather do one thing than another thing if you would prefer to do it • *I would rather wait until tomorrow.* ❸ more exactly; instead of • *She lay down or rather fell, on the bed.* • *He is lazy rather than stupid.* ❹ (*informal*) definitely, yes • *'Will you come?' 'Rather!'*

ratify *VERB* ratifies, ratifying, ratified
to confirm or agree to something officially • *They ratified the treaty.*
➤ **ratification** *NOUN*

rating *NOUN* **ratings**
❶ the way something is rated ❷ a sailor who is not an officer

ratio (say **ray**-shee-oh) *NOUN* **ratios**
❶ the relationship between two numbers, showing how many times one number goes into the other • *The ratio of 2 to 10 = 2:10 = ²⁄₁₀ = ⅕* ❷ proportion • *Mix flour and butter in the ratio of two to one.* (= two measures of flour to one measure of butter)

ration *NOUN* **rations**
❶ a fixed amount allowed to one person ❷ rations are a fixed daily amount of food given to a soldier or member of an expedition

ration *VERB* **rations, rationing, rationed**
to share something out in fixed amounts • *We had to ration the water carefully.*

rational *ADJECTIVE*
❶ reasonable or sensible; based on reason • *There must be a rational explanation for this.* ❷ able to reason and make sensible decisions • *No rational person would ever behave like that.*
➤ **rationally** *ADVERB*
➤ **rationality** *NOUN*

rationalize (also **rationalise**) *VERB* **rationalizes, rationalizing, rationalized**
❶ to make a thing logical and consistent • *Attempts to rationalize English spelling have failed.* ❷ to justify something by inventing a reasonable explanation for it • *She rationalized her meanness by calling it economy.* ❸ to make a company or industry more efficient by reorganizing it
➤ **rationalization** *NOUN*

rat race *NOUN*
a continuous struggle for success in a career or business

rattle *VERB* **rattles, rattling, rattled**
❶ to make a series of short sharp hard sounds • *The windows were rattling in the wind.* ❷ to move quickly with a rattling noise • *A train rattled by.* ❸ to make a person feel nervous or flustered
➤ **rattle something off** to say or recite something rapidly

rattle *NOUN* **rattles**
❶ a rattling sound ❷ a device or baby's toy that rattles

rattlesnake *NOUN* **rattlesnakes**
a poisonous American snake with a tail that rattles

rattling *ADJECTIVE*
vigorous or brisk • *a rattling pace*

ratty *ADJECTIVE* **rattier, rattiest** (*informal*)
angry or irritable

raucous (say **raw**-kus) *ADJECTIVE*
sounding loud and harsh • *raucous laughter*

ravage *VERB* **ravages, ravaging, ravaged**
to do great damage to something; to devastate a place or thing • *The country has been ravaged by war.*

ravages *PLURAL NOUN*
damaging effects • *the ravages of war*

rave *VERB* **raves, raving, raved**
❶ to talk wildly or angrily or madly ❷ to talk enthusiastically about something • *He's been raving about the band he saw last night.*

rave *NOUN* **raves** (*informal*) a large party or event with dancing to loud fast electronic music
➤ **rave review** a very enthusiastic review

raven *NOUN* **ravens**
a large black bird, related to the crow

ravenous *ADJECTIVE*
very hungry
➤ **ravenously** *ADVERB*

ravine (say ra-**veen**) *NOUN* **ravines**
a deep narrow gorge or valley
WORD ORIGIN French, = a rush of water (because a ravine is cut by rushing water)

ravings *PLURAL NOUN*
wild talk that makes no sense

ravioli *NOUN*
small squares of pasta filled with meat and served with a sauce

ravishing *ADJECTIVE*
very beautiful

raw *ADJECTIVE*
❶ not cooked ❷ in the natural state; not yet processed • *raw sugar* ❸ without much experience • *raw recruits* ❹ with the skin removed • *a raw wound* ❺ cold and damp • *a raw morning*
➤ **a raw deal** unfair treatment
➤ **rawness** *NOUN*

raw material *NOUN* **raw materials**
natural substances used in industry • *iron ore, coal and other raw materials*

ray *NOUN* **rays**
❶ a thin line of light, heat or other radiation ❷ each of a set of lines or parts extending

a
b
c
d
e
f
g
h
i
j
k
l
m
n
o
p
q
r
s
t
u
v
w
x
y
z

from a centre ❸ a trace of something • *a ray of hope* ❹ ray or rays a large sea fish with a flat body and a long tail

rayon *NOUN*
a synthetic fibre or cloth made from cellulose
(**WORD ORIGIN**) a made-up word, probably based on French *rayon* = a ray of light (because of its shiny surface)

raze *VERB* **razes, razing, razed**
to destroy a building or town completely
• *The fort was razed to the ground.*

razor *NOUN* **razors**
a device with a very sharp blade, especially one used for shaving
➤ **razor blade** *NOUN*

razzmatazz *NOUN* (*informal*)
showy publicity or activity

RC *ABBREVIATION*
Roman Catholic

re- *PREFIX*
again (as in *rebuild*)

reach *VERB* **reaches, reaching, reached**
❶ to go as far as a place or point; to arrive at a place or thing ❷ to stretch out your hand to get or touch something ❸ to succeed in achieving something • *The cheetah can reach a speed of 70 mph.* • *Have you reached a decision?*

reach *NOUN* **reaches**
❶ the distance a person or thing can reach ❷ a distance you can easily travel • *We live within reach of the sea.*

react *VERB* **reacts, reacting, reacted**
❶ to respond to something; to have a reaction • *How did she react to the news?* ❷ to undergo a chemical change

reaction *NOUN* **reactions**
❶ an effect or feeling produced in one person or thing by another • *My immediate reaction was one of shock.* ❷ a chemical change caused when substances act upon each other
➤ **reactions** your ability to move quickly in response to something • *Racing drivers need to have quick reactions.*

reactor *NOUN* **reactors**
an apparatus for producing nuclear power in a controlled way

read *VERB* **reads, reading, read** (say red)
❶ to look at something written or printed and understand it or say it aloud ❷ a computer reads data when it copies, searches

or extracts it ❸ to show a particular number or amount • *The thermometer reads 20° Celsius.* ❹ to study a subject at university

(**SPELLING**)
The past tense of **read** is the same spelling but rhymes with **red**.

readable *ADJECTIVE*
❶ easy or enjoyable to read • *The book is very readable.* ❷ clear and able to be read • *The writing was faint but still readable.*

reader *NOUN* **readers**
❶ a person who reads ❷ a device that reads or displays data ❸ a book that helps someone learn to read

readership *NOUN* **readerships**
the readers of a newspaper or magazine; the number of these

readily (say **red**-il-ee) *ADVERB*
❶ willingly or eagerly • *She readily agreed to help.* ❷ easily; without any difficulty • *All the ingredients you need are readily available.*

readiness *NOUN*
❶ being ready or prepared for something
• *All was in readiness for the journey.*
❷ being willing to do something • *She expressed her readiness to help them.*

reading *NOUN* **readings**
❶ the activity of reading books and other forms of writing • *He loves reading.* ❷ the figure shown on a meter, gauge or other instrument ❸ a gathering of people at which something is read aloud • *a poetry reading*

ready *ADJECTIVE* **readier, readiest**
❶ fully prepared to do something; completed and able to be used • *Are you ready to go?*
• *The meal's ready.* ❷ willing to do something ❸ quick and clever • *a ready wit*
➤ **at the ready** ready for use or action

ready *ADVERB*
beforehand • *This meat is ready cooked.*

ready–made *ADJECTIVE*
made already and so able to be used or served immediately

reagent *NOUN* **reagents**
a substance used in a chemical reaction, especially to detect another substance

real *ADJECTIVE*
❶ actually existing, not imaginary • *The character is based on a real person.* ❷ actual or true • *That isn't his real name.* ❸ genuine; not an imitation • *real pearls*

real estate *NOUN* (*North American*)
property consisting of land and buildings

realism *NOUN*
seeing or showing things as they really are
➤ **realist** *NOUN*

realistic *ADJECTIVE*
❶ true to life • *a realistic painting* ❷ seeing things as they really are • *She is realistic about her chances of winning.*
➤ **realistically** *ADVERB*

reality *NOUN* **realities**
❶ what is real • *You must face reality.*
❷ something real • *Her worst fears had become a reality.*

reality TV *NOUN*
television shows that are based on real people, not actors, in real situations

realization (also **realisation**) *NOUN*
realizing something • *Then came the realization of what he had done.*

realize (also **realise**) *VERB* **realizes, realizing, realized**
❶ to be fully aware of something; to accept something as true • *He suddenly realized that he was sitting on an ants' nest.* ❷ to make a hope or plan happen • *She realized her ambition to become a racing driver.* ❸ to obtain money in exchange for something by selling it

really *ADVERB*
❶ truly or in fact • *Tell me what really happened.* ❷ very • *She's really clever.*

> SPELLING
> There is a double l in **really**.

realm (say **relm**) *NOUN* **realms**
❶ a kingdom ❷ an area of knowledge or interest • *the realms of science*

reams *PLURAL NOUN*
a large quantity of writing or information

reap *VERB* **reaps, reaping, reaped**
❶ to cut down and gather corn when it is ripe ❷ to gain something as the result of something you have done • *They are now reaping the benefits of all that training.*
➤ **reaper** *NOUN*

reappear *VERB* **reappears, reappearing, reappeared**
to appear again
➤ **reappearance** *NOUN*

reappraise *VERB* **reappraises, reappraising, reappraised**

to think about or examine something again
➤ **reappraisal** *NOUN*

rear *NOUN*
the back part of something

rear *ADJECTIVE*
placed or found at the back • *a rear wheel*

rear *VERB* **rears, rearing, reared**
❶ to care for and bring up young children or animals ❷ a horse rears when it rises up on its hind legs so that its front legs are in the air • *My horse reared up in fright.* ❸ to rise up over you • *A huge crane reared up in front of us.*

rearguard *NOUN* **rearguards**
troops protecting the rear of an army
➤ **fight a rearguard action** to go on defending or resisting something even though you are losing

rearrange *VERB* **rearranges, rearranging, rearranged**
to arrange something in a different way or order • *Will you help me rearrange the furniture?*
➤ **rearrangement** *NOUN*

reason *NOUN* **reasons**
❶ a cause or explanation of something; why something happens • *What is the reason for the delay?* ❷ reasoning; common sense • *He wouldn't listen to reason.*

reason *VERB* **reasons, reasoning, reasoned**
❶ to use your ability to think and draw conclusions ❷ to try to persuade someone by giving reasons • *It's no use trying to reason with her.*

reasonable *ADJECTIVE*
❶ ready to use or listen to reason; sensible or logical ❷ fair or moderate; not expensive • *These are reasonable prices for what you get.* ❸ acceptable or fairly good • *a reasonable standard of living*

reasonably *ADVERB*
❶ in a reasonable way; sensibly • *They were behaving quite reasonably.* ❷ fairly or quite • *They get on reasonably well.*

reassure *VERB* **reassures, reassuring, reassured**
to restore someone's confidence by removing doubts and fears • *I tried to reassure them that there was nothing wrong.*
➤ **reassurance** *NOUN*

rebate *NOUN* **rebates**
a reduction in the amount to be paid; a partial refund

rebel (say rib-**el**) *VERB* rebels, rebelling, rebelled
to refuse to obey someone in authority, especially the government; to fight against the rulers of your own country

rebel (say **reb**-el) *NOUN* rebels
❶ someone who rejects accepted standards of behaviour ❷ someone who fights against their country's government because they want things to change (**WORD ORIGIN**) from Latin *bellum* = war (originally referring to a defeated enemy who began to fight again)

rebellion *NOUN* rebellions
❶ rebelling against authority ❷ organized armed resistance to the government; a revolt

rebellious *ADJECTIVE*
often refusing to obey authority; likely to rebel • *a rebellious child*

rebirth *NOUN*
a return to life or activity; a revival of something • *the seasonal cycle of death and rebirth*

rebound *VERB* rebounds, rebounding, rebounded
to bounce back after hitting something

rebound *NOUN*
➤ **on the rebound** to hit a ball on the rebound is to hit it when it has bounced up or back

rebuff *NOUN* rebuffs
an unkind refusal; a snub

rebuff *VERB* rebuffs, rebuffing, rebuffed
to give someone a rebuff

rebuild *VERB* rebuilds, rebuilding, rebuilt
to build something again after it has been destroyed

rebuke *VERB* rebukes, rebuking, rebuked
to speak severely to a person who has done wrong

rebuke *NOUN* rebukes
a sharp or severe criticism

recalcitrant *ADJECTIVE*
disobedient or uncooperative
➤ **recalcitrance** *NOUN*

recall *VERB* recalls, recalling, recalled
❶ to remember something from the past • *Can you recall exactly what happened?* ❷ to tell a person to come back ❸ to ask for a product to be returned because it is faulty

recall *NOUN*
❶ the ability to remember; remembering

something ❷ an order for a person to return or for a thing to be returned

recap *VERB* recaps, recapping, recapped (*informal*)
to summarize what has been said
➤ **recap** *NOUN*

recapitulate *VERB* recapitulates, recapitulating, recapitulated
to state again the main points of what has been said
➤ **recapitulation** *NOUN*

recapture *VERB* recaptures, recapturing, recaptured
❶ to catch a person or animal that has escaped ❷ to take back a place that was taken from you • *Saladin recaptured Jerusalem in 1187.* ❸ to bring or get back a mood or feeling • *He was trying to recapture the happiness of his youth.*
➤ **recapture** *NOUN*

recede *VERB* recedes, receding, receded
❶ to move back or away • *The floods have receded.* ❷ to become less strong or severe • *His fear began to recede.* ❸ a man's hair is receding when he starts to go bald at the front of his head

receipt (say ris-**eet**) *NOUN* receipts
❶ a written statement that money has been paid or something has been received ❷ receiving something

receive *VERB* receives, receiving, received
❶ to take or get something that is given or sent to you ❷ to experience something • *He received injuries to his face and hands.* ❸ to react to something in a certain way • *The play was well received by the critics.* ❹ to greet a guest or visitor

SPELLING
In receive, e before i is the right way round.

receiver *NOUN* receivers
❶ a person or thing that receives something ❷ a radio or television set that receives broadcasts ❸ the part of a telephone that receives the sound and that you hold to your ear ❹ an official who takes charge of a bankrupt person's property ❺ a person who buys and sells stolen goods

recent *ADJECTIVE*
happening or made or done a short time ago • *Please enclose a recent photograph.*

recently ADVERB
not long ago • *I received an email from her recently.*

receptacle NOUN **receptacles**
something for holding or containing what is put into it

reception NOUN **receptions**
❶ the type of welcome that a person or thing receives • *We were given a friendly reception.* ❷ a formal party to receive guests • *a wedding reception* ❸ a place in a hotel or office where visitors are greeted and registered ❹ the first class in an infant school ❺ the quality of television or radio signals • *We have poor reception because of the surrounding hills.*

receptionist NOUN **receptionists**
a person whose job is to greet and deal with visitors, clients or patients

receptive ADJECTIVE
quick or willing to receive ideas

recess (say ris-**ess**) NOUN **recesses**
❶ a section of a wall that is set back from the main part; an alcove ❷ a time when work or business is stopped for a while

recession NOUN **recessions**
a reduction in a country's trade or prosperity

recharge VERB **recharges, recharging, recharged**
to put more electrical power into a battery
➤ **rechargeable** ADJECTIVE

recipe (say **ress**-ip-ee) NOUN **recipes**
a list of ingredients and instructions for preparing or cooking food
WORD ORIGIN Latin, = take (which was used at the beginning of a list of ingredients)

recipient NOUN **recipients**
a person who receives something

reciprocal (say ris-**ip**-rok-al) ADJECTIVE
given or done in return for the same thing that is given to or done for you; mutual • *The arrangement is reciprocal: they help us and we help them.*

reciprocal NOUN **reciprocals**
a reversed fraction • *$\frac{3}{2}$ is the reciprocal of $\frac{2}{3}$*

reciprocate VERB **reciprocates, reciprocating, reciprocated**
to behave or feel towards someone in the same way as they behave or feel towards you; to do the same thing in return • *She did not reciprocate his love.*

recital NOUN **recitals**
❶ reciting something ❷ a musical entertainment given by one performer or group

recite VERB **recites, reciting, recited**
to say a poem or other piece of writing aloud from memory
➤ **recitation** NOUN

reckless ADJECTIVE
rash; ignoring risk or danger • *He was a reckless driver.*
➤ **recklessly** ADVERB
➤ **recklessness** NOUN

reckon VERB **reckons, reckoning, reckoned**
❶ to have something as an opinion; to think or believe something • *I reckon it's going to rain.* ❷ to calculate an amount or total
➤ **reckon on something** to expect something and base your plans on it • *They hadn't reckoned on it being so expensive.*
➤ **reckon with something** to think about or deal with something • *We didn't reckon with the rail strike when we planned our journey.*

reclaim VERB **reclaims, reclaiming, reclaimed**
❶ to claim or get something back • *I reclaimed my umbrella from the lost property office.* ❷ to reclaim land is to make it suitable for farming or building on again by clearing or draining it
➤ **reclamation** NOUN

recline VERB **reclines, reclining, reclined**
to lean or lie back

recluse NOUN **recluses**
a person who lives alone and avoids mixing with people
➤ **reclusive** ADJECTIVE

recognition NOUN
recognizing someone or something • *She looked at me with no sign of recognition on her face.*

recognize (also **recognise**) VERB **recognizes, recognizing, recognized**
❶ to know who someone is or what something is because you have seen that person or thing before ❷ to realize or admit something • *She recognized the truth of what he was saying.* ❸ to accept something as genuine, valid or lawful • *Nine countries recognized the island's new government.*
➤ **recognizable** ADJECTIVE

recoil VERB **recoils, recoiling, recoiled**
❶ to move back suddenly in shock or disgust

a
b
c
d
e
f
g
h
i
j
k
l
m
n
o
p
q
r
s
t
u
v
w
x
y
z

• *He recoiled in horror.* ❷ a gun recoils when it jerks backwards when it is fired

recollect VERB recollects, recollecting, recollected
to remember something

recollection NOUN recollections
❶ being able to remember something • *I have no recollection of seeing her before.* ❷ something you remember

recommend VERB recommends, recommending, recommended
❶ to suggest something because you think it is good or suitable • *I recommend the strawberry ice cream.* ❷ to advise someone to do something • *We recommend that you wear strong boots on the walk.*

recommendation NOUN recommendations
❶ saying that something is good and should be tried or used ❷ a statement about what should be done

recompense VERB recompenses, recompensing, recompensed
to give a person money to make up for a loss or to reward them for something they have done for you
➤ **recompense** NOUN

reconcile VERB reconciles, reconciling, reconciled
❶ to be reconciled with someone is to become friendly with them again after quarrelling or fighting with them ❷ to be reconciled to something is to be persuaded to put up with it • *He soon became reconciled to wearing glasses.* ❸ to make things agree • *I cannot reconcile what you say with what you do.*
➤ **reconciliation** NOUN

reconnaissance (say rik-**on**-i-sans) NOUN
an exploration of an area, especially in order to gather information about it for military purposes

reconnoitre VERB reconnoitres, reconnoitring, reconnoitred
to make a reconnaissance of an area

reconsider VERB reconsiders, reconsidering, reconsidered
to consider something again and perhaps change an earlier decision
➤ **reconsideration** NOUN

reconstitute VERB reconstitutes, reconstituting, reconstituted
❶ to form something again, especially in a

different way ❷ to make dried food edible again by adding water

reconstruct VERB reconstructs, reconstructing, reconstructed
❶ to construct or build something again ❷ to create or act out past events again • *Police reconstructed the robbery.*
➤ **reconstruction** NOUN

record (say **rek**-ord) NOUN records
❶ information kept in a permanent form, e.g. in writing or stored on a computer ❷ the best performance in a sport etc. or the most remarkable event of its kind • *She holds the record for the high jump.* ❸ what is known about a person's past life or career • *He has an impressive record as a football manager.* ❹ a disc on which sound has been recorded

record (say **rek**-ord) ADJECTIVE
best, highest or most extreme recorded up to now • *A record crowd watched the match.*

record (say rik-**ord**) VERB records, recording, recorded
❶ to keep information by writing it down or storing it on a computer ❷ to store sounds or scenes (e.g. television pictures) using electronic equipment so that you can play or show them later

recorder NOUN recorders
❶ a kind of flute held downwards from the player's mouth ❷ a person or thing that records something

record player NOUN record players
a machine that plays records

recount VERB recounts, recounting, recounted
❶ (say ri-**kownt**)
to give an account of something • *We recounted our adventures.* ❷ (say ree-kownt) to count something again

recount (say **ree**-kownt) NOUN recounts
counting something again, especially votes in an election

recoup (say ri-**koop**) VERB recoups, recouping, recouped
to recover the cost of an investment or of a loss

recourse NOUN
a source of help
➤ **have recourse to someone or something**
to go to a person or thing for help

recover VERB recovers, recovering, recovered
❶ to get well again after being ill or weak • *The driver is recovering in hospital.* ❷ to

get something back again after losing it • *The police have recovered the stolen paintings.*

recovery *NOUN* **recoveries**
❶ getting well again after being ill or weak ❷ getting something back again after losing it

recreation *NOUN* **recreations**
❶ enjoying yourself and relaxing when you are not working ❷ a game or hobby that is an enjoyable activity
➤ **recreational** *ADJECTIVE*

recrimination *NOUN* **recriminations**
an accusation made against a person who has criticized or blamed you

recruit *NOUN* **recruits**
❶ a person who has just joined the armed forces ❷ a new member of a society, company or other group

recruit *VERB* **recruits, recruiting, recruited**
❶ to get someone to join something you belong to ❷ to get someone to join the armed forces
➤ **recruitment** *NOUN*

rectangle *NOUN* **rectangles**
a shape with four straight sides and four right angles
➤ **rectangular** *ADJECTIVE*

rectify *VERB* **rectifies, rectifying, rectified**
to correct a mistake or put something right

rectitude *NOUN*
morally correct behaviour

rector *NOUN* **rectors**
a member of the Church of England clergy in charge of a parish

rectum *NOUN* **rectums** or **recta**
the last part of the large intestine, ending at the anus

recumbent *ADJECTIVE*
lying down

recuperate *VERB* **recuperates, recuperating, recuperated**
to get better after an illness
➤ **recuperation** *NOUN*

recur *VERB* **recurs, recurring, recurred**
to happen again or keep on happening • *a recurring dream*
➤ **recurrent** *ADJECTIVE*
➤ **recurrence** *NOUN*

recurring decimal *NOUN* **recurring decimals**
(*in mathematics*) a decimal fraction in

which a digit or group of digits is repeated indefinitely, e.g. 0.666 ...

recycle *VERB* **recycles, recycling, recycled**
to convert waste material into a form in which it can be used again • *Plastic bottles can be recycled.*
➤ **recycling** *NOUN*

red *ADJECTIVE* **redder, reddest**
❶ of the colour of blood or a colour rather like this ❷ red hair or fur is of a reddish brown colour ❸ having communist or socialist views
➤ **redness** *NOUN*

red *NOUN*
❶ a red colour ❷ a communist or socialist
➤ **in the red** in debt
➤ **see red** to become suddenly angry

red deer *NOUN* **red deer**
a kind of large deer with a reddish-brown coat, found in Europe and Asia

redden *VERB* **reddens, reddening, reddened**
to become red; to blush • *He reddened with embarrassment.*

reddish *ADJECTIVE*
fairly red

redeem *VERB* **redeems, redeeming, redeemed**
❶ to make up for faults • *His one redeeming feature is his generosity.* ❷ to get something back by paying for it or handing over a voucher ❸ to save a person from damnation, as in some religions
➤ **redeemer** *NOUN*
➤ **redemption** *NOUN*
➤ **redeem yourself** to do something good to make up for an earlier mistake

redevelop *VERB* **redevelops, redeveloping, redeveloped**
to develop a place or area in a different way
➤ **redevelopment** *NOUN*

red-handed *ADJECTIVE*
➤ **catch someone red-handed** to catch someone while they are actually committing a crime or doing something wrong

redhead *NOUN* **redheads**
a person with reddish hair

red herring *NOUN* **red herrings**
something that draws attention away from the main subject; a misleading clue
WORD ORIGIN because a red herring (= a kipper) put hounds off the scent when it was dragged across the path of the fox being hunted

a
b
c
d
e
f
g
h
i
j
k
l
m
n
o
p
q
r
s
t
u
v
w
x
y
z

A
B
C
D
E
F
G
H
I
J
K
L
M
N
O
P
Q
R
S
T
U
V
W
X
Y
Z

red-hot *ADJECTIVE*
very hot; so hot that it has turned red

red meat *NOUN*
meat, such as beef, lamb or mutton, which is red when raw

redolent (say **red**-ol-ent) *ADJECTIVE*
❶ smelling strongly of something • *The air was redolent of onions.* ❷ strongly suggesting or reminding you of something • *a castle redolent of romance*

redoubtable *ADJECTIVE*
formidable, especially as an opponent

redress *VERB* redresses, redressing, redressed
to correct something that is unfair or wrong • *It is time to redress this injustice.*
➤ **redress the balance** to make things equal again

redress *NOUN*
compensation for something wrong that has been done • *You should seek redress for this damage.*

red tape *NOUN*
all the rules and forms that make it difficult to get official business done quickly
WORD ORIGIN because bundles of official papers used to be tied up with red or pink tape

reduce *VERB* reduces, reducing, reduced
❶ to make something smaller or less • *We can reduce pollution by cycling instead of travelling by car.* ❷ to become smaller or less ❸ to force someone into a condition or situation • *He was reduced to borrowing the money.*

reduction *NOUN* reductions
❶ when something becomes smaller or less ❷ the amount by which a thing is reduced • *There were massive reductions in the sale.*

redundant *ADJECTIVE*
❶ no longer needed ❷ someone is made redundant when they lose their job because it is no longer needed
➤ **redundancy** *NOUN*

reed *NOUN* reeds
❶ a tall plant that grows in water or marshy ground ❷ a thin strip that vibrates to make the sound in a clarinet, saxophone, oboe, etc.

reedy *ADJECTIVE* reedier, reediest
❶ full of reeds ❷ a reedy voice has a thin high tone like a reed instrument

reef *NOUN* reefs
a ridge of rock, coral or sand, especially one near the surface of the sea

reef *VERB* reefs, reefing, reefed
to shorten a sail by drawing in a strip (called a **reef**) at the top or bottom to reduce the area exposed to the wind

reef knot *NOUN* reef knots
(*chiefly British*) a symmetrical double knot that is very secure

reek *VERB* reeks, reeking, reeked
to smell strongly or unpleasantly

reek *NOUN* reeks
a strong unpleasant smell • *the reek of sweat*

reel *NOUN* reels
❶ a round device on which cotton, thread or film is wound ❷ a lively Scottish dance or the music for this

reel *VERB* reels, reeling, reeled
❶ to wind something onto or off a reel ❷ to stagger ❸ to feel dizzy or confused • *I am still reeling from the shock.*
➤ **reel something off** to repeat something from memory quickly

re-elect *VERB* re-elects, re-electing, re-elected
to elect someone again

re-enter *VERB* re-enters, re-entering, re-entered
to enter a place or contest again
➤ **re-entry** *NOUN*

re-examine *VERB* re-examines, re-examining, re-examined
to examine someone or something again

ref *NOUN* refs (*informal*)
a referee

refectory *NOUN* refectories
the dining room of a college or monastery etc.

refer *VERB* refers, referring, referred
❶ to refer to someone or something is to mention them or speak about them • *I wasn't referring to you.* ❷ to refer to a dictionary or other source of information is to look in it so that you can find something out ❸ to refer a question or problem to someone else is to pass it on to them to deal with • *My doctor referred me to a specialist.*
➤ **referral** *NOUN*

referee *NOUN* referees
the person who has the job of seeing that people keep to the rules of a game

referee *VERB* referees, refereeing, refereed
to act as a referee

> SPELLING
> There is only one f and one r in referee.

reference *NOUN* references
❶ a mention of something • *There was no reference to recent events.* ❷ a direction to a book or page or file where information can be found ❸ a letter from a previous employer describing someone's abilities and qualities
➤ **in** or **with reference to** concerning or about

reference book *NOUN* reference books
a book (such as a dictionary or encyclopedia) that gives information about a subject

reference library *NOUN* reference libraries
a library where books can be used but not taken away

referendum *NOUN* referendums or referenda
a vote on a particular question by all the people of a country

refill *VERB* refills, refilling, refilled
to fill something again • *Can I refill your glass?*

refill *NOUN* refills
a container holding a substance which is used to refill something • *My pen needs a refill.*

refine *VERB* refines, refining, refined
❶ to remove impurities from a substance ❷ to improve something, especially by making small changes

refined *ADJECTIVE*
❶ made pure by having other substances taken out of it • *refined sugar* ❷ polite, educated and well-mannered

refinement *NOUN* refinements
❶ good manners and polite behaviour ❷ something added to improve a thing

refinery *NOUN* refineries
a factory for refining something • *an oil refinery*

reflect *VERB* reflects, reflecting, reflected
❶ to send back light, heat or sound from a surface ❷ to form an image of something as a mirror does ❸ to think deeply or carefully about something • *He spent some time reflecting on what had happened.* ❹ to be a sign of something or to make it clear • *Her hard work was reflected in her exam results.*
➤ **reflector** *NOUN*

reflection *NOUN* reflections
❶ an image you can see in a mirror or other reflecting surface ❷ reflecting light ❸ a spell of thinking about something • *I think, on reflection, that I was wrong.*

reflective *ADJECTIVE*
❶ reflecting light or heat • *reflective clothing* ❷ suggesting or showing serious thought • *a reflective expression*
➤ **reflectively** *ADVERB*

reflex *NOUN* reflexes
a movement or action that you do without any conscious thought • *The doctor tested her reflexes.*

reflex angle *NOUN* reflex angles
an angle of more than 180°

reflexive pronoun *NOUN* reflexive pronouns
(*in grammar*) any of the pronouns *myself, herself, himself,* etc. (as in 'She cut *herself*.'), which refer back to the subject of the verb

reflexive verb *NOUN* reflexive verbs
a verb where the subject and the object are the same person or thing, as in 'She *cut herself*.', 'The cat *washed itself*.'

reform *VERB* reforms, reforming, reformed
❶ to make changes in something in order to improve it ❷ to give up a criminal or immoral lifestyle or to make someone do this

reform *NOUN* reforms
❶ reform is changing something in order to improve it ❷ a reform is a change made in order to improve something

Reformation *NOUN*
the Reformation was a religious movement in Europe in the 16th century intended to reform certain teachings and practices of the Roman Catholic Church, which resulted in the establishment of the Reformed or Protestant Churches

reformer *NOUN* reformers
someone who makes reforms

refract *VERB* refracts, refracting, refracted
to bend a ray of light at the point where it enters water or glass at an angle
➤ **refraction** *NOUN*
➤ **refractive** *ADJECTIVE*

refractory *ADJECTIVE*
❶ difficult to control; stubborn ❷ a refractory substance is resistant to heat

refrain *VERB* refrains, refraining, refrained
to stop yourself from doing something
• *Please refrain from talking.*

a b c d e f g h i j k l m n o p q **r** s t u v w x y z

refrain *NOUN* refrains
the chorus of a song

refresh *VERB* refreshes, refreshing, refreshed
to make someone feel less tired or less
hot and full of energy again • *She looked
refreshed after a good night's sleep.*
➤ **refresh someone's memory** to remind
someone of something by going over previous
information

refresher course *NOUN* refresher courses
a training course to bring people's knowledge
up to date

refreshing *ADJECTIVE*
❶ producing new strength or energy • *a
refreshing sleep* ❷ pleasantly different or
unusual • *refreshing honesty*

refreshment *NOUN*
❶ food and drink • *Can we offer you some
refreshment?* ❷ the state of feeling strong
and energetic again

refreshments *PLURAL NOUN*
drinks and snacks provided at an event

refrigerate *VERB* refrigerates, refrigerating,
refrigerated
to make food or drink extremely cold,
especially in order to preserve it and keep it
fresh
➤ **refrigeration** *NOUN*

refrigerator *NOUN* refrigerators
a cabinet in which food or drink is stored at a
very low temperature

refuel *VERB* refuels, refuelling, refuelled
to supply a ship or aircraft with more fuel

refuge *NOUN* refuges
a place where a person can go to be safe
from danger
➤ **take refuge** to go somewhere or do
something so that you are protected • *We
had to take refuge from the rain under a tree.*

refugee *NOUN* refugees
a person who has been forced to leave their
home or country and live somewhere else, e.g.
because of war or persecution or famine

refund *VERB* refunds, refunding, refunded
to pay money back

refund *NOUN* refunds
money that is paid back to you

refurbish *VERB* refurbishes, refurbishing,
refurbished
to redecorate a room or building and make

repairs to it
➤ **refurbishment** *NOUN*

refusal *NOUN* refusals
saying that you are unwilling to do or give or
accept something • *I can't understand her
refusal to see me.*

refuse (say ri-**fewz**) *VERB* refuses, refusing,
refused
to say that you are unwilling to do, give or
accept something • *He refuses to talk about
it.*

refuse (say **ref**-yooss) *NOUN*
rubbish or waste material • *Lorries collected
the refuse.*

refute *VERB* refutes, refuting, refuted
to prove that a person or statement is wrong

> **USAGE**
> This word is sometimes used as if it
> meant 'deny', but this meaning is not fully
> accepted as part of standard English and
> should be avoided.

regain *VERB* regains, regaining, regained
to get something back after losing it • *She
managed to regain her balance.*

regal (say **ree**-gal) *ADJECTIVE*
❶ by or to do with a monarch ❷ dignified
and splendid; fit for a king or queen

regale (say rig-**ayl**) *VERB* regales, regaling,
regaled
to amuse or entertain someone with a story
• *She regaled us with tales of her life in the
theatre.*

regalia (say rig-**ayl**-i-a) *PLURAL NOUN*
the emblems of royalty or rank • *The royal
regalia include the crown, sceptre and orb.*

regard *VERB* regards, regarding, regarded
❶ to think of a person or thing in a certain
way; to consider someone or something to
be • *We regard the matter as serious.* ❷ to
look closely at someone or something • *She
regarded us suspiciously.*

regard *NOUN*
❶ consideration or heed • *You acted without
regard to people's safety.* ❷ respect • *We
have a great regard for her.*
➤ **as regards** concerning; in connection with
• *He is innocent as regards the first charge.*
➤ **with** or **in regard** to concerning; in
connection with

regarding *PREPOSITION*
concerning; about • *For more information
regarding our products, visit our website.*

regardless *ADVERB*
without considering something; in spite of
something • *Do it, regardless of the cost.*

regards *PLURAL NOUN*
kind wishes you send in a message • *Give
your parents my regards.*

regatta *NOUN* regattas
a meeting for boat or yacht races

regency *NOUN* regencies
❶ being a regent ❷ a period when a country
is ruled by a regent

regenerate *VERB* regenerates, regenerating,
regenerated
to give new life or strength to something
➤ **regeneration** *NOUN*

regent *NOUN* regents
a person appointed to rule a country while
the monarch is too young or unable to rule

reggae (say **reg**-ay) *NOUN*
a West Indian style of music with a strong
beat

regime (say ray-zh **eem**) *NOUN* regimes
a system of government or organization • *a
Fascist regime*

regiment *NOUN* regiments
an army unit, usually divided into battalions
or companies
➤ **regimental** *ADJECTIVE*

region *NOUN* regions
❶ a part of a country or of the world • *in
tropical regions* ❷ an area of someone's body
• *pain in the lower back region*
➤ **in the region of** near; approximately • *The
cost will be in the region of €200.*

regional *ADJECTIVE*
belonging to a particular region • *a regional
accent*

register *NOUN* registers
❶ an official list of names or items ❷ a
book in which information about school
attendances is recorded ❸ the range of a
voice or musical instrument

register *VERB* registers, registering, registered
❶ to list names or items in a register
❷ to indicate or show something • *The
thermometer registered 100°.* • *His face
registered deep suspicion.* ❸ to make an
impression on someone's mind • *Does that
name register at all?* ❹ to pay extra for a
letter or parcel to be sent with special care

register office *NOUN* register offices
an office where marriages are performed and
records of births, marriages and deaths are
kept

registrar *NOUN* registrars
an official whose job is to keep written
records or registers

registration *NOUN*
putting someone's name on an official list

registration number *NOUN* registration
numbers
a series of letters and numbers identifying a
motor vehicle

registry *NOUN* registries
a place where registers are kept

registry office *NOUN* registry offices
a register office

regret *NOUN* regrets
a feeling of sorrow or disappointment about
something that has happened or been done

regret *VERB* regrets, regretting, regretted
to feel sorry or disappointed about something
• *He regretted his decision at once.*

regretful *ADJECTIVE*
feeling sorry or disappointed about
something
➤ **regretfully** *ADVERB*

regrettable *ADJECTIVE*
that you are sorry about and wish had not
happened • *a regrettable mistake*
➤ **regrettably** *ADVERB*

regular *ADJECTIVE*
❶ always happening or doing something
at certain times • *Try to eat regular meals.*
❷ even or symmetrical • *regular teeth*
❸ normal, standard or correct • *the regular
procedure* ❹ belonging to a country's
permanent armed forces • *a regular soldier*
➤ **regularity** *NOUN*

regularly *ADVERB*
❶ at regular times or intervals • *Railway
tracks are regularly checked.* ❷ often • *I go
there regularly.*

regulate *VERB* regulates, regulating,
regulated
❶ to control something by using laws or rules
❷ to control the way a machine works • *Turn
this dial to regulate the temperature.*
➤ **regulator** *NOUN*

regulation *NOUN* regulations
❶ a rule or law ❷ regulating something

regurgitate VERB regurgitates, regurgitating, regurgitated
to bring swallowed food up again into the mouth
➤ **regurgitation** NOUN

rehearsal NOUN rehearsals
practising something before you perform it in front of an audience

rehearse VERB rehearses, rehearsing, rehearsed
to practise something before performing it in front of an audience

reign VERB reigns, reigning, reigned
❶ to rule a country as king or queen ❷ to be supreme; to be the most noticeable or important thing • *Silence reigned for a while.*

reign NOUN reigns
the time when someone is king or queen

> **SPELLING**
>
> Be careful, this sounds the same as **rein**, which means a strap used by a rider to guide a horse.

reimburse VERB reimburses, reimbursing, reimbursed
to repay money that has been spent • *Your travelling expenses will be reimbursed.*
➤ **reimbursement** NOUN

rein NOUN reins
❶ a strap used by a rider to guide a horse ❷ a harness used to guide a very young child when walking

> **SPELLING**
>
> Be careful, this sounds the same as **reign**, which means to rule a country or the amount of time for which someone rules a country.

reincarnation NOUN
the belief that after death the soul is born again in a new body

reindeer NOUN reindeer
a kind of deer that lives in Arctic regions

reinforce VERB reinforces, reinforcing, reinforced
❶ to strengthen something by adding extra people or supports ❷ to strengthen or support an idea or feeling

reinforced concrete NOUN
concrete containing metal bars or wires to strengthen it

reinforcement NOUN reinforcements
❶ making something stronger ❷ a thing that strengthens something

reinforcements PLURAL NOUN
extra troops sent to strengthen a military force

reinstate VERB reinstates, reinstating, reinstated
to put a person or thing back into a previous position
➤ **reinstatement** NOUN

reiterate VERB reiterates, reiterating, reiterated
to say something again or repeatedly
➤ **reiteration** NOUN

reject (say ri-**jekt**) VERB rejects, rejecting, rejected
❶ to refuse to accept a person or thing • *They rejected all offers of help.* ❷ to throw away or discard something • *Faulty parts are rejected at the factory.*
➤ **rejection** NOUN

reject (say **ree**-jekt) NOUN rejects
a person or thing that is rejected, especially because of being faulty or poorly made

rejoice VERB rejoices, rejoicing, rejoiced
to feel or show great joy

rejoin VERB rejoins, rejoining, rejoined
to join someone or something again after leaving them

rejoinder NOUN rejoinders
a sharp or witty reply

rejuvenate VERB rejuvenates, rejuvenating, rejuvenated
to make a person seem young again
➤ **rejuvenation** NOUN

relapse VERB relapses, relapsing, relapsed
❶ to return to a previous condition • *After these words he relapsed into silence.* ❷ to become worse after improving
➤ **relapse** NOUN

relate VERB relates, relating, related
❶ to tell a story or give an account of something ❷ things relate to each another when there is a link or connection between them ❸ to make a connection between one thing and another ❹ to understand someone and get on well with them • *Some people cannot relate to children.*

related ADJECTIVE
❶ belonging to the same family ❷ connected or linked

relation *NOUN* relations
① a relative ② the way one thing is related to another
➤ **in relation to** in connection with

relationship *NOUN* relationships
① how people or things are related ② how people get on with each other ③ a loving or sexual friendship between two people

relative *NOUN* relatives
a person who is related to another

relative *ADJECTIVE*
connected or compared with something; compared with the average • *They live in relative comfort.*

relative density *NOUN* relative densities
the ratio of the density of a substance to that of a standard substance (usually water for liquids and solids and air for gases)

relatively *ADVERB*
to a fairly large degree when compared with other things • *It is a relatively easy language to learn.*

relative pronoun *NOUN* relative pronouns
a word used instead of a noun to introduce a clause that gives more information about the noun. The relative pronouns are *what, who, whom, whose, which* and *that.*

> **GRAMMAR**
>
> Relative pronouns (*what, who, whom, whose, which* and *that*) introduce a clause which gives more information about a noun, e.g. *the artist who painted this portrait; the song that I love.*
>
> See also the panel on **pronouns**.

relax *VERB* relaxes, relaxing, relaxed
① to rest or stop working ② to become less anxious or worried ③ to make a rule less strict or severe ④ to make a limb or muscle less stiff or tense • *Try to relax your arm.*
➤ **relaxed** *ADJECTIVE*
➤ **relaxation** *NOUN*

relay (say ri-**lay**) *VERB* relays, relaying, relayed
to pass on a message or broadcast

relay (say **re**-lay) *NOUN* relays
① a fresh group taking the place of another • *The firefighters worked in relays.* ② a relay race ③ a device for relaying a broadcast

relay race *NOUN* relay races
a race between teams in which each person covers part of the distance

release *VERB* releases, releasing, released
① to set someone or something free or unfasten them • *Eventually he was released from prison.* ② to let a thing fall or fly or go out • *Hundreds of balloons were released at the ceremony.* ③ to make information available • *The name of the victim has not yet been released.* ④ to make a film or recording available to the public

release *NOUN* releases
① being released ② something released, such as a new film or recording ③ a device that unfastens something

relegate *VERB* relegates, relegating, relegated
① a sports team is relegated when it goes down into a lower division of a league ② to put something into a lower group or position than before
➤ **relegation** *NOUN*

relent *VERB* relents, relenting, relented
to finally agree to something that you had refused; to become less severe • *In the end Mum and Dad relented and let me go to the party.*

relentless *ADJECTIVE*
not stopping or letting up • *Their criticism was relentless.*
➤ **relentlessly** *ADVERB*

relevant *ADJECTIVE*
connected with what is being discussed or dealt with. (The opposite is **irrelevant**.)
➤ **relevance** *NOUN*

reliable *ADJECTIVE*
able to be relied on or trusted • *Is he a reliable witness?*
➤ **reliably** *ADVERB*
➤ **reliability** *NOUN*

reliance *NOUN*
relying or depending on someone or something
➤ **reliant** *ADJECTIVE*

relic *NOUN* relics
something that has survived from an earlier time

relief *NOUN* reliefs
① a good feeling you get because something unpleasant has stopped or is not going to happen • *It was such a relief when we reached dry land.* ② the ending or lessening of pain, trouble or suffering ③ something that gives relief or help ④ help given to people in need • *The charity is involved in famine relief.* ⑤ a person who takes over a turn of duty when another finishes ⑥ a

a b c d e f g h i j k l m n o p q r s t u v w x y z

method of making a map or design that stands out from a flat surface • *The model shows hills and valleys in relief.*

relief map *NOUN* relief maps
a map that shows hills and valleys by shading or moulding

relieve *VERB* relieves, relieving, relieved
to make an unpleasant feeling or situation stop or get better • *We played cards to relieve the boredom.*
➤ **relieve someone of something** to take something from a person • *The thief relieved him of his wallet.*

relieved *ADJECTIVE*
feeling happy because something unpleasant has stopped or has not happened • *I was relieved to hear that nobody was hurt.*

religion *NOUN* religions
❶ what people believe about God or gods and how they worship ❷ a particular system of beliefs and worship

religious *ADJECTIVE*
❶ to do with religion ❷ believing firmly in a religion and taking part in its customs

religiously *ADVERB*
very carefully or regularly • *He wrote up his diary religiously every night.*

relinquish *VERB* relinquishes, relinquishing, relinquished
to give something up; to let something go

relish *NOUN* relishes
❶ great enjoyment • *He told me all the gory details with obvious relish.* ❷ a tasty sauce or pickle that adds flavour to plainer food

relish *VERB* relishes, relishing, relished
to enjoy something greatly; to look forward to something with great pleasure • *I didn't relish the idea of getting up so early.*

relive *VERB* relives, reliving, relived
to remember something that happened very vividly, as though it was happening again

relocate *VERB* relocates, relocating, relocated
to move to a new place or to make someone or something do this

reluctant *ADJECTIVE*
not willing or not keen to do something • *She was reluctant to talk about what had happened.*
➤ **reluctantly** *ADVERB*
➤ **reluctance** *NOUN*

rely *VERB* relies, relying, relied
❶ to rely on someone is to trust them to help or support you • *You can rely on me not to tell anyone.* ❷ to rely on something is to need it for a particular purpose • *Many people rely on this local bus service.*

remain *VERB* remains, remaining, remained
❶ to be left after other parts have gone or been dealt with • *One big problem remained.* ❷ to continue to be in the same place or condition; to stay • *It will remain cloudy all day.*

remainder *NOUN*
❶ the remaining part of people or things ❷ the number left after subtraction or division

remains *PLURAL NOUN*
❶ all that is left over after other parts have been removed or destroyed ❷ ancient ruins or objects that have survived to the present day • *the remains of a Roman fort* ❸ a dead body

remand *VERB* remands, remanding, remanded
to send a prisoner back into custody while further evidence is being gathered
➤ **remand** *NOUN*
➤ **on remand** in prison while waiting for a trial

remark *NOUN* remarks
something you say; a comment

remark *VERB* remarks, remarking, remarked
to make a remark; to say something

remarkable *ADJECTIVE*
unusual or extraordinary in a way that people notice • *It was a remarkable achievement.*
➤ **remarkably** *ADVERB*

remedial *ADJECTIVE*
❶ helping to cure an illness or deficiency ❷ (*old use*) to do with the teaching of school students who are not doing as well as expected

remedy *NOUN* remedies
something that cures or relieves a disease or that puts a matter right

remedy *VERB* remedies, remedying, remedied
to be a remedy for something; to put something right

remember *VERB* remembers, remembering, remembered
❶ to keep something in your mind • *Please remember to switch off the lights.* ❷ to bring

something back into your mind • *I can't remember her name.*

> **SPELLING**
> To make the past tense, remember + ed, remembered.

remembrance *NOUN*
you do something in remembrance of someone or something when you do it as a way of remembering them

remind *VERB* reminds, reminding, reminded
❶ to help or make a person remember something • *Remind me to buy some stamps.*
❷ to make a person think of something because of being similar • *The girl in that painting reminds me of you.*

reminder *NOUN* reminders
❶ a thing that reminds you of something ❷ a letter sent to remind you to pay a bill

reminiscences *PLURAL NOUN*
a person's memories of their past life

reminiscent *ADJECTIVE*
reminding you of something • *The book's style is reminiscent of 'The Hobbit'.*

remission *NOUN*
❶ a period during which a serious illness improves for a time ❷ the reduction of a prison sentence, especially for good behaviour while in prison

remit *VERB* remits, remitting, remitted
❶ to reduce or cancel a punishment or debt ❷ to send money in payment

remittance *NOUN* remittances
❶ sending money ❷ the amount of money sent

remnant *NOUN* remnants
a part or piece left over from something

remonstrate *VERB* remonstrates, remonstrating, remonstrated
to make a protest • *We remonstrated with him about his behaviour.*

remorse *NOUN*
deep regret for something wrong you have done
➤ **remorseful** *ADJECTIVE*
➤ **remorsefully** *ADVERB*

remorseless *ADJECTIVE*
relentless; not stopping or ending
➤ **remorselessly** *ADVERB*

remote *ADJECTIVE*
❶ far away in place or time • *remote stars*

• *the remote past* ❷ far away from where most people live; isolated • *a remote beach* ❸ unlikely or slight • *a remote chance*
➤ **remoteness** *NOUN*

remote *NOUN* remotes
a remote control device

remote control *NOUN* remote controls
❶ controlling something from a distance, usually by electricity or radio ❷ a device for doing this

remotely *ADVERB*
❶ to a very slight degree; slightly • *That is not even remotely funny.* ❷ from a distance

removable *ADJECTIVE*
able to be removed

removal *NOUN*
removing or moving something

remove *VERB* removes, removing, removed
❶ to take something away or take it off ❷ to get rid of something • *This should remove all doubts.*
➤ **be far removed from something** to be very different from something

remunerate *VERB* remunerates, remunerating, remunerated
to pay or reward someone
➤ **remuneration** *NOUN*

Renaissance (say ren-**ay**-sans) *NOUN*
the revival of classical styles of art and literature in Europe in the 14th-16th centuries

renal (say **reen**-al) *ADJECTIVE*
to do with the kidneys

rename *VERB* renames, renaming, renamed
to give a new name to a person or thing

rend *VERB* rends, rending, rent (*poetical use*)
to rip or tear something

render *VERB* renders, rendering, rendered
❶ to cause a person or thing to become something • *This news rendered us speechless.* ❷ to give or perform something • *The local community was quick to render help to the victims.*

rendezvous (say **rond**-ay-voo) *NOUN*
rendezvous (say **rond**-ay-vooz)
❶ a meeting with someone at an agreed time and place ❷ a place arranged for this

rendition *NOUN* renditions
the way a piece of music, a poem or a dramatic role is performed

a
b
c
d
e
f
g
h
i
j
k
l
m
n
o
p
q
r
s
t
u
v
w
x
y
z

renegade (say **ren**-ig-ayd) *NOUN* **renegades**
a person who deserts a group or cause and
joins another

renew *VERB* **renews, renewing, renewed**
❶ to replace a thing with something new or
arrange for it to be valid for a further period
• *I need to renew my bus pass.* ❷ to begin or
make or give something again • *We renewed
our request.*
➤ **renewal** *NOUN*

renewable *ADJECTIVE*
able to be renewed

renewable resource *NOUN* **renewable
resources**
a resource (such as power from the sun, wind
or waves) that can never be used up or which
can be renewed

renounce *VERB* **renounces, renouncing,
renounced**
to give up or reject something
➤ **renunciation** *NOUN*

renovate *VERB* **renovates, renovating,
renovated**
to repair an old building and make it look new
➤ **renovation** *NOUN*

renown *NOUN*
great fame

renowned *ADJECTIVE*
famous • *The area is renowned for it beauty.*

rent *NOUN* **rents**
❶ a regular payment for the use of
something, especially a house that belongs to
another person ❷ a torn place; a split

rent *VERB* **rents, renting, rented**
❶ to have or allow the use of something in
return for rent ❷ past tense of **rend**

rental *NOUN*
❶ the amount paid as rent ❷ renting
something

renunciation *NOUN*
renouncing something

reorganize (also **reorganise**) *VERB*
reorganizes, reorganizing, reorganized
to change the way in which something is
organized
➤ **reorganization** *NOUN*

repair *VERB* **repairs, repairing, repaired**
❶ to put something into good condition after
it has been damaged or broken ❷ (*formal*) to
repair to a place is to go there • *The guests*
repaired to the dining room.
➤ **repairable** *ADJECTIVE*

repair *NOUN* **repairs**
❶ repairing something • *The bridge is in need
of repair.* ❷ a place where something has
been mended • *The repair is hardly visible.*
➤ **in good** or **bad repair** in good or poor
condition; well or badly maintained

reparation *NOUN* **reparations** (*formal*)
making amends; paying for damage or loss
➤ **make reparations** to make amends or
compensate for something

reparations *PLURAL NOUN*
compensation for war damage paid by the
defeated nation

repartee *NOUN*
witty replies and remarks

repast *NOUN* **repasts** (*formal*)
a meal

repay *VERB* **repays, repaying, repaid**
❶ to pay back money that you owe ❷ to do
something for someone in return for kindness
or help • *How can I ever repay you for all you
have done?*
➤ **repayment** *NOUN*

repeal *VERB* **repeals, repealing, repealed**
to cancel a law officially
➤ **repeal** *NOUN*

repeat *VERB* **repeats, repeating, repeated**
❶ to say or do the same thing again ❷ to tell
another person about something told to you
• *You mustn't repeat this to anyone.*

repeat *NOUN* **repeats**
❶ the action of repeating something
❷ something that is repeated • *There are too
many repeats on television.*

repeatedly *ADVERB*
many times; again and again • *She hit him
repeatedly.*

repel *VERB* **repels, repelling, repelled**
❶ to drive someone back or away • *They
fought bravely and repelled the attackers.*
❷ to push something away from itself
by means of a physical force • *One north
magnetic pole repels another.* ❸ to disgust
someone

repellent *ADJECTIVE*
causing a strong feeling of disgust

repellent *NOUN* **repellents**
a chemical substance used to keep something
away • *an insect repellent*

repent VERB repents, repenting, repented
to be sorry for what you have done
➤ **repentance** NOUN
➤ **repentant** ADJECTIVE

repercussion NOUN repercussions
a consequence or effect of an event or action

repertoire (say **rep**-er-twahr) NOUN
a stock of songs or plays etc. that a person or company knows and can perform

repetition NOUN repetitions
❶ repeating something ❷ something repeated
➤ **repetitious** ADJECTIVE

repetitive ADJECTIVE
involving too much repetition • *The story is slightly repetitive in places.*
➤ **repetitively** ADVERB

replace VERB replaces, replacing, replaced
❶ to put a thing back where it was before • *She replaced the book on the shelf.* ❷ to take the place of another person or thing • *I replaced him as captain of the team.* ❸ to put a new or different thing in place of something • *I promise I'll replace the bowl I broke.*

replacement NOUN replacements
❶ a person or thing that takes the place of another ❷ when a person or thing is replaced by another

replay NOUN replays
❶ a sports match played again after a draw ❷ the playing or showing again of a recording

replay VERB replays, replaying, replayed
❶ to play a match again ❷ to play back a recording

replenish VERB replenishes, replenishing, replenished
to make something full again by replacing what has been used
➤ **replenishment** NOUN

replete ADJECTIVE
❶ well stocked or supplied ❷ feeling full after eating

replica NOUN replicas
an exact copy
➤ **replicate** VERB

reply NOUN replies
something you say or write to deal with a question, letter, etc.; an answer • *She said nothing in reply.*

reply VERB replies, replying, replied
to give a reply to someone; to answer • *'No, thank you,' he replied.*

report VERB reports, reporting, reported
❶ to describe something that has happened or that you have done or studied ❷ to make an official complaint or accusation against someone ❸ to go and tell someone that you have arrived or are ready for work

report NOUN reports
❶ a description or account of something ❷ a regular statement of how someone has worked or behaved, e.g. at school ❸ an explosive sound

reported speech NOUN
indirect speech

reporter NOUN reporters
a person whose job is to collect and report news for a newspaper, radio or television programme, etc.

repose NOUN
calm, rest or sleep

repose VERB reposes, reposing, reposed
to rest or lie somewhere

repository NOUN repositories
a place where things are stored

repossess VERB repossesses, repossessing, repossessed
to take something back because it has not been paid for

reprehensible ADJECTIVE
extremely bad and deserving blame or criticism

represent VERB represents, representing, represented
❶ to help someone by speaking or doing something on their behalf ❷ to symbolize or stand for something • *In Roman numerals, V represents 5.* ❸ to be an example or equivalent of something ❹ to show a person or thing in a picture or play etc. ❺ to describe a person or thing in a particular way

representation NOUN representations
❶ a thing that shows or describes something • *This sculpture is a representation of a human figure.* ❷ being represented by someone or something

representative NOUN representatives
a person or thing that represents another or others

representative ADJECTIVE
❶ representing others ❷ typical of a group

a b c d e f g h i j k l m n o p q r s t u v w x y z

repress VERB represses, repressing, repressed
❶ to control or hold back a feeling • *She tried to repress her anger.* ❷ to control or restrain people by force
➤ **repression** NOUN
➤ **repressive** ADJECTIVE

reprieve NOUN reprieves
postponement or cancellation of a punishment, especially the death penalty

reprieve VERB reprieves, reprieving, reprieved
to give a reprieve to someone

reprimand NOUN reprimands
a telling-off, especially a formal or official one

reprimand VERB reprimands, reprimanding, reprimanded
to scold someone or tell them off

reprisal NOUN reprisals
an act of revenge

reproach VERB reproaches, reproaching, reproached
to tell someone you are upset and disappointed by something they have done

reproach NOUN
blame or criticism • *His behaviour was beyond reproach.*

reproachful ADJECTIVE
expressing blame or criticism • *a reproachful look*
➤ **reproachfully** ADVERB

reproduce VERB reproduces, reproducing, reproduced
❶ to cause something to be seen or heard or happen again ❷ to make a copy of something ❸ animals, people and plants reproduce when they produce offspring

reproduction NOUN reproductions
❶ a copy of something, especially a work of art ❷ the process of producing offspring

reproductive ADJECTIVE
to do with reproduction • *the reproductive system*

reproof NOUN
something you say to someone when you do not approve of what they have done • *words of mild reproof*

reprove VERB reproves, reproving, reproved
to tell someone that you do not approve of something that they have done • *He reproved her for rushing away.*

reptile NOUN reptiles
a cold-blooded animal that has a backbone

and very short legs or no legs at all, e.g. a snake, lizard, crocodile or tortoise
WORD ORIGIN from Latin *reptilis* = crawling

republic NOUN republics
a country that has a president, especially one who is elected. Compare with **monarchy**.
➤ **republican** ADJECTIVE & NOUN

Republican NOUN Republicans
a supporter of the Republican Party in the USA

repudiate VERB repudiates, repudiating, repudiated
to reject or deny a suggestion or accusation

repugnant ADJECTIVE
very unpleasant or disgusting
➤ **repugnance** NOUN

repulse VERB repulses, repulsing, repulsed
❶ to drive back an attacking force ❷ to reject an offer firmly ❸ to make someone feel disgust

repulsion NOUN
❶ a feeling of disgust ❷ repelling or repulsing something

repulsive ADJECTIVE
❶ disgusting or revolting ❷ repelling things • *a repulsive force*
➤ **repulsively** ADVERB
➤ **repulsiveness** NOUN

reputable (say **rep**-yoo-ta-bul) ADJECTIVE
having a good reputation; respected • *a reputable company*

reputation NOUN reputations
what most people say or think about a person or thing • *She has a reputation for being late.* • *He started to build a reputation as a painter.*

repute NOUN
reputation • *a writer of international repute*

reputed ADJECTIVE
said or thought to be something • *The house is reputed to be haunted.*
➤ **reputedly** ADVERB

request VERB requests, requesting, requested
❶ to ask for a thing ❷ to ask a person to do something

request NOUN requests
❶ asking for something ❷ a thing asked for • *Does the prisoner have any last requests?*

requiem (say **rek**-wee-em) NOUN requiems
❶ a special Mass for someone who

has died ❷ music for the words of this
WORD ORIGIN Latin, = rest

require *VERB* requires, requiring, required
❶ to need something • *The situation requires
a lot of tact.* ❷ to officially demand or order
something; to make someone do something
• *Drivers are required to pass a test.*

requirement *NOUN* requirements
what is required; a need

requisite (say **rek**-wiz-it) *ADJECTIVE*
required or needed for something • *Does he
have the requisite patience for the job?*

requisite *NOUN* requisites
a thing needed for something

requisition *VERB* requisitions, requisitioning,
requisitioned
to take something over for official use

reread *VERB* rereads, rereading, reread
to read something again

rescue *VERB* rescues, rescuing, rescued
to save a person or thing from danger or
harm; to free someone from captivity
➤ **rescuer** *NOUN*

rescue *NOUN* rescues
the action of rescuing a person or thing
• *Thank you for coming to my rescue.*

research *NOUN*
careful study or investigation to discover
facts or information

research (say ri-**serch**) *VERB* researches,
researching, researched
to carry out research into something • *The
team has been researching into dolphin
behaviour.*
➤ **researcher** *NOUN*

resemblance *NOUN* resemblances
likeness or similarity • *He bears a remarkable
resemblance to my brother.*

resemble *VERB* resembles, resembling,
resembled
to be or look like another person or thing
• *She closely resembles my sister.*

resent *VERB* resents, resenting, resented
to feel bitter and angry about something
done or said to you • *He resented being
treated like an idiot.*
➤ **resentment** *NOUN*

resentful *ADJECTIVE*
feeling bitter and angry about something
done or said to you
➤ **resentfully** *ADVERB*

reservation *NOUN* reservations
❶ reserving something ❷ something reserved
• *a hotel reservation* ❸ an area of land kept
for a special purpose ❹ a doubt or feeling
of unease ❺ a limit on how far you agree
with something; a doubt or condition • *I
accept the plan in principle but have certain
reservations.*

reserve *VERB* reserves, reserving, reserved
to keep or order something for a particular
person or a special use in the future • *I'd like
to reserve three tickets for the show.*
➤ **reserve judgement** to leave your decision
until you have had time to consider it
properly

reserve *NOUN* reserves
❶ a person or thing kept ready to be used if
necessary ❷ an extra player chosen in case
a substitute is needed in a team ❸ an area
of land kept for a special purpose • *a nature
reserve* ❹ shyness; being reserved
➤ **in reserve** not used but kept available if
needed

reserved *ADJECTIVE*
❶ kept for someone's use • *This table is
reserved.* ❷ shy or unwilling to show your
feelings

reservoir (say **rez**-er-vwar) *NOUN* reservoirs
a place where water is stored, especially an
artificial lake

reshuffle *NOUN* reshuffles
a rearrangement, especially an exchange of
jobs between members of a group • *a Cabinet
reshuffle*
➤ **reshuffle** *VERB*

reside *VERB* resides, residing, resided
to live in a particular place

residence *NOUN* residences
❶ a place where a person lives ❷ living in a
particular place • *Some pigeons have taken
up residence in our roof.*

resident *NOUN* residents
❶ a person living in a particular place ❷ a
person staying in a hotel

resident *ADJECTIVE*
living in a particular place

residential *ADJECTIVE*
❶ containing people's homes • *a residential
area* ❷ providing accommodation • *a
residential course*

residue *NOUN* residues
what remains or is left over • *The washing*

a
b
c
d
e
f
g
h
i
j
k
l
m
n
o
p
q
r
s
t
u
v
w
x
y
z

powder left a white residue on her clothes.
➤ **residual** *ADJECTIVE*

resign *VERB* resigns, resigning, resigned
to give up your job or position
➤ **be resigned** or **resign yourself to something** to accept that you must put up with something • *She resigned herself to her fate.*

SPELLING

There is a silent **g** before the **n** in **resign**.

resignation *NOUN* resignations
❶ accepting a difficulty without complaining ❷ resigning a job or position; a letter saying you wish to do this

resilient *ADJECTIVE*
able to recover quickly from illness or trouble
➤ **resilience** *NOUN*
WORD ORIGIN from Latin *resilire* = jump back

resin *NOUN* resins
a sticky substance that comes from plants or is manufactured, used in varnish, plastics, etc.
➤ **resinous** *ADJECTIVE*

resist *VERB* resists, resisting, resisted
❶ to oppose or refuse to accept something; to fight or act against something ❷ to stop yourself having or doing something • *I couldn't resist having a quick peek.*

resistance *NOUN*
❶ resisting something • *The troops came up against armed resistance.* ❷ the ability of a substance to hinder the flow of electricity

resistant *ADJECTIVE*
❶ not affected or damaged by something • *This watch is water-resistant.* ❷ not willing to accept something • *They are resistant to new ideas.*

resistor *NOUN* resistors
a device that increases the resistance to an electric current

resit *NOUN* resits
(*British*) an examination that you sit again because you did not do well enough the first time
➤ **resit** *VERB*

resolute *ADJECTIVE*
showing great determination
➤ **resolutely** *ADVERB*

resolution *NOUN* resolutions
❶ being resolute; great determination ❷ something you have resolved to do • *New Year resolutions* ❸ a formal decision made

by a committee ❹ the solving of a problem ❺ the last part of a story where we find out how the story comes to an end and how difficulties are sorted out

resolve *VERB* resolves, resolving, resolved
❶ to decide something firmly or formally ❷ to solve or settle a problem ❸ to overcome doubts or disagreements

resolve *NOUN*
great determination to do something

resonant *ADJECTIVE*
❶ resounding or echoing • *His voice was deep and resonant.* ❷ suggesting or bringing to mind a feeling or memory
➤ **resonance** *NOUN*

resonate *VERB* resonates, resonating, resonated
to make a deep continuing sound; to echo

resort *VERB* resorts, resorting, resorted
to turn to or make use of something, especially when everything else has failed • *In the end they resorted to violence.*

resort *NOUN* resorts
a place where people go for relaxation or a holiday
➤ **the last resort** something to be tried when everything else has failed

resound *VERB* resounds, resounding, resounded
to fill a place with sound; to echo • *Laughter resounded through the house.*

resounding *ADJECTIVE*
❶ loud and echoing ❷ very great; outstanding • *a resounding victory*

resource *NOUN* resources
❶ something that can be used; an asset • *The country's natural resources include coal and oil.* ❷ a person's resources are their natural qualities and abilities

resourceful *ADJECTIVE*
clever at finding ways of doing things
➤ **resourcefully** *ADVERB*
➤ **resourcefulness** *NOUN*

respect *NOUN* respects
❶ admiration for a person's or thing's good qualities ❷ politeness or consideration • *Have respect for people's feelings.* ❸ a detail or aspect • *In this respect he is like his sister.*
➤ **with respect to** with reference to; concerning • *The rules with respect to bullying are quite clear.*

respect *VERB* respects, respecting, respected
to have respect for a person or thing

respectable *ADJECTIVE*
❶ having good manners and character; decent ❷ fairly good; adequate • *a respectable score*
➤ **respectably** *ADVERB*
➤ **respectability** *NOUN*

respectful *ADJECTIVE*
showing respect
➤ **respectfully** *ADVERB*

respecting *PREPOSITION*
concerning; to do with

respective *ADJECTIVE*
belonging to each one of several • *We went to our respective rooms.*

respectively *ADVERB*
in the same order as the people or things already mentioned • *Ruth and Emma finished first and second respectively.*

respiration *NOUN*
breathing
➤ **respiratory** *ADJECTIVE*

respirator *NOUN* respirators
❶ a device that fits over a person's nose and mouth to purify air before it is breathed ❷ an apparatus for giving artificial respiration

respire *VERB* respires, respiring, respired
to breathe

respite *NOUN* respites
a short break from something unpleasant or difficult • *There was no respite from the blistering heat.*

resplendent *ADJECTIVE*
impressively bright and colourful

respond *VERB* responds, responding, responded
❶ to reply ❷ to act in answer to, or because of, something; to react ❸ to show a good reaction to something • *The disease did not respond to treatment.*

respondent *NOUN* respondents
the person answering

response *NOUN* responses
❶ a reply or answer ❷ a reaction to something • *The news provoked an angry response.*

responsibility *NOUN* responsibilities
❶ being responsible • *I take full responsibility for the mistake.* ❷ something for which a person is responsible • *It is your responsibility to make sure the doors are locked.*

responsible *ADJECTIVE*
❶ looking after a person or thing and having to take the blame if something goes wrong ❷ reliable and trustworthy ❸ with important duties • *a responsible job* ❹ causing something • *Faulty wiring was responsible for the fire.*
➤ **responsibly** *ADVERB*

responsive *ADJECTIVE*
responding well or quickly to something

rest *NOUN* rests
❶ a time of sleep or freedom from work as a way of regaining strength ❷ a support, especially on a piece of furniture • *an armrest* ❸ an interval of silence between notes in music
➤ **at rest** not moving
➤ **come to rest** to stop moving
➤ **the rest** the remaining part; the others

rest *VERB* rests, resting, rested
❶ to have a rest; to be still ❷ to allow a part of your body to rest • *Sit down and rest your feet.* ❸ to lean or place something so it is supported; to be supported • *Rest the ladder against the wall.* ❹ to stop moving and stay in one place • *His eyes rested on the picture.* ❺ to be left without further investigation • *And there the matter rests.*
➤ **rest assured** to be confident or certain about something • *Rest assured, it will be a success.*
➤ **rest with someone** to be left to someone to deal with • *It rests with you to suggest a date.*

restaurant *NOUN* restaurants
a place where you can buy a meal and eat it

restaurateur (say rest-er-a-**tur**) *NOUN* restaurateurs
a person who owns or manages a restaurant

SPELLING

Note the spelling of this word. Unlike 'restaurant' there is no 'n' in it.

restful *ADJECTIVE*
giving rest or a feeling of rest • *a restful holiday*

restitution *NOUN*
❶ restoring something ❷ compensation for injury or damage

restive *ADJECTIVE*
restless or impatient because of delay, anxiety or boredom **WORD ORIGIN** from an earlier meaning = refusing to move, used to describe a horse

restless *ADJECTIVE*
unable to rest or keep still
➤ **restlessly** *ADVERB*
➤ **restlessness** *NOUN*

restoration *NOUN*
returning something to its original condition

restore *VERB* restores, restoring, restored
❶ to put something back to its original place or condition ❷ to clean and repair a work of art or building so that it looks as good as it did originally

restrain *VERB* restrains, restraining, restrained
to hold a person or thing back; to keep a person or animal under control • *I had to restrain myself from saying something rude.*

restraint *NOUN* restraints
❶ a limit or control on something ❷ calm and controlled behaviour

restrict *VERB* restricts, restricting, restricted
to keep someone or something within certain limits • *Fog severely restricted visibility.*
➤ **restrictive** *ADJECTIVE*

restriction *NOUN* restrictions
a rule or situation that limits what you can do
• *parking restrictions*

result *NOUN* results
❶ a thing that happens because something else has happened; an effect or consequence ❷ the score or situation at the end of a game, competition or race ❸ the answer to a sum or calculation

result *VERB* results, resulting, resulted
❶ to happen as a result ❷ to have something as a particular result • *The match resulted in a draw.*

resume *VERB* resumes, resuming, resumed
❶ to begin something again after stopping for a while • *They turned away from me and resumed their conversation.* ❷ to take or occupy something again • *After the interval we resumed our seats.*
➤ **resumption** *NOUN*

résumé (say **rez**-yoo-may) *NOUN* résumés
a summary

resurgence *NOUN* resurgences
a rise or revival of something • *a resurgence of interest in Latin*

resurrect *VERB* resurrects, resurrecting, resurrected
to bring something back into use or existence
• *It may be time to resurrect this old custom.*

resurrection *NOUN*
❶ coming back to life after being dead ❷ the revival of something
➤ **the Resurrection** in the Christian religion, the resurrection of Jesus Christ three days after his death

resuscitate *VERB* resuscitates, resuscitating, resuscitated
to revive a person who has become unconscious or stopped breathing
➤ **resuscitation** *NOUN*

retail *VERB* retails, retailing, retailed
to sell goods to the general public
➤ **retailer** *NOUN*

retail *NOUN*
selling goods to the general public. Compare with **wholesale**.

retain *VERB* retains, retaining, retained
❶ to continue to have something; to keep something in your possession or memory
• *Retain your tickets for inspection.* ❷ to hold something in place

retainer *NOUN* retainers
❶ a sum of money regularly paid to someone so that they will work for you when needed ❷ a servant who has worked for a person or family for a long time

retake *VERB* retakes, retaking, retook, retaken
to take a test or examination again

retake *NOUN* retakes
❶ a test or examination taken again ❷ a scene filmed again

retaliate *VERB* retaliates, retaliating, retaliated
to repay an injury or insult with a similar one; to attack someone in return for a similar attack
➤ **retaliation** *NOUN*

retard *VERB* retards, retarding, retarded
to slow down or delay the progress or development of something
➤ **retarded** *ADJECTIVE*

retch *VERB* retches, retching, retched
to strain your throat as if you are being sick

SPELLING
Take care not to confuse with **wretch**.

retention *NOUN*
retaining or keeping something

retentive ADJECTIVE
able to retain facts and remember things
easily • *She has a retentive memory.*

reticent (say **ret**-i-sent) ADJECTIVE
not willing to tell people what you feel or
think
➤ **reticence** NOUN

retina NOUN retinas
a layer of membrane at the back of the
eyeball, sensitive to light

retinue NOUN retinues
a group of people accompanying an
important person

retire VERB retires, retiring, retired
❶ to give up your regular work because you
have reached a certain age ❷ to go to bed
❸ to leave a place and go somewhere more
private • *The jury retired to consider their
verdict.*

retired ADJECTIVE
no longer working • *a retired teacher*

retirement NOUN
the time when someone gives up regular work
• *My grandfather is approaching retirement.*

retiring ADJECTIVE
shy; avoiding company

retort NOUN retorts
❶ a quick, witty or angry reply ❷ a glass
bottle with a long downward-bent neck, used
in distilling liquids

retort VERB retorts, retorting, retorted
to make a quick, witty or angry reply • *'Don't
be ridiculous!' he retorted.*

retrace VERB retraces, retracing, retraced
to go back over the route that you have just
taken • *We retraced our steps and returned
to the ferry.*

retract VERB retracts, retracting, retracted
❶ to pull something back or in • *All cats
except cheetahs can retract their claws.* ❷ to
withdraw a statement or accusation
➤ **retraction** NOUN
➤ **retractable** ADJECTIVE

retreat VERB retreats, retreating, retreated
to go back after being defeated or to avoid
danger or difficulty

retreat NOUN retreats
❶ retreating ❷ a quiet place to which
someone can go to relax

retribution NOUN
a deserved punishment

retrieve VERB retrieves, retrieving, retrieved
❶ to bring or get something back • *I went
next door to retrieve the ball.* ❷ to find
information stored in a computer ❸ to rescue
or save a situation
➤ **retrieval** NOUN

retriever NOUN retrievers
a kind of dog originally trained to find and
bring back birds and animals that have been
shot

retrospect NOUN
➤ **in retrospect** when you look back at what
has happened • *In retrospect, I can see it was
a terrible mistake.*

retrospective ADJECTIVE
❶ looking back on the past ❷ applying to the
past as well as the future • *The law could not
be made retrospective.*

return VERB returns, returning, returned
❶ to come back or go back ❷ to bring, give,
put or send something back

return NOUN returns
❶ returning to a place ❷ giving or sending
something back ❸ profit • *He gets a good
return on his savings.* ❹ a return ticket
➤ **in return** as payment or in exchange

return match NOUN return matches
a second match played between the same
teams

return ticket NOUN return tickets
a ticket for a journey to a place and back
again

reunify VERB reunifies, reunifying, reunified
to make a divided country into one again
• *How long has Germany been reunified?*
➤ **reunification** NOUN

reunion NOUN reunions
❶ a meeting of people who have not met
for some time • *a family reunion* ❷ coming
together again after being apart

reunite VERB reunites, reuniting, reunited
to come together again or bring people
together again after a period of separation

reuse (say ree-**yooz**) VERB reuses, reusing,
reused
to use something again • *I try to reuse plastic
bags.*
➤ **reusable** ADJECTIVE

reuse (say ree-**yooss**) NOUN
using something again

a
b
c
d
e
f
g
h
i
j
k
l
m
n
o
p
q
r
s
t
u
v
w
x
y
z

rev *VERB* revs, revving, revved (*informal*)
to make an engine run quickly, especially when starting

rev *NOUN* revs (*informal*) a revolution of an engine

Rev. *ABBREVIATION*
Reverend

reveal *VERB* reveals, revealing, revealed
❶ to make something known • *Police have not yet revealed the identity of the victim.*
❷ to show something that was hidden

reveille (say riv-**al**-ee) *NOUN* reveilles
a military waking signal sounded on a bugle or drums (**WORD ORIGIN**) from French *réveillez* = wake up!

revel *VERB* revels, revelling, revelled
❶ to take great delight in something • *She was revelling in all the attention.* ❷ to enjoy yourself with others in a lively and noisy celebration
➤ **reveller** *NOUN*

revelation *NOUN* revelations
❶ something revealed, especially something surprising • *startling revelations about her private life* ❷ revealing something

revelry *NOUN*
❶ revelling ❷ lively and noisy celebration

revels *PLURAL NOUN*
lively and noisy celebrations

revenge *NOUN*
harming someone in return for harm that they have done to you

revenge *VERB* revenges, revenging, revenged
to take revenge on someone

revenue *NOUN* revenues
❶ a country's income from taxes etc., used for paying public expenses ❷ a company's income

reverberate *VERB* reverberates, reverberating, reverberated
to be repeated as an echo; to resound • *His voice reverberated around the hall.*
➤ **reverberation** *NOUN*

revere (say riv-**eer**) *VERB* reveres, revering, revered
to respect or admire someone deeply

reverence *NOUN*
a feeling of awe and deep or religious respect

Reverend *NOUN*
the title of a member of the clergy • *the Reverend John Smith*

reverent *ADJECTIVE*
feeling or showing reverence
➤ **reverently** *ADVERB*
➤ **reverential** *ADJECTIVE*

reverie (say **rev**-er-ee) *NOUN* reveries
a daydream

reversal *NOUN* reversals
❶ a change to an opposite direction, position or course of action ❷ a piece of bad luck or misfortune

reverse *ADJECTIVE*
❶ facing or moving in the opposite direction
❷ opposite in character or order • *I will announce the results in reverse order.*

reverse *NOUN* reverses
❶ the opposite of something ❷ the reverse side or face of something ❸ a piece of misfortune • *They suffered several reverses.*
❹ the reverse gear of a vehicle
➤ **in reverse** the opposite way round

reverse *VERB* reverses, reversing, reversed
❶ to turn something upside down or the other way round ❷ to change round the usual order, position or function of two things ❸ to drive a vehicle backwards ❹ to cancel a decision; to change an opinion to the opposite one
➤ **reversible** *ADJECTIVE*

reverse gear *NOUN*
a gear that allows a vehicle to be driven backwards

revert *VERB* reverts, reverting, reverted
to return to a former state, habit or subject
• *After her divorce she reverted to her maiden name.*
➤ **reversion** *NOUN*

review *NOUN* reviews
❶ an inspection or survey of something ❷ a published description and opinion of a book, film, play, etc.

review *VERB* reviews, reviewing, reviewed
❶ to write a review of a book, film, play, etc.
❷ to reconsider a matter or decision ❸ to inspect or survey something
➤ **reviewer** *NOUN*

SPELLING

Take care not to confuse the noun **review** with **revue**, which means an entertainment consisting of songs and sketches.

revile *VERB* reviles, reviling, reviled
to criticize someone angrily in abusive language

revise VERB revises, revising, revised
❶ to go over work that you have already done, especially in preparing for an examination ❷ to correct or change something • *I have since revised my opinion.*

revision NOUN revisions
❶ a change in something in order to correct or improve it ❷ going over work that you have already done, especially in preparing for an examination

revitalize (also **revitalise**) VERB revitalizes, revitalizing, revitalized
to put new strength or vitality into something

revival NOUN revivals
❶ an improvement in the condition or strength of something • *an economic revival* ❷ a renewal of interest or popularity

revive VERB revives, reviving, revived
❶ to bring someone or something back to life, strength or use • *Attempts were made to revive him but he was already dead.* ❷ to restore interest in or the popularity of something

revoke VERB revokes, revoking, revoked
to withdraw or cancel a decree, licence or right

revolt VERB revolts, revolting, revolted
❶ to disgust someone ❷ to take part in a rebellion

revolt NOUN revolts
a rebellion

revolting ADJECTIVE
disgusting or horrible • *a revolting smell*

revolution NOUN revolutions
❶ a rebellion that overthrows the government ❷ a complete or drastic change ❸ a movement around something; one complete turn of a wheel or engine

revolutionary ADJECTIVE
❶ involving a great change • *a revolutionary idea* ❷ to do with a political revolution

revolutionary NOUN revolutionaries
a person who supports a political revolution

revolutionize (also **revolutionise**)
VERB revolutionizes, revolutionizing, revolutionized
to make a great change in something • *The Internet has revolutionized the way we shop.*

revolve VERB revolves, revolving, revolved
❶ to turn in a circle round a central point or make something do this ❷ to have something

as the most important element • *Her life revolves around her work.*

revolver NOUN revolvers
a pistol with a revolving mechanism that can be fired a number of times without reloading

revue NOUN revues
an entertainment consisting of songs and sketches, often about current events

> **SPELLING**
> Take care not to confuse **revue** with the noun **review**, which means a survey or a piece of writing.

revulsion NOUN
a feeling of strong disgust

reward NOUN rewards
❶ something given in return for something good you have done ❷ a sum of money offered for help in catching a criminal or finding lost property

reward VERB rewards, rewarding, rewarded
to give a reward to someone • *I promise you will be well rewarded for your efforts.*

rewarding ADJECTIVE
giving satisfaction and a feeling of achievement • *a rewarding job*

rewind VERB rewinds, rewinding, rewound
to wind a cassette or videotape back to or towards the beginning

rewrite VERB rewrites, rewriting, rewrote, rewritten
to write something again or differently

rhapsody (say **rap**-so-dee) NOUN rhapsodies
❶ a statement of great delight about something ❷ a romantic piece of music
WORD ORIGIN from Greek *rhapsoidos* = someone who stitches songs together

rhesus monkey NOUN rhesus monkeys
a kind of small monkey from Northern India

rhesus positive ADJECTIVE
having a substance (*rhesus factor*) found in the red blood cells of many humans and some other primates, first found in the rhesus monkey
➤ **rhesus negative** ADJECTIVE
without rhesus factor

rhetoric (say **ret**-er-ik) NOUN
❶ the art of using words impressively, especially in public speaking ❷ language that is used for its impressive effect but is not sincere or meaningful

a b c d e f g h i j k l m n o p q **r** s t u v w x y z

> **rhetorical** *ADJECTIVE*
> **rhetorically** *ADVERB*

rhetorical question *NOUN* rhetorical questions
a question that you ask for dramatic effect without expecting to get an answer, e.g. 'Who cares?' (= nobody cares)

rheumatism *NOUN*
a disease that causes pain and stiffness in joints and muscles
> **rheumatic** *ADJECTIVE*
> **rheumatoid** *ADJECTIVE*

rhino *NOUN* rhino or rhinos (*informal*)
a rhinoceros

rhinoceros *NOUN* rhinoceros or rhinoceroses
a large heavy animal with a horn or two horns on its nose **WORD ORIGIN** from Greek *rhinos* = of the nose + *keras* = horn

rhizome *NOUN* rhizomes
a thick underground stem which produces roots and new plants

rhododendron *NOUN* rhododendrons
an evergreen shrub with large clusters of trumpet-shaped flowers **WORD ORIGIN** from Greek *rhodon* = rose + *dendron* = tree

rhomboid *NOUN* rhomboids
a shape with four straight sides, with only the opposite sides and angles equal to each other

rhombus *NOUN* rhombuses
a shape with four equal sides but no right angles, like the diamond on playing cards

SPELLING
There is a silent h after the r in rhombus.

rhubarb *NOUN*
a plant with thick reddish stalks that are used as fruit

rhyme *NOUN* rhymes
❶ a similar sound in the endings of words, e.g. *bat/fat/mat, batter/fatter/matter* ❷ a poem with rhymes ❸ a word that rhymes with another

rhyme *VERB* rhymes, rhyming, rhymed
❶ to form a rhyme • *'Tough' rhymes with 'stuff'.* ❷ to have rhymes • *Some poems rhyme and some don't.*

SPELLING
There is a silent h in rhyme.

rhythm *NOUN* rhythms
a regular pattern of beats, sounds or movements • *He tapped his foot in rhythm*

with the music.

SPELLING
Try learning the phrase 'rhythm helps your two hips move' to spell rhythm.

rhythmic *ADJECTIVE*
having a regular pattern of beats, sounds or movements • *the rhythmic ticking of the clock*
> **rhythmical** *ADJECTIVE*
> **rhythmically** *ADVERB*

rib *NOUN* ribs
❶ each of the curved bones round the chest ❷ a curved part that looks like a rib or supports something • *the ribs of an umbrella*
> **ribbed** *ADJECTIVE*

ribald (say **rib**-ald) *ADJECTIVE*
funny in a rude or disrespectful way
> **ribaldry** *NOUN*

riband *NOUN* ribands
(*old use*) a ribbon

ribbon *NOUN* ribbons
❶ a narrow strip of silk, nylon or other material, used for decoration or for tying something ❷ a long narrow strip of inked material used in some printers and typewriters

rice *NOUN*
a cereal plant grown in flooded fields in hot countries or its seeds

rich *ADJECTIVE*
❶ having a lot of money or property; wealthy ❷ having a large supply of something • *The country is rich in natural resources.* ❸ a rich colour, sound or smell is pleasantly deep or strong ❹ rich food contains a lot of fat, butter or eggs ❺ expensive or luxurious • *The room was decorated with rich fabrics.*
> **richness** *NOUN*

riches *PLURAL NOUN*
great wealth

richly *ADVERB*
❶ in a rich or luxurious way • *a richly decorated room* ❷ fully or thoroughly • *This award is richly deserved.*

Richter scale *NOUN*
a scale (from 0-10) used to show the force of an earthquake **WORD ORIGIN** named after an American scientist, C. F. *Richter*, who studied earthquakes

rick *NOUN* ricks
a large neat stack of hay or straw

rick *VERB* ricks, ricking, ricked
(*British*) to sprain or wrench your neck or back

rickets *NOUN*
a disease caused by lack of vitamin D, causing deformed bones

rickety *ADJECTIVE*
poorly made and likely to break or fall down • *a rickety wooden bridge*

rickshaw *NOUN* rickshaws
a two-wheeled carriage pulled by one or more people, used in the Far East
WORD ORIGIN from Japanese *jin-riki-sha* = person-power-vehicle

ricochet (say **rik**-osh-ay) *VERB* ricochets, ricocheting, ricocheted
to bounce away from a surface after hitting it • *The bullets ricocheted off the wall.*
➤ **ricochet** *NOUN*
WORD ORIGIN French, = the skipping of a flat stone on water

ricotta *NOUN*
a kind of soft Italian cheese made from sheep's milk

rid *VERB* rids, ridding, rid
to make a person or place free from something unwanted • *He rid the town of rats.*
➤ **get rid of something** to remove something or throw it away

riddle *NOUN* riddles
a puzzling question, especially as a joke

riddle *VERB* riddles, riddling, riddled
to make a lot of holes in something • *The car was riddled with bullets.*
➤ **be riddled with something** to be full of something bad or unpleasant • *The book is riddled with mistakes.*

ride *VERB* rides, riding, rode, ridden
❶ to sit on a horse, bicycle, etc. and control it as it carries you along ❷ to travel in a car, bus, train, etc. ❸ to float or be supported on something • *The ship rode the waves.*

ride *NOUN* rides
❶ a journey on a horse, bicycle, etc. or in a vehicle ❷ a roundabout etc. that you ride on at a fair or amusement park

SPELLING
The past tense of **ride** is **rode** and the past participle is **ridden**.

rider *NOUN* riders
❶ a person who rides something, especially a horse ❷ an extra comment or statement

ridge *NOUN* ridges
❶ a long narrow part higher than the rest of something ❷ a long narrow range of hills or mountains
➤ **ridged** *ADJECTIVE*

ridicule *VERB* ridicules, ridiculing, ridiculed
to make fun of a person or thing

ridicule *NOUN*
unkind words or behaviour that make a person or thing look ridiculous

ridiculous *ADJECTIVE*
so silly or foolish that it makes people laugh or despise it • *You look ridiculous in those trousers.*
➤ **ridiculously** *ADVERB*

rife *ADJECTIVE*
widespread; happening frequently • *Crime was rife in the town.*

riff-raff *NOUN*
the rabble; disreputable people
WORD ORIGIN from old French *rif et raf* = everybody and everything

rifle *NOUN* rifles
a long gun with spiral grooves (called *rifling*) inside the barrel that make the bullet spin and so travel more accurately

rifle *VERB* rifles, rifling, rifled
to search quickly through a place in order to find or steal something • *They had rifled through his desk.*

rift *NOUN* rifts
❶ a crack or split in something ❷ a disagreement that separates friends

rift valley *NOUN* rift valleys
a steep-sided valley formed where the land has sunk

rig *VERB* rigs, rigging, rigged
❶ to fit a ship with ropes, spars, sails, etc. ❷ to arrange the result of an election or contest dishonestly
➤ **rig someone out** to provide someone with clothes or equipment
➤ **rig something up** to set up a structure quickly or out of makeshift materials • *We managed to rig up a shelter for the night.*

rig *NOUN* rigs
❶ a framework supporting the machinery for drilling an oil well ❷ the way a ship's masts and sails etc. are arranged ❸ (*informal*) an outfit of clothes

a b c d e f g h i j k l m n o p q r s t u v w x y z

rigging NOUN
the ropes etc. that support a ship's mast and sails

right ADJECTIVE
❶ on or towards the east if you think of yourself as facing north ❷ correct; true • *the right answer* ❸ morally good; fair or just • *It's not right to cheat.* ❹ conservative; not in favour of socialist reforms
➤ **rightness** NOUN

right ADVERB
❶ on or towards the right • *Turn right here.* ❷ straight; directly • *Go right on.* ❸ all the way; completely • *Turn right round.* ❹ exactly • *right in the middle* ❺ correctly or appropriately • *Did I do that right?*
➤ **right away** immediately

right NOUN **rights**
❶ the right-hand side or part of something ❷ what is morally good or fair or just ❸ something that people are allowed to do or have • *People over 18 have the right to vote in elections.*

right VERB **rights, righting, righted**
❶ to make a thing upright • *The crew managed to right the boat.* ❷ to put something right • *The fault might right itself.*

right angle NOUN
an angle of 90°

righteous ADJECTIVE
doing what is right; virtuous • *He was filled with righteous indignation.*
➤ **righteously** ADVERB
➤ **righteousness** NOUN

rightful ADJECTIVE
deserved or proper • *The bike was returned to its rightful owner.*
➤ **rightfully** ADVERB

right-hand ADJECTIVE
on the right side of something • *the top right-hand corner of the page*

right-handed ADJECTIVE
using the right hand in preference to the left hand

right-hand man NOUN **right-hand men**
the person you depend on the most to help you in your work

rightly ADVERB
correctly or justifiably • *She is rightly proud of her achievements.*

right-minded ADJECTIVE
having ideas and opinions which are sensible and morally good

right of way NOUN **rights of way**
❶ a public path across private land ❷ the right of one vehicle to pass or cross a junction before another

rigid ADJECTIVE
❶ stiff or firm; not bending easily • *a rigid support* ❷ strict and difficult to change • *rigid rules*
➤ **rigidly** ADVERB
➤ **rigidity** NOUN

rigmarole NOUN **rigmaroles**
❶ a long rambling statement ❷ a complicated procedure **WORD ORIGIN** from Middle English *ragman* = a legal document

rigor mortis (say ri-ger **mor**-tis) NOUN
stiffening of the body after death
WORD ORIGIN Latin, = stiffness of death

rigorous ADJECTIVE
❶ strict or severe • *a rigorous diet* ❷ careful and thorough • *rigorous tests*
➤ **rigorously** ADVERB

rigour NOUN **rigours**
❶ doing something carefully with great attention to detail • *The tests were carried out with rigour.* ❷ strictness or severity ❸ harshness of weather or conditions • *the rigours of winter*

rile VERB **riles, riling, riled** (*informal*)
to annoy or irritate someone

rill NOUN **rills**
a very small stream

rim NOUN **rims**
the outer edge of a cup, wheel or other round object

rime NOUN **rimes**
the part of a syllable that contains the vowel and, if there is one, the final consonant or group of consonants, e.g. *og* in *dog*

rimmed ADJECTIVE
having an edge or border • *Her eyes were rimmed with red.*

rind NOUN
the tough skin on bacon, cheese or fruit

ring NOUN **rings**
❶ a circle; a circular band • *The coffee cup left a ring on the table.* • *a key ring* ❷ a thin circular piece of metal you wear on a finger ❸ the space where a circus performs ❹ a square area in which a boxing match or wrestling match takes place ❺ the act or sound of ringing

➤ **give someone a ring** (*informal*) to telephone someone

ring *VERB* **rings, ringing, rang, rung**
❶ to telephone someone • *Please ring me tomorrow.* ❷ to cause a bell to sound ❸ to make a loud clear sound like that of a bell ❹ to be filled with sound • *The hall rang with cheers.*
➤ **ring a bell** to sound faintly familiar • *His name rings a bell.*

ring *VERB* **rings, ringing, ringed**
❶ to put a ring round something • *Ring the answer that you think is the right one.* ❷ to surround something • *The whole area was ringed with police.*

ringleader *NOUN* **ringleaders**
a person who leads others in rebellion, mischief or crime

ringlet *NOUN* **ringlets**
a tube-shaped curl of hair

ringmaster *NOUN* **ringmasters**
the person in charge of a performance in a circus ring

ring road *NOUN* **ring roads**
(*British*) a road that runs around the edge of a town so that traffic does not have to go through the centre

ringtone *NOUN* **ringtones**
the sound your mobile phone makes when it receives a call

ringworm *NOUN*
a fungal skin infection that causes itchy circular patches, especially on the scalp

rink *NOUN* **rinks**
a place made for skating

rinse *VERB* **rinses, rinsing, rinsed**
❶ to wash something in clean water to remove soap ❷ to wash something lightly

rinse *NOUN* **rinses**
❶ rinsing ❷ a liquid for colouring the hair

riot *NOUN* **riots**
wild or violent behaviour by a crowd of people in a public place
➤ **run riot** to behave or spread in a wild or uncontrolled way • *Her imagination began to run riot.*

riot *VERB* **riots, rioting, rioted**
to take part in a riot
➤ **rioter** *NOUN*

riot gear *NOUN*
protective clothing, helmets, shields, etc.

worn or carried by the police or army dealing with a riot

riotous *ADJECTIVE*
❶ noisy and uncontrolled; boisterous • *riotous laughter* ❷ disorderly or unruly

RIP *ABBREVIATION*
may he or she (or they) rest in peace
WORD ORIGIN short for Latin *requiescat* (or *requiescant*) *in pace*

rip *VERB* **rips, ripping, ripped**
❶ to tear something roughly ❷ to become torn ❸ to remove something quickly by pulling hard • *He ripped off his tie.* ❹ to rush along • *A tornado ripped through the town.*
➤ **rip someone off** (*informal*) to swindle someone or charge them too much

rip *NOUN* **rips**
a torn place

ripe *ADJECTIVE* **riper, ripest**
❶ ready to be harvested or eaten ❷ ready and suitable • *The time is ripe for revolution.*
➤ **ripeness** *NOUN*
➤ **a ripe old age** a great age

ripen *VERB* **ripens, ripening, ripened**
to become ripe or to make something ripe • *The grapes were ripening in the sun.*

rip-off *NOUN* **rip-offs**
(*informal*) something that costs a lot more than it should

riposte (say rip-**ost**) *NOUN* **ripostes**
❶ a quick clever reply ❷ a quick return thrust in fencing

ripple *NOUN* **ripples**
❶ a small wave or series of waves ❷ a gentle sound that rises and falls • *a ripple of applause*

ripple *VERB* **ripples, rippling, rippled**
to form ripples

rise *VERB* **rise, rising, rose, risen**
❶ to go upwards • *Smoke was rising from the fire.* • *The sun rises in the east.* ❷ to increase • *Prices are expected to rise.* ❸ to get up from lying, sitting or kneeling ❹ to get out of bed ❺ to rebel • *They rose in revolt against the tyrant.* ❻ bread or cake rises when it swells up by the action of yeast ❼ a river rises when it begins its course ❽ wind rises when it begins to blow more strongly

rise *NOUN* **rises**
❶ the action of rising; an upward movement ❷ an increase in amount or in wages ❸ an upward slope

➤ **give rise to something** to cause something to happen

rising *NOUN* **risings**
a revolt against a government

risk *NOUN* **risks**
a chance that something bad will happen
• *There's a risk that the river might flood.*

risk *VERB* **risks, risking, risked**
❶ to take the chance of damaging or losing something • *They risked their lives to rescue the children.* ❷ to accept the risk of something unpleasant happening • *He risks injury each time he climbs.*

risky *ADJECTIVE* **riskier, riskiest**
full of risk • *That was a risky thing to do.*

risotto *NOUN*
an Italian dish of rice cooked with vegetables and, usually, meat

rissole *NOUN* **rissoles**
(*British*) a fried cake of minced meat or fish

rite *NOUN* **rites**
a religious ceremony; a solemn ritual
• *funeral rites*

ritual *NOUN* **rituals**
the series of actions used in a religious or other ceremony

ritual *ADJECTIVE*
done as part of a ritual • *ritual chanting*

rival *NOUN* **rivals**
a person or thing that competes with another or tries to do the same thing

rival *VERB* **rivals, rivalling, rivalled**
to be as good as another person or thing
• *Nothing can rival the taste of home-made ice cream.* **WORD ORIGIN** from Latin *rivalis* = someone using the same stream (from *rivus* = stream)

rivalry *NOUN* **rivalries**
competition between people or groups
• *There was a lot of rivalry between the sisters.*

river *NOUN* **rivers**
a large stream of water flowing in a natural channel

rivet *NOUN* **rivets**
a strong nail or bolt for holding pieces of metal together. The end opposite the head is flattened to form another head when it is in place.

rivet *VERB* **rivets, riveting, riveted**
❶ to fasten something with rivets ❷ to hold

someone still • *He stood riveted to the spot.*
❸ to hold someone's attention completely • *I was riveted by her story.*
➤ **riveter** *NOUN*

riveting *ADJECTIVE*
so fascinating that it holds your attention completely • *It's a riveting story.*

rivulet *NOUN* **rivulets**
a small stream

roach *NOUN* **roach**
a small freshwater fish

road *NOUN* **roads**
❶ a level way with a hard surface made for traffic to travel on ❷ a way or course • *She seems to be well on the road to recovery.*

roadblock *NOUN* **roadblocks**
a barrier across a road, set up by the police or army to stop and check vehicles

road rage *NOUN*
aggressive or violent behaviour by a driver towards other drivers

roadside *NOUN*
the side of a road

roadway *NOUN*
the middle part of the road, used by traffic

roadworthy *ADJECTIVE*
safe to be used on roads

roam *VERB* **roams, roaming, roamed**
to wander widely • *Sheep roam freely on the hillside.*

roan *ADJECTIVE*
a roan horse has a brown or black coat with many white hairs

roar *NOUN* **roars**
❶ a loud deep sound like that made by a lion ❷ loud laughter

roar *VERB* **roars, roaring, roared**
❶ to make a roar ❷ to laugh loudly
➤ **do a roaring trade** to sell a lot of something quickly

roast *VERB* **roasts, roasting, roasted**
❶ to cook meat etc. in an oven or over a fire ❷ to be roasting is to feel very hot

roast *ADJECTIVE*
cooked by roasting • *roast beef*

roast *NOUN* **roasts**
a piece of meat that has been roasted

rob *VERB* **robs, robbing, robbed**
❶ to steal something from a person or place, often using force • *He robbed me of*

my watch. • *The bank's been robbed.* ❷ to prevent someone from having something that they should have • *Injury robbed her of a place in the final.*

robber *NOUN* **robbers**
a person who steals from a place, often using force

robbery *NOUN* **robberies**
the crime of stealing from a place, often using force

robe *NOUN* **robes**
a long loose piece of clothing, especially one worn in ceremonies

robe *VERB* **robes, robing, robed**
to dress someone in a robe or ceremonial robes

robin *NOUN* **robins**
a small brown bird with a red breast

robot *NOUN* **robots**
❶ a machine that looks or acts like a person ❷ a machine operated by remote control ❸ (*S. African*) a set of traffic lights
WORD ORIGIN from Czech *robota* = forced labour

robotic *ADJECTIVE*
to do with robots; like a robot • *a robotic voice*

robust *ADJECTIVE*
strong and healthy
➤ **robustly** *ADVERB*
WORD ORIGIN from Latin *robur* = strength, an oak tree

rock *NOUN* **rocks**
❶ a large stone or boulder ❷ the hard part of the earth's crust, under the soil ❸ a hard sweet usually shaped like a stick and sold at the seaside ❹ rock music ❺ a rocking movement

rock *VERB* **rocks, rocking, rocked**
❶ to move gently backwards and forwards or from side to side; to make something do this ❷ to shake someone or something violently • *The earthquake rocked the city.* ❸ to shock or upset someone • *We were rocked by the news of her death.*

rock and roll, rock 'n' roll *NOUN*
a kind of popular dance music with a strong beat, originating in the 1950s

rock-bottom *ADJECTIVE*
at the lowest level • *rock-bottom prices*

rocker *NOUN* **rockers**
❶ a curved support for a chair or cradle ❷ a

rocking chair
➤ **off your rocker** (*informal*) mad or crazy

rockery *NOUN* **rockeries**
a mound or bank in a garden, where plants are made to grow between large rocks

rocket *NOUN* **rockets**
❶ a firework that shoots high into the air ❷ a tube-shaped structure that is pushed up into the air by burning gases, used to send up a missile or a spacecraft

rocket *VERB* **rockets, rocketing, rocketed**
to move quickly upwards or away

rocking chair *NOUN* **rocking chairs**
a chair that can be rocked by a person sitting in it

rocking horse *NOUN* **rocking horses**
a model of a horse that can be rocked by a child sitting on it

rock music *NOUN*
popular music with a heavy beat

rocky *ADJECTIVE* **rockier, rockiest**
❶ covered with or made of rocks • *a rocky landscape* ❷ unsteady or unstable

rod *NOUN* **rods**
❶ a long thin stick or bar ❷ a stick with a line attached for fishing

rodent *NOUN* **rodents**
an animal that has large front teeth for gnawing things. Rats, mice and squirrels are rodents **WORD ORIGIN** from Latin *rodens* = gnawing

rodeo (say roh-**day**-oh) *NOUN* **rodeos**
a display of cowboys' skill in riding wild horses, controlling cattle, etc.

roe *NOUN*
❶ a mass of eggs or reproductive cells in a fish's body ❷ **roes** or **roe** a kind of small deer of Europe and Asia. The male is called a **roebuck**.

rogue *NOUN* **rogues**
❶ a dishonest person ❷ a mischievous but likeable person

rogue *ADJECTIVE*
behaving in a way that is different from the rest and causing trouble • *a rogue agent*
➤ **roguery** *NOUN*

roguish *ADJECTIVE*
playful and mischievous • *a roguish smile*
➤ **roguishly** *ADVERB*

role *NOUN* **roles**
❶ an actor's part in a play or film

❷ someone's or something's purpose or function • *the role of computers in education* **WORD ORIGIN** from French *rôle* = roll (originally the roll of paper on which an actor's part was written)

role model *NOUN* role models
a person looked to by others as an example of how to behave

roll *VERB* rolls, rolling, rolled
❶ to move along by turning over and over, like a ball or wheel; to make something do this **❷** to form something into the shape of a cylinder or ball **❸** to flatten something by rolling a rounded object over it • *Roll out the pastry into a large circle.* **❹** a ship or boat rolls when it rocks from side to side **❺** to pass steadily • *The years rolled by.* **❻** thunder rolls when it makes a long rumbling sound

roll *NOUN* rolls
❶ a cylinder made by rolling something up **❷** a small individual portion of bread baked in a rounded shape **❸** an official list of names **❹** a long vibrating or rumbling sound • *a drum roll*

roll-call *NOUN* roll-calls
the calling of a list of names to check that everyone is present

roller *NOUN* rollers
❶ a cylinder used for flattening or spreading things or on which something is wound **❷** a long swelling sea wave

Rollerblade *NOUN* Rollerblades
(*trademark*) a boot like an ice-skating boot, with a line of wheels in place of the skate, for rolling smoothly on hard ground
➤ **rollerblading** *NOUN*

roller coaster *NOUN* roller coasters
a type of railway ride in fairgrounds and amusement parks with a series of alternate steep descents and ascents

roller skate *NOUN* roller skates
a boot with small wheels fitted under it so that you can roll smoothly over the ground
➤ **roller-skating** *NOUN*

rollicking *ADJECTIVE*
boisterous and full of fun **WORD ORIGIN** from **romp** + **frolic**

rolling pin *NOUN*
a heavy cylinder for rolling over pastry to flatten it

rolling stock *NOUN*
the railway engines, carriages and wagons used on a railway

roly-poly *NOUN* roly-polies
a pudding of paste covered with jam, rolled up and boiled

ROM *ABBREVIATION*
read-only memory, a type of computer memory with contents that can be searched or copied but not changed

Roman *ADJECTIVE*
to do with ancient or modern Rome or its people

Roman *NOUN* Romans
a person from ancient or modern Rome

Roman alphabet *NOUN*
this alphabet, in which most European languages are written

Roman candle *NOUN* Roman candles
a tubular firework that sends out coloured sparks

Roman Catholic *ADJECTIVE*
belonging to or to do with the Christian Church that has the Pope (bishop of Rome) as its head
➤ **Roman Catholicism** *NOUN*

Roman Catholic *NOUN* Roman Catholics
a member of this Church

romance (say ro-**manss**) *NOUN* romances
❶ tender feelings, experiences and qualities connected with love **❷** a love story **❸** a love affair **❹** mystery and excitement • *the romance of the East* **❺** a medieval story about the adventures of heroes • *a romance of King Arthur's court*

Romance language *NOUN* Romance languages
any of the group of European languages descended from Latin, such as French, Italian and Spanish

Roman numerals *PLURAL NOUN*
letters that represent numbers (I = 1, V = 5, X = 10, etc.), used by the ancient Romans. Compare with **Arabic numerals**.

romantic *ADJECTIVE*
❶ to do with love or romance **❷** sentimental or idealistic; not realistic or practical • *She has a romantic view of life in the countryside.*
➤ **romantically** *ADVERB*

Romany *NOUN* Romanies
❶ a member of a people who live in travelling communities; a gypsy **❷** the language of these people

romp *VERB* **romps, romping, romped**
to play in a rough or lively way
➤ **romp** *NOUN*

rompers *PLURAL NOUN*
a piece of clothing for a baby or young child, covering the body and legs

roof *NOUN* **roofs**
❶ the part that covers the top of a building, shelter or vehicle ❷ the top inside surface of something • *the roof of your mouth*

roofing *NOUN*
material used to construct the roof of a building

roof rack *NOUN* **roof racks**
a framework for carrying luggage on top of a vehicle

rook *NOUN* **rooks**
❶ a black crow that nests in large groups ❷ a chess piece shaped like a castle

rookery *NOUN* **rookeries**
❶ a place where many rooks nest ❷ a breeding place of penguins or seals

room *NOUN* **rooms**
❶ a part of a building with its own walls and ceiling ❷ enough space • *Is there room for me?*
➤ **roomful** *NOUN*

roomy *ADJECTIVE* **roomier, roomiest**
containing plenty of room; spacious • *a roomy car*

roost *VERB* **roosts, roosting, roosted**
birds roost when they perch or settle for sleep

roost *NOUN* **roosts**
a place where birds roost

rooster *NOUN* **roosters** (*North American*)
a cockerel

root *NOUN* **roots**
❶ the part of a plant that grows under the ground and absorbs water and nourishment from the soil ❷ a source or basis of something • *We are trying to get to the root of the problem.* ❸ a number which, when multiplied by itself a particular number of times, produces another number • *9 is the square root of 81 (9 × 9 = 81).*
➤ **take root** ❶ to grow roots ❷ to become established • *Gradually the idea took root.*

root *VERB* **roots, rooting, rooted**
❶ to take root in the ground; to cause something to take root ❷ to fix someone firmly in one place • *Fear rooted us to the spot.* ❸ to search for something by moving

things • *She rooted around in her handbag.*
❹ a pig or other animal roots when it turns up ground in search of food
➤ **root for someone** to support someone enthusiastically
➤ **root something out** to find something and get rid of it

rope *NOUN* **ropes**
a strong thick cord made of twisted strands of fibre
➤ **show someone the ropes** to show someone how to do a job

rope *VERB* **ropes, roping, roped**
to fasten something with a rope • *We roped ourselves together for safety.*
➤ **rope someone in** to persuade someone to take part in something

rosary *NOUN* **rosaries**
a string of beads for keeping count of a set of prayers as they are said

rose *NOUN* **roses**
❶ a scented flower with a long thorny stem; the bush this flower grows on ❷ a deep pink colour ❸ a sprinkling nozzle with many holes, e.g. on a watering can or hosepipe

rose *VERB*
past tense of **rise**

rosemary *NOUN*
an evergreen shrub with fragrant leaves, used in cooking

rosette *NOUN* **rosettes**
a large circular badge or ornament, made of ribbon

Rosh Hashanah, Rosh Hashana *NOUN*
the Jewish New Year festival

roster *NOUN* **rosters**
a list showing people's turns to be on duty

rostrum *NOUN* **rostra**
a platform for one person, e.g. for giving a speech or conducting an orchestra
(**WORD ORIGIN**) Latin, = beak, prow of a warship (because a rostrum in ancient Rome was decorated with the prows of captured enemy ships)

rosy *ADJECTIVE* **rosier, rosiest**
❶ deep pink • *rosy cheeks* ❷ hopeful or cheerful • *a rosy future*

rot *VERB* **rots, rotting, rotted**
to go soft or bad and become useless; to decay

rot *NOUN*
❶ rotting or decay ❷ (*informal*) nonsense

rota (say **roh**-ta) NOUN **rotas**
a list of people to do things or of things to be done in turn

rotate VERB **rotates, rotating, rotated**
❶ to turn or spin in circles round a central point; to revolve • *A day is the time it takes the Earth to rotate once on its axis.* ❷ to happen or make something happen in a fixed order; to take turns at doing something • *The job of treasurer rotates.*
➤ **rotary** ADJECTIVE

rotation NOUN **rotations**
❶ movement in circles round a central point • *one rotation every 24 hours* ❷ happening or making things happen in a certain order • *the rotation of crops*

rote NOUN
➤ **by rote** by repeating something again and again, but without full understanding of its meaning • *We used to learn French songs by rote.*

rotor NOUN **rotors**
a rotating part of a machine or helicopter

rotten ADJECTIVE
❶ rotted or decayed • *rotten apples* ❷ (*informal*) very bad or unpleasant • *rotten weather*
➤ **rottenness** NOUN

Rottweiler NOUN **Rottweilers**
a breed of powerful black-and-tan dog, sometimes used as a guard dog
(WORD ORIGIN) German, from *Rottweil*, a town in Germany where the dog was bred

rotund ADJECTIVE
rounded or plump
➤ **rotundity** NOUN

rouble (say **roo**-bul) NOUN **roubles**
the unit of money in Russia

rouge (say roozh) NOUN
a reddish cosmetic for colouring the cheeks
➤ **rouged** ADJECTIVE
(WORD ORIGIN) French, = red

rough ADJECTIVE **rougher, roughest**
❶ not smooth or level; uneven ❷ not gentle or careful; violent • *a rough push* ❸ not exact or detailed • *It's only a rough guess.* ❹ rough sea or weather is wild and stormy ❺ difficult and unpleasant • *He's been through a rough time recently.*
➤ **roughness** NOUN

rough VERB **roughs, roughing, roughed**
➤ **rough it** to do without ordinary comforts
➤ **rough something out** to draw or plan

something without including all the details
➤ **rough someone up** (*informal*) to beat someone up

roughage NOUN
fibre in food, which helps digestion

roughen VERB **roughens, roughening, roughened**
to make something rough • *Cold weather roughens your skin.*

roughly ADVERB
❶ approximately; not exactly • *There were roughly a hundred people there.* ❷ in a rough way; not gently • *She pushed him roughly out of the way.*

roulette (say roo-**let**) NOUN
a gambling game where players bet on where the ball on a revolving wheel will come to rest

round ADJECTIVE
❶ shaped like a circle, ball or cylinder; curved ❷ full or complete • *a round dozen* ❸ a round number is expressed to the nearest whole number or the nearest ten, hundred, etc.
➤ **roundness** NOUN
➤ **in round figures** approximately, without giving exact units

round ADVERB (*chiefly British*)
❶ in a circle or curve; surrounding something • *Go round to the back of the house.* ❷ in every direction or to every person • *Hand the cakes round.* ❸ in a new direction • *Turn your chair round.* ❹ from place to place • *We wandered round for a while.* ❺ to someone's house or place of work • *Come round after lunch.*
➤ **come round** to become conscious again
➤ **round about** ❶ near by ❷ roughly or approximately

round PREPOSITION (*chiefly British*)
❶ on all sides of • *We put a fence round the field.* ❷ in a curve or circle at an even distance from • *The earth moves round the sun.* ❸ to all parts of a place • *Show them round the house.* ❹ on or to the further side of a place • *The shop is round the corner.*

round NOUN **rounds**
❶ a series of visits made by a doctor, postman, etc. ❷ one section or stage in a competition • *Winners go on to the next round.* ❸ the playing of all the holes on a golf course ❹ a shot or series of shots from a gun; ammunition for this ❺ (*British*) a whole slice of bread; a sandwich made with two slices of bread ❻ a song in which people sing the same words but start at different times ❼ a

set of drinks bought for all the members of a group
➤ **do the rounds** to be passed round among a lot of people

round *VERB* **rounds, rounding, rounded** to travel round something • *The car rounded the corner.*
➤ **round something off** to finish or complete something • *We rounded the evening off with some music.*
➤ **round something up** to gather people or animals together • *The teacher rounded up the children.*
➤ **round something up** or **down** to increase or decrease a number to the next highest or lowest whole number

roundabout *NOUN* **roundabouts**
❶ a road junction where traffic has to pass round a circular structure in the road ❷ a circular revolving ride in a playground or at a funfair

roundabout *ADJECTIVE*
indirect; not using the shortest way of going or of saying or doing something • *I heard the news in a roundabout way.*

rounded *ADJECTIVE*
round in shape

rounders *NOUN*
a game in which players try to hit a ball and run round a circuit

Roundhead *NOUN* **Roundheads**
a supporter of the Parliamentary party in the English Civil War (1642-9) **WORD ORIGIN** so called because many of them wore their hair cut short at a time when long hair was in fashion for men

roundly *ADVERB*
thoroughly or severely • *We were roundly told off for being late.*

round-shouldered *ADJECTIVE*
with the shoulders bent forward, so that the back is rounded

round-the-clock *ADJECTIVE*
lasting or happening all day and all night

round trip *NOUN* **round trips**
a trip to one or more places and back to where you started

round-up *NOUN* **round-ups**
❶ a gathering up of cattle or people • *a police round-up of suspects* ❷ a summary • *a round-up of the news*

roundworm *NOUN* **roundworms**
a kind of worm that lives as a parasite in the intestines of animals and birds

rouse *VERB* **rouses, rousing, roused**
❶ to wake someone up • *I was roused by a knock on the door.* ❷ to make someone excited, angry or active • *Many people watching the programme were roused to action.*

rousing *ADJECTIVE*
exciting and powerful • *a rousing speech*

rout *VERB* **routs, routing, routed**
to defeat an enemy completely and force them to retreat

rout *NOUN* **routs**
a complete defeat; a disorderly retreat of defeated troops

route (say root) *NOUN* **routes**
the way you have to go to get to a place

router (say **roo**-ter) *NOUN* **routers**
a device that connects computer networks and sends information between them

routine (say roo-**teen**) *NOUN* **routines**
❶ a regular or fixed way of doing things • *A morning run is part of her daily routine.* ❷ a set sequence in a performance • *a dance routine*
➤ **routinely** *ADVERB*

rove *VERB* **roves, roving, roved**
to roam or wander • *His eyes roved around the room.*
➤ **rover** *NOUN*

row (rhymes with go) *NOUN* **rows**
a line of people or things

row (rhymes with go) *VERB* **rows, rowing, rowed**
to make a boat move by using oars

row (rhymes with cow) *NOUN* **rows** (*British*)
❶ a loud noise or uproar ❷ a quarrel or noisy argument

row (rhymes with cow) *VERB* **rows, rowing, rowed** (*British*)
to have a noisy argument

rowan (say **roh**-an) *NOUN* **rowans**
a tree that bears hanging bunches of red berries

rowdy *ADJECTIVE* **rowdier, rowdiest**
noisy and disorderly • *a rowdy group of teenagers*
➤ **rowdiness** *NOUN*

rower *NOUN* **rowers**
a person who rows a boat

rowing boat *NOUN* rowing boats
(*British*) a small boat that you move forward by using oars

rowlock (say **rol**-ok) *NOUN* rowlocks
(*British*) a device on the side of a boat, keeping an oar in place

royal *ADJECTIVE*
to do with a king or queen
➤ **royally** *ADVERB*

Royalist *NOUN* Royalists
a supporter of the monarchy in the English Civil War (1642-9)

royalist *NOUN* royalists
a person who supports the idea of a monarchy

royalty *NOUN*
❶ being royal ❷ a royal person or royal people • *We found ourselves in the presence of royalty.* ❸ **royalties** a payment made to an author or composer for each copy of a work sold or for each performance

RSVP *ABBREVIATION*
please reply (often written at the end of an invitation) **(WORD ORIGIN)** short for a French phrase *répondez s'il vous plaît*

rub *VERB* rubs, rubbing, rubbed
to move something backwards and forwards while pressing it on something else • *He rubbed his hands together.*
➤ **rub off** to be passed from one person to another • *I hope some of your good luck rubs off on me.*
➤ **rub something off** or **out** to remove something by rubbing it

rub *NOUN* rubs
rubbing something • *Give it a quick rub.*

rubber *NOUN* rubbers
❶ a strong elastic substance used for making tyres, balls, hoses, etc. ❷ a piece of rubber for rubbing out pencil or ink marks

rubber plant *NOUN* rubber plants
❶ a tall evergreen plant with tough shiny leaves, often grown as a house plant ❷ a rubber tree

rubber stamp *NOUN* rubber stamps
a small device with lettering or a design on it, which is inked and used to mark paper

rubber-stamp *VERB* rubber-stamps, rubber-stamping, rubber-stamped
to give official approval to a decision without thinking about it

rubber tree *NOUN* rubber trees
a tropical tree from which rubber is obtained

rubbery *ADJECTIVE*
looking or feeling like rubber • *rubbery lips*

rubbish *NOUN* (*chiefly British*)
❶ things that are not wanted and are to be thrown away ❷ nonsense; something of very poor quality • *Don't talk such rubbish.*

rubbish *ADJECTIVE*
(*British*) (*informal*) very poor in quality • *I thought the film was rubbish.*

rubble *NOUN*
broken pieces of brick or stone

rubella *NOUN*
an infectious disease which causes a red rash and which can damage a baby if the mother catches it early in pregnancy

rubric *NOUN*
a set of instructions at the beginning of an official document or an examination paper **(WORD ORIGIN)** from Latin *rubeus* = red (because rubrics used to be written in red)

ruby *NOUN* rubies
a red jewel

ruby wedding *NOUN*
a couple's fortieth wedding anniversary

ruck *VERB* rucks, rucking, rucked
cloth rucks up when it forms untidy creases or folds

rucksack *NOUN* rucksacks
a bag with shoulder straps for carrying on your back

ructions *PLURAL NOUN* (*informal*)
angry protests or arguments

rudder *NOUN* rudders
a hinged upright piece at the back of a ship or aircraft, used for steering

ruddy *ADJECTIVE* ruddier, ruddiest
a ruddy complexion is red and healthy-looking

rude *ADJECTIVE* ruder, rudest
❶ impolite or bad-mannered • *It was rude of me to interrupt.* ❷ to do with sex or the body in a way that might offend people; indecent • *a rude joke* ❸ roughly made • *a rude shelter* ❹ unexpected and unpleasant • *I think you may be in for a rude shock.*
➤ **rudely** *ADVERB*
➤ **rudeness** *NOUN*

rudimentary *ADJECTIVE*
1 very basic or simple • *a rudimentary knowledge of Arabic* 2 not fully developed • *Penguins have rudimentary wings.*

rudiments (say **rood**-i-ments) *PLURAL NOUN*
the elementary principles of a subject • *She taught me the rudiments of chemistry.*

rueful *ADJECTIVE*
showing sad regret • *The boy gave a rueful smile.*
➤ **ruefully** *ADVERB*

ruff *NOUN* ruffs
1 a starched pleated frill worn round the neck in the 16th century 2 a collar-like ring of feathers or fur round a bird's or animal's neck

ruffian *NOUN* ruffians
a rough or violent person

ruffle *VERB* ruffles, ruffling, ruffled
1 to disturb the smoothness of a thing • *He ruffled the boy's hair.* • *The chicken ruffled up its feathers.* 2 to upset or annoy someone

ruffle *NOUN* ruffles
a gathered ornamental frill

rug *NOUN* rugs
1 a small carpet or thick mat for the floor 2 a piece of thick fabric used as a blanket

rugby, rugby football *NOUN*
a kind of football game using an oval ball that players may carry or kick
WORD ORIGIN named after *Rugby* School in Warwickshire, where it was first played

rugged (say **rug**-id) *ADJECTIVE*
1 having a rough or uneven surface or outline • *His face was rugged.* • *a rugged coastline* 2 strong and tough

ruin *VERB* ruins, ruining, ruined
to damage or spoil a thing so severely that it is useless or no longer enjoyable • *My new shoes are completely ruined.*

ruin *NOUN* ruins
1 a building that is so badly damaged that it has almost fallen down 2 severe damage or destruction to something • *The city was in a state of ruin.*
➤ **be in ruins** to have failed completely • *My hopes were now in ruins.*
➤ **ruination** *NOUN*

ruinous *ADJECTIVE*
1 causing ruin 2 in ruins; ruined

rule *NOUN* rules
1 something that people have to obey

2 ruling or governing • *The country used to be under French rule.* 3 a carpenter's ruler
➤ **as a rule** usually; more often than not

rule *VERB* rules, ruling, ruled
1 to govern or reign 2 to make a decision • *The referee ruled that it was a foul.* 3 to draw a straight line with a ruler or other straight edge
➤ **rule something out** to say that something is not a possibility

ruler *NOUN* rulers
1 a person who governs 2 a strip of wood, metal or plastic with straight edges, used for measuring and drawing straight lines

ruling *NOUN* rulings
a judgement or decision

rum *NOUN*
a strong alcoholic drink made from sugar or molasses

rumble *VERB* rumbles, rumbling, rumbled
to make a deep heavy continuous sound • *I was so hungry that my stomach was rumbling.*

rumble *NOUN* rumbles
a deep heavy continuous sound • *There was a rumble of thunder in the distance.*

ruminant *NOUN* ruminants
an animal that chews the cud (see **cud**), such as cattle, sheep, deer, etc.
➤ **ruminant** *ADJECTIVE*

ruminate *VERB* ruminates, ruminating, ruminated
1 to chew the cud 2 to think deeply about something; to ponder
➤ **rumination** *NOUN*
➤ **ruminative** *ADJECTIVE*

rummage *VERB* rummages, rummaging, rummaged
to turn things over or move them about while looking for something • *She rummaged in her backpack and found the torch.*
➤ **rummage** *NOUN*

rummy *NOUN*
a card game in which players try to form sets or sequences of cards

rumour *NOUN* rumours
news or information that spreads to a lot of people but may not be true

rumour *VERB*
➤ **be rumoured** to be spread as a rumour • *It was rumoured that she was a witch.*

a b c d e f g h i j k l m n o p q r s t u v w x y z

rump *NOUN* rumps
the hind part of an animal

rumple *VERB* rumples, rumpling, rumpled
to make something untidy or no longer smooth • *The bed was rumpled where he had slept.*

rump steak *NOUN* rump steaks
a piece of meat from the rump of a cow

rumpus *NOUN* rumpuses (*informal*)
an uproar; an angry protest

run *VERB* runs, running, ran, run
❶ to move with quick steps so that both or all feet leave the ground at each stride ❷ to go or travel; to flow • *Tears ran down his cheeks.* ❸ to move something over or through a thing • *She ran her fingers through her hair.* ❹ to produce a flow of liquid • *Run some water into it.* • *My nose is running.* ❺ to work or function • *The engine was running smoothly.* ❻ to start or use a computer program ❼ to manage or organize something • *She runs a corner shop.* ❽ to compete in a contest or election • *He ran for President.* ❾ to extend • *A fence runs round the estate.* ❿ to last or continue for a certain amount of time • *The play ran for six months.* ⓫ to take a person somewhere in a vehicle • *I'll run you to the station.*
➤ **run across someone** to happen to meet or find someone
➤ **run a risk** to take a chance
➤ **run away** to leave a place secretly or quickly
➤ **run down** to stop gradually or decline
➤ **run someone down** ❶ to knock someone down with a moving vehicle ❷ (*informal*) to say unkind or unfair things about someone
➤ **run into someone** to happen to meet someone
➤ **run out of something** to have used up your stock of something
➤ **run someone out** to knock over the wicket of a running batsman in cricket
➤ **run someone over** to knock someone down with a moving vehicle
➤ **run through something** to examine or rehearse something

run *NOUN* runs
❶ the action of running; a time spent running • *Let's go for a run.* ❷ a point scored in cricket or baseball ❸ a continuous series of events • *She had a run of good luck.* ❹ an enclosure for animals • *a chicken run* ❺ a series of damaged stitches in a pair of tights or stockings ❻ a track • *a ski run*

➤ **on the run** running away, especially from the police

runaway *NOUN* runaways
someone who has run away

runaway *ADJECTIVE*
❶ having run away or out of control • *a runaway train* ❷ won easily • *a runaway victory*

rundown *ADJECTIVE*
❶ tired and in bad health ❷ in bad condition • *a rundown cottage*

rung *NOUN* rungs
one of the crossbars on a ladder

rung *VERB*
past participle of **ring** *VERB*

runner *NOUN* runners
❶ a person or animal that runs, especially in a race ❷ a stem that grows away from a plant and roots itself ❸ a rod or strip on which something slides; each of the long strips under a sledge ❹ a long narrow strip of carpet or covering

runner bean *NOUN* runner beans
(*British*) a kind of climbing bean with long green pods which are eaten

runner-up *NOUN* runners-up
someone who comes second in a race or competition

running
present participle of **run**
➤ **in the running** competing and with a chance of winning

running *ADJECTIVE*
continuous or consecutive; without an interval • *It rained for four days running.*

runny *ADJECTIVE* runnier, runniest
❶ flowing like liquid • *runny honey* ❷ producing a flow of liquid • *a runny nose*

run-of-the-mill *ADJECTIVE*
ordinary, not special

runway *NOUN* runways
a long hard surface on which aircraft take off and land

rupee *NOUN* rupees
the unit of money in India and Pakistan

rupture *VERB* ruptures, rupturing, ruptured
to break or burst suddenly or to cause something to do this
➤ **rupture** *NOUN*

rural *ADJECTIVE*
to do with or belonging to the countryside
• *a rural scene*

ruse *NOUN* ruses
a deception or trick

rush *VERB* rushes, rushing, rushed
❶ to move or do something quickly; to hurry
• *We rushed back as soon as we heard the news.* ❷ to take someone to a place very quickly • *The injured people were rushed to hospital.* ❸ to make someone hurry
• *Don't rush me – I'm thinking.* ❹ to attack or capture someone by dashing forward suddenly

rush *NOUN* rushes
❶ a hurry • *I can't stop – I'm in a rush.* ❷ a sudden quick movement • *All my words came out in a rush.* ❸ a sudden great demand for something ❹ a plant with a thin stem that grows in marshy places

rush hour *NOUN* rush hours
the time when traffic is busiest

rusk *NOUN* rusks
(*chiefly British*) a kind of hard dry biscuit for babies to chew

russet *NOUN*
a reddish-brown colour

rust *NOUN*
❶ a red or brown substance that forms on iron or steel exposed to damp and corrodes it ❷ a reddish-brown colour

rust *VERB* rusts, rusting, rusted
to make something rusty or to become rusty

rustic *ADJECTIVE*
❶ to do with life in the countryside; rural ❷ made of rough timber or branches • *a rustic bridge*

rustle *VERB* rustles, rustling, rustled
❶ to make a sound like dry leaves moving or paper being crumpled • *The trees rustled in the breeze.* ❷ (*North American*) to steal horses or cattle
➤ **rustler** *NOUN*
➤ **rustle something up** (*informal*) to produce something quickly • *I'll see if I can rustle up a snack.*

rustle *NOUN*
a rustling sound

rusty *ADJECTIVE* rustier, rustiest
❶ coated with rust ❷ weakened by lack of use or practice • *My French is a bit rusty these days.*

rut *NOUN* ruts
❶ a deep track made by wheels in soft ground ❷ a settled and usually dull way of life • *We are getting into a rut.*
➤ **rutted** *ADJECTIVE*

ruthless *ADJECTIVE*
determined to get what you want and not caring if you hurt other people
➤ **ruthlessly** *ADVERB*
➤ **ruthlessness** *NOUN*
WORD ORIGIN from Middle English *ruth* = pity

rye *NOUN*
a cereal used to make flour and whisky

Ss

S. *ABBREVIATION*
❶ south ❷ southern

sabbath *NOUN* sabbaths
a weekly day for rest and prayer, Saturday for Jews, Sunday for Christians
WORD ORIGIN from Hebrew *shabat* = rest

sable *NOUN*
❶ a kind of dark fur ❷ (*poetical use*) black

sabotage *NOUN*
deliberately damaging machinery or equipment to hinder an enemy or large organization

sabotage *VERB* sabotage, sabotaging, sabotaged
to deliberately damage something by an act of sabotage

saboteur *NOUN* saboteurs
a person who carries out sabotage

sabre *NOUN* sabres
❶ a heavy sword with a curved blade ❷ a light fencing sword

sac *NOUN* sacs
a bag-shaped part in an animal or plant

saccharin (say **sak**-er-in) *NOUN*
a very sweet substance used as a substitute for sugar

saccharine (say **sak**-er-een) *ADJECTIVE*
unpleasantly sweet or sentimental • *a saccharine smile*

a b c d e f g h i j k l m n o p q r s t u v w x y z

sachet (say **sash**-ay) *NOUN* sachets
a small sealed packet or bag containing a small amount of shampoo, sugar, etc.

sack *NOUN* sacks
a large bag made of strong material
➤ **get the sack** (*informal*) to be dismissed from a job

sack *VERB* sacks, sacking, sacked
❶ to dismiss someone from a job ❷ (*old use*) to plunder and destroy a captured town

sacking *NOUN*
rough cloth used to make sacks

sacrament *NOUN* sacraments
an important Christian religious ceremony such as baptism or Holy Communion

sacred *ADJECTIVE*
holy; to do with God or a god • *The Koran is the sacred book of Muslims.*

sacrifice *NOUN* sacrifices
❶ giving up a thing you value, so that something good may happen • *We will have to make a few sacrifices if we want to save enough money.* ❷ killing an animal or person as an offering to a god ❸ a thing sacrificed
➤ **sacrificial** *ADJECTIVE*

sacrifice *VERB* sacrifices, sacrificing, sacrificed
❶ to give something up so that something good may happen • *She sacrificed her career to bring up the children.* ❷ to kill an animal or person as an offering to a god

sacrilege (say **sak**-ril-ij) *NOUN*
disrespect or damage to something people think of as sacred or valuable
➤ **sacrilegious** *ADJECTIVE*

sad *ADJECTIVE* sadder, saddest
unhappy; showing or causing sorrow
➤ **sadness** *NOUN*

sadden *VERB* saddens, saddening, saddened
to make a person sad • *The news of his death saddened her greatly.*

saddle *NOUN* saddles
❶ a seat for putting on the back of a horse or other animal ❷ the seat of a bicycle ❸ a ridge of high land between two peaks

saddle *VERB* saddles, saddling, saddled
to put a saddle on a horse or other animal for riding
➤ **saddle someone with something** to burden someone with a task or problem

sadist (say **say**-dist) *NOUN* sadists
a person who enjoys hurting or humiliating other people
➤ **sadism** *NOUN*
➤ **sadistic** *ADJECTIVE*
WORD ORIGIN named after a French novelist, the Marquis de *Sade*, noted for the cruelties in his stories

sadly *ADVERB*
❶ in a sad way • *He shook his head sadly.*
❷ unfortunately • *Sadly, I won't be able to come.*

sae *ABBREVIATION*
(*British*) stamped addressed envelope

safari *NOUN* safaris
an expedition to watch or hunt wild animals
WORD ORIGIN from Arabic *safar* = a journey

safari park *NOUN* safari parks
a large park where wild animals can roam around freely and visitors can watch them from their cars

safe *ADJECTIVE*
❶ not in danger • *He felt safe up in the tree.*
❷ not dangerous • *Drive at a safe speed.*

safe *NOUN* safes
a strong cupboard or box in which valuables can be locked away safely

safeguard *NOUN* safeguards
something that protects against possible dangers

safeguard *VERB* safeguards, safeguarding, safeguarded
to protect something from danger

safely *ADVERB*
❶ without harm or danger • *The plane landed safely.* ❷ without risk • *I can safely say that she was pleased with her present.*

safe sex *NOUN*
sexual activity in which precautions, such as using a condom, are taken to prevent the spread of infections

safety *NOUN*
being safe; freedom from danger, harm or risk • *a talk on road safety*

safety pin *NOUN* safety pins
a U-shaped pin with a clip fastening over the point

saffron *NOUN*
❶ a deep yellow spice used to colour or flavour food, made from the dried stigmas of a crocus ❷ a deep yellow colour

sag *VERB* sags, sagging, sagged
❶ to go down in the middle because

something heavy is pressing on it • *The tent began to sag under the weight of the rain.*
❷ to hang down loosely; to droop • *His shoulders sagged.*

saga (say **sah**-ga) *NOUN* sagas
a long story with many episodes or adventures

sagacious (say sa-**gay**-shus) *ADJECTIVE*
shrewd and wise
➤ **sagaciously** *ADVERB*
➤ **sagacity** *NOUN*

sage *NOUN* sages
❶ a kind of herb used in cooking and formerly used in medicine ❷ a wise and respected person

sage *ADJECTIVE*
wise and experienced
➤ **sagely** *ADVERB*

sago *NOUN*
a starchy white food used to make puddings

said
past tense of **say**

sail *NOUN* sails
❶ a large piece of strong cloth attached to a mast to catch the wind and make a ship or boat move ❷ a short voyage • *We went for a sail around the island.* ❸ an arm of a windmill
➤ **set sail** to start on a voyage in a ship

sail *VERB* sails, sailing, sailed
❶ to travel in a ship or boat ❷ to start out on a voyage • *We sail at noon.* ❸ to control a ship or boat ❹ to move quickly and smoothly • *The ball sailed over the fence.*

sailboard *NOUN* sailboards
a flat board with a mast and sail, used in windsurfing

sailing ship *NOUN* sailing ships
a ship with sails

sailor *NOUN* sailors
a person who sails; a member of a ship's crew or of a navy

saint *NOUN* saints
a holy or very good person
➤ **saintly** *ADJECTIVE*

sake *NOUN*
➤ **for the sake of something** in order to get or achieve something • *She is taking more exercise for the sake of her health.*
➤ **for someone's sake** in order to help or please someone • *Don't go to any trouble for my sake.*

salad *NOUN* salads
a mixture of vegetables eaten raw or cold

salamander *NOUN* salamanders
a lizard-like amphibian

salami *NOUN*
a spiced sausage, originally made in Italy

salary *NOUN* salaries
a regular wage, usually for a year's work, paid in monthly instalments **WORD ORIGIN** from Latin *salarium* = salt-money, money given to Roman soldiers to buy salt

sale *NOUN* sales
❶ the selling of something ❷ a time when things are sold at reduced prices
➤ **for sale** or **on sale** available to be bought

salesperson *NOUN* salespersons
a person employed to sell goods
➤ **salesman** *NOUN* salesmen
➤ **saleswoman** *NOUN* saleswomen

salient (say **say**-lee-ent) *ADJECTIVE*
most noticeable or important • *the salient features of the plan*

saline *ADJECTIVE*
containing salt

saliva *NOUN*
the natural liquid in a person's or animal's mouth
➤ **salivary** *ADJECTIVE*

salivate (say **sal**-iv-ayt) *VERB* salivates, salivating, salivated
to form saliva, especially a large amount

sallow *ADJECTIVE*
sallow skin is slightly yellow

sally *NOUN* sallies
❶ a lively or witty remark ❷ a sudden attack by an enemy

sally *VERB* sallies, sallying, sallied
➤ **sally forth** or **out** to set out in a determined way

salmon (say **sam**-on) *NOUN* salmon
a large edible fish with pink flesh

salmonella (say sal-mon-**el**-a) *NOUN*
a bacterium that can cause food poisoning
WORD ORIGIN named after an American scientist, Elmer *Salmon*, who studied the causes of disease

salon *NOUN* salons
❶ a large elegant room ❷ a room or shop where customers go for hair or beauty treatment

a
b
c
d
e
f
g
h
i
j
k
l
m
n
o
p
q
r
s
t
u
v
w
x
y
z

saloon *NOUN* saloons
❶ a car with a hard roof and a separate boot
❷ a place where alcoholic drinks are bought and drunk, especially a comfortable bar in a pub

salsa *NOUN*
❶ a hot spicy sauce ❷ a kind of modern Latin American dance music; a dance to this

salt *NOUN* salts
❶ sodium chloride, the white substance that gives sea water its taste and is used for flavouring food ❷ a chemical compound of a metal and an acid

salt *VERB* salts, salting, salted
to flavour or preserve food with salt

salt cellar *NOUN* salt cellars
a small dish or perforated pot holding salt for use at meals **WORD ORIGIN** *cellar* from old French *salier* = salt-box

salts *PLURAL NOUN*
a substance that looks like salt • *bath salts*

salty *ADJECTIVE* saltier, saltiest
containing or tasting of salt

salutary *ADJECTIVE*
beneficial; having a good effect • *She gave us some salutary advice.*

salutation *NOUN* salutations
(*formal*) a greeting • *He raised his hand in salutation.*

salute *VERB* salutes, saluting, saluted
❶ to raise your right hand to your forehead as a sign of respect, especially in the armed forces • *The sergeant saluted and left the room.* ❷ to greet someone ❸ to say that you respect or admire something • *We salute this achievement.*

salute *NOUN* salutes
❶ the act of saluting ❷ the firing of guns as a sign of respect

salvage *VERB* salvages, salvaging, salvaged
to save or rescue something such as a damaged ship's cargo so that it can be used again
➤ **salvage** *NOUN*

salvation *NOUN*
❶ in Christian teaching, being saved by God from the power of evil ❷ something that rescues a person from danger or disaster

salve *NOUN* salves
❶ a soothing ointment ❷ something that soothes

salve *VERB* salves, salving, salved
➤ **salve your conscience** to make you feel less guilty about something

salver *NOUN* salvers
a small metal tray

salvo *NOUN* salvoes or salvos
firing a number of guns at the same time

same *ADJECTIVE*
❶ of one kind, exactly alike or equal • *We are the same age.* ❷ not changing; not different • *I get up at the same time every morning.*
➤ **sameness** *NOUN*

samosa *NOUN* samosas
a triangular fried pastry case filled with spicy meat or vegetables

samovar *NOUN* samovars
a Russian tea urn **WORD ORIGIN** Russian, = self-boiler

sampan *NOUN* sampans
a small flat-bottomed boat used in China **WORD ORIGIN** from Chinese *sanpan* (*san* = three, *pan* = boards)

sample *NOUN* samples
a small amount that shows what something is like

sample *VERB* samples, sampling, sampled
❶ to take a sample of something • *Scientists sampled the lake water.* ❷ to try part of something • *She sampled the cake.*

sampler *NOUN* samplers
a piece of embroidery worked in various stitches to show skill in needlework

samurai (say **sam**-oor-eye) *NOUN* samurai
a member of an ancient Japanese warrior class

sanatorium *NOUN* sanatoriums or sanatoria
a hospital where people who need a long period of treatment for an illness can stay

sanctify *VERB* sanctifies, sanctifying, sanctified
to make a place holy or sacred

sanctimonious *ADJECTIVE*
making a show of being virtuous or pious

sanction *NOUN* sanctions
❶ action taken against a nation that is considered to have broken an international law • *Sanctions against that country include refusing to trade with it.* ❷ a penalty for disobeying a law ❸ official permission or approval for something

sanction *VERB* sanctions, sanctioning, sanctioned
to officially permit or authorize something

sanctity *NOUN*
being sacred; holiness

sanctuary *NOUN* sanctuaries
❶ a safe place where people can be protected; a refuge ❷ an area where wildlife is protected • *a bird sanctuary* ❸ a sacred place; the part of a church where the altar stands

sanctum *NOUN* sanctums
a person's private room

sand *NOUN*
the tiny grains of rock that cover the ground on beaches, river beds and deserts

sand *VERB* sands, sanding, sanded
to smooth or polish a surface with sandpaper or some other rough material
➤ **sander** *NOUN*

sandal *NOUN* sandals
a lightweight shoe with straps over the foot
➤ **sandalled** *ADJECTIVE*

sandalwood *NOUN*
a scented wood from a tropical tree

sandbag *NOUN* sandbags
a bag filled with sand, used to build defences against flood water or bullets

sandbank *NOUN* sandbanks
a bank of sand under water

sandpaper *NOUN*
strong paper coated with sand or a similar substance, rubbed on rough surfaces to make them smooth

sands *PLURAL NOUN*
a beach or sandy area

sandstone *NOUN*
rock made of compressed sand

sandwich *NOUN* sandwiches
two or more slices of bread with a filling (e.g. of meat or cheese) between them

sandwich *VERB* sandwiches, sandwiching, sandwiched
to put a person or thing in a narrow space between two others • *The boy sat sandwiched between the two women on the sofa.* **WORD ORIGIN** invented by the Earl of Sandwich (1718-92) so that he could eat while gambling

sandwich course *NOUN* sandwich courses
(*British*) a college or university course which includes periods in industry or business

sandy *ADJECTIVE*
❶ like sand ❷ covered with sand ❸ yellowish-red • *sandy hair*

sane *ADJECTIVE*
❶ having a healthy mind; not mad ❷ sensible or reasonable
➤ **sanely** *ADVERB*

sanguine (say sang-gwin) *ADJECTIVE*
cheerful and optimistic • *a sanguine temperament* **WORD ORIGIN** from Latin *sanguis* = blood (because good blood was believed to be the cause of cheerfulness)

sanitary *ADJECTIVE*
❶ free from germs and dirt; hygienic ❷ to do with sanitation

sanitary towel *NOUN* sanitary towels
an absorbent pad worn by women to absorb blood during menstruation

sanitation *NOUN*
arrangements for drainage and the disposal of sewage

sanity *NOUN*
being sane; sensible behaviour

Sanskrit *NOUN*
the ancient and sacred language of the Hindus in India

sap *NOUN*
the liquid inside a plant, carrying food to all its parts

sap *VERB* saps, sapping, sapped
to sap someone's strength or energy is to use it up or weaken it gradually • *The heat had sapped all my energy.*

sapling *NOUN* saplings
a young tree

sapphire *NOUN* sapphires
a bright-blue jewel

Saracen *NOUN* Saracens
an Arab or Muslim of the time of the Crusades

sarcasm *NOUN*
being sarcastic • *There was a hint of sarcasm in his voice.*

sarcastic *ADJECTIVE*
saying the opposite of what you mean in order to insult someone or make fun of them • *She said she liked my singing but I think she*

a b c d e f g h i j k l m n o p q r s t u v w x y z

was being sarcastic.
➤ **sarcastically** *ADVERB*
WORD ORIGIN from Greek *sarkazein* = tear the flesh

sarcophagus *NOUN* sarcophagi
a stone coffin, often decorated with carvings
WORD ORIGIN from Greek *sarkos* = of flesh + -*phagos* = eating (because people used to think that the stone from which ancient coffins were made caused the bodies inside to decay)

sardine *NOUN* sardines
a small sea fish, usually sold in tins, packed tightly in oil

sardonic *ADJECTIVE*
showing amusement in a bitter or mocking way • *a sardonic smile*
➤ **sardonically** *ADVERB*

sari *NOUN* saris
a length of cloth worn wrapped round the body as a dress, especially by Indian women and girls

sarong *NOUN* sarongs
a large piece of cloth worn around the body, originally in SE Asia

sartorial *ADJECTIVE*
to do with clothes

sash *NOUN* sashes
a strip of cloth worn round the waist or over one shoulder

sash window *NOUN* sash windows
a window that slides up and down

SAT *ABBREVIATION*
standard assessment task

satanic (say sa-**tan**-ik) *ADJECTIVE*
to do with or like Satan, the Devil in Jewish and Christian teaching

satchel *NOUN* satchels
a bag you wear on the shoulder or the back, especially for carrying books to and from school **WORD ORIGIN** from Latin *saccellus* = little sack

sate *VERB* sates, sating, sated
to satisfy an appetite or desire fully

satellite *NOUN* satellites
❶ a spacecraft put in orbit round a planet to collect information or transmit communications signals ❷ a moon moving in an orbit round a planet **WORD ORIGIN** from Latin *satelles* = a guard (because astronomers compared the moons of Jupiter to guards or attendants of an important person)

satellite dish *NOUN* satellite dishes
a bowl-shaped aerial for receiving broadcasting signals transmitted by satellite

satellite television *NOUN*
television broadcasting in which the signals are transmitted by means of a communications satellite

satiate (say **say**-shee-ayt) *VERB* satiates, satiating, satiated
to satisfy an appetite or desire fully

satin *NOUN*
a silky material that is shiny on one side
➤ **satiny** *ADJECTIVE*

satire *NOUN* satires
❶ the use of humour or exaggeration to show what is bad or weak about a person or thing, especially the government ❷ a play, poem or other piece of writing that does this
➤ **satirist** *NOUN*
➤ **satirize** *VERB*

satirical *ADJECTIVE*
using satire to mock or show the faults of a person or thing • *a satirical cartoon*
➤ **satirically** *ADVERB*

satisfaction *NOUN*
❶ the feeling of pleasure you have when you achieve something or get what you need or want • *He stood back and looked at his work with a sense of satisfaction.* ❷ giving someone what they need or want

satisfactory *ADJECTIVE*
good enough; acceptable • *That is not a satisfactory explanation.*
➤ **satisfactorily** *ADVERB*

satisfy *VERB* satisfies, satisfying, satisfied
❶ to give someone what they need or want ❷ to make someone feel certain; to convince someone • *The police are satisfied that the death was accidental.* ❸ to fulfil or achieve something • *You have satisfied all our requirements.*

satsuma *NOUN* satsumas
a kind of mandarin orange originally grown in Japan **WORD ORIGIN** named after *Satsuma*, a province of Japan

saturate *VERB* saturates, saturating, saturated
❶ to make a thing thoroughly wet • *The continuous rain has saturated the soil.* ❷ to make a place or thing take in as much as possible of something • *The town is saturated with tourists in the summer.*

➤ **saturation** *NOUN*
➤ **saturated** *ADJECTIVE*

Saturday *NOUN*
the day of the week following Friday
(**WORD ORIGIN**) from Old English *Saeternesdaeg*
= day of Saturn, a Roman god

saturnine *ADJECTIVE*
looking gloomy and forbidding • *a saturnine
face* (**WORD ORIGIN**) because people born under
the influence of the planet Saturn were believed
to be gloomy

satyr (say **sat**-er) *NOUN* satyrs
in Greek myths, a woodland god with a man's
body and a goat's ears, tail and legs

sauce *NOUN* sauces
❶ a thick liquid served with food to
add flavour ❷ (*informal*) being cheeky;
impudence

saucepan *NOUN* saucepans
a metal cooking pan with a handle at the side

saucer *NOUN* saucers
a small curved plate for a cup to stand on

saucy *ADJECTIVE* saucier, sauciest
rude or cheeky
➤ **saucily** *ADVERB*
➤ **sauciness** *NOUN*

sauerkraut (say **sour**-krowt) *NOUN*
chopped and pickled cabbage, originally made
in Germany (**WORD ORIGIN**) from German *sauer*
= sour + *Kraut* = cabbage

sauna *NOUN* saunas
a room filled with steam where people sit and
sweat a lot, used as a kind of bath

saunter *VERB* saunters, sauntering, sauntered
to walk slowly and casually • *She sauntered
over to greet me.*

sausage *NOUN* sausages
a tube of skin or plastic stuffed with minced
meat and other filling

savage *ADJECTIVE*
wild and fierce; cruel
➤ **savagely** *ADVERB*
➤ **savagery** *NOUN*

savage *NOUN* savages
❶ a savage person ❷ (*old use*) a member of a
people thought of as primitive or uncivilized

savage *VERB* savages, savaging, savaged
an animal savages a person or another animal
when it attacks them and bites or scratches
them fiercely • *The sheep was savaged by a
dog.* (**WORD ORIGIN**) from Latin *silvaticus* = of

the woods, wild (because people who lived in
the woods were thought of as wild and unruly)

savannah, **savanna** *NOUN* savannahs or
savannas
a grassy plain in a hot country, with few or
no trees

save *VERB* saves, saving, saved
❶ to keep a person or thing safe; to free a
person or thing from danger or harm ❷ to
keep something, especially money, so that
it can be used later ❸ to avoid wasting
something • *This will save time.* ❹ (*in
computing*) to keep data by storing it in the
computer's memory or on a disk ❺ to stop a
goal being scored
NOUN
➤ **saver** *NOUN*

save *NOUN*
preventing a goal from being scored • *The
goalkeeper made a great save.*

save *PREPOSITION* (*formal*) except • *All the trains
save one were late.*

savings *PLURAL NOUN*
your savings are the money that you have
saved

saviour *NOUN* saviours
a person who saves someone
➤ **the** or **our Saviour** in Christianity, Jesus
Christ

savour *VERB* savours, savouring, savoured
❶ to enjoy the taste or smell of something
• *He was savouring every mouthful.* ❷ to
enjoy a feeling or experience • *She was
determined to savour every moment.*

savour *NOUN* savours
the taste or smell of something • *the savour
of fresh bread*

savoury *ADJECTIVE*
❶ tasty but not sweet ❷ having an
appetizing taste or smell

savoury *NOUN* savouries (*chiefly British*) a
savoury dish

saw *NOUN* saws
a tool with a zigzag edge for cutting wood or
metal etc.

saw *VERB* saws, sawing, sawed, sawn
❶ to cut something with a saw • *He sawed
the log in half.* ❷ to move something
backwards and forwards as if you were using
a saw • *She began sawing at the rope with
her knife.*

a
b
c
d
e
f
g
h
i
j
k
l
m
n
o
p
q
r
s
t
u
v
w
x
y
z

saw *VERB*
past tense of see

> **SPELLING**
> A saw is a tool for cutting wood. If a part of your body is sore, it hurts.

sawdust *NOUN*
powder that comes from wood cut by a saw

sawmill *NOUN* sawmills
a mill where timber is cut into planks etc. by machinery

Saxon *NOUN* Saxons
❶ a member of a people who came from Europe and occupied parts of England in the 5th-6th centuries ❷ an Anglo-Saxon

saxophone *NOUN* saxophones
a brass wind instrument with a reed in the mouthpiece
➤ **saxophonist** *NOUN*
WORD ORIGIN named after a Belgian instrument maker, Adolphe *Sax*, who invented it

say *VERB* says, saying, said
❶ to speak or express something in words ❷ to give an opinion • *I can't say I blame you.* ❸ to show something or give information • *The look on her face said it all.* • *His bedside clock said 9.30.*

say *NOUN*
➤ **have a say** to be able to give your opinion or help decide something • *I have no say in the matter.*

> **SPELLING**
> The past tense of say is said.

saying *NOUN* sayings
a well-known phrase or proverb that gives advice or says something true about life

scab *NOUN* scabs
a hard crust that forms over a cut or graze while it is healing
➤ **scabby** *ADJECTIVE*

scabbard *NOUN* scabbards
the sheath of a sword or dagger

scabies (say **skay**-beez) *NOUN*
a contagious skin disease with severe itching, caused by a parasite **WORD ORIGIN** Latin, from *scabere* = to scratch

scaffold *NOUN* scaffolds
a platform on which criminals are executed

scaffolding *NOUN*
a structure of poles or tubes and planks

making platforms for workers to stand on while building or repairing a house

scald *VERB* scalds, scalding, scalded
❶ to burn yourself with very hot liquid or steam ❷ to heat milk until it is nearly boiling

scald *NOUN* scalds
a burn from very hot liquid or steam

scale *NOUN* scales
❶ a series of units, degrees or qualities for measuring something ❷ a series of musical notes going up or down in a fixed pattern ❸ the relationship between the size of something on a map or model and the actual size of the thing in the real world • *The scale of this map is one centimetre to the kilometre.* ❹ the relative size or importance of something • *They organize parties on a large scale.* ❺ each of the thin overlapping parts on the outside of fish, snakes, etc.; a thin flake or part like this ❻ a hard substance formed in a kettle or boiler by hard water or on teeth
➤ **to scale** with the parts in the same proportions as those of an original • *The plans have been drawn to scale.*

scale *VERB* scales, scaling, scaled
❶ to climb to the top of something steep • *We will have to scale the wall.* ❷ to remove scales or scale from something
➤ **scale something down** or **up** to reduce or increase something at a fixed rate or in proportion to something else

scale model *NOUN* scale models
a model of something, made to scale

scalene (say **skay**-leen) *ADJECTIVE*
a scalene triangle has unequal sides

scales *PLURAL NOUN*
a device for weighing things

scallop *NOUN* scallops
❶ a shellfish with two hinged fan-shaped shells ❷ each curve in an ornamental wavy border
➤ **scalloped** *ADJECTIVE*

scalp *NOUN* scalps
the skin on the top of the head

scalp *VERB* scalps, scalping, scalped
to cut or tear the scalp from a person

scalpel *NOUN* scalpels
a small knife with a thin, sharp blade, used by a surgeon or artist

scaly *ADJECTIVE* scalier, scaliest
covered in scales or scale

scam *NOUN* scams (*informal*)
a dishonest scheme or a swindle

scamp *NOUN* scamps
a rascal or mischievous child

scamper *VERB* scampers, scampering, scampered
to run quickly with short light steps • *The two girls scampered across the grass.*

scampi *PLURAL NOUN*
large prawns eaten in batter or breadcrumbs

scan *VERB* scans, scanning, scanned
❶ to look at every part of something • *He scanned the horizon for any sign of land.*
❷ to glance at something • *She scanned the list quickly for her name.* ❸ poetry scans when it is correct in rhythm • *This line doesn't scan.* ❹ to use a scanner to read data from something into a computer ❺ to sweep a radar or electronic beam over an area to examine it or in search of something

scan *NOUN* scans
❶ scanning something ❷ an examination using a scanner • *a brain scan*

scandal *NOUN* scandals
❶ something shameful or disgraceful
❷ gossip about people's faults and wrongdoing

scandalize (also **scandalise**) *VERB*
scandalizes, scandalizing, scandalized
to shock a person by something considered shameful or disgraceful

scandalmonger *NOUN* scandalmongers
a person who invents or spreads scandal
WORD ORIGIN from **scandal** + an old word *monger* = trader

scandalous *ADJECTIVE*
shocking or disgraceful

Scandinavian *ADJECTIVE*
from or to do with the countries of Scandinavia (Norway, Sweden and Denmark and sometimes also Finland and Iceland)
➤ **Scandinavian** *NOUN*

scanner *NOUN* scanners
❶ a machine that examines things by means of light or other rays ❷ a machine that converts printed text, pictures, etc. into a form that can be put into a computer

scant *ADJECTIVE*
barely enough or adequate • *I paid scant attention to what she was saying.*

scanty *ADJECTIVE* scantier, scantiest
small in amount or extent; meagre • *Details of his life are scanty.*
➤ **scantily** *ADVERB*

scapegoat *NOUN* scapegoats
a person who is made to bear the blame or punishment for what others have done
WORD ORIGIN named after the **goat** which the ancient Jews allowed to **escape** into the desert after the priest had symbolically laid the people's sins upon it

scar *NOUN* scars
❶ the mark left by a cut or burn after it has healed ❷ a lasting effect left by an unpleasant experience

scar *VERB* scars, scarring, scarred
to make a scar or scars on skin • *His face was badly scarred.*

scarab *NOUN* scarabs
an ancient Egyptian ornament or symbol carved in the shape of a beetle

scarce *ADJECTIVE* scarcer, scarcest
not enough to supply people • *Food was becoming scarce.*
➤ **scarcity** *NOUN*
➤ **make yourself scarce** (*informal*) to go away or keep out of the way

scarcely *ADVERB*
only just; only with difficulty • *She could scarcely walk.*

scare *VERB* scares, scaring, scared
to frighten someone

scare *NOUN* scares
❶ a fright • *You gave me quite a scare.* ❷ a sudden widespread sense of alarm about something • *a bomb scare*

scarecrow *NOUN* scarecrows
a figure of a person dressed in old clothes, put in a field to frighten birds away from crops

scared *ADJECTIVE*
frightened or afraid • *My brother is scared of the dark.*

scaremonger *NOUN* scaremongers
a person who spreads scare stories
WORD ORIGIN from **scare** + an old word *monger* = trader

scare story *NOUN* scare stories
an inaccurate or exaggerated account of something which makes people worry unnecessarily

a
b
c
d
e
f
g
h
i
j
k
l
m
n
o
p
q
r
s
t
u
v
w
x
y
z

scarf *NOUN* **scarves**
a strip of material that you wear round your neck or head

scarlet *ADJECTIVE & NOUN*
bright red

scarlet fever *NOUN*
an infectious fever producing a scarlet rash

scarp *NOUN* **scarps**
a steep slope on a hill

scarper *VERB* **scarpers, scarpering, scarpered**
(*British*) (*informal*)
to run away or leave in a hurry
WORD ORIGIN probably from Italian *scappare* = escape

scary *ADJECTIVE* **scarier, scariest** (*informal*)
frightening

scathing (say **skay** th-ing) *ADJECTIVE*
severely criticizing a person or thing

scatter *VERB* **scatters, scattering, scattered**
❶ to throw or send things in all directions
❷ to run or leave quickly in all directions • *At the first gunshot, the crowd scattered.*

scatterbrain *NOUN* **scatterbrains**
a careless forgetful person
➤ **scatterbrained** *ADJECTIVE*

scattered *ADJECTIVE*
spread over a large area or happening several times over a period of time • *sunshine with scattered showers*

scattering *NOUN*
a small number of things spread over an area • *a scattering of houses*

scavenge *VERB* **scavenges, scavenging, scavenged**
❶ to search in rubbish for useful things ❷ a bird or animal scavenges when it searches for decaying flesh as food

scavenger *NOUN* **scavengers**
a bird, animal or person that scavenges

scenario *NOUN* **scenarios**
❶ a summary of the plot of a play or story
❷ an imagined series of events or set of circumstances

scene *NOUN* **scenes**
❶ the place where something has happened • *the scene of the crime* ❷ a part of a play or film ❸ a view someone sees • *a painting of a street scene* ❹ an angry or noisy outburst • *He made a scene about the money.* ❺ stage

scenery ❻ an area of activity • *the local music scene*

SPELLING

A **scene** is a place or part of a play. **Seen** is the past participle of **see**.

scenery *NOUN*
❶ the natural features of a landscape • *We were admiring the scenery.* ❷ things put on a stage to make it look like a place

scenic *ADJECTIVE*
having fine natural scenery • *a scenic road along the coast*

scent *NOUN* **scents**
❶ a pleasant smell • *the scent of wild flowers*
❷ a liquid perfume ❸ an animal's smell that other animals can detect

scent *VERB* **scents, scenting, scented**
❶ to discover something by its scent • *The dog scented a rabbit.* ❷ to give something a pleasant smell • *Roses scented the night air.*
❸ to feel that something is about to happen • *She could scent trouble.*
➤ **scented** *ADJECTIVE*

sceptic (say **skep**-tik) *NOUN* **sceptics**
a sceptical person

sceptical (say **skep**-tik-al) *ADJECTIVE*
doubting whether something is true; not believing things easily • *She gave him a sceptical look.*
➤ **sceptically** *ADVERB*
➤ **scepticism** *NOUN*

sceptre *NOUN* **sceptres**
a rod carried by a king or queen as a symbol of power

schedule (say **shed**-yool) *NOUN* **schedules**
a programme or timetable of things that will happen or have to be done
➤ **on schedule** on time according to a plan

schedule *VERB* **schedules, scheduling, scheduled**
to arrange something for a certain time • *We've scheduled the meeting for Monday morning.* **WORD ORIGIN** from Latin *scedula* = little piece of paper

schematic (say skee-**mat**-ik) *ADJECTIVE*
in the form of a diagram or chart

scheme *NOUN* **schemes**
a plan of what to do • *He told us about his latest money-making scheme.*

scheme *VERB* **schemes, scheming, schemed**
to make secret plans; to plot • *She felt they were all scheming against her.*
➤ **schemer** *NOUN*

scherzo (say **skairts**-oh) *NOUN* **scherzos**
a lively piece of music **WORD ORIGIN** Italian,
= joke

schism (say skizm or sizm) *NOUN* **schisms**
the splitting of a group into two opposing
sections because they disagree about
something important

schizophrenia (say skid-zo-**free**-nee-a) *NOUN*
a kind of mental illness in which people
cannot relate their thoughts and feelings to
reality
➤ **schizophrenic** *ADJECTIVE & NOUN*

scholar *NOUN* **scholars**
❶ a person who has studied a subject
thoroughly ❷ a person who has been
awarded a scholarship **WORD ORIGIN** from
Latin *scholaris* = to do with a school

scholarly *ADJECTIVE*
showing knowledge and learning

scholarship *NOUN* **scholarships**
❶ a grant of money given to someone to help
to pay for their education ❷ serious study of
an academic subject and the knowledge you
get

scholastic *ADJECTIVE*
to do with schools or education; academic

school *NOUN* **schools**
❶ a place where teaching is done, especially
of pupils aged 5-18 ❷ the pupils in a school
❸ the time when teaching takes place in a
school • *School ends at 4.30 p.m.* ❹ a group
of people who have the same beliefs or style
of work ❺ a large group of fish, whales or
dolphins

school *VERB* **schools, schooling, schooled**
to teach or train a person or animal • *She was
schooling her horse for the competition.*

schoolchild *NOUN* **schoolchildren**
a child who goes to school
➤ **schoolboy** *NOUN*
➤ **schoolgirl** *NOUN*

schooling *NOUN*
education at a school

schoolteacher *NOUN* **schoolteachers**
a person who teaches in a school
➤ **schoolmaster** *NOUN*
➤ **schoolmistress** *NOUN*

schooner (say **skoon**-er) *NOUN* **schooners**
❶ a sailing ship with two or more masts ❷ a
tall glass for serving sherry

science *NOUN* **sciences**
❶ the study of the physical world by means
of observation and experiment ❷ a branch
of this, such as chemistry, physics or biology
WORD ORIGIN from Latin *scientia* = knowledge

science fiction *NOUN*
stories about imaginary scientific discoveries
or space travel and life on other planets,
often set in the future

science park *NOUN* **science parks**
an area set up for industries using science or
for organizations doing scientific research

scientific *ADJECTIVE*
❶ to do with science or scientists • *scientific
instruments* ❷ studying things in an
organized, logical way and testing ideas
carefully • *a scientific study of the way we
use language*
➤ **scientifically** *ADVERB*

scientist *NOUN* **scientists**
❶ an expert in science ❷ someone who uses
scientific methods

scimitar (say **sim**-it-ar) *NOUN* **scimitars**
a curved oriental sword

scintillating *ADJECTIVE*
❶ sparkling ❷ lively and witty • *The
conversation was scintillating.*
WORD ORIGIN from Latin *scintilla* = spark

scion (say **sy**-on) *NOUN* **scions**
a descendant, especially of a noble family

scissors *PLURAL NOUN*
a cutting instrument used with one hand,
with two blades joined so that they can close
against each other

> **SPELLING**
> There is a tricky bit in **scissors**—it begins
> with **sc**.

scoff *VERB* **scoffs, scoffing, scoffed**
❶ to laugh or speak in a mocking way about
something you think is silly • *She scoffed
at my superstitions.* ❷ (*informal*) to eat
something greedily or to eat it all up
➤ **scoffer** *NOUN*

scold *VERB* **scolds, scolding, scolded**
to speak angrily to someone because they
have done wrong; to tell someone off
➤ **scolding** *NOUN*

scone (say skon or skohn) *NOUN* **scones**
a soft flat cake, usually eaten with butter

scoop *NOUN* **scoops**
❶ a kind of deep spoon for serving ice cream

etc. **②** an amount picked up with a scoop
• *How many scoops of ice cream do you want?* **③** a deep shovel for lifting grain, sugar, etc. **④** an important piece of news published by only one newspaper

scoop *VERB* **scoops, scooping, scooped**
① to lift or hollow something out with a scoop, spoon or the palm of your hand • *I scooped up handfuls of water and began to drink.* • *Scoop out the middle of the pineapple.* **②** to lift something with a broad sweeping movement • *He scooped her up in his arms.*

scoot *VERB* **scoots, scooting, scooted**
① to make a bicycle or scooter move along by sitting or standing on it and pushing it along with one foot **②** (*informal*) to run or go away quickly

scooter *NOUN* **scooters**
① a kind of motorcycle with small wheels **②** a board with wheels and a long handle, which you ride on by scooting

scope *NOUN*
① opportunity or possibility for something • *There is scope for improvement.* **②** the range or extent of a subject • *Those questions are outside the scope of this essay.*

scorch *VERB* **scorches, scorching, scorched**
to make something go brown by burning it slightly

scorching *ADJECTIVE* (*informal*)
very hot

score *NOUN* **scores** or, in sense 2, **score**
① the number of points or goals made in a game; a result • *What's the score?* **②** (*old use*) twenty • *'Three score years and ten' means 3 x 20 + 10 = 70 years.* **③** written or printed music
➤ **on that score** for that reason, because of that • *You needn't worry on that score.*

score *VERB* **scores, scoring, scored**
① to get a point or goal in a game **②** to keep a count of the score in a game • *I thought you were scoring.* **③** to cut or mark a line on a surface with something sharp **④** to write out a musical score

scorer *NOUN* **scorers**
① a person who scores a goal or point **②** a person who keeps a count of the score in a game

scores *PLURAL NOUN*
many; a large number

scorn *NOUN*
contempt or lack of respect for someone

scorn *VERB* **scorns, scorning, scorned**
① to treat someone with contempt **②** to refuse something because you are too proud
• *She scorned all offers of help.*

scornful *ADJECTIVE*
feeling or showing scorn • *scornful laughter*
➤ **scornfully** *ADVERB*

scorpion *NOUN* **scorpions**
an animal that looks like a tiny lobster, with a poisonous sting in its curved tail

Scot *NOUN* **Scots**
a person who comes from Scotland

scotch *NOUN*
whisky made in Scotland

scotch *VERB* **scotches, scotching, scotched**
to put an end to an idea or rumour

Scotch egg *NOUN* **Scotch eggs**
(*British*) a hard-boiled egg enclosed in sausage meat and fried

Scotch terrier *NOUN* **Scotch terriers**
a breed of terrier with rough hair

scot-free *ADJECTIVE*
avoiding the punishment that is deserved
• *They got away scot-free.*

Scots *ADJECTIVE*
from or belonging to Scotland

Scots *NOUN*
the form of English used in Scotland

> **USAGE**
> See the note at **Scottish**.

Scottish *ADJECTIVE*
to do with or belonging to Scotland

> **USAGE**
> **Scottish** is the most widely used word for describing things to do with Scotland: *Scottish education, Scottish mountains.* **Scots** is less common and is mainly used to describe people: *a Scots girl.* **Scotch** is only used in fixed expressions like *Scotch egg* and *Scotch terrier.*

scoundrel *NOUN* **scoundrels**
a wicked or dishonest person

scour *VERB* **scours, scouring, scoured**
① to search a place thoroughly • *Police are scouring the countryside.* **②** to rub something until it is clean and bright **③** to clear a channel or pipe by the force of water flowing

through it
➤ **scourer** *NOUN*

scourge (say skerj) *NOUN* **scourges**
❶ a whip for flogging people ❷ something that causes a lot of suffering or trouble

Scout *NOUN* **Scouts**
a member of the Scout Association, an organization for boys

scout *NOUN* **scouts**
someone sent out ahead of a group to collect information

scout *VERB* **scouts, scouting, scouted**
to search an area thoroughly • *We began scouting around for firewood.*

scowl *NOUN* **scowls**
a bad-tempered frown

scowl *VERB* **scowls, scowling, scowled**
to have an angry or bad-tempered look

scrabble *VERB* **scrabbles, scrabbling, scrabbled**
❶ to scratch or claw at something with the hands or feet • *The dog scrabbled at the door.*
❷ to move your fingers quickly, trying to find or get hold of something • *She scrabbled about on the ground for the coins.*

scraggy *ADJECTIVE*
thin and bony

scram *VERB* (*informal*)
go away!

scramble *VERB* **scrambles, scrambling, scrambled**
❶ to move quickly and awkwardly • *We scrambled up the rocks.* ❷ to struggle to do or get something ❸ military aircraft or their crew scramble when they take off quickly to go into action ❹ to cook eggs by mixing them up and heating them in a pan ❺ to alter a radio or telephone signal so that it cannot be used without a decoding device
➤ **scrambler** *NOUN*

scramble *NOUN* **scrambles**
❶ a climb or walk over rough ground ❷ a struggle to do or get something • *There was a mad scramble for the best seats.* ❸ a motorcycle race over rough country

scrap *NOUN* **scraps**
❶ a small piece of something • *a scrap of paper* ❷ unwanted metal or paper that can be used again • *The car was sold for scrap.*
❸ (*informal*) a fight or argument

scrap *VERB* **scraps, scrapping, scrapped**
❶ to get rid of something that is not wanted

any more • *I think we should scrap that idea.*
❷ (*informal*) to fight or quarrel

scrape *VERB* **scrapes, scraping, scraped**
❶ to remove something from a surface by moving a sharp edge across it • *Scrape the mud off your boots.* ❷ to damage or hurt something by rubbing it against something rough or hard • *She scraped her arm on a rock.* ❸ to make a harsh sound by rubbing against something rough or hard • *The branches scraped against the window.*
❹ to get something by great effort or care • *They scraped together enough money for a holiday.*
➤ **scraper** *NOUN*
➤ **scrape through** to succeed or pass an examination by only a small margin

scrape *NOUN* **scrapes**
❶ a scraping movement or sound ❷ a mark made by scraping something • *I got a nasty scrape on my knee.* ❸ (*informal*) an awkward situation caused by mischief or foolishness

scrappy *ADJECTIVE*
done carelessly or untidily

scratch *VERB* **scratches, scratching, scratched**
❶ to mark or cut the surface of a thing with something sharp ❷ to rub the skin with fingernails or claws because it itches ❸ to make a noise by rubbing a surface with something sharp • *The dog was scratching at the door.*

scratch *NOUN* **scratches**
❶ a mark made by scratching ❷ the action of scratching • *I need to have a scratch.*
➤ **start from scratch** to start from the beginning or with nothing prepared
➤ **up to scratch** up to the proper standard

scratch card *NOUN* **scratch cards**
a card you buy as part of a lottery and scratch off part of the surface to see whether you have won a prize

scratchy *ADJECTIVE*
❶ scratchy clothes are rough and itchy
❷ making a harsh sound like something being scratched over a surface • *a scratchy recording*

scrawl *NOUN* **scrawls**
untidy handwriting

scrawl *VERB* **scrawls, scrawling, scrawled**
to write in a scrawl • *He scrawled his name on a piece of paper.*

scrawny *ADJECTIVE*
thin and bony

scream *NOUN* screams
❶ a loud cry of pain, fear, anger or excitement ❷ a loud piercing sound ❸ (*informal*) a very amusing person or thing

scream *VERB* screams, screaming, screamed
to let out a scream

scree *NOUN*
a mass of loose stones on the side of a mountain

screech *NOUN* screeches
a harsh high-pitched scream or sound

screech *VERB* screeches, screeching, screeched
to make a harsh high-pitched scream or sound

screed *NOUN* screeds
a very long piece of writing

screen *NOUN* screens
❶ a surface on which films or television pictures or computer data are shown ❷ a movable panel used to hide, protect or divide something ❸ a vehicle's windscreen

screen *VERB* screens, screening, screened
❶ to show a film or television pictures on a screen ❷ to protect, hide or divide something with a screen ❸ to carry out tests on someone to find out if they have a disease ❹ to check whether a person is suitable for a job

screenplay *NOUN* screenplays
the script of a film, with instructions about how scenes should be acted and filmed

screw *NOUN* screws
❶ a metal pin with a spiral ridge (the **thread**) round it, holding things together by being twisted in ❷ a twisting movement ❸ a propeller, especially for a ship or motor boat

screw *VERB* screws, screwing, screwed
❶ to fasten something with a screw or screws ❷ to fit or turn something by twisting • *Screw the lid on to the jar.*
➤ **screw something up** to twist or squeeze something into a tight ball

screwdriver *NOUN* screwdrivers
a tool for turning screws

scribble *VERB* scribbles, scribbling, scribbled
❶ to write something quickly or untidily or carelessly ❷ to make meaningless marks
➤ **scribble** *NOUN*

scribe *NOUN* scribes
a person who made copies of writings before printing was invented

scrimmage *NOUN* scrimmages
a confused struggle

scrimp *VERB* scrimps, scrimping, scrimped
to spend as little money as possible on the things you need so that you can save it for something else • *to scrimp and save*

script *NOUN* scripts
❶ handwriting ❷ the text of a play, film or broadcast

scripture *NOUN* scriptures
❶ sacred writings ❷ the Christian writings in the Bible

scroll *NOUN* scrolls
❶ a roll of paper or parchment used for writing on ❷ a spiral design

scroll *VERB* scrolls, scrolling, scrolled
to move the display on a computer screen up or down to see what comes before or after it

scrotum (say **skroh**-tum) *NOUN* scrota or scrotums
the pouch of skin behind the penis, containing the testicles

scrounge *VERB* scrounges, scrounging, scrounged
to get something without paying for it
➤ **scrounger** *NOUN*

scrub *VERB* scrubs, scrubbing, scrubbed
❶ to clean something with water by rubbing it hard, especially with a brush ❷ (*informal*) to cancel something

scrub *NOUN*
❶ scrubbing something • *You'll need to give your face a good scrub.* ❷ low trees and bushes ❸ land covered with these

scrubby *ADJECTIVE*
❶ scrubby trees and bushes are small and not fully developed ❷ scrubby land is covered with low bushes and trees

scruff *NOUN*
the back of the neck

scruffy *ADJECTIVE*
shabby and untidy • *a scruffy jacket*
➤ **scruffily** *ADVERB*
➤ **scruffiness** *NOUN*

scrum *NOUN* scrums
❶ (also **scrummage**) a group of players from each side in rugby football who push against each other and try to win the ball with their feet ❷ a crowd pushing against each other

scrumptious *ADJECTIVE* (*informal*)
delicious

scrunch VERB scrunches, scrunching, scrunched
❶ to make a loud crunching sound • *The snow scrunched underfoot.* ❷ to squeeze or crumple something into a smaller shape • *She scrunched up the letter and threw it in the bin.*

scrunchy, scrunchie NOUN scrunchies
a band of elastic covered in fabric, used to tie up your hair

scruple NOUN scruples
a feeling of doubt or hesitation when your conscience tells you that an action would be wrong • *I have no scruples about spying on him.*

scruple VERB scruples, scrupling, scrupled
to have scruples about something • *She would not scruple to betray us.*

scrupulous ADJECTIVE
❶ very careful about paying attention to every detail ❷ strictly honest or honourable
➤ **scrupulously** ADVERB

scrutinize (also **scrutinise**) VERB scrutinizes, scrutinizing, scrutinized
to look at or examine something carefully
• *He leaned forward and scrutinized my face.*

scrutiny NOUN
a careful look at or examination of something

scuba diving NOUN
swimming underwater using a tank of air strapped to your back (**WORD ORIGIN**) from the initials of *self-contained underwater breathing apparatus*

scud VERB scuds, scudding, scudded
to move quickly and lightly; to skim along
• *Clouds scudded across the sky.*

scuff VERB scuffs, scuffing, scuffed
❶ to drag your feet while walking ❷ to mark your shoes by scraping your feet on something

scuffle NOUN scuffles
a confused fight or struggle

scuffle VERB scuffles, scuffling, scuffled
to take part in a scuffle

scull NOUN sculls
a small or lightweight oar

scull VERB sculls, sculling, sculled
to row with sculls

scullery NOUN sculleries
a room for washing dishes and other kitchen work

sculpt VERB sculpts, sculpting, sculpted
to carve something; to make sculptures • *This huge figure has been sculpted in marble.*

sculptor NOUN sculptors
a person who makes sculptures

sculpture NOUN sculptures
❶ a figure or object that is carved or shaped out of a hard material such as stone, clay or metal ❷ the art of making sculptures

sculptured ADJECTIVE
❶ made as a sculpture or decorated with sculptures • *a sculptured arch* ❷ having a strong smooth shape • *sculptured cheekbones*

scum NOUN
❶ froth or dirt on top of a liquid ❷ worthless people

scupper NOUN scuppers
an opening in a ship's side to let water drain away

scupper VERB scuppers, scuppering, scuppered
❶ to sink a ship deliberately ❷ (*informal*) to wreck something or make it fail • *It scuppered our plans.*

scurrilous ADJECTIVE
rude, insulting and probably untrue
• *scurrilous attacks in the newspapers*
➤ **scurrilously** ADVERB

scurry VERB scurries, scurrying, scurried
to run quickly with short steps • *She could see beetles scurrying around.*

scurvy NOUN
a disease caused by lack of vitamin C from not eating enough fruit and vegetables

scuttle VERB scuttles, scuttling, scuttled
❶ to run with short quick steps; to hurry away • *The crab scuttled away.* ❷ to sink a ship deliberately by letting water into it

scuttle NOUN scuttles
❶ a bucket or container for coal in a house ❷ a small opening with a lid in a ship's deck or side

scythe NOUN scythes
a tool with a long curved blade for cutting grass or corn

scythe VERB scythes, scything, scythed
to cut something with a scythe

SE ABBREVIATION
❶ south-east ❷ south-eastern

sea NOUN seas
❶ the salt water that covers most of the

a b c d e f g h i j k l m n o p q r s t u v w x y z

earth's surface • *We live by the sea.* ❷ a large area of salt water; a large lake • *the Mediterranean Sea* • *the Sea of Galilee* ❸ a large area of something • *Across the table we saw a sea of faces.*
➤ **at sea** ❶ travelling on the sea ❷ not knowing what to do

sea anemone *NOUN* sea anemones
a sea creature with short tentacles round its mouth

seabed *NOUN*
the bottom of the sea

seabird *NOUN* seabirds
a bird that lives close to the sea and gets its food from it

seaboard *NOUN* seaboards
a coastline or coastal region

sea breeze *NOUN* sea breezes
a breeze blowing from the sea onto the land

sea change *NOUN* sea changes
a dramatic change

seafaring *ADJECTIVE & NOUN*
working or travelling on the sea
➤ **seafarer** *NOUN*

seafood *NOUN*
fish or shellfish from the sea eaten as food

seagull *NOUN* seagulls
a seabird with long wings

sea horse *NOUN* sea horses
a small fish that swims upright, with a head rather like a horse's head

seal *NOUN* seals
❶ a sea mammal with thick fur or bristles, that breeds on land ❷ something designed to close an opening and prevent air or liquid from getting in or out ❸ a piece of metal with an engraved design for pressing on a soft substance to leave an impression ❹ this impression, especially one made on a piece of wax ❺ a small decorative sticker • *Christmas seals*

seal *VERB* seals, sealing, sealed
❶ to close something by sticking two parts together • *Now seal the envelope.* ❷ to close or cover something securely so that no air or liquid can get in or out • *The food is packed in sealed bags.* ❸ to settle or decide something • *His fate was sealed.*
➤ **seal something off** to prevent people getting to an area • *Police have sealed off the building.*

sea level *NOUN*
the level of the sea halfway between high and low tide

sealing wax *NOUN*
a substance that is soft when heated but hardens when cooled, used for marking or closing something with a seal

sea lion *NOUN* sea lions
a kind of large seal that lives in the Pacific Ocean

seam *NOUN* seams
❶ the line of stitches where two edges of cloth join ❷ a layer of coal in the ground

seaman *NOUN* seamen
a sailor

seamanship *NOUN*
skill in sailing a boat or ship

seamy *ADJECTIVE*
➤ **seamy side** the less attractive side or part • *Police see a lot of the seamy side of life.*
WORD ORIGIN originally, the 'wrong' side of a piece of sewing, where the rough edges of the seams show

seance (say **say**-ahns) *NOUN* seances
a meeting at which people try to make contact with the spirits of dead people

seaplane *NOUN* seaplanes
an aeroplane that can land on and take off from water

seaport *NOUN* seaports
a port on the coast

sear *VERB* sears, searing, seared
to scorch or burn the surface of something

search *VERB* searches, searching, searched
❶ to look very carefully in a place in order to find something ❷ to examine the clothes and body of a person to see if something is hidden there

search *NOUN* searches
❶ a very careful look for someone or something ❷ looking for information in a computer database or on the Internet • *I need to do a couple of Internet searches.*
➤ **searcher** *NOUN*

search engine *NOUN* search engines
(*in computing*) a computer program that allows you to search the Internet for information

searching *ADJECTIVE*
examining closely and thoroughly • *searching questions*

searchlight *NOUN* searchlights
a light with a strong beam that can be turned in any direction

search party *NOUN* search parties
a group of people organized to search for a missing person or thing

search warrant *NOUN* search warrants
an official document giving the police permission to search private property

searing *ADJECTIVE*
a searing pain is sharp and burning

seascape *NOUN* seascapes
a picture or view of the sea

seashore *NOUN*
the land close to the sea

seasick *ADJECTIVE*
sick because of the movement of a ship
➤ **seasickness** *NOUN*

seaside *NOUN*
a place by the sea where people go for holidays

season *NOUN* seasons
❶ each of the four main parts of the year (spring, summer, autumn, winter) ❷ the time of year when something happens • *the football season*
➤ **in season** available and ready for eating • *Strawberries are in season in the summer.*

season *VERB* seasons, seasoning, seasoned
❶ to give extra flavour to food by adding salt, pepper, herbs or spices ❷ to dry and treat timber to make it ready for use

seasonable *ADJECTIVE*
suitable for the time of year • *seasonable weather*

USAGE
Take care not to confuse with seasonal.

seasonal *ADJECTIVE*
❶ for or to do with a season ❷ done or happening only at certain times of year • *Fruit-picking is seasonal work.*
➤ **seasonally** *ADVERB*

USAGE
Take care not to confuse with seasonable.

seasoning *NOUN* seasonings
a substance used to season food

season ticket *NOUN* season tickets
a ticket that you can use as often as you like throughout a period of time

seat *NOUN* seats
❶ a thing made or used for sitting on ❷ a place as a member of a council, committee or parliament • *She won the seat ten years ago.* ❸ a person's bottom; the part of a skirt or trousers covering this ❹ the place where something is based or located • *London is the seat of our government.*

seat *VERB* seats, seating, seated
❶ to place someone in or on a seat ❷ to have seats for a certain number of people • *The theatre seats 3,000 people.*

seat belt *NOUN* seat belts
a strap to hold a person securely in a seat

seating *NOUN*
❶ the seats in a place • *There is seating for 400.* ❷ the arrangement of seats • *a seating plan*

sea urchin *NOUN* sea urchins
a sea animal with a spherical shell covered in sharp spikes **WORD ORIGIN** from an old meaning of *urchin* = hedgehog

seaward *ADJECTIVE* & *ADVERB*
towards the sea
➤ **seawards** *ADVERB*

seaweed *NOUN*
a plant or plants that grow in the sea

seaworthy *ADJECTIVE*
a ship is seaworthy when it is fit for a sea voyage
➤ **seaworthiness** *NOUN*

sebum *NOUN*
the natural oil produced by glands (*sebaceous glands*) in the skin to lubricate the skin and hair

secateurs *PLURAL NOUN*
clippers held in the hand for pruning plants

secede (say sis-**seed**) *VERB* secedes, seceding, seceded
to officially leave an organization of countries or states and become independent
➤ **secession** *NOUN*

secluded *ADJECTIVE*
quiet and sheltered from view • *a secluded beach*
➤ **seclusion** *NOUN*

second *ADJECTIVE*
❶ next after the first ❷ another • *a second chance*
➤ **have second thoughts** to wonder whether a decision you have made was the right one

second *NOUN* seconds
❶ a person or thing that is second ❷ an attendant of a fighter in a boxing match or duel ❸ one-sixtieth of a minute of time or of a degree used in measuring angles ❹ (*informal*) a short time • *Wait a second.*

second *VERB* seconds, seconding, seconded
❶ to support a proposal that someone else has put forward • *I second that!* ❷ to act as a fighter's second ❸ (say sik-**ond**) (*British*) to transfer a person temporarily to another job or department

secondary *ADJECTIVE*
❶ coming after or from something ❷ less important.
Compare with **primary**.

secondary colour *NOUN* secondary colours
a colour made by mixing two primary colours

secondary school *NOUN* secondary schools
a school for children of more than about 11 years old

second-hand *ADJECTIVE*
❶ bought or used after someone else has owned it ❷ selling used goods • *a second-hand shop*

secondly *ADVERB*
in the second place; as the second thing • *Secondly, I'd like to thank my parents.*

second nature *NOUN*
behaviour that has become automatic or a habit • *Lying is second nature to him.*

second-rate *ADJECTIVE*
inferior; not very good

seconds *PLURAL NOUN*
❶ goods that are not of the best quality, sold at a reduced price ❷ a second helping of food at a meal

second sight *NOUN*
the ability to foresee the future

secrecy *NOUN*
being secret; keeping things secret • *Everyone involved was sworn to secrecy.*

secret *ADJECTIVE*
❶ that must not be told or shown to other people ❷ not known by everyone ❸ working secretly

secret *NOUN* secrets
❶ something secret • *I don't like keeping secrets.* ❷ a way of achieving something that is not widely known • *What is the secret of your success?*

➤ in secret without other people knowing • *They used to meet in secret.*

secret agent *NOUN* secret agents
a spy acting for a country

secretary (say **sek**-rit-ree) *NOUN* secretaries
❶ a person whose job is to help with letters, keep files, answer the telephone and make business arrangements for a person or organization ❷ the person in a club or society who whose job is to keep records and write letters ❸ the head of a government department
➤ secretarial *ADJECTIVE*
WORD ORIGIN from Latin *secretarius* = an officer or servant allowed to know your secrets

secrete (say sik-**reet**) *VERB* secretes, secreting, secreted
❶ to hide something ❷ to produce a substance in the body • *Saliva is secreted in the mouth.*

secretion *NOUN* secretions
a substance that is secreted

secretive (say **seek**-rit-iv) *ADJECTIVE*
liking or trying to keep things secret • *He is very secretive about his past.*
➤ secretively *ADVERB*
➤ secretiveness *NOUN*

secretly *ADVERB*
without other people knowing • *She was secretly pleased to see him.*

secret police *NOUN*
a police force which works in secret for political purposes, not to deal with crime

secret service *NOUN*
a government department responsible for espionage

sect *NOUN* sects
a group of people whose beliefs differ from those of others in the same religion

sectarian (say sekt-**air**-ee-an) *ADJECTIVE*
to do with disagreements between different religious groups • *sectarian violence*

section *NOUN* sections
❶ one of the parts that something is divided into • *Our school library has a large history section.* • *The tail section of the plane broke off.* ❷ a cross-section

sector *NOUN* sectors
❶ one part of an area ❷ a part of something • *the private sector of industry* ❸ (*in mathematics*) a section of a circle between

two lines drawn from its centre to its circumference

secular *ADJECTIVE*
not connected with religion at all

secure *ADJECTIVE*
❶ well locked or protected • *Check that all the doors and windows are secure.* ❷ firmly fixed and certain not to slip • *Is that ladder secure?* ❸ feeling safe and confident and not worried ❹ certain or reliable

secure *VERB* **secures, securing, secured**
❶ to make a thing secure ❷ to fasten something firmly • *The load was secured with ropes.* ❸ to obtain or achieve something • *We secured two tickets for the show.*

securely *ADVERB*
firmly or tightly, so that something will not open or move or is protected • *Make sure your seat belt is securely fastened.*

security *NOUN* **securities**
❶ being secure or safe; safety ❷ precautions against theft, spying or terrorism ❸ something you give as a guarantee that you will pay back a loan ❹ investments such as stocks and shares

security guard *NOUN* **security guards**
a person employed to guard a building or its contents against theft and vandalism

sedan chair *NOUN* **sedan chairs**
an enclosed chair for one person, mounted on two horizontal poles and carried by two men, used in the 17th-18th centuries

sedate *ADJECTIVE*
calm and dignified
➤ **sedately** *ADVERB*

sedate *VERB* **sedates, sedating, sedated**
to give a sedative to someone
➤ **sedation** *NOUN*

sedative (say **sed**-a-tiv) *NOUN* **sedatives**
a medicine that makes a person calm or helps them sleep

sedentary (say **sed**-en-ter-ee) *ADJECTIVE*
done sitting down • *sedentary work*

Seder *NOUN* **Seders**
in Judaism, a ritual and a ceremonial meal to mark the beginning of Passover

sedge *NOUN*
a grass-like plant growing in marshes or near water

sediment *NOUN*
fine particles of solid matter that float in liquid or sink to the bottom of it

sedimentary *ADJECTIVE*
sedimentary rocks are formed from particles that have settled on a surface

sedition *NOUN*
speeches or actions intended to make people rebel against the authority of the state
➤ **seditious** *ADJECTIVE*

seductive *ADJECTIVE*
❶ sexually attractive ❷ temptingly attractive • *It's certainly a seductive idea.*

see *VERB* **sees, seeing, saw, seen**
❶ to use your eyes to notice or be aware of something ❷ to meet or visit someone • *You should see a doctor about that cough.* ❸ to understand something • *I see what you mean.* ❹ to imagine or regard something in a certain way • *Can you see yourself as a teacher?* ❺ to consider something before deciding • *'Can I go to the party?' 'We'll see.'* ❻ to make sure of something • *See that the windows are shut.* ❼ to check or discover something • *See who is at the door.* ❽ to escort or lead someone • *I'll see you to the door.*
➤ **see through something** to not be deceived by something
➤ **see to something** to make sure that something is done

see *NOUN* **sees**
the district of which a bishop or archbishop is in charge • *the see of Canterbury*

seed *NOUN* **seeds** or **seed**
❶ a tiny, hard part of a plant, capable of growing into a new plant ❷ a seeded player

seed *VERB* **seeds, seeding, seeded**
❶ to plant or sprinkle seeds in something ❷ to name the best players and arrange for them not to play against each other in the early rounds of a tournament

seedling *NOUN* **seedlings**
a very young plant growing from a seed

seedy *ADJECTIVE* **seedier, seediest**
shabby and not respectable • *a seedy hotel*

seeing *CONJUNCTION*
considering • *Seeing that we have all finished, let's go.*

seek *VERB* **seeks, seeking, sought**
❶ to search for something ❷ to try to do or obtain something • *She is seeking fame.*

a b c d e f g h i j k l m n o p q r s t u v w x y z

seem VERB seems, seeming, seemed
to give the impression of being something
• *She seems like a nice girl.*

seemingly ADVERB
apparently, but perhaps not • *a seemingly stupid question*

seemly ADJECTIVE (old use)
seemly talk or behaviour is proper or suitable

seep VERB seeps, seeping, seeped
to ooze slowly out or through something
• *Water seeped from a crack in the pipe.*
➤ **seepage** NOUN

seer NOUN seers
a person who claims they can see into the future; a prophet

see-saw NOUN see-saws
a plank balanced in the middle so that two people can sit, one on each end and make it go up and down (WORD ORIGIN) from an old rhyme which imitated the rhythm of a saw going to and fro, later used by children on a see-saw

seethe VERB seethes, seething, seethed
❶ you are seething when you are very angry
❷ to be full of people or animals moving around • *The streets were seething with tourists.* ❸ to bubble and surge like water boiling

segment NOUN segments
a part that is cut off or separates naturally from other parts • *the segments of an orange*
➤ **segmented** ADJECTIVE

segregate VERB segregates, segregating, segregated
❶ to separate people of different religions or races ❷ to isolate a person or thing
➤ **segregation** NOUN
(WORD ORIGIN) from Latin *segregare* = separate from the flock, from *gregis* = from a flock

seismic (say **sy**-zmik) ADJECTIVE
to do with earthquakes or other vibrations of the earth (WORD ORIGIN) from Greek *seismos* = earthquake

seismograph (say **sy**-zmo-grahf) NOUN
seismographs
an instrument for measuring the strength of earthquakes

seize VERB seizes, seizing, seized
❶ to take hold of a person or thing suddenly or firmly ❷ to take control or possession of something by force or by legal authority
• *Customs officers seized the smuggled*

goods. ❸ to take advantage of a chance or opportunity • *Seizing his chance, he slipped out of the door.* ❹ to have a sudden effect on someone • *Panic seized us.*
➤ **seize up** to become jammed or stuck

(SPELLING)
Seize the right spelling and put the **e** before the **i**.

seizure NOUN seizures
❶ seizing something ❷ a sudden fit, as in epilepsy or a heart attack

seldom ADVERB
rarely; not often • *He seldom spoke.*

select VERB selects, selecting, selected
to choose a person or thing carefully
➤ **selector** NOUN

select ADJECTIVE
❶ small and carefully chosen • *They have a select group of friends.* ❷ a select club or organization is exclusive and chooses its members carefully

selection NOUN selections
❶ selecting something or being selected
• *The manager is responsible for team selection.* ❷ a person or thing selected ❸ a group selected from a larger group ❹ a range of goods from which to choose • *a wide selection of toys*

selective ADJECTIVE
choosing or chosen carefully • *She is selective about what she watches on TV.*
➤ **selectively** ADVERB

self NOUN selves
❶ a person as an individual ❷ a person's particular nature • *She has recovered and is her old self again.*

(SPELLING)
Change the **f** to **ves** to make the plural **selves**.

self-addressed ADJECTIVE
addressed to yourself

self-assured ADJECTIVE
confident of your abilities

self-catering NOUN
catering for yourself, instead of having meals provided

self-centred ADJECTIVE
selfish; thinking about yourself too much

self-confident *ADJECTIVE*
confident of your own abilities
➤ **self-confidence** *NOUN*

self-conscious *ADJECTIVE*
embarrassed or worried about how you look
or what other people think of you • *She used
to feel self-conscious wearing glasses.*
➤ **self-consciously** *ADVERB*

self-contained *ADJECTIVE*
accommodation is self-contained when
it is complete in itself and contains all
the necessary facilities • *a self-contained
apartment*

self-control *NOUN*
the ability to control your own behaviour or
feelings
➤ **self-controlled** *ADJECTIVE*

self-defence *NOUN*
❶ defending yourself against attack • *He
claims he was acting in self-defence.*
❷ techniques for doing this

self-denial *NOUN*
deliberately going without things you would
like to have

self-determination *NOUN*
a country's right to rule itself and choose its
own government

self-employed *ADJECTIVE*
working independently, not for an employer

self-esteem *NOUN*
your own opinion of yourself and your own
worth

self-evident *ADJECTIVE*
obvious and not needing proof or explanation

selfie *NOUN* selfies (*informal*)
a photograph that you take of yourself,
usually using a mobile phone, and send to a
social media website

self-important *ADJECTIVE*
having a high opinion of yourself; pompous

self-interest *NOUN*
your own personal advantage

selfish *ADJECTIVE*
doing what you want and not thinking of
other people; keeping things for yourself
➤ **selfishly** *ADVERB*
➤ **selfishness** *NOUN*

selfless *ADJECTIVE*
thinking of other people rather than yourself;
unselfish

self-made *ADJECTIVE*
rich or successful because of your own
efforts

self-pity *NOUN*
too much sorrow and pity for yourself and
your own problems

self-portrait *NOUN* self-portraits
a portrait in which the artist is the subject

self-possessed *ADJECTIVE*
calm and confident in a difficult situation

self-raising *ADJECTIVE*
self-raising flour makes cakes rise without
needing to have baking powder added

self-respect *NOUN*
your own proper respect for yourself

self-righteous *ADJECTIVE*
smugly sure that you are behaving virtuously

selfsame *ADJECTIVE*
the very same • *I had been wondering that
selfsame thing.*

self-satisfied *ADJECTIVE*
very pleased with yourself

self-seeking *ADJECTIVE*
selfishly trying to benefit yourself

self-service *ADJECTIVE*
where customers help themselves to things
and pay a cashier for what they have taken

self-sufficient *ADJECTIVE*
able to produce or provide what you need
without help from others

self-willed *ADJECTIVE*
obstinately doing what you want; stubborn

sell *VERB* sells, selling, sold
❶ to give something in exchange for money
❷ to have something available for people to
buy • *Do you sell stamps?* ❸ to be on sale at
a certain price • *It sells for £5.99.*
➤ **sell out** ❶ to sell all your stock of
something ❷ (*informal*) to give up your
beliefs or principles in order to get an
advantage

sell *NOUN*
➤ **hard sell** *NOUN*
forceful selling; putting pressure on someone
to buy
➤ **soft sell** selling by suggestion or gentle
persuasion

sell-by date *NOUN* sell-by dates
(*British*) a date, marked on the packaging of
food, by which it must be sold

a
b
c
d
e
f
g
h
i
j
k
l
m
n
o
p
q
r
s
t
u
v
w
x
y
z

A B C D E F G H I J K L M N O P Q R S T U V W X Y Z

seller NOUN sellers
a person or business that sells something

sell-out NOUN sell-outs
an entertainment, sporting event, etc. for which all the tickets have been sold

selves
plural of self

semantic (say sim-**an**-tik) ADJECTIVE
to do with the meanings of words
➤ **semantically** ADVERB

semaphore NOUN
a system of signalling by holding flags out with your arms in positions that indicate letters of the alphabet

semblance NOUN
an outward appearance or apparent likeness

semen (say **seem**-en) NOUN
a white liquid produced by males and containing sperm

semi NOUN semis (informal)
a semi-detached house

semibreve NOUN semibreves
(British) the longest musical note normally used (○), lasting four times as long as a crotchet

semicircle NOUN semicircles
half a circle
➤ **semicircular** ADJECTIVE

semicolon NOUN semicolons
a punctuation mark (;) used to separate two sentences or main clauses that are linked or of equal importance

> **PUNCTUATION**
>
> You use a **semicolon** to separate two sentences or main clauses that are linked or of equal importance:
>
> *The castle was desolate; no one had lived there for centuries.*
>
> *I know you don't eat meat, fish or eggs; but what about cheese?*
>
> *You bring cups and plates; I'll bring juice and sandwiches*
>
> Semicolons can also be used instead of a comma to separate a series of clauses or phrases in a list, introduced by a colon:
>
> *There were three clues: there was mud on the carpet; the door had been forced; and the air in the room smelled of fish.*

semiconductor NOUN semiconductors
a substance that can conduct electricity but not as well as most metals do

semi-detached ADJECTIVE
a semi-detached house is joined to another house on one side only

semi-final NOUN semi-finals
a match or round whose winner will take part in the final
➤ **semi-finalist** NOUN

seminar NOUN seminars
a meeting for advanced discussion and research on a subject

seminary NOUN seminaries
a training college for priests or rabbis

semiquaver NOUN semiquavers
(British) a note in music (♪), equal in length to one quarter of a crotchet

semi-skimmed ADJECTIVE
(British) semi-skimmed milk has had some of the cream taken out

Semitic (say sim-**it**-ik) ADJECTIVE
to do with the Semites, the group of people that includes the Jews and Arabs
➤ **Semite** (say **see**-myt) NOUN

semitone NOUN semitones
(British) half a tone in music

semolina NOUN
hard round grains of wheat used to make milk puddings and pasta

senate NOUN senates
❶ the governing council in ancient Rome
❷ the upper house of the parliament of the United States, France and certain other countries

senator NOUN senators
a member of a senate

send VERB sends, sending, sent
❶ to make something go or be taken somewhere • *He sent me an email this morning.* ❷ to tell someone to go somewhere • *She sent the children to bed early.* ❸ to make a person or thing move quickly in a certain direction • *The punch sent him flying.* ❹ to affect someone in a certain way • *The noise is sending me crazy.*
➤ **sender** NOUN
➤ **send for** someone or something to ask someone to come to you • *We sent for the doctor.*
➤ **send** someone **up** (informal) to make fun of someone by imitating them

senile (say **seen**-yl) *ADJECTIVE*
weak or confused and forgetful because of old age
➤ **senility** *NOUN*

senior *ADJECTIVE*
❶ older than someone else ❷ higher in rank or importance • *senior officers* ❸ for older children • *a senior school*
➤ **seniority** *NOUN*

senior *NOUN* seniors
❶ a person who is older or higher in rank than you are • *He is my senior.* ❷ a member of a senior school

senior citizen *NOUN* senior citizens
an elderly person, especially a pensioner

senna *NOUN*
the dried pods or leaves of a tropical tree, used as a laxative

sensation *NOUN* sensations
❶ a physical feeling • *a tingling sensation* ❷ great excitement or interest or something that causes this • *The news caused a great sensation.*

sensational *ADJECTIVE*
❶ causing great excitement, interest or shock ❷ (*informal*) very good; wonderful
➤ **sensationally** *ADVERB*

sense *NOUN* senses
❶ the ability to see, hear, smell, touch or taste things ❷ the ability to feel or appreciate something • *a sense of guilt* • *a sense of humour* ❸ the power to think or make wise decisions • *He hasn't got the sense to come in out of the rain.* ❹ the meaning of a word or phrase • *The word 'run' has many senses.*
➤ **come to your senses** to finally realize that you have not been behaving sensibly
➤ **make sense** ❶ to have a meaning you can understand ❷ to be a sensible idea

sense *VERB* senses, sensing, sensed
❶ to feel or be aware of something • *I sensed that she did not like me.* ❷ to detect or record something • *This device senses radioactivity.*

senseless *ADJECTIVE*
❶ stupid; not showing good sense ❷ unconscious

sensibility *NOUN* sensibilities
sensitiveness or delicate feeling • *The criticism hurt the artist's sensibilities.*

> **USAGE**
> Note that this word does not mean 'being sensible' or 'having good sense'.

sensible *ADJECTIVE*
wise; having or showing good sense
➤ **sensibly** *ADVERB*

sensitive *ADJECTIVE*
❶ easily affected or damaged by something • *Photographic paper is sensitive to light.* ❷ easily hurt or offended • *She is very sensitive about her age.* ❸ considerate about other people's feelings ❹ needing to be deal with tactfully • *a sensitive subject* ❺ able to measure very small changes • *a sensitive instrument*
➤ **sensitively** *ADVERB*
➤ **sensitivity** *NOUN*

sensitize (also **sensitise**) *VERB* sensitizes, sensitizing, sensitized
to make a thing sensitive to something

sensor *NOUN* sensors
a device or instrument for detecting a physical property such as light, heat or sound

sensory *ADJECTIVE*
❶ to do with the senses ❷ receiving physical sensations • *sensory nerves*

sensual *ADJECTIVE*
❶ to do with physical pleasure ❷ liking or suggesting physical or sexual pleasures

sensuous *ADJECTIVE*
giving pleasure to the senses, especially by being beautiful or delicate

sentence *NOUN* sentences
❶ a group of words that express a complete thought and form a statement, question, exclamation or command ❷ the punishment announced to a convicted person in a law court

sentence *VERB* sentences, sentencing, sentenced
to give someone a sentence in a law court • *He was sentenced to two years in prison.*

> **GRAMMAR**
> A **sentence** is a group of words that typically contains a main verb. It begins with a capital letter and ends in a full stop, a question mark or an exclamation mark. It can contain a single clause or several clauses joined by conjunctions or punctuation:
>
> *Bats are nocturnal creatures.*
>
> *Desert animals are often nocturnal because it is cooler for hunting at night.*

a
b
c
d
e
f
g
h
i
j
k
l
m
n
o
p
q
r
s
t
u
v
w
x
y
z

If a sentence is a **statement**, it ends with a full stop:

The students wrote their answers on their whiteboards.

A sentence which is a **question** ends with a question mark, and one which is an **exclamation** or **command** often ends with an exclamation mark:

Have you written your answers on your whiteboards?

Write your answers on your whiteboards.

What a good answer!

A single verb can form a sentence, especially if it is a command, like *Help!* or *Stop!* Sometimes, short sentences can be formed without a verb; for example, in direct speech:

'Where are you, Lieutenant?' 'Over here!'

or in stories to create a special effect:

In every direction lay the expanse of outer space. Vast. Empty. Desolate.

See also the panel on **clauses**.

sentient *ADJECTIVE*
able to feel and perceive things • *sentient beings*

sentiment *NOUN* sentiments
❶ an attitude or opinion • *I agree with those sentiments.* ❷ a show of feeling or emotion; sentimentality • *He never lets sentiment get in the way of business.*

sentimental *ADJECTIVE*
showing or making you feel tenderness, romantic feeling or foolish emotion
➤ **sentimentally** *ADVERB*
➤ **sentimentality** *NOUN*

sentinel *NOUN* sentinels
a guard or sentry

sentry *NOUN* sentries
a soldier guarding something

sepal *NOUN* sepals
each of the leaves forming the calyx of a bud

separate (say **sep**-er-at) *ADJECTIVE*
❶ apart; not joined to something else • *The school is housed in two separate buildings.* ❷ different; not connected • *They lead separate lives.*

separate (say **sep**-er-ayt) *VERB* separates, separating, separated
❶ to make or keep people or things separate or to divide them • *The two sides of the city are separated by a river.* ❷ to become separate • *We separated into two groups.* ❸ to stop living together as a couple

SPELLING
There is a tricky bit in **separate**—there is an **a** between the **p** and the **r**.

separately *ADVERB*
apart; not together • *They arrived together but left separately.*

separation *NOUN*
❶ separating or being separated; time spent apart ❷ an agreement when a couple decide to stop living together

sepia *NOUN*
reddish-brown, like the colour of early photographs

September *NOUN*
the ninth month of the year
WORD ORIGIN from Latin *septem* = seven, because it was the seventh month of the ancient Roman calendar

septet *NOUN* septets
❶ a group of seven musicians ❷ a piece of music for seven musicians

septic *ADJECTIVE*
infected with harmful bacteria that cause pus to form

sepulchral (say sep-**ul**-kral) *ADJECTIVE*
❶ to do with a sepulchre ❷ a sepulchral voice sounds deep and hollow

sepulchre (say **sep**-ul-ker) *NOUN* sepulchres
a tomb

sequel *NOUN* sequels
❶ a book or film etc. that continues the story of an earlier one ❷ something that follows or results from an earlier event

sequence *NOUN* sequences
❶ the following of one thing after another; the order in which things happen • *Arrange these playing cards in sequence, the highest first.* ❷ a series of things

sequin *NOUN* sequins
a tiny bright disc sewn on clothes to decorate them
➤ **sequinned** *ADJECTIVE*

seraph *NOUN* seraphim or seraphs
a kind of angel

seraphic (say ser-**af**-ik) *ADJECTIVE*
a seraphic smile or look is very pure and beautiful

serenade *NOUN* serenades
a song or tune of a kind played by a man under his lover's window

serenade *VERB* serenades, serenading, serenaded
to sing or play a serenade to someone

serendipity *NOUN*
the ability to make pleasant or interesting discoveries by accident
➤ **serendipitous** *ADJECTIVE*
(WORD ORIGIN) made up by an 18th-century writer, Horace Walpole, from the title of a story *The Three Princes of Serendip* (who had this ability)

serene *ADJECTIVE*
calm and peaceful • *a serene smile*
➤ **serenely** *ADVERB*
➤ **serenity** (say ser-**en**-iti) *NOUN*

serf *NOUN* serfs
a farm labourer who worked for a landowner in the Middle Ages and who was not allowed to leave
➤ **serfdom** *NOUN*

serge *NOUN*
a kind of strong woven fabric

sergeant (say **sar**-jent) *NOUN* sergeants
a soldier or police officer who is in charge of others

sergeant major *NOUN* sergeant majors
a soldier who is two ranks higher than a sergeant

serial *NOUN* serials
a story that is broadcast or published in separate parts over a period of time • *a 10-part drama serial*
SPELLING
Take care not to confuse with cereal.

serialize (also **serialise**) *VERB* serializes, serializing, serialized
to broadcast or publish a story as a serial
➤ **serialization** *NOUN*

serial killer *NOUN* serial killers
a person who commits a series of murders

serial number *NOUN* serial numbers
a number put onto an object by the manufacturers to distinguish it from other identical objects

series *NOUN* series
❶ a number of things following or connected with each other • *a series of events* ❷ a number of separate radio or television programmes with the same characters or on the same subject ❸ a number of games or matches between the same competitors

serious *ADJECTIVE*
❶ a person or look is serious when they are solemn and thoughtful and not smiling ❷ needing careful thought; important • *We need a serious talk.* ❸ sincere; not casual or light-hearted • *a serious attempt* ❹ causing anxiety, not trivial • *a serious accident*
➤ **seriousness** *NOUN*

seriously *ADVERB*
in a serious way • *Three people were seriously injured.*
➤ **take something seriously** to treat something as important

sermon *NOUN* sermons
a talk given by a preacher, especially as part of a religious service

serpent *NOUN* serpents
a snake **(WORD ORIGIN)** from Latin *serpens* = creeping

serpentine *ADJECTIVE*
twisting and curving like a snake • *a serpentine road*

serrated *ADJECTIVE*
having a notched edge

serried *ADJECTIVE*
arranged in rows close together • *serried ranks of troops*

serum (say **seer**-um) *NOUN* sera or serums
❶ the thin pale-yellow liquid that remains from blood when the rest has clotted ❷ this fluid used medically, usually for the antibodies it contains

servant *NOUN* servants
a person whose job is to work or serve in someone else's house

serve *VERB* serves, serving, served
❶ to sell things to people in a shop ❷ to give out food to people at a meal ❸ to work for a person or organization or country ❹ to spend time doing or suffering something • *He served a prison sentence.* ❺ to be suitable for something • *This tree stump will serve as a table.* ❻ to start play in tennis etc. by hitting the ball
➤ **it serves you right** you deserve it

a b c d e f g h i j k l m n o p q r s t u v w x y z

serve *NOUN* serves
serving in tennis etc.

server *NOUN* servers
❶ a person or thing that serves ❷ (*in computing*) a computer or program that controls or supplies information to several computers connected to a network

service *NOUN* services
❶ working for a person, organization or country ❷ something that helps people or supplies what they want • *a bus service* ❸ the army, navy or air force • *the armed services* ❹ a religious ceremony ❺ providing people with goods, food, etc. • *The service at the restaurant was slow.* ❻ a set of dishes and plates for a meal • *a dinner service* ❼ the checks and repairs that are needed to keep a vehicle or machine in working order ❽ the action of serving in tennis or badminton

service *VERB* services, servicing, serviced
to repair or keep a vehicle or machine in working order

serviceable *ADJECTIVE*
usable; suitable for ordinary use or wear • *It's an old coat, but it's still serviceable.*

service charge *NOUN* service charges
an amount added to a restaurant or hotel bill to reward the waiters and waitresses for their service

service industry *NOUN* service industries
an industry which sells a service, not goods

serviceman *NOUN* servicemen
a man serving in the armed forces

services *PLURAL NOUN*
an area beside a motorway with a garage, shop, restaurant, toilets, etc. for travellers to use

service station *NOUN* service stations
a place beside a road, where petrol and other services are available

servicewoman *NOUN* servicewomen
a woman serving in the armed forces

serviette *NOUN* serviettes
(*British*) a piece of cloth or paper that you use to keep your clothes or hands clean at a meal

servile *ADJECTIVE*
like a slave; too willing to serve or obey others
➤ **servility** *NOUN*

serving *NOUN* servings
a helping of food

servitude *NOUN*
the condition of being obliged to work for someone else and having no independence; slavery

sesame *NOUN*
an African plant whose seeds can be eaten or used to make an edible oil

session *NOUN* sessions
❶ a time spent doing one thing • *a recording session* ❷ a meeting or series of meetings • *The Queen will open the next session of Parliament.*

set *VERB* sets, setting, set
❶ to set something somewhere is to put it into position • *Set the vase on the table.* ❷ to set a date or time is to arrange or decide when something will happen • *Have they set a date for the wedding?* ❸ to make something ready to work • *I'd better set the alarm.* ❹ to become firm or hard • *Leave the jelly to set.* ❺ to give someone a task or problem to deal with • *We've been set a lot of homework this weekend.* ❻ to make something happen • *Set them free.* • *Her remarks set me thinking.* ❼ the sun sets when it goes down below the horizon
➤ **set about someone** (*informal*) to attack someone
➤ **set about something** to start doing something
➤ **set off** to begin a journey
➤ **set something off** ❶ to start something happening ❷ to cause something to explode
➤ **set out** to begin a journey
➤ **set something out** to display something or make it known • *She set out her reasons for leaving.*
➤ **set to** ❶ to begin doing something vigorously ❷ to begin fighting or arguing
➤ **set something up** ❶ to place something in position, ready for use • *Can you set up the table-tennis table?* ❷ to get something started • *We want to set up a website for local artists.*

set *NOUN* sets
❶ a group of people or things that belong together ❷ a radio or television receiver ❸ (*British*) a group of school students with the same level of ability in a particular subject ❹ (*in mathematics*) a collection of things that have a common property ❺ the scenery or stage for a play or film ❻ a group of games in a tennis match ❼ the way something is placed • *the set of his jaw* ❽ a badger's burrow

set *ADJECTIVE*
❶ fixed or arranged in advance • *The evening meal is served at a set time.* ❷ ready or prepared to do something • *I'm all set to go.*
➤ **be set on something** to be determined about doing something

setback *NOUN* setbacks
something that stops progress or slows it down

set book *NOUN* set books
a book that must be studied for a literature examination

set square *NOUN* set squares
(*British*) a device shaped like a right-angled triangle, used to draw straight lines and angles

settee *NOUN* settees
(*British*) a long soft seat with a back and arms

setter *NOUN* setters
a dog of a long-haired breed that can be trained to stand rigid when it scents game

set theory *NOUN*
the branch of mathematics that deals with sets and the relations between them

setting *NOUN* settings
❶ the place and time in which a story happens ❷ the land surrounding something • *The hotel is in a beautiful setting, close to the sea.* ❸ one of the positions of the controls of a machine ❹ a set of cutlery or crockery for one person at a meal ❺ music for the words of a song

settle *VERB* settles, settling, settled
❶ to arrange something; to decide or solve something • *That settles the problem.* ❷ to become calm or comfortable or orderly; to stop being restless • *Stop chattering and settle down!* ❸ to go and live somewhere • *They settled in Canada.* ❹ to come to rest on something • *Dust had settled on his books.* • *A bird flew down and settled on the fence.* ❺ to pay a bill or debt

settle *NOUN* settles
a long wooden seat with a high back and arms

settlement *NOUN* settlements
❶ a small number of people or houses established in a new area ❷ an agreement to end an argument

settler *NOUN* settlers
one of the first people to settle in a new country; a pioneer or colonist

set-up *NOUN* (*informal*)
the way something is organized or arranged

seven *NOUN* & *ADJECTIVE* sevens
the number 7
➤ **seventh** *ADJECTIVE* & *NOUN*

seventeen *NOUN* & *ADJECTIVE* seventeens
the number 17
➤ **seventeenth** *ADJECTIVE* & *NOUN*

seventy *NOUN* & *ADJECTIVE* seventies
the number 70
➤ **seventieth** *ADJECTIVE* & *NOUN*

sever *VERB* severs, severing, severed
to cut or break something off • *The builders accidentally severed a water pipe.*

several *DETERMINER* & *PRONOUN*
more than two but not many

severally *ADVERB*
separately; one by one

severe *ADJECTIVE*
❶ strict; not gentle or kind ❷ extremely bad or serious • *He suffered severe injuries.* ❸ intense or forceful • *severe gales* ❹ very plain • *a severe style of dress*
➤ **severely** *ADVERB*
➤ **severity** *NOUN*

sew *VERB* sews, sewing, sewed, sewn or sewed
❶ to join things together by using a needle and thread ❷ to work with a needle and thread or with a sewing machine

> **SPELLING**
> To sew is to work with a needle and thread. To sow seed means to put it in the ground.

sewage (say **soo**-ij) *NOUN*
liquid waste matter carried away in drains

sewer (say **soo**-er) *NOUN* sewers
a large underground drain for carrying away sewage

sewing machine *NOUN* sewing machines
a machine for sewing things

sex *NOUN* sexes
❶ each of the two groups (*male* and *female*) into which people and animals are divided ❷ sexual activity, especially sexual intercourse

sexism *NOUN*
the unfair or offensive treatment of people of a particular sex, especially women

sexist *NOUN* sexists
a person who treats people of a particular

a b c d e f g h i j k l m n o p q r s t u v w x y z

sex, especially women, in an unfair or offensive way

sexist *ADJECTIVE*
offensive to people of a particular sex, especially women • *sexist remarks*

sextant *NOUN* sextants
an instrument for measuring the angle of the sun and stars, used for finding your position when navigating (WORD ORIGIN) from Latin *sextus* = sixth (because early sextants consisted of an arc of one-sixth of a circle)

sextet *NOUN* sextets
❶ a group of six musicians ❷ a piece of music for six musicians

sexton *NOUN* sextons
a person whose job is to take care of a church and churchyard

sextuplet *NOUN* sextuplets
each of six children born to the same mother at one time

sexual *ADJECTIVE*
❶ to do with sex ❷ to do with the difference between males and females • *sexual equality* ❸ sexual reproduction happens by the fusion of male and female cells
➤ **sexually** *ADVERB*
➤ **sexuality** *NOUN*

sexual intercourse *NOUN*
an intimate physical act between two people, especially one in which a man puts his penis into the woman's vagina, to express love, for pleasure or to conceive a child

sexy *ADJECTIVE* sexier, sexiest (*informal*)
❶ sexually attractive ❷ concerned with sex

SF *ABBREVIATION*
science fiction

shabby *ADJECTIVE* shabbier, shabbiest
❶ in a poor or worn-out condition • *a shabby suit* ❷ poorly dressed ❸ unfair or dishonourable • *That was a shabby trick.*
➤ **shabbily** *ADVERB*
➤ **shabbiness** *NOUN*

shack *NOUN* shacks
a roughly-built hut

shackle *NOUN* shackles
an iron ring for fastening a prisoner's wrist or ankle to something

shackle *VERB* shackles, shackling, shackled
❶ to put shackles on a prisoner ❷ to be shackled by something is to be restricted or limited by it • *They felt shackled by tradition.*

shade *NOUN* shades
❶ slight darkness produced where something blocks the sun's light ❷ a device that reduces or shuts out bright light ❸ a colour; how light or dark a colour is • *four different shades of blue* ❹ a slight difference • *This word has several shades of meaning.* ❺ (*poetical use*) a ghost

shade *VERB* shades, shading, shaded
❶ to shelter something from bright light ❷ to make part of a drawing darker than the rest ❸ to move gradually from one state or quality to another • *The afternoon was shading into evening.*

shading *NOUN*
the parts of a drawing that you make darker then the rest

shadow *NOUN* shadows
❶ the dark shape that falls on a surface when something is between the surface and a light ❷ an area of shade • *His face was in shadow.* ❸ a slight trace • *a shadow of doubt*

shadow *VERB* shadows, shadowing, shadowed
❶ to cast a shadow on something ❷ to follow a person secretly

Shadow Cabinet *NOUN*
(*British*) members of the Opposition in Parliament who each have responsibility for a particular area of policy

shadowy *ADJECTIVE*
❶ dark and full of shadows • *a shadowy forest* ❷ difficult to see because there is not much light • *He saw a shadowy figure standing in the doorway.*

shady *ADJECTIVE* shadier, shadiest
❶ giving shade • *a shady tree* ❷ in the shade • *Let's find a shady spot by the river.* ❸ not completely honest or legal • *a shady deal*

shaft *NOUN* shafts
❶ a long slender rod or straight part • *the shaft of an arrow* ❷ a ray of light ❸ a deep narrow hole • *a mine shaft*

shaggy *ADJECTIVE* shaggier, shaggiest
❶ having long rough hair or fibre ❷ rough, thick and untidy • *shaggy hair*

shah *NOUN* shahs
the title of the former ruler of Iran

shake *VERB* shakes, shaking, shook, shaken
❶ to move something quickly up and down or from side to side • *Have you shaken the bottle?* ❷ to move in this way • *The whole house shakes when a train goes past.* ❸ to shock or upset someone • *The news shook us.*

❹ to tremble or be unsteady • *His voice was shaking.*
➤ **shake hands** to clasp a person's right hand with yours as a way of greeting them or as a sign of agreement

shake *NOUN* **shakes**
❶ a quick movement up and down or from side to side **❷** (*informal*) a milkshake
➤ **in two shakes** very soon

shaky *ADJECTIVE* **shakier, shakiest**
unsteady or wobbly • *Her voice was shaky.*
➤ **shakily** *ADVERB*

shale *NOUN*
a kind of stone that splits easily into layers

shall *AUXILIARY VERB*
❶ used, especially with I and **we**, to refer to the future • *I shall arrive tomorrow.* **❷** used with I and **we** in questions when making a suggestion or offer or asking for advice • *Shall I shut the door?*

> **GRAMMAR**
>
> The auxiliary verb **shall** can be used to form the future tense of verbs, although it is much more common to use **will**. In the past, **shall** was only used after *I* and *we* (*I shall be leaving tonight*) and **will** was used in all other cases (*They will be leaving tonight*), but most people ignore this distinction now.
>
> **Shall** is still quite commonly used when you want to ask a question or make a suggestion:
>
> *Shall we go now?*

shallot *NOUN* **shallots**
a kind of small onion

shallow *ADJECTIVE*
❶ not deep • *The stream is quite shallow here.* **❷** not capable of deep feelings • *a shallow character*
➤ **shallowness** *NOUN*

shallows *PLURAL NOUN*
a shallow part of a stretch of water

sham *NOUN* **shams**
something that is not genuine; a pretence
• *Their marriage was a sham.*

sham *ADJECTIVE*
not real or genuine, but intended to seem so

sham *VERB* **shams, shamming, shammed**
to pretend or fake something • *Are you really ill or are you shamming?*

shamble *VERB* **shambles, shambling, shambled**
to walk in a lazy or awkward way, dragging your feet along the ground

shambles *NOUN*
a scene of great disorder or confusion
• *The rehearsal was a complete shambles.*
WORD ORIGIN from an old word **shamble** = a slaughterhouse or meat market

shambolic (say sham-**bol**-ik) *ADJECTIVE* (*British*) (*informal*)
chaotic or disorganized

shame *NOUN*
❶ a feeling of great sorrow or guilt because you have done something wrong **❷** dishonour or disgrace **❸** something you regret; a pity
• *It's a shame you have to go so soon.*

shame *VERB* **shames, shaming, shamed**
to make a person feel ashamed

shamefaced *ADJECTIVE*
looking ashamed

shameful *ADJECTIVE*
causing shame; disgraceful
➤ **shamefully** *ADVERB*

shameless *ADJECTIVE*
feeling or showing no shame
➤ **shamelessly** *ADVERB*

shampoo *NOUN* **shampoos**
❶ a liquid substance for washing the hair **❷** a substance for cleaning a carpet etc. or washing a car **❸** a wash with shampoo

shampoo *VERB* **shampoos, shampooing, shampooed**
to wash or clean something with a shampoo
WORD ORIGIN originally = to massage: from Hindi *champo* = press

shamrock *NOUN* **shamrocks**
a plant rather like clover, the national emblem of Ireland

shandy *NOUN* **shandies**
(*British*) a mixture of beer and lemonade or some other soft drink

shank *NOUN* **shanks**
❶ the leg, especially the part from knee to ankle **❷** a long narrow part • *the shank of a pin*

shan't (*mainly spoken*)
shall not

shanty *NOUN* **shanties**
❶ a shack **❷** a sailors' song with a chorus

shanty town *NOUN* **shanty towns**
a settlement consisting of shanties

a
b
c
d
e
f
g
h
i
j
k
l
m
n
o
p
q
r
s
t
u
v
w
x
y
z

shape *NOUN* **shapes**
① what a thing's outline looks like
② something that has a definite or regular form, such as a square, circle or triangle
③ a person's physical condition • *She goes swimming to keep in shape.* ④ the general form or condition of something • *the shape of British industry*
➤ **out of shape** ① no longer having the normal shape • *The front wheel was twisted out of shape.* ② not physically fit
➤ **take shape** to start to develop properly

shape *VERB* **shapes, shaping, shaped**
to make something into a particular shape
➤ **shape up** to develop well • *The plan is shaping up nicely.*

shaped *ADJECTIVE*
having a particular shape • *an L-shaped room*

shapeless *ADJECTIVE*
having no definite shape

shapely *ADJECTIVE* **shapelier, shapeliest**
having an attractive shape

share *NOUN* **shares**
① a part given to one person or thing out of something that is being divided ② each of the equal parts into which the ownership of a business company is divided, giving the person who holds it the right to receive a portion (a **dividend**) of the company's profits

share *VERB* **shares, sharing, shared**
① to give portions of something to two or more people • *We shared out the pizza between the three of us.* ② to have, use or experience something jointly with others • *She shared a room with me.*

shareholder *NOUN* **shareholders**
a person who owns shares in a company

shareware *NOUN*
computer software which is given away or which you can use free of charge

shark *NOUN* **sharks**
① a large sea fish with sharp teeth ② a person who exploits or cheats people

sharp *ADJECTIVE*
① with an edge or point that can cut or make holes ② quick at noticing or learning things • *sharp eyes* ③ changing direction suddenly; not gradual • *a sharp bend* • *a sharp rise in temperature* ④ forceful or severe • *a sharp frost* ⑤ distinct and easy to see clearly • *a sharp outline* ⑥ loud and shrill • *a sharp cry* ⑦ slightly sour ⑧ (*in music*) one semitone

higher than the natural note • *C sharp*
➤ **sharpness** *NOUN*

sharp *ADVERB*
① with a sudden change of direction • *Turn sharp right.* ② punctually or precisely • *I'll see you at six o'clock sharp.* ③ (*in music*) above the correct pitch • *You were singing sharp.*

sharp *NOUN* **sharps** (*in music*) a note one semitone higher than the natural note; the sign (#) that indicates this

sharpen *VERB* **sharpens, sharpening, sharpened**
to make something sharp or to become sharp
• *I need to sharpen my pencil.*
➤ **sharpener** *NOUN*

sharply *ADVERB*
① suddenly and by a large amount • *The road bends sharply to the left.* ② in a critical or severe way • *'Just shut up,' she said sharply.*

sharp practice *NOUN*
dishonest or barely honest dealings in business

sharpshooter *NOUN* **sharpshooters**
a person who is skilled at shooting a gun

shatter *VERB* **shatters, shattering, shattered**
① to break violently into small pieces or to make something do this ② to destroy something • *It shattered our hopes.* ③ to upset someone greatly • *We were shattered by the news.*

shattered *ADJECTIVE* (*informal*)
completely exhausted

shave *VERB* **shaves, shaving, shaved**
① to scrape growing hair off the skin with a razor ② to cut or scrape a thin slice off something
➤ **shaver** *NOUN*

shave *NOUN* **shaves**
the act of shaving the face • *Dad was having a shave.*
➤ **close shave** (*informal*) a narrow escape

shaven *ADJECTIVE*
with all the hair shaved off • *a shaven head*

shavings *PLURAL NOUN*
thin strips shaved off a piece of wood or metal

shawl *NOUN* **shawls**
a large piece of material worn round the shoulders or head or wrapped round a baby

she *PRONOUN*
the female person or animal being talked about

sheaf *NOUN* **sheaves**
❶ a bundle of papers or other objects held together ❷ a bundle of corn stalks tied together after reaping

shear *VERB* **shears, shearing, sheared, sheared** or, in sense 1, **shorn**
❶ to cut the wool off a sheep ❷ to break because of a sideways or twisting force • *One of the bolts sheared off.*
➤ **shearer** *NOUN*

> **SPELLING**
> Take care not to confuse with **sheer**, which can mean steep and vertical or thin and transparent.

shears *PLURAL NOUN*
a cutting tool shaped like a very large pair of scissors and worked with both hands

sheath *NOUN* **sheaths**
❶ a cover for the blade of a knife or sword ❷ a close-fitting cover ❸ a condom

sheathe *VERB* **sheathes, sheathing, sheathed**
❶ to put something into a sheath • *He sheathed his sword.* ❷ to put a close covering on something

shed *NOUN* **sheds**
a simply-made building used for storing things, sheltering animals or as a workshop

shed *VERB* **sheds, shedding, shed**
❶ to let something fall or flow • *The trees are shedding their leaves.* • *We all shed tears.* ❷ to shed light is to give it out ❸ to get rid of people or things • *The company has shed 200 workers.*

sheen *NOUN*
a shine or gloss on a surface

sheep *NOUN* **sheep**
an animal that eats grass and has a thick fleecy coat, kept in flocks for its wool and its meat

> **SPELLING**
> The plural is the same as the singular: • *a woolly sheep* • *We've got cows, sheep and pigs.*

sheepdog *NOUN* **sheepdogs**
a dog trained to guard and herd sheep

sheepish *ADJECTIVE*
embarrassed or shamefaced because you have done something silly • *He had a sheepish grin on his face.*
➤ **sheepishly** *ADVERB*

sheepshank *NOUN* **sheepshanks**
a knot used to shorten a rope

sheer *ADJECTIVE*
❶ complete or thorough • *sheer stupidity* ❷ vertical, with almost no slope • *a sheer drop* ❸ sheer material is very thin and transparent

sheer *VERB* **sheers, sheering, sheered**
to swerve or move sharply away • *The speedboat sheered off to one side.*

> **SPELLING**
> **Sheer** is different from **shear**: • *sheer luck* • *shear the sheep*

sheet *NOUN* **sheets**
❶ a large piece of lightweight material used on a bed in pairs for a person to sleep between ❷ a whole flat piece of paper, glass or metal ❸ a wide area of water, ice or flame ❹ a rope or chain fastening a sail

sheikh (say shayk) *NOUN* **sheikhs**
the leader of an Arab tribe or village

shelf *NOUN* **shelves**
❶ a flat piece of wood, metal or glass fixed to a wall or in a piece of furniture so that things can be placed on it ❷ a flat level surface that sticks out from a cliff or under the sea

shelf life *NOUN* **shelf lives**
the length of time something can be kept in a shop before it becomes too old to sell • *Newspapers have a shelf life of only a day.*

shell *NOUN* **shells**
❶ the hard outer covering of an egg or nut or of an animal such as a snail, crab or tortoise ❷ the walls or framework of a building, ship or other large structure ❸ a metal case filled with explosive, fired from a large gun

shell *VERB* **shells, shelling, shelled**
❶ to take something out of its shell ❷ to fire explosive shells at something • *They shelled the city all night.*
➤ **shell out** (*informal*) to pay out money

shellfish *NOUN* **shellfish**
a sea animal that has a shell

shelter *NOUN* **shelters**
❶ a place or structure that protects people from rain, wind or danger ❷ protection from the weather or from danger • *We took shelter from the rain.*

shelter *VERB* **shelters, sheltering, sheltered**
❶ to find a shelter somewhere • *They sheltered under the trees.* ❷ to provide someone with shelter ❸ to protect or cover a

a b c d e f g h i j k l m n o p q r s t u v w x y z

person or thing • *The hill shelters the house from the wind.*

shelve *VERB* shelves, shelving, shelved
❶ to put things on a shelf or shelves ❷ to postpone or reject a plan or piece of work ❸ to slope • *The bed of the river shelves steeply.*

shelving *NOUN*
a set of shelves

shepherd *NOUN* shepherds
a person whose job is to look after sheep

shepherd *VERB* shepherds, shepherding, shepherded
to guide or direct people

SPELLING
There is a silent **h** after the **p** in **shepherd**.

shepherdess *NOUN* shepherdesses
(*now usually poetical*) a woman whose job is to look after sheep

shepherd's pie *NOUN*
a dish of minced beef or lamb under a layer of mashed potato

sherbet *NOUN*
a fizzy sweet powder or drink
WORD ORIGIN from Arabic *sharbat* = a drink

sheriff *NOUN* sheriffs
the chief law officer of a county, whose duties vary in different countries

sherry *NOUN* sherries
a kind of strong wine **WORD ORIGIN** named after Jerez de la Frontera, a town in Spain, where it was first made

Shetland pony *NOUN* Shetland ponies
a kind of small, strong, shaggy pony, originally from the Shetland Isles

shield *NOUN* shields
❶ a large piece of metal or wood carried to protect the body in fighting ❷ a model of a triangular shield used as a trophy ❸ a protection from harm

shield *VERB* shields, shielding, shielded
to protect a person or thing from harm or from being discovered • *He shielded his eyes from the sun.*

shift *VERB* shifts, shifting, shifted
❶ to move, or move something, from one position or place to another • *Could you help me shift some furniture?* ❷ an opinion or situation shifts when it changes slightly
➤ **shift for yourself** to manage without help from other people

shift *NOUN* shifts
❶ a change of position or condition ❷ a group of workers who start work as another group finishes; the time when they work • *She's on the night shift this month.* ❸ a straight dress with no waist

shifty *ADJECTIVE*
looking dishonest or as if you are hiding something
➤ **shiftily** *ADVERB*

Shiite (say **shee**-eyt) *NOUN* Shiites
a member of one of the two main branches of Islam, based on the teachings of Muhammad and regarding his son-in-law Ali as his successor. Compare with **Sunni**.

shilling *NOUN* shillings
a former British coin, equal to 5p

shilly-shally *VERB* shilly-shallies, shilly-shallying, shilly-shallied
to be unable to make up your mind
WORD ORIGIN from *shall I? shall I?*

shimmer *VERB* shimmers, shimmering, shimmered
to shine with a quivering light • *The sea shimmered in the moonlight.*

shimmer *NOUN*
a quivering light

shin *NOUN* shins
the front of your leg between your knee and your ankle

shin *VERB* shins, shinning, shinned
to climb up or down something vertical by using the arms and legs • *He shinned down the drainpipe and ran off.*

shindig *NOUN* shindigs (*informal*)
a noisy party

shine *VERB* shines, shining, shone or, in sense 3, shined
❶ to give out or reflect light; to be bright ❷ to aim a light somewhere • *Shine your torch on it.* ❸ to polish shoes or a surface • *Have you shined your shoes?* ❹ to be very good at something • *He doesn't shine in maths.*

shine *NOUN*
❶ brightness on a surface ❷ a polish • *Give your shoes a good shine.*

shingle *NOUN*
pebbles on a beach

shingles *NOUN*
a disease caused by the chicken pox virus, producing a painful rash

Shinto *NOUN*
a Japanese religion which includes worship of ancestors and nature

shiny *ADJECTIVE* shinier, shiniest
shining or glossy • *a shiny new car* • *shiny black hair*

ship *NOUN* ships
a large boat, especially one that goes to sea

ship *VERB* ships, shipping, shipped
to transport goods, especially by ship

shipment *NOUN* shipments
❶ the process of shipping goods ❷ the amount shipped

shipping *NOUN*
❶ all the ships of a country ❷ the business of transporting goods by ship

shipshape *ADJECTIVE*
in good order; tidy

shipwreck *NOUN* shipwrecks
❶ the wrecking of a ship by storm or accident ❷ the remains of a wrecked ship

shipwrecked *ADJECTIVE*
someone is shipwrecked when they are left somewhere after their ship has been wrecked at sea • *a shipwrecked sailor*

shipyard *NOUN* shipyards
a place where ships are built or repaired

shire *NOUN* shires
a county
➤ **the Shires** the country areas of (especially central) England, away from the cities

shire horse *NOUN* shire horses
a kind of large, strong horse used for ploughing or pulling carts

shirk *VERB* shirks, shirking, shirked
to avoid a task or duty selfishly or unfairly
➤ **shirker** *NOUN*

shirt *NOUN* shirts
a piece of clothing you wear on the top half of the body, made of light material and with a collar and sleeves
➤ **in your shirtsleeves** not wearing a jacket over your shirt

shirty *ADJECTIVE* (*British*) (*informal*)
annoyed or bad-tempered

shiver *VERB* shivers, shivering, shivered
to tremble with cold or fear

shiver *NOUN* shivers
the act of shivering • *I felt a shiver down my spine.*

shivery *ADJECTIVE*
shaking with cold, illness or fear

shoal *NOUN* shoals
❶ a large number of fish swimming together ❷ an underwater sandbank

shock *NOUN* shocks
❶ a sudden unpleasant surprise ❷ a serious medical condition of great weakness caused by damage to the body ❸ the effect of a violent shake or knock • *the shock of the earthquake* ❹ an effect caused by electric current passing through the body ❺ a bushy mass of hair

shock *VERB* shocks, shocking, shocked
❶ to give someone a shock; to surprise or upset a person greatly ❷ to make someone feel disgusted or offended

shocking *ADJECTIVE*
❶ horrifying or disgusting • *shocking behaviour* ❷ (*informal*) very bad • *shocking weather*

shock wave *NOUN* shock waves
a sharp change in pressure in the air around an explosion or an object moving very quickly

shod
past tense of **shoe**

shoddy *ADJECTIVE* shoddier, shoddiest
of poor quality; badly made or done • *This is shoddy work.*
➤ **shoddily** *ADVERB*

shoe *NOUN* shoes
❶ a strong covering for the foot ❷ a horseshoe ❸ something shaped or used like a shoe
➤ **be in someone's shoes** to be in their situation

shoe *VERB* shoes, shoeing, shod
to fit a horse with a horseshoe

shoehorn *NOUN* shoehorns
a curved piece of stiff material for easing your heel into the back of a shoe

shoelace *NOUN* shoelaces
a cord for lacing up and fastening a shoe

shoestring *NOUN*
➤ **on a shoestring** using only a small amount of money • *The website tells you how you can travel the world on a shoestring.*

shoo *EXCLAMATION*
a word used to frighten animals away

shoo *VERB* shoo, shooing, shooed
to frighten or drive away an animal or person

a
b
c
d
e
f
g
h
i
j
k
l
m
n
o
p
q
r
s
t
u
v
w
x
y
z

shoot *VERB* shoots, shooting, shot
❶ to fire a gun or missile ❷ to hurt or kill a person or animal by shooting ❸ to move at great speed • *The car shot past us.* ❹ to kick or hit a ball at a goal ❺ to film or photograph something • *The film was shot in Africa.* ❻ to slide the bolt of a door into or out of its fastening ❼ to shoot someone a glance is to look at them sharply

shoot *NOUN* shoots
❶ a young branch or new growth of a plant ❷ an expedition for shooting animals

> SPELLING
>
> **Shoot** is different from **chute**, which means a channel for sliding down.

shooting star *NOUN* shooting stars
a meteor

shop *NOUN* shops
❶ a building or room where goods or services are on sale to the public ❷ a workshop
➤ **talk shop** to talk about your own work or job in a way that other people find boring

shop *VERB* shops, shopping, shopped
❶ to visit shops in order to buy things ❷ to buy things • *My sister is always shopping online.*
➤ **shopper** *NOUN*
➤ **shop around** to look around for the best bargain

shop floor *NOUN* (*British*)
❶ the workers in a factory, not the managers ❷ the place where they work

shopkeeper *NOUN* shopkeepers
a person who owns or manages a shop

shoplifter *NOUN* shoplifters
a person who steals goods from a shop after entering as a customer
➤ **shoplifting** *NOUN*

shopping *NOUN*
❶ buying goods in shops • *I like shopping.* ❷ the goods bought • *I'll put the shopping in the car.*

shop-soiled *ADJECTIVE*
(*British*) dirty, faded or slightly damaged through being displayed in a shop

shop steward *NOUN* shop stewards
a trade-union official who represents a group of fellow workers

shop window *NOUN* shop windows
a window in a shop where goods are displayed

shore *NOUN* shores
the land along the edge of a sea or of a lake

shore *VERB* shores, shoring, shored
to prop something up with a piece of wood or other support

shorn
past participle of **shear**

shorn *ADJECTIVE*
with hair cut very short • *his shorn head*
➤ **be shorn of something** to have something taken away from you • *Shorn of his power, the king went into exile.*

short *ADJECTIVE*
❶ not long; not lasting long • *I went for a short walk.* ❷ not tall • *He is a short man.* ❸ not enough; not having enough of something • *Water is short.* • *We are short of water.* ❹ speaking to someone in a bad-tempered and impatient way • *She was rather short with me.* ❺ short pastry is rich and crumbly because it contains a lot of fat
➤ **shortness** *NOUN*
➤ **for short** as an abbreviation • *Joanna is called Jo for short.*
➤ **in short** in a few words
➤ **short for** an abbreviation of • *Jo is short for Joanna.*
➤ **short of** without going to the length of • *I'll do anything to help, short of robbing a bank.*

short *ADVERB*
suddenly • *She stopped short.*

shortage *NOUN* shortages
there is a shortage of something when there is not enough of it • *a water shortage*

shortbread *NOUN*
a rich sweet biscuit, made with butter

shortcake *NOUN*
❶ shortbread ❷ a light cake usually served with fruit

short circuit *NOUN* short circuits
a fault in an electrical circuit in which current flows along a shorter route than the normal one

short-circuit *VERB* short-circuits, short-circuiting, short-circuited
to have or cause a short circuit

shortcoming *NOUN* shortcomings
a fault or failure to reach a good standard

short cut *NOUN* short cuts
a route or method that is quicker than the usual one • *We took a short cut across the fields.*

shorten *VERB* shortens, shortening, shortened
to make something shorter or to become
shorter • *Most people shorten Janet's name
to Jan.*

shortfall *NOUN* shortfalls
a shortage; an amount lower than needed or
expected

shorthand *NOUN*
a set of special signs for writing words down
as quickly as people say them

short-handed *ADJECTIVE*
not having enough workers or helpers

shortlist *NOUN* shortlists
a list of the most suitable people or things,
from which a final choice will be made

shortlist *VERB* shortlists, shortlisting,
shortlisted
to put someone on a shortlist

shortly *ADVERB*
❶ in a short time; soon • *They will arrive
shortly.* ❷ in an impatient and angry way
• *'None of your business,' he said shortly.*

shorts *PLURAL NOUN*
trousers with legs that do not reach to the
knee

short-sighted *ADJECTIVE* (*British*)
❶ unable to see things clearly when they are
further away ❷ not thinking enough about
what may happen in the future

short-staffed *ADJECTIVE*
not having enough workers or staff

short-tempered *ADJECTIVE*
easily becoming angry

short-term *ADJECTIVE*
to do with or happening over a short period
of time

short wave *NOUN*
a radio wave of a wavelength between 10 and
100 metres and a frequency of about 3 to 30
megahertz

shot *NOUN* shots
❶ the firing of a gun or missile or the sound
this makes ❷ lead pellets for firing from small
guns ❸ a person judged by skill in shooting
• *He's a good shot.* ❹ a hit or stroke in a
game with a ball, such as football, tennis,
golf or snooker • *a shot at goal* • *Good shot!*
❺ a heavy metal ball thrown as a sport ❻ a
photograph or a filmed scene ❼ an attempt
to do something • *Have a shot at this puzzle.*
❽ an injection of a drug or vaccine

shot *ADJECTIVE*
shot fabric is woven so that different colours
show at different angles • *shot silk*

shot *VERB*
past tense of **shoot**

shotgun *NOUN* shotguns
a gun for firing small lead pellets at close
range

shot put *NOUN*
an athletic contest in which competitors
throw a heavy metal ball
➤ **shot putter** *NOUN*

should *AUXILIARY VERB*
❶ used to say what someone ought to do
• *You should have told me.* ❷ used to say
what someone expects • *They should be here
by ten o'clock.* ❸ used to say what might
happen • *If you should happen to see him, tell
him to come.* ❹ used with *I* and *we* to make a
polite statement (*I should like to come.*) or in
a conditional clause (*If they had supported us
we should have won.*)

> **USAGE**
> In sense 4, although **should** is strictly
> correct, many people nowadays use
> **would** and this is not regarded as wrong.

shoulder *NOUN* shoulders
the part of your body between your neck and
your arm

shoulder *VERB* shoulders, shouldering,
shouldered
❶ to take something on your shoulder or
shoulders ❷ to push something with your
shoulder ❸ to accept responsibility or blame
for something

shoulder blade *NOUN* shoulder blades
either of the two large flat bones at the top
of your back

shouldn't (*mainly spoken*)
should not

shout *NOUN* shouts
a loud cry or call

shout *VERB* shouts, shouting, shouted
to give a shout; to speak or call very loudly

shove *VERB* shoves, shoving, shoved
to push something roughly
➤ **shove off** (*informal*) to go away

shove *NOUN* shoves
a rough push

a b c d e f g h i j k l m n o p q r s t u v w x y z

shovel *NOUN* shovels
a tool like a spade with the sides turned up, used for lifting coal, earth, snow, etc.

shovel *VERB* shovels, shovelling, shovelled
❶ to move or clear things with a shovel ❷ to scoop or push something roughly • *He was shovelling food into his mouth.*

show *VERB* shows, showing, showed, shown
❶ to allow or cause something to be seen • *Show me your new bike.* ❷ to make a person understand something; to explain or demonstrate something • *Can you show me how to do it?* ❸ to guide or lead someone to a place • *I'll show you to your seat.* ❹ to treat someone in a certain way • *She showed them great kindness.* ❺ to be visible • *That scratch won't show.* ❻ to prove your ability to someone • *We'll show them!*
➤ **show off** to try to impress people
➤ **show something off** to display something proudly
➤ **show up** ❶ to be clearly visible • *Nothing showed up on the X-ray.* ❷ (*informal*) to arrive

show *NOUN* shows
❶ an entertainment • *a TV game show*
❷ a display or exhibition • *a flower show*
❸ (*informal*) something that happens or is done • *He runs the whole show.*

show business *NOUN*
the entertainment industry; the theatre, films, radio and television

showcase *NOUN* showcases
❶ a glass case for displaying something in a shop, museum or gallery ❷ an event that is designed to present someone's good qualities or abilities attractively • *The programme is a showcase for new acts.*

showdown *NOUN* showdowns
a final test or confrontation

shower *NOUN* showers
❶ a brief fall of rain or snow ❷ a lot of small things coming or falling like rain • *a shower of stones* ❸ a device or cabinet for spraying water to wash a person's body; a wash in this

shower *VERB* showers, showering, showered
❶ to fall or drop things like rain • *Ash from the volcano showered down on the town.*
❷ to give someone a lot of things • *He showered her with presents.* ❸ to wash under a shower

showery *ADJECTIVE*
raining often in showers

showjumping *NOUN*
a competition in which riders make their horses jump over fences and other obstacles, with penalty points for errors
➤ **showjumper** *NOUN*

showman *NOUN* showmen
❶ a person who presents entertainments
❷ someone who is good at entertaining and getting a lot of attention
➤ **showmanship** *NOUN*

show-off *NOUN* show-offs (*informal*)
a person who tries to impress people boastfully

showpiece *NOUN* showpieces
a fine example of something for people to see and admire

showroom *NOUN* showrooms
a large room where goods are displayed for people to look at

showy *ADJECTIVE* showier, showiest
likely to attract attention; brightly or highly decorated • *showy flowers*
➤ **showily** *ADVERB*

shrapnel *NOUN*
pieces of metal scattered from an exploding shell (**WORD ORIGIN**) named after H. *Shrapnel*, a British officer who invented it in about 1806

shred *NOUN* shreds
❶ a tiny piece torn or cut off something • *His cloak had been ripped to shreds.* ❷ a very small amount of something • *There is not a shred of evidence to support this claim.*

shred *VERB* shreds, shredding, shredded
to tear or cut something into shreds
➤ **shredder** *NOUN*

shrew *NOUN* shrews
❶ a small mouse-like animal ❷ (*old use*) a bad-tempered woman who is constantly scolding people
➤ **shrewish** *ADJECTIVE* .

shrewd *ADJECTIVE*
clever and showing good judgement • *a shrewd decision*
➤ **shrewdly** *ADVERB*
➤ **shrewdness** *NOUN*
(**WORD ORIGIN**) from old sense of **shrew** = spiteful or cunning person

shriek *NOUN* shrieks
a shrill cry or scream

shriek *VERB* shrieks, shrieking, shrieked
to give a shriek

shrift *NOUN*
➤ **give someone short shrift** to give someone little attention or sympathy

shrill *ADJECTIVE*
sounding very high and piercing • *a shrill voice*
➤ **shrilly** *ADVERB*
➤ **shrillness** *NOUN*

shrimp *NOUN* shrimps
a small shellfish, pink when boiled

shrine *NOUN* shrines
an altar, chapel or other sacred place

shrink *VERB* shrinks, shrinking, shrank, shrunk
❶ to become smaller ❷ to make something smaller, especially by washing it ❸ to move back or away because you are frightened or shocked • *He shrank back into a corner of the room.* ❹ to avoid doing something unpleasant or difficult • *We will not shrink from telling them the truth.*
➤ **shrinkage** *NOUN*

shrivel *VERB* shrivels, shrivelling, shrivelled
to become dry and wrinkled or to make something like this

shroud *NOUN* shrouds
❶ a cloth in which a dead body is wrapped ❷ each of a set of ropes supporting a ship's mast

shroud *VERB* shrouds, shrouding, shrouded
❶ to wrap a dead body in a shroud ❷ to cover or conceal something • *The town was shrouded in mist.*

Shrove Tuesday *NOUN*
the day before Lent begins, when people eat pancakes **WORD ORIGIN** from the past tense of the old word *shrive* = to hear a person's confession (because it was the custom to go to confession on this day)

shrub *NOUN* shrubs
a woody plant smaller than a tree; a bush
➤ **shrubby** *ADJECTIVE*

shrubbery *NOUN* shrubberies
an area planted with shrubs

shrug *VERB* shrugs, shrugging, shrugged
to raise your shoulders slightly as a sign that you do not care or do not know about something
➤ **shrug something off** to treat something as unimportant

shrug *NOUN* shrugs
a gesture of shrugging the shoulders

shrunken *ADJECTIVE*
having shrunk; small and shrivelled • *a shrunken old woman*

shudder *VERB* shudders, shuddering, shuddered
❶ to shiver violently with horror, fear or cold ❷ to make a strong shaking movement • *The engine shuddered and then stopped.*

shudder *NOUN* shudders
a strong shivering or shaking movement

shuffle *VERB* shuffles, shuffling, shuffled
❶ to walk without lifting your feet from the ground ❷ to move your body or feet around because you are uncomfortable or nervous • *The audience began to shuffle in their seats.* ❸ to mix up playing cards by sliding them over each other several times ❹ to move things around • *She shuffled the papers on her desk.*

shuffle *NOUN*
the act of shuffling • *Give the cards a quick shuffle.*

shun *VERB* shuns, shunning, shunned
to deliberately avoid or keep away from someone or something • *She was shunned by her family when she married him.*

shunt *VERB* shunts, shunting, shunted
❶ to move a train or wagons onto another track ❷ to divert something or someone to a less important place or position

shut *VERB* shuts, shutting, shut
❶ to move a door, window, lid or cover so that it blocks an opening ❷ to become closed • *The door shut suddenly* ❸ to bring or fold parts together • *She shut the book as he came in.*
➤ **shut down** to stop business
➤ **shut something down** to stop a machine working
➤ **shut up** (*informal*) to stop talking or making a noise
➤ **shut something up** to shut something securely

shut *ADJECTIVE*
closed • *Keep your eyes shut.*

shutter *NOUN* shutters
❶ a panel or screen that can be closed over a window ❷ the device in a camera that opens and closes to let light fall on the film
➤ **shuttered** *ADJECTIVE*

shuttle *NOUN* shuttles
❶ a train, bus or aircraft that makes frequent short journeys between two points ❷ a space

a b c d e f g h i j k l m n o p q r s t u v w x y z

shuttle ❸ the part of a loom that carries the thread from side to side

shuttle *VERB* shuttles, shuttling, shuttled
to move or travel continuously between two places

shuttlecock *NOUN* shuttlecocks
a small rounded piece of cork or plastic with a crown of feathers, struck to and fro by players in badminton

shy *ADJECTIVE* shyer, shyest
afraid to meet or talk to other people; timid
➤ **shyly** *ADVERB*
➤ **shyness** *NOUN*

shy *VERB* shies, shying, shied
❶ to jump or move suddenly in alarm ❷ to throw a stone or other object
➤ **shy away from something** to avoid doing something because you are nervous or afraid

shy *NOUN* shies
a throw

SI *NOUN*
an internationally recognized system of metric units of measurement, including the metre and kilogram (**WORD ORIGIN**) short for French *Système International d'Unités* = International System of Units

Siamese cat *NOUN* Siamese cats
a cat with short pale fur with darker face, ears, tail and feet

sibilant *ADJECTIVE*
having a hissing sound • *a sibilant whisper*

sibilant *NOUN* sibilants
a speech sound that sounds like hissing, e.g. *s, sh*

sibling *NOUN* siblings
a brother or sister

sibyl *NOUN* sibyls
a prophetess in ancient Greece or Rome

sick *ADJECTIVE*
❶ ill; physically or mentally unwell
❷ vomiting or likely to vomit • *I feel sick.*
❸ disgusted, angry or anxious • *People like him make me sick.* • *She was sick with worry.* ❹ making fun of death, disability or misfortune in an unpleasant way
➤ **be sick of something** to be tired of something or fed up with it

sicken *VERB* sickens, sickening, sickened
❶ to make someone feel upset or disgusted • *We were all sickened by this vandalism.*
❷ to start feeling ill

sickening *ADJECTIVE*
shocking or disgusting

sickle *NOUN* sickles
a tool with a narrow curved blade, used for cutting crops or grass

sickle-cell anaemia *NOUN*
a severe form of anaemia which is passed on in the genes and which causes pain in the joints, fever, jaundice and sometimes death
(**WORD ORIGIN**) so called because the red blood cells become sickle-shaped

sickly *ADJECTIVE*
❶ often ill; unhealthy • *a sickly child*
❷ making people feel sick • *a sickly smell*
❸ weak or sentimental • *a sickly smile*

sickness *NOUN* sicknesses
❶ illness ❷ a disease ❸ vomiting

side *NOUN* sides
❶ a surface, especially one joining the top and bottom of something ❷ a line that forms part of the boundary of a triangle, square, etc. ❸ either of the two halves into which something can be divided by a line down its centre ❹ one of the surfaces of something except the top, bottom, front or back • *I went round the side of the building.*
❺ the part near the edge and away from the centre ❻ the right or left part of your body, especially from under your arm to the top of your leg • *I've got a pain down my right side.*
❼ the place or region next to a person or thing • *He stood at my side.* ❽ one aspect or view of something • *There is another side to the problem.* ❾ one of two groups or teams who oppose each other • *They are on our side.*
➤ **on the side** as a sideline
➤ **side by side** next to each other
➤ **take sides** to support one person or group in a dispute or disagreement and not the other

side *ADJECTIVE*
at or on a side • *the side door*

side *VERB* sides, siding, sided
➤ **side with someone** to take a person's side in an argument

sideboard *NOUN* sideboards
a long piece of furniture with drawers and cupboards and a flat top

sideburns *PLURAL NOUN*
the strips of hair growing on each side of a man's face in front of his ears

sidecar *NOUN* sidecars
a small compartment for a passenger, fixed to the side of a motorcycle

side effect *NOUN* side effects
an effect, especially an unpleasant one, that a medicine has on you as well as the effect intended

sideline *NOUN* sidelines
❶ something that you do in addition to your main work or activity ❷ each of the lines on the two long sides of a sports pitch

sidelong *ADJECTIVE*
towards one side; sideways • *a sidelong glance*

sideshow *NOUN* sideshows
a small entertainment forming part of a large one, e.g. at a fair

sidetrack *VERB* sidetracks, sidetracking, sidetracked
to take someone's attention away from the main subject or problem

sidewalk *NOUN* sidewalks
(*North American*) a pavement

sideways *ADVERB & ADJECTIVE*
❶ to or from one side • *Crabs walk sideways.*
❷ with one side facing forwards • *We sat sideways in the bus.*

siding *NOUN* sidings
a short railway line by the side of a main line

sidle *VERB* sidles, sidling, sidled
to walk in a shy or nervous manner • *She sidled up to me and whispered in my ear.*

siege *NOUN* sieges
the surrounding of a place in order to capture it or force someone to surrender
➤ **lay siege to somewhere** to begin a siege of a place

sienna *NOUN*
a kind of clay used in making brownish paints

sierra *NOUN* sierras
a range of mountains with sharp peaks, in Spain or parts of America
WORD ORIGIN Spanish, from Latin *serra* = a saw (because the peaks look like the teeth of a saw)

siesta (say see-**est**-a) *NOUN* siestas
an afternoon rest, especially in a hot country
WORD ORIGIN from Latin *sexta hora* = sixth hour, midday

sieve (say siv) *NOUN* sieves
a device made of mesh or perforated metal

or plastic, used to separate the smaller or soft parts of something from the larger or hard parts

sieve *VERB* sieves, sieving, sieved
to put something through a sieve

sift *VERB* sifts, sifting, sifted
❶ to pass a fine or powdery substance through a sieve in order to remove any lumps
❷ to examine and analyse facts or evidence carefully

sigh *NOUN* sighs
a sound made by breathing out heavily when you are sad, tired or relieved

sigh *VERB* sighs, sighing, sighed
to make a sigh • *He sighed with disappointment at the news.*

sight *NOUN* sights
❶ the ability to see ❷ a view or glimpse • *I caught sight of her in the crowd.* ❸ a thing that can be seen or is worth seeing • *Our garden is a lovely sight.* • *Visit the sights of Paris.* ❹ something silly or ridiculous to look at • *You do look a sight in those clothes!* ❺ a device looked through to help aim a gun or telescope
➤ **at sight** or **on sight** as soon as a person or thing has been seen
➤ **in sight** ❶ visible ❷ clearly near; about to happen • *Victory was in sight.*
➤ **out of sight** no longer able to be seen

sight *VERB* sights, sighting, sighted
❶ to see or observe something ❷ to aim a gun or telescope

SPELLING
Sight is different from **site**, which means the place where something is.

sighted *ADJECTIVE*
able to see; not blind

sightless *ADJECTIVE*
blind

sight-reading *NOUN*
playing or singing music at sight, without preparation

sightseeing *NOUN*
visiting interesting places in a town as a tourist
➤ **sightseer** *NOUN*

sign *NOUN* signs
❶ something that shows that a thing exists • *There are signs of decay.* ❷ a mark or symbol that stands for something • *a minus sign* ❸ a board or notice that tells or

a
b
c
d
e
f
g
h
i
j
k
l
m
n
o
p
q
r
s
t
u
v
w
x
y
z

shows people something • *a road sign* ❹ an action or movement giving information or a command • *She made a sign to them to be quiet.* ❺ any of the twelve divisions of the zodiac, represented by a symbol

sign VERB **signs, signing, signed**
❶ to make a sign or signal • *He signed to them to follow him.* ❷ to write your signature on something; to accept a contract or agreement by doing this ❸ to give someone a contract for a job, especially in a professional sport • *They have signed three new players.* ❹ to use signing
➤ **sign on** ❶ to accept a job by signing a contract ❷ to sign a form to say that you are unemployed and want to claim benefit

SPELLING
There is a silent **g** before the **n** in **sign**.

signal NOUN **signals**
❶ a device, gesture or sound that gives information or a command ❷ a message made up of such things ❸ a sequence of electrical impulses or radio waves

signal VERB **signals, signalling, signalled**
to give someone a signal

signal ADJECTIVE
remarkable or striking • *It was a signal victory for him.*
➤ **signally** ADVERB

signal box NOUN **signal boxes**
(*British*) a building from which railway signals and points are controlled

signalman NOUN **signalmen**
a person who controls railway signals

signature NOUN **signatures**
❶ the form in which a person writes their own name ❷ (*in music*) a set of sharps and flats after the clef in a score, showing the key the music is written in (the *key signature*) or the sign, often a fraction such as ¾ (the *time signature*), showing the number of beats in the bar and their rhythm

signature tune NOUN **signature tunes**
(*British*) a special tune always used to announce a particular programme or performer on television or radio

signet ring NOUN **signet rings**
a ring with a person's initials or a design engraved on it

significance NOUN
the meaning or importance of something • *I did not realize the significance of this discovery at first.*

significant ADJECTIVE
❶ having a meaning; full of meaning ❷ important • *a significant event*
➤ **significantly** ADVERB

signification NOUN
the meaning of something

signify VERB **signifies, signifying, signified**
❶ to be a sign or symbol of something; to mean something ❷ to indicate something • *She signified her approval with a nod.* ❸ to be important; to matter

signing, sign language NOUN
a way of communicating by using movements of your hands instead of sounds, used mainly by deaf people

signpost NOUN **signposts**
a sign at a road junction showing the names and distances of the places that each road leads to

Sikh (say seek) NOUN **Sikhs**
a follower of Sikhism

Sikhism (say **seek**-izm) NOUN
a religion founded in Punjab in the 15th century by Guru Nanak and based on belief in one God

silage NOUN
fodder made from green crops stored in a silo

silence NOUN **silences**
❶ absence of sound ❷ not speaking
➤ **in silence** without speaking or making a sound • *She watched him in silence for a long time.*

silence VERB **silences, silencing, silenced**
to make a person or thing silent • *He silenced her with a glare.*

silencer NOUN **silencers**
a device for reducing the sound made by a gun or a vehicle's exhaust system

silent ADJECTIVE
❶ without any sound ❷ not speaking
➤ **silently** ADVERB

silhouette (say sil-oo-**et**) NOUN **silhouettes**
❶ a dark shadow seen against a light background ❷ a portrait of a person in profile, showing the shape and outline only in solid black

silhouette VERB **silhouettes, silhouetting, silhouetted**
to show an outline as a silhouette • *A figure stood in the doorway, silhouetted against the light.* **WORD ORIGIN** named after a French

author, É. de *Silhouette*, who made paper cut-outs of people's profiles from their shadows

silica *NOUN*
a hard white mineral that is a compound of silicon, used to make glass

silicon *NOUN*
a substance found in many rocks, used in making microchips

silicone *NOUN*
a compound of silicon used in paints, varnish and lubricants

silk *NOUN* silks
❶ a fine soft thread or cloth made from the fibre produced by silkworms for making their cocoons ❷ a length of silk thread used for embroidery

silken *ADJECTIVE*
made of silk • *a silken gown*

silkworm *NOUN* silkworms
the caterpillar of a kind of moth, which feeds on mulberry leaves and spins itself a cocoon

silky *ADJECTIVE*
soft, smooth and shiny like silk • *silky hair*

sill *NOUN* sills
a strip of stone, wood or metal underneath a window or door

silly *ADJECTIVE* sillier, silliest
foolish or unwise
➤ **silliness** *NOUN*
WORD ORIGIN from Old English *saelig* = happy or fortunate, later = innocent or feeble

silo (say **sy**-loh) *NOUN* silos
❶ a pit or tower for storing green crops (see **silage**) or corn or cement ❷ an underground place for storing a missile ready for firing

silt *NOUN*
fine sand and mud that is laid down by a river or the sea

silt *VERB* silts, silting, silted
➤ **silt up** to become blocked with silt

silver *NOUN* silvers
❶ a shiny white precious metal ❷ the colour of silver ❸ coins or objects made of silver or silver-coloured metal ❹ a silver medal, usually given as second prize

silver *ADJECTIVE*
❶ made of silver ❷ coloured like silver

silver *VERB* silvers, silvering, silvered
to make something silvery or to become silvery • *Moonlight silvered the lake.*

silver wedding *NOUN* silver weddings
a couple's 25th wedding anniversary

silvery *ADJECTIVE*
shiny like silver or silver in colour • *silvery light* • *silvery hair*

SIM card *NOUN* SIM cards
a small piece of plastic inside a mobile phone that stores information about the person using the phone

similar *ADJECTIVE*
❶ nearly the same as another person or thing; of the same kind ❷ (*in mathematics*) having the same shape but not the same size • *similar triangles*
➤ **similarly** *ADVERB*

similarity *NOUN* similarities
❶ the quality of being alike • *She bears a striking similarity to her mother.* ❷ a feature that makes one thing like another • *There are many similarities between the two planets.*

simile (say **sim**-il-ee) *NOUN* similes
a way of describing something by comparing it with something else, e.g. *He is as strong as a horse.* and *We ran like the wind.*

simmer *VERB* simmers, simmering, simmered
to boil very gently over a low heat
➤ **simmer down** to calm down after being angry or excited

simper *VERB* simpers, simpering, simpered
to smile in a silly and annoying way
➤ **simper** *NOUN*

simple *ADJECTIVE* simpler, simplest
❶ easy to answer or solve • *a simple question* ❷ not complicated or elaborate • *It was a simple plan, but it worked.* ❸ plain, not showy • *a simple black dress* ❹ without much sense or intelligence

simple-minded *ADJECTIVE*
naive or foolish

simpleton *NOUN* simpletons (*old use*)
a foolish person

simplicity *NOUN*
the quality of being simple • *The beauty of this plan is its simplicity.*

simplify *VERB* simplifies, simplifying, simplified
to make a thing simple or easy to understand
➤ **simplification** *NOUN*

simply *ADVERB*
❶ in a simple way • *I'll try to explain it simply.* ❷ without doubt; completely • *The*

a b c d e f g h i j k l m n o p q r s t u v w x y z

view is simply wonderful. ❸ only or merely
• *It's simply a question of time.*

simulate *VERB* simulates, simulating,
simulated
❶ to reproduce the appearance or conditions
of something • *This machine simulates a
space flight.* ❷ to pretend to have a certain
feeling • *They simulated fear.*
➤ **simulation** *NOUN*

simulator *NOUN* simulators
a machine or device for simulating actual
conditions or events, often used for training
• *a flight simulator*

simultaneous (say sim-ul-**tay**-nee-us)
ADJECTIVE
happening at the same time • *The two
explosions were simultaneous.*
➤ **simultaneously** *ADVERB*

sin *NOUN* sins
❶ the breaking of a religious or moral law
❷ a very bad action

sin *VERB* sins, sinning, sinned
to commit a sin
➤ **sinner** *NOUN*

since *CONJUNCTION*
❶ from the time when • *Where have you
been since I last saw you?* ❷ because • *Since
you refuse to come, I'll have to go on my own.*

since *PREPOSITION*
from a certain time • *She has been here since
Christmas.*

since *ADVERB*
between then and now • *He ran away and
hasn't been seen since.*

sincere *ADJECTIVE*
you are being sincere when you mean what
you say and express your true feelings
• *Please accept our sincere thanks.*
➤ **sincerely** *ADVERB*
➤ **sincerity** *NOUN*
➤ **Yours sincerely** see **yours**

sine *NOUN* sines
in a right-angled triangle, the ratio of the
length of a side opposite one of the acute
angles to the length of the hypotenuse.
Compare with **cosine**.

sinecure (say **sy**-nik-yoor) *NOUN* sinecures
a paid job that requires no work

sinew *NOUN* sinews
strong tissue that connects a muscle to a
bone

sinewy *ADJECTIVE*
slim, muscular and strong

sinful *ADJECTIVE*
❶ guilty of sin ❷ bad or wicked
➤ **sinfully** *ADVERB*
➤ **sinfulness** *NOUN*

sing *VERB* sings, singing, sang, sung
❶ to make musical sounds with your voice
❷ to perform a song

SPELLING

The past tense of **sing** is **sang** and the past
participle is **sung**.

singe (say sinj) *VERB* singes, singeing, singed
to burn something slightly

singer *NOUN* singers
a person who sings or whose job is singing • *a
pop singer*

single *ADJECTIVE*
❶ one only; not double or multiple ❷ suitable
for one person • *single beds* ❸ distinct or
separate • *I answered every single question
correctly.* ❹ not married ❺ for the journey to
a place but not back again • *a single ticket*

single *NOUN* singles
❶ a single person or thing ❷ a single ticket
❸ a record with one short piece of music on
it
➤ **singles** a game of tennis between two
players

single *VERB* singles, singling, singled
➤ **single someone out** to pick someone out
or distinguish them from other people

single file *NOUN*
➤ **in single file** in a line, one behind the
other

single-handed *ADJECTIVE*
by your own efforts; without any help

single-minded *ADJECTIVE*
with your mind set on one purpose only

single parent *NOUN* single parents
a person bringing up a child or children
without a partner

singlet *NOUN* singlets
a man's vest or similar piece of clothing worn
under or instead of a shirt

singly *ADVERB*
in ones; one by one • *These stamps are
available singly or in books of twelve.*

singsong *ADJECTIVE*
having a monotonous tone or rhythm • *a singsong voice*

singsong *NOUN* **singsongs**
❶ informal singing by a gathering of people • *Come on, let's have a singsong.* ❷ a singsong tone

singular *NOUN* **singulars**
the form of a noun or verb used when it stands for only one person or thing • *The singular is 'man' and the plural is 'men'.* Compare with **plural**.

singular *ADJECTIVE*
❶ in the singular; meaning only one • *'Mouse' is a singular noun.* ❷ uncommon or extraordinary • *a woman of singular courage*
➤ **singularity** *NOUN*

singularly *ADVERB*
remarkably or unusually • *a singularly handsome man*

sinister *ADJECTIVE*
❶ looking or seeming evil or harmful ❷ wicked; intending to do harm • *a sinister motive* **WORD ORIGIN** from Latin, = on the left (which was thought to be unlucky)

sink *VERB* **sinks, sinking, sank, sunk**
❶ to fall under the surface of water or to the bottom of the sea or to make something do this • *The ship sank in a storm.* • *They fired on the ship and sank it.* ❷ to go or fall slowly downwards • *He sank to his knees.* ❸ to push something sharp deeply into something • *The dog sank its teeth into my leg.* ❹ to dig or drill a hole or well ❺ to invest money in something
➤ **sink in** to become understood

sink *NOUN* **sinks**
a fixed basin with a tap or taps to supply water, especially one in a kitchen

sinuous *ADJECTIVE*
with many bends or curves • *the sinuous movement of a snake*

sinus (say **sy**-nus) *NOUN* **sinuses**
a hollow part in the bones of the skull, connected with the nose • *My sinuses are blocked.*

sip *VERB* **sips, sipping, sipped**
to drink something in small mouthfuls

sip *NOUN* **sips**
a small amount of a drink that you take into your mouth

siphon *NOUN* **siphons**
❶ a pipe or tube in the form of an upside-down U, arranged so that liquid is forced up it and down to a lower level ❷ a bottle containing soda water which is released through a tube

siphon *VERB* **siphons, siphoning, siphoned**
to draw out liquid through a siphon

sir *NOUN*
❶ a word used when speaking or writing politely to a man • *Can I help you, sir?* ❷ the title given to a knight or baronet • *Sir Francis Drake*

sire *NOUN* **sires**
a word formerly used when speaking to a king

sire *VERB* **sires, siring, sired**
to be the male parent of a horse or dog • *This stallion has sired several winners.*

siren *NOUN* **sirens**
❶ a device that makes a long loud sound as a signal ❷ a dangerously attractive woman **WORD ORIGIN** named after the *Sirens* in Greek legend, women who by their sweet singing lured seafarers to shipwreck on the rocks

sirloin *NOUN*
beef from the upper part of the loin

sirocco *NOUN* **siroccos**
a hot dry wind that reaches Italy from Africa

sisal (say **sy**-sal) *NOUN*
fibre from a tropical plant, used for making ropes

sissy *NOUN* **sissies**
a timid or cowardly person

sister *NOUN* **sisters**
❶ a daughter of the same parents as another person ❷ a female friend or associate ❸ a nun ❹ a senior hospital nurse, especially one in charge of a ward
➤ **sisterly** *ADJECTIVE*

sisterhood *NOUN* **sisterhoods**
❶ companionship and mutual support between women ❷ a society or association of women

sister-in-law *NOUN* **sisters-in-law**
the sister of a married person's husband or wife; the wife of a person's brother or sister

sit *VERB* **sits, sitting, sat**
❶ to rest on your bottom, as you do when you are on a chair • *We were sitting in the front row.* ❷ to put someone in a sitting position ❸ to be situated or positioned in a certain place • *The house sits on top of a hill.* ❹ to take a test or examination

a b c d e f g h i j k l m n o p q r s t u v w x y z

❺ a parliament or law court sits when it has assembled for business ❻ to act as a babysitter

sitar *NOUN* sitars
an Indian musical instrument that is like a guitar

sitcom *NOUN* sitcoms (*informal*)
a situation comedy

site *NOUN* sites
the place where something happens or happened or is built or positioned • *a building site* • *This is the site of a famous battle.*

site *VERB* sites, siting, sited
to site something somewhere is to locate or build it there

> **SPELLING**
> **Site** is different from **sight**, which means your ability to see or something that you see.

sit-in *NOUN* sit-ins
a protest in which people sit down in a public place and refuse to move

sitter *NOUN* sitters
❶ a person who poses for a portrait ❷ a person who looks after children, pets or a house while the owners are away

sitting *NOUN* sittings
❶ the time when people are served a meal ❷ the time when a parliament or committee is conducting business

sitting room *NOUN* sitting rooms
(*chiefly British*) a room with comfortable chairs for sitting in

situated *ADJECTIVE*
in a particular place or situation • *They lived in a village situated in a valley.*

situation *NOUN* situations
❶ a state of affairs at a certain time; the way things are • *The police faced a difficult situation.* ❷ a position of a building or town, with its surroundings ❸ a job

situation comedy *NOUN* situation comedies
a comedy series on radio or television, based on how characters react to unusual or comic situations

six *NOUN* & *ADJECTIVE* sixes
the number 6
> **sixth** *ADJECTIVE* & *NOUN*
> **at sixes and sevens** in disorder or disagreement

sixteen *NOUN* & *ADJECTIVE* sixteens
the number 16
> **sixteenth** *ADJECTIVE* & *NOUN*

sixth form *NOUN* sixth forms
(*British*) a form for students aged 16-18 in a secondary school

sixth sense *NOUN*
the ability to know something by instinct rather than by using any of the five senses; intuition

sixty *NOUN* & *ADJECTIVE* sixties
the number 60
> **sixtieth** *ADJECTIVE* & *NOUN*

size *NOUN* sizes
❶ the measurements or extent of something ❷ any of the series of standard measurements in which certain things are made • *a size eight shoe* ❸ a gluey substance used to glaze or stiffen paper or cloth

size *VERB* sizes, sizing, sized
❶ to arrange things according to their size ❷ to treat something with size
> **size something up** ❶ to estimate the size of something ❷ to form an opinion or judgement about a person or thing

sizeable *ADJECTIVE*
large or fairly large

sizzle *VERB* sizzles, sizzling, sizzled
to make a crackling or hissing sound

sjambok (say **sham**-bok) *NOUN* sjamboks
(*S. African*) a strong whip originally made from the skin of a rhinoceros

skate *NOUN* skates
❶ a boot with a steel blade attached to the sole, used for sliding smoothly over ice ❷ a roller skate ❸ skate
a large flat edible sea fish

skate *VERB* skates, skating, skated
to move around on skates
> **skater** *NOUN*

skateboard *NOUN* skateboards
a small board with wheels, used for standing and riding on as a sport
> **skateboarder, skateboarding** *NOUN*

skein *NOUN* skeins
a coil of yarn or thread

skeletal *ADJECTIVE*
to do with a skeleton or like a skeleton
• *skeletal figures dressed in rags*

skeleton *NOUN* skeletons
❶ the framework of bones in a person's

or animal's body ❷ a framework, e.g. of a building

sketch NOUN **sketches**
❶ a rough drawing or painting ❷ a short account of something ❸ a short amusing play

sketch VERB **sketches, sketching, sketched**
to make a sketch • *She sketched the view from the window.*

sketchy ADJECTIVE
rough and not detailed or careful

skew, skewed ADJECTIVE
slanting; not straight or level

skewer NOUN **skewers**
a long pin pushed through meat to hold it together while it is being cooked

skewer VERB **skewers, skewering, skewered**
to fix or pierce something with a skewer or pin

ski (say skee) NOUN **skis**
each of a pair of long narrow strips of wood, metal or plastic fixed under the feet for moving quickly over snow

ski VERB **skies, skiing, skied**
to travel on skis

skid VERB **skids, skidding, skidded**
to slide accidentally, especially in a vehicle

skid NOUN **skids**
❶ a skidding movement ❷ a runner on a helicopter, for use in landing

skier NOUN **skiers**
a person who skis

ski jump NOUN **ski jumps**
a steep slope with a sharp drop where it levels out at the bottom, for skiers to jump off as a sport

skilful ADJECTIVE
having or showing great skill
➤ **skilfully** ADVERB

skill NOUN **skills**
❶ the ability to do something well • *It takes great skill to paint a picture like that.* ❷ an ability that you need in order to do something • *He's been learning some new football skills.*

skilled ADJECTIVE
❶ skilful; highly trained or experienced ❷ skilled work needs particular skills or special training

skim VERB **skims, skimming, skimmed**
❶ to remove something from the surface of a liquid; to take the cream off milk ❷ to move

quickly over a surface, almost touching it
• *The plane flew very low, skimming the tops of the buildings.* ❸ to read something quickly

skimmed milk NOUN
milk that has had the cream removed

skimp VERB **skimps, skimping, skimped**
to supply or use less than is needed • *Don't skimp on the food.*

skimpy ADJECTIVE **skimpier, skimpiest**
skimpy clothes do not cover much of the body • *a skimpy dress*

skin NOUN **skins**
❶ the flexible outer covering of a person's or animal's body ❷ an outer layer or covering, e.g. of a fruit ❸ a skin-like film formed on the surface of a liquid

skin VERB **skins, skinning, skinned**
to take the skin off something

skin diving NOUN
swimming under water with flippers and breathing apparatus but without a diving suit
➤ **skin diver** NOUN

skinhead NOUN **skinheads**
a youth with very closely cropped hair

skinny ADJECTIVE **skinnier, skinniest**
very thin

skip VERB **skips, skipping, skipped**
❶ to move along lightly, especially by hopping on each foot in turn ❷ to jump with a skipping rope ❸ to go quickly from one subject to another ❹ to miss something out
• *You can skip chapter six.*

skip NOUN **skips**
❶ a skipping movement ❷ a large open-topped metal container for taking away builders' rubbish

skipper NOUN **skippers** (*informal*)
the captain of a ship or team

skipping rope NOUN **skipping ropes**
(*British*) a rope, usually with a handle at each end, that you swing over your head and under your feet as you jump

skirmish NOUN **skirmishes**
a short rough fight

skirmish VERB **skirmishes, skirmishing, skirmished**
to take part in a skirmish

skirt NOUN **skirts**
❶ a piece of clothing for a woman or girl that hangs down from the waist ❷ the part of a dress below the waist

skirt *VERB* skirts, skirting, skirted
to go round the edge of something • *The path skirts the lake.*

skirting, skirting board *NOUN* skirtings, skirting boards
(*British*) a narrow board round the wall of a room, close to the floor

skit *NOUN* skits
a short humorous play or sketch that makes fun of something by imitating it • *He wrote a skit on 'Hamlet'.*

skittish *ADJECTIVE*
frisky; lively and excitable • *a skittish horse*

skittle *NOUN* skittles
a wooden or plastic bottle-shaped object that people try to knock down by bowling a ball in the game of **skittles**

skive *VERB* skives, skiving, skived (*British*) (*informal*)
to dodge work
➤ **skiver** *NOUN*

skulk *VERB* skulks, skulking, skulked
to move around or wait somewhere secretly, usually when you are planning to do something bad • *There was someone skulking behind the bushes.*

skull *NOUN* skulls
the framework of bones in your head

skullcap *NOUN* skullcaps
a small close-fitting cap worn on the top of the head

skunk *NOUN* skunks
a North American animal with black and white fur that can spray a bad-smelling fluid

sky *NOUN* skies
the space above the earth, appearing blue in daylight on fine days

skydiving *NOUN*
the sport of jumping from an aeroplane and performing manoeuvres before opening your parachute
➤ **skydiver** *NOUN*

skylark *NOUN* skylarks
a lark that sings while it hovers high in the air

skylight *NOUN* skylights
a window in a roof

skyline *NOUN* skylines
the outline of land or buildings seen against the sky • *the Manhattan skyline*

skyscraper *NOUN* skyscrapers
a very tall building

slab *NOUN* slabs
a thick flat piece of something

slack *ADJECTIVE*
❶ not pulled tight • *Leave the rope slack.*
❷ not busy or working hard • *Business is slack at this time of the year.*
➤ **slackly** *ADVERB*
➤ **slackness** *NOUN*

slack *NOUN*
the slack part of a rope or line

slack *VERB* slacks, slacking, slacked
to avoid work; to be lazy
➤ **slacker** *NOUN*

slacken *VERB* slackens, slackening, slackened
❶ to loosen something or to become loose
❷ to become or make something slower or less busy • *Her pace gradually slackened.*

slacks *PLURAL NOUN*
trousers for informal occasions

slag *NOUN*
waste material separated from metal in smelting

slag heap *NOUN* slag heaps
(*British*) a mound of waste matter from a mine

slain
past participle of **slay**

slake *VERB* slakes, slaking, slaked
to slake your thirst is to quench it

slalom *NOUN* slaloms
a ski race down a zigzag course
WORD ORIGIN Norwegian *sla* = sloping + *låm* = track

slam *VERB* slams, slamming, slammed
❶ to shut or make something shut loudly • *We heard the front door slam.* ❷ to hit something with great force

slam *NOUN* slams
the act or sound of slamming

slander *NOUN* slanders
a spoken statement that damages a person's reputation and is untrue. Compare with **libel.**
➤ **slanderous** *ADJECTIVE*

slander *VERB* slanders, slandering, slandered
to make a slander against someone
➤ **slanderer** *NOUN*

slang *NOUN*
words that are used very informally to add vividness or humour to what is said, especially

those used only by a particular group of people • *teenage slang*
➤ **slangy** *ADJECTIVE*

slanging match *NOUN* **slanging matches**
(*British*) a noisy quarrel, with people shouting insults at each other

slant *VERB* **slants, slanting, slanted**
❶ to slope or lean ❷ to present news or information from a particular point of view

slant *NOUN* **slants**
❶ a sloping or leaning position ❷ a way of presenting news or information from a particular point of view

slap *VERB* **slaps, slapping, slapped**
❶ to hit someone with the palm of the hand or with something flat ❷ to put something somewhere forcefully or carelessly • *We slapped paint on the walls.*

slap *NOUN* **slaps**
slapping someone • *a slap on the back*

slapdash *ADJECTIVE*
hasty and careless

slapstick *NOUN*
comedy with people hitting each other, falling over and throwing things

slash *VERB* **slashes, slashing, slashed**
❶ to make large cuts in something ❷ to cut or strike something with a long sweeping movement ❸ to reduce something greatly • *Prices were slashed.*

slash *NOUN* **slashes**
❶ a slashing cut ❷ a slanting line (/) used in writing and printing

slat *NOUN* **slats**
each of the thin strips of wood, metal or plastic arranged so that they overlap and form a screen, e.g. in a venetian blind

slate *NOUN* **slates**
❶ a kind of grey rock that is easily split into flat plates ❷ a piece of this rock used in covering a roof or (in the past) for writing on

slate *VERB* **slates, slating, slated**
❶ to cover a roof with slates ❷ (*informal*) to criticize a person or thing severely

slaughter *VERB* **slaughters, slaughtering, slaughtered**
❶ to kill an animal for food ❷ to kill people or animals ruthlessly or in great numbers

slaughter *NOUN*
the killing of a lot of people or animals

slaughterhouse *NOUN* **slaughterhouses**
a place where animals are killed for food

slave *NOUN* **slaves**
a person who is owned by someone else and has to work for them without being paid

slave *VERB* **slaves, slaving, slaved**
to work very hard • *He's been slaving away in the kitchen.*

slave-driver *NOUN* **slave-drivers**
a person who makes others work very hard

slaver (say **slav**-er or **slay**-ver) *VERB* **slavers, slavering, slavered**
to have saliva flowing from the mouth • *a slavering dog*

slavery *NOUN*
❶ being a slave • *They were sold into slavery.*
❷ the system of having slaves • *the abolition of slavery*

slavish *ADJECTIVE*
showing no independence or originality

slay *VERB* **slays, slaying, slew, slain** (*old or poetical use*)
to kill someone

sled *NOUN* **sleds** (*North American*)
a sledge

sledge *NOUN* **sledges**
(*British*) a vehicle for travelling over snow, with strips of metal or wood instead of wheels
➤ **sledging** *NOUN*

sledgehammer *NOUN* **sledgehammers**
a very large heavy hammer

sleek *ADJECTIVE*
smooth and shiny • *sleek black hair*

sleep *NOUN*
❶ the condition of rest in which your eyes are closed, your body is relaxed and your mind is unconscious • *You need some sleep.* ❷ a time when you are resting like this • *Did you have a good sleep?*
➤ **go to sleep** part of your body goes to sleep when it becomes numb
➤ **put something to sleep** to kill an animal painlessly, e.g. with an injection of a drug

sleep *VERB* **sleeps, sleeping, slept**
to have a sleep
➤ **sleep with someone** to have sexual intercourse with someone

sleeper *NOUN* **sleepers**
❶ someone who is asleep ❷ each of the wooden or concrete beams on which the rails of a railway rest ❸ a railway carriage with beds or berths for passengers to sleep in; a place in this

sleeping bag *NOUN* **sleeping bags**
a padded bag to sleep in, especially when you are camping

sleepless *ADJECTIVE*
without sleep or unable to sleep • *We had a sleepless night.*

sleepover *NOUN* **sleepovers**
a night spent away from home, after a party

sleepwalker *NOUN* **sleepwalkers**
a person who walks about while they are asleep
➤ **sleepwalking** *NOUN*

sleepy *ADJECTIVE*
❶ feeling a need or wish to sleep ❷ quiet and lacking activity • *a sleepy little town*
➤ **sleepily** *ADVERB*
➤ **sleepiness** *NOUN*

sleet *NOUN*
a mixture of rain and snow or hail

sleeve *NOUN* **sleeves**
❶ the part of a piece of clothing that covers your arm ❷ the cover of a record
➤ **up your sleeve** hidden but ready for you to use

sleeveless *ADJECTIVE*
without sleeves • *a sleeveless dress*

sleigh (say slay) *NOUN* **sleighs**
a large sledge pulled by horses

sleight of hand (say slight) *NOUN*
skilful movements of your hand that other people cannot see, especially when doing conjuring tricks

slender *ADJECTIVE*
❶ slim and graceful ❷ slight or small • *a slender chance of winning*

sleuth (say slooth) *NOUN* **sleuths**
a detective

slew
past tense of **slay**

slice *NOUN* **slices**
❶ a thin flat piece cut off something ❷ a portion of something

slice *VERB* **slices, slicing, sliced**
❶ to cut something into slices ❷ to cut something from a larger piece • *Slice the top off the egg.* ❸ to cut something cleanly • *The knife sliced through the apple.*

slick *ADJECTIVE*
❶ done quickly and cleverly, without obvious

effort ❷ clever at persuading people but not sincere ❸ smooth and slippery

slick *NOUN* **slicks**
❶ a large patch of oil floating on water ❷ a slippery place

slide *VERB* **slides, sliding, slid**
❶ to move smoothly over a flat or slippery surface or to make something do this • *She loved sliding down the bannister.* ❷ to move somewhere quietly or secretly • *I slid out of the room when nobody was looking.*

slide *NOUN* **slides**
❶ a sliding movement ❷ a structure for children to play on, with a smooth slope for sliding down ❸ a photograph that can be projected on a screen ❹ a small glass plate on which you can place things to examine them under a microscope ❺ a fastener to keep your hair tidy

slight *ADJECTIVE*
very small; not serious or important

slight *VERB* **slights, slighting, slighted**
to insult a person by treating them without respect

slight *NOUN* **slights**
an insult

slightly *ADVERB*
to a small degree; a little • *They were slightly hurt.*

slim *ADJECTIVE* **slimmer, slimmest**
❶ thin and graceful ❷ small; hardly enough • *a slim chance of winning*

slim *VERB* **slims, slimming, slimmed** (*British*)
to try to make yourself thinner, especially by dieting
➤ **slimmer** *NOUN*

slime *NOUN*
unpleasant wet slippery stuff

slimy *ADJECTIVE* **slimier, slimiest**
❶ covered in slime ❷ pretending to be friendly in a way that is not sincere

sling *NOUN* **slings**
❶ a piece of cloth tied round your neck to support an injured arm • *He had his arm in a sling.* ❷ a looped strap used to throw a stone

sling *VERB* **slings, slinging, slung**
❶ to hang something up or support it so that it hangs loosely • *He had slung the bag round his neck.* ❷ (*informal*) to throw something roughly or carelessly • *You can sling your wet clothes into the washing machine.*

slink *VERB* **slinks, slinking, slunk**
to move in a stealthy or guilty way • *He slunk off to bed.*

slip *VERB* **slips, slipping, slipped**
❶ to slide accidentally; to lose your balance by sliding ❷ to move somewhere quickly and quietly • *She slipped out of the house before anyone was awake.* ❸ to slip something somewhere is to put it there quickly without being seen • *He slipped the letter into his pocket.* ❹ to escape from something • *The dog slipped its leash.*
➤ **slip your mind** to be forgotten • *I'm sorry, it slipped my mind.*
➤ **slip up** to make a mistake

slip *NOUN* **slips**
❶ an accidental slide or fall • *One slip and you could fall into the river.* ❷ a small mistake ❸ a small piece of paper ❹ a piece of women's underwear like a thin dress or skirt ❺ a pillowcase
➤ **give someone the slip** to escape from someone or avoid them

slipper *NOUN* **slippers**
a soft comfortable shoe to wear indoors

slippery *ADJECTIVE*
smooth or wet so that it is difficult to stand on or hold
➤ **slipperiness** *NOUN*

slip road *NOUN* **slip roads**
(*British*) a road by which you enter or leave a motorway

slipshod *ADJECTIVE*
a slipshod piece of work is careless or badly done **WORD ORIGIN** originally = wearing slippers or badly fitting shoes; from **slip** + **shod**

slipstream *NOUN* **slipstreams**
a current of air driven backward as an aircraft or vehicle moves forward very fast

slit *NOUN* **slits**
a narrow straight cut or opening

slit *VERB* **slits, slitting, slit**
to make a slit or slits in something

slither *VERB* **slithers, slithering, slithered**
❶ to move along the ground like a snake • *The snake slithered away.* ❷ to slip or slide unsteadily • *We were slithering around on the ice.*

sliver (say **sliv**-er) *NOUN* **slivers**
a thin strip of something hard or brittle, such as wood or glass

slob *NOUN* **slobs** (*informal*)
a careless, untidy, lazy person

slobber *VERB* **slobbers, slobbering, slobbered**
to have saliva coming out of your mouth
WORD ORIGIN probably from old Dutch *slobberen* = paddle in mud

sloe *NOUN* **sloes**
the small dark plum-like fruit of blackthorn

slog *VERB* **slogs, slogging, slogged**
❶ to work hard • *I've been slogging away at my essay.* ❷ to walk with effort • *We slogged through the snow.* ❸ to hit something hard

slog *NOUN*
a piece of hard work or effort • *Climbing up that hill was a real slog.*

slogan *NOUN* **slogans**
a short catchy phrase used to advertise something or to sum up an idea • *Their slogan was 'Ban the bomb!'.* **WORD ORIGIN** from Scottish Gaelic *sluagh-ghairm* = battle-cry

sloop *NOUN* **sloops**
a small sailing ship with one mast

slop *VERB* **slops, slopping, slopped**
❶ to spill liquid over the edge of its container ❷ liquid slops when it spills in this way

slope *VERB* **slopes, sloping, sloped**
to be at an angle so that it is higher at one end than the other; to lean to one side • *The road slopes down to the river.*
➤ **sloping** *ADJECTIVE*
➤ **slope off** (*informal*) to go away quietly without being seen

slope *NOUN* **slopes**
❶ a surface or piece of land that slopes • *The village is built on a slope.* ❷ the amount by which something slopes

sloppy *ADJECTIVE* **sloppier, sloppiest**
❶ liquid and splashing easily ❷ careless or badly done • *sloppy work* ❸ too sentimental or romantic • *a sloppy story*
➤ **sloppily** *ADVERB*
➤ **sloppiness** *NOUN*

slops *PLURAL NOUN*
❶ waste food fed to animals ❷ dirty water or liquid waste matter

slosh *VERB* **sloshes, sloshing, sloshed** (*informal*)
❶ to splash in a messy way • *Water was sloshing around under our feet.* ❷ to pour or splash liquid carelessly

slot *NOUN* **slots**
a narrow opening to put things in
➤ **slotted** *ADJECTIVE*

slot *VERB* slots, slotting, slotted
to put something into a place where it fits

sloth (rhymes with both) *NOUN* sloths
❶ laziness ❷ a South American animal that
lives in trees and moves very slowly
➤ **slothful** *ADJECTIVE*

slot machine *NOUN* slot machines
a machine worked by putting a coin in the
slot

slouch *VERB* slouches, slouching, slouched
to stand, sit or move in a lazy awkward way,
with your shoulders and head bent forward
➤ **slouch** *NOUN*

slough (say sluf) *VERB* sloughs, sloughing,
sloughed
to shed a layer of dead skin • *A snake sloughs
its skin periodically.*

slough (rhymes with cow) *NOUN* sloughs
a swamp or marshy place

slovenly (say **sluv**-en-lee) *ADJECTIVE*
careless or untidy

slow *ADJECTIVE*
❶ not quick; taking more time than is usual
❷ showing a time earlier than the correct
time • *Your watch is slow.* ❸ not clever; not
able to understand quickly or easily
➤ **slowness** *NOUN*

slow *ADVERB*
slowly; at a slow rate • *Go slow.*

slow *VERB* slows, slowing, slowed
❶ to go more slowly ❷ to make something
go more slowly • *The storm slowed us down.*

slowly *ADVERB*
at a slow rate or speed

slow motion *NOUN*
movement in a film or on television which has
been slowed down

slow-worm *NOUN* slow-worms
a small European legless lizard that looks like
a snake and gives birth to live young

sludge *NOUN*
thick mud

slug *NOUN* slugs
❶ a small slimy animal like a snail without a
shell ❷ a pellet for firing from a gun

sluggard *NOUN* sluggards
a slow or lazy person

sluggish *ADJECTIVE*
slow-moving; not alert or lively

sluice (say slooss) *NOUN* sluices
❶ a sluice gate ❷ a channel carrying off
water

sluice *VERB* sluices, sluicing, sluiced
to wash something with a flow of water

sluice gate *NOUN* sluice gates
a sliding barrier for controlling a flow of
water

slum *NOUN* slums
an area of dirty and overcrowded houses in
a city

slumber *NOUN* slumbers
peaceful sleep

slumber *VERB* slumbers, slumbering,
slumbered
to sleep peacefully

slump *VERB* slumps, slumping, slumped
to fall or sit down heavily or suddenly • *He
slumped to the ground in agony.*

slump *NOUN* slumps
a sudden great fall in prices or trade

slur *VERB* slurs, slurring, slurred
❶ to pronounce words indistinctly by running
the sounds together • *He was drunk and his
speech was slurred.* ❷ to mark notes in music
with a slur

slur *NOUN* slurs
❶ a slurred sound ❷ an unfair comment
or insult that harms a person's reputation
❸ a curved line placed over notes in music
to show that they are to be sung or played
smoothly without a break

slurp *VERB* slurps, slurping, slurped
to eat or drink something with a loud sucking
sound

slurp *NOUN* slurps
a loud sucking sound

slurry *NOUN*
a semi-liquid mixture of water and cement,
clay or manure

slush *NOUN*
❶ partly melted snow on the ground
❷ very sentimental talk or writing
WORD ORIGIN imitating the sound when you
walk in it

slushy *ADJECTIVE*
❶ with snow partly melted on the ground
• *slushy pavements* ❷ very sentimental
• *slushy love songs*

sly *ADJECTIVE* slyer, slyest
❶ unpleasantly cunning or secret

❷ mischievous and knowing • *a sly smile*
➤ **slyness** NOUN

slyly ADVERB
in a sly way • *He glanced at her slyly.*

smack NOUN smacks
❶ a hard slap with your hand **❷** a loud sharp sound of a thing hitting something • *It hit the wall with a smack.* **❸** a loud kiss **❹** (*informal*) a hard hit or blow **❺** a slight flavour or trace of something **❻** (*British*) a small sailing boat used for fishing

smack VERB smacks, smacking, smacked
❶ to slap someone with your hand, especially as a punishment **❷** to hit something hard **❸** to have a slight flavour or trace of something • *His manner smacks of conceit.*
➤ **smack your lips** to close and then part your lips noisily in enjoyment

smack ADVERB (*informal*) forcefully or directly
• *My face landed smack in the snow.*

small ADJECTIVE
❶ not large; less than the usual size **❷** not important or significant • *She noticed a few small mistakes.*
➤ **smallness** NOUN
➤ **the small of the back** the smallest part of the back, at the waist

small hours PLURAL NOUN
the early hours of the morning, after midnight

small-minded ADJECTIVE
not willing to change your opinions or think about what is really important; petty

smallpox NOUN
a serious contagious disease that causes a fever and produces spots that leave permanent scars on the skin

small print NOUN
(*British*) the details of a contract, especially if they are in very small letters or difficult to understand

small talk NOUN
conversation about unimportant things

smarmy ADJECTIVE (*informal*)
flattering someone or being too polite to them in a way that seems false

smart ADJECTIVE
❶ neat and elegant; dressed well **❷** clever or shrewd **❸** forceful and brisk • *She set off at a smart pace.* **❹** fashionable and expensive • *a smart restaurant* **❺** controlled by a computer

• *smart bombs*
➤ **smartness** NOUN

smart VERB smarts, smarting, smarted
❶ to feel a stinging pain • *My eyes were smarting from the smoke.* **❷** to feel upset about a criticism or failure • *He was still smarting from his defeat in the final.*

smart card NOUN smart cards
a small plastic card on which information is stored in electronic form

smarten VERB smartens, smartening, smartened
to make a person or thing smarter or to become smarter • *You need to smarten yourself up a bit.*

smartly ADVERB
❶ to be smartly dressed is to be well dressed in neat clothes **❷** quickly and suddenly • *He stepped smartly forward.*

smartphone NOUN smartphones
a mobile phone that also works as a computer

smash VERB smashes, smashing, smashed
❶ to break noisily into pieces or make something break in this way **❷** to hit something or move with great force • *The truck left the road and smashed into a wall.* **❸** to strike the ball forcefully downwards in tennis and other games **❹** to destroy or defeat someone completely

smash NOUN smashes
❶ the action or sound of smashing **❷** a collision between vehicles **❸** (*informal*) a smash hit

smash hit NOUN smash hits (*informal*)
a very successful song or show

smashing ADJECTIVE (*British*) (*informal*)
excellent

smattering NOUN
a slight knowledge of a subject or a foreign language

smear VERB smears, smearing, smeared
❶ to rub something greasy or sticky or dirty on a surface **❷** to try to damage someone's reputation
➤ **smeary** ADJECTIVE

smear NOUN smears
❶ a dirty or greasy mark made by smearing **❷** material smeared on a slide to be examined under a microscope **❸** a smear test

smear test NOUN smear tests
(*British*) the taking and examination of a

a b c d e f g h i j k l m n o p q r s t u v w x y z

sample of the cervix lining, to check for faulty cells which may cause cancer

smell *VERB* smells, smelling, smelt or smelled
❶ to be aware of something by means of your nose • *I can smell smoke.* ❷ to give out a smell • *The cheese smells funny.*

smell *NOUN* smells
❶ something you can smell; a quality in something that makes people able to smell it ❷ an unpleasant quality of this kind ❸ the ability to smell things • *I have a good sense of smell.*

smelly *ADJECTIVE* smellier, smelliest
having an unpleasant smell

smelt *VERB* smelts, smelting, smelted
to melt ore to get the metal it contains

smile *NOUN* smiles
an expression on your face that shows you are pleased or amused, with your lips stretched and turning upwards at the ends

smile *VERB* smiles, smiling, smiled
to give a smile

smirk *NOUN* smirks
a self-satisfied smile

smirk *VERB* smirks, smirking, smirked
to give a smirk

smite *VERB* smites, smiting, smote, smitten (*old use*)
to strike something or someone with a hard blow

smith *NOUN* smiths
a person who makes things out of metal, especially a blacksmith

smithereens *PLURAL NOUN*
small fragments • *The house had been blown to smithereens.*

smithy *NOUN* smithies
a blacksmith's workshop

smitten
past participle of **smite**
➤ **be smitten with something** to be suddenly affected by a disease or feeling, especially love

smock *NOUN* smocks
❶ an overall shaped like a long loose shirt ❷ a loose top worn by a pregnant woman

smog *NOUN*
a mixture of smoke and fog
(WORD ORIGIN) from **smoke** + **fog**

smoke *NOUN*
❶ the mixture of gas and solid particles given

off by a burning substance ❷ a time spent smoking a cigarette • *He wanted a smoke.*

smoke *VERB* smokes, smoking, smoked
❶ to give out smoke • *a smoking chimney* ❷ someone is smoking when they have a lit cigarette between their lips and are drawing its smoke into their mouth ❸ to preserve meat or fish by treating it with smoke
• *smoked haddock*
➤ **smoker** *NOUN*

smokeless *ADJECTIVE*
burning without producing smoke
• *smokeless fuel*

smokescreen *NOUN* smokescreens
❶ a mass of smoke used to hide the movement of troops ❷ something that conceals what is happening

smoky *ADJECTIVE*
❶ full of or producing smoke • *a smoky fire* ❷ like smoke

smooth *ADJECTIVE*
❶ having a surface without any lumps, wrinkles or roughness • *smooth skin* ❷ a smooth liquid or mixture has no lumps in it ❸ moving without bumps or jolts • *We had a smooth ride.* ❹ not harsh • *a smooth flavour* ❺ without problems or difficulties
➤ **smoothness** *NOUN*

smooth *VERB* smooths, smoothing, smoothed
to make something smooth and flat • *She smoothed her hair back.*

smoothly *ADVERB*
❶ in an even and steady way • *Traffic is flowing smoothly again.* ❷ without any problems or difficulties • *I hope everything goes smoothly today.*

smote
past tense of **smite**

smother *VERB* smothers, smothering, smothered
❶ to cover someone's face so that they cannot breathe ❷ to put out a fire by covering it ❸ to cover something thickly
• *The chips were smothered in ketchup.*
❹ to hold back or conceal something • *She smothered a giggle.*

smoulder *VERB* smoulders, smouldering, smouldered
❶ to burn slowly without a flame ❷ to feel an emotion strongly without showing it • *He was smouldering with jealousy.*

smudge *NOUN* smudges
a dirty mark made by rubbing something
➤ **smudgy** *ADJECTIVE*

smudge *VERB* smudges, smudging, smudged
to make a smudge on something or to
become smudged • *The writing here was
smudged.*

smug *ADJECTIVE*
too pleased with your own good fortune or
abilities • *Don't look so smug.*
➤ **smugly** *ADVERB*
➤ **smugness** *NOUN*

smuggle *VERB* smuggles, smuggling, smuggled
❶ to bring something into a country secretly
or illegally ❷ to take something secretly into
or out of a place • *He smuggled some food
out of the house.*
➤ **smuggler** *NOUN*

smut *NOUN* smuts
❶ a small piece of soot or dirt ❷ rude or
indecent talk or pictures
➤ **smutty** *ADJECTIVE*

snack *NOUN* snacks
❶ a small meal ❷ food eaten between meals

snack bar *NOUN* snack bars
a small cafe where snacks are sold

snag *NOUN* snags
❶ an unexpected difficulty ❷ a sharp or
jagged part sticking out from something

snag *VERB* snags, snagging, snagged
to catch something you are wearing on
something sharp

snail *NOUN* snails
a small animal with a soft body and a shell

snail's pace *NOUN*
a very slow pace

snake *NOUN* snakes
a reptile with a long narrow body and no legs
➤ **snaky** *ADJECTIVE*

snake *VERB* snakes, snaking, snaked
to move or go in long twisting curves • *The
river snaked through a wooded valley.*

snap *VERB* snaps, snapping, snapped
❶ to break suddenly or with a sharp sound
or to make something do this • *The rope
snapped.* • *He snapped the branch in two.*
❷ an animal snaps when it bites suddenly
or quickly ❸ to say something quickly and
angrily • *There's no need to snap.* ❹ to move
something into a certain position with a
sharp noise • *She snapped the bag shut.* ❺ to
take a quick photograph of something

➤ **snap your fingers** to make a sharp
snapping sound with your thumb and a finger

snap *NOUN* snaps
❶ the action or sound of snapping ❷ an
informal photograph ❸ a card game in which
players shout 'Snap!' when they see two
similar cards

snap *ADJECTIVE*
made or done very quickly or suddenly • *It
was a snap decision.*

snapdragon *NOUN* snapdragons
a plant with flowers that have a mouth-like
opening

snappy *ADJECTIVE*
❶ snapping at people ❷ quick and lively

snapshot *NOUN* snapshots
an informal photograph that you take quickly

snare *NOUN* snares
❶ a trap for catching birds or small animals
❷ something that attracts someone but is a
trap or a danger

snare *VERB* snares, snaring, snared
to catch a bird or animal in a snare

snarl *VERB* snarls, snarling, snarled
❶ to growl angrily ❷ to speak in a bad-
tempered way
➤ **be snarled up** to become tangled or
jammed • *The motorway was snarled up for
miles.*

snarl *NOUN* snarls
a snarling sound

snatch *VERB* snatches, snatching, snatched
❶ to grab or take something quickly ❷ to
quickly make use of time or a chance • *I
managed to snatch some sleep.*

snatch *NOUN* snatches
❶ a short and incomplete part of a song
or conversation ❷ an act of snatching
something

sneak *VERB* sneaks, sneaking, sneaked
❶ to move somewhere quietly and secretly
❷ (*informal*) to take something secretly • *He
sneaked a biscuit from the tin.* ❸ (*informal*)
to tell tales about someone

sneak *NOUN* sneaks (*informal*) a person who
tells tales

sneakers *PLURAL NOUN*
(*North American*) soft-soled shoes

sneaky *ADJECTIVE*
dishonest or deceitful • *a sneaky trick*
➤ **sneakily** *ADVERB*

a b c d e f g h i j k l m n o p q r s t u v w x y z

sneer *VERB* sneers, sneering, sneered
to show contempt for someone by the way
you speak or the expression on your face
• *'And who would believe you?' sneered the
old man.*

sneer *NOUN* sneers
the expression on someone's face when they
sneer

sneeze *VERB* sneezes, sneezing, sneezed
to send out air suddenly and uncontrollably
through your nose and mouth in order to get
rid of something irritating the nostrils
➤ **not to be sneezed at** (*informal*) worth
having

sneeze *NOUN* sneezes
the action or sound of sneezing
WORD ORIGIN from Old English *fneosan*,
imitating the sound

snide *ADJECTIVE*
sneering in a sly way • *a snide remark*

sniff *VERB* sniffs, sniffing, sniffed
❶ to make a sound by drawing air in through
your nose ❷ to smell something

sniff *NOUN* sniffs
the act or sound of sniffing
➤ **sniffer** *NOUN*

sniffer dog *NOUN* sniffer dogs
a dog trained to find drugs or explosives by
smell

sniffle *VERB* sniffles, sniffling, sniffled
to keep sniffing because you have a cold or
are crying

sniffle *NOUN* sniffles
the act or sound of sniffling

snigger *VERB* sniggers, sniggering, sniggered
(*British*) to laugh quietly and slyly

snigger *NOUN* sniggers
(*British*) a quiet sly laugh

snip *VERB* snips, snipping, snipped
to cut something with scissors or shears in
small quick cuts

snip *NOUN* snips
an act of snipping something

snipe *NOUN* snipe
a marsh bird with a long beak

snipe *VERB* snipes, sniping, sniped
❶ to shoot at people from a hiding place
❷ to attack someone with sly critical remarks
➤ **sniper** *NOUN*
WORD ORIGIN probably from a Scandinavian
language; the verb because the birds are shot
from a hiding place

snippet *NOUN* snippets
a small piece of news or information

snivel *VERB* snivels, snivelling, snivelled
to cry or complain in a whining way

snob *NOUN* snobs
a person who despises those who have not
got wealth, power or particular tastes or
interests
➤ **snobbery** *NOUN*
➤ **snobbish** *ADJECTIVE*

snooker *NOUN*
a game played with long sticks (called *cues*)
and 22 balls on a special cloth-covered table

snoop *VERB* snoops, snooping, snooped
to look around a place secretly in order to
find something out • *I caught him snooping
around in my room.*
➤ **snooper** *NOUN*

snooty *ADJECTIVE* (*informal*)
haughty and contemptuous

snooze (*informal*) *NOUN* snoozes
a short sleep

snooze *VERB* snoozes, snoozing, snoozed
to have a short sleep

snore *VERB* snores, snoring, snored
to breathe noisily while you are sleeping

snore *NOUN* snores
noisy breathing while you are sleeping

snorkel *NOUN* snorkels
a tube through which a person swimming
under water can take in air
➤ **snorkelling** *NOUN*

snort *VERB* snorts, snorting, snorted
to make a rough sound by breathing
forcefully through your nose

snort *NOUN* snorts
a snorting noise • *She gave a little snort of
contempt.*

snout *NOUN* snouts
an animal's snout is the front part sticking
out from its head, with its nose and jaws

snow *NOUN*
frozen drops of water that fall from the sky in
small white flakes

snow *VERB* snows, snowing, snowed
it is snowing when snow is falling
➤ **be snowed under** to have more work to do
than you can easily deal with

snowball *NOUN* snowballs
snow pressed into a ball for throwing
➤ **snowballing** *NOUN*

snowball *VERB* snowballs, snowballing, snowballed
to grow quickly in size or intensity

snow-blindness *NOUN*
temporary blindness caused by the glare of light reflected by snow

snowdrift *NOUN* snowdrifts
a large heap or bank of snow piled up by the wind

snowdrop *NOUN* snowdrops
a small white flower that blooms in early spring

snowflake *NOUN* snowflakes
a flake of snow

snowline *NOUN*
the level above which snow never melts

snowman *NOUN* snowmen
a figure made of snow

snowplough *NOUN* snowploughs
a vehicle or device for clearing roads of snow

snowshoe *NOUN* snowshoes
a frame rather like a tennis racket for walking on soft snow

snowstorm *NOUN* snowstorms
a storm in which snow falls

snow white *ADJECTIVE*
pure white

snowy *ADJECTIVE*
❶ with snow falling • *snowy weather*
❷ covered with snow • *snowy mountain tops*
❸ pure white • *snowy white sheets*

snub *VERB* snubs, snubbing, snubbed
to treat someone rudely, especially by ignoring them

snub *NOUN* snubs
an insulting remark or unfriendly treatment

snub-nosed *ADJECTIVE*
having a short turned-up nose

snuff *NOUN*
powdered tobacco for taking into the nose by sniffing

snuff *VERB* snuffs, snuffing, snuffed
to put out a candle by covering or pinching the flame
➤ **snuffer** *NOUN*

snuffle *VERB* snuffles, snuffling, snuffled
to sniff in a noisy way

snuffle *NOUN* snuffles
the sound of snuffling

snug *ADJECTIVE* snugger, snuggest
❶ warm and cosy ❷ fitting closely or tightly
➤ **snugly** *ADVERB*

snuggle *VERB* snuggles, snuggling, snuggled
to curl up in a warm comfortable place • *She snuggled down under the blanket.*

so *ADVERB*
❶ in this way; to such an extent • *Why are you so cross?* ❷ very • *This programme is so boring.* ❸ also; too • *OK, I was wrong, but so were you.*
➤ **and so on** and other similar things • *They took food, water, spare clothing and so on.*
➤ **or so** or about that number • *We need about fifty or so.*
➤ **so as to** in order to
➤ **so far** up to now
➤ **so long!** (*informal*) goodbye
➤ **so what?** (*informal*) that is not important

so *CONJUNCTION*
for that reason • *They threw me out, so I came here.*

soak *VERB* soaks, soaking, soaked
to make a person or thing very wet or leave them in water
➤ **soak** *NOUN*
➤ **soak something up** to take in a liquid in the way that a sponge does

so-and-so *NOUN* so-and-sos
a person whose name you do not know or do not need to say

soap *NOUN* soaps
❶ a substance you use with water for washing and cleaning things ❷ a soap opera

soap *VERB* soaps, soaping, soaped
to put soap on something

soap opera *NOUN* soap operas
a television serial about the day-to-day lives of a group of people **WORD ORIGIN** originally American, where they were originally sponsored by soap manufacturers

soapy *ADJECTIVE*
full of soap or covered in soap • *soapy water*

soar *VERB* soars, soaring, soared
❶ to rise or fly high in the air ❷ to increase very quickly • *Prices were soaring.*

sob *VERB* sobs, sobbing, sobbed
to make a gasping sound when crying

sob *NOUN* sobs
a sound of sobbing

sober *ADJECTIVE*
❶ not drunk ❷ serious and calm • *She had*

a b c d e f g h i j k l m n o p q r s t u v w x y z

a sober expression. ❸ not bright or showy
• *sober colours*
➤ **soberly** *ADVERB*
➤ **sobriety** (say so-**bry**-it-ee) *NOUN*

sober *VERB* sobers, sobering, sobered
to become sober again or to make someone sober

sob story *NOUN* sob stories
an account of someone's experiences, told to get your help or sympathy • *She gave me some sob story about having her purse stolen.*

so-called *ADJECTIVE*
named in what may be the wrong way • *Even the so-called experts couldn't solve the problem.*

soccer *NOUN*
football (Association football, not rugby or American football)

> **USAGE**
>
> The word *soccer* is used especially in the USA.

WORD ORIGIN short for **Association football**, the official name from the late 19th century

sociable *ADJECTIVE*
friendly and liking to be with other people
➤ **sociably** *ADVERB*
➤ **sociability** *NOUN*

social *ADJECTIVE*
❶ to do with people meeting one another in their spare time • *a social club* ❷ to do with life in a community • *They were writing a social history of the town.* ❸ living in groups, not alone • *Bees are social insects.* ❹ liking to be with other people
➤ **socially** *ADVERB*

socialism *NOUN*
a political system where wealth is shared equally between people and the main industries and resources are controlled by the state. Compare with **capitalism**.

socialist *NOUN* socialists
a person who believes in socialism

socialize (also **socialise**) *VERB* socializes, socializing, socialized
to meet other people socially

social media *NOUN*
websites and computer programs that people use to communicate on the Internet using mobile phones, computers, etc.

social security *NOUN*
money and other assistance provided by the government for those in need through being unemployed, ill or disabled

social services *PLURAL NOUN*
welfare services provided by the government, for example care for vulnerable children and adults

social worker *NOUN* social workers
a person trained to help people in a community who have family or money problems
➤ **social work** *NOUN*

society *NOUN* societies
❶ a community; people living together in a group or nation • *We live in a multiracial society.* ❷ a group of people organized for a particular purpose • *the school dramatic society* ❸ company or companionship • *We enjoy the society of our friends.*

sociology (say soh-see-**ol**-o-jee) *NOUN*
the study of human society and social behaviour
➤ **sociological** *ADJECTIVE*
➤ **sociologist** *NOUN*

sock *NOUN* socks
a piece of clothing that covers your foot and the lower part of your leg

sock *VERB* socks, socking, socked
(*informal*) to hit or punch someone hard • *He socked me on the jaw.*

socket *NOUN* sockets
❶ a hollow into which something fits • *a tooth socket* ❷ a device into which an electric plug or bulb is put to make a connection

sod *NOUN* sods
a piece of turf

soda *NOUN*
❶ a substance made from sodium, such as baking soda ❷ soda water ❸ (*North American*) a sweet fizzy drink

soda water *NOUN*
water made fizzy with carbon dioxide, used in drinks

sodden *ADJECTIVE*
made very wet • *His boots were sodden.*

sodium *NOUN*
a soft white metal

sodium bicarbonate *NOUN*
a soluble white powder used in fire extinguishers and fizzy drinks and to make cakes rise; baking soda

sodium carbonate *NOUN*
white powder or crystals used to clean things; washing soda

sofa *NOUN* sofas
a long soft seat with a back and arms
(**WORD ORIGIN**) from Arabic *suffa* = long stone bench

soft *ADJECTIVE*
❶ not hard or firm; easily pressed or cut into a new shape ❷ smooth, not rough or stiff • *a soft towel* ❸ gentle and not loud • *He spoke in a soft voice.* ❹ not bright or harsh • *soft pinks and greens* ❺ soft drugs are not likely to be addictive ❻ soft water is free of minerals that prevent soap from making much lather
➤ **softness** *NOUN*

soft drink *NOUN* soft drinks
a cold drink that is not alcoholic

soften *VERB* softens, softening, softened
❶ to make something soft or to become soft • *This lotion is good for softening the skin.* ❷ to become kinder or more friendly • *His face softened a little.*
➤ **softener** *NOUN*

soft furnishings *PLURAL NOUN*
(*British*) cushions, curtains, rugs, loose covers for chairs, etc.

soft-hearted *ADJECTIVE*
sympathetic and easily moved

softly *ADVERB*
❶ in a gentle way • *She closed the door softly behind her.* ❷ quietly • *He could hear them talking softly in the next room.*

software *NOUN*
computer programs and data, which are not part of the machinery of a computer. Compare with **hardware**.

softwood *NOUN* softwoods
wood from pine trees or other conifers

soggy *ADJECTIVE* soggier, soggiest
very wet and heavy • *soggy ground*

soil *NOUN* soils
❶ the loose earth in which plants grow ❷ a nation's territory • *on British soil*

soil *VERB* soils, soiling, soiled
to make something dirty

sojourn (say **soj**-ern) *NOUN* sojourns
a temporary stay at a place

sojourn *VERB* sojourns, sojourning, sojourned
to stay at a place temporarily

solace (say **sol**-as) *NOUN*
something that makes you feel better when you are unhappy or disappointed • *He found solace in books.*

solar *ADJECTIVE*
from or to do with the sun

solar panel *NOUN* solar panels
a panel designed to catch the sun's rays and use their energy for heating or to make electricity

solar power *NOUN*
electricity or other forms of power that come from the sun's rays

solar system *NOUN*
the sun and the planets that revolve round it

solder *NOUN*
a soft alloy that is melted to join pieces of metal together

solder *VERB* solders, soldering, soldered
to join two pieces of metal together with solder

soldier *NOUN* soldiers
a member of an army
(**SPELLING**)
There is an **i** after the **d** in **soldier**.

sole *NOUN* soles
❶ the bottom surface of a foot or shoe ❷ a flat edible sea fish

sole *VERB* soles, soling, soled
to put a new sole on a shoe

sole *ADJECTIVE*
single or only • *She was the sole survivor.*

solely *ADVERB*
only; involving nothing or nobody else • *He was solely to blame.*

solemn *ADJECTIVE*
❶ not smiling or cheerful ❷ dignified or formal
➤ **solemnly** *ADVERB*
➤ **solemnity** *NOUN*
(**SPELLING**)
There is a silent **n** at the end of **solemn**.

solenoid *NOUN* solenoids
a coil of wire that becomes magnetic when an electric current is passed through it

sol-fa *NOUN*
a system of syllables (*doh, ray, me, fah, so, la, te*) used to represent the notes of the musical scale

a b c d e f g h i j k l m n o p q r s t u v w x y z

solicit *VERB* solicits, soliciting, solicited
to ask for or try to obtain something • *I've been soliciting opinions from rail users.* • *All the candidates are busy soliciting for votes.*
➤ **solicitation** *NOUN*

solicitor *NOUN* solicitors
a lawyer who advises clients, prepares legal documents and represents clients in the lower courts

solicitous *ADJECTIVE*
anxious and concerned about a person's comfort and welfare
➤ **solicitously** *ADVERB*
➤ **solicitude** *NOUN*

solid *ADJECTIVE*
❶ not hollow; with no space inside • *These bars are made of solid steel.* ❷ keeping its shape; not liquid or gas ❸ continuous • *I had to wait for two solid hours.* ❹ firm or strongly made; not flimsy • *The house is built on solid foundations.* ❺ strong and dependable • *The police have no solid evidence.*
➤ **solidity** *NOUN*

solid *NOUN* solids
❶ a solid thing ❷ a shape that has three dimensions (length, width and height or depth)

solidarity *NOUN*
unity and support between people sharing opinions and interests

solidify *VERB* solidifies, solidifying, solidified
to become solid • *The mixture soon solidified.*

solidly *ADVERB*
❶ strongly or firmly • *a solidly built house* ❷ without stopping • *It rained solidly all afternoon.*

solids *PLURAL NOUN*
solid food; food that is not liquid • *Is your baby eating solids yet?*

soliloquy (say sol-**il**-ok-wee) *NOUN* soliloquies
a speech in a play in which a person speaks their thoughts aloud when alone or without addressing anyone else

solitaire *NOUN* solitaires
❶ a game for one person, in which marbles are moved on a special board until only one is left ❷ a diamond or other precious stone set by itself

solitary *ADJECTIVE*
❶ alone, without other people • *He lived a solitary life.* ❷ single; by itself • *a solitary example*

solitary confinement *NOUN*
a form of punishment in which a prisoner is kept alone in a cell and not allowed to see other people

solitude *NOUN*
being solitary or alone • *She longed for peace and solitude.*

solo *NOUN* solos
something sung, played, danced or done by one person alone

solo *ADJECTIVE & ADVERB*
done alone; by yourself • *a solo flight* • *to fly solo*

soloist *NOUN* soloists
a person who plays, sings or performs a solo

solstice (say **sol**-stiss) *NOUN* solstices
either of the two times in each year when the sun is at its furthest point north or south of the equator
➤ **summer solstice** about 21 June in the northern hemisphere
➤ **winter solstice** about 22 December in the northern hemisphere
WORD ORIGIN from Latin *sol* = sun + *sistere* = stand still

soluble *ADJECTIVE*
❶ a soluble substance is able to be dissolved ❷ a soluble problem or puzzle is able to be solved
➤ **solubility** *NOUN*

solution *NOUN* solutions
❶ the answer to a problem or puzzle ❷ a liquid in which something is dissolved

solve *VERB* solves, solving, solved
to find the answer to a problem or puzzle • *There's a mystery we've been trying to solve.*

solvent *NOUN* solvents
a liquid used for dissolving something

solvent *ADJECTIVE*
having enough money to pay all your debts

sombre *ADJECTIVE*
❶ dark in colour • *sombre clothes* ❷ gloomy or serious • *He was in a sombre mood.*

sombrero (say som-**brair**-oh) *NOUN* sombreros
a hat with a very wide brim

some *DETERMINER*
❶ a few or a little • *some apples* • *some sugar* ❷ an unknown person or thing • *Some fool left the door open.* ❸ about • *We waited some 20 minutes.*
➤ **some time** ❶ quite a long time • *I've been*

wondering about it for some time. ❷ at some point in time • *You must come round for a meal some time.*

some *PRONOUN*
a certain number or amount that is less than the whole • *Some of them were late.*

somebody *PRONOUN*
❶ some person; someone ❷ an important or impressive person

somehow *ADVERB*
in some way or for some reason • *We must finish the work somehow.* • *Somehow I knew the door would be locked.*

someone *PRONOUN*
some person; somebody

somersault *NOUN* somersaults
a movement in which you turn head over heels before landing on your feet

somersault *VERB* somersaults, somersaulting, somersaulted
to perform a somersault

something *PRONOUN*
some thing; a thing which you cannot or do not want to name
➤ **something like** ❶ rather like • *It's something like a rabbit.* ❷ approximately • *It took something like 100 years to build.*

sometime *ADVERB*
at some point in time • *I saw her sometime last year.*

sometimes *ADVERB*
at some times but not always • *We sometimes walk to school.*

somewhat *ADVERB*
to some extent • *He was somewhat annoyed.*

somewhere *ADVERB*
in or to some place

son *NOUN* sons
a boy or man who is someone's child

sonar *NOUN*
a system for finding objects under water by the reflection of sound waves
(WORD ORIGIN) from *so*und *na*vigation and *r*anging

sonata *NOUN* sonatas
a piece of music for one instrument or two, in several movements

song *NOUN* songs
❶ a tune with words for singing ❷ a bird's song is the musical sounds it makes ❸ singing • *He burst into song.*

➤ **for a song** bought or sold very cheaply
➤ **make a song and dance** (*informal*) to make a great fuss about something

songbird *NOUN* songbirds
a bird that sings sweetly

sonic *ADJECTIVE*
to do with sound or sound waves

sonic boom *NOUN* sonic booms
a loud noise caused by the shock wave of an aircraft travelling faster than the speed of sound

son-in-law *NOUN* sons-in-law
a daughter's husband

sonnet *NOUN* sonnets
a kind of poem with 14 lines

sonny *NOUN* (*informal*)
boy or young man • *Come on, sonny!*

sonorous (say **sonn**-er-us) *ADJECTIVE*
giving a loud deep sound • *a sonorous voice*

soon *ADVERB*
❶ in a short time from now ❷ not long after something ❸ early or quickly • *Don't leave so soon.*
➤ **as soon** as much or willingly • *I'd just as soon stay here.*
➤ **as soon as** at the moment that
➤ **sooner or later** at some time in the future

soot *NOUN*
the black powder left by smoke in a chimney or on a building
➤ **sooty** *ADJECTIVE*

soothe *VERB* soothes, soothing, soothed
❶ to make someone calmer or less upset ❷ to make a part of the body or a feeling feel less painful

soothing *ADJECTIVE*
that soothes someone or something
• *soothing music*
➤ **soothingly** *ADVERB*

soothsayer *NOUN* soothsayers
a prophet

sop *NOUN* sops
something unimportant you give to a troublesome person to make them feel better

sop *VERB* sops, sopping, sopped
➤ **sop something up** to soak up liquid with a sponge

sophisticated *ADJECTIVE*
❶ a sophisticated person has refined or cultured tastes and is experienced about

life ❷ complicated and advanced • *a sophisticated machine*
➤ **sophistication** NOUN

soporific ADJECTIVE
causing sleep or drowsiness

sopping ADJECTIVE
very wet; drenched

soppy ADJECTIVE
(*British*) (*informal*) sentimental in a silly way

soprano NOUN sopranos
a woman, girl or boy with a high singing voice

sorcerer NOUN sorcerers
a person who can perform magic

sorceress NOUN sorceresses
a woman who can perform magic

sorcery NOUN
magic or witchcraft

sordid ADJECTIVE
❶ dirty and nasty ❷ dishonourable or immoral • *sordid motives*

sore ADJECTIVE
❶ painful or smarting • *a sore throat*
❷ (*informal*) annoyed or offended ❸ serious or upsetting • *The bridge is in sore need of repair.*
➤ **soreness** NOUN

sore NOUN sores
a sore place on your body

> **SPELLING**
> Do not confuse this word with saw.

sorely ADVERB
seriously; very • *I was sorely tempted to run away.*

sorrel NOUN
❶ a herb with sharp-tasting leaves ❷ a reddish-brown horse

sorrow NOUN sorrows
❶ sadness or regret caused by loss or disappointment ❷ something that causes this • *He sat down and told her all his sorrows.*

sorrow VERB sorrows, sorrowing, sorrowed
to feel sorrow; to grieve

sorrowful ADJECTIVE
feeling or showing great sadness • *a sorrowful expression*
➤ **sorrowfully** ADVERB

sorry ADJECTIVE sorrier, sorriest
❶ feeling regret for something you have done and wanting to apologize • *I'm sorry I forgot your birthday.* ❷ feeling pity or sympathy for someone • *I'm sorry you've been ill.* ❸ wretched or unattractive • *His clothes were in a sorry state.*

sort NOUN sorts
❶ a group of things or people that are similar; a kind or variety • *What sort of fruit do you like?* ❷ (*in computing*) putting data in a particular order • *Can you help me do an alphabetical sort of these names?*
➤ **out of sorts** slightly unwell or depressed
➤ **sort of** (*informal*) rather; to some extent • *I sort of expected it.*

sort VERB sorts, sorting, sorted
to arrange things in groups according to their size or type
➤ **sort someone out** (*informal*) to deal with and punish someone
➤ **sort something out** to deal with and solve a problem or difficulty

sortie NOUN sorties
❶ an attack by troops coming out of a besieged place ❷ an attacking expedition by a military aircraft

SOS NOUN SOSs
an urgent appeal for help **WORD ORIGIN** the international Morse code signal of extreme distress, chosen because it is easy to recognize, but often said to stand for Save Our Souls

sosatie NOUN sosaties
(*S. African*) a number of meat pieces that have been spiced and placed on a skewer for grilling

sought
past tense of **seek**

soul NOUN souls
❶ the invisible part of a person that some people believe goes on living after the body has died ❷ a person's mind and emotions ❸ a person • *There isn't a soul about.* ❹ a kind of popular music that developed from gospel music

soulful ADJECTIVE
having or showing deep feeling • *his soulful dark eyes*
➤ **soulfully** ADVERB

sound NOUN sounds
❶ vibrations that travel through the air and can be detected by the ear; the sensation they produce ❷ sound reproduced in a film or recording ❸ a mental impression you get from something • *We don't like the sound of his plans.* ❹ a narrow stretch of water

connecting two seas; a strait • *Plymouth Sound*

sound *VERB* sounds, sounding, sounded
❶ to make a sound • *The trumpets sounded.* ❷ to make a sound with something • *Don't forget to sound your horn.* ❸ to give a certain impression when heard • *He sounds angry.* ❹ to test something by noting the sounds you can hear from it • *A doctor sounds a patient's lungs with a stethoscope.* ❺ to test the depth of water beneath a ship
➤ **sound someone out** to try to find out what a person thinks or feels about something

sound *ADJECTIVE*
❶ in good condition; not damaged ❷ healthy; not diseased ❸ reasonable or correct • *His ideas are sound.* ❹ reliable or secure • *a sound investment* ❺ thorough or deep • *She has a sound knowledge of the subject.* • *I am a sound sleeper.*
➤ **soundness** *NOUN*

sound barrier *NOUN*
the resistance of the air to objects moving at speeds near the speed of sound

sound bite *NOUN* sound bites
a very short part of a speech or statement broadcast on radio or television because it seems to sum up the person's opinion in a few words

sound effects *PLURAL NOUN*
sounds produced artificially to make a play, film, etc. seem more realistic

soundly *ADVERB*
deeply or thoroughly • *The boys were sleeping soundly.* • *They were soundly beaten in the final.*

soundtrack *NOUN* soundtracks
the sound or music that goes with a cinema film

soup *NOUN* soups
a liquid food made from meat, fish or vegetables
➤ **in the soup** (*informal*) in trouble

sour *ADJECTIVE*
❶ tasting sharp like vinegar or lemons ❷ stale and unpleasant; not fresh • *sour milk* ❸ bad-tempered and unfriendly • *He gave me a sour look.*
➤ **sourness** *NOUN*

sour *VERB* sours, souring, soured
to become sour or to make something sour

source *NOUN* sources
❶ the place where something comes from • *This website is a great source of information on volcanoes.* ❷ the starting point of a river

sour grapes *PLURAL NOUN*
pretending that something you want is no good because you know you cannot have it
(**WORD ORIGIN**) from a fable in which a fox says that the grapes he cannot reach are probably sour

sourly *ADVERB*
in a bad-tempered and unfriendly way • *'Why are you here?' she said sourly.*

souse *VERB* souses, sousing, soused
❶ to soak or drench something ❷ to soak fish in pickle

south *NOUN*
❶ the direction to the right of a person who faces east ❷ the southern part of a country, city or other area

south *ADJECTIVE & ADVERB*
towards or in the south; coming from the south
➤ **southerly** (say **su** th-er-lee) *ADJECTIVE*
➤ **southern** *ADJECTIVE*
➤ **southerner** *NOUN*
➤ **southernmost** *ADJECTIVE*

south-east *NOUN, ADJECTIVE & ADVERB*
midway between south and east
➤ **south-easterly** *ADJECTIVE*
➤ **south-eastern** *ADJECTIVE*

southward *ADJECTIVE & ADVERB*
towards the south
➤ **southwards** *ADVERB*

south-west *NOUN, ADJECTIVE & ADVERB*
midway between south and west
➤ **south-westerly** *ADJECTIVE*
➤ **south-western** *ADJECTIVE*

souvenir (say soo-ven-**eer**) *NOUN* souvenirs
something that you keep to remind you of a person, place or event (**WORD ORIGIN**) from French *se souvenir* = remember

sou'wester *NOUN* sou'westers
a waterproof hat with a wide flap at the back
(**WORD ORIGIN**) from *south-wester*, a wind from the south-west, often bringing rain

sovereign *NOUN* sovereigns
❶ a king or queen who is the ruler of a country; a monarch ❷ an old British gold coin, originally worth £1

a
b
c
d
e
f
g
h
i
j
k
l
m
n
o
p
q
r
s
t
u
v
w
x
y
z

sovereign *ADJECTIVE*
❶ supreme • *sovereign power* ❷ a sovereign state is independent and runs its own affairs

sovereignty *NOUN*
the power a country has to govern itself and make its own laws

sow (rhymes with go) *VERB* sows, sowing, sowed, sown or sowed
❶ to put seeds into the ground so that they will grow into plants ❷ to cause feelings or ideas to develop • *Her words sowed doubt in my mind.*
➤ **sower** *NOUN*

> **SPELLING**
> Take care not to confuse with **sew**, which means to work with a needle and thread.

sow (rhymes with cow) *NOUN* sows
a female pig

soya bean *NOUN* soya beans
a kind of bean from which edible oil and flour are made

soy sauce, soya sauce *NOUN*
a Chinese or Japanese sauce made from fermented soya beans

spa *NOUN* spas
a health resort where there is a spring of water containing mineral salts

space *NOUN* spaces
❶ the whole area outside the earth, where the stars and planets are ❷ an area or volume • *This table takes too much space.* ❸ an empty area; a gap • *There is a space at the back of the cupboard.* ❹ an interval of time • *We moved house twice in the space of a year.*

space *VERB* spaces, spacing, spaced
to arrange things so that there are spaces between them • *Space the posts about a metre apart.*

spacecraft *NOUN* spacecraft
a vehicle for travelling in outer space

spaceman *NOUN* spacemen
a male astronaut

spaceship *NOUN* spaceships
a spacecraft, especially one carrying people

space shuttle *NOUN* space shuttles
a spacecraft that can travel into space and land like a plane when it returns to earth

space station *NOUN* space stations
a satellite which orbits the earth and is used as a base by scientists and astronauts

space suit *NOUN* space suits
a protective suit which enables an astronaut to survive in space

space walk *NOUN* space walks
moving about or walking by an astronaut outside the spacecraft

spacewoman *NOUN* spacewomen
a female astronaut

spacious *ADJECTIVE*
providing a lot of space; roomy • *a spacious apartment*
➤ **spaciousness** *NOUN*

spade *NOUN* spades
❶ a tool with a long handle and a wide blade for digging ❷ a playing card with black shapes like upside-down hearts on it, each with a short stem

spadework *NOUN*
hard or uninteresting work done to prepare for an activity or project

spaghetti *NOUN*
pasta made in long thin sticks, which soften into strings when you cook them
> **WORD ORIGIN** Italian, = little strings

> **SPELLING**
> There is a silent **h** after the **g** in **spaghetti**.

span *NOUN* spans
❶ the length from end to end or across something ❷ the part between two uprights of an arch or bridge ❸ the length of a period of time ❹ the distance from the tip of your thumb to the tip of your little finger when your hand is spread out

span *VERB* spans, spanning, spanned
to reach from one side or end to the other • *A wooden bridge spans the river.*

spangle *NOUN* spangles
a small piece of glittering material
➤ **spangled** *ADJECTIVE*

spaniel *NOUN* spaniels
a kind of dog with long ears and silky fur

spank *VERB* spanks, spanking, spanked
to smack a person on the bottom as a punishment

spanking *ADJECTIVE*
brisk and lively • *at a spanking pace*

spanner *NOUN* spanners
(*British*) a tool for gripping and turning a nut or bolt

spar *NOUN* **spars**
a strong pole used for a mast or boom on a ship

spar *VERB* **spars, sparring, sparred**
❶ to practise boxing ❷ to argue with someone, often in a friendly way

spare *VERB* **spares, sparing, spared**
❶ to afford to give or do without something • *Can you spare a moment?* ❷ to be merciful towards someone; to not kill, hurt or harm a person or thing • *The duke agreed to spare their lives.* ❸ to avoid making a person suffer something • *Spare me the details.* ❹ to use or treat something economically • *No expense will be spared.*
➤ **to spare** left over without being needed • *We arrived with five minutes to spare.*

spare *ADJECTIVE*
❶ not used but kept ready in case it is needed; extra • *a spare wheel* ❷ thin or lean
➤ **go spare** (*informal*) to become very angry

spare *NOUN* **spares**
a spare thing or part

spare time *NOUN*
time not needed for work

sparing (say **spair**-ing) *ADJECTIVE*
careful or economical; not wasteful
➤ **sparingly** *ADVERB*

spark *NOUN* **sparks**
❶ a tiny glowing piece of something hot ❷ a flash produced electrically ❸ a trace of something • *a spark of hope*

spark *VERB* **sparks, sparking, sparked**
❶ to give off a spark or sparks ❷ to cause something • *The arrests sparked off a riot.*

sparking plug *NOUN* **sparking plugs**
(*British*) a spark plug

sparkle *VERB* **sparkles, sparkling, sparkled**
❶ to shine with tiny flashes of light • *The river sparkled in the sunlight.* ❷ to show brilliant wit or liveliness

sparkle *NOUN* **sparkles**
❶ a lot of tiny flashes of light • *There was a sparkle of excitement in her eyes.* ❷ liveliness • *The show lacked sparkle.*

sparkler *NOUN* **sparklers**
a hand-held firework that gives off sparks

sparkling wine *NOUN* **sparkling wines**
a bubbly wine

spark plug *NOUN* **spark plugs**
a device that makes a spark to ignite the fuel in an engine

sparrow *NOUN* **sparrows**
a small brown bird

sparse *ADJECTIVE*
thinly scattered; small in number or amount • *Vegetation on the island is sparse.*

sparsely *ADVERB*
in only small numbers or amounts • *It is a sparsely populated region.*

spartan *ADJECTIVE*
simple and without comfort or luxuries
WORD ORIGIN named after the people of *Sparta* in ancient Greece, famous for their hardiness

spasm *NOUN* **spasms**
❶ a sudden involuntary movement of a muscle ❷ a sudden brief burst of something • *a spasm of rage*

spasmodic *ADJECTIVE*
❶ happening or done at irregular intervals ❷ to do with or caused by a spasm
➤ **spasmodically** *ADVERB*

spat
past tense of **spit**

spat *NOUN* **spats**
a short gaiter

spate *NOUN* **spates**
❶ a lot of things coming one after another • *a recent spate of thefts* ❷ a sudden flood in a river

spatial *ADJECTIVE*
to do with space

spatter *VERB* **spatters, spattering, spattered**
❶ to scatter something wet in small drops • *He spattered paint all over the floor.* ❷ to splash someone or something • *She was spattered with mud.*

spatter *NOUN* **spatters**
a small amount of something in small drops

spatula *NOUN* **spatulas**
a tool like a knife with a broad blunt flexible blade, used for spreading or mixing things

spawn *NOUN*
❶ the eggs of fish, frogs, toads or shellfish ❷ the thread-like matter from which fungi grow

spawn *VERB* **spawns, spawning, spawned**
❶ to produce spawn ❷ to be produced from spawn ❸ to produce something in large numbers • *The film spawned a series of sequels.*

a b c d e f g h i j k l m n o p q r s t u v w x y z

spay *VERB* spays, spaying, spayed
to sterilize a female animal by removing the ovaries

speak *VERB* speaks, speaking, spoke, spoken
❶ to say something; to talk ❷ to talk or be able to talk in a foreign language • *Do you speak French?*
➤ **speak up** ❶ to speak more loudly ❷ to give your opinion

speaker *NOUN* speakers
❶ a person who is speaking ❷ someone who makes a speech ❸ the part of a radio, CD player, computer, etc. that the sound comes out of
➤ **the Speaker** the person who is in charge of the debates in some parliaments

spear *NOUN* spears
a weapon for throwing or stabbing, with a long shaft and a pointed tip

spear *VERB* spears, spearing, speared
to pierce something with a spear or with something pointed • *They were standing in their boats spearing fish.*

spearhead *VERB* spearheads, spearheading, spearheaded
to lead a campaign or attack

spearmint *NOUN*
mint used in cookery and for flavouring chewing gum

special *ADJECTIVE*
❶ not ordinary or usual; exceptional • *a special occasion* • *Take special care of it.*
❷ meant for a particular person or purpose • *You need a special tool for this job.*

special effects *PLURAL NOUN*
illusions created for films or television by using props, trick photography or computer images

specialist *NOUN* specialists
an expert in one subject • *a skin specialist*

speciality *NOUN* specialities
❶ something in which a person specializes • *There are lots of sports I like playing but my speciality is gymnastics.* ❷ a special product, especially a food

specialize (also **specialise**) *VERB* specializes, specializing, specialized
to give particular attention or study to one subject or thing • *She specialized in biology.*
➤ **specialization** *NOUN*

specially *ADVERB*
❶ in a special way ❷ for a special purpose • *I came specially to see you.*

special needs *PLURAL NOUN*
educational requirements resulting from learning difficulties, physical disability or emotional and behavioural difficulties • *children with special needs*

species (say **spee**-shiz) *NOUN* species
❶ a group of animals or plants that have the same features and can breed with each other ❷ a kind or sort • *a species of sledge*

specific *ADJECTIVE*
❶ definite or precise • *I gave you specific instructions on what to do.* ❷ to do with a particular thing • *The money was given for a specific purpose.*

specifically *ADVERB*
❶ clearly and precisely • *I specifically said we had to go.* ❷ in a special way or for a special purpose • *The car is designed specifically for people with disabilities.*

specification *NOUN* specifications
a detailed description of how to make or do something

specific gravity *NOUN* specific gravities
relative density

specify *VERB* specifies, specifying, specified
to name or list things precisely • *The recipe specified cream, not milk.*

specimen *NOUN* specimens
❶ a sample of something ❷ an example • *a fine specimen of an oak tree*

speck *NOUN* specks
❶ a tiny piece of something • *a speck of dust* ❷ a tiny mark or spot

speckle *NOUN* speckles
a small spot or mark

speckled *ADJECTIVE*
covered with small spots or marks • *a speckled hen*

specs *PLURAL NOUN* (*informal*)
spectacles

spectacle *NOUN* spectacles
❶ an impressive sight or display ❷ a ridiculous sight

spectacles *PLURAL NOUN*
(*British*) a pair of glasses
➤ **spectacled** *ADJECTIVE*

spectacular *ADJECTIVE*
very impressive to see • *spectacular scenery*

spectator *NOUN* spectators
a person who watches a game, show or other event

spectre *NOUN* spectres
a ghost
➤ **spectral** *ADJECTIVE*

spectrum *NOUN* spectra
❶ the bands of colours seen in a rainbow
❷ a wide range of things or ideas • *a broad spectrum of interests*

speculate *VERB* speculates, speculating, speculated
❶ to form opinions without having any definite evidence ❷ to invest in stocks or property in the hope of making a profit but with the risk of loss
➤ **speculation** *NOUN*
➤ **speculator** *NOUN*
➤ **speculative** *ADJECTIVE*

sped
past tense of **speed**

speech *NOUN* speeches
❶ the ability to speak or a person's way of speaking ❷ a talk to an audience ❸ a group of lines spoken by a character in a play

speechless *ADJECTIVE*
too surprised or emotional to be able to say anything

speech marks *PLURAL NOUN*
punctuation marks " " or ' ' used to show that someone is speaking; inverted commas

speed *NOUN* speeds
❶ a measure of the time in which something moves or happens ❷ being quick or fast
➤ **at speed** quickly

speed *VERB* speeds, speeding, sped (in senses 2 and 3 speeded)
❶ to go quickly • *The train sped by.* ❷ to drive faster than the legal limit
➤ **speed up** to become quicker
➤ **speed something up** to make something go or happen faster • *This will speed things up.*

speedboat *NOUN* speedboats
a fast motor boat

speed camera *NOUN* speed cameras
a camera by the side of a road which automatically photographs any vehicle which breaks the speed limit

speed hump *NOUN* speed humps
a ridge built across a road to make vehicles slow down

speed limit *NOUN* speed limits
the maximum speed at which vehicles may legally travel on a particular road

speedometer *NOUN* speedometers
a device in a vehicle, showing its speed

speedway *NOUN* speedways
a track for motorcycle racing

speedwell *NOUN* speedwells
a wild plant with small blue flowers

speedy *ADJECTIVE* speedier, speediest
quick or swift • *Thank you for your speedy reply.*
➤ **speedily** *ADVERB*

spell *VERB* spells, spelling, spelled or spelt
❶ to put letters in the right order to make a word or words ❷ a set of letters spell a word when they form it • *C-A-T spells 'cat'* ❸ to have something as a result • *Wet weather spells disaster for crops.*
➤ **speller** *NOUN*

spell *NOUN* spells
❶ a period of time • *We're in the middle of a cold spell.* ❷ a period of a certain work or activity • *He had a brief spell in the army.*
❸ a set of words that is supposed to have magical power

spellbound *ADJECTIVE*
with your attention completely held as if by magic • *We all sat spellbound as she told her story.*

spellchecker, spellcheck *NOUN* spellcheckers or spellchecks
a computer program that you use to check your writing to see if your spelling is correct

spelling *NOUN* spellings
❶ the way a word is spelled ❷ how well someone can spell • *Her spelling is poor.*

spend *VERB* spends, spending, spent
❶ to use money to pay for things ❷ to use up time, energy or effort in doing something • *Don't spend too much time on it.* ❸ to pass time doing something • *I spent the weekend painting my bedroom.*

spendthrift *NOUN* spendthrifts
a person who spends money extravagantly and wastefully

sperm *NOUN* **sperms** or **sperm**
the male cell that fuses with an ovum to
produce offspring

spew *VERB* **spews, spewing, spewed**
❶ to vomit ❷ to send out something
unpleasant in a stream • *The volcano was
spewing out lava.*

sphere *NOUN* **spheres**
❶ a perfectly round solid shape; the shape
of a ball ❷ a field of interest, activity or
knowledge • *The history of music is her main
sphere of interest.*

> **SPELLING**
> The 'f' sound is spelt **ph** in **sphere**.

spherical *ADJECTIVE*
having the shape of a sphere

spheroid *NOUN* **spheroids**
a solid which is sphere-like but not perfectly
spherical

sphinx *NOUN* **sphinxes**
a stone statue with the body of a lion and a
human head, especially the huge one (almost
5,000 years old) in Egypt **WORD ORIGIN** from
the *Sphinx* in Greek mythology, a winged
creature with a woman's head and a lion's body

spice *NOUN* **spices**
❶ a strong-tasting substance used to flavour
food, often made from dried parts of plants
❷ something that adds interest or excitement
• *Variety is the spice of life.*

spice *VERB* **spices, spicing, spiced**
❶ to flavour food with spices ❷ to make
something more interesting or exciting

spick and span *ADJECTIVE*
neat and clean

spicy *ADJECTIVE*
spicy food tastes strongly of spices

spider *NOUN* **spiders**
a small animal with eight legs that spins webs
to catch insects on which it feeds

spidery *ADJECTIVE*
spidery handwriting has long thin lines and
sharp angles, like a spider's legs

spike *NOUN* **spikes**
a pointed piece of metal; a sharp point

spike *VERB* **spikes, spiking, spiked** to pierce
something with a spike

spiked *ADJECTIVE*
with one or more spikes • *spiked running
shoes*

spiky *ADJECTIVE*
full of spikes or sharp points • *She has short
spiky hair.*

spill *VERB* **spills, spilling, spilt** or **spilled**
❶ to let something fall out of a container
• *Careful, you're spilling your drink.* ❷ to fall
out of a container • *The coins came spilling
out.*
> **spillage** *NOUN*

spill *NOUN* **spills**
❶ spilling; something spilt • *an oil spill at sea*
❷ a fall from a horse or bicycle

spin *VERB* **spins, spinning, spun**
❶ to turn round and round quickly or to
make something do this • *The plane was
spinning out of control.* • *He was spinning
a coin on the table.* ❷ to make raw wool or
cotton into threads by pulling and twisting
its fibres ❸ a spider or silkworm spins a web
or cocoon when it forms one out of threads
from its body
> **spin a yarn** to tell a story
> **spin something out** to make something
last as long as possible

spin *NOUN* **spins**
❶ a spinning movement ❷ a short outing in
a car

spinach *NOUN*
a vegetable with dark green leaves

spinal *ADJECTIVE*
to do with the spine

spinal cord *NOUN* **spinal cords**
the thick cord of nerves enclosed in the spine,
that carries messages to and from the brain

spindle *NOUN* **spindles**
❶ a thin rod on which you wind thread ❷ a
pin or bar that turns round or on which
something turns

spindly *ADJECTIVE*
thin and long or tall • *The creature stood on
two spindly legs.*

spin doctor *NOUN* **spin doctors**
a person whose job is to make information
or events seem favourable to their employer,
usually a politician or political party

spin drier *NOUN* **spin driers**
a machine in which washed clothes are spun
to remove excess water

spindrift *NOUN*
spray blown along the surface of the sea

spine *NOUN* **spines**
❶ the line of bones down the middle of your

back ❷ a sharp point on an animal or plant
• *This cactus has sharp spines.* ❸ the back
part of a book where the pages are joined
together

spine-chilling *ADJECTIVE*
frightening and exciting • *a spine-chilling
horror film*

spineless *ADJECTIVE*
❶ without a backbone ❷ lacking in
determination or strength of character

spinet *NOUN* spinets
a small harpsichord

spinney *NOUN* spinneys
(*British*) a small wood or thicket

spinning wheel *NOUN* spinning wheels
a household device for spinning wool or
cotton into thread

spin-off *NOUN* spin-offs
something extra produced while making
something else

spinster *NOUN* spinsters
an insulting word for a woman who has
not married, especially an older woman
WORD ORIGIN the original meaning was 'one
who spins' (because many unmarried women
used to earn their living by spinning, which
could be done at home)

spiny *ADJECTIVE*
covered with spines; prickly

spiral *ADJECTIVE*
going round and round a central point and
becoming gradually closer to it or further
from it; twisting continually round a central
line or cylinder

spiral *NOUN* spirals
a spiral line or course

spiral *VERB* spirals, spiralling, spiralled
❶ to move in a spiral • *A curl of grey smoke
began to spiral upwards.* ❷ to increase or
decrease continuously and quickly • *Prices
were spiralling.*

spire *NOUN* spires
a tall pointed part on top of a church tower

spirit *NOUN* spirits
❶ a person's mood or mind and feelings
• *He was in good spirits.* ❷ the part of a
person that is thought to survive death; a
person's soul ❸ a ghost or a supernatural
being ❹ courage or liveliness • *She answered
with spirit.* ❺ a kind of quality in something
• *the romantic spirit of the book* ❻ a strong
distilled alcoholic drink

spirit *VERB* spirits, spiriting, spirited
to carry off a person or thing quickly and
secretly • *They spirited her away during the
night.*

spirited *ADJECTIVE*
brave; self-confident and lively

spirit level *NOUN* spirit levels
a device consisting of a tube of liquid with
an air bubble in it, used to find out whether
something is level

spiritual *ADJECTIVE*
❶ to do with the human soul; not physical
❷ to do with religious beliefs
➤ **spiritually** *ADVERB*
➤ **spirituality** *NOUN*

spiritual *NOUN* spirituals
a religious folk song, originally sung by black
Christians in America

spiritualism *NOUN*
the belief that the spirits of dead people
communicate with living people
➤ **spiritualist** *NOUN*

spit *VERB* spits, spitting, spat or spit
❶ to send out drops of liquid forcibly from
your mouth • *He spat at me.* ❷ to force
something out of your mouth • *The baby
spat out her dummy.* ❸ to rain lightly • *It's
spitting with rain.*

spit *NOUN* spits
❶ saliva or spittle ❷ a long thin metal spike
put through meat to hold it while it is being
roasted ❸ a narrow strip of land sticking out
into the sea

spite *NOUN*
a desire to hurt or annoy someone
➤ **in spite of something** although something
has happened or is a fact • *We went out in
spite of the rain.*

spite *VERB* spites, spiting, spited
to hurt or annoy someone from spite

spiteful *ADJECTIVE*
behaving unkindly in order to hurt or annoy
someone • *That was a spiteful thing to say.*
➤ **spitefully** *ADVERB*
➤ **spitefulness** *NOUN*

spitfire *NOUN* spitfires
a fiery-tempered person

spitting image *NOUN*
an exact likeness

spittle *NOUN*
saliva, especially when it is spat out

a b c d e f g h i j k l m n o p q r s t u v w x y z

splash *VERB* splashes, splashing, splashed
❶ to make liquid fly about in drops ❷ liquid splashes when it flies about in drops ❸ to make a person or thing wet by splashing • *The bus splashed us as it went past.*

splash *NOUN* splashes
❶ the action, sound or mark of splashing ❷ a bright patch of colour or light
➤ **make a splash** to attract a lot of attention

splatter *VERB* splatters, splattering, splattered
to splash over something • *The ground was splattered with blood.*

splay *VERB* splays, splaying, splayed
to spread wide apart or make something do this • *He splayed his fingers.*

spleen *NOUN* spleens
an organ of the body, close to the stomach, that helps to keep the blood in good condition
➤ **vent your spleen on someone** to be bad-tempered or spiteful towards them

splendid *ADJECTIVE*
❶ magnificent; full of splendour ❷ excellent; very fine
➤ **splendidly** *ADVERB*

splendour *NOUN*
a brilliant display or appearance • *the dazzling splendour of court life*

splice *VERB* splices, splicing, spliced
❶ to join pieces of rope or wire by twisting their strands together ❷ to join pieces of film, tape or wood by overlapping the ends

splint *NOUN* splints
a straight piece of wood or metal tied to a broken arm or leg to hold it firm

splinter *NOUN* splinters
a thin sharp piece of wood, glass or stone broken off a larger piece

splinter *VERB* splinters, splintering, splintered
to break into splinters • *The boat's hull began to splinter and crack.*

split *VERB* splits, splitting, split
❶ to break apart, especially along the length of something ❷ to divide something into parts ❸ to divide something among people • *I'll split the cost with you.*
➤ **split up** ❶ to end a marriage or other relationship ❷ to go off in different directions

split *NOUN* splits
❶ the splitting or dividing of something ❷ a crack or tear in something, where it has split
➤ **the splits** an acrobatic position in which your legs are stretched widely in opposite directions

split second *NOUN*
a very brief moment of time; an instant

split-second *ADJECTIVE*
❶ done very quickly • *He had to make a split-second decision.* ❷ very precise • *split-second timing*

splodge *NOUN* splodges
a dirty mark or stain

splurge *VERB* splurges, splurging, splurged (*informal*)
to spend a lot of money on something, especially a luxury • *She splurged her first week's wages on a make-over.*

splutter *VERB* splutters, spluttering, spluttered
❶ to make a quick series of spitting or coughing sounds ❷ to speak quickly and in a confused way • *'But... but... you can't!' he spluttered.*
➤ **splutter** *NOUN*

spoil *VERB* spoils, spoiling, spoilt or spoiled
❶ to damage something and make it useless or unsatisfactory ❷ to make someone selfish by always letting them have what they want ❸ to treat someone kindly • *Go on, spoil yourself!*

spoils *PLURAL NOUN*
plunder or other things gained by a victor • *the spoils of war*

spoilsport *NOUN* spoilsports
a person who spoils other people's enjoyment of things

spoke
past tense of **speak**

spoke *NOUN* spokes
each of the bars or rods that go from the centre of a wheel to its rim

spokesman *NOUN* spokesmen
a spokesperson, especially a man

spokesperson *NOUN* spokespersons
a person who speaks on behalf of a group of people

spokeswoman *NOUN* spokeswomen
a female spokesperson

sponge *NOUN* sponges
❶ a sea creature with a soft porous body ❷ the skeleton of this creature or a piece of a similar substance, used for washing or

padding things ❸ a soft lightweight cake or pudding

sponge VERB sponges, sponging, sponged
❶ to wipe or wash something with a wet sponge ❷ to get money or food off other people without giving anything in return • *He's always sponging off his friends.*
➤ **sponger** NOUN

spongy ADJECTIVE
soft and absorbent, like a sponge • *The ground was spongy under his feet.*

sponsor NOUN sponsors
❶ a person or organization that provides money for an arts or sports event or for a broadcast in return for advertising
❷ someone who gives money to a charity in return for something achieved by another person
➤ **sponsorship** NOUN

sponsor VERB sponsors, sponsoring, sponsored
to be a sponsor for a person or thing • *Many marathon runners are sponsored to raise money for charity.*

spontaneous (say spon-**tay**-nee-us) ADJECTIVE
happening or done naturally; not forced or suggested by someone else • *They burst into spontaneous applause.*
➤ **spontaneously** ADVERB
➤ **spontaneity** NOUN

spoof NOUN spoofs
an amusing imitation of a film, television programme, etc. **WORD ORIGIN** originally the name of a card game invented and named by an English comedian, Arthur Roberts (1852-1933)

spook NOUN spooks (*informal*)
a ghost

spooky ADJECTIVE spookier, spookiest
(*informal*) strange and frightening; haunted by ghosts • *The house was spooky in the dark.*
➤ **spookily** ADVERB

spool NOUN spools
a rod or cylinder on which something is wound

spoon NOUN spoons
a small device with a rounded bowl on a handle, used for lifting food to your mouth or for stirring or measuring things

spoon VERB spoons, spooning, spooned
to take or lift something with a spoon

spoonerism NOUN spoonerisms
an accidental swapping round of the initial letters of two words, e.g. by saying

a boiled sprat instead of *a spoiled brat* **WORD ORIGIN** named after the Reverend William *Spooner* (1844-1930), who often made mistakes of this kind

spoon-feed VERB spoon-feeds, spoon-feeding, spoon-fed
❶ to feed a baby or invalid with a spoon
❷ to provide someone with so much help or information that they do not have to make any effort

spoonful NOUN spoonfuls
as much as a spoon will hold

spoor NOUN spoors
the track left by an animal

sporadic ADJECTIVE
happening or found at irregular intervals; scattered
➤ **sporadically** ADVERB

spore NOUN spores
a tiny reproductive cell of a plant such as a fungus or fern

sporran NOUN sporrans
a pouch worn in front of a kilt

sport NOUN sports
❶ a game or activity that exercises your body, especially a game you play outdoors • *What sports do you play?* ❷ games of this kind • *Are you keen on sport?* ❸ (*informal*) a person who behaves well when they are defeated or teased • *Thanks for being such a good sport.*

sport VERB sports, sporting, sported
❶ to wear something in a showy way • *He sported a gold tiepin.* ❷ (*old use*) to play; to amuse yourself

sporting ADJECTIVE
❶ connected with sport; interested in sport
❷ behaving fairly and generously

sporting chance NOUN
a reasonable chance of success

sports car NOUN sports cars
an open low-built fast car

sports jacket NOUN sports jackets
a man's jacket for informal wear (not part of a suit)

sportsman NOUN sportsmen
a man who takes part in sport

sportsmanship NOUN
sporting behaviour; behaving fairly and generously to rivals

a
b
c
d
e
f
g
h
i
j
k
l
m
n
o
p
q
r
s
t
u
v
w
x
y
z

sportswoman *NOUN* sportswomen
a woman who takes part in sport

spot *NOUN* spots
❶ a small round mark ❷ a pimple on your skin ❸ a small amount of something • *We had a spot of trouble.* ❹ a place • *This is a nice spot.* ❺ a drop • *a few spots of rain*
➤ **on the spot** ❶ without delay or change of place • *We can repair your bike on the spot.* ❷ under pressure to take action • *This really puts him on the spot!*
➤ **spot on** (*informal*) exactly right or accurate

spot *VERB* spots, spotting, spotted
❶ to notice or recognize someone or something • *We spotted her in the crowd.* ❷ to watch for certain things and take note of them, as a hobby • *train-spotting*
➤ **spotter** *NOUN*

spot check *NOUN* spot checks
a check, usually without warning, on one of a group of people or things

spotless *ADJECTIVE*
perfectly clean
➤ **spotlessly** *ADVERB*

spotlight *NOUN* spotlights
❶ a strong light that can shine on one small area ❷ the centre of public attention • *The Royal Family are used to being in the spotlight.*

spotted *ADJECTIVE*
marked or decorated with spots • *a spotted handkerchief*

spotty *ADJECTIVE*
marked with spots

spouse *NOUN* spouses
a person's husband or wife

spout *NOUN* spouts
❶ a pipe or similar opening from which liquid can pour ❷ a jet of liquid

spout *VERB* spouts, spouting, spouted
❶ to come out as a jet of liquid ❷ (*informal*) to speak for a long time

sprain *VERB* sprains, spraining, sprained
to injure a joint by twisting it

sprain *NOUN* sprains
an injury by spraining

sprat *NOUN* sprats
a small edible fish

sprawl *VERB* sprawls, sprawling, sprawled
❶ to sit or lie with your arms and legs spread out loosely • *She was sprawling in*

an armchair by the fire. • *The blow sent him sprawling to the ground.* ❷ to spread out loosely or untidily • *Looking down, I could see the city sprawling beneath me.*

sprawl *NOUN*
something that spreads over a large area in an untidy way • *the sprawl of Cairo*

spray *VERB* sprays, spraying, sprayed
to scatter tiny drops of liquid over something

spray *NOUN* sprays
❶ tiny drops of liquid sent through the air ❷ a device for spraying liquid ❸ a liquid for spraying • *fly spray* ❹ a single shoot with its leaves and flowers ❺ a small bunch of flowers

spread *VERB* spreads, spreading, spread
❶ to open or stretch something out to its full size • *He spread the map on the table.* ❷ to make something cover a surface • *We spread jam on the bread.* ❸ to become longer or wider • *The stain was spreading.* ❹ to become or make something more widely known or distributed • *The story quickly spread round the village.* • *We spread the news.*

spread *NOUN* spreads
❶ a paste for spreading on bread ❷ the action or result of spreading • *Nothing could stop the spread of the disease.* ❸ a thing's breadth or extent ❹ (*informal*) a large or grand meal

spreadeagled *ADJECTIVE*
with arms and legs stretched out
• *He lay spreadeagled on the bed.*
WORD ORIGIN originally = a picture of an eagle with legs and wings stretched out, used as an emblem on a knight's shield, inn sign, etc.

spreadsheet *NOUN* spreadsheets
a computer program that allows you to set out tables of figures and to do complex calculations

spree *NOUN* sprees
a short time you spend doing something you enjoy • *a shopping spree*

sprig *NOUN* sprigs
a small branch or shoot

sprightly *ADJECTIVE* sprightlier, sprightliest
lively and full of energy

spring *VERB* springs, springing, sprang, sprung
❶ to jump or move quickly or suddenly • *He sprang to his feet.* ❷ to grow or come from something • *The trouble has sprung from carelessness.* • *Weeds have started to spring*

up. ❸ to produce something without warning • *They sprang a surprise on us.*

spring *NOUN* **springs**
❶ the season of the year when most plants begin to grow ❷ a coil of wire or metal that goes back to its original shape when you bend or squeeze it and let it go ❸ a sudden upward movement ❹ a place where water comes up naturally from the ground

springboard *NOUN* **springboards**
a springy board from which people jump in diving and gymnastics

springbok *NOUN* **springboks** or **springbok**
a South African gazelle
WORD ORIGIN Afrikaans, from Dutch *springen* = to spring + *bok* = buck, antelope

spring-clean *VERB* **spring-cleans, spring-cleaning, spring-cleaned**
to clean a house thoroughly in springtime

spring onion *NOUN* **spring onions**
(*British*) a small onion with a long green stem, eaten raw in salads

spring roll *NOUN* **spring rolls**
a Chinese pancake filled with vegetables and (sometimes) meat and fried until crisp

springtime *NOUN*
the season of spring

springy *ADJECTIVE* **springier, springiest**
able to spring back easily after being bent or squeezed
➤ **springiness** *NOUN*

sprinkle *VERB* **sprinkles, sprinkling, sprinkled**
to make tiny drops or pieces fall on something • *I like to sprinkle sugar over strawberries.*
➤ **sprinkler** *NOUN*

sprinkling *NOUN* **sprinklings**
a few here and there; a small amount • *a sprinkling of stars in the sky*

sprint *VERB* **sprints, sprinting, sprinted**
to run very fast for a short distance

sprint *NOUN* **sprints**
a short fast race
➤ **sprinter** *NOUN*

sprite *NOUN* **sprites**
an elf, fairy or goblin

sprocket *NOUN* **sprockets**
each of the row of teeth round a wheel, fitting into links on a chain

sprout *VERB* **sprouts, sprouting, sprouted**
to start to grow; to put out shoots • *New leaves were sprouting from the trees.*

sprout *NOUN* **sprouts**
❶ a shoot of a plant ❷ a Brussels sprout

spruce *NOUN* **spruces**
a kind of fir tree

spruce *ADJECTIVE*
neat and smart

spruce *VERB* **spruces, sprucing, spruced**
to smarten someone or something • *I'd better spruce myself up.*

spry *ADJECTIVE* **spryer, spryest**
active, nimble and lively • *a spry old gentleman*

spud *NOUN* **spuds** (*informal*)
a potato

spume *NOUN*
froth or foam

spur *NOUN* **spurs**
❶ a sharp device worn on the heel of a rider's boot to urge a horse to go faster ❷ something shaped like a spur, such as a hard spike on the back of a cock's leg ❸ something that encourages you to do something ❹ a ridge that sticks out from a mountain
➤ **on the spur of the moment** on an impulse; without planning

spur *VERB* **spurs, spurring, spurred**
❶ to urge someone on or encourage them to do something • *The letter spurred him into action.* ❷ to use spurs to make a horse go faster

spurious *ADJECTIVE*
not genuine

spurn *VERB* **spurns, spurning, spurned**
to refuse to accept something • *She spurned his offer of help.*

spurt *VERB* **spurts, spurting, spurted**
to gush out • *Blood spurted from the wound.*

spurt *NOUN* **spurts**
❶ a sudden gush ❷ a sudden increase in speed or effort • *He put on a spurt and caught us up.*

sputter *VERB* **sputters, sputtering, sputtered**
❶ to make a quick series of spitting or popping sounds • *The engine sputtered into life.* ❷ to speak quickly and in a confused way • *'W–What?' she sputtered.*

sputum *NOUN*
saliva or phlegm

spy *NOUN* spies
someone who works secretly for one country, person, etc. to find out things about another

spy *VERB* spies, spying, spied
❶ to be a spy ❷ to keep watch secretly • *Have you been spying on me?* ❸ to see or notice something • *She spied a house in the distance.*

squabble *VERB* squabbles, squabbling, squabbled
to quarrel or bicker

squabble *NOUN* squabbles
a minor quarrel or argument

squad *NOUN* squads
a small group of people working or being trained together

squadron *NOUN* squadrons
part of an army, navy or air force

squalid *ADJECTIVE*
dirty and unpleasant • *He lived in a squalid little room.*

squall *NOUN* squalls
❶ a sudden storm or gust of wind ❷ a baby's loud cry

squall *VERB* squalls, squalling, squalled
a baby squalls when it cries loudly

squally *ADJECTIVE*
squally weather is windy and stormy

squalor *NOUN*
dirty and unpleasant conditions • *Some families were living in squalor.*

squander *VERB* squanders, squandering, squandered
to spend money or time wastefully

square *NOUN* squares
❶ a flat shape with four equal sides and four right angles ❷ an area in a town or city, surrounded by buildings ❸ the result of multiplying a number by itself • *9 is the square of 3 (9 = 3 x 3).*

square *ADJECTIVE*
❶ having the shape of a square ❷ forming a right angle • *The desk has square corners.* ❸ equal or even • *The teams are all square with six points each.* ❹ used to give the length of each side of a square shape or object • *The carpet is four metres square.* ❺ used to give a measurement of an area • *an area of 25 square metres*
➤ **squareness** *NOUN*

square *VERB* squares, squaring, squared
❶ to make a thing have straight edges and right angles ❷ to multiply a number by itself • *5 squared is 25.* ❸ to square with something is to match it or agree with it • *His story doesn't square with yours.* ❹ to settle or pay a bill or debt

square deal *NOUN* square deals
a deal or arrangement that is honest and fair

squarely *ADVERB*
directly or exactly • *She turned and looked me squarely in the eye.*

square meal *NOUN* square meals
a good satisfying meal

square root *NOUN* square roots
the number that gives a particular number if it is multiplied by itself • *3 is the square root of 9 (3 x 3 = 9).*

squash *VERB* squashes, squashing, squashed
❶ to press something so that it becomes flat or out of shape ❷ to force something into a small space; to pack something tightly • *We squashed ourselves into the minibus.* ❸ to stop something from developing • *These rumours were quickly squashed.*

squash *NOUN* squashes
❶ a lot of people forced into a small space ❷ a fruit-flavoured soft drink ❸ a game played with rackets and a soft ball in a special indoor court ❹ a kind of gourd used as a vegetable

squat *VERB* squats, squatting, squatted
❶ to sit back on your heels; to crouch ❷ to live in an unoccupied building without permission
➤ **squatter** *NOUN*

squat *NOUN* squats
an unoccupied building that people are living in without permission

squat *ADJECTIVE*
short and fat

squaw *NOUN* squaws
a North American Indian woman or wife

USAGE
This word is offensive.

squawk *VERB* squawks, squawking, squawked
to make a loud harsh cry

squawk *NOUN* squawks
a loud harsh cry

squeak *VERB* squeaks, squeaking, squeaked
to make a short high-pitched cry or sound

squeak *NOUN* squeaks
a short high-pitched cry or sound

squeaky *ADJECTIVE*
making squeaks • *a squeaky floorboard*

squeal *VERB* squeals, squealing, squealed
to make a long shrill cry or sound • *The girls squealed with delight.*

squeal *NOUN* squeals
a long shrill cry or sound

squeamish *ADJECTIVE*
easily disgusted or shocked
➤ **squeamishness** *NOUN*

squeeze *VERB* squeezes, squeezing, squeezed
❶ to press something from opposite sides, especially to get liquid out of it ❷ to force your way into or through a place • *We squeezed through a gap in the hedge.*
➤ **squeezer** *NOUN*

squeeze *NOUN* squeezes
❶ the action of squeezing ❷ a drop of liquid squeezed out • *Add a squeeze of lemon.* ❸ a tight fit • *We all got in but it was a bit of a squeeze.* ❹ a time when money is difficult to get or borrow

squelch *VERB* squelches, squelching, squelched
to make a sound like someone treading in thick mud

squelch *NOUN* squelches
a squelching sound

squib *NOUN* squibs
a small firework that hisses and then explodes

squid *NOUN* squids
a sea animal with eight short tentacles and two long ones

squiggle *NOUN* squiggles
a short curly line

squint *VERB* squints, squinting, squinted
❶ to peer at something or look at it with half-shut eyes • *She squinted through the keyhole.* ❷ to have eyes that look in different directions at the same time

squint *NOUN* squints
a fault in someone's eyesight that makes them squint

squire *NOUN* squires
❶ the man who owns most of the land in a country parish or district ❷ a young nobleman in the Middle Ages who served a knight

squirm *VERB* squirms, squirming, squirmed
to wriggle about, especially when you feel embarrassed or awkward

squirrel *NOUN* squirrels
a small animal with a bushy tail and red or grey fur, living in trees **WORD ORIGIN** from Greek *skiouros*, from *skia* = shadow + *oura* = tail (because its long bushy tail cast a shadow over its body and kept it cool)

squirt *VERB* squirts, squirting, squirted
to send liquid out in a jet or to come out like this • *Orange juice squirted in his eye.*

squirt *NOUN* squirts
a jet of liquid

St., St *ABBREVIATION*
❶ Saint ❷ Street

stab *VERB* stabs, stabbing, stabbed
to pierce or wound someone with something sharp

stab *NOUN* stabs
❶ the action of stabbing ❷ a sudden sharp pain • *She felt a stab of fear.* ❸ (*informal*) an attempt • *I'll have a stab at it.*

stability *NOUN*
being stable or steady

stabilize (also **stabilise**) *VERB* stabilizes, stabilizing, stabilized
to make something stable or to become stable

stabilizer (also **stabiliser**) *NOUN* stabilizers
a device for keeping a vehicle or ship steady

stable *ADJECTIVE*
❶ steady and firmly fixed or balanced ❷ not likely to change or end suddenly • *a stable relationship* ❸ sensible and dependable

stable *NOUN* stables
a building where horses are kept

stable *VERB* stables, stabling, stabled
to keep a horse in a stable

staccato *ADVERB & ADJECTIVE*
(*in music*) played with each note short and separate

stack *NOUN* stacks
❶ a neat pile ❷ a haystack ❸ (*informal*) a large amount • *I have a stack of work to get through.* • *There's stacks to do.* ❹ a single tall chimney; a group of small chimneys

stack *VERB* stacks, stacking, stacked
to pile things up • *Boxes were stacked against one wall.*

stadium *NOUN* stadiums
a sports ground surrounded by seats for spectators

staff *NOUN* staffs or, in sense 4, staves
❶ the people who work in an office, shop, etc. ❷ the teachers in a school or college ❸ a stick or pole used as a weapon or support or as a symbol of authority ❹ a set of five horizontal lines on which music is written

staff *VERB* staffs, staffing, staffed
to provide a place or organization with a staff of people • *The centre is staffed by a team of volunteers.*

stag *NOUN* stags
a male deer

stage *NOUN* stages
❶ a platform for performances in a theatre or hall ❷ a point or part of a process or journey • *Now for the final stage.*
➤ **the stage** the profession of acting or working in the theatre

stage *VERB* stages, staging, staged
❶ to present a performance on a stage ❷ to organize an event • *We decided to stage a protest.*

stagecoach *NOUN* stagecoaches
a horse-drawn coach of a kind that used to run regularly from one point to another along the same route **WORD ORIGIN** so called because it ran in stages, picking up passengers at points along the route

stage fright *NOUN*
fear or nervousness before or while performing to an audience

stage-manage *VERB* stage-manages, stage-managing, stage-managed
❶ to be stage manager of a performance ❷ to organize and control an event so that it has a particular effect

stage manager *NOUN* stage managers
the person in charge of the scenery, lighting, sound, etc. during a stage performance

stage-struck *ADJECTIVE*
loving the theatre and longing to be an actor

stagger *VERB* staggers, staggering, staggered
❶ to walk unsteadily ❷ to amaze or shock someone • *I was staggered at the price.* ❸ to arrange things so that they do not all happen at the same time • *We stagger our holidays so that there is always someone here.*
➤ **stagger** *NOUN*

staggering *ADJECTIVE*
very surprising and almost unbelievable • *a staggering amount of money*

stagnant *ADJECTIVE*
❶ not flowing ❷ not active or developing • *Business is stagnant.*

stagnate *VERB* stagnates, stagnating, stagnated
❶ to be stagnant ❷ to be dull through lack of activity or variety
➤ **stagnation** *NOUN*

staid *ADJECTIVE*
steady and serious in manner

stain *NOUN* stains
❶ a dirty mark that is difficult to remove ❷ a blemish on someone's character or past record ❸ a liquid used for staining things

stain *VERB* stains, staining, stained
❶ to make a stain on something ❷ to colour material or wood with a liquid that sinks into the surface

stained glass *NOUN*
pieces of coloured glass held together in a lead framework to make a picture or pattern

stainless *ADJECTIVE*
without a stain

stainless steel *NOUN*
steel that does not rust easily

stair *NOUN* stairs
each of the fixed steps in a series that lead from one level or floor to another in a building

staircase *NOUN* staircases
a set of stairs

stairway *NOUN* stairways
a staircase

stairwell *NOUN* stairwells
the space going up through a building, which contains the stairs

stake *NOUN* stakes
❶ a thick pointed stick to be driven into the ground ❷ the post to which people used to be tied for execution by being burnt alive ❸ an amount of money bet on something ❹ an investment that gives a person a share or interest in a business
➤ **at stake** at risk of being lost

stake *VERB* stakes, staking, staked
❶ to fasten, support or mark something out with stakes ❷ to bet or risk money on an event
➤ **stake a claim** to claim or obtain a right to something

SPELLING
Be careful, this sounds the same as **steak**.

stalactite *NOUN* stalactites
a stony spike hanging like an icicle from the roof of a cave

> USAGE
>
> See note at **stalagmite**.

stalagmite *NOUN* stalagmites
a stony spike standing like a pillar on the floor of a cave

> USAGE
>
> Remember that a **stalagmite** stands up from the ground, while a **stalactite** hangs down from the ceiling.

stale *ADJECTIVE*
❶ no longer fresh ❷ bored and lacking new ideas because you have been doing something for too long

stalemate *NOUN*
❶ a drawn position in chess when a player cannot make a move without putting the king in check ❷ a deadlock; a situation in which neither side in an argument will give way

stalk *NOUN* stalks
a stem of a plant or fruit

stalk *VERB* stalks, stalking, stalked
❶ to track or hunt a person or animal stealthily ❷ to walk in a stiff or angry way • *He stalked out of the room.*

stall *NOUN* stalls
❶ a table or counter from which things are sold ❷ a place for one animal in a stable or shed

stall *VERB* stalls, stalling, stalled
❶ an engine or vehicle stalls when it stops suddenly because of lack of power ❷ to delay things or avoid giving an answer to give yourself more time

stallion *NOUN* stallions
a male horse

stalls *PLURAL NOUN*
the seats in the lowest level of a theatre

stalwart *ADJECTIVE*
strong and faithful • *my stalwart supporters*

stamen *NOUN* stamens
the part of a flower that produces pollen

stamina *NOUN*
the strength and energy you need to keep doing something for a long time

stammer *VERB* stammers, stammering, stammered
to keep repeating the same syllables when you speak

stammer *NOUN* stammers
a tendency to stammer

stamp *NOUN* stamps
❶ a small piece of gummed paper with a special design on it; a postage stamp ❷ a small device for pressing words or marks on something; the words or marks made by this ❸ a distinctive characteristic • *His story bears the stamp of truth.*

stamp *VERB* stamps, stamping, stamped
❶ to bang your foot heavily on the ground ❷ to walk with loud heavy steps ❸ to stick a postage stamp on something ❹ to press a mark or design on something • *The librarian stamped my books.*
➤ **stamp something out** to put an end to something • *We have stamped out vandalism in the area.*

stampede *NOUN* stampedes
a sudden rush by animals or people

stampede *VERB* stampedes, stampeding, stampeded
animals or people stampede when they rush fast and wildly

stance *NOUN* stances
❶ the way a person or animal stands ❷ a person's attitude to something

stanchion *NOUN* stanchions
an upright bar or post forming a support

stand *VERB* stands, standing, stood
❶ to be on your feet without moving; to rise to your feet • *We were standing at the back of the hall.* • *Please stand up.* ❷ to put something in an upright position • *We stood the vase on the table.* ❸ to be somewhere • *The castle stood on the top of a hill.* ❹ to stay the same • *My offer still stands.* ❺ to be a candidate for election • *She stood for Parliament.* ❻ to be able to bear or tolerate something • *I can't stand that noise.* ❼ to provide and pay for something • *I'll stand you a drink.*
➤ **it stands to reason** it is reasonable or obvious
➤ **stand by** to be ready for action
➤ **stand for something** ❶ to represent or mean something • *'US' stands for 'United States'.* ❷ to tolerate or put up with something • *She won't stand for any arguments.*
➤ **stand in for someone** to take someone's place
➤ **stand out** to be clear or obvious

➤ **stand up for someone** to support or defend someone
➤ **stand up to someone** to refuse to be threatened by someone
➤ **stand up to something** to stay in good condition despite rough treatment • *The bridge is designed to stand up to high winds.*

stand *NOUN* stands
❶ something made for putting things on • *a music stand* ❷ a stall where things are sold or displayed ❸ a building at a sports ground with a roof and rows of seats for spectators ❹ a standing position • *He took his stand near the door.* ❺ when someone resists an attack or defends their opinion • *The time has come to make a stand.*

standard *NOUN* standards
❶ how good something is • *a high standard of work* ❷ a thing used to measure or judge something else ❸ a special flag • *the royal standard*

standard *ADJECTIVE*
❶ of the usual or average quality or kind • *The logs are sawn into pieces of standard sizes.* ❷ regarded as the best and widely used • *the standard book on spiders*

standard assessment task *NOUN* standard assessment tasks
a standard test given to schoolchildren to assess their progress in one of the subjects of the national curriculum

Standard English *NOUN*
the form of English widely accepted as the normal and correct form. It is taught in schools and spoken and written by educated people.

standardize (also **standardise**) *VERB*
standardizes, standardizing, standardized
to make things be of a standard size or type
➤ **standardization** *NOUN*

standard lamp *NOUN* standard lamps
(*British*) a lamp on an upright pole that stands on the floor

standard of living *NOUN*
the level of comfort and wealth that a country or a person has

standby *NOUN* standbys
❶ something or someone kept to be used if needed ❷ a system by which tickets for a play or an air flight can be bought cheaply at the last minute if there are any seats left
➤ **on standby** ready to be used if needed
• *Troops were on standby during the crisis.*

stand-in *NOUN* stand-ins
a deputy or substitute

standing *NOUN*
❶ a person's status or reputation ❷ the period for which something has existed • *a contract of five years' standing*

standing order *NOUN* standing orders
an instruction to a bank to make regular payments or to a trader to supply something regularly

stand-offish *ADJECTIVE*
cold and formal; not friendly

standpipe *NOUN* standpipes
a pipe connected directly to a water supply, especially one set up in the street to provide water in an emergency

standpoint *NOUN* standpoints
a way of thinking about something; a point of view

standstill *NOUN*
a stop; an end to movement or activity • *The traffic has come to a complete standstill.*

stanza *NOUN* stanzas
a verse of poetry

staple *NOUN* staples
❶ a small piece of metal pushed through papers and clenched to fasten them together ❷ a U-shaped nail ❸ a basic or important food or product that people eat or use a lot

staple *VERB* staples, stapling, stapled
to fasten pieces of paper together with a staple

staple *ADJECTIVE*
main or usual • *Rice is their staple food.*

stapler *NOUN* staplers
a device for putting staples in paper

star *NOUN* stars
❶ a large mass of burning gas that is seen as a bright speck of light in the sky at night ❷ a shape with a number of points or rays sticking out from it; an asterisk ❸ an object or mark of this shape showing rank or quality • *a five-star hotel* ❹ a famous performer; one of the chief performers in a play, film or show

star *VERB* stars, starring, starred
❶ to be one of the main performers in a film or show • *John Wayne starred in many westerns.* ❷ to have someone as a main performer • *The film starred Robin Williams as a grown-up Peter Pan.*

starboard *NOUN*
the right-hand side of a ship or aircraft when

you are facing forward. Compare with **port**.
WORD ORIGIN from Old English *steorbord* = rudder side (because early sailing ships were steered with a paddle mounted on the right-hand side)

starch *NOUN* starches
❶ a white carbohydrate in bread, potatoes and other food ❷ a form of this substance used to stiffen clothes

starch *VERB* starches, starching, starched
to stiffen something with starch

starchy *ADJECTIVE*
❶ starchy food contains a lot of starch ❷ a starchy person behaves in a very stiff way

stardom *NOUN*
being a star performer

stare *VERB* stares, staring, stared
to look at something intensely

stare *NOUN* stares
a long fixed look • *I gave him a hard stare.*

SPELLING
Take care not to confuse this word with **stair**.

starfish *NOUN* starfish or starfishes
a sea animal shaped like a star with five points

stark *ADJECTIVE*
❶ complete or unmistakable • *They watched in stark terror.* ❷ desolate and bare • *the stark lunar landscape*
➤ **starkly** *ADVERB*
➤ **starkness** *NOUN*

stark *ADVERB*
completely or entirely • *stark naked*

starlight *NOUN*
light from the stars

starling *NOUN* starlings
a noisy black or brown bird with speckled feathers

starred *ADJECTIVE*
marked with an asterisk or star symbol • *The starred items on the list are not for sale.*

starry *ADJECTIVE*
full of stars • *a starry night*

starry-eyed *ADJECTIVE*
made happy by foolish dreams or unrealistic hopes

start *VERB* starts, starting, started
❶ to begin something or to make it begin
❷ to make an engine or machine begin

running • *I'll start the car.* ❸ to begin a journey ❹ to make a sudden movement because of pain or surprise

start *NOUN* starts
❶ the beginning of something • *We've made a good start.* ❷ the place where a race starts
❸ an advantage that someone starts with • *We gave the young ones ten minutes' start.*
❹ a sudden movement of surprise or fear • *She woke with a start.*

starter *NOUN* starters
❶ a small amount of food served before the main course of a meal ❷ someone who starts a race

startle *VERB* startles, startling, startled
to surprise or alarm a person or animal

starvation *NOUN*
suffering or death from lack of food

starve *VERB* starves, starving, starved
❶ to suffer or die from lack of food; to make someone do this • *The prisoners had been starved to death.* ❷ to deprive someone of something they need • *She was starved of love.*

starving *ADJECTIVE* (*informal*)
very hungry

stash *VERB* stashes, stashing, stashed (*informal*)
to store something safely in a secret place

state *NOUN* states
❶ the quality of a person or thing or their circumstances; the way they are
❷ an organized community under one government or forming part of a republic • *the State of Israel* • *the 50 States of the USA* ❸ a country's government • *Help for the earthquake victims was provided by the state.*
❹ (*informal*) an excited or upset condition • *Don't get into a state about the robbery.*
➤ **in state** in a grand style or with grand ceremony

state *VERB* states, stating, stated
to say or write something clearly or formally

stately *ADJECTIVE* statelier, stateliest
grand and dignified • *a stately procession*
➤ **stateliness** *NOUN*

stately home *NOUN* stately homes
(*British*) a large and magnificent house belonging to an aristocratic family

statement *NOUN* statements
❶ words stating something ❷ a formal account of something that happened • *The*

a b c d e f g h i j k l m n o p q r s t u v w x y z

witness made a statement to the police. ❸ a printed report of a financial account • *a bank statement*

> **GRAMMAR**
>
> A **statement** is a sentence that is a definite and clear expression of something and which is not a question, command or exclamation.
>
> A **statement** ends with a full stop:
>
> *The students wrote their answers on their whiteboards.*
>
> *Bats are nocturnal creatures.*
>
> See also the panel on **sentences**.

state school *NOUN* state schools
(*British*) a school which is funded by the government and which does not charge fees to pupils

statesman *NOUN* statesmen
a person, especially a man, who is important or skilled in governing a country
➤ **statesmanship** *NOUN*

stateswoman *NOUN* stateswomen
a woman who is important or skilled in governing a country

static *ADJECTIVE*
not moving or changing • *Prices have been static for a while.*

static electricity *NOUN*
electricity that is present in something but does not flow as current

station *NOUN* stations
❶ a stopping place for trains or buses with platforms and buildings for passengers and goods ❷ a building equipped for people who serve the public or for certain activities • *the police station* ❸ a broadcasting company with its own frequency ❹ a place where a person stands ready to do something ❺ (*old use*) a person's position or rank ❻ (*Australian/NZ*) a large sheep or cattle farm

station *VERB* stations, stationing, stationed
to put someone in a certain place for a purpose • *He was stationed at the door to take the tickets.*

stationary *ADJECTIVE*
not moving • *The car was stationary when the van hit it.*

> **SPELLING**
>
> **Stationary** is different from **stationery**:
> • *a stationary vehicle* • *The shop sells books and stationery.*

stationer *NOUN* stationers
a shopkeeper who sells stationery
> **WORD ORIGIN** from Latin *stationarius* = a tradesman (usually a bookseller) who had a shop or stand (as opposed to one who travelled about selling goods)

stationery *NOUN*
paper, envelopes, pens and other things used for writing

> **SPELLING**
>
> **Stationery** is different from **stationary**:
> • *The shop sells books and stationery.* • *a stationary vehicle.*

statistic *NOUN* statistics
a piece of information expressed as a number • *These statistics show that the population has doubled.*
➤ **statistical** *ADJECTIVE*
➤ **statistically** *ADVERB*

statistician (say stat-is-**tish**-an) *NOUN* statisticians
an expert in statistics

statistics *NOUN*
the study of information based on the numbers of things

statuary *NOUN*
statues

statue *NOUN* statues
a model made of stone or metal to look like a person or animal

statuesque (say stat-yoo-**esk**) *ADJECTIVE*
like a statue in stillness or dignity

statuette *NOUN* statuettes
a small statue

stature *NOUN*
❶ a person's height • *He's quite small in stature.* ❷ the importance or reputation a person has because of their ability or achievements

status (say **stay**-tus) *NOUN* statuses
❶ a person's or thing's position or rank in relation to others ❷ high rank or social position ❸ the category that a person or thing is put into • *Scientists decided that Pluto should lose its status as a planet.* ❹ a message on a social networking website that tells people what you are doing or thinking

status quo (say stay-tus **kwoh**) *NOUN*
the state of affairs as it was before a change

status symbol *NOUN* status symbols
something that you own because it shows off

your wealth or position in society, rather than because you like it or need it

statute *NOUN* statutes
a law passed by a parliament
➤ **statutory** *ADJECTIVE*

staunch *ADJECTIVE*
firm and loyal • *our staunch supporters*
➤ **staunchly** *ADVERB*

stave *NOUN* staves
❶ a set of five horizontal lines on which music is written ❷ each of the curved strips of wood forming the side of a cask or tub

stave *VERB* staves, staving, staved or stove
to dent something or break a hole in it • *The collision stove in the front of the ship.*
➤ **stave something off** to keep something away or delay it • *I ate a banana to stave off hunger.*

stay *VERB* stays, staying, stayed
❶ to continue to be in the same place or condition; to remain somewhere ❷ to spend time in a place as a visitor ❸ to keep something or someone back or in control • *Only one thing stayed her hand.*
➤ **stay put** (*informal*) to remain in place

stay *NOUN* stays
❶ a time spent somewhere • *We didn't have time for a long stay.* ❷ a postponement • *a stay of execution* ❸ a support, especially a rope or wire holding up a mast or pole

stead *NOUN*
➤ **in a person's** or **thing's stead** instead of this person or thing
➤ **stand a person in good stead** to be very useful to someone

steadfast *ADJECTIVE*
firm and not changing • *a steadfast refusal*

steadily *ADVERB*
in an even and regular way; gradually and continuously • *The snow fell steadily.* • *Things got steadily worse.*

steady *ADJECTIVE* steadier, steadiest
❶ not shaking or moving; firm ❷ regular or constant; continuing the same • *They kept up a steady pace.*
➤ **steadiness** *NOUN*

steady *VERB* steadies, steadying, steadied
to make something steady or to become steady • *She steadied herself against the wall.*

steak *NOUN* steaks
a thick slice of meat (especially beef) or fish

steal *VERB* steals, stealing, stole, stolen
❶ to take and keep something that does not belong to you; to take something secretly or dishonestly ❷ to move secretly or without being noticed • *He stole out of the room.*

> **SPELLING**
> The past tense of **steal** is **stole** and the past participle is **stolen.**

stealth (say stelth) *NOUN*
doing something in a quiet and secret way so that you are not noticed • *She approached them with great stealth.*

stealthy (say stelth-ee) *ADJECTIVE* stealthier, stealthiest
quiet and secret, so as not to be noticed
➤ **stealthily** *ADVERB*

steam *NOUN*
the gas or vapour that comes from boiling water; this used to drive machinery
➤ **run out of steam** to have no energy left

steam *VERB* steams, steaming, steamed
❶ to give off steam ❷ to move somewhere by the power of steam • *The ship steamed down the river.* ❸ to cook food with steam • *a steamed pudding*
➤ **steam up** to be covered with mist or condensation • *The windows have steamed up.*

steam engine *NOUN* steam engines
an engine driven by steam

steamer *NOUN* steamers
❶ a steamship ❷ a container in which things are steamed

steamroller *NOUN* steamrollers
a heavy vehicle with a large roller used to flatten surfaces when making roads
WORD ORIGIN because the first ones were powered by steam

steamship *NOUN* steamships
a ship driven by steam

steamy *ADJECTIVE*
full of steam • *a steamy bathroom*

steed *NOUN* steeds (*old or poetical use*)
a horse

steel *NOUN* steels
❶ a strong metal made from iron and carbon ❷ a steel rod for sharpening knives

steel *VERB* steels, steeling, steeled
➤ **steel yourself** to find courage to face something difficult

a
b
c
d
e
f
g
h
i
j
k
l
m
n
o
p
q
r
s
t
u
v
w
x
y
z

steel band *NOUN* steel bands
a West Indian band of musicians who play instruments made from oil drums

steel wool *NOUN*
a mass of fine, sharp steel threads used for cleaning a surface or rubbing it smooth

steely *ADJECTIVE*
❶ like or to do with steel ❷ cold, hard and severe • *a steely glare*

steep *ADJECTIVE*
❶ sloping very sharply, not gradually ❷ (*informal*) unreasonably high • *a steep price*
➤ **steeply** *ADVERB*
➤ **steepness** *NOUN*

steep *VERB* steeps, steeping, steeped
to soak something thoroughly
➤ **be steeped in something** to be completely filled or familiar with something • *The story is steeped in mystery.*

steepen *VERB* steepens, steepening, steepened
to become steeper • *The path began to steepen.*

steeple *NOUN* steeples
a church tower with a spire on top

steeplechase *NOUN* steeplechases
a race across country or over hedges or fences (**WORD ORIGIN**) so called because the race originally finished at a distant church steeple which was always in view

steeplejack *NOUN* steeplejacks
a person who climbs tall chimneys or steeples to do repairs

steer *VERB* steers, steering, steered
to make a car, ship or bicycle etc. go in the direction you want; to guide something
➤ **steer clear of something** to take care to avoid something

steer *NOUN* steers
a young castrated bull kept for its beef

steering wheel *NOUN* steering wheels
a wheel for steering a vehicle

steersman *NOUN* steersmen
a person who steers a boat or ship

stellar *ADJECTIVE*
to do with a star or stars

stem *NOUN* stems
❶ the main central part of a tree, shrub or plant ❷ a thin part on which a leaf, flower or fruit is supported ❸ a thin upright part, e.g. the thin part of a wine glass between the bowl and the foot ❹ (*in grammar*) the main part of a verb or other word, to which endings are attached

stem *VERB* stems, stemming, stemmed
to stop the flow of something
➤ **stem from something** to come or result from something • *Many of her problems stemmed from lack of money.*

stench *NOUN* stenches
a very unpleasant smell

stencil *NOUN* stencils
a piece of card, metal or plastic with pieces cut out of it, used to produce a picture or design

stencil *VERB* stencils, stencilling, stencilled
to produce or decorate something with a stencil

stentorian *ADJECTIVE*
very loud and clear • *a stentorian voice*
(**WORD ORIGIN**) from the name of *Stentor*, a herald in ancient Greek legend who was said to be able to shout as loud as fifty men

step *NOUN* steps
❶ a movement made by lifting the foot and setting it down ❷ the sound of a person putting down their foot when walking or running ❸ each of the level surfaces on a stair or ladder for placing the foot ❹ each of a series of things done in some process or action • *The first step is to find somewhere to practise.*
➤ **in step** ❶ stepping in time with others in marching or dancing ❷ in agreement
➤ **watch your step** to be careful

step *VERB* steps, stepping, stepped
to tread or walk
➤ **step in** to become involved in a difficult situation in order to help
➤ **step on it** (*informal*) to hurry
➤ **step up something** to increase something

stepbrother *NOUN* stepbrothers
the son of one of your parents from an earlier or later marriage

stepchild *NOUN* stepchildren
a child that a person's husband or wife has from an earlier marriage
➤ **stepdaughter** ➤ **stepson** *NOUN*

stepfather *NOUN* stepfathers
a man who is married to your mother but was not your natural father

stepladder *NOUN* stepladders
a folding ladder with flat treads

stepmother *NOUN* stepmothers
a woman who is married to your father but was not your natural mother

steppe *NOUN* steppes
a grassy plain with few trees, especially in Russia

stepping stone *NOUN* stepping stones
❶ each of a line of stones put into a shallow stream so that people can walk across ❷ a way of achieving something or a stage in achieving it • *Good exam results can be a stepping stone to a career.*

steps *PLURAL NOUN*
a stepladder

stepsister *NOUN* stepsisters
the daughter of one of your parents from an earlier or later marriage

stereo *ADJECTIVE*
stereophonic

stereo *NOUN* stereos
❶ stereophonic sound or recording ❷ a stereophonic CD player, record player, etc.

stereophonic *ADJECTIVE*
using sound that comes from two different directions to give a natural effect

stereoscopic *ADJECTIVE*
giving the effect of being three-dimensional, e.g. in photographs

stereotype *NOUN* stereotypes
a fixed image or idea of a type of person or thing that is widely held • *The stereotype of a hero is one who is tall, strong, brave and good-looking.* **WORD ORIGIN** originally = a kind of printing block, from Greek *stereos* = solid, three-dimensional (because the block always produced the same words, like the fixed idea in the modern meaning)

sterile *ADJECTIVE*
❶ clean and free from germs ❷ not able to have children or reproduce
➤ **sterility** *NOUN*

sterilize (also **sterilise**) *VERB* sterilizes, sterilizing, sterilized
❶ to make a thing free from germs, e.g. by heating it ❷ to make a person or animal unable to reproduce
➤ **sterilization** *NOUN*

sterling *NOUN*
British money

sterling *ADJECTIVE*
❶ genuine • *sterling silver* ❷ excellent; of great worth • *her sterling qualities*

stern *ADJECTIVE*
strict and severe; not smiling • *He gave them a stern look.* • *a stern warning*
➤ **sternness** *NOUN*

stern *NOUN* sterns
the back part of a ship

sternly *ADVERB*
in a stern way • *She looked at him sternly.*

steroid *NOUN* steroids
a substance of a kind that includes certain hormones and other natural secretions

stethoscope *NOUN* stethoscopes
a device used by doctors for listening to sounds in a person's body, e.g. heartbeats and breathing **WORD ORIGIN** from Greek *stethos* = breast + *skopein* = look at

stew *VERB* stews, stewing, stewed
to cook food slowly in liquid

stew *NOUN* stews
a dish of meat and vegetables cooked slowly in liquid
➤ **in a stew** (*informal*) very worried or agitated

steward *NOUN* stewards
❶ a man whose job is to look after the passengers on a ship or aircraft ❷ an official who keeps order or looks after the arrangements at a large public event

stewardess *NOUN* stewardesses
a woman whose job is to look after the passengers on a ship or aircraft

stick *NOUN* sticks
❶ a long thin piece of wood ❷ a walking stick ❸ the implement used to hit the ball in hockey, polo or other games ❹ a long thin piece of something • *a stick of celery*

stick *VERB* sticks, sticking, stuck
❶ to push a thing into something • *Stick a pin in it.* ❷ to fix something by glue or as if by glue • *I need to stick a few stamps on the parcel.* ❸ to become fixed and unable to move • *The drawer keeps sticking.* ❹ (*informal*) to bear something or put up with it • *I can't stick that noise!*
➤ **stick out** ❶ to come out from a surface or to stand out from the surrounding area ❷ to be very noticeable
➤ **stick to something** ❶ to remain faithful to a promise or agreement ❷ to keep to something and not change it • *He stuck to his story.*
➤ **stick together** ❶ to stay together ❷ to support each other
➤ **stick up for someone** (*informal*) to

support or defend someone
➤ **be stuck with something** (*informal*) to be unable to avoid something unwelcome

sticker *NOUN* **stickers**
a sticky label or sign for sticking on something

sticking plaster *NOUN* **sticking plasters**
(*British*) a strip of sticky material for covering cuts

stick insect *NOUN* **stick insects**
an insect with a long thin body and legs, which looks like a twig

stickleback *NOUN* **sticklebacks**
a small fish with sharp spines on its back

stickler *NOUN* **sticklers**
a person who insists on something • *The boss is a stickler for punctuality.*

sticky *ADJECTIVE* **stickier, stickiest**
❶ able or likely to stick to things ❷ sticky weather is hot and humid, causing perspiration ❸ (*informal*) difficult or awkward • *a sticky situation*
➤ **stickiness** *NOUN*
➤ **come to a sticky end** to die or end in a painful or unpleasant way

stiff *ADJECTIVE*
❶ not bending, moving or changing its shape easily • *The door handle is stiff.* ❷ not able to move or bend the body easily • *I woke up feeling very stiff.* ❸ thick and hard to stir • *a stiff dough* ❹ difficult • *It was a stiff climb to the top.* ❺ formal in manner; not friendly ❻ severe or strong • *a stiff breeze*
➤ **stiffness** *NOUN*

stiffen *VERB* **stiffens, stiffening, stiffened**
to become stiff or to make something stiff

stiffly *ADVERB*
❶ in a formal and unfriendly way • *'Thank you,' she said stiffly.* ❷ in a way that shows you cannot move your body easily • *He got stiffly to his feet.*

stifle *VERB* **stifles, stifling, stifled**
❶ to stop something happening or developing • *She stifled a yawn.* ❷ to make it difficult for someone to breathe because of heat or lack of fresh air

stigma *NOUN* **stigmas**
❶ a mark of disgrace; a stain on a reputation ❷ the part of a pistil that receives the pollen in pollination

stile *NOUN* **stiles**
an arrangement of steps or bars for people to climb over a fence

stiletto *NOUN* **stilettos**
a dagger with a narrow blade

stiletto heel *NOUN* **stiletto heels**
a high pointed shoe heel

still *ADJECTIVE*
❶ not moving • *the still water of a mountain lake* ❷ silent • *a still night* ❸ not fizzy • *still mineral water*

still *ADVERB*
❶ without moving • *Stand still.* ❷ up to this or that time • *He was still there.* ❸ in a greater amount or degree • *You can do still better.* ❹ nevertheless • *They've lost. Still, they tried and that was good.*

still *VERB* **stills, stilling, stilled**
to make something still • *I tried to still the trembling in my hand.*

still *NOUN* **stills**
❶ a photograph of a scene from a cinema film ❷ an apparatus for distilling alcohol or other liquid

stillborn *ADJECTIVE*
born dead

still life *NOUN* **still lifes**
a painting of an arrangement of objects, especially fruit, flowers or ornaments

stillness *NOUN*
being quiet, with nothing moving • *A bird's cry broke the stillness.*

stilted *ADJECTIVE*
stiffly formal

stilts *PLURAL NOUN*
❶ a pair of poles with supports for the feet so that the user can walk high above the ground ❷ posts for supporting a house built above marshy ground

stimulant *NOUN* **stimulants**
a drug or substance that makes you feel more awake and active for a while

stimulate *VERB* **stimulates, stimulating, stimulated**
❶ to make someone excited or enthusiastic ❷ to encourage something to develop • *The programme has stimulated a lot of interest in her work.*
➤ **stimulation** *NOUN*

stimulus *NOUN* **stimuli**
something that encourages a thing to develop or produces a reaction

sting *NOUN* stings
① a sharp-pointed part of an animal or plant, often containing a poison, that can cause a wound **②** a painful wound caused by this part

sting *VERB* stings, stinging, stung
① to wound or hurt someone with a sting **②** to feel a sharp pain **③** to make someone feel upset or hurt • *I was stung by this criticism.* **④** (*informal*) to cheat someone by charging them too much

stingray *NOUN* stingrays
a fish with a flat body, fins like wings and a poisonous spine in its tail

stingy (say **stin**-jee) *ADJECTIVE* stingier, stingiest
mean, not generous; giving or given in small amounts
➤ **stinginess** *NOUN*

stink *NOUN* stinks
① an unpleasant smell **②** (*informal*) an unpleasant fuss or protest

stink *VERB* stinks, stinking, stank or stunk
to have an unpleasant smell

stint *NOUN* stints
a fixed amount of work to be done

stint *VERB* stints, stinting, stinted
to stint on something is to be sparing with it and not use much • *Don't stint on the cream.*

stipend (say **sty**-pend) *NOUN* stipends
a salary, especially one paid to a clergyman

stipple *VERB* stipples, stippling, stippled
to paint, draw or engrave a design in small dots

stipulate *VERB* stipulates, stipulating, stipulated
to insist on something as part of an agreement
➤ **stipulation** *NOUN*

stir *VERB* stirs, stirring, stirred
① to mix a liquid or soft mixture by moving a spoon etc. round and round in it **②** to move slightly or start to move after sleeping or being still • *She didn't stir all afternoon.* **③** to make someone feel a strong emotion • *The story stirred my imagination.*
➤ **stir something up** to excite or arouse something • *They are always stirring up trouble.*

stir *NOUN*
① the action of stirring **②** strong public feeling or excitement • *The news caused a stir.*

stir-fry *VERB* stir-fries, stir-frying, stir-fried
to cook something by frying it quickly over a high heat while stirring and tossing it

stir-fry *NOUN* stir-fries
a dish cooked by stir-frying

stirring *ADJECTIVE*
making people feel strong emotion • *a stirring speech*

stirrup *NOUN* stirrups
a metal part that hangs from each side of a horse's saddle and supports the rider's foot

stitch *NOUN* stitches
① a loop of thread made in sewing or knitting **②** a method of arranging the threads • *an embroidery stitch* **③** a sudden sharp pain in your side, caused by running

stitch *VERB* stitches, stitching, stitched
to sew or fasten something with stitches

stoat *NOUN* stoats
a kind of weasel, also called an ermine

stock *NOUN* stocks
① a number of things kept ready to be sold or used **②** farm animals; livestock **③** the line of a person's ancestors • *a man of Irish stock* **④** a liquid used in cooking, made from the juices you get by stewing meat, fish or vegetables **⑤** a number of shares in a company's capital **⑥** the main stem of a tree or plant **⑦** the base, holder or handle of an implement or weapon **⑧** a garden flower with a sweet smell
➤ **take stock** to make an overall assessment of a situation

stock *VERB* stocks, stocking, stocked
① to keep a supply of goods to sell **②** to provide a place with a stock of something
➤ **stock up** to buy a supply of goods

stockade *NOUN* stockades
a fence made of stakes

stockbroker *NOUN* stockbrokers
a person who buys and sells stocks and shares for clients

stock car *NOUN* stock cars
an ordinary car strengthened for use in races where deliberate bumping is allowed

stock exchange *NOUN* stock exchanges
a country's central place for buying and selling stocks and shares

stocking *NOUN* stockings
a piece of clothing covering the foot and part or all of the leg

stock market *NOUN* stock markets
❶ a stock exchange ❷ the buying and selling of stocks and shares

stockpile *NOUN* stockpiles
a large stock of things kept in reserve
➤ **stockpile** *VERB*

stocks *PLURAL NOUN*
a wooden framework with holes for a seated person's legs, in which criminals were locked as a punishment

stock-still *ADJECTIVE*
quite still

stocktaking *NOUN*
the counting, listing and checking of the amount of stock held by a shop or business

stocky *ADJECTIVE* stockier, stockiest
short and solidly built • *a stocky man*

stodge *NOUN*
(*British*) stodgy food

stodgy *ADJECTIVE* stodgier, stodgiest (*British*)
❶ stodgy food is heavy and filling ❷ dull and boring • *a stodgy book*

stoical (say **stoh**-ik-al) *ADJECTIVE*
bearing pain or difficulties calmly without complaining
➤ **stoically** *ADVERB*
➤ **stoicism** *NOUN*
WORD ORIGIN named after ancient Greek philosophers called *Stoics*

stoke *VERB* stokes, stoking, stoked
to put fuel in a furnace or on a fire
➤ **stoker** *NOUN*

stole
past tense of **steal**

stole *NOUN* stoles
a wide piece of material worn round the shoulders by women

stolid *ADJECTIVE*
not showing much emotion or excitement
➤ **stolidly** *ADVERB*
➤ **stolidity** *NOUN*

stomach *NOUN* stomachs
❶ the part of your body where food starts to be digested ❷ the front part of your body that contains your stomach; your abdomen

stomach *VERB* stomachs, stomaching, stomached
to tolerate something or put up with it

stone *NOUN* stones
❶ a piece of rock ❷ stones or rock as material, e.g. for building ❸ a jewel ❹ the hard case round the kernel of plums, cherries, peaches, etc. ❺ a unit of weight equal to 14 pounds (6.35 kg) • *She weighs 8 stone.*

stone *VERB* stones, stoning, stoned
❶ to throw stones at someone ❷ to remove the stones from fruit

Stone Age *NOUN*
the earliest period of human history, when tools and weapons were made of stone

stone circle *NOUN* stone circles
a circle of large stones or boulders, put up in prehistoric times

stone-cold *ADJECTIVE*
extremely cold

stoned *ADJECTIVE* (*informal*)
under the influence of drugs or alcohol

stone-deaf *ADJECTIVE*
completely deaf

stoneware *NOUN*
a kind of pottery with a hard shiny surface
• *a stoneware jar*

stony *ADJECTIVE*
❶ full of stones ❷ hard like stone
❸ unfriendly and not answering • *They listened to him in stony silence.*

stooge *NOUN* stooges (*informal*)
❶ a comedian's assistant, used as a target for jokes ❷ an assistant who does dull or routine work

stool *NOUN* stools
❶ a movable seat without arms or a back ❷ a lump of faeces

stoop *VERB* stoops, stooping, stooped
❶ to bend your body forwards and down
❷ to lower your standards of behaviour • *He would not stoop to cheating.*

stoop *NOUN* stoops
❶ a way of standing or walking with your head and shoulders bent forwards ❷ (*North American & S. African*) a porch, small verandah or set of steps in front of a house

stop *VERB* stops, stopping, stopped
❶ to come to an end or bring something to an end; to no longer do something ❷ to be no longer moving or working • *A car stopped in front of us.* ❸ to prevent something happening or continuing • *They put a fence up to stop the dog getting out.* ❹ to fill a hole or gap • *We need to stop up the other end of the tube.* ❺ to stay somewhere for a short time

stop *NOUN* stops
❶ stopping; a pause or end • *She brought the car to a stop.* ❷ a place where a bus or train regularly stops ❸ a lever or knob that controls pitch in a wind instrument or allows organ pipes to sound

stopcock *NOUN* stopcocks
a valve controlling the flow of liquid or gas in a pipe

stopgap *NOUN* stopgaps
a temporary substitute

stoppage *NOUN* stoppages
❶ an interruption in the work of a factory or business ❷ a break in play during a game ❸ a blockage in something

stopper *NOUN* stoppers
a plug for closing a bottle or sealing a hole

stop press *NOUN*
(*British*) late news put into a newspaper after printing has started **WORD ORIGIN** because the printing presses are stopped to allow the late news to be added

stopwatch *NOUN* stopwatches
a watch that can be started and stopped when you wish, used for timing races

storage *NOUN*
the storing of things

store *NOUN* stores
❶ a supply of things kept for future use ❷ a place where things are kept until they are needed ❸ a shop, especially a large one ❹ (*North American*) any shop
➤ **in store** going to happen soon • *There's a surprise in store for you.*
➤ **set store by something** to value something greatly

store *VERB* stores, storing, stored
to keep things until they are needed

storey *NOUN* storeys
one whole floor of a building

SPELLING
Storey is different from **story**: • *the second storey of the building* • *Read me a story.*

stork *NOUN* storks
a large bird with long legs and a long beak

storm *NOUN* storms
❶ a period of bad weather with strong winds, rain or snow and often thunder and lightning ❷ a violent attack or outburst • *a storm of protest*

➤ **a storm in a teacup** a great fuss over something unimportant

storm *VERB* storms, storming, stormed
❶ to move or behave violently or angrily • *He stormed out of the room.* ❷ to suddenly attack and capture a place • *They stormed the castle.*

stormy *ADJECTIVE* stormier, stormiest
❶ having a storm or a lot of storms • *It was a stormy night.* ❷ loud and angry • *a stormy argument*

story *NOUN* stories
❶ an account of a real or imaginary event ❷ the plot of a novel, play or film ❸ (*informal*) a lie • *Don't tell stories!*

SPELLING
Story is different from **storey**: • *Read me a story.* • *the second storey of the building*

stout *ADJECTIVE*
❶ rather fat ❷ thick and strong • *a stout stick* ❸ brave and determined • *a stout defender of human rights*
➤ **stoutly** *ADVERB*
➤ **stoutness** *NOUN*

stout *NOUN*
a kind of dark beer

stove *NOUN* stoves
❶ a device containing an oven or ovens ❷ a device for heating a room

stove *VERB*
past tense of **stave**

stow *VERB* stows, stowing, stowed
to pack or store something away • *We stowed our backpacks above the seats.*
➤ **stow away** to hide on a ship or aircraft so that you can travel without paying

stowaway *NOUN* stowaways
someone who stows away on a ship or aircraft

straddle *VERB* straddles, straddling, straddled
❶ to sit or stand with your legs either side of something ❷ to be built across something • *A long bridge straddles the river.*

straggle *VERB* straggles, straggling, straggled
❶ to grow or spread in an untidy way • *Brambles straggled across the path.* ❷ to walk too slowly and not keep up with the rest of a group
➤ **straggler** *NOUN*
➤ **straggly** *ADJECTIVE*

straight ADJECTIVE
❶ going continuously in one direction; not curving or bending ❷ level, horizontal or upright • *Is this picture straight?* ❸ tidy; in proper order ❹ honest and frank • *Give me a straight answer.*
➤ **straightness** NOUN

straight ADVERB
❶ in a straight line or manner • *Go straight on, then turn left.* ❷ directly; without delay • *I went straight home.*

> **SPELLING**
> Take care not to confuse with **strait**.

straightaway, straight away ADVERB
immediately; at once

straighten VERB straightens, straightening, straightened
❶ to make something straight • *He straightened his tie.* ❷ to become straight; to stand up straight • *She straightened up with pride.*

straightforward ADJECTIVE
❶ easy to understand or do, not complicated ❷ honest and frank

strain VERB strains, straining, strained
❶ to injure a part of your body by stretching or using it too much ❷ to put a lot of pressure on something ❸ to stretch something tightly ❹ to make a great effort • *I was straining to see what was happening.* ❺ to put something through a sieve or filter to separate liquid from solid matter

strain NOUN strains
❶ the process or force of straining • *The rope broke under the strain.* ❷ an injury caused by straining ❸ the effect on someone of too much work or worry ❹ something that uses up strength, patience or resources ❺ a part of a tune ❻ a breed or variety of an animal, plant, etc.; a line of descent ❼ an inherited characteristic • *There's an artistic strain in the family.*

strainer NOUN strainers
a device for straining liquids • *a tea strainer*

strait NOUN straits
a narrow stretch of water connecting two seas

> **SPELLING**
> Take care not to confuse with **straight**.

straitened ADJECTIVE
➤ **in straitened circumstances** short of money

straitjacket NOUN straitjackets
a strong jacket-like piece of clothing put round a violent person to tie their arms

strait-laced ADJECTIVE
very prim and proper

straits PLURAL NOUN
a strait • *the Straits of Dover*
➤ **be in dire straits** to have severe difficulties

strand NOUN strands
❶ each of the threads or wires twisted together to form a rope, yarn or cable ❷ a single thread or hair ❸ an idea, theme or story that forms part of a whole • *a novel with several strands*

stranded ADJECTIVE
❶ left on sand or rocks in shallow water • *a stranded ship* ❷ left in a difficult or lonely position • *We were stranded when our car broke down.*

strange ADJECTIVE
❶ unusual or surprising ❷ not known or seen or experienced before • *a strange town*
➤ **strangeness** NOUN

strangely ADVERB
in a strange way • *The streets were strangely quiet.*

stranger NOUN strangers
❶ a person you do not know ❷ a person who is in a place that they do not know • *Actually, I'm a stranger here myself.*

strangle VERB strangles, strangling, strangled
❶ to kill someone by squeezing their throat to prevent them breathing ❷ to restrict something so that it does not develop
➤ **strangler** NOUN

strangulated ADJECTIVE
sounding as though the throat is being tightly squeezed • *a strangulated cry*

strangulation NOUN
killing someone by strangling them

strap NOUN straps
a flat strip of leather, cloth or plastic for fastening things or holding them in place

strap VERB straps, strapping, strapped
to fasten or bind something with a strap or straps

strapping ADJECTIVE
tall and healthy-looking • *a strapping lad*

strata
plural of **stratum**

stratagem *NOUN* **stratagems**
a cunning method of achieving something; a plan or trick

strategic *ADJECTIVE*
❶ to do with strategy ❷ giving you an advantage • *a strategic move*
➤ **strategically** *ADVERB*

strategist *NOUN* **strategists**
an expert in strategy

strategy *NOUN* **strategies**
❶ a plan or policy to achieve something • *our economic strategy* ❷ the planning of a war or campaign. Compare with **tactics**.

stratified *ADJECTIVE*
arranged in strata
➤ **stratification** *NOUN*

stratosphere *NOUN*
a layer of the atmosphere between about 10 and 60 kilometres above the earth's surface

stratum (say **strah**-tum) *NOUN* **strata**
a layer or level • *You can see several strata of rock in the cliff.*

> **USAGE**
>
> The word **strata** is a plural. It is incorrect to say 'a strata' or 'this strata'; correct use is *this stratum* or *these strata.*

straw *NOUN* **straws**
❶ dry cut stalks of corn ❷ a narrow tube for drinking through

strawberry *NOUN* **strawberries**
a small red juicy fruit, with its seeds on the outside **WORD ORIGIN** perhaps because straw is put around the plants to keep slugs away

stray *VERB* **strays, straying, strayed**
to leave a group or proper place and wander; to become lost

stray *ADJECTIVE*
❶ that has strayed; wandering around lost • *a stray cat* ❷ found on its own, separated from the others • *a stray sock*

stray *NOUN* **strays**
a stray dog or cat

streak *NOUN* **streaks**
❶ a long thin line or mark ❷ a trace or sign of something • *a streak of cruelty* ❸ a spell of success or good fortune • *on a winning streak*
➤ **streaky** *ADJECTIVE*

streak *VERB* **streaks, streaking, streaked**
❶ to mark something with streaks • *His face was streaked with tears.* ❷ to move very

quickly ❸ to run naked in a public place for fun or to get attention
➤ **streaker** *NOUN*

streaky bacon *NOUN*
(*British*) bacon with alternate strips of lean and fat

stream *NOUN* **streams**
❶ water flowing in a channel; a brook or small river ❷ liquid flowing in one direction ❸ a number of things moving in the same direction, such as traffic ❹ a group in which children of similar ability are placed in a school

stream *VERB* **streams, streaming, streamed**
❶ to move in a strong fast flow • *Traffic streamed across the junction.* ❷ to produce a stream of liquid • *Her eyes were streaming.* ❸ to arrange schoolchildren in streams according to their ability

streamer *NOUN* **streamers**
a long narrow ribbon or strip of paper

streamline *VERB* **streamlines, streamlining, streamlined**
❶ to give something a smooth shape that helps it to move easily through air or water ❷ to organize something so that it works more efficiently
➤ **streamlined** *ADJECTIVE*

street *NOUN* **streets**
a road with houses beside it in a city or village

strength *NOUN* **strengths**
❶ how strong a person or thing is; being strong ❷ an ability or good quality • *Patience is your great strength.*

> **SPELLING**
>
> There is a silent **g** after the **n** in **strength**.

strengthen *VERB* **strengthens, strengthening, strengthened**
to become stronger or to make something stronger • *These exercises will help to strengthen your stomach muscles.*

strenuous *ADJECTIVE*
needing or using great effort • *strenuous exercise*
➤ **strenuously** *ADVERB*

stress *NOUN* **stresses**
❶ a force that presses, pulls or twists something ❷ emphasis, especially the extra force with which you pronounce part of a word or phrase ❸ worry and pressure caused

by having too many problems or too much to do

stress *VERB* stresses, stressing, stressed
❶ to pronounce part of a word or phrase with extra emphasis ❷ to emphasize a point or idea • *I must stress the importance of arriving on time.* ❸ to make someone suffer stress

stressed *ADJECTIVE*
too anxious and tired to be able to relax

stressful *ADJECTIVE*
causing worry and pressure • *a stressful job*

stretch *VERB* stretches, stretching, stretched
❶ to pull something or be pulled so that it becomes longer or wider or larger ❷ to extend or be continuous • *The wall stretches all the way round the park.* ❸ to push out your arms and legs as far as you can ❹ to make use of all your ability or intelligence • *This course should really stretch you.*
➤ **stretch out** to lie down with your arms and legs at full length

stretch *NOUN* stretches
❶ the action of stretching • *I got up and had a good stretch.* ❷ a continuous period of time or area of land or water

stretcher *NOUN* stretchers
a framework for carrying a sick or injured person

strew *VERB* strews, strewing, strewed, strewn or strewed
to scatter things over a surface • *Paper cups were strewn over the floor.*

stricken *ADJECTIVE*
overcome or strongly affected by an illness or a feeling such as grief or fear

strict *ADJECTIVE*
❶ demanding that people obey rules and behave well • *a strict teacher* ❷ complete or exact • *in strict confidence* • *She left strict instructions that she wasn't to be disturbed.*
➤ **strictness** *NOUN*

strictly *ADVERB*
completely or exactly • *Eating in the library is strictly forbidden.* • *That is not strictly true.*

stride *VERB* strides, striding, strode, stridden
to walk with long steps

stride *NOUN* strides
❶ a long step when walking or running ❷ a step that helps you make progress • *Scientists are making great strides in the search for a cure.*
➤ **get into your stride** to settle into a fast

and steady pace of working
➤ **take something in your stride** to cope with something without difficulty

strident (say **stry**-dent) *ADJECTIVE*
loud and harsh
➤ **stridently** *ADVERB*

strife *NOUN*
conflict; fighting or quarrelling

strike *VERB* strikes, striking, struck
❶ to hit a person or thing ❷ to attack or afflict people suddenly • *Then disaster struck.* ❸ to make an impression on someone's mind • *She strikes me as being lazy.* ❹ to light a match by rubbing it against a rough surface ❺ to refuse to work as a protest against pay or conditions ❻ to produce coins or medals by pressing or stamping metal ❼ to sound or ring a number of times • *The clock struck ten.* ❽ to find gold or oil by digging or drilling ❾ to go in a certain direction • *We struck north through the forest.*
➤ **strike something off** or **out** to cross something out
➤ **strike up** a band strikes up when it begins playing
➤ **strike something up** to start a friendship or conversation

strike *NOUN* strikes
❶ a hit ❷ a military attack • *an air strike* ❸ refusing to work as a way of making a protest ❹ a sudden discovery of gold or oil
➤ **go on strike** to stop working as a protest

striker *NOUN* strikers
❶ a worker who is on strike ❷ a football player whose main job is to try to score goals

striking *ADJECTIVE*
❶ impressive or attractive • *Her eyes were her most striking feature.* ❷ so unusual or interesting that you cannot help noticing it • *The resemblance between them is striking.*
➤ **strikingly** *ADVERB*

string *NOUN* strings
❶ thin cord made of twisted threads, used to fasten or tie things; a piece of this or similar material ❷ a piece of wire or cord stretched and vibrated to produce sounds in a musical instrument ❸ a line or series of things • *a string of buses*

string *VERB* strings, stringing, strung
❶ to hang something on a string • *Lights were strung from tree to tree.* ❷ to fit something with a string • *The archer calmly strung his bow.* ❸ to thread pearls or beads on a string ❹ to remove the tough fibre from

beans

➤ **string someone along** to mislead someone over a period of time

➤ **string something out ❶** to spread something out in a line **❷** to make something last a long time

stringed *ADJECTIVE*
stringed instruments are ones that have strings, especially members of the violin family

stringent (say **strin**-jent) *ADJECTIVE*
strict and precise • *There are stringent rules about this.*

strings *PLURAL NOUN*
the stringed instruments of an orchestra

stringy *ADJECTIVE*
❶ long and thin, like string ❷ containing tough fibres

strip *VERB* strips, stripping, stripped
❶ to take a covering or layer off something ❷ to undress ❸ to take something away from someone as a punishment • *He was stripped of his title.*

strip *NOUN* strips
❶ a long narrow piece or area ❷ the distinctive clothes worn by a sports team while playing

strip cartoon *NOUN* strip cartoons
a series of drawings telling a story

stripe *NOUN* stripes
❶ a long narrow band of colour ❷ a strip of cloth worn on the sleeve of a uniform to show the wearer's rank

striped, stripy *ADJECTIVE*
marked with a pattern of stripes • *a red and white striped dress*

strip light *NOUN* strip lights
(*British*) a fluorescent lamp in the form of a tube

stripling *NOUN* striplings
a youth

stripper *NOUN* strippers
❶ a tool or substance used for stripping paint ❷ a person who performs striptease

striptease *NOUN* stripteases
an entertainment in which a person slowly undresses

strive *VERB* strives, striving, strove, striven
to try hard to do or get something • *He was always striving for perfection.*

strobe *NOUN* strobes (short for **stroboscope**)
a light that flashes on and off continuously

stroke *NOUN* strokes
❶ a movement of the arm when hitting something, swimming or rowing ❷ a style of swimming ❸ a movement you make when you are writing or painting • *a brush stroke* ❹ an action or effort • *a stroke of genius* ❺ the sound made by a clock striking ❻ a sudden illness that often causes paralysis ❼ an act of stroking something • *He gave the cat a stroke.*

stroke *VERB* strokes, stroking, stroked
to move your hand gently along something

stroll *VERB* strolls, strolling, strolled
to walk in a leisurely way

stroll *NOUN* strolls
a short leisurely walk
➤ **stroller** *NOUN*

strong *ADJECTIVE*
❶ having great power, energy or effect ❷ not easy to break, damage or defeat • *The gate was held by a strong chain.* ❸ great in intensity • *strong feelings* ❹ having a lot of flavour or smell ❺ having a certain number of members • *an army 5,000 strong*

strong *ADVERB*
➤ **be going strong** to be making good progress

stronghold *NOUN* strongholds
❶ a fortified place ❷ an area where many people live or think in a particular way • *a Tory stronghold*

strongly *ADVERB*
❶ in a strong way; with strength • *They fought back strongly.* ❷ very much • *The room smelt strongly of perfume.*

strong point *NOUN* strong points
a strength; something that you are very good at • *Maths is her strong point.*

strongroom *NOUN* strongrooms
a room designed to protect valuable things from fire and theft

strontium *NOUN*
a soft silvery metal (WORD ORIGIN) named after *Strontia* in the Scottish highlands, where it was discovered

strove
past tense of **strive**

structural *ADJECTIVE*
to do with the way that something is built or

constructed • *a structural fault*
➤ **structurally** *ADVERB*

structure *NOUN* **structures**
❶ something that has been constructed or built ❷ the way something is constructed or organized

structure *VERB* **structures, structuring, structured**
to organize or arrange something into a system or pattern • *You need to structure your arguments with more care.*

struggle *VERB* **struggles, struggling, struggled**
❶ to move your arms and legs and wriggle fiercely in trying to get free ❷ to try very hard to do something difficult • *She was struggling to keep up with the others.* ❸ to try to overcome an opponent or a problem

struggle *NOUN* **struggles**
❶ the act of struggling • *He lost his glasses in the struggle.* ❷ a hard fight or great effort

strum *VERB* **strums, strumming, strummed**
to sound a guitar by running your fingers across its strings

strut *VERB* **struts, strutting, strutted**
to walk proudly or stiffly • *A peacock strutted across the lawn.*

strut *NOUN* **struts**
❶ a bar of wood or metal that strengthens a framework ❷ a strutting walk

strychnine (say **strik**-neen) *NOUN*
a bitter poisonous substance

stub *NOUN* **stubs**
❶ a short stump left when the rest has been used or worn down ❷ the part of a ticket or cheque that you keep as a record

stub *VERB* **stubs, stubbing, stubbed**
to bump your toe painfully
➤ **stub something out** to put out a cigarette by pressing it against something hard

stubble *NOUN*
❶ the short stalks of corn left in the ground after the harvest is cut ❷ short hairs growing on a man's chin when he has not shaved

stubborn *ADJECTIVE*
❶ determined not to change your ideas or ways; obstinate ❷ difficult to remove or deal with • *stubborn stains*
➤ **stubbornly** *ADVERB*
➤ **stubbornness** *NOUN*

stubby *ADJECTIVE*
short and thick

stucco *NOUN*
plaster or cement used for coating walls and ceilings, often moulded into decorations
➤ **stuccoed** *ADJECTIVE*

stuck
past tense and past participle of **stick**

stuck *ADJECTIVE*
unable to move or make progress • *I'm stuck.*

stuck-up *ADJECTIVE* (*informal*)
conceited or snobbish

stud *NOUN* **studs**
❶ a small curved lump or knob ❷ a device like a button on a stalk, used to fasten a detachable collar to a shirt ❸ a number of horses kept for breeding; the place where they are kept ❹ a stallion

studded *ADJECTIVE*
❶ covered with studs or other decorations • *The necklace was studded with jewels.*
❷ scattered or sprinkled with something • *The sky was studded with stars.*

student *NOUN* **students**
a person who studies a subject, especially at a college or university

studied *ADJECTIVE*
not natural but done with deliberate effort • *She answered with studied indifference.*

studio *NOUN* **studios**
❶ the room where an artist or photographer works ❷ a place where cinema films are made ❸ a room from which radio or television broadcasts are made or recorded

studious *ADJECTIVE*
spending a lot of time studying or reading

studiously *ADVERB*
carefully and deliberately • *She studiously avoided answering the question.*

study *VERB* **studies, studying, studied**
❶ to spend time learning about something ❷ to look at something carefully • *She studied his face for a moment.*

study *NOUN* **studies**
❶ the process of studying ❷ a subject studied; a piece of research ❸ a room used for studying or writing ❹ a piece of music for playing as an exercise ❺ a drawing done for practice or in preparation for another work

stuff *NOUN*
❶ a substance or material • *What's this stuff at the bottom of the glass?* ❷ a group of things or belongings • *Leave your stuff outside.*

stuff VERB stuffs, stuffing, stuffed
❶ to fill something tightly ❷ to fill something with stuffing ❸ to push a thing roughly into something • *He stuffed the notebook into his pocket.* ❹ (*informal*) to eat greedily

stuffing NOUN
❶ material used to fill the inside of something ❷ a savoury mixture put into meat or poultry before cooking

stuffy ADJECTIVE stuffier, stuffiest
❶ a stuffy room is badly ventilated, without enough fresh air ❷ with blocked breathing passages • *a stuffy nose* ❸ formal and boring
➤ **stuffily** ADVERB
➤ **stuffiness** NOUN

stumble VERB stumbles, stumbling, stumbled
❶ to trip and lose your balance ❷ to make a mistake or hesitate while you are speaking or doing something
➤ **stumble across** or **on something** to find something by chance

stumbling block NOUN stumbling blocks
an obstacle; something that causes difficulty

stump NOUN stumps
❶ the bottom of a tree trunk left in the ground when the rest has fallen or been cut down ❷ something left when the main part is cut off or worn down ❸ each of the three upright sticks of a wicket in cricket

stump VERB stumps, stumping, stumped
❶ to be too difficult or puzzling for someone • *The last question stumped everyone.* ❷ to walk stiffly or noisily ❸ in cricket, to stump the person batting is to get them out by knocking the bails off the stumps while the person is standing out of the crease
➤ **stump up** (*informal*) to produce the money needed to pay for something

stumpy ADJECTIVE
short and thick • *stumpy legs*

stun VERB stuns, stunning, stunned
❶ to knock a person unconscious ❷ to daze or shock someone • *She was stunned by the news.*

stunning ADJECTIVE
extremely beautiful or attractive
➤ **stunningly** ADVERB

stunt NOUN stunts
❶ something daring done as a performance or as part of the action of a film ❷ something unusual done to attract attention • *a publicity stunt*

stunt VERB stunts, stunting, stunted
to prevent a thing from growing or developing normally • *a stunted tree*

stupefy VERB stupefies, stupefying, stupefied
to make a person dazed
➤ **stupefaction** NOUN

stupendous ADJECTIVE
amazing or tremendous
➤ **stupendously** ADVERB

stupid ADJECTIVE
❶ not clever or thoughtful ❷ without reason or common sense
➤ **stupidly** ADVERB
➤ **stupidity** NOUN

stupor (say **stew**-per) NOUN stupors
a state of being dazed or only partly conscious • *He was asleep, in a drunken stupor.*

sturdy ADJECTIVE sturdier, sturdiest
strong and solid • *The branch looked sturdy enough.*
➤ **sturdily** ADVERB
➤ **sturdiness** NOUN

sturgeon NOUN sturgeon
a large edible fish

stutter VERB stutters, stuttering, stuttered
to keep repeating the sounds at the beginning of words

stutter NOUN stutters
a tendency to stutter

sty NOUN sties or, in sense 2, styes
❶ a pigsty ❷ (also **stye**) a sore swelling on an eyelid

style NOUN styles
❶ the way something is done, made, said or written • *a style of architecture* ❷ fashion or elegance ❸ the part of a pistil that supports the stigma in a plant

style VERB styles, styling, styled
to design or arrange something, especially in a fashionable style

stylish ADJECTIVE
fashionable and elegant • *a stylish black dress*

stylistic ADJECTIVE
to do with the style of something

stylus NOUN styluses or styli
the device like a needle that travels in the grooves of a record to produce the sound

suave (say swahv) ADJECTIVE
polite in a charming and confident way

a b c d e f g h i j k l m n o p q r s t u v w x y z

➤ **suavely** *ADVERB*
➤ **suavity** *NOUN*

sub *NOUN* subs (*informal*)
❶ a submarine ❷ a subscription ❸ a substitute

subaltern *NOUN* subalterns
an army officer ranking below a captain

sub-aqua *ADJECTIVE*
to do with underwater sports, such as diving

subatomic *ADJECTIVE*
❶ smaller than an atom ❷ forming part of an atom

subconscious *ADJECTIVE*
to do with mental processes of which we are not fully aware but which influence our actions

subconscious *NOUN*
the hidden part of your mind that influences your actions without you being fully aware of it

subcontinent *NOUN* subcontinents
a large mass of land that forms part of a continent • *the Indian subcontinent*

subcontractor *NOUN* subcontractors
a person or company hired by another company to do a particular part of their work

subdivide *VERB* subdivides, subdividing, subdivided
to divide something again or into smaller parts
➤ **subdivision** *NOUN*

subdue *VERB* subdues, subduing, subdued
❶ to overcome someone or bring them under control ❷ to make a person or animal quieter or gentler
➤ **subdued** *ADJECTIVE*

subject *NOUN* subjects
❶ the person or thing being talked or written about or dealt with ❷ something that is studied ❸ (*in grammar*) the word or words naming who or what does the action of a verb, e.g. '*The book*' in *The book fell off the table.* ❹ someone who is ruled by a monarch or government

subject *ADJECTIVE*
ruled by a monarch or government; not independent
➤ **subject to something** depending on something or likely to be affected by it • *Our decision is subject to your approval.* • *Trains are subject to delays because of flooding.*

subject (say sub-**jekt**) *VERB* subjects, subjecting, subjected
❶ to make a person or thing undergo something • *They subjected him to hours of questioning.* ❷ to bring a country under your control
➤ **subjection** *NOUN*

subjective *ADJECTIVE*
❶ based on a person's own tastes, feelings or opinions. Compare with **objective**. ❷ existing only in a person's mind and not produced by things outside it

subjugate *VERB* subjugates, subjugating, subjugated
to defeat a country or group of people and bring the people under your control
➤ **subjugation** *NOUN*

subjunctive *NOUN* subjunctives
the form of a verb used to indicate what is imagined or wished or possible. There are only a few cases where it is commonly used in English, e.g. '*were*' in *if I were you* and '*save*' in *God save the Queen.*

sublime *ADJECTIVE*
❶ noble or impressive • *sublime poetry*
❷ extreme; not caring about the consequences • *with sublime carelessness*

submarine *NOUN* submarines
a ship that can travel under water

submarine *ADJECTIVE*
under the sea • *They laid a submarine cable.*

submerge *VERB* submerges, submerging, submerged
to go under water or to put something under water • *The boat was now partly submerged.*
➤ **submersion** *NOUN*

submission *NOUN* submissions
❶ submitting to someone • *He bowed his head in submission.* ❷ something that you submit or offer for consideration

submissive *ADJECTIVE*
willing to obey

submit *VERB* submits, submitting, submitted
❶ to give in to someone or agree to obey them ❷ to hand something in or offer it to be judged or considered • *Submit your plans to the committee.*

subordinate *ADJECTIVE*
❶ less important ❷ lower in rank

subordinate *NOUN* subordinates
a person working under someone's authority or control

subordinate *VERB* subordinates,
subordinating, subordinated
to treat something as being less important
than another thing

subordinate clause *NOUN* subordinate
clauses
a clause which adds details to the main clause
of the sentence, but cannot be used as a
sentence by itself

sub-plot *NOUN* sub-plots
a secondary plot in a play, film or novel

subpoena (say sub-**peen**-a) *NOUN* subpoenas
an official document ordering a person to
appear in a law court

subpoena *VERB* subpoenas, subpoenaing,
subpoenaed
to summon someone by a subpoena
(**WORD ORIGIN**) from Latin *sub poena* = under a
penalty (because there is a punishment for not
obeying the order to appear)

sub-post office *NOUN* sub-post offices
a small local post office, often in a shop,
which offers fewer services than a main post
office

subscribe *VERB* subscribes, subscribing,
subscribed
❶ to make a regular payment in order to
be a member of a society or to receive a
magazine or other service ❷ to apply to take
part in something • *The course is already
fully subscribed.* ❸ to contribute money to
a project or charity ❹ to say that you agree
with something • *We cannot subscribe to this
theory.*
➤ **subscriber** *NOUN*

subscription *NOUN* subscriptions
money you pay to subscribe to something

subsequent *ADJECTIVE*
coming after something in time or order; later
• *Subsequent events proved that she was
right.*
➤ **subsequently** *ADVERB*

subservient *ADJECTIVE*
prepared to obey others without question
➤ **subservience** *NOUN*

subset *NOUN* subsets
a group or set forming part of a larger group
or set

subside *VERB* subsides, subsiding, subsided
❶ to begin to sink into the ground • *The
house has subsided over the years.* ❷ to
become less intense or quieter • *Her fear
subsided.*

subsidence (say sub-**sy**-dens or **sub**-sid-ens)
NOUN
the gradual sinking or caving in of an area of
land

subsidiary
less important; secondary

subsidiary *NOUN* subsidiaries
a business company that is controlled by
another larger company

subsidize (also **subsidise**) *VERB* subsidizes,
subsidizing, subsidized
to pay a subsidy to a person or firm

subsidy *NOUN* subsidies
money paid to an industry that needs help or
to keep down the price at which its goods or
services are sold to the public

subsist *VERB* subsists, subsisting, subsisted
to manage to live with very little food or
money • *We subsisted on fruit and nuts.*
➤ **subsistence** *NOUN*

subsoil *NOUN*
soil lying just below the surface layer

substance *NOUN* substances
❶ a solid or liquid material; what something
is made of • *Glue is a sticky substance.* ❷ the
main or essential part of something • *We
agree with the substance of your report but
not with its details.*

sub-standard *ADJECTIVE*
below the normal or required standard

substantial *ADJECTIVE*
❶ of great size, value or importance • *a
substantial fee* ❷ solidly built • *substantial
houses*

substantially *ADVERB*
mostly • *The rules of the two games are
substantially the same.*

substation *NOUN* substations
a subsidiary station for distributing electric
current

substitute *NOUN* substitutes
a person or thing that acts or is used instead
of another

substitute *VERB* substitutes, substituting,
substituted
to substitute one thing or person for another
is to use the first one instead of the second
• *In this recipe you can substitute oil for
butter.*
➤ **substitution** *NOUN*

a
b
c
d
e
f
g
h
i
j
k
l
m
n
o
p
q
r
s
t
u
v
w
x
y
z

subterfuge *NOUN* subterfuges
a deception

subterranean *ADJECTIVE*
underground • *a subterranean river*

subtitle *NOUN* subtitles
❶ a secondary or additional title ❷ words shown on the screen during a film, e.g. to translate a foreign language

subtle (say **sut**-el) *ADJECTIVE*
❶ faint or delicate • *This soup has a subtle flavour.* ❷ slight and difficult to detect or describe • *a subtle distinction* ❸ ingenious but not immediately obvious • *a subtle joke*
➤ **subtly** *ADVERB*
➤ **subtlety** *NOUN*

subtotal *NOUN* subtotals
the total of part of a group of figures

subtract *VERB* subtracts, subtracting, subtracted
to subtract one number or amount from another is to take it away • *If you subtract 2 from 7, you get 5.*

subtraction *NOUN*
the process of taking one number or amount from another

subtropical *ADJECTIVE*
of regions that border on the tropics

suburb *NOUN* suburbs
a district with houses that is outside the central part of a city
➤ **suburban** *ADJECTIVE*

suburbia *NOUN*
the suburbs of a city and the people who live there

subvert *VERB* subverts, subverting, subverted
to try to destroy or weaken something by attacking it secretly and in an indirect way
➤ **subversion** *NOUN*
➤ **subversive** *ADJECTIVE*

subway *NOUN* subways
❶ an underground passage for pedestrians ❷ (*North American*) an underground railway

succeed *VERB* succeeds, succeeding, succeeded
❶ to do or get what you wanted or intended ❷ to come after another person or thing • *The bells stopped and were succeeded by a strange clanking noise.* ❸ to become the next holder of an office, especially the monarchy • *She succeeded to the throne.* • *Edward VII succeeded Queen Victoria.*

success *NOUN* successes
❶ doing or getting what you wanted or intended ❷ a person or thing that does well • *The show was a great success.*

> **SPELLING**
> There is a double **c** and double **s** in **success**.

successful *ADJECTIVE*
having success or being a success
➤ **successfully** *ADVERB*

succession *NOUN* successions
❶ a series of people or things ❷ the process of following in order ❸ succeeding to the throne; the right of doing this
➤ **in succession** one after another

successive *ADJECTIVE*
following one after another • *on five successive days*
➤ **successively** *ADVERB*

successor *NOUN* successors
a person or thing that comes after another and takes their place

succinct (say suk-**sinkt**) *ADJECTIVE*
concise; expressed briefly • *a succinct reply*
➤ **succinctly** *ADVERB*

succour (say **suk**-er) *NOUN*
help given in time of need

succour *VERB* succours, succouring, succoured
to offer help to someone in need

succulent *ADJECTIVE*
❶ juicy and tasty ❷ succulent plants have thick juicy leaves or stems

succumb (say suk-**um**) *VERB* succumbs, succumbing, succumbed
to give way to something overpowering • *He finally succumbed to curiosity and went to look.*

such *DETERMINER*
❶ of the same kind; similar • *Cakes, biscuits and all such foods are fattening.* ❷ of the kind described • *There's no such person.* ❸ so great or so much • *It gave me such a fright!*
➤ **such as** for example

such-and-such *DETERMINER*
one in particular but you are not saying which • *He promises to come at such-and-such a time but is always late.*

suchlike *PRONOUN*
of that kind

suck *VERB* sucks, sucking, sucked
❶ to take in liquid or air through almost-

closed lips ❷ to squeeze something in your mouth by using your tongue • *She was sucking a sweet.* ❸ to draw something in • *The canoe was sucked into the whirlpool.*
➤ **suck up to someone** (*informal*) to flatter someone in the hope of winning their favour

suck *NOUN* **sucks**
the action of sucking

sucker *NOUN* **suckers**
❶ a rubber or plastic cup that sticks to a surface by suction ❷ an organ on the body of an animal or insect that it uses to cling to a surface by suction ❸ a shoot coming up from a root or underground stem ❹ (*informal*) a person who is easily deceived

suckle *VERB* **suckles, suckling, suckled**
to feed on milk at the mother's breast or udder

sucrose *NOUN*
the form of sugar that is obtained from sugar cane and sugar beet

suction *NOUN*
❶ the process of sucking ❷ producing a vacuum so that things are sucked into the empty space • *Vacuum cleaners work by suction.*

sudden *ADJECTIVE*
happening or done quickly and without warning
➤ **suddenness** *NOUN*

suddenly *ADVERB*
quickly and without warning • *Suddenly, everyone started shouting.*

sudoku (say soo-**doh**-koo) *NOUN* **sudokus**
a puzzle in which you have to write the numbers 1 to 9 in a particular pattern in a grid of 81 squares

suds *PLURAL NOUN*
froth on soapy water

sue *VERB* **sues, suing, sued**
to start a lawsuit to claim money from someone

suede (say swayd) *NOUN*
leather with one side rubbed to make it soft and velvety

suet *NOUN*
hard fat from cattle and sheep, used in cooking

suffer *VERB* **suffers, suffering, suffered**
❶ to feel pain or sadness ❷ to experience something bad • *The house suffered some damage.* • *She suffers from hay fever.* ❸ to

become worse or be badly affected • *She's not sleeping and her work is suffering.*
➤ **sufferer** *NOUN*

sufferance *NOUN*
➤ **on sufferance** allowed but only reluctantly

suffering *NOUN* **sufferings**
pain or misery

suffice *VERB* **suffices, sufficing, sufficed**
to be enough for someone's needs • *A couple of hours should suffice.*

sufficient *ADJECTIVE*
enough; as much as is necessary
➤ **sufficiently** *ADVERB*

suffix *NOUN* **suffixes**
a letter or set of letters joined to the end of a word to make another word (e.g. in forget*ful*, lion*ess*, rust*y*) or a form of a verb (e.g. sing*ing*, wait*ed*)

> **GRAMMAR**
>
> **Suffixes** are groups of letters that are not themselves words, but can be combined with other words to change their meaning and form new words. Suffixes are added at the end of other words (e.g. read*able*, green*ish*, pictur*esque*).
>
> Some suffixes make words that are closely related to the original word. For example, suffixes such as *-ly*, *-ity*, *-ness*, and *-y*, are used to form derivatives which belong to a new word class (e.g. *naturally, normality, softness*).
>
> Words like *free* and *friendly* can be added to the ends of other words to form compounds (e.g. *dairy-free, user-friendly*). These are not true suffixes but separate words in their own right.

suffocate *VERB* **suffocates, suffocating, suffocated**
❶ to suffer or die because you cannot breathe ❷ to make it difficult or impossible for someone to breathe
➤ **suffocation** *NOUN*

suffrage *NOUN*
the right to vote in political elections

suffragette *NOUN* **suffragettes**
a woman who campaigned in the early 20th century for women to have the right to vote

suffuse *VERB* **suffuses, suffusing, suffused**
to spread through or over something • *A blush suffused her cheeks.*

a b c d e f g h i j k l m n o p q r s t u v w x y z

sugar *NOUN*
a sweet food obtained from the juices of various plants, such as sugar cane or sugar beet

sugar *VERB* sugars, sugaring, sugared
to add sugar to food or drink

sugary *ADJECTIVE*
sugary food or drink has a lot of sugar in it

suggest *VERB* suggests, suggesting, suggested
❶ to put forward an idea or plan for someone to consider ❷ to make an idea or possibility come into your mind • *Her smile suggested that she agreed with me.*

suggestion *NOUN* suggestions
❶ something that you mention to someone as an idea or possibility ❷ a slight amount or sign of something • *There was a suggestion of a sob in her voice.*

suggestive *ADJECTIVE*
making you think of something • *This music is suggestive of the sea.*

suicide *NOUN* suicides
❶ killing yourself deliberately • *He committed suicide.* ❷ a person who deliberately kills himself or herself
➤ **suicidal** *ADJECTIVE*

suit *NOUN* suits
❶ a matching jacket and trousers or a jacket and skirt, that are meant to be worn together ❷ a set of clothing for a particular activity • *a diving suit* ❸ any of the four sets of cards (clubs, hearts, diamonds, spades) in a pack of playing cards ❹ a lawsuit

SPELLING
Take care not to confuse with **suite**.

suit *VERB* suits, suiting, suited
❶ to be suitable or convenient for a person or thing ❷ a piece of clothing or hairstyle suits you when it looks good on you

suitable *ADJECTIVE*
satisfactory or right for a particular person, purpose or occasion
➤ **suitably** *ADVERB*
➤ **suitability** *NOUN*

suitcase *NOUN* suitcases
a rectangular container for carrying clothes, usually with a hinged lid and a handle

suite (say sweet) *NOUN* suites
❶ a set of matching furniture ❷ a set of rooms in a hotel ❸ a set of short pieces of music

SPELLING
Take care not to confuse with **suit**.

suitor *NOUN* suitors
a man who is courting a woman

sulk *VERB* sulks, sulking, sulked
to be silent and bad-tempered because you are not pleased

sulk *NOUN* sulks
a period of sulking

sulky *ADJECTIVE*
silent and bad-tempered because you are not pleased • *He sat in sulky silence.*
➤ **sulkily** *ADVERB*
➤ **sulkiness** *NOUN*

sullen *ADJECTIVE*
sulking and gloomy
➤ **sullenly** *ADVERB*
➤ **sullenness** *NOUN*

sully *VERB* sullies, sullying, sullied
to stain or spoil something; to blemish something • *The scandal sullied his reputation.*

sulphur *NOUN*
a yellow chemical used in industry and in medicine
➤ **sulphurous** *ADJECTIVE*

sulphuric acid *NOUN*
a strong colourless acid containing sulphur

sultan *NOUN* sultans
the ruler of certain Muslim countries

sultana *NOUN* sultanas
a raisin without seeds

sultry *ADJECTIVE*
hot and humid • *sultry weather*

sum *NOUN* sums
❶ a total ❷ a problem in arithmetic ❸ an amount of money

sum *VERB* sums, summing, summed
➤ **sum up** to give a summary at the end of a talk or discussion

SPELLING
Do not confuse this word with **some**.

summarize (also **summarise**) *VERB* summarizes, summarizing, summarized
to make or give a summary of something • *Let me first summarize the plot of the novel.*

summary *NOUN* **summaries**
a statement of the main points of something said or written

summary *ADJECTIVE*
❶ brief or concise • *a summary report*
❷ done or given hastily, without delay
• *summary punishment*
➤ **summarily** *ADVERB*

summer *NOUN* **summers**
the warm season between spring and autumn
➤ **summery** *ADJECTIVE*

summer house *NOUN* **summer houses**
a small building providing shade in a garden or park

summertime *NOUN*
the season of summer

summit *NOUN* **summits**
❶ the top of a mountain or hill ❷ a meeting between the leaders of powerful countries • *a summit conference*

summon *VERB* **summons, summoning, summoned**
❶ to order someone to come or appear
❷ to call people together • *A meeting of the governors was quickly summoned.*
➤ **summon something up** to gather together your strength or courage in order to do something • *I couldn't even summon up the energy to get out of bed.*

summons *NOUN* **summonses**
a command to appear in a law court

sump *NOUN* **sumps**
a metal case that holds oil round an engine

sumptuous *ADJECTIVE*
splendid and expensive-looking • *a sumptuous feast*
➤ **sumptuously** *ADVERB*

sun *NOUN* **suns**
❶ the star round which the earth travels
❷ light and warmth from the sun • *Let's sit in the sun.* ❸ any star in the universe round which planets travel

sun *VERB* **suns, sunning, sunned**
➤ **sun yourself** to sit or lie in the sunshine

sunbathe *VERB* **sunbathes, sunbathing, sunbathed**
to sit or lie in the sunshine to get a suntan

sunbeam *NOUN* **sunbeams**
a ray of the sun

sunbed *NOUN* **sunbeds**
(*British*) a bench that you lie on under a sunlamp

sunblock *NOUN*
a cream or lotion that you put on your skin to protect it from the sun's harmful rays

sunburn *NOUN*
redness of the skin someone gets if they are in the sun for too long
➤ **sunburnt** or **sunburned** *ADJECTIVE*

sundae (say **sun**-day) *NOUN* **sundaes**
a mixture of ice cream and fruit, nuts and cream **WORD ORIGIN** from **Sunday** (because sundaes were originally sold then, possibly to use up ice cream not sold during the week)

Sunday *NOUN*
the day of the week between Saturday and Monday, thought of as either the first or the last day of the week **WORD ORIGIN** from Old English *sunnandaeg* = day of the sun

sunder *VERB* **sunders, sundering, sundered** (*poetical use*)
to break or tear something apart

sundial *NOUN* **sundials**
a device that shows the time by a shadow on a dial

sundown *NOUN*
(*North American*) sunset

sundries *PLURAL NOUN*
various small things

sundry *ADJECTIVE*
various or several
➤ **all and sundry** all people; everyone

sunflower *NOUN* **sunflowers**
a very tall flower with golden petals round a dark centre **WORD ORIGIN** so called because the flower head turns to follow the sun

sunglasses *PLURAL NOUN*
dark glasses you wear to protect your eyes from strong sunlight

sunken *ADJECTIVE*
sunk deeply into a surface • *Their cheeks were pale and sunken.*

sunlamp *NOUN* **sunlamps**
a lamp which uses ultraviolet light to give people an artificial tan

sunlight *NOUN*
light from the sun

sunlit *ADJECTIVE*
lit by sunlight • *a sunlit courtyard*

Sunni NOUN Sunnis
a member of one of the two main branches of
Islam, based on the teachings of Muhammad
and regarding his father-in-law Abu Bakr
as his successor; about 90% of Muslims are
Sunnis. Compare with **Shiite**.

sunny ADJECTIVE sunnier, sunniest
❶ full of sunshine • *a sunny day* ❷ cheerful
• *She was in a sunny mood.*

sunrise NOUN sunrises
the rising of the sun; dawn • *They left at
sunrise.*

sunscreen NOUN
a cream or lotion that you put on your skin to
protect it from the sun's harmful rays

sunset NOUN sunsets
the setting of the sun

sunshade NOUN sunshades
a parasol or other device to protect people
from the sun

sunshine NOUN
warmth and light that comes from the sun

sunspot NOUN sunspots
a dark place on the sun's surface

sunstroke NOUN
an illness caused by being in the sun too long

suntan NOUN suntans
a brown colour of the skin caused by the sun
➤ **suntanned** ADJECTIVE

sun visor NOUN sun visors
a flap at the top of a vehicle's windscreen
that shields your eyes from the sun

sup VERB sups, supping, supped
to drink liquid in sips or spoonfuls

super ADJECTIVE (*informal*)
excellent or superb

superb ADJECTIVE
magnificent or excellent
➤ **superbly** ADVERB

supercilious ADJECTIVE
haughty and scornful (WORD ORIGIN) from
Latin *supercilium* = eyebrow, because raising
the eyebrows is a sign of this attitude

superficial ADJECTIVE
❶ on the surface • *It's only a superficial
cut.* ❷ not deep or thorough • *a superficial
knowledge of French*
➤ **superficially** ADVERB
➤ **superficiality** NOUN

superfluous (say soo-**per**-floo-us) ADJECTIVE
more than is wanted; not necessary • *He gave
me a look that made any words superfluous.*
➤ **superfluity** NOUN

superglue NOUN
a kind of strong glue that sticks very quickly

superhuman ADJECTIVE
❶ beyond ordinary human ability
• *superhuman strength* ❷ higher than
human; divine

superimpose VERB superimposes,
superimposing, superimposed
to place a thing on top of something else

superintend VERB superintends,
superintending, superintended
to be in charge of someone or something

superintendent NOUN superintendents
❶ a supervisor ❷ a police officer above the
rank of inspector

superior ADJECTIVE
❶ higher in position or rank • *She is your
superior officer.* ❷ better than another
person or thing ❸ showing that you think
you are better than other people

superior NOUN superiors
a person or thing that is superior to another

superiority NOUN
❶ being better than something else
❷ behaviour that shows you think you are
better than other people

superlative ADJECTIVE
of the highest degree or quality • *superlative
skill*
➤ **superlatively** ADVERB

superlative NOUN superlatives
the form of an adjective or adverb that
expresses 'most' • *The superlative of 'big'
is 'biggest' and the superlative of 'bad' is
'worst'.*

(GRAMMAR)

Superlative adjectives and adverbs are
used to compare and contrast people,
things or actions. The superlative shows
which of three or more things is greatest
or most: *Cheetahs are the <u>fastest</u> land
animals.*

For many adjectives, and some adverbs,
the superlative is formed by adding *-est*
(or *-st* if the word already ends in e). Note
that some adjectives double their final
letter, and those ending in -*y* change to -*i*

before adding -est:

This flower is the biggest and palest in the garden.

What's the scariest film you've ever seen?

For longer adjectives, and for adverbs ending in -ly, the superlative is formed with *most*:

Hot-air balloons are the most interesting way to travel.

It was the most beautifully painted picture I had ever seen.

However, some common adjectives and adverbs have irregular superlatives which in some cases are different words, e.g. *good | well* (*best*), *bad | badly* (*worst*) and *far* (*farthest* or *furthest*).

You will find guidance in this dictionary on irregular superlatives.

See also the panel on **comparatives**.

superman *NOUN* **supermen**
a man with superhuman powers

supermarket *NOUN* **supermarkets**
a large self-service shop that sells food and other goods

supernatural *ADJECTIVE*
not belonging to the natural world or having a natural explanation • *supernatural beings such as ghosts*
➤ **supernatural** *NOUN*

superpower *NOUN* **superpowers**
one of the most powerful nations of the world, such as the USA

supersede *VERB* **supersedes, superseding, superseded**
to take the place of something • *Cars superseded horse-drawn carriages.*

supersonic *ADJECTIVE*
faster than the speed of sound

superstition *NOUN* **superstitions**
a belief or action that is not based on reason or evidence, e.g. the belief that it is unlucky to walk under a ladder

superstitious *ADJECTIVE*
believing in superstitions • *I'm very superstitious about the number 13.*

superstore *NOUN* **superstores**
a very large supermarket selling a wide range of goods

superstructure *NOUN* **superstructures**
❶ a structure that rests on something else
❷ a building as distinct from its foundations

supertanker *NOUN* **supertankers**
a very large tanker

supervise *VERB* **supervises, supervising, supervised**
to be in charge of a person or thing and inspect what is done • *Your job is to supervise the building of the bridge.*
➤ **supervision** *NOUN*
➤ **supervisor** *NOUN*

superwoman *NOUN* **superwomen**
a woman with superhuman powers

supper *NOUN* **suppers**
a meal eaten in the evening

supplant *VERB* **supplants, supplanting, supplanted**
to take the place of a person or thing that has been removed

supple *ADJECTIVE*
able to bend easily; flexible, not stiff
➤ **suppleness** *NOUN*

supplement *NOUN* **supplements**
❶ something added as an extra ❷ an extra section added to a book or newspaper • *the colour supplement*

supplement *VERB* **supplements, supplementing, supplemented**
to add to something • *Some people take vitamin pills to supplement their diet.*

supplementary *ADJECTIVE*
added as an extra • *supplementary information*

suppliant (say sup-lee-ant) (or **supplicant**) *NOUN* **suppliants, supplicants**
a person who asks humbly for something

supplication *NOUN*
asking or begging humbly for something, especially when praying • *She knelt in supplication.*

supply *VERB* **supplies, supplying, supplied**
to give or sell or provide what is needed or wanted
➤ **supplier** *NOUN*

supply *NOUN* **supplies**
❶ an amount of something that is kept ready to be used when needed • *We keep a supply*

of paper in the cupboard. ❷ supplies are things like food, medicines or fuel needed by an army, expedition, etc. • *Their supplies were running out.* ❸ the action of supplying something

supply teacher NOUN supply teachers
a teacher who takes the place of a regular teacher when he or she is away

support VERB supports, supporting, supported
❶ to hold something up so that it does not fall down ❷ to give help or encouragement to someone or something • *Not many people supported this proposal.* ❸ to like a particular sports team and want it do well • *Which football team do you support?* ❹ to provide someone with the necessities of life • *She has two children to support.*

support NOUN supports
❶ the action of supporting • *You can rely on my support.* ❷ a person or thing that supports

supporter NOUN supporters
a person who supports something, especially a sports team or political party • *football supporters*

supportive ADJECTIVE
giving help or support to someone in a difficult situation • *She received many supportive emails.*

suppose VERB supposes, supposing, supposed
❶ to think that something is likely to happen or be true • *Yes, I suppose you're right.* ❷ to assume something or consider it as a suggestion • *Suppose the world were flat.*
➤ **be supposed to do something** to be expected to do something; to have to do something as a duty

supposedly ADVERB
so people believe or think • *They are supposedly the best team in the world.*

supposition NOUN suppositions
something that a person thinks is likely or true

suppress VERB suppresses, suppressing, suppressed
❶ to put an end to something using force or by authority • *Troops suppressed the rebellion.* ❷ to keep something from being known or seen • *They suppressed the truth.* • *He managed to suppress a smile.*
➤ **suppression** NOUN

supremacy (say soo-**prem**-asi) NOUN
having more authority or power than anyone else

supreme ADJECTIVE
❶ most important or highest in rank ❷ very great • *With a supreme effort, he managed not to laugh.*

supremely ADVERB
extremely • *supremely happy*

surcharge NOUN surcharges
an extra charge

sure ADJECTIVE
❶ completely confident that you are right; feeling no doubt • *Are you sure you locked the door?* ❷ certain to happen or do something • *Our team is sure to win.* ❸ reliable; that you can be certain of • *A cold wind like that is a sure sign of winter.* ❹ steady and confident • *a sure aim*
➤ **for sure** definitely
➤ **make sure** ❶ to find out exactly ❷ to make something happen or be true • *Make sure you have everything you need before you start.*

sure ADVERB (*informal*) surely; certainly
➤ **sure enough** certainly; in fact

surely ADVERB
❶ without doubt; certainly • *This will surely cause problems.* ❷ it must be true; I feel sure • *Surely I met you last year.*

sureness NOUN
the quality of being steady and confident • *the sureness of her aim*

surety NOUN sureties
❶ a guarantee ❷ a person who promises to pay a debt or fulfil a contract if another person fails to do so

surf NOUN
the white foam of waves breaking on a rock or shore

surf VERB surfs, surfing, surfed
❶ to go surfing ❷ to browse through the Internet

surface NOUN surfaces
❶ the outside of something ❷ any of the sides of an object, especially the top part ❸ an outward appearance • *On the surface he was a kindly man.*

surface VERB surfaces, surfacing, surfaced
❶ to come up to the surface from under water • *The submarine slowly surfaced.* ❷ to put a surface on a road or path

surface mail *NOUN*
letters and packages carried by sea or over land, not by air

surfboard *NOUN* surfboards
a board used in surfing

surfeit (say **ser**-fit) *NOUN*
too much of something
➤ **surfeited** *ADJECTIVE*

surfer *NOUN* surfers
a person who goes surfing

surfing *NOUN*
balancing yourself on a board that is carried to the shore on the waves

surge *VERB* surges, surging, surged
❶ to move forwards or upwards like waves ❷ to increase suddenly and powerfully

surge *NOUN* surges
❶ a sudden rush forward or upward ❷ a sudden increase in something, especially a strong feeling • *I felt a surge of panic.*

surgeon *NOUN* surgeons
a doctor who treats disease or injury by cutting or repairing the affected parts of the body

surgery *NOUN* surgeries
❶ the work of a surgeon ❷ the place where a doctor or dentist regularly gives advice and treatment to patients ❸ the time when patients can visit a doctor or dentist

surgical *ADJECTIVE*
to do with a surgeon or surgery • *surgical instruments*
➤ **surgically** *ADVERB*

surly *ADJECTIVE* surlier, surliest
bad-tempered and unfriendly • *He glared at them in surly silence.*
➤ **surliness** *NOUN*

surmise *VERB* surmises, surmising, surmised
to guess or suspect something

surmise *NOUN* surmises
a guess

surmount *VERB* surmounts, surmounting, surmounted
❶ to overcome a difficulty ❷ to get over an obstacle ❸ to be on top of something • *The museum is surmounted by a huge dome.*

surname *NOUN* surnames
the name that you share with other members of your family

surpass *VERB* surpasses, surpassing, surpassed
to do or be better than someone or something • *It surpassed her wildest dreams.*

surplus *NOUN* surpluses
an amount left over after you have spent or used what you need

surplus *ADJECTIVE*
more than you need • *Squirrels store surplus food, usually by burying it.*

surprise *NOUN* surprises
❶ something unexpected ❷ the feeling caused by something that was not expected
➤ **take someone by surprise** to happen to someone unexpectedly

surprise *VERB* surprises, surprising, surprised
❶ to be a surprise; to make someone feel surprise ❷ to come upon or attack someone unexpectedly

SPELLING
There is an **r** after the **u** in **surprise**.

surprised *ADJECTIVE*
feeling or showing surprise

surprising *ADJECTIVE*
causing surprise
➤ **surprisingly** *ADVERB*

surreal *ADJECTIVE*
strange and bizarre, like some dreams are

surrealism *NOUN*
a style of painting that shows strange objects and scenes like those seen in dreams and fantasies
➤ **surrealist** *NOUN*

surrender *VERB* surrenders, surrendering, surrendered
❶ to stop fighting and give yourself up to an enemy ❷ to hand something over to another person, especially when forced to do so

surrender *NOUN*
when someone surrenders • *They raised their hands in surrender.*

surreptitious (say su-rep-**tish**-us) *ADJECTIVE*
done secretly or quickly so other people will not notice • *a surreptitious peep*
➤ **surreptitiously** *ADVERB*

surrogate mother *NOUN* surrogate mothers
a woman who agrees to conceive and give birth to a baby for a woman who cannot have a baby herself

surround *VERB* surrounds, surrounding, surrounded

to come or be all round a person or thing
• *Police surrounded the building.*

surroundings *PLURAL NOUN*
the conditions or area around a person or thing

surveillance (say ser-**vay**-lans) *NOUN*
a close watch kept on a person or thing
• *Police kept him under surveillance.*

survey (say **ser**-vay) *NOUN* **surveys**
❶ a general look at something ❷ an inspection of an area or building

survey (say ser-**vay**) *VERB* **surveys, surveying, surveyed**
❶ to look carefully at the whole of something • *He stood in the doorway and surveyed the room.* ❷ to make a survey of an area or building
➤ **surveyor** *NOUN*

survival *NOUN* **survivals**
❶ surviving; the likelihood of surviving
• *Finding shelter was his only chance of survival.* ❷ something that has survived from an earlier time

survive *VERB* **survives, surviving, survived**
❶ to stay alive; to continue to exist ❷ to remain alive after an accident or disaster
• *Only two people survived the crash.* ❸ to continue living after someone has died

survivor *NOUN* **survivors**
a person who survives, especially after an accident or disaster

susceptible (say sus-**ept**-ib-ul) *ADJECTIVE*
likely to be affected by something • *She is susceptible to colds.*
➤ **susceptibility** *NOUN*

suspect (say sus-**pekt**) *VERB* **suspects, suspecting, suspected**
❶ to think that a person is not to be trusted or has committed a crime; to distrust someone ❷ to have a feeling that something is likely or possible • *I suspect I've sprained my ankle.*

suspect (say **sus**-pekt) *NOUN* **suspects**
a person who is suspected of a crime or doing something wrong

suspect (say **sus**-pekt) *ADJECTIVE*
possibly not true or not to be trusted

suspend *VERB* **suspends, suspending, suspended**
❶ to hang something up • *A lamp was suspended from the ceiling.* ❷ to postpone something or stop it temporarily ❸ to remove a person from a job or position for a time

• *He was suspended for three matches for hitting another player.* ❹ to keep something from falling or sinking in air or liquid
• *Particles are suspended in the fluid.*

suspender *NOUN* **suspenders**
a fastener to hold up a sock or stocking by its top

suspense *NOUN*
an anxious or uncertain feeling while waiting for something to happen or become known
• *Don't keep us all in suspense – tell us who won.*

suspension *NOUN* **suspensions**
❶ suspending something or someone ❷ the springs etc. in a vehicle that lessen the effect of rough road surfaces ❸ a liquid containing small pieces of solid material which do not dissolve

suspension bridge *NOUN* **suspension bridges**
a bridge supported by cables

suspicion *NOUN* **suspicions**
❶ a feeling that someone has done something wrong or cannot be trusted ❷ a slight feeling that something is likely or possible • *I have a suspicion that he has forgotten he invited us.*

suspicious *ADJECTIVE*
❶ making you suspect or distrust someone or something • *There are suspicious footprints along the path.* ❷ suspecting or distrusting someone or something • *I'm suspicious about what happened.*
➤ **suspiciously** *ADVERB*

SPELLING
There is a tricky bit in **suspicious** – it has ci in the middle.

sustain *VERB* **sustains, sustaining, sustained**
❶ to keep something going • *It's hard to sustain interest for such a long time.*
❷ to keep someone alive or healthy ❸ to experience or suffer something bad • *He sustained serious injuries.*

sustainable *ADJECTIVE*
❶ using natural products and energy in a way that does not harm the environment
• *sustainable forests* ❷ able to be continued for a long time

sustenance *NOUN*
food and drink; nourishment

suture (say **soo**-cher) *NOUN* **sutures**
surgical stitching of a cut

SW *ABBREVIATION*
❶ south-west ❷ south-western

swab (say swob) *NOUN* swabs
❶ a mop or pad for cleaning or wiping something; a small pad for cleaning a wound
❷ a specimen of fluid from the body taken on a swab for testing

swab *VERB* swabs, swabbing, swabbed
to clean or wipe something with a swab

swagger *VERB* swaggers, swaggering, swaggered
to walk or behave in a conceited and confident way

swagger *NOUN*
a way of walking or behaving that seems too confident

swain *NOUN* swains (*old use*)
❶ a country lad ❷ a young lover or suitor

swallow *VERB* swallows, swallowing, swallowed
❶ to make something go down your throat
❷ to believe something that ought not to be believed • *I found her excuse hard to swallow.*
➤ **swallow something up** to take something in and completely cover it • *She walked away and was soon swallowed up in the crowd.*

swallow *NOUN* swallows
a small bird with a forked tail and pointed wings

swamp *NOUN* swamps
an area of soft, wet land; a marsh
➤ **swampy** *ADJECTIVE*

swamp *VERB* swamps, swamping, swamped
❶ to flood an area ❷ to overwhelm someone with a great mass or number of things • *They have been swamped with complaints.*

swan *NOUN* swans
a large usually white swimming bird with a long neck

swanky *ADJECTIVE*
(*informal*) fashionable and expensive • *a swanky restaurant*

swansong *NOUN* swansongs
a person's last performance or work
WORD ORIGIN from the old belief that a swan sang sweetly when it was about to die

swap (*informal*) *VERB* swaps, swapping, swapped
to exchange one thing for another

swap *NOUN* swaps
❶ an act of swapping • *Let's do a swap.*
❷ something you swap for something else

WORD ORIGIN formerly = seal a bargain by slapping each other's hands; imitating the sound

swarm *NOUN* swarms
a large number of insects flying or moving about together

swarm *VERB* swarms, swarming, swarmed
❶ to gather or move in a swarm ❷ to be crowded with people • *The town is swarming with tourists in the summer.*

swarthy *ADJECTIVE*
having a dark complexion
➤ **swarthiness** *NOUN*

swashbuckling *ADJECTIVE*
a swashbuckling film is full of daring adventures and sword-fighting, set in the past

swastika *NOUN* swastikas
an ancient symbol formed by a cross with its ends bent at right angles, adopted by the Nazis as their sign **WORD ORIGIN** from Sanskrit *svasti* = well-being, luck

swat *VERB* swats, swatting, swatted
to hit or crush a fly or other insect
➤ **swatter** *NOUN*

swathe (say swawth) *NOUN* swathes
a broad strip or area • *vast swathes of countryside*
➤ **cut a swathe through something** to pass through an area causing destruction

swathe (say swayth) *VERB* swathes, swathing, swathed
to wrap a person or thing in layers of bandages, paper or clothes

sway *VERB* sways, swaying, swayed
❶ to move or swing gently from side to side • *Trees were swaying in the wind.* ❷ to influence or affect someone • *His speech swayed the crowd.*
➤ **sway** *NOUN*

swear *VERB* swears, swearing, swore, sworn
❶ to make a solemn promise • *She swore to tell the truth.* ❷ to make someone promise something • *We swore him to secrecy.* ❸ to use very rude or offensive words
➤ **swear by something** to have great confidence in something

swear word *NOUN* swear words
a word considered rude or shocking, often used by someone who is angry

sweat (say swet) *NOUN*
moisture given off by your body through the pores of your skin; perspiration

a b c d e f g h i j k l m n o p q r s t u v w x y z

sweat *VERB* sweats, sweating, sweated
to give off sweat; to perspire

sweater *NOUN* sweaters
a jersey or pullover

sweatshirt *NOUN* sweatshirts
a thick cotton jersey worn for sports or casual wear

sweaty *ADJECTIVE*
covered or damp with sweat

swede *NOUN* swedes
a large kind of turnip with purple skin and yellow flesh **WORD ORIGIN** short for *Swedish turnip* (because it originally came from Sweden)

sweep *VERB* sweeps, sweeping, swept
❶ to clean or clear an area with a broom or brush ❷ to move or remove something quickly • *The floods swept away the bridge.* ❸ to go smoothly and quickly • *She swept out of the room.* ❹ to travel quickly over an area • *A new craze is sweeping the country.*
➤ **sweeper** *NOUN*

sweep *NOUN* sweeps
❶ the process of sweeping • *Give this room a good sweep.* ❷ a sweeping movement ❸ a chimney sweep ❹ a sweepstake

sweeping *ADJECTIVE*
general or wide-ranging • *He made sweeping changes.*

sweepstake *NOUN* sweepstakes
a form of gambling on sporting events in which all the money staked is divided among the winners **WORD ORIGIN** so called because the winner 'sweeps up' all the other players' stakes

sweet *ADJECTIVE*
❶ tasting as if it contains sugar; not bitter ❷ very pleasant • *a sweet smell* ❸ charming or delightful • *What a sweet little cottage.*
➤ **sweetness** *NOUN*
➤ **a sweet tooth** a liking for sweet things

sweet *NOUN* sweets
❶ a small shaped piece of sweet food made with sugar or chocolate ❷ a pudding; the sweet course in a meal ❸ a loved person

sweetcorn *NOUN*
the juicy yellow seeds of maize

sweeten *VERB* sweetens, sweetening, sweetened
to make something sweet
➤ **sweetener** *NOUN*

sweetheart *NOUN* sweethearts
a person you love very much

sweetly *ADVERB*
in an attractive or pleasant way • *She smiled sweetly at him.*

sweetmeat *NOUN* sweetmeats (*old use*)
a sweet

sweet pea *NOUN* sweet peas
a climbing plant with sweet-smelling flowers

sweet potato *NOUN* sweet potatoes
a root vegetable with reddish skin and sweet yellow flesh

swell *VERB* swells, swelling, swelled, swollen or swelled
❶ to become larger or to make something larger • *My ankle was starting to swell.* ❷ to increase in amount, volume or force • *The music began to swell.*

swell *NOUN* swells the rise and fall of the sea's surface

swell *ADJECTIVE* (*informal*) (*North American*) very good

swelling *NOUN* swellings
a swollen place on your body

sweltering *ADJECTIVE*
uncomfortably hot

swerve *VERB* swerves, swerving, swerved
to turn to one side suddenly • *The car swerved to avoid the cyclist.*
➤ **swerve** *NOUN*

swift *ADJECTIVE*
happening or moving quickly • *He drew out his sword in one swift movement.*
➤ **swiftly** *ADVERB*
➤ **swiftness** *NOUN*

swift *NOUN* swifts
a small bird rather like a swallow

swig (*informal*) *VERB* swigs, swigging, swigged
to drink quickly, taking large mouthfuls

swig *NOUN* swigs
a large mouthful of a drink

swill *VERB* swills, swilling, swilled
to pour water over or through something; to wash or rinse something

swill *NOUN*
❶ the process of swilling something • *Give it a swill.* ❷ a sloppy mixture of waste food given to pigs

swim *VERB* swims, swimming, swam, swum
❶ to move your body through the water; to be in the water for pleasure ❷ to cross a stretch of water by swimming • *She swam the Channel.* ❸ to be covered with or full of

liquid • *Our eyes were swimming with tears.*
❹ to feel dizzy • *He felt sick and his head swam.*

swim *NOUN* swims
a spell of swimming • *Let's go for a swim.*

swimmer *NOUN* swimmers
a person who swims • *Are you a good swimmer?*

swimming bath *NOUN* swimming baths
(*British*) a public swimming pool

swimming costume *NOUN* swimming costumes
(*British*) the clothing a woman wears to go swimming; a bikini or swimsuit

swimming pool *NOUN* swimming pools
an artificial pool for swimming in

swimming trunks *PLURAL NOUN*
shorts which a man wears to go swimming

swimsuit *NOUN* swimsuits
a one-piece swimming costume

swindle *VERB* swindles, swindling, swindled
to cheat a person of their money or possessions in business

swindle *NOUN* swindles
a trick to swindle someone
➤ **swindler** *NOUN*

swine *NOUN* swine
❶ a pig ❷ a very unpleasant person
❸ (*informal*) a difficult thing • *This crossword's a real swine!*

swing *VERB* swings, swinging, swung
❶ to move back and forth while hanging
❷ to move or turn in a curve • *The door swung open.* ❸ to change from one opinion or mood to another

swing *NOUN* swings
❶ a swinging movement ❷ a seat hung on chains or ropes so that it can be moved backwards and forwards ❸ the amount by which votes or opinions change from one side to another ❹ a kind of jazz music
➤ **in full swing** full of activity or working fully

swipe *VERB* swipes, swiping, swiped
❶ to hit a person or thing with a swinging blow ❷ (*informal*) to steal something ❸ to pass a credit card through an electronic reading device when making a payment ❹ to move a finger across a touchscreen

swipe *NOUN* swipes
an attempt to hit a person or thing with a swinging blow

swirl *VERB* swirls, swirling, swirled
to move round quickly in circles • *The water swirled down the plug hole.*

swirl *NOUN* swirls
a swirling movement

swish *VERB* swishes, swishing, swished
to move with a hissing or rushing sound

swish *NOUN* swishes
a swishing sound

swish *ADJECTIVE* (*British*) (*informal*) smart and fashionable

Swiss roll *NOUN* Swiss rolls
(*British*) a thin sponge cake spread with jam or cream and rolled up

switch *NOUN* switches
❶ a device that you press or turn to start or stop something working, especially by electricity ❷ a change of opinion, policy or methods ❸ a mechanism for moving the points on a railway track ❹ a flexible rod or whip

switch *VERB* switches, switching, switched
❶ to turn something on or off by means of a switch ❷ to change something suddenly ❸ to replace a thing with something else

switchback *NOUN* switchbacks
a railway at a fair, with steep slopes up and down alternately

switchboard *NOUN* switchboards
a panel with switches for making telephone connections or operating electric circuits; the staff operating a switchboard

swivel *VERB* swivels, swivelling, swivelled
to turn round smoothly • *She swivelled round to say something.*

swollen
past participle of **swell**

swollen *ADJECTIVE*
thicker or wider than usual • *My wrist is still swollen where I bumped it.*

swoon (*old use*) *VERB* swoons, swooning, swooned
to faint

swoon *NOUN*
when someone faints

swoop *VERB* swoops, swooping, swooped
❶ to dive or come down with a rushing movement • *The eagle swooped down on its prey.* ❷ to make a sudden attack or raid

swoop *NOUN* swoops
a sudden dive or attack

a
b
c
d
e
f
g
h
i
j
k
l
m
n
o
p
q
r
s
t
u
v
w
x
y
z

swop *VERB* swops, swopping, swopped
a different spelling of **swap**

sword (say sord) *NOUN* swords
a weapon with a long pointed blade fixed in a handle or hilt
➤ **swordsman** *NOUN*

swordfish *NOUN* swordfish
a large sea fish with a long sword-like upper jaw

sworn *ADJECTIVE*
❶ sworn evidence or testimony is given under oath ❷ sworn enemies are determined to remain enemies

swot (*British*) (*informal*) *VERB* swots, swotting, swotted
to study hard

swot *NOUN* swots
a person who swots

sycamore *NOUN* sycamores
a tall tree with winged seeds, often grown for its timber

syllable *NOUN* syllables
a word or part of a word that has one vowel sound when you say it • *'Cat' has one syllable, 'el-e-phant' has three syllables.*

syllabus *NOUN* syllabuses
a list of the subjects to be studied by a class or for an examination

symbol *NOUN* symbols
❶ a thing used as a sign to stand for something • *The crescent is a symbol of Islam.* ❷ a mark or sign with a special meaning (e.g. +, – and x, in mathematics)

> SPELLING

Take care not to confuse with **cymbal**.

symbolic *ADJECTIVE*
acting as a symbol of something • *The white dove is symbolic of peace.*
➤ **symbolical** *ADJECTIVE*
➤ **symbolically** *ADVERB*

symbolism *NOUN*
the use of symbols to stand for things

symbolize (also **symbolise**) *VERB* symbolizes, symbolizing, symbolized
to be a symbol of something • *Red sometimes symbolizes danger.*

symmetrical *ADJECTIVE*
able to be divided into two halves which are exactly the same but the opposite way round
• *Wheels and butterflies are symmetrical.*
➤ **symmetrically** *ADVERB*

symmetry *NOUN*
the quality of being symmetrical or well-proportioned

> SPELLING

The 'i' sound is spelt with a **y** in **symmetry**. Do not forget to double the **m**.

sympathetic *ADJECTIVE*
feeling or showing sympathy or understanding for someone • *He gave me a sympathetic smile.*
➤ **sympathetically** *ADVERB*

sympathize (also **sympathise**) *VERB* sympathizes, sympathizing, sympathized
to show or feel sympathy • *I sympathize with her and I'll try to help.*
➤ **sympathizer** *NOUN*

sympathy *NOUN* sympathies
❶ the sharing or understanding of other people's feelings or opinions ❷ a feeling of pity or tenderness towards someone who is hurt, sad or in trouble

symphony *NOUN* symphonies
a long piece of music for an orchestra
➤ **symphonic** *ADJECTIVE*

symptom *NOUN* symptoms
a sign that a disease or condition exists • *Red spots are a symptom of measles.*
➤ **symptomatic** *ADJECTIVE*

synagogue (say sin-a-gog) *NOUN* synagogues
a place where Jews meet for worship

synchronize (also **synchronise**) (say sink-ron-yz) *VERB* synchronizes, synchronizing, synchronized
❶ to make things happen at the same time ❷ to make watches or clocks show the same time ❸ to happen at the same time
➤ **synchronization** *NOUN*

syncopated (say sink-o-payt-id) *ADJECTIVE*
a piece of music is syncopated when the strong beats are played weak and the weak beats are played strong
➤ **syncopation** *NOUN*

syndicate *NOUN* syndicates
❶ a group of people or firms who work together in business ❷ a group of people who buy something together or who gamble together, sharing the cost and any gains

syndrome *NOUN* syndromes
❶ a set of symptoms ❷ a set of opinions or ways of behaving that are characteristic of a particular condition

synod (say **sin**-od) *NOUN* **synods**
a council of senior members of the clergy

synonym (say **sin**-o-nim) *NOUN* **synonyms**
a word that means the same or almost the same as another word • *'Large' and 'great' are synonyms of 'big'.*
➤ **synonymous** (say sin-**on**-im-us) *ADJECTIVE*

> **GRAMMAR**
>
> A **synonym** is a word which has the same meaning as or a very similar meaning to, another word. For example, *unhappy, miserable, sorrowful* and *glum* are all synonyms of the word *sad.*
>
> An **antonym** is a word which has the opposite meaning to another word. For example, *visible* is an antonym of *invisible*; and *timid, cowardly* and *spineless* are antonyms of *brave.* Note that some words which look like opposites (e.g. *valuable/invaluable, different/indifferent*) are not true antonyms, because they do not have opposite meanings.
>
> A *thesaurus* is a kind of dictionary which lists synonyms and antonyms of words. You can use a thesaurus to help you find alternatives for words in your writing. For example, instead of repeating the adjective *creepy*, you could vary it with synonyms like *eerie, weird, uncanny, spooky* or *spine-chilling.*

synopsis (say sin-**op**-sis) *NOUN* **synopses**
a summary of a story or book

syntax (say **sin**-taks) *NOUN*
the way words are arranged to make phrases or sentences
➤ **syntactic** *ADJECTIVE*
➤ **syntactically** *ADVERB*

synthesis (say **sin**-thi-sis) *NOUN* **syntheses**
combining different things to make something

synthesize (also **synthesise**) (say **sin**-thi-syz) *VERB* **synthesizes, synthesizing, synthesized**
to make something by combining parts

synthesizer (also **synthesiser**) *NOUN* **synthesizers**
an electronic musical instrument that can make a large variety of sounds

synthetic *ADJECTIVE*
artificially made; not natural • *synthetic fibres*
➤ **synthetically** *ADVERB*

syringe *NOUN* **syringes**
a device for sucking in a liquid and squirting it out

syrup *NOUN*
a thick sweet liquid
➤ **syrupy** *ADJECTIVE*
WORD ORIGIN from Arabic *sharab* = a drink

system *NOUN* **systems**
❶ a set of parts, things or ideas that are organized to work together • *the digestive system* ❷ a way of doing something • *We have a new system for taking books out of the library.*

systematic *ADJECTIVE*
done using a fixed plan or method; methodical • *We began a systematic search of the area.*
➤ **systematically** *ADVERB*

tab *NOUN* **tabs**
a small flap or strip that sticks out
➤ **keep tabs on someone** (*informal*) to watch someone closely

tabard *NOUN* **tabards**
a kind of sleeveless tunic, decorated in the past with a coat of arms

tabby *NOUN* **tabbies**
a grey or brown cat with dark stripes
WORD ORIGIN originally = a kind of striped silk material: named after al-Attabiyya, a district of Baghdad where it was made

tabernacle *NOUN* **tabernacles**
❶ (in the Bible) the portable shrine used by the ancient Jews during their wanderings in the wilderness ❷ a meeting place for worship used by some groups of Christians

table *NOUN* **tables**
❶ a piece of furniture with a flat top supported on legs ❷ a list of facts or figures arranged in rows and columns ❸ a list of the results of multiplying a number by other numbers • *My little sister is learning her three times table.*

table *VERB* **tables, tabling, tabled**
to put forward a proposal for discussion at a meeting

tableau (say **tab**-loh) *NOUN* tableaux (say **tab**-lohz)
a dramatic or attractive scene, especially one posed on a stage by a group of people who do not speak or move

tablecloth *NOUN* tablecloths
a cloth for covering a table, especially at meals

tablespoon *NOUN* tablespoons
a large spoon for serving food
➤ **tablespoonful** *NOUN*

tablet *NOUN* tablets
❶ a pill ❷ a solid piece of soap ❸ a flat piece of stone or wood with words carved or written on it ❹ a small flat computer that you use by touching the screen

table tennis *NOUN*
a game played on a table divided by a net, over which you hit a small ball with bats

tabloid *NOUN* tabloids
a newspaper with pages that are half the size of larger newspapers

taboo *ADJECTIVE*
not to be done, used or talked about • *a taboo subject*

taboo *NOUN* taboos
a custom that you should avoid doing or talking about a particular thing because it might offend or embarrass other people
WORD ORIGIN from Tongan *tabu* = sacred

tabulate *VERB* tabulates, tabulating, tabulated
to arrange information or figures in a table or list

tacit (say **tas**-it) *ADJECTIVE*
implied or understood without being put into words • *tacit approval* **WORD ORIGIN** from Latin *tacitus* = not speaking

taciturn (say **tas**-i-tern) *ADJECTIVE*
saying very little • *his taciturn manner*
➤ **taciturnity** *NOUN*

tack *NOUN* tacks
❶ a short nail with a flat top ❷ the direction taken when tacking in sailing ❸ a course of action or policy • *I think we need to change tack.* • *OK, let's try a different tack.* ❹ riding equipment, such as harnesses and saddles

tack *VERB* tacks, tacking, tacked
❶ to nail something down, especially a carpet, with tacks ❷ to sew material together with long stitches ❸ to sail a zigzag course to take advantage of what wind there is

➤ **tack something on** to add something as an extra

tackle *VERB* tackles, tackling, tackled
❶ to try to do something that needs doing • *Firefighters came to tackle the blaze.* ❷ to try to get the ball from someone else in a game of football, rugby or hockey ❸ to talk to someone about a difficult or awkward matter

tackle *NOUN* tackles
❶ equipment, especially for fishing ❷ a set of ropes and pulleys ❸ tackling someone in football, rugby or hockey

tacky *ADJECTIVE*
❶ sticky or not quite dry • *The paint is still tacky.* ❷ (*informal*) showing poor taste or style; cheaply made
➤ **tackiness** *NOUN*

tact *NOUN*
taking care not to offend or upset people by saying the wrong thing • *Tact isn't one of her strong points.*

tactful *ADJECTIVE*
having or showing tact
➤ **tactfully** *ADVERB*

tactical *ADJECTIVE*
to do with tactics
➤ **tactically** *ADVERB*

tactics *NOUN*
❶ the methods you use to achieve something or gain an advantage ❷ the method of arranging military forces in battle or players in a team game
➤ **tactician** *NOUN*

> **USAGE**
> **Strategy** is a general plan for a whole campaign. **Tactics** refers to one part of this.

tactile *ADJECTIVE*
to do with the sense of touch

tactless *ADJECTIVE*
having or showing a lack of tact • *a tactless remark*
➤ **tactlessly** *ADVERB*

tadpole *NOUN* tadpoles
a young frog or toad that has developed from the egg and lives entirely in water

taffeta *NOUN*
a stiff silky material, often used for dresses

tag *NOUN* tags
❶ a label tied on or stuck to something ❷ a

tag metal or plastic point at the end of a shoelace ❸ a game in which one person chases the others

tag *VERB* **tags, tagging, tagged**
❶ to label something with a tag ❷ to add something as an extra thing • *An apology was tagged on at the end of her email.* ❸ to identify a person shown in a photograph on a social networking website
➤ **tag along** (*informal*)
to go somewhere with other people • *Her sister insisted on tagging along.*

tail *NOUN* **tails**
❶ the part that sticks out from the rear end of the body of a bird, fish or animal ❷ the part at the end or rear of something, such as an aircraft

tail *VERB* **tails, tailing, tailed**
❶ to remove stalks from fruit or vegetables • *First, top and tail the green beans.* ❷ (*informal*) to follow someone closely without them seeing you
➤ **tail off** or **away** to become quieter, smaller or weaker and then disappear • *His voice tailed off.*

tailback *NOUN* **tailbacks**
a long line of traffic stretching back from an obstruction

tailless *ADJECTIVE*
without a tail

tailor *NOUN* **tailors**
a person who makes men's clothes

tailor *VERB* **tailors, tailoring, tailored**
❶ to make or fit clothes ❷ to adapt or make something for a special purpose

tailor-made *ADJECTIVE*
specially made or suited for a purpose

tails *PLURAL NOUN*
❶ the side of a coin opposite the head • *Heads or tails?* ❷ a man's formal jacket with two long pieces hanging down at the back

taint *NOUN* **taints**
a small amount of something bad or unpleasant that spoils something

taint *VERB* **taints, tainting, tainted**
to spoil something with a taint • *His reputation was tainted by the scandal.*

take *VERB* **takes, taking, took, taken**
This word has many uses, including
❶ to get something into your hands, possession or control • *Take this cup.* • *They took many prisoners.* ❷ to carry, drive or lead a person or thing to a place • *Take this parcel*

to the post. • *Can you take me to the station?* ❸ to make use of something • *Let's take a taxi.* ❹ to have or do something • *You need to take a long holiday.* • *Let me take a look.* ❺ to take an exam is to sit it ❻ to study or teach a subject • *Who takes you for maths?* ❼ to make an effort • *Thanks for taking the trouble to see me.* ❽ to experience a feeling • *Don't take offence.* ❾ to accept or put up with something • *I'll take a risk.* ❿ to require something • *It takes a strong man to lift this.* ⓫ to write something down • *I'd better take notes.* ⓬ to use a camera to make a photograph • *I took some pictures of our new dog.* ⓭ to subtract one number from another • *Take 17 from 60.* ⓮ to assume that something is true • *I take it that you agree.*
➤ **taker** *NOUN*
➤ **I take it** I understand or suppose • *I take it that you're not coming?*
➤ **take after someone** to be like a parent or relative
➤ **take someone in** to fool or deceive someone
➤ **take something in** ❶ to understand something that you hear or read ❷ to make a piece of clothing narrower or tighter
➤ **take leave of someone** to say goodbye to someone
➤ **take off** an aircraft takes off when it leaves the ground and becomes airborne
➤ **take something off** to remove something, especially a piece of clothing
➤ **take someone on** ❶ to begin to employ someone ❷ to play or fight against someone
➤ **take something over** to take control of a business or activity
➤ **take part in something** to join in an activity
➤ **take place** to happen or occur
➤ **take to something** to develop a liking or ability for something
➤ **take something up** ❶ to start doing something regularly • *I've taken up karate.* ❷ to use or fill an amount of space or time • *Gymnastics takes up all of her time.* ❸ to accept an offer

takeaway *NOUN* **takeaways**
❶ a place that sells cooked meals for customers to take away ❷ a meal from such a place

take-off *NOUN* **take-offs**
the act of an aircraft leaving the ground and becoming airborne

takeover *NOUN* takeovers
the taking control of one business company by another

takings *PLURAL NOUN*
money that has been received, especially by a shopkeeper

talcum powder *NOUN*
a scented powder put on the skin to make it feel smooth and dry **(WORD ORIGIN)** from *talc*, the substance from which it is made

tale *NOUN* tales
a story

talent *NOUN* talents
a natural ability to do something well • *She has a talent for singing.* **(WORD ORIGIN)** from Greek *talanton* = sum of money

talented *ADJECTIVE*
having a natural ability to do something well

talisman *NOUN* talismans
an object that is supposed to bring good luck

talk *VERB* talks, talking, talked
to speak or have a conversation
➤ **talker** *NOUN*
➤ **talk down to someone** to speak to someone using simple language because you think they are less intelligent or important than you

talk *NOUN* talks
❶ a conversation or discussion ❷ an informal lecture

talkative *ADJECTIVE*
talking a lot

tall *ADJECTIVE* taller, tallest
❶ higher than the average • *a tall tree*
❷ measured from the bottom to the top • *It is 10 metres tall.*

tallow *NOUN*
animal fat used to make candles, soap, lubricants, etc.

tall story *NOUN* tall stories
(*informal*) a story that is hard to believe

tally *NOUN* tallies
the total amount of a debt or score

tally *VERB* tallies, tallying, tallied
to match or agree with something else • *Does your list tally with mine?* • *The accounts of the two witnesses did not tally.*

Talmud *NOUN*
the collection of writings that contain Jewish religious law

talon *NOUN* talons
a strong claw, especially on a bird of prey

tambourine *NOUN* tambourines
a circular musical instrument with metal discs fixed round it, so that it jingles when you tap or shake it

tame *ADJECTIVE*
❶ a tame animal is gentle and not afraid of people; not wild or dangerous ❷ not exciting; dull • *She finds village life very tame.*
➤ **tamely** *ADVERB*

tame *VERB* tames, taming, tamed
to make an animal become tame
➤ **tamer** *NOUN*

Tamil *NOUN* Tamils
❶ a member of a people of southern India and Sri Lanka ❷ their language

tam-o'-shanter *NOUN* tam-o'-shanters
a round Scottish cap with a bobble in the middle **(WORD ORIGIN)** named after *Tam o' Shanter*, hero of a poem by the Scottish poet Robert Burns

tamp *VERB* tamps, tamping, tamped
to press or pack something down firmly

tamper *VERB* tampers, tampering, tampered
➤ **tamper with something** to interfere with something or make changes to it so that it will not work properly • *Someone had tampered with the car's brakes.*

tampon *NOUN* tampons
a plug of soft material that a woman puts into her vagina to absorb the blood during her period

tan *NOUN* tans
❶ brown colour in skin that has been exposed to sun; a suntan ❷ a light brown colour

tan *VERB* tans, tanning, tanned
❶ to turn your skin brown by exposing it to the sun ❷ to make an animal's skin into leather by treating it with chemicals

tandem *NOUN* tandems
a bicycle for two riders, one behind the other
➤ **in tandem** together or at the same time
(WORD ORIGIN) Latin, = at length

tandoori *NOUN*
a style of Indian cooking in which food is cooked in a clay oven (a **tandoor**)

tang *NOUN* tangs
a strong flavour or smell • *a tang of lemon*

tangent *NOUN* tangents
a straight line that touches the outside of a

curve or circle
➤ **go off at a tangent** to move away suddenly from a subject or line of thought being considered

tangerine *NOUN* **tangerines**
a kind of small orange **WORD ORIGIN** named after *Tangier* in Morocco, where the fruit originally came from

tangible *ADJECTIVE*
❶ able to be touched ❷ that can be clearly seen; real or definite • *tangible benefits*
➤ **tangibly** *ADVERB*

tangle *VERB* **tangles, tangling, tangled**
to twist things together or become twisted into a confused mass • *My fishing line has tangled.* • *These computer cables are all tangled up.*

tangle *NOUN* **tangles**
a twisted or muddled mass of hair, wires, etc.

tango *NOUN* **tangos**
a ballroom dance with gliding steps and sudden pauses

tank *NOUN* **tanks**
❶ a large container for a liquid or gas ❷ a heavy armoured vehicle used in war

tankard *NOUN* **tankards**
a large mug for drinking beer from, usually made of silver or pewter

tanker *NOUN* **tankers**
❶ a large ship for carrying oil ❷ a large lorry for carrying a liquid

tanner *NOUN* **tanners**
a person who tans animal skins into leather
➤ **tannery** *NOUN*

tannin *NOUN*
a substance obtained from the bark or fruit of various trees (also found in tea), used in tanning and dyeing things

tantalize (also **tantalise**) *VERB* **tantalizes, tantalizing, tantalized**
to tease or torment a person by showing them something good that they cannot have **WORD ORIGIN** from the name of *Tantalus* in Greek mythology, who was punished by being made to stand near water and fruit which moved away when he tried to reach them

tantamount *ADJECTIVE*
to be tantamount to something is to be equivalent to it or virtually the same as it • *The Queen's request was tantamount to a command.* **WORD ORIGIN** from Italian *tanto montare* = amount to so much

tantrum *NOUN* **tantrums**
an outburst of bad temper

tap *NOUN* **taps**
❶ a device for letting out liquid or gas in a controlled flow ❷ a quick light hit; the sound of this • *I gave her a tap on the shoulder.* ❸ tap dancing

tap *VERB* **taps, tapping, tapped**
❶ to hit a person or thing quickly and lightly • *I tried tapping on the window.* • *He was busy tapping away at his computer.* ❷ to obtain supplies or information from a source ❸ to fix a device to a telephone line so that you can overhear conversations on it

tap dancing *NOUN*
dancing in shoes with metal caps that make sharp tapping sounds on the floor
➤ **tap dance** *NOUN*
➤ **tap dancer** *NOUN*

tape *NOUN* **tapes**
❶ a narrow strip of cloth, paper or plastic ❷ a narrow plastic strip coated with a magnetic substance and used for making recordings ❸ a tape recording ❹ a tape measure

tape *VERB* **tapes, taping, taped**
❶ to fix, cover or surround something with tape ❷ to record something on magnetic tape
➤ **have something taped** (*informal*) to understand something or be able to deal with it

tape deck *NOUN* **tape decks**
the part of a sound system on which music recorded on tape can be played

tape measure *NOUN* **tape measures**
a long strip marked in centimetres or inches for measuring things

taper *VERB* **tapers, tapering, tapered**
to become thinner or narrower towards one end
➤ **taper off** to become gradually less

taper *NOUN* **tapers**
a very thin candle, used for lighting things

tape recorder *NOUN* **tape recorders**
a machine for recording music or sound on magnetic tape and playing it back
➤ **tape recording** *NOUN*

tapestry *NOUN* **tapestries**
a piece of strong cloth with pictures or patterns woven or embroidered on it

tapeworm *NOUN* **tapeworms**
a long flat worm that can live as a parasite in the intestines of people and animals

tapioca *NOUN*
a starchy substance in hard white grains obtained from cassava, used for making milk puddings

tapir (say **tay**-per) *NOUN* **tapirs**
a pig-like animal with a long flexible snout

tar *NOUN*
a thick black liquid made from coal or wood and used in making roads

tar *VERB* **tars, tarring, tarred**
to coat something with tar

tarantula *NOUN* **tarantulas**
a large kind of spider found in southern Europe and in tropical countries. Some species of tarantula have a poisonous bite.

tardy *ADJECTIVE* **tardier, tardiest**
slow or late
➤ **tardily** *ADVERB*
➤ **tardiness** *NOUN*

target *NOUN* **targets**
something that you aim at and try to hit or reach

target *VERB* **targets, targeting, targeted**
to aim at something or have it as a target

tariff *NOUN* **tariffs**
a list of prices or charges

tarmac *NOUN*
❶ a mixture of tar and broken stone, used for making a hard surface on roads, paths, playgrounds, etc. ❷ an area surfaced with tarmac, especially on an airfield
WORD ORIGIN *Tarmac* is a trade mark

tarnish *VERB* **tarnishes, tarnishing, tarnished**
❶ metal tarnishes when it becomes stained and less shiny • *The silver has tarnished.* ❷ to spoil or damage something • *The scandal tarnished his reputation.*
➤ **tarnish** *NOUN*

tarot card (rhymes with barrow) *NOUN*
one of the cards in a special pack used for fortune-telling

tarpaulin *NOUN* **tarpaulins**
a large sheet of waterproof canvas

tarragon *NOUN*
a plant with leaves that are used to flavour salads and in cooking

tarry (say **tar**-ee) *ADJECTIVE*
covered with or like tar

tarry (say **ta**-ree) *VERB* **tarries, tarrying, tarried** (*old use*)
to stay for a while longer; to linger

tart *NOUN* **tarts**
❶ a pie containing fruit or sweet filling ❷ a piece of pastry with jam etc. on top

tart *ADJECTIVE*
❶ sour-tasting ❷ sharp in manner • *a tart reply*
➤ **tartly** *ADVERB*

tartan *NOUN*
a pattern with coloured stripes crossing each other, especially one that is used by a Scottish clan

tartar *NOUN* **tartars**
❶ a hard chalky deposit that forms on teeth ❷ a person who is fierce or difficult to deal with **WORD ORIGIN** the second sense comes from the *Tartar* warriors from central Asia in the 13th century

tartlet *NOUN* **tartlets**
a small pastry tart

task *NOUN* **tasks**
a piece of work that needs to be done
➤ **take someone to task** to tell someone off for doing something wrong

task force *NOUN* **task forces**
a group specially organized for a particular task

taskmaster *NOUN* **taskmasters**
a person who gives other people a lot of work to do • *a hard taskmaster*

tassel *NOUN* **tassels**
a bundle of threads tied together at the top and used to decorate something
➤ **tasselled** *ADJECTIVE*

taste *VERB* **tastes, tasting, tasted**
❶ to take a small amount of food or drink to try its flavour ❷ to be able to notice or recognize flavours • *Can you taste the garlic in this soup?* ❸ to have a certain flavour • *The milk tastes sour.*

taste *NOUN* **tastes**
❶ the feeling caused in the tongue by something placed on it ❷ the ability to taste things ❸ the ability to enjoy beautiful things or to choose things that are of good quality or go together well • *She shows good taste in her choice of clothes.* ❹ a liking for something • *The trip gave him a taste for foreign travel.* ❺ a very small amount of food or drink

tasteful *ADJECTIVE*
showing good taste
➤ **tastefully** *ADVERB*
➤ **tastefulness** *NOUN*

tasteless *ADJECTIVE*
❶ having no flavour ❷ showing poor taste
➤ **tastelessly** *ADVERB*
➤ **tastelessness** *NOUN*

tasty *ADJECTIVE* **tastier, tastiest**
having a strong pleasant taste

tattered *ADJECTIVE*
badly torn and ragged • *a tattered dress*

tatters *PLURAL NOUN*
rags; badly torn pieces
➤ **in tatters** torn to pieces • *My coat was in tatters.*

tattoo *NOUN* **tattoos**
❶ a picture or pattern marked on someone's skin by using a needle and dye ❷ a drumming or tapping sound • *He beat a tattoo on the table with his fingers.* ❸ an outdoor entertainment consisting of military music and marching

tattoo *VERB* **tattoos, tattooing, tattooed**
to mark a person's skin with a tattoo

tatty *ADJECTIVE*
shabby and worn • *a tatty carpet*

taunt *VERB* **taunts, taunting, taunted**
to jeer at or insult someone

taunt *NOUN* **taunts**
a taunting remark **WORD ORIGIN** from French *tant pour tant* = tit for tat

taut *ADJECTIVE*
stretched tightly • *Keep the rope taut.*
➤ **tautly** *ADVERB*
➤ **tautness** *NOUN*

tautology *NOUN* **tautologies**
saying the same thing again in different words, e.g. *You can get the book free for nothing.* (where *free* and *for nothing* mean the same)

tavern *NOUN* **taverns** (*old use*)
an inn or public house

tawdry *ADJECTIVE*
cheap and gaudy
➤ **tawdriness** *NOUN*
WORD ORIGIN from *St Audrey's lace* (cheap finery formerly sold at St Audrey's fair at Ely)

tawny *ADJECTIVE*
brownish-yellow

tax *NOUN* **taxes**
❶ money that people or business firms have to pay to the government, to be used for public purposes ❷ a strain or burden • *The long walk was a tax on his strength.*

tax *VERB* **taxes, taxing, taxed**
❶ to put a tax on something ❷ to charge someone a tax ❸ to put a strain or burden on a person or thing • *This will tax your strength.* ❹ (*formal*) to accuse someone of doing something wrong • *I taxed him with leaving the door open.*

taxation *NOUN*
money that has to be paid as taxes

taxi *NOUN* **taxis**
a car with a driver that you can hire for journeys, usually with a meter to record the fare to be paid
➤ **taxicab** *NOUN*

taxi *VERB* **taxis** or **taxies, taxiing, taxied**
an aircraft taxis when it moves slowly along the ground before taking off or after landing

taxidermist *NOUN* **taxidermists**
a person who prepares and stuffs the skins of animals in a lifelike form
➤ **taxidermy** *NOUN*

taxpayer *NOUN* **taxpayers**
a person who pays tax

TB *ABBREVIATION*
tuberculosis

tea *NOUN* **teas**
❶ a drink made by pouring hot water on the dried leaves of an evergreen shrub (the *tea plant*) ❷ these dried leaves ❸ a drink made with the leaves of other plants • *camomile tea* ❹ a meal in the afternoon or early evening

tea bag *NOUN* **tea bags**
a small bag holding about a teaspoonful of tea

teacake *NOUN* **teacakes**
(*British*) a kind of bun usually served toasted and buttered

teach *VERB* **teaches, teaching, taught**
❶ to give a person knowledge or skill; to train someone ❷ to give lessons in a subject • *She taught us history last year.* ❸ to show someone what to do or avoid • *That will teach you not to meddle!*

teachable *ADJECTIVE*
able to be taught

teacher *NOUN* **teachers**
a person who teaches others, especially in a school

a b c d e f g h i j k l m n o p q r s t u v w x y z

teaching *NOUN* teachings
things that are taught • *the teachings of Plato*

tea cloth *NOUN* tea cloths
a tea towel

teacup *NOUN* teacups
a cup for drinking tea

teak *NOUN*
the hard strong wood of an evergreen Asian tree

teal *NOUN* teal
a kind of duck

tea leaves *PLURAL NOUN*
the small leaves left in a cup or mug after you have drunk the tea

team *NOUN* teams
❶ a set of players who form one side in certain games and sports ❷ a set of people working together ❸ two or more animals harnessed to pull a vehicle or a plough

team *VERB* teams, teaming, teamed
➤ **team up with someone** to join someone in order to do something together
➤ **team someone with someone** to put people together in a team

teamwork *NOUN*
the ability of a team or group to work well together

teapot *NOUN* teapots
a pot with a lid and a handle, for making and pouring tea

tear (say teer) *NOUN* tears
a drop of the water that comes from the eyes when a person cries
➤ **in tears** crying

tear (say tair) *VERB* tears, tearing, tore, torn
❶ to make a split in something or pull it apart • *She tore the letter in half.* ❷ to pull or remove something with force • *I tore the poster off the wall.* ❸ to become torn • *Newspaper tears easily.* ❹ to run or travel hurriedly • *He tore down the street.*

tear (say tair) *NOUN* tears
a split made by tearing

> **SPELLING**
>
> The verb **tear** rhymes with **hair** and means to rip something. The past tense of the verb **tear** is **tore** and the past participle is **torn**.

teardrop *NOUN* teardrops
a single tear

tearful *ADJECTIVE*
in tears; crying easily
➤ **tearfully** *ADVERB*

tear gas *NOUN*
a gas that makes people's eyes water painfully, sometimes used by the police or army to control crowds

tease *VERB* teases, teasing, teased
❶ to make fun of someone and say things to make them annoyed ❷ to pick threads apart into separate strands

tease *NOUN* teases
a person who often teases others

teaser *NOUN* teasers
(*informal*) a difficult problem or puzzle

teaspoon *NOUN* teaspoons
a small spoon for stirring tea or measuring small amounts

teaspoonful *NOUN* teaspoonfuls
as much as a teaspoon will hold

teat *NOUN* teats
❶ one of the nipples on a female animal, through which the young suck milk ❷ the cap of a baby's feeding bottle

tea towel *NOUN* tea towels
(*chiefly British*) a cloth for drying washed dishes and cutlery

tech (say tek) *NOUN* techs (*informal*)
a technical college

technical *ADJECTIVE*
❶ to do with technology or the way things work ❷ to do with a particular subject and its methods • *the technical terms of chemistry* ❸ using words that only people who know a lot about a subject will understand
WORD ORIGIN from Greek *technikos* = skilled in an art or craft

technical college *NOUN* technical colleges
a college where technical and practical subjects are taught

technicality *NOUN* technicalities
a small detail of the law or a process

technically *ADVERB*
according to the strict facts or rules • *He was technically in charge, but no one took any notice of what he said.*

technician *NOUN* technicians
a person whose job is to look after scientific equipment and do practical work in a laboratory

technique *NOUN* **techniques**
a method of doing something skilfully

technological *ADJECTIVE*
to do with technology • *technological developments*

technology *NOUN* **technologies**
the study of machinery, engineering and how things work
➤ **technologist** *NOUN*

teddy bear *NOUN* **teddy bears**
a soft furry toy bear (**WORD ORIGIN**) named after US President Theodore ('*Teddy*') Roosevelt, who liked hunting bears

tedious *ADJECTIVE*
annoyingly slow or long; boring
➤ **tediously** *ADVERB*
➤ **tediousness** *NOUN*

tedium *NOUN*
a dull or boring time or experience

tee *NOUN* **tees**
❶ the flat area from which golfers strike the ball at the start of play for each hole ❷ a small piece of wood or plastic on which a golf ball is placed for being struck

teem *VERB* **teems, teeming, teemed**
❶ to be full of something • *The river was teeming with fish.* ❷ to rain very hard; to pour

teen *ADJECTIVE & NOUN* **teens** (*informal*)
a teenager

teenage *ADJECTIVE*
in your teens; to do with teenagers

teenaged *ADJECTIVE*
in your teens

teenager *NOUN* **teenagers**
a person in their teens

teens *PLURAL NOUN*
the time of your life between the ages of 13 and 19

teeny *ADJECTIVE* **teenier, teeniest** (*informal*)
tiny

tee-shirt *NOUN* **tee-shirts**
a T-shirt

teeter *VERB* **teeters, teetering, teetered**
to stand or move unsteadily • *She teetered along in her high-heeled shoes.*

teethe *VERB* **teethes, teething, teethed**
a baby is teething when its first teeth are beginning to grow through the gums

teetotal *ADJECTIVE*
never drinking alcohol
➤ **teetotaller** *NOUN*

Teflon *NOUN* (*trademark*)
a type of plastic used as a non-stick coating for pans (**WORD ORIGIN**) from poly*tetrafl*uoroethylene, its scientific name

telecommunications *PLURAL NOUN*
communications over long distances, e.g. by telephone, radio or television

telegram *NOUN* **telegrams**
a message sent by telegraph

telegraph *NOUN*
a way of sending messages by using electric current along wires or by radio
➤ **telegraphic** *ADJECTIVE*
➤ **telegraphy** *NOUN*

telepathy (say til-**ep**-ath-ee) *NOUN*
communication of thoughts from one person's mind to another without speaking, writing or gestures
➤ **telepathic** *ADJECTIVE*

telephone *NOUN* **telephones**
a device or system using electric wires or radio to enable one person to speak to another who is some distance away

telephone *VERB* **telephones, telephoning, telephoned**
to speak to a person by telephone
(**WORD ORIGIN**) from Greek *tele* = far off + *phone* = sound, voice

telephonist (say til-**ef**-on-ist) *NOUN* **telephonists**
(*British*) a person who operates a telephone switchboard

telescope *NOUN* **telescopes**
an instrument using lenses to magnify distant objects
➤ **telescopic** *ADJECTIVE*

telescope *VERB* **telescopes, telescoping, telescoped**
to become shorter or make something shorter, by sliding overlapping sections into each other

televise *VERB* **televises, televising, televised**
to broadcast an event or programme by television

television *NOUN* **televisions**
❶ a system using radio waves to reproduce a view of scenes or events on a screen ❷ an apparatus for receiving these pictures

❸ televised programmes • *How much television do you watch?*

tell *VERB* tells, telling, told
❶ to make a thing known to someone, especially by words • *Come on, tell me what happened.* ❷ to say something • *Don't tell lies.* ❸ to order or advise someone to do something • *Tell them to wait outside.* ❹ to reveal a secret • *Promise you won't tell.* ❺ to be certain about something or recognize it • *I could tell she was worried.* • *Can you tell the difference between the twins?* ❻ to produce an effect • *The strain was beginning to tell on him.*
➤ **all told** in all, all together • *There are ten of them, all told.*
➤ **tell someone off** (*informal*) to scold someone because they have done something wrong
➤ **tell tales** to report something naughty or bad that someone else has done

telling *ADJECTIVE*
having a strong effect or meaning • *It was a telling reply.*

tell-tale *NOUN* tell-tales
a person who tells tales

tell-tale *ADJECTIVE*
revealing or indicating something that is supposed to be secret • *There was a tell-tale spot of jam on his chin.*

telly *NOUN* tellies (*British*) (*informal*)
❶ television ❷ a television set

temerity (say tim-**e**rri-tee) *NOUN*
rashness or boldness

temp *NOUN* temps (*informal*)
a secretary or other worker who works for short periods of time in different companies

temper *NOUN* tempers
❶ a person's mood • *He is in a good temper.* ❷ an angry mood • *She was in a temper.*
➤ **lose your temper** to lose your calmness and become angry

temper *VERB* tempers, tempering, tempered
❶ to harden or strengthen metal by heating and cooling it ❷ to make something less severe or soften its effects • *Justice needs to be tempered with mercy.*

temperament *NOUN* temperaments
a person's nature as shown in the way they usually behave • *a nervous temperament*

temperamental *ADJECTIVE*
❶ likely to become excitable or moody

suddenly ❷ to do with a person's temperament

temperance *NOUN*
❶ drinking little or no alcohol ❷ the ability to control your behaviour; self-restraint

temperate *ADJECTIVE*
a temperate climate is neither extremely hot nor extremely cold **WORD ORIGIN** originally = not affected by strong emotions

temperature *NOUN* temperatures
❶ how hot or cold a person or thing is ❷ an abnormally high temperature of the body • *She's feverish and has a temperature.*

SPELLING

Do not forget the **er** in the middle of **temperature**.

tempest *NOUN* tempests
(*old use*) a violent storm

tempestuous *ADJECTIVE*
stormy; full of commotion

template *NOUN* templates
a thin sheet of shaped metal, plastic or card used as a guide for cutting or shaping things

temple *NOUN* temples
❶ a building where a god is worshipped ❷ the part of your head between your forehead and your ear

tempo *NOUN* tempos or tempi
❶ the speed or rhythm of something ❷ the speed at which a piece of music is played

temporary *ADJECTIVE*
lasting for a short time only; not permanent • *a temporary shelter*
➤ **temporarily** (say **tem**-per-er-il-ee) *ADVERB*

tempt *VERB* tempts, tempting, tempted
❶ to try to persuade or attract someone, especially into doing something wrong or unwise ❷ to be tempted to do something is to want to do it even though it may not be the right thing to do • *I was tempted to tell her the whole story.*
➤ **tempter** *NOUN*
➤ **temptress** *NOUN*

temptation *NOUN* temptations
❶ a feeling that you want to do something, even if you know it is wrong • *I managed to resist the temptation to open the letter.* ❷ something that tempts you

tempting *ADJECTIVE*
attractive in a way that makes you want to do or have something • *a tempting offer*

ten *NOUN ADJECTIVE* tens
the number 10

tenable *ADJECTIVE*
able to be held or defended • *a tenable theory* • *The job is tenable for one year only.*

tenacious (say ten-**ay**-shus) *ADJECTIVE*
❶ holding or clinging firmly to something
❷ obstinate and persistent
➤ **tenaciously** *ADVERB*
➤ **tenacity** *NOUN*

tenant *NOUN* tenants
a person who rents a house, building or land from a landlord
➤ **tenancy** *NOUN*

tend *VERB* tends, tending, tended
❶ to be likely to do something; to usually happen • *He tends to have a nap in the afternoon.* ❷ to look after something or someone • *Shepherds were tending their sheep.*

tendency *NOUN* tendencies
the way a person or thing is likely to behave • *She has a tendency to be lazy.*

tender *ADJECTIVE*
❶ easy to chew; not tough or hard ❷ easily hurt or damaged; delicate or sensitive • *tender plants* ❸ a tender part of your body is painful when touched ❹ gentle and loving • *a tender smile*
➤ **tenderly** *ADVERB*
➤ **tenderness** *NOUN*

tender *VERB* tenders, tendering, tendered
to offer something formally • *He tendered his resignation.*

tender *NOUN* tenders
❶ a formal offer to supply goods or carry out work at a stated price • *The council asked for tenders to build a school.* ❷ a truck attached to a steam locomotive to carry its coal and water ❸ a small boat carrying stores or passengers to and from a larger one
➤ **legal tender** kinds of money that are legal for making payments • *Are pound notes still legal tender?*

tendon *NOUN* tendons
a strong strip of tissue that joins muscle to bone

tendril *NOUN* tendrils
❶ a thread-like part by which a climbing plant clings to a support ❷ a thin curl of hair

tenement *NOUN* tenements
a large house or building divided into flats or rooms that are let to separate tenants

tenet (say **ten**-it) *NOUN* tenets
a firm belief held by a person or group

tenner *NOUN* tenners (*British*) (*informal*)
a ten-pound note; £10

tennis *NOUN*
a game played with rackets and a ball on a court with a net across the middle

tenon *NOUN* tenons
a piece of wood shaped to fit into a mortise

tenor *NOUN* tenors
❶ a male singer with a high voice ❷ the general meaning or drift of something • *I was encouraged by the tenor of her remarks.*

tenpin bowling *NOUN*
a game in which players try to knock over ten skittles set up at the end of a track by rolling hard balls down it

tense *NOUN* tenses
the form of a verb that shows when something happens, e.g. he *came* (**past tense**), he *comes* or *is coming* (**present tense**)

tense *ADJECTIVE*
❶ tightly stretched • *tense muscles* ❷ nervous or worried and unable to relax ❸ making people tense • *a tense moment*
➤ **tensely** *ADVERB*
➤ **tenseness** *NOUN*

tense *VERB* tenses, tensing, tensed
to have muscles that have become hard and not relaxed • *I felt myself tense up.*

GRAMMAR

The **tense** of a verb tells you when the action of the verb takes place.

The **present tense** shows that something is happening now or is true now.
The **simple present tense** describes something that is continuous or repeated. It is usually shown by having no ending, or by adding -*s*:

Titan is Saturn's biggest moon.

I hate olives.

Do you mind if I come in?

The **present progressive tense** (also called the **present continuous tense**) shows that something is in the process of happening now, either happening right now or continuing over a longer period.

It uses the auxiliary verb *be* and the

present participle (or *-ing* form) of the main verb:

What are you doing?

I am still reading the first chapter.

The **present perfect tense** is used to talk about something that happened earlier and is still relevant now, or something that started happening in the past and is still happening now. It uses *have* and the past participle (or *-ed* form) of the main verb:

They have finished their work, so they can go out now.

She has played in goal for several matches.

The **past tense** shows that something happened in the past. The **simple past tense** is used for something that happened earlier or in the past and is now finished. It is normally shown by adding *-ed*:

The Apollo 11 mission landed on the Moon in 1969.

Did you play football today?

The **past progressive tense** (also called the **past continuous tense**) shows that something was in the process of happening at some time in the past. It was not finished, or was still happening when something else happened. It is formed with the simple past of *be* and the present participle (or *-ing* form) of the main verb:

When war broke out, my grandparents were living in Austria.

She was feeling nervous.

The **past perfect tense** is used to talk about something that happened before something else in the past, or something that started happening in the past and was still happening at a later time. It is formed with the simple past of *have* and the past participle (or *-ed* form) of the main verb:

The party had finished by the time I arrived.

He had played for them for years.

To talk about something that will, or may,

happen in the **future**, you use *will*, or another modal verb before the main verb:

I will send you my email address.

Will your sister mind if I borrow her hairdryer?

To talk about something that will, or may, happen by a specific time in the future, the modal verb *will* is used with the past of *have* and the past participle of the main verb:

By tomorrow I will have finished all my work.

See also the panel on **verbs**.

tensile *ADJECTIVE*
❶ to do with tension ❷ able to be stretched

tension *NOUN* **tensions**
❶ how tightly stretched a rope or wire is
❷ a feeling of anxiety or nervousness about something that is just about to happen
❸ voltage • *high-tension cables*

tent *NOUN* **tents**
a shelter made of canvas or cloth supported by upright poles

tentacle *NOUN* **tentacles**
a long flexible part of the body of an animal such as an octopus, used for feeling or grasping things or for moving

tentative *ADJECTIVE*
cautious; trying something out • *a tentative suggestion*
➤ **tentatively** *ADVERB*

tenterhooks *PLURAL NOUN*
➤ **on tenterhooks** tense and anxious about something that is going to happen
WORD ORIGIN from *tenter* = a machine with hooks for stretching cloth to dry

tenth *ADJECTIVE & NOUN* **tenths**
next after the ninth

tenuous *ADJECTIVE*
very slight or thin • *tenuous threads* • *a tenuous connection*

tenure (say **ten**-yoor) *NOUN* **tenures**
the holding of a position of employment or of land or property

tepee (say **tee**-pee) *NOUN* **tepees**
a tent formerly used by Native Americans, made by fastening skins or mats over poles
WORD ORIGIN a Native American word

tepid *ADJECTIVE*
only slightly warm; lukewarm • *tepid water*

term *NOUN* terms
❶ the period of weeks when a school or college is open ❷ a definite period • *a term of imprisonment* ❸ a word or expression with a special meaning • *a glossary of technical terms*

term *VERB* terms, terming, termed
to describe or name something by using a certain word or expression • *These male bees are termed 'drones'.*

terminal *NOUN* terminals
❶ a building where passengers arrive or depart • *an airport terminal* ❷ a place where a wire is connected in an electric circuit or battery ❸ a computer keyboard and screen used for sending data to or from the main computer

terminal *ADJECTIVE*
a terminal illness is one that cannot be cured and that the person will die from • *terminal cancer*
➤ **terminally** *ADVERB*

terminate *VERB* terminates, terminating, terminated
to end or stop or to make something end or stop • *This train terminates here.*
➤ **termination** *NOUN*

terminology *NOUN* terminologies
the technical terms of a subject

terminus *NOUN* termini
the last station on a railway or bus route

termite *NOUN* termites
a small insect that eats wood and lives in large groups

terms *PLURAL NOUN*
❶ a relationship between people • *They ended up on friendly terms.* ❷ conditions offered or agreed, especially in a treaty or contract • *peace terms*
➤ **come to terms with something** to learn to accept a difficulty or unwelcome situation

tern *NOUN* terns
a seabird with long wings

terrace *NOUN* terraces
❶ a row of houses joined together ❷ a level area on a slope or hillside ❸ a paved area beside a house
➤ **terraced** *ADJECTIVE*

terracotta *NOUN*
❶ a kind of pottery ❷ the brownish-red colour of flowerpots

terra firma *NOUN*
dry land; the ground **WORD ORIGIN** Latin, = firm land

terrain *NOUN* terrains
a stretch of land • *hilly terrain*

terrapin *NOUN* terrapins
an edible freshwater turtle of North America

terrestrial *ADJECTIVE*
❶ to do with the earth or land ❷ terrestrial television is broadcast by aerials on the ground rather than by satellite

terrible *ADJECTIVE*
very bad; awful

terribly *ADVERB*
❶ very badly • *He was missing his parents terribly.* ❷ (*informal*) very; extremely • *I'm terribly sorry.*

terrier *NOUN* terriers
a kind of small lively dog **WORD ORIGIN** from old French *chien terrier* = earth-dog (because they were used to dig out foxes from their earths)

terrific *ADJECTIVE* (*informal*)
❶ very great • *There was a terrific bang.* ❷ very good or excellent
➤ **terrifically** *ADVERB*

terrified *ADJECTIVE*
very afraid • *I'm terrified of snakes.*

terrify *VERB* terrifies, terrifying, terrified
to make a person or animal very frightened

territorial *ADJECTIVE*
❶ to do with or belonging to a country's territory • *a territorial dispute* ❷ a territorial animal or bird guards and defends an area of land it believes to be its own • *Cats are very territorial.*

territory *NOUN* territories
❶ an area of land, especially one that belongs to a country ❷ an area of land that an animal or bird thinks of as its own and defends against others

terror *NOUN* terrors
❶ very great fear ❷ a terrifying person or thing

terrorist *NOUN* terrorists
a person who uses violence for political purposes
➤ **terrorism** *NOUN*

terrorize (also **terrorise**) *VERB* terrorizes,
terrorizing, terrorized
to frighten someone by threatening them

terse *ADJECTIVE*
using few words and not very friendly • *a
terse reply*
➤ **tersely** *ADVERB*

tertiary (say **ter**-sher-ee) *ADJECTIVE*
to do with the third stage of something;
coming after secondary

tessellated *ADJECTIVE*
decorated with shapes that fit together into a
pattern without overlapping or leaving gaps
• *a tessellated floor*
➤ **tessellation** *NOUN*
WORD ORIGIN from Latin *tessella* = a small
piece of wood, bone or glass, used as a token or
in a mosaic

test *NOUN* tests
❶ a short examination • *a spelling test* ❷ a
way of discovering the qualities, abilities or
presence of a person or thing • *a test for
radioactivity* ❸ a test match

test *VERB* tests, testing, tested
to carry out a test on a person or thing
• *Mum needs to have her eyes tested.*
➤ **tester** *NOUN*

testament *NOUN* testaments
❶ a written statement ❷ either of the two
main parts of the Bible, the Old Testament or
the New Testament

testicle *NOUN* testicles
either of the two glands in the scrotum where
semen is produced

testify *VERB* testifies, testifying, testified
❶ to give evidence or swear that something is
true ❷ to be evidence or proof of something
• *Three world titles testify to her talent.*

testimonial *NOUN* testimonials
❶ a letter describing someone's abilities and
character ❷ a gift presented to someone as a
mark of respect

testimony *NOUN* testimonies
evidence; what someone testifies

test match *NOUN* test matches
a cricket or rugby match between teams from
different countries

testosterone (say test-**ost**-er-ohn) *NOUN*
a male sex hormone

test tube *NOUN* test tubes
a tube of thin glass with one end closed, used
for experiments in chemistry

test-tube baby *NOUN* test-tube babies
a baby that develops from an egg that has
been fertilized outside the mother's body and
then placed back in the womb

testy *ADJECTIVE*
easily annoyed; irritable
➤ **testily** *ADVERB*

tetanus *NOUN*
a disease that makes the muscles become
stiff, caused by bacteria

tetchy *ADJECTIVE*
easily annoyed; irritable
➤ **tetchily** *ADVERB*

tête-à-tête (say tayt-ah-**tayt**) *NOUN* tête-à-
têtes
a private conversation between two people
WORD ORIGIN French, = head to head

tether *VERB* tethers, tethering, tethered
to tie up an animal so that it cannot move far

tether *NOUN* tethers
a rope for tethering an animal
➤ **at the end of your tether** unable to stand
something any more

tetrahedron *NOUN* tetrahedrons
a solid with four sides (i.e. a pyramid with a
triangular base)

text *NOUN* texts
❶ the words of something written or printed
❷ a text message ❸ a sentence from the
Bible used as the subject of a sermon in a
Christian church

text *VERB* texts, texting, texted
to send a text message to someone on a
mobile phone • *He texted me to tell me when
the train would arrive.*

textbook *NOUN* textbooks
a book that teaches you about a subject

textiles *PLURAL NOUN*
kinds of cloth; fabrics

text message *NOUN* text messages
a written message sent on a mobile phone

texture *NOUN* textures
the way that the surface of something
feels when you touch it • *Silk has a smooth
texture.*

thalidomide *NOUN*
a medicinal drug that was found (in 1961) to

cause babies to be born with deformed arms and legs

than *CONJUNCTION & PREPOSITION*
compared with another person or thing • *His brother is taller than he is.* • *She speaks French better than me.*

thank *VERB* thanks, thanking, thanked
to tell someone that you are grateful to them
➤ **thank you** an expression of thanks

thankful *ADJECTIVE*
❶ pleased and relieved • *I was thankful that nobody was around.* ❷ showing thanks; grateful

thankfully *ADVERB*
❶ in a grateful way ❷ fortunately; luckily • *Thankfully, it has stopped raining.*

thankless *ADJECTIVE*
a thankless task is one that you are not likely to get thanked or rewarded for doing

thanks *PLURAL NOUN*
❶ words that thank someone; gratitude ❷ (*informal*) thank you
➤ **thanks to** as a result of; because of • *Thanks to you, we succeeded.*

thanksgiving *NOUN*
an expression of gratitude, especially to God

that *DETERMINER & PRONOUN* those
the one there • *That book is mine.* • *Whose bike is that?*

that *ADVERB*
to such an extent • *I'll come that far but no further.*

that *RELATIVE PRONOUN*
which, who or whom • *This is the DVD that I wanted.* • *We liked the people that we met on holiday.*

that *CONJUNCTION*
used to introduce a wish, reason or result • *I hope that you are well.* • *The puzzle was so hard that no one could solve it.*

> **GRAMMAR**
> See also the panel at **which**.

thatch *NOUN*
straw or reeds used to make a roof

thatch *VERB* thatches, thatching, thatched
to make a roof with thatch
➤ **thatcher** *NOUN*

thaw *VERB* thaws, thawing, thawed
to melt; to stop being frozen • *The snow was beginning to thaw.*

thaw *NOUN* thaws
a period of warm weather that thaws ice and snow

the *DETERMINER* called the definite article
a particular one; that or those

> **GRAMMAR**
> The word *the* is known as the **definite article**. You use it before a noun or noun phrase when the person or thing you are talking about has already been mentioned or you want to specify which one you mean:
>
> *That is <u>the</u> cave where <u>the</u> dragon sleeps.*
>
> *Jupiter is <u>the</u> largest gas planet.*

theatre *NOUN* theatres
❶ a building where people go to see plays or shows ❷ the writing, acting and producing of plays ❸ a special room where surgical operations are done • *the operating theatre*

theatrical *ADJECTIVE*
❶ to do with plays or acting ❷ theatrical behaviour is exaggerated and done for showy effect
➤ **theatrically** *ADVERB*

theatricals *PLURAL NOUN*
performances of plays

thee *PRONOUN* (*old use*)
you (referring to one person and used as the object of a verb or after a preposition)

theft *NOUN* thefts
stealing • *He was arrested for theft.*

their *DETERMINER*
❶ belonging to them • *Their coats are over there.* ❷ (*informal*) belonging to a person • *Somebody has left their coat on the bus.*

> **SPELLING**
> **Their** is different from **there**: • *their pets* • *I'm going there soon.*

theirs *POSSESSIVE PRONOUN*
belonging to them • *These coats are theirs.*

> **USAGE**
> It is incorrect to write *their's*.

them *PRONOUN*
the form of *they* used as the object of a verb or after a preposition • *We forgot to bring them.* • *I gave it to them.*

theme *NOUN* themes
❶ the subject of a speech, piece of writing, discussion, etc. ❷ a melody

theme park *NOUN* theme parks
an amusement park where the rides and
attractions are based on a particular subject

theme tune *NOUN* theme tunes
a special tune always used to announce a
particular programme or performer

themselves *PRONOUN*
they or them and nobody else. The word
is used to refer back to the subject of a
sentence (e.g. *They blame themselves.*) or for
emphasis (e.g. *My grandparents built this
house themselves.*).
➤ **by themselves** on their own; alone

then *ADVERB*
❶ at that time • *I lived in London then.*
❷ after that; next • *I'll just get changed and
then we can go out.* • *Then a strange thing
happened.* ❸ in that case; therefore • *If this
is yours, then this must be mine.*

thence *ADVERB*
from that place

theology *NOUN*
the study of religion
➤ **theological** *ADJECTIVE*
➤ **theologian** *NOUN*

theorem *NOUN* theorems
a mathematical statement that can be proved
by reasoning

theoretical *ADJECTIVE*
based on theory, not on practice or
experience
➤ **theoretically** *ADVERB*

theorize (also **theorise**) *VERB* theorizes,
theorizing, theorized
to form a theory or theories

theory *NOUN* theories
❶ an idea or set of ideas put forward to
explain something • *Darwin's theory of
evolution* ❷ the principles of a subject rather
than its practice
➤ **in theory** according to what should
happen rather than what may in fact happen

therapeutic (say therra-**pew**-tik) *ADJECTIVE*
helping to treat or cure a disease or illness
• *Sunshine can have a therapeutic effect.*

therapy *NOUN* therapies
a way of treating a physical or mental illness,
especially without using surgery or artificial
medicines
➤ **therapist** *NOUN*

there *ADVERB*
❶ in or to that place ❷ used to call attention
to something or to talk about it • *There's
a spider in the bath.* • *There has been a
mistake.*

SPELLING
There is different from **their**: • *I'm going
there soon.* • *their pets*

thereabouts *ADVERB*
near there

thereafter *ADVERB*
from then or there onwards

thereby *ADVERB*
by that means; because of that

therefore *ADVERB*
for that reason; and so

therm *NOUN* therms
a unit for measuring heat, especially from gas

thermal *ADJECTIVE*
❶ to do with heat; worked by heat
❷ designed to keep you warm in cold weather
• *thermal underwear*

thermodynamics *NOUN*
the science dealing with the relation between
heat and other forms of energy

thermometer *NOUN* thermometers
a device for measuring temperature

Thermos *NOUN* Thermoses (*trademark*)
a kind of vacuum flask

thermostat *NOUN* thermostats
a piece of equipment that automatically
keeps the temperature of a room or piece of
equipment steady

thesaurus (say thi-**sor**-us) *NOUN* thesauruses
or thesauri
a kind of dictionary that lists words
in groups that have similar meanings
WORD ORIGIN from Greek *thesauros* =
storehouse, treasury

these *DETERMINER & PRONOUN*
plural of **this**

thesis *NOUN* theses
❶ a theory that someone has put forward
❷ a long essay written by a candidate for a
university degree

they *PRONOUN*
❶ the people or things being talked about
❷ people in general • *They say it's going to
be a mild winter.* ❸ he or she; a person • *I am
never angry with anyone unless they deserve
it.*

they're (*mainly spoken*)
they are

> **SPELLING**
>
> **They're = they + are.** Do not forget to add an **apostrophe** between the **y** and the **re**.

thick *ADJECTIVE*
❶ measuring a lot from one side to the other; broad or wide • *a thick slice of cake* ❷ measuring from one side to the other • *The wall is ten centimetres thick.* ❸ with a lot of things packed close together; dense • *thick dark hair* • *thick fog* ❹ fairly stiff; not flowing easily • *thick cream* ❺ (*informal*) stupid

thicken *VERB* thickens, thickening, thickened
to become thicker or to make something thicker • *The fog had thickened.*

thicket *NOUN* thickets
a number of shrubs and small trees growing close together

thickly *ADVERB*
❶ in thick pieces or in a deep layer • *thickly sliced bread* • *The roads were thickly covered with snow.* ❷ with a lot of things packed close together • *thickly wooded hills*

thickness *NOUN* thicknesses
how thick something is • *What thickness of board do we need?*

thickset *ADJECTIVE*
❶ having a stocky or burly body ❷ with parts placed or growing close together

thief *NOUN* thieves
a person who steals things

thieving *NOUN*
stealing things

thieving *ADJECTIVE*
behaving like a thief

thigh *NOUN* thighs
the part of your leg between your hip and your knee

thimble *NOUN* thimbles
a small metal or plastic cap that you put on the end of your finger to protect it when you are sewing

thin *ADJECTIVE* thinner, thinnest
❶ measuring a small amount from one side to the other ❷ not fat ❸ not dense or closely packed together ❹ runny or watery
➤ **thinness** *NOUN*

thin *VERB* thins, thinning, thinned
to become less thick or to make something less thick
➤ **thin out** to become less dense or crowded • *The crowd had thinned out by late afternoon.*
➤ **thin something out** to make something less dense or crowded

thine *DETERMINER & POSSESSIVE PRONOUN* (*old use*)
yours (referring to one person)

thing *NOUN* things
an object; something which can be seen, touched or thought about

things *PLURAL NOUN*
❶ personal belongings • *Can I leave my things here?* ❷ events or circumstances • *Things are looking good.*

think *VERB* thinks, thinking, thought
❶ to use your mind ❷ to have something as an idea or opinion • *Do you think we have enough time?* ❸ to intend or plan to do something • *I'm thinking of buying a guitar.*

> **SPELLING**
>
> The past tense of **think** is **thought**.

think *NOUN*
a time spent thinking about something • *I'll have a think and let you know.*

thinker *NOUN* thinkers
a person who thinks about things, especially important subjects

thinly *ADVERB*
❶ in thin pieces or in a thin layer • *thinly sliced bread* • *He spread the butter thinly on his toast.* ❷ with only a few things or people spread over a place • *a thinly populated area* ❸ in a way that is not sincere or enthusiastic • *She smiled thinly.*

third *ADJECTIVE*
next after the second
➤ **thirdly** *ADVERB*

third *NOUN* thirds
❶ the third person or thing ❷ one of three equal parts of something

Third World *NOUN*
the poorest and underdeveloped countries of Asia, Africa and South America
WORD ORIGIN originally called 'third' because they were not considered to be politically connected with the USA and its allies (the *First World*) or with the Communist countries led by Russia (the *Second World*)

a b c d e f g h i j k l m n o p q r s t u v w x y z

thirst *NOUN*
❶ a feeling of dryness in your mouth and throat that makes you want to drink ❷ a strong desire for something • *a thirst for adventure*

thirst *VERB* thirsts, thirsting, thirsted
to have a strong desire for something • *She thirsted for revenge.*

thirsty *ADJECTIVE*
feeling that you need to drink
➤ **thirstily** *ADVERB*

thirteen *NOUN & ADJECTIVE* thirteens
the number 13
➤ **thirteenth** *ADJECTIVE & NOUN*

thirty *NOUN & ADJECTIVE* thirties
the number 30
➤ **thirtieth** *ADJECTIVE & NOUN*

this *DETERMINER & PRONOUN* these
the one here • *This is my stop.* • *Have a look at this picture.*

this *ADVERB*
to such an extent • *I'm not used to getting up this early.*

thistle *NOUN* thistles
a prickly wild plant with purple, white or yellow flowers

thistledown *NOUN*
the very light fluff on thistle seeds

thither *ADVERB* (*old use*)
to that place

thong *NOUN* thongs
a narrow strip of leather used for fastening things

thorax *NOUN* thoraxes
the part of the body between the head or neck and the abdomen **WORD ORIGIN** Greek, = breastplate

thorn *NOUN* thorns
❶ a small pointed growth on the stem of a plant ❷ a thorny tree or shrub

thorny *ADJECTIVE* thornier, thorniest
❶ having many thorns; prickly ❷ causing difficulty or disagreement • *a thorny problem*

thorough *ADJECTIVE*
❶ done or doing things carefully and in detail ❷ complete in every way • *a thorough mess*
➤ **thoroughness** *NOUN*

thoroughbred *ADJECTIVE*
bred of pure or pedigree stock

thoroughbred *NOUN* thoroughbreds
an animal of of pure or pedigree stock

thoroughfare *NOUN* thoroughfares
a public road or path that is open at both ends

thoroughly *ADVERB*
❶ completely; very much • *We thoroughly enjoyed ourselves.* ❷ carefully and in detail • *She checked the figures thoroughly.*

those *DETERMINER & PRONOUN*
plural of **that** • *Where are those cards?* • *Those are the ones I want.*

thou *PRONOUN* (*old use*)
you (referring to one person)

though *CONJUNCTION*
in spite of the fact that; even if • *We can try phoning her, though she may already have left.*

though *ADVERB*
however; all the same • *She's right, though.*

thought
past tense of **think**

thought *NOUN* thoughts
❶ something that you think; an idea or opinion • *Look, I've just had a thought.* ❷ the process of thinking • *She was deep in thought.*

thoughtful *ADJECTIVE*
❶ thinking a lot • *a thoughtful expression* ❷ thinking of other people and what they need or want; considerate • *That was very thoughtful of you.*
➤ **thoughtfully** *ADVERB*
➤ **thoughtfulness** *NOUN*

thoughtless *ADJECTIVE*
❶ careless; not thinking of what may happen ❷ not thinking of others; inconsiderate
➤ **thoughtlessly** *ADVERB*
➤ **thoughtlessness** *NOUN*

thousand *NOUN & ADJECTIVE* thousands
the number 1,000
➤ **thousandth** *ADJECTIVE & NOUN*

thrall *NOUN*
➤ **in thrall to someone** in someone's power or completely under their control

thrash *VERB* thrashes, thrashing, thrashed
❶ to beat someone with a stick or whip; to keep hitting someone very hard ❷ to defeat someone completely ❸ to move about, or move a part of your body, violently • *The crocodile thrashed its tail.*
➤ **thrash something out** to discuss a matter thoroughly

thread *NOUN* threads
① a thin length of any substance ② a length of spun cotton, wool or nylon used for making cloth or in sewing or knitting ③ the spiral ridge round a screw ④ a theme or idea running through a story or argument • *I'm afraid I've lost the thread.* ⑤ a series of connected messages from an Internet discussion of a subject

thread *VERB* threads, threading, threaded
① to put a thread through the eye of a needle ② to pass something long and thin through or round something ③ to put beads on a thread

threadbare *ADJECTIVE*
threadbare cloth or clothing is old and worn thin with the threads showing

threat *NOUN* threats
① a warning that you will punish, hurt or harm a person or thing ② the possibility of trouble or danger • *The threat of war hung over the region.* ③ a person or thing causing danger

threaten *VERB* threatens, threatening, threatened
① to make threats against someone ② to be a threat or danger to a person or thing • *The quarrel threatened to turn violent.*

three *NOUN & ADJECTIVE* threes
the number 3

three-dimensional *ADJECTIVE*
having three dimensions (length, width and height or depth)

thresh *VERB* threshes, threshing, threshed
to beat corn in order to separate the grain from the husks

threshold *NOUN* thresholds
① a slab of stone or board forming the bottom of a doorway; the entrance ② the point at which something begins to happen or change • *We are on the threshold of a great discovery.*

thrice *ADVERB* (*old use*)
three times

thrift *NOUN*
being careful with money and not spending too much
➤ **thrifty** *ADJECTIVE*
➤ **thriftily** *ADVERB*

thrill *NOUN* thrills
a feeling of great excitement or pleasure

thrill *VERB* thrills, thrilling, thrilled
to give someone a feeling of great excitement or pleasure

thrilled *ADJECTIVE*
very excited and pleased • *I was thrilled to be invited.*

thriller *NOUN* thrillers
an exciting story or film, usually about crime or spying

thrilling *ADJECTIVE*
very exciting

thrive *VERB* thrives, thriving, throve, thrived or thriven
to prosper or grow strongly • *Crops thrive in this climate.*

throat *NOUN* throats
① the tube in your neck that takes food and drink down into your body ② the front of your neck

throaty *ADJECTIVE*
① produced deep in the throat • *a throaty chuckle* ② hoarse

throb *VERB* throbs, throbbing, throbbed
to beat or vibrate with a strong rhythm • *The ship's engines throbbed quietly.* • *My hand was throbbing with pain.*

throb *NOUN* throbs
a throbbing sound or feeling

throes *PLURAL NOUN*
severe pangs of pain
➤ **in the throes of something** in the middle of doing something difficult • *We are in the throes of exams.*

thrombosis *NOUN*
the formation of a clot of blood in the body

throne *NOUN* thrones
① a special chair for a king or queen at ceremonies ② the position of being king or queen • *the heir to the throne*

throng *NOUN* throngs
a large crowd of people

throng *VERB* throngs, thronging, thronged
to go somewhere in large numbers
• *Thousands of people thronged the streets.*

throttle *NOUN* throttles
a device that controls the flow of fuel to an engine; an accelerator

throttle *VERB* throttles, throttling, throttled
to strangle someone
➤ **throttle back** or **down** to reduce the

speed of an engine by partially closing the throttle

through PREPOSITION
❶ from one end or side to the other end or side of • *She climbed through the window.* ❷ during; throughout • *There will be celebrations all through the weekend.* ❸ by means of; because of • *We lost it through carelessness.* ❹ at the end of; having finished successfully • *We must be through the worst of the winter by now.*

through ADVERB
❶ through something • *We squeezed through.* ❷ with a telephone connection made • *I'll put you through to the president.* ❸ finished • *Wait till I'm through with these papers.*

through ADJECTIVE
❶ going directly all the way to a destination • *a through train* ❷ a through road leads directly from one place to another

> SPELLING
>
> **Through** is different from **threw**, which is a form of the verb *throw*: • *Climb through the window.* • *He threw a stone at the window.*

throughout PREPOSITION & ADVERB
all the way through; from beginning to end

throve
past tense of **thrive**

throw VERB throws, throwing, threw, thrown
❶ to send a person or thing through the air ❷ to put something in a place carelessly or hastily • *She came in and threw her coat on the chair.* ❸ to move part of your body quickly • *He threw his head back and laughed.* ❹ to put someone in a certain state • *It threw us into confusion.* ❺ to confuse or upset someone • *Your question threw me for a minute.* ❻ to move a switch or lever in order to operate it ❼ to shape a pot on a potter's wheel ❽ to hold a party
> **thrower** NOUN
> **throw something away** ❶ to get rid of something because it is useless or unwanted ❷ to waste something • *You threw away an opportunity.*
> **throw up** (*informal*) to vomit
> **throw yourself into something** to start doing something with energy or enthusiasm

> SPELLING
>
> The past tense of **throw** is **threw** and the past participle is **thrown**.

throw NOUN throws
a throwing action or movement • *That was a good throw.*

thrum VERB thrums, thrumming, thrummed
to make a low regular sound • *He could hear the engine softly thrumming.*
> **thrum** NOUN

thrush NOUN thrushes
❶ a songbird with a speckled breast ❷ an infection causing tiny white patches in the mouth and throat

thrust VERB thrusts, thrusting, thrust
to push something somewhere with a lot of force • *He thrust his hands into his pockets.*

thrust NOUN thrusts
a hard push

thud NOUN thuds
the dull sound of a heavy knock or fall

thud VERB thuds, thudding, thudded
to fall with a thud; to make a thud

thug NOUN thugs
a rough and violent person
> **WORD ORIGIN** from Hindi: the *Thugs* were robbers and murderers in India in the 17th-19th centuries

thumb NOUN thumbs
the short thick finger set apart from the other four
> **be under a someone's thumb** to be completely under a person's influence

thumb VERB thumbs, thumbing, thumbed
to turn the pages of a book or magazine quickly with your thumb
> **thumb a lift** to hitch-hike

thumbnail ADJECTIVE
brief; giving only the main facts • *a thumbnail sketch*

thumbnail NOUN thumbnails
a very small picture on a computer screen which shows you what a larger picture looks like

thumbscrew NOUN thumbscrews
a former instrument of torture for squeezing the thumb

thump VERB thumps, thumping, thumped
❶ to hit or knock something heavily ❷ to punch someone ❸ to make a heavy dull sound; to thud ❹ to throb or beat strongly • *My heart was thumping.*

thump NOUN thumps
an act or sound of thumping

thunder *NOUN*
❶ the loud noise that you hear with lightning during a storm ❷ a similar noise • *the thunder of horses' hooves*
➤ **thundery** *ADJECTIVE*

thunder *VERB* **thunders, thundering, thundered**
❶ to make the noise of thunder or a noise like thunder ❷ to speak loudly • *'Come here!' he thundered.*

thunderbolt *NOUN* **thunderbolts**
a lightning flash thought of as a destructive missile

thunderous *ADJECTIVE*
extremely loud • *thunderous applause*

thunderstorm *NOUN* **thunderstorms**
a storm with thunder and lightning

thunderstruck *ADJECTIVE*
amazed or shocked

Thursday *NOUN*
the day of the week following Wednesday
WORD ORIGIN from Old English *thuresdaeg* = day of thunder, named after Thor, the Norse god of thunder

thus *ADVERB*
❶ in this way • *Hold the wheel thus.* ❷ for this reason; therefore • *Thus, we must try again.*

thwart *VERB* **thwarts, thwarting, thwarted**
to frustrate a plan or attempt; to prevent someone from achieving something

thy *DETERMINER* (*old use*)
your (referring to one person)

thyme (say time) *NOUN*
a herb with fragrant leaves

thyroid gland *NOUN* **thyroid glands**
a large gland at the front of the neck
WORD ORIGIN from Greek *thyreos* = a shield (because of the shape of the gland)

thyself *PRONOUN* (*old use*)
yourself (referring to one person)

tiara (say tee-**ar**-a) *NOUN* **tiaras**
a woman's jewelled crescent-shaped ornament worn like a crown

tic *NOUN* **tics**
an unintentional twitch of a muscle, especially of the face

tick *NOUN* **ticks**
❶ (*British*) a mark (✓) put next to something to show that it is correct or has been checked or done ❷ a regular clicking sound, especially the sound made by a clock or watch ❸ (*British*) (*informal*) a moment • *I won't be a tick.* ❹ a bloodsucking insect

tick *VERB* **ticks, ticking, ticked**
❶ (*British*) to mark something with a tick • *She ticked the correct answers.* ❷ to make the sound of a tick
➤ **tick someone off** (*British*) (*informal*) to scold someone or tell them off

ticket *NOUN* **tickets**
❶ a printed piece of paper or card that allows a person to travel on a bus or train, see a show, etc. ❷ a label showing a thing's price

tickle *VERB* **tickles, tickling, tickled**
❶ to touch a person's skin lightly in order to produce a slight tingling feeling and make them laugh and wriggle ❷ a part of your body tickles when you have a slight tingling or itching feeling there • *My throat is tickling.* ❸ to amuse or please someone

ticklish *ADJECTIVE*
❶ a ticklish person is likely to laugh or wriggle when they are tickled ❷ awkward or difficult • *a ticklish situation*

tidal *ADJECTIVE*
to do with or affected by tides

tidal wave *NOUN* **tidal waves**
a huge sea wave

tiddler *NOUN* **tiddlers** (*British*) (*informal*)
a very small fish

tiddlywinks *NOUN*
a game playing by flicking a small counter into a cup by pressing on its edge with another counter

tide *NOUN* **tides**
❶ the regular rising and falling of the level of the sea, which usually happens twice a day ❷ (*old use*) a time or season • *Christmas-tide*

tide *VERB* **tides, tiding, tided**
➤ **tide someone over** to give someone what they need, especially money, for a short time

tidings *PLURAL NOUN* (*formal*)
news or information

tidy *ADJECTIVE* **tidier, tidiest**
❶ with everything in its right place; neat and orderly ❷ (*informal*) fairly large • *It costs a tidy sum.*
➤ **tidily** *ADVERB*
➤ **tidiness** *NOUN*

tidy *VERB* **tidies, tidying, tidied**
to make a place tidy

tidy NOUN
the act of tidying a place • *I'll give the house a quick tidy before they arrive.*

tie VERB ties, tying, tied
❶ to fasten something with string, rope, ribbon, etc. ❷ to arrange something into a knot or bow ❸ to make the same score as another competitor
➤ **be tied up** to be busy • *Sorry, I'm tied up all afternoon.*

tie NOUN ties
❶ a strip of material worn passing under the collar of a shirt and knotted in front ❷ a result when two or more competitors have equal scores ❸ one of the matches in a competition ❹ a close connection or bond • *the ties of friendship*

tie-break, tie-breaker NOUN tie-breaks or tie-breakers
a way to decide the winner when competitors have tied, especially an additional question in a quiz or an additional game at the end of a set in tennis

tier (say teer) NOUN tiers
each of a series of rows or levels placed one above the other
➤ **tiered** ADJECTIVE

tiff NOUN tiffs
a slight quarrel

tiger NOUN tigers
a large wild animal of the cat family, with yellow and black stripes

tight ADJECTIVE
❶ fitting very closely ❷ firmly fastened ❸ fully stretched; tense ❹ in short supply • *Money is tight at the moment.* ❺ mean or stingy • *He is very tight with his money.* ❻ severe or strict • *tight security* ❼ (*informal*) slightly drunk
➤ **tightness** NOUN

tight ADVERB
tightly or firmly • *Hold on tight.*

tighten VERB tightens, tightening, tightened
to make something tighter or to become tighter • *She tightened her grip.*

tightly ADVERB
closely and firmly; in a tight manner • *Her eyes were tightly closed.* • *Screw the lid on tightly.*

tightrope NOUN tightropes
a tightly stretched rope high above the ground, for acrobats to perform on

tights PLURAL NOUN
a piece of clothing that fits tightly over the feet, legs and lower part of the body

tigress NOUN tigresses
a female tiger

tile NOUN tiles
a thin square piece of baked clay or other hard material, used in rows for covering roofs, walls or floors

tiled ADJECTIVE
a tiled roof, wall or floor is covered with tiles

till PREPOSITION & CONJUNCTION
until

> **USAGE**
>
> It is better to use **until** when the word comes first in a sentence (e.g. *Until last year we had never been abroad*) or when you are speaking or writing formally.

till NOUN tills
a drawer or box for money in a shop; a cash register

till VERB tills, tilling, tilled
to plough land to prepare it for cultivating

tiller NOUN tillers
a handle used to turn a boat's rudder

tilt VERB tilts, tilting, tilted
to move or move something into a sloping position • *He tilted his head to one side.*

tilt NOUN
a sloping position
➤ **at full tilt** at full speed or force

timber NOUN timbers
❶ wood for building or making things ❷ a wooden beam

timbered ADJECTIVE
made of wood or with a wooden framework • *timbered houses*

timbre (say tambr) NOUN timbres
the quality of a voice or musical sound

time NOUN times
❶ a measure of the continuing existence of everything in years, months, days and other units ❷ what point in the day it is, as shown on a watch or clock • *Can you tell me the time?* ❸ a particular moment or period of things existing or happening • *There was a time when I would have agreed with you.* ❹ an occasion • *This is the first time I've been here.* ❺ a period that is suitable or available for something • *Do you have time for a quick chat?* ❻ a system of measuring time

• *Greenwich Mean Time* ❼ (*in music*) rhythm depending on the number and stress of beats in the bar
➤ **at times** or **from time to time** sometimes or occasionally
➤ **in time** ❶ not late ❷ after a while; eventually
➤ **on time** prompt or punctual • *The train left on time.*

time *VERB* times, timing, timed
❶ to measure how long something takes
❷ to arrange when something is to happen
• *You timed your arrival perfectly.*

timeless *ADJECTIVE*
not affected by the passage of time; eternal
• *It is a timeless classic.*

time limit *NOUN* time limits
a fixed amount of time within which something must be done

timely *ADJECTIVE*
happening at a suitable or useful time • *a timely warning*

timer *NOUN* timers
a device for timing things

times *PLURAL NOUN*
(*in mathematics*) multiplied by • *Five times three is 15 (5 x 3 = 15).*

time scale *NOUN* time scales
the length of time that something takes or that you need in order to do something

timetable *NOUN* timetables
a list showing the times when things happen, e.g. when buses or trains arrive and depart or when school lessons take place

timid *ADJECTIVE*
nervous and easily frightened
➤ **timidly** *ADVERB*
➤ **timidity** *NOUN*

timing *NOUN*
❶ the choice of time to do something
• *Arriving at lunchtime was good timing.*
❷ the time when something happens

timorous *ADJECTIVE*
nervous and afraid

timpani *PLURAL NOUN*
kettledrums

tin *NOUN* tins
❶ a silvery-white metal ❷ a metal container for preserving food

tin *VERB* tins, tinning, tinned
to seal food in a tin to preserve it

tincture *NOUN* tinctures
❶ a solution of medicine in alcohol ❷ a slight trace of something

tinder *NOUN*
any dry substance that catches fire easily

tine *NOUN* tines
a point or prong of a fork, comb or antler

tinge *VERB* tinges, tingeing, tinged
❶ to colour something slightly ❷ to add a slight amount of another feeling • *Our relief was tinged with sadness.*

tinge *NOUN* tinges
❶ a slight amount of a colour ❷ a slight amount of a feeling • *A tinge of jealousy crept into her voice.*

tingle *VERB* tingles, tingling, tingled
to have a slight pricking or stinging feeling
• *The cold water made my skin tingle.*

tingle *NOUN* tingles
a tingling feeling

tinker *NOUN* tinkers (*old use*)
a person travelling about mending pots and pans

tinker *VERB* tinkers, tinkering, tinkered
to work at something casually, trying to improve or mend it • *He is always tinkering with his bike.*

tinkle *VERB* tinkles, tinkling, tinkled
to make a gentle ringing sound

tinkle *NOUN* tinkles
a tinkling sound

tinny *ADJECTIVE*
a tinny sound is unpleasantly thin and high-pitched

tinsel *NOUN*
strips of glittering material used for decoration

tint *NOUN* tints
a shade of colour, especially a pale one

tint *VERB* tints, tinting, tinted
to colour something slightly
➤ **tinted** *ADJECTIVE*

tiny *ADJECTIVE* tinier, tiniest
very small

tip *NOUN* tips
❶ the part right at the top or end of something • *the tip of your nose* ❷ a small but useful piece of advice or information
❸ a small present of extra money given to someone who has served you • *a tip for the*

a b c d e f g h i j k l m n o p q r s t u v w x y z

waiter ④ a place where you can take rubbish and leave it ⑤ a very untidy place

tip *VERB* **tips, tipping, tipped**
① to turn something upside down or tilt it
• *She tipped the water out of the bucket.*
• *He tipped his head back and laughed.*
② to give a person a tip to thank them for a service ③ to name someone as likely to win or succeed • *Which team would you tip to win the championship?* ④ to be tipped with something is to have it right at the end • *The wings are tipped with yellow.* ⑤ to leave rubbish somewhere
➤ **tip someone off** to give someone a warning or special information about something

tip-off *NOUN* **tip-offs**
a warning or special piece of advice given to someone

tipple *NOUN* **tipples**
an alcoholic drink

tipsy *ADJECTIVE*
slightly drunk

tiptoe *VERB* **tiptoes, tiptoeing, tiptoed**
to walk on your toes very quietly or carefully
• *He tiptoed up the stairs.*
➤ **on tiptoe** walking or standing on your toes

tip-top *ADJECTIVE* (*informal*)
excellent; very best • *in tip-top condition*

tirade (say ty-**rayd**) *NOUN* **tirades**
a long angry or violent speech

tire *VERB* **tires, tiring, tired**
to make someone tired or to become tired

tired *ADJECTIVE*
feeling that you need to sleep or rest
➤ **be tired of something** to have had enough of something • *I'm tired of waiting.*

tireless *ADJECTIVE*
having a lot of energy; not tiring easily

tiresome *ADJECTIVE*
continually annoying

tiring *ADJECTIVE*
making you tired • *a tiring journey*

tissue *NOUN* **tissues**
① tissue paper ② a paper handkerchief ③ the substance forming any part of the body of an animal or plant • *bone tissue*

tissue paper *NOUN*
very thin soft paper used for wrapping and packing things

tit *NOUN* **tits**
a kind of small bird
➤ **tit for tat** something equal given in return; retaliation

titanic (say ty-**tan**-ik) *ADJECTIVE*
huge (**WORD ORIGIN**) from the *Titans*, gigantic gods and goddesses in Greek legend

titanium *NOUN*
a strong silver-grey metal used to make light alloys that do not corrode easily

titbit *NOUN* **titbits**
a nice little piece of something, e.g. of food, gossip or information

tithe *NOUN* **tithes**
one-tenth of a year's output from a farm etc., formerly paid as tax to support the clergy and church

title *NOUN* **titles**
① the name of a book, film, song, etc.
② a word used to show a person's rank or position, e.g. *Dr, Lord, Mrs* ③ a championship in sport • *the world heavyweight title* ④ a legal right to something, especially land or property

titled *ADJECTIVE*
a titled person has a title as a noble

titter *VERB* **titters, tittering, tittered**
to laugh quietly in a nervous or silly way

titter *NOUN*
a quiet nervous or silly laugh

tittle-tattle *NOUN*
gossip

TNT *ABBREVIATION*
trinitrotoluene; a powerful explosive

to *PREPOSITION*
① used to show direction towards a place or position • *We usually walk to school.* • *He quickly rose to power.* ② used to show the limit of something • *from noon to two o'clock* ③ used for comparison • *We won by six goals to three.* • *I prefer cats to dogs.* ④ used to show the person or thing that receives or is affected by something • *Give it to me.* • *She was always friendly to everyone.* ⑤ used before a verb to form an infinitive (*I want to see him.*) or to show purpose (*He does that to annoy us.*) or alone when the verb is understood (*We meant to go but forgot to.*)

to *ADVERB* to or in the proper or closed position or condition • *Push the door to.*
➤ **to and fro** backwards and forwards

toad *NOUN* toads
a frog-like animal that lives mainly on land

toad-in-the-hole *NOUN*
(*British*) sausages baked in batter

toadstool *NOUN* toadstools
a fungus (usually poisonous) with a round top on a stalk

toady *VERB* toadies, toadying, toadied
to flatter someone to make them want to help you
➤ **toady** *NOUN*
WORD ORIGIN short for *toad-eater*, because quack healers used to have assistants who ate toads and were then supposedly cured

toast *VERB* toasts, toasting, toasted
❶ to heat bread etc. to make it brown and crisp ❷ to warm something in front of a fire or grill ❸ to drink in honour of someone

toast *NOUN* toasts
❶ toasted bread ❷ the call to drink in honour of someone; the person honoured in this way • *Let's drink a toast to the bride and groom.*

toaster *NOUN* toasters
an electrical device for toasting bread

tobacco *NOUN*
the dried leaves of certain plants prepared for smoking in cigarettes, cigars or pipes or for making snuff

tobacconist *NOUN* tobacconists
(*chiefly British*) a shopkeeper who sells cigarettes, cigars, etc.

toboggan *NOUN* toboggans
a small sledge used for sliding downhill
➤ **tobogganing** *NOUN*

today *NOUN*
this present day • *Today is Monday.*

today *ADVERB*
❶ on this day • *Have you seen him today?*
❷ nowadays • *Young people today have far more freedom.*

toddle *VERB* toddles, toddling, toddled
❶ a young child toddles when it walks with short unsteady steps ❷ to walk or go somewhere casually

toddler *NOUN* toddlers
a young child who has only recently learnt to walk

to-do *NOUN* to-dos
a fuss or commotion

toe *NOUN* toes
❶ any of the separate parts (five in humans) at the end of each foot ❷ the part of a shoe, sock or stocking that covers the toes
➤ **on your toes** alert and ready to act

toffee *NOUN* toffees
a sticky sweet made from heated butter and sugar

toga (say **toh**-ga) *NOUN* togas
a long loose piece of clothing worn by men in ancient Rome

together *ADVERB*
with another person or thing; with each other • *They went to the party together.* • *Now glue the two parts together.*

toggle *NOUN* toggles
a short piece of wood, metal, etc. used like a button

toil *VERB* toils, toiling, toiled
❶ to work hard ❷ to move slowly and with difficulty • *We toiled up the hill.*

toil *NOUN*
hard work

toilet *NOUN* toilets
❶ a bowl-like object, connected by pipes to a drain, which you use to get rid of urine and faeces ❷ a room containing a toilet ❸ the process of washing, dressing and tidying yourself

toilet paper *NOUN*
paper for cleaning yourself after you have used a toilet

token *NOUN* tokens
❶ a piece of metal or plastic that can be used instead of money ❷ a voucher or coupon that can be exchanged for goods ❸ a sign or signal of something • *Please accept this gift as a small token of our gratitude.*

tolerable *ADJECTIVE*
able to be put up with
➤ **tolerably** *ADVERB*

tolerant *ADJECTIVE*
willing to accept or put up with other people's behaviour and opinions even if you do not agree with them
➤ **tolerantly** *ADVERB*
➤ **tolerance** *NOUN*

tolerate *VERB* tolerates, tolerating, tolerated
❶ to allow something even if you do

not approve of it • *I will not tolerate bad manners.* ❷ to bear or put up with something unpleasant • *I don't know how you tolerate all that noise.*
➤ **toleration** NOUN

toll (rhymes with hole) NOUN tolls
❶ a charge made for using a road or bridge ❷ loss or damage caused by something • *The death toll in the earthquake is rising.*
➤ **take its toll** to damage or have a bad effect on a person or thing

toll VERB tolls, tolling, tolled
to ring a bell slowly

tom, tomcat NOUN toms or tomcats
a male cat

tomahawk NOUN tomahawks
a small axe used by Native Americans

tomato NOUN tomatoes
a soft round red or yellow fruit eaten as a vegetable

tomb (say toom) NOUN tombs
a place where someone is buried; a monument built over this

tombola NOUN
(*British*) a kind of lottery **WORD ORIGIN** from Italian *tombolare* = tumble (because often the tickets are drawn from a revolving drum)

tomboy NOUN tomboys
a girl who enjoys playing rough noisy games

tombstone NOUN tombstones
a memorial stone set up over a grave

tome NOUN tomes
a large heavy book

tommy gun NOUN tommy guns
a small machine gun **WORD ORIGIN** from the name of its American inventor, J. T. *Thompson* (died 1940)

tomorrow NOUN & ADVERB
the day after today

> **SPELLING**
> Double up the r in **tomorrow** (but the m stays single).

tom-tom NOUN tom-toms
a drum beaten with the hands

ton NOUN tons
❶ a unit of weight equal to 2,240 pounds or about 1,016 kilograms ❷ a large amount • *There's tons of room.* ❸ (*informal*) a speed of 100 miles per hour

tonal ADJECTIVE
to do with tone

tone NOUN tones
❶ a sound in music or of the voice ❷ each of the five larger intervals between notes in a musical scale (the smaller intervals are **semitones**) ❸ a shade of a colour ❹ the quality or character of something • *a cheerful tone*

tone VERB tones, toning, toned
➤ **tone something down** to make a thing quieter or less bright or less harsh
➤ **tone in** to blend or fit in well, especially in colour
➤ **tone something up** to make your body firm and strong by doing exercise

tone-deaf ADJECTIVE
not able to tell the difference between different musical notes

tongs PLURAL NOUN
a tool with two arms joined at one end, used to pick up or hold things

tongue NOUN tongues
❶ the long soft muscular part that moves about inside your mouth ❷ a language ❸ the leather flap on a shoe or boot underneath the laces ❹ a pointed flame

tongue-tied ADJECTIVE
too shy to speak

tongue-twister NOUN tongue-twisters
something that is difficult to say quickly and correctly, e.g. 'She sells seashells.'

tonic NOUN tonics
❶ a medicine etc. that makes a person healthier or stronger ❷ anything that makes a person more energetic or cheerful ❸ (also **tonic water**) a fizzy mineral water with a bitter taste, often mixed with gin ❹ the first note in a scale, providing the keynote in a piece of music

tonight NOUN & ADVERB
this evening or night

tonnage NOUN
the amount a ship or ships can carry, expressed in tons

tonne NOUN tonnes
a metric ton (1,000 kilograms)

tonsil NOUN tonsils
either of two small masses of soft flesh inside your throat

tonsillitis *NOUN*
inflammation of the tonsils

too *ADVERB*
❶ also • *Take the others too.* ❷ more than is wanted or allowed etc. • *It's too hot to sit outside.*

> **SPELLING**
> Too is different from to: • *I'm going to Manchester.* • *too much food*

tool *NOUN* tools
❶ a device that helps you to do a particular job • *A saw is a tool for cutting wood or metal.* ❷ a thing used for a particular purpose • *An encyclopedia is a useful study tool.*

toolbar *NOUN* toolbars
a row of symbols on a computer screen that show the different things that you can do with a particular program

toot *NOUN* toots
a short sound produced by a horn

toot *VERB* toots, tooting, tooted
to make a toot

tooth *NOUN* teeth
❶ one of the hard white bony parts that are rooted in your gums, used for biting and chewing things ❷ one of a row of sharp parts • *the teeth of a saw*
➤ **toothed** *ADJECTIVE*
➤ **fight tooth and nail** to fight very fiercely

toothache *NOUN*
pain in your teeth or gums

toothbrush *NOUN* toothbrushes
a long-handled brush for cleaning your teeth

toothpaste *NOUN* toothpastes
a paste for cleaning your teeth

toothpick *NOUN* toothpicks
a small pointed piece of wood or plastic for removing bits of food from between your teeth

toothy *ADJECTIVE*
having large teeth or showing a lot of teeth • *a toothy grin*

top *NOUN* tops
❶ the highest part of something ❷ the upper surface of something ❸ the covering or stopper of a bottle, jar, etc. ❹ a piece of clothing you wear on the upper part of your body ❺ a toy that can be made to spin on its point
➤ **on top of something** in addition to something

top *ADJECTIVE*
highest or most important • *at top speed*

top *VERB* tops, topping, topped
❶ to put a top on something • *The cake was topped with icing.* ❷ to be at the top of something • *She tops the list.* ❸ to remove the top of something
➤ **top something up** to fill something that is partly empty • *I need to top up my mobile phone.*

topaz *NOUN* topazes
a kind of gem, often yellow

top hat *NOUN* top hats
a man's tall stiff black or grey hat worn with formal clothes

top-heavy *ADJECTIVE*
too heavy at the top and likely to overbalance

topic *NOUN* topics
a subject to write, learn or talk about

topical *ADJECTIVE*
to do with things that are happening or in the news now • *a topical film*
➤ **topicality** *NOUN*

topless *ADJECTIVE*
not wearing any clothes on the top half of the body

topmost *ADJECTIVE*
highest or tallest • *the topmost branches*

topography (say top-**og**-ra-fee) *NOUN* topographies
the position of the rivers, mountains, roads, buildings, etc. in a place
➤ **topographical** *ADJECTIVE*

topping *NOUN* toppings
food that is put on the top of a cake, dessert, pizza, etc.

topple *VERB* topples, toppling, toppled
❶ to fall over; to totter and fall ❷ to make something fall over ❸ to topple someone in power is to overthrow them

top secret *ADJECTIVE*
extremely secret • *top secret information*

topsy-turvy *ADVERB & ADJECTIVE*
upside down; muddled

Torah (say **tor**-uh) *NOUN*
in Judaism, the law of God as given to Moses and recorded in the first five books of the Bible

torch *NOUN* torches
❶ a small electric lamp that you can carry in

a
b
c
d
e
f
g
h
i
j
k
l
m
n
o
p
q
r
s
t
u
v
w
x
y
z

your hand ❷ a stick with burning material on the end, used as a light

toreador (say **to**rree-a-dor) *NOUN* toreadors
a bullfighter

torment *VERB* torments, tormenting, tormented
❶ to make someone suffer greatly ❷ to tease or keep annoying someone
➤ **tormentor** *NOUN*

torment *NOUN* torments
great suffering

torn
past participle of **tear** *VERB*

tornado (say tor-**nay**-doh) *NOUN* tornadoes
a violent storm or whirlwind
WORD ORIGIN from Spanish *tronada* = thunderstorm

torpedo *NOUN* torpedoes
a long tube-shaped missile that can be fired under water to destroy ships

torpedo *VERB* torpedoes, torpedoing, torpedoed
to attack or destroy a ship with a torpedo

torpid *ADJECTIVE*
slow-moving; not lively
➤ **torpor** *NOUN*

torrent *NOUN* torrents
❶ a rushing stream; a great flow ❷ a heavy downpour of rain

torrential *ADJECTIVE*
torrential rain pours down very heavily

torrid *ADJECTIVE*
❶ very hot and dry ❷ emotional and passionate • *a torrid love affair*

torso *NOUN* torsos
the trunk of the human body
WORD ORIGIN Italian, = stump

tortilla *NOUN* tortillas
in Mexican cookery, a flat cake made from flour or maize, often stuffed

tortoise *NOUN* tortoises
a slow-moving animal with a shell over its body

tortoiseshell (say **tort**-a-shell) *NOUN* tortoiseshells
❶ the mottled brown and yellow shell of certain turtles, used for making combs etc.
❷ a cat or butterfly with mottled brown colouring

tortuous *ADJECTIVE*
❶ full of twists and turns • *a tortuous path* ❷ complicated and not easy to follow • *tortuous logic*

torture *VERB* tortures, torturing, tortured
❶ to make a person feel great pain, especially so that they will give information ❷ to cause someone great emotional pain or worry

torture *NOUN* tortures
something done to torture a person; mental or physical suffering
➤ **torturer** *NOUN*

torturous *ADJECTIVE*
like torture; agonizing • *a torturous wait for news of survivors*

Tory *NOUN* Tories
a member of the British Conservative Party
➤ **Tory** *ADJECTIVE*
WORD ORIGIN from Irish *toraidhe* = an outlaw

toss *VERB* tosses, tossing, tossed
❶ to throw something, especially up into the air ❷ to spin a coin to decide something according to which side of it is upwards after it falls ❸ to move restlessly or unevenly from side to side • *She was tossing and turning all night.*

toss *NOUN* tosses
the act of tossing a coin or other object

toss-up *NOUN* toss-ups
❶ the tossing of a coin ❷ an even chance

tot *NOUN* tots
❶ a small child ❷ (*informal, chiefly British*) a small amount of spirits • *a tot of rum*

tot *VERB* tots, totting, totted
➤ **tot something up** (*informal, chiefly British*) to add up figures or amounts

total *ADJECTIVE*
❶ including everything • *the total amount* ❷ complete • *total darkness*

total *NOUN* totals
the amount you get by adding everything together

total *VERB* totals, totalling, totalled
❶ to add up the total ❷ to reach an amount as a total • *The cost of the damage totalled $5,000.*

totalitarian *ADJECTIVE*
using a form of government where people are not allowed to form rival political parties

totally *ADVERB*
completely • *I totally agree with you.*

totem pole *NOUN* totem poles
a pole carved or painted by Native Americans with the symbols (*totems*) of their tribes or families

totter *VERB* totters, tottering, tottered
to walk unsteadily; to wobble • *The old man tottered along beside me.*
➤ **tottery** *ADJECTIVE*

toucan (say **too**-kan) *NOUN* toucans
a tropical American bird with a huge brightly-coloured beak

touch *VERB* touches, touching, touched
❶ to put your hand or fingers on something lightly ❷ two things touch when they join together so that there is no space between ❸ to come into contact with something or hit it gently ❹ to move or meddle with something • *Don't touch anything in this room.* ❺ to reach a certain point • *The thermometer touched 30° Celsius.* ❻ to affect someone's feelings, e.g. by making them feel sympathy • *His sad story touched our hearts.*
➤ **touch and go** uncertain or risky
➤ **touch down** an aircraft or spacecraft touches down when it lands
➤ **touch on something** to discuss a subject briefly
➤ **touch something up** to improve something by making small additions or changes

touch *NOUN* touches
❶ the action of touching • *You can find the map of any city at the touch of a button.* ❷ the ability to feel things by touching them ❸ a small thing that improves something • *I'm just putting the finishing touches to the cake.* ❹ communication with someone • *We have lost touch with him.* ❺ a special skill or style of workmanship • *She hasn't lost her touch* ❻ the part of a football field outside the playing area • *He kicked the ball into touch.*

touchdown *NOUN* touchdowns
the action of touching down

touché (say **too**-shay) *EXCLAMATION*
used to acknowledge a true or clever point made against you in an argument
WORD ORIGIN French, = touched, originally referring to a hit in fencing

touching *ADJECTIVE*
making you feel sadness, pity or sympathy • *a touching scene*

touchline *NOUN* touchlines
one of the lines that mark the side of a sports pitch

touchscreen *NOUN* touchscreens
a screen on a computer or phone which allows you to interact with it by touching areas on the screen

touchstone *NOUN* touchstones
a test by which the quality of something is judged **WORD ORIGIN** formerly, a kind of stone against which gold and silver were rubbed to test their purity

touchy *ADJECTIVE* touchier, touchiest
easily offended

tough *ADJECTIVE*
❶ strong; difficult to break or damage • *You'll need tough shoes for the climb.* ❷ difficult to chew ❸ able to stand hardship and not easily hurt ❹ firm or severe • *Don't be too tough on her.* ❺ difficult • *a tough decision*
➤ **toughness** *NOUN*

toughen *VERB* toughens, toughening, toughened
to make someone or something tough or to become tough • *You need to toughen up a little.*

tour *NOUN* tours
a journey in which you visit several places

tour *VERB* tours, touring, toured
to make a tour

tourism *NOUN*
the industry of providing services for people on holiday in a place

tourist *NOUN* tourists
a person who visits a place for pleasure, especially when on holiday

tournament *NOUN* tournaments
a competition in which there is a series of games or contests

tourniquet (say **toor**-nik-ay) *NOUN* tourniquets
a strip of material pulled tightly round an arm or leg to stop bleeding from an artery

tousle (say **towz**-el) *VERB* tousles, tousling, tousled
to ruffle someone's hair

tout (rhymes with scout) *VERB* touts, touting, touted
to try to sell something or get business

a b c d e f g h i j k l m n o p q r s t u v w x y z

tout *NOUN* touts
a person who sells tickets for a sports match, concert, etc. at more than the original price

tow (rhymes with go) *VERB* tows, towing, towed
to pull a vehicle along behind you • *They towed our car to the garage.*

tow *NOUN*
an act of towing
➤ **in tow** (*informal*) following closely behind

towards, toward *PREPOSITION*
❶ in the direction of • *She walked towards the sea.* ❷ in relation to; regarding • *He behaved kindly towards his children.* ❸ as a contribution to • *Put the money towards a new bicycle.* ❹ near; close to • *It was getting on towards midnight.*

towel *NOUN* towels
a piece of absorbent cloth for drying things
➤ **towelling** *NOUN*

tower *NOUN* towers
a tall narrow building or part of a building

tower *VERB* towers, towering, towered
to be very high; to be taller than others • *Skyscrapers towered over the city.*

tower block *NOUN* tower blocks
(*British*) a tall building containing offices or flats

town *NOUN* towns
a place with many houses, shops, offices and other buildings

town hall *NOUN* town halls
a building with offices for the local council and usually a hall for public events

township *NOUN* townships
in South Africa under apartheid, a town set aside for black people to live

towpath *NOUN* towpaths
a path beside a canal or river, originally for use when a horse was towing a barge

toxic *ADJECTIVE*
poisonous; caused by poison

toxicology *NOUN*
the study of poisons
➤ **toxicologist** *NOUN*

toxin *NOUN* toxins
a poisonous substance, especially one formed in the body by germs

toy *NOUN* toys
a thing to play with

toy *ADJECTIVE*
❶ made as a toy ❷ a toy dog is one

belonging to a very small breed kept as a pet
• *a toy poodle*

toy *VERB* toys, toying, toyed
➤ **toy with something** ❶ to think about an idea casually or idly ❷ to move something about without thinking about what you are doing • *He was nervously toying with his pen.*

toyshop *NOUN* toyshops
a shop that sells toys

trace *NOUN* traces
❶ a mark or sign left by a person or thing • *He vanished without a trace.* ❷ a very small amount • *They found traces of blood on the carpet.*

trace *VERB* traces, tracing, traced
❶ to copy a picture or map etc. by drawing over it on transparent paper ❷ to find a person or thing after following tracks or other evidence • *The police have been trying to trace her.*

traceable *ADJECTIVE*
able to be traced

tracery *NOUN*
a decorative pattern of holes in stone, e.g. in a church window

track *NOUN* tracks
❶ a mark or marks left by a moving person or thing ❷ a rough path made by being used ❸ a road or area of ground specially prepared for racing ❹ a set of rails for trains or trams to run on ❺ one of the songs or pieces of music on a CD, tape, etc. ❻ a continuous band round the wheels of a heavy vehicle such as a tank or tractor
➤ **keep** or **lose track of something** to keep or fail to keep yourself aware of something or informed about it

track *VERB* tracks, tracking, tracked
❶ to follow a person or animal by following the tracks they leave ❷ to follow or observe something as it moves
➤ **tracker** *NOUN*
➤ **track someone** or **something down** to find a person or thing by searching

track events *PLURAL NOUN*
athletic events that involve racing on a running track, as opposed to field events

track record *NOUN* track records
a person's past achievements

track suit *NOUN* track suits
a warm loose suit of the kind worn by athletes before and after contests or for jogging

tract *NOUN* tracts
❶ an area of land ❷ a series of connected parts along which something passes • *the digestive tract* ❸ a pamphlet containing a short essay, especially about religion

traction *NOUN*
❶ pulling a load ❷ the ability of a vehicle to grip the ground • *The wheels were losing traction in the snow.* ❸ a medical treatment in which an injured arm or leg is pulled gently for a long time by means of weights and pulleys

traction engine *NOUN* traction engines
a steam or diesel engine for pulling a heavy load along a road or across a field etc.

tractor *NOUN* tractors
a motor vehicle for pulling farm machinery or other heavy loads

trade *NOUN* trades
❶ buying, selling or exchanging goods ❷ business of a particular kind; the people working in this ❸ a job or occupation, especially a skilled craft

trade *VERB* trades, trading, traded
to buy, sell or exchange things
➤ **trade something in** to give a thing as part of the payment for something new • *He traded in his motorcycle for a car.*

trademark *NOUN* trademarks
a symbol or name that a firm puts on its products and that other firms are not allowed to use

trader *NOUN* traders
a person who buys and sells things • *market traders*

tradesman *NOUN* tradesmen
a person employed in trade, especially one who sells or delivers goods

trade union *NOUN* trade unions
a group of workers organized to help and protect workers in their own trade or industry

tradition *NOUN* traditions
❶ the passing down of customs or beliefs from one generation to another ❷ a custom or belief passed on in this way

traditional *ADJECTIVE*
❶ passed down from one generation to another • *a book of traditional stories from all round the world* ❷ following older methods and ideas rather than modern ones • *It is a very traditional school.*
➤ **traditionally** *ADVERB*

traffic *NOUN*
❶ vehicles, ships or aircraft moving along a route ❷ trading or dealing in drugs or other illegal goods

traffic *VERB* traffics, trafficking, trafficked
to deal in something illegal, especially drugs
➤ **trafficker** *NOUN*

traffic lights *PLURAL NOUN*
coloured lights used as a signal to traffic at road junctions or roadworks

traffic warden *NOUN* traffic wardens
(*British*) an official whose job is to make sure that vehicles are parked legally

tragedian (say tra-**jee**-dee-an) *NOUN* tragedians
❶ a person who writes tragedies ❷ an actor in tragedies

tragedy *NOUN* tragedies
❶ a play with unhappy events or a sad ending ❷ a very sad or distressing event

tragic *ADJECTIVE*
❶ very sad or distressing ❷ to do with tragedies • *a great tragic actor*
➤ **tragically** *ADVERB*

trail *NOUN* trails
❶ a track or scent left behind by an animal ❷ a series of marks in a line left behind by someone or something that has passed • *a trail of footprints* ❸ a path or track for walking through the countryside or a forest

trail *VERB* trails, trailing, trailed
❶ to follow the trail of an animal or person ❷ to be dragged along behind you; to drag something along behind you • *Her long skirt trailed in the mud.* ❸ to follow someone more slowly or wearily • *A few walkers trailed behind the others.* ❹ to hang down or float loosely ❺ to become fainter • *Her voice trailed away.*

trailer *NOUN* trailers
❶ a truck or other container pulled along by a vehicle ❷ a short piece from a film or television programme, shown in advance to advertise it

train *NOUN* trains
❶ a railway engine pulling a line of carriages or trucks that are linked together ❷ a number of people or animals moving in a line • *a camel train* ❸ a series of things • *a train of events* ❹ part of a long dress or robe that trails on the ground at the back

train *VERB* trains, training, trained
❶ to give a person instruction or practice

so that they become skilled ❷ to learn how to do a job • *He's training to be a doctor.* ❸ to practise for a sporting event • *She was training for the race.* ❹ to make a plant grow in a particular direction • *We'd like to train roses up the walls.* ❺ to aim a gun, camera, etc. • *He trained his gun on the bridge.*

trainee *NOUN* trainees
a person who is being trained

trainer *NOUN* trainers
❶ a person who trains people or animals ❷ a soft rubber-soled shoe of the kind worn for running and sport

traipse *VERB* traipses, traipsing, traipsed
to walk wearily; to trudge a long distance

trait (say trayt) *NOUN* traits
one of a person's characteristics

traitor *NOUN* traitors
a person who betrays their country or friends
➤ **traitorous** *ADJECTIVE*

trajectory *NOUN* trajectories
the path taken by a moving object such as a bullet or rocket

tram *NOUN* trams
a public passenger vehicle which runs on rails in the road

tramlines *PLURAL NOUN*
❶ rails for a tram ❷ the pair of parallel lines at the side of a tennis court

tramp *NOUN* tramps
❶ a person without a home or job who walks from place to place ❷ a long walk ❸ the sound of heavy footsteps

tramp *VERB* tramps, tramping, tramped
❶ to walk with heavy footsteps ❷ to walk for a long distance

trample *VERB* tramples, trampling, trampled
to tread heavily on something; to crush something by treading on it • *Don't trample on the flowers.* • *He was trampled to death by a runaway horse.*

trampoline *NOUN* trampolines
a large piece of canvas joined to a frame by springs, used by gymnasts for jumping on

trance *NOUN* trances
a dreamy or unconscious state rather like sleep

tranquil *ADJECTIVE*
calm and quiet • *a tranquil summer day*
➤ **tranquilly** *ADVERB*

tranquillity *NOUN*
being calm and quiet • *a scene of peace and tranquillity*

tranquillizer (also **tranquilliser**) *NOUN* tranquillizers
a drug or medicine used to make a person feel calm

transaction *NOUN* transactions
a piece of business done between people
➤ **transact** *VERB*

transatlantic *ADJECTIVE*
across or on the other side of the Atlantic Ocean

transcend *VERB* transcends, transcending, transcended
to go beyond the usual limits of something

transcribe *VERB* transcribes, transcribing, transcribed
to copy or write something out
➤ **transcription** *NOUN*

transcript *NOUN* transcripts
a written copy

transept *NOUN* transepts
the part that is at right angles to the nave in a cross-shaped church

transfer *VERB* transfers, transferring, transferred
❶ to move a person or thing from one place to another ❷ to hand something over to someone else
➤ **transferable** *ADJECTIVE*

transfer *NOUN* transfers
❶ the transferring of a person or thing ❷ a picture or design that can be transferred onto another surface

transfigure *VERB* transfigures, transfiguring, transfigured
to change the appearance of something greatly
➤ **transfiguration** *NOUN*

transfixed *ADJECTIVE*
unable to move because of fear or surprise • *She stared at him, transfixed with horror.*
➤ **transfix** *VERB*

transform *VERB* transforms, transforming, transformed
to change the form, appearance or character of a person or thing to something quite different

transformation *NOUN* transformations
a complete change in the form, appearance or character of a person or thing

transformer *NOUN* transformers
a device used to change the voltage of an electric current

transfusion *NOUN* transfusions
putting blood taken from one person into another person's body

transgress *VERB* transgresses, transgressing, transgressed
to break a rule or law
➤ **transgression** *NOUN*

transient *ADJECTIVE*
not lasting or staying for long
➤ **transience** *NOUN*

transistor *NOUN* transistors
❶ a tiny electronic device that controls a flow of electricity ❷ (also **transistor radio**) a portable radio that uses transistors

transit *NOUN*
the process of travelling from one place to another • *The goods were damaged in transit.*

transition *NOUN* transitions
the process of changing from one state or form to another • *the transition from childhood to adolescence*
➤ **transitional** *ADJECTIVE*

transitive *ADJECTIVE*
a transitive verb is one that is used with a direct object after it, e.g. *change* in *change your shoes* (but not in *change into dry shoes*). Compare with **intransitive**.
➤ **transitively** *ADVERB*

transitory *ADJECTIVE*
existing for a time but not lasting

translate *VERB* translates, translating, translated
to put something into another language • *The book has been translated from Arabic into English.*
➤ **translator** *NOUN*

translation *NOUN* translations
something translated from another language

translucent (say tranz-**loo**-sent) *ADJECTIVE*
allowing light to shine through but not transparent

transmission *NOUN* transmissions
❶ transmitting something ❷ a broadcast ❸ the gears by which power is transmitted from the engine to the wheels of a vehicle

transmit *VERB* transmits, transmitting, transmitted
❶ to send or pass something on from one person or place to another ❷ to send out a signal or broadcast

transmitter *NOUN* transmitters
a device for transmitting radio or television signals

transom *NOUN* transoms
❶ a horizontal bar of wood or stone dividing a window or separating a door from a window above it ❷ a small window above a door

transparency *NOUN* transparencies
❶ being transparent ❷ a transparent photograph that can be projected onto a screen

transparent *ADJECTIVE*
able to be seen through • *The insect's wings are almost transparent.*

transpire *VERB* transpires, transpiring, transpired
❶ to become known; to turn out • *It transpired that she had known nothing at all about it.* ❷ to happen • *The police need to know what transpired on the yacht.* ❸ plants transpire when they give off watery vapour from leaves etc.
➤ **transpiration** *NOUN*

transplant *VERB* transplants, transplanting, transplanted
❶ to transfer an organ from the body of one person to another ❷ to remove a plant and put it to grow somewhere else
➤ **transplantation** *NOUN*

transplant *NOUN* transplants
❶ the process of transplanting something • *a heart transplant* ❷ something transplanted

transport *VERB* transports, transporting, transported
to take people, animals or things from one place to another
➤ **transportation** *NOUN*

transport *NOUN*
the process or means of transporting people, animals or things • *The city has a good system of public transport.*

transporter *NOUN* transporters
a heavy vehicle for transporting large objects, such as cars

transpose *VERB* transposes, transposing, transposed
❶ to change the position or order of

a
b
c
d
e
f
g
h
i
j
k
l
m
n
o
p
q
r
s
t
u
v
w
x
y
z

something ❷ to put a piece of music into a different key
➤ **transposition** NOUN

transverse ADJECTIVE
lying across something
➤ **transversely** ADVERB

transvestite NOUN transvestites
a person who likes wearing clothes intended for someone of the opposite gender

trap NOUN traps
❶ a device for catching and holding animals ❷ a plan or trick for capturing, detecting or cheating someone ❸ a two-wheeled carriage pulled by a horse ❹ a bend in a pipe, filled with water to prevent gases from rising up from a drain

trap VERB traps, trapping, trapped
❶ to catch or hold a person or animal in a trap ❷ to be trapped is to be stuck in a dangerous place or difficult situation you cannot escape from • *The driver was trapped in the wreckage.* ❸ to trick someone into doing or saying something

trapdoor NOUN trapdoors
a door in a floor, ceiling or roof

trapeze NOUN trapezes
a bar hanging from two ropes as a swing for acrobats

trapezium NOUN trapeziums or trapezia
a quadrilateral in which two opposite sides are parallel and the other two are not

trapezoid NOUN trapezoids
a quadrilateral in which no sides are parallel

trapper NOUN trappers
someone who traps wild animals, especially for their fur

trappings PLURAL NOUN
❶ the clothes or possessions that show your rank or position ❷ an ornamental harness for a horse

trash NOUN
rubbish or nonsense
➤ **trashy** ADJECTIVE

trash can NOUN trash cans
(*North American*) a dustbin

trauma (say **traw**-ma) NOUN traumas
a shock or upsetting experience that produces a lasting effect on a person's mind

traumatic ADJECTIVE
a traumatic experience is very unpleasant and upsetting

travail NOUN (*old use*)
hard or laborious work

travel VERB travels, travelling, travelled
to go from one place to another
travel NOUN
going on journeys • *air travel*

travel agent NOUN travel agents
a person whose job is to arrange travel and holidays for people

traveller NOUN travellers
❶ a person who is travelling or who often travels ❷ a gypsy or a person who does not settle in one place

traveller's cheque NOUN traveller's cheques
a cheque for a fixed amount of money that is sold by banks and that can be exchanged for money in foreign countries

traverse VERB traverses, traversing, traversed
to go across something, especially as part of a journey or expedition

travesty NOUN travesties
a bad or ridiculous form of something • *His story is a travesty of the truth.*

trawl VERB trawls, trawling, trawled
to fish by dragging a large net along the seabed

trawler NOUN trawlers
a boat used in trawling

tray NOUN trays
❶ a flat piece of wood, metal or plastic, usually with raised edges, for carrying cups, plates, food, etc. ❷ an open container for holding documents and letters in an office

treacherous ADJECTIVE
❶ betraying someone; disloyal ❷ dangerous or unreliable • *It's snowing and the roads are treacherous.*
➤ **treacherously** ADVERB

treachery NOUN
doing something that betrays someone

treacle NOUN
a thick sticky liquid produced when sugar is purified
➤ **treacly** ADJECTIVE
WORD ORIGIN originally = ointment for an animal bite; from Greek *therion* = wild or poisonous animal

tread VERB treads, treading, trod, trodden
to walk on something or put your foot on it
tread NOUN treads
❶ a sound or way of walking • *He had a*

heavy tread. ❷ the top surface of a stair; the part you put your foot on ❸ the part of a tyre that touches the ground

> **SPELLING**
> The past tense of **tread** is **trod** and the past participle is **trodden**.

treadle NOUN treadles
a lever that you press with your foot to turn a wheel that works a machine

treadmill NOUN treadmills
❶ a wide mill wheel turned by the weight of people or animals treading on steps fixed round its edge ❷ monotonous routine work

treason NOUN
betraying your country
➤ **treasonable** ADJECTIVE
➤ **treasonous** ADJECTIVE

treasure NOUN treasures
❶ a store of precious metals or jewels ❷ a precious thing or person

treasure VERB treasures, treasuring, treasured
to value greatly something that you have • I will treasure those memories forever.

treasure hunt NOUN treasure hunts
a game in which people try to find a hidden object

treasurer NOUN treasurers
a person in charge of the money of a club, society, etc.

treasure trove NOUN
gold or silver etc. found hidden and with no known owner

treasury NOUN treasuries
a place where money and valuables are kept
➤ **the Treasury** the government department in charge of a country's income

treat VERB treats, treating, treated
❶ to behave in a certain way towards a person or thing • She had always treated him with suspicion. ❷ to deal with a subject • This question is treated in more detail in the next chapter. ❸ to give medical care to a person or animal • He was treated for sunstroke. ❹ to put something through a chemical or other process • The fabric has been treated to make it waterproof. ❺ to pay for someone else's food, drink or entertainment • I'll treat you to an ice cream.

treat NOUN treats
❶ something special that gives pleasure

❷ the process of treating someone to food, drink or entertainment • This is my treat.

treatise NOUN treatises
a book or long essay on a subject

treatment NOUN treatments
❶ the way you behave towards or deal with a person, animal or thing ❷ medical care

treaty NOUN treaties
a formal agreement between two or more countries

treble ADJECTIVE
three times as much or as many

treble NOUN trebles
❶ a treble amount ❷ a person with a high-pitched or soprano voice

treble VERB trebles, trebling, trebled
to make something, or to become, three times as much or as many • The price has trebled since last year.

tree NOUN trees
a tall plant with a single very thick hard stem or trunk that is usually without branches for some distance above the ground

trefoil NOUN
a plant with three small leaves (e.g. clover)

trek NOUN treks
a long walk or journey

trek VERB treks, trekking, trekked
to go on a long walk or journey • The five-man team trekked to the South Pole.

trellis NOUN trellises
a framework with crossing bars of wood or metal to support climbing plants

tremble VERB trembles, trembling, trembled
to shake gently, especially because you are afraid

tremble NOUN trembles
a trembling movement or sound

tremendous ADJECTIVE
❶ very large; huge • a tremendous explosion ❷ excellent

tremendously ADVERB
very or very much • It is tremendously exciting.

tremor NOUN tremors
❶ a shaking or trembling movement ❷ a slight earthquake

tremulous ADJECTIVE
trembling from nervousness or weakness • a

tremulous voice
➤ **tremulously** ADVERB

trench NOUN trenches
a long narrow hole cut in the ground

trenchant ADJECTIVE
strong and effective • *trenchant criticism*

trend NOUN trends
the general direction in which something is
going or developing • *recent trends in the
fashion world*

trendy ADJECTIVE (*informal*)
fashionable; following the latest trends
• *trendy clothes*

trepidation NOUN
fear and anxiety about something that may
happen • *She entered the cave with great
trepidation.*

trespass VERB trespasses, trespassing,
trespassed
❶ to go on someone's land or property
without their permission ❷ (*old use*) to do
wrong; to sin
➤ **trespasser** NOUN

trespass NOUN trespasses (*old use*)
wrongdoing; sin

tress NOUN tresses
a lock of hair

trestle NOUN trestles
each of a set of supports on which you place
a board to form a table
➤ **trestle table** NOUN

triad (say **try**-ad) NOUN triads
❶ a group or set of three things ❷ a Chinese
secret organization involved in crime

trial NOUN trials
❶ the process of examining the evidence in
a law court to decide whether a person is
guilty of a crime ❷ testing a thing to see how
good it is or how well it works • *Scientists
are carrying out trials on the new drug.* ❸ a
test of qualities or ability • *a trial of strength*
❹ an annoying person or thing; a hardship
➤ **on trial** ❶ being tried in a law court
❷ being tested
➤ **trial and error** trying out different
methods of doing something until you find
one that works

triangle NOUN triangles
❶ a flat shape with three sides and three
angles ❷ a percussion instrument made from
a metal rod bent into a triangle

triangular ADJECTIVE
in the shape of a triangle

tribal ADJECTIVE
to do with or belonging to a tribe • *tribal
leaders*
➤ **tribally** ADVERB

tribe NOUN tribes
❶ a group of families living in one area as a
community, ruled by a chief ❷ a set of people
➤ **tribesman** NOUN
➤ **tribeswoman** NOUN

tribulation NOUN tribulations
great trouble or hardship

tribunal (say try-**bew**-nal) NOUN tribunals
a committee appointed to hear evidence and
give judgements when there is a dispute

tribune NOUN tribunes
an official chosen by the people in ancient
Rome

tributary NOUN tributaries
a river or stream that flows into a larger one
or into a lake

tribute NOUN tributes
❶ something said, done or given as a mark
of respect or admiration for someone
❷ payment that one country or ruler had to
pay to a more powerful one in the past

trice NOUN (*old use*)
➤ **in a trice** in a moment

triceps (say **try**-seps) NOUN triceps
the large muscle at the back of the upper arm
WORD ORIGIN Latin, = three-headed (because
the muscle is attached at three points)

trick NOUN tricks
❶ a crafty or deceitful action; a practical
joke • *Let's play a trick on Jo.* ❷ a skilful
action, especially one done for entertainment
• *a card trick* ❸ the cards picked up by the
winner after one round of a card game such
as whist
➤ **do the trick** (*informal*) to achieve the
result that you want

trick VERB tricks, tricking, tricked
to deceive or cheat someone by a trick
➤ **trick something out** to decorate a place
• *The building was tricked out with little
flags.*

trickery NOUN
the use of tricks; deception

trickle *VERB* **trickles, trickling, trickled**
to flow or move slowly • *Raindrops trickled down the window.*

trickle *NOUN* **trickles**
a slow gradual flow

trickster *NOUN* **tricksters**
a person who tricks or cheats people

tricky *ADJECTIVE* **trickier, trickiest**
❶ difficult to do or deal with • *There were a couple of tricky questions.* ❷ cunning or deceitful

tricolour (say **trik**-ol-er) *NOUN* **tricolours**
a flag with three coloured stripes, e.g. the national flag of France or Ireland

tricycle *NOUN* **tricycles**
a vehicle like a bicycle but with three wheels

trident *NOUN* **tridents**
a three-pronged spear, carried by Neptune and Britannia as a symbol of their power over the sea

trier *NOUN* **triers**
a person who tries hard

trifle *NOUN* **trifles**
❶ a pudding made of sponge cake covered in custard, fruit and cream ❷ a very small amount ❸ something that has very little importance or value
➤ **a trifle** (*informal*) a little bit; slightly • *He seemed a trifle anxious.*

trifle *VERB* **trifles, trifling, trifled**
to treat a person or thing without seriousness or respect • *She is not a woman to be trifled with.*

trifling *ADJECTIVE*
small in value or importance

trigger *NOUN* **triggers**
a lever that is pulled to fire a gun

trigger *VERB* **triggers, triggering, triggered**
to make something happen, especially suddenly • *The smoke must have triggered her asthma attack.*

trigonometry (say trig-on-**om**-it-ree) *NOUN*
the calculation of distances and angles by using triangles

trilby *NOUN* **trilbies**
(*chiefly British*) a man's soft felt hat
WORD ORIGIN named after *Trilby* O'Ferrall, the heroine of a popular book and play, who wore a similar hat

trill *VERB* **trills, trilling, trilled**
❶ to make a quivering musical sound ❷ to say something in a high cheerful voice • *'How lovely!' she trilled.*

trill *NOUN* **trills**
a quivering musical sound

trillion *NOUN* **trillions**
❶ a million million ❷ (*old use*) a million million million

trilogy *NOUN* **trilogies**
a group of three stories, poems or plays etc. about the same people or things

trim *VERB* **trims, trimming, trimmed**
❶ to cut the edges or unwanted parts off something ❷ to decorate a hat or piece of clothing by adding lace, ribbons, etc. • *The gown was trimmed with fur.* ❸ to arrange sails to suit the wind

trim *NOUN* **trims**
❶ cutting or trimming • *My hair needs a quick trim.* ❷ lace, ribbons, etc. used to decorate something
➤ **in good trim** in good condition; fit

trim *ADJECTIVE*
neat and orderly
➤ **trimly** *ADVERB*

Trinity *NOUN*
in Christianity, God regarded as three persons (Father, Son and Holy Spirit)

trinket *NOUN* **trinkets**
a small ornament or piece of jewellery

trio *NOUN* **trios**
❶ a group of three people or things ❷ a group of three musicians or singers ❸ a piece of music for three musicians

trip *VERB* **trips, tripping, tripped**
❶ to catch your foot on something and fall; to make someone do this ❷ to move with quick light steps ❸ to operate a switch
➤ **trip up** ❶ to stumble ❷ to make a small mistake
➤ **trip someone up** to cause a person to stumble or make a mistake

trip *NOUN* **trips**
❶ a journey or outing ❷ the action of tripping; a stumble ❸ (*informal*) hallucinations caused by taking a drug

tripe *NOUN*
❶ part of an ox's stomach used as food ❷ (*informal*) rubbish or nonsense

triple *ADJECTIVE*
❶ consisting of three parts ❷ involving three people or groups • *a triple alliance* ❸ three times as much or as many

triple *VERB* triples, tripling, tripled
to make something, or to become, three times as much or as many

triple jump *NOUN*
an athletic contest in which competitors try to jump as far as possible by doing a hop, step and jump

triplet *NOUN* triplets
each of three children or animals born to the same mother at one time

tripod (say **try**-pod) *NOUN* tripods
a stand with three legs, e.g. to support a camera or telescope

trireme (say **try**-reem) *NOUN* triremes
an ancient Greek or Roman warship with three banks of oars

trisect *VERB* trisects, trisecting, trisected
to divide something into three equal parts

trite (rhymes with kite) *ADJECTIVE*
worn out by constant repetition; hackneyed
• *a few trite remarks*

triumph *NOUN* triumphs
❶ a great success or victory ❷ a feeling of joy at success or victory • *They returned home in triumph.*

triumph *VERB* triumphs, triumphing, triumphed
❶ to be successful or victorious ❷ to rejoice in success or victory

triumphal *ADJECTIVE*
celebrating a great success or victory • *a triumphal arch*

triumphant *ADJECTIVE*
❶ victorious in a battle or contest ❷ rejoicing over a victory or success
➤ **triumphantly** *ADVERB*

triumvirate *NOUN* triumvirates
a ruling group of three people

trivet *NOUN* trivets
an iron stand for a pot or kettle, placed over a fire

trivia *PLURAL NOUN*
unimportant details or pieces of information
• *a quiz on pop trivia*

trivial *ADJECTIVE*
small in value or importance • *I'm sorry to bother you with such a trivial matter.*
➤ **triviality** *NOUN*
WORD ORIGIN from Latin *trivialis* = (originally) at a crossroads, and then commonplace

troll (rhymes with hole) *NOUN* trolls
❶ in Scandinavian mythology, a supernatural being, either a giant or a friendly but mischievous dwarf ❷ a person who writes unpleasant comments on the Internet in order to annoy people

trolley *NOUN* trolleys
❶ a small table on wheels or castors, used for serving food and drink ❷ a basket on wheels, used in supermarkets

trolleybus *NOUN* trolleybuses
(*British*) a bus powered by electricity from an overhead wire to which it is connected

trombone *NOUN* trombones
a large brass musical instrument with a sliding tube

troop *NOUN* troops
❶ an organized group of soldiers, Scouts, etc. ❷ a number of people or animals moving along together

troop *VERB* troops, trooping, trooped
to move along as a group or in large numbers
• *They all trooped in.*

trooper *NOUN* troopers
a soldier in the cavalry or in an armoured unit

troops *PLURAL NOUN*
soldiers

trophy *NOUN* trophies
❶ a cup or other prize given for winning a competition ❷ something taken in war or hunting as a souvenir of success

tropic *NOUN* tropics
a line of latitude about 23½° north of the equator (**tropic of Cancer**) or 23½° south of the equator (**tropic of Capricorn**)
➤ **the tropics** the hot regions between these two latitudes
WORD ORIGIN from Greek *trope* = turning (because the sun seems to turn back when it reaches these points)

tropical *ADJECTIVE*
to do with, or found in, the tropics • *tropical fish*

troposphere *NOUN*
the layer of the atmosphere extending about 10 kilometres upwards from the earth's surface

trot *VERB* trots, trotting, trotted
❶ a horse trots when it moves faster than when walking but more slowly than when cantering ❷ a person trots when they run gently with short steps

➤ **trot something out** (*informal*) to produce or repeat something that has been used many times before • *He trotted out the usual excuses.*

trot *NOUN*
a trotting run
➤ **on the trot** (*informal*) one after the other without a break • *She worked for ten days on the trot.*

troth (rhymes with both) *NOUN* (*old use*)
loyalty; a solemn promise

trotter *NOUN* **trotters**
a pig's foot used for food

troubadour (say **troo**-bad-oor) *NOUN* **troubadours**
a poet and singer in southern France in the 11th-13th centuries

trouble *NOUN* **troubles**
❶ a problem, difficulty or worry ❷ a cause of any of these
➤ **be in trouble** to be likely to get punished because of something you have done
➤ **take trouble** to take great care in doing something

trouble *VERB* **troubles, troubling, troubled**
❶ to cause trouble to someone ❷ to bother or disturb someone • *Sorry to trouble you, but can you spare a minute?* ❸ to make an effort to do something • *Nobody troubled to ask if I needed help.*

troublemaker *NOUN* **troublemakers**
a person who often deliberately causes trouble

troublesome *ADJECTIVE*
causing trouble or annoyance

trough (say trof) *NOUN* **troughs**
❶ a long narrow open container, especially one holding water or food for animals ❷ a channel for liquid ❸ the low part between two waves or ridges ❹ a long region of low air pressure

trounce *VERB* **trounces, trouncing, trounced**
to defeat someone heavily

troupe (say troop) *NOUN* **troupes**
a company of actors or other performers

SPELLING
Take care not to confuse with **troop**, which means a number of people or animals moving together.

trousers *PLURAL NOUN*
a piece of clothing worn over the lower half of your body, with a separate part for each leg

trousseau (say **troo**-soh) *NOUN* **trousseaus** or **trousseaux**
a bride's collection of clothing etc. to begin married life

trout *NOUN* **trout**
a freshwater fish that is caught as a sport and for food

trowel *NOUN* **trowels**
❶ a small garden tool with a curved blade for lifting plants or scooping things ❷ a small tool with a flat blade for spreading mortar or cement

truant *NOUN* **truants**
a child who stays away from school without permission
➤ **truancy** *NOUN*
➤ **play truant** to stay away from school without permission

truce *NOUN* **truces**
an agreement to stop fighting for a while

truck *NOUN* **trucks**
❶ a lorry ❷ an open container on wheels for transporting loads; an open railway wagon ❸ an axle with wheels attached, fitted under a skateboard

truculent (say **truk**-yoo-lent) *ADJECTIVE*
defiant and aggressive
➤ **truculently** *ADVERB*
➤ **truculence** *NOUN*

trudge *VERB* **trudges, trudging, trudged**
to walk slowly and heavily • *We trudged home across the fields.*

true *ADJECTIVE* **truer, truest**
❶ representing what has really happened or exists • *a true story* ❷ genuine or proper; not false • *He was the true heir.* ❸ accurate or exact ❹ loyal or faithful • *Be true to your friends.*
➤ **come true** to actually happen as hoped or predicted • *I hope your dreams come true.*

truffle *NOUN* **truffles**
❶ a soft sweet made with chocolate ❷ a fungus that grows underground and is valued as food because of its rich flavour

truly *ADVERB*
❶ truthfully ❷ sincerely or genuinely • *We*

a b c d e f g h i j k l m n o p q r s t u v w x y z

are truly grateful. ❸ (*old use*) loyally or faithfully
➤ **Yours truly** see **yours**

SPELLING
There is no e in **truly.**

trump *NOUN* **trumps**
❶ a playing card of a suit that ranks above the others for one game or round of play ❷ (*old use*) a blast of a trumpet

trump *VERB* **trumps, trumping, trumped**
to beat a card by playing a trump
➤ **trump something up** to invent an excuse or an accusation

trumpet *NOUN* **trumpets**
❶ a metal wind instrument with a narrow tube that widens near the end ❷ something shaped like this

trumpet *VERB* **trumpets, trumpeting, trumpeted**
❶ an elephant trumpets when it makes a loud sound with its trunk ❷ to blow a trumpet ❸ to shout or announce something loudly
➤ **trumpeter** *NOUN*

truncate *VERB* **truncates, truncating, truncated**
to shorten something by cutting off its beginning or end

truncheon *NOUN* **truncheons**
(*chiefly British*) a short thick stick carried as a weapon by a police officer

trundle *VERB* **trundles, trundling, trundled**
to move something along heavily, especially on wheels, or to move like this • *He was trundling a wheelbarrow.* • *A bus trundled across the bridge.*

trunk *NOUN* **trunks**
❶ the main stem of a tree ❷ an elephant's long flexible nose ❸ a large box with a hinged lid for transporting or storing clothes etc. ❹ the human body except for the head, arms and legs ❺ (*North American*) the boot of a car

trunk call *NOUN* **trunk calls** (*old use, chiefly British*)
a long-distance telephone call

trunk road *NOUN* **trunk roads**
(*British*) an important main road

trunks *PLURAL NOUN*
shorts worn by men and boys for swimming, boxing, etc.

truss *NOUN* **trusses**
❶ a framework of beams or bars supporting a roof or bridge ❷ a type of padded belt worn to support a hernia

truss *VERB* **trusses, trussing, trussed**
❶ to tie up a person or thing securely ❷ to support a roof or bridge with trusses

trust *VERB* **trusts, trusting, trusted**
❶ to believe that a person or thing is good, truthful or reliable ❷ to let a person have or use something in the belief that they will look after it • *Don't trust him with your phone!* ❸ to hope or expect something • *I trust that you are well.*
➤ **trust to something** to rely on something • *I'm just trusting to luck.*

trust *NOUN* **trusts**
❶ the belief that a person or thing can be trusted ❷ responsibility; being trusted • *a position of trust.* ❸ a legal arrangement in which a person looks after money or property for someone else with instructions about how to use it
➤ **trustful** *ADJECTIVE*
➤ **trustfully** *ADVERB*

trustee *NOUN* **trustees**
a person who looks after money or property for someone else

trustworthy *ADJECTIVE*
able to be trusted; reliable

trusty *ADJECTIVE*
trustworthy or reliable • *my trusty sword*

truth *NOUN* **truths**
❶ a true fact or statement ❷ the quality of being true

truthful *ADJECTIVE*
❶ telling the truth • *a truthful boy* ❷ true • *a truthful account of what happened*
➤ **truthfully** *ADVERB*
➤ **truthfulness** *NOUN*

try *VERB* **tries, trying, tried**
❶ to make an effort to do something; to attempt something ❷ to test something by using or doing it • *Try sleeping on your back.* ❸ to examine the evidence in a law court to decide whether a person is guilty of a crime ❹ to be a strain on something • *You really are trying my patience.*
➤ **try something on** to put on clothes to see if they fit or look good
➤ **try something out** to use something to see if it works

try *NOUN* **tries**
❶ a go at trying something; an attempt

• *Have another try.* ❷ in rugby, putting the ball down behind the opponents' goal line in order to score points

trying ADJECTIVE
putting a strain on your patience; annoying

tsar (say zar) NOUN tsars
the title of the former ruler of Russia
WORD ORIGIN Russian, from Latin *Caesar*

tsetse fly (say **tet**-see) NOUN tsetse flies
a tropical African fly which has a bite that can cause sleeping sickness in people

T-shirt NOUN T-shirts
a short-sleeved shirt shaped like a T

tsunami NOUN tsunamis
a huge sea wave caused by an underwater earthquake **WORD ORIGIN** Japanese, from *tsu* = harbour + *nami* = a wave

tub NOUN tubs
a round open container holding liquid, ice cream, soil for plants, etc.

tuba (say **tew**-ba) NOUN tubas
a large brass wind instrument that makes a deep sound **WORD ORIGIN** Italian from Latin, = war trumpet

tubby ADJECTIVE tubbier, tubbiest
short and fat

tube NOUN tubes
❶ a long hollow piece of metal, plastic, rubber, glass, etc., especially for liquids or gases to pass along ❷ a long hollow container made of soft metal or plastic, for something soft • *a tube of toothpaste* ❸ the underground railway in London

tuber NOUN tubers
a short thick rounded root (e.g. of a dahlia) or underground stem (e.g. of a potato) that produces buds from which new plants will grow

tuberculosis NOUN
a disease of people and animals, producing small swellings in parts of the body, especially in the lungs

tubing NOUN
tubes; a length of tube

tubular ADJECTIVE
shaped like a tube

tuck VERB tucks, tucking, tucked
❶ to push a loose edge into something so that it is hidden or held in place • *Now tuck the flap in the envelope.* ❷ to put something away in a small space • *She tucked the letter*

in her pocket.
➤ **tuck in** (*informal*) to eat heartily
➤ **tuck someone in** or **up** to make someone comfortable in bed by folding the edges of the bedclothes tightly

tuck NOUN tucks
❶ a flat fold stitched in a piece of clothing ❷ (*informal*) food, especially sweets and cakes etc. that children enjoy
➤ **tuck shop** NOUN

tucker NOUN (*informal*)
(*Australian/NZ*) food

Tuesday NOUN
the day of the week following Monday
WORD ORIGIN from Old English *Tiwesdaeg* = day of Tiw, a Norse god

tuft NOUN tufts
a bunch of threads, grass, hair or feathers growing or held close together
➤ **tufted** ADJECTIVE

tug VERB tugs, tugging, tugged
❶ to pull something hard or suddenly ❷ to tow a ship

tug NOUN tugs
❶ a hard or sudden pull ❷ a small powerful boat used for towing others

tug of war NOUN
a contest between two teams pulling a rope from opposite ends

tuition NOUN
teaching, especially when given to one person or a small group

tulip NOUN tulips
a large cup-shaped flower on a tall stem growing from a bulb

tulle (say tewl) NOUN
a very fine silky net material used for veils, wedding dresses, etc.

tumble VERB tumbles, tumbling, tumbled
❶ to fall or roll over suddenly or clumsily • *He tumbled down the hill.* ❷ to move or fall somewhere in an uncontrolled or untidy way • *She opened her bag and all her things tumbled out.*

tumble NOUN tumbles
a sudden fall or drop

tumbledown ADJECTIVE
falling into ruins • *a tumbledown cottage*

tumble-drier NOUN tumble-driers
a machine that dries washing by turning it over many times in heated air

a b c d e f g h i j k l m n o p q r s t u v w x y z

tumbler *NOUN* tumblers
❶ a drinking glass with no stem or handle
❷ a part of a lock that is lifted when a key is turned to open it ❸ an acrobat

tumbril *NOUN* tumbrils (*old use*)
an open cart used to carry condemned people to the guillotine during the French Revolution

tummy *NOUN* tummies (*informal*)
your stomach

tumour (say **tew**-mer) *NOUN* tumours
an abnormal lump growing on or in the body

tumult (say **tew**-mult) *NOUN*
an uproar or state of noisy confusion and agitation

tumultuous (say tew-**mul**-tew-us) *ADJECTIVE*
noisy and excited • *a tumultuous welcome*

tun *NOUN* tuns
a large cask or barrel

tuna (say **tew**-na) *NOUN* tuna
a large edible sea fish with pink flesh

tundra *NOUN*
the vast level Arctic regions of Europe, Asia and America where there are no trees and the subsoil is always frozen

tune *NOUN* tunes
a short piece of music; a pleasant series of musical notes
➤ **in tune** at the correct musical pitch

tune *VERB* tunes, tuning, tuned
❶ to put a musical instrument in tune ❷ to adjust a radio or television set to receive a certain channel ❸ to adjust an engine so that it runs smoothly
➤ **tuner** *NOUN*
➤ **tune up** an orchestra tunes up when it brings the instruments to the correct pitch

tuneful *ADJECTIVE*
having a pleasant tune

tungsten *NOUN*
a grey metal used to make a kind of steel

tunic *NOUN* tunics
❶ a jacket worn as part of a uniform ❷ a piece of clothing without sleeves, reaching from the shoulders to the hips or knees

tunnel *NOUN* tunnels
a passage made underground or through a hill

tunnel *VERB* tunnels, tunnelling, tunnelled
to make a tunnel

tunny *NOUN* tunnies
a tuna

turban *NOUN* turbans
a covering for the head made by wrapping a strip of cloth round a cap, worn especially by Muslims and Sikhs

turbid *ADJECTIVE*
turbid water is muddy and not clear

turbine *NOUN* turbines
a machine or motor that is driven by a flow of water, steam or gas

turbojet *NOUN* turbojets
a jet engine or aircraft with turbines

turbot *NOUN* turbot
a large flat edible sea fish

turbulence *NOUN*
violent and uneven movement of air or water • *We experienced turbulence during the flight.*

turbulent *ADJECTIVE*
❶ moving violently and unevenly • *turbulent seas* ❷ involving much change and disagreement and sometimes violence • *a turbulent period of history*

tureen *NOUN* tureens
a deep dish with a lid, from which soup is served at the table

turf *NOUN* turfs or turves
❶ short grass and the earth round its roots ❷ a piece of this cut from the ground
➤ **the turf** horse racing

turf *VERB* turfs, turfing, turfed
to cover ground with turf
➤ **turf someone out** (*informal*) to force someone to leave a place

turgid (say **ter**-jid) *ADJECTIVE*
pompous and boring • *a turgid speech*

turkey *NOUN* turkeys
a large bird kept for its meat
(**WORD ORIGIN**) originally the name of a different bird which was imported from Turkey

turmoil *NOUN*
wild confusion or agitation • *Her mind was in turmoil.*

turn *VERB* turns, turning, turned
❶ to move round or take a new direction; to make something move in this way • *Turn left at the lights.* ❷ to change in appearance etc.; to become • *He turned pale.* • *These caterpillars will turn into butterflies.* ❸ to make something change • *You can turn milk*

into butter. ❹ to move a switch or tap etc. to control something • *Turn that radio off.* ❺ to pass a certain time • *It has turned midnight.* ❻ to shape something on a lathe
➤ **turn something down** ❶ to fold something down ❷ to reduce the flow or sound of something ❸ to reject or refuse something • *We offered her a job but she turned it down.*
➤ **turn out** ❶ to happen • *Let's wait and see how things turn out.* ❷ to prove to be • *The visitor turned out to be my uncle.*
➤ **turn something out** to empty something, especially to search or clean it
➤ **turn to someone** to go to someone for help or advice
➤ **turn up** to appear or arrive suddenly or unexpectedly
➤ **turn something up** to increase the flow or sound of something

turn *NOUN* **turns**
❶ the action of turning; a turning movement • *Give the key three turns.* ❷ a change; the point where something turns ❸ a place where a road bends ❹ an opportunity or duty that comes to each person in succession • *It's your turn to wash up.* ❺ a short performance in an entertainment ❻ (*informal*) an attack of illness; a nervous shock • *It gave me a nasty turn.*
➤ **a good turn** a helpful action
➤ **in turn** in succession; one after another
(**WORD ORIGIN**) from Greek *tornos* = lathe

turncoat *NOUN* **turncoats**
a person who changes sides or changes what they believe

turning *NOUN* **turnings**
a place where one road meets another, forming a corner

turning point *NOUN* **turning points**
a point where an important change takes place • *This battle was a turning point in the war.*

turnip *NOUN* **turnips**
a plant with a large round white root used as a vegetable

turnout *NOUN* **turnouts**
the number of people who attend a meeting, vote at an election, etc. • *Despite the rain, there was a pretty good turnout.*

turnover *NOUN* **turnovers**
❶ the amount of money received by a firm selling things ❷ the rate at which goods are sold or workers leave and are replaced ❸ a

small pie made by folding pastry over fruit, jam, etc.

turnpike *NOUN* **turnpikes** (*old use*)
a road on which a toll was charged

turnstile *NOUN* **turnstiles**
a revolving gate that lets one person in at a time

turntable *NOUN* **turntables**
a circular revolving platform or support, e.g. for the record in a record player

turpentine *NOUN*
a kind of oil used for thinning paint, cleaning paintbrushes, etc.

turps *NOUN* (*informal*)
turpentine

turquoise *NOUN* **turquoises**
❶ a sky-blue or greenish-blue colour ❷ a bright blue jewel (**WORD ORIGIN**) from French *pierre turquoise* = Turkish stone

turret *NOUN* **turrets**
❶ a small tower on a castle or other building ❷ a revolving structure containing a gun
➤ **turreted** *ADJECTIVE*

turtle *NOUN* **turtles**
a sea animal that looks like a tortoise
➤ **turn turtle** to capsize

turtle-dove *NOUN* **turtle-doves**
a wild dove

tusk *NOUN* **tusks**
a long pointed tooth that sticks out from the mouth of an elephant, walrus, etc.

tussle *NOUN* **tussles**
a struggle or conflict over something

tussle *VERB* **tussles, tussling, tussled**
to struggle or fight over something • *The two players tussled with each another for the ball.*

tussock *NOUN* **tussocks**
a tuft or clump of grass

tutor *NOUN* **tutors**
❶ a private teacher, especially of one pupil or a small group ❷ a teacher of students in a college or university

tutorial *NOUN* **tutorials**
a meeting in which students discuss a subject with their tutor

tutu (say **too**-too) *NOUN* **tutus**
a ballet dancer's short stiff frilled skirt

TV *ABBREVIATION*
television

twaddle *NOUN* (*informal*)
nonsense

twain *NOUN & ADJECTIVE* (*old use*)
two

twang *NOUN* twangs
❶ a sharp sound like that of a wire when plucked ❷ a nasal tone in a person's voice

twang *VERB* twangs, twanging, twanged
❶ to make a sharp sound like that of a wire when plucked ❷ to play a guitar etc. by plucking its strings

tweak *VERB* tweaks, tweaking, tweaked
to pinch and twist or pull something sharply

tweak *NOUN* tweaks
a tweaking movement

tweed *NOUN*
a thick rough woollen cloth, often woven of mixed colours **WORD ORIGIN** originally a mistake; the Scottish word *tweel* (= twill) was wrongly read as *tweed* by being confused with the River Tweed

tweeds *PLURAL NOUN*
clothes made of tweed

tweet *NOUN* tweets
❶ the chirping sound made by a small bird ❷ a short message sent on the social network Twitter

tweet *VERB* tweets, tweeting, tweeted
❶ a small bird tweets when it makes a chirping sound ❷ to send a message on the social network Twitter

tweezers *PLURAL NOUN*
small pincers for picking up or pulling very small things

twelve *NOUN & ADJECTIVE* twelves
the number 12
➤ **twelfth** *ADJECTIVE & NOUN*

SPELLING
Take care: there is an **f** before the **th**.

twenty *NOUN & ADJECTIVE* twenties
the number 20
➤ **twentieth** *ADJECTIVE & NOUN*

twice *ADVERB*
❶ two times; on two occasions • *I've only been there twice.* ❷ double the amount

twiddle *VERB* twiddles, twiddling, twiddled
to turn something round or over and over in an idle way • *He tried twiddling the knob on the radio.*

twiddle *NOUN*
a twiddling movement
➤ **twiddle your thumbs** to have nothing to do

twig *NOUN* twigs
a small shoot on a branch or stem of a tree or shrub

twig *VERB* twigs, twigging, twigged (*informal*)
to realize what something means • *I suddenly twigged what she was talking about.*

twilight *NOUN*
dim light from the sky just after sunset or just before sunrise

twill *NOUN*
material woven so that there is a pattern of diagonal lines

twin *NOUN* twins
❶ either of two children or animals born to the same mother at one time ❷ either of two things that are exactly alike

twin *VERB* twins, twinning, twinned
❶ to put things together as a pair ❷ (*British*) if a town is twinned with a town in a different country, the two towns exchange visits and organize cultural events together

twine *NOUN*
strong thin string

twine *VERB* twines, twining, twined
to twist or wind one thing round another • *She twined her arms around his neck.*

twinge *NOUN* twinges
a sudden pain or unpleasant feeling • *a twinge of guilt*

twinkle *VERB* twinkles, twinkling, twinkled
❶ to shine with tiny flashes of light; to sparkle ❷ your eyes twinkle when they look bright because you are happy or amused

twinkle *NOUN* twinkles
❶ a twinkling light ❷ a bright expression in your eyes that shows you are happy or amused

twirl *VERB* twirls, twirling, twirled
❶ to twist something round quickly ❷ to turn around in a circle

twirl *NOUN* twirls
a twirling movement

twist *VERB* twists, twisting, twisted
❶ to turn the ends of something in opposite directions ❷ to turn round or from side to side • *The road twisted through the hills* ❸ to bend something out of its proper shape • *My bike's front wheel is twisted.* • *I think*

I've twisted my ankle. ❹ to pass threads or strands round something or round each other ❺ to distort the meaning of what someone says • *You're twisting my words.*

twist *NOUN* twists
❶ a twisting movement or action ❷ a strange or unexpected development in a story or series of events
➤ **twisty** *ADJECTIVE*

twister *NOUN* twisters
(*North American*) a tornado

twit *NOUN* twits (*informal, chiefly British*)
a silly or foolish person

twitch *VERB* twitches, twitching, twitched
to move suddenly with a slight jerk or to make something do this

twitch *NOUN* twitches
a twitching movement

twitter *VERB* twitters, twittering, twittered
birds twitter when they make quick chirping sounds

twitter *NOUN* twitters
a twittering sound

two *NOUN & ADJECTIVE* twos
the number 2
➤ **be in two minds** to be undecided about something

two-dimensional *ADJECTIVE*
having two dimensions (length and width); flat

two-faced *ADJECTIVE*
insincere or deceitful

tycoon *NOUN* tycoons
a rich and influential business person
(WORD ORIGIN) from Japanese *taikun* = great prince

tying
present participle of **tie**

type *NOUN* types
❶ a kind or sort • *What type of music do you like?* ❷ letters or figures etc. designed for use in printing

type *VERB* types, typing, typed
to write something by using a keyboard

typecast *VERB* typecasts, typecasting, typecast
an actor is typecast when they are always given the same kind of role to play • *She doesn't want to be typecast as a dumb blonde.*

typescript *NOUN* typescripts
a typed copy of a text or document

typewriter *NOUN* typewriters
a machine with keys that you press to print letters or figures etc. on a piece of paper
➤ **typewritten** *ADJECTIVE*

typhoid fever *NOUN*
a serious infectious disease with fever, caused by harmful bacteria in food or water

typhoon *NOUN* typhoons
a violent hurricane in the western Pacific or East Asian seas **(WORD ORIGIN)** from Chinese *tai fung* = great wind

typhus *NOUN*
an infectious disease causing fever, weakness and a rash

typical *ADJECTIVE*
❶ having the usual characteristics or qualities of a particular type of person or thing • *a typical Italian village* ❷ as you would expect from a particular person or thing • *He spoke with typical enthusiasm.* • *She's late again – typical!*
➤ **typically** *ADVERB*

typify (say **tip**-if-eye) *VERB* typifies, typifying, typified
to be a typical example of something • *He typifies the popular image of a football manager.*

typist *NOUN* typists
a person who types, especially as their job

typography (say ty-**pog**-ra-fee) *NOUN*
the style or appearance of the letters and figures etc. in printed material

tyrannize (also **tyrannise**) (say **ti**rran-yz) *VERB* tyrannizes, tyrannizing, tyrannized
to behave like a tyrant to people

tyrannosaurus *NOUN* tyrannosauruses
a huge flesh-eating dinosaur that walked upright on its large hind legs
(WORD ORIGIN) from Greek *tyrannos* = ruler + *sauros* = lizard

tyranny (say **ti**rran-ee) *NOUN* tyrannies
❶ government by a tyrant ❷ the way a tyrant behaves towards people
➤ **tyrannical** *ADJECTIVE*

tyrant (say **ty**-rant) *NOUN* tyrants
a person who rules cruelly and unjustly; someone who insists on being obeyed

tyre *NOUN* **tyres**
a covering of rubber fitted round a wheel to make it grip the road and run more smoothly

ubiquitous (say yoo-**bik**-wit-us) *ADJECTIVE*
found everywhere • *Mobile phones are ubiquitous these days.* **WORD ORIGIN** from Latin *ubique* = everywhere

U-boat *NOUN* **U-boats**
a German submarine of the kind used in the Second World War **WORD ORIGIN** short for German *Unterseeboot* = undersea boat

udder *NOUN* **udders**
the bag-like part of a cow, ewe, female goat, etc. from which milk is taken

UFO *ABBREVIATION*
unidentified flying object

ugly *ADJECTIVE* **uglier, ugliest**
❶ unpleasant to look at; not beautiful
❷ hostile and threatening • *The crowd was in an ugly mood.*
➤ **ugliness** *NOUN*
WORD ORIGIN from Old Norse *uggligr* = frightening

UHF *ABBREVIATION*
ultra-high frequency (between 300 and 3000 megahertz)

UHT *ABBREVIATION*
(*British*) ultra heat-treated; used to describe milk that has been treated at a very high temperature so that it will keep for a long time

UK *ABBREVIATION*
United Kingdom

ukulele (say yoo-kul-**ay**-lee) *NOUN* **ukuleles**
a small guitar with four strings
WORD ORIGIN Hawaiian, literally = jumping flea

ulcer *NOUN* **ulcers**
a sore on the inside or outside of the body

ulterior *ADJECTIVE*
beyond what is obvious or stated • *Perhaps he had an ulterior motive for doing this.*

ultimate *ADJECTIVE*
furthest in a series of things; final • *Our ultimate destination is London.*

ultimately *ADVERB*
in the end; finally • *Ultimately, the decision is yours.*

ultimatum (say ul-tim-**ay**-tum) *NOUN* **ultimatums**
a final demand or statement that, unless something is done by a certain time, action will be taken or war will be declared

ultra- *PREFIX*
❶ beyond (as in *ultraviolet*) ❷ extremely; excessively (as in *ultra-modern*)

ultramarine *NOUN*
a deep bright blue **WORD ORIGIN** from Latin *ultra* = beyond + *mare* = sea (because it was originally imported 'across the sea' from the East)

ultrasonic *ADJECTIVE*
an ultrasonic sound is beyond the range of human hearing

ultrasound *NOUN*
sound with an ultrasonic frequency, used in medical examinations

ultraviolet *ADJECTIVE*
ultraviolet light rays are beyond the violet end of the spectrum and so not visible to the human eye

umber *NOUN*
a kind of brown pigment **WORD ORIGIN** from Italian *terra di Ombra* = earth of Umbria (a region in central Italy)

umbilical cord (say um-**bil**-ik-al) *NOUN* **umbilical cords**
the tube through which a baby receives nourishment before it is born, connecting its body with the mother's womb

umbrage *NOUN*
➤ **take umbrage** to take offence
WORD ORIGIN originally = shadow or shade: from Latin *umbra* = shadow

umbrella *NOUN* **umbrellas**
a circular piece of material stretched over a folding frame with a central stick or pole, which you open to protect yourself from rain
WORD ORIGIN from Italian *ombrella* = a little shade (because the first umbrellas were used as protection against the sun rather than to keep off the rain)

umlaut *NOUN* umlauts
a mark (¨) placed over a vowel in German to indicate a change in its pronunciation

umpire *NOUN* umpires
a referee in cricket, tennis and some other games

umpire *VERB* umpires, umpiring, umpired
to act as an umpire

UN *ABBREVIATION*
United Nations

un- *PREFIX*
❶ not (as in *uncertain*) ❷ used before a verb to reverse its action (as in *unlock* = release from being locked)

> USAGE
> Many words beginning with this prefix are not listed here if their meaning is obvious.

unable *ADJECTIVE*
not able to do something

unaccountable *ADJECTIVE*
❶ unable to be explained • *For some unaccountable reason I completely forgot your birthday.* ❷ not accountable for what you do
➤ **unaccountably** *ADVERB*

unadulterated *ADJECTIVE*
pure; not mixed with things that are less good

unaided *ADJECTIVE*
without any help

unanimous (say yoo-**nan**-im-us) *ADJECTIVE*
with everyone agreeing • *a unanimous decision*
➤ **unanimously** *ADVERB*
➤ **unanimity** (say yoo-nan-**im**-it-ee) *NOUN*

unarmed *ADJECTIVE*
without weapons • *unarmed combat*

unassuming *ADJECTIVE*
modest; not arrogant or pretentious

unavoidable *ADJECTIVE*
not able to be avoided; bound to happen

unaware *ADJECTIVE*
not aware; not knowing about something • *She was unaware of the danger outside.*

unawares *ADVERB*
unexpectedly; without warning • *His question caught me unawares.*

unbalanced *ADJECTIVE*
❶ not balanced ❷ slightly mad or mentally ill

unbearable *ADJECTIVE*
so painful or unpleasant that you cannot bear or endure it • *The heat was almost unbearable.*
➤ **unbearably** *ADVERB*

unbeatable *ADJECTIVE*
unable to be defeated or improved on

unbeaten *ADJECTIVE*
that has not been defeated or improved on

unbecoming *ADJECTIVE*
❶ not making a person look attractive ❷ not suitable or fitting

unbeknown *ADJECTIVE*
without someone knowing about it • *Unbeknown to us, they had planned a surprise party.*

unbelievable *ADJECTIVE*
❶ difficult to believe ❷ amazing
➤ **unbelievably** *ADVERB*

unbend *VERB* unbends, unbending, unbent
❶ to change from a bent position; to straighten up ❷ to relax and become friendly

unbiased *ADJECTIVE*
not biased; impartial

unbidden *ADJECTIVE*
without being asked or invited; unexpectedly • *The phrase sprang into her head unbidden.*

unblock *VERB* unblocks, unblocking, unblocked
to remove an obstruction from something

unborn *ADJECTIVE*
not yet born

unbridled *ADJECTIVE*
not controlled or restrained • *unbridled rage*

unbroken *ADJECTIVE*
not broken or interrupted • *a minute of unbroken silence*

unburden *VERB* unburdens, unburdening, unburdened
to remove a burden from the person carrying it
➤ **unburden yourself** to tell someone your secrets or problems so that you feel better

uncalled for *ADJECTIVE*
not justified or necessary • *Such rudeness was quite uncalled for.*

uncanny *ADJECTIVE* uncannier, uncanniest
strange or mysterious • *an uncanny coincidence*
➤ **uncannily** *ADVERB*

a b c d e f g h i j k l m n o p q r s t **u** v w x y z

unceremonious *ADJECTIVE*
❶ without formality or ceremony ❷ offhand or abrupt

uncertain *ADJECTIVE*
❶ not known certainly ❷ not sure or confident about something ❸ not reliable
• *His aim is rather uncertain.*
➤ **uncertainty** *NOUN*
➤ **in no uncertain terms** clearly and forcefully

uncertainly *ADVERB*
without confidence; hesitantly • *They smiled uncertainly at one another.*

uncharitable *ADJECTIVE*
making unkind judgements about people or actions
➤ **uncharitably** *ADVERB*

uncle *NOUN* uncles
the brother of your father or mother; your aunt's husband

unclear *ADJECTIVE*
❶ not clear or definite ❷ not certain about something

unclothed *ADJECTIVE*
not wearing any clothes; naked

uncomfortable *ADJECTIVE*
❶ not comfortable ❷ uneasy or awkward about something
➤ **uncomfortably** *ADVERB*

uncommon *ADJECTIVE*
not common; unusual

uncompromising (say un-**komp**-ro-my-zing) *ADJECTIVE*
not allowing a compromise; inflexible
• *uncompromising views*

unconcerned *ADJECTIVE*
not caring about something; not worried

unconditional *ADJECTIVE*
without any conditions; complete or absolute
• *unconditional surrender*
➤ **unconditionally** *ADVERB*

unconscious *ADJECTIVE*
❶ not conscious ❷ not aware of things ❸ done without realizing it • *He gave an unconscious smile.*
➤ **unconsciously** *ADVERB*
➤ **unconsciousness** *NOUN*

SPELLING
Don't forget the sci in the middle.

uncontrollable *ADJECTIVE*
unable to be controlled or stopped
➤ **uncontrollably** *ADVERB*

uncooperative *ADJECTIVE*
not cooperative

uncouth (say un-**kooth**) *ADJECTIVE*
rude and rough in manner

uncover *VERB* uncovers, uncovering, uncovered
❶ to remove the covering from something
❷ to discover or reveal something • *They uncovered a plot to kill the king.*

unction *NOUN*
❶ anointing with oil, especially in a religious ceremony ❷ an oily manner

unctuous (say **unk**-tew-us) *ADJECTIVE*
having an oily manner; polite in an exaggerated way
➤ **unctuously** *ADVERB*
➤ **unctuousness** *NOUN*

undecided *ADJECTIVE*
❶ not yet settled; not certain ❷ not having made up your mind yet

undeniable *ADJECTIVE*
impossible to deny; undoubtedly true
➤ **undeniably** *ADVERB*

under *PREPOSITION*
❶ below or beneath • *Hide it under the desk.* ❷ less than • *under 5 years old*
❸ governed or controlled by • *The country prospered under his rule.* ❹ in the process of; undergoing • *The road is under repair.*
❺ making use of • *He wrote under the name of 'Lewis Carroll'.* ❻ according to the rules of
• *This is permitted under our agreement.*
➤ **under way** in motion or in progress

under *ADVERB*
in or to a lower place or level or condition
• *Slowly the diver went under.*

underarm *ADJECTIVE & ADVERB*
❶ moving the hand and arm forward and upwards • *an underarm throw* ❷ in or for the armpit

undercarriage *NOUN* undercarriages
an aircraft's landing wheels and their supports

underclothes *PLURAL NOUN*
underwear
➤ **underclothing** *NOUN*

undercover *ADJECTIVE*
done or doing things secretly • *an undercover agent*

undercurrent *NOUN* **undercurrents**
❶ a current that is below the surface or below another current ❷ a feeling or influence that is hidden beneath the surface but whose effects are felt • *I could sense an undercurrent of tension in the room.*

undercut *VERB* **undercuts, undercutting, undercut**
to sell something for a lower price than someone else sells it

underdeveloped *ADJECTIVE*
❶ not fully developed or grown ❷ an underdeveloped country is poor and lacks modern industrial development

underdog *NOUN* **underdogs**
a person or team in a contest that is expected to lose

underdone *ADJECTIVE*
not thoroughly done; undercooked

underestimate *VERB* **underestimates, underestimating, underestimated**
to make too low an estimate of a person or thing • *We underestimated the time it would take.*

underfoot *ADVERB*
on the ground; under your feet • *It was slippery underfoot.*

undergarment *NOUN* **undergarments**
a piece of underwear

undergo *VERB* **undergoes, undergoing, underwent, undergone**
to experience or go through something • *The new aircraft underwent intensive tests.*

undergraduate *NOUN* **undergraduates**
a student at a university who has not yet taken a degree

underground *ADJECTIVE & ADVERB*
❶ under the ground ❷ done or working in secret

underground *NOUN*
a railway that runs through tunnels under the ground

undergrowth *NOUN*
(*British*) bushes and other plants growing closely, especially under trees

underhand *ADJECTIVE*
done or doing things in a sly or secret way

underlie *VERB* **underlies, underlying, underlay, underlain**
❶ to be the basis or explanation of something • *Hard work underlies the team's success this season.* ❷ to be or lie under something

underline *VERB* **underlines, underlining, underlined**
❶ to draw a line under something you have written ❷ to emphasize something or show it clearly • *The accident underlines the need to be careful all the time.*

underling *NOUN* **underlings**
a person working under someone's authority or control

underlying *ADJECTIVE*
❶ forming the basis or explanation of something but not easy to notice • *the underlying causes of the trouble* ❷ lying under something • *the underlying rocks*

undermine *VERB* **undermines, undermining, undermined**
to weaken something gradually • *These recent defeats have undermined her confidence.*

underneath *PREPOSITION & ADVERB*
below or beneath

underpaid *ADJECTIVE*
paid too little

underpants *PLURAL NOUN*
a piece of men's underwear covering the lower part of the body, worn under trousers

underpass *NOUN* **underpasses**
a road that goes underneath another

underprivileged *ADJECTIVE*
having a lower standard of living and fewer opportunities than most other people in society

underrate *VERB* **underrates, underrating, underrated**
to have too low an opinion of a person or thing

undersigned *ADJECTIVE*
who has or have signed at the bottom of this document • *We, the undersigned, wish to protest.*

undersized *ADJECTIVE*
of less than the normal size

understand *VERB* **understands, understanding, understood**
❶ to know what something means or how it works or why it exists ❷ to know what someone is like and why they behave the

a
b
c
d
e
f
g
h
i
j
k
l
m
n
o
p
q
r
s
t
u
v
w
x
y
z

way they do ❸ to have heard or been told something • *I understand that you would like to speak to me.* ❹ to take something for granted • *Your expenses will be paid, that's understood.*

understandable *ADJECTIVE*
❶ able to be understood ❷ reasonable or natural • *She replied with understandable anger.*
➤ **understandably** *ADVERB*

understanding *NOUN*
❶ the power to understand or think; intelligence ❷ sympathy or tolerance ❸ agreement in opinion or feeling • *a better understanding between nations*

understanding *ADJECTIVE*
sympathetic and helpful • *Thanks for being so understanding.*

understatement *NOUN* **understatements**
a statement that does not say something strongly enough or give the complete truth • *To say I am not happy is an understatement; I am furious.*

understudy *NOUN* **understudies**
an actor who learns a part in order to be able to play it if the usual actor is ill or absent

understudy *VERB* **understudies, understudying, understudied**
to be an understudy for an actor or part

undertake *VERB* **undertakes, undertaking, undertook, undertaken**
❶ to agree or promise to do something ❷ to take on a task or responsibility

undertaker *NOUN* **undertakers**
a person whose job is to arrange funerals and burials or cremations

undertaking *NOUN* **undertakings**
❶ a job or task that is being undertaken ❷ a promise or guarantee ❸ the business of an undertaker

undertone *NOUN* **undertones**
❶ a low or quiet tone to someone's voice • *They spoke in undertones.* ❷ an underlying quality or feeling • *His letter has a threatening undertone.*

undertow *NOUN* **undertows**
a current below that of the surface of the sea and moving in the opposite direction

underwater *ADJECTIVE & ADVERB*
placed, used or done beneath the surface of water

underwear *NOUN*
clothes you wear next to your skin, under other clothes

underweight *ADJECTIVE*
not heavy enough

underwent
past tense of **undergo**

underworld *NOUN*
❶ the people who are regularly involved in crime ❷ in myths and legends, the place for the spirits of the dead, under the earth

undesirable *ADJECTIVE*
not wanted or liked

undeveloped *ADJECTIVE*
not yet developed

undignified *ADJECTIVE*
not dignified

undo *VERB* **undoes, undoing, undid, undone**
❶ to unfasten or unwrap something ❷ to cancel the effect of something • *He has undone all our careful work.*

undoing *NOUN*
➤ **be someone's undoing** to be the cause of someone's ruin or failure • *His greed proved to be his undoing.*

undoubted *ADJECTIVE*
certain or definite; not regarded as doubtful • *She has undoubted talent.*

undoubtedly *ADVERB*
definitely; without a doubt • *Her quick thinking undoubtedly saved their lives.*

undress *VERB* **undresses, undressing, undressed**
to take your clothes off

undue *ADJECTIVE*
more than is necessary or reasonable • *I don't want to put undue pressure on them.*

undulate *VERB* **undulates, undulating, undulated**
to move like a wave or waves; to have a wavy appearance
➤ **undulation** *NOUN*
WORD ORIGIN from Latin *unda* = a wave

unduly *ADVERB*
excessively; more than is reasonable • *She didn't seem unduly worried.*

undying *ADJECTIVE*
lasting forever • *their undying love*

unearth *VERB* **unearths, unearthing, unearthed**

1 to dig something up; to uncover something by digging **2** to find something by searching • *I've unearthed some interesting information.*

unearthly *ADJECTIVE*
1 unnatural; strange and frightening
2 (*informal*) very early or inconvenient • *We had to get up at an unearthly hour.*

uneasy *ADJECTIVE*
1 worried or anxious **2** uncomfortable • *An uneasy silence followed.*
➤ **uneasily** *ADVERB*
➤ **uneasiness** *NOUN*

uneatable *ADJECTIVE*
not fit to be eaten

unemployed *ADJECTIVE*
without a job

unemployment *NOUN*
1 being without a job **2** the number of people without a job

unending *ADJECTIVE*
not coming to an end; endless

unequal *ADJECTIVE*
1 not equal in amount, size or value **2** not giving the same opportunities to everyone
• *an unequal society*
➤ **unequalled** *ADJECTIVE*
➤ **unequally** *ADVERB*

unerring (say un-**er**-ing) *ADJECTIVE*
making no mistake • *unerring accuracy*

uneven *ADJECTIVE*
1 not level or regular • *The path was uneven.*
2 not equally balanced • *an uneven contest*
➤ **unevenly** *ADVERB*
➤ **unevenness** *NOUN*

unexceptionable *ADJECTIVE*
not in any way objectionable

unexceptional *ADJECTIVE*
not exceptional; quite ordinary

unexpected *ADJECTIVE*
not expected; coming as a surprise • *an unexpected visitor*
➤ **unexpectedness** *NOUN*

unexpectedly *ADVERB*
when you are not expecting it • *They arrived unexpectedly.*

unfair *ADJECTIVE*
not fair; unjust
➤ **unfairly** *ADVERB*
➤ **unfairness** *NOUN*

unfaithful *ADJECTIVE*
1 not faithful or loyal **2** not sexually loyal to one partner

unfamiliar *ADJECTIVE*
not familiar • *Suddenly, an unfamiliar voice called his name.*

unfasten *VERB* unfastens, unfastening, unfastened
to open the fastenings of something

unfavourable *ADJECTIVE*
not favourable or helpful
➤ **unfavourably** *ADVERB*

unfeeling *ADJECTIVE*
not caring about other people's feelings; unsympathetic

unfit *ADJECTIVE*
1 not in perfect health because you do not take enough exercise **2** not suitable for something • *The water was unfit to drink.*

unfold *VERB* unfolds, unfolding, unfolded
1 to open something out or spread it out
• *She unfolded the map.* **2** to become known gradually • *They listened as the story unfolded.*

unforeseen *ADJECTIVE*
not foreseen; unexpected • *an unforeseen problem*

unforgettable *ADJECTIVE*
not likely to be forgotten • *Getting close to a whale is an unforgettable experience.*

unforgivable *ADJECTIVE*
not able to be forgiven

unfortunate *ADJECTIVE*
1 unlucky • *an unfortunate accident* **2** that you feel sorry about; regrettable • *an unfortunate remark*

SPELLING
Look out – there is an e after the last t.

unfortunately *ADVERB*
in a way that is sad or disappointing
• *Unfortunately, I won't be able to come to your party.*

unfounded *ADJECTIVE*
not based on facts

unfreeze *VERB* unfreezes, unfreezing, unfroze, unfrozen
to thaw or to cause something to thaw

unfriendly *ADJECTIVE*
not friendly
➤ **unfriendliness** *NOUN*

unfurl VERB unfurls, unfurling, unfurled
to unroll something or spread it out • *They unfurled a large flag.*

unfurnished ADJECTIVE
without furniture • *an unfurnished flat*

ungainly ADJECTIVE
awkward-looking or clumsy • *a tall, ungainly youth*
➤ **ungainliness** NOUN

ungodly ADJECTIVE
❶ not religious ❷ (*informal*) outrageous; very inconvenient • *She woke me at an ungodly hour.*

ungovernable ADJECTIVE
impossible to control • *an ungovernable temper*

ungracious ADJECTIVE
not kindly or courteous
➤ **ungraciously** ADVERB

ungrateful ADJECTIVE
not grateful
➤ **ungratefully** ADVERB

unguarded ADJECTIVE
❶ without a guard or protection • *The gate had been left unguarded.* ❷ without thought or caution; indiscreet • *He said this in an unguarded moment.*

unhappily ADVERB
❶ in an unhappy way • *He shook his head unhappily.* ❷ unfortunately • *Unhappily, several people were hurt.*

unhappy ADJECTIVE
❶ not happy; sad ❷ not pleased or satisfied ❸ unfortunate or regrettable • *an unhappy coincidence*
➤ **unhappiness** NOUN

unhealthy ADJECTIVE
❶ not in good health ❷ not good for you • *an unhealthy diet*

unheard-of ADJECTIVE
never known or done before; extraordinary

unhinge VERB unhinges, unhinging, unhinged
to cause a person's mind to become unbalanced

unicorn NOUN unicorns
a mythical animal that is like a horse with one long straight horn growing from its forehead

uniform NOUN uniforms
special clothes showing that the wearer is a member of a certain school, army or organization

uniform ADJECTIVE
always the same; not varying • *The desks are of uniform size.*
➤ **uniformly** ADVERB
➤ **uniformity** NOUN

uniformed ADJECTIVE
wearing a uniform

unify VERB unifies, unifying, unified
to join several things together into one thing; to unite things
➤ **unification** NOUN

unilateral ADJECTIVE
done by one person, group or country and not by the others • *a unilateral decision*

uninhabitable ADJECTIVE
unfit to live in

uninhabited ADJECTIVE
with nobody living there • *an uninhabited island*

unintentional ADJECTIVE
not done deliberately
➤ **unintentionally** ADVERB

uninterested ADJECTIVE
having or showing no interest in something • *He seemed uninterested in what I had to say.*

> **USAGE**
> If you mean 'impartial', use **disinterested**.

uninteresting ADJECTIVE
not interesting

union NOUN unions
❶ the joining of things together ❷ a group of states or countries that have joined together to form one country or group ❸ a trade union

unionist NOUN unionists
❶ a member of a trade union ❷ a person who wishes to unite one country with another

Union Jack NOUN Union Jacks
the flag of the United Kingdom

unique (say yoo-**neek**) ADJECTIVE
being the only one of its kind; unlike any other • *Everyone's fingerprints are unique.*
➤ **uniquely** ADVERB

> **USAGE**
> The word **unique** is sometimes used to mean 'unusual', but many people regard this as incorrect. So it is safer to avoid saying things like *very unique* or *rather unique*.

unisex *ADJECTIVE*
designed to be suitable for both sexes • *a unisex hairdresser's*

unison *NOUN*
➤ **in unison** ❶ with all saying, singing or doing the same thing at the same time ❷ in agreement

unit *NOUN* units
❶ an amount used as a standard in measuring or counting things • *Centimetres are units of length.* ❷ a group of people who have a certain job within a larger organization • *an army unit* ❸ a device or piece of furniture regarded as a single thing but forming part of a larger group or whole • *a sink unit* ❹ (*in mathematics*) any whole number less than 10

unite *VERB* unites, uniting, united
❶ to form several people or things into one group or thing ❷ people or things unite when they join together to do something

United Kingdom *NOUN*
Great Britain and Northern Ireland

unity *NOUN*
❶ being united or being in agreement
❷ something whole that is made up of parts

universal *ADJECTIVE*
to do with, including or done by everyone or everything • *The idea met with universal agreement.*

universally *ADVERB*
by everyone; everywhere • *He was universally known as 'Big Tom'.*

universe *NOUN*
everything that exists, including the earth and living things and all the stars and planets

university *NOUN* universities
a place where people go to study at an advanced level after leaving school

unjust *ADJECTIVE*
not fair or just • *unjust laws*
➤ **unjustly** *ADVERB*

unkempt *ADJECTIVE*
looking untidy or neglected

unkind *ADJECTIVE*
not kind; harsh
➤ **unkindly** *ADVERB*
➤ **unkindness** *NOUN*

unknown *ADJECTIVE*
not known or familiar

unlawful *ADJECTIVE*
not allowed by the law or rules

unleaded *ADJECTIVE*
unleaded petrol has no added lead

unleash *VERB* unleashes, unleashing, unleashed
to let a strong feeling or force be released • *The announcement unleashed a storm of protest.*

unleavened (say un-**lev**-end) *ADJECTIVE*
unleavened bread is made without yeast or other substances that would make it rise

unless *CONJUNCTION*
except when; if … not • *We cannot go unless we are invited.*

unlike *PREPOSITION*
not like • *Unlike me, she enjoys sport.*

unlike *ADJECTIVE*
not alike; different • *The two children are very unlike.*

unlikely *ADJECTIVE* unlikelier, unlikeliest
not likely to happen or be true

unlimited *ADJECTIVE*
not limited; very great or very many

unload *VERB* unloads, unloading, unloaded
to remove the load of things carried by a ship, aircraft or vehicle

unlock *VERB* unlocks, unlocking, unlocked
to open something by undoing a lock

unluckily *ADVERB*
unfortunately; as a result of bad luck

unlucky *ADJECTIVE*
not lucky; having or bringing bad luck

unmanageable *ADJECTIVE*
difficult or impossible to control or deal with

unmarried *ADJECTIVE*
not married

unmask *VERB* unmasks, unmasking, unmasked
❶ to remove a person's mask ❷ to reveal what a person or thing is really like

unmentionable *ADJECTIVE*
too bad or embarrassing to be spoken about

unmistakable *ADJECTIVE*
that cannot be mistaken for another person or thing • *There was an unmistakable hint of triumph in her eyes.*
➤ **unmistakably** *ADVERB*

unmitigated *ADJECTIVE*
absolute • *The rehearsal was an unmitigated disaster.*

a
b
c
d
e
f
g
h
i
j
k
l
m
n
o
p
q
r
s
t
u
v
w
x
y
z

unnatural *ADJECTIVE*
not natural or normal • *His hair was an unnatural shade of yellow.*
➤ **unnaturally** *ADVERB*

unnecessary *ADJECTIVE*
not necessary; more than is necessary

unnerve *VERB* **unnerves, unnerving, unnerved**
to make someone lose courage or determination • *The silence unnerved me.*
➤ **unnerving** *ADJECTIVE*

unoccupied *ADJECTIVE*
a building or room is unoccupied when nobody is using it or living in it

unofficial *ADJECTIVE*
not official
➤ **unofficially** *ADVERB*

unorthodox *ADJECTIVE*
different from what is usual or generally accepted • *an unorthodox method*

unpack *VERB* **unpacks, unpacking, unpacked**
to take things out of a suitcase, bag, box, etc.

unpaid *ADJECTIVE*
❶ not yet paid • *an unpaid bill* ❷ not receiving payment for work you do

unparalleled *ADJECTIVE*
having no parallel or equal

unpick *VERB* **unpicks, unpicking, unpicked**
to undo the stitching of something

unpleasant *ADJECTIVE*
not pleasant; nasty
➤ **unpleasantly** *ADVERB*
➤ **unpleasantness** *NOUN*

unpopular *ADJECTIVE*
not liked or popular

unprecedented (say un-**press**-id-en-tid) *ADJECTIVE*
that has never happened before • *The flood waters have risen to unprecedented levels.*

unprejudiced *ADJECTIVE*
without prejudice; impartial

unprepared *ADJECTIVE*
not prepared beforehand; not ready or equipped to deal with something

unprincipled *ADJECTIVE*
without good moral principles; unscrupulous

unprofessional *ADJECTIVE*
not professional; not worthy of a member of a profession

unprofitable *ADJECTIVE*
not producing a profit or advantage

unprotected *ADJECTIVE*
❶ not protected or kept safe ❷ used to describe sexual activity in which a condom is not used

unqualified *ADJECTIVE*
❶ not officially qualified to do something ❷ complete; not limited in any way • *The show was an unqualified success.*

unravel *VERB* **unravels, unravelling, unravelled**
❶ to disentangle things ❷ to undo something that is knitted ❸ to look into a problem or mystery and solve it • *Fossils help scientists unravel the mysteries of prehistoric times.*

unready *ADJECTIVE*
not ready; hesitating

USAGE
In the title of the English king *Ethelred the Unready* the word means 'lacking good advice or wisdom'.

unreal *ADJECTIVE*
not real; existing only in the imagination
➤ **unreality** *NOUN*

unrealistic *ADJECTIVE*
not showing or accepting things as they really are

unreasonable *ADJECTIVE*
❶ not reasonable ❷ excessive or unjust
➤ **unreasonably** *ADVERB*

unrelieved *ADJECTIVE*
without anything to vary it • *unrelieved gloom*

unremitting *ADJECTIVE*
never stopping or relaxing; persistent

unrequited (say un-ri-**kwy**-tid) *ADJECTIVE*
unrequited love is not returned or rewarded

unreserved *ADJECTIVE*
❶ not reserved ❷ without restriction; complete • *an unreserved apology*
➤ **unreservedly** *ADVERB*

unrest *NOUN*
trouble or rioting caused by people because they are angry and dissatisfied • *a time of civil unrest*

unripe *ADJECTIVE*
not yet ripe

unrivalled *ADJECTIVE*
having no equal; better than all others • *an unrivalled collection of rare photographs*

unroll *VERB* unrolls, unrolling, unrolled
to open something that has been rolled up

unruly *ADJECTIVE*
badly behaved and difficult to control • *an unruly crowd*

unsafe *ADJECTIVE*
not safe; dangerous

unsavoury *ADJECTIVE*
unpleasant or disgusting

unscathed *ADJECTIVE*
not harmed or injured

unscrew *VERB* unscrews, unscrewing, unscrewed
to undo or remove something by twisting it or by taking out screws

unscrupulous *ADJECTIVE*
willing to do things that are dishonest or unfair in order to get what you want

unseat *VERB* unseats, unseating, unseated
to throw a person from horseback or from the seat on a bicycle

unseemly *ADJECTIVE*
not proper or suitable; indecent

unseen *ADJECTIVE*
not seen or noticed • *He managed to slip out of the room unseen.*

unseen *NOUN* unseens (*British*) a passage for translation without previous preparation

unselfish *ADJECTIVE*
not selfish; not thinking only about yourself
➤ **unselfishly** *ADVERB*
➤ **unselfishness** *NOUN*

unsettle *VERB* unsettles, unsettling, unsettled
to make someone feel uneasy or anxious
➤ **unsettling** *ADJECTIVE*

unsettled *ADJECTIVE*
❶ not settled or calm ❷ unsettled weather is likely to change

unshakeable *ADJECTIVE*
not able to be shaken or changed; strong and firm • *an unshakeable belief*

unshaven *ADJECTIVE*
an unshaven man has not shaved recently

unsightly *ADJECTIVE*
not pleasant to look at; ugly

unskilled *ADJECTIVE*
not having or not needing special skill or training

unsociable *ADJECTIVE*
not sociable or friendly

unsocial *ADJECTIVE*
not social
➤ **unsocial hours** time spent working when most people are free

unsolicited *ADJECTIVE*
not asked for • *unsolicited advice*

unsound *ADJECTIVE*
❶ not reliable; not based on sound evidence or reasoning • *unsound advice* ❷ not firm or strong ❸ not healthy • *of unsound mind*

unspeakable *ADJECTIVE*
too bad or horrid to be described

unstable *ADJECTIVE*
not stable; likely to change or become unbalanced

unsteady *ADJECTIVE*
not steady; shaking or wobbling or likely to fall • *She is still a little unsteady on her feet.*
➤ **unsteadily** *ADVERB*

unstuck *ADJECTIVE*
➤ **come unstuck** ❶ to stop sticking to something ❷ (*informal*) to fail or go wrong

unsuccessful *ADJECTIVE*
not successful; failed • *an unsuccessful attempt to reach an agreement*
➤ **unsuccessfully** *ADVERB*

unsuitable *ADJECTIVE*
not suitable or appropriate

unsung *ADJECTIVE* (*formal*)
not famous or praised but deserving to be • *the unsung heroes of the campaign*

unsure *ADJECTIVE*
not confident or certain • *He stood there, unsure what to say.*

unthinkable *ADJECTIVE*
too bad or too unlikely to be worth considering

unthinking *ADJECTIVE*
thoughtless; not thinking of other people

untidy *ADJECTIVE* untidier, untidiest
messy and not tidy • *an untidy desk*
➤ **untidily** *ADVERB*
➤ **untidiness** *NOUN*

untie *VERB* unties, untying, untied
to undo something that has been tied or to free someone who has been tied up

until *PREPOSITION & CONJUNCTION*
up to a particular time or event

See the note at **till**.

There is only one l in **until**.

untimely *ADJECTIVE*
happening too soon or at an unsuitable time
• *his untimely death*

unto *PREPOSITION (old use)*
to

untold *ADJECTIVE*
too much or too many to be counted • *untold wealth*

untoward *ADJECTIVE*
inconvenient or unfortunate • *I hope nothing untoward happens.*

untrue *ADJECTIVE*
not true; false

untruth *NOUN* untruths
an untrue statement; a lie
➤ **untruthful** *ADJECTIVE*
➤ **untruthfully** *ADVERB*

unused *ADJECTIVE*
❶ (say un-**yoozd**) not yet used • *an unused stamp* ❷ (say un-**yoost**) not familiar with something • *They were unused to seeing strangers.*

unusual *ADJECTIVE*
not usual; strange or exceptional

unusually *ADVERB*
❶ more than is usual • *an unusually cold winter* ❷ in a way that is not normal or typical • *Unusually for her, she forgot his birthday.*

unutterable *ADJECTIVE*
too great to be described • *unutterable joy*

unveil *VERB* unveils, unveiling, unveiled
❶ to remove a veil or covering from something ❷ to reveal something new that has been kept hidden or secret

unwanted *ADJECTIVE*
not wanted

unwarranted *ADJECTIVE*
not justified or reasonable

unwary *ADJECTIVE*
not cautious or careful about danger
➤ **unwarily** *ADVERB*

unwelcome *ADJECTIVE*
not welcome or wanted • *an unwelcome visitor*

unwell *ADJECTIVE*
not in good health

unwholesome *ADJECTIVE*
❶ harmful to your health ❷ unhealthy-looking

unwieldy *ADJECTIVE*
awkward to move or control because of its size, shape or weight
➤ **unwieldiness** *NOUN*

unwilling *ADJECTIVE*
not willing to do something; reluctant • *He was unwilling to say any more.*
➤ **unwillingly** *ADVERB*

unwind *VERB* unwinds, unwinding, unwound
❶ to unroll something ❷ (*informal*) to relax after you have been working hard

unwise *ADJECTIVE*
not wise; foolish
➤ **unwisely** *ADVERB*

unwitting *ADJECTIVE*
❶ not intended ❷ not realizing something
➤ **unwittingly** *ADVERB*

unwonted (say un-**wohn**-tid) *ADJECTIVE*
not customary or usual • *She spoke with unwonted rudeness.*

unworn *ADJECTIVE*
not yet worn

unworthy *ADJECTIVE*
not worthy or deserving

unwrap *VERB* unwraps, unwrapping, unwrapped
to open something that is wrapped

unzip *VERB* unzips, unzipping, unzipped
to undo something that is zipped up

up *ADVERB*
❶ to or in a higher place or position or level • *Prices went up.* ❷ so as to be in a standing or upright position • *Everyone stood up.* ❸ out of bed • *It's time to get up.* ❹ completely • *Eat up your carrots.* ❺ finished • *Your time is up.* ❻ (*informal*) happening • *Something is up.*
➤ **up against something** ❶ close to something ❷ (*informal*) faced with difficulties or dangers
➤ **ups and downs** changes of luck, sometimes good and sometimes bad
➤ **up to** ❶ until; as far as ❷ busy with or

doing something • *What are you up to?*
❸ capable of doing something • *I don't think I'm up to it.*
➤ **be up to someone** to be someone's responsibility • *It's up to us to help her.*
➤ **up to date** ❶ modern or fashionable ❷ giving the most recent information

> **USAGE**
> Use hyphens when this is used as an adjective before a noun, e.g. *up-to-date information* (but *the information is up to date*).

up *PREPOSITION*
upwards through, along or into • *Water came up the pipes.*

up-and-coming *ADJECTIVE* (*informal*)
likely to become successful

upbraid *VERB* upbraids, upbraiding, upbraided (*formal*)
to angrily tell someone off because they have done something wrong

upbringing *NOUN* upbringings
your upbringing is the way you have been brought up

update *VERB* updates, updating, updated
to bring a thing up to date

update *NOUN* updates
the version of something that has the most recent information • *a news update*

upgrade *VERB* upgrades, upgrading, upgraded
❶ to improve a machine by installing new parts in it ❷ to improve a piece of software by installing a newer version
➤ **upgrade** *NOUN*

upheaval *NOUN* upheavals
a sudden violent change or disturbance

uphill *ADVERB*
up a slope

uphill *ADJECTIVE*
❶ going up a slope ❷ difficult • *It was an uphill struggle.*

uphold *VERB* upholds, upholding, upheld
to support or agree with a decision, opinion or belief • *Police officers have a duty to uphold the law.*

upholster *VERB* upholsters, upholstering, upholstered
to put a soft padded covering on furniture

upholstery *NOUN*
covers and padding for furniture

upkeep *NOUN*
keeping something in good condition or the cost of this

uplands *PLURAL NOUN*
the higher parts of a country or region
➤ **upland** *ADJECTIVE*

uplifting *ADJECTIVE*
making you feel more cheerful or hopeful • *an uplifting speech*

upload *VERB* uploads, uploading, uploaded (*in computing*) to move data from your computer to a larger computer network or system so that it can be read by other users

upon *PREPOSITION*
on

> **SPELLING**
> There is only one **p** in **upon**.

upper *ADJECTIVE*
higher in place or rank

upper case *NOUN*
capital letters

upper class *NOUN* upper classes
the highest class in society, especially the aristocracy
➤ **upper-class** *ADJECTIVE*

uppermost *ADJECTIVE*
highest in place or importance • *This question was uppermost in her mind.*

uppermost *ADVERB*
on or to the top or the highest place • *Keep the painted side uppermost.*

upright *ADJECTIVE*
❶ standing straight up; vertical ❷ strictly honest or honourable

upright *NOUN* uprights
a post or rod placed upright, especially as a support

uprising *NOUN* uprisings
a rebellion or revolt against the government

uproar *NOUN*
an outburst of noise or excitement or anger • *The room was in uproar.*

uproarious *ADJECTIVE*
very noisy • *uproarious laughter*

uproot *VERB* uproots, uprooting, uprooted
❶ to remove a plant and its roots from the ground ❷ to make someone leave the place where they have lived for a long time

upset *ADJECTIVE*
❶ unhappy or anxious about something
❷ slightly ill • *an upset stomach*

upset *VERB* **upsets, upsetting, upset**
❶ to make a person unhappy or anxious **❷** to disturb the normal working of something • *This has really upset my plans.* **❸** to overturn something or knock it over

upset *NOUN* **upsets**
❶ a slight illness • *a stomach upset* **❷** an unexpected result or setback • *There has been a major upset in the quarter-finals.*

upshot *NOUN* **upshots**
the eventual outcome • *The upshot was that we missed the last ferry.*
WORD ORIGIN originally = the final shot in an archery contest

upside down *ADVERB & ADJECTIVE*
❶ with the upper part underneath instead of on top **❷** in great disorder; very untidy • *The thieves turned the place upside down.*

upstairs *ADVERB & ADJECTIVE*
to or on a higher floor

upstart *NOUN* **upstarts**
a person who has risen suddenly to a high position and who then behaves arrogantly

upstream *ADJECTIVE & ADVERB*
in the direction from which a stream flows

uptake *NOUN*
➤ **quick on the uptake** quick to understand
➤ **slow on the uptake** slow to understand

uptight *ADJECTIVE* (*informal*)
tense and nervous or annoyed

up-to-date *ADJECTIVE*
❶ modern or fashionable **❷** giving the most recent information

upward *ADJECTIVE & ADVERB*
going towards what is higher • *an upward current of air*
➤ **upwards** *ADVERB*

uranium *NOUN*
a heavy radioactive grey metal used as a source of nuclear energy
WORD ORIGIN named after the planet *Uranus*

urban *ADJECTIVE*
to do with a town or city

urbanize (also **urbanise**) *VERB* **urbanizes, urbanizing, urbanized**
to change a place into a town-like area
➤ **urbanization** *NOUN*

urchin *NOUN* **urchins**
a rough and poorly dressed young boy • *a street urchin* **WORD ORIGIN** from Latin *ericius* = hedgehog

Urdu (say **oor**-doo) *NOUN*
a language related to Hindi, spoken in northern India and Pakistan

urge *VERB* **urges, urging, urged**
❶ to try to persuade a person to do something **❷** to drive people or animals onward • *He urged his horse up the hill.* **❸** to recommend or advise something

urge *NOUN* **urges**
a strong desire or wish • *She felt an urge to go for a swim.*

urgent *ADJECTIVE*
needing to be done or dealt with immediately • *Come quickly – it's urgent!*
➤ **urgently** *ADVERB*
➤ **urgency** *NOUN*

urinal (say yoor-**ry**-nal) *NOUN* **urinals**
a bowl or trough fixed to the wall in a men's public toilet, for men to urinate into

urinate (say **yoor**-in-ayt) *VERB* **urinates, urinating, urinated**
to pass urine out of your body
➤ **urination** *NOUN*

urine (say **yoor**-in) *NOUN*
waste liquid that collects in the bladder and is passed out of the body
➤ **urinary** *ADJECTIVE*

urn *NOUN* **urns**
❶ a large metal container with a tap, in which water is heated **❷** a container shaped like a vase with a base, especially one for holding the ashes of a cremated person

US *ABBREVIATION*
United States (of America)

us *PRONOUN*
the form of **we** used when it is the object of a verb or after a preposition

USA *ABBREVIATION*
United States of America

usable *ADJECTIVE*
able to be used

usage *NOUN* **usages**
❶ use; the way something is used **❷** the way words are used in a language • *English usage often differs from American usage.*

use (say yooz) *VERB* **uses, using, used**
to perform an action or job with something

• *Can I use your pen?*
➤ **used to ❶** was or were in the habit of doing • *We used to go by train.* ❷ familiar with or accustomed to • *I'm used to his strange behaviour.*
➤ **use something up** to use all of something so that none is left

use (say yooss) *NOUN* **uses**
❶ the action of using something; being used • *the use of computers in schools* ❷ the purpose for which something is used • *Can you find a use for this crate?* ❸ the quality of being useful • *These scissors are no use at all.*

used *ADJECTIVE*
not new; second-hand • *used cars*

useful *ADJECTIVE*
able to be used a lot or to do something that needs doing
➤ **usefully** *ADVERB*
➤ **usefulness** *NOUN*

useless *ADJECTIVE*
❶ not having any use; producing no effect • *Their efforts were useless.* ❷ (*informal*) not very good at something • *I'm useless at drawing.*
➤ **uselessly** *ADVERB*
➤ **uselessness** *NOUN*

user *NOUN* **users**
a person who uses something

user-friendly *ADJECTIVE*
designed to be easy to use

username *NOUN* **usernames**
the name you use to log on to a computer system

usher *NOUN* **ushers**
a person who shows people to their seats in a cinema, theatre or church

usher *VERB* **ushers, ushering, ushered**
to lead someone in or out • *The guard ushered them out.*

usherette *NOUN* **usherettes**
a woman who shows people to their seats in a cinema or theatre

USSR *ABBREVIATION*
(*old use*) Union of Soviet Socialist Republics

usual *ADJECTIVE*
as happens or is done or used often or all the time • *She was late as usual.*

usually *ADVERB*
most of the time; normally • *What time do you usually go to bed?*

usurp (say yoo-**zerp**) *VERB* **usurps, usurping, usurped**
to take power or a position or right from someone wrongfully or by force
➤ **usurpation** *NOUN*
➤ **usurper** *NOUN*

usury (say **yoo**-zher-ee) *NOUN*
the lending of money at an excessively high rate of interest
➤ **usurer** *NOUN*

utensil (say yoo-**ten**-sil) *NOUN* **utensils**
a tool or device, especially one you use in the house • *cooking utensils*

uterus (say **yoo**-ter-us) *NOUN* **uteri** or **uteruses**
the womb

utilitarian *ADJECTIVE*
designed to be useful rather than decorative or luxurious; practical

utility *NOUN* **utilities**
❶ the quality of being useful ❷ an organization that supplies water, gas, electricity, etc. to the community

utilize (also **utilise**) *VERB* **utilizes, utilizing, utilized**
to make use of something • *She was able to utilize her talent for mimicry.*
➤ **utilization** *NOUN*

utmost *ADJECTIVE*
extreme or greatest • *Look after it with the utmost care.*
➤ **utmost** *NOUN*
➤ **do your utmost** to do the most that you are able to

Utopia (say yoo-**toh**-pee-a) *NOUN* **Utopias**
an imaginary place or state of things where everything is perfect
➤ **Utopian** *ADJECTIVE*
WORD ORIGIN Latin, = nowhere; used in 1516 as the title of a book by Sir Thomas More, in which he describes an ideal society

utter *VERB* **utters, uttering, uttered**
to say something or make a sound with your mouth • *He promised not to utter a word about it.*
➤ **utterance** *NOUN*

utter *ADJECTIVE*
complete or absolute • *It was utter misery.*

utterly *ADVERB*
completely or totally • *It's utterly impossible.*

uttermost *ADJECTIVE & NOUN*
extreme or greatest; utmost

a b c d e f g h i j k l m n o p q r s t u v w x y z

U-turn *NOUN* **U-turns**
❶ a U-shaped turn made in a vehicle so that it then travels in the opposite direction ❷ a complete change of ideas or policy

vacancy *NOUN* **vacancies**
❶ a position or job that has not been filled • *We have a vacancy for a shop assistant.* ❷ an available room in a hotel or guest house • *We have no vacancies.*

vacant *ADJECTIVE*
❶ empty; not filled or occupied • *a vacant seat* • *a vacant post* ❷ not showing any expression; blank • *a vacant stare*
➤ **vacantly** *ADVERB*

vacate *VERB* **vacates, vacating, vacated**
to leave or give up a place or position

vacation (say vak-**ay**-shon) *NOUN* **vacations**
a holiday, especially between the terms at a university

vaccinate (say **vak**-sin-ayt) *VERB* **vaccinates, vaccinating, vaccinated**
to protect someone from a disease by injecting them with a vaccine
➤ **vaccination** *NOUN*

vaccine (say **vak**-seen) *NOUN* **vaccines**
a substance used to give someone immunity against a disease (WORD ORIGIN) from Latin *vacca* = cow (because serum from cows was used to protect people from the disease smallpox)

vacillate (say **vass**-il-ayt) *VERB* **vacillates, vacillating, vacillated**
to keep changing your mind
➤ **vacillation** *NOUN*

vacuum *NOUN* **vacuums**
❶ a completely empty space; a space without any air in it ❷ (*informal*) a vacuum cleaner

vacuum *VERB* **vacuums, vacuuming, vacuumed**
to clean something using a vacuum cleaner

vacuum cleaner *NOUN* **vacuum cleaners**
an electrical device that sucks up dust and dirt from the floor

vacuum flask *NOUN* **vacuum flasks**
(*chiefly British*) a container with double walls that have a vacuum between them, used for keeping liquids hot or cold

vagabond *NOUN* **vagabonds**
a person with no settled home or regular work; a vagrant

vagary (say **vay**-ger-ee) *NOUN* **vagaries**
a change in something that is difficult to control or predict • *the vagaries of fashion*

vagina (say va-**jy**-na) *NOUN* **vaginas**
the passage in a female body that leads from the vulva to the womb

vagrant (say **vay**-grant) *NOUN* **vagrants**
a person with no settled home or regular work; a tramp
➤ **vagrancy** *NOUN*

vague *ADJECTIVE*
❶ not definite or clear • *I only have a vague memory of his face.* ❷ not thinking clearly or precisely
➤ **vagueness** *NOUN*

vaguely *ADVERB*
❶ in a way that is not definite or clear; slightly • *The name is vaguely familiar.* ❷ without thinking clearly • *He smiled vaguely and walked away.*

vain *ADJECTIVE*
❶ conceited, especially about how you look ❷ useless or unsuccessful • *They made vain attempts to save her.*
➤ **vainly** *ADVERB*
➤ **in vain** with no result; uselessly • *I tried in vain to call for help.*

SPELLING
Take care not to confuse with **vane** or **vein**.

valance *NOUN* **valances**
a short curtain round the frame of a bed or above a window

vale *NOUN* **vales**
a valley

valency *NOUN* **valencies**
(*in science*) the power of an atom to combine with other atoms, measured by the number of hydrogen atoms it is capable of combining with

valentine *NOUN* **valentines**
❶ a card sent on St Valentine's day (14 February) to the person you love ❷ the person you send this card to

valet (say **val**-ay or **val**-it) *NOUN* **valets**
a man's servant who takes care of his clothes and appearance

valiant *ADJECTIVE*
brave or courageous
➤ **valiantly** *ADVERB*

valid *ADJECTIVE*
❶ legally able to be used or accepted • *a valid passport* ❷ valid reasoning is sound and logical • *You make a valid point.*
➤ **validity** *NOUN*

valley *NOUN* **valleys**
❶ a long low area between hills ❷ an area through which a river flows • *the Nile valley*

valour *NOUN*
bravery, especially in battle
➤ **valorous** *ADJECTIVE*

valuable *ADJECTIVE*
❶ worth a lot of money ❷ very useful or important • *She gave me valuable advice.*

valuables *PLURAL NOUN*
valuable things

value *NOUN* **values**
❶ the amount of money that something could be sold for ❷ how useful or important something is • *They learnt the value of regular exercise.* ❸ (*in mathematics*) the number or quantity represented by a figure • *What is the value of x?*

value *VERB* **values, valuing, valued**
❶ to think that something is important or worth having • *I would value your opinion.* ❷ to work out how much something could be sold for
➤ **valuation** *NOUN*

valueless *ADJECTIVE*
having no value

valve *NOUN* **valves**
❶ a device for controlling the flow of gas or liquid through a pipe or tube ❷ a structure in the heart or in a blood vessel allowing blood to flow in one direction only ❸ a device that controls the flow of electricity in old televisions and radios

vampire *NOUN* **vampires**
in stories, a dead creature that is supposed to leave its grave at night and suck blood from living people

van *NOUN* **vans**
❶ a covered vehicle for carrying goods ❷ (*British*) a railway carriage for luggage or goods or for the use of the guard

➤ **in the van** at the front or in the leading position

vandal *NOUN* **vandals**
a person who deliberately breaks or damages things, especially public property
➤ **vandalism** *NOUN*
WORD ORIGIN named after the *Vandals*, a Germanic tribe who invaded the Roman Empire in the 5th century, destroying many books and works of art

vandalize (also **vandalise**) *VERB* **vandalizes, vandalizing, vandalized**
to damage property deliberately

vane *NOUN* **vanes**
❶ the blade of a propeller, sail of a windmill or other device that acts on or is moved by wind or water ❷ a weathervane
SPELLING
Take care not to confuse with **vain** or **vein**.

vanguard *NOUN*
❶ the leading part of an army or fleet ❷ the first people to adopt a fashion or idea

vanilla *NOUN*
a flavouring obtained from the pods of a tropical plant

vanish *VERB* **vanishes, vanishing, vanished**
to disappear completely • *The magician vanished in a puff of smoke.*

vanity *NOUN*
the quality of being too proud of your abilities or of how you look

vanquish *VERB* **vanquishes, vanquishing, vanquished**
to defeat someone completely

vantage point *NOUN* **vantage points**
a place from which you have a good view of something

vaporize (also **vaporise**) *VERB* **vaporizes, vaporizing, vaporized**
to turn into vapour or to change something into vapour

vapour *NOUN* **vapours**
a visible gas to which some substances can be converted by heat; steam or mist

variable *ADJECTIVE*
likely to vary; not staying the same
➤ **variability** *NOUN*
variable *NOUN* **variables**
something that varies or can vary; a variable quantity

a
b
c
d
e
f
g
h
i
j
k
l
m
n
o
p
q
r
s
t
u
v
w
x
y
z

variance *NOUN*
the amount by which things differ
➤ **at variance** differing or conflicting

variant *NOUN* **variants**
a thing that is a slightly different form of
something else • *The game is a variant of
baseball.*

variant *ADJECTIVE*
differing from something • *'Gaol' is a variant
spelling of 'jail'.*

variation *NOUN* **variations**
❶ varying; the amount by which something
varies • *There have been slight variations
in temperature.* ❷ a different form of
something

varicose *ADJECTIVE*
varicose veins are permanently swollen

varied *ADJECTIVE*
of different sorts; full of variety • *She has
varied interests.*

variegated (say **vair**-ig-ay-tid) *ADJECTIVE*
with patches of different colours • *a plant
with variegated leaves*

variety *ADJECTIVE* **varieties**
❶ a number of different kinds of the
same thing • *There was a variety of cakes
to choose from.* ❷ a particular kind of
something • *There are several varieties of
spaniel.* ❸ the quality of not always being the
same; variation • *You need more variety in
your diet.* ❹ a form of entertainment made
up of short performances of singing, dancing
and comedy

various *ADJECTIVE*
❶ of several different kinds • *People choose
to be vegetarians for various reasons.*
❷ several • *We met various people.*
➤ **variously** *ADVERB*

varnish *NOUN* **varnishes**
a liquid that dries to form a hard shiny usually
transparent coating

varnish *VERB* **varnishes, varnishing, varnished**
to coat something with varnish

vary *VERB* **varies, varying, varied**
❶ to keep changing • *The weather varies a lot
here.* ❷ to make changes to something ❸ to
be different from one another • *The cars are
the same, although the colours vary.*

vascular *ADJECTIVE*
consisting of tubes or similar vessels for
circulating blood, sap or water in animals or
plants • *the vascular system*

vase *NOUN* **vases**
an open usually tall container used for
holding cut flowers or as an ornament

Vaseline *NOUN* (*trademark*)
petroleum jelly for use as an ointment

vassal *NOUN* **vassals**
in feudal times, a man who was given land to
live on in return for promising loyally to fight
for the landowner

vast *ADJECTIVE*
very great, especially in area • *a vast expanse
of water*
➤ **vastly** *ADVERB*
➤ **vastness** *NOUN*

VAT *ABBREVIATION*
value added tax; a tax on goods and services

vat *NOUN* **vats**
a very large container for holding liquid

vaudeville (say **vawd**-vil) *NOUN*
a kind of variety entertainment popular in the
early 20th century

vault *VERB* **vaults, vaulting, vaulted**
to jump over something, especially while
supporting yourself on your hands or with
the help of a pole • *He vaulted over the fence
and ran off.*

vault *NOUN* **vaults**
❶ a vaulting jump ❷ an arched roof ❸ an
underground room used to store things ❹ a
room for storing money or valuables ❺ a
burial chamber

vaulted *ADJECTIVE*
having an arched roof

vaulting horse *NOUN* **vaulting horses**
a padded wooden block for vaulting over in
gymnastics

vaunt *VERB* **vaunts, vaunting, vaunted**
to boast something

VDU *ABBREVIATION*
visual display unit; a monitor for a computer

veal *NOUN*
meat from a calf

vector *NOUN* **vectors**
(*in mathematics*) a quantity that has size and
direction, such as velocity (which is speed in a
certain direction)

Veda (say **vay**-da or **vee**-da) *NOUN* **Vedas**
the most ancient and sacred literature of the
Hindus
➤ **Vedic** *ADJECTIVE*

veer VERB veers, veering, veered
to swerve or change direction suddenly • *The car veered off the road and hit a tree.*

vegan NOUN vegans
a person who does not eat or use any animal products

vegetable NOUN vegetables
a plant that can be used as food

vegetarian NOUN vegetarians
a person who does not eat meat
➤ **vegetarianism** NOUN

vegetate VERB vegetates, vegetating, vegetated
to lead a dull life doing nothing interesting
WORD ORIGIN originally = grow like a vegetable

vegetation NOUN
plants that are growing • *The hills are covered in thick vegetation.*

vehement (say vee-im-ent) ADJECTIVE
showing strong feeling • *a vehement refusal*
➤ **vehemently** ADVERB
➤ **vehemence** NOUN

vehicle NOUN vehicles
a means of transporting people or goods, especially on land

veil NOUN veils
a piece of thin material worn to cover a woman's face or head
➤ **draw a veil over something** to avoid discussing something

veil VERB veils, veiling, veiled
❶ to cover something with a veil ❷ to partially conceal something • *A mist began to veil the hills.*

veiled ADJECTIVE
partly hidden or disguised • *a thinly veiled threat*

vein NOUN veins
❶ any of the tubes that carry blood from all parts of the body to the heart. Compare with **artery**. ❷ a line or streak on a leaf, rock or insect's wing ❸ a long deposit of mineral or ore in the middle of a rock ❹ a mood or manner • *She spoke in a serious vein.*

SPELLING
Take care not to confuse with **vain** or **vane**.

veld (say velt) NOUN veld
an area of open grassland in South Africa
WORD ORIGIN from an Afrikaans word, from Dutch *veld* = field

vellum NOUN
smooth parchment or writing paper

velocity NOUN velocities
speed in a given direction

velour (say vil-**oor**) NOUN
a thick velvety material

velvet NOUN
a woven material with very short soft furry fibres on one side

velvety ADJECTIVE
smooth and soft, like velvet • *her velvety voice*

vendetta NOUN vendettas
a long-lasting bitter quarrel; a feud

vending machine NOUN vending machines
a slot machine from which you can obtain drinks, chocolate, etc.

vendor NOUN vendors
someone who is selling something, especially a house

veneer NOUN veneers
❶ a thin layer of good wood covering the surface of a cheaper wood in furniture ❷ an outward show of some good quality • *a veneer of politeness*

venerable ADJECTIVE
worthy of respect or honour because of being so old

venerate VERB venerates, venerating, venerated
to honour someone with great respect or reverence
➤ **veneration** NOUN

venetian blind NOUN venetian blinds
a window blind consisting of horizontal strips that can be adjusted to let light in or shut it out

vengeance NOUN
harming or punishing someone in return for something bad they have done to you; revenge
➤ **with a vengeance** with great force or intensity • *He set to work with a vengeance.*

vengeful ADJECTIVE
wanting to punish someone who has harmed you
➤ **vengefully** ADVERB
➤ **vengefulness** NOUN

venial (say veen-ee-al) ADJECTIVE
venial sins or faults are pardonable and not serious

venison *NOUN*
the meat from a deer

Venn diagram *NOUN* **Venn diagrams**
(*in mathematics*) a diagram in which circles
are used to show the relationships between
different sets of things **WORD ORIGIN** named
after an English mathematician, John *Venn*

venom *NOUN*
❶ the poisonous fluid produced by snakes,
scorpions, etc. ❷ a feeling of bitter hatred for
someone • *a look of pure venom*
➤ **venomous** *ADJECTIVE*

vent *NOUN* **vents**
an opening in something, especially to let out
smoke or gas
➤ **give vent to something** to express your
feelings strongly

vent *VERB* **vents, venting, vented**
to express your feelings, especially anger,
strongly • *The crowd vented their anger on
the referee.*

ventilate *VERB* **ventilates, ventilating,
ventilated**
to let air move freely in and out of a room or
building
➤ **ventilation** *NOUN*
➤ **ventilator** *NOUN*

ventriloquist *NOUN* **ventriloquists**
an entertainer who makes their voice sound
as if it comes from another source
➤ **ventriloquism** *NOUN*
WORD ORIGIN from Latin *venter* = abdomen
+ *loqui* = speak (from the ancient belief that
people who were possessed by an evil spirit
spoke from their stomachs)

venture *NOUN* **ventures**
something you decide to do that is risky or
adventurous

venture *VERB* **ventures, venturing, ventured**
to dare or be bold enough to do or say
something or to go somewhere • *We ventured
out into the snow.*

venturesome *ADJECTIVE*
ready to take risks; daring

venue (say **ven**-yoo) *NOUN* **venues**
the place where an event such as a meeting,
sports match or concert is held

veracity (say ver-**as**-it-ee) *NOUN*
truth or being truthful

veranda *NOUN* **verandas**
a terrace with a roof along the side of a house

verb *NOUN* **verbs**
a word that shows what a person or thing is
doing or what is happening, e.g. *bring, came,
sing, were*

GRAMMAR

A **verb** can describe an action or process
(e.g. *dive, chew, heal, thaw*), a feeling (e.g.
think, know, believe) or a state (e.g. *be,
remain*). A sentence usually contains at
least one verb.

Verbs change their form according to
which person (*I, you, he, she, it, we* or
they) and tense (past, present or future)
they are in. **Regular verbs** change their
endings in predictable ways, e.g. by
adding *-s* or *-ed*: *I shout, she shouts, we
shouted*, etc. **Irregular verbs** have more
varied forms, especially in the past tense:
*we swim, we swam, we have swum; I am,
we were, they have been.*

An **auxiliary verb** is used to form the
tenses of another verb, for example *have*
in *I have just received this email*, and
will in *They will never find us here*. The
auxiliary verbs *can, will, shall, may*, and
must are also called **modal verbs**; they
are used to express a wish, need, ability
or permission to do something. A **phrasal
verb** includes a preposition or adverb, for
example *drop in, fall out* and *wrap up*.

See also the panel on **tenses**.

verbal *ADJECTIVE*
❶ spoken, not written • *We had a verbal
agreement.* ❷ to do with words or in the
form of words
➤ **verbally** *ADVERB*

verbatim (say ver-**bay**-tim) *ADVERB* & *ADJECTIVE*
in exactly the same words • *He copied down
the whole paragraph verbatim.*

verdant *ADJECTIVE*
verdant grass or fields are fresh and green

verdict *NOUN* **verdicts**
a judgement or decision made after
considering something, especially one made
by a jury

verdigris (say **verd**-i-grees) *NOUN*
green rust on copper or brass
WORD ORIGIN from French *vert-de-gris*,
literally = green of Greece

verdure *NOUN*
green vegetation; its greenness

verge *NOUN* verges
❶ a strip of grass along the edge of a road or path ❷ to be on the verge of something is to be close to doing it • *I was on the verge of tears.*

verge *VERB* verges, verging, verged
➤ **verge on something** to be nearly something • *This puzzle verges on the impossible.*

verger *NOUN* vergers
a person who is caretaker and attendant in a church

verify *VERB* verifies, verifying, verified
to check or show that something is true or correct
➤ **verification** *NOUN*

veritable *ADJECTIVE*
real; rightly named • *She was a veritable mine of useless information.*

vermicelli (say verm-i-**sel**-ee) *NOUN*
pasta made in long thin threads
WORD ORIGIN Italian, = little worms

vermilion *NOUN & ADJECTIVE*
bright red

vermin *PLURAL NOUN*
animals or insects that damage crops or food or carry disease, such as rats and fleas
➤ **verminous** *ADJECTIVE*

vernacular (say ver-**nak**-yoo-ler) *NOUN*
vernaculars
the language of a country or district, as distinct from an official or formal language

vernal *ADJECTIVE*
to do with the season of spring

verruca (say ver-**oo**-ka) *NOUN* verrucas
a kind of wart on the sole of the foot

versatile *ADJECTIVE*
able to do or be used for many different things • *a versatile tool*
➤ **versatility** *NOUN*

verse *NOUN* verses
❶ writing arranged in short lines, usually with a particular rhythm and often with rhymes; poetry ❷ a group of lines forming a unit in a poem or song ❸ each of the short numbered sections of a chapter in the Bible

versed *ADJECTIVE*
➤ **versed in something** experienced or skilled in something

version *NOUN* versions
❶ a particular person's account of something

that happened • *His version of the accident is different from mine.* ❷ a different form of something • *I don't like their version of the song.* ❸ a translation • *modern versions of the Bible*

versus *PREPOSITION*
against; competing with • *The final was France versus Brazil.*

vertebra *NOUN* vertebrae
each of the bones that form your backbone

vertebrate *NOUN* vertebrates
an animal that has a backbone. (The opposite is **invertebrate**.)

vertex *NOUN* vertices, (say **ver**-tis-eez)
(*in mathematics*) the highest point of a cone or triangle.

vertical *ADJECTIVE*
going directly upwards, at right angles to something level or horizontal • *The cliff was almost vertical.*
➤ **vertically** *ADVERB*

vertigo *NOUN*
a feeling of dizziness and loss of balance, especially when you are very high up

verve (say verv) *NOUN*
enthusiasm and liveliness

very *ADVERB*
❶ to a great amount or intensity; extremely • *It was very cold.* ❷ used to emphasize something • *on the very next day* • *the very last drop*

very *ADJECTIVE*
❶ exact or actual • *It's the very thing we need.* ❷ extreme • *Our house is at the very end of the street.*

vespers *NOUN*
a church service held in the evening

vessel *NOUN* vessels
❶ a ship or boat ❷ a container, especially for liquid ❸ a tube carrying blood or other liquid in the body of an animal or plant

vest *NOUN* vests
a piece of underwear you wear on the top half of your body

vested interest *NOUN* vested interests
a strong reason for wanting something to happen, usually because you will benefit from it

vestibule *NOUN* vestibules
❶ an entrance hall or lobby ❷ a church porch

vestige *NOUN* **vestiges**
a trace; a very small amount of something that is left after the rest has gone • *Only the very last vestiges of the snow remained.*
WORD ORIGIN from Latin *vestigium* = footprint

vestment *NOUN* **vestments**
a ceremonial garment, especially one worn by the clergy or choir at a church service

vestry *NOUN* **vestries**
a room in a church where vestments are kept and where the clergy and choir put these on

vet *NOUN* **vets**
(*chiefly British*) a person trained to give medical and surgical treatment to animals

vet *VERB* **vets, vetting, vetted** (*British*) to make a careful check of a person or thing, especially of someone's background before employing them **WORD ORIGIN** short for *veterinary surgeon*

veteran *NOUN* **veterans**
a person who has long experience, especially in the armed forces

veterinary (say **vet**-rin-ree) *ADJECTIVE*
to do with the medical and surgical treatment of animals • *a veterinary surgeon*

veto (say **vee**-toh) *NOUN* **vetoes**
❶ a refusal to let something happen ❷ the right to stop something from happening

veto *VERB* **vetoes, vetoing, vetoed**
to refuse to let something happen
WORD ORIGIN Latin, = I forbid

vex *VERB* **vexes, vexing, vexed**
to annoy someone or cause them worry • *Her behaviour vexed him a good deal.*
➤ **vexation** *NOUN*

vexed question *NOUN* **vexed questions**
a problem that is difficult or much discussed

VHF *ABBREVIATION*
very high frequency

via (say **vy**-a) *PREPOSITION*
❶ going through; by way of • *The train goes from London to Edinburgh via York.* ❷ by means of; using • *You can get in touch with us via our website.*

viable *ADJECTIVE*
able to work or exist successfully • *a viable plan*
➤ **viability** *NOUN*

viaduct *NOUN* **viaducts**
a long bridge, usually with many arches,

carrying a road or railway over a valley or low ground

vial *NOUN* **vials**
a small glass bottle

viands (say **vy**-andz) *PLURAL NOUN* (*old use*)
food

vibrant *ADJECTIVE*
❶ full of energy; lively • *a vibrant city*
❷ vibrant colours are bright and strong

vibrate *VERB* **vibrates, vibrating, vibrated**
to move very quickly from side to side and with small movements • *Every time a train went past the walls vibrated.*

vibration *NOUN* **vibrations**
a continuous shaking movement that you can feel • *the vibrations of the ship's engines*

vicar *NOUN* **vicars**
a member of the Church of England clergy who is in charge of a parish

vicarage *NOUN* **vicarages**
the house of a vicar

vicarious (say vik-**air**-ee-us) *ADJECTIVE*
not experienced yourself but felt by imagining you share someone else's experience • *I got a vicarious pleasure from reading about his adventures.*

vice *NOUN* **vices**
❶ an evil or bad habit; a bad fault ❷ evil or wickedness ❸ a device for gripping something and holding it firmly while you work on it

vice- *PREFIX*
❶ authorized to act as a deputy or substitute (as in *vice-captain, vice-president*) ❷ next in rank to someone (as in *vice-admiral*)

vice versa *ADVERB*
the other way round • *Summer in the UK is winter in Australia and vice versa.*
WORD ORIGIN Latin, = the position being reversed

vicinity *NOUN*
the area near or round a place • *Is there a park in the vicinity?*

vicious *ADJECTIVE*
❶ cruel and aggressive ❷ severe or violent • *a vicious blizzard*
➤ **viciously** *ADVERB*
➤ **viciousness** *NOUN*

vicious circle *NOUN* **vicious circles**
a situation in which a problem produces

an effect which in turn makes the problem worse

victim *NOUN* **victims**
someone who is injured, killed, robbed, etc. • *a murder victim*

victimize (also **victimise**) *VERB* **victimizes, victimizing, victimized**
to single someone out for harsh or unfair treatment

victor *NOUN* **victors**
the winner of a battle or contest

Victorian *ADJECTIVE*
belong to the time of Queen Victoria (1837-1901)
➤ **Victorian** *NOUN*

victorious *ADJECTIVE*
that wins a victory • *the victorious team*

victory *NOUN* **victories**
success won against an opponent in a battle, contest or game

victuals (say **vit**-alz) *PLURAL NOUN* (*old use*)
food and drink

video *NOUN* **videos**
❶ a system of recording moving pictures and sound, especially as a digital file • *The accident was captured on video.* ❷ a short film or recording that you can watch on a computer or mobile phone, especially over the Internet ❸ a copy of a film or television programme that has been recorded

video *VERB* **videos, videoing, videoed** (*chiefly British*) to record something on video
WORD ORIGIN Latin, = I see

video game *NOUN* **video games**
a game in which you press electronic controls to move images on a screen

vie *VERB* **vies, vying, vied**
to compete with someone; to carry on a rivalry • *The boys were vying with each other to see who could tell the funniest joke.*

view *NOUN* **views**
❶ what you can see from one place, e.g. beautiful scenery • *There's a fine view from the top of the hill.* ❷ sight or range of vision • *The ship sailed into view.* ❸ an opinion • *She has strong views about art.*
➤ **in view of** because of
➤ **on view** displayed for people to see
➤ **with a view to** with the hope or intention of

view *VERB* **views, viewing, viewed**
❶ to watch or look at something • *A map is*

a plan of an area, viewed from above. ❷ to consider or regard a person or thing in a certain way • *He viewed us with suspicion.*

viewer *NOUN* **viewers**
someone who views something, especially a television programme

viewpoint *NOUN* **viewpoints**
❶ an opinion or point of view ❷ a place giving a good view

vigil (say **vij**-il) *NOUN* **vigils**
staying awake to keep watch or to pray • *a long vigil*

vigilant (say **vij**-il-ant) *ADJECTIVE*
keeping careful watch for danger or difficulties • *A pilot must remain vigilant at all times.*
➤ **vigilantly** *ADVERB*
➤ **vigilance** *NOUN*

vigilante (say vij-il-**an**-tee) *NOUN* **vigilantes**
a member of a group who organize themselves, without authority, to try to prevent crime and disorder in their community

vigorous *ADJECTIVE*
full of strength and energy • *vigorous exercise*
➤ **vigorously** *ADVERB*

vigour *NOUN*
strength and energy

Viking *NOUN* **Vikings**
a Scandinavian trader and pirate in the 8th-11th centuries

vile *ADJECTIVE*
❶ extremely disgusting • *That tastes vile.*
❷ very bad or wicked
➤ **vilely** *ADVERB*
➤ **vileness** *NOUN*

villa *NOUN* **villas**
a house, especially a holiday home abroad

village *NOUN* **villages**
a group of houses and other buildings in a country district, smaller than a town and usually having a church

villager *NOUN* **villagers**
a person who lives in a village

villain *NOUN* **villains**
a wicked person or a criminal
➤ **villainous** *ADJECTIVE*
➤ **villainy** *NOUN*

villein (say **vil**-an or **vil**-ayn) *NOUN* **villeins**
a tenant in feudal times

a b c d e f g h i j k l m n o p q r s t u v w x y z

vim NOUN (*informal*)
vigour or energy

vindicate VERB vindicates, vindicating, vindicated
① to clear a person of blame or suspicion
② to prove something to be true or worthwhile
➤ **vindication** NOUN

vindictive ADJECTIVE
showing a desire for revenge; spiteful
➤ **vindictively** ADVERB
➤ **vindictiveness** NOUN

vine NOUN vines
a climbing or trailing plant whose fruit is the grape

vinegar NOUN
a sour liquid used to flavour food or in pickling

vineyard (say **vin**-yard) NOUN vineyards
an area of land where vines are grown to produce grapes for making wine

vintage NOUN vintages
① all the grapes that are harvested in one season or the wine made from them ② the period from which something comes • *The furniture is of 1920s vintage.*

vintage car NOUN vintage cars
(*British*) a car made between 1917 and 1930

vinyl NOUN
a kind of plastic

viola (say vee-**oh**-la) NOUN violas
a musical instrument like a violin but slightly larger and with a lower pitch

violate VERB violates, violating, violated
① to break an agreement, rule or law ② to treat a person or place with disrespect and violence
➤ **violation** NOUN

violence NOUN
① physical force that does harm or damage ② strength or intensity • *the violence of the storm*

violent ADJECTIVE
① using or involving violence ② strong or intense • *a violent dislike*
➤ **violently** ADVERB

violet NOUN violets
① a small plant that often has purple flowers ② a bluish-purple colour

violin NOUN violins
a musical instrument with four strings, played with a bow
➤ **violinist** NOUN

VIP ABBREVIATION
very important person

viper NOUN vipers
a small poisonous snake

virgin NOUN virgins
a person who has never had sexual intercourse
➤ **virginal** ADJECTIVE
➤ **virginity** NOUN

virgin ADJECTIVE
not yet touched or used • *virgin snow*

virile (say **vir**-yl) ADJECTIVE
having masculine strength or vigour, especially sexually
➤ **virility** NOUN

virtual ADJECTIVE
① being something in effect though not strictly in fact • *His silence was a virtual admission of guilt.* ② existing as a computer image and not physically • *Click here to go on a virtual tour of the gallery.*

virtually ADVERB
nearly or almost • *She virtually admitted it.*

virtual reality NOUN
an image or environment produced by a computer that is so realistic that it seems to be part of the real world

virtue NOUN virtues
① moral goodness; a particular form of this • *Honesty is a virtue.* ② a good quality or advantage • *Jamie's plan has the virtue of simplicity.*
➤ **by virtue of** because of

virtuoso (say ver-tew-**oh**-soh) NOUN virtuosos or virtuosi
a person with outstanding skill, especially in singing or playing music
➤ **virtuosity** NOUN

virtuous ADJECTIVE
behaving in a morally good way
➤ **virtuously** ADVERB

virus NOUN viruses
① a very tiny living thing, smaller than a bacterium, that can cause disease ② a disease caused by a virus ③ a hidden set of instructions in a computer program that is designed to destroy data

visa (say **vee**-za) NOUN visas
an official mark put on someone's passport by

officials of a foreign country to show that the holder has permission to enter that country

visage (say **viz**-ij) NOUN visages
a person's face

viscount (say **vy**-kownt) NOUN viscounts
a nobleman ranking below an earl and above a baron
➤ **viscountess** NOUN

viscous (say **visk**-us) ADJECTIVE
thick and gluey, not pouring easily
➤ **viscosity** NOUN

visibility NOUN
the distance you can see clearly • *Visibility is down to 20 metres.*

visible ADJECTIVE
able to be seen or noticed • *The ship was visible on the horizon.*

visibly ADVERB
in a way that is easy to notice • *He was visibly shocked.*

vision NOUN visions
❶ the ability to see; sight ❷ something that you see in your imagination or in a dream ❸ the ability to make imaginative plans for the future ❹ a person or thing that is beautiful to see

visionary ADJECTIVE
extremely imaginative or fanciful

visionary NOUN visionaries
a person with extremely imaginative ideas and plans

visit VERB visits, visiting, visited
❶ to go to see a person or place ❷ to stay somewhere for a while

visit NOUN visits
❶ going to see a person or place ❷ a short stay somewhere

visitation NOUN visitations
an official visit, especially to inspect something

visitor NOUN visitors
a person who is visiting or staying at a place

visor (say **vy**-zer) NOUN visors
❶ the part of a helmet that covers the face ❷ a shield to protect the eyes from bright light or sunshine

vista NOUN vistas
a long view

visual ADJECTIVE
to do with or used in seeing; to do with sight

• *She has a good visual memory.*
➤ **visually** ADVERB

visual aid NOUN visual aids
a picture, video or film used as an aid in teaching

visual display unit NOUN visual display units
(*British*) a device that looks like a television screen and displays data being received from a computer or fed into it

visualize (also **visualise**) VERB visualizes, visualizing, visualized
to form a mental picture of something • *I'm trying to visualize what your room looked like before you decorated it.*
➤ **visualization** NOUN

vital ADJECTIVE
❶ essential; very important • *It is vital that you practise every day.* ❷ connected with life; necessary for life to continue • *vital functions such as breathing*

vitality NOUN
liveliness or energy

vitally ADVERB
extremely • *Sleep is vitally important to all of us.*

vitamin (say **vit**-a-min or **vy**-ta-min) NOUN vitamins
any of a number of substances that are present in various foods and are essential to keep people and animals healthy

vitreous (say **vit**-ree-us) ADJECTIVE
like glass in being hard, transparent or brittle • *vitreous enamel*

vitriol (say **vit**-ree-ol) NOUN
savage criticism
➤ **vitriolic** ADJECTIVE

vivacious (say viv-**ay**-shus) ADJECTIVE
happy and lively
➤ **vivaciously** ADVERB
➤ **vivacity** NOUN

vivid ADJECTIVE
❶ bright and strong or clear • *vivid colours* • *a vivid description* ❷ active and lively • *a vivid imagination*
➤ **vividly** ADVERB
➤ **vividness** NOUN

vivisection NOUN
doing experiments on live animals as part of scientific research

vixen NOUN vixens
a female fox

a
b
c
d
e
f
g
h
i
j
k
l
m
n
o
p
q
r
s
t
u
v
w
x
y
z

vizier (say viz-**eer**) *NOUN* **viziers** (*historical*)
an important Muslim official

vocabulary *NOUN* **vocabularies**
❶ all the words used in a particular subject or language ❷ the words known to an individual person • *She has a good vocabulary.*

vocal *ADJECTIVE*
to do with or using the voice
➤ **vocally** *ADVERB*

vocal cords *PLURAL NOUN*
two strap-like membranes in the throat that can be made to vibrate and produce sounds

vocalist *NOUN* **vocalists**
a singer, especially in a pop group

vocation *NOUN* **vocations**
❶ a person's job or occupation ❷ a strong desire to do a particular kind of work or a feeling of being called by God to do something

vocational *ADJECTIVE*
teaching you the skills you need for a particular job or profession • *vocational training*

vociferous (say vo-**sif**-er-us) *ADJECTIVE*
noisily and forcefully expressing your views

vodka *NOUN* **vodkas**
a strong alcoholic drink very popular in Russia

vogue *NOUN* **vogues**
the current fashion • *Very short hair for women seems to be the vogue.*
➤ **in vogue** in fashion • *Stripy dresses are definitely in vogue.*

voice *NOUN* **voices**
❶ the sounds that you make when you speak or sing ❷ the ability to speak or sing • *She has lost her voice.* ❸ someone expressing a particular opinion about something • *Emma's the only dissenting voice.* ❹ the right to express an opinion or desire • *I have no voice in this matter.*

voice *VERB* **voices, voicing, voiced**
to say something clearly and strongly • *We voiced our objections to the plan.*

voicemail *NOUN*
a system for recording and storing phone messages for people to listen to later

void *ADJECTIVE*
❶ completely lacking something • *The message seemed void of all meaning.* ❷ not legally valid • *The agreement was declared void.*

void *NOUN* **voids**
an empty space or hole

volatile (say **vol**-a-tyl) *ADJECTIVE*
❶ evaporating quickly • *a volatile liquid*
❷ changing quickly from one mood to another
➤ **volatility** *NOUN*

volcanic *ADJECTIVE*
caused or produced by a volcano • *a volcanic eruption*

volcano *NOUN* **volcanoes**
a mountain with an opening at the top from which lava, ashes and hot gases from below the earth's crust are or have been thrown out
WORD ORIGIN Italian, from *Vulcan*, the ancient Roman god of fire

vole *NOUN* **voles**
a small animal rather like a rat

volition *NOUN*
to do something of your own volition is to choose to do it • *She left of her own volition.*

volley *NOUN* **volleys**
❶ a number of bullets or shells fired at the same time ❷ in tennis and football, hitting or kicking the ball before it touches the ground

volley *VERB* **volleys, volleying, volleyed**
to hit or kick the ball before it touches the ground • *He volleyed the ball into the back of the net.*

volleyball *NOUN*
a game in which two teams hit a large ball to and fro over a net with their hands

volt *NOUN* **volts**
a unit for measuring electric force
WORD ORIGIN named after an Italian scientist, Alessandro *Volta*, who discovered how to produce electricity by a chemical reaction

voltage *NOUN* **voltages**
electric force measured in volts

voluble *ADJECTIVE*
talking very much
➤ **volubly** *ADVERB*
➤ **volubility** *NOUN*

volume *NOUN* **volumes**
❶ the amount of space filled by something ❷ an amount or quantity • *The volume of work has increased.* ❸ the strength or power of sound • *Can you turn up the volume?* ❹ a book, especially one of a set
WORD ORIGIN from Latin *volumen* = a roll (because ancient books were made in a rolled form)

voluminous (say vol-**yoo**-min-us) *ADJECTIVE*
❶ bulky; large and full • *a voluminous skirt*
❷ able to hold a lot • *a voluminous bag*

voluntary *ADJECTIVE*
❶ done or doing something because you want to do it, not because you have to do it
❷ unpaid • *voluntary work*
➤ **voluntarily** *ADVERB*

volunteer *VERB* volunteers, volunteering, volunteered
❶ to offer to do something of your own accord, without being asked or forced to ❷ to provide something willingly or freely without being asked for it • *Several people generously volunteered their time.*

volunteer *NOUN* volunteers
a person who volunteers to do something, e.g. to serve in the armed forces

voluptuous *ADJECTIVE*
❶ giving a luxurious feeling • *voluptuous furnishings* ❷ a woman is voluptuous when she has an attractively curved figure

vomit *VERB* vomits, vomiting, vomited
to bring up food from the stomach and out through the mouth; to be sick

vomit *NOUN*
food from the stomach brought back out through the mouth

voodoo *NOUN*
a form of witchcraft and magical rites, especially in the West Indies

voracious (say vor-**ay**-shus) *ADJECTIVE*
greedy; devouring things eagerly • *a voracious appetite*
➤ **voraciously** *ADVERB*
➤ **voracity** *NOUN*

vortex *NOUN* vortices
a whirlpool or whirlwind

vote *VERB* votes, voting, voted
to show which person or thing you prefer by putting up your hand or making a mark on a piece of paper

vote *NOUN* votes
❶ the action of voting ❷ the right to vote

voter *NOUN* voters
someone who votes, especially in an election

votive *ADJECTIVE*
given to fulfil a vow • *votive offerings at the shrine*

vouch *VERB* vouches, vouching, vouched
➤ **vouch for something** to guarantee that something is true or certain • *I will vouch for his honesty.*

voucher *NOUN* vouchers
a piece of paper showing that you are allowed to pay less for something or that you can get something in exchange

vouchsafe *VERB* vouchsafes, vouchsafing, vouchsafed
(*formal*) to grant or offer something • *She did not vouchsafe a reply.*

vow *NOUN* vows
a solemn promise

vow *VERB* vows, vowing, vowed
to make a solemn promise to do something • *She vowed never to speak to him again.*

vowel *NOUN* vowels
any of the letters a, e, i, o, u and sometimes y, which represent sounds in which breath comes out freely. Compare with **consonant**.

voyage *NOUN* voyages
a long journey on a ship or in a spacecraft

voyage *VERB* voyages, voyaging, voyaged
to make a voyage
➤ **voyager** *NOUN*

vulgar *ADJECTIVE*
rude; without good manners
➤ **vulgarity** *NOUN*
(**WORD ORIGIN**) from Latin *vulgus* = the common or ordinary people

vulgar fraction *NOUN* vulgar fractions
(*British*) a fraction shown by numbers above and below a line (e.g. ½, ¾), not a decimal fraction

vulnerable *ADJECTIVE*
able to be hurt or harmed or attacked • *The town was vulnerable to attack from the north.*
➤ **vulnerability** *NOUN*

vulture *NOUN* vultures
a large bird that feeds on dead animals

vulva *NOUN* vulvas
the outer parts of the female genitals

vying
present participle of **vie**

Ww

wacky *ADJECTIVE* wackier, wackiest
(*informal*)
crazy or silly

wad (say wod) *NOUN* wads
a pad or bundle of soft material or banknotes, papers, etc.

wad *VERB* wads, wadding, wadded
to pad something with soft material

waddle *VERB* waddles, waddling, waddled
to walk with short steps, swaying from side to side, as a duck does

waddle *NOUN*
a waddling walk

wade *VERB* wades, wading, waded
❶ to walk through water or mud ❷ to read through something with effort because it is dull, difficult or long

wader *NOUN* waders
❶ (also **wading bird**) any bird with long legs that feeds in shallow water ❷ waders are long rubber boots that you wear for standing in water

wafer *NOUN* wafers
a kind of thin biscuit

wafer-thin *ADJECTIVE*
very thin

waffle (say wof-el) *NOUN* waffles
❶ a small cake made of batter and eaten hot ❷ talking or writing for a long time without saying anything important or interesting

waffle *VERB* waffles, waffling, waffled
to talk or write for a long time without saying anything important or interesting

waft (say woft) *VERB* wafts, wafting, wafted
to float gently through the air • *The smell of her perfume wafted across the room.*

wag *VERB* wags, wagging, wagged
❶ a dog wags its tail when it moves it quickly from side to side because it is happy or excited ❷ you wag your finger when you move it up and down or from side to side

wag *NOUN* wags
❶ a wagging movement ❷ a person who makes jokes

wage *NOUN* (or **wages**) *PLURAL NOUN*
a regular payment to someone in return for the work they do

wage *VERB* wages, waging, waged
to carry on a war or campaign

wager (say **way**-jer) *NOUN* wagers
a bet

wager *VERB* wagers, wagering, wagered
to make a bet with someone

waggle *VERB* waggles, waggling, waggled
to move something quickly to and fro • *Can you waggle your ears?*

wagon *NOUN* wagons
❶ a cart with four wheels, pulled by a horse or an ox ❷ an open railway truck, e.g. for coal

wagoner *NOUN* wagoners
the driver of a horse-drawn wagon

wagtail *NOUN* wagtails
a small bird with a long tail that it moves up and down

waif *NOUN* waifs
a homeless and helpless person, especially a child

wail *VERB* wails, wailing, wailed
to make a long sad cry

wail *NOUN* wails
a sound of wailing

wainscot, wainscoting *NOUN*
wooden panelling on the wall of a room

waist *NOUN* waists
the narrow part in the middle of your body

> **SPELLING**
> Take care not to confuse with **waste**, which means things that are not wanted.

waistcoat *NOUN* waistcoats
(*British*) a short close-fitting jacket without sleeves, worn over a shirt and under a jacket

waistline *NOUN* waistlines
the amount you measure around your waist, which indicates how fat or thin you are

wait *VERB* waits, waiting, waited
❶ to stay somewhere or delay doing something until something happens • *Wait here – I'll be back in a minute.* ❷ to be left to be dealt with later • *This question will have to wait until our next meeting.* ❸ to be a waiter
➤ **wait on someone** ❶ to hand food and drink to people at a meal ❷ to fetch and carry for someone as an attendant

wait *NOUN*
an act or time of waiting • *We had a long wait for the train.*

waiter *NOUN* waiters
a man who serves people with food and drink in a restaurant

waiting list *NOUN* waiting lists
a list of people waiting for something to become available

waiting room *NOUN* waiting rooms
a room provided for people who are waiting for something

waitress *NOUN* waitresses
a woman who serves people with food and drink in a restaurant

waive *VERB* waives, waiving, waived
to not insist on having something • *She waived her right to a first-class seat.*

> **SPELLING**
> Take care not to confuse with **wave**.

wake *VERB* wakes, waking, woke, woken
❶ to stop sleeping • *Wake up!* *I woke when I heard the bell.* ❷ to make someone stop sleeping • *You have woken the baby.*

wake *NOUN* wakes
❶ the track left on the water by a moving ship or boat ❷ currents of air left behind a moving aircraft ❸ a party held after a funeral ➤ **in the wake of something** following or coming after something

wakeful *ADJECTIVE*
unable to sleep

waken *VERB* wakens, wakening, wakened
to wake up or to wake someone up • *He wakened from a deep sleep.*

walk *VERB* walks, walking, walked
to move along on your feet at an ordinary speed

walk *NOUN* walks
❶ a journey on foot • *We went for a walk by the river.* ❷ the way that someone walks • *He has a funny walk.* ❸ a path or route for walking

walkabout *NOUN* walkabouts
❶ an informal stroll among a crowd by an important visitor ❷ (*Australian*) a journey through a remote area taken by an Australian Aboriginal wishing to experience a traditional way of life

walker *NOUN* walkers
someone who goes for a walk, especially a long one

walkie-talkie *NOUN* walkie-talkies (*informal*)
a small portable radio transmitter and receiver

walking stick *NOUN* walking sticks
a stick used as a support while walking

walk of life *NOUN* walks of life
a person's occupation or social position • *He has friends from all walks of life.*

walkover *NOUN* walkovers
an easy victory

wall *NOUN* walls
❶ a continuous upright structure, usually made of brick or stone, forming one of the sides of a building or room or supporting something or enclosing an area ❷ the outside part of something • *the stomach wall* ❸ something that forms a barrier • *a wall of silence*

wall *VERB* walls, walling, walled
to block or surround something with a wall • *The entrance to the tomb was then walled up.*

wallaby *NOUN* wallabies
a kind of small kangaroo

walled *ADJECTIVE*
surrounded by a wall • *a walled garden*

wallet *NOUN* wallets
a small flat folding case for holding banknotes, credit cards, documents, etc.

wallflower *NOUN* wallflowers
a garden plant with fragrant flowers, blooming in spring **WORD ORIGIN** because it is often found growing on old walls

wallop (*informal*) *VERB* wallops, walloping, walloped
to hit or beat someone

wallop *NOUN* wallops
a heavy blow or punch

wallow *VERB* wallows, wallowing, wallowed
❶ to roll about in water or mud ❷ to get great pleasure by being surrounded by something • *They spent the whole weekend wallowing in luxury.*

wallow *NOUN* wallows
an area of mud or shallow water where mammals go to wallow

wallpaper *NOUN* wallpapers
❶ paper used to cover the inside walls of

a
b
c
d
e
f
g
h
i
j
k
l
m
n
o
p
q
r
s
t
u
v
w
x
y
z

rooms ❷ the background pattern or picture that you choose to have on your computer screen

walnut *NOUN* walnuts
❶ an edible nut with a wrinkled surface
❷ the wood from the tree that bears this nut, used for making furniture

walrus *NOUN* walruses
a large Arctic sea animal with two long tusks

waltz *NOUN* waltzes
a dance with three beats to a bar

waltz *VERB* waltzes, waltzing, waltzed
to dance a waltz
➤ **waltz in** to enter a place in a very casual and confident way

wan (say **wonn**) *ADJECTIVE*
❶ pale from being ill or tired ❷ a wan smile is faint and without enthusiasm
➤ **wanly** *ADVERB*

wand *NOUN* wands
a thin rod, especially one used by a magician or wizard

wander *VERB* wanders, wandering, wandered
❶ to go about without trying to reach a particular place • *We spent the afternoon wandering around the town.* ❷ to leave the right path or direction; to stray • *Don't let the sheep wander.* ❸ to be distracted or move on to other things • *He let his attention wander.*
➤ **wanderer** *NOUN*

wander *NOUN*
a wandering journey

wane *VERB* wanes, waning, waned
❶ the moon wanes when it shows a bright area that becomes gradually smaller after being full. (The opposite is **wax**.) ❷ to become less, smaller or weaker • *His popularity was waning.*

wane *NOUN*
➤ **on the wane** becoming less or weaker

wangle *VERB* wangles, wangling, wangled
(*informal*) to get or arrange something by trickery or clever planning • *He's managed to wangle himself a trip to Paris.*

want *VERB* wants, wanting, wanted
❶ to have a desire or wish for something • *What do you want for breakfast?* ❷ to need something • *Your hair wants cutting.*
➤ **want for something** to lack something that you need • *They did not want for money.*

want *NOUN* wants
❶ a wish to have something ❷ a lack or need

of something • *People were dying for want of water.*

wanted *ADJECTIVE*
a wanted person is a suspected criminal that the police wish to find or arrest

wanting *ADJECTIVE*
lacking in what is needed or usual • *He was certainly not wanting in courage.*

wanton (say **wonn**-ton) *ADJECTIVE*
done deliberately for no good reason
• *wanton damage*

war *NOUN* wars
❶ fighting between nations or groups, especially using armed forces ❷ a serious struggle or effort against crime, disease, poverty, etc.
➤ **at war** taking part in a war

warble *VERB* warbles, warbling, warbled
to sing with a gentle trilling sound, as some birds do

warble *NOUN* warbles
a warbling song or sound

warbler *NOUN* warblers
a kind of small songbird

war crime *NOUN* war crimes
a crime committed during a war that breaks international rules of war
➤ **war criminal** *NOUN*

ward *NOUN* wards
❶ a room with beds for patients in a hospital ❷ a child looked after by a guardian ❸ an area electing a councillor to represent it

ward *VERB* wards, warding, warded
➤ **ward something off** to keep something away • *He put his arms up to ward off the blows.*

warden *NOUN* wardens
an official who is in charge of a hostel, college, etc. or who supervises something

warder *NOUN* warders (*chiefly British*)
an official in charge of prisoners in a prison

wardrobe *NOUN* wardrobes
❶ a cupboard to hang clothes in ❷ a stock of clothes or costumes

ware *NOUN* wares
manufactured goods of a certain kind
• *hardware* • *silverware*
➤ **wares** goods offered for sale

warehouse *NOUN* warehouses
a large building where goods are stored

warfare *NOUN*
fighting a war • *years of siege warfare*

warhead *NOUN* **warheads**
the explosive head of a missile or torpedo

warlike *ADJECTIVE*
❶ fond of making war • *They were a warlike people.* ❷ threatening war

warm *ADJECTIVE*
❶ fairly hot; not cold or cool ❷ keeping the body warm • *a warm jumper* ❸ friendly or enthusiastic • *They gave us a warm welcome.* ❹ close to the right answer or to something hidden • *You're getting warm now.*

warm *VERB* **warms, warming, warmed** (also **warm up**)
to make something warm or to become warm • *I warmed my hands over the fire.*
➤ **warm to someone or something** to begin to like or become more interested in someone or something
➤ **warm up** to do gentle exercises to prepare yourself before playing sport

warm-blooded *ADJECTIVE*
a warm-blooded animal has blood that remains warm permanently

warmly *ADVERB*
❶ in warm clothes • *We were all warmly dressed.* ❷ in a friendly or enthusiastic way • *She greeted us warmly as we arrived.*

warmth *NOUN*
❶ being warm or keeping warm • *The cattle huddled together for warmth.* ❷ being friendly or enthusiastic • *She was touched by the warmth of their welcome.*

warn *VERB* **warns, warning, warned**
to tell someone about a danger or difficulty that may affect them or about what they should do • *I tried to warn him, but he wouldn't listen.*
➤ **warn someone off** to tell someone to keep away or to avoid a thing

warning *NOUN* **warnings**
something said or written to warn someone

warp (say worp) *VERB* **warps, warping, warped**
❶ to become bent or twisted out of shape, e.g. because of dampness; to bend or twist something in this way ❷ to distort a person's ideas or judgement • *Jealousy warped his mind.*

warp *NOUN* the lengthwise threads in weaving, crossed by the weft

warpath *NOUN*
➤ **on the warpath** angry and getting ready for a fight or argument

warrant *NOUN* **warrants**
a document that authorizes a person to do something (e.g. to search a place) or to receive something

warrant *VERB* **warrants, warranting, warranted**
❶ to justify or deserve something • *Nothing can warrant such rudeness.* ❷ to guarantee or bet that something will happen

warranty *NOUN* **warranties**
a guarantee • *a three-year warranty*

warren *NOUN* **warrens**
❶ a piece of ground where there are many burrows in which rabbits live and breed ❷ a building or place with many winding passages

warring *ADJECTIVE*
involved in a war • *the country's warring factions*

warrior *NOUN* **warriors**
a person who fights in battle; a soldier

warship *NOUN* **warships**
a ship used in war

wart *NOUN* **warts**
a small hard lump on the skin, caused by a virus

wartime *NOUN*
a time of war

wary (say **wair**-ee) *ADJECTIVE*
cautious about possible danger or difficulty • *She gave him a wary look.* • *Foxes tend to be wary of humans.*
➤ **warily** *ADVERB*
➤ **wariness** *NOUN*

wash *VERB* **washes, washing, washed**
❶ to clean something with water or other liquid ❷ to be washable • *Cotton washes easily.* ❸ to flow against or over something • *Waves washed over the deck.* ❹ to carry something along by a moving liquid • *A wave washed him overboard.* ❺ (*informal*) to be believable or acceptable • *That excuse just won't wash.*
➤ **be washed out** (*informal*) to be abandoned because of rain
➤ **wash up** to wash the dishes and cutlery after a meal

wash *NOUN* **washes**
❶ the action of washing ❷ a quantity of clothes for washing ❸ the disturbed water

a b c d e f g h i j k l m n o p q r s t u v w x y z

behind a moving ship ❹ a thin coating of colour or paint

washable *ADJECTIVE*
able to be washed without becoming damaged

washbasin *NOUN* washbasins
(*chiefly British*) a small sink for washing your hands and face

washer *NOUN* washers
❶ a small ring of rubber or metal placed between two surfaces (e.g. under a bolt or screw) to fit them tightly together ❷ a washing machine

washing *NOUN*
clothes that need to be washed or have been washed

washing machine *NOUN* washing machines
a machine for washing clothes

washing soda *NOUN*
sodium carbonate

washing-up *NOUN*
(*British*) washing the dishes and cutlery after a meal • *I'll give you a hand with the washing-up.*

wash-out *NOUN* wash-outs (*informal*)
a complete failure

wasn't (*mainly spoken*)
was not

> SPELLING
> Wasn't = was + not. Add an **apostrophe** between the **n** and the **t**.

wasp *NOUN* wasps
a stinging insect with black and yellow stripes round its body

wastage *NOUN*
loss of something by waste

waste *VERB* wastes, wasting, wasted
❶ to use more of something than you need or to use it without getting enough results ❷ to fail to use something • *You are wasting a good opportunity.*
> **waste away** to become gradually weaker or thinner • *She was wasting away for lack of food.*

waste *ADJECTIVE*
❶ left over or thrown away because it is not wanted • *waste paper* ❷ not used or usable • *an area of waste land*
> **lay waste to a place** to destroy the crops and buildings of an area

waste *NOUN* wastes
❶ wasting a thing or not using it well • *a waste of time* ❷ things that are not wanted or not used ❸ an area of desert or frozen land • *the wastes of the Siberia*

> SPELLING
> Take care not to confuse with **waist**, which means the narrow part in the middle of your body.

wasteful *ADJECTIVE*
using more than is needed; producing waste
> **wastefully** *NOUN*
> **wastefulness** *NOUN*

wasteland *NOUN* wastelands
a barren or empty area of land

watch *VERB* watches, watching, watched
❶ to look at a person or thing for some time ❷ to be on guard or ready for something to happen • *Watch for the traffic lights to turn green.* ❸ to pay careful attention to something • *Watch where you put your feet.* ❹ to take care of something • *His job is to watch the sheep.*
> **watch out** to be careful about something
> **watcher** *NOUN*

watch *NOUN* watches
❶ a device like a small clock, usually worn on the wrist ❷ the action of watching • *I'll keep watch while you have a look around.* ❸ a turn of being on duty in a ship

watchdog *NOUN* watchdogs
a dog kept to guard property

watchful *ADJECTIVE*
watching closely; alert • *She kept a watchful eye on the door.*
> **watchfully** *ADVERB*
> **watchfulness** *NOUN*

watchman *NOUN* watchmen
a person employed to look after an empty building at night

watchword *NOUN* watchwords
a word or phrase that sums up a group's policy; a slogan • *Our watchword is 'safety first'.*

water *NOUN* waters
❶ a colourless odourless tasteless liquid that is a compound of hydrogen and oxygen ❷ a lake or sea ❸ the tide • *at high water*
> **pass water** to urinate

water *VERB* waters, watering, watered
❶ to sprinkle or supply something with water • *Have you watered the plants?* ❷ to produce

tears or saliva • *It makes my mouth water.*
➤ **water something down** to dilute
something or make it weaker

watercolour *NOUN* **watercolours**
❶ paint made with pigment and water (not
oil) ❷ a painting done with this kind of paint

watercress *NOUN*
a kind of cress that grows in water

water cycle *NOUN*
the process by which water falls to the
ground as rain and snow, runs into rivers and
lakes, flows into the sea, evaporates into the
air and forms clouds and then falls to the
ground again

waterfall *NOUN* **waterfalls**
a place where a river or stream flows over the
edge of a cliff or large rock

watering can *NOUN* **watering cans**
a container with a long spout, for watering
plants

water lily *NOUN* **water lilies**
a plant that grows in water, with broad
floating leaves and large flowers

waterlogged *ADJECTIVE*
waterlogged ground is so wet that it cannot
soak up any more water

watermark *NOUN* **watermarks**
❶ a mark showing how high a river or tide
rises or how low it falls ❷ a faint design in
some kinds of paper that can be seen when
the paper is held up to the light

watermelon *NOUN* **watermelons**
a melon with a smooth green skin, red pulp
and black seeds

watermill *NOUN* **watermills**
a mill worked by a waterwheel

water polo *NOUN*
a game played by teams of swimmers with a
ball like a football

waterproof *ADJECTIVE*
that keeps out water • *a waterproof jacket*

waterproof *NOUN* **waterproofs**
(*British*) a waterproof coat or jacket

watershed *NOUN* **watersheds**
❶ a turning point in the course of events ❷ a
line of high land from which streams flow
down on each side

waterskiing *NOUN*
the sport of skimming over the surface of

water on a pair of flat boards (**waterskis**)
while being towed by a motor boat

waterspout *NOUN* **waterspouts**
a column of water formed when a whirlwind
draws up a whirling mass of water from the
sea

water table *NOUN* **water tables**
the level below which the ground is saturated
with water

watertight *ADJECTIVE*
❶ made or fastened so that water cannot get
in or out ❷ so carefully put together that it
has no mistakes and cannot be proved to be
untrue • *He has a watertight alibi.*

waterway *NOUN* **waterways**
a river or canal that ships can travel on

waterwheel *NOUN* **waterwheels**
a large wheel turned by a flow of water, used
to work machinery

waterworks *PLURAL NOUN*
a place with pumping machinery for
supplying water to a district

watery *ADJECTIVE*
❶ like water ❷ full of water or tears • *watery
eyes* ❸ made weak or thin by too much water
• *watery soup*

watt *NOUN* **watts**
a unit of electric power **WORD ORIGIN** named
after James *Watt*, a Scottish engineer, who
studied energy

wattage *NOUN* **wattages**
electric power measured in watts

wattle *NOUN* **wattles**
❶ sticks and twigs woven together to make
a fence or walls ❷ an Australian tree with
golden flowers

wave *NOUN* **waves**
❶ a ridge moving along the surface of the
sea or breaking on the shore ❷ a curling
piece of hair ❸ (*in science*) the wave-like
movement by which heat, light, sound or
electricity etc. travels ❹ a sudden build-up of
something • *She felt a wave of anger.* ❺ the
action of waving your hand • *He gave us a
little wave.*

wave *VERB* **waves, waving, waved**
❶ to move your hand from side to side as a
greeting or signal ❷ to move loosely from
side to side or up and down, or to move
something like this • *Flags were waving in the
wind.* ❸ to make a thing wavy ❹ to be wavy

waveband NOUN wavebands
a set of radio waves of similar length that are used for broadcasting radio programmes

wavelength NOUN wavelengths
❶ the distance between corresponding points on a sound wave or electromagnetic wave ❷ the length of a radio wave that a particular radio station uses to broadcast its programmes
➤ **on the same wavelength** having the same point of view as someone else • *We don't seem to be on the same wavelength at all*

wavelet NOUN wavelets
a small wave

waver VERB wavers, wavering, wavered
❶ to be unsteady or to move unsteadily • *For a second her voice wavered.* ❷ to begin to weaken • *He felt his courage start to waver.* ❸ to hesitate or be uncertain • *My mind wavered between going and staying.*

wavy ADJECTIVE
full of waves or curves • *brown wavy hair*
➤ **waviness** NOUN

wax NOUN waxes
❶ a soft substance that melts easily, used to make candles, crayons and polish ❷ beeswax

wax VERB waxes, waxing, waxed
❶ to coat or polish something with wax ❷ the moon waxes when it shows a bright area that becomes gradually larger. (The opposite is **wane.**) ❸ to become stronger or more important ❹ to speak or write in a certain way • *He waxed lyrical about his childhood.*

waxen ADJECTIVE
❶ made of wax ❷ like wax

waxwork NOUN waxworks
a lifelike model of a person made in wax

waxy ADJECTIVE
looking or feeling like wax • *He had pale waxy skin.*

way NOUN ways
❶ how something is done; a method or style • *This is the best way to make scrambled eggs.* ❷ a manner • *She spoke in a kindly way.* ❸ how to get somewhere; a route • *Can you tell me the way to the station?* • *We stopped for lunch on the way.* ❹ a direction or position • *Luckily she was looking the other way.* • *This picture is the wrong way up.* ❺ a path or road leading from one place to another ❻ a distance in space or time • *It's a long way from here.* ❼ a respect • *It's a good*

idea in some ways. ❽ a condition or state • *Things were in a bad way.*
➤ **get** or **have your own way** to make people let you do what you want
➤ **give way** ❶ to collapse ❷ to let other traffic go first ❸ to yield to someone's wishes or demands
➤ **in the way** preventing you from moving forwards or seeing something
➤ **no way** (*informal*) that is impossible!
➤ **under way** see **under**

way ADVERB (*informal*) far • *That is way beyond what we can afford.*

wayfarer NOUN wayfarers
a traveller, especially someone who is walking

waylay VERB waylays, waylaying, waylaid
to lie in wait for a person or people, especially in order to talk to them or rob them

wayside NOUN
➤ **fall by the wayside** to fail to continue doing something

wayward ADJECTIVE
disobedient; wilfully doing what you want

WC ABBREVIATION
a toilet (**WORD ORIGIN**) short for 'water closet', an old name for a toilet

we PRONOUN
a word used by a person to refer to himself or herself and another or others

weak ADJECTIVE
❶ having little strength, power or energy ❷ easy to break, damage or defeat ❸ not great in intensity • *a weak signal* ❹ poor at doing something

weaken VERB weakens, weakening, weakened
to make something weaker or to become weaker • *He could feel his grip weakening.*

weakling NOUN weaklings
a weak person or animal

weakly ADVERB
without much strength or force • *She smiled weakly.*

weakly ADJECTIVE
sickly; not strong

weakness NOUN weaknesses
❶ being weak ❷ a fault or something that you do not do well • *Our players have different strengths and weaknesses.*

weal NOUN weals
a raised mark left on someone's flesh by a whip or blow

wealth *NOUN*
❶ a lot of money or property; riches ❷ a large quantity • *The book has a wealth of illustrations.*

wealthy *ADJECTIVE* wealthier, wealthiest
having wealth; rich

wean *VERB* weans, weaning, weaned
to get a baby used to taking food other than milk
➤ **wean someone off something** to make someone give up a habit gradually

weapon *NOUN* weapons
something used to harm or kill people in a battle or fight

weaponry *NOUN*
weapons • *an exhibition of Roman armour and weaponry*

wear *VERB* wears, wearing, wore, worn
❶ to have clothes, jewellery, etc. on your body ❷ to have a certain look on your face • *She wore a frown.* ❸ to damage something by rubbing or using it often; to become damaged in this way • *The carpet has worn thin.* ❹ to last while being used • *This material wears well.*
➤ **wearable** *ADJECTIVE*
➤ **wearer** *NOUN*
➤ **wear off** ❶ to be removed by wear or use ❷ to become less strong or intense
➤ **wear on** to pass gradually • *The night wore on.*
➤ **wear out** to become weak or useless from continuous use
➤ **wear someone out** to make someone very tired

wear *NOUN*
❶ what you wear; clothes • *evening wear* ❷ (also **wear and tear**) gradual damage done by rubbing or using something

wearisome *ADJECTIVE*
causing weariness; tiring

weary *ADJECTIVE* wearier, weariest
❶ worn out and tired ❷ tiring • *It's weary work.*
➤ **wearily** *ADVERB*
➤ **weariness** *NOUN*

weary *VERB* wearies, wearying, wearied
❶ to make someone weary ❷ to grow tired of something • *The children never wearied of hearing her stories.*

weasel *NOUN* weasels
a small fierce animal with a slender body and reddish-brown fur

weather *NOUN*
the rain, snow, wind, sunshine etc. at a particular time or place
➤ **under the weather** feeling ill or depressed

weather *VERB* weathers, weathering, weathered
❶ to become worn or change colour because of the effects of the weather; to make something do this • *The wind and rain have weathered the cliffs.* ❷ to come through a difficult time or experience successfully • *The ship weathered the storm.*

weathercock, weathervane *NOUN*
weathercocks or weathervanes
a pointer, often shaped like a cockerel, that turns in the wind and shows from which direction it is blowing

weave *VERB* weaves, weaving, wove, woven
❶ to make material or baskets by crossing threads or strips under and over each other ❷ to put a story together • *She wove a thrilling tale.* ❸ (past tense also **weaved**) to move from side to side to get round things in the way • *He weaved through the traffic.*
➤ **weaver** *NOUN*

weave *NOUN* weaves
a style of weaving • *a loose weave*

web *NOUN* webs
❶ a cobweb ❷ something complicated • *a web of lies*
➤ **the Web** the World Wide Web

webbed *ADJECTIVE*
webbed feet have toes joined by pieces of skin, as ducks' and frogs' feet do

webcam *NOUN* webcams
a camera that is connected to a computer so that what it records can be seen on a website as it happens

weblog *NOUN* weblogs
a blog

web page *NOUN* web pages
a document forming part of a website

website *NOUN* websites
a place on the Internet where you can get information about a subject, company, etc. • *Visit our website to learn more.*

wed *VERB* weds, wedding, wedded
to marry someone

wedding *NOUN* weddings
the ceremony and celebration when a couple get married

a
b
c
d
e
f
g
h
i
j
k
l
m
n
o
p
q
r
s
t
u
v
w
x
y
z

A
B
C
D
E
F
G
H
I
J
K
L
M
N
O
P
Q
R
S
T
U
V
W
X
Y
Z

wedge *NOUN* wedges
1 a piece of wood or metal that is thick at one end and thin at the other. It is pushed between things to force them apart or prevent something from moving. 2 a wedge-shaped thing • *a wedge of cheese*

wedge *VERB* wedges, wedging, wedged
1 to keep something in place with a wedge • *I wedged the door open.* 2 to pack things tightly together • *Ten of us were wedged in the lift.*

wedlock *NOUN*
the state of being married

Wednesday *NOUN*
the day of the week following Tuesday
WORD ORIGIN from Old English *Wodnesdaeg* = day of Woden or Odin, the chief Norse god
SPELLING
Take care, there is a **d** before the **n** and an **e** after it.

wee *ADJECTIVE* (*Scottish*)
little or small

weed *NOUN* weeds
a wild plant that grows where it is not wanted

weed *VERB* weeds, weeding, weeded
to remove weeds from the ground

weedy *ADJECTIVE* weedier, weediest
1 full of weeds 2 thin and weak

week *NOUN* weeks
1 a period of seven days, especially from Sunday to the following Saturday 2 the part of the week that does not include the weekend

weekday *NOUN* weekdays
a day other than Saturday or Sunday

weekend *NOUN* weekends
Saturday and Sunday

weekly *ADJECTIVE & ADVERB*
happening or done once a week

weeny *ADJECTIVE* (*informal*)
tiny

weep *VERB* weeps, weeping, wept
1 to shed tears; to cry 2 to ooze moisture in drops
➤ **weepy** *ADJECTIVE*

weeping willow *NOUN* weeping willows
a willow tree that has drooping branches

weevil *NOUN* weevils
a kind of small beetle

weft *NOUN*
the threads on a loom that are woven across the warp

weigh *VERB* weighs, weighing, weighed
1 to measure the weight of something 2 to have a certain weight • *What do you weigh?* 3 to be important or have influence • *Her evidence weighed heavily with the jury.*
➤ **weigh anchor** to raise the anchor and start a voyage
➤ **weigh someone down** to depress or trouble someone
➤ **weigh something down** to hold something down with something heavy
➤ **weigh something out** to take a certain weight of a substance from a larger quantity
➤ **weigh something up** to think about something carefully before deciding what to do

weight *NOUN* weights
1 how heavy something is; the amount that something weighs 2 a piece of metal of known weight, especially one used on scales to weigh things 3 a heavy object, used to hold things down 4 importance or influence

weight *VERB* weights, weighting, weighted
to attach a weight to something • *The fishing nets are weighted with lead.*
SPELLING
The 'ay' sound is spelt **eigh**.

weightless *ADJECTIVE*
having no weight, for example when travelling in space
➤ **weightlessness** *NOUN*

weightlifting *NOUN*
the sport or exercise of lifting heavy weights
➤ **weightlifter** *NOUN*

weighty *ADJECTIVE* weightier, weightiest
1 heavy 2 serious and important • *These are weighty matters.*

weir (say weer) *NOUN* weirs
a small dam across a river or canal to control the flow of water

weird *ADJECTIVE*
very strange or unnatural • *I had a weird dream last night.*
➤ **weirdly** *ADVERB*
➤ **weirdness** *NOUN*
SPELLING
In weird, **e** before **i** is the right way round.

welcome *NOUN* welcomes
a greeting or reception, especially a kind or friendly one

welcome *ADJECTIVE*
❶ that you are glad to receive or see • *This is a welcome surprise.* ❷ allowed or invited to do or take something • *You are welcome to come.*

welcome *VERB* welcomes, welcoming, welcomed
❶ to show that you are pleased when a person arrives ❷ to be glad to receive or hear of something • *We welcome this decision.*

weld *VERB* welds, welding, welded
to join pieces of metal or plastic by heating and pressing or hammering them together

welfare *NOUN*
people's health, happiness and comfort

welfare state *NOUN*
a system in which a country's government provides money to pay for health care, social services, benefits, etc.

well *ADVERB* better, best
❶ in a good or suitable way • *She swims well.* ❷ thoroughly; to a great extent • *Make sure it is well cooked.* ❸ probably or reasonably • *This may well be our last chance.*
➤ **well off** ❶ fairly rich ❷ in a good situation

well *ADJECTIVE* better, best
❶ in good health • *He is not well.* ❷ satisfactory; fine • *All is well.*

well *NOUN* wells
❶ a deep hole dug to bring up water or oil from underground ❷ a deep space in a building, e.g. containing a staircase

well *VERB* wells, welling, welled
to rise or flow up • *Tears welled up in our eyes.*

well-being *NOUN*
good health, happiness and comfort

wellies *PLURAL NOUN* (*informal*)
wellingtons

wellingtons *PLURAL NOUN*
rubber or plastic waterproof boots
WORD ORIGIN named after the first Duke of *Wellington*, who wore long leather boots

well-known *ADJECTIVE*
known by many people • *a well-known actor* • *a well-known fact*

well-mannered *ADJECTIVE*
having good manners

well-meaning *ADJECTIVE*
having good intentions

well-nigh *ADVERB*
almost or nearly • *Passing the test seems well-nigh impossible.*

well-read *ADJECTIVE*
having read a lot of good books

well-to-do *ADJECTIVE*
fairly rich

welt *NOUN* welts
a raised mark left on someone's flesh by a whip or blow; a weal

welter *NOUN*
a confused mixture; a jumble • *a welter of information*

wench *NOUN* wenches (*old use*)
a girl or young woman

wend *VERB* wends, wending, wended
➤ **wend your way** to go somewhere slowly or by an indirect route

weren't (*mainly spoken*)
were not

werewolf *NOUN* werewolves
in legends and stories, a person who changes into a wolf when the moon is full

west *NOUN*
❶ the direction where the sun sets, opposite east ❷ the western part of a country, city or other area

west *ADJECTIVE & ADVERB*
towards or in the west; coming from the west • *We sailed west.* • *the west coast* • *a west wind*
➤ **westerly** *ADJECTIVE*

western *ADJECTIVE*
of or in the west

western *NOUN* westerns
a film or story about cowboys or American Indians in western North America during the 19th and early 20th centuries
➤ **westerner** *NOUN*
➤ **westernmost** *ADJECTIVE*

westward *ADJECTIVE & ADVERB*
towards the west
➤ **westwards** *ADVERB*

wet *ADJECTIVE* wetter, wettest
❶ soaked or covered in water or other liquid ❷ not yet dry • *wet paint* ❸ rainy • *It's been wet here all day.*
➤ **wetness** *NOUN*

wet *VERB* wets, wetting, wet or wetted
to make something wet • *Wet the brush slightly before putting it in the paint.*

wet suit *NOUN* wet suits
a close-fitting rubber suit, worn by skin divers and windsurfers to keep them warm and dry

whack (*informal*) *VERB* whacks, whacking, whacked
to hit someone or something hard

whack *NOUN* whacks
a hard hit or blow

whale *NOUN* whales
a very large sea mammal
➤ **have a whale of a time** (*informal*) to enjoy yourself very much

whaler *NOUN* whalers
a person or ship that hunts whales

whaling *NOUN*
hunting whales

wharf (say worf) *NOUN* wharves or wharfs
a quay where ships are loaded and unloaded

what *DETERMINER*
❶ used to ask the amount or kind of something • *What kind of music do you like?* ❷ used to say how strange or great a person or thing is • *What an idiot!*

what *PRONOUN*
❶ what thing or things • *What did you say?* ❷ the thing that • *This is what you must do.*
➤ **what's what** (*informal*) which things are important or useful • *She knows what's what.*

SPELLING
There is a silent **h** after the **w** in **what**.

whatever *PRONOUN*
❶ anything or everything • *Do whatever you like.* ❷ no matter what • *Keep calm, whatever happens.*

whatever *DETERMINER*
of any kind or amount • *Take whatever books you need.*

whatever *ADVERB*
at all • *There is no doubt whatever.*

whatsoever *ADVERB*
at all • *There is no chance whatsoever.*

wheat *NOUN*
a cereal plant from which flour is made

wheedle *VERB* wheedles, wheedling, wheedled
to persuade someone to do something by coaxing or flattering them • *She was good at wheedling money out of her mother.*

wheel *NOUN* wheels
❶ a round device that turns on a shaft that passes through its centre ❷ a steering wheel ❸ a horizontal revolving disc on which clay is made into a pot

wheel *VERB* wheels, wheeling, wheeled
❶ to push a bicycle or trolley etc. along on its wheels ❷ to move or fly in a wide circle or curve • *Birds wheeled above the ship.*
➤ **wheel round** to turn round quickly to face another way

wheelbarrow *NOUN* wheelbarrows
a small cart with one wheel at the front and legs at the back, pushed by handles

wheelchair *NOUN* wheelchairs
a chair on wheels, used by a person who cannot walk

wheel clamp *NOUN* wheel clamps
(*British*) a device that can be locked around a vehicle's wheel to stop it from moving, used especially on cars that have been parked illegally

wheelie *NOUN* wheelies
(*informal*) the stunt of riding a bicycle or motorcycle for a short distance with the front wheel off the ground

wheelie bin *NOUN* wheelie bins
(*British*) a large dustbin on wheels

wheeze *VERB* wheezes, wheezing, wheezed
to make a hoarse whistling sound as you breathe

wheeze *NOUN* wheezes
the sound of wheezing
➤ **wheezy** *ADJECTIVE*

whelk *NOUN* whelks
a shellfish that looks like a snail

whelp *NOUN* whelps
a young dog; a pup

when *ADVERB*
at what time; at which time • *When does the film start?*

when *CONJUNCTION*
❶ at the time that • *The bird flew away when I moved.* ❷ although; considering that • *Why are you going canoeing when you can't swim?*

whence *ADVERB*
(*formal*)
from where; from which

whenever CONJUNCTION
at whatever time; every time • *Whenever I go there, it's raining.*

where ADVERB & CONJUNCTION
in or to what place or that place • *Where did you put it?* • *Leave it where it is.*

where PRONOUN
❶ what place • *Where does she come from?*
❷ the place that • *This is where I belong.*

whereabouts ADVERB
in or near what place • *Whereabouts are you going?*

whereabouts PLURAL NOUN
the place where something is • *Do you know the whereabouts of my radio?*

whereas CONJUNCTION
but in contrast • *Some people enjoy sport, whereas others hate it.*

whereby ADVERB
by which; by means of which • *I have a plan whereby such accidents can be avoided in the future.*

wherefore ADVERB (old use)
why; for what reason

whereupon CONJUNCTION
after which; and then

wherever ADVERB
in or to whatever place; no matter where • *You can sit wherever you like.*

whet VERB whets, whetting, whetted
to sharpen a blade or edge by rubbing it against a stone
➤ **whet your appetite** to make you feel hungry
> SPELLING
> Take care not to confuse with **wet**.

whether CONJUNCTION
used to show a doubt or choice between two possibilities; if • *I don't know whether to believe her or not.*

whetstone NOUN whetstones
a shaped stone for sharpening tools

whey (say way) NOUN
the watery liquid left when milk forms curds

which DETERMINER
what particular • *Which way did he go?*

which PRONOUN
❶ what person or thing • *Which is your desk?*
❷ the person or thing referred to • *The*

film, which is a western, will be shown on Saturday.

> GRAMMAR
> You use the relative pronoun **which** when it begins a clause giving additional information that you could leave out: *The book, which is now out of print, was a bestseller in its day.* You use **that** or **which** when it begins a clause that defines or identifies something important and which cannot be left out: *The book which I'm looking for is now out of print. The book I'm looking for is now out of print.*
>
> See also the panel on **clauses**.

> SPELLING
> There is a silent **h** after the **w** in **which**.

whichever PRONOUN & DETERMINER
no matter which; any which • *Choose whichever colour you like.*

whiff NOUN whiffs
a slight smell of something • *a whiff of perfume*

Whig NOUN Whigs
a member of a political party in the 17th-19th centuries, opposed to the Tories

while CONJUNCTION
❶ during the time that; as long as • *He was humming a tune while he worked.*
❷ although; but • *She is dark, while her sister is fair.*

while NOUN
a period of time • *We haven't been on touch for a while.*

while VERB whiles, whiling, whiled
➤ **while away time** to pass time in a leisurely way • *We whiled away the afternoon on the river.*

whilst CONJUNCTION
during the time that; while

whim NOUN whims
a sudden wish to do or have something • *He gave in to his daughter's every whim.*

whimper VERB whimpers, whimpering, whimpered
to cry or whine softly

whimper NOUN whimpers
a sound of whimpering

whimsical ADJECTIVE
slightly odd and playful • *His writing has a*

a b c d e f g h i j k l m n o p q r s t u v w x y z

whimsical quality.
➤ **whimsically** *ADVERB*

whine *VERB* whines, whining, whined
❶ to make a long high miserable cry or a shrill sound ❷ to complain in a petty or feeble way

whine *NOUN* whines
a whining sound or cry

SPELLING
There is a silent **h** after the **w** in **whine**.

whinge *VERB* whinges, whinging or whingeing, whinged
(*British*) (*informal*) to grumble persistently

whinny *VERB* whinnies, whinnying, whinnied
a horse whinnies when it neighs gently or happily

whinny *NOUN* whinnies
a gentle neigh

whip *NOUN* whips
a cord or strip of leather fixed to a handle and used for hitting people or animals

whip *VERB* whips, whipping, whipped
❶ to beat a person or animal with a whip
❷ to beat cream until it becomes thick
❸ (*informal*) to steal something
➤ **whip something out** (*informal*) to take something out quickly or suddenly • *He whipped out a gun.*
➤ **whip something up** to stir up people's feelings • *They quickly whipped up support for the idea.*

whippet *NOUN* whippets
a small dog rather like a greyhound, used for racing

whirl *VERB* whirls, whirling, whirled
to turn or spin very quickly or to make something do this

whirl *NOUN* whirls
a quick turn or spin

whirlpool *NOUN* whirlpools
a whirling current of water, often drawing floating objects towards its centre

whirlwind *NOUN* whirlwinds
a strong wind that whirls round a central point

whirr *VERB* whirrs, whirring, whirred
to make a continuous buzzing sound • *The motor started to whirr.*

whirr *NOUN* whirrs
a continuous buzzing sound

whisk *VERB* whisks, whisking, whisked
❶ to move or brush something away quickly and lightly • *A waiter whisked away our plates.* ❷ to take a person somewhere very quickly • *After the performance she was whisked away in a limousine.* ❸ to beat eggs, etc. until they are frothy

whisk *NOUN* whisks
❶ a kitchen tool used for whisking things ❷ a whisking movement

whisker *NOUN* whiskers
❶ whiskers are the long stiff hairs growing near the mouth of a cat ❷ a man's whiskers are the hair growing on his face, especially on his cheeks

whisky *NOUN* whiskies
a strong alcoholic drink **WORD ORIGIN** from Scottish Gaelic *uisge beatha* = water of life

whisper *VERB* whispers, whispering, whispered
❶ to speak very softly ❷ to talk secretly; to spread a rumour

whisper *NOUN* whispers
❶ a whispering tone of voice ❷ a rumour

SPELLING
There is a silent **h** after the **w** in **whisper**.

whist *NOUN*
a card game usually for four people

whistle *VERB* whistles, whistling, whistled
❶ to make a shrill or musical sound by blowing through your lips ❷ to make a shrill sound • *The kettle was whistling away.* • *An arrow whistled through the air.*

whistle *NOUN* whistles
❶ a whistling sound ❷ a device that makes a shrill sound when air or steam is blown through it

whit *NOUN*
the least possible amount • *He could not have a done a whit better himself.*

white *NOUN* whites
❶ the very lightest colour, like snow or salt
❷ the transparent substance (**albumen**) round the yolk of an egg, which turns white when it is cooked ❸ a person with light-coloured skin

white *ADJECTIVE*
❶ of the colour white ❷ having light-coloured skin ❸ very pale from the effects of illness, fear or worry ❹ white coffee is made with milk
➤ **whiteness** *NOUN*

whitebait *NOUN* whitebait
a small silvery-white fish

white elephant *NOUN* white elephants
a useless possession, especially one that is expensive to keep

white-hot *ADJECTIVE*
extremely hot; so hot that heated metal looks white

white lie *NOUN* white lies
a harmless or trivial lie that you tell in order to avoid hurting someone's feelings

white meat *NOUN*
poultry, veal, rabbit and pork

whiten *VERB* whitens, whitening, whitened
to become white or to make something white • *His face whitened.* • *A fall of snow had whitened the tops of the trees*

whitewash *NOUN*
❶ a white liquid containing lime or powdered chalk, used for painting walls and ceilings ❷ concealing mistakes or other unpleasant facts so that someone will not be punished

whitewash *VERB* whitewashes, whitewashing, whitewashed
to coat a wall or ceiling with whitewash

whither *ADVERB* (old use)
to what place • *They did not know whither they were going.*

whiting *NOUN* whiting
a small edible sea fish with white flesh
WORD ORIGIN from Dutch *wijt* = white

whittle *VERB* whittles, whittling, whittled
to shape wood by trimming thin slices off the surface
➤ **whittle something down** to reduce something by removing various things from it • *We need to whittle down the cost.*

whizz, whiz *VERB* whizzes, whizzing, whizzed
to move very quickly, often making a sound like something rushing through the air • *Bullets whizzed past my ear.* • *A police car whizzed by.*

who *PRONOUN*
❶ which person or people • *Who threw that?* ❷ the particular person or people • *This is the boy who stole the apples.*

whoa *EXCLAMATION*
a command to a horse to stop or stand still

whoever *PRONOUN*
❶ any or every person who • *Whoever comes is welcome.* ❷ no matter who • *I don't want to see anyone, whoever it is.*

whole *ADJECTIVE*
❶ complete; all of • *Could you eat a whole pizza?* • *I spent the whole day in bed.* ❷ not broken or cut; in one piece • *Snakes swallow their prey whole.*

whole *NOUN*
❶ the full amount ❷ a complete thing
➤ **as a whole** in general
➤ **on the whole** considering everything; mainly

SPELLING
Whole is different from hole, which is a gap or opening.

wholefood *NOUN* wholefoods
(*British*) food that has been processed as little as possible

wholehearted *ADJECTIVE*
given without doubts or reservations • *You have my wholehearted support.*

wholemeal *ADJECTIVE*
(*British*) made from the whole grain of wheat

whole number *NOUN* whole numbers
a number without fractions

wholesale *NOUN*
the business of selling goods in large quantities to be resold by others. Compare with **retail**.
➤ **wholesaler** *NOUN*

wholesale *ADJECTIVE & ADVERB*
❶ on a large scale; including everybody or everything • *wholesale destruction* ❷ in the wholesale trade

wholesome *ADJECTIVE*
healthy and good for you • *simple wholesome food*
➤ **wholesomeness** *NOUN*

wholly *ADVERB*
completely or entirely • *She is not wholly to blame.*

whom *PRONOUN*
the form of **who** used when it is the object of a verb or comes after a preposition, as in *the*

a
b
c
d
e
f
g
h
i
j
k
l
m
n
o
p
q
r
s
t
u
v
w
x
y
z

boy whom I saw or to whom we spoke

USAGE

Whom can sound rather formal. In modern English, especially in speech and less formal writing, it often sounds more natural to use who, as in the boy who you saw last night (or simply the boy you saw last night) and Who were you referring to?

whoop (say woop) NOUN **whoops**
a loud cry of excitement

whoop VERB **whoops, whooping, whooped**
to give a whoop

whoopee EXCLAMATION
a cry of joy

whooping cough (say **hoop**-ing) NOUN
an infectious disease that causes spasms of coughing and gasping for breath

whopper NOUN **whoppers** (informal)
❶ something very large ❷ a blatant lie

whopping ADJECTIVE (informal)
very large or remarkable • He has scored a whopping 72 points.

whorl NOUN **whorls**
❶ a coil or curved shape ❷ a ring of leaves or petals

who's (mainly spoken)
who is; who has

SPELLING

Who's is different from **whose**: • Who's next in the queue? • Whose coat is this?

whose DETERMINER & PRONOUN
belonging to what person or persons; of whom; of which • Whose bike is that? • That is the girl whose party we went to.

SPELLING

Do not confuse this word with **who's**: • Whose coat is this? • Who's next in the queue?

why ADVERB
for what reason or purpose; the particular reason on account of which • Why didn't you tell me? • This is why I came.

wick NOUN **wicks**
❶ the string that goes through the middle of a candle and is lit ❷ the strip of material that you light in a lamp or heater that uses oil

wicked ADJECTIVE
❶ morally bad or cruel ❷ mischievous

• He gave me a wicked grin. ❸ (informal) excellent; very good
➤ **wickedly** ADVERB
➤ **wickedness** NOUN
WORD ORIGIN from Old English wicca = witch

wicker NOUN
thin canes or twigs woven together to make baskets, fences or furniture
➤ **wickerwork** NOUN

wicket NOUN **wickets**
❶ a set of three stumps and two bails used in cricket ❷ the strip of ground between the wickets

wicket-gate NOUN **wicket-gates**
a small gate used to save opening a much larger one

wicketkeeper NOUN **wicketkeepers**
the fielder in cricket who stands behind the batsman's wicket

wide ADJECTIVE
❶ measuring a lot from side to side; not narrow • The river was wide. ❷ measuring from side to side • The cloth is one metre wide. ❸ covering a great range • My uncle has a wide knowledge of birds. ❹ fully open • staring with wide eyes ❺ missing the target • The shot was wide of the mark.

wide ADVERB
❶ to the full extent; far apart • The door was wide open. ❷ missing the target • The shot went wide. ❸ over a large area • She travelled far and wide.
➤ **wide awake** fully awake

widely ADVERB
commonly; among many people • They are widely admired.

widen VERB **widens, widening, widened**
to make something wider or to become wider • His eyes widened in amazement.

widespread ADJECTIVE
existing in many places or over a wide area • a widespread belief

widow NOUN **widows**
a woman whose husband has died

widowed ADJECTIVE
made a widow or widower

widower NOUN **widowers**
a man whose wife has died

width NOUN **widths**
❶ how wide something is • The room is eight metres in width. ❷ the distance of a swimming pool from one side to the other

wield *VERB* wields, wielding, wielded
❶ to hold and use a weapon or tool • *a knight wielding a sword* ❷ to have and use power or influence

wife *NOUN* wives
the woman someone is married to

wi-fi *NOUN*
the system for connecting computers, mobile phones, etc. to the Internet without using wires

wig *NOUN* wigs
a covering made of real or artificial hair, worn on the head

wiggle *VERB* wiggles, wiggling, wiggled
to move something from side to side • *They wiggled their hips in time to the music.*

wiggle *NOUN* wiggles
a wiggling movement
➤ **wiggly** *ADJECTIVE*

wigwam *NOUN* wigwams
a tent formerly used by Native Americans, made by fastening skins or mats over poles

wild *ADJECTIVE*
❶ wild animals and plants live or grow in their natural state and are not looked after by people ❷ wild land is in its natural state and has not been changed by people • *a wild landscape* ❸ not controlled; very violent or excited • *There were wild celebrations in the streets.* • *She went wild when she saw the mess.* ❹ very foolish or unreasonable • *You do have wild ideas.* ❺ a wild guess has not been thought about carefully and is unlikely to be correct
➤ **wildness** *NOUN*

wild *NOUN* wilds
❶ the wild is the natural environment in which animals live • *I would love to see a herd of elephants in the wild.* ❷ the wilds are remote areas far from towns and cities

wildebeest *NOUN* wildebeest or wildebeests
a gnu

wilderness *NOUN* wildernesses
an area of natural land which is wild and uncultivated

wildfire *NOUN*
➤ **spread like wildfire** to spread or become known over a large area very fast • *News of his arrival spread like wildfire.*

wildlife *NOUN*
wild animals in their natural setting

wildly *ADVERB*
❶ in a way that is not controlled • *My heart was beating wildly.* ❷ extremely; very • *The story has been wildly exaggerated.*

Wild West *NOUN*
the western states of the USA during the period when the first Europeans were settling there and there was not much law and order

wiles *PLURAL NOUN*
clever tricks that someone uses to get what they want

wilful *ADJECTIVE*
❶ obstinately determined to do what you want • *a wilful child* ❷ done deliberately • *This is wilful disobedience.*
➤ **wilfully** *ADVERB*
➤ **wilfulness** *NOUN*

will *AUXILIARY VERB*
used to talk about what will happen in the future and in questions or promises • *They will arrive soon.* • *Will you shut the door?* • *I will get my revenge.*

will *NOUN* wills
❶ the mental power to decide and control what you do ❷ a desire; a chosen decision • *I wrote the letter against my will.* ❸ determination to do something • *She has a strong will to succeed.* ❹ a legal document saying what is to be done with someone's possessions when they die
➤ **at will** whenever you like • *You can come and go at will.*

will *VERB* wills, willing, willed
to use your will power to try to influence something • *I was willing you to win!*

> **GRAMMAR**
> See also the panel at **shall**.

willing *ADJECTIVE*
ready and happy to do what is wanted • *Are you willing to help?*
➤ **willingly** *ADVERB*
➤ **willingness** *NOUN*

will-o'-the-wisp *NOUN* will-o'-the-wisps
❶ a flickering spot of light seen on marshy ground ❷ something that is impossible to achieve **WORD ORIGIN** from *Will*, short for *William*, + an old sense of *wisp* = small bundle of straw burned as a torch

willow *NOUN* willows
a tree or shrub with flexible branches, usually growing near water

A

B

C

D

E

F

G

H

I

J

K

L

M

N

O

P

Q

R

S

T

U

V

W

X

Y

Z

will power *NOUN*
strength of mind to control what you do

willy–nilly *ADVERB*
❶ whether you want to or not ❷ without planning; haphazardly **WORD ORIGIN** from *will I, nill I* (= will I, will I not)

wilt *VERB* wilts, wilting, wilted
❶ a flower or plant wilts when it loses freshness and droops ❷ to lose your strength or energy • *After two hours in the sun, we were beginning to wilt.*

wily (say **wy**-lee) *ADJECTIVE*
cunning or crafty
➤ **wiliness** *NOUN*

wimp *NOUN* wimps
(*informal*) a weak or timid person

wimple *NOUN* wimples
a piece of cloth folded round the head and neck, worn by women in the Middle Ages

win *VERB* wins, winning, won
❶ to defeat your opponents in a game, contest or battle ❷ to get or achieve something by a victory or by using effort or skill • *She won second prize.* ❸ to gain someone's favour or support • *By the end he had won over the audience.*

win *NOUN* wins
a victory in a game or contest

wince *VERB* winces, wincing, winced
to make a slight movement because you are in pain or embarrassed

winch *NOUN* winches
a device for lifting or pulling things, using a rope or cable that winds onto a revolving drum or wheel

winch *VERB* winches, winching, winched
to lift or pull something with a winch

wind (rhymes with tinned) *NOUN* winds
❶ a current of air ❷ gas in the stomach or intestines that makes you feel uncomfortable ❸ the breath that you need to do something, e.g. for running or speaking ❹ the wind instruments of an orchestra
➤ **get wind of something** to hear a rumour about something
➤ **put the wind up someone** (*informal*) to frighten or alarm someone

wind (rhymes with tinned) *VERB* winds, winding, winded
to make a person out of breath • *The climb had winded us.*

wind (rhymes with find) *VERB* winds, winding, wound
❶ to have a lot of bends or curves • *The river winds down the valley.* ❷ to wrap or twist a thing round something else • *She wound a bandage round her finger.* ❸ to move something up or down by turning a handle • *I can't wind the window down.* ❹ (also **wind up**) to make a clock or watch work by tightening its spring
➤ **winder** *NOUN*
➤ **wind up** (*informal*) to end up in a place or situation • *He wound up in jail.*
➤ **wind something up** to close a business

windbag *NOUN* windbags (*informal*)
a person who talks too much

windfall *NOUN* windfalls
❶ a piece of unexpected good luck, especially a sum of money ❷ a fruit blown off a tree by the wind

wind farm *NOUN* wind farms
a group of windmills or wind turbines for producing electricity

wind instrument *NOUN* wind instruments
a musical instrument played by blowing, e.g. a trumpet or flute

windlass *NOUN* windlasses
a machine for pulling or lifting things (e.g. a bucket from a well), with a rope or cable that is wound round an axle by turning a handle

windmill *NOUN* windmills
a mill worked by the wind turning its sails

window *NOUN* windows
❶ an opening in a wall or roof or in the side of a vehicle to let in light and air, usually filled with glass ❷ (*in computing*) a framed area on a computer screen used for a particular purpose **WORD ORIGIN** from Old Norse *vind* = wind, air + *auga* = eye

window–shopping *NOUN*
looking at things in shop windows but not buying anything

windpipe *NOUN* windpipes
the tube by which air passes from the throat to the lungs

windscreen *NOUN* windscreens
(*British*) the glass in the window at the front of a motor vehicle

windshield *NOUN* windshields
(*North American*) a windscreen

windsurfing *NOUN*
the sport of surfing on a board that has a sail

fixed to it
➤ **windsurfer** *NOUN*

wind turbine *NOUN* wind turbines
a large modern windmill used for producing electricity

windward *ADJECTIVE*
facing the wind • *the windward side of the ship*

windy *ADJECTIVE*
with much wind • *It's windy outside.*

wine *NOUN* wines
❶ an alcoholic drink made from grapes or other plants ❷ a dark red colour

> SPELLING
Do not confuse this word with **whine**.

wing *NOUN* wings
❶ one of the pair of parts of a bird, bat or insect, that it uses for flying ❷ one of the pair of long flat parts that stick out from the side of an aircraft and support it while it flies ❸ a part of a large building that extends from the main part ❹ the part of a motor vehicle's body above a wheel ❺ a player whose place is at one of the far ends of the forward line in football or hockey ❻ a section of a political party, with more extreme opinions than the others
➤ **on the wing** flying
➤ **take wing** to fly away
➤ **under your wing** under your protection
➤ **the wings** the sides of a theatre stage out of sight of the audience

wing *VERB* wings, winging, winged
❶ to fly somewhere • *The bird winged its way home.* ❷ to wound a bird in the wing or a person in the arm

winged *ADJECTIVE*
having wings • *Pegasus was a mythical winged horse.*

wingless *ADJECTIVE*
without wings • *wingless insects*

wingspan *NOUN*
the length between the two wing tips of a bird or aircraft

wink *VERB* winks, winking, winked
❶ to close and open your eye quickly, especially as a signal to someone ❷ a light winks when it flickers or twinkles

wink *NOUN* winks
❶ the action of winking ❷ a very short period of sleep • *I didn't sleep a wink that night.*

winkle *NOUN* winkles
a kind of edible shellfish

winkle *VERB* winkles, winkling, winkled
➤ **winkle something out** (*chiefly British*) to get information from someone with difficulty • *I managed to winkle the truth out of him eventually.*

winner *NOUN* winners
❶ a person, team or animal that wins something ❷ something very successful • *Her latest book is a winner.*

winning *ADJECTIVE*
attractive and charming • *a winning smile*

winnings *PLURAL NOUN*
the money someone wins in a game or by gambling

winnow *VERB* winnows, winnowing, winnowed
to toss or fan grain so that the loose dry outer part is blown away

winsome *ADJECTIVE*
charming and attractive

winter *NOUN* winters
the coldest season of the year, between autumn and spring

winter *VERB* winters, wintering, wintered
to spend the winter somewhere

wintry *ADJECTIVE*
❶ wintry weather is cold, like winter ❷ a wintry smile is cold and unfriendly

wipe *VERB* wipes, wiping, wiped
❶ to dry or clean something by rubbing it ❷ to remove something by rubbing it • *She wiped away her tears.*
➤ **wipe something out** ❶ to cancel something • *He's wiped out the debt.* ❷ to destroy something completely

wipe *NOUN* wipes
the action of wiping • *Give the window a quick wipe.*

wiper *NOUN* wipers
a device for wiping something, especially on a vehicle's windscreen

wire *NOUN* wires
❶ a strand or thin flexible rod of metal ❷ a piece of wire used to carry electric current ❸ a fence made from wire

wire *VERB* wires, wiring, wired
❶ to fit or connect something with wires to carry electric current ❷ to fasten or strengthen something with wire

wireless ADJECTIVE
able to send and receive signals without using wires • *a wireless Internet connection*

wireless NOUN wirelesses
(*old use*) a radio set

wiring NOUN
the system of wires carrying electricity in a building or in a device

wiry ADJECTIVE
❶ a wiry person is lean and strong ❷ wiry hair is tough and stiff

wisdom NOUN
❶ being wise ❷ wise sayings or writings

wisdom tooth NOUN wisdom teeth
a molar tooth that may grow at the back of the jaw of a person aged about 20 or more

wise ADJECTIVE
❶ able to make sensible decisions and give good advice because of the experience and knowledge that you have • *a wise old woman* ❷ sensible and showing good judgement • *a wise decision*
➤ **wisely** ADVERB
➤ **be none the wiser** to not know any more about something than you did before

wish VERB wishes, wishing, wished
❶ to feel or say that you would like to have or do something or would like something to happen ❷ to say that you hope someone will get something • *Wish me luck!*

wish NOUN wishes
❶ something you wish for; a desire • *I have no wish to see see him again.* ❷ the action of wishing • *Close your eyes and make a wish.*

wishbone NOUN wishbones
a forked bone between the neck and breast of a chicken or other bird

wishful thinking NOUN
belief in something based on what you would like, not on the facts

wisp NOUN wisps
❶ a few strands of hair or bits of straw etc. ❷ a small streak of smoke or cloud
➤ **wispy** ADJECTIVE

wisteria, wistaria (say wist-**eer**-ee-a or wist-**air**-ee-a) NOUN
a climbing plant with hanging blue, purple or white flowers (**WORD ORIGIN**) named after an American professor, Caspar *Wistar*

wistful ADJECTIVE
sadly longing for something • *There was a wistful look in her eyes.*

➤ **wistfully** ADVERB
➤ **wistfulness** NOUN

wit NOUN wits
❶ the ability to think quickly and clearly and make good decisions • *The game was a long battle of wits.* • *No one had the wit to ask for help.* ❷ a clever kind of humour ❸ a witty person
➤ **at your wits' end** not knowing what to do
➤ **keep your wits about you** to stay alert

witch NOUN witches
a person, especially a woman, who is thought to have magic powers

> **SPELLING**
> Do not confuse this word with **which**.

witchcraft NOUN
the use of magic, especially for evil purposes

witch doctor NOUN witch doctors
a magician who belongs to a tribe and is believed to use magic to heal people

witch-hunt NOUN witch-hunts
a campaign to find and punish people who hold views that are thought to be unacceptable or dangerous

with PREPOSITION
used to indicate
❶ being in the company or care of someone • *I came with a friend.* ❷ having or wearing something • *Who's that man with the beard?* ❸ using something • *Hit it with a hammer.* ❹ because of something • *He shook with laughter.* ❺ feeling or showing something • *She heard the news with great sadness.* ❻ towards or concerning something • *I was angry with him.* ❼ against someone or something • *There's no point in arguing with her.*

withdraw VERB withdraws, withdrawing, withdrew, withdrawn
❶ to take something away or take it back • *She withdrew her hand from his.* ❷ to go away from a place or stop taking part in something • *The troops withdrew from the frontier.* • *His injury meant he had to withdraw from the race.*

withdrawal NOUN withdrawals
❶ withdrawing something • *the withdrawal of troops from the region* ❷ an amount of money taken out of an account ❸ the process of stopping taking drugs to which you are addicted, often with unpleasant reactions • *withdrawal symptoms*

withdrawn *ADJECTIVE*
very shy or reserved

wither *VERB* withers, withering, withered
❶ a plant withers when it shrivels or wilts
❷ to become weaker then disappear

withering *ADJECTIVE*
scornful or sarcastic • *a withering remark*

withers *PLURAL NOUN*
the ridge between a horse's shoulder blades

withhold *VERB* withholds, withholding,
withheld
to refuse to give something to someone • *He
has withheld his permission.*

within *PREPOSITION & ADVERB*
inside; not beyond something • *I'll be back
within an hour.*

without *PREPOSITION*
❶ not having or using • *You can't get in
without a key.* ❷ free from • *She looked
at him without fear.* ❸ (old use) outside
• *without the city wall*

withstand *VERB* withstands, withstanding,
withstood
to resist something or put up with it
successfully • *The bridge is designed to
withstand high winds.*

witness *NOUN* witnesses
❶ a person who sees or hears something
happen • *There were no witnesses to the
accident.* ❷ a person who gives evidence in a
law court

witness *VERB* witnesses, witnessing, witnessed
❶ to be a witness of something • *Did anyone
witness the accident?* ❷ to sign a document
to confirm that it is genuine

witted *ADJECTIVE*
having wits of a certain kind • *quick-witted*

witticism *NOUN* witticisms
a witty remark

witty *ADJECTIVE* wittier, wittiest
clever and amusing; full of wit
➤ **wittily** *ADVERB*

wizard *NOUN* wizards
❶ a man with magic powers; a magician ❷ a
person with amazing abilities • *She's a real
computer wizard.* **WORD ORIGIN** from an old
sense of *wise* = a wise person

wizardry *NOUN*
❶ the clever and impressive things that a
person or thing can do • *The film's special
effects were created using the latest*

computer wizardry. ❷ the powers that a
wizard has

wizened (say **wiz**-end) *ADJECTIVE*
full of wrinkles • *a wizened face*

woad *NOUN*
a kind of blue dye formerly made from a plant

wobble *VERB* wobbles, wobbling, wobbled
to move unsteadily from side to side or to
make something do this • *Careful, this chair
wobbles.*

wobble *NOUN* wobbles
a wobbling movement

wobbly *ADJECTIVE*
moving unsteadily from side to side • *a
wobbly tooth*

woe *NOUN* woes
❶ great sorrow ❷ someone's woes are their
troubles and misfortunes

woebegone *ADJECTIVE*
looking unhappy

woeful *ADJECTIVE*
❶ very sad; full of woe ❷ very bad;
disgraceful • *a woeful lack of information*
➤ **woefully** *ADVERB*

wok *NOUN* woks
a Chinese cooking pan shaped like a large
bowl

wolf *NOUN* wolves
a fierce wild animal of the dog family, often
hunting in packs

wolf *VERB* wolfs, wolfing, wolfed
to eat something greedily

woman *NOUN* women
a grown-up female human being

womanhood *NOUN*
the condition of being a woman • *She soon
grew to womanhood.*

womanly *ADJECTIVE*
having qualities that are thought to be typical
of women

womb (say woom) *NOUN* wombs
the hollow organ in a female's body where
babies develop before they are born

wombat *NOUN* wombats
an Australian animal rather like a small bear

wonder *VERB* wonders, wondering, wondered
❶ to feel that you want to know something;
to try to decide about something • *We are
still wondering what to do next.* ❷ to feel
great surprise and admiration

a b c d e f g h i j k l m n o p q r s t u v w x y z

wonder NOUN wonders
❶ a feeling of surprise and admiration • *He stared in wonder at the stunning landscape.*
❷ something that fills you with surprise and admiration; a marvel • *It is one of the wonders of modern science.*
➤ **no wonder** it is not surprising

wonderful ADJECTIVE
marvellous or excellent
➤ **wonderfully** ADVERB

wonderment NOUN
a feeling of wonder

wondrous ADJECTIVE (*old use*)
wonderful; marvellous

wont (say wohnt) ADJECTIVE (*old use*)
accustomed; used to doing something • *Most afternoons he was wont to practise the trumpet.*

wont NOUN
a habit or custom • *She got up early, as was her wont.*

won't (*mainly spoken*)
will not

> **SPELLING**
>
> Won't is short for **will** + **not**. Do not forget to add an **apostrophe** between the **n** and the **t**.

woo VERB woos, wooing, wooed (*old use*)
❶ to try to win the love of a woman ❷ to seek someone's favour or support

wood NOUN woods
❶ the substance that trees are made of ❷ many trees growing close together

woodcock NOUN woodcock
a bird with a long bill, often shot for sport

woodcut NOUN woodcuts
an engraving made on wood; a print made from this

wooded ADJECTIVE
covered with growing trees • *wooded hills*

wooden ADJECTIVE
❶ made of wood ❷ stiff and showing no expression or liveliness
➤ **woodenly** ADVERB

woodland NOUN woodlands
wooded country

woodlouse NOUN woodlice
a small crawling creature with seven pairs of legs, living in rotten wood or damp soil

woodpecker NOUN woodpeckers
a bird that taps tree trunks with its beak to find insects

woodwind NOUN
wind instruments that are usually made of wood, e.g. the clarinet and oboe

woodwork NOUN
❶ making things out of wood ❷ things made out of wood

woodworm NOUN woodworms
the larva of a kind of beetle that bores into wooden furniture; the damage done to wood by this

woody ADJECTIVE
❶ like wood; consisting of wood ❷ full of trees

woof NOUN woofs
the gruff bark of a dog

wool NOUN wools
❶ the thick soft hair of sheep and goats ❷ thread or cloth made from this

woollen ADJECTIVE
made of wool

woollens PLURAL NOUN
clothes made of wool

woolly ADJECTIVE
❶ covered with wool or wool-like hair ❷ like wool or made of wool ❸ not thinking clearly; vague or confused • *woolly ideas*
➤ **woolliness** NOUN

word NOUN words
❶ a set of sounds or letters that has a meaning and when written or printed has no spaces between the letters ❷ a brief conversation • *Can I have a word with you?* ❸ a promise • *He kept his word.* ❹ a command or spoken signal • *Run when I give the word.* ❺ a message or piece of news • *We sent word of our safe arrival.*
➤ **have words** to quarrel
➤ **word for word** in exactly the same words

word VERB words, wording, worded
to express something in words • *You will need to word the question carefully.*

word class NOUN word classes
any of the groups into which words are divided in grammar (noun, pronoun,

determiner, adjective, verb, adverb, preposition, conjunction, exclamation)

> **GRAMMAR**
>
> The **word classes** of English are the different types of words you use in making sentences. Each word class has a special job to do: for example, a noun names things and a verb tells you what someone or something is doing. The names of the main word classes are: *noun, verb, adjective, adverb, pronoun, determiner, conjunction, preposition,* and *exclamation* (also sometimes called *interjection*). Word classes are also called **parts of speech**.
>
> A word can belong to more than one word class, depending on its position and purpose in a sentence. For example, the word *back* can be a noun (*a sore back*), an adjective (*the back seat*), an adverb (*to fall back*) or a verb (*to back a plan*).
>
> See also the panels for **adjectives, adverbs, conjunctions, determiners, nouns, prepositions, pronouns** and **verbs**.

wording *NOUN*
the way something is worded

word of honour *NOUN*
a solemn promise

word-perfect *ADJECTIVE*
having memorized every word perfectly • *He was word-perfect at the rehearsal.*

word processor *NOUN* **word processors**
a type of computer or program used for editing and printing letters and documents

wore
past tense of **wear**

work *NOUN* **works**
❶ something you have to do that needs effort or energy • *Digging is hard work.* ❷ a job; employment ❸ something you write or produce at school • *Please get on with your work quietly.* ❹ (*in science*) the result of applying a force to move an object ❺ a piece of writing, painting, music, etc. • *the works of William Shakespeare*
➤ **at work** busy working
➤ **out of work** having no work; not able to find a job

work *VERB* **works, working, worked**
❶ to spend time doing something that needs effort or energy ❷ to have a job or be employed • *She works in a bank.* ❸ to act or operate correctly or successfully • *Is the lift working?* ❹ to make something function or operate • *Can you work the lift?* ❺ to shape or press something • *Work the mixture into a paste.* ❻ to gradually move into a particular position • *The screw had worked loose.*
➤ **work out** to have a particular result, especially a good one • *I hope things work out well.*
➤ **work something out** to find an answer by thinking or calculating
➤ **work someone up** to make someone become excited, angry or anxious • *I could see she was getting really worked up.*
➤ **work up to something** to gradually progress to something more difficult or advanced

workable *ADJECTIVE*
that can be used or will work • *a workable plan*

worker *NOUN* **workers**
❶ a person who works ❷ a member of the working class ❸ a bee or ant that does the work in a hive or colony but does not produce eggs

workforce *NOUN* **workforces**
the number of people who work in a particular factory, industry, country, etc.

working class *NOUN* **working classes**
people who work for wages, especially in manual or industrial work
➤ **working-class** *ADJECTIVE*

workman *NOUN* **workmen**
a man who works with his hands, especially at building or making things

workmanship *NOUN*
a person's skill in making or producing something

work of art *NOUN* **works of art**
something produced by an artist, especially a painting or sculpture

workout *NOUN* **workouts**
a session of physical exercise or training

works *PLURAL NOUN*
❶ the moving parts of a machine ❷ a factory or industrial site

worksheet *NOUN* **worksheets**
a sheet of paper with a set of questions about a subject for students, often used with a textbook

workshop *NOUN* **workshops**
a place where things are made or mended

a b c d e f g h i j k l m n o p q r s t u v w x y z

A
B
C
D
E
F
G
H
I
J
K
L
M
N
O
P
Q
R
S
T
U
V
W
X
Y
Z

world *NOUN* **worlds**
❶ the earth with all its countries and peoples ❷ all the people on the earth; everyone • *He felt that the world was against him.* ❸ a planet • *creatures from another world* ❹ everything to do with a certain subject or activity • *He knows a lot about the world of sport.*
➤ **do someone the world of good** to have a very good effect on someone
➤ **think the world of someone** to have the highest possible opinion of someone

worldly *ADJECTIVE*
❶ to do with life on earth, not spiritual ❷ interested only in money, possessions and pleasure ❸ experienced about people and life
➤ **worldliness** *NOUN*

worldwide *ADJECTIVE & ADVERB*
over the whole world • *The success of these books brought her worldwide fame.*

World Wide Web *NOUN*
(*in computing*) a vast extensive information system that connects related sites and documents which can be accessed using the Internet

worm *NOUN* **worms**
❶ an animal with a long small soft rounded or flat body and no backbone or limbs ❷ (*informal*) an unimportant or unpleasant person

worm *VERB* **worms, worming, wormed**
to move along by wriggling or crawling • *I managed to worm my way under the fence.*
➤ **worm something out of someone** to gradually get someone to tell you something by constantly and cleverly questioning them • *We eventually managed to worm the truth out of them.*

wormwood *NOUN*
a woody plant with a bitter taste

worn
past participle of **wear**

worn *ADJECTIVE*
damaged because it has been rubbed or used too much • *worn tyres*

worn-out *ADJECTIVE*
❶ tired and exhausted ❷ damaged by too much use

worried *ADJECTIVE*
feeling or showing worry

worry *VERB* **worries, worrying, worried**
❶ to feel anxious or troubled about something ❷ to make someone feel anxious

or troubled about something ❸ an animal worries its prey when it holds it in its teeth and shakes it • *The dog was worrying a rat.*
➤ **worrier** *NOUN*

worry *NOUN* **worries**
❶ worrying or being anxious ❷ something that makes a person worry

worse *ADJECTIVE & ADVERB*
more bad or more badly; less good or less well
➤ **worse off** less fortunate or well off

worsen *VERB* **worsens, worsening, worsened**
to become worse or to make something worse • *The weather worsened.*

worship *VERB* **worships, worshipping, worshipped**
❶ to give praise or respect to God or a god ❷ to love or respect a person or thing greatly • *He worshipped his wife.*
➤ **worshipper** *NOUN*

worship *NOUN* **worships**
❶ worshipping; religious ceremonies ❷ a title of respect for a mayor or certain magistrates • *his worship the mayor*

worshipful *ADJECTIVE*
in titles, a word that means 'respected' • *the Worshipful Company of Goldsmiths*

worst *ADJECTIVE & ADVERB*
most bad or most badly; least good or least well

worsted *NOUN*
a kind of woollen material

worth *ADJECTIVE*
❶ having a certain value • *This stamp is worth £100.* ❷ deserving something; good or important enough for something • *That book is worth reading.*

worth *NOUN*
❶ a person's or thing's value or usefulness • *He has proved his worth to the team.* ❷ the amount that a certain sum will buy • *five pounds' worth of stamps*

worthless *ADJECTIVE*
having no value; useless
➤ **worthlessness** *NOUN*

worthwhile *ADJECTIVE*
important or good enough to deserve the time or effort needed • *a worthwhile job*

worthy *ADJECTIVE*
deserving respect or support • *The sale is for a worthy cause.*
➤ **worthiness** *NOUN*

➤ **worthy of** deserving • *This charity is worthy of your support.*

would *AUXILIARY VERB*
❶ as the past tense of **will** • *The guide said he would meet us here.* ❷ used in questions and polite requests • *Would you like some more soup?* ❸ used with I and we and the verbs *like, prefer, be glad*, etc. • *I would like to come.* • *We would be glad to help.* ❹ used of something to be expected • *That's just what he would do!*

would-be *ADJECTIVE*
wanting or pretending to be • *a would-be comedian*

wouldn't (*mainly spoken*)
would not

> **SPELLING**
> Wouldn't = would + not. Do not forget to add an **apostrophe** between the **n** and the **t**.

wound (say woond) *NOUN* **wounds**
❶ an injury done to someone's body, especially one in which the skin is cut ❷ a hurt to a person's feelings

wound (say woond) *VERB* **wounds, wounding, wounded**
❶ to cause a wound to a person or animal ❷ to hurt a person's feelings • *She was wounded by these remarks.*

wound (say wownd) *VERB*
past tense of **wind** *VERB*

wraith *NOUN* **wraiths**
a ghost

wrangle *VERB* **wrangles, wrangling, wrangled**
to have a noisy argument or quarrel

wrangle *NOUN* **wrangles**
a noisy argument or quarrel

wrap *VERB* **wraps, wrapping, wrapped**
to put paper or some other covering round something
➤ **be wrapped up in something** to be very involved and interested in something
➤ **wrap up** to put on warm clothes

wrap *NOUN* **wraps**
❶ a shawl or cloak worn to keep you warm ❷ a flour tortilla rolled around a filling and eaten as a sandwich

wrapper *NOUN* **wrappers**
a piece of paper or plastic wrapped round something

wrapping *NOUN*
material used to wrap something, especially a present

wrath (rhymes with cloth) *NOUN*
extreme anger
➤ **wrathful** *ADJECTIVE*
➤ **wrathfully** *ADVERB*

wreak (say reek) *VERB* **wreaks, wreaking, wreaked**
to cause great damage or harm • *Fog wreaked havoc with the flow of traffic.*

> **USAGE**
> The past form of **wreak** is **wreaked** not **wrought**. The adjective **wrought** is used to describe metal that has been shaped by hammering or rolling.

wreath (say reeth) *NOUN* **wreaths**
❶ flowers or leaves fastened into a circle • *a holly wreath* ❷ a curving line of mist or smoke

wreathe (say reeth) *VERB* **wreathes, wreathing, wreathed**
❶ to surround or decorate something with a wreath ❷ to cover something • *Their faces were wreathed in smiles.* ❸ to move in a curve • *Smoke wreathed upwards.*

wreck *VERB* **wrecks, wrecking, wrecked**
to damage or ruin something so badly that it cannot be used again

wreck *NOUN* **wrecks**
❶ a ship that has sunk or been very badly damaged ❷ the remains of a badly damaged vehicle or building ❸ a person who is in a bad mental or physical state • *a nervous wreck*

wreckage *NOUN*
the pieces of a wreck

wren *NOUN* **wrens**
a very small brown bird

wrench *VERB* **wrenches, wrenching, wrenched**
to twist or pull something violently • *The door had been wrenched off its hinges.* • *She wrenched herself free.*

wrench *NOUN* **wrenches**
❶ a wrenching movement ❷ pain caused by parting • *Leaving home was a great wrench.* ❸ an adjustable tool rather like a spanner, used for gripping and turning nuts or bolts

wrest *VERB* **wrests, wresting, wrested**
to take something away using force or effort • *They wrested the sword from his grasp.*

a b c d e f g h i j k l m n o p q r s t u v w x y z

A
B
C
D
E
F
G
H
I
J
K
L
M
N
O
P
Q
R
S
T
U
V
W
X
Y
Z

wrestle *VERB* wrestles, wrestling, wrestled
❶ to fight someone by grasping them and trying to throw them to the ground ❷ to struggle with a problem or difficulty • *All night he wrestled with his conscience.*

wrestle *NOUN* wrestles
❶ a wrestling match ❷ a hard struggle

wrestler *NOUN* wrestlers
a person who wrestles for sport

wretch *NOUN* wretches
❶ a person who is very unhappy or who you pity ❷ a person who is disliked

wretched *ADJECTIVE*
❶ miserable or unhappy • *a wretched beggar* ❷ of bad quality • *They were living in wretched conditions.* ❸ not satisfactory; causing a nuisance • *This wretched car won't start.*
➤ **wretchedly** *ADVERB*
➤ **wretchedness** *NOUN*

wriggle *VERB* wriggles, wriggling, wriggled
to move with short twisting movements • *The baby was wriggling around on my lap.*
➤ **wriggle out of something** to avoid work or blame cunningly

wriggle *NOUN* wriggles
a wriggling movement
➤ **wriggly** *ADJECTIVE*

wring *VERB* wrings, wringing, wrung
❶ to twist and squeeze a wet thing to get water out of it ❷ to squeeze something firmly or forcibly • *I'll wring your neck!* ❸ to get something by a great effort • *We managed to wring a promise out of him.*
➤ **wringing wet** so wet that water can be squeezed out of it

> **SPELLING**
> The past tense of **wring** is **wrung**. Do not forget the silent w before the r. Do not confuse this word with **ring**.

wringer *NOUN* wringers
a device with a pair of rollers for squeezing water out of washed clothes

wrinkle *NOUN* wrinkles
❶ wrinkles are the small lines and creases that appear in your skin as you get older ❷ a small crease in something

wrinkle *VERB* wrinkles, wrinkling, wrinkled
❶ to make wrinkles in something • *She wrinkled her nose in disgust.* ❷ to form wrinkles

wrinkled, **wrinkly** *ADJECTIVE*
having wrinkles

wrist *NOUN* wrists
the joint that connects your hand to your arm

wristwatch *NOUN* wristwatches
a watch that you wear on your wrist

writ (say rit) *NOUN* writs
a formal written command issued by a law court
➤ **Holy Writ** the Bible

write *VERB* writes, writing, wrote, written
❶ to put letters or words on paper or another surface ❷ to be the author or composer of something ❸ to send a letter to someone • *I promise that I'll write once a week.* ❹ to enter data into a computer memory
➤ **write something off** to think something is lost or useless
➤ **write something up** to write an account of something

> **SPELLING**
> There is a silent w at the start of **write**. The past tense of **write** is **wrote** and the past participle is **written**.

writer *NOUN* writers
a person who writes; an author

writhe *VERB* writhes, writhing, writhed
❶ to twist your body about because of pain or discomfort ❷ to wriggle

writing *NOUN* writings
❶ something you write ❷ the way you write

wrong *ADJECTIVE*
❶ incorrect; not true • *That's the wrong answer.* ❷ not fair or morally right • *It is wrong to cheat.* ❸ not working properly • *There's something wrong with the engine.*

wrong *ADVERB*
wrongly • *I must have typed your name in wrong.*

wrong *NOUN* wrongs
something morally wrong; an injustice
➤ **in the wrong** having done or said something wrong

wrong *VERB* wrongs, wronging, wronged
to do wrong to someone; to treat a person unfairly

wrongdoer *NOUN* **wrongdoers**
a person who does something dishonest or illegal
➤ **wrongdoing** *NOUN*

wrongful *ADJECTIVE*
unfair or unjust; illegal • *wrongful arrest*
➤ **wrongfully** *ADVERB*

wrongly *ADVERB*
in a way that is unfair or incorrect • *He was wrongly accused of stealing.*

wrought *ADJECTIVE*
wrought iron or other metal is worked by being beaten out or shaped by hammering or rolling **WORD ORIGIN** the old past participle of **work**

wry *ADJECTIVE* **wryer, wryest**
slightly mocking or sarcastic • *He gave a wry smile.*
➤ **wryly** *ADVERB*

xenophobia (say zen-o-**foh**-bee-a) *NOUN*
strong dislike or distrust of foreigners
WORD ORIGIN from Greek *xenos* = foreigner + **phobia**

Xmas *NOUN* (*informal*)
Christmas **WORD ORIGIN** the X represents the Greek letter called chi, the first letter of *Christos* = Christ

X-ray *NOUN* **X-rays**
a photograph or examination of the inside of something, especially a part of the body, made by a kind of radiation (called **X-rays**) that can penetrate solid things

X-ray *VERB* **X-rays, X-raying, X-rayed**
to make an X-ray of something

xylophone (say **zy**-lo-fohn) *NOUN* **xylophones**
a musical instrument made of wooden bars of different lengths that you hit with small hammers **WORD ORIGIN** from Greek *xylon* = wood + *phone* = sound

yacht (say yot) *NOUN* **yachts**
❶ a sailing boat used for racing or cruising
❷ a private ship
➤ **yachting** *NOUN*
➤ **yachtsman** *NOUN*
➤ **yachtswoman** *NOUN*
WORD ORIGIN from Dutch *jaghtschip* = fast pirate ship

yak *NOUN* **yaks**
an ox with long hair, found in central Asia

yam *NOUN* **yams**
the edible root of a tropical plant, also known as a sweet potato

Yank *NOUN* **Yanks** (*informal*)
a Yankee

yank (*informal*) *VERB* **yanks, yanking, yanked**
to pull something with a sudden sharp tug • *I yanked the door open.*

yank *NOUN* **yanks**
a sudden sharp tug

Yankee *NOUN* **Yankees**
an American, especially of the northern USA
WORD ORIGIN probably from Dutch *Janke* = Johnny

yap *VERB* **yaps, yapping, yapped**
to bark in a noisy shrill way

yap *NOUN* **yaps**
a shrill bark

yard *NOUN* **yards**
❶ a measure of length, 36 inches or about 91 centimetres ❷ a long pole stretched out from a mast to support a sail ❸ an enclosed area beside a building or used for a certain kind of work • *a timber yard*

yardstick *NOUN* **yardsticks**
a standard by which something is measured

yarn *NOUN* **yarns**
❶ thread spun by twisting fibres together, used in knitting, etc. ❷ (*informal*) a tale or story

yashmak *NOUN* **yashmaks**
a veil covering all of the face except for the eyes, worn by some Muslim women in public

a b c d e f g h i j k l m n o p q r s t u v w x y z

yawl *NOUN* yawls
a kind of sailing boat or fishing boat

yawn *VERB* yawns, yawning, yawned
❶ to open your mouth wide and breathe in deeply because you feel sleepy or bored ❷ to form a wide opening • *A pit yawned in front of us.*

yawn *NOUN* yawns
an act of yawning • *I stifled a yawn.*

ye *PRONOUN* (*old use*)
you (referring to two or more people)

yea (say yay) *ADVERB* (*old use*)
yes

year *NOUN* years
❶ the time the earth takes to go right round the sun, about 365¼ days ❷ the time from 1 January to 31 December ❸ any period of twelve months ❹ a group of students of roughly the same age • *Is she in your year?*

yearling *NOUN* yearlings
an animal between one and two years old

yearly *ADJECTIVE & ADVERB*
happening or done once a year

yearn *VERB* yearns, yearning, yearned
to long for something • *People yearned for peace.*
➤ **yearning** *NOUN*

yeast *NOUN*
a substance that causes alcohol and carbon dioxide to form as it develops, used in making beer and wine and in baking bread

yell *VERB* yells, yelling, yelled
to give a loud cry; to shout

yell *NOUN* yells
a loud cry; a shout

yellow *NOUN* yellows
the colour of egg yolks and ripe lemons

yellow *ADJECTIVE*
❶ of yellow colour ❷ (*informal*) cowardly

yellow *VERB* yellows, yellowing, yellowed
to become yellow, especially with age
➤ **yellowness** *NOUN*

yelp *VERB* yelps, yelping, yelped
to give a shrill bark or cry, especially in pain

yelp *NOUN* yelps
a shrill bark or cry

yen *NOUN*
❶ yens a longing for something ❷ yen
a unit of money in Japan

yeoman (say **yoh**-man) *NOUN* yeomen
(*old use*) a man who owned and ran a small farm
➤ **yeomanry** *NOUN*

yes *EXCLAMATION*
used to agree to or accept something or as an answer meaning 'I am here'

yesterday *NOUN & ADVERB*
the day before today

yet *ADVERB*
❶ up to this time; by this time • *Have you checked your email yet?* ❷ eventually • *I'll get even with him yet!* ❸ in addition; even • *She became yet more excited.*

yet *CONJUNCTION*
nevertheless • *It is strange, yet it is true.*

yeti *NOUN* yetis
a very large animal thought to live in the Himalayas, sometimes called the 'Abominable Snowman'

yew *NOUN* yews
an evergreen tree with dark green needle-like leaves and red berries

yield *VERB* yields, yielding, yielded
❶ to give in or surrender ❷ to agree to do what is asked or ordered; to give way • *He yielded to persuasion.* ❸ to produce a crop, profit or result • *These trees yield plenty of apples every year.*

yield *NOUN* yields
the amount yielded or produced • *What is the yield of wheat per acre?*

yodel *VERB* yodels, yodelling, yodelled
to sing or shout with your voice continually going from a low note to a high note and back again

yoga (say **yoh**-ga) *NOUN*
a Hindu system of meditation and self-control; a system of physical exercises based on this

yoghurt, **yogurt** (say **yog**-ert) *NOUN*
milk thickened by the action of certain bacteria, giving it a sharp taste

yoke *NOUN* yokes
❶ a curved piece of wood put across the necks of animals pulling a cart or plough ❷ a shaped piece of wood fitted across a person's shoulders, with a pail or load hung at each end ❸ a close-fitting upper part of a piece of clothing, from which the rest hangs

yoke *VERB* yokes, yoking, yoked
to harness or join animals by means of a yoke

> **SPELLING**
> Take care not to confuse with yolk.

yokel (say **yoh**-kel) *NOUN* yokels
a simple country fellow

yolk (rhymes with coke) *NOUN* yolks
the round yellow part inside an egg

Yom Kippur (say yom kip-**oor**) *NOUN*
the Day of Atonement, a solemn Jewish
religious festival, a day of fasting and
repentance

yon *ADJECTIVE & ADVERB* (*dialect*)
over there; yonder

yonder *ADJECTIVE & ADVERB* (*old use*)
over there

yore *NOUN*
> of yore of long ago • *in days of yore*

Yorkshire pudding *NOUN* Yorkshire puddings
baked batter, usually eaten with roast beef

you *PRONOUN*
❶ the person or people being spoken to
• *Who are you?* ❷ anyone or everyone; one
• *You can never be sure what will happen.*

young *ADJECTIVE*
having lived or existed for only a short time;
not old

young *PLURAL NOUN*
children or young animals or birds • *The robin
was feeding its young.*

youngster *NOUN* youngsters
a child or young person

your *DETERMINER*
belonging to you • *Don't forget your book.*

> **SPELLING**
> Your is different from you're: • *It is your
> turn.* • *You're next.*

you're (*mainly spoken*)
you are • *You're late.*

> **SPELLING**
> Do not confuse you're and your: • *You're
> next.* • *It is your turn.*

yours *POSSESSIVE PRONOUN*
belonging to you • *Is this book yours?*
> **Yours faithfully, Yours sincerely, Yours
> truly** ways of ending a letter before you sign
> it

> **USAGE**
> It is incorrect to write *your's*.

yourself *PRONOUN* yourselves
you and nobody else. The word is used to
refer back to the subject of a sentence (e.g.
Have you hurt yourself?) or for emphasis (e.g.
You told me so yourself.)
> **by yourself** or **by yourselves** alone; on
> your own

youth *NOUN* youths
❶ being young; the time when you are young
❷ a young man ❸ young people

youth club *NOUN* youth clubs
a club providing leisure activities for young
people

youthful *ADJECTIVE*
❶ typical of young people • *youthful
enthusiasm* ❷ young or looking young
> **youthfulness** *NOUN*

youth hostel *NOUN* youth hostels
a place where young people can stay cheaply
when they are hiking or on holiday

yowl *VERB* yowls, yowling, yowled
to wail or howl loudly

yowl *NOUN* yowls
a loud wailing cry or howl

yo-yo *NOUN* yo-yos
a round wooden or plastic toy that moves up
and down on a string that you hold

Yule *NOUN* (*old use*)
the Christmas festival, also called **Yuletide**

yummy *ADJECTIVE*
(*informal*) good to eat; delicious

Zz

zany *ADJECTIVE* zanier, zaniest
funny in a weird or crazy way
WORD ORIGIN from Italian *zanni* = a type of
clown

zap *VERB* zaps, zapping, zapped (*informal*)
❶ to attack or destroy something, especially
in computer games ❷ to use a remote control
to change television channels quickly
> **zapper** *NOUN*

zeal *NOUN*
enthusiasm or keenness

zealot (say **zel**-ot) *NOUN* zealots
a zealous person; a fanatic

zealous (say **zel**-us) *ADJECTIVE*
very keen or enthusiastic
➤ **zealously** *ADVERB*

zebra (say **zeb**-ra) *NOUN* zebras
an African animal of the horse family, with
black and white stripes all over its body

zebra crossing *NOUN* zebra crossings
(*British*) a place for pedestrians to cross a
road safely, marked with broad white stripes

zebu (say **zee**-bew) *NOUN* zebus
an ox with a humped back, found in India,
East Asia and Africa

zenith *NOUN*
❶ the part of the sky directly above you
❷ the highest point of something • *His power
was at its zenith.*

zephyr (say **zef**-er) *NOUN* zephyrs
a soft gentle wind **WORD ORIGIN** from Greek
Zephyros = god of the west wind

zero *NOUN* zeros
❶ nought; the figure 0 ❷ the point marked 0
on a thermometer or other scale

zero *VERB* zeros, zeroing, zeroed
➤ **zero in on something** to focus your aim or
attention on something

zero hour *NOUN*
the time when something is planned to start

zest *NOUN*
❶ great enjoyment or enthusiasm ❷ the
coloured part of orange or lemon peel

zigzag *NOUN* zigzags
a line or route that turns sharply from side
to side

zigzag *VERB* zigzags, zigzagging, zigzagged
to move in a series of sharp turns from one
side to the other • *A path zigzagged up the
hill.*

zinc *NOUN*
a white metal

zip *NOUN* zips
❶ a fastener consisting of two strips of
material, each with rows of small teeth that
fit together when a sliding tab brings them
together ❷ liveliness or energy

zip *VERB* zips, zipping, zipped
❶ to fasten or close something with a zip
❷ to move quickly with a sharp sound • *A
police car zipped past.* ❸ (*in computing*) to
compress a computer file in order to email it
at a higher speed or for long-term storage

zither *NOUN* zithers
a musical instrument with many strings
stretched over a shallow box-like body

zodiac (say **zoh**-dee-ak) *NOUN*
a strip of sky where the sun, moon and
main planets are found, divided into
twelve equal parts (called **signs of the
zodiac**), each named after a constellation
WORD ORIGIN from Greek *zoidion* = image of
an animal

zombie *NOUN* zombies
❶ (*informal*) a person who seems to be doing
things without thinking, usually because they
are very tired ❷ in voodoo and horror films, a
corpse that has been brought back to life by
witchcraft

zone *NOUN* zones
an area of a special kind or for a particular
purpose • *a war zone* • *a no-parking zone*

zoo *NOUN* zoos
a place where wild animals are kept so that
people can look at them or study them
WORD ORIGIN short for *zoological gardens*

zoology (say zoh-**ol**-o-jee) *NOUN*
the scientific study of animals
➤ **zoological** *ADJECTIVE*
➤ **zoologist** *NOUN*

zoom *VERB* zooms, zooming, zoomed
❶ to move or travel very quickly ❷ to rise or
increase quickly • *Prices had zoomed.* ❸ to
use a zoom lens to change from a distant
view to a close-up • *The camera zoomed in
on her face.*

zoom lens *NOUN* zoom lenses
a camera lens that can be adjusted to focus
on things that are close up or far away

zucchini (say **zoo**-keen-ee) *NOUN* zucchini or
zucchinis
(*North American*) a courgette

Zulu *NOUN* Zulus
a member of a South African people; the
language spoken by this people

Vocabulary Toolkit

✓ Prefixes and suffixes

Common prefixes

A **prefix** is a group of letters joined to the beginning of a word to change its meaning, e.g.

re-	**re**capture	= to capture again
un-	**un**known	= not known

Some **prefixes** already form part of the word, e.g.

com-	**com**municate	= to make contact with

Once you know how **prefixes** work, you can use them to give existing words new meanings. Because there are so many possible combinations, not all words that begin with prefixes can be included in this dictionary.

Here are some examples of the more common English prefixes:

prefix	meaning	example
an–	not, without	anarchy
anti–	against	anti-British
arch–	chief	archbishop
auto–	self	automatic
co–	together	coeducation
com–, con–	together, with	communicate
contra–	against	contradict
cyber–	to do with electronic communication	cyberspace, cybercafe
de–	undoing or taking away	derail
dis–	not	dishonest
dis–	taking away	disconnect
eco–	to do with ecology and the environment	ecosystem
em–, en–	in, into	embark, entrust

prefix	meaning	example
ex–	that used to be, former	ex-president
extra–	beyond, outside	extraordinary, extraterrestrial
fore–	before, in front of	forefinger, foregoing
giga–	times 10^9 or (in ICT) 2^{30}	gigabyte
in–	not	incorrect
il–	not	illegal
im–	not	impossible
ir–	not	irrelevant
inter–	between	international
mega–	times 10^6 or (in ICT) 2^{20}	megabyte
mis–	wrong	misbehave
mono–	one, single	monotone
multi–	many	multimedia
non–	not	non-existent
over–	too much	overdo
poly–	many	polygon
post–	after	post-war
pre–	before	prehistoric
pro–	supporting	pro-British
re–	again	recapture
semi–	half	semicircle
sub–	below	submarine
super–	over, beyond	superstore
tele–	at a distance	telecommunications
trans–	across	transport, transatlantic
ultra–	beyond	ultrasonic
un–	not, the opposite of	unknown, undo

Common suffixes

A **suffix** is a group of letters joined to the end of a word to change its meaning, e.g.

-able	eatable	= able to be eaten
-er	maker	= a person or machine that makes something
-ness	happiness	= the state of being happy

Suffixes often change the way that the word functions in the sentence, e.g.

work – verb	worker – noun	workable – adjective

Suffixes can be used to make many different combinations and not all of them are included in this dictionary. You can also make words with more than one suffix, e.g. *childishness* and *childishly*.

Here are some examples of the more common English suffixes:

suffix	meaning	example
–able –ible –uble	able to be able to be able to be	eatable accessible soluble
–ant –ent	someone who does something someone who does something	attendant superintendent
–dom	used to make nouns to do with condition or rank	martyrdom
–ee	someone who is affected	employee, refugee
–er	a person or thing that does something	maker, opener
–er	more	faster
–esque	in the style of	picturesque
–ess	a female person or animal	actress, lioness
–est	most	fastest
–ful	full (of)	beautiful, cupful
–hood	used to make nouns to do with state or condition	childhood, motherhood

suffix	meaning	example
–ic	belonging to, associated with	Islamic, terrific
–ish	rather like, somewhat	childish, greenish
–ism	used to make nouns to do with systems and beliefs	capitalism, Hinduism
–ist	someone who does something or believes something	dentist, Communist
–itis	used to make nouns for illnesses involving inflammation	appendicitis, tonsillitis
–ize or –ise	used to make verbs / used to make verbs	criticize televise
–less	not having, without	senseless
–let	small	booklet
–like	like, resembling	childlike
–ling	a small person or thing	seedling
–ly	used to make adverbs and adjectives	bravely, leisurely
–ment	used to make nouns	amusement
–ness	used to make nouns	kindness, happiness
–oid	like or resembling	celluloid
–or	a person or thing that does something	sailor, escalator
–ous	used to make adjectives	dangerous
–ship	used to make nouns	friendship, citizenship
–some	full of	loathsome
–tion	used to make nouns	abbreviation, ignition, completion
–ty	used to make nouns	ability, anxiety
–ward –wards	in a particular direction in a particular direction	backward northwards

✓ Confusable words and phrases

Common errors

These words and phrases are easy to confuse. A dictionary will help you to choose the correct meaning for any words that you are unclear about.

all right / alright

➤ *Are you **all right**?*
➤ *It's cold **all right**.*

The correct spelling is as two words: *all right*.

advice / advise

Advice is a noun.

➤ *She gave me one piece of **advice**: ignore the email.*

Advise is a verb.

➤ *She **advised** me to ignore the email.*

affect / effect

Affect is a verb. It means 'to make a difference to something'. It can also mean 'to pretend'.

➤ *My asthma **affects** my breathing.*
➤ *She **affected** ignorance about the test.*

Effect is a noun. It means 'a result'. It can also be used as a verb meaning 'to bring about'.

➤ *The weather has a big **effect** on my mood.*

breath / breathe

Breath is a noun. It sounds similar to 'bread'.

➤ *I am out of **breath**.*
➤ *Take a big **breath**.*

Breathe (which sounds like 'breethe') is a verb.

➤ *I can **breathe** underwater.*
➤ *Don't **breathe** a word of this to anyone.*

past / passed

Past is a noun meaning 'the time gone by'.
➤ *It happened in the **past**.*

It is also a preposition meaning 'beyond a certain place' or 'after a certain time'.
➤ *I walk **past** the bus stop everyday.*
➤ *It is **past** six now.*

Passed is the past tense of the verb 'to pass'.
➤ *She **passed** me a sweet.*
➤ *I **passed** my exam!*

stationery / stationary

Stationery is a noun meaning papers, pencils and envelopes.
➤ *I got my pen in the **stationery** section.*

The word 'envelope' begins with an 'e', so you can use it to remind you that stationery also has an 'e' in it.

Stationary is an adjective meaning 'not moving'.
➤ *The car was **stationary** when it was hit by the van.*

double negatives

You should never use **two negative words** together to make a **negative** statement:
➤ *I **don't** want **no** more.*
➤ *They **never** said **nothing** about it.*

The correct versions are:
➤ *I **don't** want any more.*
➤ *They **never** said anything about it.*

But you can use a **negative word** with a word beginning with a **negative prefix** like *in-* or *un-*. The **two negatives** cancel each other out and produce a **positive** meaning:
➤ *The town is not **un**attractive.*
This means that the town is fairly attractive.

I / me

You use **I** when it is the subject of a verb:
> ➤ *I want to see you.*

Strictly speaking you should use **I** also in sentences such as *It is I who saw you.* This is because what comes after the verb *be* should 'agree' with what comes before. I is the subject of the verb *be* (here in the form *is*). But in informal conversation it is acceptable to say *It is me* or *It was him*.

You use **me** when it is the object of a verb or comes after a preposition such as *to* or *with*:
> ➤ *Give it to me.*
> ➤ *He came with me.*

You may be unsure whether to use **you and I** or **you and me** when you have more than one pronoun together.

The rule is exactly the same: use **you and I** when it is the subject of the verb 'be' in the sentence.
> ➤ **You and I** *were both there.*
> ➤ *This is a picture of **you and me**.*

it's / its

It is very important to remember the difference the apostrophe makes.
It's (with an apostrophe) is short for 'it is' or 'it has':
> ➤ ***It's*** *(= it is) very late now.*
> ➤ *I think **it's** (= it has) been raining.*

Its (without an apostrophe) is a word like *his* and *their* (called a possessive determiner) and means 'belonging to it':
> ➤ *The cat licked **its** paw.*
> ➤ *The class wrote **its** own dictionary.*

Homophones

These are words that sound the same but they have different meanings and spellings. Because they sound the same, they are easy to get confused. If you are not sure which word to use in a particular sentence, check both spellings in the dictionary.

new	—	knew	no	—	know
right	—	write	through	—	threw
hole	—	whole	great	—	grate
for	—	four, fore	heard	—	herd
see	—	sea	be	—	bee
blue	—	blew	bare	—	bear
one	—	won	cheap	—	cheep
night	—	knight	hear	—	here
vain	—	vein, vane	currant	—	current
dessert	—	desert	yolk	—	yoke

✓ Phrases from different languages

Sometimes foreign phrases are used to express an idea which is tricky to give in English.

ad infinitum (in-fi-ny-tum)
without limit; for ever *(Latin = to infinity)*

à la carte
ordered and paid for as separate items from a menu *(French = from the menu)*

alfresco
in the open air *an alfresco meal (from Italian al fresco = in the fresh air)*

alter ego
another, very different, side of someone's personality *(Latin = other self)*

angst
a strong feeling of anxiety or dread about something *(German = fear)*

au fait (oh fay)
knowing a subject or procedure etc. well *(French = to the point)*

au revoir (oh rev-wahr)
goodbye for the moment *(French = until seeing again)*

avant-garde (av-ahn-gard)
people who use a modern style in art or literature etc. *(French = vanguard)*

bona fide (boh-na fy-dee)
genuine; without fraud *(Latin = in good faith)*

bon voyage (bawn vwah-yahzh)
(have a) pleasant journey! *(French)*

carte blanche (kart blahnsh)
freedom to act as you think best *(French = blank paper)*

c'est la vie (say la vee)
life is like that *(French = that is life)*

coup de grâce (koo der grahs)
a stroke or blow that puts an end to something *(French = mercy blow)*

coup d'état (koo day-tah)
the sudden overthrow of a government *(French = blow of State)*

crème de la crème (krem der la krem)
the very best of something *(French = cream of the cream)*

déjà vu (day-zha vew)
a feeling that you have already experienced what is happening now *(French = already seen)*

dolce vita (dol-chay-vee-ta)
life of pleasure and luxury *(Italian = sweet life)*

doppelgänger (doppel-geng-er)
someone who looks exactly like someone else; a double *(German = double-goer)*

en bloc (ahn blok)
all at the same time; in a block *(French)*

en masse (ahn mass)
all together *(French = in a mass)*

en route (ahn root)
on the way *(French)*

entente (ahn-tahnt or on-tont)
a friendly understanding between nations *(French)*

eureka (yoor-eek-a)
I have found it (i.e. the answer)! *(Greek)*

faux pas (foh pah)
an embarrassing blunder *(French = false step)*

gung-ho (gung-hoh)
eager to fight or take part in a war *(Chinese gonghe = work together, used as a slogan)*

hara-kiri (hara-kee-ri)
ritual suicide by cutting open the stomach with a sword *(Japanese = belly cutting)*

Homo sapiens
human beings regarded as a species of animal *(Latin = wise man)*

honcho
a leader *(Japanese = group leader)*

hors-d'oeuvre (or-dervr)
food served as an appetizer at the start of a meal *(French = outside the work)*

in memoriam
in memory (of) *(Latin)*

in situ (sit-yoo)
in its original place *(Latin)*

joie de vivre (zhwah der veevr)
a feeling of great enjoyment of life *(French = joy of life)*

kowtow (rhymes with cow)
to obey someone slavishly *(Chinese = knock the head, from the old practice of kneeling and touching the ground with the forehead as a sign of submission)*

laissez-faire (lay-say-fair)
not interfering *(French = let (them) act)*

luau (loo-ow)
a party or feast *(Hawaiian lu'au = feast)*

macho (mach-oh)
masculine in an aggressive way *(Spanish = male)*

mano a mano (mah-noh a mah-noh)
(of a meeting, fight, etc.) between two people only; face to face *(Spanish = hand to hand)*

modus operandi (moh-dus op-er-and-ee)
❶ a person's way of working. ❷ the way a thing works *(Latin = way of working)*

nota bene (noh-ta ben-ee)
(usually shortened to NB) note carefully *(Latin = note well)*

par excellence (par eks-el-ahns)
more than all the others; to the greatest degree *(French = because of special excellence)*

per annum
for each year; yearly *(Latin)*

pièce de résistance (pee-ess der ray-zees-tahns)
the most important item *(French)*

quid pro quo
something given or done in return for something *(Latin = something for something)*

raison d'être (ray-zawn detr)
the purpose of a thing's existence *(French = reason for being)*

rigor mortis (ry-ger mor-tis)
stiffening of the body after death *(Latin = stiffness of death)*

RIP
may he or she (or they) rest in peace (short for Latin *requiescat* (or *requiescant*) *in pace*)

sang-froid (sahn-frwah)
calmness in danger or difficulty *(French = cold blood)*

Schadenfreude (shah-den-froi-da)
pleasure at seeing someone else in trouble or difficulty *(German = harm joy)*

sotto voce (sot-oh voh-chee)
in a very quiet voice *(Italian = under the voice)*

status quo (stay-tus kwoh)
the state of affairs as it was before a change *(Latin = the state in which)*

terra firma
dry land; the ground *(Latin = firm land)*

tête-à-tête (tayt-ah-tayt)
a private conversation, especially between two people *(French = head to head)*

verboten (fer-boh-ten)
not allowed; forbidden *(German = forbidden)*

vis-à-vis (veez-ah-vee)
❶ in a position facing one another; opposite to. ❷ as compared with *(French = face to face)*

✓ Idioms

Idioms are groups of words that have a meaning that is often impossible to work out on your own. This is frequently because they refer to ideas or beliefs that are no longer current. In a dictionary an idiom will often be listed at the end of the entry of its key word. Below are some interesting examples.

an Achilles' heel
a weak or bad point in a person who is otherwise strong or good
(From the story of the Greek hero Achilles: his mother Thetis had dipped him in the River Styx because the water would prevent him from harm, but the water did not cover the heel by which she held him. So when the Trojan prince Paris killed Achilles he did it by throwing a spear into his heel.)

an albatross round someone's neck
something that is a constant worry or cause of feeling guilty
(An albatross was supposed to bring good luck to sailors at sea. In Coleridge's 1798 poem The Rime of the Ancient Mariner, the mariner (= sailor) shoots an albatross and this brings a curse on the ship. The crew force the mariner to wear the dead albatross round his neck as a punishment.)

in seventh heaven
blissfully happy
(In some religions, the seventh heaven is the last in a series of heavens that people's souls pass through after death.)

get out of bed on the wrong side
to be irritable all day
(The idea is that you are irritable from the moment you get up in the morning.)

a stiff upper lip
you are said to have a stiff upper lip when you are brave and self-controlled when life is difficult or dangerous
(Because the upper lip trembles when you are nervous or frightened. The phrase sounds British but in fact it occurs earliest in American writing.)

eat humble pie
to have to apologize or admit you were wrong about something
(A play on the words humble and umbles, which were the inner organs of deer or other animals used in pies.)

under the weather
feeling unwell or fed up
(A ship at sea was under the weather when a storm was overhead, making it uncomfortable for the people on board.)

the spitting image
a person who looks exactly like someone else
(From a strange old idea that a person could spit out an identical person from their mouth.)

have a chip on your shoulder
to feel jealous and resentful about life and the way you are treated compared with other people
(From an old American custom in which a person would place a chip of wood on their shoulder as a challenge to another person, who would accept the challenge by knocking the chip off.)

not turn a hair
to show no feeling or reaction
(Originally used about horses, whose hair becomes ruffled when they sweat.)

once in a blue moon
very rarely; hardly ever
(A blue moon is a second full moon in a month, which occurs rarely.)

out of the blue
without any warning; as a complete surprise
(Like something coming suddenly out of the blue of the sky.)

back to square one
back to the starting point after a failure or mistake
(Probably from the idea of going back to the first square as a penalty in a board game. Some people think the phrase is connected with early football commentaries, but this is unlikely.)

go hell for leather
at full speed
(From horse-riding, because the reins were made of leather, and people thought that going to hell must be very fast and reckless.)

break the ice
to make the first move in a conversation or undertaking
(From the idea of ships in very cold regions having to break through the ice to pass through.)

let the cat out of the bag
to reveal a secret by mistake
(Because cats do not like being confined, and it would be be hard to keep one in a bag in this way.)

full of beans
lively and energetic
(Horses used to be fed on beans to make them healthy.)

by hook or by crook
somehow or other; by any means possible
(From a practice in medieval times of allowing tenants to take as much firewood as they could from the trees by using these two tools.)

like water off a duck's back
having no effect on a person; making no impression
(Because water runs off the feathers of a duck without soaking through.)

from the horse's mouth
you get information straight from the horse's mouth when it comes from the person or people who originated it or who are most likely to know about it
(The idea is of someone wanting to make a bet asking the horses themselves which one is likely to win the race.)

a wild goose chase
a pointless and hopeless search for something
(Originally a kind of horse race in which a leading horse had to run an erratic course which the other horses had to follow: wild geese run about in all directions.)

the lion's share
the largest share or part of something
(Because lions, being very strong and fierce, get the largest share of a killed animal's carcass; originally this expression meant 'all of something' as lions were not thought to share.)

have your cake and eat it

you say someone wants to have their cake and eat it when they seem to want to have or do two things when only one of them is possible

(Because if you eat your cake you cannot still 'have' it: have here means 'keep'.)

come up to scratch

to be good or strong enough for what is needed

(Scratch is the line marking the start of a race or other sports event.)

on the ball

alert and quick to act

(A player in a game is on the ball when they have possession of it and are playing it well.)

show somebody the ropes

to give someone basic instruction in a task or activity

(From the days of sailing ships, when ropes were used to control the ship's rigging.)

hit the nail on the head

to say something exactly right or suitable

(From the idea of hitting a nail squarely on the head with a hammer, so that it goes in well.)

pass the buck

to leave something you should take responsibility for for someone else to deal with

(In the game of poker the buck was a small piece placed in front of the dealer.)

rain cats and dogs

to rain very hard

(We cannot be sure where this phrase comes from and it may just be fanciful; originally it was the other way round: rain dogs and cats. One of the earliest uses is by Jonathan Swift, the author of Gulliver's Travels, in the 18th century.)

at sixes and sevens

with everything very confused and muddled

(The phrase is very old and is probably connected with throwing dice, because there is no 'seven' on a dice and so sixes and sevens would be impossible.)

Proverbs

A proverb is a sentence that gives a piece of advice or says something wise or true.

all's well that ends well
If things succeed in the end then it doesn't matter so much about the troubles or difficulties experienced on the way.

an apple a day keeps the doctor away
If you eat well you will stay healthy and you won't need to see the doctor.

better late than never
Something done at the last moment is better than not doing it at all.

better safe than sorry
If in doubt it is better to be cautious than to take an unnecessary risk.

a bird in the hand is worth two in the bush
Something you already have is more valuable than something you might get or have been promised.

every cloud has a silver lining
Bad situations can often have some benefits.

don't count your chickens before they hatch
Do not assume that something will happen until you are sure about it.

one good turn deserves another
If you do someone a favour you can expect another in return.

once bitten, twice shy
Someone who has had a bad experience will avoid the same situation another time.

every picture tells a story
You can often tell what has happened from things you can see.

there's no time like the present
It is best to get on with a task straight away and not delay.

the proof of the pudding is in the eating
You can often only tell how good or useful something is by trying it.

a rolling stone gathers no moss
Someone who does not settle down in one place does not become important or wealthy. (Moss does not start to grow on stones that are moving.)

there's no smoke without fire
Rumours and reports usually have some truth about them. (If you can see smoke it usually means there is a fire near.)

a stitch in time saves nine
If you act promptly you will save yourself trouble later. (From the idea of mending clothes with stitches: *nine* is used because it makes a good rhyme with *time*.)

strike while the iron's hot
to act at the right moment
(From metalwork, in which iron is shaped when hot by hitting it with a hammer.)

two heads are better than one
You can usually do things better if you listen to advice.

where there's a will there's a way
You often need to be determined to overcome difficulties.

Some proverbs seem to contradict one another:

many hands make light work
A job can be done more easily if more people help to do it.

too many cooks spoil the broth
An activity might be badly done if too many people are involved in it.

more haste, less speed
If you rush or hurry over a task you will find it more difficult to do well.

time waits for no man
Do not delay in doing things that are important.

great minds think alike
Clever people often get the same ideas at the same time (often used jokingly when two people have the same idea or say the same thing).

fools seldom differ
Foolish or silly people will usually act or speak in the same way.

absence makes the heart grow fonder
People miss each other when they are apart.

out of sight out of mind
People forget each other or their problems when they are not immediately in front of them.

the squeaking wheel gets the grease
You often need to make a lot of noise or fuss to get attention.

silence is golden
It is often best to say nothing and keep quiet.

birds of a feather flock together
People of the same kind tend to like each other's company. 'Birds of a feather' are birds of the same species.

opposites attract
People often like other people who are very different in character from themselves.

the pen is mightier than the sword
Writing about people or things you do not like is often more effective than attacking them.

actions speak louder than words
It is often better to do something positive rather than just talk or think about doing it.